de Smith, Woolf & Jowell's

PRINCIPLES
OF
JUDICIAL REVIEW

The Rt Hon The Lord Woolf
Master of the Rolls
Bencher of the Inner Temple
Fellow of University College London
Pro-Chancellor of London University

Jeffrey Jowell, Q.C., M.A., LL.M., S.J.D.
Dean of the Law Faculty
Professor of Public Law and Vice Provost, University College London
Hon. Bencher of the Middle Temple

A.P. Le Sueur, LL.B.
Barrister
Reader in Laws, University College London

LONDON
SWEET & MAXWELL
1999

Published in 1999 by Sweet & Maxwell Limited of
100 Avenue Road, London NW3 3PF
http://www.smlawpub.co.uk.
Phototypeset by Tradespools Ltd, Frome, Somerset
Printed in Great Britain by Clays Ltd, St Ives plc

*No natural forests were destroyed to make this product; only farmed timber
was used and replanted.*

ISBN: 0421 62020 X

A CIP catalogue record for this book is available from the British
Library

PREFACE

The role of a judge in common law systems has been likened to that of an author of a chain novel.[1] Each author interprets the chapters (cases) previously written by others, before adding a new chapter to continue the story. The book you are reading may be thought of in the same way.

It was begun by Stanley de Smith in the 1950s as a doctoral thesis and then published in 1959. The book quickly established a reputation as a groundbreaking work. It was the first in the United Kingdom to describe and analyse this field of law with coherence. Professor de Smith produced two further editions in 1968 and 1973. After de Smith's untimely death, John Evans (now Mr Justice Evans) edited the fourth edition in 1980.

Prompted by reforms to the procedures and remedies, and also by a changing intellectual climate, the 1980s and early 1990s saw dramatic changes in judicial review: the number of applications increased from a few hundred a year to several thousand; the judicial reasoning which creates the grounds for challenging the validity of governmental action grew in its sophistication; and there was by then a burgeoning academic literature engaging in theoretical, empirical and doctrinal debates about this area of law. During this time, responsibility for continuing the book passed to Lord Justice Woolf (as he then was) and Jeffrey Jowell, with the assistance of Andrew Le Sueur. The fifth edition of the work (ISBN 0 420 46620 7) was published in 1995 (and a supplement, updating the text, was published in 1998 (ISBN 0 421 60790 4)).

The 1995 edition necessitated a radical restructuring of the work, with new chapters and necessary revision of de Smith's original positions. Chapters were added in the last part of the book on the impact of judicial review in different areas of the law (housing, immigration, planning, etc.) Nevertheless, the 1995 edition sought to be faithful to de Smith's approach in the following respects. First, by setting out principles underlying each area of judicial review: de Smith's hallmark was, above all, the elucidation of principle. Never content merely to describe a line of cases, he would invariably sum up their underlying rationale through a series of "propositions".

Secondly, we retained de Smith's unmatched historical researches, which are so important to a proper understanding of the context of judicial review today. As he wrote in his first Preface, "many of the peculiarities of judicial review in English administrative law are unintelligible unless viewed in the light of their historical origins". Finally, without pretending to be a work in comparative law, we tried

---

[1] Ronald Dworkin, *Law's Empire* (1986), Chap 7.

to refer where possible to appropriate material from other countries—especially the Commonwealth. We were assisted in that exercise by helpful advice from "foreign correspondents" who kept us informed of parallel developments in other countries.[2]

This edition is an abridged and updated version of the fifth edition, published in soft covers, and intended primarily to be used in university law schools, although we hope others will also find it of value. 1999 is a difficult time to produce such a work as the law is in flux. The new Civil Procedure Rules, which bring about radical changes to the litigation practices, have recently been put in place—but Order 53 (the procedural rules for making applications for judicial review) has still to be reformed and it is not yet clear how far the overriding objectives of the Civil Procedure Rules will influence the ways in which judicial review litigation is conducted. We were able, at proof stage, to incorporate references to the Civil Procedure Rules, including its new terminology.

Further, even more profound changes are in train. The Human Rights Act 1998 has been enacted, but most of its provisions have yet to be brought into force. We have included some basic explanations of the Act, and in places we speculate on how some questions may be decided differently by the courts once the Act is fully implemented. It is, however, too early to provide a detailed assessment of the impact of codified human rights on judicial review. Many of the other constitutional reforms instituted by the new Labour government since May 1997 will, in due course, reshape the reach and content of judicial review, not least those contained in the Scotland Act 1998, the Government of Wales Act 1998 and the Northern Ireland Act 1998. Again, only passing reference could be made to these. The Treaty of Amsterdam came into force on May 1, 1999; the book uses the re-numbered provision in the E.C. Treaty and Treaty of European Union.

Principal changes

The text of the 1995 edition has been both edited and updated and contains the following major changes. Chapter 1 ("Judicial Review and Administrative Law") has omitted a large section on extra-judicial safeguards and the sections on official disclosure of information and public interest immunity. This is because these issues are well-described in most textbooks on Administrative Law and we felt—since space was of the essence—that this work should concentrate upon the subject of its title, namely review by the courts.

---

[2] They and others who were generous in their advice and assistance are listed and thanked in the Preface to the 5th edition and its Supplement.

Chapter 2 considers the question of who may bring judicial review proceedings. Its focus is on the requirement of sufficient interest under section 31 of the Supreme Court Act 1981 and it omits discussion of standing in relation to other types of proceedings.

In Chapter 3 ("Who and What May be Subject to Judicial Review?") discussion of the exclusivity principle has been amended to reflect the new terminology required by the Civil Procedure Rules 1999. References to "writs", "actions" and "originating summons" have been replaced, unless it would be unduly anachronistic, with the term "general civil proceedings". This refers to civil litigation under the general part of the Civil Procedure Rules. Consideration of the special position of the Crown (a chapter in its own right in the 1995 edition) has been incorporated into this chapter.

Chapter 4 of the 1995 edition ("Jurisdiction, *Vires*, Law and Fact") is largely retained, except the section on "Disregard of Statutory Requirements" (paras 5–057–5–096).

Chapters 5 to 12 of the 1995 edition, the core of the work on grounds of judicial review, are retained pretty well intact and updated.

Chapters 13 to 16 deal with the procedures and remedies of judicial review. Points of detail and practice, unless they are of constitutional importance, have largely been excised. The historical study in Chapter 13 has been abridged. Chapter 14 on procedures now deals only with Order 53 applications—discussion of habeas corpus, statutory review and other public law procedures has been omitted. The terminology of the Civil Procedure Rules ("permission to apply for judicial review", to take one example) has been adopted. Chapter 15 brings together exposition on remedies that in the 1995 edition were treated separately. The scope of Chapter 16 is confined to damages in tort, rather than pecuniary remedies more generally. The final Chapter, while drawing upon parts of Chapter 21 in the 1995 edition, presents European Community Law in a substantially re-written format. We are grateful for the assistance there of Professor Takis Tridimas. The final section (on Judicial Review in context) is omitted.

The de Smith project continues. Work is now underway on the sixth edition of the main text. In the mean time, we offer the book you are reading as interim relief. The law is stated as of May 1, 1999.

Harry Woolf   June 1999
Jeffrey Jowell
Andrew Le Sueur

CONTENTS

PART 1—THE SCOPE OF JUDICIAL REVIEW

Contents

Contents

Contents

Contents

Contents

Contents

Contents

PART IV—EUROPEAN COMMUNITY LAW AND JUDICIAL REVIEW

Contents

TABLE OF CASES

References are to paragraph numbers

Table of Cases

Table of Cases

Table of Cases

Table of Cases

Table of Cases

Table of Cases

Table of Cases

Table of Cases

Table of Cases

xliii

Table of Cases

Table of Cases

Table of Cases

Table of Cases

Table of Cases

Table of Cases

Table of Cases

Table of Cases

Table of Cases

Table of Cases

Table of Cases

Table of Cases

Table of Cases

Table of Cases

Table of Cases

Table of Cases

Table of Cases

Table of Cases

Decisions of the European Court of Justice are listed below numerically. These decisions are also included in the preceding alphabetical table.

Table of Cases

Table of Cases

Table of Cases

TABLE OF STATUTES

References are to paragraph numbers

Table of Statutes

TABLE OF STATUTORY INSTRUMENTS

References are to paragraph numbers

Directives

Regulations

PART I

THE SCOPE OF JUDICIAL REVIEW

CHAPTER 1

THE PLACE OF JUDICIAL REVIEW IN ADMINISTRATIVE LAW

INTRODUCTION

This book is concerned with judicial review of the acts, decisions, determinations, orders and omissions of individuals and bodies performing public functions. In all developed legal systems there has been recognition of a fundamental requirement for principles to govern the exercise by public authorities of their powers. These principles provide a basic protection for individuals and prevent those exercising public functions from abusing their powers to the disadvantage of the public. During the last quater of the twentieth century, the circumstances in which the courts have been prepared to intervene to provide relief for unlawful administrative action have expanded in spectacular fashion. Coherent principles have steadily evolved in a number of areas of administrative law and disfiguring archaisms have been removed.[1] **1–001**

This is not a general work on administrative law in England. Judical review provides just one of a number of legal controls of administrative action. The administrative process is not, and cannot be, a succession of justiciable controversies. Public authorities are set up to govern and administer, and if their every act or decision were to be reviewable on unrestricted grounds by an independent judicial **1–002**

---

[1] See Lord Diplock's statement in R. v. Inland Revenue Commissioners, ex p. National Federation of Self Employed [1982] A.C. 617 where he said, at p. 641, that '[T]he progress towards a comprehensive system of administrative law ... I regard as having been the greatest achievement of the English courts in my judicial lifetime.' In 1971, Lord Denning, himself an imaginative architect, had asserted: 'It may truly now be said that we have a developed system of administrative law', Breen v. Amalgamated Engineering Union [1971] 2 Q.B. 175, 189. Cf. Ridge v. Baldwin [1964] A.C. 40, 72, per Lord Reid: 'We do not have a developed system of administrative law— perhaps because until fairly recently we did not need it.' For what is thought to be the first appearance in an English statute of the term 'administrative law', see State Immunity Act 1978, s. 3(2).

body, the business of administration could be brought to a standstill. The prospect of judicial relief cannot be held out to every person whose interests may be adversely affected by administrative action. Nevertheless, judicial review does lay down general principles governing the fair and legal and reasonable exercise of power by all those exercising such power in a democracy. And even though challenges to the decisions of officials may be relatively scarce, the principles established in leading cases will have an impact on a wide variety of decision-makers at all levels.[2]

1–003 Judicial review should therefore be seen in the context of the general administrative system, where different mechanisms are employed to hold public bodies accountable in different ways.[3] Political accountability, for example, is sought through regular elections, or the convention of ministerial responsibility; the ombudsmen aim to control "maladministration"; complaints by individuals against public bodies may be determined by means of an appeal tribunal or inquiry, or by means of internal review; Members of Parliament attend to the grievances of their constituents, and accountability in matters of financial probity and efficiency is sought by means of the National Audit Office, the Comptroller and Auditor General, the Public Accounts Committee and the Audit Commission. Regulatory agencies control the activity of the privatised utilities.

1–004 Institutions such as courts allow individuals to challenge a decision already made. This form of retrospective "check"[4] is just one technique of controlling discretion. Although decisions of courts may have an impact on future administrative practice, there are additional ways to control the exercise of discretion in advance, by techniques that seek to enhance the openness of and access to official bodies, in order to encourage their responsiveness and accountability to the interests they serve. English administrative law is becoming increasingly interested in different forms of regulation and in prophylactic rather than exclusively curative techniques of control.[5]

---

[2] On the impact of judicial review on official decision-making, see further para. 1–037, below.

[3] There is now a large number of textbooks dealing with aspects of administrative law from a wider perspective than this book. The following are all good starting points for students: H.W.R. Wade and C.F. Forsyth, *Administrative Law*, (7th ed., 1994); Andrew Le Sueur and Maurice Sunkin, *Public Law* (1997); A.W. Bradley and K. Ewing, *Constitutional and Administrative Law*, (12th ed., 1998).

[4] In his influential work *Discretionary Justice, a Preliminary Inquiry* (1969), Professor K. C. Davis put forward three principal techniques of controlling discretion: confining, structuring and checking.

[5] There is a growing literature on official discretion. See, *e.g.* K. Hawkins (ed.), *The Uses of Discretion* (1992), and the comprehensive review by David Feldman in [1994] P.L. 279.

ENGLISH ATTITUDES TOWARDS ADMINISTRATIVE LAW

Most legal systems demarcate sets of relationships between the **1–005** governors and the governed, and permit claims and controversies between them to be resolved and grievances redressed through the medium of courts.[6] These courts are not necessarily the ordinary courts of law; they may be special administrative courts. If they are special administrative courts, they will almost certainly apply substantive and procedural rules distinct from the "ordinary law of the land", rules which recognise the disparities between the administration and the citizen, between the situations that characteristically arise in public law and in private law: for example, the general law of contract and tort may be substantially modified in relation to public authorities. The content of administrative law in such a system will be readily identifiable and its development is likely to be coherent and reasonably symmetrical. It is possible, though perhaps more difficult, to evolve and apply a distinct and coherent body of administrative law without having separate administrative courts, just as it is possible for the ordinary courts to interpret a written constitution and in the process of interpretation to develop rules that have no counterpart in private law.

England has no Conseil d'Etat, no *Bundesverwaltungsgericht*, no **1–006** separate administrative or constitutional court exercising a broad jurisdiction; though it has some specialised courts, such as the Employment Appeal Tribunal, whose membership combines legal and non-legal expertise and which many foreign observers would call administrative courts, and more than 2,000 "administrative" tribunals. In so far as courts have general jurisdiction in administrative matters, that jurisdiction is vested in the ordinary courts of law and usually exercised by nominated judges of the Crown Office List of the Queen's Bench Division of the High Court. As we shall see[7] the absence of superior administrative courts of general jurisdiction in England is to be explained above all by constitutional history and the influence of Professor Albert Venn Dicey.[8]

---

[6] Article 6(1) of the European Convention on Human Rights seeks to protect access to the courts for, *inter alia*, people wishing to challenge the legality of government action: 'In the determination of his civil rights and obligations or of any criminal charge against him, everyone is entitled to a fair and public hearing within a reasonable time by an independent and impartial tribunal established by law...'.

[7] See para. 14–001.

[8] As in his *Introduction to the study of the Law of the Constitution* (10th ed.). For a critical account of the baleful influence of Dicey's insistence that the legality of governmental action was to be determined by the ordinary courts applying the general law of the land, see H.W. Arthurs 'Rethinking Administrative Law: a Slightly Dicey Business' (1979) 170 Osgoode Hall L.J. 1. For other illuminating accounts of Dicey's contribution to modern administrative law, see I. Harden and N. Lewis, *The Noble Lie:*

Judicial self-restraint

1–007   In 1959, when Professor de Smith wrote the first edition of this book, judicial review of administrative action lacked breadth and depth, except in so far as administrative action comprised determinations by tribunals. Non-appellate review of decisions by local authorities tended, on the whole, to be superficial outside the areas of licensing and spending powers. Review of the administrative acts and decisions of Ministers was little more than perfunctory on matters of substance. Although the courts would insist on compliance with statutory requirements as to form and procedure, it was extremely difficult to persuade them that a Minister had acted *ultra vires* by erring in law or fact, or that he was under an implied obligation to observe the rules of natural justice, or that in exercising a discretionary power he had been influenced by legally improper considerations. If a Minister was not under an express statutory duty to give reasons for his decisions, it was almost impossible to persuade a court to draw adverse inferences from his silence. If a Minister (or indeed a local authority) was empowered to take a given course of action when "satisfied" that a prescribed state of affairs existed, the courts generally interpreted such a grant of power literally and would refuse to go behind the assertion of the competent authority that it was honestly satisfied as to the existence of the conditions precedent, even if their existence was potentially ascertain able by a court. In the 1950s judicial self-restraint appeared to have won a decisive victory over judicial activism, in a field where the contest might well have been an even one.

1–008   Judicial self-restraint was even more marked in cases where attempts were made to impugn the exercise of discretionary powers by alleging abuse of the discretion itself, rather than alleging non-existence of the state of affairs on which the validity of its exercise was predicated. Quite properly, the courts were slow to read implied limitations into grants of wide discretionary powers which might have to be exercised on the basis of broad considerations of national policy. But in some instances they were too ready to disclaim power to review an exercise of discretion in which the policy element was comparatively small. This excess of caution was traceable to various causes. It was certainly influenced by

---

The British Constitution and the Rule of Law (1986); P. McAuslan and J. McEldowney (eds) 'Legitimacy and the Constitution: The dissonance between theory and practice' in *Law, Legitimacy and the Constitution*, Chap. 1 (1985); P.P. Craig, *Public Law and Democracy in the U.K. and USA. (1990)*; M. Loughlin, *Public Law and Political Theory* (1992). See also R.A. Cosgrove, *The Rule of Law: Albert Venn Dicey, Victorian Junst* (1980). Dicey's attitude was not always, however, shared in Scotland. See Professor J.D.D. Mitchell's work epitomised in 'The causes and effects of the absence of a system of public law in the United Kingdom' [1965] P.L. 95. See also his *Constitutional Law* (1964) and de Smith, *The Lawyers and The Constitution* (1960).

the experience of two world wars and their immediate aftermaths, when judicial zeal for the protection of the individual by means of restrictive interpretation of executive powers might have proved harmful to the public interest; precedents laid down in wartime and emergency cases continued to colour judicial attitudes in normal times. Many judges, moreover, showed a particular solicitude not to prejudice the status of their office by adopting attitudes which might justify political radicals in dubbing them as conservative obstructionists.[9] Lord Devlin, for instance, observed that "the efficacy of the judicial process requires that judgments should be immune from the sort of comment that is appropriate to the hustings".[10] Lord Parker, when Lord Chief Justice, put the same point more strongly: "in modern Britain, where no agreement exists on the ends of Society and the means of achieving those ends, it would be disastrous if courts did not eschew the temptation to pass judgment on an issue of policy. Judicial self-preservation may alone dictate restraint;. ... "[11] Judges did, of course, pass judgment on issues of "policy" from time to time; but the simplest way of passing judgment on such an issue was to defer to the opinion being advanced by the Executive, and where the opinion was that of a Minister responsible to Parliament the judges found reassurance in the awareness of potential, if often inefficacious, political checks.[12] This cautious approach was fully compatible with

---

[9] *cf.* Professor Griffith's observation (in Morris and Ginsberg (eds) (*Law and Opinion in England in the Twentieth Century* (1959), 120). "Judges were not restrictive in their attitudes to the measures of the Labour Government [when it was in office from 1945 to 1951]. Sometimes they seemed to be leaning over back wards almost to the point of falling off the Bench, to avoid the appearance of hostility...". See also Brian Abel Smith and Robert Stevens, *Lawyers and the Courts* (1966), 285. But the modern phase of judicial activism, beginning in the early 1960s, actually gathered impetus while the Wilson Government was in office (1964–70). By that time the political complexion of the Government was seen to be irrelevant.

[10] *Samples of Lawmaking* (1962), 23. This point is, of course, still valid in its proper context. For instance, in 1972 Lord Devlin and many other lawyers were deprecating the fact that under the Industrial Relations Act 1971 the National Industrial Relations Court (presided over by a High Court judge) and the superior appellate courts had to pronounce on highly sensitive issues arising out of and even giving rise to major industrial disputes: see also J.A.G. Griffith, *The Politics of the Judiciary* (5th ed., 1997), pp. 87–93.

[11] *Recent Developments in the Supervisory Powers of the Courts over Inferior Tribunals* (1959), pp. 27–28. The argument for a judicial attitude of rigorous self-restraint in the interpretation of legislation has been cogently put by Lord Devlin in (1976) 39 M.L.R. 1, esp. 13–16. For a recent plea on behalf of 'the constitutional imperative of judicial self-restraint which must inform judicial decision-making in public law', see Lord Irvine of Lairg, Q.C., 'Judges and Decision-Makers: the Theory and Practice of Wednesbury Review' [1996] P.L. 59.

[12] See, *e.g. Sparks v. Edward Ash Ltd* [1943] K.B. 223, 229–230; *Johnson (B.) & Co. (Builders) Ltd v. Minister of Health* [1947] 2 All E.R. 395, 404; David G.T. Williams in *Welsh Studies in Public Law* (ed. J.A. Andrews, 1970), 127–128. And see *Gouriet v. Union of Post Office Workers* [1978] A.C. 435, 524; *cf. Lord Advocate v. Glasgow Corp.*, 1973 S.L.T.

forthright opposition to what were conceived to be improper encroachments by the Legislature or the Executive on the territorial preserves of the Judiciary.[13] When a Government Bill was introduced into Parliament to reverse a decision given by the House of Lords (sitting as a court)[14] with retroactive effect,[15] Lord Devlin and Lord Parker were among its most emphatic critics. If the judges ought not to set themselves up as politicians, the politicians ought not to set themselves up as judges. Despite the rhetoric sometimes to be found in judicial pronouncements, judges did not, on the whole, regard themselves, or wish to be regarded as fervent defenders of the individual against the Executive.[16] The maintenance of law and order, the security of the state and the ability of government to conduct its business in an orderly manner are clearly matters of judicial concern.[17]

1–009   In a number of leading decisions over the years the judges voluntarily curbed their own power to review administrative action. That the rules of natural justice did not require the disclosure to an appellant of an inspector's report to a government department on an inquiry into an order for the closure of a house[18]; that the Home Secretary's decision to deport an alien was unreviewable and that the alien had no implied right to be heard before being deported[19]; that a Minister could withold any document or class of document from disclosure in judicial proceedings merely by certifying that its

---

33, HL.

[13] *cf. Liyanage v. R.* [1967] 1 A.C. 259.

[14] *Burmah Oil Co. v. Lord Advocate* [1965] A.C. 75.

[15] The Bill became the War Damage Act 1965. For a defence of this measure, see A.L. Goodhart (1966) 82 L.Q.R. 97.

[16] Devlin (*op. cit.* n. 10 above), 8. And on the social, political and educational background of judges of the superior courts, see Griffith (*op. cit.* n. 10 above), Chap. 1; see also Henry Cecil, *The English Judge* (2nd ed., 1972) 33–38.

[17] See Griffith (*op. cit.* n. 10 above), Chap. 9. The dangers inherent in encouraging a climate of indiscriminate judicial activism have been cogently exposed by Devlin L.J., when writing of judicial obstruction of statutory schemes: "They [*sc* judges] looked for the philosophy behind the Act and what they found was a Victorian Bill of Rights, favouring (subject to the observance of the accepted standards of morality) the liberty of the individual, the freedom of contract and the sacredness of property, and which was highly suspicious of taxation. If the Act interfered with these notions, the judges tended either to assume that it could not mean what it said or to minimise the interference by giving the intrusive words the narrowest possible construction, even to the point of pedantry." Devlin, *Samples of Lawmaking* (1962), p.8. For a modern account of the dangers of judicial activism see R. Cranston, "Reviewing Judicial Review" in G. Richardson and H. Genn (eds), *Administrative Law and Government Action* (1994), Ch. 3.

[18] *Local Government Board v. Arlidge* [1915] A.C. 120.

[19] *R. v. Leman Street Police Station Inspector, ex p. Venicoff* [1920] 3 K.B. 72; see also *R. v. Brixton Prison Governor, ex p. Soblen* [1963] 2 Q.B. 243; *R. v. Home Secretary, ex p. Hosenball* [1977] 1 W. L. R. 766.

production would be contrary to the public interest[20];—all these propositions were established by courts which were not obliged to reach such conclusions.

Change of approach

The sea-change in attitudes towards administrative law that we shall see later in this book began with a good deal of attention being given to the working of statutory tribunals and to the improvement of procedural safeguards for persons affected by departmental decisions taken after a hearing or an inquiry. The tribunals were more closely integrated with the general legal system; the process of departmental decision-making, particularly in the field of town and country planning law, was partly judicialised (some would say over-judicialised[21]); statutory tribunals and judicialised administration came under regular scrutiny. These developments, all begun in the late 1950s, are directly traceable to the Report of the Franks Committee on *Administrative Tribunals and Enquiries.*[22] **1–010**

At about the same time the role of the courts in reviewing administrative acts and decisions has become far more active and creative. This is a phenomenon of the past 30 years, and its origins are not so easily identifiable, but it must have owed something to the post-Franks ethos, to an increase in awareness of the more impressive performance of courts in the United States, France and some Commonwealth countries, to a judicial willingness to adopt a more purposive approach to the interpretation of statutes, to the indirect influence of academic literature upon practitioners, to the resourcefulness of individual judges, and to a period when the consumer began to assert his rights against bodies, whether trades unions, large corporations or governmental bodies of various kinds, that had previously seemed immune from any accountability or control. The "zone of immunity"[23] around a great deal of governmental action was progressively reduced. **1–011**

In 1967 another important development took place when a distant relative of the Scandinavian Ombudsman was introduced (via New **1–012**

---

[20] *Duncan v. Cammell, Laird & Co.* [1942] A.C. 624: see below.

[21] See generally, G. Ganz, *Administrative Procedures* (1974).

[22] Cm. 218 (1957). And other factors set out in J. Jowell, 'Restraining the State: Politics, Principle and Judicial Review' *Law of Opinion in Twentieth Century England* (1997) 50 C.L.P. 189.

[23] A phrase used by L. Friedman, *Total Justice* (1985) in respect of a great deal of action previously protected and then rendered vulnerable to legal attack. For a recent account of the influence of the United States of America, see I. Loveland (ed.), *A Special Relationship? American Influences on Public Law in the United Kingdom* (1995).

Zealand) under the style of Parliamentary Commissioner for Administration.[24] to investigate and report on complaints of injustice caused by maladministration on the part of the central government and its officials in respect of matters where recourse to the courts or tribunals was not normally available. Since then analogous functions have been conferred upon a Health Service Commissioner[25] and the Commissions for Local Administration.[26]

1–013   In 1966 the Law Commission,[27] began to take soundings on administrative law reform, with special reference to the role of the courts. In 1967 it published an exploratory working paper, and after extensive consultations it formally recommended to the Lord Chancellor in May 1969 that a wide-ranging inquiry be conducted by a Royal Commission or a body of similar status into the following questions: (i) whether the form and procedure of existing judicial remedies in administrative law needed to be altered; (ii) whether changes in the scope of judicial review were required; (iii) how far remedies in respect of administrative acts and omissions should include the right to damages; (iv) whether special principles should govern administrative contracts and torts; (v) how far changes should be made in the organisation and personnel of the courts for the purposes of administrative law.[28] At this time the civil service was beginning to adjust to the appointment of the Parliamentary Commissioner for Administration and was also about to undergo re-organisation in the light of the recommendations of the Fulton Committee (1968).[29] Many prominent civil servants, moreover, were uneasy at the spontaneous revival of judicial activism. And some lawyers thought that procedural reform was too urgent to be deferred till the conclusion of a large-scale inquiry. In December 1969 the Lord Chancellor rejected the Law Commission's recommendations and requested it to undertake its own inquiry into question (i), the form and procedure of judicial remedies; changes in the scope of review were to be outside the Commission's terms of reference.[30] The Commission, impeded by this unrealistically narrow limitation on its powers, produced its final report in 1976,[31] some four and a half years

---

[24] Parliamentary Commissioner Act 1967.

[25] National Health Service Reorganisation Act 1973, ss. 31–39, Sched. 3.

[26] Local Government Act 1974, ss. 23–34, Scheds 4 and 5.

[27] Constituted as a permanent advisory body on law reform in pursuance of the Law Commissions Act 1965. For a short account of the Commission's method of work, see generally J. H. Farrar, *Law Reform and the Law Commission* (1974).

[28] Cmnd. 4059 (1969).

[29] Report of the Committee on the Civil Service (Cmnd. 3638 (1968)).

[30] 306 H.L. Deb. 189–190 (December 4, 1969).

[31] Cmnd. 6407 (1976).

after the publication of a detailed working paper.[32] The principal proposal of the Commission was that the existing non-statutory remedies in administrative law should be sought in a unified application for judicial review. And this was implemented, with an expedition previously absent from this project, by amendments to the Rules of the Supreme Court that took effect in January 1978.[33]

Much of what follows in this book charts the development of judicial review since the 1978 reforms to litigation procedures and remedies.[34] Easier access to the courts was one factor leading to a steady increase in the number of applications heard by the High Court.[35] The grounds of judicial review also grew in their sophistication and their reach.[36]

1–014

The influence of human rights

In the 1970s, insular attitudes towards the protection of individual rights from governmental incursions underwent marked changes. In the Hamlyn Lectures of 1974, Sir Leslie Scarman (as he then was) concluded that the common law was ill-equipped to meet modern challenges and that the enactment of an entrenched Bill of Rights was required to ensure, in particular, that the United Kingdom was able to meet the international commitments that were assumed on its ratification of the European Convention for the Protection of Human Rights and Fundamental Freedoms (the Convention): "In other words there must be a constitutional restraint placed upon the legislative power which is designed to protect the individual citizen from instant legislation, conceived in fear or prejudice and enacted in panic."[37] Although no attempt to codify the fundamental rights of the citizen in the United Kingdom was successful until 1998, the United Kingdom is a signatory to a number of international codes, of which the most influential is the European Convention for Human Rights and

1–015

---

[32] *Remedies in Administrative Law* (Law Com. No. 40). A similar working paper on the corresponding remedies in Scots law was issued by the Scottish Law Commission (Memorandum No.14). The working paper's modest proposals evoked a surprising amount of criticism, both on technical grounds and because they would indirectly expand the scope of judicial review, which would be undesirable.

[33] Rules of the Supreme Court (Amendment No. 3) 1977, S.I. 1977 No. 1955 (I., 30). *Cf.* Judicature (Northern Ireland) Act 1978, ss. 18–25. See also Supreme Court Act 1981, s. 31.

[34] These are discussed in more detail in Chaps 13 to 16, below.

[35] For the statistics, see para. 1–035 below.

[36] The grounds of review are considered in Chaps 5 to 12, below.

[37] *English Law — The New Dimension* (1974), 20.

Fundamental Freedoms.[38] These codes protect individuals, as a matter of international law, against the misuse of legislative, executive or judicial powers within the United Kingdom.[39] The European Convention and the International Covenant on Civil and Political Rights oblige the United Kingdom to secure the rights and freedoms they guarantee in domestic law and to provide effective remedies before national authorities for breaches of their provisions. However, so long as the rights contained in these international codes were not incorporated into domestic law, English courts had no power to enforce them directly.[40]

1–016   Nevertheless, the European Convention became especially influential because citizens of the United Kingdom, where they have exhausted their remedies under domestic law, could then apply to the European Commission and Court and if a decision is given in their favour it was invariably recognised by the department of government concerned.[41] It was also established that English courts would allow reference both to the text of the Convention and its interpretation by the European Commission and Court of Human Rights in order to resolve an ambiguity in English primary or secondary legislation. In such a case the courts would presume that Parliament intended to legislate in conformity with its treaty obligations under the Convention, and not in conflict with it.[42] Both the existence, therefore, of the catalogue of rights codified under the Convention, and the reasoning employed in determining the circumstances in which such rights may be asserted (employing concepts adapted from continental legal systems such as

---

[38] 1950, Rome, November 4, 1950; T.S. 71 (1953); Cmd. 8969. The Convention is to a large extent based upon the Universal Declaration of Human Rights (Paris, December 10, 1948; UN 2 (1949); Cmd. 7662). The United Kingdom has ratified all the protocols to the Convention, other than the fourth, sixth, seventh, eighth, and ninth. The other influential code of human rights to which the U.K. is a party is the International Covenant on Civil and Political Rights (New York, December 19, 1966; T.S. 6 (1977): Cmnd. 6702). The U.K. is not a party to the Optional Protocol to that Covenant. See also Recommendation No. R(80)2 concerning exercise of discretionary powers adopted by Committee of Ministers of Council of Europe, March 11, 1980.

[39] The first international human rights code to which the United Kingdom became a party after the Second World War was the Convention on the Prevention and Punishment of the Crime of Genocide, approved by the UN General Assembly in 1948, which came into force in 1951 and was incorporated into domestic law by the Genocide Act 1969.

[40] See, *e.g. Rantzen v. Mirror Group Newspapers Ltd* [1994] Q.B. 670, 690, *per* Neill L.J.

[41] Under article 25. See also Resolution (77) 31 of Committee of Ministers of Council of Europe (Sept. 28, 1977).

[42] *R. v. Secretary of State for the Home Department, ex p. Brind* [1991] 1 A.C. 696, HL, at pp. 747–48, *per* Lord Bridge; pp. 7449–50, *per* Lord Roskill, pp. 760–61, *per* Lord Ackner.

proportionality and equality—which will be discussed later in the book)[43] affected judicial review in the United Kingdom.[44]

In November 1998 the Human Rights Act received the Royal assent. **1–017** Section 6(1) of the Act makes it unlawful for all public authoriies in the United Kingdom to act in a way which is incompatible with the rights set out in the European Convention on Human Rights.[45] When the act comes into force on October 2, 2000, its effect will be that all officials exercising a "public function,"[46] and who act in breach of the Convention rights, will be amenable to judicial review on that ground by any "victims"[47] of their decisions or actions.

The impact of the new Act will be significant in that it will, for the **1–018** first time, provide a written catalogue of rights which all public officials must respect. At present some of these rights, such as free expression, are recognised at common law unless they are incompatible with an Act of Parliament.[48] Other rights, such as the right not to be discriminated against, are provided by statute. In future a host of rights will be added to those and our domestic courts, taking into account the case-law of the European Court of Human Rights, will enforce them directly. This will add considerably to the armoury of judicial review of administrative action.

The other major change introduced by the Human Rights Act is the **1–019** capacity of the higher courts to review primary legislation in order to test its conformity with the European Convention on Human Rights. Outside of European Community law, the courts do not have that power at present. Where there is a clash between them, the sovereignty of Parliament now prevails over the rule of law. The new Act introduces a subtle compromise between those two constitutional principles. It permits courts to review primary legislation, requiring them to interpret that legislation "where possible" in conformity with the European Convention.[49] In cases, however, where there is a clear conflict between the two, the courts may not strike that legislation

---

[43] See Chap. 12 below; A. Boyle in Richardson and Genn (eds.), *op. cit.* n. 17 above, pp. 96–101.

[44] See, *e.g.* the approach of Steyn L.J. in *R. v. Secretary of State for the Home Department, ex p. Leech (No. 2)* [1994] Q.B. 198, CA. See also *Tavita v. Minister of Immigration* [1994] 2 N.Z.L.R. 257; Murray Hunt, *Using Human Rights in English Courts* (1997) and see further paras 5-047–5-057 and 12-057–12-061, below.

[45] Those rights are set out in Schedule 1 of the Act and exclude those set out in ss. 14–17.

[46] S. 6(3). Which includes courts and tribunals.

[47] S. 7(3) and (4).

[48] The techniques of the courts in applying these rights is described in the section below.

[49] S. 3 of the Act. This applies also to subordinate legislation.

down, but only make a "declaration of incompatiblity", after which it will be up to Parliament to decide whether it wants to bring its legislation into line with the European Convention rights.[50]

1–020   These changes will sharpen the grounds of judicial review. They will make breaches of Convention rights "illegal" rather than merely "unreasonable", under the present grounds of review that will be discussed later in the book.[51] However, the Human Rights Act is unlikely to be treated as just another statute. It is likely to assume constitutional significance. This is because the rights it embraces are inherent in a democratic society worthy of its name—rights to basic dignity (such as the right not to be tortured); rights to participation in decisions affecting your freedom (rights to fair trial), and the fundamental rights of expression and equality.

1–021   The fundamental changes that the Human Rights Act will introduce to judicial review should not, however, blind us to the fact that there are a number of principles of good and lawful administration that are not contained within the ambit of the European Convention. Much of judicial review will proceed as it has in the past, and with the same techniques, principles and procedures. It therefore remains necessary to consider the methods of judicial reasoning adopted by the courts which has permitted them to reach the stage they have.

The influence of the European Community

1–022   The international recognition of human rights has not been the only challenge to insular attitudes. Since 1973 the United Kingdom has been a member of the European Community, a truly remarkable supranational organisation. This has brought about profound changes to the whole constitutional system[52] and to the grounds, procedures and remedies of judicial review. The impact of Community law will be considered in Chapter 17.

LEGAL REASONING AND JUDICIAL REVIEW

1–023   In the chapters that follow we shall see how, over a relatively short period, English courts reduced the zone of immunity formerly surrounding a great deal of administrative action. That task involved

---

[50] And if so, may amend the existing incompatible legislation by means of a 'fast track' procedure—by means of statutory instrument rather than new primary legislation (ss. 10 and 20 of the Act).

[51] Illegality is discussed in Chap. 5, unreasonableness in Chap. 12.

[52] For an overview, see Patrick Birkinshaw, 'European Integration and United Kingdom Constitutional Law' (1997) 3 *European Public Law* 57.

the jettisoning of many of the conceptual barriers which had inhibited the development of effective judicial review for so long. It also required the courts to justify and articulate acceptable principles governing the exercise of public functions and the vindication of the rights of the individual against the state.

What justifies such changes in judicial attitude? And what is the correct approach to judicial review? As we have seen, there have been times when judicial review has been said to be founded on the principle that courts are the mere handmaidens of public officials; [53] there to facilitate the work of bodies charged with acting in the public interest. An alternative view asserts that the courts' role is to protect individual rights against the abuse of official power.[54]   **1–024**

The standards applied by the courts in judicial review must ultimately be justified by constitutional principles, which govern the proper exercise of public power in any democracy.[55] This is so irrespective of whether the principles are set out in a formal, written document. The sovereignty or supremacy of Parliament is one such principle, which accords primacy to laws enacted by the elected legislature. The rule of law is another such principle of the greatest importance. It acts as a constraint upon the exercise of all power. The scope of the rule of law is broad. It has managed to justify— albeit not always explicitly—a great deal of the specific content of judicial review, such as the requirements that laws as enacted by Parliament be faithfully executed by officials; that orders of courts should be obeyed; that individuals wishing to enforce the law should have reasonable access to the courts; that no person should be condemned unheard, and that power should not be arbitrarily exercised. In addition, the rule of law embraces some internal qualities of all public law: that it should be certain, that is, ascertainable in advance so as to be predictable and not   **1–025**

---

[53] A phrase used in 1962 by the former Chief Justice Parker, quoted in G.F. Williams, 'The Donoughmore Report in Retrospect", (1982) 60 Pub.Admin. 273, 291. See also the views of Lord Devlin, n. 11 above. And see generally J.A.G. Griffith, *The Politics of the Judiciary* (5th ed., 1997) and *Judicial Politics Since 1920* (1993).

[54] See, *e.g.* T.R.S. Allan, *Law, Liberty and Justice* (1993), and the account of the 'liberal normativists' in M. Loughlin, *Public Law and Political Theory* (1992). See generally the useful account of what they call the 'green light' as opposed to 'red light' approaches to judicial review in C. Harlow and R. Rawlings, *Law and Administration* (1997) Chaps 1 and 2.

[55] For recent accounts that seek to base administrative law on political theory see M. Loughlin, n. 54 above; P.P. Craig, *Public Law and Democracy in the U.K. and the USA* (1990), esp. Chap. 2.

retrospective in its operation; and that it be applied equally, without unjustifiable differentiation.[56]

1–026   Other constitutional principles are perhaps less clearly identified but nevertheless involve features inherent in a democratic state. These include the requirements of political participation,[57] equality of treatment[58] and freedom of expression.[59]

1–027   A constitutional principle achieves practical effect as a constraint upon the exercise of all public power. Where the principle is violated it is enforced by the courts which define and articulate its precise content. As we shall see, English law now recognises three principal "grounds" of judicial review, known as "procedural propriety", "rationality" and "legality".[60] These grounds are not isolated requirements of a discrete area of law; they refer to and attempt to impose upon all decision-makers standards that are inherent in a democracy. Procedural propriety imposes fair decision-making procedures necessary to the degree of participation which democracy requires. Rationality seeks the accuracy of decisions and prohibits excessive burdens being imposed on individuals. The ground of legality involves the application both of the sovereignty of Parliament and the rule of law, by requiring Parliament's will to be respected and

---

[56] We are not here joining the perennial debate as to whether Dicey's meaning of the rule of law is either sound or accurate, but are suggesting that these qualities fit comfortably enough with the rule of law as it has been practically applied.

[57] An important debate about the United States' Constitution, but which has relevance in the United Kingdom, is the extent to which the constitution seeks to further 'process values' (permitting effective participation in the democratic process) or also deals in substantive or moral rights against the state. The argument for the former is put by J.H. Ely, *Democracy and Distrust* (1980). For criticism, see P. Brest, 'The substance of protest' (1982) 42 Ohio S.L.J. 131; L. Tribe, 'The puzzling persistence of process-based constitutional theories' (1980) 89 Yale L.J. 1037; R. Dworkin, 'The forum of principle' (1982) 56 N.Y.U.L.R. 469; M. Tushnet, 'Darkness on the edge of town' (1980) 89 Yale L.J. 1037. See also G. Richardson, 'The Legal Regulation of Process', in Richardson and Genn (eds), *Administrative Law and Government Action* (1994), p. 10.

[58] See J. Jowell, 'Is Equality a Constitutional Principle?', (1994) 47 C.L.P. vol. 2 p. 3; 'The Rule of Law Today' in J. Jowell and D. Oliver (ed.) *The Changing Constitution* (3rd ed., 1994), Chap. 3. *Cf.* T.R.S. Allen, *Law, Liberty and Justice* (1993) for a view that equality is inherent in the rule of law.

[59] See *Derbyshire C.C. v. Times Newspapers Ltd* [1993] A.C. 534, where the House of Lords held that the Council was not entitled to bring a libel action against the newspaper. It was made clear that such an entitlement would have a chilling effect on free expression and that the right to free expression was derived from the principle that, in a democracy, necessary criticism of government should not be unjustifiably restrained. In *Goldsmith v. Bhoyrul* [1998] 2 W.L.R. 435 Buckley J. extended the *Derbyshire* principle to prevent a political party (the Referendum Party) from bringing a libel action.

[60] Terms employed by Lord Diplock in *Council of Civil Service Union v. Minister for the Civil Service* [1985] A.C. 374 and since employed widely by the courts.

official action to be congruent with legislative purpose. In applying the ground of legality the courts are effectively acting as guardians of Parliament's intent.[61] Parliamentary sovereignty and the rule of law are therefore not inevitably mutually opposed, since a great deal of judicial review (and indeed the rule of law) is concerned with enforcing Parliament's will.

In some cases, however, courts have been faced with the challenge **1–028** of having to adjudicate when the principle of the rule of law and the principle of the sovereignty of Parliament are in competition. This can occur when Parliament attempts to oust or limit the jurisdiction of the courts to determine the scope of an inferior body's powers.[62] One of the live issues today is the extent to which the courts—both in judging the exercise of administrative power and the substance of primary legislation—are required to acquiesce in the view that the rule of law must fail in that competition and give way to parliamentary supremacy.[63] The apparent inconsistency between the rule of law and parliamentary supremacy may be resolved by the courts making the presumption that Parliament intended its legislation to conform to the rule of law as a constitutional principle. This presumption is powerful and is not easily rebutted; only express words or possibly necessary implication will suffice. If it is alleged that the courts' jurisdiction is entirely excluded, even this may not suffice.[64] If officials refuse an individual reasonable access to the courts, or discriminate against a class of individuals, the courts will usually intervene to correct such breaches of the rule of law unless the language of the statute clearly and unambiguously prohibits this.[65]

---

[61] See Craig, n. 55 above, pp. 47–55 on the development of the courts' role in interpreting Parliamentary 'intention'.

[62] See Chap. 4, below.

[63] Here it should be noted that English courts are now called upon to judge the legality of primary legislation as well as administrative action, if it is alleged that it conflicts with directly effective European Community law: *e.g. R. v. Secretary of State for Transport, ex p. Factortame Ltd (No. 1)* [1990] 2 A.C. 85 and *R. v. Secretary of State for Employment ex p. Equal Opportunities Commission* [1995] 1 A.C. 1. This, together with the possibility of a declaration of incompatibility under the Human Rights Act, may create a climate which alters the practice in purely domestic law. For a robust defence of orthodox views on parliamentary supremacy, and a justification of judicial review on the basis of implied parliamentary intent, see Christopher Forsyth, 'Of Fig Leaves and Fairy Tales: the Ultra Vires Doctrine, the Sovereignty of Parliament and Judicial Review' [1996] C.L.J. 122.

[64] See the discussion about ouster clauses in Chap. 4 below.

[65] See, *e.g. R. v. Secretary of State for the Home Department, ex p. Leech (No. 2)* [1994] Q.B. 198, where regulations prohibiting a prisoner's unimpeded access to a solicitor were held unlawful. Steyn L.J. referred to the right of access to a solicitor as being part of the right of access to the courts themselves. This he called a 'constitutional right' which could not be taken away except by express words or necessary implication. See also *R. v. Secretary of State for Social Security, ex p. Joint Council for the Welfare of*

1–029   In general the presumption of constitutionality operates in the following way: Parliament, when enacting legislation, is presumed to intend that the future implementation and enforcement of its legislation should conform with the fundamental principles of the constitution as elucidated in standards set by the common law. All legislation is enacted in the context of these standards (which are still being elaborated by the courts) which govern the exercise of all official power.

1–030   It would, however, be incomplete and misleading to view the exercise of judicial review as being restricted solely to the application of canons of interpretation governing the weighing of presumptions when construing statutory power.[66] The principles of public law are not confined to the exercise of statutory powers: they apply to the Crown's prerogatives[67] and to the exercise of non-statutory powers.[68] Furthermore, imputing intentions to the legislature can give the impression of artificiality, and obscures the role of the courts themselves in resorting to "the justice of the common law" to "supply the omissions of the legislature".[69] The concrete application and elucidation of broad constitutional principles are not self-evident or static. It is for the courts to articulate them as rules and standards of good administration. The general principles are specifically implemented in the context of contemporary standards of fairness as well as other values.[70] For example, that aspect of the rule of law that requires legal certainty and predictability is practically applied through the emerging requirement that "legitimate expectations" should

---

Immigrants [1997] 1 W.L.R. 275 (regulations denying asylum seekers welfare benefits held to be unlawful; the effect of this decision was later reversed by the Immigration and Asylum Act 1996, s. 9); *R. v. Lord Chancellor, ex p. Witham* [1997] 2 All E.R. 779 (Laws J. held new rules on court fees to be *ultra vires;* access to the courts is a constitutional right which could only be denied by the government if it persuaded Parliament to pass legislation with express provision permitting the executive to turn poor people away from the court door. Such rights were not 'the consequence of the democratic political process but would be logically prior to it'). And see further para. 12–058, below.

[66] See, *e.g. Kioa v. West* (1986) 62 A.L.R. 321, 366, *per* Brennan S. who denied that any 'free-standing common law rights' in relation to administrative law existed independently of statute. See also *Gai v. Commonwealth* (1982) 150 C.L.R. 113, 115. But see for the possibility that some common law rights lie so deep that even Parliament cannot override them *Fraser v. State Services Commission* [1984] 1 N.Z.L.R. 116 at 121; and *Taylor v. New Zealand Poultry Board* [1984] 1 N.Z.L.R. 394 at 398, *per* Cooke J.

[67] As established in *Council of Civil Servants Union v. Minister for the Civil Service* [1985] A.C. 374.

[68] See D. Oliver 'Is the *Ultra Vires* Rule the Basis of Judicial Review?' [1987] P.L., 543.

[69] *per* Byles J. in *Cooper v. Wandsworth Board of Works* (1863) 14 C.B. (N.S.) 180, 194.

[70] See, *e.g.* Lord Diplock's definition of the ground of review of irrationality as reflecting 'accepted moral standards'. *Council for Civil Service Unions v. Minister for the Civil Service*, n. 67 above at 71.

be fulfilled in appropriate circumstances.[71] Values such as these are part of our general legal system, developed in accordance with accepted norms as to the proper role of the democratic state and the rights of individuals within it.[72]

Many of the standards applied through judicial review are **1–031** necessarily open-textured. It has been claimed that some of them, such as natural justice, fairness, or reasonableness, are so vague as to be practically meaningless. Lord Reid rightly regarded these claims as "tainted by the perennial fallacy that because something cannot be cut and dried or nicely weighed or measured therefore it does not exist".[73] Judicial review will naturally search for precision, as an aid to the prediction and prescription of administratively fair and correct practices. Yet it cannot afford entirely to abandon flexibility (a principle by no means inferior to that of certainty, aimed at individuated justice).[74] The search for precise standards will always need to be accompanied by a recognition of the particular circumstances of a special case, depending upon the breadth of the power conferred upon the decision-maker; the conditions of its exercise; the availability of alternative procedural protections, and the fairness to the parties involved (and to others affected by the decision). It is for these reasons that the courts themselves retain discretion in the grant of remedies in judicial review.[75]

Is the reasoning in cases involving "public law" fundamentally **1–032** different from those involving "private law"?[76] The general principles of justice contained within the common law apply to both. Yet in public law cases the quest for the lawful exercise of power will take

---

[71] See Chaps. 8 and 12 below. For an account that claims much for the rule of law's scope in deepening, accountability in administrative law, see I. Harden and N. Lewis, *The Noble Lie: The British Constitution and the Rule of Law* (1986). *Cf.* R. Cotterell in Richardson & Genn, *op. cit.* n. 17 above, p. 13.

[72] In a series of recent essays several English judges, writing extra-judicially, have sought to place judicial review within the context of democratic rights: Lord Scarman, "The Development of Administrative Law: Obstacles and Opportunities" [1990] P.L. 490; Lord Browne-Wilkinson, "The Infiltration of a Bill of Rights" [1992] P.L. 397; Sir John Laws, "Judicial Remedies and The Constitution" (1994) 57 M.L.R. 213, and "Law and Democracy" [1995] P.L., 72; Lord Woolf, "Droit Public—English Style" [1995] P.L. 57; Sir Stephen Sedley, "The Sound of Silence: Constitutional Law Without a Constitution" (1994) 110 L.Q.R. 270; Sedley, "Human Rights: a Twenty-first Century Agenda" [1995] P.L. 356; Laws, "The Constitution: morals and rights" [1996] P.L. 622; Lord Irvine of Lairg, "Response to Sir John Laws" [1996] P.L. 636. For an excellent overview of the recent contributions by members of the judiciary to constitutional theory, see Murray Hunt, *Using Human Rights in English Courts* (1997), Chap. 5.

[73] *Ridge v. Baldwin* [1964] A.C. 40 at p. 64–65.

[74] See generally, D.J. Galligan, *Discretionary Powers* (1986).

[75] See para. 15–048.

[76] For a further discussion of the distinction between public and private law, see Chap. 3.

into account both the rights of the person challenging government action (who may be an individual, a group of individuals or another public body) and the fact that the body challenged is frequently acting on behalf of the public. Neither side should be favoured on the basis of their status as litigants. Yet at the heart of a system of public law should be the recognition of the need to strike the appropriate balance between the need for public authorities to be free to perform their proper functions on behalf of the public and the corresponding requirement that they should have due regard for the legitimate rights and interests of the individual and groups of individuals. When performing their functions[77] public authorities should recognise their responsibility to strike this balance. When this does not happen there needs to be a means of redress.

1–033   There is another sense too in which the courts, in resolving cases of public law, are subject to limitations that apply less frequently, if at all, in private law disputes. In articulating the standards of proper administrative practice in the way we have described, the courts have a clearly defined and authoritative role. It is for them to adjudicate both upon the scope of a power and the manner of its exercise. This role may be confidently assumed by the courts. It is also a constitutional role under the democratic principle of the separation of powers.[78] Courts, like other institutions, including Parliament, are subject to institutional constraints and must take care not to trespass upon the decision-making functions best suited to other branches of government. Public law cases are replete with instances where officials have been conferred very broad discretionary powers. Judicial review does permit the courts to interfere with the exercise of those powers on the ground of the way the decision was reached (the procedure employed as well as the process of arriving at the decision—the factors taken into account or ignored). It also permits in some cases interference with the substance of the decision itself.[79] Courts should, however, avoid interfering with the exercise of official discretion when

---

[77] For a 'functionalist' approach to administrative law (and an excellent intellectual history of the subject) see M. Loughlin, *Public Law and Political Theory* (1992).

[78] On separation of powers more generally, see M.C.J. Vile, *Constitutionalism and the Separation of Powers* (1967); G. Marshall, *Constitutional Theory* (1971), Chap. 5; now Eric Barendt, "Separation of Powers and Constitutional Government" [1995] P.L. 599; Sir Stephen Sedley, "Autonomy and the Rule of Law", Chap. 14, in R. Rawlings (ed.), *Law, Society and Economy* (1997). See also the debate in the House of Lords on the relationship between the judiciary, the legislature and the executive, and on judicial participation in public controversy: H.L. Deb., Vol. 572, col. 1449 (July 3, 1996) and col. 1581 (July 4, 1996) and Robert Stevens, "Judges, Politics, Politicians and the Confusing Role of the Judiciary", Chap. 11 in Keith Hawkins (ed.), *The Human Face of Law* (1997).

[79] See further the discussion in Chap. 12 below.

its aim is the pursuit of policy.[80] Courts are not institutionally suited to engage in the task of weighing utilitarian calculations of social, economic or political preference. These tasks are best suited to institutions in the political arena. Nevertheless, despite this important limitation on their capacity, courts are able, and indeed obliged, to require the observance of those principles that govern lawful public decision-making. In so doing they seek to reinforce representative government, not to oppose it—and to promote, not to undermine, the inherent features of a democracy.

THE IMPORTANCE OF JUDICIAL REVIEW

Although this and previous editions of this book published between 1959 and 1980 warned that judicial review of administrative action was "inevitably sporadic and peripheral",[81] caution is now needed before relegating judicial review to a minor role in the control of official power. There are two reasons for this. First, the number of applications for judicial review has grown annually, is still growing and is unlikely to diminish. Secondly, empirical research suggests a heightened awareness of the potential impact of judicial review among officials and politicians has altered the ways in which some types of decisions are taken.

1–034

The growing case load

In 1996 there were 3,901 applications for permission to apply for judicial review.[82] The number of applications considered at a full hearing was only a fraction of this, over half of all permission applications being refused and many of those granted permission being withdrawn during the wait for the full hearing. In relation to the number of potentially challengeable governmental decisions made each year, the number of review challenges commenced is very small. Nevertheless the growth in the caseload, in part at least a product of the procedural reforms of 1978, places considerable pressure on the

1–035

---

[80] In accordance with the meaning (now well known, but by no means uncontroversial) of that term employed by Ronald Dworkin. See in particular his Maccabean lecture 'Political Judges and the Rule of Law' (1978) Pr.B.Acad. 64. For Dworkin's distinction between 'principle' and 'policy' see R. Dworkin, *Taking Rights Seriously*, (1977) pp. 82–87.

[81] J.M. Evans (ed.), *de Smith's Judicial Review of Administrative Action*, (4th ed., 1980), p.3. This statement is discussed in G. Richardson and M. Sunkin, 'Judicial Review: Questions of Impact' [1996] P.L. 79.

[82] Formerly called 'leave': see para. 14–020.

courts and resulted in backlogs and delays.[83] To focus on the overall number of applications for permission is, however, to hide the fact that most of the growth occurred in particular subject areas.[84] In the years between 1987 and 1991, cases concerning immigration[85] represented between 45 per cent and 20 per cent of the annual caseload and applications in respect of the statutory responsibilities of local authorities to provide accommodation for homeless people grew to nearly 25 per cent of all cases annually.[86] In relation to both of these categories of case, there have been calls for the supervisory jurisdiction of the High Court to be replaced either by appeals to the county court or to a tribunal.[87] Up to 15 per cent of applications for judicial review each year concern judicial review of magistrates and Crown Court proceedings.

1–036   Local authorities are the most numerous category of respondent, being the object of around 35 per cent of the challenges each year. A handful of government departments, most notably the Home Office, make up about 25 per cent.

Local authorities are also the applicants in a significant number of cases (between 15 and 35 per cent in the years 1987 to 1991), though individual applicants are by far the most common, typically accounting for over 80 per cent of applications.

The response of government

1–037   Central and local government have became increasingly aware of the potency of judicial review challenge. Although the numbers of challenges remained relatively small, and most were confined to narrow issues, a handful of cases during the 1980s had a significant impact on the way judicial review was perceived. Among these were the challenges to the public transport fares policy of the GreaterLondon

---

[83] See para. 13–057; and see H. Woolf, 'Judicial Review: A Possible Programme for Reform' [1992] P.L. 221.

[84] See M. Sunkin, L. Bridges and G. Mészáros, *Judicial Review in Perspective: An Investigation of Trends in the Use and Operation of the Judicial Review Procedure in England and Wales* (1995). The authors summarise some of their findings in 'Trends in Judicial Review' [1993] P.L. 443. This section draws heavily upon that research. See also Sunkin, 'What is Happening to Applications to Judicial Review?' (1987) 50 M.L.R. 432 and [1991] P.L. 490 and B. Hadfield and E. Weaver, 'Trends in Judicial Review in Northern Ireland' [1994] P.L. 12.

[85] On immigration, see further Chap. 25 of the main edition of this text.

[86] In 1996 alternative remedies were created for people wishing to challenge decisions about homelessness: see para. 13–066.

[87] See Woolf, *op. cit.* n. 83 above, pp. 226–227. This has happened in homeless cases. Housing Act 1996, ss. 202, 204.

Council in 1981[88] and to the lawfulness of a statutory instrument implementing government policy on entitlement to board and lodging payments to welfare claimants in 1985.[89]

Central government

During the 1980s, central government became increasingly concerned **1–038** at the number of successful judicial review challenges and that departments seemed ill-equipped to respond effectively to actual or potential judicial reviews. Writing in 1983, the Treasury Solicitor drew attention to the fact that "senior administrators show a surprising ignorance of elementary legal principles" and "a lack of appreciation of the impact of legal considerations on administrative problems involving either considerable financial loss or embarrassment to Ministers".[90] A cabinet committee endorsed this view and a strategy was formulated to deal with these problems. One aspect of the response was for the Treasury Solicitor's department and the Cabinet Office to distribute over 35,000 copies of a pamphlet called *The Judge Over Your Shoulder* to civil servants in 1987.[91] This set out some basic information about the judicial review process and some of the precautions which administrators could take to avoid the risk of challenge. A programme of legal awareness training was also organised for civil servants. Another aspect of the strategy was that departments were urged to ensure that legislation was "expressed in the clearest possible language, even at the cost of drafting terms that are presentationally or politically unattractive."[92]

In the years which followed, a marked change in the ethos of departments occurred. Law and lawyers were no longer seen as peripheral to the process of administration. Administrators became

---

[88] *Bromley L.B.C. v. Greater London Council* [1983] 1 A.C. 768. For an analysis of the impact of this decision on local government decision-making, see further L. Bridges *et al., Legality and Local Politics* (1987).

[89] *R. v. Secretary of State for Social Security ex p. Colton, The Times,* August 5, 1985, DC and December 14, 1985, CA. On the impact of this case on central government, see Maurice Sunkin and A.P. Le Sueur, 'Can Government Control Judicial Review?' (1991) 44 C.L.P. 161.

[90] Sir Michael Kerry, 'Administrative Law and the Administrator' (1983) 3 *Management in Government,* pp. 170–171.

[91] See A. W. Bradley, 'The Judge Over Your Shoulder' [1987] P.L. 485. A second edition of the pamphlet was prepared in 1994, on which see D. Oliver [1994] P.L. 514. Compare the booklet issued by the Commonwealth Secretariate, *Good Government and Administrative Law: an International Guide* (1996) and that published by the Australian Government, *Legal Issues: a Guide for Policy Development and Administration* (October 1994).

[92] See Bradley, *op. cit.,* n. 91.

more aware of the legal implications of their decisions and departmental lawyers tended to become involved at earlier stages of the policy-making process.[93]

Local authorities

1–039 In respect of local authorities as well, the 1980s marked a greatly increased awareness on the part of local authority officers and councillors of the potency of judicial review as both a challenge to their decisions and as a weapon to be employed by them against central government. As a result, relationships between central and local government altered, with increased emphasis being given to the definition of legal powers and duties, and adjudication given greater prominence alongside administrative bargaining and negotiation as a method of dispute resolution.[94] In short, "the courts and the legal process have become, seemingly, a necessary part of the political debate and decision-making".[95] In some authorities, this has involved a trend towards greater formality in decision-making, particularly in committees, where councillors and officers are anxious to be able to demonstrate, should a decision be challenged, that all and only relevant factors were considered.[96] The opinions of independent counsel are now frequently sought and some concern has been expressed that "these can supplant the decision-making powers of an elected body unless there are members with the confidence and political will to resist".[97]

---

[93] See Sunkin and Le Sueur, (1991) 44 C.L.P. 161, p. 171. There seems to have been an 'absorption of the prospect of legal challenge into ... departments' political and administrative bloodstream': A. Barker, 'The Impact of Judicial Review: Perspectives from Whitehall and the Courts' [1996] P.L. 612, 613. During the mid-1990s, government ministers also became more ready publicly to criticise unfavourable judgments in a confrontational manner, aided by a partisan press: see A.P. Le Sueur, 'The Judicial Review Debate: From Partnership to Friction' (1996) 31 *Government and Opposition* 8; Diana Woodhouse, 'Politicians and Judges: A Conflict of Interest' (1996) 49 Parl. Aff. 423 and, *In Pursuit of Good Administration: Ministers, Civil Servants and Judges* (1997); and Robert Stevens, 'Judges, Politics, Politicians and the Confusing Role of the Judiciary', Chapter 11 in Keith Hawkins (ed.), *The Human Face of Law: Essays in Honour of Donald Harris* (1997).

[94] See M. Loughlin, *Local Government in the Modern State* (1986), pp. 193–201. See also: Martin Loughlin, *Legality and Locality: the Role of Law in Central Government Relations* (1996); Davina Cooper, 'Institutional Illegality and Disobedience–Local Government Narratives' (1996) 16 O.J.L.S. 255.

[95] Bridges *et al.*, *op. cit.*, n. 88 above, p. 3.

[96] Bridges *et al.*, *op. cit.*, n. 88 above, p. 92. They comment that members are 'deluged with paper on all aspects of the subject' under consideration and matters previously implicitly understood are now recorded.

[97] Bridges *et al.*, *op. cit.* n. 88 above, p. 99.

The extent to which this picture is commonplace is unclear. The **1–040** trends described are likely to be strongest in those authorities with recent and direct experience of a judicial review challenge to a significant decision in an important policy area. The impact of judicial review is also likely to be concentrated in the upper echelons of an organisation. For case workers and line bureaucrats, even those working in policy areas with a history of judicial review challenge, law in general and the principles of judicial review in particular, may still find little place in administrative culture and decision-making.[98]

Evaluation

An evaluation of the practical impact of judicial review on the quality **1–041** of government decisions is still constrained by the limited empirical research in the field. The whole picture is likely to be a patchy one. In some contexts, the principles of judicial review may play a role in promoting high standards of public administration[99] but this will happen routinely only where officials and politicians invest resources in translating and transposing the words handed down in judgments to their own day-to-day administrative practices and ethos. The judges, too, have an important role to play. If the spirit of their judgments is to be embraced they need to show sensitivity to the tasks of officials in particular contexts[1] and a willingness to articulate intelligible and relatively precise principles. The abandonment of the many nice technical distinctions which have for many years beset judicial review will also assist the process.

---

[98] See the empirical research of Ian Loveland on the implementation by local authorities of the homeless persons legislation: 'Housing Benefit: Administrative Law and Administrative Practice' (1988) 66 Pub. Admin. 57 and 'Administrative Law, Administrative Processes, and the Housing of Homeless Persons: A View from the Sharp End' [1991] Jnl. Soc. Welfare and Fam. Law 4. He notes in the former that in one of the authorities studied 'decision-making processes are entirely uninformed by explicit reference to administrative law as such. Mention of the *Wednesbury* principles draws a blank stare from most officers' (p. 73).

[99] See David Feldman, 'Judicial Review: A Way of Controlling Government?' (1988) 66 Pub. Admin. 21. *Cf.* Report of Justice/All Souls Review of Administrative Law in the UK, *Administrative Justice: Some Necessary Reforms* (1988), Chap. 2 on the need for codes setting out in a positive form principles of good administration.

[1] Lord Donaldson M.R. has spoken in several judgments of the need to establish a partnership between the courts and the administration 'based on a common aim, namely the maintenance of the highest standards of public administration': see *R. v. Lancashire C.C., ex p. Huddleston* [1986] 2 All E. R. 941, 945; also *R. v. Monopolies and Mergers Commission, ex p. Argyll Group plc* [1986] 1 W.L.R. 763. 774.

In other contexts the effect of judicial review on the quality of decision-making in public authorities may be less obvious. The anticipation of legal challenge may lead to greater formalism in decision-making and increased bureaucratisation.[2]

Judicial review and political action

1–042 Even before the procedural reforms of 1979, litigation had for many years been employed by individuals and groups as a way of seeking change in government policy.[3] From the 1970s onwards a number of pressure groups consciously adopted "test case strategies" in which judicial review, in conjunction with other forms of legal proceedings[4] and together with conventional forms of political action, was used to seek change in government policy and methods of decision-making. Test cases by way of judicial review caused change in areas including entitlement to welfare benefits, prisoners' rights and immigration. Success, however, was often temporary, limited and indirect: judicial review generated publicity and was capable of inflicting political embarrassment on ministers. The response of government, however, was often quickly to nullify or sidestep the effects of an unpalatable judicial decision by enacting primary legislation or amending delegated legislation. Sometimes administrative practices were changed, but judicial review had limited success in bringing about significant and lasting change in substantive government policy.

THE CHAPTERS WHICH FOLLOW IN PART 1

1–043 The Chapters which follow this one seek to examine some of the central issues in judicial review. Section 31(3) of the Supreme Court Act 1981 purports to limit the right to apply for judicial review to those people who have "a sufficient interest in the matter to which the application relates". Chapter 2 charts the changing attitude of the courts to this prerequisite and concludes that few people today will be denied access to the courts because they lack such standing.

---

[2] See further Bridges *et al., op. cit.* n. 88 above, Chap. 8. See further G. Richardson and M. Sunkin, 'Judicial Review: Questions of Impact' [1996] P.L. 79 and Simon James, 'The Political and Administrative Consequences of Judicial Review' (1996) 74 Pub. Admin. 613.

[3] See C. Harlow and R. Rawlings, *Pressure Through Law* (1992); R. Rawlings, 'Litigation as Political Action' in I. Loveland (ed.), *A Special Relationship? American Influences on Public Law in the United Kingdom* (1995).

[4] Including tribunals, litigation on rights conferred by European Community law and proceedings under the European Convention on Human Rights.

Chapter 3 then poses the questions who and what decisions are **1–044**
subject to challenge by way of judicial review. The answers
demonstrate both the virtues and the infelicities that characterise the
development of the judicial review case law. On the positive side, the
courts have been adept at sweeping away anachronistic technicalities
in the law which once demarcated which types of governmental
decisions were amenable to challenge — and erecting, in their place, a
broad approach based on whether or not a public function is being
carried out by the decision-maker.[5] The negative side has been the
common law's failure to state with clarity the procedural aspect of the
public/private divide.[6] The courts have correctly recognised that the
Order 53 procedure[7] creates protections for public authorities against
frivolous or misconceived litigation. The general policy of the law is
therefore to require public law litigation to be initiated and conducted
according to the rules of Order 53 rather than those that apply to
general civil proceedings. The search for a precise and certain way of
formulating such a rule of "procedural exclusivity" proved for many
years to be elusive and, alas, a great deal of time and money has been
spent on procedural wrangling.

Finally, in this Part of the book, Chapter 4 examines the difficult
concept of jurisdictional error. In the past, the doctrine of *ultra vires*
was widely used to explain the constitutional function of judicial
review: the court struck down decisions of bodies exercising public
functions which those bodies had no power to make. We shall need
therefore to consider both the nature of the court's own power and
that of the bodies which it supervises.

---

[5] See para. 3–021.

[6] See para. 3–046.

[7] Now contained in Civil Procedure Rules 1999, Sched. 1. For detailed discussion, see
Chap. 14. below.

CHAPTER 2

WHO MAY BRING PROCEEDINGS?

Locus Standi

INTRODUCTION

This Chapter considers the issue of standing, that is whether an **2–001** applicant's interests have been sufficiently affected by the decision which he seeks to challenge. In the absence of standing, or *locus standi*, the court has no jurisdiction to exercise its supervisory power over the impugned action of a public body. How issues of standing are decided determines who has access to justice and it therefore has a constitutional significance. At its heart is the question whether it can ever be right, as a matter of principle, for a person with an otherwise meritorious challenge to the validity of a public body's action to be turned away by the court on the ground that his rights or interests are not sufficiently affected by the impugned decision? To put this another way, are there some decisions of public bodies, the legality of which is otherwise justiciable, but in respect of which no one person has been sufficiently affected to enable a legal challenge to be made? To answer yes to these questions presupposes that the primary function of the court's supervisory jurisdiction is to redress individual grievances, rather than that judicial review is concerned, more broadly, with the maintenance of the rule of law. In recent years there has been a marked trend towards the court approaching standing issues in a more flexible and liberal way than once was the case.

THE REASON FOR HAVING RULES OF STANDING

All developed legal systems have had to face the problem of resolving **2–002** the conflict between two aspects of the public interest—the desirability of encouraging individual citizens to participate actively in the enforcement of the law, and the undesirability of encouraging the professional litigant and the meddlesome interloper invoking the

29

jurisdiction of the courts in matters in which he is not concerned.[1] The conflict has been resolved by developing principles which determine who is entitled to bring proceedings; that is who has *locus standi* or standing to bring proceedings. If those principles are satisfactory they should only prevent a litigant who has no legitimate reason for bringing proceedings from doing so.

2–003   A number of arguments are traditionally advanced for not allowing totally unrestricted access to the court to any member of the public for the purpose of challenging an administrative action of which he does not approve. First, it would be unwise to assume that the effect of the doctrine of precedent and the power of the courts to award costs, even on an idemnity basis, will sufficiently deter unmeritorious challenges. Secondly, the courts' resources should not be dissipated by the need to provide a forum for frivolous proceedings. Thirdly, the proper function of central and local government and other public bodies should not be disrupted unnecessarily to the disadvantage of other members of the public by having to contest proceedings. Fourthly, there is something to be said for the courts, as a matter of prudence, reserving their power to interfere with the workings of public bodies to those occasions when there is an application before them by someone who has been adversely affected by the unlawful conduct of which complaint is made. Fifthly, particularly in relation to administrative action which can affect sections of the public, it is important that the proceedings should be brought by a person who, because he is sufficiently interested in the outcome of the proceedings or otherwise, is in a position to ensure that full argument in favour of the remedy which is sought is deployed before the court. Sixthly, it is important that the courts confine themselves to their correct constitutional role, and do not become involved in determining issues which are not justiciable by giving unlimited access to the courts.[2]

2–004   There are substantial arguments in favour of adopting a generous approach to standing. This is particularly true in judicial review proceedings since here it is frequently important, in the interests of the public generally, that the law should be enforced. The policy should

---

[1] How serious this conflict actually is, is open to question. As Professor K.F. Scott has written, 'The idle and whimsical plaintiff, a litigant who litigates for a lark, is a spectre which haunts the legal literature, not the courtroom': 'Standing in the Supreme Court—A Functional Analysis' (1973) 86 Harv. L.R. 645.

[2] See further Sir Konrad Schiemann, 'Locus Standi', [1990] P.L. 342 and his judgment in *R. v. Secretary of State for the Environment, ex p. Rose Theatre Trust Ltd* [1990] 1 Q.B. 504; L. Bridges, M. Sunkin and G. Mészáros, *Judicial Review in Perspective* (revised ed., 1995), contains an interesting analysis of applicants for judicial review. Applications were made in 84–88 per cent of cases by individuals; of the remainder 50–60 per cent are by companies, 6 per cent by central government, 14–35 per cent by local authorities and only 1–2 per cent by non-governmental organisations (see pp. 34–35).

therefore be to encourage and not discourage public-spirited individuals and groups, even though they are not directly affected by the action which is being taken, to challenge unlawful administrative action. Other safeguards, besides restrictive rules as to standing, exist to protect the courts and administrators from unmeritorious challenges. (In the case of judicial review there is the requirement that applicants obtain permission from the court and in proceedings without that requirement there is the ability to apply to have the proceedings struck out if there is no cause of action or the proceedings are an abuse of the court.) Where there are strict rules as to standing there is always the risk that no one will be in a position to bring proceedings to test the lawfulness of administrative action of obvious illegality or questionable legality. It is hardly desirable that a situation should exist where because all the public are equally affected no one is in a position to bring proceedings. The fears that are sometimes voiced of the courts being overwhelmed by a flood of frivolous actions are unsupported by any evidence of this happening in practice. The costs of litigation are now so heavy that it is only the most determined vexatious litigant who will indulge in legal proceedings which are without merit. The arguments in favour of a restrictive approach to standing nearly always confuse the question of the merits of the litigation with the question of who should be entitled to bring the proceedings. If there is a satisfactory mechanism for dealing with unmeritorious or frivolous claims most of the arguments for a restrictive approach fall away.

THE HIGH COURT'S JURISDICTION

The issue of whether an applicant has sufficient interest in the matter to which the application relates goes to the court's jurisdiction to entertain the application for judicial review.[3] The respondent may not therefore merely agree to the applicant having standing, as the parties are not entitled to confer jurisdiction, which the court may not have, by consent.[4] This said, the broad test of sufficient interest creates considerable scope for differing judgments on the same facts as to whether an applicant has standing.[5]

2–005

---

[3] *R. v. Secretary of State for Social Services, ex p. Child Poverty Action Group* [1990] 2 Q.B. 540; *R. v. Secretary of State for Foreign and Commonwealth Affairs, ex p. World Development Movement Ltd* [1995] 1 W.L.R. 386 (noted by P. Cane, "Standing up for the Public" [1995] P.L. 276).

[4] *R. v. Secretary of State for Social Services, ex p. Child Poverty Action Group* [1990] 2 Q.B. 540.

[5] *e.g.* in *Inland Revenue Commissioners v. National Federation for the Self-Employed and Small Business Ltd* [1982] A.C. 617, Lord Diplock, dissenting on the issue, held that the pressure group had standing; and in *Equal Opportunities Commission v. Secretary of*

When and how is standing a relevant issue?

2–006 In English law, the jurisdictional requirement of a "sufficient interest" for an applicant to apply for judicial review is stipulated by section 31(3) of the Supreme Court Act 1981 and, in almost identical terms, by RSC, Ord. 53, rule 3.[6] These provisions refer expressly to the court refusing permission or leave unless it considers that the applicant has standing.[7] In the *National Federation* case, however, the House of Lords held that except in an obvious case, questions as to sufficient interest ought not to be dealt with as a preliminary issue at the permission stage but should be postponed until the full hearing of the application.[8] Given that an applicant's sufficient interest (or lack of it) can usually only be determined by considering the whole legal and factual matrix of the case, it may well be desirable to consider standing at this later stage. It has, however, compounded a confusion as to the relevance of standing. Suggestions have been made that the degree of "interest" required by an applicant will depend on the remedy which is claimed, *e.g.* a greater degree of interest is needed for an order of mandamus than for a declaration, but it is argued below that this approach is misconceived and that the test of standing is the same irrespective of the remedy which is claimed.[9] It therefore follows that if standing has any role to play at the full hearing of a judicial review application, it is confined to whether the court has jurisdiction to entertain the application at all. Standing should have no relevance to questions as to the grant or refusal of particular forms of remedy.

The relevance of the pre-1978 authorities

2–007 When, in 1978, the new RSC, Ord. 53 procedure for judicial review was introduced[10] it included for the first time a statutory test of standing of general application. A new general test was highly desirable since, up to 1978 the courts had not managed to clarify what was the test of standing in the case of any of the principal prerogative orders which were still in current use (*i.e.* certiorari, prohibition and

---

State for Employment [1995] 1 A.C. 1 Lord Jauncey dissented on the issue whether the E.O.C. had standing.

[6] See para. 2–009, below. RSC, Ord. 53 is now a Schedule to the Civil Procedure Rules.

[7] On the permission stage more generally, see para. 14–003.

[8] See further para. 2–015 below. An empirical study of the leave stage has shown that it is extremely rare for leave to be refused on the sole ground that an applicant lacks standing: see A.P. Le Sueur and M. Sunkin. 'Applications for Judicial Review: The Requirement of Leave' [1992] P.L. 102.

[9] See further para. 2–017, below.

[10] See further para. 13–057.

mandamus).[11] Different tests were applied depending on the order which was sought and those tests were in turn different from those which applied in private law proceedings for an injunction or a declaration.

One of the objects of the new test was to save the courts from **2–008** having to reconcile the multiplicity of often conflicting authorities which governed the principles of *locus standi* under the previous procedure for obtaining the prerogative orders. However the pre-1978 authorities should not always be ignored as being merely of historic interest. First of all, it can be stated with confidence that as the reforms introduced in 1978 were intended to liberalise the procedure for obtaining the prerogative orders, the approach to standing on an application for judicial review is now at least as generous to the applicant as that which previously existed. So, if the pre-1978 authorities indicate that an appellant would have standing, this is almost certainly still the position. Then the pre-1978 authorities can provide a useful embarkation point from which to set out to discover the principles which should now apply. This can be valuable where the present requirements of standing are unclear because the new test prescribed by the statute and the Rules is not precise and does no more than, by using words different from those current prior to 1978, signal that a fresh approach should be adopted by the courts.[12] For example, some of the old cases are of interest in so far as they indicate that prior to 1978 a very generous approach to standing was already being adopted. Thus proceedings could be brought even by "strangers" for an order of prohibition. In addition many of the pre-1978 judgments used language to describe what was required to establish standing which is identical to that which is still current in statutes which specify who is entitled to appeal against or make a statutory application to the High Court involving administrative action, under a specific procedure laid down by legislation. The old authorities are still of value in indicating what those statutes require in order to establish standing. However in general on an application for judicial review, the old authorities provide no assistance and can be misleading. For example, the old authorities indicate that the test varied depending on which prerogative order or area of the law was involved (the standard appeared to be higher if the application for the prerogative order related to a criminal cause or matter than if the

---

[11] On the prerogative orders, see paras 15-003–15-015.
[12] The Law Commission explained the use of the new test of sufficient interest (Cmnd. 6407 (1976), para. 48) by saying: '... any attempt to define in precise terms the nature of the standing required would run the risk of imposing an undesirable rigidity ... what is needed is a formula which allows for further development of the requirement of standing by the courts having regard to the relief which is sought.'

application related to a planning matter).[13] This, it is suggested later, should no longer be the position.[14]

THE REQUIREMENT OF SUFFICIENT INTEREST

2–009   Rules 3(1) and 3(7) of RSC, Order 53 are in the following terms:

"(1) No application for judicial review shall be made unless the permission of the Court has been obtained in accordance with this rule. . ..

(7) The Court shall not grant permission unless it considers that the applicant has a sufficient interest in the matter to which the application relates."

Section 31(3) of the Supreme Court Act 1981 restates these provisions in similar words:

"(3) No application for judicial review shall be made unless the leave of the court has been obtained in accordance with the Rules of Court; and the court shall not grant leave to make such an application unless it considers that the applicant has a sufficient interest in the matter to which the application relates."

2–010   The language of Order 53 and section 31(3) make it clear that the statutory requirement that the applicant has a "sufficient interest" is a threshold test of standing which applies when the applicant is seeking permission to apply. If the applicant has an insufficient interest at that stage, the court is prohibited from granting permission. Order 53 and section 31(3) do not contain any express guidance as to when permission should, as opposed to should not, be granted.[15] However it is reasonably obvious that it is intended that if the applicant has what the courts regard as being sufficient interest leave cannot be refused on the ground of lack of standing alone. Nonetheless the extent of the applicant's interest remains a factor which can play a part in influencing a court as to whether or not to grant permission to a

---

[13] Such a distinction could be justified perfectly logically because in criminal proceedings there are normally only two parties, the prosecutor and the defendant, whereas planning procedures under the planning legislation allow for generous representation before the inquiry which the legislation normally contemplated would precede a decision on an appeal.

[14] See para. 2–017.

[15] This court is in contrast with RSC, Ord. 53, r.1(2) and s. 31(2) which require the court when considering whether to grant declaratory or injunctive relief to have regard to the persons and bodies *against* whom relief may be granted by prerogative orders.

particular applicant. If, for example, there were to be more than one applicant who was wishing to raise the same issue at the same time, the court would naturally be inclined to give preference to the applicant who has the more substantial interest in the outcome of the proceedings and might only give leave to that applicant or adjourn the application of the applicant with the lesser interest pending the outcome of the other application.

The requirement of "sufficient interest" was intended to provide a **2–011** wholly new test although in some of the earlier authorities similar terms were used to indicate what would suffice.[16] As the words of Order 53, rule 3(7) and section 31(3) do not provide any guidance as to what will or will not be a "sufficient interest", the courts are left to set the parameters of what does and does not constitute a "sufficient interest" and to decide whether to apply different standards depending upon the precise remedy which is being claimed. Rule 3(7) and section 31(3) only apply expressly to the grant of permission. They do not address the question as to whether standing can play any, and if so what, part in determining if the applicant should be granted a remedy at the conclusion of the hearing.

It is clear that the term "sufficient interest" is being given a generous **2–012** interpretation by the courts. They will assess the extent of the applicant's interest against all the factual and legal circumstances of the application. If the administrative action which the applicant wishes to challenge interferes directly with the applicant's personal or public rights or has adverse financial consequences for him then this will be an obvious case in which he will have standing. The statute which governs the administrative action which is the subject of the application may expressly or impliedly indicate that the applicant has an interest in the subject matter of the application. Thus if the statute gives the applicant the right to make representations before the decision is reached this will be a strong indication that he has standing to challenge the decision when it is made. There are however many less obvious situations where an applicant can qualify as having sufficient interest. In fact the range of situations in which an applicant will have the necessary interest are so vast it is impossible to list them all. However, by way of example, parents and governors have sufficient interest in the proposed closure or reorganisation of a school[17]; potential contractors may seek review of restrictive clauses in

---

[16] For example, in *R. v. Customs and Excise Commissioners, ex p. Cooke and Stevenson* [1970] 1 All E.R. 1068 Lord Parker C.J. had referred to the need for a sufficient interest. The test precribed by the Charities Act 1993 is 'persons interested in the charity' and there is a helpful examination of the test by Nicholls L.J. in *Re Hampton Fuel Allotment Charity* [1989] Ch. 484, 493H–494H.

[17] See, *e.g. R. v. Secretary of State for Education and Science, ex p. Threapleton* [1988] C.O.D. 102 and *R. v. Gwent C.C., ex p. Bryant* [1988] C.O.D. 19.

local authority contracts[18]; a company in liquidation and its creditors can challenge the decision of the Registrar of Companies to register a bank charge[19]; members of a union can challenge a directive to their employers[20]; and an unsuccessful applicant for planning permission has been held able to challenge the decision to grant permission to another developer.[21]

The National Federation of Self-Employed case

2–013 The wording of Order 53, rule 3(7), and section 31(3) was subject to close scrutiny by the House of Lords in *Inland Revenue Commissioners v. National Federation of Self-Employed and Small Businesses Ltd.*[22] The speeches adopt a radically different approach to the whole question of *locus standi* from that which had applied prior to 1977. However the emphasis in all the speeches was not the same and the case does not remove all the difficulties which are inherent in determining what are the principles which should govern the question of standing on an application for judicial review. The approach of the House of Lords does however enable the court, except in exceptional circumstances, to investigate any serious breach of public duty notwithstanding an applicant's alleged lack of standing.

2–014 The *National Federation* case provides a good illustration of the type of situation in which issues as to standing can arise. The Federation, a limited company, represented members of the public who were either self-employed or ran small businesses. The Federation was concerned about an arrangement which had been reached between the Inland Revenue and employers of some 6,000 casual workers in Fleet Street and their union. The arrangement involved casual workers ceasing the practice of evading paying tax by using false names, such as Mickey Mouse, and, in return, the Revenue not conducting investigations into the tax lost as a result of the practice in previous years. The Federation's

---

[18] *R. v. Enfield L.B.C., ex p. Unwin (Roydon) Ltd* [1989] C.O.D. 466 but *cf. R. v. Avon C.C., ex p. Terry Adams Ltd* [1993] C.O.D. 35 (a tenderer whose tender for a waste disposal contract fell to be invalidated automatically had no interest in the grant of a contract to another tenderer whose tender was also liable to be invalidated) and (CA) *The Times*, January 20, 1994.

[19] *R. v. Registrar of Companies, ex p. Esal (Commodities) Ltd* [1986] Q.B. 1114.

[20] *R. v. Secretary of State for the Home Department, ex p. Brind* [1991] 2 A.C. 696.

[21] *R. v. St Edmundsbury B.C., ex p. Investors in Industry Commercial Properties* [1985] 1 W.L.R. 1168 and *Save Britain's Heritage v. Number One Poultry* [1991] 1 W.L.R. 153.

[22] [1982] A.C. 617. The effect of the decision is happily described by Sir William Wade Q.C. and C.F. Forsyth in *Administrative Law* (7th ed., 1994) p. 709 as being 'to crystallise the elements of a generous and public orientated doctrine of standing which had previously been sporadic and uncoordinated'. For a helpful analysis of the case see P. Cane, 'Standing, Legality and the Limits of Public Law' [1981] P.L. 322.

complaint was that the Revenue was treating the casual workers differently from the way in which other taxpayers guilty of tax evasion were treated. It claimed a declaration that the Revenue had acted unlawfully in granting this "amnesty" and an order of mandamus directing the Revenue to assess and collect the income tax due from the casual workers for the previous years. In the Divisional Court the question of the Federation's *locus standi* was taken as a preliminary issue. It was held that the Federation did not have sufficient interest to support their application and the application was dismissed. The Federation's appeal to the Court of Appeal was allowed and the Revenue then successfully appealed to the House of Lords.

The first important message to be derived from the decision of the **2–015** House of Lords is that, except in an obvious case, questions as to standing should not be dealt with at the permission to apply stage. This is an important safeguard against the adoption of a too restrictive approach to access by the courts. The message follows from the House of Lords conclusion that it was unfortunate that the question of *locus standi* had been taken as a preliminary issue at first instance. Their Lordships made clear that while in obvious cases it was appropriate at the permission stage for a court to find that an applicant had no sufficient interest to support his application and to refuse leave, this did not apply to the *National Federation* case where the question of sufficient interest had to be considered together with the legal and factual context of the application, which included the whole question of the statutory duties of the Revenue and the alleged breach of those duties. The House of Lords investigated the merits of the application as fully as was possible on the information which was before them and only dismissed the application having done so. It is important to note that all members of the House were treating the sufficiency of the Federation's interest in the subject matter of the application as being a factor which it was relevant to take into account in deciding both the threshold issue of whether permission should be granted and the final decision as to whether relief could be granted. If it was a clear case the question of standing would be disposed of at the permission stage. Otherwise the issue should be dealt with at the hearing. In deciding whether it was a clear case one had to take into account the merits. This means that at the final stage the question of *locus standi* is inevitably going to be absorbed into the question of whether, as a matter of discretion, relief should be granted. Lord Wilberforce (with whose speech Lords Fraser and Roskill agreed) pointed out that except in the "simple" case "the question of sufficient interest cannot ... be considered in the abstract, or as an isolated point: it must be taken together with legal and factual context."[23]

---

[23] Lord Diplock described r.3(5) as raising—'[a] threshold question in the sense that the court must direct its mind to it and form prima facie view about it on the material

2–016   Their Lordships accepted that the purpose of the procedure under Order 53 was to avoid the old technical rules which applied to the prerogative orders prior to its introduction in 1977.[24] Lord Diplock drew attention to the fact that the draughtsman of the Order "avoided using the expression 'a person aggrieved', although it lay ready to his hand. He chose instead to get away from any formula that might be thought to have acquired, through judicial exposition, a particular meaning as a term of legal art."[25] The new procedure was intended to be and is in fact "more flexible than that which it supersedes".[26] An example of the difference in approach of the court at leave stays and at the full hearing is provided by the case of *R. v. Legal Aid Board, ex p. Bateman.*[27] The case arose out of Miss Bateman's attempt to increase the costs payable to her solicitor by the legal aid authorities for acting on her behalf in litigation. The solicitor had exhausted his statutory remedies without success. Miss Bateman then made an application for judicial review of the final decision of the Board. Leave (now "permission") to apply for judicial review was granted and an application to set aside leave failed on the ground that the question of standing should be considered at the substantive hearing together with the merits. Although the application failed on the merits, the Divisional Court also decided she lacked the necessary standing. Miss Bateman was not personally affected by the Board's decision and she was seeking on legal aid to advance her solicitors' cause. Nolan L.J. accepted her interest in order to be sufficient need not be financial, but "her feelings of gratitude and sympathy" did not "afford any sufficient

---

that is available at the first stage. The prima facie view so formed, if favourable to the applicant, may alter on further consideration in the light of further evidence that may be before the court at the second stage, the hearing of the application ... itself.' He added (at 643–64): The whole purpose of requiring that leave [now permission] should first be obtained to make the application for judicial review would be defeated if the court were to go into the matter (that is of *locus standi*) in any depth at that stage. If, on a quick perusal of the material then available, the court thinks that it discloses what might on further consideration turn out to be an arguable case in favour of granting to the applicant the relief claimed, it ought in the exercise of a judicial discretion to give him leave to apply for that relief. The discretion the court is exercising at that stage is not the same as that which it is called on to exercise when all the evidence is in and the matter has been fully argued at the hearing of the application.' See also Lord Roskill at 656D–E, 662E–G.

[24] Lord Wilberforce, at 631A.

[25] At 642D.

[26] Lord Scarman at 647H. Flexibility is illustrated by the decision in *R. v. Secretary of State for Social Services, ex p. CPAG and GLC, The Times,* August 16, 1984 in which the CPAG were regarded as having standing but not the Greater London Council (a local authority), who could only argue that some of their rate payers would be affected by the decision. In the Court of Appeal the point was left open: *The Times,* August 8, 1985.

[27] [1992] 1 W.L.R. 711.

justification for her, either in her own interest, or in the public interest, to enter the lists on their behalf... her attempt to intervene is at best quixotic and cannot be upheld".

The relevance of the relief claimed

It is contended that the test of sufficient interest is intended to be the same irrespective of the remedy which is claimed on the application for judicial review. This is contrary to the views expressed by Lord Wilberforce and possibly those of Lord Scarman in the *National Federation* case.[28] However it would be difficult in practice to apply different principles of standing to different remedies at the permission stage. This is because applicants tend to include all possible remedies in an application for permission and usually it is only after the hearing, often after judgment, that an applicant decides the remedy which he will ask the court to grant. It would also be inconsistent with the intended comprehensive nature of the procedure of judicial review to have to apply different tests of standing for the different remedies. There is no binding authority in which a court is recorded as being prepared to grant permission to apply for one remedy rather than another on an application for permission and there appears to be no enthusiasm to revive the technical distinctions between different remedies which were drawn in some of the cases prior to 1978.

2–017

If Lords Wilberforce and Scarman were referring to the end of the hearing, then their views are perfectly acceptable since when it comes to deciding in its discretion whether to grant relief, a court is going to be more hesitant in some situations in granting, for example, an order of mandamus or an injunction, the disobedience of which can amount to contempt, than a declaration.[29] At this stage of the hearing the extent of the interest of the applicant is a factor to be considered when deciding what, if any, relief to grant. A good illustration of this is provided by *R. v. Felixstowe JJ., ex p. Leigh*.[30] In that case it was held

2–018

---

[28] 'The fact that the same words used to cover all forms of remedy allowed by the rule does not mean that the test is the same in all cases'. It was, however, not a 'technical rule ... but a rule of commonsense, reflecting the different character of the relief asked for.' Lord Scarman stressed that 'the applicant's interest has to be judged in relation to the subject matter of his application' and added that 'this relationship has always been of importance in the law. It is well illustrated by the history of the development of the prerogative writs, notably the difference of approach to mandamus and certiorari, and it remains a factor of importance in the exercise of discretion today' (at 648E). It is not clear to what stage of the proceedings these statements referred.

[29] See Zamir and Woolf, *The Declaratory Judgment* (2nd ed., 1993), paras 5–066 *et seq.* as to the importance of the discretionary nature of a declaratory relief.

[30] [1987] Q.B. 582.

after the full hearing that a journalist, who had not been present at the hearing, had sufficient standing under Order 53, rule 3(7), to claim a declaration that a policy of not disclosing names of Justices who had heard certain types of case was contrary to public interest and unlawful. On the other hand he was refused an order of mandamus, ordering the court to reveal the names of the justices who had heard a particular case: the applicant was sufficiently interested in the point of principle but not in what had happened in the particular case which had given rise to the application.[31]

The broad and flexible approach

2–019 As Lord Roskill in the *National Federation* case pointed out, the phrase "sufficient interest" was selected by the Rules Committee of the Supreme Court in 1977 "as one which could sufficiently embrace all classes of those who might apply and yet permit sufficient flexibility in any particular case to determine whether or not 'sufficient interest' was in fact shown."[32] This is precisely the approach which has been adopted in the vast majority of the cases which have come before the courts since that time. Indeed it is difficult to find any case where an applicant has been refused relief on the grounds that he has no *locus standi* where relief would have been granted but for his lack of *locus standi*. In the *National Federation* case itself the applicants were entitled to be accorded standing in order to obtain permission to apply for judicial review but failed on the merits.[33]

2–020 "Sufficient interest" should therefore be regarded as being an extremely flexible test of standing.[34] The more important the issue and the stronger the merits of the application, the more ready will the courts be to grant permission notwithstanding the limited personal involvement of the applicant; thus a reporter and the National Union of Journalists have been regarded as having sufficient interest to apply

---

[31] In the only judgment, Watkins L.J. indicated that the court was exercising its 'undoubted discretion ... primarily in its factual context'. While declining to decide whether a stricter test applied to applications for mandamus than other remedies, he indicated that he was 'inclined to think it does not'. See P. Cane, 'Statutes, Standing and Representation' [1990] P.L. 307.

[32] At 658B. In keeping with the flexible approach to standing the courts adopt a relaxed attitude to errors. See, *e.g. R. v. Life Assurance and Unit Trust Regulatory Organisation, ex p. Ross* [1993] 1 Q.B. 17 at 45B. But see *R. v. Hereford and Worcester C.C., ex p. Smith* [1994] C.O.D. 129 where an appropriate body had not intervened and relief was inappropriate.

[33] [1982] A.C. 617 at 664.

[34] There has been a similar liberalisation of the requirements as to standing in other parts of the Commonwealth: see G.L. Perris. 'The Doctrine of Locus Standi in Commonwealth Administrative Law' [1983] P.L. 342.

for judicial review to quash an order prohibiting the publication of a report of committal proceedings made by magistrates under the Contempt of Court Act 1981.[35] The prohibition interfered with the freedom of the press. A person whose telephone was tapped, but not someone who had telephoned him, can seek judicial review of a possible warrant issued by the Secretary of State authorising the interception of communications.[36] In *R. v. Department of Transport, ex p. Presvac Engineering Ltd*,[37] the Court of Appeal considered that Presvac had *locus standi* to apply for judicial review in relation to the grant by the Department of a certificate to a competitor company of Presvac that valves manufactured by that company were acceptable for the purposes of Merchant Shipping Regulations 1984.[38] A head of chambers has standing to make an application to challenge the decision of the Bar Council not to proceed with an investigation of a member of chambers for whom he had been responsible.[39]

In the case of one taxpayer seeking to become involved in the affairs of another taxpayer normally the applicant would rarely have sufficient merit to justify the application being made. This is because of the statutory structure under which the Commissioners operate which requires them to treat information obtained by them from a taxpayer as confidential. However, if any case disclosed serious wrongdoing by the Revenue then one taxpayer is entitled to intervene **2–021**

---

[35] *R. v. Horsham JJ., ex p. Farquharson* [1982] Q.B. 762.

[36] *R. v. Secretary of State for the Home Department, ex p. Ruddock* [1987] 1 W.L.R. 1482. Taylor J. suggested that if those who telephoned the person to whom the warrant related could apply this would mean that if a terrorist's telephone was tapped the issue of the warrant could be attacked on an application for judicial review by 'his butcher, his baker and whichever other innocents were intercepted on his line'. The judge regarded the duty not to issue an unlawful warrant as being owed to the person whose telephone was the subject of the warrant alone so that only that person alone could make the application. However it is suggested this is too narrow an approach to be applied generally. In many situations it could be the person who is making the call to the tapped phone whose need for privacy is the greater.

[37] (1992) 4 Admin. L.R. 121; see also *R. v. Att.-Gen., ex p. ICI* [1985] 1 C.M.L.R. 588; *R. v. Department of Social Security, ex p. Overdrive Credit Card Ltd* [1991] 1 W.L.R. at 641.

[38] (1992) 4 Admin. L.R. 121. In his judgment Purchas L.J. said: I see nothing in these speeches' (in the *National Federation* case) 'to indicate that a person who is directly and financially affected by the unlawful or erroneous performance by a public authority of its statutory functions cannot as a general rule be said to qualify as having a sufficient interest. The emphasis is on the subject matter of the alleged misfeasance, not upon the possible differential effects upon various people affected by the misfeasance.' In *R. v. International Stock Exchange, ex p. Else* [1993] Q.B. 534, Sir Thomas Bingham M.R. considered that investors in a company could not challenge the cancellation of a company's registration by relying on a European directive, but recognised the possibility of their being able to do so under domestic law.

[39] *R. v. General Council of the Bar, ex p. Percival* [1991] 1 Q.B. 212, 230–231.

in the affairs of another taxpayer.[40] Thus in determining the question of standing both the importance of the issue involved and the framework in which the administrative role is performed is of importance.

The scope of the duty or the statutory right to complain test

2–022   The *National Federation* case involved an application for mandamus of an alleged failure by the Revenue to perform a duty. It was probably because of this that their Lordships stressed the importance, in determining issues of standing, of whether the statutory language created a duty and whether the applicant was within the scope or ambit of that duty.[41] Lord Frazer considered that one should "look at the statute under which the duty arises and see whether it gives any express or implied right to persons in the position of the applicant to complain of the alleged unlawful act or omission."[42] It is suggested that this is an unhelpful approach except in a limited class of cases where the applicant's interest would in any event be obvious. An example of this class of case is where the statute gives the body seeking to make the application special responsibility in the field of activity to which the application relates. Thus in an application involving alleged sexual discrimination the Equal Opportunities

---

[40] Lord Roskill recognised that: 'It is possible to envisage a case where because of some grossly improper pressure or motive (the Revenue) have failed to perform their statutory duty as respects a particular taxpayer or class of taxpayer. In such a case ... judicial review might be available to other taxpayers. But it will require to be a most extreme case for ... having regard to the nature of the appellant's statutory duty and the degree of confidentiality enjoined by statute attaches to the performance ... in general it is not open to individual taxpayers or to a group of taxpayers to seek to interfere between the appellants and other taxpayers ... and ... the court should, by refusing relief by way of judicial review, firmly discourage such attempted interference by other taxpayers.' ([1982] A.C. 617, 662G–663B). *Cf. R. v. Att.-Gen., ex p. ICI* [1985] C.M.L.R. 588; where ICI was able to challenge an arrangement reached between the Revenue and competing chemical companies as a favourable petroleum tax regime.

[41] Lord Wilberforce, at [1982] A.C. 617, 631F–G. If the language of the statute is being considered in determining standing then again the approach should not be too restrictive. Thus under the Immigration Act 1971 the Home Secretary gives directions to the airline in respect of the removal of immigrants who are to be deported, but the deportee is entitled to challenge the directions since the directions were clearly of concern to the deportee.

[42] At 646B.

Commission would have standing.[43] However applications for judicial review are usually made in situations where the statute does not provide a remedy for the unlawful exercise of the statutory discretion or power which is being challenged. In those situations it is difficult, if not impossible, to apply satisfactorily the implied right to complain test which Lord Frazer suggested.

The standing of a representative body or a pressure group

Particular problems to do with standing may arise in cases where the applicant is a representative body (such as a resident's amenity group or trade union) or a campaigning pressure group. The first difficulty concerns the *capacity* of the body to commence legal proceedings. This is distinct from the issue of standing. In one case it was held that an unincorporated association had no legal personality and so could not apply for judicial review in its own name, even if each member of the association had standing to apply personally.[44] In its 1994 report, the Law Commission described this approach as unfortunate in principle and recommended that unincorporated associations should be permitted to make applications for judicial review in their own name through one or more of their members applying in a representative capacity where the court is satisfied that members of the applicant association have been, or would be, adversely affected or are raising an issue of public interest warranting judicial review, and that the members of the association are appropriate persons to bring that challenge.[45] This must surely be correct, especially given that the unincorporated status of a respondent has not been regarded as a bar to being subject to and defending judicial review proceedings.[46]

2–023

Other more general difficulties may arise to do with the standing of representative and pressure groups. Lord Wilberforce considered that a body which represents a group of applicants, such as the Federation of

2–024

---

[43] In the Court of Appeal in *R. v. Secretary of State for Employment, ex p. Equal Opportunities Commission* [1993] 1 W.L.R. 872, the majority of the Court took a different view from that expressed in the text, but in the House of Lords [1995] 1 A.C. 1 the judgment of Dillon L.J. was preferred and it was decided that the EOC had standing in view of its statutory responsibilities.

[44] *R. v. Darlington B.C., ex p. Association of Darlington Taxi Owners* [1994] C.O.D. 424; see also *Alwoodly Golf Club v. Leeds City Council* [1995] N.P.C. 149. Cf. *R. v. Tower Hamlets L.B.C., ex p. Tower Hamlets Combined Traders Association* [1994] C.O.D. 325 and *R. v. Traffic Commissioner for the North Western Traffic Area, ex p. BRAKE* [1996] C.O.D. 248 in which Turner J. disapproved *Darlington Taxi Owners* and refused to set aside leave to move for judicial review which had been granted to an unincorporated association the aim of which was to promote greater safety in the use of lorries on public roads.

[45] Law Com. No. 226, para. 5.41.

[46] See, *e.g. R. v. Panel on Takeovers and Mergers, ex p. Datafin plc* [1987] Q.B. 815.

the Self-Employed and Small Business Ltd, who are seeking to establish standing are in no better position than an individual, "since an aggregate of individuals, each of whom has no interest, cannot of itself have an interest".[47] In *R. v. Secretary of State for the Environment, ex p. Rose Theatre*,[48] Schiemann J. applied the same principle to a body of individuals who, because they were interested in preserving a site of historical theatrical remains from development, formed a company to challenge the failure of the minister to prevent the development. The company failed in its application on the merits but the judge carefully considered the question of standing before coming to the conclusion the company did not have standing. In his judgment Schiemann J. identified eight principles which were "not inconsistent" with the speeches in the *National Federation* case. Two of those principles were:

> "7. The fact that some thousands of people join together and assert that they have an interest does not create an interest if the individuals did not have an interest.
>
> 8. The fact that those without an interest incorporate themselves and give the company in its memorandum power to pursue a particular object does not give the company an interest."

2–025   No doubt there can be circumstances where both of these principles can be applied without producing undesirable results. However it would be wrong to regard them as being of general application. The simple act of incorporation may not improve the status of an applicant. There is no magic in the act of incorporation for public law purposes. However the fact that a group of persons combine to make an application may give them enhanced authority to speak on a subject on behalf of a section of the public. As a group or a company

---

[47] Lord Wilberforce at [1982] A.C. 617, 633D. In the USA a restrictive approach is adopted in relation to pressure groups being accorded standing. In *Lujan v. Defenders of Wildlife* (1992) 112 S.Ct. 2135 an action by wildlife conservation and other environmental groups challenging a decision to limit the application of the Endangered Species Act 1973 was dismissed for lack of standing. Justice Scalia said (at 2136) that the irreducible minimum of standing contains three elements: first, the plaintiff must have suffered an 'injury in fact'—an invasion of a legally-protected interest which is (a) concrete and particularised and (b) 'actual or imminent, not conjectural or hypothetical'. Secondly, there must be a causal connection between the injury and the conduct complained of—the injury has to be 'fairly ... trace[able] to the challenged action and not th[e] result [of] the independent action of some third party not before the court'. Thirdly, it must be 'likely', as opposed to merely 'speculative', that the injury will be 'redressed by a favourable decision'. He said that 'particularised' means the 'injury must affect the plaintiff in a personal and individual way.' See Bernard Schwartz, (1993) Admin. L.R. 273.

[48] [1990] 1 Q.B. 504. *Cf. R. v. Stroud D.C., ex p. Goodenough* (1980) 43 P. & C.R. 59.

they may acquire a special status of acknowledged expertise.[49] It is possible for there to be situations where there are persons who are directly affected by administrative action who are for reasons of poverty, ignorance or lack of an incentive incapable of bringing proceedings. There are other situations where if a public interest body or pressure group are not in the position to bring proceedings nobody would be in a position to do so, as no individual is affected to a greater extent than any other individual. In such situations an appropriate body or, if necessary, an appropriate individual should be regarded by the court as having the necessary standing. In the *Rose Theatre* case, counsel for the applicant did not submit that an "agglomeration of individuals might have a standing which any one individual lacked". It is suggested he was wrong not to do so. Indeed that there were individuals who were involved in the Rose Theatre company of acknowledged distinction in the field of archaeology who should, because of the nature of the issue before the court, have been regarded as being a significant factor in favour of there being standing.[50] A specialist body which has the authority to speak collectively on behalf of its membership can carry greater weight than any one individual, no matter how distinguished. Similarly a trade union or a professional body is the obvious litigant to make an application as to an administrative decision which affects its members generally.[51] The preferable approach was adopted by Otton J. in *R. v. H.M. Inspectorate of Pollution, ex p. Greenpeace Ltd (No. 2).*[52] He decided that Greenpeace was entitled to challenge the Secretary of State's decision as to the discharge and disposal of radioactive waste at Sellafield. He pointed out if Greenpeace did not have standing an application would have to be made by an employee or neighbour of the establishment who would not be as well qualified as Greenpeace to make the application. The judge declined to follow the decision in the *Rose Theatre* case.

A subsequent case took the trend of liberalising the requirement of standing a step further. In *R. v. Secretary of State for Foreign Affairs, ex p. World Development Movement Ltd*[53] the Divisional Court held that the

2–026

---

[49] *R. v. Inspectorate of Pollution, ex p. Greenpeace Ltd (No. 2)* [1994] 4 All E.R. 239; *R. v. Secretary of State for Social Security, ex p. Joint Council for the Welfare of Immigrants* [1997] 1 W.L.R. 275.

[50] In the later case of *R. v. Poole B.C., ex p. BeeBee* [1991] 2 P.L.R. 27. Schiemann J. took a more generous view of standing in a public interest case. See also, for a more generous approach, *R. v. Secretary of State for Employment, ex p. Equal Opportunities Commission* [1995] 1 A.C. 1 and *New Zealand Maori Council v. Att.-Gen. of New Zealand* [1994] 2 W.L.R. 255, 257B.

[51] See n. 20 above.

[52] [1994] 4 All E.R. 239. Greenpeace's primary objectives include the protection of wildlife and the elimination of threats to the environment. See also, *R. v. Secretary of State for the Environment, ex p. Friends of the Earth Ltd* (1995) 7 Admin. L.R. 26.

[53] [1995] 1 W.L.R. 386.

applicant had sufficient interest to apply for judicial review. The W.D.M. was a non-partisan pressure group, over 20 years old, which campaigned to improve the quality and quantity of overseas aid given by the British government. In the past it had given evidence to Parliamentary select committees, had regular contact with the Overseas Development Administration (the government department responsible for overseas aid) and internationally it had consultative status with United Nations organisations. In one respect, however, the W.D.M. differed from Greenpeace; whereas in the *Greenpeace* application challenging the legality of testing THORP, individual members of Greenpeace who lived in Cumbria would have been directly affected by the testing, and so have sufficient interest to make an application themselves, no individual member of the W.D.M. was any more or less affected by the grant to build a power station on the Pergau dam in Malaysia than other members of the public. Nevertheless, the court held that the W.D.M. had sufficient interest, referring to a range of factors: the merits of the application (here the impugned decision was held to be unlawful); the importance of vindicating the rule of law; the importance of the issue raised; the likely absence of any other challenger; the nature of the breach of duty against which relief was sought; and the prominent role of these applicants in giving advice, guidance and assistance with regard to all.

2–027   The process of liberalising the standing requirements for pressure groups has now reached the stage where in *R. v. Secretary of State for Trade and Industry, ex p. Greenpeace*[54] Laws J. commented that litigation of this kind was now an "accepted and greatly valued dimension of the judicial review jurisdiction". The corollary of this, however, is that a pressure group bringing a public interest challenge had to "act as a friend to the court," meaning that its conduct in making an application has to be controlled with particular strictness—especially as regards the requirement that applications for leave be made promptly and in any event within three months of the impugned decision.

2–028   The courts have also been willing to confer standing on individuals to pursue applications for judicial review in the public interest. In *R. v. Somerset C.C. and ARC Southern Ltd, ex p. Dixon*[55] the applicant sought permission to apply for judicial review of the conditional grant of planning permission to extend a limestone quarry. He was, *inter alia*, a local resident, a parish councillor and a member of more than one body concerned with the environment. The local planning authority contended that the applicant, having no interest as a landowner or as possessor of a personal right or interest threatened by the proposed

---

[54] [1998] Env. L.R. 415.

[55] (1998) 75 P. & C.R. 175; but *cf. R. v. North Somerset DC, ex p. Garnett* [1998] Env. L.R. 91.

quarrying, had no "sufficient interest" to be granted leave (*i.e.* permission) to apply for judicial review within the meaning of section 31(3) of the Supreme Court Act 1981. Sedley J. rejected these submissions and the notion that there always exists a simple dichotomy between, on the one hand, the generality of the public which has a general interest in seeing public bodies comply with the law and, on the other, the person who has a particular interest in the matter above the generality (a distinction drawn in *R. v. Canterbury C.C., ex p. Spingimage Ltd*[56]). There was, Sedley J. held, no authority for a proposition that a court is necessarily compelled to refuse permission where the interest of the applicant is shared with the generality of the public (and if dicta of Schiemann J. in *R. v. Secretary of State for the Environment, ex p. Rose Theatre Co. Ltd*[57] suggested otherwise they were not to be followed). While accepting that in the majority of cases such a greater interest may be necessary to establish that an applicant is more than a mere busybody, Sedley J. stated that "there will be, in public life, a certain number of cases of apparent abuse of power in which any individual, simply as a citizen, has a sufficient interest to bring the matter before the court". One such case is *R. v. Secretary of State for Foreign and Commonwealth Affairs, ex p. Rees-Mogg* where there was no dispute as to the applicant's *locus standi* (he was *inter alia* a former editor of *The Times* newspaper) and the Divisional Court accepted "without question that Lord Rees-Mogg brings the proceedings because of his sincere concern for constitutional issues".[58]

In summary, it can be said that today the court ought not to decline jurisdiction to hear an application for judicial review on the ground of lack of standing to any responsible person or group seeking, on reasonable grounds, to challenge the validity of governmental action.

LAW COMMISSION PROPOSALS FOR REFORM

In its 1994 report, the Law Commission noted that "the fluid nature of the requirement of sufficiency means that it is uncertain what precisely is required."[59] It recommended that RSC, Ord. 53 and section 31 of the Supreme Court Act be amended to make special provision for the standing requirements in cases where the applicant is a representative or pressure group or where there is a public interest in a matter being litigated but no individual has standing. It proposed that a "two track"

2–029

---

[56] (1994) 68 P. &. C.R. 171.
[57] [1990] Q.B. 505 at 506.
[58] [1994] Q.B. 552.
[59] Law Com. No. 226, para. 5.16.

system be established.[60] The first track would cover situations where a person has a direct interest in the impugned decision, in the sense that he has had his legal rights or legitimate expectations affected or there has been a refusal to confer some discretionary benefit. Here standing should be accorded as a matter of course. The second track would cover public interest challenges, *i.e.* applications in which no person is affected more than the public generally and also challenges by a group rather than an individual where the decision nevertheless affects an individual.[61] In such cases, the court would have regard to a wider range of factors than under the first track in deciding whether there is standing, including: the importance of the legal point: the chances of the issue being raised in any other proceedings; the allocation of scarce judicial resources; and the concern that in the determination of issues the courts should have the benefit of the conflicting points of view of those most directly affected by them.

Implementation of the Law Commission proposals will require amendment of primary legislation and the Rules of Court. In the meantime, the *W.D.M.* and other cases mentioned above have moved the court's approach under the existing rules to a position which is not dissimilar.

THIRD PARTY INTERVENTION

2–030 The court has a discretion to hear representations from persons other than the applicant and respondent when it considers this will assist to dispose of an application. Order 53, rule 5(7) enables the court to require a third person to be served and rule 9(1) gives the court power to allow any person to be heard who wishes to be heard in *opposition* to the motion whom the court considers a proper person to do so. These provisions, which are rarely resorted to in practice, could enable the court to hear a wide range of arguments (including those from pressure groups) in complex public interest litigation.[62]

---

[60] *Op. cit.*, para. 5.20. A proposal supported by Lord Woolf in *Access to Justice—final report* (1995), p. 255.

[61] The report gives as an illustration of this type of challenge *R. v. Chief Adjudication Office, ex p. Bland and the T.U.C.*, *The Times*, February 6, 1985 where the Trades Union Congress was held not to have standing to challenge the legality of reductions of state welfare benefits to striking miners.

[62] See further Sir Konrad Schiemann, 'Interventions in Public Interest Cases' [1996] P.L. 240.

Standing and the Full Hearing

The distinction between the requirements of *locus standi* in order to   2–031
obtain permission to apply for judicial review and the standard which
has to be complied with in order to obtain relief after the merits of the
application have been fully investigated has been affirmed in several
decisions. A helpful approach was indicated by Lord Donaldson M.R.,
in *R. v. Monopolies and Mergers Commission, ex p. Argyll Group*[63] when
stating that:

> "The first stage test, which is applied upon the application for
> [permission], will lead to a refusal if the applicant has no interest
> whatsoever and is, in truth, no more than a meddlesome
> busybody. If, however, an application appears otherwise to be
> arguable and there is no other discretionary bar, such as
> dilatoriness on the part of the applicant, the applicant may expect
> to get [permission] to apply, leaving the test of interest or standing
> to be re-applied as a matter of discretion on the hearing of the
> substantive application. At this stage, the strength of the
> applicant's interest is one of the factors to be weighed in the
> balance ..."

This approach was endorsed by Purchas L.J. in his judgment, with   2–032
which the other members of the court agreed, in *R. v. Department of
Transport, ex p. Presvac Engineering Ltd*[64] when, after considering
extensively the decision of the House of Lords in the *National
Federation* case, he said:

> "Personally I would prefer to restrict the use of the expression *locus
> standi* to the threshold exercise and to describe the decision at the
> ultimate stage as an exercise of discretion not to grant relief
> because the applicant has not established that he had been or
> would be sufficiently affected."

The approach of Purchas L.J. of confining the use of the expression   2–033
locus standi to the application for permission stage has much to
commend it. It accords with what appears to be the policy behind
Order 53, rule 3(7), and section 31(3) which links the requirement of
"sufficient interest" to the application for permission stage. The
emphasis on the discretion of the court in relation to the extent of the
interest of the applicant after leave has been granted is also in accord

---

[63] [1986] 1 W.L.R. 763, at 773–774; and also *R. v. Somerset C.C., ex p. Dixon* (1998) 75 P. &.
C.R. 175.
[64] (1992) 4 Admin. L.R. 121.

with the approach adopted by Lord Diplock and Lord Scarman, but not all their Lordships, in the *National Federation* case.[65] The court always has a discretion to refuse a particular form of relief or any relief on an application for judicial review. In deciding whether or not to grant relief, the court is required to have regard to all the circumstances. It is therefore sensible for the court not to isolate the question of the applicant's interest for separate treatment, but to take it into account when it comes to decide what, if any, relief it should grant, as a matter of discretion. The weight or importance which will be attached to the applicant's interest will differ depending on the circumstances. If the application relates to a decision which only affects a single individual other than the applicant and no great harm will be done if relief is not granted, then the court is likely to attach greater significance to the applicant not having a direct interest in the outcome. On the other hand if the decision which is the subject of the application affects the public at large or for some other reason its validity is of general public consequence, then the extent of the applicant's personal involvement is going to be of less importance.

Summary

2–034   The general approach to the issue of standing can be summarised as follows:

(1) "Sufficient interest" has to receive a generous interpretation. It has to be treated as a broad and flexible test.

(2) Only where the answer is obvious should issues as to standing be resolved on the application for permission. In other cases lack of standing should not prevent leave being granted.

(3) Issues as to standing at the leave stage do not depend on the remedy which is then being claimed.

(4) If the applicant has a special expertise in the subject matter of the application that will be a factor in establishing sufficient interest. This applies whether the applicant is an individual or some type of association. The fact that the applicant's

---

[65] [1982] A.C. 617, 643–644, Lord Scarman at 648D/E and 653H, and *cf.* approach of Lord Wilberforce at 631C (but note he was dealing the threshold requirement), and Lord Frazer at 646A/B. Lord Roskill, at 656D, emphasises the discretionary nature of judicial review.

responsibility in relation to the subject of the application is recognised by statute is a strong indication of sufficient interest.

(5) A great variety of factors are capable of qualifying as sufficient interest. They are not confined to property or financial or other legal interests. They can include civic (or community), environmental and cultural interests. The interests can be future or contingent.

(6) The gravity of the issue which is the subject of the application is a factor taken into account in determining the outcome of questions of standing. The more serious the issue at stake, the less significance will be attached to arguments based on the applicant's alleged lack of standing.

(7) In deciding what, if any, remedy to grant as a matter of discretion, the court will take into account the extent of the applicant's interest. At this stage different remedies may require a different involvement by the applicant.[66]

---

[66] Under the Human Rights Act 1998, which will come into force on October 2, 2000, section 7(1) and (7) provide that for a person to bring proceedings under that Act he must be (or would be) a 'victim' of an unlawful act. This is the test under Article 34 of the Convention and the case-law of the European Court of Human Rights. During the passage of the legislation through Parliament it was argued that the same test of standing as is provided for judicial review should be inserted in the Act. The government, however, did not accept the arguments of its critics who said that the dual test would create problems for the parties and the courts.

CHAPTER 3

WHO AND WHAT MAY BE SUBJECT TO JUDICIAL REVIEW?

INTRODUCTION

The existence of a divide separating public and private law probably causes more controversy between distinguished commentators than any other aspect of English administrative law. The nature of that controversy and the explanation for it will be considered later but it probably goes deeper than the divide itself. Some regard its creation as being regrettable, retrograde and unnecessary; others consider that it is an essential prerequisite for the development of effective public law procedures and coherent public law principles.[1]

3–001

Despite this controversy, what the commentators do agree on is the difficulty in identifying the path which the divide follows and its extensive influence on many aspects of administrative law. The distinction between public and private law now plays a crucial role in determining:

3–002

(1) when it is necessary to bring proceedings by way of judicial review, under Order 53, with its distinct procedural requirements[2];

(2) by whom and against whom proceedings which raise public law issues can be brought[3];

---

[1] 'Public Law principles', when used in this sense will normally refer to those common law principles, standards and rules applied by the courts in determining judicial review proceedings. These principles should therefore be complied with by bodies when performing public law functions (on which, see below). These bodies may also be subject to principles established in contexts other than judicial review, e.g. the requirement to avoid 'maladministration' enforced by the ombudsmen and the need for 'efficiency'.

[2] See Chap. 14 and in particular the requirement of permission to commence the proceedings, restricted time limits, limited disclosure and oral evidence and cross examination and the fact that the proceedings are almost always heard in London.

[3] On standing, see Chap. 2 above.

(3) the principles which the court will apply and the role it will play in order to determine those issues[4]; and

(4) the remedies which may be granted.[5]

THE HISTORICAL DEVELOPMENT OF "PUBLIC LAW" IN ENGLAND AND WALES

3–003 The most striking distinction between the common law and civil law legal systems on the continent, of which the French is a prime example (having the Conseil d'Etat, and a system of *tribuneaux administratifs*) is the absence within the common law systems of any separate court applying a universally applicable body of concepts and rules, quite distinct from the general law of the land, regulating justiciable administrative activity.

3–004 The absence of superior administrative courts of general jurisdiction is to be explained by the common lawyer's interpretation of constitutional history. The early Stuarts had endeavoured to withdraw matters of State from the courts of common law,[6] and had enforced their will primarily through the medium of their prerogative courts, in which substantive and procedural rules unknown to the common law were applied. The common lawyers joined in alliance with the parliamentarians to bring about the downfall of the Court of Star Chamber and other prerogative courts in 1641, and their alliance was renewed in 1655 to thwart the arbitrary pretensions of James II. The traditions handed down from the constitutional struggles of the seventeenth century created an all but invincible prejudice against encroachments upon the province annexed by the common-law courts in the field of public law. Public law and private law were in the future to be undivided and indivisible. These traditions were reinforced by the exceptional degree of public esteem earned by the superior judges after the Act of Settlement 1701 had ensured their independence of the Executive, and they led naturally to a general tendency to exaggerate the practical efficacy of the functions exercised by the ordinary courts in controlling the activities of government bodies and office holders.[7]

---

[4] The major question is as to whether the court will be limited to a supervisory role.

[5] It is only on an application for judicial review that the prerogative orders can be granted (on which, see para. 15–003). In addition the circumstances in which a declaration may be granted can be affected; see para. 15–030.

[6] In particular by the writ *de non procedendo rege inconsulto*.

[7] Echoed even today in the argument that it is unnecessary, and indeed undesirable, to have a specialised Administrative Division of the High Court because the Crown

New prejudices were added to the old by Dicey's unsound critique **3–005**
of the exclusive administrative jurisdiction vested in the French
Conseil d'Etat, which he stigmatised as being opposed to the
fundamental principles of the rule of law that pervaded the British
Constitution.[8] To him the rule of law involved the proposition that
every person, including Ministers and officials, was subject to the
ordinary law of the realm and amenable to the jurisdiction of the
ordinary courts; *droit administratif*, on the other hand, implied the
exemption of the Government and its servants from personal legal
responsibility for official acts before the ordinary courts; instead, they
were subject to "official" law applied by special and more or less
official bodies.[9] Since the rule of law was a good thing, what was
incompatible with the rule of law was obviously a bad thing. English
lawyers were readily persuaded to regard administrative law, or *droit
administratif*, as a misfortune inflicted upon the benighted folk across
the Channel. In 1932 the Committee on Ministers' Powers thought it
sufficient to condemn as "inconsistent with … the supremacy of the
Law" a proposal to take away the existing supervisory and appellate
jurisdiction of the High Court and to vest it in new and distinct
administrative courts.[10] As recently as 1935 the then Lord Chief Justice
of England could still dismiss the term "administrative law" as
"Continental jargon".[11] In so far as it was being brought into existence

---

Office and the nominated judges of the Queen's Bench Division do the job so
excellently: see para. 14–001.

[8] *Introduction to the Study of the Law of the Constitution* (10th ed., 1959), pp. 328–405. The
Justice/All Souls Committee report *Administrative Justice, Some Necessary Reforms*
(1988), Chap. 7, considered whether it would be desirable to introduce a Conseil
d'Etat model into the U.K. and it concluded it would not, pointing out, 'it is not
possible as it were, to pick up such an institution, set it down in alien soil, and
expect it to flourish'. See further J.W.F. Allison, *A Continental Distinction in the Common
Law: a Historical and Comparative Perspective on English Public Law* (1996).

[9] Dicey, *op. cit.* n. 8 above, pp. 193–195, 202–203. For a sympathetic re-appraisal of
Dicey's formulation in its historical setting, see F. H. Lawson, 'Dicey Revisited' (1959)
7 *Political Studies* 109, 207. *Cf.* Trowbridge H. Ford, 'Dicey as a Political Journalist'
(1970) 18 *Political Studies* 220. See also M. Loughlin, *Public Law and Political Theory*
(1992) Chap. 7; P. Craig, *Public Law and Democracy in the United Kingdom and The
United States of America* (1990), Chap. 2.

[10] Cmd. 4060 (1932), 110. A somewhat similar proposal was rejected by the Franks
Committee on Administrative Tribunals and Enquiries, but in less forthright terms
(Cmnd. 218 (1957), 28–29).

[11] Lord Hewart of Bury, *Not Without Prejudice*, p. 96. And see Salmon L.J.'s observation
in *Re Grosvenor Hotel, London (No. 2)* [1965] Ch. 1210, 1261: 'I do not believe that the
court would be … obliged to accept the *ipse dixit* of the Minister just because he was
a member of the executive. There is no *droit administratif* in England.' During the
passage of the Immigration Act 1971, the then Home Secretary, Mr Maudling,
expressed his scepticism of the value of empowering appeal tribunals to review the
exercise of discretion, as follows: 'I have never seen the sense of administrative law
in our country, because it is only someone else taking the Government's decision for

by Parliament (by confiding justiciable issues to special statutory tribunals and delegating unreviewable powers to Ministers) it was to be resisted as un-English. A climate of opinion in which administrative law was treated as an alien intrusion that was not (or at least ought not to be) part of the law of England was inimical to objective research into the problems posed by the developing law of public administration.[12] The inter-war years in particular was largely dominated by impassioned but often sterile controversies concerning the constitutional propriety of administrative tribunals and delegated legislation.

British insularity

3–006   Serious inquiry into the experience of other countries was also inhibited by conservative insularity—an attitude of mind that has always been widely diffused among English politicians, administrators and lawyers. Insularity, even complacency, could easily be understood. The British Constitution—a constitution which had evolved empirically over the centuries, owing next to nothing to the example of foreign countries, embodying no general guarantee of individual rights and characterised above all by the sovereignty of Parliament—stood resolutely unique. Representative and responsible government was securely founded; political and administrative morality was unusually high; the administration of justice by the ordinary courts was even-handed and incorrupt; the common law, itself pre-eminently pragmatic, was tenacious but adaptable. Such an environment bred the assumption that England had little to learn from other countries in matters of public law. Moreover, the absence of judicial review of the constitutionality of legislation was conducive to a lack of informed interest among practising lawyers in the juridical problems of government. The role assigned to constitutional and administrative law in legal education was modest.[13]

---

them' (H.C. Official Report, Stdg. Ctte. B, 1508 (May 25, 1971)). *Cf.* The Report of the Select Committee on Legal Education in 1846, urging that administrative law was a subject fit to be taught at universities (quoted by Brian Abel-Smith and Robert Stevens, *Lawyers and the Courts*, p. 69).

[12] For a critical account of the baleful influence of Dicey's insistence that the legality of governmental action was to be determined by the ordinary courts applying the general law of the land, see H.W. Arthurs, 'Rethinking Administrative Law: a Slightly Dicey Business' (1979) 170 O.H.L.J. 1 and *Without the Law: Administrative Justice and Legal Pluralism in Nineteenth Century England* (1985); and M. Loughlin, 'Courts and Governance', Chap. 9 in P. Birks (ed.), *The Frontiers of Liability* vol. 1 (1994).

[13] de Smith, *The Lawyers and the Constitution*, pp. 17–29.

The change in attitude

Although Anglo-Saxon attitudes were too deeply ingrained to be **3–007**
suddenly transformed, over the years since the end of the 1960s the
situation has dramatically changed. While in 1964 a distinguished
judge could say "We do not have a developed system of
administrative law—perhaps because until fairly recently we did not
need it",[14] in 1971 Lord Denning, himself a leading architect of our
public law, asserted "It may truly now be said that we have a
developed system of administrative law"[15] and in 1981 in *R. v. Inland
Revenue Commissioners, ex p. National Federation of the Self-Employed and
Small Businesses Ltd*,[16] Lord Diplock, a principal builder of the system,
proudly proclaimed, "that progress towards a comprehensive system
of administrative law ... I regard as having been the greatest
achievement of the English Courts in my judicial lifetime".[17]

These developments were assisted by the existence of some features **3–008**
of a public law system long before the developments in which Lords
Denning and Diplock took such pride had happened. Thus proceedings
for the prerogative orders always had their own procedure, and prior to
the introduction of judicial review, they were heard before the
Divisional Court, which was normally presided over by the Lord Chief
Justice of the day. The use of that Court is now reserved for the most
important applications for judicial review, but all applications
continued to be controlled by the historic Crown Office; today, as in the
past, public law proceedings are normally on the "Crown side" of the
High Court. In addition the fact that private rights could be modified
under English law by being affected by the public interest goes back at
least to Sir Matthew Hale's *Treatise de Portibus Maris*.[18] In a passage,
cited in *Allnutt v. Inglis*,[19] he stated in respect of a wharf licensed by the

---

[14] *Ridge v. Baldwin* [1964] A.C. 40, 72, *per* Lord Reid.
[15] *Breen v. Amalgamated Engineering* [1971] 2 Q.B. 175 at 189. See J. Jowell,
'Administrative Law" in J. Jowell and P. McAuslan (eds) *Lord Denning, The Judge and
The Law* (1984).
[16] [1982] A.C. 617.
[17] *R. v. Inland Revenue Commissioners, ex p. National Federation of Self-Employed and Small
Businesses Ltd* [1982] A.C. 617, 641C. In 1974 he also stated at a meeting to pay tribute
to the work of the late author of this book, that the effect of recent developments
'has been to provide this country with a system of administrative law which is in
substance nearly as comprehensive in its scope as *droit administratif* in France and
gives effect to principles which, though not derived from Gallic concepts of *legalité*
and *détournement de pouvoir*, are capable of achieving the same result': [1974] C.L.J.
233, 244.
[18] Vol. 2. of Tracts published by Hargrave, Part 2, Chap. 6, pp. 77.
[19] (1810) 12 East 526 at 530, 104 E.R. 206 at 208. See also *Boct v. Stennet*, 8 Term Rep. 606
and *Munn v. Illinois* 94 U.S. (1877) where Waite C.J. after citing Hale said at p. 130:
'when private property is devoted to public use, it is subject to public regulation'
and *Minister of Justice for Canada v. Levis* [1919] A.C. 505.

Queen or where there was no other wharf in the locality: "there cannot be taken arbitrary and excessive duties...but the duties must be reasonable and moderate...for now the wharf and crane...are affected with a public interest, and they cease to be *juris privati* only".

This is an approach to monopolistic power, requiring it to be exercised reasonably, which has been adopted and applied in other parts of the Commonwealth.[20]

3–009   Many factors contributed to the change of attitude. The public were resorting to the courts with increasing frequency in order to obtain protection against alleged abuse by public bodies of their greatly expanded powers. The 1970s and 1980s were a period of confrontation between central and local government which resulted frequently in bitter disputes coming before the courts.[21] There were by then over 2,000 administrative tribunals whose decisions were either subject to appeal to the High Court or judicial review. Many decisions of ministers, for example in relation to planning appeals, could be quashed on a statutory application to the High Court. The resulting increase in litigation of an administrative law nature gave the courts the opportunity to develop principles which enabled them to hold the ring between members of the public and central and local government. Additional factors were the citation of decisions of the European Court of Human Rights and the impact of Community law. However the most important influence was the introduction of a new procedure of judicial review in 1978.[22] The new procedure acted as a catalyst. The safeguards built into the new procedure meant that the Courts could extend the scope of review without it resulting in abuse.[23] It was however the decision of the House of Lords in *O'Reilly v. Mackman*[24] in 1983, which highlighted the importance of the distinction between public and private law. It did so by laying down that, as a general rule, it would be contrary to public policy, and as such an abuse of the process of the court not to bring disputes as to public law issues before the courts by way of the Order 53 judicial review procedure. Up to that time it had been thought the litigant had a choice. He could either begin, at his election, general civil proceedings for an injunction, a declaration or, in some situations, damages; or he could

---

[20] See 5th ed. of this text, at para. 3–051.

[21] *Secretary of State for Education and Science v. Tameside M.B.C.* [1977] A.C. 1014 provides an early example of what was to follow. Central Government was in favour of abolishing the grammar schools and some local authorities did everything in their power to thwart Central Government. See further M. Loughlin, *Legality and Locality: the Role of Law in Central-Local Government Relations* (1996).

[22] On which, see para. 13–057.

[23] See generally Chap. 14 on the permission requirement, requirement of promptness, restrictive stance on disclosure. As to rules of standing, see Chap. 2.

[24] [1983] 2 A.C. 237.

apply for judicial review.[25] After *O'Reilly v. Mackman*[26] if you wrongly classified an issue as appropriate for judicial review when it should have been initiated by general civil proceedings or vice versa, and as a result commenced the wrong type of proceedings, this could be fatal to the success of a claim.[27]

Initially, disputes as to whether a public or private law issue was **3–010** involved occurred when a person issued general civil proceedings instead of an application for judicial review under Order 53. In later cases where the position was reversed and it was argued that the proceedings should have been made by general civil proceedings.[28]

It is not surprising that this situation has resulted in the principle **3–011** established in *O'Reilly v. Mackman* being the subject of considerable criticism.[29] However most, if not all developed legal systems recognise

---

[25] In *Davy v. Spelthorne B.C.* [1984] A.C. 262, 276, Lord Wilberforce said:'the expressions 'private law' and 'public law' have recently been imported into the law of England from countries which, unlike our own, have separate systems concerning public law and private law. No doubt they are convenient expressions for descriptive purposes. In this country they must be used with caution, for, typically English law fastens, not upon principles but upon remedies.' This oft-quoted statement underestimates the distinction, usually unexpressed, which was long established between the 'public law' situations where the prerogative orders were available and the 'private law' situations where they were not (on which, see below, para. 15–003.)

[26] See n. 24, above.

[27] There were decisions which anticipated the decision in *O'Reilly v. Mackman*. In *Heywood v. Hull Prison Board of Visitors* [1980] 1 W.L.R. 1386 an action was struck out and dicta by Roskill L.J. (at 1395) (in *Uppal v. Home Office* [1980] 3 All E.R. 594, 601) that the proceedings should be brought by judicial review were referred to. Reservations were also expressed by Lords Wilberforce and Bridge in *Din v. Wandsworth London Borough Council* [1983] 1 A.C. 657, 666C and 68SE. See generally Woolf, 'Public Law—Private Law: Why the Divide?' [1986] P.L. 220.

[28] An example is provided by *R. v. Disciplinary Committee of the Jockey Club, ex p. H.H. Aga Khan* [1993] 1 W.L.R. 909. Although in the Divisional Court the judges suggested that the applicant should avoid the need to resolve the issue of jurisdiction by starting a second set of proceedings which could be consolidated with the existing proceedings for judicial review the Aga Khan preferred to have the issue of principle as to whether proceedings for judicial review were appropriately decided. For a case where both public and private law proceedings were commenced, see *R. v. Football Assoc. Ltd, ex p. Football League Ltd* [1993] 2 All E.R. 833.

[29] See Sir Patrick Neill Q.C. *Administrative Law: Snakes and Ladders* (1985) and Wade and Forsyth, *Administrative Law* (7th ed., 1994) p. 681. In the preface to the 6th edition, Sir William Wade comments that within a fortnight of the 5th edition of his book the House of Lords had created 'the most seismic disturbance that the subject had suffered in many years. By declaiming a rigid dichotomy between public and private law' while at 677, he states that the 'rigid dichotomy which has been imposed...must be accounted a serious setback for administrative law'. *Cf.* Woolf, *Protection of the Public—A New Challenge* (1990) pp. 25 *et seq.* Although the Law Commission in their 1976 report which led to the introduction of judicial review (Cmnd. 6407, para. 34) did not intend judicial review to be an exclusive procedure it should have been appreciated that, unless it was in the majority of cases, the safeguards provided for the administration, such as the requirement of leave, would

some degree of distinction between public and private law.[30] As was pointed out by Lord Goff in *Re Norway's Application*, "the identification of public law matters differs from country to country, sometimes in minor respects and sometimes in major respects".[31]

3–012   For a great many years the way in which the courts have identified the activities which are subject to public law is by deciding whether or not they are activities to which the High Court's supervisory jurisdiction of judicial review may be invoked by aggrieved persons. In the past this was mainly done by asking what was the *source of the power* being exercised by the decision-maker whose action was impugned. Where the power was statutory or, more recently, derived from the prerogative,[32] then that jurisdiction could be invoked. Where, however, powers were conferred solely by a contract (such as an arbitration agreement or an agreement governing the relationship between members of an unincorporated association), judicial review generally was not available.[33] Today, the courts recognise such an approach is too restrictive and they are now influenced by the type of *function performed* by the decision-maker whose action is challenged.[34] Where a body is carrying out a public function (such as that undertaken by a non-government regulatory organisation in relation to the area of activity which is subject to its control), the courts will consider intervening to require compliance with the principles of judicial review. This is the case even if the body is non-statutory, exercising powers which are not derived either from legislation or the prerogative. The following sections consider, first, the source-based approach and, secondly, the function-based approach.

JUDICIAL REVIEW AND SOURCES OF POWER

3–013 The English courts have often focused upon the legal source of a body's powers, rather than the function it is performing, in order to determine whether a decision is subject to judicial review. In many situations this continues to be a helpful, though limited, approach.

---

[30] See Szladits, *International Encyclopaedia of Comparative Law*, Vol. 2, paras 25, 31, 57.

[31] [1990] 1 A.C. 723, 802–803.

[32] On judicial review of prerogative powers, see Chap. 5, para. 5–037 *et seq.*

[33] The position is, however, complex: on judicial review of powers connected with contracts, see below, paras 3-018–3-019 and 3–040. See also Chap. 5, para. 5–035.

[34] Notably in *R. v. Panel on Takeovers and Mergers, ex p. Datafin plc* [1987] 1 Q.B. 815, CA; see also *R. v. Criminal Injuries Compensation Board, ex p. Lain* [1967] 2 Q.B. 864.

Statutory bodies and office holders

There are a vast number of bodies which derive their authority and **3–014** obligation to perform their functions from a statutory source and in consequence are referred to as public bodies. They include local authorities, courts (from the House of Lords to magistrates' courts), tribunals, regulatory bodies and the holders of a public office, including Ministers of the Crown, the Parliamentary and Local Commissioners for Administration. Even the Master of the Rolls, when exercising his powers in relation to appeals under the Solicitors Act 1974, is subject to judicial review.[35]

A large proportion of all applications for judicial review are **3–015** concerned with the exercise of statutory power and discretion conferred upon Secretaries of State and local authorities by specific Acts of Parliament; about these there is little difficulty. Merely to assert, however, as a general proposition that a decision is taken by a statutory body or is the exercise of a statutory power, does not provide a great deal of general guidance as to whether or not it will be controlled by the principles of judicial review. The scope for complexities may be illustrated by reference to judicial review of decisions taken by the courts: although they are statutory bodies[36] exercising statutory (and common law) powers, their decisions are not necessarily subject to judicial review. Of the superior courts, only the Crown Court is amenable to judicial review, and even here the scope for judicial review is limited. Section 29(3) of the Supreme Court Act 1981 provides:

"In relation to the jurisdiction of the Crown Court, other than its jurisdiction in matters relating to trial on indictment, the High Court shall have jurisdiction to make orders of mandamus, prohibition or certiorari as the High Court possesses in relation to the jurisdiction of an inferior court".[37]

And while decisions of inferior courts, such as magistrates' courts, are notionally subject to judicial review, in practice statutes so often provide for *appeals* against their determinations that judicial review is the exception rather than the rule; the High Court does not exercise its

---

[35] See *R. v. Master of the Rolls, ex p. McKinnell* [1993] 1 W.L.R. 88.

[36] As to the Court of Appeal, High Court and the Crown Court (collectively the Supreme Court of Judicature), see Supreme Court Act 1981, s. 1. As to magistrates' courts, see Magistrates' Court Act 1980.

[37] The phrase 'matters relating to trials on indictment' has proved problematic: see, *e.g.* *R. v. Crown Court at Leeds, ex p. Hussain* [1995] 1 W.L.R. 1329. See further R. Ward, 'Judicial Review and Trials on Indictment' [1990] P.L. 50.

supervisory jurisdiction where an alternative remedy exists.[38] So, in short, while the fact that a decision or action is authorised by statute is always relevant in determining whether or not it is regulated by the principles of judicial review, a classification of a body or decision as "statutory" in general may provide only an uncertain touchstone to what happens in practice.[39]

Bodies established and decisions taken under the prerogative

3–016   Action which has as its source prerogative power is now potentially subject to judicial review—though in this context much government action may be non-justiciable. While it is arguable as to whether the Criminal Injuries Compensation Board is correctly regarded as being a body established under the Royal Prerogative or merely as a body established by the Crown which is non-statutory, it was so regarded by the Divisional Court in *R. v. Criminal Injuries Compensation Board, ex p. Lain*[40] and treated as being amenable to certiorari. In explaining why this was the position Diplock L.J. stated that the jurisdiction of the High Court had "not in the past been dependent upon the source of the tribunals' authority to decide issues submitted to its determination, except where such authority is derived solely from agreement of the parties to the determination".[41] The emphasis placed by Lord Diplock on the source of a power not usually being decisive in determining whether a body is subject to judicial review is in accord with what it is suggested should be the position today. Bodies deriving their existence from the prerogative do however have an obvious link with the Crown which makes it likely that they may

---

[38] *cf. R. v. Hereford Magistrates' Court, ex p. Rowlands* [1998] Q.B. 110 in which the Divisional Court held that the existence of a right of appeal by way of retrial in the Crown Court did not preclude a person convicted in the Magistrates' Court from applying for judicial review on the grounds of procedural impropriety, unfairness or bias.

[39] Thus in *R. v. The National Trust for Places of Historic Interest or Natural Beauty, ex p. Scott and Others* [1998] 1 W.L.R. 228 Tucker J. refused permission to apply for judicial review in respect of the National Trust's decision to ban deer hunting on Trust land. The Trust, a statutory body established by the National Trust Act 1971, was exercising public functions in making its decision. However, the Trust was also a charity, its Council members were charity trustees, and accordingly it was protected by the provisions of the Charities Act 1993, s. 33 which regulated legal proceedings against charities. The applicants had neither obtained an order of the Charity Commissioners authorising the proceedings nor the leave of a judge of the Chancery Division. The present application was in the nature of 'charity proceedings' and as consent had not been obtained in accordance with the 1993 Act, the court had no jurisdiction over the matter.

[40] [1967] 2 Q.B. 864, 881 *per* Lord Parker C.J. and, 883 *per* Diplock L.J.

[41] *ibid.* at 884. It is suggested this statement accurately reflects the position.

qualify as public bodies. However, while many obvious public bodies derive their powers from a Royal Charter, for example boroughs, some purely commercial corporations still exist, for example London Assurance Corporation and the Peninsular and Oriental Steam Navigation Company, so it cannot be assumed that because a company has been established by Royal Charter it is a public body.

It is unlikely that any significance will now be attached, in determining whether a body is subject to public law, to the fact that the source of its power is derived from the prerogative. This reflects the approach of the House of Lords in *Council of Civil Service Unions v. Minister for the Civil Service* where statutory and prerogative powers were assimilated and in *Hazell v. Hammersmith L.B.C.* where the powers of corporations created by Royal Charter were held to be restricted to their statutory powers.[42]

3–017

Contract and judicial review

In addition to statutory and prerogative powers, bodies may seek to perform their functions by basing action on contractual power. The scope for judicial review of such action is considered in more detail in a later Chapter.[43]

3–018

Here it is sufficient to note that—as with statute and the prerogative—merely to assert that a decision has its legal *source* of authority in contract provides little general guidance as to whether or not such action will or ought to be subject to judicial review. The picture is complex. In some situations the courts have been prepared to use their supervisory jurisdiction and apply judicial review principles to what may be characterised as contractual relationships,[44] whereas in other cases the existence of a contract or potential contractual relationship has been given as a reason for action *not* being susceptible to judicial review.[45]

---

[42] *Council of Civil Service Unions v. Minister for the Civil Service* [1985] A.C. 374, 399A–E, 400C, 407A–F, 410C, 411A, F–H, 417G–H, 418C–D, 419B–C, 423G, 424B and *Hazell v. Hammersmith L.B.C.* [1992] A.C. 1, 21G–22A.

[43] See paras 5-035–5-036.

[44] See, *e.g. R. v. Wear Valley D.C., ex p. Binks* [1985] 2 All E.R. 699 (termination of informal licence to run take-away food stall subject to review).

[45] See, *e.g. R. v. Lord Chancellor, ex p. Hibbit & Saunders (A Firm)* [1993] C.O.D. 326 DC (firm alleged that procedure for inviting tenders to provide court reporting services to the Lord Chancellor's Department was unfair); *R. v. Panel of the Federation of Communication Services Ltd, ex p. Kubis* [1998] C.O.D. 5 (application for judicial review refused to applicant who, while not a member of the self-regulatory organisation, was nevertheless in contractual relationship with it in respect of an anti-theft scheme). *cf. Andreou v. Institute of Chartered Accountants in England and Wales* [1998] 1 All E.R. 14.

3–019   It is submitted that the court ought to have regard to the function being performed by body whose decision is impugned, rather than the formal source of its power,[46] this should be so whether or not the body in question is ostensibly a "public" or "private" one. If a public function is being performed, and contract law does not provide an aggrieved person with an appropriate remedy,[47] then action taken under or in pursuance of a contract should be subject to control by judicial review principles. Where a public body enters into a contract with a supplier, a dispute about the rights and duties arising out of the contract will often be determined by private law. However, the decision of a public body to enter, or not enter, into a contract may be subject to judicial review. This involves the exercise of a statutory discretion which therefore must be taken lawfully and must not constitute an abuse of power. If it is a purely commercial decision it is unlikely that there will be any ground of domestic judicial review for a court to intervene[48] but if there is some ulterior purpose or excess or abuse of power the court will do so. The court is entitled to examine the motives of a public body.[49] When, for example, a local authority resolves not to contract in future with a company, on the ground of its links with South Africa during the apartheid era,[50] or to boycott the publications of a particular news company on the ground of the company's labour practices or attitudes[51] such a decision is far from being a purely commercial decision and will therefore be required to comply with public law principles. If it uses its powers in order to punish a body who has done nothing wrong according to English law or in a manner which is procedurally improper or unfair, the courts

---

[46] *cf.* S. Arrowsmith, 'Judicial Review of the Contractual Powers of Public Authorities' (1990) 106 L.Q.R. 277, 291 where it is argued that: 'the way forward now is for the courts to adopt the same approach to the judicial review of contractual powers as they do to the review of other activities of government. Under the Human Rights Act 1998, 'public authority' is defined, under s. 6, as '(a) a court or tribunal, and (b) any person certain of whose functions are functions of a public nature.'

[47] *e.g.* because the aggrieved person, such as an individual who seeks to participate in an activity regulated by a non-statutory self-regulatory body, does not have a contract with the body or because private law does not provide a particular form of relief (such as certiorari).

[48] *cf.* the power of the court to intervene under the public procurement regulations which require stipulated procedures to be followed in awarding a contract and impose duties to provide reasons to justify the choice of a particular contractor: para. 3–027, n. 88.

[49] On the difference between purpose and motive, see paras 6–080–6–083 of the principal edition of this work.

[50] *R. v. Lewisham L.B.C., ex p. Shell UK Ltd* [1988] 1 All E.R. 938. See also *Bromley v. G.L.C.* [1983] 1 A.C. 768, 813 and *Wheeler v. Leicester C.C.* [1985] A.C. 1054.

[51] *R. v. Ealing L.B.C., ex p. Times Newspapers Ltd* (1987) 85 L.G.R. 316.

may intervene.[52] A public body may be under additional responsibilities in relation to its contractual obligations.[53]

Again, the establishment of wages and salaries for public sector **3–020** workers is usually a matter of commercial judgment for public authorities. In exceptional cases, however, judicial review may be appropriate to determine a challenge to a wage settlement when it is claimed that the authority exceeded or abused its conferred powers.[54]

JUDICIAL REVIEW AND PUBLIC FUNCTIONS

Having considered the limits of the source-based approach, we now **3–021** examine the preferable functions-based approach to determining whether a decision taken by a body is amenable to judicial review.

A body is performing a "public function" when it seeks to achieve **3–022** some collective benefit for the public or a section of the public and is accepted by the public, or a section of it, as having authority to do so. Such legitimacy may be conferred by the fact that the body is established by Parliament; it may also arise in other ways. In the case of a self-regulatory body, the general consent to the exercise of its powers by businesses in a particular sector establishes its legitimacy. The existence of a contract between the applicant and the respondent body may also confer legitimacy upon an assertion of regulatory or other power, but (as had been noted) where a contract is the *sole* source of authority and a contractual remedy is adequate, the court will be unlikely to intervene by way of judicial review.[55] Public bodies exercise public functions when they intervene or participate in social or economic affairs in the public interest. This may happen in a wide variety of ways. For instance, a body is performing a public function when it provides "public goods"[56] or other collective services, such as

---

[52] *R. v. Lewisham L.B.C.*, n. 50, above, at 951.

[53] The principle that a public body may not fetter its discretion, by contract or otherwise (see discussion below, Chap. 10) does not apply to private bodies. A local authority when determining whether to terminate a tenancy or when fixing the rent its tenants have to pay must act reasonably. See *Wandsworth B.C. v. Winder* [1985] A.C. 461 and para. 3–015, above.

[54] *Pickwell v. Camden L.B.C.* [1983] Q.B. 962.

[55] See para. 3–018. Where a contract does exist between a person and a regulatory body, a term will normally be implied that the body act fairly and an injunction or declaration may be obtained by means of an ordinary civil action to enforce this duty. There will not, however, necessarily be liability for loss caused as a result of careless exercise of decision-making power: see *Wright v. Jockey Club, The Times*, June 16, 1995.

[56] This is a term used by economists to refer to services such as defence, lighthouses and public street lighting for which a free market cannot operate efficiently. "A public good is one for which consumption of the good by one individual does not detract from that of any other individual"—in other words, if such services were provided

health care, education and personal social services, from funds raised by taxation. A body may perform public functions in the form of adjudicatory services (such as those of the criminal and civil courts and tribunal system).[57] They also do so if they regulate commercial and professional activities to ensure compliance with proper standards.[58] For all these purposes, a range of legal and administrative techniques may be deployed, including: rule-making; adjudication (and other forms of dispute resolution); inspection; and licensing.[59]

3–023   Public functions need not be the exclusive domain of the state. Charities, self-regulatory organisations and other nominally private institutions (such as universities, the Stock Exchange, Lloyd's of London, churches) may also perform some types of public function. As Sir John Donaldson M.R. urged, it is important for the courts to "recognise the realities of executive power" and not allow "their vision to be clouded by the subtlety and sometimes complexity of the way in which it can be exerted".[60] Non-governmental bodies such as these are just as capable of abusing their powers as is government.[61]

There is much to commend a function-based approach to determining the scope of judicial review. Not only does it enable the courts to articulate more explicitly the modern constitutional role of judicial review—the common law control of public functions[62]—but it may provide redress for grievance where no other remedy exists.[63] As

---

by a private business and sold to individuals, there would be no effective way of excluding other people who had not paid for it from also enjoying the service: see C.G. Veljanovski, *The New Law and Economics* (1982), p. 45.

[57] The role of the court in supervising 'judicial' activity has played a central role in the development of judicial review principles. On the one vital distinction between judicial, quasi-judicial and administrative action, see below, Appendix. Findings by arbitrators acting under contractual agreements between parties to submit disputes to arbitration are not subject to judicial review, though under the Arbitration Acts 1950 to 1979 the High Court does have a special supervisory role.

[58] See generally Anthony Ogus, *Regulation: Legal Form and Economic Theory* (1994).

[59] In the United States, the procedures of administrative agencies are normally classified as simply 'rule making and adjudication'. See, *e.g.* S. Breyer and R. Stewart, *Administrative Law and Regulatory Policy* (1979), Chap. 1.

[60] *R. v. Panel on Takeovers and Mergers, ex p. Datafin plc* [1987] 1 Q.B. 815, 838–839.

[61] For an interesting overview, see Sir Gordon Borrie, 'The Regulation of Public and Private Power' [1989] P.L. 552. See also Julia Black, 'Constitutionalising Self-Regulation' (1996) 59 M.L.R. 24; A.I. Ogus, 'Rethinking Self-Regulation' (1995) 15 O.J.L.S. 95; Colin Munro, 'Self-regulation in the Media' [1997] P.L. 6.

[62] See further D. Oliver, 'Is the *Ultra Vires* Rule the Basis of Judicial Review?' [1987] P.L. 543; *cf.* C. Forsyth, 'Of Fig Leaves and Fairy Tales: the ultra vires doctrine, the sovereignty of Parliament and Judicial Review' [1996] C.L.J. 122.

[63] *e.g.* to a member of the public directly affected by action of a non-statutory regulatory body with which he has no contractual relationship. Of course, the mere fact that there may be no remedy other than judicial review (such as in contract or tort) is not in itself a sufficient reason for the court to apply judicial review principles and remedies; the body must be exercising a public function.

it is through the principles of judicial review that the rule of law and other constitutional principles are given practical effect,[64] the supervisory jurisdiction of the High Court should ensure that bodies, whether nominally public or private, when performing public functions comply with the law and achieve acceptable standards of administration. While some public functions fall outside the scope of judicial review,[65] nevertheless there exists a wide and growing—if sometimes uncertain—range of public functions which are potentially subject to the supervisory scrutiny of the courts.

Even where the courts do employ the broad test based on the existence of public functions, it is not always clear what criteria are relevant to that test. In the leading case of *R. v. Panel on Takeovers and Mergers, ex p. Datafin plc*, Sir John Donaldson M.R. suggested that possibly "the only essential elements are what can be described as a public element, which can take many different forms, and the exclusion from jurisdiction of bodies where the sole source of power is the consensual submission to its jurisdiction".[66] He warned that even as the law then stood, in the law reports it was possible to find enumerations of factors giving rise to the jurisdiction, but it was a fatal error to regard the presence of all those factors as essential or as being exclusive of other factors. In subsequent cases, the courts have gone on to elaborate a variety of overlapping criteria designed to particularise the broad-based functional approach of the Master of the Rolls in *Datafin*. They include the following[67]:

3–024

---

[64] On constitutional principles and judicial reasoning, see further Chap. 1.

[65] The courts may be ill-equipped to intervene where an activity is not justiciable, for example the allocation of public health care resources, where no objective standards which can be applied by the courts: see below Chap. 5. Nor are decisions of officers of the House of Commons itself amenable to judicial review: (*R. v. Parliamentary Commissioner for Standards, ex p. Fayed* [1998] 1 All E.R. 93; the Court of Appeal held that the Commissioner for Standards, an officer established by the Standing Orders of the House of Commons, was part of Parliament's own processes and as such outside the court's jurisdiction).

[66] [1987] 1 Q.B. 815, 838.

[67] The very extensive body of authority includes: *Law v. National Greyhound Racing Club Ltd* [1983] 1 W.L.R. 1302, CA; *R. v. Panel on Takeovers and Mergers, ex p. Datafin plc* [1987] Q.B. 815, CA; *R. v. Advertising Standards Authority, ex p. Insurance Service plc* (1989) 9 Tr.L.R. 169, (1990) 2 Admin. L.R. 77, DC; *R. v. Disciplinary Committee of the Jockey Club, ex p. Massingberd-Mundy* (1989) [1993] 2 All E.R. 207, DC; *R. v. Jockey Club, ex p. RAM Racecourses Ltd* (1990) [1993] 2 All E.R. 225, DC; *R. v. Chief Rabbi of the United Hebrew Congregations, ex p. Wachmann* [1992] 1 W.L.R. 1036; *R. v. Football Association Ltd, ex p. Football League Ltd* [1993] 2 All E.R. 833 (Rose J.); *R. v. Disciplinary Committee of the Jockey Club, ex p. Aga Khan* [1993] 1 W.L.R. 909, CA; *R. v. Insurance Ombudsman, ex p. Aegon Life Assurance Ltd* [1994] C.O.D. 426; *R. v. Press Complaints Commission, ex p. Stewart-Brady* (1997) 9 Admin. L.R. 247; *R. v. London Beth Din (Court of Chief Rabbi), ex p. Bloom* [1998] C.O.D. 131; *R. v. Panel of the Federation of Communication Services Ltd, ex p. Kubis* [1998] C.O.D. 56; *Andreou v. Institute of Chartered Accountants in England and Wales* [1998] 1 All E.R. 14. See further: C.

(1) The "but for" test—whether, but for the existence of a non-statutory body, the government would itself almost inevitably have intervened to regulate the activity in question.[68] Here the court poses a hypothetical question. Evidence as to the position of comparable bodies in other countries has sometimes been regarded as relevant, and sometimes not.[69]

(2) Whether the government has acquiesced or encouraged the activities of the body under challenge by providing "underpinning" for its work, has woven the body into the fabric of public regulation[70] or that the body was established "under the authority of government".[71] Here the court is concerned not with what might happen, but with what has actually occurred. The mere fact that existence of the body is explicitly or implicitly recognised in legislation is insufficient.[72]

Forsyth, 'The Scope of Judicial Review: 'public duty' not 'source of power'" [1987] P.L. 356; M. Beloff, 'Pitch, Pool, Rink ... Court? Judicial Review in the Sporting World' [1989] P.L. 95; D. Pannick, 'Who is Subject to Judicial Review and in Respect of What?' [1992] P.L. 1; N. Bamforth, 'The Scope of Judicial Review: Still Uncertain' [1993] P.L. 239.

[68] A factor present in, *e.g. R. v. Advertising Standards Authority, ex p. Insurance Service plc* (above n. 67) where it was held that in the absence of a self-regulatory body such as the ASA, its functions "would no doubt be exercised by the Director General of Fair Trading" (*per* Glidewell L.J. at 86). *Cf., e.g. R. v. Football Association Ltd, ex p. Football League Ltd* (above, n. 67) (television or other commercial company more likely than government to step in to regulate football if the F.A. did not exist). The but-for test is not conclusive. In *ex p. Aga Khan* (above, n. 67), the Master of the Rolls was "willing to accept that if the Jockey Club did not regulate horse racing the government would probably be driven to create a public body to do so," but went on to hold that the Club "is not in its origin, its history, its constitution or (least of all) its membership a public body" (at 923); the other members of the CA differed, holding that the government would not have intervened.

[69] The fact that outside England some governments regulated the sport of horse racing was not regarded as significant in *ex p. Aga Khan* (n. 67, above) at 932. *Cf. Datafin* (n. 67, above) where the Panel's lack of a direct statutory base was regarded as "a complete anomaly, judged by the experience of other comparable markets world wide" (at 835).

[70] An expression used by Sir Thomas Bingham M.R. in *ex p. Aga Khan* (above, n. 67) at 921.

[71] See Diplock L.J. in *ex p. Lain* [1967] 2 Q.B. 864 at 884 cited with approval by Lloyd L.J. in *ex p. Datafin plc* (above, n. 67) at 849.

[72] See, *e.g.: ex p. Wachmann* (above, n. 67) (existence and some functions of Chief Rabbi recognised by United Synagogues Act 1870 and Slaughter Houses Act 1974); *ex p. Aegon Life Insurance Ltd* (above n. 67) (under Financial Services Act 1986 LAUTRO recognised by Secretary of State as self-regulatory organisation; rather than itself carrying out a complaints investigation function, as required by the Act, LAUTRO recognised the Insurance Ombudsman as performing that task); *ex p. Football Association Ltd* (above, n. 67) where the F.A. had been recognised by Football Spectators Act 1989, s. 4. In none of these cases was the presence of the legislation

(3) Whether the body was exercising extensive or monopolistic powers, for instance by effectively regulating entry to a trade, profession or sport.[73] The Panel on Takeovers and Mergers was said to have "a giant's strength".[74] Monopolistic power is not, however, necessarily to be equated with the performance of public functions. Extensive power over others is often exercised in the private sphere and here judicial review is not available.[75] The seriousness of the impact of the decision on those affected,[76] or the number of people affected by the action,[77] have not been regarded as relevant; nor is the importance of the body in national life.[78]

(4) Whether the aggrieved person has consensually submitted to be bound by the decision-maker. This is closely linked to the previous criterion. In considering the position of the Panel on Takeovers and Mergers in *Datafin*, Lloyd L.J. stated that "the City is not a club which one can join or not at will ... The panel regulates not only itself, but all others who have no alternative but to come to the market in a case to which the code applies."[79] The question of whether there has been

---

sufficient to make the body reviewable.

[73] As with the other criteria, the existence of monopolistic power is not in itself sufficient to make a decision-maker subject to judicial review. Rose J. accepted that the F.A. had 'virtually monopolistic powers' (see *ex p. Football League Ltd*, n. 67 above, at 848), and so did the Court of Appeal in *ex p. Aga Khan* (n. 67 above).

[74] *Datafin* (above, n. 67) at 845, *per* Lloyd L.J.

[75] See, *e.g. Aga Khan* (above, n. 67) at 932–933 where Hoffman L.J. stated: 'the mere fact of power, even over a substantial area of economic activity, is not enough. In a mixed economy, power may be private as well as public. Private power may affect the public interest and livelihoods of many individuals. But that does not subject it to the rules of public law. If control is needed, it must be found in the law of contract, the doctrine of restraint of trade, the Restrictive Trade Practices Act 1976, articles 85 and 86 of the EEC treaty and all the other instruments available in law for curbing excesses of private power.'

[76] See, *e.g. R. v. Chief Rabbi, ex p. Wachmann* (above, n. 67) (whether or not a decision had 'public law consequences' must be determined otherwise than by reference to the seriousness of its impact upon those affected).

[77] *e.g.* in *ex p. Football League Ltd* (above, n. 67), Rose J. noted at 841 that 'FA's powers extend beyond contract to affect the lives of many hundreds of thousands who are not in any contractual relationship ... though the same could be said about large public companies'.

[78] See *ex p. Football League Ltd* (above, n. 67) where Rose J. at 840 notes that the important role of the F.A. had been recognised by official government reports. *Cf. ex p. Massingberd-Mundy* (above, n. 67) where Neill L.J. stated that, had the matter been free of authority, he would have held that the Jockey Club was judicially reviewable because it held a position of major public importance and 'near monopolistic powers in an area in which the public generally have an interest and many persons earn their livelihoods'.

[79] *Datafin* (above, n. 67) at 846.

consensual submission ought not to be merged with that of whether a contract *entirely* regulates the relationship between the parties. It has always been the case that private or domestic tribunals are performing no public function when their "authority is derived solely from contract, that is the agreement of the parties concerned".[80] Their functions are therefore outside the scope of judicial review. Whether or not a contract exists between the aggrieved person and the body, in some situations the body may be performing regulatory or other functions which create a situation where the person is left with the stark choice of either submitting himself to the control of the body or not participating in the activity concerned.[81] Here, it is submitted, judicial review ought in principle to be available to an aggrieved person, though if a contract exists a contractual claim will normally be an appropriate alternative remedy which may bar judicial review.

(5) Suggestions have also been made from time to time that the court ought to have regard to the limited number of judges and the growing judicial review case load in deciding whether a class of body is susceptible to judicial review.[82] To take account of this factor appears to be wrong in principle and creates potential problems as to the independence of the judiciary. The number of the judiciary is of no relevance to the scope of judicial review. By failing to fill vacancies the executive could reduce the number of judges and thus, if the factor is relevant, theoretically reduce the scope of judicial review.

---

[80] See, *e.g. R. v. Criminal Injuries Compensation Board, ex p. Lain* [1967] 2 Q.B. 864, 882 (*per* Lord Parker C.J.) and 884–885 (*per* Diplock L.J.).

[81] See, *e.g. ex p. Wachmann* (above, n. 67) (judicial review not excluded because the applicant had consensually submitted to the Chief Rabbi's jurisdiction; the exclusion from judicial review of those who consensually submit to some subordinate jurisdiction properly applied only to arbitrators or private and domestic tribunals. Other reasons were, however, given for not subjecting the Chief Rabbi's decision to judicial review). There is much to be said for this view. *Cf.* the statement of Farquharson L.J. in *ex p. Aga Khan* (above, n. 67) at 928: 'The fact is that if the applicant wishes to race his horses in this country he had no choice but to submit to the Jockey Club's jurisdiction. This may be true but nobody is obliged to race his horses in this country and it does not destroy the element of consensuality'. See also *R. v. Code of Practice Committee of the Association of British Pharmaceutical Industry, ex p. Professional Counselling Aids Ltd* (1990) 3 Admin. L.R. 697; [1991] C.O.D. 228.

[82] See comments by Rose J. in *ex p. Football League Ltd* (above, n. 67) at 849 that it would be 'a misapplication of scarce judicial resources' to hold the F.A. amenable to the court's public law supervisory jurisdiction' and dicta of Lord Donaldson M.R. in *R. v. Panel on Take-overs and Mergers, ex p. Guinness plc* [1990] 1 Q.B. 146, 177–178. *Cf.* D. Pannick [1992] P.L. 1, 6–7.

Undue reliance upon any one of the above criteria—while perhaps **3–025** helpful in promoting certainty in this area of law[83]—should be avoided. The test of public function should be overriding and the qualities enumerated in the criteria should be weighed and balanced in the context of each specific case. This will avoid the formalism that might otherwise develop and that has, in the past, inhibited the proper development of so much of administrative law.[84]

The application of the principles of judicial review can have the **3–026** effect of extending the rights of the individual. For example, it can give an individual a right to be consulted which he would not have in private law.[85] On the other hand, the extent of redress that is available in judicial review may be less extensive than that available in private law.[86]

Not all decisions of public bodies are or should be governed by **3–027** distinct principles of public law. For instance, when a public authority enters into a contract the same principles of private law apply as those which govern similar transactions between private corporations, though if in making a contract a public body acts in an arbitrary or unreasonable manner, or exceeds its statutory powers, its decision may be subject to judicial review.[87] A complex body of legislation also now regulates public procurement and other contracting functions of public bodies.[88] English law recognises, however, that a public body can act

---

[83] Bodies ought to be able to know what, if any, legal standards will be applied to their activities. Certainty is also desirable for applicants whose legal advisors need to know whether to use public law or private law proceedings to redress a grievance. As to procedure, the divide between public and private law may become less important in the future for applicants and their legal advisors if recent proposals of the radical reform of the civil justice system in England and Wales are implemented. The court itself rather than the parties will take on responsibility for making decisions about the form and management of litigation: see *Access to Justice* (1996), Final Report to the Lord Chancellor on the Civil Justice System in England and Wales by Lord Woolf. The procedural implications of the public/private law divide are considered below, para. 3–035.

[84] Consider, *e.g.*, the judicial/administrative/quasi-judicial categories (below, Chap. 6).

[85] *Council for Civil Service Unions v. Minister for the Civil Service* [1985] A.C. 374.

[86] See the discussion on estoppel and substantive legitimate expectations in Chap. 12.

[87] See para. 3–018.

[88] See, *e.g.* Public Supply Contracts Regulations 1991 (S.I. 1991 No. 2679). Public Works Contracts Regulations 1991 (S.I. 1991 No. 2680), Utilities and Works Contracts Regulations 1992 (S.I. 1992 No. 3279) and Local Government Act 1988.

in more than one capacity.[89] This is unlike the situation in most civil legal systems, such as the French system, where all the activities of public bodies are governed by public law.

3–028   Conversely, not all the activities of private bodies (such as private companies) are subject only to private law. For example, the activities of a private body (such as a recently privatised company) may be governed by the standards of public law when its decisions are subject to duties conferred by statute[90] or when, by virtue of the function it is performing or possibly its dominant position in the market, it is under an implied duty to act in the public interest.[91] A private company selected to run a prison, for example, although motivated by considerations of commercial profit should be regarded, at least in relation to some of its activities, as subject to public law because of the nature of the function it is performing.[92] This is because the prisoners, for whose custody and care it is responsible, are in the prison in consequence of an order of the court, and the purpose and nature of their detention is a matter of public concern and interest.

3–029   The jurisprudence of the European Court of Justice is instructive. In a number of cases the question has arisen whether a body was to be regarded as exercising the powers of a "State". This is of course a narrower question than that considered here, namely, whether a body is subject to the regime of domestic judicial review. But the principles behind each question are similar. In *Foster v. British Gas plc*[93] it was held that a directive could be directly effective against bodies, whatever their legal form, (a) "which have been made responsible, pursuant to a measure adopted by the State for providing a public service" or (b) where the service it provided was at the material time "under the control of the state", or (c) where the body has "special

---

[89] In particular in relation to the activities of the Crown a distinction has to be drawn between the sovereign's personal activities (and personal capacity) and those activities which are performed as the personification of the State. The distinction has been underlined by the Queen's decision to pay tax on her private income. Furthermore, although there can be situations where, because of the special status of the Crown, the Crown is under no liability this does not mean that Ministers and other officers of the Crown will not be under any personal liability for their activities performed on behalf of the Crown. See *M. v. Home Office* [1994] 1 A.C. 377; and also *Raymond v. Honey* [1983] A.C. 1, *Victoria v. Australian Building Construction Employees' and Builders Labourers' Federation* (1982) 152 C.L.R. 25 and *Bhatnager v. Minister of Employment* (1990) 71 D.L.R. 84. Government bodies cannot sue for libel, *Derbyshire C.C. v. Times Newspapers Ltd* [1993] A.C. 534, HL but a Minister can do so.
[90] *e.g.* Gas Act 1986, s. 9 (to supply gas).
[91] See below, para. 3–032, and *Foster v. British Gas plc* (n.93, below) and *Nationalised and Privatised Industries*, and *Mercury Energy Ltd v. Electricity Corp. of N.Z. Ltd* [1994] 1 W.L.R. 521.
[92] See above, para. 3–018.
[93] *Foster v. British Gas plc* [1991] 2 A.C. 306, HL; Case C-188/89 [1991] 1 Q.B. 405, E.C.J. and below, Chap. 17.

powers beyond those which result from the normal rules applicable in relations between individuals". These three criteria go much further than a definition of state power which confines itself to the nominal and formal classification of a "public" body. The first and third criteria in particular are practical indicators of the circumstances in which nominally "private" bodies may be said to be performing "public" functions.[94]

Summary

The position described can be summarised in the following propositions: **3–030**

(1) The test of whether a body is performing a public function, and is hence amenable to judicial review, may not depend upon the source of its power or whether the body is ostensibly a "public" or a "private" body.

(2) The principles of judicial review prima facie govern the activities of bodies performing public functions.

(3) However, not all decisions taken by bodies in the course of their public functions are the subject matter of judicial review. In the following two situations judicial review will not normally be appropriate even though the body may be performing a public function:

  (a) Where some other branch of the law more appropriately governs the dispute between the parties. In such a case, that branch of the law and its remedies should and normally will be applied; and

  (b) Where there is a contract between the litigants. In such a case the express or implied terms of the agreement should normally govern the matter. This reflects the normal

---

[94] The United States Supreme Court has over the years wrestled with the question whether action by nominally private bodies constitutes 'state action' under the 14th Amendment to the US Constitution (forbidding any State to deprive any person of due process of law or equal protection of the law). The tests for when private action qualifies as State action have varied. Sometimes a 'public function' test has been employed, *e.g.* in relation to a park managed by private trustees (*Evans v. Newton* (1966) 382 U.S. 296; 86 S.Ct. 496). This test has recently been restricted to functions which are 'traditionally and exclusively reserved to the State' (*Blum v. Yanetsky* (1982) 457 U.S. 991; 102 S.Ct. 2777). although state action is implied whenever there is a significant element of state coercion or regulation behind the decision or action of the 'private' body (*Layar v. Edmondson Oil Co.* (1982) 457 U.S. 922; 102 S.Ct. 2744; *cf.* *Jackson v. Metropolitan Edison Co.* (1974) 419 U.S. 345; 95 S.Ct. 449).

approach of English law, namely, that the terms of a contract will normally govern the transaction, or other relationship between the parties, rather than the general law.[95] Thus, where a special method of resolving disputes (such as arbitration or resolution by private or domestic tribunals) has been agreed by the parties (expressly or by necessary implication), that regime, and not judicial review, will normally govern the dispute.

SPECIAL SITUATIONS

3–031 The general principles, set out above, for determining whether a body is carrying out public functions, and thus subject to judicial review, do not apply universally. Some bodies are regarded as having unique characteristics, to which special considerations apply.

Regulation in higher education: University Visitors

3–032 Until a recent majority decision of the House of Lords[96] the position of a University Visitor was in doubt. The House of Lords had to consider whether the decision of a Visitor as to the construction of the statutes of a University was subject to judicial review. The majority decided it was not. Not because a Visitor's jurisdiction was based on contract but because a University was an eleemosynary or charitable foundation and the Visitor was the sole judge of the law of the foundation which was law peculiar to the University or domestic rather than the general law of the land. The Visitor was treated as having exclusive jurisdiction to determine disputes arising under the domestic law of the University and the proper application of those laws to those persons within his jurisdiction. However, the majority of their Lordships were of the opinion that although the court had no jurisdiction to review a decision made by the Visitor as to questions of either fact or law, whether right or wrong, provided his decision was made within his jurisdiction (in the narrowest sense of acting within his power under the regulating documents to enter upon the

---

[95] *R. v. CICB, ex p. Lain* [1967] 2 Q.B. 864. A contractual nexus is not necessarily fatal but if the source of the power is contractual, that is consensual, this can be: *R. v. Insurance Ombudsman, ex p. Aegon Life Assurance Ltd* [1994] C.O.D. 426; *R. v. Jockey Club, ex p. Aga Khan* [1993] 1 W.L.R. 909; *R. v. Panel on Takeovers and Mergers, ex p. Datafin* [1987] Q.B. 815, 835, 838, 847A–C; *cf. R. v. Lloyds of London, ex p. Briggs* [1993] 1 Lloyd's Rep. 176, 185 *per* Legatt L.J. (all the powers were exercised by Lloyd's over its members by agreement.)

[96] (Three to two) *Page v. Hull University Visitor* [1993] A.C. 682.

adjudication of the dispute), judicial review would lie against the Visitor if he acted outside his jurisdiction or if he abused his power in a manner wholly incompatible with his judicial role or acted in breach of the rules of natural justice.[97] The fact that the majority considered that the decisions of the Visitor could be subject to judicial review but only if he went outside his jurisdiction, means that he could be regarded as performing a public function. The justification for putting him in this anomalous position, where only certain of his decisions are reviewable, was based upon a long line of authorities which were regarded as creating, so far as the Visitor was concerned, a "unique" position.[98] A position in which it was highly desirable that there should be finality of decision.[99]

Not all universities have Visitors, though where comparable   3–033
appellate committees exist, an applicant will be required to exhaust those alternative remedies before making an application for judicial review. Nor are all disciplinary and other decisions taken by universities which do have a Visitor necessarily within the ambit of the Visitor's jurisdiction.[1]

---

[97] See also *Thomas v. University of Bradford* [1987] A.C. 795, 825, as explained in *Page v. Hull University Visitor* [1993] 1 All E.R. 97, 100. In *R. v. University of Nottingham, ex p. Ktorides* [1998] C.O.D. 26 the Court of Appeal rejected submissions that the court should accept jurisdiction over a challenge to a decision that the applicant failed part of her postgraduate teacher training course (and about which no complaint had been made to the Visitor) because there had been a statutory intrusion into the University's role in the provision of teacher training by virtue of the Education (Teachers) Regulations 1993 which enabled a minister to withdraw accreditation of an institution. This was not sufficient to remove the Visitor's exclusive jurisdiction.

[98] Lord Slynn of Hadley, in rejecting the distinction drawn by the majority, referred to the speech of Lord Diplock in *Re Racal Communications Ltd* [1981] A.C. 374 in which he referred to *Anisminic Ltd v. Foreign Compensation Commission* [1969] 2 A.C. 147 and added that 'the breakthrough made by *Anisminic* was that, in respect of administrative tribunals and authorities, the old distinctions between errors of law that went to jurisdiction and errors of law that did not, was for practicable purposes abolished'. He also referred to a similar statement by Lord Diplock in *O' Reilly v. Mackman* [1983] 2 A.C. 237, 278. These comments have considerable force and it is to be hoped that the Visitor will indeed be treated as being in a unique position and the same distinction will not be drawn in relation to other persons performing public functions. However, the decision has already been applied to decisions of Visitors to the Inns of Court. *R. v. Visitors to the Inns of Courts, ex p. Calder* [1993] 3 W.L.R. 287.

[99] See [1993] 1 All E.R., 101a, b. 109h *per* Lords Griffiths and Browne-Wilkinson and *cf.* Lord Slynn at 114f and g.

[1] See, *e.g. R. v. University College London, ex p. Christofi* (September 12, 1997, CA, unrep.) (Court considered and rejected on its merits a judicial review challenge brought by a former student against findings of an *ad hoc* committee of senior academics from outside UCL that he had falsified scientific data published in international journals while engaged in post-doctoral research).

The Crown

3–034   Statutes only rarely impose public law duties or confer discretions on the Crown itself; instead it is normal for the Secretary of State to be given such responsibilities.[2] Most prerogative powers are now also exercised by Ministers of the Crown.[3] For this reason, it is of little practical importance that neither the prerogative remedies (certiorari, prohibition and mandamus) nor injunctions can be obtained against the Crown directly because they will clearly issue against Ministers of the Crown.[4] The constitutional justification for immunity of the Crown itself from public law remedies, perhaps now best described as an outdated fiction, is "both because there would be an incongruity in the Queen commanding herself to do an act, and also because the disobedience to a writ of mandamus is to be enforced by attachment."[5] The Crown is the nominal applicant (*R. v. Respondent, ex p. Applicant*) in applications for judicial review.[6] The provisions of the Crown Proceedings Act 1947 do not apply to applications for judicial review or other public law proceedings on the Crown side of the Queen's Bench Division of the High Court.[7]

PROCEDURAL EXCLUSIVITY

3–035   Having considered the question of which decisions of what bodies are subject to judicial review, we now turn to examine the procedural

---

[2] See *M. v. Home Office* [1994] 1 A.C. 377, 417. As to the status and significance of the office of Secretary of State, see A. Simcock, 'One and Many—the Office of Secretary of State' (1992) 70 Pub. Admin. 535. On the changing nature of the legal status of the Crown, see further Joseph M. Jacob, *The Republican Crown: Lawyers and the Making of the State in Twentieth Century Britain* (1996) and M. Sunkin and S. Payne (eds), *The Nature of the Crown* (1999).

[3] As to judicial review of prerogative powers, see para. 3–016 and para. 5–037 *et seq.*

[4] See *M. v. Home Office* (n.2, above). One interesting example of a statute placing a public law power directly on the Crown, see the Import, Export and Customs Powers (Defence) Act 1939, s. 9(3): 'This Act shall expire on such date as His Majesty may declare by Order in Council to be the end of the emergency that was the occasion of the passing of this Act.' Even if an applicant successfully argued that the Crown had (say) unlawfully refused to declare an end to the emergency, the court would have no power to grant a prerogative order or an injunction as the public law discretion is placed directly in the hands of the Crown. *Cf. R. v. Blackledge and Others* (1996) 8 Admin. L.R. 361.

[5] *R. v. Powell* (1841) 1 Q.B. 352, 361, *per* Lord Denman C.J. quoted with approval by Lord Woolf in *M. v. Home Office* (n.2, above) at 415.

[6] See Chap. 14.

[7] s. 38(2). The confusion which arose as to whether the court had jurisdiction to order an interim injunction against a Minister on an application for judicial review was rectified by the House of Lords in *M. v. Home Office* (n. 2, above).

aspects of the public-private divide. The issue here is whether a litigant wishing to challenge the legality of a decision made by a body amenable to judicial review is *required* to use the Order 53 application for judicial review procedure.[8] Circumstances may arise where a litigant instead wishes to proceed using the general code set out in the Civil Procedure Rules in order to obtain a declaration, injunction or damages. A defendant may also wish to raise issues of public law by way of a defence in general civil proceedings or in a criminal trial. The extent to which public law submissions may be advanced outside Order 53 proceedings continues to be highly contentious.

The justification for the divide

When recommending in 1976 the creation of a new procedure for judicial review, the Law Commission contemplated the co-existence of judicial review proceedings and actions brought by issuing a writ or originating summons for a declaration (private law proceedings) in relation to public law issues.[9] This was not, however, a realistic approach. The application for judicial review procedures had the safeguard of the requirement for leave (now called "permission") and a limited period in which to make applications, which would serve no purpose if they could be bypassed by issuing an ordinary claim for a declaration which was not subject to the same safeguards. It is true that in private law proceedings there are also safeguards. For example, once a claim is issued (not before) it is possible for the statement of case to be struck out as disclosing no reasonable grounds or being an abuse of the process of the court. However, the protection provided in Order 53 proceedings is greater than that provided in general civil proceedings. In an application for judicial review under Order 53, the onus is on the applicant to show that he has a prima facie case, while in general civil proceedings the onus is on the defendant to show that the applicant has either no cause of action or the proceedings are otherwise unmeritorious.

3–036

---

[8] The main features of the Order 53 application for judicial review procedure are described in Chap. 14, below.

[9] Remedies in Administrative Law (Law Commission No. 73 (1976)) paras 34, 58(a). (The issue of 'writs' and 'summons' has been replaced by 'claim forms' in the Civil Procedure Rules enacted in 1999).

The general rule

3–037   The much criticised decision in the House of Lords in, *O'Reilly v. Mackman*[10] was therefore the logical consequence[11] of the procedure included in Order 53. In that case Lord Diplock set out the general rule.

> "Now ... all remedies for infringement of rights protected by public law can be obtained upon an application for judicial review, as can also remedies for infringement of rights under private law if such infringement should also be involved, it would in my view as a general rule be contrary to public policy, and as such an abuse of the process of the court, to permit a person seeking to establish that a decision of a public authority infringed rights to which he was entitled to protection under public law to proceed by way of ordinary action and by this means to evade the provisions of Order 53 for the protection of such authorities... I have described this as a general rule; for, though it may normally be appropriate to apply it by the summary process of striking out the action, there may be exceptions, particularly where the invalidity of the decision arises as a collateral issue in a claim for infringement of a right of the plaintiff arising under private law, or where none of the parties object to the adoption of the procedure by writ or originating summons. Whether there should be other exceptions should, in my view, at this stage in the development of procedural public law, be left to be decided on a case to case basis."

3–038   It is important to note that in the passage of his speech just cited Lord Diplock was setting out a general rule and a rule which was to be the subject of exceptions which were to be worked out on a case-by-case basis.[12] In addition *O'Reilly v. Mackman* typified the sort of case which it could be expected would result in the misgivings which had been expressed in earlier cases about the undesirability of bypassing judicial review being reiterated. It involved four prisoners

---

[10] [1983] 2 A.C. 237.

[11] *cf.* for example, the report of Justice/All Souls, *Administrative Justice—Some Necessary Reforms* (1988) para. 6.18, which describes it as 'an unfortunate decision'. Wade and Forsyth say it 'must be accounted a serious setback for administrative law...a step back towards the time of the old forms of action which were so deservedly buried in 1852.' (*Administrative Law* (7th ed., 1994), p. 682.) See also Sir Patrick Neill Q.C., *Administrative Law: Snakes and Ladders* (1985) but *cf.* Woolf, 'Public Law—Private Law, Why the Divide?' [1986] P.L. 220 and *Protection of the Public—A New Challenge* (1990), pp. 24 *et seq.*

[12] [1983] 2 A.C. 237, 284–285.

who, after the Hull Prison Riots, brought an action claiming declarations that the disciplinary awards which had been made against them by the Prison Visitors were invalid as being in breach of the Prison Rules and as contravening the principles of natural justice. If the proceedings had been by way of judicial review, it is most unlikely that permission would have been granted for them to be commenced since the applicants were short on merits.

Homogenised decisions

In the *Irish Dairy Board* case[13] the Irish Dairy Board sought damages   3–039
and an injunction to restrain the Milk Marketing Board from selling milk for making butter at different prices to an intervention agency or into the United Kingdom. The action was based upon breaches of E.C. and U.K. legislation. The Milk Marketing Board contended that the action should have been brought by way of judicial review but as Sir John Donaldson M.R., said, it was not an abuse or, as the court preferred to style it, "a misuse" of the process of the court since in so far as public law issues were involved they were "inextricably mixed—'homogenised' ... in the context of the subject matter of the dispute". So where public and private law decisions are not separate and distinct, but homogenised the principle of exclusivity laid down in *O'Reilly v. Mackman* need not be followed. However, presumably the company, if it wished, could have brought judicial review proceedings and obtained damages and an injunction under the powers contained in Order 53.[14]

Collateral public law qualities

In accordance with Lord Diplock's recommendation[15] in *O'Reilly v.*   3–040
Mackman other exceptions have been subsequently identified. One exception is where the public law aspect of the proceedings is collateral to an issue which is the proper subject matter of private law proceedings. In *Davy v. Spelthorne B.C.*[16] the Court of Appeal did not

---

[13] *An Bord Bainne Coop Ltd v. Milk Marketing Board* [1984] 2 C.M.L.R. 584, 587–588. *Cf. Guevara v. Hounslow B.C., The Times.* April 17, 1987.

[14] Another situation where it would be appropriate to proceed either by issue of a claim form or judicial review would be where it was alleged that a public body has exceeded or abused its public law powers and wrongfully detained the applicant and his property and as a result damages are sought as well as the declaring invalid or the quashing of the decision. See Chap. 16, below.

[15] [1983] 2 A.C. 237, 284–285.

[16] (1983) 81 L.G.R. 580.

permit the plaintiff to proceed with a claim for an injunction in ordinary civil proceedings to prevent the implementation of an enforcement notice and the setting aside of the notice, but did allow a claim for damages for negligent advice by the Council to proceed arising out of the same matter. The House of Lords dismissed the authority's appeal in relation to the claim for damages since liability for damages did not directly raise any question of public law.[17]

3–041   In *Mercury Communications Ltd v. Director General of Telecommunications and another* the House of Lords refused to strike out an originating summons where it was argued that the matters in question ought to have been raised in an application for judicial review. Lord Slynn of Hadley stated that it was:

> "of particular importance ... to retain some flexibility, as the precise limits of what is called 'public law' and what is called 'private law' are by no means worked out. ... It has to be borne in mind that the overriding question is whether the proceedings constitute an abuse of the process of the court."[18]

In the instant case, the dispute as to the correct interpretation by the Director General of a condition in a licence granted to British Telecommunications plc was "in substance as well as form" a dispute over terms of a contract. In *British Steel plc v. Customs and Excise Commissioners* Laws J. at first instance struck out a writ claiming restitution and repayment of excise duty on hydrocarbon oils.[19] The plaintiffs claimed that the demands for payment of duty were unlawful because the plaintiffs were entitled to relief from paying duty under the relevant legislation. The plaintiffs had neither sought to challenge the defendants' demands by way of judicial review, nor declined to pay and await action by the commissioners with a view to pleading a defence to the effect that they were entitled to relief under the legislation. Laws J. held that whereas the illegality of the tax demands was the premise of *Woolwich Building Society v. I.R.C. (No. 2),*[20] in the instant case it was the very question falling for decision:

---

[17] [1984] A.C. 262. See also the speech of Lord Scarman in *Gillick v. West Norfolk and Wisbech A.H.A.* [1986] A.C. 112, 178. Lord Scarman considered that it was sufficient if the private law content of a claim was sufficiently great to override the public law element. In the Court of Appeal in *Wandsworth L.B.C. v. Winder* [1985] A.C. 461, 480, he said: 'I find it difficult to conceive of a case where a citizen's invocation of the ordinary procedure of the courts in order to enforce his private law rights, or his reliance on his private law rights by way of defence in an action brought against him, could as such amount to an abuse of the process of the court.'

[18] [1996] 1 W.L.R. 48 at 578D. See further P.P. Craig, 'Proceeding Outside Order 53: A Modified Test?' (1996) 112 L.Q.R. 531.

[19] [1996] 1 All E.R. 1002.

[20] [1992] A.C. 70.

"Where the statute confers what it plainly a private right, if on the Act's true construction the right enures only after and in consequence of a purely public law decision in favour of the claimant, any complaint directed to the public decision-making stage must be brought by Order 53."

The Court of Appeal allowed an appeal against Laws J.'s decision.[21] It held that applying the reasoning in *Woolwich* to the facts of the instant case justified the conclusion that a demand for tax following an unlawful refusal to grant relief from tax was an "unlawful demand" for the purposes of Lord Goff's reformulation of the law. The writ action could continue as British Steel might be able to prove that it was an "approved person" and, if it could, it would have a restitutionary claim.

Relying on public law as a defence to private law proceedings

A closely related situation arises where a defendant seeks to avoid **3–042** liability in general civil proceedings by challenging the validity of a public law decision on which the proceedings are based. This is the position, apparently, even though if the defendant wished to initiate proceedings himself to challenge the decision he would have to do so by judicial review. It appears that if, instead, he waits for a claim to be made against him he is perfectly entitled to raise the invalidity of the decision in his defence.[22] A difficulty about this exception to the *O'Reilly v. Mackman* principle is that it could result in differing decisions of the court depending upon who commenced proceedings first. For example, if because of delay the applicant for judicial review is refused relief, any other applicant who subsequently applies for judicial review would almost certainly be in the same position. However, the principle of *res judicata* does not normally apply to

---

[21] [1997] 2 All E.R. 366.

[22] This was the position in *Wandsworth L.B.C. v. Winder* [1985] A.C. 461. At 509–510 Lord Fraser of Tullybelton said: "It would in my opinion be a very strange use of language to describe the respondent's behaviour in relation to this litigation as an abuse or misuse by him of the process of the court. He did not select the procedure to be adopted. He is merely seeking to defend proceedings brought against him by the appellant. In so doing he is seeking only to exercise an ordinary right of any individual to defend an action against him on the ground that he is not liable for the whole sum claimed by the plaintiff. Moreover he puts forward his defence as a matter of right, whereas an application for judicial review, success would require an exercise of the court's discretion in his favour." The *Winder* case was distinguished in *Tower Hamlets v. Abdi*, *The Times*, October 26, 1992.

judicial review,[23] so if the applicant, who had failed in his application for judicial review, because of his culpable delay, is sued he could still rely on the same matters as those on which he relied in his application for judicial review as a defence to any proceedings in which those matters are relevant. As in the majority of public law disputes a number of members of the public are affected by the outcome of the proceedings this is hardly satisfactory. There should not be differing consequences for different members of the public depending upon who was responsible for initiating the proceedings.[24] However an alleged invalidity cannot be relied upon if, assuming it were to be established, it would not constitute a defence.[25]

The position in criminal proceedings

3–043   At one time, the courts drew a distinction between alleged patent or substantive defects in the subordinate legislation or administrative decisions upon which a prosecution was based—which could be raised at a criminal trial—and latent or procedural defects (for instance that a decision was reached in breach of natural justice) which could not be raised.[26] This approach has since been rejected by the House of Lords.[27] There is a strong presumption that a defendant in criminal proceedings is entitled to argue that the subordinate legislation or administrative decision upon which a prosecution is founded is *ultra vires*; there is, however, also a presumption in favour of the lawfulness of subordinate legislation. It is open to the court, having construed the legislation upon which a prosecution is brought and considered the nature of the defendant's submissions, to hold that

---

[23] The extent to which it is applicable at all is unclear. See Wade and Forsyth, *Administrative Law* (7th ed., 1994), pp. 276–283.

[24] For a criticism of the *Winder* decision see Woolf, *Protection of the Public: A New Challenge* (1990), pp. 29–32.

[25] In *Avon C.C. v. Buscott* [1988] Q.B. 656 an attempt was made by gypsies to avoid being evicted from a site where they were undoubtedly trespassers by contending that the local authority was in breach of its duty to provide sites for them and was therefore acting unreasonably, but this defence was regarded as being of no avail, *Cf. Doyle v. Northumbria Probation Committee* [1991] 1 W.L.R. 1340.

[26] *Bugg v. DPP* [1993] Q.B. 437, Div. Ct.

[27] *R. v. Wicks* [1998] A.C. 92 (*Bugg* doubted); *Boddington v. British Transport Police* [1998] 2 W.L.R. 639 (*Bugg* overruled).

Parliament intends to prohibit collateral challenges during the course of criminal trials.[28] The court will, however, be loathe to do this.[29]

Where there is no dispute as to the appropriate procedure

If the parties do not contest the appropriateness of the procedure which is being used, then it is unlikely that the court will interfere with what the parties regard as being the appropriate procedure though parties cannot by consent confer jurisdiction on the courts which they do not possess. However, the use of the wrong procedure should not be regarded as affecting the court's jurisdiction.[30]

3–044

Where private law dominates the proceedings

A broad approach was adopted in *Roy v. Kensington, Chelsea and Westminster Family Practitioners Committee*.[31] The case concerned a claim

3–045

---

[28] In *Wicks* (note above), the defendant was prosecuted for failure to comply with an enforcement notice served upon him pursuant to Town and Country Planning Act 1990, s.172. He elected for trial on indictment and his counsel sought to argue that the local planning authority had had regard to immaterial considerations in its decision to serve the enforcement notice, which was accordingly invalid. On appeal, their Lordships held that it was not possible to lay down a general rule; the question whether issues could be raised at a criminal trial to impugn a decision or legislation depended entirely on the construction of the statute under which the prosecution was bought. In the instant case, it was held that 'enforcement notice' meant a notice issued by the planning authority that was formally valid and had not been quashed. One important factor which compelled this conclusion was that the 1990 Act contained an elaborate code with detailed provisions regarding appeals. Parliament had intended the Divisional Court, not criminal proceedings arising from a failure to comply with an enforcement notice, to be the appropriate forum to question such notices. It was therefore not permissible for the defendant to seek to impugn the enforcement notice in the Crown Court.

[29] *Dilieto v. Ealing LBC* [1998] 2 All E.R. 885 (no reason in principle why defendant in prosecution for failing to comply with a breach of a condition notice contrary to Town and Country Planning Act 1990, s. 187A should not be able to challenge its validity by way of defence; unlike *Wicks* there was no statutory appeal procedure and no allegation of *Wednesbury* unreasonableness was made); *Boddington v. British Transport Police* (note 27 above) (nothing in Transport Act 1962 or British Rail Byelaws to rebut presumption that person prosecuted for smoking on train entitled to defend himself on basis of the invalidity of the decision to put 'no smoking' notices in every carriage).

[30] This could be considered as being the explanation for the ability of the plaintiffs in *Gillick v. West Norfolk and Wisbech A.H.A.* [1986] A.C. 112 and *Royal College of Nursing v. Department of Health and Social Security* [1982] A.C. 800 to make claims and not apply for permission to seek judicial review when challenging ministerial guidance.

[31] [1992] 1 A.C. 624. See also the later cases of *Mercury Communications Ltd. v. Director General of Telecommunications* [1996] 1 W.L.R. 48; *British Steel plc v. Customs of Excise*

by a general medical practitioner for his full practice allowance, notwithstanding the fact that the Committee had decided that that practice allowance should be reduced because the practitioner was devoting a substantial amount of time to his private practice. It was argued by the Committee that the proceedings should have been by way of Order 53 judicial review because of the nature of the allegations which were being made. However, Dr Roy was allowed to continue his proceedings by way of a claim in general civil proceedings since the House of Lords took the view that the court had jurisdiction to entertain such a claim either because the *O'Reilly v. Mackman* principle did not apply or because his private law rights dominated the proceedings and the order sought for the payment of money could not be granted on judicial review. Lord Bridge asserted that the principle to be applied was that where "a litigant asserts his entitlement to a subsisting right in private law, whether by way of claim or defence, the circumstances that the existence and extent of the private right asserted may incidentally involve the examination of a public law issue cannot prevent the litigant from seeking to establish his right by action commenced by writ or originating summons" (*i.e.* by making a claim). Lord Lowry, who gave the main speech, took a similar view, asserting—

> "the arguments for excluding the present case from the ambit of the rule or, in the alternative, making an exception of it are similar and to my mind convincing. Dr Roy has either a contractual or statutory private law right to his remuneration in accordance with his statutory terms of service. Although he seeks to enforce performance of a public law duty under paragraph 12(1), his private law rights dominate the proceedings ... Unless the procedure adopted by the moving party is ill-suited to dispose of the question at issue, there is much to be said in favour of the proposition that a court having jurisdiction ought to let a case be heard rather than entertain a debate concerning the form of the proceedings."

The disadvantages of the present situation

3–046 The decision in *Roy* has been criticised on the grounds that it reflects a mode of piecemeal retreat from the full rigour of *O'Reilly* and is likely

---

Commrs. [1997] 2 All E.R. 366; *Trustees of the Dennis Rye Pension Fund v. Sheffield City Council* [1997] 4 All E.R. 747; *Andreou v. Institute of Chartered Accountants in England and Wales* [1998] 1 All E.R. 14.

to create anomaly and confusion.[32] However, in fact the *Roy* approach will have much to commend it if it enables public authorities to be protected from proceedings when this is desirable without generating unhelpful disputes as to whether the correct procedure has been adopted. The regrettable aspect of the present situation is that parties frequently engage in ferocious litigation as to whether the right procedure has been adopted purely for tactical purposes. Their indulging in this activity is made worthwhile by the fact that, depending on the nature of the issue involved, there can be substantial advantages in an applicant choosing one form of procedure rather than another. Unfortunately, although the House of Lords has had a number of opportunities to improve the situation, the case by case approach has prevented the development of a formula which would inject some commonsense into the present position. Undue reliance has been placed upon Viscount Simmonds' well-known dicta in *Pyx Granite Co. Ltd v. Ministry of Housing and Local Government*[33] that:

"The principle is not by any means to be whittled down that the subject's recourse to Her Majesty's courts for the determination of his rights is not to be excluded except by clear words."[34]

While Viscount Simmonds' principle certainly should never be undervalued, it should be remembered that it was made in the context of a case where the Minister was suggesting that a litigant was not entitled to seek any remedy from the courts and that instead the issues had to be determined by the Minister. That is not the situation which is being considered here, where the issue is not whether there shall be access to Her Majesty's courts but the procedure which should be adopted within those courts. It is important to remember that in *O'Reilly v. Mackman* there was no question of any mistake having been made as to which procedure should be used. It was, to use Lord Diplock's words, a "blatant attempt to avoid protection of the respondent for which Order 53 provides", or, in Lord Wilberforce's words in *Davy v. Spelthorne B.C.*,[35] it was a case where "the plaintiffs were improperly and flagrantly seeking to evade the protection which the rule confers on public authorities".

3–047

The requirement of procedural exclusivity was considered by the Law Commission in its 1994 report.[36] The Commission supported the

3–048

---

[32] See Ivan Hare, [1992] C.L.J. 202.

[33] [1960] A.C. 260, 286.

[34] See, *e.g. Davy v. Spelthorne B.C.* [1984] A.C. 262 at 274; *Wandsworth v. Winder* [1985] A.C. 461; and *Roy v. Kensington and Chelsea Family Practitioners Committee* [1992] 1 A.C. 624, 638 and 654; *Raymond v. Honey* [1983] 1 A.C. 1.

[35] [1984] A.C. 262, 278.

[36] Law Com. No. 226, Pt III.

"broad" approach adopted by Lord Lowry in *Roy's* case, believing "that the present position whereby a litigant is required to proceed by way of Order 53 only when (a) the challenge is on public law and no other grounds, *i.e.* where the challenge is solely to the validity or legality of a public authority's acts or omissions, and (b) the litigant does not seek either to enforce or defend a completely constituted private law right, is satisfactory".[37]

3–049   To an extent the existing Order 53 allows for some flexibility by allowing proceedings started by judicial review to continue as if made under the general provisions of the Civil Procedure Rules.[38] However, there is no express provision dealing with the alternative situation, where the proceedings are started under Part 7 of the Rules but would have been better dealt with under Order 53.

3–050   Although the present position is an unhappy one, what is needed is a revision of the present situation, not the overruling of the *O'Reilly* decision. That decision has served administrative law in England well since it has encouraged the judiciary to extend the scope of judicial review by preserving the effectiveness and the safeguards which are an important part of the present system of judicial review. In any reform of the present situation, consideration will also have to be given to the lack of certainty as to the consequences of a decision being *ultra vires*. If a decision remains ostensibly effective until set aside, then it is possible to have procedural safeguards. If, however, decisions which are *ultra vires* have no effect, then the procedural safeguards serve no purpose.[39]

3–051   Until the position is changed by statutory intervention or otherwise (if change there is to be) it is suggested that a substantial improvement could be achieved in the present position if the courts adopted the following policy: courts should decline to allow parties to litigate as to whether the right procedure has been adopted as a preliminary issue unless the case is one where the choice of procedure would be conclusive as to the substantive outcome of the case. In other situations, the courts should usually require the parties to defer the issues as to the procedure which should have been adopted until the trial of the substantive issues. In the meantime, courts should treat the proceedings as having been initiated both under Order 53 and Part 7 of the Civil Procedure Rules. If necessary the courts should give such directions as are necessary to achieve this result. At the trial, it will then only be necessary to investigate the procedural issue if it

---

[37] *Op. cit.*, para. 3–15.

[38] See Order 53, r. 9(5), which has been described as an anti-technicality rule by Sir John Donaldson M.R. in *R. v. East Berkshire Health Authority, ex p. Walsh* [1985] Q.B. 152, 166.

[39] See Chap. 4 and *R. v. Hendon JJ., ex p. DPP* [1993] 1 All E.R. 411, 415.

may have a material effect on the outcome. In this way sterile and expensive procedural disputes which may be of no practical significance to the outcome of a case may be avoided.[40]

---

[40] Peter Cane in 'Mapping the Frontiers' *The Frontiers of Liability*, Vol. 1 (1994) describes a similar proposal as a 'common getaway'; see also Lord Woolf, *Access to Justice* (1996).

CHAPTER 4

JURISDICTION, *VIRES*, LAW AND FACT

INTRODUCTION

Judicial review of administrative action was founded upon the premise **4–001** that an inferior tribunal or administrative body is entitled to decide wrongly, but is not entitled to exceed the jurisdiction it was given by statute. The statutory jurisdiction (later referred to also as *"vires"*) permitted the body to make errors of fact, or errors of law *within* its jurisdiction, provided that such an error of law was not manifest "on the face of the record". In this respect judicial review is to be distinguished from an appeal. It was largely restricted to review for *excess* of jurisdiction, while an appeal would usually enable errors both of fact or of law to be rectified. *Ultra vires*, or excess of jurisdiction, in the narrow or strict sense, was thus the organising principle which both justified judicial review (by declaring all power to be derived power) and constrained it (by permitting a degree of autonomy to the reviewed body).

The concept of jurisdictional error has become one of the most **4–002** elusive in administrative law, largely because it calls for analytical distinctions which have, as judicial review has developed, become difficult if not impossible to sustain. There is the vexed distinction between jurisdictional error and error of law within jurisdiction. There is also a related distinction between "preliminary" or "collateral" requirements[1] which have to be fulfilled before a body's jurisdiction exists (which therefore go to a body's jurisdiction, being preliminary or collateral to the "merits" of the decision), and requirements (of law or fact or merits) which do not. Finally, there is the equally contested distinction between "void" and "voidable" decisions: that is a decision

---

[1] Collateral in this sense should not be confused with collateral used in another sense involving jurisdiction, namely, a challenge of the lawfulness of a decision in collateral or indirect proceedings, that is, other than by judicial review, *e.g.* by way of a defence in criminal or civil proceedings. See para. 4–047 below.

which is invalid or void in the sense that it is a nullity, or voidable in that it can be set aside but until it is set aside gives rise to legal consequences.

4–003   At the heart of these seemingly technical distinctions there lie fundamental constitutional issues concerning the rule of law (to what extent should administrative bodies be able to determine the scope of their own powers? To what extent ought invalid decisions be able to survive once successfully challenged?); the relationship between the courts and the administration (to what extent should courts exercising powers of review refrain from correcting the administration's factual or legal errors?), and the sovereignty of Parliament (to what extent do the courts possess an inherent power to review the legality of official action despite Parliamentary legislation purporting to exclude or limit such review?).

4–004   Although these traditional distinctions and labels cannot yet be declared obsolete, they are today largely of historic interest for three reasons. First, after a stage during which the courts only tentatively asserted their right to insist on the legality of administrative action, they have now become more confident in their constitutional responsibility of enforcing the rule of law, thus generally requiring all administrative action to be simply lawful, whether or not it is technically outwith a body's so-called jurisdiction in the narrow sense. Secondly, the procedures contained in the application for judicial review have enabled the courts to conduct more thorough investigation of the way in which administrative decisions are reached—the decision-making process—than was previously possible by means of an application for the prerogative writs. The existence of such procedures means that there is little sense in retaining the former distinction between errors of law that are and those that are not patent—on the face of the record—since latent errors are accessible to investigation. Thirdly, the courts have now developed a series of principles, under the rubric of a number of "grounds" of review, that are accepted as governing the exercise of official power and which the courts legitimately enforce upon all bodies exercising public functions. Judicial review is therefore today primarily concerned with those principles rather than with any notion of jurisdictional rectitude or *vires*, in the narrow sense of those terms. Yet because the old distinctions do occasionally arise it is still necessary to consider their history and background, which supply the intellectual foundations of so much of modern judicial review.

4–005   Before doing so, however, it should be borne in mind that the terms "jurisdiction" and *"vires"* are both at times confused by the fact that they can refer to the power either of the body reviewed or of the reviewing court. The assertion that the courts have no jurisdiction to review non-jurisdictional error committed by an administrative tribunal raises questions both about the power to review of the court and the power to err of the tribunal. When Parliament seeks to oust the jurisdiction of the courts to review decisions of an inferior body, the question arises as to whether the intention was to preclude the court reviewing even for a jurisdictional error committed by the inferior body. Here again two questions are raised: (a) the power of the court to review, and (b) the kind of determination (or non-determination) that the inferior body is entitled to make with impunity. These different senses of jurisdiction interlock and overlap. Although they may be kept conceptually distinct, we believe that they require common treatment and cannot be fully understood in isolation one from the other.[2]

The following issues are discussed in this Chapter: **4–006**

(1) the historical development of the concepts of jurisdiction and *vires;*

(2) jurisdiction and *vires* today in respect of (a) the powers of public bodies, and (b) the powers of the courts in the face of a statute seeking to oust their jurisdiction (our view of the situation today is summarised in para. 4–041 below);

(3) the distinction between decisions that are "void" or a "nullity" and those that are "voidable";

(4) the extent to which a litigant may seek to challenge an official decision by means of collateral proceedings;

(5) the power of the courts to review findings of law and findings of fact.

HISTORICAL DEVELOPMENT

From the earliest times the influence of the common law permeated **4–007** the local courts and the local communities, and proceedings instituted before borough courts were removable into the King's courts at Westminster.[3] Usurpations of authority by municipal corporations gave rise to actions to impugn the validity of byelaws,[4] *quo warranto* proceedings,[5] and later, applications for writs of *scire facias* to repeal

---

[2] We are therefore in this edition conflating the previous treatment of jurisdiction (Chap. 3 of the 4th edition) and that of statutory restriction of judicial review (Chap. 7).

[3] Holdsworth, *History of English Law,* ii, 395–405.

[4] *ibid.* 398, 400, giving illustrations from the fourteenth and fifteenth centuries.

[5] Replaced by injunctions by the Administration of Justice (Miscellaneous Provisions) Act 1938, s. 9.

borough charters.[6] When the justices of the peace emerged as the principal organ of local administration, the Court of King's Bench (which of all the common-law courts was the one most closely associated with the business of government) assumed superintendence over their proceedings—a superintendence that was facilitated by the fact that the administrative functions of the justices were discharged in a judicial form. During the course of the seventeenth century a distinction gradually came to be drawn, as we shall see, between acts done without jurisdiction, which might be collaterally impeached in civil proceedings brought against the justices for trespass and which could be quashed by a writ of certiorari, and erroneous acts done within jurisdiction, which could not ordinarily be impugned in collateral proceedings and which were immune from the reach of certiorari unless an error was apparent on the face of the "record". The essential features of this distinction survived to condition the scope of judicial control over the successors of the justices of the peace in the work of public administration.

4–008   The courts of common law had at the outset asserted a right to determine the proper jurisdiction of courts administering other systems of law and to contain them within that jurisdiction by writs of prohibition.[7] But it was not until the seventeenth century that what was to become the modern conception of judicial review took shape.[8] In actions for trespass and other civil wrongs against the Commissioners of Sewers and the judges and officers of other inferior courts, a distinction began to be drawn between a court which proceeded erroneously or *inverso ordine* within its jurisdiction, and a court which proceeded without jurisdiction of the cause. Only in the latter class of case could the order of the court be collaterally impeached and its judges or officers subjected to civil liability.[9] The jurisdiction of a court might be limited with respect to place, persons or subject-matter; and the conferment of a limited or stinted jurisdiction, so Hale held, implied a negative, namely, that the court should not proceed at all in other cases. "But if they should commit a

---

[6] Now obsolete, or abolished by the Crown Proceedings Act, 1947.

[7] See Chap. 13 below.

[8] See the illuminating contributions by Amnon Rubinstein, *Jurisdiction and Illegality* (1965), Chap. 4; Edith G. Henderson, *Foundations of English Administrative Law* (1963); Louis L. Jaffe, *Judicial Control of Administrative Action* (1933), 205–208, 329–334, 624–629; Geoffrey Sawer (1954) 3 U. of W. Aust.Ann.L.R. 24; Jaffe and Henderson (1956) 72 L.Q.R. 345; and Jaffe (1957) 70 Harv.L.R., 953–963.

[9] See esp. Coke's dicta in the case of the *Marshalsea* (1613) 10 Co.Rep. 68b, 76. But Coke himself did not always follow this distinction; see *Dr Bonham's case* (1610) 8 Co.Rep. 113b.

mistake in a matter that were within their power, that would not be examinable here."[10]

After 1700 certiorari to quash became the regular mode of **4–009** impugning the decisions of inferior courts. At first it was not easy to distinguish between certiorari to quash for want of jurisdiction and certiorari to quash for a defect on the face of the record.[11] The inferior court was required to incorporate in its record all the facts which invested it with jurisdiction, and often a wide range of other facts besides,[12] and if any material fact was omitted the record was bad on its face. In so far as the exercise of the power to quash was clearly referable to jurisdictional defects, errors committed by inferior courts were almost invariably assumed to go to jurisdiction.[13] That a distinction between errors within jurisdiction and errors going to jurisdiction was still recognised was demonstrated by the establishment in the latter part of the eighteenth century of the practice that findings on jurisdictional matters, though not on other matters, could be impugned by affidavit evidence.[14] But it was not until the first half of the nineteenth century that a reaction set in against the prevalent tendency to treat nearly all of an inferior court's findings as touching its jurisdiction.[15] This reaction made it possible to

---

[10] *Terry v. Huntington* (1668) Hardres 480, 483; see also *Commins v. Massam* (1643) March 196, 197–198, *per* Heath J.; *Groenvelt v. Burwell* (1700) 1 Ld.Raym. 454, 467–468; *per* Holt C.J.

[11] It has been plausibly suggested that certiorari to quash was developed mainly as a means of impugning errors within jurisdiction for which no other remedy (*e.g.* an action for trespass against magistrates or enforcement officers) was available, and that certiorari came to be regarded primarily as a remedy for jurisdictional defects because of the need for giving meaning to non-certiorari clauses (Rubinstein, *op. cit.* n. 8 above, 64–68, 71–73).

[12] Both in summary convictions and in orders the adjudication had to be stated, and in summary convictions the court was also required to set out the evidence and its conclusions drawn therefrom.

[13] Not till about 1720 was it clearly settled that not every statutory requirement was to be treated as jurisdictional (Henderson, *op. cit.* n. 8 above, 157). For the development of the distinction between jurisdictional and non-jurisdictional matters in prohibition and in mandamus cases, see *ibid.* Chap. 4.

[14] As late as 1735 extrinsic evidence to disprove the existence of jurisdictional facts was held inadmissible (*R. v. Oulton Inhabitants* (1735) Cas.t.Hard. 169). The distinction between the two classes of errors came to be drawn more sharply in the second half of the nineteenth century, when the recital of evidential facts was omitted from the records of summary convictions. For a recent affirmation of this distinction, see *R. v. West Sussex Quarter Sessions, ex p. Johnson Trust Ltd* [1974] Q.B. 24.

[15] See esp. *Brittain v. Kinnaird* (1819) 1 B. & B. 432; *Cave v. Mountain* (1840) 1 Mon. & G. 257; *R. v. Bolton* (1841) 1 Q.B. 66; *R. v. Rotherham (Inhabitants)* (1842) 3 Q.B. 776; *R. v. Buckinghamshire JJ.* (1843) 3 Q.B. 800. The relevant authorities are examined very fully in *R. v. Mahony* [1910] 2 J.R. 695, and more briefly in *R. v. Nat Bell Liquors Ltd* [1922] 2 A.C. 128. See generally Jaffe, *Judicial Control of Administrative Action*, 624–630.

construct a coherent theory of the concept of jurisdiction which, had it but prevailed, would have seriously limited the scope of judicial review both in magisterial law and in administrative law.

The pure theory of jurisdiction

4–010 This "pure" theory of jurisdiction may be stated as follows.[16] Jurisdiction means authority to decide. Whenever a judicial tribunal is empowered or required to inquire into a question of law or fact for the purpose of giving a decision, its findings thereon cannot be impeached collaterally or on an application for judicial review but are binding until reversed on appeal. Moreover, "Where a court has jurisdiction to entertain an application, it does not lose its jurisdiction by coming to a wrong conclusion, whether it was wrong in law or in fact".[17] It does not lose its jurisdiction even if its conclusion on any aspect of its proper field of inquiry is entirely without evidential support.[18] The question whether a tribunal has jurisdiction depends not on the truth or falsehood of the facts into which it has to inquire, or upon the correctness of its findings on these facts, but upon their nature, and it is determinable "at the commencement, not at the conclusion, of the inquiry".[19] A preliminary or collateral question is

---

[16] It is expounded with great ability by D.M. Gordon in 'The Relation of Facts to Jurisdiction' (1929) 45 L.Q.R. 459. See also (1944) 60 L.Q.R. 250 and (1960) 1 U. of B.C.L. Rev. 185. For his replies to criticisms of his views by the late author of this book, Dr Rubinstein and Professor H. W. R. Wade, see (1960) 76 L.Q.R. 506; (1966) 82 L.Q.R. 263, 515.

[17] *R. v. Central Criminal Court JJ.* (1886) 17 QBD 598, 602; *R. v. Grant* (1850) 19 L.J.M.C. 59; *Kemp v. Neville* (1862) 10 C.B.(n.s.) 523,; 549–552; *R. v. St Olave's Southwark, District Board of Works* (1857) 8 E. & B. 659; *R. v. Bradley* (1894) 70 L.T. 349; *Shridramappa Pasare v. Narhari Bin Shivappa* (1900) L.R. 27 I.A. 216, 225; *R. v. Cheshire JJ., ex p. Heaver* (1913) 108 L.T. 374; *R. (Limerick Corp.) v. L.G.B.* [1922] 2 I.R. 76, 93; *R. v. Weston-Super-Mare JJ., ex p. Barkers (Contractors) Ltd* [1944] 1 All E.R. 747; *R. v. Minister of Health* [1939] 1 K.B. 232; *R. v. Minister of Transport, ex p. Beech-Allen (W.H.) Ltd* (1964) 62 L.G.R. 76; *Punton v. Ministry of Pensions and National Insurance (No. 2)* [1964] 1 W.L.R. 226; *The State (Davidson) v. Farrell* [1960] I.R. 438; *Permanent Trustee Co. of N.S.W. v. Campbelltown Corp.* (1960) 105 C.L.R. 401, 408, 413; *R. v. District Court, ex p. White* (1967) 116 C.L.R. 644; *Whiting v. Archer* [1964] N.Z.L.R. 742, 747; *R. v. Brixton Prison Governor, ex p. Armah* [1968] A.C. 192, 234, per Lord Reid (but see his explanation in *Anisminic Ltd v. Foreign Compensation Commission* [1969] 2 A.C. 147, 171). See also, *R. v. Governor of Pentonville Prison, ex p. Sotiriadis* [1975] A.C. 1, 30, where Lord Diplock stated that on habeas corpus applications in extradition cases the courts have assimilated acting on no evidence with excess of jurisdiction.

[18] *R. v. Shropshire JJ., ex p. Blewitt* (1866) 14 L.T. 598; *Ex p. Hopwood* (1850) 15 Q.B. 121; *R. v. Mahony* [1910] 2 I.R. 695; *R. v. Nat Bell Liquors Ltd* [1922] 2 A.C. 128; *R. v. Ludlow, ex p. Barnsley Corp.* [1947] K.B. 634, 639; *Rural Co-operative Society Ltd v. Thomson* [1969] N.Z.L.R. 300.

[19] *R. v. Bolton* (1841) 1 Q.B. 66, 74.

said to be one that is collateral to "the merits"[20] or to "the very essence of the inquiry"[21]; it is "not the main question which the tribunal have to decide".[22] Thus, a tribunal empowered to determine claims for compensation for loss of office has jurisdiction to determine all questions of law and fact relating to the measure of compensation and the tenure of the office, and it does not exceed its jurisdiction by determining any of those questions incorrectly; but it has no implied jurisdiction to entertain a claim for reinstatement or damages for wrongful dismissal, and it will exceed its jurisdiction if it makes an order in such terms, for it has no legal power to give any decision whatsoever on those matters. A tribunal may also lack jurisdiction if it is improperly constituted, or (possibly) if it fails to observe certain essential preliminaries to the inquiry.[23] But it does not exceed its jurisdiction by basing its decision upon an incorrect determination of any question that it is empowered or required (*i.e.* has jurisdiction) to determine.[24]

THE *ULTRA VIRES* DOCTRINE

In essence, the doctrine of *ultra vires* permits the courts to strike down 4–011 decisions made by bodies exercising public functions which they have no power to make. Acting *ultra vires* and acting without jurisdiction have essentially the same meaning, although in general the term "*vires*" has been employed when considering administrative decisions and subordinate legislative orders, and "jurisdiction" when considering judicial decisions, or those having a judicial flavour.[25]

The evolution of a specific concept of *ultra vires* did not take place 4–012 in the context of the power of public authorities. The term was first

---

[20] *Bunbury v. Fuller* (1853) 9 Ex. 111, 140; *R. v. Lincolnshire JJ., ex p. Brett* [1926] 2 K.B. 192, 202; *R. (Limerick Corp.) v. L.G.B.* [1922] 2 I.R. 76, 93.

[21] *Ex p. Vaughan* (1866) L.R. 2 Q.B. 114, 116.

[22] *R. v. Fulham, etc. Rent Tribunal, ex p. Zerek* [1951] 2 K.B. 1, 6. A tribunal that proceeds in a matter that is *res judicata* has also been said to exceed its jurisdiction: *Jowett v. Bradford (Earl)* [1977] 2 All E.R. 33.

[23] *Colonial Bank of Australasia Ltd v. Willan* (1874) L.R. 5, PC at 417, 422. Gordon has even challenged the validity of the last-mentioned proposition in 'Observance of Law as a Condition of Jurisdiction' (1931) 47 L.Q.R. 386, 557.

[24] This approach to jurisdiction corresponds with the court's approach to jurisdiction on arbitration not only in the past but as it is today. See the historical survey of jurisdictional control of arbitration in Mustill and Boyd, *Commercial Arbitration* (2nd ed., 1989), Chap. 20.

[25] But see *R. v. Secretary of State for the Environment, ex p. Ostler* [1977] Q.B. 122, 135, 138, where a distinction was drawn between the effect of a breach of the rules of natural justice and fraud upon the jurisdiction of a judicial tribunal and upon the *vires* of an administrative decision, albeit one to which the rules of natural justice applied.

generally used to denote excess of legal authority by independent statutory bodies and railway companies in the middle years of the nineteenth century[26]; though the main features of the doctrine to which this name was given had already been taking shape over a long period in relation to the powers of common-law corporations.[27] The term came to be used in relation to municipal corporations, then to the other new types of local government authorities,[28] and finally to the Crown and its servants and even to inferior judicial bodies.

4–013 The *ultra vires* doctrine has had a restricted application to corporations created otherwise than by or under statute. Although such corporations are subject to the doctrine in areas regulated by legislation, they seem to be as capable of performing other transactions (*e.g.* entering into contracts, acquiring land or providing new services) as any natural person.[29] But they may be restrained from committing acts infringing their charter of incorporation[30]; they cannot perpetrate any direct interference with the rights of individuals without specific legal authority; and in the case of such municipal corporations as owed their origin to the royal prerogative, it was doubtful whether they could expend money save in circumstances defined by statute.[31]

Subordinate legislative instruments, as well as administrative acts and decisions, may be *ultra vires* on substantive as well as procedural grounds.[32]

---

[26] H.A. Street, *A treatise on the doctrine of Ultra Vires,* (1930) 1–3. *Ultra Vires* has been largely eroded in modern company law except for some 'ghostly relics'. See generally, L.C.B. Gower, *Principles of Modern Company Law,* (5th ed., 1992) pp. 165–198. And see Companies Act, 1985, ss. 35(1) and 35A. And see H. Rajak, 'Judicial Control: Corporations and the Decline of Ultra Vires' [1995] Cambrian L.R. 9.

[27] Holdsworth, *op. cit.* n. 3 above, viii, 59–61.

[28] W.I. Jennings in *A Century of Municipal Progress* (ed. Laski, Jennings and Robson (1978)), 418.

[29] *Sutton Hospital* case (1612) 10 Co.Rep. 23a, 30b; *Wenlock (Baroness) v. River Dee Co.* (1887) 36 Ch.D. 675, 685; *Att.-Gen. v. Manchester Corp.* [1906] 1 Ch. 643, 651; *Att.-Gen. v. Leeds Corp.* [1929] 2 Ch. 291, 295; *Att.-Gen. v. Leicester Corp.* [1943] Ch. 86, 93. The authority of the rule was strongly criticised by Street, *op. cit.* n. 26 above, at 18–22.

[30] A member of the incorporated body may sue: *Jenkin v. Pharmaceutical Society of Great Britain* [1921] 1 Ch. 392; *Dickson v. Pharmaceutical Society of Great Britain* [1970] A.C. 403. Violation of the charter will entitle the Crown to institute proceedings for a *scire facias* to revoke the charter.

[31] Under the Local Government Act 1972, almost all local authorities are statutory bodies. In *Hazell v. Hammersmith & Fulham L.B.C.* [1992] A.C. 1, although the local authority had been incorporated by royal charter, the charter did not confer on the borough any greater power than the statutory power exercisable by any other local authority, since the grant of incorporation had been made by virtue of the royal prerogative and in pursuance of the 1963 Act, the combined effect of which was to create a statutory corporation. It followed that the council had no power to carry out the swap transaction whether in its own name or in the name of the borough.

[32] Cases in which ministerial or departmental regulations have been held wholly or partly *ultra vires* on substantive grounds include *Customs and Excise Commissioners v.*

STATUTORY RESTRICTION OF JUDICIAL REVIEW

Before considering the extent to which the "pure" theory of jurisdiction **4–014** has any relevance today, and, if so, the type of legal error that constitutes an error of jurisdiction in the strict sense, we consider the way the courts approached statutory restrictions upon judicial review.[33] This will allow us to view in tandem the two interlocking aspects of jurisdiction that we have identified—the jurisdiction of the body reviewed to commit errors of law or fact (the issue we have just been considering) and the jurisdiction of the court to review the decision of inferior bodies in the face of legislation which attempts to restrict such review.

In matters of public law, the role of the ordinary courts is of high **4–015** constitutional importance. It is a function of the judiciary to determine the lawfulness of the acts and decisions and orders of the Executive, tribunals and other officials exercising public functions, and to afford protection to the rights of the citizen. Legislation which deprives them of these powers is inimical to the principle of the rule or supremacy of law.

The courts have, therefore, long been zealous to resist **4–016** encroachments upon their jurisdiction. An attitude which may have originally been conditioned by the solicitude of the judges for their emoluments (which were dependent largely on fees paid by suitors) has been reinforced by traditions stemming from the battles successfully waged against the prerogative courts in the seventeenth century and by the authority that the superior judges have since acquired. The view is widely held that "the proper tribunals for the determination of legal disputes in this country are the courts, and they are the only tribunals which, by training and experience, and assisted by properly qualified advocates, are fitted for the task."[34] It is a common-law presumption of legislative intent[35] that access to the

---

Cure & Deeley Ltd [1964] 1 Q.B. 340; *Utah Construction & Engineering Pty Ltd v. Pataky* [1966] A.C. 629, PC; *Hotel and Catering Industry Training Board v. Automobile Pty Ltd* [1969] 1 W.L.R. 697; *Malloch v. Aberdeen Corp. (No. 2)* 1974 S.L.T. 253.

[33] This question was considered separately in Chap. 7 of the 4th edition of the principal work.

[34] *Lee v. Showmen's Guild of Great Britain* [1952] 2 Q.B. 329, 354, *per* Romer L.J. *Cf.* his dictum in *R. v. Medical Appeal Tribunal, ex p. Gilmore* [1957] 1 Q.B. 574, 587.

[35] Reaffirmed in a number of cases; see *e.g. Goldsack v. Shore* [1950] 1 K.B. 708, 712; *Bennett & White (Calgary) Ltd v. Municipal District of Sugar City (No. 5)* [1951] A.C. 786, 808–809, 812; *London Hospital Governors v. Jacobs* [1956] 1 W.L.R. 662, 669, 676; *R. v. Medical Appeal Tribunal, ex p. Gilmore* (above, n. 34); *Francis v. Yiewsley & West Drayton U.D.C.* [1957] 2 Q.B. 136, 148; *Pyx Granite Co. v. Ministry of Housing and Local Government* [1958] 1 Q.B. 554, 571; [1960] A.C. 260, 286; *Re Parliamentary Privilege Act 1770* [1958] A.C. 331, 353; *Customs and Excise Commissioners v. Cure & Deeley Ltd* [1962] 1 Q.B. 340, 357–359, 369 (but *cf. Marsh (B.) (Wholesale) Ltd v. Customs and Excise*

Queen's courts in respect of justiciable issues is not to be denied save by clear words in a statute. Subordinate legislation purporting to restrict or exclude access to the courts has been held to be *ultra vires* in the absence of express authorisation of such provisions in the enabling Act.[36]

4–017   Section 11 of the Tribunals and Inquiries Act 1958 reinforced judicial attitudes towards "finality clauses" by enacting that, subject to four exceptions,[37] any provision in an Act passed before August 1, 1958, to the effect that an order or determination was not to be "called into question in any court" (and any such provision which "by similar words" excluded any of the powers of the High Court), was not to prevent the issue of certiorari or mandamus.[38] This section was re-enacted as section 14 of the Tribunals and Inquiries Act 1971 and section 12(1) of the 1992 Act.

The section applies to all forms of finality clauses, howsoever worded (subject to the exceptions listed), and covers other remedies (such as the declaratory judgment[39]) as well as certiorari and mandamus. It may not extend to exclusionary clauses contained in statutes passed after July 1958.

4–018   Various means have been devised by Parliament to seek to restrict judicial review. Indirect means include the establishment of a prescribed appeals procedure, or the conferring of wide "subjective" discretion upon the decisionmaker. These indirect means are considered elsewhere.[40] Direct means have included legislation

---

Commissioners [1970] 2 Q.B. 206); *Baron v. Sunderland Corp*, [1966] 2 Q.B. 56, 66; *Ealing L.B.C. v. Race Relations Board* [1972] A.C. 342. See also *Re Boaler* [1915] 1 K.B. 21, 36; *R. v. Secretary of State for the Home Department, ex p. Leech* [1994] Q.B. 198.

[36] *Chester v. Bateson* [1920] 1 K.B. 829; *Newcastle Breweries Ltd v. R., ibid.,* 854; *Paul (R. & W.) Ltd v. Wheat Commission* [1937] A.C. 139; *Cure & Deeley case* (above, n.35); though *cf. Postmaster-General v. Wadsworth* [1939] 4 All E.R. 1, an unsatisfactory decision of the Court of Appeal. See also *Re Bachand v. Dupuis* [1946] 2 D.L.R. 641, BC (orders purporting to make execution of court judgments dependent on administrative approval, held invalid); and *Re Kellner's Will Trusts* [1949] 2 All E.R. 43. See also *Leech* (above, n. 35); *Raymond v. Honey* [1983] 1 A.C. 1.

[37] Now there are only two exceptions under s. 12(3) of the Tribunals and Inquiries Act 1992: (a) an order or determination of a court of law, and (b) where an Act makes special provision for application to the High Court within a specified time.

[38] The Franks Committee on Administrative Tribunals and Enquiries had recommended in 1957 that no statute should contain words purporting to oust certiorari, prohibition or mandamus in respect of statutory tribunals (Report, Cmnd. 218 (1957), 27, 93). The House of Commons Select Committee on Statutory Instruments was already required to consider whether to draw the attention of the House to instruments made under statutes purporting to exclude them from challenge in the courts.

[39] *Anisminic Ltd v. Foreign Compensation Commission* [1969] 2 A.C. 147, where the plaintiffs successfully claimed a declaration.

[40] The question of whether alternative remedies are exclusive or must first be exhausted before seeking judicial review is considered in Chap. 15, 15–046 *et seq.* below. Subjective discretion is considered in Chaps. 5 and 12.

employing a variety of formulae—"finality clauses", "no certiorari" clauses, "conclusive evidence" clauses, time-limited clauses and general formulae purporting to exclude review. These will now be considered in turn.

Finality clauses

By the end of the seventeenth century it had been settled that a **4–019** conviction or order made by any inferior tribunal could be removed by certiorari into the Court of King's Bench to be quashed for excess or want of jurisdiction or error on the face of the record. The court, viewing with disfavour the process of conviction without indictment,[41] and applying the principle that statutes creating new jurisdictions ought to be strictly construed[42] tended to combine lack of discrimination with excess of zeal and quashed convictions and orders for minor technical defects. Parliament therefore incorporated into a number of statutes conferring summary jurisdiction provisions that were designed to take away the right to apply for certiorari to quash decisions, either by using express words to that effect,[43] or by providing that the matter was to be finally determined by the justices.

The King's Bench, however, held that a general finality clause was **4–020** insufficient to deprive the courts of their power to award the beneficial remedy of certiorari for patent errors of law[44] or for jurisdictional defects,[45] unless the right to a certiorari had itself been conferred by statute.[46] These precedents were followed in later cases, and it became settled law that a finality clause did not restrict in any way whatsoever the power of the courts to issue certiorari to quash either for jurisdictional defects[47] or for error of law on the face of the record.[48] It was clear, furthermore, that a finality clause did not affect

---

[41] *R. v. Corden* (1769) 4 Burr. 2279.

[42] *Warwick v. White* (1722) Bunb. 106.

[43] This practice began towards the end of the seventeenth century, shortly after it had become usual to give a right of appeal from justices sitting out of sessions to Quarter Sessions: *Paley on Summary Convictions* (9th ed.), 800. See generally *R. v. Mahony* [1910] 2 I.R. 695, 730 *et seq., per* Gibson J.

[44] As distinct from errors on questions of fact: *R. v. Plowright* (1686) 3 Mod. 95.

[45] See, *e.g. R. v. Plowright* (above, n. 44); *R. v. Moreley* (1760) 2 Burr. 1041; *R. v. Jukes* (1800) 8 T.R. 542.

[46] *R. v. Hunt* (1856) 6 E. & B. 408. See generally D.C.M. Yardley (1957) 3 U. of Queensld.L.J. 103.

[47] *R. v. Nat Bell Liquors Ltd* [1922] A.C. 128, 159–160; *R. v. Minister of Transport, ex p. H.C. Motor Works Ltd* [1927] 2 K.B. 401; *R. v. Minister of Health* [1939] 1 K.B. 232, 246, 249; *R. v. Medical Appeal Tribunal, ex p. Gilmore* [1957] 1 Q.B. 574, 583–585, 588.

[48] See *Gilmore's* case (above, n. 47) and Notes [1957] P.L. 89 and 20 M.L.R. 394. As a result of this decision a right of appeal on questions of law was statutorily provided

their power to award a declaration that a decision or order made by a statutory body is invalid.[49] Even such words as "final and conclusive" were ineffective to abridge or attenuate judicial review.[50] The only practical effects of a finality clause were to take away a right of appeal where one already exists—*e.g.* rights of appeal to the High Court by way of case stated from inferior courts[51]—and to preclude a body from rescinding or rectifying one of its own valid decisions.[52]

"No certiorari" clauses

4–021 Even where the right to certiorari had been expressly taken away by statute, the courts relying on one or other of the restrictive rules of interpretation already mentioned, or upon the proposition that Parliament could not have intended a tribunal of limited jurisdiction to be permitted to exceed its authority without the possibility of direct correction by a superior court, persistently declined to construe the words of the statute literally. It was held that certiorari would issue, notwithstanding the presence of words taking away the right to apply for it, if the inferior tribunal was improperly constituted (as where some of its members had a disqualifying interest),[53] or if it lacked or exceeded jurisdiction because of the nature of the subject-matter or failure to observe essential preliminaries,[54] or if a conviction or order

---

to the Industrial Injuries Commissioner by the Family Allowance and National Insurance Act 1959, s.2.

[49] *Taylor v. National Assistance Board* [1956] P. 470; [1957] P. 101, 111 (dictum); *Pyx Granite Co. v. Ministry of Housing and Local Government* [1958] 1 Q.B. 554; [1960] A.C. 260; *Ridge v. Baldwin* [1964] A.C. 40. See also *Watt v. Lord Advocate*, 1977 S.L.T. 130; *Smith v. East Sussex C.C.* (1977) 76 L.G.R. 332.

[50] See *Fenwick v. Croydon Union Rural Sanitary Authority* [1891] 2 Q.B. 216 and *Att.-Gen. v. Hanwell U.D.C.* [1900] 1 Ch. 51; [1900] 2 Ch. 377 ('binding and conclusive'). In so far as any effect at all was attributable to a finality clause, it could often be circumvented by limiting its operation to matters other than those in issue before court: see *St Lucia Usines Co. v. Colonial Treasurer* [1924] A.C. 508, 513; *Gateshead Union Guardians v. Durham C.C.* [1918] 1 Ch. 146; *Seabrooke v. Grays Thurrock Local Board* (1891) 8 T.L.R. 19; *Gillow v. Durham C.C.* [1913] A.C. 54, 57.

[51] *Westminster Corp. v. Gordon Hotels Ltd* [1907] 1 K.B. 910; [1908] A.C. 142; *Hall v. Arnold* [1950] 2 K.B. 543; *Kydd v. Liverpool Watch Committee* [1908] A.C. 327; *Piper v. St Marylebone Licensing JJ.* [1928] 2 K.B. 221. See also *Re McCosh's Application* [1958] N.Z.L.R. 731; *Dean v. District Auditor for Ashton-in-Makerfield* [1960] 1 Q.B. 149. But see *Tehrani v. Rostron* [1972] 1 Q.B. 182.

[52] *R. v. Agricultural Land Tribunal (South Eastern Area), ex p. Hooker* [1952] 1 Q.B. 182.

[53] *R. v. Cheltenham Commissioners* (1841) 1 Q.B. 467; *R. v. L. & N.W. Ry.* (1863) 9 L.T. (N.S.) 423.

[54] *R. v. Somersetshire JJ.* (1826) 5 B. & C. 816; *R. v. St Albans JJ.* (1853) 22 L.J.M.C. 142; *R. v. Wood* (1855) 3 E. & B. 49; *ex p. Bradlaugh* (1878) 3 Q.B.D. 509, 512; *R. v. Hurst, ex p. Smith* [1960] 2 Q.B. 133; *R. v. Worthington-Evans, ex p. Madan* [1959] 2 Q.B. 145, 152; *R. v. Bloomsbury and Marylebone County Court, ex p. Villerwest Ltd* [1975] 1 W.L.R. 1175.

had been procured by fraud or collusion.[55] Such language would also be ineffective to exclude certiorari or a declaration of invalidity for breach of either rule of natural justice.[56] Legislation purporting to exclude review by other named remedies (*e.g.* prohibition, injunction) was equally ineffective to prevent the courts from containing inferior tribunals within the limits of their jurisdiction.[57]

Conclusive evidence clauses

A clause making the confirmation of a compulsory purchase order **4–022** final and of effect as if enacted in the Act and "conclusive evidence that the requirements of this Act have been complied with, and that the order is duly made and is within the powers of this Act," has been held to exclude any inquiry into the *vires* of the order on an application for certiorari,[58] despite the absence of any words expressly taking away the right to a certiorari. The Committee on Ministers' Powers doubted whether even this type of clause (which appeared in

---

[55] *R. v. Gillyard* (1848) 12 Q.B. 527; *Colonial Bank of Australasia Ltd v. Willan* (1874) L.R. 5 PC 417. Nor does an express privative clause affect the right of the Crown, or of a private prosecutor in criminal proceedings, to apply for the order.

[56] See dicta in *Ridge v. Baldwin* [1964] A.C. 40, 120–121.

[57] On prohibition, see *Jacobs v. Brett* (1875) L.R. 20 Eq. 1. On injunctions, see *Andrews v. Mitchell* [1905] A.C. 78; contrast *Catt v. Wood* [1910] A.C. 404 (where the error of law did not go to jurisdiction); see also *Wayman v. Perseverance Lodge* [1917] 1 K.B. 677. There appears to be no statute expressly excluding review by an action for a declaration, but the same principles would surely have applied; see *Ridge v. Baldwin* [1964] A.C. 40; *Anisminic Ltd v. Foreign Compensation Commission* [1969] 2 A.C. 147, although it was assumed throughout *Anisminic* that a no certiorari clause would remove the power to quash for patent error of law not going to jurisdiction.

[58] *Ex p. Ringer* (1909) 73 J.P. 436; see also *Reddaway v. Lancs C.C.* (1925) 41 T.L.R. 422; *Minister of Health v. R., ex p. Yaffe* [1931] A.C. 494, 520, 532–533 (dicta). In *Merricks v. Heathcoat-Amory* [1955] Ch. 567, Upjohn J. found it unnecessary to consider the legal effect of a similar formula. In *London Parochial Charities Trustees v. Att.-Gen.* [1955] 1 W.L.R. 42, Roxburgh J. held that a formula providing that an Order in Council approving a statutory scheme 'shall be conclusive evidence that such scheme was within the scope of and made in conformity with' the Act, and that 'the validity of such scheme and order shall not be questioned in any legal proceedings whatsoever,' precluded the courts from undertaking any inquiry into *vires*. And see *Graddage v. Haringey L.B.C.* [1975] 1 W.L.R. 241 (statutory provision that subject to a right of appeal, a notice 'shall be final and conclusive as to any matters which could have been raised on such an appeal' precluded a declaration of invalidity for latent defects, but not if flawed *ex facie*. See J. Alder (1975) 38 M.L.R. 573 for a critical comment. See also *Armstrong v. Whitfield* [1974] Q.B. 16 (declaration by Quarter Sessions conclusive on existence of public rights of way); *County and Nimbus Estates Ltd v. Ealing L.B.C.* (1978) 76 L.G.R. 624 (magistrates barred by conclusive evidence clause from considering alleged invalidity of proposal to increase rateable value); *Suffolk C.C. v. Mason* [1979] A.C. 705 (definitive map conclusive evidence of status of public right of way); *Ellett v. Manukau City Corp.* [1976] 1 N.Z.L.R. 345.

a number of statutes passed before 1931)[59] would protect an order that was manifestly unrelated to the scheme of the Act.[60] However, conclusive evidence clauses in statutes were successful to endow with finality an executive pronouncement as to the existence of a state of affairs peculiarly within the knowledge of the executive branch of government,[61] or to cure a defect in the proceedings of a statutory body[62]; and to preclude such a body from revoking or varying its own decisions.[63]

Time-limited clauses

4–023   A number of statutes, particularly in the areas of housing, town and country planning and compulsory acquisition, preclude challenge to the validity of decisions made outside a limitation period within which statutory appeals are available. The Town and Country Planning Act, for example, has, since its inception in 1947, allowed applications to the High Court within six weeks only, on the ground that the relevant decision is "not within the power of this Act" or that any of the Act's "relevant requirements" have been breached.[64] After the six-week period the validity of the action "shall not be questioned in any legal proceedings whatsoever".[65]

4–024   Once the period in which a statutory remedy is available has expired, the circumstances in which a decision or order protected by a preclusive clause has been successfully challenged in proceedings for a non-statutory remedy are extremely limited, if they exist at all. In

---

[59] See John Willis, *The Parliamentary Powers of English Government Departments*, 101–106; and the Housing Act 1930, Sched. III, para. 2.

[60] Cmd. 4060 (1932), 40. Conclusive evidence clauses containing an element of ambiguity could be circumvented. See *Waterford Corp. v. Murphy* [1920] 2 I.R. 165; *Damodhar Gordhan v. Deoram Kanji* (1875) 1 App. Cas. 332.

[61] See the provisions exempting from statutory schemes acts certified by the Minister to be in the interests of national security; *e.g.* Employment Protection Act 1975, s. 121(4); Sex Discrimination Act 1975, s. 52; Race Relations Act 1976, ss. 42, 69(2), (3).

[62] See *Woollett v. Minister of Agriculture and Fisheries* [1955] 1 Q.B. 103.

[63] *R. v. Agricultural Land Tribunal (South Eastern Area), ex p. Hooker* [1952] 1 K.B. 1. See also *Broxbourne B.C. v. Secretary of State for the Environment* [1979] 2 W.L.R. 846 (established use certificate conclusive of matters contained in it so as to preclude on appeal against enforcement notice further inquiry about actual use of land).

[64] Now s.288(3) of the Town and Country Planning Act 1990.

[65] For current examples of statutes with time limitation clauses see R. Gordon, *Crown Office Proceedings*, Section H, and the Law: Commission Report No. 226, *Administrative Law: Judicial Review and Statutory Appeals*, proposing (para. 12.20) that a list should be maintained of those statutory appeals where a different time limit applies to the normal 28 days.

Smith v. East Elloe R.D.C.,[66] the House of Lords held a compulsory purchase order immune from judicial review on the ground of alleged bad faith after a time limit had expired.

The principal justification for regarding a clause containing a time **4–025** limit as an effective bar to review after the time limit has expired is that the legislator, having created a statutory remedy, is entitled to limit the availability of that remedy. This can be the case even where the time limit is too short to enable the order or decision to be challenged in some situations. The use of limitation periods to prevent the assertion of legal rights is, after all, a perfectly familiar feature of the legal system. Furthermore, there can be an obvious public interest in enabling public or private works to be commenced and resources to be committed in reliance upon the legal invulnerability of an apparently valid order. In *East Elloe* it was suggested that an order that is patently *ultra vires* may be impugned outside the six-week period.[67]

Formulae purporting to exclude judicial review by general but comprehensive language

Formulae of this character were the principal statutory device adopted **4–026** for giving the impress of finality to administrative action by the direct prohibition of judicial review. The legal effects attributable to such formulae varied according to the contexts in which they appeared.

Where exclusionary formulae were contained in statutes dealing with foreign relations or the working of the parliamentary system, there was a much stronger probability that the courts would give the prohibitive words a literal interpretation.[68] In other contexts, however, the courts have declined to give literal effect to generally worded clauses apparently intended totally to exclude from judicial review the determinations of administrative tribunals. This question was raised in

---

[66] [1956] A.C. 736 (action for declaration).

[67] See *Smith v. East Elloe R.D.C.* [1956] A.C. 736 (*per* Viscount Simonds), 769–770 (*per* Lord Radcliffe); *cf. Graddage v. Haringey L.B.C.* [1975] 1 W.L.R. 241, 250. See also *R. v. Secretary of State for the Environment, ex p. Ostler* [1977] Q.B. 122.

[68] Such provisions were, for example, contained in s.5 of the Extradition Act 1870, relating to Orders in Council that apply the provisions of the Act to any foreign State; s.3 of the Parliament Act 1911, making a certificate given by the Speaker under the Act conclusive for all purposes and immune from challenge in any court of law; and s.3(7) of the House of Commons (Redistribution of Seats) Act 1949, which provides that the validity of an Order in Council (for the delimitation of constituencies) purporting to be made under the Act and reciting that a draft thereof has been approved by both Houses shall not be questioned in any legal proceedings whatsoever; *cf. Harper v. Home Secretary* [1955] Ch. 238.

the case of *Anisminic*,[69] which also dealt a blow to the distinction between jurisdictional and non-jurisdictional error from which it has scarcely recovered.

The *Anisminic* case

4–027   The *Anisminic* case concerned decisions of the Foreign Compensation Commission (which hears and determines claims for compensation out of payments received by the Crown from foreign governments for measures taken by them against the property of British subjects). The statute stated that the Commission's decisions were not to be "called in question in any court of law".[70] The reasons for excluding judicial review were that payments awarded to claimants were *ex gratia* and that it would be undesirable for the calculations made by the Commission for distribution of the limited sums at its disposal to be upset by successful applications to the courts. More important, perhaps, instituting judicial proceedings might seriously retard distribution to successful claimants. Nevertheless, the House of Lords held that the exclusionary formula did not apply to a purported "determination" that was a nullity because it was not one that the Commission had jurisdiction to make. The effect of the clause was merely to protect valid decisions that might otherwise have been impugned for a non-jurisdictional error of law on the face of the record.[71]

4–028   The most important breakthrough[72] in *Anisminic* was the emphatic rejection by the House of Lords[73] of the idea[74] that the jurisdiction of an inferior tribunal was determinable only at the outset of its inquiry. It was observed[75] that a tribunal having jurisdiction over a matter in

---

[69] *Anisminic v. Foreign Compensation Commission* [1969] 2 A.C. 147.
[70] Foreign Compensation Act 1950, s.4(4). The Tribunals and Inquires Act 1958, s. 11(3) exempted the Commission from the scope of the section.
[71] The 1950 Act was subsequently amended to provide a right of appeal from the Commission to the Court of Appeal on jurisdictional and other questions of law. Foreign Compensation Act 1969; the former provision exempting decisions of the Commission from the scope of the 1958 Act was omitted from the Tribunals and Inquiries Act 1971, s. 14(3).
[72] A term used by Lord Diplock about *Anisminic* in *O'Reilly v. Mackman* [1982] 2 A.C. 237 at 278. He also referred to it there as 'a landmark decision'. *Ibid.*
[73] *Anisminic Ltd v. Foreign Compensation Commission* [1969] 2 A.C. 147 (Lords Reid, Pearce and Wilberforce; Lords Morris and Pearson dissenting). For comment on the decision see H.W.R. Wade (1969) 85 L.Q.R. 198, Lord Diplock (1971) 24 C.L.P. 1; D.M. Gordon (1971) 34 M.L.R. 1; B.C. Gould [1970] P.L. 358; de Smith [1969] C.L.J. 161.
[74] Already rejected in a number of earlier cases: see, *e.g. R. v. Nat Bell Liquors Ltd* [1922] 2 A.C. 128, 156.
[75] Most of the observations about to be noted were strictly *obiter*, since their Lordships held that the appellants, who had claimed to be entitled to a share in a compensation

the first instance might exceed its jurisdiction by breaking the rules of natural justice,[76] applying a wrong legal test and answering the wrong question,[77] failing to take relevant considerations into account or basing the decisions on legally irrelevant considerations.[78] Although they accepted the survival of the rule that a judicial tribunal has power to err within the limits of its jurisdiction, it was not easy to identify errors of law which, in the light of their analyses, would not be held to go to jurisdiction.

Subsequent cases

In *Pearlman v. Keepers and Governors of Harrow School*[79] the relevant statute provided that the determination of a county court judge on the question of the rateable value of a house was to be "final and conclusive". The Court of Appeal nevertheless, by a majority, overruled the county court's holding that a new central heating system was not a "structural alteration or addition to the house". The county court judge's misconstruction of those words was held to be an error of law which went to his jurisdiction. Lord Denning, however, made it clear that the difference between jurisdictional and non-jurisdictional error could not be sustained logically, and considered that no inferior court or administrative tribunal has jurisdiction to make an error of law "on which the decision of the case depends".[80]

4–029

---

fund for British-owned property nationalised in Egypt had established their claim on the true construction of the relevant legislation, and that the Commission had erred in applying to the claimants a test of eligibility that they were not required to comply with and had dismissed the claim on this preliminary point. However, Lord Morris and all the members of the Court of Appeal ([1968] 2 Q.B. 862) agreed that if the Commission had erred, its error went to the merits and not to jurisdiction. See also Gordon, *loc. cit.* n. 73 above.

[76] [1969] 2 A.C. 147, 171, 195, 207, 215.

[77] *ibid.* 171, 195, 215; *cf.* the more guarded formulation by Lord Wilberforce at 210.

[78] *ibid.* 171, 195, 198, 215. See also *R. v. Southampton JJ., ex p. Green* [1976] Q.B. 11 (decision that recognisance should be forfeit held to be in excess of jurisdiction because magistrates ignored a relevant factor and took into account an irrelevant consideration: but Browne L.J. (at 22) doubted whether an exercise of discretion on wrong legal principles could be brought within *Anisminic*. *Cf. R. v. Secretary of State for the Environment, ex p. Ostler* [1977] Q.B. 122, where a distinction appears to have been drawn between the jurisdictional control exercised over judicial tribunals and the application of the *ultra vires* doctrine to administrative decisions made in the exercise of a wide discretion, although Lord Denning has extra-judicially expressed regret at 'some unguarded' statements made by him in this case: *The Discipline of Law* (1979), 108.

[79] [1979] Q.B. 56.

[80] *per* Lord Denning at pp. 69–70. Eveleigh L.J., agreeing, held, at p. 77 that 'before the tribunal could embark on its inquiry, it was necessary for it to decide the meaning of the question it was required to answer. This was a collateral matter. It had nothing to

4–030 *Pearlman* was considered in two cases decided within a short time of each other the following year. In the first, the Privy Council held[81] that a clause that provided that an award of the Industrial Court in Malaysia shall be "final and conclusive"[82] was effective to preclude judicial review if the inferior tribunal "made an error of law which does not affect its jurisdiction". Lord Denning's view in *Pearlman* of the coincidence of error of law and error of jurisdiction was therefore not accepted and Lord Lane's dissent in that case preferred. In the second case, *Re Racal Communications Ltd,*[83] the House of Lords considered a challenge to an order of the High Court under the Companies Act 1948 to authorise the inspection of the company's books. The majority held that the ouster calause[84] was effective to exclude the power of the Court of Appeal to review the High Court judge's decision. Lord Diplock made a distinction, however, between cases where a legal error is made by an administrative tribunal or authority and the case of an error made by a court of law. In the former case, there is a presumption that Parliament did not intend the administrative body to be the final arbiter of questions of law. There is, however, no such presumption in relation to courts of law. In respect of administrative bodies the distinction between errors of law that went to jurisdiction and errors of law that did not "was for practical purposes abolished". In respect of inferior courts, however, the "subtle distinctions...that did so much to confuse English administrative law before *Anisminic*" might survive and the superior court conducting the review "should not be astute to hold that Parliament did not intend the inferior court to have jurisdiction to decide for itself the meaning of ordinary words used in the statute involving, as many do, inter-related questions of law, fact and degree."[85]

4–031 It should be noted that *Racal Communications* by no means exempted all courts or judicial decisions from review for non-jurisdictional error

---

do with the merits of the case'. But see the dissent of Geoffrey Lane L.J. who said, at pp. 75–76: 'The question is not whether he had made a wrong decision, but whether he inquired into and decided a matter which he had no right to consider.'

[81] *South East Asia Fire Bricks Sdn Bhd v. Non-Metallic Mineral Prouducts Manufacturing Employees Union* [1981] A.C. 363.

[82] s.29(3)(a) of the Malaysian Industrial Relations Act 1967, continuing that 'no award shall be challenged, appealed against, reviewed, quashed or called in question in any court of law'.

[83] [1981] A.C. 374.

[84] s.441(3) of the Companies Act 1948: 'The decision of a judge of the High Court...on an application under this section shall not be appealable.'

[85] *Re Racal Communications,* n. 83 above, at p. 383. In evaluating what was said in *Re Racal,* it is important to remember that decisions of High Court judges are not subject to judicial review and the Court of Appeal's jurisdiction is statutory and so can be limited by statute.

of law. The case was limited to a consideration of the scope of a statutory provision attempting to oust the jurisdiction of the courts to review mistakes of law made by a judge of the High Court, which it was held could only be corrected by means of appeal to an appellate court.[86]

Two years later, Lord Diplock, in his celebrated *obiter* in *O'Reilly v.* **4–032** *Mackman*,[87] emphasised this point. He referred to *Anisminic* as:

"A landmark decision...which has liberated English public law from the fetters that the courts had therefore imposed on themselves so far as determinations of *inferior courts and statutory tribunals* were concerned, by drawing esoteric distinctions between errors of law committed by such tribunals that went to their jurisdiction, and errors of law committed by them within their jurisdiction. The breakthrough that *Anisminic* made was the recognition by the majority of this House that if a tribunal...mistook the law applicable to the facts as it had found them, it must have asked itself the wrong question, *i.e.* one into which it was not empowered to inquire and so had no jurisdiction to determine. Its purported 'determination', not being a 'determination' within the meaning of the empowering legislation, was accordingly a nullity."[88]

In *R. v. Manchester Coroner, ex p. Tal*[89] the question was raised as to **4–033** whether a decision of a coroner's inquest was subject to judicial review for jurisdictional error alone. Despite the statement by Lord Diplock in *Re Racal Communications* to the effect that courts would be so treated, his clearer statement in *O'Reilly v. Mackman* was preferred, Goff L.J. stating that "Lord Diplock did not intend to say [in *Racal Communications*] that the *Anisminic* principle did not extend to inferior courts as well as tribunals".[90] It was therefore held that all errors of law committed during the course of the coroner's inquest were reviewable by the court,[91] and that "as a matter of principle, the *Anisminic* principle applies to inferior courts as well as inferior

---

[86] Lord Salmon said that the *Anisminic* principle was confined 'to decisions made by commissioners, tribunals or inferior courts which can now be reviewed by the High Court of Justice, just as the decisions of inferior courts used to be reviewed by the old Court of King's Bench under the prerogative writs'. *Ibid.* at 386.

[87] [1982] 2 A.C. 237, 278, and agreed to by the remainder of their Lordships.

[88] *ibid.* at 278 (emphasis added). In *Racal Communications*, n. 83 above at 386.

[89] [1984] 3 All E.R. 240.

[90] *ibid.* at 248.

[91] Contrary to an earlier decision of the Divisional Court, *R. v. Surrey Coroner, ex p. Campbell* [1982] Q.B. 661. In *Renfrew D.C. v. McGourlick* [1987] S.L.T. 538; [1987] P.L. 631 a total ouster clause did not present challenge to a decision of the Sheriff.

tribunals, nevertheless we do not wish to be understood as expressing any opinion that the principle will apply with full force in the case of every inferior court".[92]

4–034   In the more recent decision of *R. v. Hull University Visitor, ex p. Page*[93] the majority of the House of Lords accepted "the general rule" that any misdirection or error of law made by an administrative tribunal or inferior court in reaching its decision can be quashed for error of law.[94] In the case of an ouster clause, however, the majority in *Page* accepted the distinction made by Lord Diplock in *Racal Communications* that the presumption that a "final and conclusive" clause was not intended to oust the power to review the decision (including errors of law) applied to administrative bodies but not to courts. These comments were, however, strictly *obiter*, since the question to be decided in *Page*, was not that of an ouster clause but whether a University Visitor had exclusive jurisdiction to determine disputes arising under the domestic law of the university. It was held that the visitor of an eleemosynary charity, applying the internal laws of the charity, and not applying the "general law of the land" occupied an "exceptional" and "anomolous" position and was therefore not subject to the general rule that judicial review would lie to impeach decisions taken within a body's jurisdiction in the narrow sense.[95] Judicial review would only lie to the visitor "in cases where he has acted outside his jurisdiction (in the narrow sense) or abused his powers or acted in breach of the rules of natural justice."[96]

---

[92] The case of *R. v. Ipswich Justices, ex p. Edwards* (1979) 143 J.P. 699 was cited, where the principle was not applied in the case of committing justices.

[93] [1993] A.C. 682.

[94] *per* Lord Browne-Wilkinson at 702. See also *R. v. Chancellor of Chichester Consistory Court, ex p. News Group Newspapers, The Times,* July 15, 1991; [1992] C.O.D. 48.

[95] A similar view has been taken in respect of decisions of judges of the High Court acting as visitors to the Inns of Court. *R. v. Visitors to the Inns of Court, ex p. Calder* [1994] Q.B. 1 and *R. v. Honourable Society of the Middle Temple, ex p. Bullock* [1996] C.O.D. 376 (in an educational matter the judges qualified to sit as Visitors did not have an unfettered power to overrule decisions made by an expert review body under statutorily approved regulations and the Visitor was therefore right to conclude that he should only interfere if satisfied that the review board had acted irrationally or unlawfully). On the powers of Visitors, see *R. v. Visitor of the University of London, ex p. Vijayatunga* [1990] 2 Q.B. 444; *R. v. University of Nottingham, ex p. Ktorides* [1998] C.O.D. 26; *R. v. University College London, ex p. Christofi,* September 12, 1997, CA (unreported).

[96] *Page,* n. 93 above, at 704, Lord Griffiths (at pp. 692–694) agreeing, would permit judicial review of the visitor decision which amounted to an 'abuse of his powers' (a term he had used in *Thomas v. University of Bradford* [1987] A.C. 795, 825.) Abuse of power was contrasted by Lord Griffiths with a 'mistake of law', which, in the case of the university visitor, was not reviewable. 'In such a case the judge is not abusing his powers: he is exercising them to the best of his ability albeit some other court thinks he was mistaken. I used the phrase 'abuse of his powers' to connote some form of misbehaviour that was wholly incompatible with the judicial role that the judge was

There are other situations where some important principle will **4–035** permit review for jurisdictional error alone. One such principle is the avoidance of double jeopardy in relation to criminal proceedings.[97] Normally when a person has been acquitted, the prosecution is not entitled to go behind that acquittal, and if they do the defendant will be entitled to rely on a plea of *autrefois acquit*. This is, however, subject to where the previous proceedings were a "nullity".[98] For the proceedings to be a nullity they will have to be shown to be "no trial at all".[99] For this to happen the decision has to be made without jurisdiction in the narrow sense. Thus in *R v. Hendon JJ., ex p. DPP*[1] the decision of the magistrate was held to be a nullity when the defendant was quite irrationally acquitted because of the late arrival in the court of the prosecuting lawyer through no fault of his own.

There have been isolated suggestions that the scope of review in **4–036** habeas corpus is confined to want of jurisdiction in the narrow sense. In *R. v. Secretary of State for the Home Department, ex p. Cheblak*[2] Lord Donaldson M.R. drew a distinction, *obiter*, between habeas corpus and judicial review. In his view "A writ of habeas corpus will issue where someone is detained without any authority or the purported authority is beyond the powers of the person authorising the detention and so is unlawful".[3] In *R. v. Secretary of State for the Home Department, ex p.*

---

expected to perform. I did not intend it to include a mere error of law*. (At 693.) Compare the dissent of Lord Slynn, with whom Lord Mustill agreed, who could see no reason in principle for limiting the availability of certiorari to a patent excess of power and *excluding review on other grounds recognised by law*, and no reason for excluding review on grounds generally available in the case of the decision of a visitor (at p. 710). He also said that 'If the individual's rights are affected he should be entitled to the same protection by the courts as he would be in respect of the decisions of a wide range of other tribunals and bodies to whom decisions involving questions of law are assigned* (*ibid.*).

[97] A judge of a superior court, when acting as a statutory tribunal, has no such immunity. See *R. v. Master of the Rolls, ex p. McKinnell* [1993] 1 W.L.R. 88. Crown Courts are exempt by statute from review in matters relating to trial or indictment. See *Re Smalley* [1985] A.C. 622; Supreme Court Act 1981, s.29(3); *R. v. Central Criminal Court, ex p. Raymond*, [1986] 1 W.L.R. 710; [1986] P.L. 338; *R. v. Chichester Crown Court, ex p. Abodunrin* (1984) 79 Cr.App.R. 295; [1985] P.L. 318; *Re Sampson* [1987] 1 W.L.R. 194; Ward, 'Judicial Review and Trials on Indictment: Section 29(3) of the SCA 1981* [1990] P.L. 50.

[98] See paras 4-042–4-046.

[99] See Lord Roskill in *Harrington v. Roots* [1984] A.C. 743, 753.

[1] [1994] Q.B. 167.

[2] [1991] 1 W.L.R. 890.

[3] *ibid.* at 894. Judicial review on the other hand was available where the decision 'is within the power of the person taking it but, due to procedural error, a misappreciation of the law, failure to take account of relevant matters, a taking account of irrelevant matters or the unreasonableness of the decision or action, it should never have been taken'; *ibid.*

Muboyayi[4] it was held[5] that, where the applicant for habeas corpus was not alleging the absence of precedent fact[6] but was challenging the reasons for the underlying decision, then habeas corpus could not lie.

4–037   This view is, however, contradicted by the recent Law Commission Report[7] and other strong authority to the effect that both habeas corpus and judicial review are dealt with "under a common principle".[8] There is also good reason in principle why the writ of habeas corpus, which is the most renowned contribution of the English common law to the protection of human liberty, should not be anomalously confined in its scope—to the detriment of such liberty.[9]

4–038   In respect of time-limited ouster clauses, although the logic of *Anisminic* cast doubt upon their efficacy to preclude review for excess of jurisdiction (as defined in that case) the courts have been inclined to prevent all challenges after the expiration of a reasonable limitation period,[10] even in cases where the applicant does not or is not able to discover the grounds for challenging the decision until after the statutory period has elapsed,[11] or because he does not learn of the

---

[4] [1992] 1 Q.B. 244.

[5] *per* Lord Donaldson M.R., with whom Glidewell and Taylor L.JJ. agreed. *Ibid.* at 254–55.

[6] See para. 4–040 below.

[7] Law Com. No. 226 *Administrative Law: Judicial Review and Statutory Appeals* (1994) Part XI.

[8] *per* Lord Scarman in *R. v. Secretary of State for the Home Department, ex p. Khawaja* [1984] A.C. 74, 99. See also Sharpe, *The Law of Habeas Corpus* (1989) pp. 21–23, 53; R. Gordon, *Crown Office Proceedings* (1990) D1–021. Case law supports this view. See, *e.g. Armah v. Government of Ghana* [1968] A.C. 192 (not referred to in *Muboyayi*—although cited to the Court—and not before the Court in *Cheblak*). See also *R. v. Governor of Brixton Prison, ex p. Mourat Mehmet* [1962] 2 Q.B. 1. See also *R. v. Miller* 2 All E.R. 613.

[9] Confining its scope to jurisdictional error could also, as the Law Commission Report (n. 7 above) recognises, offend against the European Convention on Human Rights. See. *e.g. Brogan v. United Kingdom* (1991) 13 E.H.R.R. 439.

[10] See, *e.g. R. v. Secretary of State for the Environment, ex p. Ostler* [1977] Q.B. 122; *R. v. Secretary of State for the Environment, ex p. Kent* [1988] J.P.L. 706; *R. v. Cornwall C.C., ex p. Huntington* [1994] All E.R. 694; *Martin v. Bearsden and Milngavie D.C.* 1987 S.L.T. 300. But see *Greater London Council v. Secretary of State for the Environment* [1985] J.P.L. 868 (reasoning underpinning the decision which was otherwise in the applicant's favour could be challenged when it damaged some further interest of the applicant); *Lenlyn Ltd v. Secretary of State for the Environment* (1985) 50 P. & C.R. 129 (failure of the decision-maker to exercise his discretion by refusing to make a decision); *R. v. Carmarthen D.C., ex p. Blewin Trust Ltd, The Times,* July 3, 1989; [1990] C.O.D. 5; *cf. Pollway Nominees Ltd v. Croydon L.B.C.* [1987] A.C. 79 (21-day limitations clause ineffective). But see *Renfrew D.C. v. McCorlick* [1987] S.L.T. 538. See *Century National Merchant Bank Ltd v. Omar Davies,* Privy Council, March 16, 1998 (10-day appeal from minister's action to Court of Appeal carried 'a necessary implication' of finality. *Barraclough v. Brown* [1897] A.C. 615 applied).

[11] As in *Smith v. East Elloe,* and *Ostler,* nn. 67 and 10 above, respectively.

decision until it is too late to challenge it.[12] As a matter of principle the objection to such a challenge is the absence of a discretion in the court to extend the time limit.

JURISDICTION AND *VIRES* TODAY

It has been suggested that *Anisminic* freed the courts to adopt a "functional"[13] or "pragmatic"[14] approach to the question of jurisdiction. This approach, it will be suggested below,[15] may be helpful in those few instances where those "subtle distinctions"[16] between jurisdictional or non-jurisdictional error survive today.[17] There is, however, a preliminary question that must be asked: namely, under what circumstance does the distinction between jurisdictional and non-jurisdictional error survive? That preliminary question, it is submitted, should not be approached on the basis of pragmatism. It should rather be based upon principle.[18] The apposite principles are deeply embedded in our constitutional law, but have rarely been explicitly applied to administrative law. The principle of the rule of law is one such, which addresses two relevant issues. The first of these is the legality of decisions of administrative bodies; the rule of law does not permit inferior bodies by determining their own powers to alter their scope. Any excess of their powers should be subject to restraint. The second issue addressed by the rule of law relates to legal certainty; where possible, individuals ought to be able to rely upon the validity of official decisions. Another constitutional principle is the sovereignty of Parliament. Under this principle Parliament may (in the interest perhaps of certainty and finality) permit an inferior body to determine its own powers. The courts should attempt to reconcile these various

4–039

---

[12] As in *Kent*, n. 10 above. Similarly, if the applicant wrongly begins judicial review proceedings and loses time, there is nothing to be done. Note that the time limits for judicial review are elastic (see Chap. 15 below, para. 15–019).

[13] L. Jaffe, (1957) 70 Harv.L.Rev. 953; *Judicial Control of Administrative Action*, pp. 631–663 See also J. Beatson, 'The scope of judicial review for error of law' (1984) O.J.L.S. 22.

[14] G.L. Peiris, 'Judicial review and judicial policy: the evolving mosaic' (1987) 103 L.Q.R. 66. See also C.T. Emery and B. Smythe, 'Error of Law in Administrative Law' (1984) 100 L.Q.R. 612. See *British Columbia (Milk Board) v. Grisnich (c.o.b. Mountainview Acres)* [1995] 2 S.C.R. 895.

[15] Para. 4–040.

[16] *per* Lord Diplock in *Re Racal Communications*, n. 83 above, at 390–391.

[17] See paras 4–033–4–035 above.

[18] Note that Goff L.J. in *Tal* (n. 89 above) considered that 'as a matter of principle' the *Anisminic* principle applied to both inferior courts and tribunals. See also Sir John Laws, 'Illegality: The Problem of Jurisdiction', in M. Supperstone and J. Goudie (eds), *Judicial Review* (1992), p. 51.

principles when they appear superficially to compete. The courts thus presume, in the absence of clear words to the contrary, that Parliament does not intend to offend the rule of law.

4–040   Identifying the relevant principles does not of course automatically solve the difficult problems in this area, particularly those relating to interpretation of Parliamentary intent and to the scope and context of particular powers. Nevertheless, reference back to these principles will allow the issues to be resolved in a more coherent manner than can be achieved through a purely functional or pragmatic approach that leads to confusion and a "wilderness of single instances".[19]

4–041   Attempting to refer to and utilise these principles in the light of the recent developments, the following propositions can now be advanced.

> (1) The doctrine of *ultra vires*, to the extent that it implies that all administrative power is derived from a specific statutory source, can no longer be considered the sole justification for review of the powers of bodies exercising public functions. Certain of these functions are today carried out under common law powers or under powers, like that of self-regulatory bodies, with "no visible means of legal support."[20] These powers "do not lend themselves to the language of *ultra vires*".[21] A previous chapter discusses when such powers may be amenable to judicial review and the extent to which they are therefore governed by "public law" principles. Insistence upon *ultra vires* as the basis for judicial review inhibits review when the powers of the body are not derived from a defined statutory source. As has been noted,[22] these days an increasing amount of regulatory activity is carried out by the use of powers created by contract, or by means of the manipulation of rights to property. Even prerogative powers, formerly immune from judicial review, have been brought within its ambit.[23] The review of such powers cannot easily be justified by the *ultra vires* principle. Yet, the courts have recognised that it is important to the rule of law that the abuse of those powers be controlled irrespective of their source and that the nature of the control should be the same as the control of more conventional administrative powers conferred by statute.

---

[19] H.W.R. Wade, 'Crossroads in Administrative Law' (1968) 21 C.L.P. 75, 85. See also D.J. Galligan, 'Judicial Review and the Textbook Writers' (1982) 2 O.J.L.S. 257 and Jack Beatson, 'The Scope of Judicial Review for Error of Law' (1984) 4 O.J.L.S. 22.

[20] *per* Sir John Donaldson M.R. in *R. v. Panel on Takeovers and Mergers, ex p. Datafin* [1987] 1 Q.B. 815, 824.

[21] Dawn Oliver, 'Is the *ultra vires* rule the basis of judicial review?' [1987] P.L. 543, 545.

[22] Chap. 3 above, paras 3-015–3-022.

[23] See Chap. 5, below, paras 5-037–5-046.

(2) Accordingly, the foundation for judicial review should no longer be regarded as *ultra vires*. In general therefore, upon an application for judicial review it is no longer of any significance whether the source of alleged invalidity of administrative action is based upon an excess of jurisdiction or error of law within jurisdiction. Nor does it matter whether the error is or is not an error disclosed on the face of the record.[24]

(3) Therefore, all power can be appropriately reviewed today under what might be described as the principles of lawful or legitimate administration. These principles enunciated as "grounds" of judicial review, were conveniently set out by Lord Diplock in the *GCHQ* case[25] (a case itself involving review of prerogative power) as "legality", "procedural propriety" and "rationality". These requirements form a firm foundation upon which to review the public functions of modern administration and do not depend upon the limited notion of jurisdiction or *vires* in its narrow sense.[26]

---

[24] 'In my judgment the decision in *Anisminic Ltd v. Foreign Compensation Commission* ... rendered obsolete the distinction between errors of law on the face of the record and other errors of law by extending the doctrine of *ultra vires*. Thenceforward it was to be taken that Parliament had only conferred the decision making power on the basis that it was to be exercised on the correct legal basis: a misdirection in law in making the decision rendered the decision *ultra vires*." *per* Lord Browne-Wilkinson in *R. v. Hull University Visitor, ex p. Page* [1993] A.C. 682, 701.

[25] *Council for Civil Service Unions v. Minister for the Civil Service* [1985] A.C. 374.

[26] This view has much recent support. See, *e.g.* Lloyd L.J. in the *Takeover Panel* case, n. 20 above: 'The express powers conferred on inferior tribunals were of critical importance in the early days when the sole or main ground for intervention by the courts was that the inferior tribunal had exceeded its powers. But those days are long since past' [1987] 1 Q.B. 815. See also Oliver, *op. cit.* n. 21 above. See also Sir John Laws, 'Illegality: The Problem of Jurisdiction' in Supperstone and Goudie (eds), *Judicial Review* (1992), Chap. 4. But see Sir William Wade and C.F. Forsythe, *Administrative Law*, 7th ed., pp. 340 *et seq.* See also C. Forsyth, 'Of Fig Leaves and Fairy Tales, The Ultra Vires Doctrine, The Sovereignty of Parliament and Judicial Review' [1996] C.L.J. 122; Sir William Wade, 'Habeas Corpus and Judicial Review' (1997) 113 L.Q.R. 55. *Cf.* P. Craig [1998] C.L.J. 63. And see the helpful discussion by Lord Cooke of the concept of jurisdiction in *R. v. Bedwellty JJ, ex p. Williams* [1997] A.C. 225 (although remedy for error of law at court's discretion, where a committal procedure was so influenced by inadmissible evidence as to amount to an irregularity, a remedy would normally follow (although express use of 'jurisdiction' was avoided). And see Michael Taggart, 'The Contribution of Lord Cooke to Scope of Review Doctrine in Administrative Law: A Comparative Common Law Perspective', in *The Struggle for Simplicity in the Law: Essays for Lord Cooke of Thorndon* (1997), p. 189. And see D. Dyzenhaus, 'The Politics of Deference: Judicial Review and Democracy' in M. Taggart (ed.), *The Province of Administrative Law* (1997), p. 279.

(4) Nor does it matter whether the body being reviewed is an inferior administrative or judicial body. In the absence of a statute attempting to exclude judicial review, decisions of both inferior courts and judicial-type bodies are subject to the same principles as administrative bodies and tribunals.[27]

(5) There are, however, very exceptional situations where the court's powers of review may be limited to jurisdictional errors in the narrow sense. These include decisions involving the acquittal of a criminal offence (where the principle of double jeopardy is in play) and cases governed by a special historical tradition in relation to a particular institution (such as a university over which, because it is an eleemosynary charitable foundation, the visitor of the university has exclusive jurisdiction).[28] These are, however, strictly exceptional and anomalous situations. Habeas corpus is not one of them.[29] In general the rule of law requires that "there must be no Alsatia in England where the King's writ does not run".[30]

(6) *Precedent fact* One of the exceptions to the prohibition on courts reviewing the facts upon which decisions of inferior bodies are based is where it is alleged that there is an absence of required "jurisdictional fact". Where a set of facts must exist for the exercise of the jurisdiction of the body (in the strict sense of permitting the body to enter into its inquiry) the courts are entitled to inquire into the existence of those facts.[31] The language of jurisdiction is not necessary to justify such intervention.[32] The statute in such a case imposes a condition

---

[27] See para. 4–031 above. In New Zealand it has been said that, assuming Parliament can (at least within unexplored limits) empower an administrative tribunal to determine some questions of law conclusively, such power must at least be given clearly and it would be surprising if an administrative officer were not to be given such power. Hence a privative clause would not protect a statutory misinterpretation by such an officer. *Bulk Gas Users Group v. Attorney-General* [1983] N.Z.L.R. 129. In *Regan v. Lousich* [1995] 2 N.Z.L.R. 620 Tipping J., after a full examination of modern authorities, held that a privative clause does not protect a decision of an inferior court if it is erroneous in *law*, unfair or unreasonable.

[28] See *Page* (n. 24 above) and *R. v. Visitors to the Inns of Court, ex p. Calder* (n. 95 above). See *New Zealand Rail Ltd v. Employment Court* [1995] 3 N.Z.L.R. 179 (privative clause confines judicial review to jurisdictional errors in Lord Reid's 'narrow and original sense', but provision for appeal on questions of law).

[29] See paras 4-035–4-037 above.

[30] *Czarnikow v. Roth Schmidt and Co.* [1922] 2 K.B. 478, 488, *per* Scrutton L.J.

[31] See the discussion above at para. 5–030 and cases such as *White and Collins v. Minister of Health* [1934] 2 K.B. 838.

[32] For support in this view see Sir John Laws 'Illegality: The problem of jurisdiction' in M. Supperstone and J. Goudie, (eds), *Judicial Review* (1992), Chap. 4.

as precedent to the exercise of the body's power and it is the duty of the court to ensure that the condition has been met. The exercise of the decision-maker's power is dependent upon the existence of a fact or set of facts; the court is entitled to ensure that those facts exist.

This point was not fully appreciated in *Zamir v. Secretary of State for Home Affairs*,[33] where the question for the House of Lords was whether an appellant was an "illegal entrant".[34] It was held that the matter was one for the immigration officer although the court could "see whether there was evidence on which the immigration officer, acting reasonably, could decide as he did".[35] This approach was, however, overruled in *R. v. Secretary of State for the Home Department, ex p. Khawaja*[36] where it was held that it was the court's duty to inquire whether the immigration officer's belief that the entry had been illegal was correct.[37]

(7) Where a statute seeks to oust the jurisdiction of the courts to review the decisions of an inferior body, there is a compelling inference that Parliament did not intend that body to be the final arbiter of its own powers. There is therefore a presumption that any error of law committed by that body is reviewable, whether or not the error is one of jurisdiction in the narrow sense.[38]

---

[33] [1980] A.C. 930.

[34] Under the Immigration Act 1971, s.33(1).

[35] *per* Lord Wilberforce, at 949D.

[36] [1984] A.C. 74.

[37] Where precedent fact is a condition to the exercise of power, the courts are not confined to intervening only when the fact-finding body has acted 'unreasonably'. They should themselves assess whether, on the balance of probabilities, those facts are justified by sufficient evidence. For recent cases where precedent fact was held not to be present see *R. v. Secretary of State for the Home Department, ex p. Naheed Ejaz* [1994] Q.B. 496, CA; *Silver Mountain Investments Ltd v. Att.-Gen. of Hong Kong* [1994] 1 W.L.R. 925, PC; *R. v. Secretary of State for the Home Department, ex p. Onibiyo* [1996] Q.B. 768 (*Bugdaycay* and *Khawaja* considered; court no power to review as an objective precedent fact whether fresh 'claim for asylum' had been made). But see *Tan Te Lam v. Superintendent of Tai A Chau Detention Centre* [1997] A.C. 97, PC (question whether applicant could be repatriated to Vietnam from Hong Kong is a matter of jurisdiction for the court) and see also, *Re Rahman (Saidur)* [1998] Q.B. 136.

[38] 'It is hard to conceive that a legislature would create a tribunal with a limited jurisdiction and yet bestow on such tribunal an unlimited power to determine the extent of its jurisdiction.' Dickson J., dissenting in *Jacmain v. Att.-Gen. of Canada* [1978] 25 C.R. 1529 (Can.). In *R. v. Hereford Magistrate's Court ex p. Rowlands* [1998] Q.B. 110 it was held that the existence of a right of appeal by way of a retrial in the Crown Court did not preclude a person convicted in the Magistrate's Court from applying for judicial review. And see *British Steel plc v. Customs and Excise Commissioners* [1997] 2 All E.R. 366, CA.

In this situation two equally important principles can be involved, neither of which is subservient to the other. These principles are, first, that the exercise of any power should be subject to the rule of law (and so subject in the final analysis to the supervision of the courts), and secondly that, Parliament is sovereign. While the courts will give effect to the language used by Parliament, they do so in a manner which presumes that Parliament intended to act consistently with the rule of law. Such is the strength of this presumption that it can prevail over apparently clear language to the effect that the inferior body's decisions were to be final and conclusive. The courts are loath to relinquish their inherent power to review for jurisdictional error. While it may be possible for Parliament to bar judicial review for "any determination or purported determination", the fact that this has never been done indicates the persuasive force of the rule of law as a principle endorsing the power of the courts to require administrative legality.

Parliamentary draftsmen have, however, recently devised a variety of formulae to restrict judicial review. Some simply provide that a document issued shall be "final and conclusive".[39] Others provide that a statutory duty imposed by the Act shall not "be read as imposing either directly or indirectly, any form of duty or liability enforceable by proceedings before any court".[40] The Local Government

---

[39] *e.g.* in *R. v. Registrar of Companies, ex p. Central Bank of India* [1986] Q.B. 1114 it was held by the Court of Appeal that a certificate of the registration of a charge provided by the Registrar of Companies was 'conclusive evidence' under the Companies Act 1948, s.98 (2) and was therefore not reviewable by the court even if the Registrar had made an error of fact or law or mixed fact and law in the course of determining the question. The words of the statute were held thus to override s.14(1) of the Tribunals and Inquiries Act (1971), which in effect itself overrides provisions in a pre-1958 statute seeking to oust the court's jurisdiction. The court was informed in that case that there were about 300 such clauses ('conclusive evidence' clauses) in existence. See J. Beatson and M.H. Mathews, *Administrative Law: Cases and Materials* (1989) p. 534; Emery and Smythe, *Judicial Review* (1986), p. 54. See also *R. v. Secretary of State for Foreign and Commonwealth Affairs, ex p. Trawnik, The Times,* February 21, 1986.

[40] s.2(6) of the London Regional Transport Act 1984. The Act provides various duties, *e.g.* to provide for efficient, economic and safe transportation (s.2(1) and (2)) and to provide for the needs of the disabled (s.2(7)). Section 139 of the Mental Health Act 1983 provides that '(1) No person shall be liable, whether on the ground of want of jurisdiction or on any other ground, to any civil or criminal proceedings to which he would have been liable apart from this section in respect of any act purporting to be done in pursuance of this Act or any regulations or rules made under this Act...unless the act was done in bad faith or without reasonable care'. In *Re Waldron* [1986] Q.B. 824 it was held that 'civil proceedings' did not refer to judicial review.

Finance Act 1987 even seeks to confer validity on action taken by the Secretary of State that might otherwise be held unlawful.[41]

In these situations, when assessing the effect of the language used by Parliament, a number of factors will have to be taken into account, such as: the need in the circumstances for legal certainty on which the affected person may rely[42]; the degree of expertise of the decision-making body; the esoteric nature of the traditions or legal provisions decided by the decision-making body; and the extent to which interrelated questions of law, fact and degree are often best decided by the body which hears the evidence at first hand, rather than the courts on judicial review.

(8) As we have seen,[43] there are two situations where the presumption that a statute does not seek to oust the court's jurisdiction has substantially reduced force:

(a) where the statute seeks to preclude judicial review of the decision of a court; and

(b) where a statute permits a reasonable time to challenge a decision of an inferior body but then purports, in the interest of finality, there-after to preclude challenge to its validity.

As to the first of these exceptions, the question of what is a court is not always clear cut, and the distinction between courts and other bodies invites a resuscitation of the discredited dichotomy between "judicial" and "administrative"

---

[41] s.13(1) of the Act provides that 'the validity of anything done, whether before or after the passing of this Act, by the Secretary of State under or for the purposes of paragraph 1 or 3 of Schedule 1 to the Local Government (Scotland) Act 1966 in relation to the financial years 1983–84 or any subsequent financial year shall not be called into question in any legal proceedings on the ground that in ascertaining the actual expenditure or the estimated expenditure of a local authority the Secretary of State took into account the transfer of any sum between the authority's general fund and any special account or account maintained by them under any enactment.'
The same Act provides in s.4(1) that 'Anything done by the Secretary of State before the passing of this Act for the purposes of the relevant provisions in relation to any of the initial years or intermediate years shall be deemed to have been done in compliance with those provisions.'

[42] The need for certainty in commercial dealings was very much a factor influencing the court in *Central Bank of India*, n. 39 above. See also the importance attached to certainty in respect of the assumption of management of a bank in *Century National Merchant Bank Ltd*, n. 10 above.

[43] Paras 4–023 *et seq.*

decisions.[44] Nevertheless, where an inferior body has undoubted legal expertise, and where a right of appeal against its decisions has not been provided, it is perhaps not unacceptable for that body to be accorded a broader degree of deference and autonomy than that accorded to a body lacking those attributes.[45]

As to the second exception, the requirement of the rule of law, although compromised, is met to the extent that an affected person has some reasonable time to challenge the decision. The time limit is imposed in order to accommodate the needs of legal certainty. Nevertheless, and despite authority to the contrary,[46] not all decisions of lower courts, nor all decisions taken by other bodies after the expiry of a time-limited ouster clause, should be exempt from judicial review. It would seem right in principle that decisions that lack jurisdiction in "the narrow and original sense of not being entitled to enter on the inquiry in question"[47] (for example, if a body is wrongly constituted) should be amenable to judicial review.

It is also suggested, despite the authorities to the contrary,[48] that if it is not possible for an applicant to ascertain the existence of a ground for challenging a decision during the period in which a challenge is permitted, the applicant should be permitted, at least for excess of jurisdiction, to apply for judicial review.[49] The court could then decide whether, in all circumstances, leave should be granted.

---

[44] See the discussion in respect of natural justice and the fair hearing in Chaps 7 and 8 below.

[45] See para. 4–033 above.

[46] See n. 10 above.

[47] *per* Lord Reid in *Anisminic* [1969] 2 A.C. 147.

[48] See, *e.g. Ostler*, n. 10 above.

[49] For a review of statutory exclusion of judicial review in Australian, Canadian and New Zealand law, see the article by that name by G.C. Peiris in [1982] P.L. 451. Peiris concludes that in all three jurisdictions "the function of the court is to give effect to the terms of the privative provision while retaining, whenever practicable, supervisory jurisdiction within a narrower compass". For an account of the Canadian approach to questions both of jurisdiction and exclusionary clauses, see J. Evans, H. Janisch, D. Mullan and R. Risk, *Administrative Law; Cases Texts and Materials* (1989), Chaps. 11 and 12. In the past, judicial restraint to "curial deference" was exercised in the face of privative and no certiorari clauses (see, *e.g.* Laskin C.J. in *Canada Labour Relations Board v. Halifax Longshoremen's Assoc.* [1983] 1 S.C.R. 245, 256; *Canadian Union of Public Employees Local 963 v. The New Brunswick Liquor Corp.* [1979] 2 S.C.R. 227 (S.C.C.); (1979) 97 D.L.R. (3d) 417. But the attitude seems to be changing. See, *e.g. Re Ontario Public Service Employers Union and Forer, etc.* (1985) 23 D.L.R. (4th) 97, Ont. CA. In the last few years the Supreme Court of Canada has developed a new "pragmatic and functional" approach. If, under that approach, a tribunal has

(9) In those few remaining situations, identified above, where the distinction between jurisdictional and non-jurisdictional error survives, the question as to what is a non-jurisdictional error cannot be based upon any clear predetermined criteria that will serve as a test for all bodies.

As we have seen,[50] no satisfactory test has ever been formulated for distinguishing findings which go to jurisdiction from findings which go to the merits. The test is therefore not based so much upon logic or principle but upon pragmatism and must depend upon the context of the particular power and the function being performed.

After *Anisminic* virtually every error of law is a jurisdictional error, and the only place left for non-jurisdictional error is where the components of the decision made by the inferior body included matters of fact and policy as well as law, or where the error was evidential (concerning for example the burden of proof or admission of evidence).[51] Perhaps the most precise indication of jurisdictional error is that advanced by Lord Diplock in *Racal Communications*, when he suggested that a tribunal is entitled to make an error when the matter "involves, as many do inter-related questions of law, fact and degree".[52] Thus it was for the county court judge in *Pearlman*[53] to decide whether the installation of central heating in a dwelling amounted to a "structural alteration extension or addition". This was a "typical question of mixed law, fact and degree which only a scholiast would think it appropriate to dissect into two separate questions, one for decision by the superior court, *viz.* the meaning of these words, a question which must entail considerations of degree, and the other for decision by a county court, *viz.* the application of words to the particular installation, a question which also entails considerations of degree."

It is, however, doubtful whether any test of jurisdictional error will prove satisfactory. The distinction between jurisdictional and non-jurisdictional error is ultimately based upon

---

jurisdiction, the court goes on to consider whether the decision was 'patently unreasonable'. See, *e.g. Public Service Alliance of Canada v. H.M. the Queen as Represented by the Att.-Gen. of Canada and Econosult Inc.* [1991] 1 S.C.R. 619, 80 D.L.R. (4th) 520. And see A. J. Roman, 'The Pendulum Swings Back-Case Comment on *W. W. Lester*', (1991) 48 Admin. L.R. 274.

[50] Para. 4–028 above.
[51] Para. 4–028 above.
[52] *Re Racal Communications* [1981] A.C. 374, 390–391.
[53] [1979] Q.B. 56.

foundations of sand. Much of the superstructure has already crumbled. What remains is likely quickly to fall away as the courts rightly insist that all administrative action should be, simply, lawful, whether or not jurisdictionally lawful.

VOIDNESS AND NULLITY

The position in the past

4–042   Behind the simple dichotomy of void and voidable acts (invalid and valid until declared to be invalid) lurk terminological and conceptual problems of excruciating complexity.[54] The problems arose from the premise that if an act, order or decision is *ultra vires* in the sense of outside jurisdiction, it was said to be invalid, or null and void. If it is *intra vires* it was, of course, valid. If it is flawed by an error perpetrated within the area of authority or jurisdiction, it was usually said to be voidable[55]; that is, valid till set aside on appeal or in the past quashed by certiorari for error of law on the face of the record.[56]

4–043   Is it correct to say that "there are no degrees of nullity"?[57] If so, does it follow that *ex nihil fit*-out of nothing comes nothing? The notion that void acts are destitute of legal effect is and always has been subject to major qualifications. Thus, although the courts refused to entertain appeals against void decisions because they were nugatory,[58] and have

---

[54] For the fullest analysis, see Amnon Rubinstein, *Jurisdiction and Illegality* (1963). See also D.M. Gordon (1931) 47 L.Q.R. 386, 557; W.R. Wade (1967) 83 L.Q.R. 499; (1968) 84 L.Q.R. 95; M.B. Akehurst (1968) 31 M.L.R. 2, 131.

[55] Compare the discussion of acts mapped by non-compliance with 'directory' requirements set out in the principal work at paras 5–057 *et seq.*

[56] Unless an error on the face of the record goes to jurisdiction, the decision in question was undoubtledly voidable, not void (see, *e.g. Punton v. Ministry of Pensions and National Insurance (No. 2)* [1964] 1 W.L.R. 226; *DPP v. Head* [1959] A.C. 83, 109, 112); but in *R. v. Paddington Valuation Officer, ex p. Peachey Property Corp. Ltd* [1966] 1 Q.B. 380, 402, Lord Denning M.R. appeared to assume that patent error would have rendered the impugned decision void.

[57] *Anisminic Ltd v. Foreign Compensation Commission* [1969] 2 A.C. 147, 170, *per* Lord Reid.

[58] *R. v. Jones (Gwyn)* [1969] 2 Q.B. 33. See also *Chapman v. Earl* [1968] 1 W.L.R. 1315; *Metropolitan Properties Co. (F.G.C.) Ltd v. Lannon* [1969] 1 Q.B. 577, where an application for certiorari was regarded as the appropriate means of challenge rather than an appeal; *Campbell v. Rochdale General Commissioners* [1975] 2 All E.R. 385 (breach of rules of natural justice: court could only affirm or reverse on appeal, thus rendering the matter *res judicata* on the merits: certiorari regarded as the appropriate

even refused to award certiorari to quash such acts and decisions,[59] it was inappropriate for a court to decline to hear an appeal or an application to set aside an ostensibly valid act which was in reality void.[60] In a few cases the courts accorded full legal recognition, in the public interest, to decisions by *de facto* officers, who because of the informality of their appointment, were not strictly entitled to exercise any jurisdiction at all.[61]

Again, although an *ultra vires* decision was ineffective against the **4–044** party aggrieved, he might need, for his own protection, a formal pronouncement of a court setting the decision aside or declaring it to be void. Meanwhile, he could be enjoined from disregarding the decision until its validity had been finally determined.[62] If he took no judicial proceedings at all within a prescribed statutory time-limit, the void decision could become as impregnable as if it had been valid in the first place.[63] And until he obtained such a judicial pronouncement in an appropriate form of proceedings, third parties (unable to impugn the invalid decision) would be obliged to treat it as if it were valid.[64]

In addition, the courts have in practice had sufficient room for **4–045** manoeuvre to be able to avoid being driven to reach unsatisfactory

---

remedy); see, however, Bernard Schwartz and H.W.R. Wade, *Legal Control of Government* (1972), 159–160. See also *Hanson v. Church Commissioners for England* [1978] Q.B. 823, where relief both by way of appeal and certiorari was sought for breach of the rules of natural justice. Certiorari was granted, and the matter remitted to a differently constituted tribunal: *semble* the appeal was dismissed. An appeal was allowed for breach of the rules of natural justice by an industrial tribunal in *Wilcox v. H.G.S.* [1976] I.C.R. 306.

[59] See, *e.g. R. v. Barnstaple JJ., ex p. Carder* [1938] 1 K.B. 385.

[60] *e.g.* where X has been invalidly removed from an office and Y has been appointed in his place; or where P's licence has been invalidly revoked and allocated to Q, it may be futile for X and P to carry on as if nothing has happened. And see *Lakhani v. Hoover Ltd* [1978] I.C.R. 1063 (appellant dismissed for non-membership of trade union; a court subsequently held his expulsion from union invalid. *Held*, ground for dismissal nonetheless fair, as if he had not been a union member).

[61] *e.g. Scadding v. Lorant* (1851) 3 H.L.C. 418; *Re Aldridge* (1893) 15 N.Z.L.R. 361; *cf. R. v. Bedford Level Corp.* (1805) 6 East 356; *Adams v. Adams* [1971] P. 188; *R. v. Cawthorne, ex p. Public Service Association, etc.* (1977) 17 S.A.S.R. 321, 329–335; Rubinstein, *op. cit.* n.54 above, 205–208; Sir Owen Dixon, *Jesting Pilate*, 229.

[62] *Hoffmann-La Roche (F.) & Co. AG v. Secretary of State for Trade and Industry* [1975] A.C. 295 (defendants failed to rebut presumption of validity of ministerial order).

[63] See *Re Gale, deed* [1966] Ch. 236, 242, 247. See also *Ridge v. Baldwin* [1964] A.C. 40, 125, *per* Lord Morris.

[64] See *Re F. (Infants)* [1977] Fam. 165.

conclusions by the pressure exerted by conceptual reasoning. They often employed the elasticity provided by the discretionary nature of most of the judicial remedies, particularly where the applicant had not been prejudiced.[65]

The situation today

4–046 The erosion of the distinction between jurisdictional errors and non-jurisdictional errors has, as we have seen, correspondingly eroded the distinction between void and voidable decisions. The courts have become increasingly impatient with the distinction,[66] to the extent that the situation today can be summarised as follows:

> (1) All official decisions are presumed to be valid until set aside or otherwise held to be invalid by a court of competent jurisdiction.[67]

---

[65] See *Miller v. Weymouth and Melcombe Regis Corp.* (1974) 27 P. & C.R. 468, 480–481; *Kent C.C. v. Secretary of State for the Environment* (1977) 75 L.G.R. 452, 460–461. Contrast, however, *Goddard v. Minister of Housing and Local Government* [1958] 1 W.L.R. 1151, 1153; *de Savoury v. Secretary of State for Wales* (1976) 31 P. & C.R. 344, 347.

[66] *e.g.* Lord Diplock in *Hoffmann-La Roche*, n.62 above, who considered the terms 'concepts developed in the private law of contract which are ill adapted to the field of public law' [1975] A.C. 295, 366. In *London and Clydeside Estates Ltd v. Aberdeen D.C.* [1980] 1 W.L.R. 182, Lord Hailsham considered the existence of 'stark categories such as 'mandatory' and 'directory', 'void' and 'voidable', a 'nullity' and 'purely regulatory' ... useful but ... misleading in so far as it may be supposed to present a court with the necessity of fitting a particular case into one or other of mutually exclusive and starkly contrasted compartments, ... which in some cases (*e.g.* 'void' and 'voidable') are borrowed from the language of contract or status and are not easily fitted to the requirements of administrative law', *ibid.* at 189–190. Lord Denning, as we have seen, initially supported the void-voidable distinction and terminology but in *Lovelock v. Minister of Transport* (1980) 40 P. & C.R. 336, 345 said 'I have got tired of all the discussion about 'void' and 'voidable'. It seems to be a matter of words—of semantics—and that is all.' See also Lord Denning in *The Discipline of Law* (1979) p. 77 where he said: 'I confess that at one time I used to say that such a decision was not void but only voidable. But I have seen the error of my ways'. See also his retraction of remarks in the *Ostler* case, n. 10 above, at p. 108.

[67] Lord Radcliffe in *Smith v. East Elloe R.D.C.* (cited above; Lord Denning in *Lovelock* (n. 66 above) went on to say that 'The plain fact is that, even if such a decision as this is 'void' or a 'nullity', it remains in being unless and until some steps are taken before the courts to have it declared void'. Lord Diplock in *Hoffmann-La Roche*, n. 62 above, said that 'the presumption that subordinate legislation is *intra vires* prevails in the absence of rebuttal, and ... it cannot be rebutted except by a party to legal proceedings in a court of competent jurisdiction who has locus standi to challenge the validity of the subordinate legislation in question.' *Ibid.* at 366. See also Cooke J. in *A. J. Burr Ltd v. Blenheim Borough* [1980] 2 N.Z.L.R. 1 at 4. See also the decision of the Privy Council in *Calvin v. Carr* [1980] A.C. 574 where Lord Wilberforce stated (at pp. 589–590) that a decision made contrary to natural justice is void, 'but that, until it is so declared by a competent body or court, it

Under the terminology of void and voidable decisions, this proposition raises a paradox, namely, that a decision, although technically void, is in practice voidable. Such a paradox is, however, circumvented if we abandon those terms which "lead to confusion"[68] and instead use the terms lawful and unlawful decisions. Decisions are thus presumed lawful unless and until a court of competent jurisdiction declares them unlawful. There is good reason for this: the public must be entitled to rely upon the validity of official decisions and individuals should not take the law into their own hands.[69] These reasons are built into the procedures of the application for judicial review, which requires for example an application to quash a decision to be brought within a limited time.[70] A decision not challenged within that time, whether or not it would have been declared unlawful if challenged, and whether or not unlawful for jurisdictional error, retains legal effect. So does a decision found to be unlawful but where a remedy is, in the court's discretion, withheld. The language of void and voidable cannot, however, accommodate such an effect, as it would insist that a void decision, being void *ab initio*, is devoid of legal consequences and that a voidable decision is capable of being set aside.[71]

---

may have some effect, or existence, in law." He preferred the term "invalid or vitiated" to void, and felt that it would be "wholly unreal" to hold that the decision made was totally void in the sense of being legally non-existent. The Master of the Rolls in *R. v. Panel on Takeovers and Mergers, ex p. Datafin plc* [1987] Q.B. 815 referred to "a very special feature of public law decisions" to be the fact that "however wrong they may be, however lacking in jurisdiction they may be, they subsist and remain fully effective unless and until they are set aside by a court of competent jurisdiction." See also *Bugg v. DPP* [1993] Q.B. 473.

[68] *per* Lord Diplock in *Hoffmann-La Roche*, n. 62 above, at 366.

[69] For a consideration of the presumption of regularity (*ommia praesumantur rite et solemniter esse acta donec probetur in contrarium*), see *R. v. Inland Revenue Commissioners, ex p. T. C. Coombs & Co.* [1991] 2 A.C. 283. Although an individual in the case in which "a fundamental obligation may have been so outrageously and flagrantly ignored or defied", may "safely ignore what has been done and treat it as having no legal consequences upon himself. In such a case it may be that the subject is entitled to use the defect in procedure simply as a shield or defence without having taken any positive action of his own". *Per* Lord Hailsham in *London and Clydeside Estates Ltd v. Aberdeen D.C.*, n. 66 above, at 190.

[70] See Chap. 14 below.

[71] *cf.* Professor Sir William Wade who, although agreeing that the term 'void' is 'meaningless in any absolute sense" says too that "so long as the *ultra vires* doctrine remains the basis, of administrative law, the correct epithet must be 'void'." H.W.R. Wade and C.F. Forsyth, *Administrative Law* (7th ed., 1994), p. 342.

(2) Outside of the rare exceptions we have identified,[72] decisions may be unlawful whether or not they exceed a body's jurisdiction in the narrow sense, or are flawed by an error of law within the body's jurisdiction or an error of law on the face of the record. This argument has already been made[73] and it is not necessary to repeat it now.

(3) Where the court has discretion to refuse to provide a remedy, or is only prepared to provide a remedy that is prospective and not retrospective in effect (in the form of a declaration), it may in appropriate situations refuse to quash an unlawful decision. This can happen where there is a lack of prejudice to the applicant,[74] or where to quash the decision would prejudice third parties who have relied on the validity of the decision.[75]

(4) There are a limited number of situations where the use of the word "nullity", coupled with the distinction between jurisdictional and non-jurisdictional error, survives. Here, some important principle justifies the retention of these concepts. We have seen that one such principle is the need to avoid double jeopardy in relation to criminal proceedings.[76] Thus a previous acquittal may only be challenged where it is a nullity in the sense of being made without jurisdiction in the narrow sense.[77]

(5) In some cases a person who has been adversely affected by an unlawful official decision may be entitled to restitution for consequential loss. The House of Lords have held that money paid to the Inland Revenue Commission pursuant to a demand based upon an invalid regulation was prima facie recoverable.[78] The majority of the Lords held that the claimant

---

[72] Paras 4-040–4-041.

[73] *ibid.*

[74] See para. 15–046 below.

[75] See, *e.g R. v. Panel on Takeovers and Mergers, ex p. Datafin plc,* n. 67 above; *R. v. Panel on Takeovers and Mergers, ex p. Guinness plc* [1990] 1 Q.B. 146; *R. v. Secretary of State for Social Services, ex p. Association of Metropolitan Authorities* [1986] 1 W.L.R. 1. See Lewis [1988] P.L. 78; P. P. Craig. *Administrative Law* (3rd ed., 1994), pp. 597–600.

[76] See para. 4–035 above.

[77] See *Harrington v. Roots* [1984] A.C. 743, 753, and *R. v. Hendon JJ., ex p. DPP* [1994] Q.B. 167. In planning law the distinction between 'invalidity' and 'nullity' survives. See, *e.g. McKay v. Secretary of State for the Environment* [1994] J.P.L. 806. And see the new distinction between 'procedural' and 'substantive' invalidity discussed below at para. 4–051.

[78] *Woolwich Equitable Building Society v. Inland Revenue Commission (No. 2)* [1993] A.C. 70. It was held that interest on the amount paid was also recoverable.

was entitled in "common justice" to restitution[79] and that the court should seek to "do justice between the parties".[80]

Lord Goff's *obiter* in that case, to the effect that the principle of recovery may not apply in cases where the authority had "misconstrued a relevant statute or regulation" or had "simply ... paid the money under a mistake of law"'[81] fails to recognise the full effect of the collapse of the distinction between jurisdictional and non-jurisdictional error. As Lord Slynn said in that case, it is where the demand is based upon a mistake of law that the principle of recovery is "most likely to be needed".[82]

COLLATERAL CHALLENGE

To what extent may a litigant seeking to challenge the validity of an **4–047** official decision do so in proceedings not specially "designated by law for the purpose of having ... a[n] official decision set aside, reversed or modified"?[83] Is the litigant permitted to raise the validity indirectly or "collaterally", perhaps as a defence in an action for damages or in criminal proceedings? May the matter be raised in a tribunal of limited jurisdiction?

In principle it would for example seem wrong for a person to be **4–048** prosecuted for breach of a decision or a byelaw or a regulation that was invalid whatever the source of its invalidity. Two difficulties, however, arise: first, the proceedings may be inappropriate to handle public law questions (for example, by not, as in judicial review possessing discretion to refuse relief; or having time limits, or because of lack of expertise).[84] Secondly, in the past, because of the distinction between void and voidable, the only decisions open to collateral attack were void decisions; errors of law within a body's jurisdiction—even

---

[79] *per* Lord Goff at 759. In addition, it was held that the Bill of Rights (1688) applied, forbidding taxes to be levied without the consent of Parliament. See P. Birks, "When Money is Paid in Pursuance of a Void Authority" [1992] P.L. 580.

[80] *per* Lord Goff at 761. For a discussion of the opportunity to be compensated for unlawful official action, see Chap. 16 below. *British Steel plc v. Customs and Excise Commission* [1997] 2 All E.R. 366 (where there was an unlawful demand for tax, the taxpayer was entitled to a common law restitutionary right to repayment unless removed by legislation. Therefore the plaintiff was not restricted to judicial review proceedings but entitled to bring common law action for restitution).

[81] *ibid.* at 763–764.

[82] *ibid.* at 787.

[83] A. Rubinstein, *Jurisdiction and Illegality* (1963) 37–38.

[84] See H. Woolf, *Protection of the Public: a New Challenge* (1990).

including those on the face of the record—were regarded as valid and effective for all purposes unless successfully impugned through direct attack. Thus, here again the issue of jurisdictional and non-jurisdictional error of law raises its head.

4–049   Although over the years the courts have not been entirely consistent on the point, in general, collateral challenges have been allowed.[85] And even after *O'Reilly v. Mackman*[86] which, as we have seen,[87] held that challenges to the validity of action by public authorities must be brought by way of judicial review, and that it is an abuse of process not to do so, it was recognised both in *O'Reilly v. Mackman* and in *Cocks v. Thanet B.C.*[88] that a public law challenge could be permitted if it arose collaterally in the course of an ordinary action.[89]

4–050   Whatever the limits today upon collateral challenge (and we shall see these shortly), the distinction between void and voidable decisions is no longer one of them. In *London & Clydeside Estates v. Aberdeen D.C.*,[90] Lord Hailsham, attacking that "misleading" language, made it clear that except in "flagrant" and "outrageous" cases, a statutory order such as a byelaw remains effective until it is quashed.[91] The question

---

[85] For examples of successful impeachments of decisions in collateral proceedings. see *DPP v. Head* [1959] A.C. 83; *Customs and Excise Commissioners v. Cure & Deeley Ltd* [1962] 1 Q.B. 340; *R. v. Commissioners of Customs and Excise, ex p. Hedges and Butler Ltd* [1986] 2 All E.R. 164; *Musson v. Emile* [1964] 1 W.L.R. 337. See also *Heptulla Bros Ltd v. Thakore* [1956] 1 W.L.R. 289; *R. v. Pugh (Judge), ex p. Graham* [1951] 2 K.B. 623; *R. v. Sheffield Area Rent Tribunal, ex p. Purshouse* (1957) 121 J.P. 553. *West Glamorgan C.C. v. Rafferty* [1987] 1 W.L.R. 457. And for collateral attack by way of habeas corpus, see *R. v. Brixton Prison Governor, ex p. Ahsan* [1969] 2 Q.B. 222. See also *R. v. Rose, ex p. Wood* (1885) 19 J.P. 676; *May v. Beattie* [1927] 2 K.B. 353; *Margate Pier Co. v. Hannam* (1819) 3 B. & Ald. 266.

[86] [1983] 2 A.C. 237.

[87] Chap. 3 above.

[88] [1983] 2 A.C. 286.

[89] See also *Davy v. Spelthorne B.C.* [1984] A.C. 262. But see *Wandsworth L.B.C. v. Winder* [1985] A.C. 461, where the challenge was held not to be a 'central issue' in the case. See, however, H.W.R. Wade and C.R. Forsyth, *Administrative Law* (7th ed., 1994), p. 321 who says that 'any decisive issue is necessarily central'. See also J. Beatson (1987) 103 L.Q.R. 34, 58 who points out that the way the issue arose in Wandsworth was a classic example of a collateral challenge. See now *Roy v. Kensington Family Practitioners Committee* [1992] 1 A.C. 624.

[90] [1980] 1 W.L.R. 182.

[91] *ibid.* at 189–190. See also Lord Radcliffe in *Smith v. East Elloe R.D.C.* [1956] A.C. 736, 769–770 who said that 'An order, even if not made in good faith, is still an act capable of legal consequences. It bears no brand of invalidity upon its forehead. Unless the necessary proceedings are taken at law to establish the cause of invalidity and to get it quashed or otherwise upset, it will remain as effective for its ostensible purpose as the most impeccable of orders'. See also Lord Diplock in *Hoffmann-La*

today therefore is whether the court or tribunal in question is competent to be seised of a collateral challenge to the validity of an official decision, rather than whether the decision challenged is or is not a jurisdictional error.

The matter has received attention in the context of criminal **4–051** enforcement of official decisions, regulations and byelaws. In *Quietlynn Ltd v. Plymouth City Council*[92] it was held that a licence for a sex establishment challenged collaterally before justices for procedural irregularity was presumed to be valid unless it was invalid on its face, and that in the case of such a challenge the correct proceedings was for the matter to be adjourned to enable an application for judicial review to be made and determined. However, in *R. v. Reading Crown Court, ex p. Hutchinson*,[93] the Court of Appeal held that "justices have always had jurisdiction to inquire into the validity of a byelaw. They are not only entitled, but bound to do so when the defendant relies on the invalidity of the byelaw by way of defence."[94]

In *Bugg v. DPP*[95] the defendants, charged with entering a military **4–052** area contrary to byelaws,[96] pleaded not guilty on the ground, *inter alia*, that the byelaws were not valid because of non-compliance with certain procedural requirements. The Divisional Court held that all subordinate legislation, whether "void" or "voidable", was in principle open to collateral challenge on the grounds of "substantive invalidity" (where the byelaws were on their face outside the scope of their powers or patently unreasonable). A challenge, however, on the

---

Roche and Co. A.G. v. Secretary of State for Trade and Industry [1975] A.C. 295, 366 who said that 'the presumption that subordinate legislation is *intra vires* prevails in the absence of rebuttal, and ... cannot be rebutted except by a party to legal proceedings in a court of competent jurisdiction who has *locus standi* to challenge [its] validity.'

[92] [1988] Q.B. 114.

[93] [1988] Q.B. 384.

[94] *per* Lloyd L.J. at 391. This case went to the House of Lords [1990] 2 A.C. 783, but the issue of invalidity was not there considered, but see Lord Bridge at 804. See also *R. v. Oxford Crown Court, ex p. Smith* (1989) 154 J.P. 422, following the approach of Lloyd L.J. in *ex p. Hutchinson*, n. 93 above. see also *R. v. Parking Adjudicator for London, ex p. Bexley L.B.C.* [1998] C.O.D. 116 (parking adjudicator exercising appellate functions under Road Traffic Act 1984, s. 32 was entitled and bound to consider validity of byelaw; he had correctly held that a provision was *Wednesbury* unreasonable).

[95] [1993] Q.B. 473.

[96] Byelaw 2(b) of the R.A.F. Alconbury Byelaws 1985 under s.17(2) of the Military Lands Act 1892 (the 'Greenham Common byelaws').

ground of "procedural invalidity" was not normally an appropriate matter to be investigated in a magistrates' court since such an investigation required evidence in proceedings to which the byelaw-making authority was not to be a party. In such a case, the byelaws were, until set aside, to be treated as valid.[97] However, strong doubts were expressed about *Bugg* in *R. v. Wicks*[98] and in *Boddington v. British Transport Police*[99] the House of Lords held that a defendant in criminal proceedings was entitled to challenge the invalidity of a byelaw whether on procedural or substantive grounds.

4–053   In *Chief Adjudication Officer v. Foster*,[1] the House of Lords considered whether a social security commissioner had jurisdiction to determine any challenge to the validity of regulations made by the Secretary of State when they were given statutory jurisdiction under an Act[2] to hear an appeal on the ground that the decision of a social security appeal tribunal was erroneous on a "point of law".[3] Leaving open the question of whether procedural and substantive validity should receive different treatment, it was held that the commissioners did have such jurisdiction "whenever it is necessary to do so in determining whether a decision under appeal was erroneous in point of law."[4] Lord Bridge, for a unanimous House, held that such a conclusion avoids a "cumbrous duplicity of proceedings" and welcomed the prior view of one of the commissioners "who have great expertise in this esoteric area of the law" which would benefit the superior court upon appeal or review. He also explained why the commissioners and indeed the tribunal were not an inappropriate body to determine such an issue, and the Secretary of State's views could be put before the tribunal by the adjudicating officer.

---

[97] This distinction was adopted by Lord Taylor C.J. in respect of regulations in *R. v. Blackledge & others*, (1996) 8 Admin. L.R. 316.

[98] [1997] 2 W.L.R. 876. See further A.W. Bradley, 'Collateral challenge to enforcement decisions—a duty to apply for judicial review?' [1997] P.L. 365.

[99] [1998] 2 All E.R. 203.

[1] [1993] A.C. 754.

[2] Social Security Act 1975, s. 101.

[3] The Court of Appeal held that the commissioners did not have such jurisdiction. See also *Aspin v. Estill* (1987) 60 T.C. 549, purporting to follow *R. v. Inland Revenue Commissioners, ex p. Preston* [1985] A.C. 836.

[4] *per* Lord Bridge at 712. Lord Bridge referred to the distinction between substantive and procedural invalidity in *Bugg*, but considered it unnecessary to decide that point since the issue in *Foster* was 'one of pure statutory construction unaffected by evidence.' *Ibid.* See *Re Jamison* (N.I.Q.B.D.) unreported October 14, 1996. Kerr J. referring to *Foster* said 'I would be slow to conclude, on the authority of that decision alone, that a Social Security Commissioner does not have jurisdiction to decide whether the refusal of an adjournment amounted to a breach of natural justice'.

The position in relation to collateral attack appears today to be as 4–054
follows[5]:

(1) Except possibly for a decision which is clearly invalid on its face, all official decisions are presumed to be valid until impugned by a court of competent jurisdiction.

(2) An individual should in principle be able to rely on, as a defence in collateral proceedings before an appellate body, any invalidity, whether or not the source of invalidity is alleged to arise out of a jurisdictional or non-jurisdictional error (or whether the decision or instrument is "void" or "voidable").

(3) To avoid "cumbrous duplicity of proceedings", that challenge should where possible take place in the forum in which it is made, without adjournment to enable an application to be made for judicial review.[6]

(4) In some situations collateral challenge may not be permitted on the ground that the particular proceedings are inappropriate to decide the matter in question (for example, where evidence is needed to substantiate the claim, or where the decision-maker is not a party to the proceedings, or where the claimant has not suffered any direct prejudice as a result of the alleged invalidity).

SCOPE OF REVIEW OF FINDINGS OF LAW AND FINDINGS OF FACT

In its ideal conception, judicial review is essentially confined to review 4–055
of legal error. The body reviewed has jurisdiction to determine
questions of fact. Statutory appeal from most tribunals and inquiries is

---

[5] For recent comments on the above cases see C. Emery, 'Collateral Attack—Attacking *Ultra Vires* Action Indirectly in Courts and Tribunals' (1993) 56 M.L.R. 643; Neville Harris, 'Challenging the *Vires* of Social Security Regulations: *Chief Adjudication Officer v. Foster*' (1993) 56 M.L.R.; David Feldman, 'Collateral Challenge and Judicial Review: the Boundary Dispute Continues' [1993] P.L. 37; A.W. Bradley, 'Judicial Review by Other Routes' [1988] P.L. 169; C. Emery, 'The *Vires* Defence—*Ultra Vires* as a Defence to Criminal or Civil Proceedings' [1992] C.L.J. 308.

[6] The situation could of course change if a procedure were introduced to permit reference between tribunals and different branches of the High Court. Compare the EEC Treaty Art. 177 reference procedure, discussed in Chap. 21 of the 5th edition to this work. See the suggestions in this regard of Woolf, 'Judicial Review: A Possible Programme for Reform' [1992] P.L. 221, at 229; C. Emery, (1993) 56 M.L.R. 643, 667–668; Law Commission Consultation Paper No. 26, s. 18.32.

also largely confined to appeal on points of law alone. In practice, however, the boundary between law and fact is not always easy to perceive.

4–056   There is often no difficulty in distinguishing a question of law from one of fact. A finding of fact may be defined as an assertion that a phenomenon exists, has existed or will exist, independently of any assertion as to its legal effect.[7] The meaning that a lawyer should attribute to the terms of a policy of insurance is a question of law; the question whether the holder of a policy has renewed the policy before its expiry is one of fact.

4–057   Perplexing problems may, however, arise in analysing the nature of the process by which a tribunal determines whether a factual situation falls within or without the limits of a category or standard prescribed by a statute or other legal instrument. Every finding by a tribunal postulates a process of abstraction and inference, which may be conditioned solely by the adjudicator's practical experience and knowledge of affairs, or partly or wholly by his knowledge of legal principle. He hears evidence and, by satisfying himself as to its reliability, finds what were the "true" facts; it may then be necessary for him to draw a series of inferences from these primary findings in order to determine what were the material facts on which he has to base his decision; in order to draw certain of these inferences correctly he may need to apply his knowledge of legal rules. At what point does an inference drawn from facts become an inference of law? Is the application of a statutory norm to the material facts always to be classified as the determination of a question of law? And where in this spectrum lie questions of policy?[8]

4–058   The criteria adopted by the courts for distinguishing between questions of law and questions of fact have not been uniform. It has been noted that where an appellate court has power to review questions of law only, it is apt to hold that a finding or inference was one of law if satisfied that it was wrong but that it was one of fact if satisfied that it was right.[9] Moreover, criteria applied in one branch of

---

[7] Louis L. Jaffe, *Judicial Control of Administrative Action*, 548. For another analysis of the various distinctions drawn between questions of law and questions of fact, see *Salmond on Jurisprudence* (12th ed.), 65–75.

[8] For a particularly searching analysis, see W.A. Wilson, "A Note on Fact and Law" (1963) 26 M.L.R. 609. And see K.J. Keith. "Appeals from Administrative Tribunals" (1969) 5 Victoria U. of Wellington L.Rev. 123; P.H. Clarke, "Law and Fact in the Assessment of Compensation" [1979] J.P.L. 277. For a helpful review of these issues see E. Mureinik (1982) L.Q.R. 621. See also C. Emery and B. Smythe, *Judicial Review* (1986), Chap. 3; P. Cane, *An Introduction to Administrative Law* (1992) Chap. 6; D. Galligan, *Discretionary Powers* (1986), pp. 314–320.

[9] See John Dickinson, *Administrative Justice and the Supremacy of the Law in the United States* (1959).

the law may be largely irrelevant in another.[10] Much may depend upon the view adopted by the court of the ability of the tribunal, the degree of technicality or detail of the legislation and the nature of the interests affected by the tribunal's determinations. Subject to these qualifications, it is possible to make some meaningful generalisations about the tests applied by the courts to discriminate between law and fact in administrative law. But we must first enter another linguistic maze.

Suppose the question is whether an object is a cube. Laymen and lawyers alike will probably say that this is purely a question of fact. One knows the mathematical definition of a cube; one measures the object and finds out whether it conforms to the definition. This is, however, a particular application of a mathematical law; and if the term "cube" were defined in an Act of Parliament[11] a lawyer might possibly be heard to say that the application of the statutory definition was partly or wholly a matter of law. If the question is whether X is a "British subject", as defined by statute, a lawyer is likely to call it a question of law or mixed law and fact. The meaning of "British subject" is a question of law. Particular facts about X are ascertained. A correct answer to the question can only be given by a person with some legal knowledge. If the question is whether a particular transaction constitutes a breach of contract, only a person with legal knowledge and expertise can be relied upon to give a correct answer. The layman as well as the lawyer is likely to call this a question of law.

Suppose now that the question is whether an injury sustained by Y arose "out of or in the course of employment" for the purpose of his entitlement to industrial injury benefit. Here one is dealing with a

4–059

4–060

---

[10] A tribunal may err in law by applying the same criteria to determine whether a single statutory standard has been satisfied in different factual contexts: *Hampton (Dick) (Earth Moving) Ltd v. Lewis (Valuation Officer)* [1976] Q.B. 254. Nevertheless, the important decision of the House of Lords in *Edwards v. Bairstow* [1956] A.C. 14, a tax case in which the concept of a question of law was given a broad interpretation, has been influential in other contexts. It has been applied, *e.g. in R. v. Medical Appeal Tribunal, ex p. Gilmore* [1957] 1 Q.B. 574, a case of certiorari to quash for patent error of law, and in rating (*Solihull Corp. v. Gas Council* [1961] 1 W.L.R. 619) and arbitration (*Tersons Ltd v. Stevenage Development Corp.* [1965] 1 Q.B. 37) cases, and in a case involving the scope of the obligation to pay social security contributions (*Global Plant Ltd v. Secretary of State for Social Services* [1972] 1 Q.B. 139), and in a case concerning the registration of common land (*C.E.G.B. v. Clwyd C.C* [1976] 1 W.L.R. 151, 158–159, 160–161), and in unfair dismissal cases (*e.g. Palmer v. Vauxhall Motors Ltd* [1977] I.C.R. 24). Similarly, the decision in *Brutus v. Cozens* [1973] A.C. 854, a criminal appeal in which the House of Lords held that the application of a statutory term that conformed to its ordinary linguistic usage was a question of fact, has been widely used in administrative law.

[11] The term 'cubic yard' is so defined (Weights and Measures Act 1985, Sched. 1, Pt. VI).

concept less precise than "cube", "British subject" or breach of contract". It will not be profitable for the adjudicator deciding that question to begin by trying to formulate an exact definition of the pharse "course of employment"; the texture of the concept is too open, though under the old Workman's Compensation Acts the courts did their best to close it. He may ask various questions in order to establish the facts that he thinks material in answering the ultimate question. Where was Y at the relevant time? What was he doing? What were his instructions about the time, place and method of work? Having made his primary findings the adjudicator may then go on to draw inferences from them, *e.g.* so as to determine whether Y was deviating from his instructions, and if so by how much. These inferences will normally be called inferences of fact. Finally, he will decide whether the circumstances in which Y sustained his injury fall within the legal concept of "course of employment". This ultimate finding or inference could as well be styled one of law as one of fact. The courts have tended to characterise the question of "course of employment" as one of "fact and degree".[12] They are, however, prepared to intervene to correct clear errors and where questions of general principle are raised that are likely to recur.[13]

---

[12] See *R. v. Industrial Injuries Commissioner, ex p. A.E.U. (No. 2)* [1966] 2 Q.B. 31, 49, 50, 51 (*per* Davies L.J.), 52 (*per* Salmon L.J.). The court's attitude to rent assessment committees is, however, less easy to predict: see *Mason v. Skilling* [1974] 1 W.L.R. 1437; *Palmer v. Peabody Trust* [1975] Q.B. 604; but *cf. Metropolitan Property Holdings Ltd v. Finegold* [1975] 1 W.L.R. 349. The courts may also rely on the discretionary nature of remedies, see *e.g. R. v. National Insurance Commissioner, ex p. Michael* [1977] 1 W.L.R. 109, 122 (*per* Lord Denning M.R.).

[13] *A.E.U.* case (n. 12 above) at 49–50, 51 (*per* Davies L.J.), 52 (*per* Salmon L.J.); see also *R. v. West London Supplementary Benefits Appeal Tribunal, ex p. Clarke* [1975] 1 W.L.R. 1396; *Michael's* case (n. 12 above) at 1 12, 115–116. In this case (at 1 12) and elsewhere, Lord Denning has tended to the view that the application of a statute to particular facts always involves the determination of a question of law, although courts should also guard against undue involvement with the merits of routine decisions that raise no wider issues, provided, of course, that the tribunal has not adopted an interpretation that the words of the statute cannot linguistically carry, and the tribunal's procedure is fair: see, *e.g. R. v. Preston Supplementary Benefits Appeal Tribunal, ex p. Moore* [1975] 1 W.L.R. 624, 631: *R. v. Criminal Injuries Compensation Board, ex p. Ince* [1973] 1 W.L.R. 1334; *H.T.V. Ltd v. Price Commission* [1976] I.C.R. 170, 185–186; and in the context of appeals, see, *e.g. Hampton (Dick) (Earth Moving) Ltd v. Lewis (Valuation Officer)* [1976] Q.B. 254; *Halfdan Greig & Co. A/S v. Sterling Coal and Navigation Corp.* [1973] 1 Q.B. 843; *British Railways Board v. Customs and Excise Commissioners* [1977] 1 W.L.R. 588; *Pearlman v. Harrow School Keepers and Governors* [1979] Q.B. 56, 66–67. *Cf.*, however, *Dyson Holdings Ltd v. Fox* [1976] Q.B. 503 (where his Lordship preferred to regard the question whether a mistress was a member of a tenant's 'family', and so a statutory tenant under the Rent Acts, as one of law; but in order to avoid earlier decisions by the Court of Appeal that he wished not to follow, he was prepared to regard it as one of fact: he warned county court judges, however, that whilst they were final finders of fact, they should not in future disregard this

A matter is usually held to be one of degree (and therefore of fact) **4–061** if it is one on which reasonable persons may arrive at discrepant conclusions on the evidence before them.[14] Examples of such questions are whether a house is "unfit for human habitation" or whether a "substantial part" of premises is to be reconstructed,[15] whether a house has changed its character because of structural alteration.[16] whether operations on land involve a "material change of use" constituting development for which planning permission is required.[17] Courts may nonetheless lay down guidelines or criteria within which the tribunal of fact must normally approach its task.[18] The standard of "fair rent", for example, may be specified over time by reference to criteria such as the age of the premises, its locality, character and state of repair.[19] The vaguer the statutory standard, the more closely does a determination that the facts found confirm (or do not conform) to that

---

ruling from the Court of Appeal! But *cf. Joram Developments Ltd v. Sharratt* [1979] 1 W.L.R. 3; *Helby v. Rafferty, ibid.*, 13). See *R. v. Nat. Ins. Comm., ex p. Stratton* [1979] Q.B. 361, 369.

[14] For a fuller analysis, see W.A. Wilson, 'Questions of Degree' (1969) 32 M.L.R. 361.

[15] *Re Bowman* [1932] 2 K.B. 621; *Daly v. Elstree R.D.C.* [1949] 2 All E.R. 13; *Hall v. Manchester Corp.* (1915) 84 L.J.Ch. 732; *Atkinson v. Bettinson* [1955] 1 W.L.R. 1127; *Bewlay (Tobacconists) Ltd v. British Bata Shoe Co.* [1959] 1 W.L.R. 45. Similarly, whether a building is a 'dwelling-house' is a question of fact: *Scurlock v. Secretary of State for Wales* (1977) 33 P. & C.R. 202.

[16] *Mitchell v. Barnes* [1950] 1 K.B. 448; *Solle v. Butcher* [1950] 1 K.B. 671; but *cf. Pearlman's* case, n. 13 above.

[17] One question that arises in this context is whether intensification of use can amount to a change of use. See, *e.g. Brooks and Burton Ltd v. Secretary of State for the Environment* [1978] 1 All E.R. 733; *Guildford R.D.C. v. Fortescue* [1959] 2 Q.B. 112. See also *Marshall v. Nottingham Corp.* [1960] 1 W.L.R. 707; *East Barnet U.D.C. v. British Transport Commission* [1962] 2 Q.B. 484; *Bendles Motors Ltd v. Bristol Corp.* [1963] 1 W.L.R. 247; *Snook v. Secretary of State for the Environment* (1975) 33 P. & C.R. 1. See also in other contexts, *Bean v. Doncaster Amalgamated Collieries Ltd* [1944] 2 All E.R. 279, 284; *Bracegirdle v. Oxley* [1947] K.B. 349, 358. Yet the questions whether a trade unionist has been guilty of 'unfair competition' within the meaning of the union's rules (*Lee v. Showmen's Guild of Great Britain* [1952] 2 Q.B. 329) and whether a dentist or doctor has been guilty of 'infamous conduct in a professional respect' (*Felix v. General Dental Council* [1960] A.C. 704; *Bhattacharya v. General Medical Council* [1967] 2 A.C. 259; *Faridian v. General Medical Council* [1971] A.C. 995) have been held to be questions of law although they might well have been labelled questions of fact and degree. See also *O'Kelly v. Trusthouse Forte plc* [1984] Q.B. 90 where it was held that the question whether the applicants were 'employees' was one of law, but the answer turned on issues of fact and degree which were for the industrial tribunal, and not the employment appeal tribunal to decide.

[18] See, *e.g. Burdle v. Secretary of State for the Environment* [1972] 4 W.L.R. 1207; *Johnston v. Secretary of State for the Environment* (1974) 28 P. & C.R. 424; *de Mulder v. Secretary of State for the Environment* [1974] Q.B. 792; *Brooks and Burton Ltd v. Secretary of State for the Environment* [1977] 1 W.L.R. 1294 (planning cases); see also in another context, *Capper Pass Ltd v. Lawton* [1977] Q.B. 852.

[19] For an account of the process of evaluation in respect of rules and standards and criteria, see J. Jowell. 'The Legal Control of Administrative Discretion' [1973] P.L. 178.

standard approximate to an exercise of discretion or value judgment rather than a finding of fact. What are to the judges questions of fact and degree (as opposed to questions of law) are often to the layman matters of personal opinion.[20] Nevertheless, the discretion is weak as the range of factors that may be taken into account is limited by the statutory purpose and not the whim of the decision-maker.[21]

4–062 It does not follow, however, that either the judge or the layman will regard every determination of such a question as unassailable. If, for example, a statute were to ascribe legal consequences to tallness, a body deciding that an Englishman of 5′6″ was not tall, or that one of 6′2″ was not tall, would be clearly in error; and a court would doubtless find a verbal formula such as "irrationality" for characterising the error as one of law. But if the same body were to hold a man of 5′10″ to be tall (or not tall), the judge and the layman would agree that the application of the standard of tallness to the facts was not a legal question, though they might use different terminology to describe the decision.[22]

4–063 One way of explaining the problem that has enjoyed considerable popularity in the courts is as follows. The initial question of whether statutory words conform to their ordinary linguistic usage or are to be understood in some technical or artificial sense is always a question of law for the courts.[23] If they fall into the latter category and do not have the meaning that a layman would ascribe to them because, for example, they have acquired some wider or narrower meaning as a

---

[20] But a Minister's opinion as to the best application of planning policy to the facts found by an inspector in a planning appeal has been held not to be a 'finding of fact'; hence, although the Minister has rejected the inspector's recommendations on this point and dismissed the appeal, the appellant was not entitled to make further written representations on account of the Minister's disagreement with his inspector: *Luke of Pavenham v. Minister of Housing and Local Government* [1968] 1 Q.B. 172; *Vale Estates (Acton) Ltd v. Secretary of State for the Environment* (1971) 69 L.G.R. 543, *French Kier Developments Ltd v. Secretary of State for the Environment* [1977] 1 All E.R. 296; *Wholesale Mail Order Supplies Ltd v. Secretary of State for the Environment* [1976] J.P.L. 163; *Pyrford Properties Ltd v. Secretary of State for the Environment* (1977) 36 P. & C.R. 28; *Meravale Builders Ltd v. Secretary of State for the Environment* (1978) 36 P. & C.R. 87. See also *Lithgow v. Secretary of State for Scotland*, 1973 S.L.T. 81; *cf. Fairmount Investments Ltd v. Secretary of State for the Environment* [1976] 1 W.L.R. 1255. See also *Hambledon and Chiddingfold P.C. v. Secretary of State for the Environment* [1976] J.P.L. 502.

[21] See Dworkin's distinction between strong discretion (the sergeant who may pick 'any five men' for patrol) and weak discretion (the sergeant may pick 'the five most experienced men') in R. Dworkin, *Taking Rights Seriously* (1977) p.32.

[22] 'A tall child may be the same height as a short man, a warm winter the same temperature as a cold summer and a fake diamond may be a genuine antique': H.L.A. Hart, *The Concept of Law* (1961) at p.156.

[23] *Brutus v. Cozens* [1973] A.C. 854; *Customs and Excise Commissioners v. Mechanical Services (Trailer Engineers) Ltd* [1978] 1 W.L.R. 56.

result of prior judicial interpretation or are given a statutory definition that deviates from normal usage, then their application in individual cases will more readily be reviewed by the courts.[24] If, however, they bear their "ordinary" meaning, then their application will normally be regarded as raising a question of fact,[25] because, presumably, judges are no better acquainted with the English language than the body entrusted with the primary responsibility for decision-making. But a tribunal will err in law if it finds that a statutory term, albeit one to be understood in its "ordinary" sense, applies to a factual situation to which no reasonable person who understands English would think the words were capable of applying. The error of law might be described as a finding of fact wholly unsupported by the evidence; alternatively, the court might say that the tribunal must have asked itself the wrong question (*i.e.* it could only have reached the result that it did by assuming, erroneously, that the words bore some "special" meaning). There is, however, another way in which an application of "ordinary" language may raise a question of law. Even within their ordinary linguistic usage words can have different shades (or registers) of meaning: a proper appreciation of their statutory context may, however, indicate that as a matter of statutory interpretation they do not bear their full range of meaning.[26] For example, under the Social Security Act 1973 a disabled person was entitled to an attendance allowance, if he requires, *inter alia*, attention during the night. Now although "night" is being used in its "ordinary" meaning (so that its application to particular facts will generally raise no question of law), its statutory context indicates that it should be understood to mean

---

[24] See, for example, *Taylor v. Provan* [1975] A.C. 194 (whether expenses have been 'necessarily' incurred in the performance by a taxpayer of the duties of his office); *Munby v. Furlong* [1977] Ch. 359 (whether a barrister's law books are 'plant' for the purpose of claiming an income tax deduction). *Cf.*, however, *R. v. General Commissioners for Income Tax, ex p. Rind Trusters* [1975] Q.B. 517. Whether a 'profit' has arisen for tax purposes is generally regarded as a question of fact, subject to the legal principle that no tax is payable on a 'profit' until it actually accrues; *Willingale v. International Commercial Bank Ltd* [1978] A.C. 834.

[25] *e.g. Brutus v. Cozens* (n. 23 above); *W. v. L.* [1974] Q.B. 711, 719 (whether a person is suffering from 'mental illness': note that words may still be 'ordinary' in this context, although their proper application may require in part an expertise of a non-legal kind); *Evans v. Godber* [1974] 1 W.L.R. 1317; *R. v. National Insurance Commissioners, ex p. Secretary of State for Social Services* [1974] 1 W.L.R. 1290; *Dyson Holdings Ltd v. Fox* [1976] Q.B. 503; *LTSS Ltd v. Hackney L.B.C.* [1976] Q.B. 663 (whether a building was used as a 'warehouse'); *Simmons v. Pizzey* [1979] A.C. 37 ('household').

[26] See *R. v. National Insurance Commissioners* (n.25 above); *Price v. Civil Service Commission* [1977] 1 W.L.R. 1417 (whether women 'can comply with' a job requirement refers, in the context of the Sex Discrimination Act 1975, s. 1(1)(b), to practical, not theoretical, ability). See also the views expressed by Lord Simon of Glaisdale in *Ransom v. Higgs* [1974] 1 W.L.R. 1594, 1618–1620, and in *Maunsell v. Olins* [1975] A.C. 373, 390–395.

that time during which households normally sleep (when rendering services to a disabled person would be more onerous), and not the hours of darkness or the latter part of the day, even though the word "night" in its ordinary sense could well describe these periods. Once the appropriate shade or "register" of meaning has been identified as a matter of law, its application remains a question of fact. The House of Lords held that the question of "accommodation" was a matter of fact as it involved a "broad spectrum ranging from the obvious to the debatable to the just conceivable."[27] In such cases it was the duty of the court to leave the decision to the public body to whom Parliament has intrusted the decision-making power "save in a case where it is obvious that the public body, consciously or unconsciously are acting perversely".[28] The House of Lords has recently held that the meaning of the phrase "substantial part of the United Kingdom" was open to a "spectrum of possible meanings" ranging from "not trifling" to "nearly complete".[29] The Court would only substitute its opinion on that matter if the decision was "so aberrant that it cannot be classed as rational".

4–064   A tribunal which has made a finding of primary fact wholly unsupported by evidence, or which has drawn an inference wholly unsupported by any of the primary facts found by it, will be held to have erred in point of law.[30] Again, such a finding could be held to be "irrational" or "unreasonable" and, as we shall discuss later,[31] the courts presume that, as a matter of law, Parliament did not intend any decision-maker so to act.

4–065   Lawyers also speak of questions of "mixed law and fact". Thus, whether the facts in issue are capable of falling within a category prescribed by statute may be treated as a question of law, since it entails a determination of the legal ambit of that category; whether they do fall within that category may be treated as a question of fact.[32]

---

[27] *Pulhofer v. Hillingdon L.B.C.* [1986] A.C. 484 at pp. 517–518 (*per* Lord Brightman).

[28] *ibid.*

[29] *R. v. Monopolies and Mergers Commission, ex p. South Yorkshire Transport Ltd* [1993] 1 W.L.R. 23, *per* Lord Mustill.

[30] See, *e.g. Allinson v. General Council of Medical Education and Registration* [1894] 1 Q.B. 750, 760, 773; *American Thread Co. v. Joyce* (1913) 108 L.T. 353; *Smith v. General Motor Cab Co.* [1911] A.C. 188; *Doggett v. Waterloo Taxi Cab Co.* [1910] 2 K.B. 336; *Jones v. Minister of Health* (1950) 84 Ll.L.Rep. 416; *Cababe v. Walton-on-Thames U.D.C.* [1914] A.C. 102, 114; *Rowell v. Minister of Pensions* [1946] 1 All E.R. 664, 666; *Davies v. Price* [1958] 1 W.L.R. 434, 441–442; *R. v. Birmingham Compensation Appeal Tribunal, ex p. Road Haulage Executive* [1952] 2 All E.R. 100; *Maradana Mosque Trustees v. Mahmud* [1967] 1 A.C. 13; *Global Plant Ltd v. Secretary of State for Social Services* [1972] 1 Q.B. 139, 155.

[31] Chap. 12 below.

[32] See, *e.g. White v. St Marylebone B.C.* [1915] 3 K.B. 249; *Re Butler* [1939] 1 K.B. 570, 579; *R. v. Supplementary Benefits Commission, ex p. Singer* [1973] 1 W.L.R. 713; *Brooks and Burton Ltd v. Secretary of State for the Environment* [1977] 1 W.L.R. 1294; *Clarks of Hove*

But the latter question can also be treated as a question of law; the factual part of a question of "mixed law and fact" is then confined to the ascertainment of the primary facts and perhaps the drawing of certain inferences from the facts.[33] Another way of expressing the distinction that is sometimes obscured by these terminological ambiguities[34] is to say that whilst a question of statutory interpretation, normally raising an issue of significance that is not confined to the particular facts of the case, is always one of law, the application of the statute, properly interpreted, to those facts may or may not be.[35]

Finally, mention might be made of the distinction between law and   **4–066**
fact and policy. These distinctions were sharply illustrated in the case of *R. v. Secretary of State for the Home Department, ex p. Bugdaycay*[36] which involved two decisions made by immigration authorities. The first raised the question whether immigrants should be given asylum in the United Kingdom on the ground that they were political refugees. The second was the question whether an immigrant would be in danger of persecution if deported. The House of Lords held the first question not normally open to judicial review, as it contained issues of policy and diplomacy which the courts were not suited to resolving. On the second question it was held that the courts could overturn the decision, which had not given sufficient weight to a letter showing the likelihood of persecution. This distinction is similar to that drawn in United States administrative law between "legislative facts" (matters pertaining to question of policy or discretion, and not appropriate for trial-type hearings) and "adjudicative facts" (matters pertaining to the particular parties) which are so appropriate.[37] In

---

Ltd. v. Bakers' Union [1978] 1 W.L.R. 1207, 1217. See also *Bocking v. Roberts* [1974] Q.B. 307. *Burton v. Field & Sons Ltd* [1977] I.C.R. 106; *R. v. West London Supplementary Benefits Appeal Tribunal, ex p. Wyatt* [1978] 1 W.L.R. 240. See also *Willingale v. International Commercial Bank Ltd* [1978] A.C. 834, where it was stated that whether something amounted to a 'profit' for tax purposes was generally a matter of fact to be determined in accordance with the principles of commercial accounting, but as a matter of law no profit could arise for tax purposes until it was realised.

[33] See, *e.g. Felix v. General Dental Council* [1960] A.C. 704, 717; *Bhattacharya v. General Medical Council* [1967] 2 A.C. 259, 265; *Faridian v. General Medical Council* [1971] A.C. 995.

[34] American courts have also experienced difficulty with this matter. For a 'practical' approach to the problem, see K.C. Davis, *Administrative Law Treatise*, iv, paras 30.00 *et seq.* (and Supplements). For an 'analytical' solution to the distinction between law, fact and discretion, see Louis L. Jaffe, *Judicial Control of Administrative Action*, Chap. 14.

[35] *cf. Pearlman v. Harrow School Keepers and Governors* [1979] Q.B. 56; *A.C.T. Construction Ltd v. Commissioners of Customs and Excise* [1979] 1 W.L.R. 870.

[36] [1987] A.C. 514.

[37] See K.C. Davis, *Administrative Law Treatise* (2nd ed., 1960), Chap. 6.

adequately on matters outside the normal range of judicial expertise.[50]

(5) The concept of error of law includes the giving of reasons that are bad in law[51] or (where there is a duty to give reasons[52]) inconsistent, unintelligible[53] or substantially inadequate.[54] It includes also the application of a wrong legal test to the facts found, taking irrelevant considerations into account and failing to take relevant considerations into account,[55] exercising a discretion on the basis of any other incorrect legal principles,[56] misdirection as to the burden of proof,[57] and wrongful admission or exclusion of evidence,[58] as well as arriving at a

---

[50] *Baldwin & Francis* case (n.49 above); *R. v. Patents Appeal Tribunal, ex p. Swift & Co.* [1962] 2 Q.B. 647. Contrast the earlier approach adopted in *R v. Appeal Tribunal, ex p. Champion Fibre & Paper Co.* [1956] R.P.C. 223 and *Re Baldwin & Francis' Application* [1957] R.P.C. 465. Possibly the willingness of the superior courts to intervene in patent cases is a response to special factors; the existence of a patent bar and the fact that the Patents Appeal tribunal (now the Patents Court) consists of High Court judges. Despite the technical expertise required to administer the Price Code the courts have not shrunk from intervening when they have detected errors of law committed by the Price Commission: *G.E.C. Ltd v. Price Commission* [1975] I.C.R. 1; *H.T.V. Ltd v. Price Commission* [1976] I.C.R. 170.

[51] See Chap. 12 below.

[52] See Chap. 9 below.

[53] *cf. Givaudan & Co. v. Minister of Housing and Local Government* [1967] 1 W.L.R. 250 (this being failure to comply with statutory requirements to give reasons); *Hope v. Secretary of State for the Environment* (1976) 31 P. & C.R. 120; *French Kier Developments Ltd v. Secretary of State for the Environment* [1977] 1 All E.R. 296; *Accountancy Tuition Centre v. Secretary of State for the Environment* [1977] J.P.L. 792. See esp. *Save Britain's Heritage v. Number One Poultry Ltd* [1991] 1 W.L.R. 153.

[54] *Re Poyser and Mills' Arbitration* [1964] 2 Q.B. 467. This decision was distinguished, however, in *Re Allen and Matthews' Arbitration* [1971] 2 Q.B. 518; and in *Mountview Court Properties Ltd v. Devlin* (1970) 21 P. & C.R. 686 the Divisional Court held that a complete failure to comply with a statutory duty to give reasons was not in itself an error of law. But see *Nudds v. Eastwood (W. & J.B.) Ltd* [1978] I.C.R. 171 and *U.K.A.P.E. v. ACAS* [1979] I.C.R. 303, *contra*. See further, *Save Britain's Heritage*, n. 53 above, and Chap. 9 below.

[55] See Chap. 5 below.

[56] *Wootton v. Central Land Board* [1957] 1 W.L.R. 424; *Instrumatic Ltd v. Supabrase Ltd* [1969] 1 W.L.R. 519; *Pepys v. London Transport Executive* [1975] 1 W.L.R. 234; *R. v. A Wreck Commissioner, ex p. Knight* [1976] 3 All E.R. 8; *Melwood Units Pty Ltd v. Commissioner of Main Roads* [1978] 3 W.L.R. 520, PC.

[57] *R. (Hanna) v. Ministry of Health and Local Government* [1966] N.I. 52, 61; *R. v. Secretary of State for the Home Department, ex p. Khawaja* [1984] A.C. 74 (overruling on this point *Zamir v. Secretary of State for the Home Department* [1980] A.C. 930).

[58] See *R. v. Industrial Injuries Commissioner, ex p. Ward* [1965] 2 Q.B. 112; *Devis (W.) & Sons Ltd v. Atkins* [1977] A.C. 931; *Merseyside and North Wales Electricity Board v. Taylor* [1975] I.C.R. 185. Or insufficient weight attached to evidence. See *R. v. Secretary of State for the Home Department, ex p. Bugdaycay* [1987] A.C. 514.

conclusion without any supporting evidence.[59] Error of law also includes decisions which are unreasonably burdensome or oppressive.[60] Thus whether or not the drawing of an inference from the primary facts, or the application of a statutory term to the facts and inferences drawn therefrom, is held or assumed to be a matter of fact (or fact and degree) or a matter of law, the court may still hold the decision erroneous in point of law if any of the above defects is present.

(6) Despite dicta attempting to restrict judicial review on questions of fact to situations where the public body is acting "perversely"[61] there have been isolated suggestions that review of fact should be permitted. Lord Denning contended on at least three occasions that a misdirection in fact or law could form the basis of review.[62] In the *Tameside* case,[63] judgments in both the Court of Appeal[64] and the House of Lords made similar suggestions. In particular, Lord Wilberforce said:

"In many statutes a minister or other authority is given a discretionary power and in these cases the court's power to review any exercise of the discretion, though still real is limited. In these cases it is said that the courts cannot substitute their opinion for that of the minister: they can interfere on such grounds as that the minister has acted right outside his powers or outside the purpose of the Act, or unfairly, or upon an incorrect basis of fact."

---

[59] See Chap. 12 below.

[60] See Chap. 12 below.

[61] Lord Brightman in *Pulhofer v. Hillingdon L.B.C.* [1986] A.C. 484, 518 said that "it is the duty of the court to leave the decision [of the existence or non-existence] of a fact to the public body to whom Parliament has entrusted the decision-making power save in a case where it is obvious that the public body, consciously or unconsciously, are acting perversely".

[62] In *Secretary of State for Employment v. ASLEF (No. 2)* [1972] 2 Q.B. 455, 493; in *Laker Airways v. Department of Trade* [1977] 1 Q.B. 643, 705–706. In *Smith v. Inner London Education Authority* [1978] 1 All E.R. 411, 415 he said: "It is clear that, if the education authority or the Secretary of State have exceeded their powers or misused them, the courts can say: 'Stop'. Likewise, if they have misdirected themselves in fact or in law. I go further. If they have exercised their discretion wrongly, or for no good reason, then too the courts can interfere."

[63] *Secretary of State for Education and Science v. Tameside M.B.C.* [1977] A.C. 1014.

[64] *e.g.* Lord Scarman who said that "misunderstanding or ignorance of an established and relevant fact" was within the "scope of judicial review"; [1977] A.C. 1014, 1047.

A number of English planning decisions have assumed that a material mistake of fact is a proper ground for the courts to quash the decision of a planning inspector[65]

Similar suggestions that a mistake of fact could invalidate a decision have been provided in New Zealand by Sir Robin Cooke. In *Daganayasi v. Minister of Immigration*[66] he said (as Cooke J.): "If...the Minister is led into a mistake and a failure to take into account the true facts, it is not right that the appellant should suffer".[67] Although more recently he has said that a mistake of fact, in order to jeopardise the validity of a decision must be "an established one or an established and recognised opinion; and it cannot be said to be a mistake to adopt one of two differing points of view of the facts, each of which may be reasonably held."[68] The Australian Administrative Decisions (Judicial Review) Act 1977 provides that an administrative decision may be reviewed where the decision is based "on the existence of a particular fact, and that fact did not exist".[69]

In general it is right that courts do leave the assessment of fact to bodies which are primarily suited to gathering and assessing the evidence. Review must not become appeal. On the other hand it should be presumed that Parliament intended inferior bodies rationally to relate the evidence and their reasoning to the decision with which they are charged with making.[70] The taking into account of a mistaken fact can

---

[65] *e.g. Mason v. Secretary of State for the Environment and Bromsgrove D.C.* [1984] J.P.L. 332 (inspector based decision on miscalculation of distance between two properties; but not material); *Jagendorf and Trott v. Secretary of State and Krasucki* [1985] J.P.L. 771 (material error that extension would not obstruct premises when clearly would do so); *Hollis v. Secretary of State for the Environment* (1984) 47 P. & C.R. 351 Glidewell J. assumes incorrect conclusion by inspector that land never had green belt status a ground for quashing the decision. For further discussion of this point see the useful article on this subject by Timothy H. Jones 'Mistake of fact in Administrative Law' [1990] P.L. 507. But see *R. v. Independent Television Commission, ex p. TSW Broadcasting Ltd,* [1996] E.M.L.R. 291, HL where Lord Templeman said: 'Judicial review does not issue merely because a decision-maker has made a mistake' See generally, Ian Yeats, 'Findings of Fact: The Role of the Courts', in G. Richardson and H. Genn, (eds), *Administrative Law and Government Action* (1994), Chap. 6.

[66] [1980] 2 N.Z.L.R. 130.

[67] *ibid.* at 149.

[68] *New Zealand Fishing Industry Association Inc. v. Minister of Agriculture and Fisheries* [1988] 1 N.Z.L.R. 544, at 552.

[69] s. 5(3)(b). The section has, however, been held to be declaratory of the common law and referring to the taking into account of irrelevant considerations; Mason J. in *Minister for Aboriginal Affairs v. Peko-Wallsend Ltd* (1985–86) 162 C.L.R. 24, 39.

[70] See further, Chap. 12 below.

just as easily be absorbed into a traditional legal ground of review by referring to the taking into account of an irrelevant consideration; or the failure to provide reasons that are adequate or intelligible, or the failure to base the decision upon any evidence. In this limited context material error of fact has always been a recognised ground for judicial intervention.

Should we now go further and adopt a general rule empowering the courts to set aside findings of fact by statutory tribunals and administrative authorities if "unsupported by substantial evidence"[71] If such a rule were to become meaningful, it would require bodies which at present conduct their proceedings informally to have verbatim transcripts or to keep detailed notes of evidence.[72] If the administrative findings were made partly on the basis of inspections and views, a body of super-inspectors would be needed. It should be noted that in the United States the courts have occasionally supplemented the substantive evidence rule with the "hard look doctrine" under which an agency making rules must be prepared to show the court the factual and empirical data on which the rule was based, so that opposing parties could offer responses and the court judge the rigour of the decision-making process.[73] In some contexts the substantive evidence rule has much to commend it; and, as we have noted, some judges have already asserted jurisdiction to set aside decisions based on clearly erroneous inferences of fact either by classifying this type of error as an error of law

---

[71] As in the federal administrative law of the United States (Administrative Procedure Act of 1946, s. 10(e)), and of Canada (Federal Court Act 1970, s. 28(1)(c)).

[72] Thus the challenge to a clearance order failed in *Savoury v. Secretary of State for Wales* (1976) 31 P. & C.R. 344 because of the difficulty in establishing upon what evidence (if any) the local authority decided that there was 'suitable accommodation available' for those displaced. Cf. *Sabey (H.) & Co. Ltd v. Secretary of State for the Environment* [1978] 1 All E.R. 586 (affidavit evidence admissible to show that there was no evidence upon which the inspector or the Minister could base a finding of fact).

[73] The 'hard look doctrine' received a hard knock in *Vermont Yankee Nuclear Power Corp. v. Natural Resources Defence Council* (1978) 435 US 519. See R. Stewart, 'Vermont Yankee and the Evolution of Administrative Procedure' (1978) 91 Harv.L.R. 1805. For a plea for the doctrine in the U.K., see N. Lewis and I. Harden, and N. Lewis, *The Noble Lie* (1986). Chap. 9. And see J. Beatson, 'A British View of *Vermont Yankee*" (1981) 55 Tulane L.R. 435.

or merely by proceeding on the assumption that manifest error of fact makes a decision unlawful.[74]

Finally, mention should be made of the area of directly effective European Community law where courts might have to satisfy themselves as to the existence of fact. This issue is discussed more fully in Chapters 12 and 17, where we shall see that where the breach of Community law is alleged the courts, in many cases, have to consider the facts of the case, for example whether a provision unlawfully discriminates, or interferes with the free movement of goods or persons.[75]

---

[74] Above, notes 62–68. See also Wade and Forsyth, *op. cit.* (7th ed.), pp. 311–312; 316 *et seq.* Scarman, *English Law, The New Dimension*, 48–50; D.W. Elliott (1972) 37 Sask. L.R. 48 (review for 'no evidence' in Canada). In the context of precedent fact (above, para. 4–041) the substantive evidence test is applied.

[75] See, *e.g.* Forbes J. in *R. v. Minister of Agriculture, ex p. Bell Lines* [1984] 2 C.M.L.R. 502: *Thomas v. Adjudication Officer* [1991] 2 Q.B. 164. Sir John Laws considers this kind of investigation by the courts no different than an investigation of illegality (as opposed to irrationality). Sir John Laws, 'Illegality: the Problem of Jurisdiction' in M. Supperstone and J. Goudie (eds), *Judicial Review* (1992) at pp. 76–77.

PART II

THE GROUNDS OF JUDICIAL REVIEW

THE GROUNDS OF JUDICIAL REVIEW

Introduction

Judicial review may now be sought to impugn any unlawful decision. **II–001**
As we saw in Chapter 4, the notion that judicial review is confined
to jurisdictional error and error of law on the face of the record has
been seriously eroded, if not destroyed. In his classic dictum in the
GCHQ case, Lord Diplock provided a useful structure to help
delineate the bounds of the unlawful decision. He classified under
three heads what he called "the grounds upon which administrative
action is subject to control by judicial review".[1] He called these
illegality, irrationality and procedural impropriety, with
proportionality as a possible fourth ground that may be applied in
the future. The first three grounds were defined by Lord Diplock as
follows:

> "By illegality...I mean that the decision-maker must understand
> correctly the law that regulates his decision-making power and
> give effect to it...By 'irrationality' I mean what can now be
> succinctly referred to as '*Wednesbury* unreasonableness'...It
> applies to a decision which is so outrageous in its defiance of
> logic or of accepted moral standards that no sensible person who
> had applied his mind to the question to be decided could have
> arrived at it...I have described the third head as 'procedural
> impropriety' rather than the failure to observe basic rules of
> natural justice or failure to act with procedural fairness towards
> the person who will be affected by the decision. This is because
> susceptibility to judicial review under this head covers also
> failure by an administrative tribunal to observe procedural rules
> that are expressly laid down in the legislative instrument by
> which its jurisdiction is conferred, even where such failure does
> not involve any denial of natural justice."[2]

---

[1] *Council of Civil Service Unions v. Minister for the Civil Service* [1985] A.C. 374, 410.
[2] *ibid.* at 410–411.

II–002 This classification has been generally adopted in practice and usefully provides three distinct ways in which decisions may fall short of lawful standards. The classification will therefore be followed in the chapters in this Part. Chapter 5 will consider "illegality" (where the decision-maker exceeds the authorised terms or the purposes for which the power has been conferred). Chapters 6–11 will consider the procedural standards which are appropriate to or required by statue for the exercise of the power). Chapter 12 will consider the unreasonable exercise of power, including various ways in which power may be abused. Proportionally, although not yet firmly (or explicitly) entrenched in English law outside of directly effective European Community law, is considered as a principle by which to evaluate different aspects of an unreasonable decision, in Chapter 12.

II–003 Adopting this classification does not mechanically assign any particular administrative offence to any one of the categories. Nor does it claim that there is no overlap between them. For example, the principle that discretion should not be fettered is discussed in Chapter 10 below under the general ground of procedural fairness. This is because the essence of the "no-fettering" principle is that the decision-maker should always be prepared to listen to someone with something new to say; a principle closely allied to the fair hearing and addressing the participation of affected parties in the process of decision-making. But it could also be said that a decision-maker who fetters his powers has misinterpreted or ignored his legal duty to use and not confine the discretion conferred on him. This approach would label the no-fettering principle as "illegality". Again, the label "irrationality" may more accurately describe the obstinate refusal to depart from a self-created rule or policy. Similarly, the failure to give reasons, or the failure to base a decision upon any evidence, could fall equally comfortably into the category of procedural impropriety or irrationality.[3]

II–004 It should be borne in mind that these "grounds" of review are not exhaustive,[4] that they may overlap, and that they are simply

---

[3] Failure to give any reasons for a decision is considered in Chap. 8 under procedural fairness, and inadequate or incomprehensible reasons in Chap. 12, under irrationality. The failure to provide any evidence for a decision is considered as an example of irrationality in Chap. 12. However, the wrongful failure to admit evidence could amount to a failure to take into account a relevant consideration and thus fall into the category of illegality.

[4] As was pointed out by Lord Scarman in *R. v. Secretary of State for the Environment, ex p. Nottinghamshire C.C.* [1986] A.C. 240, 249.

convenient grouping or "chapter headings"[5] in which to consider the variety of principles which govern the variety of ways in which power may be unlawfully exercised or abused.

---

[5] *per* Lord Donaldson M.R. in *R. v. Secretary of State for the Home Department, ex p. Brind* [1991] 1 A.C. 696, 722. Under South Africa's new constitution (Act 108 of 1996, s.33(1)): 'Everyone has the right to administrative action that is lawful, reasonable and procedurally fair'. See further H. Corder and T. Malawa (eds), *Administrative Justice in Southern Africa* (1997).

CHAPTER 5

ILLEGALITY

INTRODUCTION

An administrative decision is flawed if it is illegal. A decision is illegal **5–001**
if:

(1) it contravenes or exceeds the terms of the power which
authorises the making of the decision; or

(2) it pursues an objective other than that for which the power to
make the decision was conferred.

The task for the courts in evaluating whether a decision is illegal is
essentially one of construing the content and scope of the instrument
conferring the power in order to determine whether the decision falls
within its "four corners". In so doing the courts enforce the rule of law,
requiring administrative bodies to act within the bounds of the powers
they have been given. They also act as guardians of Parliament's
will—seeking to ensure that the exercise of power is what Parliament
intended.

At first sight the application of this ground of review seems a fairly **5–002**
straightforward exercise of statutory interpretation, for which courts
are well suited. Yet there are a number of issues that arise in public
law that make the courts' task more complex. The principal difficulty
is the fact that power is often conferred, and necessarily so in a
complex modern society, in terms which appear to afford the decision-
maker a broad degree of discretion. Statutes abound with expressions
such as: "the minister may"; conditions may be imposed as the
authority "thinks fit"; action may be taken "if the Secretary of State
believes". These formulae, and others like them, appear on their face
to grant the decision-maker infinite power, or at least the power to
choose from a wide range of alternatives, free of judicial interference.
Yet the courts insist that such seemingly unconstrained power is
confined by the purpose for which the statute conferred the power.
This task is made easier where the purpose is clearly defined, but this
is not always so, and in many cases the purposes are difficult to

ascertain. For example, the Town and Country Planning Act, which controls the use and development of land, has not since its inception in 1947 ever contained a definition of the scope of planning. The task of demarcating the purpose of planning has thus been left to those who are charged with implementing the Act; subject to final authoritative interpretation by the courts.

5–003   This Chapter will consider the question of legality in relation to the following issues:

(1) review by the courts of discretionary power;

(2) the review of prerogative powers;

(3) the extent to which statutory powers may be confined by fundamental human rights;

(4) the evaluation of purpose and relevant considerations;

(5) partial illegality;

(6) the delegation of discretionary powers.

REVIEW OF DISCRETIONARY POWER

5–004   The legal concept of discretion implies power to make a choice between alternative courses of action or inaction.[1] If only one course can lawfully be adopted, the decision taken is not the exercise of a discretion but the performance of a duty. To say that somebody has a discretion presupposes that there is no uniquely right answer to a problem. There may, however, be a number of answers that are wrong in law.[2] And there are degrees of discretion—varying scope for decisional manoeuvre afforded to the decision-maker.[3] This section will consider the limits set by the courts to the exercise of statutory discretionary powers.

---

[1] *cf.* K.C. Davis, *Discretionary Justice* (1969), p.4: 'A public officer has discretion whenever the effective limits of his power leave him free to make a choice among possible courses of action or inaction.'

[2] And even cases where the power is discretionary but in the circumstances which exist, the discretion can only be exercised in one way.

[3] Ronald Dworkin makes the distinction between 'strong discretion' (the sergeant's discretion to pick 'any five men' for a patrol) and 'weak discretion' (the sergeant's discretion to pick 'the most five experienced men'): *Taking Rights Seriously,* (1977) p. 32. See also D.J. Galligan, *Discretionary Powers* (1986). For some useful empirical studies of discretion see G. Richardson, A. Ogus and P. Burrows, *Policing Pollution: A Study of Regulation and Enforcement* (1982); K. Hawkins, *Environment and Enforcement: Regulation and the Social Definition of Pollution* (1984); B. M. Hutter, *The Reasonable Arm*

At the outset it should be emphasised that the scope of judicial **5–005** review of a discretion will be determined mainly by the wording of a power and the context in which it is exercised.[4] It would be absurd for the courts to apply identical criteria in determining the validity of a Minister's designation of a particular area as the site of a nuclear power station, the increase in the rents of council houses, the attachment of conditions to the grant of planning permission, and a Minister's allocation of aid to a foreign country.

Parliament may, by apt words, specify exhaustively the ways in **5–006** which a discretion may be exercised, as by enumerating the types of conditions which an authority may, if it thinks fit, attach to the grant of a licence; the attachment of any other type of condition will then be *ultra vires*. Again, it may lay down standards to which the exercise of a power must conform.[5] The crucial question, however, is: in what circumstances and to what extent will the courts review the merits of the exercise of a statutory discretion which is not limited by the express provisions of the Act? The courts have repeatedly affirmed their incapacity to substitute their own judgment for that of an authority in which the discretion has been confided, and there are many matters which the courts are indisposed to question. Though they are the ultimate judges of what is lawful and what is unlawful, there are certain questions which the courts are ill-equipped to decide.[6] But while emphasising the reluctance of the courts to interfere

---

of the Law: The Law Enforcement Procedures of Environmental Health Officers (1988). See also: K. Hawkins (ed.) *The Uses of Discretion* (1992). And see its review by D. Feldman, 'Discretion, Choices and Values' [1994] P.L. 279.

[4] See *Secretary of State for Education and Science v. Tameside M.B.C.* [1977] A.C. 1014, 1047, per Lord Wilberforce: 'there is no universal rule as to the principles on which the exercise of a discretion may be reviewed: each statute or type of statute must be individually looked at.'

[5] The extent to which discretionary power *should* be confined by rule in any particular context will not be considered here. For concern with the 'optimal precision' of rules, see R.H. Posner, *An Economic Analysis of Law* (1986), Chap. 20; D. Oliver, 'Regulating Precision' in A. Hawkins and J. Thomas, *Making Regulatory Policy* (1985); C. McRudden, 'Codes in a Cold Climate: Administrative Rule-Making by the Commissions for Racial Equality' (1988) 51 M.L.R. 409; R. Baldwin 'Why Rules Don't Work' (1990) 53 M.L.R. 321; D. McBarnet and C. Whelan, 'The Elusive Spirit of the Law: Formalisation and the Struggle for Legal Control' (1991) 54 M.L.R. 848. For earlier accounts of the need to confine discretion, see C. Reich, 'The New Property' 73 Yale L.J. 733; J. Jowell, *Law and Bureaucracy* (1975) and 'The Legal Control of Administrative Discretion' [1973] P.L. 178. See also R. Baldwin and K. Hawkins, 'Discretionary Justice: Davis Reconsidered' [1984] P.L. 570. *Cf.* G. Mashaw *Bureaucratic Justice* (1983).

[6] *Roberts v. Hopwood* [1925] A.C. 578, 606–607, per Sumner L.J. See also, on judicial deference to local authorities exercising discretion in matters where elected representatives are likely to be particularly well equipped to determine what is desirable in the interests of local inhabitants, *R. v. Brighton Corp., ex p. Tilling (Thomas) Ltd* (1916) 85 L.J.K.B. 1552, 1555 (public transport licensing); *Re T (A.J.J.) (An Infant)*

in some situations, the courts maintain the right to determine what is lawful. The principle that discretions must be exercised "according to law" is, indeed, deeply entrenched in the common law.

5–007   The criteria by which the exercise of a discretion could be judged were indicated early in the seventeenth century. Lambard's advice to justices—"no way better shall the Discretion of a Justice of the Peace appear than if he (remembering that he is *lex loquens*) do contain himself within the listes of the law, and (being soberly wise) do not use his own discretion, but only where both the law permitteth, and the present case requireth it"[7] —was fortified by dicta and decisions of the courts. Discretion, said Coke, was *scire per legem quod sit justum*[8]; it was "a science or understanding to discern between falsity and truth, between right and wrong, between shadows and substance, between equity and colourable glosses and pretences, and not to do according to their wills and private affections".[9] In 1647 it was laid down by the King's Bench that "wheresoever a commissioner or other person hath power given to do a thing at his discretion, it is to be understood of sound discretion, and according to law, and that this Court hath power to redress things otherwise done by them".[10] The concept of a judicial discretion, which was not confined to courts in the strict sense, was later stated by Lord Mansfield to import a duty to be "fair, candid, and unprejudiced; not arbitrary, capricious, or biased; much less, warped by resentment, or personal dislike".[11] In 1591 the discretion of licensing justices was expressed to mean that they were to act "according to the rules of reason and justice, not according to private opinion ...according to law, and not humour". Their discretion was to be "not arbitrary, vague, and fanciful, but legal and regular".[12]

[1970] Ch. 688 (child custody decision); *Sagnata Investments Ltd v. Norwich Corp.* [1971] 2 Q.B. 614 (amusement arcade permit); *Cumings v. Birkenhead Corp.* [1972] Ch. 12 (local educational policy); *R. v. Barnet and Camden Rent Tribunal, ex p. Frey Investments Ltd* [1972] 2 Q.B. 342 (whether to refer tenancies to rent tribunal); *Bristol D.C. v. Clark* [1975] 1 W.L.R. 1443; *Thompson v. Thompson* [1976] Fam. 25; *Cannock Chase D.C. v. Kelly* [1978] 1 W.L.R. 1 (allocation of tenancies of council houses); *Elliott v. Southwark L.B.C.* [1976] 1 W.L.R. 499 (whether to make rehabilitation order on houses compulsorily required). *Pickwell v. Camden L.B.C.* [1983] Q.B. 962 (allocation of salaries and wages). And see the discussion on justiciability at paras 5-029–5-034 below.

[7] *Eirenarcha*, 58.

[8] *Keighley's* case (1609) 10 Co.Rep. 139a. 140a.

[9] *Rooke's* case (1598) 5 Co.Rep. 99b, 100a (assessment by Commissioners of Sewers). See also Callis, *Readings upon the Statute of Sewers* (2nd ed.), p. 112–113; *Hetley v. Boyer* (1614) Cro. Jac. 336: case of *Commendams* (1617) Hob. 140, 158–159.

[10] *Estwick v. City of London* (1647) Style 42, 43 (suspension of a councillor).

[11] *R. v. Askew* (1768) 4 Burr. 2186, 2189 (determination by College of Physicians as to competence to practise medicine).

[12] *Sharp v. Wakefield* [1891] A.C. 173, 179, *per* Lord Halsbury L.C. (substantially recapitulating a dictum of Lord Mansfield C.J., in *R. v. Wilkes* (1770) 4 Burr. 2528, 2539, concerning discretions exercised by courts of justice). See further W. A. Robson,

It follows that a discretionary power which is prima facie unfettered **5–008** may be held to be subject to implied limitations set by the common law.[13] Indeed, at an early date the courts drew a distinction between judicial discretions and executive discretions, recognising that it would be inappropriate to apply the same criteria to all classes of discretions[14]; and the courts would sometimes characterise a discretion as judicial when they wish to assert powers of review[15] but as executive or administrative when they wished to explain their inability or unwillingness to measure it by reference to any objective standard.[16]

Scope of review enlarged by right of appeal

The scope of review may be conditioned by a variety of factors: the **5–009** wording of the discretionary power, the subject-matter to which it relates, the character of the authority to which it is entrusted, the purpose for which it is conferred, the particular circumstances in which it is in fact exercised. The power of the courts to control abuses of discretion may vary according to whether there is a right of appeal to a court of law from the exercise of a discretion. In many cases the right of appeal by a party aggrieved is to be construed as empowering the court to substitute its own opinion for the opinion of the authority which made the decision if it is satisfied that the decision was

---

Justice and Administrative Law (3rd ed., 1951), pp. 400 *et seq.*; *Roncarelli v. Duplessis* [1959] S.C.R. 122, 140; *Ward v. James* [1966] 1 Q.B. 273, 293–295; and *Birkett v. James* [1978] A.C. 297, 317 (discretion on interlocutory order reviewable on appeal to promote consistency).

[13] For a comprehensive account of this question see A. Barak, *Judicial Discretion* (1989).

[14] See Holdsworth, *History of English Law*, x, 248–249, 252; and D.M. Gordon, "'Administrative' Tribunals and the Courts" (1933) 49 L.Q.R., 419–428 (where, however, the degree of immunity of discretionary powers from judicial review is overstated).

[15] As in *R. v. Manchester Legal Aid Committee, ex p. Brand (R. A.) & Co.* [1952] 2 Q.B. 413.

[16] As in *Johnson (B.) & Co. (Builders) Ltd v. Minister of Health* [1947] 2 All E.R. 395, 399–400 (Minister's decision whether or not to confirm a compulsory purchase order) and *Att.-Gen. v. Bastow* [1957] 1 Q.B. 514 (Attorney-General's decision to sue for injunction to restrain continuance of criminal offence); *Robinson v. Minister of Town and Country Planning* [1947] K.B. 702; *Holmes (Peter) & Son v. Secretary of State for Scotland* 1965 S.C. 1 (designation of large areas as subject to comprehensive redevelopment and compulsory purchase). See also *Webb v. Minister of Housing and Local Government* [1964] 1 W.L.R. 1295, 1301. And *cf. R. v. Secretary of State for the Environment, ex p. Ostler* [1977] Q.B. 122, where the administrative nature of the Minister's discretion to confirm a compulsory purchase order was offered as one reason for the court's inability to review its legality outside the statutory time limitation for impugning it.

wrong,[17] though due regard ought to be paid to the competence of the authority in arriving at its original decision.[18] Thus, inferior courts have been held to have power to determine *de novo* on appeal whether the opinion of a borough council that a street trader was unfit to hold a licence was well founded,[19] whether a local authority was correct to conclude that it was in the public interest to suspend a pleasure boat licence,[20] whether proposed private street works were unreasonable,[21] whether a local authority should have made a compulsory purchase order on a house unfit for human habitation, rather than a demolition, or closing order,[22] whether a local authority's decision to grant or refuse a permit to provide amusements with prizes was a right one,[23] and whether a local authority should refund the overpayment of

---

[17] See, *e.g. Stepney B.C. v. Joffe* [1949] 1 K.B. 599, 603; *Godfrey v. Boumemouth Corp.* [1969] 1 W.L.R. 47; *Sagnata Investments Ltd v. Norwich Corp.* [1971] 2 Q.B. 614; *Victoria Square Property Co. Ltd v. Southwark L.B.C.* [1978] 1 W.L.R. 463.

[18] The *Sagnata Investments* case (n. 17 above), commenting on dictum in *Godfrey's* case (n. 17 above) at 52.

[19] *Stepney B.C. v. Joffe* (n. 17 above); see also *Fulham B.C. v. Santill* [1933] 2 K.B. 357. But the magistrates' court has no appellate jurisdiction when an applicant has been refused a licence to trade on a particular pitch because the local authority has decided to award it to another: *R. v. Thames Magistrates' Court, ex p. Greenbaum* (1957) 55 L.G.R. 129; *R. v. Tower Hamlets L.B.C., ex p. Kayne-Levenson* [1975] Q.B. 431.

[20] *Weymouth Corp. v. Cook* (1973) 71 L.G.R. 458.

[21] *Mansfield Corp. v. Butterworth* [1898] 2 Q.B. 274; *Southgate B.C. v. Park Estates (Southgate) Ltd* [1954] 1 Q.B. 359; Private Street Works Act 1892, s. 7 (repd.); Highways Act 1959, ss. 173–178. But the discretion of the magistrates is not unfettered: *Bognor Regis U.D.C. v. Boldero* [1962] 2 Q.B. 448. The statutory provisions in question, though not strictly conferring a right of appeal against the local authority's decision, amounted to much the same thing, empowering magistrates to decide on the merits of objections to the local authority's proposals.

[22] *Victoria Square* case (n. 17 above). See also *Fletcher v. Ilkeston Corp.* (1932) 96 J.P. 7.

[23] *Godfrey's* case; the *Sagnata Investments* case, n. 17 above. But applicants' opportunities for appeal will be reduced if the local authority has exercised its statutory power to resolve not to grant permits of a specified class: see *R. v. Herrod, ex p. Leeds City Council* [1978] A.C. 403. See also *Owen Cooper Estates Ltd v. Lexden & Winstree R.D.C.* (1965) 63 L.G.R. 66 (whether conditions attached to caravan site licence unduly burdensome); *Croydon Corp. v. Thomas* [1947] K.B. 386; *Peterborough Corp. v. Holdich* [1956] 1 Q.B. 124 (whether it was reasonable for local authority to require occupier of house to supply dustbin); *Middlesex C.C. v. Miller* [1948] 1 K.B. 438 (whether conditions attached to grant of licence to conduct nursing agency necessary for securing the proper conduct of the agency); and see *Greenly v. Lawrence* [1949] 1 All E.R. 241; *Kavanagh v. Chief Constable of Devon and Cornwall* [1974] Q.B. 624 (police refusal of firearms certificate); *Allender v. Royal College of Veterinary Surgeons* [1951] 2 All E.R. 859; *Hughes v. Architects' Registration Council of the U.K.* [1957] 2 Q.B. 550 (full review of decisions of statutory domestic tribunals in appeal to a Divisional Court). And contrast *Stamp Duties Commissioner (N.S.W.) v. Pearse* [1954] A.C. 91 (opinion of commissioners fully reviewable in appellate proceedings) with *Att.-Gen. v. Gamage (A. W.) Ltd* [1949] 2 All E.R. 732 (opinion of commissioners not reviewable at all in collateral proceedings).

rates.[24] The powers of those appellate courts must still not be exercised on the basis of legally irrelevant considerations,[25] but power to entertain an appeal on the merits may endow a court with authority far wider than the inherent but residual supervisory jurisdiction of the High Court,[26] wider also than statutory power to entertain appeals on matters of law.[27]

Discretion and duty

Sometimes the question before a court is whether words which apparently confer a discretion are instead to be interpreted as imposing a duty. Such words as "may" and "it shall be lawful" are prima facie to be construed as permissive, not imperative.[28] Exceptionally, however, they may be construed as imposing a duty to act, and even a duty to act in one particular manner.[29]   **5–010**

---

[24] *R. v. Rochdale M.B.C., ex p. Cromer Ring Mill Ltd* [1982] 3 All E.R. 761.

[25] *Esdell Caravan Parks Ltd v. Hemel Hempstead R.D.C.* [1966] 1 Q.B. 895 (caravan site licence); *Pocklington v. Melksham U.D.C.* [1964] 2 Q.B. 673 (demolition order); the *Victoria Square* case (n. 17 above).

[26] The distinction is well brought out in *Retarded Children's Aid Society Ltd v. Barnet L.B.C.* [1969] 2 Q.B. 22, 28–29, *per* Lord Parker C.J. See also *Hammond v. Hutt Valley & Metro-Bays Politan Milk Board* [1958] N.Z.L.R. 720.

[27] See Law Commission Report 226 *Administrative Law; Judicial Review and Statutory Appeals* (1994) Pt. XII.

[28] *Julius v. Bishop of Oxford* (1880) 5 App.Cas. 214. Students may wish to consider the following problem: 'I learned afterwards that in the scholarship examination another man had obtained more marks than I had, but Whitehead had the impression that I was the abler of the two. He therefore burned the marks before the examiners' meeting, and recommended me in preference to the other man' (*The Autobiography of Bertrand Russell, 1872–1914* (1967), 57). *Discuss.*
(Notes for Guidance: (1) Assuming that there were no formal rules prescribing criteria for the award of scholarships, do you think the examiners had an implied duty to award them to the highest placed candidates, or did they have a discretion? (2) If the former, what legal remedy, if any, would the candidate with higher marks have had, and against whom? (3) If the latter, did the exercise of White-head's discretion taint the subsequent proceedings with invalidity? (4) If not, why not? (5) If yes, what legal remedies would the other candidate have had, and against whom? (The answers to these questions are not provided in this book.))

[29] See *Alderman Blackwell's* case (1683) 1 Vent. 152; and authorities cited in *Stroud's Judicial Dictionary* (4th ed.), Vol. 3 ('May') and examined in *Julius v. Bishop of Oxford* (n. 28 above). See also *Shelley v. L.C.C.* [1949] A.C. 56; *Peterborough Corp. v. Holdich* [1956] 1 Q.B. 124; *Labour Relations Board of Saskatchewan v. R.* [1956] S.C.R. 82; *Re Shuter* [1960] 1 Q.B. 142; *Annison v. District Auditor for St Pancras B.C.* [1962] 1 Q.B. 489; *R. v. Derby JJ., ex p. Kooner* [1971] 1 Q.B. 147; *Lord Advocate v. Glasgow Corp.* 1973 S.L.T. 3 (HL, Sc.); *Re Pentonville Prison Governor, ex p. Narang* [1978] A.C. 247. See also *R. v. Home Secretary, ex p. Phansopkar* [1976] Q.B. 606. And see the discussion at para. 5–029 and n. 82, below. For a recent analysis of the uses of 'may' and 'shall', 'duty' and 'power', see, *R. v. Berkshire County Council, ex p. Parker* [1997] C.O.D. 64.

5–011   This can be the situation where a power is given to a public officer for the purpose of being used for the benefit of persons who are specifically pointed out.[30] Thus, licensing authorities empowered to renew the licences of taxi-cab drivers and stevedores were held to be obliged to do so when an applicant had complied with prescribed procedural requirements[31]; and local authorities empowered to approve building plans were held to be obliged to approve plans that were in conformity with their byelaws.[32]

5–012   Conversely, an apparently absolute duty cast by statute upon a public authority may be interpreted as granting a discretion as to the manner and extent of its performance. Thus, a local authority required by statute to provide suitable alternative accommodation for those displaced by a closing order was held not to be obliged to place them at the top of its housing waiting list.[33] The local authority was in effect given discretion in relation to which it had to use its best endeavours to deal with the result of a housing shortage in the most satisfactory way. Similarly, the manner and timing of the performance by a highway authority of its statutory duty to remove obstructions from the highway are to a large extent within the discretion of the authority.[34] And the duty cast upon various public authorities to enforce the law is subject to a significant degree of discretion at the levels both of general policy and in individual cases.[35] Courts are likely to interpret broad statutory duties in this way when they involve the allocation of scarce resources amongst competing claims. Finally, a court may explain its unwillingness to review for error of

---

[30] *Julius v. Bishop of Oxford* (n. 28 above) at 225, *per* Earl Cairns L.C.

[31] *R. v. Metropolitan Police Commissioner, ex p. Holloway* [1911] 2 K.B. 1131; *R. v. Mahony, ex p. Johnson* (1931) 46 C.L.R. 131.

[32] *R. v. Newcastle-upon-Tyne Corp.* (1889) 60 L.T. 963; *R. v. Ormesby Local Board of Health* (1894) 43 W.R. 96; *R. v. Tynemouth R.D.C.* [1896] 2 Q.B. 219 though *cf. R. v. Eastbourne Corp.* (1900) 83 L.T. 338. See further, para. 5–027 below.

[33] *R. v. Bristol Corp., ex p. Hendy* [1974] 1 W.L.R. 498; *Thornton v. Kirklees M.B.C.* [1979] 3 W.L.R. 1. Contrast, however, *Salford City Council v. McNally* [1976] A.C. 379; *R. v. Kerrier D.C., ex p. Guppys (Bridport) Ltd* (1976) 32 P. & C.R. 411, where it was held that local authorities have no discretion to serve abatement notices under the Public Health Act 1936 or to discharge their obligations under the Housing Act 1957 in respect of houses unfit for human habitation: the duties imposed by both statutes are cumulative. See also *R. v. Hillingdon Area Health Authority, ex p. Wyatt, The Times,* December 12, 1977 (1978) 76 L.G.R. 727 (duty to provide home nurses).

[34] See *Haydon v. Kent C.C.* [1978] Q.B. 343.

[35] *R. v. Metropolitan Police Commissioner, ex p. Blackburn* [1968] 2 Q.B. 118; *R. v. Metropolitan Police Commissioner, ex p. Blackburn (No. 3)* [1973] Q.B. 241. See also *Buckoke v. G.L.C.* [1971] Ch. 655; *R. v. Kensington and Chelsea L.B.C., ex p. Birdwood* (1976) 74 L.G.R. 424. The statute itself may permit a broad degree of discretion to enforce. For example, the Town and Country Planning Act 1990, s. 172 gives power to planning authorities to enforce against a breach of permission when it appears to them 'expedient' to do so.

law an inference drawn by an administrative tribunal from primary facts to a statutory standard when no uniquely correct answer is indicated by saying that the matter is one of fact, degree or opinion.[36] Discretion, in other words, may be conferred implicitly as well as expressly.

Are there unreviewable discretionary powers?

The exercise of statutory powers directly affecting individual interests is nearly always potentially reviewable, albeit that it may be on narrow grounds, at the instance of a person having appropriate *locus standi*, and the courts at different times have shown a variable degree of enthusiasm about intervening.   **5–013**

Wartime and immediate post-war decisions ought now to be treated with caution. The emergency legislation of the Second World War gave the Executive vast powers over persons and property. The wording of the grants of power was sufficient, on a literal interpretation, to support the validity of almost any act purporting to be done under their authority, yet not only did the courts give a strictly literal interpretation to subjectively worded formulae[37]; in their anxiety not to impede the war effort they declined to give a literal interpretation to a formula which prima facie enabled them to review the reasonableness of the grounds for exercising a discretionary power authorising summary deprivation of personal liberty.[38] Such a measure   **5–014**

---

[36] See the discussion in Chap. 4, above, para. 4–066.

[37] Apart from enunciating perfunctory dicta about the need for the competent authority to act in good faith.

[38] *Liversidge v. Anderson* [1942] A.C. 206 (see para. 5–016 below). For decisions in similar vein, see *Bhagat Singh v. King-Emperor* (1931) L.R. 58 I.A. 169; *King-Emperor v. Benoari Lal Sarma* [1945] A.C. 14; *Uganda v. Commissioner of Prisons, ex p. Matovu* [1966] E.A. 514. See also *McEldowney v. Forde* [1971] A.C. 632 (Northern Ireland Minister's power to make regulations for preservation of peace and maintenance of order held to import only limited powers of judicial review; *Att.-Gen. for Canada v. Hallet & Carey Ltd* [1952] A.C. 427 applied; but *cf.* dicta by Lord Diplock, dissenting, at 659–661); and see *R. v. Halliday* [1917] A.C. 260, for judicial self-restraint in the First World War. See also dicta in *Laker Airways Ltd v. Department of Trade* [1977] Q.B. 643, 699, 712 (power of Minister to give directions to the Civil Aviation Authority overriding specific provisions in the statute in time of war, in the interests of national security or international relations or for the protection of the environment: Civil Aviation Act 1971, s. 4(1)(3)).
Where power to declare a state of emergency is conferred in subjective language, the courts are likely to show great self-restraint: see *Ningkan v. Government of Malaysia* [1970] A.C. 379; *Dean v. Att.-Gen. of Queensland* [1971] Qd.R. 391. For the formulation of broader tests of legality to determine whether it appeared to a Minister that facts existed justifying him in seeking from the courts a 'cooling-off' order or a compulsory ballot in connection with an industrial dispute, see *Secretary of State for*

of judicial self-restraint it is to be hoped will not be repeated except possibly in conditions of grave emergency.[39] But a literal construction of the subjective type of formula was to reappear in a number of immediate post-war cases having only a remote connection with national emergency. Happily, a shift in approach to judicial interpretation has taken place since these cases were decided. Below we shall consider the main groups of subjectively worded formulae, bearing in mind this change of approach.

Where the competent authority is empowered to take a prescribed course of action if satisfied that it is necessary in the public interest

5–015 Initially in this situation the courts held that they could not go behind a statement by the competent authority (in the absence of proof of bad faith) that it was satisfied that the statutory condition for the exercise of the power existed.[40] But it was later conceded that if prima facie grounds could be established for the proposition that the authority could not have been so satisfied, a court will be entitled to hold the act or decision to be invalid unless the authority itself persuades the court that it did in fact genuinely form the opinion which it claims to have held.[41] However, in any event, the burden cast upon a person seeking to impugn such an act or decision is likely to be a heavy one to discharge.[42]

Employment v. ASLEF [1972] 2 Q.B. 443; *Secretary of State for Employment v. ASLEF (No.2), ibid.* 455.

[39] See paras 5-025–5-026 below.

[40] *Re Beck & Pollitzer's Application* [1948] 2 K.B. 339 (order stopping up a highway); *Land Realisation Co. v. Postmaster-General* [1950] Ch. 435 (compulsory purchase order). See also *Shand v. Minister of Railways* [1971] N.Z.L.R. 615 (closure of railway line). And see the comment of Lord Denning M.R. in *Secretary of State for Education and Science v. Tameside M.B.C.* [1977] A.C. 1014, 1025 to the effect that the statements in the war-time and post-war cases 'do not apply to-day'.

[41] *cf.* dicta in *R. v. Brixton Prison Governor, ex p. Soblen* [1963] 2 Q.B. 243, 302, 307–308 (a case in which the Home Secretary was alleged to have used his power to order the deportation of an alien, a power exercisable whenever he deemed it to be 'conductive to the public good', for the ulterior purpose of effecting an unlawful extradition).

[42] In *Soblen's* case (n. 41 above), evidence relating to intergovernmental communications was withheld from production when the Secretary of State certified that its production would be injurious to good diplomatic relations.

Where the competent authority is empowered to act upon reasonable conduct or cause

In *Liversidge v. Anderson*[43] the House of Lords held that the Secretary   **5–016** of State's power to order the detention of any person whom he had "reasonable cause to believe" to be of hostile origins or associations, and over whom it was therefore necessary to exercise control, was validly exercised unless it was shown that he had not honestly considered that he had had reasonable cause for his belief.[44] This interpretation of the words "reasonable cause to believe" cannot be said to be logically impossible[45]; but it is contrary to the traditional attitude of the courts towards such formulae,[46] and it is unlikely to be repeated save in extraordinary circumstances, where the courts consider that judicial review of executive discretion would be highly detrimental to the national interest.[47]

In 1970 powers were given to the tax authorities to issue a warrant   **5–017** to enter premises where they have "reasonable ground" for suspecting an offence. Having entered the premises they had the power to seize and remove items found there which they had "reasonable cause to believe" may be required as evidence of the offence.[48] Suspecting tax

---

[43] [1942] A.C. 206. See also *Uganda v. Commissioner of Prisons, ex p. Matovu* [1966] E.A. 514.

[44] The only other admissible ground for challenge was that the detention order was improperly made out; see *R. v. Home Secretary, ex p. Budd* [1942] 2 K.B. 14, 22.

[45] *Pace* Lord Atkin, who delivered a powerful dissenting judgment, at 225–247. The nature of the 'objective' test that Lord Atkin thought appropriate has sometimes been misrepresented; see 246–247 of his judgment, in which he gave his reasons for agreeing with the other members of the House in the analogous case of *Green v. Home Secretary* [1942] A.C. 284.

[46] On the meaning of 'reasonable cause' in various contexts, see *Shelley v. L.C.C.* [1949] A.C. 56; *Osgood v. Nelson* (1872) L.R. 5 H.L. 636, 647; *Wilson v. Esquimalt & Nanaimo Ry.* [1922] 1 A.C. 202, 212. For the jurisdiction of the courts to determine whether compulsory acquisition of property was 'reasonably necessary' for redevelopment, see *Coleen Properties Ltd v. Minister of Housing and Local Government* [1971] 1 W.L.R. 433; *cf. Migdale Investments Ltd v. Secretary of State for the Environment* [1976] J.P.L. 365; *R. v. Secretary of State for Transport, ex p. de Rothschild* [1989] 1 All E.R. 933.

[47] In a case arising in Trinidad the court emphatically refuted a suggestion that a power vested in an immigration officer to detain a person whom he had 'reason to suspect' of being a prohibited immigrant imported a purely subjective test of reasonableness. *Cedeno v. O'Brien* (1964) 7 W.I.R. 192. Contrast *Boucaut Bay v. Commonwealth* (1927) 40 C.L.R. 98; see also *Belfast Corp. v. O.D. Cars Ltd* [1960] A.C. 490, 520–521, 526–527 (provisions of a planning scheme which 'the Ministry considers reasonable' held not amenable to judicial review); See also *Nakkuda Ali v. Jayaratne* [1951] A.C. 66, 76–77 (controller could cancel textile dealer's licence when he had reasonable grounds for believing dealer to be unfit to hold a licence; held (*obiter* at 77) that there had in fact to exist reasonable grounds, known to the controller, before he could exercise the power of cancellation).

[48] Taxes Management Act 1970, s. 20C.

fraud, the Inland Revenue officials obtained search warrants, entered premises and seized documents without informing the applicants of the offences suspected or the persons suspected of having committed them. The House of Lords upheld the Inland Revenue's actions and held that the applicants had no right to be informed of the alleged offences, or of the "reasonable ground" for suspecting an offence.[49] Nevertheless, it was held that the existence of "reasonable cause to believe" was a question of objective fact, to be tried on evidence, and Lord Diplock said that "the time has come to acknowledge openly that the majority of this House in *Liversidge v. Anderson* were expediently and, at that time perhaps, excusably wrong and the dissenting speech of Lord Atkin was right."[50] The police officer who has a common-law or statutory power to arrest on reasonable suspicion, and the public official who has power to cancel a licence when he has reasonable grounds to believe the licensee to be unfit to hold a licence, must be prepared to justify in court the reasonableness of their beliefs; they cannot defeat an attack upon the grounds on which they have exercised their discretion merely by proving that they honestly thought that their beliefs had been reasonable.[51] The criterion of reasonableness is not subjective, but objective in the sense that it is subject to independent scrutiny.

5–018   A number of provisions of the Police and Criminal Evidence Act 1984 give powers to search persons or premises or to arrest where there exists a "reasonable cause" or "reasonable grounds" for suspecting an offence.[52] Both the case law[53] and the Code of Practice under the Act[54] provide that there must be some "objective basis" for reasonable grounds of suspicion to exist. Such suspicion must therefore be based on factors such as a description of an article being carried by the suspected offender. Reasonable suspicion cannot,

---

[49] *R. v. I.R.C., ex p. Rossminster* [1980] A.C. 952.

[50] *ibid.* at 1011.

[51] See, *e.g. Liversidge v. Anderson* [1942] A.C. 206, 228–229; *Nakkuda Ali v. Jayaratne* [1951] A.C. 66. See also *R. v. Secretary of State for the Home Department, ex p. Khawaja* [1984] A.C. 74. (Insufficient for the immigration officer to show some reasonable grounds for his action. The standard should be higher when a power to affect liberty was in issue. Therefore a high degree of probability that the immigrant had practised deception had to be shown.)

[52] s. 1(3) gives a constable the power to search a person or vehicle if he has 'reasonable cause' for suspecting that he will find stolen or prohibited articles. S. 24(5) provides that a person may be arrested by any person who has 'reasonable grounds for suspecting' a person to be guilty of an arrestable offence. And s. 25(1) provides that a constable may arrest a person for a non-arrestable offence if he has 'reasonable grounds for suspecting' that an offence has been committed by that person.

[53] *Dumbell v. Roberts* [1944] 1 All E.R. 326; *Ward v. Hogg* (1858) 157 E.R. 533; *Dallison v. Caffery* [1965] 1 Q.B. 348; *Hussein v. Chong Fook Kam* [1970] A.C. 942; *Castorina v. Chief Constable of Surrey* (1988) New L.J. 180.

[54] *Code of Practice of the Police & Criminal Evidence Act 1984* (HMSO 1991) paras 1.5–1.7.

however, be supported upon the basis of personal factors alone (such as the fact that the arrested person is known to have had a previous conviction, or the person's race).[55]

This is not to say that the courts will readily interfere with the **5–019** exercise of discretion if, from the nature of the subject-matter or the surrounding circumstances (*e.g.* the necessity for taking swift action for the preservation of public order), it would be difficult for anyone but the repository of the power to form an opinion as to the occasion for its exercise, or if, in a doubtful case, it would be unfair to penalise the authority for a possible error of judgment. In such a situation if there are reasonable grounds, the opinion of the judge as to whether he would have formed the same belief is of no more relevance than the opinion of the judge as to the guilt of a defendant, if there is reasonable evidence to go to a jury.[56]

On the whole, the courts have been circumspect in reviewing the **5–020** remuneration paid by a local authority to its officers and employees,[57] even where statutory criteria of reasonableness have been prescribed. The modern judicial tendency has been to move towards a position of self-restraint,[58] abstaining from *de novo* review and leaning in the direction of non-interference, save where no reasonable body of persons could have arrived at the decision in question—a test of validity which could have been applied had the word "reasonable" been absent from the grant of power.[59]

---

[55] See generally, M. Zander, *The Police and Criminal Evidence Act 1984* (1990) pp. 6–7, 59–61.

[56] *Liversidge v. Anderson* (n. 51 above) at 239, *per* Lord Atkin.

[57] Local Government Act 1933, s. 106(2) (duty to pay 'reasonable remuneration'; see now Local Government Act 1972, s. 112(2) (duty to appoint subject to 'reasonable terms and conditions, including conditions as to remuneration')).

[58] *Re Walker's Decision* [1944] K.B. 173, 644; *Luby v. Newcastle-under-Lyme Corp.* [1964] 2 Q.B. 64, 70–72; [1965] 1 Q.B. 214, 230–231. But the courts used to assert a wider jurisdiction to review the reasonableness of rents, though they did not in fact hold charges to be invalid in any reported case (see *Belcher v. Reading Corp.* [1950] Ch, 580; *Smith v. Cardiff Corp. (No. 2)* [1955] Ch. 159; *Summerfield v. Hampstead B.C.* [1957] 1 W.L.R. 467) until *Backhouse v. Lambeth L.B.C.* (1972) 116 S.J. 802.

[59] In the *Luby* and *Backhouse* cases, the *Wednesbury* test of unreasonableness (see Chap. 12, below) was applied. See also *Evans v. Collins* [1965] 1 Q.B. 380. And compare the discussion in paras 12-066–12-067 below on the interpretation of the term 'unreasonable' in a statute. See also *Pickwell v. Camden L.B.C.* [1983] Q.B. 962.

Where the connection between the subject-matter of the power to be exercised and the purposes prescribed by statute was expressed to be determinable by the opinion of the competent authority

5–021 Section 1(1) of the Emergency Powers (Defence) Act 1939 empowered His Majesty in Council to make such regulations as appeared to him to be necessary or expedient for securing the public safety, the defence of the realm, the maintenance of public order or the efficient prosecution of the war, or for maintaining supplies and services essential to the life of the community.[60] The courts held that it was not open to anyone to canvass in the courts the necessity or expediency for making any such regulation that was good on its face,[61] or any order made in virtue of a regulation which reproduced similar enabling words.[62]

5–022 All that the courts were then willing to do was to see that the power which it was claimed to have been exercised was one which fell within the four corners of the powers given by the legislature and to see that the power was exercised in good faith. Apart from that, the courts did not abrogate to themselves any power to inquire into the reasonableness, the policy, the sense, or any other aspect of the transaction.[63]

5–023 The burden of establishing that the competent authority did not honestly believe that its conduct was directed to the furtherance of any of these comprehensive purposes, but was in pursuance of an ulterior motive, would be almost impossible to discharge. Dicta to the effect that regulations purporting to be made in virtue of similar powers had to be capable of being related to the prescribed purposes[64] were disregarded.

---

[60] See further, the Emergency Powers (Defence) Act 1940, s.1; and the Supplies and Services Acts 1945–51.

[61] *R. v. Comptroller-General of Patents, ex p. Bayer Products Ltd* [1941] 2 K.B. 306.

[62] *Progressive Supply Co. v. Dalton* [1943] Ch. 54 (trading restrictions); *Point of Ayr Collieries Ltd v. Lloyd-George* [1943] 2 All E.R. 547; *Carltona Ltd v. Commissioners of Works, ibid.* 560; *Pollok School Co. v. Glasgow Town Clerk*, 1946 S.C. 373, 386; 1947 S.C. 605 (requisitioning); *Demetriades v. Glasgow Corp.* [1951] 1 All E.R. 457 (use of requisitioned property). A like interpretation was given to similarly worded Canadian emergency legislation: *Reference Re Chemical Regulations* [1943] S.C.R. 1. See also *Underhill v. Ministry of Food* [1950] 1 All E.R. 591 (orders for rationing of sweets made in virtue of s.1 of the Supplies and Services (Transitional Powers) Act 1945).

[63] *Carltona Ltd v. Commissioners of Works* (n. 62 above) at 564, *per* Lord Greene M.R.; *cf.* though, *Teh Cheng Poh v. Public Prosecutor, Malaysia* [1980] A.C. 458, PC (distinguished in *Ali v. R.* [1992] 2 A.C. 93).

[64] *Att.-Gen. for Canada v. Hallet & Carey Ltd* [1952] A.C. 427, 450; *Ross-Clunis v. Papadopoullos* [1958] 1 W.L.R. 546, 559, PC. *Cf. Lipton Ltd v. Ford* [1917] 2 K.B. 647, 654 for a like test for ascertaining the validity of regulations made under the Defence of the Realm Acts in the First World War.

In the atmosphere of the war and its immediate aftermath, judicial **5–024** activism was still imperceptible, even where the statutory purposes were defined with closer precision. In cases involving public control over land use and housing accommodation, one could point to dicta to the effect that an order shown to be perverse or otherwise lacking in any evidentiary support might be held *ultra vires* because the competent authority could not be deemed to have been genuinely satisfied that it was appropriate for a purpose sanctioned by legislation.[65] Yet if persons claimed to be aggrieved they invariably failed in the courts; and the judgments persistently laid a heavier emphasis on the amplitude of the discretionary power than on the need to relate it to the purposes of the Act.[66] The incantation of statements denying the absoluteness of administrative discretion in such cases was little more than a perfunctory ritual to satisfy the consciences of the judges.

Change of approach

More than a decade was to elapse after the Second World War before **5–025** the pendulum swung and the emphasis shifted. In New Zealand in 1959 a power vested in the Governor-General to make such regulations as he "thinks necessary to secure the due administration" of an Education Act was held to be invalidly exercised in so far as his opinion as to the necessity for such a regulation was not reasonably tenable.[67] In England in 1962 the power of the Commissioners of Customs and Excise to make regulations for "any matter for which provision appears to them necessary for the purpose of giving effect" to the Act was not construed as constituting them as the sole judges of what was in fact necessary for the purposes of the Act; and a regulation in which they gave themselves power to determine conclusively the amounts of tax payable was held to be *ultra vires*.[68] Again, in 1964, the courts were not deterred by a subjectively worded formula from holding that a compulsory purchase order made

---

[65] *Robinson v. Minister of Town and Country Planning* [1947] K.B. 702, 724; *Demetriades v. Glasgow Corp.* [1951] 1 All E.R. 457, 463.

[66] *Minister of Agriculture and Fisheries v. Price* [1941] 2 K.B. 116; *Robinson's* case (n. 65 above); *Taylor v. Brighton Corp.* [1947] K.B. 736; *Swindon Corp. v. Pearce* [1948] 2 All E.R. 119. See also *Holmes (Peter) & Son v. Secretary of State for Scotland*, 1965 S.C. 1.

[67] *Reade v. Smith* [1959] N.Z.L.R. 996; see also *Low v. Earthquake Commission* [1959] N.Z.L.R. 1198, 1207–1208 (dicta).

[68] *Customs and Excise Commissioners v. Cure and Deeley Ltd* [1962] 1 Q.B. 340. A number of the authorities referred to in the preceding pages were considered in the judgment at 366–368. But on different facts, a similarly worded provision of a subsequent Act was interpreted literally in *Marsh (B.) (Wholesale) Ltd v. Customs and Excise Commissioners* [1970] 2 Q.B. 206.

ostensibly for the purpose of coast protection work was invalid because the land in question was not in fact required for such a purpose.[69] As was observed in a leading Canadian case, "there is always a perspective within which a statute is intended to operate."[70]

5–026 The decision in 1968 of the House of Lords in *Padfield's* case[71] was an important landmark.[72] The Minister had refused to appoint a committee, as he was statutorily empowered to do at his discretion, to investigate complaints made by members of the Milk Marketing Board that the majority of the Board had fixed milk prices in a way that was unduly unfavourable to the complainants. The House of Lords held that the Minister's discretion was not unfettered and that the reasons that he had given for his refusal showed that he had acted *ultra vires* by taking into account factors that were legally irrelevant and by using his power in a way calculated to frustrate the policy of the Act.[73] The view was also expressed by four of their Lordships that even had the Minister given no reasons for his decision, the court would not have been powerless to intervene: for once a prima facie case of misuse of power had been established, it would have been open to the court to infer that the Minister had acted unlawfully if he had declined to supply any justification at all for his decision.[74] In the years that followed the Court of Appeal[75]

---

[69] *Webb v. Minister of Housing and Local Government* [1964] 1 W.L.R. 1295; [1965] 1 W.L.R. 755—a complicated case, in which the enabling legislation was couched partly in subjective and partly in objective terms. See J. Bennett Miller [1966] P.L. 330; A.W. Bradley [1965] C.L.J. 161.

[70] *Roncarelli v. Duplessis* [1959] S.C.R. 122, 140, *per* Rand J. See also *Rogers v. Jordan* (1965) 112 C.L.R. 580 (dicta).

[71] *Padfield v. Minister of Agriculture, Fisheries and Food* [1968] A.C. 997.

[72] For some critical comments upon this decision and, more generally, upon judicial willingness to imply limitations upon the scope of subjectively worded discretion, see R.C. Austin, 'Judicial Review of Subjective Discretion' (1975) 28 C.L.P. 150, esp. 167–173.

[73] The Minister's reasons for refusing to accede to the complainants' request had been that it was the purpose of the statutory scheme that issues of the kind raised by the complainants should be settled by the representatives of the producers from the different regions who sat on the Board, and that were the committee to uphold the complainants, it would be politically embarrassing for him if he decided not to implement the committee's recommendations. After the decision of the House of Lords the Minister complied with the order by referring the complaint to a committee of investigation. The committee reported in favour of the complainants; the Minister declined to follow the recommendation.

[74] [1968] A.C., at 1032–1933 (*per* Reid L.J.), 1049 (*per* Hodson L.J.), 1053–1054 (*per* Pearce L.J.), 1061–1062 (*per* Upjohn L.J.).

[75] See, *e.g. Congreve v. Home Office* [1976] Q.B. 629 (subjective power to revoke television licences not validly exercisable to prevent avoidance of prospectively announced fee increase); *Laker Airways Ltd v. Department of Trade* [1977] Q.B. 643 (neither statutory power to give directions to Civil Aviation Authority nor non-statutory power conferred by treaty validly exercisable to defeat legislative scheme). See also *R. v.*

and the House of Lords[76] set aside as *ultra vires* the exercise of discretion that included a substantial subjective element. It is interesting to note that important as the decision in *Padfield* has been in the evolution of judicial attitudes, the Minister was ultimately able to uphold the Board's decision without resorting to legislation. Another feature of those decisions was the willingness of the courts to assert their power to scrutinise the factual basis upon which discretionary powers have been exercised.[77]

Where the competent authority is empowered to take such action or to impose such conditions as it thinks fit in relation to a matter directly impinging on individual interests

The courts have generally declined to construe such words as investing the authority with an absolute discretion to do as it pleases. The Minister of Transport, when empowered to make such order as he thought fit on a licensing appeal, was obliged to confine himself to matters raised in the course of the appeal and to disregard irrelevant

5–027

Home Secretary, ex p. Phansopkar [1976] Q.B. 606 (Minister had no discretion to insist that applicants for certificates of partiality obtain them abroad when this would involve burdensome delay upon the exercise of their right to enter the United Kingdom).

[76] See, *e.g. Daymond v. Plymouth City Council* [1976] A.C. 609 (statutory power to make charges for sewerage services as the authority thought fit did not authorise charging those not in receipt of the services): *Secretary of State for Education and Science v. Tameside M.B.C.* [1977] A.C. 1014 (Minister improperly exercised power to give directions to a local education authority when satisfied that the authority was proposing to act unreasonably).

[77] See, particularly, the *Tameside* case (n. 76 above), especially at 1047, 1065–1066, 1072; but the statutory standard on which the Minister had to be satisfied was by no means wholly subjective. Their Lordships did not indorse the wider scope of inquiry into the underlying facts advanced in the Court of Appeal by Scarman L.J. at 1030–1031. *Cf.* Sir Leslie Scarman, *English Law—The New Dimension*, Chap. 3, especially at pp. 48–50. See also *Laker Airways* (n. 75 above) at 706. But see the 'Draconian' powers given to the Secretary of State under s. 23 of the Housing Act 1980 to intervene to exercise the powers of a local housing authority to do 'all such things as appear to him necessary or expedient' to enable tenants to exercise the right to buy. Under that statute he may exercise those powers 'Where it appears [to him] that [the tenants] have or may have difficulty in exercising their right to buy effectively or expeditiously'. In *R. v. Secretary of State for the Environment, ex p. Norwich C.C.* [1982] Q.B. 808 it was held that this formula did not require the Secretary of State to intervene only when the authority had acted 'unreasonably' but, it seems, there had to be some objective evidence that the tenants were experiencing 'difficulty' (*per* Kerr L.J.).

considerations in exercising his discretion.[78] A local authority empowered to attach such conditions as it thinks fit to the grant of a licence or permit had to have regard to relevant considerations and disregard the irrelevant, even though the factors which it is to take into account were not mentioned in the Act.[79] The authority had also genuinely to address itself to the application before it, consider it on its individual merits, and not promote a purpose alien to the spirit of the Act.

5–028   The courts also reversed their previous reluctance to scrutinise the exercise of discretions by Ministers and local authorities in the field of town planning and housing law[80] by being willing to determine the validity of conditions annexed as a matter of discretion to grants of planning permission and caravan site licences by reference to criteria formulated in the context of licensing decisions and byelaws.[81]

Discretion and justiciability

5–029   Later in this Chapter we shall see the more precise techniques by which the courts today review decisions on the ground of illegality by insisting that powers pursue legitimate purposes and relevant considerations. Meanwhile, our brief excursus into the judicial control of discretionary power indicates that no statutory power is any

---

[78] *R. v. Minister of Transport, ex p. H.C. Motor Works Ltd* [1927] 2 K.B. 401; *R. v. Minister of Transport, ex p. Upminster Services Ltd* [1934] 1 K.B. 277. See also *Whitehead v. Haines* [1965] 1 Q.B. 200 (irrelevant conditions attached to justices' licence).

[79] *R. v. L.C.C., ex p. Entertainments Protection Association* [1931] 2 K.B. 215; *R. v. G.L.C., ex p. Blackburn* [1976] 1 W.L.R. 550 (condition invalid because it did not prohibit licensee from exhibiting a film in breach of the criminal law). However, not every administrative order that apparently authorises a technical violation of the criminal law is invalid: *Buckoke v. G.L.C.* [1971] Ch. 655; *cf. Johnson v. Phillips* [1976] 1 W.L.R. 65.

[80] See, *e.g. Robins (E.) & Son Ltd v. Minister of Health* [1939] 1 K.B. 520; *R. v. East Kesteven R.D.C.* [1947] 1 All E.R. 310; *Robinson v. Minister of Town and Country Planning* [1947] K.B. 702 (appl'd. in *Holmes (Peter) & Son v. Secretary of State for Scotland*, 1965 S.C. 1); *Taylor v. Brighton Corp.* [1947] K.B. 736; *Johnson (B.) & Co. (Builders) Ltd v. Minister of Health* [1947] 2 All E.R. 395, 398–400; *Swindon Corp. v. Pearce* [1948] 2 All E.R. 119.

[81] *Pyx Granite Co. v. Ministry of Housing and Local Government* [1958] 1 Q.B. 554, 572, *per* Lord Denning M.R., approved in *Fawcett Properties Ltd v. Buckingham C.C.* [1961] A.C. 636; *Hall & Co. v. Shoreham-by-Sea U.D.C.* [1964] 1 W.L.R. 240; *Mixnam's Properties Ltd v. Chertsey U.B.C.* [1965] A.C. 735; *Hartnell v. Minister of Housing and Local Government* [1965] A.C. 134; *R. v. Hillingdon L.B.C., ex p. Royco Homes Ltd* [1974] Q.B. 720; *Lowe (David) & Sons Ltd v. Provost, etc. of Burgh of Musselburgh*, 1974 S.L.T. 5. For a recent decision outside of this area see *Singh v. Secretary of State for the Home Department* [1992] 1 W.L.R. 1052, HL (s.18(1) of the Immigration Act 1971 provides that the Secretary of State 'may' make regulations to providing rights of appeal. *Held:* Secretary of State was under a duty to make regulations so that interested persons could exercise an effective appeal).

longer inherently unreviewable.[82] As was said by Lord Upjohn in *Padfield*,[83] even if a statute were to confer upon a decision-maker an "unfettered discretion".

> "[T]he use of that adjective [unfettered], even in an Act of Parliament, can do nothing to unfetter the control which the judiciary have over the executive, namely, that in exercising their powers the latter must act lawfully and that is a matter to be determined by looking at the Act and its scope and object in conferring a discretion upon the Minister rather than by the use of adjectives."[84]

Yet there are some decisions which the courts are ill-equipped to review; those which are not justiciable,[85] either because they admit of no objective justification or because the issues they determine are polycentric[86] in effect. Such decisions include those that necessitate the

5–030

---

[82] The same could be said for prerogative powers, which will be considered below—paras 5–037 *et seq.* It has recently been held that even a Minister's power to bring into force the provisions of a statute, while not to be interpreted as a duty, was not 'absolute or unfettered'. *R. v. Secretary of State for the Home Department, ex p. Fire Brigades Union* [1995] 2 All E.R. 244, 252 (*per* Lord Browne-Wilkinson).

[83] *Padfield v. Minister of Agriculture Fisheries and Food* [1968] A.C. 997. In the United States, deference may be shown to the interpretation of a statute by an administrative body where the statute is ambiguous under the *Chevron* doctrine (*Chevron v. Natural Resources Defense Council* (1984) 467 U.S. 837. The court then only interferes where the body's interpretation was not 'rational'. But *Chevron* may be losing its force. See T. W. Merrill, 'Judicial Deference to Executive Precedent' 101 Yale L.J. 969.

[84] *ibid.* at 1060. For interpretation of a statute which came close to conferring unfettered discretion, but which nevertheless permitted judicial review, see *R. v. Secretary of State for the Environment, ex p. Norwich C.C.* [1982] Q.B. 808 ('Where it appears to the Secretary of State that tenants ... have or may have difficulty in exercising the right to buy [council houses]'. *Held:* evidence of such difficulty existed). The power of the Parliamentary Commission for Administration to 'act in his own discretion' was reviewed in *R. v. Parliamentary Commission for Administration, ex p. Dyer* [1994] 1 W.L.R. 621.

[85] Or 'not amenable to the judicial process' (*per* Lord Roskill in *Council for the Civil Service Unions v. Minister for the Civil Service* [1985] 1 A.C. 374, 418. For further discussion of justiciability, see Chap. 7 below, paras 7–031–7–036 and paras 12–054–12–056 below.

[86] In the sense that an alteration or quashing of the decision will require a rearrangement of other decisions, each of which have interacting points of influence. See Lon Fuller, 'The Forms and Limits of Adjudication' (1978–79) 92 Harv. L.R. 395, who likens a polycentric problem to that of a spider's web: 'A pull on one strand will distribute tensions after a complicated pattern throughout the web as a whole. Doubling the original pull will, in all likelihood, not simply double each of the resulting tensions but rather create a different complicated pattern of tensions. This would certainly occur, for example, if the double pull caused one or more of the weaker strands to snap.' These words were quoted by Neill L.J. in the recent case *R. v. Secretary of State for the Home Department, ex p. P* [1995] 1 All E.R. 870. See J. Allison

evaluation of social and economic policy,[87] or the allocation of scarce resources among competing claims.[88] Courts are institutionally unsuited to resolving these kinds of problem, which are best left to be decided in the political arena.[89] Thus it was held that it would be quite futile to impugn the government's decision that Foulness should be developed as the third London airport, merely by contending that the decision was unreasonable or that Cublington was more suitable.[90]

'Fuller's Analysis of Polycentric Disputes and The Limits of Adjudication' (1994) C.L.J. 367. See generally, A. Chayes, 'The Role of the Judge in Public Law Litigation' (1976) 89 Harv. L.R. 1281, esp. 1288 *et seq.*

[87] In the sense employed by Ronald Dworkin. See his 'Political Judges and the Rule of Law' (1978) *Proceedings of the British Academy,* 64. For his distinction between 'principle' and 'policy', see *Taking Rights Seriously* (1977) pp. 82–87. Compare two aspects of policy decisions considered not to be justiciable. Questions of 'high policy' (identified by Taylor L.J. in *R. v. Secretary of State for the Home Department, ex p. Everett* [1989] Q.B. 811—such as making treaties, dissolving Parliament, mobilising the armed forces) and questions of a lower order but involving 'competing policy considerations', which Lord Diplock in the GCHQ case considered to involve 'a balancing exercise which judges by their upbringing and their experience are ill-qualified to perform'. *Council of Civil Service Unions v. Minister for the Civil Service* [1985] A.C. 374, 411.

[88] In *Buttes Gas v. Hammer* [1982] A.C. 888, a case involving relations with a foreign state, Lord Diplock said that the court has 'no justiciable or manageable standards by which to judge' the issue. To attempt such review, he said, the court would be in a 'judicial no-man's land'. See also Lord Bridge in *R. v. Secretary of State for the Environment, ex p. Hammersmith and Fulham L.B.C.* [1991] 1 A.C. 521, 593, on the need for an 'objective criterion' in order for a decision to be amenable to judicial review. See also S. Sorabjee 'Decisions of the Supreme Court in *S. R. Rommai v. Union of India*' (1994) 3 S.C.C. (Jour) 2.

[89] But the fact that Ministers may be accountable to Parliament for their actions, and that local authorities are elected, ought not in itself to inhibit review of the legality of a decision. See, *e.g. R. v. Inland Revenue Commissioners, ex p. National Federation of Self-Employed and Small Businesses Ltd* [1982] A.C. 617, 644. Lord Diplock: 'It is not, in my view, a sufficient answer to say that judicial review of the actions of officers or departments of central governments is unnecessary because they are accountable to Parliament for the way in which they carry out their functions. They are accountable to Parliament for what they do so far as regards efficiency and policy, and of that Parliament is the only judge; they are responsible to a court of justice for the lawfulness of what they do, and of that the court is the only judge.' But *cf.* Lord Keith in *R. v. Secretary of State for Trade and Industry, ex p. Lonrho Plc* [1989] 1 W.L.R. 525, 536: 'These provisions [that the Secretary of State may act against a proposed merger after a report by the Monopolies and Mergers Commission has so advised to Parliament and the Secretary of State acts by a draft order laid before Parliament] ensure that a decision which is essentially political in character will be brought to the attention of Parliament and subject to scrutiny and challenge therein, and the courts must be carful not to invade the political field and substitute their own judgment for that of the Minister. The courts judge the lawfulness not the wisdom of the decision.'

[90] *Essex C.C. v. Ministry of Housing and Local Government* (1967) 66 L.G.R. 23. *Cf.* Lord Bridge in *Gillick v. West Norfolk & Wisbech Area Health Authority* [1986] 1 A.C. 112, 193 (the court should exercise its jurisdiction with the 'utmost restraint' in cases involving 'questions of social and ethical controversy'. See also Lord Mustill in

Courts have recently declined to review decisions about the **5–031**
allocation of scarce governmental resources in the area of health care
and education. The parents of a child requiring an urgent heart
operation submitted that the excessive delay (although at the top of
the waiting list, the operation had been postponed on three occasions)
breached the duty of the Secretary of State for Health to provide "the
effective provision of health services".[91] It was held that it was not for
the court to "substitute its own judgment for the judgment of those
who are responsible for the allocation of resources". Nor was it "for
the courts of this country to arrange the lists in the hospital".[92] The
allocation of school places was the subject of an application for judicial
review when some parents alleged that the Inner London Education
Authority failed to carry out its duty to provide sufficient school
places.[93] It was held that the duty was intended to enure for the
public in general and not to give the individual litigant a cause of
action.[94] Where the Secretary of State had the power to decide
whether the expenditure of local authorities had been "excessive" and
to penalise them if it had been, the House of Lords held that decision
not suited to judicial determination because of the lack of "objective
criteria" by which to determine the content of excessive expenditure.[95]

Airedale NHS Trust v. Bland [1993] A.C. 789, 891. See also *R. v. Higher Education
Funding Council, ex p. Institute of Dental Surgery* [1994] 1 W.L.R. 242 where Sedley J.
considered the question of rating the research of a university department not
amenable to review on the ground of lack of the court's expertise.

[91] National Health Services Act 1977, s. 3. The duty is subject to the "extent as he
considers necessary to meet all reasonable requirements …".

[92] *R. v. Central Birmingham Health Authority, ex p. Collier, Lexis,* January 6, 1988, CA, *per*
Stephen Brown L.J. Nevertheless, all the judges agreed that if it could be shown that
the health authority had acted unreasonably then the courts may intervene. However,
no evidence of the reasons for the postponements and delay was before the court. A
case on similar facts was referred to in *Collier,* namely *R. v. Central Birmingham Health
Authority, ex p. Walker* (November 25, 1987, unreported). See also *R. v. Cambridge H.A.,
ex p. B* [1995] 2 All E.R. 129, CA. On similar facts see the recent case in the South
African Constitutional Court, *T. Soobramoney v. Minister of Health Kwazula Natal,* 1997
(12) B.C.C.R. 1696, CC.

[93] s. 8 of the Education Act 1944 imposes duties on local education authorities to secure
the availability of "sufficient schools … for all pupils".

[94] *R. v. Inner London Education Authority, ex p. Ali and Murshid* (1990) 2 Admin.L.Rev.
822. For a consideration of the distinction between a duty imposed for the benefit of
a particular class of individuals as opposed to a general duty to the public as a
whole see *Lonrho Ltd v. Shell Petroleum (No. 2)* [1982] A.C. 173, HL and *R. v. Deputy
Governor of Parkhurst Prison, ex p. Hague* [1992] 1 A.C. 58.

[95] *R. v. Secretary of State for the Environment, ex p. Hammersmith and Fulham L.B.C.,* n. 88
above, *per* Lord Bridge at 593, 597. And where it was alleged that the proposals of
the Boundary Commission resulted in an "excessive disparity" between the number
of electors in each constituency and the "electoral quota" (as required by the Rules), it
was held that this was a question on which the courts should be reluctant to decide,
there being "more than one answer", particularly since any adjustment to the

5–032   A recent case considered the justiciability of the exercise of a prerogative power in establishing a scheme to provide compensation for criminal injuries. The scheme excluded claims resulting from crimes where the victim and the offender were members of the same household. Although it was held that the power was potentially reviewable for unreasonableness, including bad faith, Neill L.J. considered the decision not justiciable because it involved "a balance of competing claims on the public purse and the allocation of economic resources which the court is ill equipped to deal with".[96]

5–033   Apart from non-justiciable decisions, the courts will no longer in principle refrain from reviewing any decision. Even the managerial decisions of a prison governor may be reviewed, and the courts have rejected the old distinction between "judicial" and "administrative" decisions (the latter being held not amenable to review).[97] It can now be said that "it is not the label of 'administration' or 'management' that determines the existence of jurisdiction but the quality and attributes of the decision."[98]

5–034   However, the intensity of review, what is called in European law the "margin of appreciation"[99] may differ in accordance with a number of factors such as the nature of the power, the rights and interests affected, the degree of expertise of the decision-maker[1] and the

---

boundaries would necessitate other compensating adjustments to the proposals (a typical polycentric problem, although not directly referred to as such): *R. v. Boundary Commission for England, ex p. Foot* [1983] Q.B. 600.

[96] *R. v. Secretary of State for the Home Department, ex p. P*, n. 86 above. Evans L.J. disagreed on that point, considering the issue not to involve the allocation of resources. He said that the decision 'to introduce and continue a Scheme to be administered by an independent body of persons on a judicial or quasi-judicial basis seems to me to be almost the epitome of an executive or administrative decision which is amenable to review by the Courts'. Peter Gibson L.J. felt that the appeals should not be dismissed as attempts to impugn non-justiciable decisions, but nevertheless agreed with Neill L.J.'s comments 'that the Court is ill-equipped to deal with questions of this sort'.

[97] See *Leech v. Parkhurst Prison Deputy Governor* [1988] A.C. 533. See G. Richardson, *Law, Process and Custody: Prisoners and Patients* (1993) pp. 48 *et seq.*

[98] *ibid.*, per Lord Oliver, at 579. But 'judicial review is not the way to obtain co-operation between two authorities' (the local housing authority and social services authority): *per* Lord Templeman in *R. v. Northavon D.C., ex p. Smith* [1994] 3 All E.R. 313, 320.

[99] Preferably 'margin of evaluation' or 'margin of discretion', but margin of appreciation seems to have infiltrated English law now. For a further discussion see Chap. 12, paras 12–053–12–061 below.

[1] See, *e.g. R. v. Monopolies and Mergers Commission, ex p. Argyll Group plc* [1986] 1 W.L.R. 763 where Lord Donaldson M.R. held, in the context of the administration of the monopolies legislation by the Commission and the Secretary of State, that good public administration requires 'proper consideration of the public interest. In this context, the Secretary of State is the guardian of the public interest'. He also said that good public administration requires, in the financial field at least, 'decisiveness and finality'. *Ibid.* at 266.

opportunity for internal review or alternative means of appeal.[2] Although a question involving national security is no longer a reason in itself to suspend review, the intensity of review is likely in such cases to be low, especially in times of war or conflict.[3]

Contractual powers

It has sometimes been suggested that contractual powers are not amenable to judicial review. As we have seen, government at all levels is increasingly employing contractual techniques to achieve its regulatory aims. If those powers were free of judicial review the zone of immunity surrounding the exercise of government powers would substantially increase. In 1975, in an attempt to enforce its anti-inflationary policy, the government, without seeking statutory approval, employed its existing discretionary powers to put pressure on firms whose wage settlements were considered too high. A "blacklist" of such firms was compiled and the government exhorted a variety of public bodies not to place contracts with those on the list. It also refused various grants (such as export credit guarantees) to those on the blacklist.[4] The policy was not fully tested in the courts and was abandoned in 1978.[5] This kind of exercise of power has been called the "new prerogative"[6] because it is seemingly outside the reach of judicial review. The argument is that the applicants for the grants or contracts have no right or legitimate expectation to receive them, and the government has discretion to refuse the grants on broad grounds of

5–035

---

[2] The courts do not in general refrain from reviewing a case on the ground that the Minister has powers to intervene and has decided not to do so. See, *e.g. R. v. Hereford and Worcester L.E.A., ex p. Jones* [1981] 1 W.L.R. 768; *R. v. Ealing L.B.C., ex p. Times Newspapers Ltd* (1986) 85 L.G.R. 316. But see *R. v. Chief Constable of the Merseyside Police, ex p. Calveley* [1986] 1 Q.B. 424.

[3] *e.g. R. v. Secretary of State for the Home Department, ex p. Cheblak* [1991] 1 W.L.R. 890 (decided at the time of the Gulf War). But see also *Balfour v. Foreign and Commonwealth Office* [1994] 2 All E.R. 588.

[4] Under the Export Guarantees Act 1975. Also under the Industry Act 1972.

[5] See C. Turpin, *British Government and the Constitution* (1985) 337; Furguson and Page, 'Pay Restraint; The Legal Constraints' (1978) 128 N.L.J. 515; Page, 'Public Law and Economic Policy: The United Kingdom Experience' (1982) 9 J. Law & Soc. 25.

[6] T. Daintith, 'Regulation by Contract: The New Prerogative' [1979] C.L.P. 41. See also T. Daintith, 'The Techniques of Government', in J. Jowell and D. Oliver *The Changing Constitution* (3rd ed. 1994) p. 209 where Daintith distinguishes two techniques of governmental regulation, the one based on *imperium* (ordinary command of law) the other on *dominium* (use of government's command of resources). See also M. Freeland, 'Government by Contract and Public Law' [1994] P.L. 86.

public policy.[7] This argument rests, however, on shaky ground. Where the contractual power is being used for public purposes, and is thus amenable to judicial review,[8] the recipient of the power must use it for a lawful purpose and not unreasonably. The power to award grants for the purpose of export credit guarantees surely does not contain within it a power to penalise firms which have done no legal wrong (since the government's pay policy was not at the time enacted into law). The courts have had no hesitation in invalidating the attempts of both central and local government to impose penalties or sanctions upon recipients of licences and contracts when the recipients had done no legal wrong or when the decisions were based on irrelevant considerations.[9]

5–036   The power to regulate by means of contract is sometimes specifically provided by statute. For example, under town and country planning powers, the planning authority may, by imposing a condition to a planning permission[10] achieve some wider benefit to the area (such as landscaping of the site). The scope of such a condition is, however, limited. The condition must achieve a planning purpose, may not be unreasonable, and must "fairly and reasonably relate" to the development[11] (a swimming pool at the other end of town could not be achieved by means of a condition).[12] The governing statute also, however, provides another way in which benefits may be achieved: by way of an agreement, now known as a "planning obligation".[13] Because the promised benefits under a planning obligation are *agreed*

---

[7] The Local Government Act 1988, s. 17, severely restricts the ability of local authorities to take into account non-commercial considerations when awarding contracts. See generally, C. Turpin, *Government Procurement and Contracts* (1989); S. Arrowsmith, *Government Procurement and Judicial Review* (1988). See the full account of government contracting in P. Craig, *Administrative Law* (3rd ed. 1994) Chap. 19. Contracting has been subjective to regulation through the application of European Community procurement directives and U.K. legislation. See, *e.g.* Public Works Directive 71/305; Public Supplies Directive 77/62; Public Works Contracts Regulations 1991, S.I. 1991 No. 2680; Public Supply Contracts Regulations 1991, S.I. 1991 No. 2679; Utilities and Works Contracts Regulations 1992, S.I. 1992 No. 3279. See also S. Arrowsmith (1990) 106 L.Q.R. 277.

[8] See para. 3–018.

[9] See, *e.g. Congreve v. Home Office* [1976] Q.B. 629 (cancellation of television licences); *Wheeler v. Leicester City Council* [1985] A.C. 1054 (withdrawal of licence to use sports ground); *R. v. Lewisham L.B.C., ex p. Shell UK Ltd* [1988] 1 All E.R. 938 (boycott of company's products); *R. v. Wear Valley D.C., ex p. Binks* [1985] 2 All E.R. 699 (withdrawal of licence to operate in informal market).

[10] Town and Country Planning Act 1990, s.70(1).

[11] Tests laid down in *Newbury D.C. v. Secretary of State for the Environment* [1981] A.C. 578.

[12] An example given in *R. v. Westminster City Council, ex p. Monahan* [1990] 1 Q.B. 87.

[13] Town and Country Planning Act 1990, s.106 (formerly s.52 of the Town and Country Planning Act 1971).

rather than *imposed*, it seems at first sight that they may be immune from legal challenge, even where the benefit has scant connection with the development (such as the swimming pool at the other end of town). Indeed it has been recently held by the House of Lords that a planning obligation need not "fairly and reasonably relate" to the permission.[14] This, however, does not mean that an obligation is entirely exempt from judicial control. Its content must still qualify as a material planning consideration—fulfilling planning and not extraneous purposes—and must not be manifestly unreasonable.

REVIEW OF THE PREROGATIVE POWERS

The previous limits on reviewing prerogative powers

In the past, it was doubted whether prerogative powers were capable of being the subject of judicial review except in the narrowest sense of determining whether the prerogative power exists, as to its extent, as to whether it is being exercised in the appropriate form and as to how far it has been superseded by statute.[15] The courts were not normally prepared to examine the appropriateness or adequacy of the grounds for exercising the power,[16] or the fairness of the procedure followed   5–037

---

[14] *Tesco Stores Ltd v. Secretary of State for the Environment* [1995] 2 All E.R. 636.

[15] See, *e.g. Willion v. Berkley* (1561) Plow. 223; case of *Monopolies* (1602) 11 Co.Rep. 84b; *Prohibitions del Roy* (1607) 12 Co.Rep. 63; case of *Proclamations* (1611) 12 Co.Rep. 74; *Burmah Oil Co. v. Lord Advocate* [1965] A.C. 75; *Att.-Gen. v. De Keyser's Royal Hotel Ltd* [1920] A.C. 508; *Walwin (L.E.) and Partners Ltd v. West Sussex C.C.* [1975] 3 All E.R. 604; *Laker Airways Ltd v. Department of Trade* [1977] Q.B. 643; *Johnson v. Kent* (1974) 132 C.L.R. 164.

[16] See, *e.g. R. v. Allen* (1862) 1 B.&S. 850 (*nolle prosequi*); *Musgrove v. Chun Teeong Toy* [1891] A.C. 272 (exclusion of alien); *Bugsier Reederei-und-Bergungs A/G v. S.S. Brighton* [1951] 2 T.L.R. 409 (licence granted to enemy company to sue in British court); *Chandler v. DPP* [1964] A.C. 763, 790–792, 796, 800–801, 814 (disposition of forces); *Hanratty v. Lord Butler of Saffron Walden* (1971) 115 S.J. 386 and *de Freitas v. Benny* [1976] A.C. 239 (prerogative of mercy); *Jenkins v. Att.-Gen.* (1971) 115 S.J. 674 (dissemination of official information); *Blackburn v. Att.-Gen.* [1971] 1 W.L.R. 1037 (treatymaking power); *Secretary of State for the Home Department v. Lakdawalla* [1972] Imm. A.R. 26 (issue of passport). Lord Denning M.R. in *Laker Airways* (n. 15 above) at 705–707 anticipated a change in the law by assimilating the review of the prerogative with that of statutory power, so that its exercise may be impugned for 'misdirection in fact or in law'. The majority, however, procceded on a narrower basis, concluding

before the power was exercised,[17] and they would not allow bad faith
to be attributed to the Crown.[18] The unwillingness of the courts to
review prerogative powers could be explained partly on the basis of
the close relationship those powers were regarded as having with the
Sovereign personally, the Crown being the source of the powers, and
partly because the courts regarded prerogative powers as being those
common law powers of the Crown which had no statutory source.[19]

---

that the Civil Aviation Act 1971 had impliedly superseded the Crown's prerogative in
foreign affairs, and that the holder of a licence under the statute could not be
deprived of its commercial value by a decision on the part of the Secretary of State to
revoke the licensee's status as a designated carrier under the Bermuda Agreement. In
other respects the majority accepted the orthodox position on the unreviewability of
the exercise of the prerogative (at 718, *per* Roskill L.J. and, *semble*, at 727–728, *per*
Lawton L.J.).

[17] *de Freitas v. Benny* (n.16 above) at 247–248.

[18] *Duncan v. Theodore* (1917) 23 C.L.R. 510, 544; *Australian Communist Party v.
Commonwealth* (1951) 83 C.L.R. 1, 257–258.

[19] Professor Sir William Wade is critical of this approach as to what is a prerogative
power. See Wade & Forsyth, *Administrative Law* (7th ed.) p. 248:

'prerogative power is properly speaking, legal power which appertains to the
Crown but not to its subjects. Blackstone explained the correct use of the term.
It signifies, in its etymology (from prae and rogo) something that is required or
demanded for, or in preference to, all others. Hence it follows, that it must be in
its nature singular and eccentrical; that it can only be applied to those rights and
capacities which the King enjoys alone, in contradistinction to others and not to
those which he enjoys in common with any of his subjects; for if once any one
prerogative of the Crown could be held in common with a subject, it would cease
to be prerogative any longer.'

The definition of the prerogative as given by Dicey (*Introduction to the Study of the
Law of the Constitution* (8th ed. 1915) p. 421) was:

'The prerogative is the name for the remaining portion of the Crown's original
authority, and is therefore, as already pointed out, the name for the residue of
discretionary power left at any moment in the hands of the Crown, whether such
power be in fact exercised by the King himself or by his ministers.'

This definition was quoted with approval in *Att.-Gen. v. de Keyser's Royal Hotel Ltd*
[1920] A.C. 508, 526, and by Lord Fraser in *The Civil Service Unions v. The Minister for
the Civil Service* [1985] A.C. 374.

Prerogative discretions which were immune from review and which **5–038**
may have directly affected the interests of individuals included the
refusal and withdrawal of passports,[20] the internment[21] and
expulsion[22] of enemy aliens, (possibly) refusal of entry to friendly
aliens,[23] decisions relating to the disposition and use of the armed
forces,[24] decisions on promotion, dismissal, pay and pensions in
relation to members of the armed forces[25] and perhaps members of
the civil service too,[26] and a wide range of acts done during wartime
(*e.g.* the requisitioning of property[27] and the destruction of property to
deny its use to the enemy).[28] Nor were acts of State (acts done by the
Crown in the conduct of foreign relations,[29] or acts done by or with
the authority, antecedent or subsequent, of the Crown in relation to an
alien outside Her Majesty's dominions) cognisable by the courts.[30]

The courts would also accept the conclusiveness of a certificate **5–039**
entered by a responsible Minister on certain matters of State into
which they are not prepared to conduct any independent inquiry—*e.g.*
whether another State is independent, whether the Crown is at war
with it, whether its government is recognised *de jure* or *de facto* or not
at all, whether a defendant in legal proceedings is entitled to
sovereign immunity or to diplomatic status.[31]

---

[20] *Secretary of State for the Home Department v. Lakdawalla*, n.16 above, a decision of the
Immigration Appeal Tribunal on the absolute discretionary power of the Crown to
withhold a United Kingdom passport.
[21] *R. v. Vine Street Police Station Superintendent, ex p. Lichmann* [1916] 1 K.B. 268.
[22] *Netz v. Chuter Ede* [1946] Ch. 224; *R. v. Bottrill, ex p. Kuechenmeister* [1947] K.B. 41.
[23] *Musgrove v. Chun Teeong Toy* [1891] A.C. 272.
[24] *China Navigation Co. v. Att.-Gen.* [1932] 2 K.B. 197: *The Zamora* [1916] 1 A.C. 77, 107;
Chandler v. DPP [1964] A.C. 763. See also Crown Proceedings Act 1947, s.11(2).
[25] Glanville Williams, *Crown Proceedings* (1948), Chap. 3.
[26] See GCHQ case.
[27] Discussed in the *De Keyser* case [1920] A.C. 508.
[28] *Burmah Oil Co. v. Lord Advocate* [1965] A.C. 75; see now War Damage Act 1965.
[29] See, *e.g. West Rand Central Gold Mining Co. v. R.* [1905] 2 K.B. 391; *Salaman v. Secretary
of State for India* [1906] 1 K.B. 613, 639–640.
[30] *Buron v. Denman* (1848) 2 Ex. 167; *cf. Nissan v. Att.-Gen.* [1970] A.C. 179, where the
plaintiff was a British subject.
[31] But the courts retained jurisdiction to determine related questions not covered by
such certificates (see, *e.g. Empson v. Smith* [1966] 1 Q.B. 426 and *Agbor v. Metropolitan
Police Commissioner* [1969] 1 W.L.R. 703 (diplomatic immunities), *Trendtex Trading Corp.
v. Central Bank of Nigeria* [1977] Q.B. 529 (sovereign immunity: see now State
Immunity Act 1978)) and to determine what legal implications flow from a fact
conclusively certified (*Carl Zeiss Stiftung v. Rayner & Keeler Ltd (No. 2)* [1967] 1 A.C.
853 (unrecognised status of East Germany)): and even to determine the basic issue in
the absence of a certificate covering the point (*Re Al-Fin Corporation's Patent* [1970] Ch.
160 (whether North Korea a state)). See also *Adams v. Adams* [1971] P. 188, 205–206
(status of Rhodesian 'Government').

5–040   This is not to say that English courts would decline jurisdiction over all "political questions".[32] There are matters, some but not all having a strongly political flavour, which they had decided for historical or policy reasons to treat as non-justiciable.[33] In addition, certain enforcement powers had been held to be exclusively non-reviewable. One such was the Attorney-General's discretion to bring relator proceedings, at least in the case of private law proceedings.[34]

The present approach

5–041   In 1967 the Court of Appeal decided that decisions of the Criminal Injuries Compensation Board could be quashed for error of law. The Criminal Injuries Compensation Scheme was established by the government of the day to make *ex gratia* payments to those suffering personal injuries as a result of criminal offences. The compensation was payable by the Board out of money voted by Parliament, but neither the Board nor the scheme had any statutory authority; accordingly it was said that the Board was exercising prerogative powers.[35] However, the question of whether or not prerogative powers could be reviewed was authoritatively determined in favour of their being reviewable by the House of Lords in the *GCHQ* case.[36] The majority of their Lordships[37] were of the opinion that the exercise of powers authorised by the prerogative may be reviewable when their exercise is open to judicial review. It depended on the subject-matter.

---

[32] See *Adegbenro v. Akintola* [1963] A.C. 614, where, in a pre-eminently political case, the Privy Council gave a decision adverse to the claims of the *de facto* Premier of Western Nigeria. The decision was reversed in Nigeria by retroactive constitutional amendment.

[33] G. Sawer, 'Political Questions' (1963) 15 U.T.L.J. 49. Among the 'political' questions in respect of which English courts have declined jurisdiction are matters falling within the ambit of parliamentary privilege (*Bradlaugh v. Gossett* (1884) 12 QBD 271), but the courts reserve the right (as with the royal prerogative) to determine the existence and extent of an alleged privilege (*Stockdale v. Hansard* (1839) 9 A. & E. 1).

[34] *Gouriet v. Union of Post Office Workers* [1978] A.C. 435. *cf. McWhirter v. Independent Broadcasting Authority* [1973] Q.B. 629; *R. v. Solicitor General, ex p. Taylor and Taylor* (1996) 8 Admin. L.R. 206; *R. v. Attorney-General ex p. Edey* (Transcript February 26, 1992); *R. v. Attorney-General ex p. Ferrante* [1995] C.O.D. 18.

[35] This was not accepted by Professor Sir William Wade since 'anyone may set up a trust or organisation to distribute money, and for the Government to do so involves no 'prerogative' power.' See Wade and Forsyth, n. 19 above, *ibid.*

[36] *The Council of Civil Service Unions v. The Minister for the Civil Service* [1985] A.C. 374. The case concerned the decision of the Minister for the Civil Service (the Prime Minister) to give instructions to affect the terms and conditions of Civil Servants at GCHQ so as to exclude them from membership of any trade union other than a department staff association approved by the Director of GCHQ.

[37] Lords Scarman, Diplock and Roskill.

The minority[38] preferred to leave open the question as to whether prerogative powers were reviewable until it had to be determined.[39] Prerogative powers may, however, relate to areas which because of their nature are not justiciable. As Lord Roskill said in the course of his speech in the *GCHQ* case:

> "Prerogative powers such as those relating to the making of treaties, the defence of the realm, the prerogative of mercy, the grant of honours, the dissolution of Parliament and the appointment of Ministers as well as others are not, I think, susceptible to judicial review because their nature and subject matter is such as not to be amenable to judicial process."

Lord Scarman considered that:

> "The controlling factor in determining whether the exercise of prerogative power is subjected to judicial review is not its source but its subject matter."[40]

And Lord Diplock considered that a prerogative power may be subject to judicial review if its exercise will have consequences for some person either:

> "(a) by altering the rights or obligations of that person which are enforceable by or against him in private law; or (b) by depriving him of some benefit or advantage which either (i) he has in the past been permitted by the decision-maker to enjoy and which he can legitimately expect to be permitted to continue to do until there has been communicated to him some rational grounds for withdrawing it on which he has been given an opportunity to comment or (ii) he has received assurances from the decision-maker will not be withdrawn without giving him first an opportunity of advancing reasons for contending that they should not be withdrawn."[41]

Since the *GCHQ* case, some prerogative powers have been reviewed. **5–042** The courts have been prepared to review but not grant relief as to a decision of the Home Secretary to refuse to make an *ex gratia* payment

---

[38] Lords Fraser and Brightman.

[39] The application for judicial review in GCHQ ultimately failed not because the power which was being exercised was a prerogative power but because the power was being exercised in the interests of national security, which overrode any rights which the applicants would otherwise have had to be granted judicial review.

[40] Lord Scarman, at 407.

[41] Lord Diplock, at 408.

to a person who had been convicted and imprisoned and then subsequently acquitted on appeal.[42] The powers of the Home Secretary in relation to immigrants which are not statutory and the power to issue passports are reviewable.[43] Taylor L.J. distinguished those acts at "the top of the scale of executive functions under the prerogative" involving "high policy", which were not justiciable, from "administrative decisions, affecting the rights of individuals and their freedom of travel", which are justiciable. It has even been held that it is open to the courts to review the issue of a warrant to intercept telephone communications signed by the Secretary of State for the Home Department, notwithstanding the policy of the Secretary of State to maintain silence in the interests of national security to confirm or deny the existence of any warrant.[44] In so far as civil servants' conditions of service are regulated by the prerogative and not by a contract of employment, then judicial review is available.[45]

5–043   In *Chief Constable of Kent, ex p. Land; R. v. Director of Public Prosecutions, ex p. B,*[46] it was held that the broad discretion of the Crown Prosecution Service to continue or discontinue criminal proceedings was subject to judicial review where it could be demonstrated that the decision had been made regardless of or clearly contrary to settled policy of the Director of Public Prosecutions.

5–044   What remains today of the prerogative powers which Lord Roskill identified as not being amenable to judicial review in the *GCHQ* case?[47] There will be some questions of "high policy" such as the making of treaties,[48] the defence of the realm, the dissolution of

---

[42] *R. v. Secretary of State for the Home Department, ex p. Harrison* [1988] 3 All E.R. 86.

[43] *R. v. Secretary of State for the Home Department, ex p. Beedassee* [1989] C.O.D. 525; *R. v. Secretary of State for Foreign and Commonwealth Affairs, ex p. Everett* [1989] Q.B. 811.

[44] *R. v. Secretary of State for the Home Department, ex p. Ruddock and Ors* [1987] 1 W.L.R. 1482. The power is now governed by the Interception of Communications Act 1985. For recent cases where national security has been relevant see *R. v. Secretary of State for the Home Department, ex p, McQuillan* [1995] 4 All E.R. 400; *R. v. Secretary of State for the Home Department, ex p. Adams* [1995] All E.R. 177 E.C.; *R. v. Secretary of State for the Home Department, ex p. Chahal* [1995] 1 W.L.R. 526, CA and *Chahal v. United Kingdom* (1997) 23 E.H.R.R. 413.

[45] [1978] A.C. 435 *cf. McWhirter v. Independent Broadcasting Authority* [1973] Q.B. 629.

[46] [1993] 1 All E.R. 756. See also *R. v. DPP, ex p. C.,* [1995] 1 Cr. App. R. 136. For a further discussion of prosecutorial discretion see Chap. 10 below, para. 10–007 and n. 35. See also *R. v. Inland Revenue Commissioners ex p. Mead* [1993] 1 All E.R. 772; and *R. v. Haringey Justices, ex p. DPP* [1996] Q.B. 351 (in both the Crown Court and in magistrates' courts the prosecution had an 'unfettered discretion' which witnesses to call).

[47] [1985] A.C. 374, 418.

[48] However, see Lord Denning in *Laker Airways Ltd v. Department of Trade* [1977] Q.B. 643; but *cf. J.H. Rayner (Mincing Lane) Ltd v. DTI* [1990] 2 A.C. 418.

Parliament and the appointment of Ministers where the courts as a matter of discretion do not intervene, because the matters are simply not justiciable.

Other former prerogative powers should not any more, however, **5–045** automatically be assumed to be non-justiciable. It is noticeable that one of the prerogative powers assumed by Lord Roskill in the *GCHQ* case to be non-justiciable, the prerogative of mercy, has since been judicially reviewed. In *R. v. Secretary of State for the Home Department. ex p Bentley,*[49] the applicant applied for review of the Home Secretary's decision not to pardon her brother who had been sentenced to death and hanged 39 years earlier. The applicant contended that the Home Secretary had erred in law in his approach to the issue in that he considered that the grant of free pardon required the finding that her brother was morally and technically innocent, where the right question to be asked was whether in all the circumstances the punishment imposed should have been suffered. It was held that the decision ought to be based upon accepted public law principles and not be immune from legal challenge, despite the element of policy in the decision. The Home Secretary's failure to consider the grant of a posthumous pardon when the previous Home Secretary's decision had been wrong was held to be a clear error of law.[50] The court broke new ground in this case, guided only by a recent decision of the New Zealand Court of Appeal. In *Burt v. Governor-General,*[51] it was said that although the prerogative of mercy is a—

"prerogative power in the strictest sense of that term, for it is peculiar to the Crown and its exercise directly affects the rights of persons ... there is nothing heteredox ... in asserting that the rule of law requires that challenges shall be permitted ... of a kind which the Courts are competent to deal ... In attempting such a judgment it must be right to exclude any lingering thought that the prerogative of mercy is no more than an arbitrary monarchial right of grace and favour. As developed it has become an integral element in the criminal justice system, a constitutional safeguard against mistakes."[52]

The court in *Bentley* held that the powers of the court could not any longer be ousted simply by invoking the word "prerogative":

---

[49] [1994] Q.B. 349.
[50] Although the court made no order and simply invited the Home Secretary to reconsider his decision (which he did).
[51] [1992] 3 N.Z.L.R. 672.
[52] *ibid.,* at 681.

"The question is simply whether the nature and subject matter of the decision is amenable to the judicial process. Are the courts qualified to deal with the matter or does the decision involve such questions of policy that they should not intrude because they are ill-equipped to do so?"[53]

The court concluded that "some aspects of the exercise of the Royal prerogative are amenable to the judicial process".

5–046   The result of these recent cases is that it can no longer be said that the prerogative power is *ipso facto* immune from judicial review. Like other discretionary powers, it all depends upon whether the impugned decision is "justiciable".[54] The courts, in assessing this question, must be sensitive to their own limits to evaluate questions of high policy[55] and questions involving the allocation of scarce social and economic resources. Yet the courts should also take a realistic view of the distinction between an act of the "Crown-as-monarch" and that of "Crown-as-executive".[56] The New Zealand Court of Appeal was surely right to point out the need, in the interest of the rule of law, for challenge to be permitted to issues on which the courts are competent to pronounce. The courts ought not to allow the prerogative to be raised as a bar to intervention without further consideration of that issue. In a recent case the House of Lords held, by a majority, that the Home Secretary could not, under his prerogative power, introduce a scheme for compensation for victims of crime that was inconsistent with a scheme contemplated by a statute. The Home Secretary's actions were "unlawful and an abuse of the prerogative power".[57]

---

[53] *Bentley,* n. 50 above, *per* Watkins L.J. at 453. An example was given: "If ... it was clear that the Home Secretary had refused to pardon someone solely on the grounds of their sex, race or religion, the courts would be expected to interfere and, in our judgment, would be entitled to do so."*Bentley* was distinguished in *R. v. Reckley ex p. Minister for Public Safety and Immigration* [1996] 1 A.C. 527 where the Privy Council held that the prerogative of mercy was not reviewable under the particular procedures of the Bahamas' Constitution.

[54] See the discussion at paras 5-029–5-034 above.

[55] Such as the making of treaties, held to be an unreviewable prerogative power in the recent case of *R. v. Secretary of State for Foreign and Commonwealth Affairs, ex p. Rees-Mogg* [1994] Q.B. 552.

[56] *per* Lord Templeman in *M. v. Home Office* [1994] 1 A.C. 377, 395. This paragraph was cited with approval by Baragwanath J. in the High Court of New Zealand in *Patel v. Chief Executive of the Department of Labour* [1997] 1 N.Z.L.R. 102, 108. In *New Zealand Maori Council v. Attorney-General* [1996] 3 N.Z.L.R. 140, a majority of the Court of Appeal held that a Cabinet approval of a course of action was not reviewable (but see the dissent of Thomas J.).

[57] *R. v. Secretary of State for the Home Department, ex p. Fire Brigades Union,* [1995] 2 A.C. 583 *per* Lord Browne-Wilkinson. It was held that the purported scheme was unlawful even though the statutory provision providing for the scheme was not yet in force and the Secretary of State was not under any duty to bring the statutory scheme into

FUNDAMENTAL HUMAN RIGHTS

Up to now there has been no code of fundamental rights in United **5–047** Kingdom law. This will change when The Human Rights Act 1998 comes into force. The changes to be introduced by that statute have been briefly outlined above[58] and will be considered further below. However, it should not be assumed that in the absence of a domestic bill of rights that individuals have no legal entitlements against the state. For a start, the United Kingdom is, as we have seen, a signatory to a number of international human rights codes, of which the European Convention on Human Rights and Fundamental Freedoms has been the most influential.[59] The fundamental rights specified by the Convention, while not specifically incorporated into domestic law, have been protected as a matter of international law against encroachment by the government of the United Kingdom. That is not to say, however, that fundamental rights and freedoms have not been recognised in English law. The United Kingdom citizen is free to do what he or she wishes unless that freedom is curtailed by the common law or statute. These freedoms were indeed the source of much of the European Convention.[60] But without constitutional status, as specific statutory protection, to what extent could these rights and freedoms survive incursion by governmental action? This has been achieved in three ways: first, by the application of safeguards applied in European Community law; secondly, by the application of the Convention as a treaty obligation in international law, and thirdly, by inference that fundamental rights and freedoms prevail in domestic common law

---

effect. Noted by Barendt [1995] P.L. 357 and E.W. Thomas (1996) 112 L.Q.R. 177). In *R. v. Secretary of State for the Home Department, ex p. Launder (No. 2)* [1997] 1 W.L.R. 839 (the House of Lords held that the Home Secretary's discretion under Extradition Act 1989 was normally justiciable); *R. v. Secretary of State for Foreign and Commonwealth Affairs, ex p. Manelfi* [1996] 12 C.L. 65 (judicial review of decision that M was ineligible for employment at GCHQ because of the foreign nationalities of his parents—M claimed application of the rules without waiver were *Wednesbury* unreasonable and contrary to the common law and the International Covenant on Civil and Political Rights 1996, Art. 26. *Held*, dismissing the application: the decision in the making of the rules and their application were made in the interests of national security and were non-justiciable); see also *R. v. Lord Chancellor ex p. Maxwell* [1997] 1 W.L.R. 104 (allocation of judges between High Court and Court of Appeal justiciable but not normally reviewable).

[58] See Chap. 1.
[59] See further Chap. 1, paras 1-015–1-022.
[60] See Lord Lester Q.C. 'European Human Rights and The British Constitution', in J. Jowell and D. Oliver (eds) *The Changing Constitution* (1994) Chap. 2 and see G. Marston, 'The United Kingdom's part in the Preparation of the European Convention on Human Rights', 1950, Vol. 42 1 C.L.Q. (1993) 796.

unless expressly, or by necessary implication, curtailed or extinguished by statute.[61]

Fundamental rights in European Community law

5–048 Although the European Union has not acceded to the European Convention of Human Rights, the European Court of Justice has held that "fundamental rights form an integral part of the general principles of law, the observance of which ... [the Court] ensures."[62] The principles of the Convention thus form an integral part of Community law, and when Community law is directly effective in the United Kingdom, the Convention too is directly applicable.[63]

The European Convention as the source of a treaty obligation in international law

5–049 Where Community law is not directly effective, obligations contained in the provisions of the Convention have not been the direct source of legal rights enforceable in the United Kingdom. United Kingdom statutes, however, could, under a principle of statutory construction "be construed, if they are reasonably capable of bearing such a meaning, as intended to carry out the obligation[s specified in the Convention] and not to be inconsistent with it".[64] In other words, there

---

[61] In Chap. 12 below the extent to which a decision violating human rights may be considered 'unreasonable' will be considered.

[62] *Nold KG v. Commission* Case 4/73 [1974] E.C.R. 491; *Orkem v. Commission* Case 374/87 [1989] E.C.R. 3283. See A. Barav, 'Omnipotent Courts', in Curtin and Heukels (eds) *The Institutional Dynamics of European Integration; Liber Amicorum Henry G. Schermers* (1994); N. Grief 'The Domestic Impact of the European Convention of Human Rights as Mediated Through Community Law' [1991] P.L. 555; C. Barnard and R. Greave, 'The Application of Community Law in the United Kingdom 1986–93' [1994] C.M.L.R. 1055.

[63] See, *e.g.* Case 63/83 *R. v. Kirk* [1984] E.C.R. 2689; [1985] 1 All E.R. 453; Case 222/84 *Johnston v. Chief Constable of the Royal Ulster Constabulary* [1986] E.C.R. 1651. For an excellent account of the extent of the use of human rights in English courts see Murray Hunt, *Using Human Rights Law in English Courts* (1997); and see M. Beloff and H. Mountfield, 'Unconventional Behaviour? Judicial Uses of the European Convention on Human Rights in England and Wales' 1996 E.H.R.L.R. 467.

[64] *per* Lord Diplock in *Garland v. British Rail Engineering Ltd* [1983] 2 A.C. 751, 771 see also Lord Kilbrandon's dissenting speech in *Broome v. Cassell* [1972] A.C. 1027 at 1133, HC; Lord Reid's speeches in *Waddington v. Miah* [1974] 1 W.L.R. 692 at 694, HC and in *Blathwayt v. Baron Cawley* [1976] A.C. 397 at 426, HC. see A. Lester, 'Fundamental Rights: The United Kingdom Isolated?' [1984] P.L. 46, at 66–68. But *cf.* the review of the authorities by Ackner L.J. in *R. v. Secretary of State for the Home Department, ex p. Brind* [1991] 1 A.C. 696, especially at 761 *et seq.* And see Chap. 12 below. Compare the

is a presumption that Parliament intends its legislation to comply with the United Kingdom's treaty obligations. These obligations can be overridden, but only by clear language or necessary implication. Where the words are ambiguous, that is, capable of bearing more than one meaning, the treaty obligation prevails.

In *R. v. Home Secretary, ex p. Brind*[65] the applicants sought to invoke this principle in the face of a ban by the Home Secretary on the broadcasting of the direct spoken words of members of certain terrorist organisations in Northern Ireland (their words could be spoken by actors or others not representatives of their organisations). The powers of the Home Secretary, while not specifically permitting any kind of censorship, conferred on him broad discretion to require the broadcasting authorities "to refrain from broadcasting any matter".[66] The applicants argued that that power was inconsistent with Art. 10 of the Convention which protects freedom of speech and that, in the circumstances, the provisions of the Convention should be applied. The House of Lords, however, rejected this argument, holding that the presumption that legislation complies with a treaty obligation only applies in the case of a true ambiguity and does not apply to limit the meaning of clear general words. To hold otherwise would, they thought, amount to the use of a "mere canon of construction" to incorporate "international law into the domestic field".[67] It was held that the broad discretion conferred on the Home Secretary was thus sufficient to refute the presumption in favour of the application of a treaty obligation. It was also held that the Home Secretary was not under any duty to have regard to the Convention as a relevant

5–050

---

approach in New Zealand, where it was held that the International Convention for the Elimination of all forms of Racial Discrimination 1965 was not directly applicable. *Ashby v. Minister of Immigration* [1981] 1 N.Z.L.R. 222. But see now *Tavita v. Minister of Immigration* [1994] 2 N.Z.L.R. 257.

See also *Governor of Pitcairn v. Sutton* [1995] 1 N.Z.L.R. 426, 430 ('generally worded statutory discretions are not to be exercised without taking into account international obligations' per Cooke P.); *Rajan v. Minister of Immigration* [1996] 3 N.Z.L.R. 543. As a result of the *Tavita* judgment, immigration policies were introduced in New Zealand to give better effect to Art. 23 of the International Covenant on Civil and Political Rights. In Australia, where legislation implements an international commitment, it is appropriate for the courts to have regard to the interpretation of the international instrument by the international community in settling the domestic interpretation; *Rocklea Spinning Mills Ltd v. Anti-Dumping Authority* (1995) 129 A.L.R. 401 (Federal Court of Australia). And see the discussion of *Minister for Immigration and Ethnic Affairs v. Teoh* (1995) 183 C.L.R. 273 below Chaps 7 and 12.

[65] [1991] 1 A.C. 696.

[66] s.24(3) of the Broadcasting Act 1981 (in relation to the IBA), and clause 13(4) of the BBC's licence and agreement, both provide that the Home Secretary 'may require the IBA or BBC to refrain from broadcasting matters specified'.

[67] *per* Lord Bridge at 748. International law was held to involve not only the Convention but also the jurisprudence of the European Court of Human Rights.

consideration,[68] for to do so would be to incorporate "by the back door" the Convention which Parliament had not yet incorporated.[69]

5–051   Despite this unanimous judgment, it does not necessarily follow that the exercise of power under legislation conferring broad discretionary powers will always be sufficient to exclude the obligations contained in the Convention or other treaty. The test adopted in *Brind* to assess whether the obligation under a treaty was overridden by a statutory power was unorthodox. The focus was upon the question whether the statutory words were "ambiguous". Since they were not ambiguous, in the sense of being open to two or more constructions, the presumption of conformity with the treaty obligation was held to have been rebutted. The orthodox test is somewhat different. It asks whether the statutory words are "reasonably capable of bearing... a meaning"[70] that is consistent with the treaty obligation. The presumption is that they are consistent unless the words clearly rebut the presumption, with ambiguous words not being sufficient to have that effect.[71] If the words as construed fail to address the issue either way, expressly or by necessary implication, then they should normally be presumed to be in conformity with the Convention as a treaty obligation.[72] Be that as it may, the enactment of the Human Rights Act will preempt this controversy at least in respect of the application of the European Convention on Human Rights.

---

[68] Lord Templeman dissented on this point. And see now *R. v. Secretary of State for the Home Department, ex p. Launder* [1997] 1 W.L.R. 839 at 867 (Lord Hope).

[69] *per* Lord Ackner, *ibid.*, at 761–762.

[70] [1983] 2 A.C. 751. See *R. v. Secretary of State for The Home Department, ex p. Simms,* July 8, 1999, HL.

[71] The Court of Appeal followed the approach in *Brind* in *National and Local Government Officers Association v. Secretary of State for the Environment, The Times,* December 2, 1992. (Regulations which invaded freedom of expression upheld. The regulations restricted the rights on members, officers and staff of local authorities holding a politically restricted post from becoming or remaining a member of a local authority. Since no 'ambiguity' in the statute, no application of ECHR Art. 10, nor did the Secretary of State have to have regard to Art. 10.) See also *R. v. General Medical Council, ex p. Colman* [1990] 1 All E.R. 489. (Guidance issued by G.M.C. pursuant to power conferred by s.35A of the Medical Act 1983 to provide advice on standards of professional conduct, prohibited the distribution of promotional information about holistic medicine. 'No ambiguity' in the section which could be regarded as the subject matter of an international obligation.)

[72] This is the position taken by Lord Browne-Wilkinson, 'The Infiltration of a Bill of Rights' [1992] P.L. 406. Critical of *Brind* for similar reasons as the above, he asks: 'Can it really be suggested that Parliament intended to authorise, for example (under the provisions above and employed in *Brind*) a directive prohibiting broadcasts which are critical of the government for the time being in power, or of the Home Secretary himself?' *Ibid.* at 406. Powerful judicial *ex cathedra* support is growing for this position. See also Sir John Laws, 'Is the Constitution the Guardian of Fundamental Rights?' [1993] P.L. 59; 'Law and Democracy' [1995] P.L. 72; Sir Stephen Sedley, 'The Sound of Silence: Constitutional Law without a Constitution' (1994) 110 L.Q.R. 270.

Fundamental rights in English common law

Despite the absence until now of codified human rights in the United **5–052**
Kingdom, a number of fundamental rights have been independently
protected by the common law.

An example is the right to freedom of speech and expression. In
relation to the law of confidentiality, in the "Spycatcher" case, Lord
Goff remarked that in the field of freedom of speech there is no
difference in principle between English law on the subject and Art. 10
of the Convention.[73] Recently, when a local authority sought to sue a
newspaper in libel, the House of Lords refused to entertain the action.
It was said that:

> "it is of the highest public importance that a democratically elected
> body should be open to uninhibited criticism. The threat of a civil
> action for defamation must inevitably have an inhibiting effect on
> free Speech."[74]

As was made clear in that case, the right to free speech was derived
not from international obligations but from the fact that, in a
democracy, criticism of government should not be unjustifiably
restrained.[75]

As with treaty obligations, the courts make a presumption or an **5–053**
inference that Parliament does not intend to deprive the subject of
his or her common-law rights except where this is made clear by
express words or by necessary implication. This is the generic
presumption of which the following are species[76]: that, in the
absence of express words or necessary intendment, statutes are not
to be interpreted so as to authorise the interference with the liberty
of the person,[77] or the deprivation of the property rights of the

---

[73] *Att.-Gen. v. Guardian Newspapers Ltd (No. 2)* [1990] 1 A.C. 109, 283–284.

[74] *Derbyshire C.C. v. Times Newspapers Ltd* [1993] A.C. 534, 547, *per* Lord Keith.

[75] The House of Lords sought persuasive guidance here not from European sources but
principally from United States and South African sources: *New York Times v. Sullivan*
(1964) 376 U.S. 254; *Die Spoorbond v. South African Railways* 1946 A.D. 999. Compare
the approach of the Court of Appeal in *Derbyshire*, where Balcombe, Butler-Sloss and
Ralph Gibson L.JJ. held that under Art. 10 of the Convention there was no pressing
social need that a corporate public authority should have the right to sue in
defamation for the protection of its reputation. See *Ex p. Simms*, note 70 above.

[76] See further, H.L.E. (3rd ed.), xxxvi. pp. 412–414.

[77] *R. v. Halliday, ex p. Zadig* [1917] A.C. 260, 274; *R. v. Cannon Row Police Station
Inspector, ex p. Brady* (1921) 126 L.T. 9, 13; *R. v. Thames Magistrate, ex p. Brindle* [1975] 1
W.L.R. 1400. But this presumption may yield to the maxim *salus populi suprema lex* in
wartime: *R. v. Halliday* (above); *Ronnfeldt v. Phillips* (1918) 35 T.L.R. 46, 47; *Liversidge v.
Anderson* [1942] A.C. 206.

subject without compensation,[78] or so as to abrogate existing contractual rights[79]; and that statutory powers must, as far as is reasonably practicable, be so exercised as to avoid injury, or to minimise the scope of any injury that must inevitably be caused, to the rights of others.[80] Among other rules of construction, the following are especially important for the interpretation of statutory powers of public authorities: that express words are necessary to empower a public authority to raise money from the subject[81]; that in the absence of contrary intendment, the power is to be exercised only by the

---

[78] *Central Control Board v. Cannon Brewery Co.* [1919] A.C. 744, 752; *Bournemouth-Swanage Motor Road & Ferry Co. v. Harvey & Sons* [1929] 1 Ch. 686, 697; *Colonial Sugar Refining Co. v. Melbourne Harbour Trust Commrs.* [1927] A.C. 343; *Consett Iron Co. v. Clavering Trustees* [1935] 2 K.B. 42, 65; *Foster Wheeler Ltd v. Green (E.) & Son Ltd* [1946] Ch. 101, 108; *Hall v. Shoreham-by-Sea U.D.C.* [1964] 1 W.L.R. 240; *Hartnell v. Minister of Housing and Local Government* [1965] A.C. 1134. See also *Langham v. City of London Corp.* [1949] 1 K.B. 208, 212, 213. And see *Burmah Oil Co. v. Lord-Advocate* [1965] A.C. 75 (prerogative powers; *cf.* War Damage Act 1965). The presumption is still stronger where powers conferred by delegated legislation are in question: *Newcastle Breweries Ltd v. R.* [1920] 1 K.B. 854. But the force of the presumption is weak in the context of modern planning legislation (*Westminster Bank Ltd v. Beverley B.C.* [1971] A.C. 508; *Hoveringham Gravels Ltd v. Secretary of State for the Environment* [1975] Q.B. 754; *cf.*, however, *Hall and Co. Ltd v. Shoreham-by-Sea U.D.C.* [1964] 1 W.L.R. 240; *R. v. Hillingdon L.B.C., ex p. Royco Homes Ltd* [1974] Q.B. 720). See further *Aquilina v. Depasquale* [1971] A.C. 728; *Limb & Co. (Stevedores) Ltd v. British Transport Docks Board* [1971] 1 W.L.R. 311; and generally, on the conferment of powers of expropriation even with compensation, *Att.-Gen. for Canada v. Hallet & Carey Ltd* [1952] A.C. 427, 449–451. See also *Sovmots Investments Ltd v. Secretary of State for the Environment* [1979] A.C. 144; *cf. Hutton v. Esher U.D.C.* (1973) 26 P. & C.R. 17. See now, Local Government (Miscellaneous Provisions) Act 1976, s. 13.

[79] *Allen v. Thorn Electrical Industries Ltd* [1968] 1 Q.B. 487. Cf. *Grunwick Processing Laboratories Ltd v. ACAS* [1978] A.C. 655 (limitations upon the exercise of discretion construed as mandatory because, *inter alia*, of its potential impact upon the freedom of employer and employee to agree the terms of the contract of employment); and see *Powley v. ACAS* [1978] I.C.R. 123, 135.

[80] See paras 12–044 *et seq.*

[81] *Att.-Gen. v. Wilts United Dairies Ltd* (1921) 37 T.L.R. 884; *Brocklebank (T. & J.) Ltd v. R.* [1924] 1 K.B. 647 (*rev'd.* on other grounds, [1925] 1 K.B. 252); *Liverpool Corp. v. Maiden (Arthur) Ltd* [1938] 4 All E.R. 200; *Ministry of Town and Country Planning Bulletin of Selected Appeal Decisions,* 1948, 111/16; *Davey Paxman & Co. v. Post Office, The Times,* November 16, 1954, which made it necessary to pass the Wireless Telegraphy (Validation of Charges) Act 1954; *City Brick & Terra Cotta Co. v. Belfast Corp.* [1958] N.I. 44; *Daymond v. Plymouth City Council* [1976] A.C. 609 (see Water Charges Act 1976, ss. 1, 2); *Congreve v. Home Office* [1976] Q.B. 629; *Clark v. University of Melbourne* [1978] V.R. 457, 463–465. Unparliamentary taxation for the use of the Crown contravenes the Bill of Rights 1689 (*cf. Cobb & Co. v. Kropp* [1967] 1 A.C. 141), although it has been judicially opined that the presumption may have outlived its usefulness and that 'A modern Hampden would in many quarters be pilloried as a tax-evader' (*Customs and Excise Commissioners v. Thorn Electrical Industries Ltd* [1975] 1 W.L.R. 1661, 1673, *per* Kilbrandon L.J.). For a similar sentiment, see G. Ganz [1976] P.L. 14, in a comment on *Congreve's* case. See also *McCarthy and Stone (Developments) Ltd v. Richmond-upon-Thames L.B.C.* [1992] 2 A.C. 48.

authority upon which it has been conferred[82]; that express words or necessary implication are required to warrant the exercise of a statutory power with retroactive effect.[83] More recent cases have recognised the privilege against self-incrimination,[84] limitations on searches of premises and seized documents,[85] and even the ancient right to fish in tidal waters.[86] Perhaps more fundamentally, the right to life has been recognised as meriting "the most anxious scrutiny" of an administrative decision.[87] Judicial recognition has recently also been accorded to freedom of movement (in relation to an order excluding a resident of Northern Ireland from Great Britain).[88]

Of the common-law presumptions, the most influential in modern administrative law is that which preserves the ultimate jurisdiction of the courts to pronounce on matters of law. Accordingly, only in the most exceptional circumstances will the courts construe statutory language so as to endow a public body with exclusive authority to determine the ambit of its own powers.[89] Access of the individual to the courts, another fundamental requirement of the rule of law, is similarly recognised. In *Raymond v. Honey*[90] it was held that the Home Secretary had no power to make prison rules to "authorise hindrance

5–054

---

[82] See paras 5–107 *et seq.* below.

[83] *Master Ladies Tailors Organisation v. Minister of Labour and National Service* [1950] 2 All E.R. 525, 528; *Howell v. Falmouth Boat Construction Co.* [1951] A.C. 837. Cf. *Sabally and Njie v. Att.-Gen.* [1965] 1 Q.B. 273. See also *R. v. Pentonville Prison Governor, ex p. Azam* [1974] A.C. 18; *Scott v. Aberdeen Corp.*, 1976 S.L.T. 141.

[84] *Re O* [1991] 2 W.L.R. 475, 480.

[85] *Marcel v. Commissioner of Police* [1992] 2 W.L.R. 50, approving the words of Lord Browne-Wilkinson in *ibid.* [1991] 2 W.L.R. 1118, 1124. And see Lord Browne-Wilkinson, above, [1992] P.L. at 407.

[86] *Anderson v. Alnwick D.C.* [1993] 1 W.L.R. 1156 (byelaws invalid for restricting digging for lugworms—if not ragworms—from the foreshore as bait). Another ancient right, the right to hunt, was referred to by Laws J. in *R. v. Somerset C.C., ex p. Fewings* (1994) L.G.R. 674; [1995] 1 All E.R. 513. In the late 19th century the validity of a number of byelaws prohibiting the playing of musical instruments in the street was challenged by the Salvation Army. Sometimes the challenges were successful—see, *e.g. Powell* (1884) 51 L.T. 92 where Stephen J. said: 'the liberty of the subject always consists in doing something that a man is not forbidden to do.' But see *Johnson v. Croydon Corp.* (1886) 16 QBD 708; *Slee v. Meadows* (1911) 75 J.P. 246; *Kruse v. Johnson* [1898] 2 Q.B. 91.

[87] In *R. v. Secretary of State for the Home Department, ex p. Bugdaycay* [1987] A.C. 514, 531, Lord Bridge said (in relation to a deportation case): 'The most fundamental of human rights is the individual's right to life and when an administrative decision under challenge is said to be one which may put the applicant's life at risk, the basis of the decision must surely call for the most anxious scrutiny.' See also Lord Scarman in *R. v. Secretary of State for the Home Department, ex p. Khawaja* [1984] A.C. 74, 110–111.

[88] *R. v. Secretary of State for the Home Department, ex p. McQuillan* [1995] 4 All E.R. 400 (*per* Sedley J.).

[89] See Chap. 4 above, paras 4–014 *et seq.*

[90] [1983] A.C. 1.

or interference with so basic a right" as the citizen's right of access to the court.[91] In *Leech (No. 2)*,[92] the Court of Appeal held unlawful a regulation which permitted a prison governor to read and stop correspondence between a prisoner and his legal advisor. Despite a generally worded governing statute,[93] it was held, following *Raymond v. Honey*,[94] that a prisoner retains all his rights which are not taken away expressly or by necessary implication. It was also held that a prisoner's right of unimpeded access to his solicitor was an inseparable part of the right of access to the courts themselves.[95] Lord Wilberforce in *Raymond v. Honey*[96] had called such a right a "basic right". Steyn L.J. in *Leech* called it a "constitutional right", and reaffirmed the presumption against a statute's authorising interference with those rights by subordinate legislation.[97]

---

[91] *ibid.* at 11.

[92] *R. v. Secretary of State for Home Affairs, ex p. Leech (No. 2)* [1994] Q.B. 198.

[93] The Prison Act 1952, s. 47(1), conferring power on the Home Secretary to make rules for the 'regulation and management' of prisons and for the 'classification, treatment, employment, discipline and control of persons required to be detained therein'. The material part of the disputed rules 33(3) and 37A of the Prisons Rules 1964 provided that the prison governor could read every letter to or from a prisoner and stop any letter that was 'objectionable or of inordinate length', except for correspondence between a prisoner who was party to proceedings in which a writ had been issued and his legal advisor.

[94] [1982] A.C. 1, 10.

[95] *Golder v. U.K.* (1975) 1 E.H.R.R. 524.

[96] n. 94 above at 10.

[97] For the aspects of proportionality contained in Steyn L.J.'s judgment, see Chap. 12. The approach in *Leech* was expressly followed by Laws J. in *R. v. Lord Chancellor, ex p. Witham* [1998] Q.B. 575 (court fees deprived the citizen of his constitutional right of access to the courts. Such rights were not 'the consequence of the democratic political process but would be logically prior to it'). *Leech* was also followed by Latham J. in *R. v. Secretary of State for the Home Department, ex p. Simms* [1997] C.O.D. 217 (prohibition on the use by a journalist of material gathered on a visit to a prisoner violated prisoners' right to free speech and the restriction not necessary or justified; now updated by the House of Lords on July 8, 1999. *Leech* was taken a step further in *R. v. Secretary of State for Social Security ex p. Joint Council for the Welfare of Immigrants* [1997] 1 W.L.R. 275 where it was held that regulations excluding from income support entitlement those who sought asylum otherwise than on immediate arrival in the U.K. or whose claims were rejected and awaiting appeal, both conflicted with and rendered rights in other legislation nugatory and were so Draconian to an extent that 'no civilised nation can tolerate.' *per* Simon Brown L.J. Dictum of Lord Ellenborough C.J. was in *R. v. Eastbourne (Inhabitants)* (1803) 4 East 103 at 107 approved: 'the law of humanity, which is anterior to all positive laws obliges us to afford [poor foreigners] relief, to save them from starving'. And see also Lord Steyn's acceptance of the concept of 'substantive fairness', based on the rule of law in *Pierson v. Secretary of State for the Home Department* [1998] A.C. 539. Cf. *R. v. Lord Chancellor, ex p. Lightfoot* [1998] 4 All E.R. 764 (*Witham* distinguished in challenge to statutory instrument imposing deposit for official receivers' fees).

The foundation in precedent for the presumption against the **5–055** infringement of human rights in English domestic law is therefore solid. The foundation in theory is less apparent and barely discussed. It is unnecessary to seek the source of human rights in natural law when they can be properly viewed as integral features of a democratic state. Freedom of speech is an obvious component of any democratic society, as are other rights, both those which address democratic procedures and those which address the treatment of individuals in a democracy.[98] Courts in other countries have recognised this explicitly.[99]

Associated with the presumption of implied human rights is the **5–056** presumption that Parliament intends the powers it confers to be exercised in accordance with "public policy". Public policy is an "unruly horse"[1] which must be ridden with care, but it is the public law equivalent of private law equitable principles, such as that which states that no person may benefit from his own wrong. Thus the courts will presume that Parliament did not intend to imperil the welfare of the state or its inhabitants. In a recent case public policy has even been held to override the clear terms of a statute, when to conform with the letter of the statute might have endangered a life.[2]

Finally, it should be noted that the courts may be placing too **5–057** restrictive an interpretation upon the view of the majority in

---

[98] See, *e.g.* R. Dworkin, 'Equality, Democracy and the Constitution', (1990) Alberta Law Rev. 324; T.R.S. Allan, *Law, Liberty and Justice* (1993); C. McCrudden and G. Chambers, *Individual Rights and the Law in Britain* (1994), esp. Chaps. 1 and 16; D. Feldman, *Civil Liberties and Human Rights in England and Wales* (1993).

[99] For examples in Israel, see David Kretzmer, 'The New Basic Laws and Human Rights: A Mini-Revolution in Israeli Constitutional Law?' (1992) *Israel Law Review* 238; S. Goldstein, 'Protection of Human Rights by Judges: The Israeli Experience' (1994) St Louis U.L.J. 605; *Kol Ha'am v. Minister of Interior* (1953) 7 P.D. 871; *Kahane v. Broadcasting Authority* (1987) 4 (iii) P.D. 255. See also H.P. Lee, 'The Australian High Court and Implied Fundamental Guarantees' [1993] P.L. 606.

[1] In *Enderby Town Football Club v. Football Association* [1971] Ch. 591, Lord Denning M.R. said: 'I know that over 300 years ago Hobart C.J. said that 'Public policy is an unruly horse'. It has often been repeated since. So unruly is the horse, it is said [*per* Burrough J. in *Richardson v. Mellish* (1824) 2 Bing 229, 252], that no judge should ever try to mount it lest it run away with him. I disagree. With a good man in the saddle, the unruly horse can be kept in control. It can jump over obstacles. It can leap the fences put up by fictions and come down on the side of justice, as indeed was done in *Nagle v. Feilden* [1966] 2 Q.B. 633. It can hold a rule to be invalid even though it is contained in a contract.'

[2] *R. v. Registrar-General, ex p. Smith* [1991] 2 Q.B. 393 (applicant detained in a mental hospital following conviction for murder of a cellmate in belief he was killing his adoptive mother. Application under s.51A of the Adoption Act 1976 to Registrar-General for copy of his birth certificate refused on ground that his natural mother might be endangered if her identity was known to him). For other examples of application of public policy, see *Nagle v. Feilden* [1966] 2 Q.B. 633 (Jockey Club's refusal of horse trainer's licence to woman held against public policy); *Edwards v. SOGAT* [1971] Ch. 354 (unfair discrimunation in withdrawal of collective bargaining rights).

Brind[3] that, in construing the exercise of power in purely domestic law, regard may not be had to the European Convention of Human Rights. In some cases it has been assumed that English legislation was intended to implement the Convention's designs.[4] In *Leech*, the Court of Appeal extended its consideration of the "settled principles of our domestic law"[5] to consider also the jurisprudence of the European Court of Human Rights[6] which, although not directly binding, "reinforces a conclusion that we have arrived at...".[7] According to the European Court of Human Rights, the United Kingdom government itself has asserted in that court that a rationality argument is available against the Home Secretary in relation to a challenge to his decision to deport a fugitive "where it was established that there was serious risk of inhuman or degrading treatment" (the words of Art. 3 of the Convention).[8] And in a recent judgment Sedley J., while not seeking to contradict the authority of *Brind*, said that:

> "the principles and standards set out in the Convention can certainly be said to be a matter of which this country now takes notice in setting its own standards .... Once it is accepted that the standards articulated in the European Convention ... march with the common law and inform the jurisprudence of the European Union, it becomes unreal and potentially unjust to continue to develop English public law without reference to them."[9]

The Human Rights Act 1998

5–058 When the Human Rights Act comes into force, all public authorities will be required to act in conformity with the provisions of the European Convention on Human Rights referred to in the Act.[10] Where they do not do so, the courts may strike down their decisions. In effect, the ground of review will be illegality, since the authority will have contravened or exceeded the terms of the statute. However,

---

[3] n. 65 above.

[4] *R. v. Canon Park Mental Health Review Tribunal, ex p. A* [1993] 1 All E.R. 481, DC. Generally approved in the Court of Appeal [1994] C.O.D. 480.

[5] *Leech (No. 2)* n. 92 above, at 217, *per* Steyn L.J.

[6] In *Campbell v. U.K.* (1993) 15 E.H.R.R. 137.

[7] *Leech*, n. 92 above, at 217.

[8] *Vilvarajah v. U.K.* (1991) 14 E.H.R.R. 248.

[9] *R. v. Secretary of State for the Home Department, ex p. McQuillan* [1995] 4 All E.R. 400. And see Lord Hope in *Launder*, n. 68 above.

[10] Sched 1 and ss.14–17. See Lester and Pannick (eds) *Human Rights Law and Practice* (1999).

the process by which the courts will then decide is more complex than is the case with other statutes because the standards to be applied are those set out in an international treaty, namely, the European Convention on Human Rights. Furthermore, in interpreting those standards, our domestic courts "must take into account" any judgments of the European Court of Human rights in Strasbourg.[11]

The task before the courts will therefore be more demanding than in the run-of-the-mill case of illegality and is complicated further by the fact that the rights set out in the Convention are perhaps more fundamental than entitlements provided in other statutes. This is because the Convention rights seek to delineate the limits of governmental power in a democratic society. In incorporating the Convention into domestic law, we are expressly departing from the model of democracy so far adopted in the United Kingdom, a model which equates democracy with majority rule, and therefore in theory allows Parliament, elected by the majority, to authorise anything from slavery to torture to detention without trial. The new model provides that there are some areas which even a majority may not invade in a democracy worthy of its name. The result is therefore that, although the Human Rights Act is not entrenched (subject, for example, to alteration by a two-thirds majority in Parliament), and although it appears to be a statute like any other, it is likely to gain special significance and to be treated over the years as having the status of a basic constitutional provision—setting standards necessary in a democratic society properly so called. **5–059**

Not only will it be open to the courts to review the actions of officials exercising public functions. The Act, significantly, innovates the possibility of judicial review[12] of primary legislation, (including Orders in Council made under the royal prerogative).[13] However, in a compromise between the rule of law and Parliamentary sovereignty, the courts may here only issue a declaration of incompatibility,[14] which will not affect the validity, continuing operation or enforcement of the provision in the incompatible statute.[15] Here too, a tradition of constitutional interpretation is likely to emerge. The Act specifically requires the courts to read and give effect to legislation in a way that is compatible with the Convention rights "so far as it is possible to do so". This requirement will effectively over-rule the *Brind* decision; the conferment of a broad discretion on a decision-maker will not be **5–060**

---

[11] Section 2. And the other decisions or opinions set out there.
[12] By the higher courts only: s. 4(5).
[13] s. 3
[14] s. 4.
[15] Although it will trigger the power of Parliament to remedy the defect under section 10 of the Act, which may be done by a 'fast track' procedure, by means of statutory instrument (see also s. 20).

enough to imply that Parliament intended to exclude the Convention's provisions. The courts are also likely to imply words into an enactment to save it being declared incompatible with Convention rights.[16]

5–061   Both in respect of the decisions of public officials and legislation, the courts are likely to adopt an approach that will give a restrictive interpretation to legislation that conflicts with Convention rights. But note that the rights under the Convention are not always self-evident and will sometimes clash with each other. For example, the right to expression under Article 10 of the Convention may be in conflict with the right to respect for privacy under Article 8. Nor are all the rights couched in absolute terms; some permit a degree of limitation or derogation.[17] In those cases the Convention permits the right in question to be infringed where the measure is—in respect, for example of Article 10 (freedom of expression):

> "prescribed by law and necessary in a democratic society, in the interests of national security, territorial integrity or public safety, for the prevention of disorder or crime, for the protection of health or morals, for the protection of the reputation or rights of others, for preventing the disclosure of information received in confidence, or for maintaining the authority and impartiality of the judiciary."

In deciding whether such a test has been met, the courts will have to apply the principle of proportionality.[18] Under that principle measures interfering with rights will have to be justified by an important counter-objective; be rationally connected to that objective and, finally, be no more that is necessary to accomplish that objective.

5–062   Above all, however, the courts will have in future to assess what degree of freedom from governmental interference is "necessary in a democratic society". Such a calculation should not release the courts to make policy decisions that are not appropriate for them to make and that are in the proper realm of an elected legislature. But it will introduce into judicial review a new constitutional dimension.

---

[16] The courts are also unlikely to treat provisions of the Act as impliedly repealed or amended by subsequent legislation. Express intention will be required, and Ministers in charge of Bills will have to make an express statement of compatibility: s. 19.

[17] These include Articles 8–11.

[18] For which see further, para. 12–068 below.

EXERCISE OF A DISCRETIONARY POWER FOR EXTRANEOUS PURPOSE

If a power granted for one purpose is exercised for a different **5–063**
purpose, that power has not been validly exercised. In administrative law[19] this elementary proposition was first laid down in cases concerning the exercise of powers of compulsory acquisition. These cases held that when persons embarking in great undertakings, for the accomplishment of which those engaged in them have received authority from the legislature to take compulsorily the lands of others, paying to the latter proper compensation, the persons so authorised cannot be allowed to exercise the powers conferred on them for any collateral object; that is, for any purposes except those for which the legislature has invested them with extraordinary powers.[20]

An expression of judicial solicitude for private property rights[21] was **5–064**
thus enlarged into a fundamental principle of English administrative law, possibly even based upon an unwritten constitutional principle. Most of the reported cases deal with the misapplication of powers by local authorities, though the same general principle governed the exercise of subordinate legislative power experienced by the executive.[22]

The principle has been expressed in different ways. Sometimes it is **5–065**
said that decision-makers should not pursue "collateral objects", or that they should not pursue ends which are outside the "objects and purposes of the statute". On other occasions it is said that power should not be "exceeded" or that the purposes pursued by the decision-maker should not be "improper", "ulterior", or "extraneous" to those required by the statute in question. It is also said that

---

[19] The doctrine of a fraud upon a power is, of course, well known in equity.
[20] *Galloway v. London Corp.* (1866) L.R. 1 HL 34, 43.
[21] For other early dicta, see *Webb v. Manchester & Leeds Ry.* (1839) 4 Myl. & Cr. 116. 118; *Dodd v. Salisbury & Yeovil Ry.* (1859) 1 Giff. 158; *Stockton & Darlington Ry. v. Brown* (1860) 9 H.L.C. 246, 254, 256; *Biddulph v. St George's, Hanover Square, Vestry* (1863) 33 L.J.Ch. 411, 417; *Hawley v. Steele* (1877) 6 Ch.D. 521, 527–529. See also *Marshall Shipping Co. v. R.* (1925) 41 T.L.R. 285: 'You can never beat into the heads of people exercising bureaucratic authority that they must exercise their powers singly, and not for collateral objects.'
[22] For byelaws, see, *e.g. Scott v. Glasgow Corp.* [1899] A.C. 470, 492; *Baird (Robert) Ltd v. Glasgow Corp.* [1936] A.C. 32, 42; *Boyd Builders Ltd v. City of Ottawa* (1964) 45 D.L.R. (2d) 211; *Re Burns and Township of Haldimand* (1965) 52 D.L.R. (2d) 101; *Prince George (City of) v. Payne* [1978] 1 S.C.R. 458; see also *Paul v. Ayrshire C.C.*, 1964 S.L.T. 207 (dicta). There are many instances of challenges to departmental legislation on this ground; see, generally, *Yates (Arthur) & Co. Pty Ltd v. Vegetable Seeds Committee* (1945) 72 C.L.R. 37.

"irrelevant considerations" should not be taken into account in reaching a decision. All these terms of course "run into each other" and "overlap".[23]

5–066   However, the designation of a purpose as "improper" is distinct because of its connotation of *moral* impropriety. In most cases where the term "improper" has been employed the decision-maker either knowingly pursues a purpose that is different from the one that is ostensibly being pursued, or the motive behind the decision is illicit (based for example on personal factors such as revenge or prejudice). Because, therefore, of its adverse moral imputation, the notion of improper purposes is more akin to that of bad faith (a notion which directly imputes motives involving dishonesty, fraud or malice) which is considered in Chapter 12 below as an instance of the ground of the "unreasonable" exercise or abuse of power.[24]

5–067   When a decision-maker pursues a purpose outside of the four corners of his powers, he mostly does so by taking an "irrelevant consideration" into account (the term "relevant" referring to the purpose of the statute). The interpretation of purpose, and the relevance of considerations taken into account in pursuing that purpose, are therefore often inextricably linked. However, in some cases neither the motive for the decision, nor the considerations taken into account in reaching that decision, are apparent. In such a case the purpose pursued is judged alone, without reference to the considerations by which it was influenced. The definition of purpose and the relevance of considerations must therefore be considered as separate aspects of the illegal decision.[25]

Where purposes are specified in the statute

5–068   The law reports abound with cases involving challenges to the interpretation by public officials of statutory power. Sometimes the exercise of interpretation by the courts of the statutory provision in question involves no more than a search for the "natural and ordinary meaning" of a word or term. For example, a number of cases under various statutes requiring local authorities to house the homeless have

---

[23] *per* Lord Greene in *Associated Provincial Picture Houses v. Wednesbury Corp.* [1948] 1 K.B. 223, 228.

[24] *e.g* where a local authority acquired a property ostensibly to widen the street—an authorised purpose—but in reality to sell it at a profit. *Gard v. Commissioners for Sewers of the City of London* (1885) 28 Ch.D. 486. In French law a similar distinction is made. The improper purpose as defined above and a decision taken in bad faith fall under the ground of 'détournement de pouvoir'. See L. Neville Brown and J. Bell, *French Administrative Law* (1993), pp. 229 *et seq.*

[25] Irrelevant considerations are discussed further para. 5–083 below.

considered the meaning of terms such as "homelessness",[26] or "intentionally homeless".[27] Others have considered the duty to provide "adequate accommodation" to gypsies "residing in or resorting to the area".[28] The term "ordinarily resident in the United Kingdom" has also been construed in various contexts.[29] Planning authorities, when deciding whether to grant permission in "conservation areas", are required to pay special attention to the desirability of "preserving or enhancing the character or appearance" of the designated conservation area.[30] Do those words require that permission be granted only for development which positively improves the area, or do they merely require that the standards of amenity in the area are maintained at their existing level and not harmed? The House of Lords, after various interpretations in the courts below,[31] held the latter interpretation to be correct.[32]

More often than not, even apparently straightforward terms need to be understood in the context of the purpose of the statute as a whole. In the recent case *Pepper v. Hart*,[33] the term in dispute was that of "cost" in section 63 of the Finance Act 1976. The question was whether teachers at independent schools whose children were educated at the school at very reduced fees should be taxed on the "marginal cost" to the school of educating those children (which would be a small sum), or on the "average cost" (which would be significantly higher). The issue had implications for the in-house benefits of many other employees as well. It was decided that the statutory purpose favoured the interpretation most favourable to the teachers. Departing from previous authority,[34] the House of Lords referred to parliamentary

5–069

---

[26] See, *e.g. R. v. Hillingdon L.B.C., ex p. Islam* [1981] 1 A.C. 688.

[27] See, *e.g. R. v. Secretary of State for the Environment, ex p. Tower Hamlets L.B.C.* [1993] Q.B. 632.

[28] Under s. 6 Caravan Sites Act, 1968. See *W. Glamorgan v. Rafferty* [1987] 1 W.L.R. 457; *R. v. Gloucester C.C., ex p. Dutton* [1992] C.O.D. 1.

[29] See, *e.g. Shah v. Barnet L.B.C.* [1983] 2 A.C. 309 (in the context of a student seeking non-overseas status).

[30] Planning (Listed Buildings and Conservation Areas) Act 1990, s.72.

[31] See, *e.g. Steinberg v. Secretary of State for the Environment* (1988) 58 P. & C.R. 453.

[32] *South Lakeland D.C. v. Secretary of State for the Environment* [1992] A.C. 141.

[33] [1993] A.C. 593. A distinction should be made between the use of *Hansard* to resolve an ambiguity in a statutory provision, and its use to determine the general purpose of a statutory scheme. In the latter case, *Pepper v. Hart* is not relevant and the court accordingly is not bound by its restrictions and thus, for example, may look at statements other than those of the Minister promoting the bill: see *Three Rivers D.C. v. Bank of England (No. 2)* [1996] 2 All E.R. 363.

[34] Specifically, the *Practice Statement (Judicial Precedent)* [1966] 1 W.L.R. 1234; *Davis v. Johnson* [1979] A.C. 264; *Hadmor Productions Ltd v. Hamilton* [1983] A.C. 191. *Hansard* reports have been directly referred to in some cases, *e.g. Pickstone v. Freemans plc* [1989] A.C. 66, and *Owen Bank v. Bracco* [1992] A.C. 443 and in others (mainly involving national security issues) the Crown has referred to *Hansard*. See, *e.g. Ex p.*

material to assist the construction of the ambiguous provision. Reference may now therefore be made to the parliamentary record to aid the construction of legislation which is ambiguous or obscure and where the material clearly discloses the mischief aimed at or the legislative intention underlying the meaning of the words in question.[35] This important step will aid the "purposive" or "teleological" approach to statutory interpretation. It might, however, encourage the artificial manufacture of parliamentary intent, and may at times confound the presumption of parliamentary respect for certain fundamental constitutional principles where the intention clearly reveals that Parliament wished, say, to oust the court's jurisdiction or to breach the rule of law.[36] Reference to the parliamentary record may also perhaps encourage too much weight to be attached to the original intention behind a regulatory scheme when the implementation of that scheme may benefit by the alteration of objectives over time.[37]

5–070   Even when purposes are clearly specified in a statute, the authority may undertake tasks that are "reasonably incidental" to the achievement of those purposes.[38] In respect of the activities of local authorities, section 111 of the Local Government Act 1972 gives statutory recognition to that rule of common law, authorising them to do any thing which is "calculated to facilitate, or is conducive or incidental to, the discharge of any of their functions." This phrase has itself been the subject of statutory construction in cases where, for example, local authorities have attempted to raise revenue by charging fees or speculating on the financial markets. When a local education authority decided to charge fees for individual and group music tuition, that decision was held unlawful as the duty under the statute to provide "education" without charge[39] included the duty to provide music tuition.[40] Similarly, a local authority was held not entitled to charge for consultations with developers prior to applications for

---

[35] *Brind* [1991] A.C. 696.

[35] *per* Lord Browne-Wilkinson, *ibid.* at 1056, who could not foresee that any statement other than that of the Minister or other promoter of the bill was likely to met those criteria.

[36] See Dawn Oliver. "*Pepper v. Hart*: A Suitable Case for Reference to Hansard?" [1993] P.L. 5.

[37] See the discussion of the changing objectives of planning law, at paras 5-079–5-081 below.

[38] *Ashbury Railway Carriage and Iron Co. Ltd v. Riche* (1875) L.R. 7 HL 653; *Att.-Gen. v. Great Eastern Railway Company* (1880) 5 App. Cas. 473; *Att.-Gen. v. Fulham Corp.* [1912] 1 Ch. 440.

[39] Under s.61 of the Education Act 1949.

[40] *R. v. Hereford and Worcester Local Education Authority, ex p. Jones* [1981] 1 W.L.R. 768. In general authorities require specific authorisation to raise revenue. *Att.-Gen. v. Wilts United Dairies Ltd* (1921) 37 T.L.R. 884.

planning permission being lodged. The House of Lords held that, although pre-application advice was not a duty or a discretionary power, but an incidental power authorised by section 111 of the Local Government Act, the power to charge for that incidental power was not authorised.[41] The courts also struck down the power of a London local authority to enter into interest rate swap transaction, which involved speculation as to future interest trends, with the object of making a profit to increase the available resources of the authority. That activity was held inconsistent with the borrowing powers of local authorities and not "conducive or incidental" to the discharge of those limited powers.[42]

Where a statute conferred power upon local authorities to incur expenditure for the "publication within their area of information on matters relating to local government", an expensive media and poster campaign mounted by the Inner London Education Authority was invalidated on the ground that it was made with the dual purpose both of informing the public of the detail of the education service and also of persuading the public to support the authority's opposition to the government's "rate-capping" policy. The first objective of the campaign (information) was lawful, but the second objective (persuasion) was held to be an unlawful purpose, which materially influenced the decision.[43]   **5–071**

Outside of the area of public expenditure, the relevance of sanctions imposed by local authorities for various motives has arisen in a number of cases. Where a statute imposed a duty upon every library authority to provide a "comprehensive and efficient library service",[44] the action of three London local authorities in banning from their libraries all publications of the Times Newspaper Group was held unlawful.[45] The ban was imposed to demonstrate support for the trade unions involved in a long and bitter dispute with the newspaper's proprietors. It was held that the ban pursued an "ulterior purpose"   **5–072**

---

[41] *McCarthy and Stone (Developments) Ltd v. Richmond-upon-Thames L.B.C.* [1992] 2 A.C. 48.

[42] *Hazell v. Hammersmith & Fulham L.B.C.* [1992] 2 A.C. 1. Some recent cases holding various financial or housing schemes of local authorities to be *ultra vires* include: *Credit Suisse v. Allerdale B.C.* [1997] Q.B. 306; *Credit Suisse v. Waltham Forest L.B.C.* [1997] Q.B. 362; *Sutton London L.B.C. v. Morgan Grenfell and Co. Ltd* (1997) 9 Admin L.R. 145. But see *R. v. Greater Manchester Police Authority, ex p. Century Motors (Farnworth) Ltd, The Times,* May 31, 1996 (necessary implication that power to levy charges for vehicle recovery operation); *R. v. Powys C.C. ex p. Hambidge, The Times,* November 5, 1997 (Local authority may charge for services under section 2 of the Chronically Sick and Disabled Persons Act 1970).

[43] *R. v. Inner London E.A., ex p. Westminster City Council* [1986] 1 W.L.R. 28. In relation to dual purposes, see para. 5–082.

[44] The Public Libraries and Museums Act 1964. s. 7(1).

[45] *R. v. Ealing L.B.C., ex p. Times Newspapers Ltd* (1986) 85 L.G.R. 316.

which was "set by a political attitude to a so-called workers' struggle against a tyrannical employer with the object of punishing the employer".[46] In an earlier case Lord Denning indicated that the closure of schools during a prolonged labour dispute could, if influenced by trade union pressure, amount to an unlawful extraneous purpose.[47]

5–073   Where local authorities have sought to impose conditions upon the use of their land, the courts have required them to further the purposes authorised by the statutes under which the land was acquired. A London authority attached a condition to permission for the holding of a community festival in a park.[48] The condition required the banning at the festival of "any political party or organisation seeking to promote or oppose any political party or cause". It was held that those restrictions were extraneous to the purpose of the statute under which the authority had purchased the park, namely "for the purpose of being used as public walks or a pleasure ground".[49] A recent case concerned the controversial question of hunting deer with hounds. The Somerset County Council had passed a resolution to ban hunting on their (council-owned) land on the Quantock Hills. The ban was motivated by the "moral repugnance" of the majority of the council towards hunting. The land had been acquired under a statute generally authorising acquisition of land for "the benefit, improvement or development of their area".[50] That purpose was interpreted as permitting the council to pursue objects which would "conduce to the better management of the estate". Had the ban been introduced to protect rare flora damaged by the hunt, or to eliminate physical interference with the enjoyment of others of the amenities offered on the land, it might have been lawful. However, since the ban was fuelled by the "ethical perceptions of the Councillors about the rights and wrongs of hunting", the purposes it sought were outwith that of the governing statute.[51]

5–074   The power of the Foreign Secretary to grant assistance to overseas countries was subjected to recent judicial scrutiny. The Overseas Development and Co-operation Act 1980 confers such power on the Secretary of State "for the purpose of promoting the economy of a

---

[46] The ban was also held to be unreasonable. See Chap. 12 below. And see discussion at paras 5–094–5–096.

[47] *Meade v. Haringey L.B.C.* [1979] 1 W.L.R. 637.

[48] *R. v. Barnet L.B.C., ex p. Johnson* [1989] C.O.D. 538.

[49] Public Health Act 1865, s.164. The ban was also held on unreasonable infringement of the right of association.

[50] Local Government Act 1972, s. 120(1).

[51] *R. v. Somerset C.C., ex p. Fewings* [1995] 1 All E.R. 513 (*per* Laws J.). The Court of Appeal upheld this decision, although on different grounds [1995] 1 W.L.R. 1037. And see Davina Cooper, 'For the Sake of the Deer: Land, Local Government and the Hunt (1997) 45 *Sociological Review* 668.

country or territory outside the United Kingdom, or the welfare of its people. . .".[52] It was clear that the project which had been funded, the Pergau dam hydro-electric project in Malaysia, was not itself economically "sound" and was a "very bad buy". However, it was contended for the Secretary of State that wider political and economic interest were and could have been taken into account, including an alleged undertaking by the Prime Minister to provide the assistance (perhaps, as alleged in the press—although not directly alluded to in the judgments—as part of a wider arrangement involving an agreement to purchase defence items in the United Kingdom). The court, however, held that these wider purposes were not sufficient in themselves to qualify as a project for assistance under the statute. Although the statute did not specifically require an assisted project to be economically "sound", so much had to be implied. Had there been a "developmental promotion purpose" within section 1 of the Act, only then would it have been proper to take into account the wider political and economic considerations, including the impact which withdrawing from the offer would have had on commercial relations with Malaysia. In the circumstances, however, there was, at the time when assistance was provided, "no such purpose within the section".[53]

The power of the Home Secretary in respect of the continuing **5–075** detention of life prisoners has been the subject of particular recent attention, both by Parliament and the courts. In respect of discretionary life-sentenced prisoners, detainees and those detained during Her Majesty's pleasure, the "danger to the public" was the only ground on which to justify the Home Secretary continuing the prisoner's detention after the punitive term set for his release. The relevant statute under which the Home Secretary was acting was the Criminal Justice Act 1991 (especially sections 34 and 35). A series of cases thus set out that matters extraneous to the danger to the public are unlawful considerations which the Home Secretary may not take into account.[54] In 1997, however, the Home Secretary's powers were revised by section 29 of the Crime (Sentences) Act. It has recently been held that these powers permit the Home Secretary to take into account, in his decision, whether or not to release a mandatory life prisoner, factors broader than public risk; in this case whether or not the prisoner was likely to commit an imprisonable offence fail to comply with the terms of his release. The Lord Chief Justice in that

---

[52] Overseas Development and Co-operation Act 1980, s.1(1).

[53] *R. v. Secretary of State for Foreign Affairs, ex p. The World Development Movement Ltd* [1995] 1 W.L.R. 386.

[54] See for example, the two most recent cases in the House of Lords, both overturning the Home Secretary's exercise of his power. *Secretary of State for the Home Department, ex p. Venables and Thompson* [1997] 3 W.L.R. 23; *R. v. Secretary of State for the Home Department ex p. Pierson* [1997] 3 W.L.R. 492.

case held that the discretion conferred on the Home Secretary was "extraordinarily wide" and, although lawfully exercised, it "lay uneasily with the rule of law."[55]

Unspecified purposes

5–076 If a discretionary power is conferred without express reference to purpose, it must still be exercised in accordance with such implied purposes as the courts attribute to the legislation.[56] We have seen that the Minister who, in reliance upon an ostensibly unfettered discretionary power, refused to refer a complaint by milk producers to a committee of investigation because this might lead him into economic and political difficulties, was held to have violated the unexpressed purpose, or the "policy and objects" of the Act, for which the power of reference had been conferred[57] and (according to a somewhat hyperbolical interpretation of their Lordships' comments) "was roundly rebuked by the House of Lords for his impudence".[58] In order to avoid paying an announced (but not yet enacted) increase in the fee for a television licence, some licence-holders obtained another licence at the old rate before their existing licence expired. The Court of Appeal held that the Minister could not use his power to revoke licences, albeit conferring no apparent limits on that power, in order to deprive licensees of the advantage that they had secured from the gap between the Government's announcement and Parliamentary authorisation of the change in fees.[59]

5–077 Subsequent cases made it clearer that the imposition of a penalty in the absence of a legal wrong pursues an extraneous purpose. Purporting to be acting under the general duty under the Race

---

[55] *R. v. Secretary of State for the Home Department ex p. Stafford, The Times,* Nov. 28, 1997.

[56] See, *e.g. Liversidge v. Anderson* [1942] A.C. 206, 220, 248, 261, 278; *Barber v. Manchester Regional Hospital Board* [1958] 1 W.L.R. 181, 193; *Potato Marketing Board v. Merricks* [1958] 2 Q.B. 316, 331; dicta cited in argument in *Smith v. East Elloe R.D.C.* [1956] A.C. 736, 740. The proposition stated in the text has nevertheless been doubted or contradicted (see *Yates (Arthur) & Co. Pty Ltd v. Vegetable Seeds Committee* (1946) 72 C.L.R. 37, 68, *per* Latham C.J.) by some authorities. The decision in *R. v. Paddington & St Marylebone Rent Tribunal, ex p. Bell London & Provincial Properties Ltd* [1949] 1 K.B. 666 (block reference of 555 tenancies by local authority to rent tribunal without considering wishes of tenants or circumstances of particular cases; reference held invalid in that council was using tribunal as a general rent-fixing agency) has generally been regarded as a good illustration of the proposition in the text, but the case has now been explained as an example of a merely capricious reference: *R. v. Barnet & Camden Rent Tribunal, ex p. Frey Investments Ltd* [1972] 2 Q.B. 342, CA.

[57] *Padfield v. Minister of Agriculture, Fisheries and Food* [1968] A.C. 997; see para. 5–026 above.

[58] *Breen v. Amalgamated Engineering Union* [1971] 2 Q.B. 175, 191, *per* Lord Denning M.R.

[59] *Congreve v. Home Office* [1976] Q.B. 629.

Relations Act 1976 to "promote good race relations",[60] and also purporting to act under its broad powers to manage its own land, Leicester City Council withdrew the licence of a local rugby club to use the council-owned recreation ground. The council did this as a mark of their disapproval that the club had been unable to persuade some of its members to withdraw from the English rugby footballers' tour of South Africa, at the time of apartheid and as a demonstration of their effort to "promote good relations between persons of different racial or ethnic groups". The House of Lords held the council's action unlawful, Lord Templeman considering it to be a "misuse of power ... punishing the club where it had done no wrong".[61] Similar reasons (the opposition to apartheid and the promotion of good race relations) motivated the London Borough of Lewisham which decided to boycott the products of Shell U.K. Ltd so as to put pressure on the parent companies of the group to withdraw their interests from South Africa. It was held that the dominant purpose of the boycott was to penalise the applicant for the fact that the group to which it belonged had trading links with South Africa. These links were not unlawful and the council's decision had therefore been influenced by an "extraneous and impermissible purpose"[62] Another boycott was considered by the courts when Liverpool City Council threatened to withdraw grant aid from organisations which might consider joining a (voluntary) employment training scheme introduced by the Government. The Court of Appeal held the purpose (punishment or coercion) to be unlawful.[63]

When two school governors were removed by the Inner London **5–078** Education Authority because they had opposed the Authority's educational policy, the House of Lords considered whether the broad discretion conferred on the authority permitted this action. The statute

---

[60] s.61.

[61] *Wheeler v. Leicester City Council* [1985] A.C. 1954. *Cf.* the approach of Lord Browne-Wilkinson in his dissenting judgment in the Court of Appeal, *ibid.* at 1064–1065, where he raised the conflict between 'two basic principles of a democratic society', one that allowed a 'democratically elected body to conduct its affairs in accordance with its own views' and the other 'the right to freedom of speech and conscience enjoyed by each individual'. Basing his decision on illegality rather than on unreasonableness (the council having taken a 'legally irrelevant factor' into account), he came close to deciding the matter on the ground of the council's acting inconsistently with 'fundamental freedoms of speech and conscience'. *Cf.* the New Zealand decision of *Ashby v. Minister of Immigration* [1981] 1 N.Z.L.R. 222 where the refusal of the Minister to bar the entry of the South African rugby football team into New Zealand was upheld on the ground that the public interest (a relevant consideration in the context of the Minister's power) allowed the decision.

[62] *R. v. Lewisham L.B.C., ex p. Shell U.K. Ltd* [1988] 1 All E.R. 938.

[63] *R. v. Liverpool City Council, ex p. Secretary of State for Employment, The Times,* November 12, 1988; [1988] C.O.D. 404.

simply provided that a governor "shall be removable by the authority by whom he was appointed".[64] It was held that the power could not be exercised in a way that usurped the governor's independent function and that such a usurpation was in effect extraneous to the power conferred.[65]

Planning powers and the notion of changing purpose

5–079 Since 1947, when the systematic control of land use and development was introduced by the Town and Country Planning Act of that year, local authorities, and the Secretary of State for the Environment[66] on appeal, have possessed seemingly unlimited power to grant and refuse planning permission. The governing statute[67] requires "regard to be had" to the development plan as drafted by the local authority, but it has always allowed "other material considerations" also to be considered.[68] Conditions may be imposed upon permissions as the authority "think fit".[69] This apparently broad discretionary power has, however, not permitted conditions to be used for the purpose of requiring an applicant to construct a road, to be dedicated to the public, without compensation, if he would be entitled to compensation were the normal procedure for road construction laid down by another Act to be followed.[70] Nor can it be used to enable the authority to discharge its responsibility to house those on its waiting list for council accommodation; the proper course for the authority to take is compulsory acquisition subject to the payment of compensation

[64] Education Act 1944, s. 21(1).

[65] *Brunyate v. Inner London Education Authority* [1989] 1 W.L.R. 542. But when eight recalcitrant councillors were removed from a local authority housing committee ostensibly to reduce the size of that committee (and not to punish their behaviour), the decision was not held unlawful. *R. v. Greenwich L.B.C., ex p. Lovelace* [1990] 1 W.L.R. 18; *aff'd* [1991] 1 W.L.R. 506. See also *Champion v. Chief Constable of the Gwent Constabulary* [1990] 1 W.L.R. 1 (refusal of membership of school appointments committee to police constable governor held unlawful as it was not 'likely' to give the appearance of partiality). See also *R. v. Warwickshire C.C., ex p. Dill-Russell* (1991) 3 Admin. L.R. 415; *aff'd* (1991) 3 Admin. L.R. 415 (lawful for all governors of school to resign simultaneously so as to achieve proportionality with political representation on reappointment).

[66] Formerly the Minister of Housing and Local Government.

[67] Now the Town and Country Planning Act 1990.

[68] Formerly the development plan and other material considerations had equal influence. Since 1991, however, the development plan shall be followed unless other material considerations 'indicate otherwise'; s.54A, Town and Country Planning Act 1990.

[69] Town and Country Planning Act 1990, s.70(1).

[70] *Hall & Co. v. Shoreham-by-Sea U.D.C.* [1964] 1 W.L.R. 240.

and to provide the housing under its powers under the appropriate Act.[71] Planning powers cannot therefore be used for non-material, that is, non-planning purposes.[72]

The judicial construction of the Town and Country Planning Act **5–080** over time shows that the purposes pursued by a statutory scheme may not be static. When first enacted, the act was concerned largely with what have been called physical criteria: questions such as access to the site, siting of the buildings, their height, bulk, set-back, mass, design and external appearance. It was held unequivocally that the "character of the use of the land, not the particular purposes of a particular occupier"[73] was the concern of planning, and therefore the authority could not seek to favour any particular occupant or class of occupant. Over the years, however, the emphasis in planning policy has changed and a local plan providing for the protection from development of certain traditional industries necessary to maintain the diverse social character of the area was upheld by the House of Lords as pursuing a legitimate planning purpose. Lord Scarman held that, in considering the "character of the use of the land", it would be "inhuman pedantry" to ignore the "human factor" in planning. Therefore, as an exception to the general rule, account could be taken of "the personal circumstances of the occupier, personal hardship [and] the difficulties of businesses which are of value to the community ...".[74] While earlier cases made it clear that the identity of the occupier or class of occupier (*e.g.* rich or poor) of housing was not a material planning consideration.[75] government policy has changed and

---

[71] *R. v. Hillingdon L.B.C., ex p. Royco Homes Ltd* [1974] Q.B. 720.

[72] The fact that one means of achieving a lawful statutory purpose appears to the court to be more appropriate than another will not usually justify the selection of that route as uniquely legitimate. *Cf. C.C. Auto Port Pty Ltd v. Minister of Works* (1966) 113 C.L.R. 365; *Hanks v. Minister of Housing and Local Government* [1963] 1 Q.B. 999. See also *Westminster Bank Ltd v. Beverley B.C.* [1971] A.C. 508; *Hoveringham Gravels Ltd v. Secretary of State for the Environment* [1975] Q.B. 754 (planning powers wide enough to restrict use of land for a purpose specifically dealt with in other legislation which contained compensation provisions). And see *Associated Minerals Consolidated Ltd v. Wyong Shire Council* [1975] A.C. 538, PC: *Vancouver (City of) v. Simpson* [1977] 1 S.C.R. 71. See also in a different context, *Asher v. Secretary of State for the Environment* [1974] Ch. 208 (choice of procedure to be taken against the recalcitrant councillors of Clay Cross).

[73] *per* Lord Parker C.J. in *East Barnet U.D.C. v. British Transport Commission* [1962] 2 Q.B. 484.

[74] *Westminster City Council v. Great Portland Estates plc* [1985] A.C. 661.

[75] *Royco Homes*, n.71 above. An exception was allowed for agricultural occupancy conditions in green belts or rural areas. *Fawcett Properties Ltd v. Buckingham C.C.* [1961] A.C. 636. See the decision of the Secretary of State for the Environment discharging a condition imposed by the London Borough of Brent providing that 25 per cent of the housing in a residential development be occupied on a tenancy basis for a period of 10 years. The reason was "To ensure that new residential

"affordable housing" now features in the policy guidelines issued by the Department of Environment as a permissible goal of planning.[76] Recent cases have held that "affordable housing" may be a material planning consideration.[77]

5–081   The experience of the interpretation of planning powers over time provides a salient reminder of the fluid nature of statutory purposes and the danger of freezing their purpose for all time through undue reliance upon the so-called "original intention" of the legislature (even if such intention is capable of discovery).[78] The goals of a scheme of public regulation are inevitably influenced by what the administrators do, and by what they need to do to keep abreast of changing social and professional expectations. When a statute provides broad discretion it is often for the purpose of permitting the objectives of the enterprise to be shaped over time.

Plurality of purposes

5–082   We now take hold of a legal porcupine which bristles with difficulties as soon as it is touched. In a case where the actor has sought to achieve unauthorised as well as authorised purposes, what test should be applied to determine the validity of his act?

At least six separate tests have been applied where plural purposes or motives are present. The choice of one test in preference to another can materially affect the decision. Despite this, it is not uncommon to

---

developments contribute to meeting the needs of the borough's residents for low-cost housing ...' [1988] J.P.L. 222.

[76] Department of the Environment, Planning Policy Guidelines 3: 'The community's need for affordable housing is a material planning consideration which may properly be taken into account in formulating development plan policies.'

[77] See *Mitchell v. Secretary of State for the Environment* [1994] J.P.L. 916, CA, which upheld the refusal of permission to change the use of a house in multiple occupation to self-contained flats in order to meet the need for cheap rental accommodation. Saville L.J. made it clear that the case was not (as *Royco* may have been) an attempt to impose upon the private owner the statutory obligations of the council with regard to the provision of housing. Balcombe L.J. held that the retention of housing of a type and cost available to a particular section of the community was a matter relating to the 'character and the use of land', and cited PPG 3, n. 76 above, in support of his view. See also *ECC Construction Ltd v. Secretary of State for the Environment* (1994) 69 P. & C.R. 51. In *Mitchell* the policy in favour of affordable housing was included in the council's published policies. This was not the case, nor was considered necessary, in *ECG Construction*.

[78] If parliamentary records are resorted to in cases such as these they may well inhibit, if not used sensibly, the kind of incremental development of purpose seen in planning law.

find two or more of the tests applied in the course of a single judgment.[79] The following tests, none of which is entirely satisfactory, have been formulated:

(1) What was the true purpose for which the power was exercised? If the actor has in truth used his power for the purpose for which it was conferred, it is immaterial that he achieved as well a subsidiary object. Thus, if a power to construct an underground public convenience is exercised in such a way as to provide a subway leading to the convenience that can also be used by pedestrians who do not wish to take advantage of its facilities, the power has been validly exercised. The position would have been different if the construction of the conveniences was a colourable device adopted in order to enable a subway to be built.[80] A local authority empowered to spend money upon altering and repairing streets "as and when required" acts lawfully in resurfacing a road that is in fact in need of repair, although the immediate occasion for carrying out the work is the hope of attracting an automobile club to use it for racing trials.[81] If the Home Secretary is honestly satisfied that the deportation of an alien is conducive to the public good and there is some basis for his belief, his deportation order is valid although the practical effect (and perhaps a secondary desired effect) of the order is to secure the extradition of the alien to another country seeking his rendition for a non-extraditable offence.[82]

(2) What was the dominant purpose for which the power was exercised? If the actor pursues two or more purposes where only one is expressly or impliedly permitted, the legality of the act is determined by reference to the dominant purpose. This test, based on an analogy with the law of tortious conspiracy,[83] has been applied in several cases.[84] In substance

---

[79] See, *e.g. Webb v. Minister of Housing and Local Government* [1965] 1 W.L.R. 755, 773–774, 777H (test (5), below), 778G (test (2)); *Grieve v. Douglas-Home*, 1965 S.C. 313 (tests (1) and (2)—a particularly interesting case. *R. v. Inner London Education Authority, ex p. Westminster City Council* [1986] 1 W.L.R. 28 (tests (1) and (5)).

[80] *Westminster Corp. v. L. & N.W. Ry.* [1905] A.C. 426.

[81] *R. v. Brighton Corp., ex p. Shoosmith* (1907) 96 L.T. 762.

[82] *R. v. Brixton Prison Governor, ex p. Soblen* [1963] 2 Q.B. 243. It is to be noted that the Home Secretary's discretion was couched in subjective terms and was exercisable on 'policy' grounds. For discussions of the case, see C.H.R. Thornberry (1963) 121 C.L.Q. 414; Paul O'Higgins (1963) 27 M.L.R. 521; J.M. Evans, *Immigration Law*, pp. 106–108.

[83] *Crofter Hand Woven Harris Tweed Co. v. Veitch* [1942] A.C. 435.

[84] *Earl Fitzwilliam's Wentworth Estates Co. v. Minister of Town and Country Planning* [1951] 2 K.B. 284, 307, *per* Denning L.J. (dissenting). The House of Lords did not give any

it may often prove to be nothing more than a different verbal formulation of the "true purpose" test. Where several purposes coexist, attempts to single out the "true" purpose have an air of unreality. If, of course, the avowed purpose is shown to be a mere sham, the "true purpose" test can readily be applied. It is of some interest that in *Soblen's* case (above) the courts concentrated their analysis on the question of whether the deportation order was a sham, or a pretext for procuring an unlawful extradition; they abstained from asking themselves what was the Home Secretary's dominant purpose in making the order, though this would not appear to have been an irrelevant question.

In the Pergau dam case[85] it was held that the Minister's dominant purpose in funding the uneconomic project was not the authorised one of furthering the "economy" or "welfare" of the people of Malaysia. In the stag hunting ban case[86] it was held that the dominant purpose of fulfilling the "ethical perceptions" of the councillors did not fulfil the statute's authorised purpose—that of improvement of the amenity of the area.[87]

(3) Would the power still have been exercised if the actor had not desired concurrently to achieve an unauthorised purpose?[88]

(4) Was any of the purposes pursued an authorised purpose? If so, the presence of concurrent illicit purposes does not affect the validity of the act. This test appears to have been applied in only one English case, and even then somewhat equivocally.[89] It is submitted that in English law the existence

---

ruling on this point on appeal ([1952] A.C. 362). For subsequent formulations of a similar test, see *Webb's* case (n. 79 above) at 778; *Grieve v. Douglas-Home* (n. 79 above); *R. v. Immigration Appeals Adjudicator, ex p. Khan* [1972] 1 W.L.R. 1058 (whether primary purpose of entering U.K. as full-time student was to take up permanent residence); *R. v. Ealing L.B.C., ex p. Times Newspapers Ltd* (1986) 85 L.G.R. 316 (dominant purpose in imposing ban on purchase of publications for library was to interfere in industrial dispute).

[85] *R. v. Secretary of State for Foreign Affairs, ex p. The World Development Movement*, n.53 above.

[86] *R. v. Somerset C.C., ex p. Fewings* [1995] I W.L.R. 1037.

[87] Perhaps in both these cases the *sole* purpose was unauthorised.

[88] This test was applied by the High Court of Australia. *Thompson v. Randwick Municipal Council* (1950) 81 C.L.R. 87, 106. It may have the disadvantage of requiring the courts to speculate about motives for which it is ill-equipped, but it is not very different from test (6) below.

[89] *Earl Fitzwilliam's* case [1951] 1 K.B. 203, 217–219, *per* Birkett J. See also Lord MacDermott's observations in the House of Lords [1952] A.C. 362, 385; but *cf.* Denning L.J. 's test, n.84 above.

of one legitimate purpose among illegitimate purposes will only save the validity of an act if the purpose for which the power was granted has been substantially fulfilled.

(5) Were any of the purposes pursued an unauthorised purpose? If so, and if the unauthorised purpose has materially influenced the actor's conduct, the power has been invalidly exercised because irrelevant considerations have been taken into account. The effect of applying such a test may be directly opposed to that produced by the preceding test.[90] This is a curious state of affairs, for the concepts of improper purpose and irrelevancy are intimately related and are often analytically indistinguishable.[91] That the possibility of a sharp conflict between them exists has seldom been recognised. The question was considered in a case where the validity of a compulsory purchase order was impugned—the court preferred the test of irrelevancy: had the making of the order been significantly or substantially influenced by irrelevant considerations.[92]

Recent cases have affirmed this approach. When irrelevant considerations have been taken into account, the courts have invalidated the decision if those considerations have had a "substantial" or "material" influence upon the decision.[93]

---

[90] Thus, in *Sadler v. Sheffield Corp.* [1924] 1 Ch. 483, where notices of dismissal served on teachers were held to be invalid because they have been served not on 'educational grounds' (as was required by the Act) but in reality on financial grounds, P. O. Lawrence J. said *obiter* (at 504–505) that even if bona fide educational grounds for dismissal had coexisted with the financial grounds, it would have been wrong to try to separate them, and that mixed educational and financial grounds were not educational grounds within the meaning of the Act, which were the only grounds that could lawfully be taken into account (applying dictum in *R. v. St Pancras Vestry* (1890) 24 QBD, 375.

[91] As in *Padfield's* case (paras 5–026 and 5–076, above). See G.D.S. Taylor [1976] C.L.J. 272.

[92] *Hanks v. Minister of Housing and Local Government* [1963] 1 Q.B. 999, 1018–1020, *per* Megaw J.; *cf. Meravale Builders Ltd v. Secretary of State for the Environment* (1978) 36 P. & C.R. 87. In practice the result of analysing a situation by reference to the effect of irrelevant considerations will often be the same as that produced by applying the 'dominant purpose' test (test (2), above). *Cf. Fawcett Properties Ltd v. Buckingham C.C.* [1958] 1 W.L.R. 1161, 1167–1168.

[93] See, *e.g. R. v. Inner London Education Authority, ex p. Westminster City Council* [1986] 1 W.L.R. 28 (advertising campaign for the purposes of: (a) information about rate-capping and (b) persuasion against it. Persuasion held an extraneous purpose which materially influenced the decision); *R. v. Lewisham L.B.C., ex p. Shell U.K. Ltd* [1983] 1 All E.R. 938 (boycott in order to induce Shell to sever its trading links with South Africa held 'substantial influence' on decision). See also *R. v. Ealing L.B.C., ex p. Times Newspapers Ltd* (1986) 85 L.G.R. 316.

(6) Would the decision-maker have reached the *same decision* if regard had only been had to the relevant considerations or to the authorised purposes? This is a subtle variation of the previous (material influence) test. It was applied when the Broadcasting Complaints Commission refused to investigate a complaint for a number of reasons, only one of which was bad (that the investigation would impose too great a burden on the Commission's limited staff). It was held that where the bad reason was not mixed and could be disentangled from the good, then the decision could stand if the Commission would have reached "precisely the same decision on the other valid reasons".[94] This test accords with the current French approach to the issue of plurality of purposes.

EXERCISE OF A DISCRETIONARY POWER ON IRRELEVANT GROUNDS OR WITHOUT REGARD TO RELEVANT CONSIDERATIONS

5–083 If the exercise of a discretionary power has been influenced by considerations that cannot lawfully be taken into account, or by the disregard of relevant considerations required to be taken into account, a court will normally hold that the power has not been validly exercised. It may be immaterial that an authority has considered irrelevant matters in arriving at its decision if it has not allowed itself to be influenced by those matters[95]; and it may be right to overlook a minor error of this kind even if it has affected an aspect of the decision.[96] The influence of extraneous matters will be manifest if they

---

[94] *R. v. Broadcasting Complaints Commission, ex p. Owen* [1985] Q.B. 1153. See also *R. v. Rochdale M.B.C., ex p. Cromer Ring Mill Ltd* [1982] 3 All E.R. 761 (misconceived guidelines 'substantially influenced' decision not to refund rates, despite good reasons which could not be disentangled).

[95] See *R. v. London (Bishop)* (1890) 24 QBD 213, 226–227 (*aff'd.* on grounds not identical, *sub nom. Allcroft v. Bishop of London* [1891] A.C. 666); *Ex p. Rice; Re Hawkins* (1957) 74 W.N. (N.S.W.) 7, 14; *Hanks v. Minister of Housing and Local Government* [1963] 1 Q.B. 999, 1018–1020; *Re Hurle-Hobbs' Decision* [1944] 1 All E.R. 249.

[96] *Hounslow L.B.C. v. Twickenham Garden Developments Ltd* [1971] Ch. 233, 271. In *R. v. Barnet & Camden Rent Tribunal, ex p. Frey Investments Ltd* [1972] 2 Q.B. 342 the Court of Appeal would have upheld the validity of a reference of private tenancies by a local authority to a rent tribunal even if relevant factors had been disregarded and irrelevant factors taken into account, provided that the reference was not arbitrary or capricious. See Note (1972) 35 M.L.R. 415. See also *Bristol D.C. v. Clark* [1975] 1 W.L.R. 1443, 1449–1450 (*per* Lawton L.J.); *Asher v. Secretary of State for the Environment* [1974] Ch. 208, 221, 227.

have led the authority to make an order that is invalid *ex facie*, or if the authority has set them out as reasons for its order[97] or has otherwise admitted their influence.

In cases where the reasons for the decision are not available, and there is no material either way to show by what considerations the authority was influenced, the court may determine whether their influence is to be inferred from the surrounding circumstances. In such cases the courts may infer either that an extraneous purpose was being pursued or that the exercise of discretion was unreasonable. The matter was succinctly put by Lord Keith, who said that where reasons for a decision were absent "and if all other known facts and circumstances appear to point overwhelmingly in favour of a different decision, the decision-maker ... cannot complain if the court draws the inference that he had no rational reason for his decision."[98]   **5–084**

If the influence of irrelevant factors is established, it does not appear   **5–085** to be necessary to prove that they were the sole or even the dominant influence. As a general rule it is enough to prove that their influence was material or substantial. For this reason there may be a practical advantage in founding a challenge to the validity of a discretionary act on the basis of irrelevant considerations rather than extraneous purpose, though the line of demarcation between the two grounds of invalidity is often imperceptible.[99]

If the ground of challenge is that relevant considerations have not   **5–086** been taken into account, the court will normally try to assess the actual or potential importance of the factor that was overlooked,[1] even though this may entail a degree of speculation. It will often be absurd for a court to hold that a discretion had been invalidly exercised because a trivial factor had been overlooked. But in some situations the validity of administrative action will be contingent on strict observance of antecedent requirements. In determining what factors may or must be taken into account by the competent authority, the courts are again faced with problems of statutory interpretation. If relevant factors are specified in the enabling Act it is for the courts to

---

[97] As in *Pilling v. Abergele U.D.C.* [1950] 1 K.B. 636.

[98] *Lonrho plc v. Secretary of State for Trade and Industry* [1989] 1 W.L.R. 525, 539. See also *R. v. Civil Service Appeal Board, ex p. Cunningham* [1991] 4 All E.R. 310 (where there was an absence of reasons for low compensation award and no reasons given inference made that decision irrational). See also *Padfield v. Minister of Agriculture, Fisheries and Food* [1968] A.C. 997, 1032–1033, 1049, 1053–1054, 1061–1062 (*per* Lords Reid, Hodson, Pearce and Upjohn).

[99] As in *Marshall v. Blackpool Corp.* [1935] A.C. 16 and *Padfield's* case (n.13 below). See also *R. v. Rochdale M.B.C., ex p. Cromer Ring Mill Ltd* [1992] 2 All E.R. 761. And compare the discussion above, paras 5–082 and 5–083 *et seq.*

[1] See *R. v. London (Bishop)* (1890) 24 QBD at 266–227, 237, 244; *Baldwin & Francis Ltd v. Patents Appeal Tribunal* [1959] A.C. 663, 693, *per* Lord Denning; dicta in *R. v. Paddington Valuation Officer, ex p. Peachey Property Corp. Ltd* [1966] 1 Q.B. 380.

determine whether they are factors to which the authority is compelled to have regard[2] and, if so, whether they are to be construed as being exhaustive. This question arose in a case where members of the Labour Party challenged the recommendations of the Boundary Commission.[3] The Commission was under a duty to make recommendations to the Home Secretary about the boundaries of parliamentary constituencies (though the final decision rests with Parliament).[4] The statute set out a series of rules to which the Commission were required to give effect. These included the requirements (a) that "so far as practicable" the constituencies are not to cross London borough boundaries and (b) that the electorate shall be as near to the "electoral quota" as possible.[5] If it appeared, however, that it was desirable to avoid an "excessive disparity" between the electoral quota and the actual electorate of any constituency, the Commission had a discretion to take (c) "geographical considerations" into account.[6] The Commission were also permitted to take account, in so far as they reasonably could, of (d) "inconvenience attendant on alterations of constituencies and of any local ties broken by such alterations."[7] The applicants considered that the Commission had laid undue emphasis on the requirement of not crossing local boundaries and insufficient emphasis on the requirement of achieving equality of numbers in the electorates of their constituents. It was held that although the Acts set out requirements to which the Commission had to have regard, the burden on the applicants of showing that the commission had exercised their powers wrongly was heavy as the rules themselves were no more than guidelines. Despite the wide disparity in some constituency boundaries, there was no evidence that the Commission had misunderstood or ignored Parliament's instructions.

5–087   If the relevant factors are not specified (*e.g.* if the power is merely to grant or refuse a licence, or to attach such conditions as the competent authority thinks fit), it is for the courts to determine whether the permissible considerations are impliedly restricted, and, if so, to what extent,[8] although when the courts conclude that a wide range of

---

[2] See *Yorkshire Copper Works Ltd v. Registrar of Trade Marks* [1954] 1 W.L.R. 554, where the House of Lords held that the Registrar was bound to have regard to specific factors to which he was prima facie empowered to have regard. See *R. v. Shadow Education Committee of Greenwich B.C., ex p. Governors of John Ball Primary School* (1989) 88 L.G.R. 589 (failure to have regard to parental preferences).

[3] *R. v. Boundary Commission for England, ex p. Foot* [1983] 1 Q.B 600, CA.

[4] House of Commons (Redistribution of Seats) Act 1949, s.2(1)(a).

[5] Rules 4(1) and 5 set out in Sched. 2 to the Act.

[6] *ibid.*, rr. 4 and 5.

[7] House of Commons (Redistribution of Seats) Act 1958, s.2(2).

[8] See generally paras 5-027–5-029.

factors may properly be considered, they will be reluctant to lay down a list with which the authority will be required to comply in every case.[9]

It is now open to a court when granting certiorari to remit the   **5–088** matter to the authority with a direction to reconsider and to decide in accordance with the findings of the court.[10] Apart from this, the role of the courts is limited to ensuring that discretion has been exercised according to law.[11] If, therefore, a party aggrieved by the exercise of discretionary power seeks an order of mandamus to compel the authority to determine the matter on the basis of legally relevant considerations, the proper form of the mandamus will be one to hear and determine according to law[12]; though by holding inadmissible the considerations on which the original decision was based, the court may indirectly indicate the particular manner in which the discretion ought to be exercised.[13]

Examples of discretionary powers having been unlawfully exercised   **5–089** on legally irrelevant grounds are multitudinous. Many of the earlier cases are concerned with magistrates refusing to issue summonses for extraneous reasons,[14] or failing to consider relevant factors before ordering a surety to forfeit a recognisance,[15] with tribunals improperly

---

[9] *e.g. Elliott v. Southwark L.B.C.* [1976] 1 W.L.R. 499, 507. In *Bristol D.C. v. Clark* [1975] 1 W.L.R. 1443, the court looked for guidance on the factors relevant to the exercise of a statutory discretion to a departmental circular issued after the enactment of the legislation.

[10] RSC, Ord. 53, r. 9(4). (See Civil Procedure Rules, Sched. 1).

[11] See, *e.g. Smith v. Chorley U.D.C.* [1897] 1 Q.B. 678, 680–681; *R. v. L.C.C.* [1915] 2 K.B. 466; *R. v. Brighton Corp.* (1916) 85 L.J.K.B. 1552, 1555–1556; *Roberts v. Hopwood* [1925] A.C. 578, 606; *Short v. Poole Corp.* [1926] Ch. 66; *Att.-Gen. v. Manchester Corp.* [1931] 1 Ch. 254, 270; *Dormer v. Newcastle-upon-Tyne Corp.* [1940] 2 K.B. 204, 218; *Associated Provincial Picture Houses Ltd v. Wednesbury Corp.* [1948] 1 K.B. 223; *Fraser (D.R.) & Co. v. Minister of National Revenue* [1949] A.C. 24, 36.

[12] *cf. R. v. Kingston JJ., ex p. Davey* (1902) 86 L.T. 589.

[13] *cf.* in a slightly different context, *R. v. Manchester JJ.* [1899] 1 Q.B. 571, 576. See also *R. v. Flintshire C.C. County Licensing (Stage Plays) Committee* [1957] 1 Q.B. 350; *Padfield v. Minister of Agriculture, Fisheries and Food* [1968] A.C. 997. If the statutory conditions needed to obtain a permit or licence have been complied with, but the competent authority refuses the application on irrelevant grounds or attaches invalid conditions to the permit, the court will sometimes award mandamus to grant the application though strictly mandamus to hear and determine according to law is the correct order unless the authority has no discretion at all once the conditions precedent have been fulfilled: *R. v. London (City of) Licensing JJ., ex p. Stewart* [1954] 1 W.L.R. 1325.

[14] *R. v. Adamson* (1875) 1 QBD 201; *R. v. Boteler* (1864) 33 L.J.M.C. 101; *R. v. Mead, ex p. National Health Insurance Commrs* (1916) 85 L.J.K.B. 1065 (refusals based on disapproval of conduct of complainants or of the policy or application of the legislation concerned); *R. v. Bennett and Bond* (1908) 72 J.P. 362; *R. v. Nuneaton Borough JJ.* [1954] 1 W.L.R. 1318 (refusal on ground that other proceedings more appropriate).

[15] *e.g. R. v. Southampton JJ., ex p. Green* [1976] Q.B. 11; *R. v. Horseferry Road Stipendiary Magistrate, ex p. Pearson* [1976] 1 W.L.R. 511.

refusing or agreeing to adjourn proceedings before them,[16] and with licensing justices refusing applications,[17] granting them subject to irrelevant conditions,[18] or even granting them unconditionally on irrelevant grounds.[19] There are decisions on the unlawful expenditure of public funds by local authorities,[20] and a miscellany of decisions which illustrate the general rule in a wide range of contexts.[21]

5–090   As we have seen, the interpretation of statutory purpose and that of the relevancy of considerations are closely related, since the question in regard to the considerations taken into account in reaching a decision is normally whether that consideration is relevant to the statutory purpose. This is seen in respect of the considerations taken into account by planning authorities as a basis of a refusal of planning permission. Is it relevant to refuse an application for permission to change the use on the site from use A to use B on the ground that the authority wishes to preserve the use of site as A (and have no inherent objection to use B)? It has been held that the preservation of an existing use may be a material planning consideration, but only if, on the balance of probabilities, there is a fair chance of use A being continued.[22] Where, however, the authority wished to retain the existing use so that it could be kept in their own occupation, it was held that that consideration was not a legitimate planning consideration.[23] Other disputed considerations in the area of planning law involve the regard that has been had to factors such as precedent

---

[16] On the question whether a tribunal is entitled to adjourn a matter because a change in the law is pending, see *R. v. Whiteway, ex p. Stephenson* [1961] V.R. 168, 171; *Boyd Builders Ltd v. Ottawa* (1964) 45 D.L.R. (2d) 211 (adjournment improper); but the position may be different if the change in the law is imminent and reasonably certain; *cf. Clifford Sabey (Contractors) Ltd v. Long* [1959] 2 Q.B. 290, 298–300. For non-judicial exercise of discretion to postpone operation of demolition order, see *Pocklington v. Melksham U.D.C.* [1964] 2 Q.B. 673. See also *Royal v. Prescott-Clarke* [1966] 1 W.L.R. 788; *Walker v. Walker* [1967] 1 W.L.R. 327.

[17] *e.g. R. v. de Rutzen* (1875) 1 QBD 55.

[18] *e.g. R. v. Bowman* [1898] 1 Q.B. 663. See also *R. v. Birmingham Licensing Planning Committee, ex p. Kennedy* [1972] 2 Q.B. 140 (refusal to allow application to proceed unless irrelevant condition complied with); see too *Fletcher v. London (Metropolis) Licensing Committee* [1976] A.C. 150.

[19] *e.g. R. v. Cotham* [1898] 1 Q.B. 802.

[20] *Att.-Gen. v. Tynemouth Poor Law Union Guardians* [1930] 1 Ch. 616; *Roberts v. Hopwood* [1925] A.C. 578; *Prescott v. Birmingham Corp.* [1955] Ch. 210; *Taylor v. Munrow* [1960] 1 W.L.R. 151.

[21] See, *e.g. Padfield's* case (para. 5–026 above); and many of the cases on improper purpose (para. 5–068 *et seq.*, above).

[22] *Westminster City Council v. British Waterways Board* [1985] A.C. 676: *London Residuary Body v. Lambeth L.B.C.* [1990] 1 W.L.R. 744. See also *Clyde & Co. v. Secretary of State for the Environment* [1977] 1 W.L.R. 926 (desirability of maintaining the possibility that land would be used to relieve housing shortage a material consideration); *cf. Granada Theatres Ltd v. Secretary of State for the Environment* [1976] J.P.L. 96.

[23] *per* Lord Bridge in *Westminster City Council v. British Waterways Board*, n.22 above.

(it has been held that permission may be refused because it would be difficult to resist similar applications in the future)[24]; to the fact that alternative sites would be more appropriate for the development, or to the personal circumstances of the applicant.

Where a university, after consultation with the police, refused to   **5–091** permit a meeting on its premises addressed by members of the South African Embassy during the apartheid regime, it did so in the belief that the meeting would provoke public violence in the neighbouring area. The statute required universities to ensure that freedom of speech was secured and that the use of university premises was not denied to any individual body on the ground of their beliefs, policy or objectives. It was held that in taking into account the likelihood of violence outside of their premises the decision had been influenced by an irrelevant consideration and was therefore *ultra vires*.[25] The action of a local trading standards officer was held to have been unlawful when, three days after a children's toy was found to have been dangerous, he suspended the manufacturer from supplying the toy for six months. He claimed to have had regard to a regulation which would have permitted the suspension, but which was not yet in force. The court held that consideration to be irrelevant.[26] Where a statute gave the power to the minister to licence medicines for importation into the United Kingdom when it was "expedient" to do so, it was held that his taking into account of trade mark (private) rights was a consideration irrelevant to the public law powers in the circumstances of that case.[27]

Financial considerations

A number of cases have reviewed the question of the relevance of the   **5–092** level of expenditure undertaken by an authority—the excessive cost of a project, or its failure to devote sufficient resources to a project. The cases show that it is not possible in the abstract to say whether financial considerations are relevant to the particular decision; it all depends on the nature of the power, and the context in which it is exercised.

---

[24] *Collis Radio Ltd v. Secretary of State for the Environment* (1975) 29 P. & C.R. 390.

[25] *R. v. Liverpool University, ex p. Caesar Gordon* [1991] 1 Q.B. 124. See also *R. v. Coventry Airport and ors., ex p. Phoenix Aviation and ors.,* [1995] 3 All E.R. & 37, DC (unlawful surrender to the dictates of pressure groups opposed to the export of live animals). But see *R. v. Chief Constable of Sussex ex p. International Traders Ferry* [1998] 3 W.L.R. 1260.

[26] *R. v. Birmingham C.C., ex p. Ferrero Ltd* (1991) 3 Admin. L.R. 613.

[27] *R. v. Secretary of State for Social Services, ex p. Wellcome Foundation* [1987] 2 All E.R. 1025.

5–093 First, there are cases challenging an authority's decision not to undertake expenditure on the ground of excessive cost. In one such case a company had overpaid rates to a local authority. The local authority claimed unfettered discretion whether to refund the rates and was reluctant to do so because of its own poor financial situation and the adverse effect of the expenditure on the situation of the ratepayers. It was held that, in the circumstances, the authority should, as a prime consideration, have had regard to the unfairness to the company, a consideration which had been ignored in favour of the financial considerations which were not relevant.[28] In the context of a different statutory scheme, however, it was held that delay in processing claims for social security benefit could be excused by the lack of sufficient funds or resources, although it was also said that the manifest misallocation of funds could render a decision unreasonable.[29] When the Broadcasting Complaints Commission

---

[28] *Tower Hamlets L.B.C. v. Chetnik Developments Ltd* [1988] A.C. 858. See also *R. v. Rochdale M.B.C., ex p. Cromer Ring Mill Ltd* [1982] 3 All E.R. 761.

[29] *R. v. Secretary of State for Social Services, ex p. Child Poverty Action Group* [1990] 2 Q.B. 570, CA. And see *R. v. Secretary of State for Social Services, ex p. Child Poverty Action Group, The Times,* August 8, 1985, CA where although (as had been held at first instance) local staff of the Social Security Inspectorate were not carrying out certain procedures correctly so that some 1,600 claimants did not receive refunds to which they were entitled, s.27(1) of the Supplementary Benefits Act 1976 did not impose a mandatory duty to every individual case, but only to provide 'workable administrative arrangements'. The question of the relevance of resources has been decided in a large number of cases. Cases where resources were held to be relevant considerations were: *R. v. Gloucestershire C.C., ex p. Barry* [1997] A.C. 584 (duty to assess need for care arrangements made under Chronically Sick and Disabled Persons Act 1970, s.2. Financial resources may lawfully be taken into account in determining whether the obligation exists at all). This case was followed in *R. v. East Sussex CC ex p. Tandy* [1997] 3 W.L.R. 884. See also *R. v. Southwark L.B.C., ex p. Udu* (1996) 8 Admin. L.R. 25 (policy of refusing grants to courses at private colleges, including the College of Law. Held: the Local Authority was a political body with limited funds, and it was entitled to have policies and to decide how to allocate those funds). *R. v. Chief Constable of Sussex, ex p. International Trader's Ferry* [1998] 3 W.L.R. 1260 (a Chief Constable's decision to provide policing on only two days a week to protect the transport of livestock where animal rights' protestors were demonstrating was reasonable under domestic and E.C. law because of restraints on resources); *R. v. Registered Homes Tribunal, ex p. Hertfordshire C.C., The Times,* February 28, 1996 (financial considerations relevant to the registration of homes). Cases where resources were held not relevant were: *R. v. Sefton MBC ex p. Help the Aged* [1997] 4 All E.R. 532, CA (lack of financial resources does not entitle a local authority to defer compliance with their duty under section 2 of the Chronically Sick and Disabled Persons Act 1970); *R. v. Cheshire C.C., ex p. C, The Times,* August 8, 1996 (the decision about special educational needs should be made on purely educational grounds without reference to financial considerations); Case C-44/95, *R. v. Secretary of State for the Environment, ex p. RSPB* [1997] Q.B. 206. (On Art. 234 reference from House of Lords), ECJ held that economic considerations are not relevant to determining wild bird protection areas under Directive 79/409; *R. v.*

decided not to investigate a complaint on the ground that to do so would be burdensome and perhaps require the employment of additional staff, this was held not to be a good reason.[30] In a recent case, Parliament had enacted a statute to implement a new criminal injuries compensation scheme. The statute conferred upon the Home Secretary discretion as to when to bring the new scheme into effect. Before implementing the new scheme, the Home Secretary sought to introduce, under his prerogative powers (by means of which the previous scheme had been administered), a scheme different from that envisaged by the legislation. The House of Lords held that the courts should "hesitate long" before holding the Home Secretary under a duty to implement the scheme contemplated by the statute. However, he did not have absolute and unfettered discretion not to do so. The cost of implementing the statutory scheme was a factor relevant to his decision as to when the new scheme might be implemented. But he could not frustrate the statutory purpose by introducing a scheme inconsistent with that approved by Parliament.[31]

At the other extreme are cases where an authority's expenditure has been challenged for being excessive.[32] The attempt of the Poplar

5–094

Secretary of State for the Environment, ex p. Kingston-Upon-Hull City Council [1996] C.O.D. 289 (the cost of the treatment of waste water was not a relevant consideration); but see *R. v. National Rivers Authority, ex p. Moreton* [1996] Env. L.R. D17 (investment budget relevant to decision of NRA to allow discharge); *R. v. Hillingdon L.B.C., ex p. Governing Body of Queensmead School* [1997] E.L.R. 331 (Collins J. held that budgetary constraints and lack of funds could play no part in the assessment of a child's special educational needs); *R. v. Social Fund Inspector, ex p. Taylor* [1998] C.O.D. 152. It is important in the above cases to note that under any given statutory scheme a distinction is often made between (a) determining whether a person's need exists and (b) whether that need can be satisfied within available resources. Normally (depending upon the statutory scheme) need should be initially determined without regard to resources.

[30] *R. v. Broadcasting Complaints Commission, ex p. Owen* [1985] Q.B. 1153.

[31] *R. v. Secretary of State for the Home Department, ex p. Fire Brigades Union* [1995] 2 A.C. 583. *Cf. R. v. Blackledge* (1995) 92 L.S.G. 32 (prosecutions made under orders made pursuant to a statute contemplating their existence only for the period of the 'emergency' (following the declaration of war in 1939) not *ultra vires*). See also *Willcock v. Muckle* [1951] 2 K.B. 844.

[32] An education authority is not obliged to provide a child with free transport to a school of his parents' choice irrespective of the distance involved *R. v. Essex C.C., ex p. C., The Times,* December 9, 1993, 1 F.C.R. 773, CA. See also *R. v. Dyfed C.C., ex p. S* [1995] 1 F.C.R. 113, CA; *R. v. Secretary of State for the Home Department, ex p. Wynne* [1992] Q.B. 406, CA (ability of prisoner to pay full cost not relevant to decision whether to allow production in court); *R. v. Legal Aid Committee No. 10 (East Midlands), ex p. McKenna* (1990) 2 Admin.L.R. 585 (cost of litigation irrelevant to legal aid). On a related question of cost, see *R. v. Highgate JJ., ex p. Petrou* [1954] 1 W.L.R. 485 (power to award cost does not give power to impose a fine). In *R. v. Secretary of State for Health, ex p. Keen* (1991) 3 Admin. L.R. 180 it was held lawful for resources to be allocated in anticipation of a new scheme proposed in a Parliamentary Bill (provided the authority's discretion was not fettered).

Borough Council in 1925 to raise the wages and salaries of its employees, and to pay women employees rates equal to that of men, was held contrary to law. The House of Lords in that case came close to holding that expenditure unreasonable,[33] but the *ratio decidendi* was based upon the view that the amounts paid were at a time of falling cost of living, more in the nature of a gratuity than the wages and salaries which the authority was authorised to pay.[34] In 1983 the question of local authority expenditure arose again in respect of the decision of the Greater London Council to reduce transport fares by 25 per cent.[35] The fare cuts would have lost the council approximately £50 million of the rate support grant which they would otherwise have been entitled to receive from the central government sources. Although the governing statute gave wide discretion to promote the provision of "integrated, efficient and economic transport facilities",[36] it also required the authorities[37] to make up any deficit incurred in one accounting period in the next such period.[38] This provision was held to limit the authorities' discretion and subject them to a duty to run the system on ordinary business principles, which the drastic reductions in the fares contravened.[39]

5–095   The courts have, from time to time, invoked the principle that local authorities owe an implied "fiduciary duty" to their ratepayers. The breach of such a duty has rarely formed the *ratio* of a decision to strike down the expenditure concerned.[40] The fiduciary duty could be interpreted in two ways: First, it could imply a duty to act on ordinary business principles and not to be "thriftless"[41] with ratepayers' money. Such a meaning of the fiduciary duty comes close to permitting the courts themselves to decide the levels of expenditure which meet those standards. As the House of Lords has reminded us in a different

---

[33] *Roberts v. Hopwood* [1925] A.C. 578.

[34] A point made by Ormrod L.J. in *Pickwell v. Camden L.B.C.* [1983] Q.B. 962. See also Sir David Williams, 'Law and Administrative Discretion' (1994) Indiana J. of Global Legal Studies 191. For a consideration of the 'fiduciary principle' raised in *Roberts v. Hopwood* and other cases, see Chap. 12, paras 12-065–12-064 below. See also *Prescott v. Birmingham Corp.* [1955] Ch. 210; *Taylor v. Monrou* [1960] 1 W.L.R. 151.

[35] *Bromley L.B.C. v. Greater London Council* [1983] 1 A.C. 768.

[36] Section 1 of the Transport (London) Act 1969.

[37] The Greater London Council and the London Transport Executive.

[38] Transport (London) Act 1969, s.7(3)(b).

[39] A subsequent scheme, known as the 'balanced fare scheme' was held to be lawful. *R. v. London Transport Executive, ex p. Greater London Council* [1983] Q.B. 484.

[40] e.g. in *Roberts v. Hopwood* (n.33 above), or *Bromley L.B.C. v. G.L.C.* (n.35 above). Both these cases were decided on the basis of 'illegality'. See also *Re Westminster City Council* [1986] A.C. 668 (grants by G.L.C. unlawful but not unreasonable). But see *Prescott v. Birmingham*, n.34 above.

[41] *per* Lord Diplock in *Bromley L.B.C. v. G.L.C.*, n.35 above at 899; *cf. Hazell v. Hammersmith and Fulham L.B.C.* [1992] 2 A.C. 1, where Lord Templeman referred to the duty of the local authority to be 'prudent' with ratepayers' money (at 37).

context, courts are not, in judicial review, equipped to make such decisions.[42] A second interpretation views the fiduciary duty as a duty to take into account, in reaching a decision on expenditure, the interests of the ratepayers.[43] Since the ratepayers' interests are likely to be adversely affected by a decision to increase expenditure, it is surely right that those interests should be considered by the local authority (although not necessarily slavishly followed). This second meaning of the fiduciary duty does not involve the courts in a function to which, in judicial review, they are unsuited. It merely involves them in requiring that considerations which are relevant to the local authority's powers, namely, the interests of the ratepayers, be taken into account. This function is perfectly suited to judicial review.

In the *Bromley* case, a further question concerned the relevance to   **5–096** the decision of the council's so-called "mandate". It was argued that the promise to reduce transport fares was the major part of the manifesto on which the new ruling party had fought the recent election. The House of Lords clearly held, however, that a so-called mandate from the electorate can have no influence on the *legality* of a decision, which must fulfil the purposes authorised by the statute which governs the power in question.[44]

Planning cases show how financial considerations may be relevant   **5–097** or irrelevant, depending upon the different context in which the decision is made. The question of whether cost is a "material consideration" has arisen in a number of contexts. It has been held that the likelihood that a development would, because of its excessive cost, never be implemented, may be a material consideration in refusing planning permission.[45] Yet the question of whether a development was a good investment proposition for the developer was held not to be material.[46] The refusal of planning permission

---

[42] *R. v. Secretary of State for the Environment, ex p. Hammersmith and Fulham L.B.C.* [1991] 1 A.C. 521. Per Lord Bridge, at least in relation to unreasonableness. See the discussion on justiciability, paras 5–029–5–034 above. And see Chap. 12 below, paras 12–053–12–056. See also *Pickwell v. Camden* (n.34 above) where Ormrod L.J. said levels of expenditure were best left to the decision of the electors rather than the courts.

[43] Today, commercial ratepayers and domestic council taxpayers.

[44] Compare the influence of the mandate upon the *reasonableness* of a decision, discussed in Chap. 12, para. 12–063, below. And *cf. R. v. Merseyside C.C. ex p. Great Universal Stores Ltd.* (1982) 80 L.G.R. 639. In New Zealand there is a line of cases in which the fiduciary concept has been applied: see *Lovelock v. Waitakere City Council* [1996] 3 N.Z.L.R. 310.

[45] *Sovmots Investments Ltd v. Secretary of State for the Environment* [1979] A.C. 144.

[46] *Murphy (J.) & Sons Ltd v. Secretary of State for the Environment* [1973] 1 W.L.R. 560; *Walters v. Secretary of State for Wales* [1979] J.P.L. 171 (cost of development not a material planning consideration); but see *Sovmots Investments Ltd v. Secretary of State for the Environment* [1977] Q.B. 411, 422–425; *Hambledon and Chiddingfold P.C. v. Secretary of State for the Environment* [1976] J.P.L. 502; *Niarches (London) Ltd v. Secretary of State for the Environment* (1978) 35 P. & C.R. 259). On the relevance of cost to the making of a compulsory purchase order under the Housing Act 1957, Pt III, see

because of the absence in the proposal of any "planning gain" (a benefit by means of a material contribution to the authority) has also been held to be a non-material consideration.[47] On the other hand, in a case where the Directors of the Covent Garden opera house sought planning permission for an office development near its site, the Court of Appeal held that the fact that the profits from the development would be devoted to improving the facilities of the opera house was a consideration that could properly be taken into account in deciding whether to grant permission for the office development.[48]

Government policy as a relevant consideration

5–098 In a number of cases the question has arisen of whether regard may or must be had to various forms of government advice or indication of government policy. Normally such policy will be expressed through a government circular which lacks statutory force.[49] A number of questions may arise in respect of non-statutory guidance which are addressed elsewhere in this work, such as their possible effect in creating legitimate expectations,[50] or whether their effect is to fetter the decision-maker's discretion.[51] The question has also arisen as to whether or not a circular may amount to an authoritative account of the law at all, and thus be subject to judicial review.[52]

---

[47] *Eckersley v. Secretary of State for the Environment* (1977) 34 P. & C.R. 124. See further, Michael Purdue [1979] J.P.L. 146.

[47] *Westminster Renslade Ltd v. Secretary of State for the Environment* [1983] J.P.L. 454.

[48] *R. v. Westminster City Council, ex p. Monahan* [1990] 1 Q.B. 87, although it was doubted whether such a consideration would be material or relevant if the benefit was not in physical proximity to the development (*e.g.* if the benefit was in the form of a swimming pool at the other end of the town). For the use of planning obligations (formerly planning agreements) to achieve this kind of benefit, see para. 5–036 above. *Cf. R. v. Camden L.B.C., ex p. Cram and Ors, The Times,* January 25, 1995 (it was relevant for Council to seek to make a profit from a car parking scheme).

[49] See R. Baldwin and J. Houghton, 'Circular Arguments: The Status and Legitimacy of Administrative Rules', [1986] P.L. 239; G. Ganz, *Quasi-legislation* (1986). For the distinction between direction and guidance see *Laker Airways v. Department of Trade* [1977] Q.B. 643, 714. See also *R. v. Secretary of State for Social Services and the Social Fund Inspector, ex p. Stitt* (1992) 4 Admin. L.R. 713. And for what constitutes 'policy', see further para. 12–028 below.

[50] See Chap. 12 below, para. 12–033. See also para. 12–015.

[51] See Chap. 10 below.

[52] See *Gillick v. West Norfolk & Wisbech Area Health Authority* [1986] A.C. 112. Lord Bridge *dubitante*: in appropriate circumstances a misleading or manifestly inaccurate circular may be reviewed. But see *R. v. Secretary of State for the Environment, ex p. Greenwich L.B.C.* [1989] C.O.D. 530, where the applicants sought judicial review to prohibit the distribution by the Secretary of State for the Environment of a leaflet on the community charge. The application was refused on the ground that the document, although perhaps misleading by omission, was not literally inaccurate.

To what extent can a failure to have regard to a government non-statutory policy invalidate a decision for disregard of a material consideration? A local authority is entitled to ignore or act contrary to a policy circular which misstates the law.[53] On the other hand, circulars or Planning Policy Guidance Notes issued by the Department of the Environment, although only advisory in nature, have been held to be material planning considerations to which regard must be had by both local authorities and the Secretary of State in making decisions about development control.[54] Yet policy cannot make a matter which is otherwise a material consideration an irrelevant consideration or vice versa. However, if the decision-maker departs from the policy, clear reasons for doing so must be provided, in order that the recipient of the decision will know why the decision is made as an exception to the policy and the grounds upon which the decision is taken.[55]

5–099

PARTIAL ILLEGALITY AND SEVERANCE

What if an act or decision is partly legal and partly illegal? Suppose that a tribunal has power to revoke occupational licences. It revokes X's licence, and proceeds to order that he shall be disqualified from applying for a new licence for five years. It has no power to impose such a disqualification. In this case, X will be able to obtain an order of certiorari to quash the five-year disqualification, or a declaration that the disqualification is void; but the court can still hold that the revocation of his licence is valid, for the two limbs of the tribunal's order are severable from one another.

5–100

Cases of partial invalidity are often more complicated than this because the good and the bad elements are not clearly distinct. The

5–101

---

[53] *R. v. Secretary of State for the Environment, ex p. Tower Hamlets L.B.C.* [1993] Q.B. 632 (Code of Guidance to Local Authorities on Homelessness by Department of the Environment held to misstate the law). See also *R. v. Secretary of State for the Environment, ex p. Lancashire C.C.* [1994] 4 All E.R. 165 (policy guidance issued to local government Commissioners to replace their authorities with unitary authorities held more in the nature of directions than guidance and therefore unlawful).

[54] A policy need not normally have been promulgated in any particular way, but after-dinner speeches do not qualify: *Dinsdale Developments Ltd. v. Secretary of State for the Environment* [1986] J.P.L. 276. Draft policy statements may qualify: *Richmond-upon-Thames L.B.C. v. Secretary of State for the Environment* [1984] J.P.L. 24; but may not: *Pye J.A. (Oxford) Estates Ltd. v. Secretary of State for the Environment* [1982] J.P.L. 577.

[55] *E.C. Gransden & Co. Ltd v. Secretary of State for the Environment* (1987) 54 P. & C.R. 86. See also *Carpets of Worth Ltd v. Wye Forest D.C.* (1991) 62 P. & C.R. 334. For application of these principles outside of planning law, in relation to police negotiating machinery, see *R. v. Secretary of State for the Home Department, ex p. Lancashire Police Authority* [1992] C.O.D. 161. For a further discussion see paras 10-009–10-013 below. For prosecutorial policy see para. 5–043 above.

typical problem in this area of the law arises where a permit or licence has been granted subject to void conditions. Three approaches may be followed by the court, assuming that the jurisdiction of the court (*e.g.* to enter in an appeal against the conditions alone) has not been demarcated by statute. First, it may set aside the entire decision because the competent authority might well have been unwilling to grant unconditional permission; the applicant must therefore start again.[56] Secondly, it may simply sever the bad from the good. In such a case the effect will be to give unconditional permission if all the conditions are struck down, and this may frustrate the intentions of the competent authority.[57] Thirdly, the court may adopt an intermediate position, and sever the invalid condition only if it is trivial, or if it is quite extraneous to the subject-matter of the grant, or perhaps if there are other reasons for supposing that the authority would still have granted permission had it believed that the conditions might be invalid. This approach has recommended itself to the House of Lords in a case involving the validity of planning conditions.[58] But it involves the courts in a speculative attribution of intent to an administrative body. Until recently, it was difficult to elicit any clear principle from the cases on partly invalid byelaws, though the courts had fewer compunctions about striking out only the invalid words if the character of what remained was unaltered by a decision to sever the bad from the good.[59] In *DPP v.* Hutchinson,[60] the House of Lords considered the validity of byelaws prohibiting entry onto the Greenham Common where there were military installations. The

---

[56] As in *Hall & Co. v. Shoreham-by-Sea U.D.C.* [1964] 1 W.L.R. 240. *Pyx Granite Co. v. Ministry of Housing and Local Government* [1958] 1 Q.B. 554, 578–579, *per* Hodson L.J.; *R. v. Hillingdon L.B.C., ex p. Royco Homes Ltd* [1974] Q.B. 720.

[57] Nevertheless, this course has been adopted in a number of cases; see. *e.g. Ellis v. Dubowski* [1921] 3 K.B. 621 (though this was a prosecution for breach of a invalid condition and the question of severability did not directly arise); *Mixnam's Properties Ltd v. Chertsey U.D.C.* [1965] A.C., 735; *Hartnell v. Minister of Housing and Local Government* [1965] A.C. 1134. See also *Lowe (David) & Sons Ltd v. Provost, etc. of Burgh of Musselburgh.* 1974 S.L.T. 5.

[58] *Kingsway Investments (Kent) Ltd v. Kent C.C.* [1971] A.C. 72, 90–91, 102–103, 112–114; though *cf.* [1971] A.C. 106–107, *per* Guest L.J. See also *Allnatt London Properties Ltd v. Middlesex C.C.* (1964) 62 L.G.R. 304. A similar approach was recently adopted in *Transport Ministry v. Alexander* [1978] 1 N.Z.L.R. 306, 311–312 (invalid part severable because it was 'not fundamental or part of the structure of the regulation').

[59] See generally, *Potato Marketing Board v. Merricks* [1958] 2 Q.B. 316, 333, *per* Devlin J. (a case of a partly unauthorised demand for information under the threat of a penalty). The cases on byelaws are generally unhelpful. See, *e.g. R. v. Lundie* (1862) 31 L.J.M.C. 157; *Reay v. Gateshead Corp.* (1886) 55 L.T. 92, 103; *Strickland v. Hayes* [1896] 1 Q.B. 290, 292; *Rossi v. Edinburgh Corp.* [1905] A.C., 21: *Craies on Statute Law* (7th ed.), 336. There is a better discussion of principle in *Olsen v. City of Camberwell* [1926] V.L.R. 58.

[60] [1990] 2 A.C. 783. See A.W. Bradley 'Judicial Enforcement of *Ultra Vires* Byelaws: The Proper Scope of Severance' [1990] P.L. 293.

enabling legislation permitted such byelaws to be made, provided that rights of common were not interfered with. The appellants claimed that the byelaws did interfere with the rights of common and this contention was upheld. Could the bad parts of the byelaw be severed from the good? The House of Lords considered whether, in order to be severable, the test was that of "textual severability" or "substantial severability" If textual severability was the correct test, then the bad part of the instrument could be disregarded as exceeding the lawmaker's power, provided what remained was still "grammatical and coherent".[61] If, however, the proper test was that of substantial severability, then what remained after severance could survive as lawful provided that is was "essentially unchanged in its legislative purpose, operation and effect."[62] The majority of their Lordships accepted the test of "substantial severability" and it was held that this could be achieved in the following two situations:

(1) Where the text could be severed so that the valid part could operate independently of the invalid part, then the test of substantial severability would be satisfied when the valid part is unaffected by, and independent of, the invalid part.

(2) Where severance could only be effected by modifying the text, this can only be done "when the court is satisfied that it is effecting no change in the substantial purpose and effect of the impugned provision".[63]

---

[61] Sometimes called the 'blue pencil test'. See *R. v. Company of Fisherman of Faversham* (1799) 8 Dwrn & E. 352, 356.

[62] As applied in *Dunkley v. Evans* [1981] 1 W.L.R. 1522. See also *Daymond v. Plymouth City Council* [1976] A.C. 609. See also the Australian approach followed in *R. v. Commonwealth Court of Conciliation and Arbitration, ex p. Whybrow and Co.* (1910) 11 C.L.R. 1.

[63] *per* Lord Bridge at 811. But see Lord Lowry, dissenting, at 819: 'To liberalise the [severance] test would be anarchic, not progressive'. For a recent example of the severance of an invalid part of a statutory instrument (void for unreasonableness) under situation (1) above, see *R. v. Immigration Appeal. Tribunal, ex p. Begum Manshoora* [1986] Imm. A.R. 385. Cf. *R. v. Inland Revenue Commissioners, ex p. Woolwich Equitable Building Society* [1990] 1 W.L.R. 1400, HL (alteration of substance by textual severance too great); *R. v. North Hertfordshire D.C., ex p. Cobbold* [1985] 3 All E.R. 486 (unreasonable conditions attached to license for pop concert. Severance would alter whole character of licence). See also *Mouchell Superannuation Fund Trustees v. Oxfordshire C.C.* [1992] 1 P.L.R. 97, CA.

DELEGATION OF POWERS

The rule against delegation

5–102   A discretionary power must, in general, be exercised only by the authority to which it has been committed. It is a well-known principle of law that when a power has been confided to a person in circumstances indicating that trust is being placed in his individual judgment and discretion, he must exercise that power personally unless he has been expressly empowered to delegate it to another. This principle, which has often been applied in the law of agency, trusts and arbitration as well as in public law, is expressed in the form of the maxim *delegatus non potest delegare* (or *delegan*), a maxim which, it has been suggested, "owes its origin to medieval commentators on the Digest and the Decretals, and its vogue in the common law to the carelessness of a sixteenth-century printer".[64] The former assumption that it applies only to the sub-delegation of delegated legislative powers and to the sub-delegation of other powers delegated by a superior administrative authority is unfounded. It applies to the delegation of all classes of powers, and it was indeed originally invoked in the context of delegation of judicial powers. It is therefore convenient to travel beyond the delegation of discretionary powers in the strict sense and to view the problem as a whole.

5–103   The cases on delegation have arisen in diverse contexts, and many of them turn upon unique points of statutory interpretation. The terminology of the judgments is not always consistent. The maxim *delegatus non potest delegare* does not enunciate a rule that knows no exception; it is a rule of construction which makes the presumption that "a discretion conferred by statute is prima facie intended to be exercised by the authority on which the statute has conferred it and by no other authority, but this presumption may be rebutted by any contrary indications found in the language, scope or object of the statute".[65] But the courts have some-times assumed that the maxim does lay down a rule of rigid application, so that devolution of power cannot (in the absence of express statutory authority) be held to be

---

[64] P.W. Duff and H. Whiteside (1929) 14 Cornell L.Q. 168, 173. The authors suggest that the maxim, recited by Coke in his *Institutes* (ii, 597), was probably taken from an incorrect rendering in a passage in an early printed edition of Bracton. But see Horst P. Ehmke (1961) 47 Cornell L.Q. 50, 54–55, pointing out that Bracton was indeed addressing himself to the impropriety of sub-delegating judicial power delegated by the King.

[65] John Willis, 'Delegatus non potest delegare' (1943) 21 Can. B.R. 257, 259. This article contains an excellent review of the earlier authorities.

valid unless it is held to fall short of delegation. In this way an unreasonably restricted meaning has often been given to the concept of delegation.[66]

Delegation of "judicial" powers

The maxim is applied with the utmost rigour to the proceedings of the ordinary courts, and in the entire process of adjudication a judge must act personally,[67] except in so far as he is expressly absolved from this duty by statute.[68] Special tribunals and public bodies exercising functions broadly analogous to the judicial are also precluded from delegating their powers of decision unless there is express authority to that effect,[69] or the legislation can be construed to define the tribunal (subject to any requirement of a quorum) as those members who sit to-decide a particular case.[70] Generally, in spite of the retreat from a rigid conceptual distinction between administrative, judicial, and quasi-judicial functions, it is still the case that the courts will be more ready to find a necessary implication of delegation in respect of a body that does not exercise strictly "judicial" functions.[71]

5–104

---

[66] See cases cited by Willis, *op. cit.* n. 65 above, 257–258.

[67] *Caudle v. Seymour* (1841) 1 Q.B. 889 (depositions taken by justices' clerk). *Cf.*, however, *Hunt v. Allied Bakeries Ltd (No. 2)* [1959] 1 W.L.R. 50, 56; *R. v. Brentford JJ., ex p. Catlin* [1975] Q.B. 455. See also *R. v. Majewski* [1977] A.C. 443, 449–451 (registrar's power to refer criminal appeals for summary dismissal); *R. v. Gateshead JJ., ex p. Tesco* [1981] Q.B. 470 (power of single justice or justices' clerk to issue summonses could not be delegated to court official); approved in *Hill v. Alderton* (1982) 75 Cr. App. R. 346, HL. And see *Olympia Press Ltd v. Hollis* [1973] 1 W.L.R. 1520 where it was held that each magistrate did not have to read all the books that were the subject of forfeiture proceedings provided that they collectively discussed them before making a decision (*Burke v. Copper* [1962] 1 W.L.R. 700 distinguished).

[68] An arbitrator too must discharge his functions personally: *Russell on Arbitration* (20th ed.), pp. 252 *et seq.* Generally, on implied power to sub-delegate ministerial functions, *Allam & Co. v. Europa Poster Services Ltd* [1968] 1 W.L.R. 638 (where the sub-delegated function, though not the decisions culminating in it, was merely "ministerial").

[69] *G.M.C. v. U.K. Dental Board* [1936] Ch 41; *Barnard v. National Dock Labour Board* [1953] 2 Q.B. 18; *Vine v. National Dock Labour Board* [1957] A.C. 488; *Labour Relation Board of Saskatchewan v. Speers* [1948] 1 D.L.R. 340; *Turner v. Allison* [1971] N.Z.L.R. 833. *Cf. Re S. (a Barrister)* [1970] 1 Q.B. 160 (jurisdiction to disbar, though ostensibly delegated, was in truth original). And see *Re Schabas and Caput of University of Toronto* (1975) 52 D.L.R. (3d) 495; *Re Bortolotti and Ministry of Housing* (1977) 76 D.L.R. (3d) 408 (chairman of tribunals has no inherent power to make rulings on points of law that bind the other members).

[70] *Howard v. Borneman (No. 2)* [1976] A.C. 301.

[71] See *Young v. Fife Regional Council* 1986 S.L.T. 331 (Scottish Teachers Salaries Committee and no power to delegate decision regarding teachers' pay to sub-committee, because since functions was "at least" quasi judicial, there was no implied power of delegation); *R. v. Gateshead JJ., ex p. Tesco* (n.67 above) (court officials could lawfully

5–105   But, as we shall see in the discussion on procedural propriety,[72] the courts will sometimes concede that a public body has an implied power to entrust a group of its own members with authority to investigate, to hear evidence and submissions and to make recommendations in a report, provided that (a) it retains the power of decision in its own hands and receives a report full enough to enable it to comply with its duty to "hear" before deciding,[73] and (b) the context does not indicate that it must perform the entire "adjudicatory" process itself. Determinations by Ministers, however, stand in a special class; not only may the hearing be conducted by a person authorised in that behalf, but the decision may be made by an authorised official in the Minister's name. The House of Lords has recently affirmed that a decision required to be taken by the Home Secretary on the period which a life sentence prisoner should serve for the purposes of retribution and deterrence may be taken by a Minister of state at the Home Office on his behalf. However, any advice on that question given by the Lord Chief Justice must be given by the holder of that office, as his function cannot be delegated.[74]

---

carry out non-judicial duties of justices' clerk, but no judicial duties). South African courts allowed implied delegation of 'purely administrative' or 'ministerial' functions but not of 'legislative' or 'judicial' functions: *United Democratic Front v. Staatspresident* 1987 (4) S.A. 649 (W).

[72] *Cf. Osgood v. Nelson* (1872) L.R. 5 HL 636 (council could validly empower one of its committees to investigate charges against an official, the council itself retaining the power of decision); and see *Devlin v. Barnett* [1958] N.Z.L.R. 828 (promotions board entitled to entrust another body with conduct of tests): *Att.-Gen. (ex rel. McWhirter) v. Independent Broadcasting Authority* [1973] Q.B. 629, 651, 657–658 (Authority normally able to rely on staff reports except when credible evidence contradicting a report is received): *R. v. Commission for Racial Equality, ex p. Cottrell and Rothon* [1980] 1 W.L.R. 1580 (C.R.E. allowed to delegate formal investigation into alleged discrimination and hence could rely and act on evidence received in reports). See also *Vine's case* (n.69 above) at 512. *Cf. Re Sarran* (1969) 14 W.L.R. 361.

[73] *Semble*, if a local authority is required to be satisfied of the existence of certain facts before exercising a power but is not obliged to afford any hearing beforehand, its satisfaction may be sufficiently expressed by formally adopting findings made by its committees even though these findings do not fully record the materials on which they were based: *Goddard v. Minister of Housing and Local Government* [1958] 1 W.L.R. 1151; *Savoury v. Secretary of State for Wales* (1976) 31 P. & C.R. 344. This latter decision also illustrates the difficulty of reviewing the validity of the resolution for lack of evidence when the applicant is unable to discover upon what evidence the council acted: but see, however, *Electronic Industries Ltd v. Oakleigh Corp.* [1973] V.R. 177 where the court was prepared to infer that the council had not considered a particular matter. See also *Agnew v. Manchester Corp.* (1902) 67 J.P. 174. But in some contexts (*e.g.* where bodies making decisions significantly affecting individual rights perfunctorily adopt findings by officials) the courts may hold that failure to exercise independent judgment or discretion constitutes an unlawful abdication of authority; *R. v. Chester City Council, ex p. Quietlynn Ltd* (1984) 83 L.G.R. 308; *R. v. Birmingham City Council, ex p. Quietlynn Ltd* (1985) 83 L.G.R. 461.

[74] *Doody v. Secretary of State for the Home Department* [1994] 1 A.C. 531.

Delegation of "legislative" powers

There is a strong presumption against construing a grant of delegated   **5–106**
legislative power as empowering the delegate to sub-delegate the
whole or any substantial part of the law-making power entrusted to
it.[75] In New Zealand cases this presumption was invoked as a ground
for holding regulations and orders made by the sub-delegate to be
invalid.[76] But the presumption is not irrebuttable, and in a Canadian
wartime case the power of the Governor-General in Council to make
such regulations as he might by reason of the existence of war deem
necessary or advisable for the defence of Canada was held to be wide
enough to enable him to sub-delegate to the Controller of Chemicals
power to make regulations.[77] There seems to be no English authority
directly in point in constitutional or administrative law. In the First
World War the sweeping legislative powers vested by the Defence of
the Realm Acts in the King in Council were extensively sub-delegated
to Ministers and others; the validity of such sub-delegation was not,
apparently, challenged in the courts. In the Second World War the King
in Council was expressly empowered by section 1(3) of the Emergency
Powers (Defence) Act 1939 to sub-delegate his legislative powers
under the Act. It is doubtful whether implied authority to sub-
delegate legislative powers would ever be conceded by the English
courts save in time of grave emergency.[78] For when Parliament has
specifically appointed an authority to discharge a legislative function,
a function normally exercised by Parliament itself, it cannot readily be

---

[75] See *King-Emperor v. Benoari Lal Sarma* [1945] A.C. 14, 24; *R. v. Lampe, ex p. Maddolozzo*
[1966] A.L.R. 144 (dicta). See also H.C. 187 (1947–46), paras 16–17, H.C. 201 (1947–48),
paras 3–4; Fox and Davies, 'Sub-Delegated Legislation' (1955) 28 A.L.J. 486.

[76] *Geraghty v. Porter* [1917] N.Z.L.R. 554 (distinguished in *Hookings v. Director of Civil
Aviation* [1957] N.Z.L.R. 929); *Godkin v. Newman* [1928] N.Z.L.R. 593; *Jackson (F.E.) &
Co. v. Collector of Customs* [1939] N.Z.L.R. 682, 732–734; *Hawke's Bay Raw Milk
Producers' Co-operative Co. v. New Zealand Milk Board* [1961] N.Z.L.R. 218
(distinguished in *Van Gorkom v. Att.-Gen.* [1977] 1 N.Z.L.R. 535). See C.C. Aikman in
(1960) 3 Victoria Univ. of Wellington L. Rev. 69 for an authoritative analysis of the
case law.

[77] Reference *Re Chemicals Regulations* [1943] S.C.R. 1. But see *Att.-Gen. of Canada v. Brent*
[1956] S.C.R. 318 (powers of Governor-General in Council to make regulations with
respect to immigration restrictions not validly exercised by making of regulations
which in substance transferred to public officers the effective power to make the
necessary rules); with which contrast *Hookings v. Director of Civil Aviation* [1957]
N.Z.L.R. 929. And see *Arnold v. Hunt* (1943) 67 C.L.R. 429; with which contrast *Croft
v. Rose* [1957] A.L.R. 148. *Cf.* Merralls, Note (1957) 1 Melbourne Univ. L.R. 105.

[78] Reference to extrinsic documents in delegated legislation is common, and is not
considered to involve sub-delegation unless the document is not in existence when the
instrument is approved, and its content is beyond the control of the Minister; see
criticisms of the Joint Committee on Statutory Instruments, 26th Report, H.C. 21-XI,
1974–75; *cf. R. v. Secretary of State for Social Services, ex p. Camden L.B.C.* [1987] 1 W.L.R. 819.

presumed to have intended that its delegate should be free to empower another person or body to act in its place. Nevertheless, one can envisage circumstances in which a carefully delimited sub-delegation of rule-making power could more reasonably be upheld than a sub-delegation of uncontrolled administrative discretion to be exercised in relation to individual cases.[79]

Delegation of "administrative" powers

5–107 Most of the practical problems concerned with sub-delegation have been related to the exercise of powers of a discretionary character— powers to regulate, to grant licences and permits, to requisition, to require the abatement of nuisances and to institute legal proceedings.

Delegation and agency

5–108 In this context, sharp differences of opinion have been expressed on the relationship between the concepts of delegation and agency. They have sometimes been treated as being virtually indistinguishable[80] but in many cases a distinction has been drawn between them, particularly where the court is acting on the assumption that an authority can validly employ an agent but cannot delegate its powers.

5–109 The correct view seems to be that the distinctions drawn between delegation and agency are frequently misconceived in so far as they are based on the erroneous assumption that there is never an implied power to delegate, but that some forms of relationship that are properly included within the concept of delegation are substantially different from those which typify the relationship of principal and agent. There are three main characteristics of agency. First, the agent acts on behalf of his principal and in his name, and the acts done by the agent within the scope of his authority are attributable to the principal. These principles are an broadly applicable to delegation in administrative law, and it would generally by held to be unlawful for an authority to invest a delegate with powers exercisable in his own name. But where legislative powers are delegated by Parliament, or validly sub-delegated by Parliament's delegate, the delegate or sub-delegate exercises his powers in his own name. And in the schemes of administrative delegation drawn up in local government law, the

---

[79] Aikman, *loc. cit.* n.76 above, at 82–83.

[80] See, *e.g. Huth v. Clarke* (1890) 25 QBD 391; *Lewisham Borough v. Roberts* [1949] 2 K.B. 608, 622; *Gordon, Dadds & Co. v. Morris* [1945] 2 All E.R. 616; R.M. Jackson (1952) 68 L.Q.R. 363, 376–377.

relationships between the local authorities concerned have often been far removed from those connoted by the relationship of principal and agent.[81] Secondly, the agent can be given detailed directions by his principal and does not usually have a wide area of discretion. On the other hand one to whom statutory discretionary powers are delegated often has a substantial measure of freedom from control in exercising them. But the degree of freedom from control with which he is vested may be a decisive factor in determining the validity of the delegation made to him. The more significant are the effective powers of control retained by the delegating authority, the more readily will the courts uphold the validity of the delegation; and they may choose to uphold its validity by denying that there has been any delegation at all,[82] on the ground that in substance the authority in which the discretion has been vested by statute continues to address its own mind to the exercise of the powers.[83] Thirdly, in agency the principal retains concurrent powers. This principle was generally applicable to delegation by a local authority to its committees. Thus, the local authority retained power to make decisions in relation to matters comprised within the delegation[84]—a rule now expressly restated by statute[85]—and it could (and presumably still can) revoke the authority of a delegate.[86] Nevertheless, it has sometimes been stated that delegation implies a denudation of authority.[87] This cannot be accepted as an accurate general proposition. On the contrary, the general rule is that an authority which delegates its powers does not divest itself of them—indeed, if it purports to abdicate it may be imposing a legally ineffective fetter on its own discretion[88]—and can

---

[81] Peter G. Richards, *Delegation in Local Government*, 35–39, 63 *et seq.* Inter-delegation between local authorities has been considerably diminished by the Local Government Act 1972.

[82] As in *Devlin v. Barnett* [1958] N.Z.L.R. 828; *cf. Winder v. Cambridgeshire C.C.* (1978) 76 L.G.R. 549.

[83] A distinction between the valid appointment of an 'agent' and the invalid appointment of a 'delegate' (*sc.* one to whom wide discretionary powers are entrusted) is traceable in the law of trusts; see, however, Trustees Act 1925, s. 23.

[84] *Huth v. Clarke* (1890) 25 QBD 391. See *Gordon, Dadds & Co. v. Morris* [1945] 2 All E.R. 616, 621.

[85] Local Government Act 1972, s.101(4).

[86] *Manton v. Brighton Corp.* [1951] 2 K.B. 393 (power of council to revoke authority of member of sub-committee).

[87] *Blackpool Corp. v. Locker* [1948] 1 K.B. 349, 377–378, *per* Scott and Asquith L.JJ. See also H.A. Street, *Ultra Vires*, 277; J.F. Garner (1949) 27 Pub.Admin. 115. *Cf. Winder v. Cambridgeshire C.C.* (1978) 76 L.G.R. 549 (local authority retained residual discretion to exercise a power that it had delegated under a statutorily required instrument of college government, when the refusal of the delegate to act would otherwise frustrate the discharge of the authority's overall educational responsibilities).

[88] For the general rule that a public authority cannot fetter itself in the exercise of discretionary powers, see Chap. 10 below.

resume them. But if it has validly delegated an executive power to make decisions, it will normally be bound by a particular decision, conferring rights on individuals (and possibly one derogating from those rights), made in pursuance of the delegated power and will be incapable of rescinding or varying it[89]; nor will it be competent to "ratify" with retroactive effect a decision encroaching on individual rights made by the delegate in excess of the powers so delegated, even though the delegating authority could validly have made the decision itself in the first place.[90]

5–110   It must be explained that in local government law there may be delegation either of executive power[91] (in which case the delegating authority may be bound by the delegate's decisions and the degree of supervision exercisable over the delegate may sometimes be minimal) or of power to make recommendations or decisions subject to the approval of the delegating authority. In the latter class of case (which is not always categorised as true delegation) difficult marginal problems of interpretation have arisen where a delegate or sub-delegate has taken action (*e.g.* to require the execution of works on private property or to institute legal proceedings) without antecedent approval and the authority whose approval is required has purported to ratify the action already taken.[92] Other difficult problems,

---

[89] *Battelley v. Finsbury B.C.* (1958) 56 L.G.R. 165. See also *Morris v. Shire of Morwell* [1948] V.L.R. 83. *Cf.* the unsettled question of whether the Home Secretary may disregard a decision by an immigration officer to grant leave to enter that is not consistent with the immigration rules: *R. v. Home Secretary, ex p. Choudhary* [1978] 1 W.L.R. 1 177; *R. v. Home Secretary, ex p. Ram* [1979] 1 W.L.R. 148.

[90] This appears to be the best explanation of the decision in *Blackpool Corp. v. Locker* (n. 89 above). A Minister delegated requisitioning powers, subject to restrictive conditions, to local authorities or their clerks by a departmental circular. A town clerk requisitioned L.'s house without complying with certain conditions. It was unsuccessfully contended that a subsequent letter from the Minister had cured the invalidity by ratification. It was doubtful, moreover, whether the purported ratification was to be construed as anything more than an act of affirmance, or whether the local authority or its clerk was to be regarded as an agent of the Minister, who was himself acting 'on behalf of His Majesty'. But the assertion (at 379) that the Minister was incompetent to requisition the house anew because he had not reserved powers to himself in the instrument of delegation cannot be supported. See also *Att.-Gen., ex rel. Co-operative Retail Services Ltd v. Taff-Ely B.C.* (1979) 39 P. & C.R. 223, CA, *aff'd* 42 P. & C.R. 1, HL (council could not ratify purported grant of planning permission by district clerk, since *ultra vires* act could not be ratified; *quaere* whether in any case council had power to grant planning permission). And see the discussion on estoppel, Chap. 12, paras 12-025–12-026 below.

[91] The power of local authorities to delegate to committees, sub-committees and officers, and of committees to sub-delegate was greatly extended by the Local Government Act 1972, Pt VI, esp. s. 101.

[92] See, on the one hand, *Firth v. Staines* [1897] 2 Q.B 70; *R. v. Chapman, ex p. Arlidge* [1918] 2 K.B. 298; and *Warwick R.D.C. v. Miller-Mead* [1962] Ch. 441 applied by the Court of Appeal in *Stoke on Trent City Council v. B & Q Retail Ltd* [1984] Ch. 1; and,

peripheral to the general question of delegation, have arisen in cases where it has been contended that a local government officer, acting without a formal grant of authority, has imposed legally binding obligations on his employers by virtue of undertakings, assurances or other conduct.[93]

General principles of delegation

The following are some of the principles elicited from the cases in which devolution of statutory discretions has been considered. **5–111**

(1) Where an authority vested with discretionary powers affecting private rights empowers one of its committees or sub-committees, members or officers to exercise those powers independently without any supervisory control by the authority itself, the exercise of the powers is likely to be held invalid. Thus, where the Minister of Agriculture had validly delegated to a war agricultural executive committee power to give directions with respect to the cultivation, management or use of land, and the committee sub-delegated to its officer power to determine in which fields a specified crop should be grown and to issue a direction to the farmer without reference to the committee, a direction issued by the officer was held to be invalid.[94] A byelaw by which a local authority hands over its own regulatory powers to an official by vesting him with virtually unrestricted discretion may be held to be void.[95] A delegation of power to review prosecutions to decide whether there was sufficient evidence to proceed, from the Director of Public Prosecutions to non-lawyers, was held unlawful since the statute by giving the power to the DPP clearly contemplated that it would only be delegated to a member of

---

on the other hand, *St Leonard's Vestry v. Holmes* (1885) 50 J.P. 132 and *Bowyer, Philpott & Payne Ltd v. Mather* [1919] 1 K.B. 419. Cf. *Att.-Gen., ex rel. Co-operative Retail Services Ltd v. Taff-Ely B.C.*, n.90 above. Cf. C. Cross and S. Bailey *Cross on Local Government Law* (8th ed., 1991) pp. 74–79; D. Lanham 'Ratification in Public Law' (1981) Otago Law Rev. 35.

[93] See Chap. 12 paras, 12-025–12-033 and Mark Freedland, 'The Rule Against Delegation and the Carltona doctrine in an Agency Context' [1996] P.L. 19.

[94] *Allingham v. Minister of Agriculture and Fisheries* [1948] 1 All E.R. 780. See also *High v. Billings* (1903) 67 J.P. 388. For the wide powers of sub-delegation conferred by the Local Government Act 1972, see C. Cross and S. Bailey *Cross on Local Government Law* (8th ed., 1991) pp. 74–79.

[95] See *Madoc Township v. Quinlan* (1972) 21 D.L.R. (3d) 136; *R. v. Sandler, ibid.* 286.

the Crown Prosecution Service, who would be a lawyer.[96] The powers to determine the state of health of a child, in relation to the question of whether free transport to school should be provided, could not be delegated to the school medical officer but had to be exercised by the education committee as a whole.[97]

(2) The degree of control (*a priori* or *a posteriori*) maintained by the delegating authority over the acts of the delegate or sub-delegate may be a material factor in determining the validity of the delegation. In general the control preserved (*e.g.* by a power to refuse to ratify an act or to reject a recommendation) must be close enough for the decision to be identifiable as that of the delegating authority.[98] That the decision of the delegate is not final or conclusive because of control exerted by a third party, in the form of an appeal or review from the decision of the delegating authority and/or delegate, may also be an important factor in determining the validity of the delegation.[99]

(3) How far, if at all delegation of discretionary power is impliedly authorised may also depend on the amplitude of the power, the impact of its exercise upon individual interests and the importance to be attached to the efficient transaction of public business by informal delegation of responsibility.[1]

---

[96] *R. v. DPP ex p. Association of First Division Civil Servants, The Times*, May 24, 1988. However, the House of Lords did not hold invalid power exercised by a subordinate officer of a rating authority when the power was conferred on the authority itself: *Provident Mutual Life Assurance Association v. Derby C.C.* [1981] 1 W.L.R. 173, HL.

[97] *R. v. Devon C.C., ex p. G.* [1989] A.C. 573.

[98] See dicta in *Hall v. Manchester Corp.* (1915) 84 L.J. Ch. 734, 741 and *Cohen v. West Ham Corp.* [1933] Ch. 814, 826–827 on the duty of local authorities to exercise independent discretion before acting on reports by their officers. And see *R. v. Board of Assessment, etc.* (1965) 49 D.L.R. (2d) 156 (tax assessment board, by simply adopting valuations made by official, failed to perform statutory duties).

[99] *Provident Mutual Life Assurance Assn. v. Derby City Council* [1981] 1 W.L.R. 173, 181, HL (principal rating assistant could serve completion notice without consulting borough treasurer; right of appeal to county court existed).

[1] See generally *Ex p. Forster, re University of Sydney* (1963) S.R. (N.S.W.) 723, 733–734; John Willis, *loc. cit.*, n.65 above. In *R. v. Monopolies and Mergers Commission, ex p. Argyll Group plc* [1986] 1 W.L.R. 763, CA it was held that the Chairman of the M.M.C. did not have authority to act on his own to request the Secretary of State to lay the reference about the company aside. However, a properly constituted group of M.M.C. members would have reached the same conclusion and therefore the act was valid. But where a chairman of a local education committee designated the date for the closure of a school, that was held an unlawful delegation: *R. v. Secretary of State for Education and Science, ex p. Birmingham C.C.* (1984) 83 L.G.R. 79.

(4) It is improper for an authority to delegate wide discretionary powers to another authority over which it is incapable of exercising direct control, unless it is expressly empowered so to delegate.[2] Thus, the Minister of Works could not allocate to the Minister of Health part of his functions in the system of building licensing.[3] A Canadian provincial marketing board, exercising delegated authority, could not sub-delegate part of it regulatory powers to an inter-provincial authority.[4] Nor could a local authority, empowered to issue cinematograph licences subject to conditions, attach a condition that no film shall be shown which had not been certified for public exhibition by the British Board of Film Censors,[5] unless the authority has expressly reserved to itself power to dispense with that requirement in any individual case.[6] It is doubtful how far a Minister would be held to have an implied power to devolve discretionary functions upon local authorities and their officers, over whom he is constitutionally enabled to exercise indirect control. One may surmise that the courts would not readily uphold the validity of a devolution of very wide discretionary powers, but that if the devolution of discretion covered a relatively narrow field they might characterise the relationship as agency rather than delegation and hold that it had been validly created.[7]

---

[2] *cf. Kyle v. Barbor* (1888) 58 L.T. 229.

[3] *Jackson, Stansfield & Sons v. Butterworth* [1948] 2 All E.R. 558, 564–566 (dicta); *sed quaere* whether the Minister of Works in that case had done anything more than use the Minister of Health as a convenient channel of communication with local authorities; see de Smith (1949) 12 M.L.R. 29, 38. See further, on transfer of powers between Ministers, Ministers of the Crown (Transfer of Functions) Act 1946. And see *Lavender (H.) & Son Ltd v. Minister of Housing and Local Government* [1970] 1 W.L.R. 1231 (Minister X determining planning appeal by mechanically applying policy of Minister Y; decision in effect that of Minister Y, and therefore *ultra vires*). *Cf.,* however, *Kent C.C. v. Secretary of State for the Environment* (1977) 75 L.G.R. 452, where the Minister was held to have decided a planning appeal himself although he had had regard to the opinion of another Minister on an important issue in the appeal. If a Minister delays the making or implementation of a discretionary decision till the matter has been debated in Parliament he is not, of course, delegating his power of decision at all: *R. v. Brixton Prison Governor, ex p. Enaharo* [1963] 2 Q.B. 455.

[4] *Prince Edward Island Potato Marketing Board v. Willis (H.B.) Inc.* [1952] 2 S.C.R. 391.

[5] *Ellis v. Dubowski* [1921] 3 K.B. 621. See also *R. v. Burnley JJ.* (1916) 85 L.J.K.B. 1565. But see Cinematograph Act 1952, s.3(1), which authorises a licensing authority to delegate to another body (including the Board) the function of designating films as unsuitable for children. But general licensing functions may no longer be delegated to magistrates (Local Government Act 1972, s.204(5)).

[6] *Mills v. L.C.C.* [1925] 1 K.B. 213; *R. v. G.L.C., ex p. Blackburn* [1976] 1 W.L.R. 550.

[7] This approach is suggested by dicta in *Jackson, Stansfield & Sons v. Butterworth* [1948] 2 All E.R., 564–565.

(5) Where the exercise of a discretionary power is entrusted to a named officer—*e.g.* a chief officer of police, a medical officer of health or an inspector—another officer cannot exercise his powers in his stead unless express statutory provision has been made for the appointment of a deputy or unless in the circumstances the administrative convenience of allowing a deputy or other subordinate to act as an authorised agent very clearly outweighs the desirability of maintaining the principle that the officer designated by statute should act personally.[8] But where statute permitted discharge of disciplinary functions of the Law Society Council to "an individual (whether or not a member of the Society's staff)", there was nothing which required the Council to familiarise itself with the name of the delegatee; the Council could delegate to the holder from time to time of an office.[9] The principle of *delectus personae*—the presumption of deliberate selection—is not an independent normative principle, but is merely a principle of statutory construction which will readily give way to legislative indications to the contrary.[10]

(6) The maxim *delegatus non potest delegare* has on the whole been applied more strictly to the further sub-delegation of sub-delegated powers than to the sub-delegation of primary delegated powers.[11] This is in accordance with the maxim *expressio unius est exclusio alterius*: where Parliament has expressly authorised sub-delegation of a specific character, it can generally be presumed to have intended that no further sub-delegation shall be permissible.

(7) Again, it may generally be presumed that express authority to sub-delegate powers is to be construed as impliedly excluding authority to sub-delegate the performance of duties involving the exercise of deliberate judgment, unless the performance of the duty is inextricably interwoven with the exercise of the power.[12]

(8) Where power to sub-delegate prescribed functions has been conferred by statute, the delegation must be conveyed in an

---

[8] *Nelms v. Roe* [1970] 1 W.L.R. 4, 8; *Mason v. Pearce, The Times,* October 7, 1981; *R. v. Majewski* [1977] A.C. 443, 449–451.

[9] *R. v. The Law Society, ex p. Curtin* (1994) 6 Admin. L.R. 657.

[10] *ibid., per* Steyn L.J.

[11] See, *e.g. Cook v. Ward* (1877) 2 C.P.D. 255. Powers of sub-delegation are greatly extended by the Local Government Act 1972, s. 101.

[12] *Mungoni v. Att.-Gen. of Northern Rhodesia* [1960] A.C. 336; *R. v. DPP, ex p. Association of First Division Civil Servants, The Times,* May 24, 1988.

authorised form[13] to the designated authority,[14] and must identify sufficiently what are the functions thus delegated instead of leaving the sub-delegate to decide the ambit of his own authority.[15]

(9) Canadian courts have in the past taken a restrictive view of the competence of local authorities to confer a free discretion on their members or officials to dispense with prohibitions embodied in byelaws. Thus, Montreal could not make a byelaw providing that nobody was to run a business in the city without an official permit; this was analysed as an invalid sub-delegation.[16] And in another case,[17] a marketing board (itself a sub-delegate) was empowered to make regulations on certain matters; the regulations that it made were held invalid on the ground that they contained no standards, but reserved to the board the power to exercise its discretion case by case. The board was said not to have exercised the legislative function delegated to it but to have sub-delegated to itself an administrative function.[18] The New Zealand decisions are

---

[13] For the manner of conveying such authorisation within a police force, see *Nelms v. Roe* [1970] 1 W.L.R. 4; *Pamplin v. Gorman* [1980] R.T.R. 54; *cf. Record Tower Cranes Ltd v. Gisbey* [1969] 1 W.L.R. 148.

[14] *cf. Esmonds Motors Pty Ltd v. Commonwealth* (1970) 120 C.L.R. 463 (Minister acted *ultra vires* by designating himself); *R. v. Secretary of State for the Environment, ex p. Hillingdon L.B.C.* [1986] 1 W.L.R. 192, *aff'd* [1986] 1 W.L.R. 807 (power under s.101(1) of the Local Government Act 1972 to delegate to a committee does not give the power to delegate to a committee of one); *cf. R. v. Secretary of State for Education and Science, ex p. Birmingham C.C.* (1984) 83 L.G.R. 79 (no power to delegate to a member of an authority).

[15] *Ratnagopal v. Att.-Gen.* [1970] A.C. 972 (Governor-General, empowered to appoint a commissioner of inquiry, left terms of reference excessively vague). But see *R. v. Law Society, ex p. Curtin* (n.9 above); delegation to a named official may not be required. See also the situations in which the authority may be estopped from denying the authority of an officer to whom power has not been officially delegated discussed in Chap. 12 paras 12-025–12-026, below. See esp. *Lever Finance Ltd v. Westminster L.B.C.* [1971] 1 Q.B. 222. *Cf. Western Fish Products Ltd v. Penwith D.C.* (1978) 38 P. & C.R. 7. [1981] 2 All E.R. 204.

[16] *Vic Restaurant Inc. v. Montreal* [1959] S.C.R. 58 (distinguished in *Lamoureux v. City of Beaconsfield* [1978] 1 S.C.R. 134).

[17] *Brant Dairy Co. Ltd v. Milk Commission of Ontario* [1973] S.C.R. 131; *Re Canadian Institute of Public Real Estate Companies and City of Toronto* (1979) 25 N.R. 108 (S.C.C.). *Cf.*, however, *Re Bedesky and Farm Products Marketing Board on Ontario* (1976) 58 D.L.R. (3d) 484, 502–504.

[18] This reasoning reflects to a limited degree the argument advanced in K.C. Davis, *Discretionary Justice*, esp. pp. 57–59, that bodies and officials in whom discretion is vested should be under an obligation to confine and structure it by the promulgation of decisional criteria so as to strike the best balance in the context between rules and discretion. See further, n. 3 above. This is a variation on the non-delegation doctrine at one time used by the Supreme Court of the United States to render invalid statutes

conflicting; sometimes such provisions have been construed as valid conditional prohibitions, and sometimes as sub-delegations the validity of which may be dependent on the prescription of standards governing the exercise of the dispensing power.[19] Issues such as these have seldom arisen in the English courts.[20] If an absolute prohibition would be valid, then prima facie a conditional prohibition should be upheld[21]; but it may be relevant in some cases to consider the context, the persons to whom the dispensing or regulatory power are delegated and the scope of the authority "delegated" to them.

The *Carltona* principle

5–112   Special considerations arise where a statutory power vested in a Minister or a department of state is exercised by a departmental official. The official is not usually spoken of as a delegate, but rather

---

that delegated legislative power without setting sufficiently precise limits upon its exercise: see, *e.g. Field v. Clark* 143 U.S. 649 (1892). See Jaffe, 'An Essay on Delegation of Legislative Power' (1947) 47 Colum. L. Rev. 359, 561. In later reappeared in other contexts; see, *e.g. Shuttlesworth v. Birmingham* (1969) 394 U.S. 147 (byelaw requiring that permit be obtained before holding public demonstration, invalid because of the broad discretion entrusted to an official); *Furman v. Georgia* (1972) 408 U.S. 238; *Proffitt v. Florida* (1976) 428 U.S. 242, where the constitutionality of capital punishment was attacked in part because of the broad discretion 'delegated' to the judge and jury in imposing it. *Cf. Francis v. Chief of Police* [1973] A.C. 761, 773, where the Privy Council held that a statutory requirement that the permission of the Chief of Police be obtained before 'noisy instruments' could lawfully be used at public meetings did not delegate so much discretion as to infringe the freedom of speech and assembly provisions of a constitution of St Christopher, Nevis and Anguilla.

[19] See *Mackay v. Adams* [1918] N.Z.L.R. 518; *Jackson (F.E.) & Co. v. Collector of Customs* [1939] N.Z.L.R. 682; *Hazeldon v. McAra* [1948] N.Z.L.R. 1087; *Ideal Laundry Ltd v. Petone Borough* [1957] N.Z.L.R. 1038; *Hookings v. Director of Civil Aviation, ibid.*, 929. For a penetrating review of these and other Commonwealth decisions, see Aikman in (1960) 3 Victoria Univ. of Wellington L. Rev. at 85–95. See also *Att.-Gen. and Robb v. Mount Roskill Borough* [1971] N.Z.L.R. 1030.

[20] See, however, the cinema licensing decisions cited at n.6 above, and the decision of the Privy Council in *Francis v. Chief of Police* (n.18 above). In England licensing powers are nearly always conferred directly by statute or under explicit statutory authority.

[21] *Williams v. Weston-super-Mare U.D.C.* (1907) 98 L.T. 537, 540. Specific authority to grant dispensations from certain statutory requirements has been vested in Ministers or local authorities. See Public Health Act 1961, ss. 6–8 (building regulations). However, a statutory power to regulate will not normally be construed as authorising total prohibition: *Tarr v. Tarr* [1973] A.C. 254, 265–268.

as the *alter ego* of the Minister or the department[22]; power is devolved rather than delegated.[23] (A different analysis must, of course, be adopted where powers are explicitly conferred upon or delegated to an official by a law-making instrument.[24]) Under the *"Carltona* principle" the courts have recognised that "the duties imposed on Ministers and the powers given to Ministers are normally exercised under the authority of the Ministers by responsible officials of the department. Public business could not be carried on if that were not the case."[25] In general, therefore, a Minister is not obliged to bring his own mind to bear upon a matter entrusted to him by statute but may act through a duly authorised officer[26] of his department.[27] The officer's authority need not be conferred upon him by the Minister personally[28]; it may be conveyed generally and informally by the officer's hierarchical superiors in accordance with departmental practice.[29] Whether it is necessary for the authorised officer explicitly to profess to act on behalf of the Minister is not certain.[30]

---

[22] See, *e.g. Lewisham Borough v. Roberts* [1949] 2 K.B. 608, 629; *R. v. Skinner* [1968] 2 Q.B. 700; *Re Golden Chemical Products Ltd* [1976] Ch. 300, 307; *cf. Woollett v. Minister of Agriculture and Fisheries* [1955] 1 Q.B. 103. The harmless fiction of the *'alter ego* principle' (see Lanham 'Delegation and the Alter Ego Principle' (1984) 100 L.Q.R. 587) does, however, have its limits. Admissions by a civil servant will not necessarily be treated as admissions by his Minister, *Williams v. Home Office* [1981] 1 All E.R. 1121. Similarly, evidence of receipt of a letter by a Minister's department will not satisfy a requirement that advice be received by a Minister of the Crown, although evidence of receipt by an official with responsibility for the matter in question will suffice: *Air 2000 Ltd v. Secretary of State for Transport (No. 2),* 1990 S.L.T. 335.

[23] *R. v. Secretary of State, ex p. Oladehinde* [1991] 1 A.C. 254, 283–284, CA (see n.33 below, for HL).

[24] As where power to decide certain classes of planning appeals have been vested in inspectors by legislation.

[25] *Carltona Ltd v. Commissioners of Works* [1943] 2 All E.R. 560, 563, *per* Lord Greene, M.R. See also *West Riding C.C. v. Wilson* [1941] 2 All E.R. 827, 831, *per* Viscount Caldecote C.J.; *Re Golden Chemical Products Ltd* (n.22 above). *Cf.,* however, *R. v. Home Secretary, ex p. Phansopkar* [1976] Q.B. 606 where the Minister was held to have no power to require applicants for certificates of partiality to obtain them from British Government officials in the applicant's country of origin rather than from the Home Office in London.

[26] *cf. Customs & Excise Commissioners v. Cure & Deeley Ltd* [1962] 1 Q.B. 340 (manner of authorisation prescribed by statute; *held,* not complied with). Section 7 of the Emergency Powers (Defence) Act 1939 also made express provision for the manner and form of delegation; *cf. Carlish v. East Ham Corp.* [1948] 2 K.B. 380.

[27] *West Riding* case (n.25 above); *Point of Ayr Collieries Ltd v. Lloyd-George* [1943] 2 All E.R. 546; *Carltona* case (n.25 above); *Lewisham* case (n.22 above); *Woollett's* case (n.22 above).

[28] *Lewisham* case (n.22 above); *Woollett's* case (n.22 above); *R. v. Skinner* (n.22 above); *cf. Horton v. St Thomas Elgin General Hospital* (1982) 140 D.L.R. (3d) 274.

[29] *ibid.*; see esp. *Woollett's* case (n.22 above) at 124–126, *per* Jenkins L.J.; see also the *Golden Chemical* case (n.22 above) at 305.

[30] *cf. Woollett's* case (n.22 above) at 120–121, 132, 134 *per* Denning and Morris L.JJ.; *Re Reference Under Section 11 of the Ombudsman Act* (1979) 2 A.L.D. 86, 94. In the *Golden*

5–113   It may be that there are, however, some matters of such importance
that the Minister is legally required to address himself to them
personally. There appears to be no English case in which an exercise of
discretion was held invalid on this ground[31] and many of the dicta
that appear to support the existence of such an obligation are at best
equivocal.[32] It is, however, possible that orders drastically affecting the
liberty of the person—*e.g.* deportation orders,[33] detention orders made
under wartime security regulations[34] and perhaps discretionary orders
for the rendition of fugitive offenders[35] require the personal attention
of the Minister.[36] On the other hand, the Minister was not required
personally to approve breath-testing equipment, despite its importance
to the liberty of motorists suspected of driving after consuming
alcohol,[37] and a decision on the question of a life sentence prisoner's
tariff period may be taken on behalf of the Home Secretary by a
Minister of state at the Home Office.[38] Objection to the production of
documentary evidence in legal proceedings on the ground that its
production would injurious to the public interest must be taken by the

---

Chemical case (n.22 above) at 311, it was said to be preferable for the departmental
officer who had in fact taken the decision to state that he had been satisfied that the
statutory criterion for exercising the power had been met.

[31] Indeed in the *Golden Chemicals* case (n.22 above) the judge denied that such a
category existed. But see *Ramawad v. Minister of Manpower and Immigration* [1978] 2
S.C.R. 375.

[32] In *Golden Chemicals* (n.22 above) at 309–310, Brightman J. concluded that the dicta in
Liversidge Anderson (n.34 below) should be understood as referring to political
expediency and to the Minister's personal responsibility to Parliament, rather than to
his legal obligation.

[33] *R. v. Chiswick Police Station Superintendent, ex p. Sacksteder* [1918] 1 K.B. 578, 585–586,
591–592 (dicta). The decision has in fact been taken by the Home Secretary personally
(Cmnd. 3387 (1967), 16). In *Oladehinde v. Secretary of State for the Home Department*
[1991] 1 A.C. 254, which concerned the provisional decision to deport, the House of
Lords appeared to accept that the final decision to deport had to be taken by the
Secretary of State personally or by a junior Home Office minister if he was
unavailable. *R. v. Secretary of State for the Home Department, ex p. Mensah* [1996] Imm.
A.R. 223.

[34] *Liversidge v. Anderson* [1942] A.C. 206, 223–224, 265, 281; *Point of Ayr* case (n.27 above)
at 548 (dicta).

[35] *R. v. Brixton Prison Governor, ex p. Enahoro* [1963] 2 Q.B. 455, 466.

[36] Had he believed that such a category existed, the judge in *Re Golden Chemicals* might
well have included in it the power to present a petition for the compulsory winding
up of a company (Companies Act 1967, s.10. See Lanham, 'Delegation and the Alter
Ego Principle' (1984) 100 L.Q.R. 587, 592–594, who argues that where life or personal
liberty are at stake, the *alter ego* principle may not apply.

[37] *R. v. Skinner* [1968] 2 Q.B. 700: it might, of course, be argued that the reliability of the
equipment raises technical questions to which the Minister will normally bring no
special expertise.

[38] *Doody v. Secretary of State for the Home Department* [1994] 1 A.C. 531.

Minister or the permanent head of the department, certifying that personal consideration has been given to the documents in question.[39] It has been said that when a Minister is required to consider an inspector's report, he must in fact genuinely consider the report and the objections[40]; but it is not clear that the devolution of such a function upon a senior departmental officer would invalidate the order. Indeed, as has already been pointed out[41] there seems to be no general rule that Ministers when discharging functions of a judicial character must direct their own minds to the cases before them. Nor is it necessary for a Minister to act personally in the exercise of powers of a legislative character; in some departments statutory instruments are signed by senior officials acting under a general grant of authority from the Minister.[42]

Similarly, it is uncertain whether the courts will examine the 5–114 suitability of the official who performs the work. The *Carltona* case emphasised that Parliament, not the, courts, was the forum for scrutiny of the Minister's decision,[43] but more recently it has been accepted that the courts may also examine the devolvement of authority, by way of judicial review.[44] At the very least, it would seem that the official must satisfy the test of *Wednesbury* unreasonableness: he must not be so junior that no reasonable minister would allow him to exercise the power.[45] It is thus possible that the conferment of full responsibility for the performance of an important act upon a minor departmental official might invalidate the performance of the act.

---

[39] *Duncan v. Cammell, Laird & Co.* [1942] A.C. 624, 638.

[40] *Franklin v. Minister of Town and Country Planning* [1948] A.C. 87, 103, *per* Thankerton L.J. (dictum).

[41] At para. 5–104 above.

[42] See Griffith and Street, *Principles of Administrative Law* (5th ed.), pp. 64–66. Departmental practice varies; in some departments all or nearly all statutory instruments are signed by the Minister personally (Report of the Joint Committee on Delegated Legislation (1971–72 H.C. 475), Minutes of Evidence, 196–203). In *Lewisham Borough v. Roberts* [1949] 2 K.B. 608, 621–622 Denning L.J. indicated that legislative functions had to be performed by the Minister personally; but Bucknill and Jenkins L.JJ. (at 619, 629–630) were of the contrary opinion. (Note, Lanham (*op. cit.* n. 36 above) says Bucknill's judgment was not clear on the point.) The majority of the Quebec Court of Appeal has held that a legislative power cannot be devolved: *R. v. Carrieres Ste Therese Ltee* (1982) 69 C.C.C. (2d) 251; and see Lanham (n. 36 above) at 594–595.

[43] *Carltona* (n. 25 above) at 563. Canadian courts have been more inclined to examine the suitability of the official; see *R. v. Wiens* (1970) 74 W.W.R. 639; *R. v. Harrison* (1976) 66 D.L.R. (3d) 660.

[44] *Oladehinde,* (n. 23 above) CA, at 281–282.

[45] *Oladehinde* (n. 23 above), QBD at 260; CA at 282. In the House of Lords, Lord Griffiths perhaps went further in stating that devolvement of authority to officials under the *Carltona* principle was permissible "providing ... that the decisions are suitable to their grading and experience" (n. 23 above, HL at 303). See also Lanham, *loc. cit.* n. 36 above at p. 590.

5-115   The *Carltona* principle may be expressly excluded by legislation,[46] but whether it may in addition be excluded by statutory implication remains uncertain. Two situations should be distinguished. Where a power of delegation is expressly conferred by Parliament on a Minister, it may compel the inference that Parliament intended to restrict devolution of power to the statutory method, thus impliedly excluding the *Carltona* principle.[47] Commonwealth authority, however, suggests that such an implication will not readily be drawn.[48] It has also been suggested that the principle may be impliedly excluded where it appears inconsistent with the intention of Parliament as evinced by a statutory framework of powers and responsibilities.[49] However, where the Immigration Act 1971 apparently clearly divided responsibilities between immigration officers and the Secretary of State, the Court of Appeal and House of Lords held that the *Carltona* principle enabled powers of the Secretary of State to be exercised by immigration officers. In the Court of Appeal it was said that the *Carltona* principle was not merely an implication which would be read into a statute in the absence of any clear contrary indication, but was a common law constitutional principle, which could not be excluded by implication unless "a challenge could be mounted on the possibly broader basis that the decision to devolve authority was *Wednesbury* unreasonable".[50] The House of Lords allowed the devolution of power on the narrower ground that the implication to exclude could not be drawn; the devolution did "not conflict with or embarrass [the officers] in the discharge of their specific statutory duties under the Act".[51] Although their statutory analysis may be questioned,[52] the approach of the House of Lords accorded greater weight than the Court of Appeal to the intention of Parliament.

---

[46] See, *e.g.* the Immigration Act 1971, ss.13(5), 14(3) and 15(4), all of which refer to action by the Minister 'and not by a person acting under his authority'.

[47] *Customs and Excise Cmrs v. Cure and Deeley Ltd* [1962] 1 Q.B. 340 (conferment by Parliament of express power of delegation on Commissioners deprived them of previously existing benefit of *Carltona* principle): but compare *Carltona* itself (n.25 above), where express power did not lead to exclusion of principle.

[48] *O'Reilly v. Commissioner of State Bank of Victoria* (1982) 44 A.L.R. 27; compare *Re Reference Under Section 11 of the Ombudsman Act* (1979) 2 A.L.D. 86, but see Lanham (n.36 above) pp. 600–603.

[49] *Ramawad v. Minister of Manpower and Immigration* (1978) 81 D.L.R. (3d) 687; *Sean Investments v. Minister of Health* (1981) 39 A.L.R. 363.

[50] *Oladehinde* (n.23 above) CA, at 282 (Lord Donaldson M.R.).

[51] *Oladehinde* (n.23 above) HL, at 303 (Lord Griffiths). This conclusion was influenced by the fact that the Minister retained a personal role in reviewing and signing each deportation order.

[52] Weight was placed on several explicit limitations of the Minister's powers to him personally, as excluding further implicit limitations; yet it was surely consistent of Parliament to intend some powers to be exercised by the Minister personally, some to be exercised by the Minister or his civil servants in the department, and others

It is sometimes suggested that other public bodies or officers besides **5–116**
ministers are entitled to the benefit of the *Carltona* principle,[53] in cases
where the argument of administrative necessity compels the inference
that delegation or devolution must have been contemplated. Such
cases are better analysed in terms of ordinary delegation or agency,
since the rationale of the *Carltona* principle rests not only on the
argument from administrative necessity,[54] but also on the possibility of
parliamentary control of devolution of power. Nevertheless, there are
some further circumstances in which the *Carltona* principle is properly
invoked. Powers of the Queen or Governor in Council may be
exercised by a Minister or official in his department, although any
formal decision necessary will be made by the Queen in Council.[55]
Powers conferred on senior departmental officers may be devolved to
more junior officials in the department.[56]

Acting under dictation

An authority entrusted with a discretion must not, in the purported **5–117**
exercise of its discretion, act under the dictation of another body or
person. In at least two Commonwealth cases, licensing bodies were
found to have taken decisions on the instructions of the heads of
government who were prompted by extraneous motives.[57] But, as less
colourful cases illustrate, it is enough to show that a decision which
ought to have been based on the exercise of independent judgment
was dictated by those not entrusted with the power to decide,[58]

---

to be exercised by immigration officers—as the statutory scheme appeared to
require.
[53] *e.g. Lanham* (n.36 above) at 604 *et seq.*
[54] *Nelms v. Roe* [1970] 1 W.L.R. 4, 8 (Lord Parker C.J.).
[55] *FAI Insurances Ltd v. Winneke* (1982) 41 A.L.R. 1; *South Australia v. O'Shea* (1987) 163
C.L.R. 378; *cf. Att.-Gen. v. Brent* [1956] 2 D.L.R. (2d) 503.
[56] *Commissioners of Customs and Excise v. Cure and Deeley* [1962] 1 Q.B. 340; *O'Reilly v.
Commissioners of State Bank of Victoria* (1982) 44 A.L.R. 27. *R. v. Secretary of State for the
Home Department, ex p. Sherwin* (1996) 32 B.M.L.R. 1. (*Carltona* applied to the Benefits
Agency which was held to be part of the Department of Social Security and the
agency staff belonged to the Civil Service). See also *R. v. Greater Manchester Police
Authority ex p. Century Motors (Farnworth) Ltd, The Times,* May 31, 1996. But see, *R. v.
Oxfordshire C.C., ex p. Pittick* [1995] C.O.D. 397 (Education Act 1981, s. 7(2)—council
had not improperly delegated its duty to provide special needs education to the
school); *R. v. Harrow L.B.C., ex p. M* [1997] 3 F.C.R. 761 (obligations on a local
education authority under Education Act 1993, s.168 to arrange that special
educational provision be made for a child was not delegable); *MFI Furniture Centre
Ltd v. Hibbert* [1996] C.O.D. 100 (validity of council's Minutes of Delegation).
[57] *Roncarelli v. Duplessis* [1959] S.C.R. 121: *Rowjee v. State of Andhra Pradesh, A.I.R.,* 1964
S.C. 962.
[58] See *McLoughlin v. Minister for Social Welfare* [1958] I.R. 1, 27.

although it remains a question of fact whether the repository of discretion abdicated it in the face of external pressure.[59] And it is immaterial that the external authority has not sought to impose its policy. For instance, where a local authority, in assessing compensation for loss of office, erroneously made certain deductions because it thought it was obliged to do so, having regard to the practice followed in such cases by the Treasury (to which an appeal lay from its decisions), mandamus issued to compel it to determine the claim according to law.[60] Where a Minister entertaining a planning appeal dismissed the appeal purely on the strength of policy objections entered by another Minister, it was held that his decision had to be quashed because he had, in effect, surrendered his discretion to the other Minister.[61] Authorities directly entrusted with statutory discretions, be they executive officers or members of distinct tribunals, are usually entitled and are often obliged to take into account considerations of public policy, and in some contexts the policy of a Minister or of the Government as a whole may be a relevant factor in weighing those considerations[62]; but this will not absolve them from their duty to exercise their personal judgment in individual cases,[63] unless explicit statutory provision has been made for them to be given binding instructions by a superior,[64] or (possibly) unless the cumulative effect of the subject-matter and their hierarchical

---

[59] See, *e.g. Hlookoff v. City of Vancouver* (1968) 65 D.L.R. (2d) 71; 63 W.W.R. 129; *Malloch v. Aberdeen Corp. (No. 2)*, 1974 S.L.T. 253, 264.

[60] *R. v. Stepney Corp.* [1902] 1 K.B. 317. See also *Buttle v. Buttle* [1953] 1 W.L.R. 1217.

[61] *Lavender (H.) & Son Ltd v. Minister of Housing and Local Government* [1970] 1 W.L.R. 1231 (where the other Minister might be said to have imposed his policy); *cf. Kent C.C. v. Secretary of State for the Environment* (1977) 75 L.G.R. 452.

[62] *cf. R. v. Mahony, ex p. Johnson* (1931) 46 C.L.R. 131, 145; *R. v. Anderson, ex p. Ipec-Air Pty Ltd* (1968) 113 C.L.R. 177; *Ansett Transport Industries (Operations) Pty Ltd v. Commonwealth* (1977) 17 A.L.R. 513; *Re Innisfi (Township of) and Barrie (City of)* (1977) 80 D.L.R. (3d) 85. See also *Roberts v. Dorset C.C.* (1977) 75 L.G.R. 462 (adoption by local authority of central government circular). But see *Re Multi-Malls Inc. and Minister of Transportation and Communications* (1977) 73 D.L.R. (3d) 18 (Minister's refusal of permit for proposed development invalid because he had regard to general government planning policy, rather than limiting his decision to road traffic matters).

[63] See the judgments in the *Ipec-Air* case (n. 62 above) for divergent expressions of opinion on the question of how far a decision of the Director-General of Civil Aviation (a public officer) to refuse permission to import aircraft and to refuse a charter licence to operate an inter-state air service could properly be predetermined by current government policy. See also the discussion of government policy as a 'relevant consideration', paras 5-098–5-099 above.

[64] *e.g.* by s.4(3) of the Civil Aviation Act 1971 (power of Secretary of State to give specific directions to licensing authority for certain purposes); *cf.*, however, s.3(2) authorising the Secretary of State to issue guidance to the authority on the performance of its statutory functions which it must perform 'as it considers is in accordance with the guidance': see *Laker Airways Ltd v. Department of Trade* [1977] Q.B. 643, 698–700, 713, 714, 724–725.

subordination[65] (in the case of civil servants and local government officers) [66] make it clear that it is constitutionally proper for them to receive and obey instructions conveyed in the proper manner and form.[67]

Needless to say, a duty not to comply with executive instructions to decide individual cases in a particular way is cast upon courts *stricto sensu*.[68]

---

[65] See I. Zamir (1969) 57 California L.R. 866.

[66] But in local government, treasurers have been obliged to obey the law and to disobey the council's instructions if contrary to law.

[67] *cf. Simms Motor Units Ltd v. Minister of Labour and National Service* [1946] 2 All E.R. 201 (where instructions were communicated to the officers in an unauthorised form).

[68] *Evans v. Donaldson* (1909) 9 C.L.R. 140; *Ex p. Duncan* (1904) 4 S.R. (N.S.W.) 217; *R. (Courtney) v. Emerson* [1913] 2 I.R. 377. See also *Buttle v. Buttle* [1953] 1 W.L.R. 1217.

CHAPTER 6

PROCEDURAL FAIRNESS: INTRODUCTION AND HISTORY

INTRODUCTION

The following Chapters[1] deal with the procedures for arriving at   **6–001**
administrative decisions, rather than with their substance. They
therefore consider the structures of decision-making and not the
quality or impact of the decisions themselves. An important concern of
procedural justice is to provide the opportunity for individuals to
participate in decisions that affect them. Another is to promote the
quality, accuracy and rationality of the decision-making process. Both
concerns aim at enhancing the legitimacy of that process.

While substantive justice aims to ensure that decisions are kept   **6–002**
within the scope of conferred powers, and to ensure the proper
exercise of those powers, procedural justice aims to provide
individuals with a fair opportunity to influence the outcome of a
decision, and deals with issues such as the requirement to consult, to
hear representations, and to hold hearings. It addresses also the
content and proper manner of those consultations, representations and
hearings, so as to ensure that they are appropriate in the
circumstances, meaningful, and that they assist and do not hinder the
administrative process.

Some administrative decisions do not permit any participation; those   **6–003**
for example that require speed and despatch and cannot be delayed. A
hearing could not be held about whether a fire brigade, in the course
of a fire, should destroy a building. In cases where participation is
appropriate, the content of the procedures will vary in accordance
with the nature of the decision to be made. Thus in some
circumstances a full public inquiry may be required, whereas in others
there will only be a bare entitlement to consultation. Courts, in
deciding the scope and limits of procedural fairness, must be alert to

---

[1] Chaps 6–11.

the interests of administration, and therefore sensitive to the subject-matter of the decision to be made. Participation should not however be seen as opposed to the interests of effective administration. It can greatly improve the quality of official decisions by providing the decision-makers with information they might not otherwise receive; information about the quality of the decision, as well as its perceived impact upon individuals or groups.

6–004   The interest of individuals in participation in decisions by which they are to be affected is obvious: they will wish to influence the outcome of the decision. Fairness requires that, in appropriate circumstances, they should have the opportunity of doing so.[2] Procedural fairness does not however guarantee that the exercise of the opportunity to make representations will automatically result in the representations made being accepted. Nor does the existence of fair procedures guarantee the open mind of the decision maker. There is always room for "symbolic reassurance",[3] and for the cynical manipulation of procedural forms on the part of a decision maker who has no intention of being persuaded and whose mind is closed. In order to overcome this, some procedural rules aim at making the decision-making process meaningful and not merely ritualistic. One such rule prohibits biased decision-makers. Another prohibits the fettering of discretion, thus ensuring that the decision-maker keeps an open mind. The duty to give reasons for decisions, where it exists, aims at ensuring the rationality of the decision. It attempts to ensure that the arguments presented to the decision-maker will be taken into account, and be seen to be taken into account.

6–005   Historically, the principle of natural justice appropriated most of procedural fairness, and, as we shall see, eventually unnecessarily confined itself to situations where a body was acting "judicially", and where "rights" rather than "privileges", were in issue. Although often

---

[2] John Rawls, *A Theory of Justice* (1972), p. 239 states that 'the rule of law requires some form of due process ... designed to ascertain the truth ... The precepts of natural justice are to insure that the legal order will be impartially and regularly maintained'. Fair proceedings aim however at more than instrumental ends (accuracy for example). They are also a constituent element of the legal and democratic process which should treat individuals with concern and respect. For this point of view see R.M. Dworkin, *Taking Rights Seriously* (1977), Chap 4. See also G. Maher, 'Natural Justice as Fairness' in *The Legal Mind* (N. MacCormick and P. Birks (eds) (1986). For a full account of fair procedures in discretionary decisions see D.J. Galligan, *Discretionary Powers* (1986), Chap. 7. For two important American contributions see R. Stewart, 'The Reformation of American Law' (1974–5) 88 Harv. L.R. 1667; J.L. Mashaw, *Due Process in the Administrative State* (Yale, 1985), esp. pp. 202–206. See G. Richardson, 'The Legal Regulation of Process,' in G. Richardson and Genn (eds) *Administrative Law and Government Action* (1990), p. 105 and D.J. Galligan, *Due Process and Fair Procedures* (1996).

[3] See M. Edelman, *The Symbolic Uses of Politics* (1964).

retained as a general concept, the term natural justice has since been largely replaced and extended by the more general duty to act "fairly". More recently, Lord Diplock adopted the term "procedural propriety" to describe one of the three "grounds" of judicial review.[4] Such a term extends the exclusively common law ambit of natural justice and fair hearings to situations where procedures are also provided by statute. His term fails, however, to include other aspects of fair procedures, such as the duty not to fetter discretion, a duty which requires a decision-maker, even where a policy has been announced, to be willing to consider representations arguing for exceptions (thus ensuring the continuous possibility of effective participation in the decision-making process).[5]

The following issues will now be dealt with under the general head **6–006** of procedural propriety or fairness:

(1) The circumstances giving rise to an entitlement to procedural fairness. This Chapter will explain the historical development of natural justice and fairness. Chapter 7 will consider the situations giving rise to a procedural entitlement. That entitlement can arise from a statutory duty to provide a particular procedure, or from a relationship recognised by the common law, involving the deprivation or diminution of a right or protectable interest. It may also, these days, arise out of a "legitimate expectation" encouraged by the decision-maker;

(2) Chapter 8 will consider the content of the procedural protection to which the individual may be entitled. Depending upon the situation, this may range from the mere right to be consulted, to that of a full public hearing containing most of the features of a judicial trial;

(3) Chapter 9 will consider the situations in which there would normally be an entitlement to fair procedures, but where the

---

[4] *Council of Civil Service Unions v. Minister for the Civil Service* [1985] A.C. 374, 410.

[5] The previous editions of this work dealt with fettering of discretion under "Review of Discretionary Powers" (4th ed.), Chap. 6. The 'grounds' of review may overlap. Indeed, some principles may fall under two grounds. Fettering of discretion is one of these. It constitutes illegality to the extent that the decision-maker has wrongly interpreted his rule or policy as permitting no deviation. To the extent however that a situation where discretion has been fettered permits no representations to the decision maker whose 'ears are closed', the issue is one of procedural propriety, and has parallels with other issues concerning the fair hearing. For a case where fettering of discretion and the absence of natural justice were closely connected see *R. v. Secretary of State for the Environment, ex p. Brent L.B.C.* [1982] Q.B. 593.

circumstances (such as those involved in a decision concerning questions of national security) may negate the right to some or all of those procedures;

(4) Chapters 10 and 11 will consider the principal techniques to ensure that procedures provided are meaningful. These include the rule against the fettering of discretion[6] and the entitlement to an unbiased decision-maker.[7]

HISTORICAL DEVELOPMENT

The concept of natural justice

6–007 The expression "natural justice", which is the source from which procedural fairness now flows, has been described as one "sadly lacking in precision".[8] It has been consigned more than once to the lumber room. Thus, it has been said that in so far as it "means that a result or process should be just, it is harmless though it may be a high-sounding expression; in so far as it attempts to reflect the old *jus naturale*, it is a confused and unwarranted transfer into the ethical sphere of a term employed for other distinctions; and, in so far as it is resorted to for other purposes, it is vacuous."[9] No one who has the slightest acquaintance with the medieval English legal system[10] or with legal systems in other parts of the world[11] will suggest that those elements of judicial procedure which are now regarded as the hallmark of a civilised society have been generally enforced or even generally regarded as proper. But courts and commentators who decline to accept any form of justice as natural may take their choice from among "substantial justice,"[12] "the essence of justice,"[13]

---

[6] Chap. 10, below.

[7] Chap. 11, below.

[8] *R. v. Local Government Board* [1914] 1 K.B. 160. In *Norwest Holst Ltd v. Secretary of State for Trade* [1978] Ch. 201, 226, Ormrod L.J. commented that 'natural' added nothing to justice 'except perhaps a hint of nostalgia'.

[9] *Local Government Board v. Arlidge* [1915] A.C. 120, 138, *per* Lord Shaw. See also *Maclean v. Workers' Union* [1929] 1 Ch. 602, 624; and see *McInnes v. Onslow-Fane* [1978] 1 W.L.R. 1520, 1530; *Norwest Holst Ltd v. Secretary of State for Trade* [1978] Ch. 201, 226, where a 'mesmerising' effect is attributed to the phrase 'the requirements of natural justice.'

[10] See D.M. Gordon (1931) 47 L.Q.R. 386, 403–404.

[11] See Wigmore, *A Kaleidoscope of Justice* (1941).

[12] *Smith v. R.* (1878) 3 App. Cas. 614, 623.

[13] *Spackman v. Plumstead District Board of Works* (1885) 10 App. Cas. 229, 240.

"fundamental justice,"[14] "universal justice,"[15] "rational justice,"[16] the "principles of British justice,"[17] or simply "justice without any epithet,"[18] "fair play in action"[19] or "fairness writ large and juridically"[20] as phrases which express the same idea. And in any event "natural justice" was written into the statute book in 1969.[21] Moreover, "natural justice" is said to express the close relationship between the common law and moral principles,[22] and in addition it has an impressive ancestry. That no man is to be judged unheard was a precept known to the Greeks,[23] inscribed in ancient times upon images in places where justice was administered,[24] proclaimed in Seneca's Medea,[25] enshrined in the scriptures,[26] mentioned by St. Augustine,[27] embodied in Germanic[28] as well as African[29] proverbs,

---

[14] *Hopkins v. Smethwick Local Board of Health* (1890) 24 QBD 712, 716.

[15] *Drew v. Drew* (1855) 2 Macq. 1, 8.

[16] *R. v. Russell* (1869) 10 B. & S. 91, 117.

[17] *Errington v. Minister of Health* [1935] 1 K.B. 249, 280.

[18] *Green v. Blake* [1948] I.R. 242, 248; or 'the ordinary principles of justice' (*Norwest Holst* (n. 9 above) at 226, *per* Ormrod L.J.).

[19] *Ridge v. Baldwin* [1963] 1 Q.B. 539, 578, *per* Harman L.J., a much-quoted phrase, See also *Fairmount Investments Ltd v. Secretary of State for the Environment* [1976] 1 W.L.R. 1255, 1266, for another vaguely sporting metaphor ('a fair crack of the whip').

[20] *Furnell v. Whangarei High Schools Board* [1973] A.C. 660, 679, *per* Lord Morris of Borth-y-Gest; he added that it was not 'a leaven to be associated only with judicial or quasi-judicial occasions.'

[21] Foreign Compensation Act 1969, s.3(10) (ground for impugning purported determination by Foreign Compensation Commission); and in Canada, see Federal Court Act, 1970, s. 28(1)(a).

[22] See A. L. Goodhart, *English Law and the Moral Law*, p.65.

[23] J.M. Kelly in (1964) 9 *Natural Law Forum* 103; he points out, however, that the Greeks tended to regard the principle as a practical aid to making good decisions rather than an abstract principle of justice. But since equal application of the law to similar situations is an important aspect of justice, there is a significant overlap betwen good decision-making and justice. See also A.R.W. Harrison, *The Law of Athens* (1971) Vol. 2.

[24] G. Del Vecchio, *Justice*, pp. 172–173.

[25] 'Qui statuit aliquid, parte inaudita altera, Aequum, licet statuerit, haud aequus fuerit,' lines 199–200, cited in *Boswell's Case* (1606) 6 Co. Rep. 48b, 52a, *Bagg's Case* (1615) 11 Co. Rep. 93b, 99a, and in several nineteenth-century cases.

[26] 'Doth our law judge any man, before it hear him, and know what he doeth?' (John, vii, 51). But *cf.* n. 32, below.

[27] *De Duabus Animabus*, xiv, ii.

[28] 'Eines Mannes Rede ist Keines Mannes Rede, Man soll sie billig hören beede'; 'Richter sollen zwei gleiche Ohren haben' (Lotmar, *Die Gerechtigkeit*, 77, 92).

[29] Thus, it is commended in proverbs and songs of the Lozi tribe in Barotseland (Max Gluckman, *The Judicial Process Among the Barotse of Northern Rhodesia*, p.102). See also the Kiganda proverb referred to by E.S. Haydon in *Law and Justice in Buganda*, p.333. The Kiganda proverb corresponding to the maxim *nemo judex in causa sua* means literally 'a monkey does not decide an affair of the forest' (*ibid.*). Practice did not always conform to precept.

ascribed in the Year Books to the law of nature,[30] asserted by Coke to be a principle of divine justice,[31] and traced by an eighteenth-century judge to the events in the Garden of Eden.[32] The historical and philosophical foundations of the English concept of "natural" justice may be insecure; but it is not therefore the less worthy of preservation. If it is vulnerable to rational criticism, so too are the "unalienable rights" of the Founding Fathers of the American Constitution or the notion of "due process".[33] And the view that "natural justice is so vague as to be practically meaningless" is tainted by "the perennial fallacy that because something cannot be cut and dried or nicely weighed or measured therefore it does not exist."[34]

6–008   Certainly it did exist in English law. It became identified with the two constituents of a fair hearing; (a) that the parties should be given a proper opportunity to be heard and to this end should be given due notice of the hearing[35] and (b) that a person adjudicating should be disinterested and unbiased.[36]

Early development of the right to a fair hearing

6–009   In 1850 it was said that "No proposition can be more clearly established than that a man cannot incur the loss of liberty or property for an offence by a judicial proceeding until he has had a fair opportunity of answering the case against him,[37] unless indeed the Legislature has expressly or impliedly given an authority to act

---

[30] 'In lege naturae requiritur ques les parties soient presentes ou que ils soient absentes per contumacie' ((1469) Y.B. 9 Edw. 4, Trin. pl. 9). *Cf. R. v. Clegg* (1721) 8 Mod. 3 at 4. See also H.H. Marshall, *Natural Justice*, Chap. 2.

[31] *Institutes*, iii, 35. Rhadamanthus, the cruel judge of Hell, punished before he heard. 'But far otherwise doth Almighty God proceed … 1. Vocat 2. Interrogat, 3 Judicat.'

[32] *R. v. Chancellor of the University of Cambridge* (1723) 1 Str. 557, 567, *per* Fortescue J. ' … even God himself did not pass sentence upon Adam before he was called upon to make his defence. 'Adam' (says God) 'where art thou? Hast thou not eaten of the tree, whereof I commanded thee that thou shouldst not eat?' ' But the biblical precedents are conflicting: see R.F.V. Heuston, *Essays in Constitutional Law* (2nd ed., 1964), 185, and J. M. Kelly in (1964) 9 *Natural Law Forum* at 110.

[33] The term 'due process' has recently been invoked in a number of English decisions. See, *e.g. R. v. Secretary for State for the Home Department ex p. Moon* (1996) & Admin. L.R. 477 at 485 c.

[34] *Ridge v. Baldwin* [1964] A.C. 40, 64–65, *per* Lord Reid.

[35] *Audi alterem partem.*

[36] *Nemo judex in causa sua.* Bias will be dealt with in Chap. 11.

[37] The rule was said by Hawkins to be implied in the construction of all penal statutes (*Pleas of the Crown*, i, 420). See also *Painter v. Liverpool Oil Gas Light Co.* (1836) 3 A. & E. 433, 448–449: 'a party is not to suffer in person or in purse without an opportunity of being heard.'

without that necessary preliminary".[38] Most of the earliest reported decisions in which natural justice was applied[39] concerned summary proceedings before justices. Service of a summons upon the party affected was regarded as a condition of the validity of such proceedings,[40] not only in criminal matters but also in applications for the issue of distress warrants and orders for the levying of taxes and the charges imposed by public authorities upon the subject.[41] Justices who adjudicated summarily without having issued a summons were at one time punishable in the Court of King's Bench for misdemeanour.[42] Decisions on the effect of non-service of process were numerous and not always reconcilable,[43] but instances were not wanting of the strict application of the general principle that service is mandatory in civil as well as criminal proceedings before judicial tribunals.[44]

A second line of cases relates to the deprivation of offices and other   **6–010** dignities. Here the effective starting-point is 1615, when James Bagg, a chief burgess of Plymouth, who had been disfranchised for singularly unbecoming conduct,[45] was reinstated by mandamus because he had been removed without notice or hearing[46] In 1723 mandamus was issued to restore Dr Bentley to his academic degrees in the University of Cambridge, of which he had been deprived without a summons.[47] It became established with respect to offices that removal had to be preceeded by notice and hearing if the office was a freehold or was to

---

[38] *Bonaker v. Evans* (1850) 16 Q.B. 162, 171 *per* Parke B.

[39] See cases collected in note (a) to 8 Mod. 154.

[40] *R. v. Dyer* (1703) 1 Salk. 181; *R. v. Benn and Church* (1795) 6 T.R. 198. A more modern example is *R. v. Dudley J.J., ex p. Payne* [1979] 1 W.L.R. 891 (no notice of hearing given to a defendant before sentence).

[41] *R. v. Benn and Church* (n.40 above); *Harper v. Carr* (1797) 7 T.R. 270; *Gibbs v. Stead* (1828) 8 B. & C. 528; *Painter v. Liverpool Oil Gas Light Co.* (n.37 above); *R. v. Totnes Union* (1854) 14 Q.B. 349; *R. v. Cheshire Lines Committee* (1873) L.R. 8 Q.B. 344; see also Hankins (1940) 25 Iowa L.Rev. 457, 460–462.

[42] *R. v. Venables* (1725) 2 Ld.Raym. 1405; *R. v. Alington* (1726) 2 Str. 678.

[43] Early authorities are reviewed in *Marsh v. Marsh* [1945] A.C. 271 and more fully in *Posner v. Collector for Inter-State Destitute Persons (Victoria)* (1946) 74 C.L.R. 461. See also Gordon (1931) 47 L.Q.R., 557–563, 579–582.

[44] *e.g. R. v. North, ex p. Oakey* [1927] 1 K.B. 491; *Craig v. Kanssen* [1943] K.B. 256: *Chettiar v. Chettiar* [1962] 1 W.L.R. 279; *R. v. London County Q.S. Appeals Committee, ex p. Rossi* [1956] 1 Q.B. 682 (appealed in *R. v. Industrial Court, ex p. George Green & Thomson Ltd* (1967) 2 K.I.R. 259); *R. v. Havering JJ., ex p. Smith* [1974] 3 All E.R. 484. But statutorily prescribed detail on the manner of service may not be mandatory: *R. v. Devon and Cornwall Rent Tribunal, ex p. West* (1973) 29 P. & C.R. 316. In criminal matters the law is now largely governed by the Magistrates' Courts Act 1952.

[45] As by saying to the mayor 'You are a cozening knave' and 'I will make thy neck crack'; and by 'turning the hinder part of his body in an inhuman and uncivil manner' towards the mayor, saying 'Come and kiss'.

[46] *Bagg's Case* (1615) 11 Co.Rep. 93b.

[47] *R. v. Chancellor of the University of Cambridge* (1723) 1 Str. 557.

be forfeited only for cause,[48] but not if there was a discretionary power to remove the holder at pleasure.[49] These principles, which extended even to dismissals of schoolmasters and parish clerks, came to be largely forgotten, partly, perhaps, because of the decline of the concept of a freehold office, and partly because the tenure of public office was usually determinable either at pleasure or in accordance with specific statutory, contractual or customary procedures. In 1963 they were rescued from oblivion, dressed in modern garb, by the House of Lords.[50] Since then, they have been expanded to cover some categories of employees of public and quasi-public bodies.[51]

6–011   Linked with this group of cases are the decisions on the regulation of the clergy. Where a bishop issued an order for the sequestration of the profits of a benefice without having given the vicar notice of the charges of neglect that had been made against him or an opportunity to refute them, and where the Archbishop of Canterbury dismissed an appeal by a curate against the revocation of his licence without having afforded him an adequate hearing, the courts gave redress for violation of natural justice.[52] One of the most remarkable illustrations of the *audi alteram partem* principle in a reported case was *Capel v. Child*,[53] where a bishop, empowered by statute to order a vicar to appoint a curate (to be paid by the vicar) when satisfied, either of his own knowledge or by affidavit, that the vicar had neglected his duties, was held to be under an absolute duty to give the vicar notice and opportunity to be heard before making the order. This was a high-water mark of judicial intervention; in later cases the courts generally showed themselves disinclined inclined to require investigations conducted by ecclesiastical authorities to conform to judicial standards.[54]

---

[48] *Bagg's Case* (n. 46 above); *Protector. v. Colchester* (1655) Style 446, 452; *R. v. Wilton (Mayor)* (1697) 2 Salk. 428; *R. v. Ipswich (Bailiffs)* (1705) 2 Ld.Raym. 1233; *R. v. Smith* (1844) 5 Q.B. 614; *Re Fremington School* (1846) 10 Jur. (o.s.) 512; *Ex p. Ramshay* (1852) 21 L.J.Q.B, 238, 239; *Osgood v. Nelson* (1872) L.R. 5 HL 636; *Fisher v. Jackson* [1891] 2 Ch. 84.

[49] *R. v. Stratford-on-Avon (Mayor)* (1671) 1 Lev. 291; *R. v. Andover* (1701) 1 Ld.Raym. 710; *R. v. Darlington Free Grammar School Governors* (1844) 6 Q.B. 682; *Re Poor Law Commissioners* (1850) 19 L.J.M.C. 70. See, generally, *Dickson v. Viscount Combermere* (1863) 3 F. & F. 527, 548, note (a).

[50] *Ridge v. Baldwin* [1964] A.C. 40 (chief constable, removable only for statutory cause, dismissed without notice of charges against him or adequate opportunity to be heard; dismissal declared invalid).

[51] *Malloch v. Aberdeen Corp.* [1971] 1 W.L.R. 1578, esp. 1594–1599; *Stevenson v. United Road Transport Union* [1977] I.C.R. 893. However, the principles will normally only apply to 'public' bodies: *see* Chap. 3, above.

[52] *Bonaker v. Evans* (1850) 16 Q.B. 163; *R. v. Canterbury (Archbishop)* (1859) 1 E. & E. 545.

[53] (1832) 2 Cr. & J. 558, but *cf. Re Hammersmith Rent Charge* (1849) 4 Ex. 87, 94, 100.

[54] *Abergavenny (Marquis) v. Llandaff (Bishop)* (1888) 20 QBD 460; *R. v. Canterbury (Archbishop), ex p. Morant* [1944] K.B. 282, contrast *R. v. North, ex p. Oakey* [1927] 1 K.B. 491.

Nineteenth-century decisions established that the *audi alteram partem* **6–012**
rule was to govern the conduct of arbitrators,[55] of professional bodies
and voluntary associations in the exercise of their disciplinary
functions,[56] and indeed of "every tribunal or body of persons invested
with authority to adjudicate upon matters involving civil consequences
to individuals."[57] An individual who was expelled from membership
of a club[58] or similar association,[59] or from a trade union,[60] or who
was excluded from pursuing his calling by removal from a register[61]
or revocation of a licence for misconduct[62] or a direction by his trade
association to withhold from him essential supplies,[63] was prima facie
entitled to have the decision set aside by the courts unless he had
been given adequate notice of the allegations made against him and a
fair opportunity to reply to them. This principle was applied with
particular vigour where the sanction imposed would deprive a person
of his livelihood[64] or where there was a charge of discreditable

---

[55] *Re Brook* (1864) 16 C.B. (N.S.) 403; *Russell on the Law of Arbitration* (20th ed., 1982), pp.
213–218, 233.

[56] See Dennis Lloyd (1950) 13 M.L.R. 281; Z. Chafee (1930) 43 Harv.L.R. 993; Lloyd, *Law
Relating to Unincorporated Associations* 1938, pp. 127–129; W.A. Robson, *Justice and
Administrative Law* (3rd ed.), Chap. 4.

[57] *Wood v. Woad* (1874) L.R. 9 Ex. 190, 196.

[58] *Innes v. Wylie* (1844) 1 Car. & Kir. 257; *Dawkins v. Antrobus* (1881) 17 Ch.D. 615; *Fisher
v. Keane* (1878) 11 Ch.D. 353; *Gray v. Allison* (1909) 25 T.L.R. 531; *Lamberton v. Thorpe*
(1929) 141 L.T. 638.

[59] *Wood v. Woad* (n.57, above) (mutual insurance society); see also *Lapointe v.
L'Association de Bienfaisance et de Retraite de la Police de Montreal* [1906] A.C. 535 (denial
of pension to member of police friendly society). See also *John v. Rees* [1970] Ch. 345
(suspension or explusion from political party). This decision was distinguished in
Lewis v. Heffer [1978] 1 W.L.R. 1061 on the ground that the suspension was imposed
pending an inquiry and not as a punishment. Nor was the rule applied in *Gaiman v.
National Association for Mental Health* [1971] Ch. 317 (exclusion from membership of a
company).

[60] *Parr v. Lancashire & Cheshire Miners' Federation* [1913] 1 Ch. 366; *Burn v. National
Amalgamated Labourers' Union* [1920] 2 Ch. 364; *Abbott v. Sullivan* [1952] 1 K.B. 189,
199; *Annamunthodo v. Oilfield Workers' Trade Union* [1961] A.C. 945; *Lawlor v. Union of
Post Office Workers* [1965] Ch. 712; *Taylor v. National Union of Seamen* [1967] 1 W.L.R.
532; *Hiles v. Amalgamated Society of Woodworkers* [1968] Ch. 440; *Leary v. National Union
of Vehicle Builders* [1971] Ch. 34; *Edwards v. SOGAT* [1971] Ch. 354; see also *Roebuck v.
National Union of Mineworkers* [1977] I.C.R. 573 (bias).

[61] *Leeson v. General Medical Council* (1889) 43 Ch.D. 366, 383–384; *G.M.C. v. Spackman*
[1943] A.C. 627.

[62] *cf. Green v. Blake* [1948] I.R. 242. See also *Davis v. Carew-Pole* [1956] 1 W.L.R. 833;
McInnes v. Onslow-Fane [1978] 1 W.L.R. 1520; and Lloyd in (1958) 21 M.L.R. 661 and
(1963) 26 M.L.R. 412.

[63] *Byrne v. Kinematograph Renters Society Ltd* [1958] 1 W.L.R. 762.

[64] *Russell v. Duke of Norfolk* [1949] 1 All E.R. 109, 119; *Abbott v. Sullivan* [1952] 1 Q.B.
189, 199, *per* Denning L.J.; *Edwards v. SOGAT* [1971] Ch. 354.

conduct.[65]

6–013   With the extension of the franchise and the decline of the doctrine of laissez faire in the latter half of the nineteenth century came a vast increase in the regulatory functions of public authorities, especially in the fields of housing and public health. Where a statute authorising interference with property or civil rights was silent on the question of notice and hearing, the courts, drawing upon the authority of the older cases, invoked "the justice of the common law" to "supply the commission of the legislature."[66] In a long line of cases on demolition orders, beginning with *Cooper v. Wandsworth Board of Works*,[67] the rule, said to be "of universal application and founded on the plainest principles of justice,"[68] was laid down that public authorities must either give the person concerned "notice that they intend to take this matter into their consideration with a view to coming to a decision, or, if they have come to a decision, that they propose to act upon it, and give him an opportunity of showing cause why such steps should not be taken".[69] An authority empowered to postpone the operation of a demolition order on the owner's application had to permit him adequately to present his case for postponement.[70] The general rule, which was applied in a variety of legislative contexts,[71] might be satisfied if an opportunity was available of obtaining a full review of the initial decision[72] or of making other representations[73] before the

---

[65] *G.M.C. v. Spackman* [1943] A.C. 627, 637–638, *per* Lord Atkin; *Breen v. A.E.U.* [1971] 2 Q.B. 175 (dicta). Compare, as a possible modern parallel, *R v. Secretary of State for the Home Department, ex p. Fayed* [1997] 1 All E.R. 228, CA.

[66] *Cooper v. Wandsworth Board of Works* (1863) 14 C.B. (N.S.) 180, 194.

[67] *ibid.*; *Brutton v. St. George's, Hanover Square, Vestry* (1871) L.R. 13 Eq. 339; *Masters v. Pontypool Local Government Board* (1878) 9 Ch.D. 677; *Hopkins v. Smethwick Board of Health* (1890) 24 QBD. 712; *Sydney Municipal Council v. Harris* (1912) 14 C.L.R. 1; *Urban Housing Co. v. Oxford City Council* [1940] Ch. 70; see also *Delta Properties Pty Ltd v. Brisbane City Council* (1956) 95 C.L.R. 11, 18; *Police Commissioner v. Tanos* (1958) 98 C.L.R. 383, 395–396.

[68] *Cooper v. Wandsworth Board of Works* (n. 66, above) at 190.

[69] *Urban Housing Co. v. Oxford City Council* (n. 67 above) at 85, *per* Sir Wilfrid Greene M.R. For local colour and the aftermath of this case, see R.F.V. Heuston, *Essays in Constitutional Law* (2nd ed., 1964), 186–188.

[70] *Broadbent v. Rotherham Corp.* [1917] 2 Ch. 31.

[71] *e.g.* closing orders in respect of houses unfit for human habitation (*Hall v. Manchester Corp.* (1915) 84 L.J.Ch. 732, 741–742, HL): forfeiture of a lease of Crown land in Australia (*Smith v. R.* (1878) 3 App.Cas. 614); transfer of indentures of immigrants from one employer to another in Trinidad (*De Verteuil v. Knaggs* [1918] A.C. 557); applications to present a case before a wages board (*R. v. Amphlett (Judge)* [1915] 2 K.B. 223): confirmation of grant of liquor licence (*R. v. Huntingdon Confirming Authority* [1929] 1 K.B. 698).

[72] *St. James and St. John, Clerkenwell, Vestry v. Feary* (1890) 24 QBD 703 (order to supply sanitary installations): but this exception is untypical.

[73] *Att.- Gen. v. Hooper* [1893] 3 Ch. 483 (removal of projection over highway); *Robinson v. Sunderland Corp.* [1899] 1 Q.B. 751, 757–758 (supply of sanitary installation); *De*

order became finally operative or was enforced; and it was, of course, displaced by express statutory provisions dispensing with the need to serve notice.[74]

Maitland had pointed out in 1888 that England was becoming "a much governed nation, governed by all manner of councils and boards and officers, central and local, high and low, exercising the powers which have been committed to them by modern statutes," and that half the reported cases in the Queen's Bench. Division had to do with aspects of administrative law such as rating, licensing, public health and education.[75] At this time it was usual to confer new adjudicatory functions upon the existing departments of State and local authorities: special tribunals had been established for the regulation of railway traffic and the determination of income tax appeals, but the proliferation of ad hoc tribunals was to be a twentieth-century phenomenon. The courts, while recognising that it would be hopeless to require government departments, making institutional decisions, to follow the procedure of courts of justice, nevertheless superimposed upon their statutory responsibilities the duty to act judicially, in certain situations, in the manner prescribed by the rules of natural justice. The best-known statement of the *audi alteram partem* rule in English administrative law was formulated by the House of Lords in relation to the appellate functions of a government department but it is of broad application.

> "Comparatively recent statutes have extended, if they have not originated, the practice of imposing upon departments or officers of State the duty of deciding or determining questions of various kinds ... In such cases ... they must act in good faith and fairly listen to both sides, for that is a duty lying upon everyone who decides anything. But I do not think they are bound to treat such a question as though it were a trial ... They can obtain information in any way they think best, always giving a fair opportunity to those who are parties in the controversy for

6–014

Verteuil v. Knaggs (n. 71 above). See also *Knuckey v. Peirce* [1964] W.A.R. 200 (notice requiring removal of rubbish from site). In principle however, a duty to give prior notice and opportunity to be heard arises when an individual will suffer direct detriment from the act of decision (*Delta* case, n. 67, above).

[74] *Cheetham v. Mayor of Manchester* (1875) L.R. 10 C.P. 249.

[75] *Constitutional History of England* (1888), pp. 501, 505; and see H.W. Arthurs, *"Without the Law": Administrative Justice and Legal Pluralism in Nineteenth Century England* (1985).

correcting or contradicting any relevant statement prejudicial to their view.[76]"

Operation of the rule reviewed

6–015 These dicta by Lord Loreburn in *Board of Education v. Rice* must nevertheless be viewed with caution. The Board in that case had been required to determine a *lis inter partes* between a local education authority and the managers of a school. Had the education authority complied with its statutory duty to maintain the school efficiently when it was discrimnating against the teachers in the school by paying them lower salaries than those paid to teachers in other schools doing similar work? The determination of this question involved the ascertainment of questions of law and fact as well as the exercise of judicial discretion. It is doubtless true to say that in such situations the deciding authority is under an implied duty to listen fairly to both sides. It does not follow that "everyone who decides anything" is subject to a similar duty, or that persons involved in a controversy must always be given an opportunity of rebutting statements prejudicial to them. A decision to increase the rate of income tax, to arrest a participant in an armed robbery, to pull down a building to prevent the spread of a fire, may have serious adverse effects on those directly concerned, but there is no duty to give prior notice or opportunity to be heard. Nor does such a duty necessarily arise where numerous persons are competing for scarce resources: the allocation of government contracts and university places may cause great hardship to the unsuccessful contenders, but it has not yet been held in this country that they have any common-law remedy on the ground that their applications have been summarily rejected, even if the rejection has been based on an adverse undisclosed report.[77]

---

[76] *Board of Education v. Rice* [1911] A.C. 179, 182 *per* Lord Loreburn L.C. See also *Local Government Board v. Arlidge* [1915] A.C. 120, 132–134p; *Spackman v. Plumstead District Board of Works* (1885) 10 App.Cas. 229, 240; *Parsons v. Lakenheath School Board* (1889) 58 L.J.Q.B. 371, 372.

[77] *cf. Re Raney and the Queen* (1974) 47 D.L.R. (3d) 533. A policy of the British Government to impose as a term in contracts with public authorities that the contractor would observe the Government's income policy was criticised, *inter alia*, on the ground that no provision was made for a hearing before the contract was terminated for breach. And see *Central Council for Education and Training in Social Work v. Edwards, The Times*, May 5, 1978 (no hearing required to consider application for admission to educational institution, but if interview held, it must be conducted fairly). Compare the position in relation to Local Government contractors: *R. v. Birmingham City Council, ex p. Dredger* (1994) 6 Admin. L.R. 553, and see below, at paras 7-029–7-036.

Only four years after the decision in *Board of Education v. Rice*,[78] the   **6–016**
House of Lords held in *Arlidge's* case[79] that a government department
determining a housing appeal was not obliged to divulge one of its
inspector's reports to the appellant, even though the report might well
have contained relevant statements prejudicial to his case which he
might have wished to controvert. This decision marked the beginning
of a partial retreat by the English courts from their earlier position—a
retreat which was not halted till the 1960s. For nearly half a century
they were to show a marked reluctance to hold that an implied duty
to give prior notice and opportunity to be heard was imposed on
persons and authorities empowered to make decisions in the general
field of administrative law.

The path of deviation

The state of the law at the outbreak of the First World War can be   **6–017**
briefly restated. Judicial tribunals empowered to deprive persons of
their liberty, impose financial burdens on them and ascertain their
legal rights had to observe the *audi alteram partem* rule. So did
arbitrators and government departments when called upon to decide
questions of law and fact in situations resembling *lites inter partes*. The
rule would also normally be held to apply where the trappings of
adjudication were present although the decision involved the exercise
of wide discretion. It was prima facie applicable in various other
situations where there was nothing resembling a *lis inter partes*
determinable by a third party: removal from an office not merely at
pleasure, the disciplining of the clergy, the exercise of disciplinary
powers by professional bodies and voluntary organisations, and
administrative intrusions (*e.g.* by demolition, destruction and
compulsory execution of work upon private property rights.

The first leading case in which the courts refused to apply the rule   **6–018**
at all in a situation where it clearly ought to have been applied was
Venicoff's case.[80] The Home Secretary had been empowered by recent
legislation to deport an alien whenever he deemed this to be
"conducive to the public good."[81] When a deportation order was
impugned, it was held that he was exercising purely executive
functions, importing no duty to act judicially. The court laid emphasis

---

[78] [1911] A.C. 179.
[79] [1915] A.C. 120.
[80] *R. v. Leman Street Police Station Inspector, ex p. Venicoff* [1920] 3 K.B. 72.
[81] Art. 12(1) of the Aliens Order 1919, made under the Aliens Restriction Act 1914
(passed immediately after the outbreak of war).

on the amplitude of the Secretary of State's discretion, the context of emergency[82] and the impracticability of giving prior notice in such a case; the impact of a deportation order on personal liberty was treated as an irrelevant consideration,[83] and the feasibility of requiring a hearing after the order had been made but before it had been executed was not canvassed in the judgments.[84] In 1962 the Court of Appeal nevertheless reaffirmed the unsatisfactory rule that an alien deportee has no implied legal right to any hearing.[85] This rule has now been modified by statute.[86]

6–019   The tenor of the judgments in the *Venicoff* case foreshadowed the debilitation of *audi alteram partem* rule as a common-law standard applied by the court to administrative decision-making.[87] In the first place, there were the references to emergency situations. During wartime, enormous powers over persons and property were vested in

---

[82] *The King v. Inspector of Leman Street Police Station, ex p. Venicoff; The King v. Secretary of State for Home Affairs, ex p. Same* [1920] 3 K.B. 72, 80 *per* Earl of Reading C.J.

[83] It was observed that the validity of a still more drastic curtailment of personal freedom, the summary preventive detention of British subjects by administrative order, had been upheld only three years earlier: *R. v. Halliday* [1917] A.C. 260.

[84] Though the Home Secretary had offered to entertain representations informally ([1920] 3 K.B. 72, 78).

[85] *R. v. Brixton Prison Governor, ex p. Soblen* [1963] 2 Q.B. 243 (interpreting Art. 20(2)(b) of the Aliens Order 1953 (S.I. 1953 No. 1671), which reproduced the words construed in *Venicoff*'s case). Lord Denning M.R. (at 298–299) reserved his opinion on the question whether the deportee might have a legal right to be heard after the order had been made but before it had been executed. See also, for dicta to the same effect, *Schmidt v. Home Secretary* [1969] 2 Ch. 149, 171, where it was held that an alien had no right to a hearing before a refusal of either initial entry or renewal of leave to remain.

[86] If a deportation order is made against a non-patrial person (otherwise than on the recommendation of a court), or if the Home Secretary refuses to revoke a deportation order already in force against him, he may appeal to an adjudicator or the Immigration Appeal Tribunal (Immigration Act 1971, ss.3(5), 5, 7, 15), subject to certain exceptions (deportation on ground that it is conducive to the public good for security, diplomatic or political reasons (s.15(3)). in which case he may be entitled to a written notice of the reasons for the decision to deport (regulation 4(1)(a), Immigration Appeals (Notices) Regulations 1984), and he is entitled to a non statutory reference to the 'Three Advisers' (819 H.C. Deb. 375–377); or where revocation of deportation order is refused on grounds of public good or by Home Secretary personally (s.15(4)). For the extremely limited extent to which the rules of natural justice may apply in these situations, see *R. v. Home Secretary, ex p. Hosenball* [1977] 1 W.L.R. 766; *R. v. Secretary of State for the Home Office ex p. Cheblak* [1991] 1 W.L.R. 890. See also J. M. Evans, *Immigration Law* (2nd ed., 1983), Chaps. 6 and 7. See also Prevention of Terrorism (Temporary Provisions) Act 1989, Sched. 2, (right to make written objections to Home Secretary upon the making of an exclusion order, and to be given a personal interview by persons nominated by Minister who must take their report into account when reconsidering the case).

[87] The distinctions made between 'administrative', 'judicial' and 'executive' decisions are set out in the Appendix to the 5th edition of this work.

the Government, and the courts showed an understandable eluctance to scrutinise the exercise of essential powers in such a way as to make it more difficult for the Government to govern. Not surprisingly, it was hard to persuade the courts that war emergency powers were subject to an implied qualification that persons adversely affected by their exercise were entitled to prior notification and an opportunity to be heard.[88] But the climate of judicial opinion engendered by the exigencies of war tended to persist long after hostilities had ended.[89]

Secondly, the existence of a wide policy discretion vested in a 6–020 minister responsible to Parliament was thought to dictate not only abstention from judicial review of the merits of particular decisions but also (and with less justification) the impropriety of setting minimum procedural standards to be observed in the course of reaching or before executing such decisions.

Thirdly, there was the implicit assumption that the role of the courts 6–021 in relation to the administrative process should be one of rigorous self-restraint, the administration ought not to be embarrassed by well-meaning judicial intruders. Such an assumption had already been clearly articulated in the *Arlidge* case.[90] It was to be revealed in other contexts.

Fourthly, the characterisation of the Secretary of State's functions as 6–022 executive and non-judicial was understood to exclude any implied obligation on his part to act in accordance with natural justice, despite the impact of his decisions on individual rights. The importance of analytical labels in restricting the scope of the obligation to act judicially was to be underlined in the years that followed. Its importance was probably enhanced by Atkin L.J.'s much-quoted judgment in the *Electricity Commissioners* case, defining the circumstances in which the writ of certiorari would issue to quash the decisions of public bodies. Certiorari (and prohibition) would issue to "any body of persons having legal authority to determine questions affecting the rights of subjects, and having the duty to act judicially."[91] In natural justice cases this dictum was generally understood to mean that a duty to act judicially was not to be inferred merely from the impact of a decision on the "rights of subjects"; such a duty would

---

[88] See, esp. the following cases where persons aggrieved by the exercise of executive powers were held to be unprotected by the *audi alteram partem rule*: *Irving v. Paterson* [1943] Ch. 180; *Howell v. Addison* [1943] 1 All E.R. 29, 32 (consent by Minister to determination of agricultural tenancy; though *cf. West Riding C.C. v. Wilson* [1941] 2 All E.R. 827,832); *Carltona Ltd v. Commissioners of Works* [1943] 2 All E.R. 560, 562 (requisitioning of factory).

[89] See paras 5–021–5–026 above, in connection with the legality of discretionary powers.

[90] [1915] A.C. 120.

[91] *R. v. Electricity Commissioners* [1924] 1 K.B. 171, 204–205 (where the contention was not that natural justice had been contravened, but that the impugned order was *ultra vires*).

arise only if there were "superadded" an express obligation to follow a judicial-type procedure in arriving at the decision.[92] In pursuit of a circuitous (and sometimes circular) line of reasoning the courts lost sight of the older cases[93] in which a duty to act judicially in accordance with natural justice had been held to arise by implication from the nature and effect of the powers exercised.[94]

6–023   Paradoxically, the decline of the *audi alteram partem* principle as an implied common-law requirement of administrative procedure was hastened by its embodiment in statutory forms. Twentieth-century statute law has reflected the disfavour with which the common law viewed administrative claims to be entitled to take direct action against private property without giving prior notice or opportunity to be heard. Public health, housing, highways and town planning legislation in particular spell out the procedural conditions under which enforcement powers are exercisable.[95] Where no statutory provision is made for prior notice to be given, it may sometimes be assumed that the omission is deliberate; so, too, where statutory provision is made for a hearing that falls short of the requirements of natural justice, the statutory procedure can often be assumed to be exhaustive. In Victorian times detailed codes were exceptional, and the courts supplied the omissions, in the interests of justice to individuals, by importing common-law principles.

6–024   Of more general significance in the reshaping of judicial attitudes was the fact that in the 1930s and 1940s the typical administrative law controversy in the superior courts was a challenge directed against the validity of a slum clearance or compulsory purchase order. The procedure for the compulsory acquisition of land by public authorities almost invariably provides for prior notice and opportunity to be heard. It was largely standardised by the Acquisition of Land (Authorisation Procedure) Act 1946 (which substantially reproduced earlier legislation on the matter), supplemented by statutory rules.[96] The acquiring authority (normally a local authority) must give public notice of its intentions, and must also notify owners, lessees and

---

[92] See, especially, *Nakkuda Ali v. Jayaratne* [1951] A.C. 66, a decision which gave the most influential support for this approach.

[93] See para. 6–013 above; through the ratio of *Cooper v. Wandsworth Board of Works* was momentarily glimpsed in 1939; *Urban Housing Co. v. Oxford City Council* [1940] Ch. 70.

[94] A point emphasised by H.W.R. Wade in 'The Twilight of Natural Justice?' (1951) 67 L.Q.R. 103 and later elaborated by Lord Reid in *Ridge v. Baldwin* [1964] A.C. 40, 74–76.

[95] See paras 9-011–9-014 below.

[96] Now see the Acquisition of Land Act 1981; Compulsory Purchase by Public Authorities (Inquiries Procedure) Rules 1976 (S.I. 1976 No. 746); and Compulsory Purchase by Non-Ministerial Acquiring Authorities (Inquiry Procedure) Rules 1990 (S.I. 1990 No. 512); See also Compulsory Purchase of Land Regulations 1990 (S.I. 1990 No. 613); *Cross on Local Government Law* (1991); DoE Circ. 6/85, Compulsory Purchase Orders: Procedures.

occupiers individually. Objections to the order may be lodged within a prescribed period by the period by the persons individually served. If an objection so made is not withdrawn, the Minister who will have to decide whether or not to confirm the order must (unless the objection relates only to compensation) either cause a public local inquiry to be held or afford the objector an opportunity of being heard before a person appointed for the purpose, and must consider the objections and the report on the inquiry or hearing. Broadly similar rules govern clearance orders to secure the demolition of slum property in an area.[97]

Persons who had not expressly been given the right to prior notice or opportunity to be heard found difficulty in persuading the courts. that implications affording them such a right ought to be read into the enabling Acts.[98] As far as the courts were concerned, the obligations of the acquiring authority had been codified by statute. To be sure, the inspector conducting the public local inquiry or private hearing had to act in conformity with natural justice even though he had no power to make an initial decision[99] but for the rest, judicial review was to be interstitial; and to the courts the interstices seemed very narrow.

6–025

Between 1935 and 1947 a number of property-owners endeavoured, with scant success, to impugn compulsory purchase orders and clearance orders on the ground that the Minister as confirming authority had failed to observe the rules of natural justice. The courts held that the Minister's functions were essentially administrative, but that once objections were lodged he assumed a quasi-judicial role which imposed upon him the duty to follow the rules of natural

6–026

---

[97] See Housing Act 1985. Pt. IX. The power under that Act to designate Housing Action Areas and General Improvement Areas has been repealed by the Housing Act 1988, which provides for the designation of Housing Actions Trusts in areas designated by the Secretary of State. S. 89 of the Local Government and Housing Act 1989 provides for the designation of Renewal Areas.

[98] An owner was not entitled to be heard by the local authority before it declared a building to be included in a clearance area: *Fredman v. Minister of Health* (1935) 154 L.T. 240. See also *Cohen v. West Ham Corp.* [1933] Ch. 814, 827 (a somewhat anomalous decision; no right to be heard before issue of notice to execute works). For the position today in which natural justice may supplement a statutory code, see paras 7–013–7–020 below.

[99] *Marriott v. Minister of Health* (1935) 154 L.T. 47, 50; *Denby (William) & Sons Ltd v. Minister of Health* [1936] 1 K.B. 337, 342–343. Where the holding of a hearing or a local inquiry was provided for by statute, it was always open to the courts to hold that the proceedings were too defective to constitute a hearing (see *Ealing Borough Council v. Minister of Housing and Local Government*; [1952] Ch. 856) or an inquiry within the meaning of the Act, even though the functions of the Minister under the Act in question were characterised as purely administrative (*Franklin v. Minister of Town and Country Planning* [1948] A.C. 87, 102, 105–106; *Wednesbury Corp. v. Ministry of Housing and Local Government (No. 2)* [1966] 2 Q.B. 275, 302–303 (dicta)). See, generally, para. 12–019 below.

justice when considering the objections and the report on the inquiry.[1] Before objections were lodged he could offer advice to the local authority on housing matters[2] and even express tentative approval of the proposed order.[3] He could obtain information from other departments[4] or from the local authority,[5] which he was not obliged to disclose to the objector although it might be prejudicial to the latter's case.[6] To this extent the objector was denied part of the protection afforded by the *audi alteram partem* rule.[7] After objections had been lodged the Minister had to hold himself aloof from the parties, in so far as he was not to receive *ex parte* statements from the local authority relating to the subject-matter of objections examined at the inquiry.[8] But he was not precluded from discussing with the local authority matters not related to the order,[9] or (possibly) matters related to the order but not made the subject of objections at the inquiry. He was apparently entitled after the inquiry to consult with other departments on matters relevant to his decision whether or not to confirm the order, but—the point was never cleared up by the courts—the character of the information thus obtained might be such as to impose on him an obligation to disclose it to the objector to enable him to challenge its accuracy.[10] He was under no implied legal

---

[1] Where under a temporary Act the Minister was empowered to dispense with a local inquiry, he was still obliged in considering objections to act in conformuty with natural justice: *Stafford v. Minister of Health* [1946] K.B. 621.

[2] *Frost v. Minister of Health* [1935] 1 K.B. 286; *Offer v. Minister of Health* [1936] 1 K.B. 40.

[3] *Re Manchester (Ringway Airport) Compulsory Purchase Order* (1935) 153 L.T. 219.

[4] *Miller v. Minister of Health* [1946] K.B. 626; *Summers v. Minister of Health* [1947] 1 All E.R. 184.

[5] *Price v. Minister of Health* [1947] 1 All E.R. 47; *Summers'* case (n. 4, above); *Johnson (B) & Co. (Builders) Ltd v. Minister of Health* [1947] 2 All E.R. 395.

[6] *Johnson's* case (n. 5, above). This is the leading case on the duties of the Minister; and for a decision in similar vein, see *Bushell v. Secretary of State for the Environment* [1981] A.C. 75 (Minister both proposing and affirming authority for compulsory purchase order under Highways Act 1959).

[7] cf. *Board of Education v. Rice* [1911] A.C. 179, 182; *R. v. City of Westminster Assessment Committee* [1941] 1 K.B. 53.

[8] *Errington v. Minister of Health* [1935] 1 K.B. 249.

[9] *Horn v. Minister of Health* [1937] 1 K.B. 164.

[10] *Darlassis v. Minister of Education* (1954) 118 J.P. 452, 466 (dictum). This issue was directly raised in *Buxton v. Minister of Housing and Local Government* [1961] 1 Q.B. 278 (arising out of a planning appeal), but the application was dismissed on a preliminary point of law because the applicant lacked locus standi). The circumstances in which information obtained by the Minister after the inquiry must be disclosed, and the consequences of disclosure, are now specified by regulations; see, *e.g.* Town and Country Planning (Inquiries Procedure) Rules 1992 (S.I. 1992 No. 2038), and Town and Country Planning Appeals (Determination by Inspectors) (Inquiry Procedures) Rules 1992 (S.I. 1992 No. 2039). The Secretary of State is now required to go back to the parties where he (a) differs from the inspector or on any matter of fact mentioned in, or appearing to him to be material to, a conclusion

duty to disclose the contents of the inspector's report to the parties[11] here again the courts diluted the *audi alteram partem* rule. His decision whether or not to confirm the order was "administrative," inasmuch as it could not be impeached for lack of evidence to support it.[12] If no objections were lodged his function was said to be administrative throughout.[13]

Where the Minister was both confirming authority and initiator of the order the courts showed an even stronger disinclination to review the discharge of his statutory duties in terms of judicial standards. Under the New Towns Act 1946 the Minister was empowered to make orders designating areas as the sites of satellite towns. If objections were lodged against a draft order, he had to cause a public local inquiry to be held with respect thereto and to consider the inspector's report before finally making the order.[14] Before the New Towns Bill had been introduced into Parliament, the Government had expressed its intention of designating Stevenage as the first of the new towns. In *Franklin v. Minister of Town and Country Planning*[15] an attempt was made to impugn an order relating to Stevenage in that the Minister had not called evidence at the inquiry in support of the draft order and had been biased in favour of the order when he had finally made it. The House of Lords rejected these contentions; the inquiry, it held, was directed to the objections, not to the order itself, and was prescribed for the further information of the Minister[16] and the criterion of bias, appropriate to measure the conduct of a quasi-judicial officer, had no relevance to the functions of the Minister which were "purely administrative". Provided that a properly conducted inquiry had been held, the only grounds of challenge could be that the

6–027

---

reached by the inspector, or (b) takes into consideration any new evidence or new matter of fact (not being a matter of government policy).

[11] *Denby (William) & Sons Ltd v. Minister of Health* [1936] 1 K.B. 337, and *Steele v. Minister of Housing and Local Government* (1956) 6 P. & C.R. 386, following *Local Government Board v. Arlidge* [1915] A.C. 120. Disclosure of the report can now be required: S.I. 1992 No. 2038, rr. 10.13.

[12] *Johnson's* case (n. 5, above); *Re Falmouth Clearance Order 1936* [1937] 3 All E.R. 308: *Re L.C.C. Order 1938* [1945] 2 All E.R. 484; *quaere* whether an order might be set aside for total absence of evidence to support it: *Re Bowman* [1932] 2 K.B. 621, 634; *cf. Robinson v. Minister of Town and Country Planning* [1947] K.B. 702, 723–724; and see *Goddard v. Minister of Housing and Local Government* [1958] 1 W.L.R. 1151; *Savoury v. Secretary of State for Wales* (1976) 31 P. & C.R. 344.

[13] *Errington v. Minister of Health* [1935] 1 K.B. 249, 259; *Johnson's* case (n. 5, above).

[14] Sched. I. The 1946 Act was replaced by the New Towns Act 1965, now the New Towns Act 1981.

[15] [1948] A.C. 87.

[16] Following *Re Trunk Roads Act 1936* [1939] 2 K.B. 515: distinguished in the Scottish case of *Magistrates of Ayr v. Lord Advocate*, 1950 S.C. 102. See also *Wednesbury Corp. v. Ministry of Housing and Local Government (No. 2)* [1966] 2 Q.B. 275 (inquiries in connection with objections to proposals for review of local government).

Minister had not in fact considered the report or the objections or "that his mind was so foreclosed that he gave no genuine consideration to them".[17] Whilst it was undoubredly proper to conclude from the nature of the legislative scheme that the Minister was entitled to approach his statutory duty to consider objections with a strong inclination to implement his own policy, the House of Lords used terminology which could be regarded as lending countenance to the view that a public authority did not act in a judicial capacity, in the sense of being required to observe the rules of natural justice, unless it occupied the role of an adjudicator determining something approximating to a *lis inter partes*, in which case a duty to observe natural justice might be superimposed upon the procedural requirements already prescribed by statute.[18]

6–028   These lines of cases profoundly influenced the attitude of English courts towards the procedural duties of public authorities invested with statutory powers in relation to individual rights. The courts tended to assume that a duty to observe the rules of natural justice arose only where the authority was already under a statutory duty to consider objections or conduct an inquiry in a "triangular" situation with two other contending parties before it; and that where no such statutory duty was imposed the functions of the authority could not be characterised as judicial for this purpose.[19] They overlooked the reasons that lay behind the some-what artificial system of

---

[17] [1948] A.C. 87, 102, 103. See, to like effect, *Robinson v. Minister of Town and Country Planning* [1947] K.B. 702; but contrast *Magistrates of Ayr v. Lord Advocate*, n. 16. above. And see now n. 19. below.

[18] *cf.* H.W.R. Wade, *Towards Administrative Justice*, p. 67: 'the right result was reached by the wrong road.' Contrast K.C. Davis in [1962] P.L. at 154–155, approving the terminology used.

[19] Statutory rules imposed upon Ministers who *initiate* compulsory purchase orders almost exactly the same procedural duties as were prescribed in connection with orders initiated by local authorities: Compulsory Purchase by Ministers (Inquiries Procedure) Rules 1967 (S.I. 1967 No. 720); *cf.* Compulsory Purchase of Land Regulations 1976 (S.I. 1976 No. 300) (local authorities), and see n. 95, above. Analogous rules now also apply to the confirmation of highway schemes initiated by the Minister: (S.I. 1976 No. 721). See also the further proposals for increasing the openness and the appearance of impartiality of highway inquiries contained in Cmnd. 7133 (1978). But a duty to act with procedural properiety is not invariably cast on a Minister initiating an order which derogates from private rights; see, *e.g. Essex County Council v. Ministry of Housing and Local Government* (1967) 66 L.G.R. 23. In *Binney and Anscomb v. Secretary of State for the Environment* [1984] J.P.L. 871, the High Court quashed the Secretary of State's decision not to hold a public inquiry into a highway improvement scheme on the ground that he believed that he was sufficiently informed by the representations already received. *Cf. Rea v. Minister of Transport* [1984] J.P.L. 876. See also the dubious decision in *Bushell v. Secretary of State for the Environment* [1981] A.C. 75 (Minister entitled to resort to Departmental sources after the inquiry on any question of fact or policy without re-opening the inquiry or, *semble*, according objectors an opportunity to rebut the additional information).

characterisation adopted in the Housing Act cases. There the courts had a threefold purpose in stressing the "essentially administrative" nature of the Minister's functions: to emphasise that the Minister had an overriding political responsibility for matters of housing policy, for which he was answerable to Parliament so that in reviewing his functions in confirming individual orders it would be inappropriate to impose upon him standards appropriate to a judge determining *lites inter partes;* to protect from disclosure departmental files and communications made to and by him in his political capacity; and to resist the contention that his final decision upon an order involved the exercise of a "quasi-judicial" discretion that might be reviewed on its merits. Viewed in the context of the British political and administrative system, most of the decisions were acceptable except in so far as they failed to ensure that the objectors were given adequate information about the case they had to meet, and failed to impose a duty in any circumstances to disclose the content of inspectors' reports.[20] But the terminology used to justify the results may have had unfortunate effects.

These housing and town planning cases achieved so much **6–029** prominence that older cases establishing a right to notice and hearing despite the absence of a *lis inter partes* or express procedural requirements lurked, neglected and half-forgotten, in the shadows of the past. Decisions in the 1940s and 1950s showed a persistent tendency to substitute for the presumption that the *audi alteram partem* principle conditioned the exercise of powers in relation to persons and property a still stronger presumption that unless a procedural duty was expressed (*e.g.* to consider objections,[21] or to decide "after due inquiry"[22]), none was to be implied.[23] Power to obtain information

---

[20] For subsequent legislative reforms, see para. 6–031, below.

[21] *cf. R. v. British Columbia Pollution Control Board* (1967) 61 D.L.R. (2d) 221.

[22] This is generally understood to mean an inquiry conducted in accordance with natural justice: *Leeson v. General Medical Council* (1890) 43 Ch.D. 366, 383; *General Medical Council v. Spackman* [1943] A.C. 627; *Memudu Lagunju v. Olubadan-in-Council* [1952] A.C. 387, 399; contrast *Patterson v. District Commissioner of Accra* [1948] A.C. 341 ('after inquiry, if necessary'); and see *Beetham v. Trinidad Cement Co.* [1960] A.C. 132 (government's power to 'inquire' into facts of trade dispute and then appoint a board of inquiry, held purely administrative); *Abergavenny (Marquis) v. Llandaff (Bishop)* (1880) 20 QBD 460, 472; *R. v. Staines Union* (1893) 69 L. 714. And *cf. Ross-Clunis v. Papadopoullos* [1958] 1 W.L.R. 546, 560–562 (power of Commissioner to conduct inquiry as he thinks fit, subject to his being satisfied as to its fairness limited scope of judicial review). See further cases cited at n. 99 above.

[23] See, esp. wartime cases cited at n. 88, above; *Patterson v. District Commissioner of Accra* (n. 22, above) (levying of differential charges on inhabitants of colonial riot area for extra police protection); *Nakkuda Ali v. Jayaratne* [1951] A.C. 66 (revocation of trader's licence); *Musson v. Rodriguez* [1953] A.C. 530 (deportation of prohibited immigrant); *R. v. Metropolitan Police Commissioner, ex p. Parker* [1953] 1 W.L.R. 1150 (revocation of taxi-cab driver's licence); *R. v. St. Lawrence's Hospital, Caterham, Statutory Visitors, ex p. Pritchard* [1953] 1 W.L.R. 1158, 1162.

from any source was assumed to be inconsistent with the existence of any duty to notify the person affected by the information obtained.[24] A sharp distinction moreover, was drawn between the deprivation of a right and the deprivation of a mere privilege, the latter function importing no judicial duty.[25] Finally, views were expressed by Lord Goddard C.J. that it was undesirable for the courts to control the exercise of disciplinary powers by characterising them as judicial.[26]

6–030   Some of these trends were illustrated by the decision in *Nakkuda Ali v. Jayaratne*.[27] The Controller of Textiles in Ceylon had cancelled a textile dealer's licence in pursuance of a power to revoke a licence when he had "reasonable grounds" for believing its holder to be unfit to continue as a dealer. The dealer applied for certiorari to quash the order, contending that the Controller had not held an inquiry conducted in conformity with natural justice. The Judicial Committee of the Privy Council dismissed his appeal, holding that the Controller, although obliged to act on reasonable grounds,[28] was under no duty to act judicially, so that certiorari could not issue and compliance with natural justice was unnecessary. Two reasons were given for the decision: that certiorari would issue only to an authority that was required to follow a procedure analogous to the judicial in arriving at its decision, and that the Controller was not determining a question affecting the rights of subjects but was merely "taking executive action to withdraw a privilege."[29] Yet the first assertion was contradicted in

---

[24] *R. v. Central Professional Committee for Opticians, ex p. Brown* [1949] 2 All E.R. 519, 521; (*Musson v. Rodriguez* (n. 23, above); *R. v. Metropolitan Police Commissioner* (n. 23, above). Contrast *Capel v. Child* (1832) 2 Cr. & J. 558.

[25] *Nakkuda Ali v. Jayaratne* (n. 23, above); and (*semble*) *R. v. Metropolitan Police Commissioner* (n. 23 above).

[26] *R. v. Metropolitan Police Commissioner, ex p. Parker* (n. 23, above) at 1155; *ex p. Fry* [1954] 1 W.L.R. 730, DC (discipline of members of the National Fire Service).

[27] [1951] A.C. 66.

[28] Distinguishing *Liversidge v. Anderson* [1942] A.C. 206 on this point.

[29] [1951] A.C. 66, at 78. The Judicial Committee also held that the dealer had in fact been given an adequate opportunity to put his case against revocation; but this finding clearly did not reduce the other grounds for the decision to the status of *obiter dicta*.
The reasons for holding that there was no duty to observe natural justice have been almost universally criticised by academic writers. They were trenchantly criticised by Lord Reid in *Ridge v. Baldwin* [1964] A.C. 40 at 77–79; his Lordship was prepared, however, to explain the decision as one resting on the wording of defence regulations (at 73, 78). The decision was restrictively distinguished by Lord Parker C.J. in *Re H.K. (An Infant)* [1967] 2 Q.B. 617, 630, 631, and disapproved by Lord Denning M.R. in *R. v. Gaming Board for Great Britain, ex p. Benaim and Khaida* [1970] 2 Q.B. 417 at 430; though in *Durayappah v. Fernando* [1967] 2 A.C. 337 at 349, PC, the Judicial Committee observed, rather opaquely, that it did not 'necessarily agree' with Lord Reid's comments.

many cases on the scope of certiorari[30]; and the second served only to demonstrate the limitations of a conceptualistic approach to administrative law. Demolition of a property-owner's uninhabitable house might be for him a supportable misfortune; deprivation of a licence to trade might mean a calamitous loss of livelihood; but the judicial flavour detected in the former function was held to be absent from the latter. The decision, whilst not unique[31] was inconsistent with the general attitude of the English courts towards the licensing and regulation of trades and occupations[32] and in general towards the right to earn one's living.[33]

Revisionism revised

By this stage valedictory addresses to the *audi alteram partem* rule in English administrative law were becoming almost commonplace. It was nevertheless suggested in the first edition of this work that the time had "not yet arrived to think of pronouncing obsequies or writing obituary notices," and that "the comatose must not be assumed to be moribund." In the 1960s the rule recovered much of its former vitality as an implied common-law requirement of fair administrative procedure. Perhaps the state of its debility had been slightly exaggerated. Its revival was indirectly stimulated by a growing awareness among practitioners and judges of old forsaken paths, of more imaginative judicial achievements in other English-speaking countries, and of academic legal literature. Undoubtedly the enactment of the Tribunals and Inquiries Act 1958, which extended the scope of judicial review in other directions, modified the general climate of judicial opinion. Above all, there had been a growth of informed interest in problems of administrative adjudication and judicialised administration generated by the publication of the Franks Report (1957), the establishment of the Council on Tribunals, the proliferation of statutory procedural rules in administrative law and the controversies aroused by the decision-making process in town and country planning. Judges do not inhabit an intellectual vacuum, and they were impelled to do some hard thinking about their own role in administrative law.

6–031

---

[30] See, *e.g. R. v. Manchester Area Legal Aid Committee, ex p. Brand (R.A.) & Co.* [1952] 2 Q.B. 413 and cases there cited at 427–428.

[31] See also *R. v. Metropolitan Police Commissioner, ex p. Parker* [1953] 1 W.L.R. 1150; and *cf. ex p. Fry* [1954] 1 W.L.R. 730.

[32] See paras 7-009–7-010, below.

[33] *e.g. Abbott v. Sullivan* [1952] 1 K.B. 189.

Decisions in other jurisdictions

6–032   Here it must suffice to take note of the large body of American case-law, and the impressively sophisticated writings of leading American commentators[34] on the right to a hearing in administrative law. The impact of American experience and thought on the decisions of English courts was neither immediate nor even obviously perceptible, but English academic lawyers were influenced.

6–033   That the *audi alteram partem* rule had not been forgotten in Commonwealth countries was made clear in the 1950s. The High Court of Australia reaffirmed the presumption in favour of the maxim in two cases where summary action derogating from private property rights had been taken in reliance on legislation which afforded no procedural safeguard.[35] The Supreme Court of Ceylon, although bound by *Nakkuda Ali v. Jayaratne*,[36] contrived to give effect to the maxim in a range of situations extending from the disqualification of a university student for misconduct[37] to the removal of local councillors.[38] The vitality of the maxim survived, too. in Canada where the Supreme Court applied the *audi alteram partem* rule to a decision of a Labour Relations Board to decertify a trade union as the bargaining agent for employees.[39] And in a striking decision the Appellate Division of the South African Supreme Court demonstrated its independence by

---

[34] See, *e.g.* K.C. Davis, *Administrative Law Treatise*, Chaps 6–8, 11, 15; Walter Gellhorn and Clark Byse, *Administrative Law: Cases and Comments* (6th ed.), Chaps 5–8.

[35] *Delta Properties Pty. Ltd v. Brisbane City Council* (1956) 95 C.L.R. 11, 18 (resolution prohibiting erection of dwellings on land); *Police Commissioner v. Tanos* (1958) 98 C.L.R. 383, 385–386 (judge declaring restaurant a disorderly house on an *ex parte* application). See also *Ex p. Wilson, re Cuff (No. 2)* (1940) 40 S.R. (N.S.W.) 559 at 564; *Re Gosling* (1943) 43 S.R. (N.S.W.) 312, 316–317; *Election Importing Co. Pty Ltd v. Courtice* (1949) 80 C.L.R. 657. 672; *R. v. Melbourne Corp, ex p. Whyte* [1949] V.L.R. 257.

[36] [1951] A.C. 66.

[37] The rule was said by Hawkins to be implied in the construction of all penal statutes (*Pleas of the Crown*. i. 420). See also *Painter v. Liverpool Oil Gas Light Co.* (1836) 3 A. & E. 433, 448–449: 'a party is not to suffer in person or in purse without an opportunity of being heard.'

[38] See, *e.g.* *del Mel v. de Silva* (1949) 51 N.L.R. 105; *Subramanian v. Minister of Local Government and Cultural Affairs* (1957) 59 N.L.R. 254; but contrast *Sugathadasa v. Jayasinghe* (1958) 59 N.L.R. 459 (dissolution of municipal council), overruled in *Durayappah v. Fernando* [1967] 2 A.C. 337.

[39] *Alliance des Professeurs Catholiques de Montréal v. Labour Relations Board of Quebec* [1953] 2 S.C.R. 140. The rule has been applied by the Supreme Court in other situations as well (see, *e.g.* *Saltfleet Board of Health v. Knapman* [1956] S.C.R. 877; *Wiswell v. Metropolitan Corp. of Greater Winnipeg* [1965] S.C.R. 512; *Re Nicholson and Haldimand-Norfolk Police Commissioners* (1979) 88 D.L.R. (3d) 671). But the line has not always been firmly held (see, *e.g.* *Calgary Power Ltd v. Copithorne* [1959] S.C.R. 24; *Howarth v. National Parole Board* [1976] 1 S.C.R. 453; *Martineau and Butters v. Matsqui Institution Inmate Disciplinary Board* [1978] 1 S.C.R. 118 (but the latter two cases turn specifically on the interpretation of the Federal Court Act 1979, s. 28(1)).

invalidating a restriction order served by a minister under the Suppression of Communism Act, the person affected not having been given the opportunity of making representations against it in accordance with the "sacred maxim," *audi alteram partem.*[40] Finally, the New Zealand courts, whilst regarding themselves bound by *Nakkuda Ali,* were nonetheless prepared to apply the rule to situations far removed from that of a judge deciding a *lis inter partes,* by finding statutory indications of a duty to act judicially, albeit that the legislation did not expressly require notice or hearing.[41]

English and Privy Council decisions

There were some indications in the first years of the 1960s, both from English courts[42] and the Privy Council, that considerations of the need for fairness in the administrative process had not been entirely eliminated from judicial thinking. Particular mention should be made of Lord Denning who, in a series of cases involving the powers of voluntary associations was concerned to ensure that these powers were tempered by corresponding responsibilities, of which the duty to hold fair inquiries was one.[43] Characteristically, Lord Denning was not

6–034

---

[40] *R. v. Ngwevela,* 1954 (1) S.A. 123 (rule not excluded by Parliament expressly or by necessary implication, and no exceptional circumstances, such as paramount need for swift preventive action, present). See also *Saliwa v. Minister of Native Affairs,* 1956 (2) S.A. 310; contrast, however, *South African Defence and Aid Fund v. Minister of Justice,* 1967 (1) S.A. 263, indicating a retreat by the judges from their bold attitude towards executive encroachments on individual freedom.

[41] See, especially, *New Zealand Dairy Board v. Okitu Co-operative Dairy Co. Ltd* [1953] N.Z.L.R. 366, 403–405, 417, 422; *New Zealand United Licensed Victuallers' Association of Employers v. Price Tribunal* [1957] N.Z.L.R. 167, 203–205, 207; *Low v. Earthquake Commission* [1959] N.Z.L.R. 1198.

[42] *R. v. Registrar of Building Societies* [1960] 1 W.L.R. 669; *Hoggard v. Worsbrough U.D.C.* [1962] 2 Q.B. 93. In a number of other cases, proceedings before courts and regularly constituted tribunals were set aside for non-compliance with the *audi alteram partem* rule: *Chettiar v. Chettiar* [1962] 1 W.L.R. 279; *R. v. Birkenhead JJ., ex p. Fisher* [1962] 1 W.L.R. 1410; *Brinkley v. Brinkley* [1963] 2 W.L.R. 822; *Fowler v. Fowler* [1963] P. 311; *Abraham v. Jutsun* [1963] 1 W.L.R. 658; *Disher v. Disher* [1965] P. 31; *Appuhamy v. R.* [1963] A.C. 474; *Sheldon v. Bromfield JJ.* [1964] 2 Q.B. 573; *S. v. S. (1964)* [1965] 1 W.L.R. 21; *Hodgkins v. Hodgkins* [1965] 1 W.L.R. 1448; *R. v. Aylesbury JJ., ex p. Wisbey* [1965] 1 W.L.R. 339 (courts); *The Seistan* [1960] 1 W.L.R. 186; *R. v. Deputy Industrial Injuries Commissioner, ex p. Jones* [1962] 2 Q.B. 677; *R. v. Industrial Tribunal, ex p. George Green & Thomson Ltd* (1967) 2 K.I.R. 259 (other statutory tribunals). Decisions on non-statutory arbitrations and domestic tribunals have been omitted.

[43] See, *e.g. Russell v. Duke of Norfolk* (1949) 65 T.L.R. 225 (withdrawal of horse trainer's licence by Jockey Club); *Abbott v. Sullivan* [1952] 1 K.B. 189 (dockworker struck off Union's register and therefore could no longer be employed); *Lee v. Showman's Guild* [1952] 2 Q.B. 329 (expulsion from a trade association). See generally, J. Jowell 'Administrative Law' in J. Jowell and P.W. McAuslan, *Lord Denning: The judge and The Law* (1983).

concerned with the formal nature of the decision but with the fact that voluntary associations have monopoly powers and that their decisions in effect deprived individuals of their livelihoods.

6–035 Then in 1963 the House of Lords restored the law to the path from which it had deviated. For in *Ridge v. Baldwin*,[44] it was held by a majority that a chief constable, dismissible only for cause prescribed by statute,[45] was impliedly entitled to prior notice of the charge against him and a proper opportunity of meeting it before being removed by the local police authority for misconduct.[46] In an illuminating review of the authorities,[47] Lord Reid repudiated the notions that the rules of natural justice applied only to the exercise of those functions which were analytically judicial, and that a "superadded" duty to act judicially had to be visible before an obligation to observe natural justice could arise in the exercise of a statutory function affecting the rights of an individual. He emphasised that the duty to act in conformity with natural justice could, in some situations, simply be inferred from a duty to decide "what the rights of an individual should be."[48]

6–036 This decision gave a powerful impetus to the emergent trend.[49] an impetus which is not yet spent in administrative law. It opened an era of activism in which the courts have subjected the working of

---

[44] [1964] A.C. 40.

[45] Negligence or other unfitness (Municipal Corporations Act 1882, s. 191(4)), repealed by Police Act 1964, s. 64(3) and Sched. 10; see now Police Act 1964, ss. 5(4), (5), 29 (compulsory retirement in interests of efficiency; express right to make representations against requirement), 33 (dismissibility for disciplinary offence; right to hearing conferred by regulations: S.I. 1985 No. 519. See also Police Act 1976, s. 10; Police and Criminal Evidence Act 1984, s. 119 and Sched. 6.

[46] The implications of the decision were much discussed: see, *e.g.* A.W. Bradley [1964] Camb.L.J. 83; A. L. Goodhart (1964) 80 L.Q.R. 105. The decision was criticised by some New Zealand writers because of the omission of a 'superadded' requirement to act judicially; J. F. Northey [1963] N.Z.L.J. 448; D.E. Patterson [1966] N.Z.L.J. 107; but see J. A. Farmer (1967) 2 N.Z.U.L.Rev. 282.

[47] [1964] A.C. 40, 71–79.

[48] *ibid.* at 75–76.

[49] Privy Council decisions in the 1960s applying the *audi alteram partem* rule to set aside administrative action included *Kanda v. Government of Malaya* [1962] A.C. 322; *Shareef v. Commissioner for Registration of Indian and Pakistani Residents* [1966] A.C. 47; *Maradana Mosque Trustees v. Mahmud* [1967] 1 A.C. 13; *Jeffs v. New Zealand Dairy Production and Marketing Board* [1967] 1 A.C. 551. See also *Durayappah v. Fernando* [1967] 2 A.C. 337 (implied duty to observe natural justice, but appeal dismissed on a technical point). See, on the other hand, *Vidyodaya University Council v. Silva* [1965] 1 W.L.R. 77; *Pillai v. Singapore City Council* [1968] 1 W.L.R. 1278.

government to a degree of judicial scrutiny, on substantive as well as procedural grounds, which shows little sign yet of diminishing.

The duty to act fairly

In the case law since the late 1960s, the courts have demonstrated **6–037** considerable flexibility in their manipulation of the principal criteria used for determining the circumstances in which a duty to observe the rules of natural justice would be implied. And as long as it was remembered that the degree of procedural formality required by the rules was capable of considerable variation according to the context,[50] an extension of the range of situations to which they were applied did not attract the criticism that the courts were "over judicialising" administrative procedures. Since 1967 the courts began to employ the term "duty to act fairly" to denote an implied procedural obligation— the contents of which may fall considerably short of the essential elements of a trial or a formal inquiry—accompanying the performance of a function that cannot, without overly straining linguistic usage,[51] be characterised as judicial in nature.

Thus, before refusing leave to enter, immigration officers are not **6–038** required to hold a judicial hearing at which the individual can produce witnesses and evidence to support his claim: this would unduly burden the administration of the system of immigration control in which officers at the ports are required, within a relatively short period of time, to make a large number of decisions. However, they are under a legal obligation to exercise their powers fairly, and this means that they must inform a person who claims a legal right to enter why they are disposed to refuse and allow him an opportunity

---

[50] Dicta to this effect in *Russell v. Duke of Norfolk* [1949] 1 All E.R. 109, 118 were cited with predictable regularity.

[51] Similar developments have occurred in other jurisdictions: see, *e.g.* in Canada *Nicholson v. Haldimand-Norfolk Regional Board of Commissioners of Police* [1979] 1 S.C.R. 311 (probationary constable entitled to procedural fairness before being let go, even though the statutory rules prescribing a hearing before dismissal did not apply to a power to dispense with services of a probationer). And in the United States, the Supreme Court has held that, while the constitutional guarantee of due process sometimes require an evidentiary trial, it may on other occasions be satisfied by a much more informal procedure: see, for instance, *Goss v. Lopez* (1975) 419 U.S. 565 (pupil entitled to reasons and opportunity to explain before being suspended from school for misconduct); Davis, *Administrative Law Treatise* (2nd ed), Chap. 13.

to allay their suspicions.[52] Similar obligations were imposed upon inspectors conducting inquiries into allegations of improprieties committed against companies by their officers.[53] While the damage to reputations that might be suffered as a result of the publication of a report containing adverse criticisms requires that affected individuals have a prior opportunity to be informed of and to comment upon any serious allegations made against them, to insist on an adjudicative hearing would be inconsistent with the public interest in protecting the confidentiality of evidence given to the inspector, and in ensuring that the inquiry is conducted with reasonable expedition. Moreover, an adverse report does not directly deprive a person of any legal rights in the strict sense. The duty to act fairly also extended the scope of the hearing to situations where a "privilege" rather than a "right" was in issue. For example, an applicant for a renewal of gaming licence cannot be refused on grounds of personal unacceptability unless the board has first intimated to him its concerns in such a way that allows the applicant to respond, but without prejudicing the confidentiality of the board's sources of information.[54]

6–039   The principal value of the introduction of the duty to act fairly into the court's vocabulary has been to assist them to extend the benefit of

---

[52] *Re H.K. (An Infant)* [1967] 2 Q.B. 617, where the applicant had a legal right to enter if he could establish his claim to be the son, under the age of 16, of a Commonwealth citizen settled in the United Kingdom. The reason for Lord Parker C.J.'s doubt over the proper characterisation of the immigration officer's function arose from the exigencies of the administration of immigration control at the ports of entry, rather than from the nature of the decision to be made. Those without a legal entitlement (or, it should now be added, a legitimate expectation) to enter or remain in the United Kingdom may be refused without the benefit of any implied procedural rights: *Schmidt v. Home Office* [1969] 2 Ch. 149.
Since 1969, there has been a right to a hearing on an appeal against many immigration decisions to independent tribunals. This is one context in which statutory justice has, to an extent at least, supplied the omission of the common law. However, the statutory duty to give reasons for refusal, before a notice of appeal is given, has been construed narrowly: *R. v. Secretary of State for the Home Department, ex p. Swati* [1986] 1 W.L.R. 477.

[53] See now Companies Act 1985, Pt. XIV; *Re Pergamon Press Ltd* [1971] Ch. 388; *Maxwell v. Department of Trade and Industry* [1974] Q.B. 523. But see *Norwest Holst Ltd v. Secretary of State for Trade* [1978] Ch. 201 (appointment of inspectors), and *R. v. Secretary of State for Trade, ex p. Perestrello* [1981] Q.B. 19 (exercise of power under Companies Act 1967, s.109 (now 1985 Act, s.447), to require the production of corporate documents), where the duty to act fairly was given hardly any independent content.

[54] *R. v. Gaming Board of Great Britain, ex p. Benaim and Khaida* [1970] 2 Q.B. 417.

basic procedural protections to situations where it would be both confusing to characterise as judicial, or even quasi-judicial, the decision-makers' functions, and inappropriate to insist on a procedure analogous to a trial.[55]

---

[55] On the relationship between classification of a function as administrative and importation of a duty to act 'fairly' rather than 'judicially,' see, *e.g. Pearlberg v. Varty* [1972] 1 W.L.R. 534, 547, *per* Lord Pearson; *Bates v. Lord Hailsham of St. Marylebone* [1972] 1 W.L.R. 1373, 1378, *per* Megarry J.; *R. v. Liverpool Corp., ex p. Liverpool Taxi Fleet Operators' Association* [1972] 2 Q.B. 299, 307–308, 310 *per* Lord Denning M.R., and Roskill L.J.; *Herring v. Templeman* [1973] 3 All E.R. 569, 584 (no duty to disclose academic assessments to student liable to expulsion); *R. v. Race Relations Board, ex p. Selvarajan* [1975] 1 W.L.R. 1686, 1695–1696. 1700 (delegation of decision-making by a body whose functions were largely investigative and conciliatory). While judges may adopt different characterisations of the same power, and use different terms to describe the applicable procedural duty, they can still agree on whether the authority was obliged to afford to the applicant the procedural right in question: see, *e.g. Re H.K.* [1967] 2 Q.B. 617, 630–631 (Lord Parker C.J., 'fairly'), 632–633 (Salmon L.J., 'natural justice'). 636 (Blain J., neutral). *Re Pergamon Press Ltd* [1971] Ch. 388, 399–400 (Lord Denning M.R., 'fairly'), 402–403 (Sachs L.J. 'natural justice'), 407 (Buckley L.J., 'not a judicial function'); *Breen v. A.E.U.* [1971] 2 Q.B. 175, 190 (Lord Denning M.R., 'fairly'), 195 (Edmund Davies L.J., 'natural justice'), 200 (Megaw L.J., neutral). See also *Grunwick Processing Laboratories Ltd v. ACAS* [1978] A.C. 655, 660, 667, *per* Lord Denning M.R. ('judicial', 'natural justice'), 677, *per* Geoffrey Lane L.J. ('unfair or contrary to the rules of natural justice'); but on appeal Lord Diplock, speaking for the majority in the House of Lords, disposed of the questions of statutory interpretation in issue without reference to either term. But see para. 7–001 below, n. 3.

CHAPTER 7

PROCEDURAL FAIRNESS: ENTITLEMENT

Natural Justice and the Duty to Act Fairly Today

Procedural fairness, as we have seen, is no longer restricted by **7–001** distinctions between "judicial" and "administrative" functions or between "rights" and "privileges". This "heresy was scotched"[1] in *Ridge v. Baldwin*.[2] The term "natural justice" is being increasingly replaced by a general duty to act fairly, which is a key element of procedural propriety.[3]

Whichever term is used, the time has come to make a break with **7–002** the artificial constraints surrounding the situations in which natural justice or the duty to act fairly are required. The previous distinctions were already comatose and should be formally declared moribund. The entitlement to fair procedures no longer depends upon the adjudicative analogy, nor whether the authority is required or empowered to decide matters analogous to *lites inter partes*. The law has moved on; not to the state where the entitlement to procedural protection can be extracted with certainty from a computer, but to where the courts are able to insist upon some degree of participation

---

[1] *R. v. Gaming Board for Great Britain, ex p. Benaim and Khaida* [1970] 2 Q.B. 417, 430 *per* Denning M.R.

[2] [1964] A.C. 40. The distinction has been abandoned in Australia since *Bankes v. Transport Regulation Board* (1968) 119 C.I.R. 222.

[3] In *O'Reilly v. Mackman* [1983] 2 A.C. 237, 275, Lord Diplock said that the rules of natural justice 'mean no more than the duty to act fairly...and I prefer so to put it'. See also *Chandra v. Minister of Immigration* [1978] 2 N.Z.L.R. 559, 564 *et seq.* reviewing authorities on the relationship between fairness and natural justice. In Australia the term 'procedural fairness' has normally been invoked in preference to 'natural justice'. *Kioa v. West* (1985) 159 C.I.R. 550, 583, although the Australian Administrative Decisions (Judicial Review) Act 1977 (AD (JR) Act), ss. 5(1)(a); 6(1)(a) prescribes natural justice as a ground of review. The applicability and content of natural justice under the Act are however the same as at common law. *Kioa, ibid.* at 583.

in reaching most official decisions by those whom the decisions will affect in widely different situations, subject only to well-established exceptions.

7–003 Procedural fairness is therefore not these days rationed at its source—blocked at the outset on the ground of a decision being administrative rather than judicial, or governing a privilege rather than a right. It may, in exceptional situations, be diverted during the course of its flow—where special circumstances, such as national security, excuse a right to a fair hearing. And the breadth of the flow will depend upon the circumstances surrounding the decision. Some decisions require full adjudicative-type hearings, others only narrowly permit the mere right to make representations.

7–004 Increasing resort to the open-textured standard of fairness is not, though, without its drawbacks. There is a point at which the benefits of its flexible application may be outweighed by the costs of uncertainty. The courts are perhaps creating "a surrogate political process to ensure the fair representation of a wide range of affected interests in the administrative process".[4] Doubts have been expressed whether the courts are institutionally equipped for such tasks,[5] and whether the unconstrained expansion of participation might paralyse effective administration.[6]

7–005 In response to these doubts, various attempts have been made to devise categories or criteria of relative precision to determine the bounds of procedural fairness in the modern era. In *Ridge v. Baldwin*[7] it was stated that the duty to observe the rules of natural justice

---

[4] R. Stewart, 'The Reformation of American Administrative Law' (1975) 88 Harv. L.R. 1669, 1670.

[5] *cf.* Martin Loughlin, 'Procedural Fairness: A Study in the Crisis of Administrative Law Theory' (1978) 28 U. Tor. L.J. 215; R.A. Macdonald, 'Procedural Fairness in Administrative Law' (1979) 25 McGill L.J. 520, and (1980) 26 McGill L.J. 1, where the development of the duty to act fairly is regarded as a major theoretical departure in the law of procedural review, but see P.P. Craig, *Administrative Law* (3rd ed., 1994), pp. 288–292. And for a judicial recognition of the limited nature of the courts' role, see *R. v. Brent L.B.C., ex p. Gunning* (1985) 84 L.G.R. 168, 180. See also Denis Galligan, *Due Process and Fair Procedures* (1996); Nick Wikeley, 'Natural Justice and non-disclosure of medical evidence' (1996) J.S.S.L. 98–99 (proper approach to non-disclosure in Social Security Appeal Tribunal hearings).

[6] See, *e.g.* the comments of Mr Michael Barnes Q.C. who conducted an inquiry into the proposal for a nuclear reactor at Hinkley Point in Somerset under the Electricity Act 1957 and the Electricity Generating Stations and Overhead Lines (Inquiries Procedures) Rules 1987 (S.I. 1987 No. 2182) (now the 1990 Rules (S.I. 1990 No. 528)). The inquiry lasted 182 days and there were nearly 10,000 objectors ('section 34 parties') with a right to appear. In Chapter 4 of his Report on the inquiry Mr Barnes warned that in the effort to ensure a proper hearing in inquiries of this scale there is a danger that the inquiry will become an 'engine of delay in reaching administrative decisions'.

[7] [1964] A.C. 40, 76.

should be inferred from the nature of the power conferred upon the authority. It has been suggested[8] that whether the nature of the power requires such an inference to be drawn may be determined by considering the following three factors: first, the nature of the complainant's interest; secondly, the conditions under which the administrative authority is entitled to encroach on those interests; and thirdly, the severity of the sanction that can be imposed. These factors offer some guidance as to which interests should be protected by fair procedures, but leave a great deal open to speculation.

A more precise classification was provided in *McInnes v. Onslow*   **7–006**
Fane,[9] where the following three situations were distinguished:

(1) "forfeiture" or "deprivation" cases, where a vested interest (such as a licence to trade) has been withdrawn;

(2) "application" cases, where no interest yet exists, but is merely being sought (such as an application for a licence, passport or a council house); and

(3) "expectation" cases, where there is a reasonable expectation of a continuation of an existing benefit which falls short of a right.

A fair hearing, it was suggested, should be granted in cases involving "forfeiture" and (normally) "expectation", but not in those involving a mere "application".

This analysis would, if strictly applied, result in anomalies and   **7–007**
injustice for there are situations where the refusal of an application could adversely affect an interest deserving of protection by means of a fair hearing. For example, the refusal of an application for a passport not only prevents the exercise of a basic liberty to travel, but may also cast aspersions on a person's character.[10] It would seem unfair to deny

---

[8] *Durayappah v. Fernando* [1967] 2 A.C. 337, 349. See also Lord Bridge in *Lloyd v. McMahon* [1987] A.C. 625, 702–703. *Cf. The Board of Education of the Indian Head School Division No. 19 of Saskatchewan v. Knight* [1990] 1 S.C.R. 653.

[9] [1978] 1 W.L.R. 1520.

[10] See *R. v. Secretary of State for Foreign and Commonwealth Affairs, ex p. Everett* [1989] Q.B. 811, where it was said that a passport was a 'normal expectation of every citizen' (*per* Taylor L.J.) and that, despite the fact that the issuance of passports was within the royal prerogative, such a power was subject to judicial review; *cf. R. v. Huntingdon D.C., ex p. Cowan* [1984] 1 W.L.R. 501. In *R. v. Secretary of State for the Home Department, ex p. Fayed* [1997] 1 All E.R. 228, the Court of Appeal held: (Woolf M.R., Phillips L.J.—Kennedy L.J. dissenting), that the applicants for British citizenship were wrongly deprived of an opportunity to make representations in advance of the refusal of their applications. The statute itself precludes a requirement for reasons. The *ratio* appears to be (*per* Lord Woolf at 237–238; Phillips L.J. at 251) that, although the applicants had no vested rights to citizenship (as in *Attorney-General v. Ryan*

---

an applicant for planning permission procedural protection (as is provided by statute)[11] so that he may argue in favour of his interest in developing his land. It would also seem unfair to deny an applicant for a licence to export goods the opportunity to make representation in support of his application (such an opportunity *not* presently provided by statute[12]).

7–008   In addition, some decisions deserving of a fair hearing do not fall into any of the three categories set out in *McInnes*. For example, it has been held that in some circumstances an interested person such as a neighbour is entitled to object to a proposed development of land despite the absence of a statutory right to make representations and the absence of any legitimate expectation of so doing.[13] That kind of situation fits none of the categories in *McInnes*, as the interested person is neither in the position of an applicant, nor someone deprived of an existing right, interest or legitimate expectation.

7–009   In general there are practical reasons why a hearing cannot be given to every applicant for a licence, for the same reason that the hearing cannot be given to all applicants for scarce resources (such as hospital beds, or university places). The task of allocation in these circumstances requires despatch, and the class of applicant may be entirely open-ended. However, one can imagine situations where the unfairness of the summary refusal of a licence or the summary award of a licence to a competitor will be so manifest (*e.g.* because the worthiness of the applicant rather than the availability of resources is the dominant factor shaping a decision),[14] that it will be right for a

---

[1980] A.C. 718, PC—constitutional entitlement to citizenship of the Bahamas), the refusal of the application would in the circumstances of this case lead to adverse inferences being drawn about the applicants' characters. *Quaere* whether the applicants would have been successful simply because their interest in citizenship was in issue. For a recent case where 'serious allegations of misconduct' against the applicant grounded a right to make representations (despite the lack of a finding of any adverse public inferences on the applicant's character), see *R. v. Immigration Board, ex p. Kirk Freeport Plaza Ltd and Island Companies Ltd* Cayman Island Court of Appeal, November 28, 1997. For another case where an applicant was afforded the right to a fair hearing see *R. v. Secretary of State for the Home Department, ex p. Moon* (1996) 8 Admin. L.R. 477.

[11] Town & Country Planning Act, 1990, s.78.

[12] The system of licensing in relation to exports to Iraq was the subject of an inquiry under Scott L.J. See Richard Scott (*Report of the Inquiry into the Export of Dual Use Goods to Iraq and Related Prosecutions*, H.C. Paper 115 1995/96). The power to control the removal of goods from the United Kingdom and to require the licensing of the exports was contained in the Import, Export and Customs Powers (Defence) Act 1939, as amended by the Import and Export Control Act 1990.

[13] *R. v. Great Yarmouth B.C., ex p. Botton Bros.* (1988) 56 P. & C.R. 99; [1988] J.P.L. 18.

[14] See, *e.g. Stininato v. Auckland Boxing Assocation (Inc.)* [1978] 1 N.Z.L.R. 1; *Trivett v. Nivison* [1976] 1 N.S.W.L.R. 312. See also Henry J. Friendly, 'Some Kind of Hearing' (1975) 123 U. Penn.L.Rev. 1267.

court to hold that the deciding body is under a duty to give the applicant an opportunity to make representations (whether in writing or orally) and of being apprised of all information on which the decision may be founded.[15]

Other situations where applicants may be accorded the benefits of a   **7–010**
fair hearing include those where the licensing authority is constituted as a distinct tribunal, or is expressly required to entertain representations or objections or appeals, or to conduct hearings or inquiries, when deciding whether or not to grant a licence.[16] A duty to act fairly may also be imposed even upon "application" cases when policy guidelines have been established (especially if published) within which discretion will normally be exercised. They may raise an expectation of benefit in those who believe that they fall within the guidelines.[17] In addition, an opportunity to be heard, both on the application and the merits of the policy, may be required in order to prevent a fettering of discretion.[18]

There are, therefore, situations which are not covered by the *McInnes*   **7–011**
approach which, like other attempts at classification, has its shortcomings. Would it, therefore, not be preferable to adopt a more comprehensive approach? Surely the time has come to recognise that the duty of fairness cannot and should not be restricted by artificial barriers or confined by inflexible categories. The duty is a general one, governed by the following propositions:

(1) Whenever a public function is being performed there is an inference, in the absence of an express requirement to the contrary, that the function is required to be performed fairly.[19]

---

[15] In *R. v. Huntingdon D.C., ex p. Cowan* [1984] 1 W.L.R. 501 it was held that an applicant for an entertainments licence was entitled to know the substance of objections and to have an opportunity of responding to those objections in writing; *cf. R. v. Independent Television Commission, ex p. T.S.W. Broadcasting Ltd, The Times,* March 30, 1992, HL.

[16] Though the obligation may be qualified by a right to refrain from disclosing the source and precise content of highly confidential information: *R. v. Gaming Board for Great Britain, ex p. Benaim and Khaida* [1970] 2 Q.B. 417, 431.

[17] See discussion at paras 7-037–7-066 below.

[18] *British Oxygen Co. Ltd v. Board of Trade* [1971] A.C. 610, 625; see also *R. v. Criminal Injuries Compensation Board, ex p. Ince* [1973] 1 W.L.R. 1334, 1345.

[19] See the discussion on the public function at para. 3–021. Thus a passage in a decision or a public report criticising a person who has not had a fair opportunity of answering the allegation may be reviewable: *O'Regan v. Lousich* [1995] 2 N.Z.L.R. 620, developing *Mahon v. New Zealand Ltd* [1984] A.C. 808. English law must now take note of the European Convention on Human Rights, Art. 6, which requires a fair hearing in the 'determination' of 'civil rights and obligations' or of 'criminal charges'. The fairness of a number of procedures in English law and practice have recently been under scrutiny in the European Court of Human Rights. See, *e.g. Benham v. United Kingdom* (1996) 22 E.H.R.R. 293 (no provision for legal aid for committals to prison for non-payment of community charge. Held, upholding the

(2) The inference will be more compelling in the case of any decision which may adversely affect a person's rights or interests or when a person has a legitimate expectation of being fairly treated.

(3) The requirement of a fair hearing will not apply to all situations of perceived or actual detriment. There are clearly some situations where the interest affected will be too insignificant, or too speculative, or too remote to qualify for a fair hearing.[20] Whether this is so will depend on all the circumstances but a fair hearing ought no longer to be rejected out of hand, for example, simply because the decision-maker is acting in a "legislative" capacity.[21]

(4) Special circumstances may create an exception which vitiates the inference of a duty to act fairly. The inference can be

---

complaint: there had been a breach of Art. 6 of the E.C.R.R.); *Pullar v. United Kingdom* (1996) 22 E.H.R.R. 391 (dismissed complaint about juror being an employee of a prosecution witness). *Bryan v. United Kingdom* (1996) 21 E.H.R.R. 342 (appeal to inspector in planning matter did not satisfy Art. 6—but subsequent review by the High Court did); *Saunders v. United Kingdom* (1997) 23 E.H.R.R. 313; *Findlay v. United Kingdom* (1997) 24 E.H.R.R. 221. (Court Martial was not a fair hearing); (leave to apply for judicial review had been refused); *Gregory v. United Kingdom*, (1998) 25 E.H.R.R. 577 (judge's direction sufficient to counter bias); *Murray v. United Kingdom* (1996) 22 E.H.R.R. 29 (access to solicitor). After the Human Rights Act 1998 comes into force, English courts will be required to have regard to such judgments of the Strasbourg Court.

[20] In such cases where there has been an application for judicial review the applicant may not qualify for standing on the ground of not possessing a 'sufficient interest' in the matter to which the application relates. Alternatively, the applicant may have failed to suffer any 'substantial prejudice' from any lack of procedural propriety where the statute requires it. See, *e.g. Save Britain's Heritage v. Number One Poultry Ltd* [1991] 1 W.L.R. 153, HL and Chap. 9 below, para. 9–030 *et seq.*

[21] But see Lord Oliver in *Leech v. Parkhurst Prison Deputy Governor* [1988] A.C. 533, 538. The Australian Administrative Appeals Tribunal has recently stated that it is a clear principle that all parties whose interests may be affected have a right to be heard by a decision-maker. *Hawker de Havilland v. Australian Securities Commission* (1992) 10 A.C.L.C. 34, 38. See also *Annetts v. McCann* (1991) 65 A.L.J.R. 167, citing with approval Deane J. in *Haoucher v. Minister for Immigration and Ethnic Affairs* (1990) 169 C.L.R. 648 that the law was 'moving towards a...position where the common law requirements of procedural fairness will, in the absence of clear contrary legislative intent, be recognised as applying generally to governmental executive decision-making'. *Annetts, ibid.,* at 168. Compare the formulation of the Supreme Court of Canada: 'There is as a general common law principle a duty of procedural fairness lying on every public authority making an administrative decision which is not of a legislative nature and affects the rights, privileges or interests of an individual' *Cardinal v. Director of Kent Institution* [1985] 2 S.C.R. 643 *per* Le Dain J. In South Africa a legislative decision recently attracted the duty of audi alteram partem. *S.A. Roads Board v. Johannesburg City Council,* 1991 (4) S.A. 1(A). See also *Hailowsky Estates Ltd v. Harlow D.C.* [1997] J.P.L. 541 (fairness required in local plan inquiry).

rebutted by the needs of national security, or because of other characteristics of the particular function. For example, a decision to allocate scarce resources amongst a large number of contenders which needs to be made with despatch may be inconsistent with an obligation to hold a fair hearing.[22] The inference may also not be drawn if the protection is to be achieved another way. For example, in the case of a "legislative" decision, at least where participation is built into the decision-making process elsewhere, the safeguard which would be provided by a fair hearing can be achieved by other means; as in cases where the decision is taken by democratically elected representatives accountable to Parliament or to the electorate for the exercise of the relevant power.[23]

(5) What fairness requires will vary according to the circumstances. The question of the content of the fair hearing is considered in Chapter below. We shall see that some decisions, while attracting the duty to be fair, will permit no more to the affected person than a bare right to submit representations.[24] In other cases however there will be a right to an oral hearing with the essential elements of a trial.[25] In between these extremes come a large variety of decisions which, because of the nature of the issues to be determined or the seriousness of their impact upon important interests,

---

[22] On the other hand, local authorities are now statutorily required to maintain for public inspection their rules for determining priority among applicants for council housing and their procedural rules for allocating it: Housing Act 1985, s. 106. A local authority that has made and published its rules of procedure may well be held to have acted unlawfully if, in some material respect, it does not apply them fairly (*e.g.* by an officer's failing to disclose some unfavourable impression gained as a result of a home visit or from the third party and to allow the applicant an opportunity to respond). See also paras 7–031 and 7–032 below.

[23] The exceptions to the fair hearing are considered fully in Chap. 9 below.

[24] For a minimalist view of fairness, as involving no more than a duty to act without bias, see, for example, *R. v. Secretary of State for Trade, ex p. Perestrello* [1981] Q.B. 19.

[25] Decision-making that formerly would have been characterised as 'judicial' fall into this category. *Cf. Mathews v. Eldridge* (1976) 424 U.S. 319, where it was said that whether the constitutional guarantee of due process requires an evidentiary hearing depends on the individual interest at stake, the extent to which a trial procedure was more likely than the procedure actually used to avoid an erroneous decision, and the government's interest, including the extra cost of the procedure requested. It has been argued that this kind of utilitarian approach fails adequately to take account of the moral harm or sense of injustice suffered by a person who is wrongly deprived of a *right* without a hearing, as opposed, for example, to the reaction engendered by a contested policy decision such as the siting of a motorway: see R. Dworkin, 'Principle, policy, procedure' in C.F.H. Tapper (ed.), *Crime Proof and Punishment: Essays in Memory of Sir Rupert Cross* (1981), pp. 193 and 221 *et seq.*

require some kind of a hearing (which may not even involve oral representations), but not anything that has all the characteristics of a full trial.[26]

(6) Whether fairness is required and what is involved in order to achieve fairness is for the decision of the courts as a matter of law. The issue is not one for the discretion of the decision-maker. The test is not whether no reasonable body would have thought it proper to dispense with a fair hearing.[27] The *Wednesbury*[28] reserve has no place in relation to procedural propriety.

7–012   The significance of this approach is that it prima facie imposes on all administrators an obligation to act fairly. Without acknowledging this expressly, the majority of the recent decisions of the courts are in practice no more than conscious or unconscious illustrations of the approach. They can be conveniently examined under the following three headings:

A. Where the terms of a statute confirm the inference of a fair hearing;

B. Where the inference of a fair hearing is confirmed by the need to safeguard a right or interest;

---

[26] See, *e.g. Edwin H. Bradley and Sons Ltd v. Secretary of State for the Environment* (1982) 47 P. & C.R. 443 (examination in public of structure plan an 'administrative' matter and therefore objectors' procedural rights limited). *Cf. R. v. Commission for Racial Equality, ex p. Cottrell and Rothon (A Firm)* [1980] 1 W.L.R. 1580, 1587, emphasising that the procedural content of judicial hearings may vary considerably according to context, and that it is not necessary to attempt to fit a function into a pigeon-hole labelled 'administrative' or 'judicial'. A similar approach has been adopted in Canada: *Martineau v. Matsqui Institution Disciplinary Board* [1980] 1 S.C.R. 602, 628–629. See also Lord Bridge in *Lloyd v. McMahon* [1987] A.C. 625, 702: 'the so-called rules of national justice are not engraved on tablets of stone.'

[27] See *R. v. Panel on Takeovers and Mergers, ex p. Guinness* [1990] Q.B. 146, *per* Woolf and Lloyd L.JJ. who said that 'the court is the arbiter of what is fair'. *Cf. R. v. Monopolies and Mergers Commission, ex p. Mathew Brown plc* [1987] 1 W.L.R. 1235, where the test was whether the MMC 'had adopted a procedure so unfair that no reasonable MMC would have adopted it'. And see *R. v. Monopolies and Mergers Commission, ex p. Stagecoach Holdings Ltd, The Times,* July 23, 1996. Application to quash MMC decisions recommending that applicant should limit its percentage holdings in rival bus companies. Applicant contended that MMC had failed to clarify certain evidential material upon which the recommendations were based. Held, dismissing the application: the propriety of the MMC's decision was to be decided on the basis of natural justice and fairness and not (as the MMC contended) by the principles of *Wednesbury* unreasonableness. 'The court is the arbiter of what is fair', although the court would give great weight to the MMC's own view of fairness.

[28] See Chap. 12 below for discussion of the *Wednesbury* case and the margin of appreciation accorded the decision-maker in cases involving abuse of discretion.

C. Where the inference of a fair hearing is confirmed by the need to safeguard an expectation induced by the decision-maker.

A. STATUTORY REQUIREMENTS AND THE FAIR HEARING

When a mandatory procedure is set out in a statute, it must be followed.[29] Many areas of public administration provide elaborate procedural codes. Town and country planning legislation, for example, permits public participation at the stage of drafting development plans,[30] requires notification of applications for planning permission,[31] requires consultation with given bodies[32] and provides the opportunity for applicants to appeal a refusal of a planning application or a condition attached to an application.[33] The appeal may be by way of written representations or a full structured inquiry.[34]

7–013

Even where the procedural code is comprehensive in its scope, the courts are called upon to adjudicate on the extent to which the statutory procedure has been fulfilled. For example, are the reasons, required of the Secretary of State on a planning appeal, "proper adequate and intelligible"?[35] Has the consultation required been "genuine"?[36] In these cases there are no express statutory requirements

7–014

---

[29] For the distinction between requirements which are 'mandatory' and 'directory' see Chap. 5 of the principal work, paras 5–057 *et seq.*

[30] Town and Country Planning Act 1990, ss. 12, 33 & 40; Town and Country Planning (Development Plan) Regulations 1991 (S.I. 1991 No. 2794).

[31] Town and Country Planning Act 1990, s.71; Town and Country Planning General Development Order 1988, art. 2B; Planning (Listed Buildings and Conservation Areas) Act 1990, s. 73.

[32] Town and Country Planning General Development Order 1988, arts. 18–21.

[33] Town and Country Planning Act 1990, ss. 78–79.

[34] See Town and Country Planning (Appeals) (Written Representations Procedure) Regulations 1987 (S.I. 1987 No. 701).

[35] *Save Britain's Heritage v. Number One Poultry Ltd* [1991] 1 W.L.R. 153, 166. See also *Westminster City Council v. Great Portland Estates plc* [1985] A.C. 661 at 663.

[36] See *R. v. Secretary of State for Social Services, ex p. Association of Metropolitan Authorities* [1986] 1 W.L.R. 1, *per* Webster J. In *R. v. Lambeth L.B.C., ex p. N* [1996] E.L.R. 299. There was a challenge to a decision to close a maintained boarding school for children with special educational needs. N argued that the authority had failed to comply with the statutory obligation to consult parents as to the closure under section 184, Education Act 1993. Held, allowing the application: section 184(1) provided that an authority had a duty to consult such persons as were appropriate, and parents were clearly intended to be consulted under Circular 3.94 issued by the Secretary of State for Education. The authority also had an obligation to ensure that parents were invited to make oral or written representations on the proposed closure and its impact on their children. The failure to do so vitiated the consulation process and the notice of closure was quashed accordingly. *R. v. Brent L.B.C., ex p. Gunning*

in relation to the adequacy, intelligibility or genuineness of the reasons or consultations, but the courts employ these criteria so as to ensure the correct standards of fairness. In doing so, the courts are not imposing additional requirements but are instead ensuring the effectiveness of existing requirements.

7–015   Can the courts supplement the statutory procedures with requirements over and above those specified? For example, can the courts impose a requirement upon a local planning authority to consult on a planning application with neighbours where no such requirement is provided in the statute? There have been cases where the courts have supplemented a statutory scheme.[37] However, in others the maxim *expressio unius exclusio alterius* has been invoked to avoid doing so.[38] Lord Reid, unusually, expressed an inclination in favour of judicial restraint when he warned against the use by the courts of "this unusual kind of power" (extending statutory procedures) which he felt should be exercised only when it is "clear

---

(1985) 84 L.G.R. 168; and *R. v. Secretary of State for Social Services, ex p. A.M.A.* [1986] 1 W.L.R. 1 considered.

[37] See *Fairmount Investments Ltd v. Secretary of State for the Environment* [1976] 1 W.L.R. 1255; *Lake District Special Planning Board v. Secretary of State for the Environment* [1975] J.P.L. 220; *Hambledon and Chiddingfold Parish Council v. Secretary of State for the Environment* [1976] J.P.L. 502; *Reading B.C. v. Secretary of State for the Environment* [1986] J.P.L. 115; *Nicholson v. Secretary of State for Energy* (1977) 76 L.G.R. 693. See also *Rich v. Christchurch Girls' High School Board of Governors (No. 1)* [1974] 1 N.Z.L.R. 1, 9, 18–20; *Coleen Properties Ltd v. Minister of Housing and Local Government* [1971] 1 W.L.R. 433; *Lithgow v. Secretary of State for Scotland*, 1973 S.L.T. 81; *Heatley v. Tasmanian Racing and Gaming Commission* (1977) 137 C.L.R. 487; *R. v. Huntingdon L.C., ex p. Cowan* [1984] 1 W.L.R 501; *Birss v. Secretary of State for Justice* [1984] 1 N.Z.L.R. 116; *Stratford-upon-Avon D.C. v. Secretary of State for the Environment* [1994] J.P.L. 741 (*aff'd.* CA January 30, 1995).

[38] See, *e.g. Bird v. St. Mary Abbotts Vestry* (1895) 72 L.T. 599; *Hutton v. Att.-Gen.* [1927] 1 Ch. 427, 437–438; *Taylor v. Prime Minister*, 1954 (3) SA. 965 (S. Rhod.); *R. v. Moloyi*, 1956 (1) S.A. 390; *Waitemata County v. Local Government Commission* [1964] N.Z.L.R. 689; *Brettingham-Moore v. St. Leonards Municipality* (1969) 121 C.L.R. 509; *Wiseman v. Borneman* [1971] A.C. 297; *Pearlberg v. Varty* [1972] 1 W.L.R. 534; *Furnell v. Whangarei High Schools Board* [1973] A.C. 660, 679; *French v. Law Society of Upper Canada* [1975] 2 S.C.R. 767, 783–786; *Maynard v. Osmond* [1977] Q.B. 240; *Salemi v. McKellar (No. 2)* (1977) 137 C.L.R. 396; *Bourke v. State Services Commission* [1978] 1 N.Z.L.R. 633, 644–646; *Lewis v. Heffer* [1978] 1 W.L.R. 1061; *R. v. Raymond* [1981] Q.B. 910; *CREEDNZ Inc. v. Governor General* [1981] 1 N.Z.L.R. 172, 1780; *Re Findlay* [1985] A.C. 318. *Cf.*, however, *Re Cardinal and Board of Commissioners of Police of the City of Cornwall* (1974) 42 D.L.R. (3d) 323; *R. v. Crown Court at Bristol, ex p. Cooper* [1990] 1 W.L.R. 1031 (*per* Bingham L.J.). See also *R. v. Secretary of State for the Environment, ex p. Hammersmith and Fulham L.B.C.* [1991] 1 A.C. 521. In the United States the Supreme Court, in a landmark case, *Vermont Yankee Nuclear Power Corp. v. Natural Resources Defense Council, Inc.*, (1978) 435 U.S. 519, it was held that, except in extremely rare circumstances, courts may force agencies to utilise rulemaking procedures beyond those prescribed in the Administrative Procedure Act 1946 or other statutory or constitutional provisions.

that the statutory procedure is insufficient to achieve justice and that to require additional steps would not frustrate the apparent purpose of the legislation".[39]

On the other hand the maxim *expressio unius*, like other aids to interpretation may be "a valuable servant, but a dangerous master to follow ... [and] ought not to be applied when it leads to inconsistency or injustice.[40] A bolder approach has been suggested more recently by Lord Bridge, who said that "the courts will not only require the procedure prescribed by the statute to be followed, but will readily imply so much and no more to be introduced by way of additional procedural safeguards as will ensure the attainment of fairness".[41]   7–016

The test today of whether to supplement statutory procedures is no longer whether the statutory procedure alone could result in manifest unfairness.[42] The preferable view is that fairness *tout court* must be attained, and that the "justice of the common law" may supplement that of the statute unless by necessary implication the procedural code must be regarded as exclusive.[43] Under either test, similar factors are likely to be relevant: the comprehensiveness of the code, the degree of deviation from the statutory procedure required, and the overall fairness of the procedures to the individual concerned.[44]   7–017

Where legislation, instead of placing a duty on a body to hold a hearing, merely gives a *discretion* to do so, the inference must normally   7–018

---

[39] *Wiseman v. Borneman* [1971] A.C. 297, 308.

[40] *Colquhoun v. Brooks* (1887) 19 QBD 400, 406; on appeal (1888) 21 QBD 52.

[41] *Lloyd v. McMahon* [1987] A.C. 625, 702–3.

[42] *Furnell's* case (above, n.38) at 679; (see J. M. Evans (1973) 36 M.L.R. 439. *Cf. Lake District Special Planning Board v. Secretary of State for the Environment* [1975] J.PL. 220); *Nicholson v. Secretary of State for Energy* (1977) 76 L.G.R. 693; *cf. Payne v. Lord Harris of Greenwich* [1981] 1 W.L.R. 754, 757; *R. v. Raymond* [1981] Q.B. 910, 920 (nothing 'inherently unjust' in absence of hearing from statutory scheme) although in this case Watkins L.J. was prepared to regard the statutory scheme as evincing a deliberate intention by Parliament to exclude a right to be heard; approved in *Grant v. Director of Public Prosecutions* [1982] A.C. 190, PC *Payne* (above) has now been expressly overruled by *R. v. Secretary of State for the Home Department, ex p. Doody* [1994] 1 A.C. 531, HL.

[43] *Furnell's* case (above, n.38) at 686 (*per* Viscount Dilhorne and Lord Reid, dissenting). See also J. F. Northey [1972] N.Z.L.J. 307; D.J. Mullan [1973] N.Z.L.J. 41. And see *Heatley's* case (above, n. 37); *Twist v. Randwick Municipal Council* (1976) 136 C.L.R. 106; and see *Re Hamilton; Re Forrest* [1981] A.C. 1038. In Australia the rules of procedural fairness are regarded as fundamental requirements of the common law and therefore their exclusion by statute will normally require a clear expression of legislative intent. See *Kioa v. West* (1985) 159 C.L.R. 550, 585; *South Australia v. O'Shea* (1987) 163 C.L.R. 378, 415. See also *Doody* (above, n. 42).

[44] In a recent case, however, the Court of Appeal held that the existence of a statutory scheme, coupled with the need for urgency vitiated a fair hearing which would otherwise have been required in a case of this kind: *R. v. Birmingham City Council, ex p. Ferrero Ltd* [1993] 1 All E.R. 530, *per* Taylor L.J. See also Lord Bridge in *Lloyd v. McMahon* [1987] A.C. 625.

be that no duty to hear exists in that context, particularly if the legislation explicitly requires that body to conduct hearings or inquiries in the performance of other functions.[45] However, where the merits of a planning proposal were the subject of intense controversy, it was held that the minister's refusal to hold a hearing was an improper exercise of discretion.[46]

Statute and legitimate expectations

7–019 Where the claim to procedural fairness is based upon a legitimate expectation,[47] and especially upon an expectation, induced by the decision-maker, of a hearing or other procedural safeguard, then the procedures should normally be granted as a supplement to the statutory scheme. In such cases the decision-maker's claim that the statutory scheme is exclusive will be difficult to justify in opposition to an express or implied representation on his part that additional procedures would be granted. However, the expectation cannot prevail where the code itself prohibits the promised procedure or makes clear that the procedures provided are exclusive.[48]

7–020 Under the planning statutes, for example, there was until recently no duty on the planning authority to consult with neighbours about applications for permission to develop land outside specially protected areas. Most local authorities, however, nevertheless routinely consulted adjacent neighbours as a matter of courtesy. In a case where a tradition of consultation had created an expectation of being consulted, and where by oversight or design a particular neighbour was not consulted, the legitimate expectation of consultation could result in the formal provisions of the act being supplemented.[49]

B. WHERE A HEARING IS REQUIRED TO SAFEGUARD RIGHTS AND INTERESTS

7–021 There is a presumption that procedural fairness is required whenever the exercise of a power adversely affects an individual's rights protected by common law or created by statute. These include rights

---

[45] *cf. Ronaki v. No. 1 Town and Country Planning Appeal Board* [1977] 2 N.Z.L.R. 174.

[46] *Binney v. Secretary of State for the Environment* [1984] J.P.L. 871.

[47] Considered below, at paras 7-037–7-066.

[48] See, *e.g. Clyde Cablevision v. Cable Authority,* 1990 S.C.L.R. 28. Timothy H. Jones [1990] P.L. 156.

[49] However, a past practice of consultation in these circumstances will not necessarily give rise to a legitimate expectation: see *R. v. Secretary of State for the Environment, ex p. Kent* [1988] J.P.L. 706; *aff'd* [1990] J.P.L. 124, CA

in property, personal liberty, status and immunity from penalties or other fiscal impositions. The right or immunity may be enjoyed by either a private person (including a corporation) or a public body.[50]

The duty to afford procedural fairness is not however limited to the   **7–022** protection of legal rights in the strict sense: it also applies to more general interests, of which the interest in pursuing a livelihood and in personal reputation have received particular recognition.[51] The interests also extend, however, to personal freedom (of a prisoner seeking parole)[52] and other benefits and advantages the conferral of which are in the discretion of the decision-maker (and were formerly regarded as "privileges",[53] and thus not meriting procedural protection).

Because the interest of the applicant, rather than the discretionary   **7–023** power of the decision maker, now founds a right to a fair hearing, a hearing is required in most situations where licences or other similar benefits are revoked, varied, suspended or refused; even where the decision-making power affords wide discretion to the decision maker. Thus a strong presumption exists that a person whose licence is threatened with revocation should receive prior notice of that fact and an opportunity to be heard. The presumption should be especially strong where revocation causes deprivation of livelihood or serious pecuniary loss, or carries an implication of misconduct. For example, in a recent case the applicants, a United States company, had been encouraged by the Department of Trade and Industry to set up a factory in the United Kingdom manufacturing oral snuff. After an inquiry into its possible carcinogenic effects the Secretary of State for Health made regulations banning the product without providing the company with an opportunity to confront the evidence provided by external witnesses. It was held that although the applicants had no

---

[50] See, *e.g. Durayappah v. Fernando* [1967] 2 A.C. 337; *R. v. Secretary of State for the Environment, ex p. Norwich City Council* [1982] Q.B. 808, 824 (dicta): *R. v. Secretary of State for the Environment, ex p. Brent L.B.C.* [1982] Q.B. 593, 642–643; *R. v. Secretary of State for Transport, ex p. Greater London Council* [1986] Q.B. 556.

[51] See generally, *Ridge v. Baldwin* [1964] A.C. 40; *McInnes v. Onslow-Fane* [1978] 1 W.L.R. 1520, 1527–1528; *R. v. Barnsley M.B.C., ex p. Hook* [1976] 1 W.L.R. 1052; *Re Pergamon Press Ltd* [1971] Ch. 388, 399; *Rees v. Crane* [1994] 2 A.C. 173, PC. Compare Lord Bridge in *Lloyd v. McMahon* [1987] A.C. 625, 702–703, where fairness appears confined to decisions which "affect the rights of individuals". But see Lord Oliver in *Leech v. Parkhurst Prison Deputy Governor* [1988] A.C. 533, 578.

[52] See, *e.g. Doody,* n. 42 above. See also *R. v. Secretary of State for the Home Department, ex p. Duggan* [1994] 3 All E.R. 277 (a classification of a prisoner directly affected his liberty and thus a fair hearing was required).

[53] See especially *Nakkudo Ali v. Jayarante* [1951] A.C. 66; *R. v. Metropolitan Police Commissioner, ex p. Parker* [1953] 1 W.L.R. 1150; *Merchants Bank Ltd v. Federal Minister of Finance* (1961) 1 All N.L.R. 598 (Nigeria).

legitimate expectation of a continuation in government policy, the adverse affects of the ban on their business interests required a fair hearing the absence of which rendered the regulations void.[54]

7–024   Variation of the terms of an existing licence to the licensee's detriment will also prima facie attract the duty to act fairly.[55] A decision to increase the number of licences, with the effect of diminishing the value of existing licences, may in some situations also attract the duty.[56]

7–025   Whether a suspension of a licence should be preceded by notice and opportunity to be heard may depend on various factors, for example, the degree of urgency involved, the duration of the suspension, whether suspension implies a finding of guilt, whether it entails material financial loss and whether it is a purely temporary measure pending full review.[57]

7–026   Non-renewal of an existing licence is usually a more serious matter than refusal to grant a licence in the first place.[58] Unless the licensee has already been given to understand when he was granted the licence that renewal is not to be expected, non-renewal may seriously upset his plans, cause him economic loss and perhaps cast a slur on his reputation. It may therefore be right to imply a duty to hear before a decision not to renew irrespective of whether there is a legitimate expectation of renewal,[59] even though no such duty is implied in the making of the original decision to grant or refuse the licence.[60]

---

[54] *R. v. Secretary of State for Health, ex p. U.S. Tobacco International Inc.* [1992] Q.B. 353.

[55] *White v. British Transport Commission* (1955) 30 Traf. Cas. 234; *Re North Coast Air Services Ltd* [1972] F.C. 390 at 404 (Can.).

[56] *R. v. Liverpool Corp., ex p. Liverpool Taxi Fleet Operators' Association* [1972] 2 Q.B. 299 per Lord Denning whose view was not expressed by the other members of the Court of Appeal.

[57] See, *e.g. Hlookoff v. City of Vancouver* (1968) 67 D.L.R, (2d) 119 (summary suspension of licence of premises for publishing newspaper on account of gross misconduct; suspension invalid). *Cf. Furnell v. Whangarei High Schools Board* [1973] A.C. 660; and see discussion on preliminary hearings, below Chap. 9, paras 9-024–9-031.

[58] This point was well brought out by the sharp decline in the value of TWW's shares when the Independent Television Authority decided in June 1967 not to renew its programme contract.

[59] See below, paras 7-037–7-066.

[60] This paragraph was cited with approval by Scarman L.J. in *Hook* (n. 51, above), at 1058. See dicta in *Schmidt v. Secretary of State for Home Affairs* [1969] 2 Ch. 149, 170–171, 173, and *Breen v. A.E.U.* [1971] 2 Q.B. 175, 191. See also the *Liverpool Taxi* case (n. 56, above) (reduction in value of existing licences), *Hook (ibid.)* at 1057 and *McInnes v. Onslow-Fane* [1978] 1 W.L.R. 1520 supporting this distinction. *Cf. Salemi v. MacKellar (No. 2)* (1977) 137 C.L.R. 396. See also *Re Holden* (1957) Tas. S.R. 16; *Delmonico v. Director of Wildlife* (1969) 67 W.W.R. 340, and s. 5(c) of the American Administrative Procedure Act 1946; though *cf. Board of Regents v. Roth* (1972) 408 U.S. 564 (denial of tenure to university teacher).

B. Where a Hearing is Required to Safeguard Rights and Interests

Applicants for new licences are in a different position from those **7–027** whose existing licences are revoked, suspended, varied or not renewed. The reason why applicants for new licences or other permissions may be denied a hearing is because in many cases there is no vested interest involved to defend. The applicant will be adversely affected by a refusal of something which he does not yet have only to the extent that he is disappointed and may have suffered some "transaction costs" in the process of the application.[61]

Nevertheless, as has been discussed,[62] there may be a number of **7–028** situations in which the decision to grant or refuse an application for a licence may attract a fair hearing. Even in the absence of a legitimate expectation, the refusal of an application may cast aspersions on a person's character. In such a case fairness dictates that the individual ought to be able to defend his interest in his reputation.[63]

---

[61] That the considerations applicable to the revocation of licences may be different from those applicable to the refusal of licences has been recognised in a number of cases, *e.g. McInnes v. Onslow Fane* (n.60, above), and particularly in Canadian provincial cases, holding that licensees have an implied right to be heard before revocation, *e.g. Fairbairn v. Highway Traffic Board of Saskatchewan* (1958) 11 D.L.R. (2d) 709; *Re Watt and Registrar of Motor Vehicles* (1958) 13 D.L.R. (2d) 124 (driving licences); *Klymchuk v. Cowan* (1964) 45 D.L.R. (2d) 587 (used car dealer's permit); *R. v. Calgary, ex p. Sanderson* (1966) 53 D.L.R. (2d) 477 (store licence); *Re Halliwell and Welfare Institutions Board* (1966) 56 D.L.R. (2d) 754 (rest home licence); though *cf. Re Foremost Construction Co. and Registrar of Companies* (1967) 61 D.L.R. (2d) 528. And see *Re North Coast Air Services Ltd* [1972] F.C. 390, 404. See also the interesting decision of the Supreme Court of Pakistan in *Faridsons Ltd v. Government of Pakistan*, P.L.D. 1961 S.C. 537 for an analysis of grounds for holding that an implied duty to give opportunity to be heard existed before revocation of a trading licence. For Australian decisions applying the rule, see *Bankes v. Transport Regulation Board (Vic.)* (1968) 119 C.L.R. 222 (taxi driver's licence); *Stollery v. Greyhound Racing Control Board* (1972) 128 C.L.R. 509 (revocation of greyhound owner's licence for misconduct). See also *James v. Pope* [1931] S.A.S.R. 441 (licence for dried fruit packing shed); *R. v. Melbourne Corp., ex p. Whyte* [1949] V.L.R. 257 (taxi driver's licence); contrast *Election Importing Co. v. Courtice* (1949) 80 C.L.R. 657, 663 (import licence). See also *Hecht v. Monaghan* (1954) 307 N.Y. 461, where, on facts almost identical to those in *Parker's* case, the court reached the opposite conclusion.

[62] See above, paras 7–008–7–010. See the discussion of the *Fayed* case above at para. 7–007 n. 10.

[63] Where the applicant is treated differently from other similarly placed applicants it has been suggested that the applicant has a right to a hearing in order to defend his interest in equal treatment. See Lord Mustill in *Doody v. Secretary of State for the Home Department* [1994] 1 A.C. 531, 566. The right to a hearing in such a situation is, it is submitted, more naturally based upon a legitimate expectation (for which discussion see below, paras 7–037–7–066) of being treated similarly to other 'like' cases.

The scope of interests attracting a right to a hearing

7–029   The right to a fair hearing is not confined to those who are direct parties to a decision.[64] However, the right does not extend to every vested right or interest. Some may be too remote or too speculative to justify their having an opportunity of being heard.[65] However, care should be exercised that decision-makers do not prejudge the impact of the decision which is in issue.[66]

7–030   To what extent should a fair hearing be provided to individuals whose interests in library use is threatened by a local authority's proposal to close a local public library? Or to shopkeepers whose business interests may be threatened by a proposed car parking scheme?[67] Before a decision is taken to increase the number of taxi licences, should a local authority hear representations from the existing licensees, who have a private interest in preserving the

---

[64] In a recent case it was held that a self-regulatory body was required to consult a non-member who was not a party to the decision but whose reputation could have been adversely affected by the decision: *R. v. LAUTRO, ex p. Ross* [1993] Q.B. 17, DC and CA. *Cf. Cheall v. Association of Professional, Executive and Computer Staff* [1983] 2 A.C. 180. See A. Lidbetter, 'Financial Services: The Right to Make Representations' [1992] P.L. 533.

[65] Some jurisdictions appear to have afforded procedural protection to the right to drink. *R. v. McArthur, ex p. Cornish* [1966] Tas. S.R. 157 (police superintendent, empowered to order licensees to stop serving alcohol to habitual drunkard on basis of information supplied, issues orders in respect of C upon information supplied by C's wife; held orders void because C was denied opportunity to rebut accusation); *Re Liquor Control Board of Ontario and Keupfer* 47 D.L.R. (3d) 326. See also *Wisconsin v. Constantineau* (1971) 400 U.S. 433.

[66] Where the applicant has been granted standing to sue in an application for judicial review it may be assumed that the impact of the decision is sufficiently serious to qualify as adversely affecting his interests (see Chap. 2 above). It is settled law in India that natural justice must be observed in all administrative decisions involving 'civil consequences'. These have been construed to cover 'infraction of not merely property or personal rights but of civil liberties, material deprivations and non-pecuniary damages. In its comprehensive connotation, everything that affects a citizen in his civil life inflicts civil consequences'. *Mohiner Singh Gill v. Chief Election Commissioner* AIR 1978 S.C. 851, 870. See also *Erusian Equipment and Chemicals v. State of West Bengal* AIR 1975 S.C. 266 (trader on government blacklist involves civil consequences because it tarnishes reputation and prevents trading with government). See Soli J. Sorabjee, 'Obliging Government to Control Itself: Recent Developments in Indian Administrative Law' [1994] P.L. 39. See also *R. v. Ealing Justices, ex p. Fanneran* (1996) 8 Admin. L.R. 351 (applicant was not informed of a hearing before justices at which they made a destruction order in relation to her pit bull terrier following her nephew's conviction of having the dog in a public place without a muzzle. Held that even though the applicant's presence at a hearing may not have made any difference to the outcome, it was important that justices acted in accordance with the rules of natural justice. The destruction order was quashed).

[67] See *R. v. Camden L.B.C., ex p. Cran and Ors., The Times*, January 25, 1995 (failure adequately to consult residents on proposed car-parking zone).

commercial value of their licences?[68] Should the authority also be required to hear from those concerned that any increase in traffic may add to congestion and levels of pollution, and adversely affect public transport?[69]

In the past, exemption from the duty of fairness has been accorded   **7–031** to decisions regarded as essentially allocative,[70] or inherently non-justiciable[71] because of their substantial policy content or "managerial" qualities.[72] However, the courts are increasingly insisting that even decisions of this kind ought to provide those whose interests are affected the opportunity to participate at least in some degree. For example, decisions of prison governors, formerly considered as falling outside the ambit of judicial review, have recently been brought within its ambit,[73] as have decisions of the Home Secretary on whether to

---

[68] See *R. v. Liverpool Corp., ex p. Liverpool Taxi Fleet Operators' Association* [1972] 2 Q.B. 299, where it was held that the Corporation's assurance created what was in essence a legitimate expectation of a hearing. Lord Denning M.R., alone in the Court of Appeal, further suggested that even in the absence of any legitimate expectation, the taxi drivers would have a sufficient interest by virtue of their existing licences to be entitled to consultation before a decision to increase the number of licences was taken. On the distinction between interests and legitimate expectations, see further paras 7-050–7-052 below.

[69] Of course, those motivated by self-interest to make representations may bring to the attention of the decision-maker whatever considerations support their position, including matters relevant to the wider public interest that might otherwise have been overlooked: see *R. v. Bromley Licensing JJ., ex p. Bromley Licensed Victuallers' Association* [1984] 1 W.L.R. 585, 589.

[70] A term used by L. Fuller, *The Morality of Law,* (1969) pp.46–47, 170–177.

[71] 'Justiciable' here means appropriate for determination by courts or bodies closely analogous to courts. For discussions of the concept of justiciability, viewed from different aspects, see L. Fuller, 'The Forms and Limits of Adjudication' (1978–79) 92 Harv. L.R. 395 (ed. A. G. Guest), Chap. 10; Robert S. Summers (1963) 26 M.L.R. 530; R. B. Stevens and B. S. Yamey, *The Restrictive Practices Court,* Chap. 3; Alfred Witkon (1966) 1 Israel L. Rev. 40; B. A. Hepple (1971) 34 M.L.R. 501; G. Ganz, 'Allocation of Decision-Making Functions' [1972] P.L. 215, 299; J. Jowell, *Law and Bureaucracy* (1975). In relation to a case involving relations with a foreign state, it has been held that the court has 'no judicial or manageable standards by which to judge' the issue, and if it tried would be 'in a judicial no-man's land'. Lord Wilberforce in *Buttes v. Hammer* [1982] A.C. 888. See also Lord Diplock in *Council of Civil Service Unions v. Minister for Civil Service* [1985] A.C. 374, 411D and 418. For a fuller discussion on justiciability see Chap. 5, paras 5-029–5-035 above.

[72] See Lord Bridge in *R. v. Secretary of State for the Environment, ex p. Hammersmith and Fulham L.B.C.* [1991] A.C. 521. For a definition of justiciability in a different context see Lord Mustill in *Airedale NHS Trust v. Bland* [1993] A.C. 789, 887–888. For a recent attempt to grapple with the issue of justiciability, referring to Fuller's article 'The Forms and Limits of Adjudication' 92 Harv. L.R. 395, see Neill L.J. in *R. v. Home Secretary, ex p. P* [1995] 1 All E.R. 870.

[73] *Leech v. Deputy Governor of Parkhurst Prison, Prevot v. Deputy Governor of Long Lartin Prison* [1988] 1 A.C. 533; *R. v. Governor of Maze Prison, ex p. McKiernan* [1985] 6 N.I.J.B. 6. (*Cf. R. v. Deputy Governor of Camphill Prison, ex p. King* [1985] Q.B. 735). See

follow the judicial view of the "penal" element or "tariff" of a mandatory life sentence when deciding whether to grant parole.[74]

7–032 In the previous edition of this work it was contended that the decision of a minister to close a coal pit would, because government economic policy was involved, not attract the duty to act fairly.[75] In a recent case, however, it has been held that just such a decision was void for failure to consult the unions and others who had a legitimate expectation of being consulted prior to the pit closures.[76] Nevertheless, decisions such as these, and others categorised as "legislative", have remained relatively immune from the assault that has been made upon the distinction between duties that are analytically "judicial" and those that are "purely administrative". English courts have been reluctant to impose the duty to consult on ministers exercising powers delegated under legislation to issue orders or directions.[77] Nor is such a duty imposed upon the procedures for making policy of a less formal kind,[78] although where consultation is required by statute the courts will police its implementation and insist that it is adequate and genuine.[79] By contrast, in the United States full opportunity for notice and comment for most administrative rule-making is provided by statute.[80]

M. Leech, *The Prisoner's Handbook* (1995), pp. 309–329.

[74] *Doody.* n. 42 above. *Cf. R. v. Secretary of State for the Home Department. ex p. McCartney* [1994] C.O.D. 528.

[75] de Smith (4th ed., 1979), p. 180.

[76] *R. v. British Coal Corporation and Secretary of State for Trade and Industry, ex p. Vardy* [1993] I.C.R. 720, DC.

[77] See, *e.g. Bates v. Lord Hailsham of Marylebone* [1972] 1 W.L.R. 1373.

[78] See generally G. Ganz, *Quasi Legislation: Recent Developments in Secondary Legislation* (1987).

[79] For instance an express statutory obligation to consult has been held to require the public authority to give to those entitled to be consulted a fair opportunity to participate in a meaningful way in the exercise of the power to which the duty relates. See, *e.g. R. v. Brent L.B.C., ex p. Gunning* (1985) 84 L.G.R. 168; *R. v. Secretary of State for Social Services, ex p. Association of Metropolitan Authorities* [1986] 1 W.L.R. 1. Thus, the authority must give to those consulted sufficient information and explanation of its proposals, and enough time to enable a considered response to be provided. In addition, it may also be necessary to discharge the duty to consult to satisfy a court that reasonable efforts have been made to identify those whom it is appropriate to consult, that the consultation occurred early enough in the decision-making process to be capable of influencing the outcome, and that the authority genuinely considered the views of those considered. See further, Chap. 8 below.

[80] For the American position, S. Breyer and R. Stewart *Administrative Law and Regulatory Policy* (1979), Chaps. 6 and 7; and see K. C. Davis, *Administrative Law Treaties* (2nd ed., 1960), Chap. 6, in which the distinction is drawn between trial-type hearings which are appropriate for the determination of 'adjudicative facts' (facts about particular parties) and argument-type hearings to help a tribunal determine 'legislative facts' (matters pertaining to questions of law, policy or discretion). This distinction is broadly acceptable in an English context, and although it has not fully

B. Where a Hearing is Required to Safeguard Rights and Interests

There are two reasons why "legislative" decisions have been held **7–033** exempt from the duty to provide a fair hearing: first, where the decision is taken by a minister or other elected official who is accountable to Parliament or a local authority, the courts will be chary of adding an additional forum of participation where one is already in place as part of the process of political accountability. The second reason is a practical one: bodies may be exempt from the duty to provide a hearing where the potential of adversely affected interests is too diverse or too numerous to permit each individual to participate.

The participation of both representative public interest groups and **7–034** individuals asserting general interests, for example, in the environment, is accepted in areas such as planning law. The planning legislation allows interested parties the opportunity to participate in planning appeals.[81] Where, however, discretion exists to deny a hearing the courts have intervened, for example to require the Secretary of State for the Environment not to dispense with an inquiry as unnecessary, when the merits of the proposal were the subject of acute local controversy among the champions of conflicting facets of the public interest.[82] It has also been held that a prominent objector to a proposed development had a right to be positively consulted prior to the holding of an appeal.[83]

When it is appropriate for the courts, rather than the legislature or **7–035** the administration, to extend rights of participation to these kind of situations is an issue of some difficulty. Undoubtedly, increasing public participation in decision-making causes delay, hinders the conferral of the intended benefits of a particular programme and imposes burdens

---

been adopted by the law its effect can be seen, for example, in the inquiry procedure followed in the making of planning, compulsory purchase and highway decisions; see, *e.g. Bushell v. Secretary of State for the Environment* [1981] A.C. 75. A duty to consult specified or other interested bodies before a regulation-making power is exercised is not an uncommon feature of British legislation: see, *e.g.* Town and Country Planning General Development Order 1988 (S.I. 1988 No. 1813) art. 12B; Social Security and Housing Benefits Act 1982, s.36(1). See generally, M. Asimov, 'Delegated Legislation: United States and United Kingdom' (1983) 3 O.J.L.S. 253 and Baruch Bracha 'The Right to be Heard in Rule Making Proceedings in England and Israel: Judicial Policy Reconsidered' (1987) Fordham International Law J. 613.

[81] Although the opportunity to participate in structure plan inquiries, through the examination in public is limited. Town and Country Planning Act 1990, s.35B.

[82] *Binney v. Secretary of State for the Environment* [1984] J.P.L. 871. But see *R. v. Secretary of State for the Environment, ex p. Greenpeace Ltd* [1994] 4 All E.R. 352.

[83] *Wilson v. Secretary of State for the Environment* [1988] P.L. 540. See also *Mancetter Developments Ltd v. Secretary of State for the Environment, Peterborough City Council and Kesteven Fruit Company* [1993] J.P.L. 439. Interested parties have a right to be consulted when a decision to hold a new inquiry is made. *R. v. Secretary of State for the Environment, ex p. Fielder Estates (Canvey) Ltd* (1989) 57 P. & C.R. 424.

upon governmental resources.[84] The preparation and presentation of effective representations also takes time and money, commodities that are not evenly spread among all segments of society. Whether, and how, procedural arrangements should be made to enable broader ranges of interest to be represented raises fundamental issues about the adequacy of existing institutional arrangements for ensuring that government hears the concerns of the governed, and is sufficiently responsive and accountable to them.

7–036   While taking care not to hamper unduly effective administration, the common law duty of fairness surely has a useful role in opening new channels of public participation, while leaving their precise contours to be defined by legislative or administrative action. As the *British Coal* case shows,[85] a legislative-type decision, and one involving issues of national economic policy, is not *ipso facto* exempt from the duty to act fairly. Even in the absence of a legitimate expectation of a hearing, it would seem fair to allow representations by at least some of those objecting to the decisions whose interests are substantially threatened by an adverse outcome.

C. The Legitimate Expectation

Introduction

7–037   Since the early 1970s one of the principles justifying the imposition of procedural protection has been the legitimate expectation. Such an expectation arises where a person responsible for taking a decision has induced in someone who may be affected by the decision a reasonable expectation that he will receive or retain a benefit or that he will be granted a hearing before the decision is taken. In such cases the courts have held that the expectation ought not to be summarily disappointed.

7–038   The scope of the legitimate expectation has been the subject of intense discussion[86]; it is still in the process of evolution. It is founded

---

[84] See n. 6, above.

[85] [1993] I.C.R. 720.

[86] See generally, Elias, 'Legitimate Expectation and Judicial Review' in *New Directions in Judicial Review* (1988); Forsyth, 'The Provenance and Protection of Legitimate Expectations' (1988) 47 C.L.J. 238; Ganz, 'Legitimate Expectation' in Harlow (ed.), *Public Law and Politics* (1986); Sharpston, 'Legitimate Expectation and Economic Reality' (1990) 15 E.L.Rev. 103; Craig, 'Legitimate Expectations: A Conceptual Analysis' (1992) 108 L.Q.R. 79; Hodgson, 'The Current Status of Legitimate Expectation in Administrative Law' (1984) 14 Melb. U.L.Rev. 686; Johnson, 'Natural Justice and Legitimate Expectations in Australia' (1985) 15 F.L.Rev. 39; Caldwell, 'Legitimate Expectation and the Rules of Natural Justice' (1983) 2 Canterbury L.Rev. 45; Hlophe, 'Legitimate Expectations and Natural Justice: English, Australian, and

upon a basic principle of fairness that legitimate expectations ought not to be thwarted.[87] The protection of legitimate expectations is at the root of the constitutional principle of the rule of law, which requires regularity, predictability, and certainty in government's dealings with the public.[88] "Legal certainty" is also a basic principle of European law.[89] For these reasons the existence of a legitimate expectation may, even in the absence of a right in private law, justify in public law an entitlement to some form of procedural protection.

The legitimate expectation should not be regarded as the sole route **7–039** to entitlement under the common law to procedural fairness. The courts' approach to legitimate expectations is more clearly identified if its role is distinguished from other principles giving rise to an entitlement to procedural propriety. Thus a fair hearing may be required in the absence of a legitimate expectation and, conversely, a legitimate expectation may confer procedural protection when it would not otherwise be required.

Development

The term "legitimate expectation" first made an appearance in English **7–040** law in *Schmidt v. Secretary of State for Home Affairs*,[90] in which a foreign student sought review of the Home Secretary's decision not to grant an extension of his temporary permit to stay in the United Kingdom. In rejecting his contention that he ought to have been afforded a hearing, Lord Denning M.R. said *obiter* that the question of a hearing "...all depends on whether he has some right or interest, or, I would

---

South African Law (1987) 104 S.A.L.J. 165. P.P. Craig, "Substantive Legitimate Expectations in Domestic and Community Law" [1996] C.L.J. 289.

[87] J. Rawls, *A Theory of Justice* (1972), pp. 235–43. A recently published article by Jeremy Bentham, written in June 1828, entitled on 'On Retrenchment' advances the 'disappointment-prevention principle', as connected with Bentham's greatest happiness principle. In judging a case a judge should, to achieve justice, weigh the relative 'strengths of expectation' of the parties: Bentham, 'On Retrenchment' in Schofield (ed.), *Official Aptitude Maximised; Expense Minimised* (1993), p. 342.

[88] See generally Raz, *The Authority of Law* (1979), Chap. 11.

[89] J. Schwarze, *European Administrative Law* (1992). The European law is based upon the concept of 'Vertrauensschutz' (the honouring of a trust or confidence). See generally, J. Usher, 'The Influence of National Concepts on Decisions of the European Court' (1976) 1 E.L.Rev. 359. See also C. Forsyth, (1988) Camb. L.J. 238; Eleanor Sharpston, 'Legitimate Expectations and Economic Reality' (1990) E.L.Rev. 103. For a useful account of the case law on the legitimate expectation in E.C. law, see *R. v. Ministry of Agriculture, Fisheries & Food, ex p. Hamble Offshore Fisheries Ltd* [1995] 2 All E.R. 714, 726–28 *per* Sedley J.

[90] [1969] 2 Ch. 149.

add, some legitimate expectation, of which it would not be fair to deprive him without hearing what he has to say".[91]

7–041   *Schmidt* and the line of early cases following it referred to the term "legitimate expectation" without analysing its scope or basis, and in particular without distinguishing it from the right to a hearing arising from the existence of a protectable interest.[92] In *R. v. Liverpool Corporation, ex p. Liverpool Taxi Fleet Operators' Association*,[93] it was held that the Corporation's decision to increase the number of taxi licences without consulting the Operator's Association was unfair because the decision was in breach of an assurance to the contrary. Although the duty to hear was not expressly justified by the doctrine of legitimate expectation in that case, later cases adopted and explained the decision on that basis.[94]

7–042   The first attempt at a comprehensive definition of the principle was provided in *Council of Civil Service Unions v. Minister for the Civil Service*.[95] A bare majority of their Lordships rested their conclusion on the fact that, but for national security, there would have been a duty on the Minister to consult, on the ground that the civil servants had a legitimate expectation that they would be consulted before trade union rights were taken away.[96] Lord Diplock stated that, for a legitimate expectation to arise, the decision:

---

[91]   *ibid.* at 170. Lord Denning's dicta were not supported by the other members of the Court. Russell L.J. dissenting, simply thought that the case was not sufficiently clear to warrant an order to strike out the action, and Widgery J. classified a situation where the renewal of a licence might 'reasonably be expected' as being 'tantamount to the withdrawal of a right.' *Ibid.* at 353.

[92]   In *Schmidt*, Lord Denning suggested that a *revocation* of an existing permit would have given the applicant 'an opportunity of making representations: for he would have a legitimate expectation of being allowed to stay for the permitted time'. See also *Breen v. Amalgamated Engineering Union* [1971] 2 W.L.R. 742; *McInnes v. Onslow-Fane* [1978] 1 W.L.R. 1520; *Smitty's Industries Ltd v. Att.-Gen.* [1980] 1 N.Z.L.R. 355; *O'Reilly v. Mackman* [1983] 2 A.C. 237 (*per* Lord Diplock).

[93]   [1972] 2 Q.B. 299; see the analysis of Ganz (n. 86, above) at pp. 149 *et seq.*

[94]   Lord Denning M.R. did not refer to the nascent doctrine, but to the 'private law' principle of equitable estoppel, discussed below, paras 7-059–7-060. For cases which have adopted the doctrine of legitimate expectation as the basis for a duty to be heard, see: *Salemi v. MacKellar (No. 2)* (1977) 137 C.L.R. 396, *per* Stephen J., dissenting; *Att.-Gen. of Hong Kong v. Ng Yuen Shiu* [1983] 2 A.C. 629; and *R. v. Secretary of State for the Home Department, ex p. Asif Mahmood Khan* [1984] 1 W.L.R. 1337.

[95]   [1985] A.C. 374. This was not, it should be noted, the first time that the House of Lords had considered the doctrine; see *O'Reilly v. Mackman* [1983] 2 A.C. 237, 275 *per* Lord Diplock (*obiter*, a prisoner has a legitimate expectation that he will not be awarded a forfeiture of remission by board of visitors without being heard in accordance with the procedures of natural justice); *Re Findlay* [1985] A.C. 318 (a prisoner has no legitimate expectation that he will be granted parole under policy which has been superseded by a more restrictive one). See also *Att.-Gen. of Hong Kong v. Ng Yuen Shiu* [1983] 2 A.C. 629.

[96]   Lords Diplock (at 408–9), Fraser (at 401B) and Roskill (at 1204H) all expressed a

"must affect [the] other person...by depriving him of some benefit or advantage which either (i) he had in the past been permitted by the decision-maker to enjoy and which he can legitimately expect to be permitted to continue to do until there has been communicated to him some rational grounds for withdrawing it on which he has been given an opportunity to comment; or (ii) he has received assurance from the decision-maker will not be withdrawn without giving him first an opportunity of advancing reasons for contending that they should not be withdrawn."[97]

As Lord Fraser put it, a legitimate expectation may arise "either from an express promise given on behalf of a public authority or from the existence of a regular practice which the claimant can reasonably expect to continue."[98]

Lord Diplock's definition of legitimate expectation makes clearer the circumstances in which it may arise, namely, from an expectation of a benefit or from an expectation of a hearing. However, the reference by Lord Diplock to *past* advantage or benefit is unduly restrictive. The expectation may also surely extend to a benefit in the future which has not yet been enjoyed but which has been promised. **7–043**

Legitimate expectations have arisen in many different circumstances over the last decade. Gypsies have had a legitimate expectation that a council would not evict them without finding an alternative site.[99] Contractors on a council's list of approved contractors had a legitimate expectation that they would not be removed from the list without a hearing.[1] An applicant submitting a tender for council land enjoyed a legitimate expectation that he would be given a further opportunity to tender following the failure of the favoured bid, since he had been **7–044**

---

preference for the term 'legitimate' over the term 'reasonable' expectation. Lords Scarman and Brightman affirmed the duty to consult without resting on the doctrine of legitimate expectation (*ibid.* at 1193G and 1208E).

[97] *ibid.* at 408–9.

[98] *ibid.* at 401B.

[99] *R. v. Brent L.B.C., ex p. MacDonagh* [1990] C.O.D. 3; 21 H.L.R. 494. The legitimate expectation arose both from an express promise of the Council, and because of a past practice of letting the gypsies stay on the land, providing services, etc.

[1] *R. v. Enfield L.B.C., exp. T. F. Unwin (Roydon) Ltd* (1989) 1 Admin. L.R. 51. The legitimate expectation would seem to be as a result of past practice: the contractors had been on the council's list 'for many years'. But see *R. v. Lord Chancellor, ex p. Hibbit and Saunders* [1993] C.O.D. 326 (shorthand writers on list of Lord Chancellor's Department).

"left with that impression".[2] A prisoner serving his sentence in Scotland where remission is one half of the sentence had a legitimate expectation when transferred to England, where remission was only one third of sentence, that the earlier release date would be applied.[3] The Commission for the New Towns had a legitimate expectation (based on a representation more than 15 years earlier) that if a local council constructed a highway, it would do so without charge.[4] The coal miners' unions had a legitimate expectation of being consulted on pit closures.[5] Litigants given an assurance by the Crown that a proposal made in the course of litigation would be honoured enjoyed a legitimate expectation that the Crown would act in accordance with the assurance.[6]

7–045   A number of other jurisdictions have recognised the legitimate expectation as founding a right to a fair hearing (although the requirements of the legitimate expectation may not always exactly coincide with those that are described immediately below).[7]

---

[2] *R. v. Barnet L.B.C., ex p. Pardes House School* [1989] C.O.D 512.

[3] *Walsh v. Secretary of State for Scotland*, 1990 S.L.T. 526.

[4] *R. v. Northamptonshire C.C., ex p. Commission for the New Towns* [1991] N.P.C. 109; [1992] C.O.D. 123.

[5] *R. v. British Coal Corp. and Secretary of State for Trade and Industry, ex p. Vardy* (1994) 6 Admin. L.R. 1.

[6] *New Zealand Maori Council v. Att.-Gen. of New Zealand* [1994] 1 A.C. 466. See also *R. v. Devon C.C., ex p. Baker* [1995] 1 All E.R. 73 (legitimate expectation of residents of home for elderly to be consulted about closure). See also *R. v. Wandsworth L.B.C., ex p. Beckwith, The Times*, June 5, 1995 (duty to consult extends to residents of other homes only indirectly affected by closure).

[7] In Ireland and the principle was accepted in *Webb v. Ireland* [1988] I.R. 353; and see the comprehensive discussion on legitimate expectations in G. Hogan and D. Morgan, *Administrative Law in Ireland* (2nd ed., 1991), Chap. 13. See also Hilary Delaney, 'The Doctrine of Legitimate Expectation in Irish Law' (1990) Dublin U.L.R. 1. For India see *Selvi Travels v. Union of India & Amir AIR* 1993 Madras 216; *Assistant Commissioner, Commercial Taxes v. Dharmendra Trading Co. AIR* 1988 SC 1247. In Australia legitimate expectation was adopted in *Heatley v. Tasmanian Racing & Gaming Commission* (1977) 137 C.L.R. 487; *cf. Salemi v. MacKellar (No. 2)* (1977) 137 C.L.R. 396, 404. While it clearly applies and has been interpreted broadly in *Annetts v. McCann* (1991) 65 A.L.J.R. 167, its precise status and meaning have been complicated by conflicting judicial pronouncements. See *South Australia v. O'Shea* (1987) 163 C.L.R. 378; *Haoucher v. Minister for Immigration and Ethnic Affairs* [1990] 169 C.L.R. 648. See also *Att.-Gen. for New South Wales v. Quinn* (1990) 170 C.L.R. 1 (discussed by P. Craig (1992) 108 L.Q.R. 79, above, n. 84). In South Africa the legitimate expectation giving rise to a fair hearing was accepted in *Administrator, Transvaal v. Traub* (1989) 4 SA 731(A). See also *Hlongwa v. Minister of Justice, Kwazulu Government* (1992) 13 I.L.J. 338 (D). The new interim South African constitution contained a 'fundamental right' (Chapter 3) to 'administrative justice'. Article 24 of Chapter 3 provided that 'Every person shall have the right to ... procedurally fair administrative action where any of his or her rights or legitimate expectations is affected or threatened.' The 1996 South African constitution simply gives a right to administrative action that is 'lawful, reasonable and procedurally fair'. In New Zealand the term 'reasonable expectation' is often

C. The Legitimate Expectation

The scope of the legitimate expectation

Expectation of what?

The terms of the representation by the decision-maker (whether   7–046
express or implied from past practice) must entitle the party to whom
it is addressed to expect, legitimately, one of two things:

(1) that a hearing or other appropriate procedures will be
    afforded before the decision is made; or

(2) that a benefit of a substantive nature will be granted or, if the
    person is already in receipt of the benefit, that it will be
    continued and not be substantially varied.

In the first case, fairness dictates that the expectation of a *hearing* be   7–047
fulfilled. The expectation may extend to the opportunity to make
representations or to any other component part of a fair hearing, for
example, the duty to give reasons.[8] In the second case, fairness
dictates that the expectation of the *benefit* should not be summarily
disappointed and that the recipient of the benefit should at least be
permitted to argue for its fulfilment.

In either of the above cases the substantive benefit or advantage   7–048
may not in the end be granted. All that is required at this stage is that
the opportunity be given to participate in the decision about whether
or not it should be granted (or not withdrawn or varied). However, in
the second case (relating to the expectation of a benefit), the law may
sometimes go further and require the expectation to be fulfilled by the
actual grant of what was promised. The principle underlying such a
decision will be discussed when we consider substantive, rather than
procedural judicial review.[9]

In the *GCHQ* case Lord Fraser held that the civil servants enjoyed a   7–049
legitimate expectation that they would be consulted before their trade
union membership was withdrawn. The expectation was in his view

---

preferred. See, *e.g. Birss v. Secretary for Justice* [1984] 1 N.Z.L.R. 56, 74; *Daganayasi v. Minister of Immigration* [1980] 2 N.Z.L.R. 130, 143–145; *Fowler & Roderique v. Att.-Gen.* [1987] 2 N.Z.L.R. 56 at 74; *Bradley v. Att.-Gen.* [1988] 2 N.Z.L.R. 454; *Petrocorp Exploration Ltd v. Butcher*, August 14, 1990, CA transcript 240/89; *aff'd* PC March 18, 1991. Canadian courts have not been greatly interested in the legitimate expectation although an agency is required to honour an undertaking to give a hearing even when not required by statute to give a hearing. See, *e.g. Gaw v. Commissioner of Corrections* (1986) 19 Admin.L.R. 137, (Fed.Ct.TD). In *Re Canada Assistance Plan (B.C.)* [1991] 2 S.C.R. 525 it was held that the doctrine of legitimate expectation does not create substantive rights but is part of procedural fairness.

[8] *R. v. Secretary of State for the Home Department, ex p. Duggan* [1994] 3 All E.R. 277.
[9] See Chap. 12 below.

grounded on the fact that prior consultation had in the past been the standard practice when conditions of service were significantly altered.[10] In Lord Diplock's view, however, the civil servants had alegitimate expectation that they would continue to enjoy the benefits of trade union membership.[11]

Expectation induced by the decision-maker

7–050 A legitimate expectation must be induced by the conduct of the decision-maker. It does not flow from any generalised expectation of justice, based upon the scale or context of the decision.[12] This quality is the essence of the distinction between an entitlement to a hearing based upon the legitimate expectation and that based upon other interests.[13] It is therefore misleading to classify under the head of

---

[10] [1985] A.C. 374, 401–403. Similarly, when British Coal and the Secretary of State were held in breach of their duty to consult with the unions on the question of pit closures (see above, n. 5), the applicants argued successfully that they were deprived of a legitimate expectation of a *hearing*. The expectation was in that case based upon an agreement establishing review procedures (known as the Modified Colliery Review Procedure) and procedures to refer pit closures to an independent tribunal.

[11] [1985] A.C. 374.

[12] As was insisted by Lords Diplock and Fraser in the *GCHQ* case above, thus indorsing the Privy Council decision in *Shiu* (n. 94, above and impliedly rejecting, insofar as it conflicted, the approach of earlier cases such as *Schmidt, Breen*, and *McInnes* (n. 92, above). Ganz, n. 86, above, at pp. 156 *et seq.*, criticises the 'confusion' which GCHQ imports into the law, but it is contended that GCHQ in fact resolves the confusion which previously existed. For criticism of the analysis of the legitimate expectation as resting on the conduct of the decision-maker, see the judgment of Brennan J. in *Kioa v. Minister for Immigration and Ethnic Affairs* (1986) 62 A.L.R. 321, 370–375, where he argues that since the principles of judicial review have their basis in the presumed intentions of Parliament, therefore 'legitimate expectation' could not be based on expectations engendered by decision-makers, which would be irrelevant to the construction of the statutory framework; *cf.* Barwick C.J. in *Salemi v. Mackellar (No. 2)* (1977) 137 C.L.R. 396, 404. But for criticism of this view see Elias, n. 86, above, at 45.

[13] See, *e.g.* the view of Lord Bridge in *Re Westminster City Council* [1986] A.C. 668. Rejecting an argument that 'the scale of [the] decisions [in respect of which natural justice was sought] and the context in which they were taken were such that the [affected] bodies would clearly have a legitimate expectation to be consulted', he warned that 'if the courts were to extend the doctrine of legitimate expectation [beyond the foundation of 'either a promise or a practice of consultation'] to embrace expectations arising from the 'scale' or 'context' of particular decisions, the duty of consultation would be entirely open-ended and no public authority could tell with any confidence in what circumstances a duty of consultation was cast upon them [and] the suggested development of the law would, in my opinion, be wholly lamentable'. Lord Bridge clearly sought to limit the doctrine to situations arising out of representations of the decision-maker and argues against its expansion to take in a class of interests (of a certain 'scale' or 'context') independent of this basis. See also

legitimate expectation interests which may require procedural protection irrespective of the conduct of the decision-maker.[14] Thus, for example, while the Court of Appeal in *R. v. Liverpool Corporation, ex p. Liverpool Taxi Fleet Operators' Association*[15] rightly held that the express assurance of consultation by the Corporation created a legitimate expectation, the *obiter* view of Lord Denning M.R. that even in the absence of an assurance the applicants' interest in maintaining the value of their licences would have entitled them to a hearing before the number of licences was increased, identifies a protectable interest quite separate from that derived from the legitimate expectation.[16]

More recent authorities confirm the conceptual distinction between **7–051** protectable interests and legitimate expectations. For example, it has been held that objectors to an application for planning permission had no legitimate expectation of being able to make representations on the matter because no conduct of the planning authority had induced such an expectation. Nevertheless, the objectors were entitled to be heard in order to defend their interests[17] as the proposed action would affect them adversely.[18] Further, in *R. v. Secretary of State for Health, ex p. U.S. Tobacco International Inc.*,[19] while it was held that the applicants could have no (substantive) legitimate expectation that the Minister would not change his policy regarding the production and sale of oral snuff, it was held that the Minister was in breach of his (statutory) duty to consult by refusing to reveal the contents of an independent report.

---

the clear distinction between legitimate expectations and protectable interests made by Taylor J. in *R. v. Secretary of State for the Environment, ex p. GLC* [1985] J.P.L. 543 (Secretary of State's exercise of discretion to delay consideration of the GLC's proposed amendments to the Greater London Development Plan not vitiated by lack of natural justice: not requirement to consult *either* on basis of a legitimate expectation, *or* under the *audi altarem partem* rule or because of a duty to act fairly, considering *Durayappah v. Fernando* [1967] 2 A.C. 337).

[14] A view taken by commentators such as Hlophe, Wade, Craig and Ganz, n.86, above. But see Elias, n.86, above.

[15] [1972] 2 Q.B. 299.

[16] Of course, it is possible that a requirement of procedural fairness may flow from *both* causes: for example, the revocation of a licence without a hearing may well infringe the interest protectable in itself *and* disappoint a legitimate expectation derived from the past conduct of the body which granted the licence.

[17] *R. v. Great Yarmouth B.C., ex p. Botton Brothers Arcades Ltd* [1988] J.P.L. 18; 56 P. & C.R. 99. See also cases cited above, n. 83.

[18] It was held that the circumstances of this case were however unique because the council had reversed its previously declared policy as to the amusement arcades in coming to the decision complained of. There was at that time no general duty on councils to consult or notify those affected by a grant of planning permission: see also *R. v. Secretary of State for the Environment, ex p. Kent* [1968] J.P.L. 706; [1990] J.P.L. 124.

[19] [1992] 1 All E.R. 212; see [1991] P.L. 163 (analysis, Schwehr and Brown).

The "high degree of fairness and candour" to the applicants was based upon the "catastrophic" effect of the ban on the applicants' financial interests.

7–052   The distinction between the legitimate expectation and protectable interest may not always be clear, particularly if the two overlap.[20] However, the underlying principles justifying one or the other are distinct. The legitimate expectation derives its justification from the principle of allowing the individual to rely on assurances given, and to promote certainty and consistent administration. Such a principle is distinct from that which permits a person to participate in the process of reaching a decision which may threaten his rights or interests. Both principles under ie the right to a fair hearing.

The nature of the representation

7–053   An expectation will be derived from *either*:

(1) an express promise or representation[21]; or

(2) a representation implied from established practice based upon the past actions or the settled conduct of the decision-maker.[22]

---

[20] An example of this situation is *R. v. Assistant Commissioner of Police of the Metropolis, ex p. Howell* [1985] RTR 52, CA where the Assistant Commissioner refused to renew the taxi licence of H, a cab driver, without first having given him an indication of the objections to renewal and without having given him a fair chance to meet the objections. In holding that the action of the Assistant Commissioner was unfair, and that the decision should be set aside, the Court of Appeal used both strands of reasoning. On the one hand, a protectable interest was taken away without consultation: 'I think natural justice required that the Assistant Commissioner, before reaching a final decision on a matter of such momentous importance to [H], should at the very least have given him the opportunity to comment...' (*per* Slade L.J. at 61k); on the other hand, 'given the doctor's view [that] he was fit to drive taxi cabs, and having been told [in the regulations] by the Assistant Commissioner that before he could grant him a further licence he would need a certificate to that effect, [H] had a reasonable expectation that the licence would be granted to him on the provision by his doctor of that certificate' (*per* Ackner L.J. at 60b).

[21] As in *Att.-Gen. of Hong Kong v. Ng Yuen Shiu* [1983] 2 A.C. 629 (assurance of interview prior to deportation); *Liverpool Taxi* [1972] 2 Q.B. 299; *R. v. Secretary of State for the Home Department, ex p. Asif Mahmood Khan* [1984] 1 W.L.R. 1337.

[22] See, *e.g.* GCHQ, n.12, above; *R. v. Brent L.B.C., ex p. Gunning* (1985) 84 L.G.R. 168 (parents' legitimate expectation of consultation prior to school closures and amalgamations based on past practice). A legitimate expectation could be simultaneously derived both from an express assurance and from past conduct: see, *e.g. R. v. Brent L.B.C., ex p. MacDonagh* [1990] C.O.D. 3. In *R.v. Secretary of State for the Home Department, ex p. Ruddock* [1987] 1 W.L.R. 1482, successive Home Secretaries had made public criteria and guidelines indicating the manner in which they proposed to exercise their discretion in relation to telephone tapping. It was held that the expectation arose from an express promise as well as the existence of a regular

C. The Legitimate Expectation

Not all past practice however may justify a legitimate expectation that the practice will continue. For example, a general, though informal, practice of notification of applications for planning permission to neighbours on adjacent sites was held not to create a legitimate expectation of consultation in a case where an individual had not been notified because of the council's oversight.[23] An alien with leave to remain in the United Kingdom for a limited period who, within that period, temporarily left the country in reliance upon first, the leave and a stamp stating that the holder was exempt from having to obtain a visa,[24] and secondly, an oral assurance by a Home Office official that she would have "no trouble returning", had a legitimate expectation that she would be allowed to re-enter the United Kingdom.[25] However, another alien who relied on the effect of the stamp alone could not establish a legitimate expectation that he was allowed to re-enter even though the use of the stamp appeared "almost calculated to mislead".[26]

Whether the representation is express or implied, it must be "clear, unambiguous, and devoid of relevant qualification".[27] It is important to look at the factual context in which the promise, assurance or other representation is made. The person seeking to rely on the

---

practice which the claimant could reasonably expect to continue. See also *R. v. IRC, ex p. Unilever plc* [1996] C.O.D. 369; [1996] S.T.C. 681, CA. (claim for tax relief made in similar from to that accepted in previous years and therefore unfair for the IRC to resile from previous practice without notice).

[23] *R. v. Secretary of State for the Environment, ex p. Kent* [1988] J.P.L. 706: *aff'd*. [1990] J.P.L. 124, CA (individual affected by planning application who was not notified either of council hearing of application, or of appeal to Secretary of State, could not challenge the decision since (1). jurisdiction was ousted by a six-week limitation clause, and (2), there was no legitimate expectation of notification, nor a protectable interest in consultation).

[24] And a stamp imposed pursuant to s. 3(3)(b) of the Immigration Act 1971, stating that the leave granted would apply unless superseded by any subsequent leave obtained by the holder.

[25] *R. v. Secretary of State for the Home Department, ex p. Oloniluyi* [1989] Imm. A.R. 135.

[26] *R. v. Secretary of State for the Home Department, ex p. Islam* [1990] Imm. A.R. 220; see also *R. v. Secretary of State for the Home Department, ex p. Patel* (1990) 3 Admin. L.R. 89.

[27] *per* Bingham L.J. in *R. v. Inland Revenue Commissioners, ex p. MFK Underwriting Agencies Ltd* [1990] 1 W.L.R. 1545; *R. v. Secretary of State for the Home Department, ex p. Sakala* [1994] Imm. A.R., 142 (statement by minister in Parliament that Secretary of State would 'almost invariably' accept the recommendation of a special adjudicator could not give rise to a legitimate expectation that the recommendation of an adjudicator would be followed). Compare the approach of the United States Supreme Court in *Board of Regents of State Colleges v. Roth* (1972) 408 U.S. 564, where it was held that the loss of a governmental benefit is a deprivation of 'property', and thus requiring 'due process' only if the individual has a 'legitimate claim of entitlement' to the benefit, rather than a mere 'unilateral expectation' of it.

representation must therefore "put all his cards face up on the table".[28]

7–056   It has been held that an expectation cannot arise simply from a misinterpretation of the words or actions of an authority.[29] It would, however, seem unfair to deny an applicant the benefits of an expectation based upon a "confident and not unreasonable hope"[30] induced by a representation that is objectively clear, albeit one that the decision-maker does not intend to encourage.[31] But there may be circumstances where the decision-maker may resile from an objectively clear, but erroneously made, representation, where it can be shown that it would not be unfair or inconsistent with good administration for the decision-maker to be permitted to withdraw the representation.[32]

Representation personally directed or general?

7–057   As the examples above make clear, where the legitimate expectation derives from an express representation, that representation need not be made to the applicant personally or directly; a general policy which affects the applicant as a member of a class is sufficient.[33] Similarly, a

---

[28] *per* Bingham L.J. in *Ex p. MFK Underwriting Agencies Ltd*, above. In *Matrix Securities Ltd v. Inland Revenue Commissioners* [1994] 1 W.L.R. 334, HL the taxpayer, in seeking advance clearance to a scheme from the Revenue, failed to make full disclosure of the relevant circumstances. In the event the Revenue were not acting unfairly in seeking to extract tax contrary to an advance clearance. Note that a document raising legitimate expectations must be prospective and cannot sustain a requirement, *e.g.*, for reasons to be given in relation to events prior to the document's publication: *R. v. Secretary of State for the Home Department, ex p. Duggan* [1994] 3 All E.R. 277.

[29] See *Islam*, and *Patel*, n. 26 above.

[30] A term used in relation to proprietory estoppel, discussed below. See *Att.-Gen. of Hong Kong v. Humphreys Estates (Queen's Gardens)* [1987] 1 A.C. 114, 124.

[31] In *R. v. Jockey Club, ex p. RAM Racecourses* [1993] 2 All E.R. 225, 238 it was held that the Jockey Club 'had neither actually or presumptively intended to reach and affect' the applicants by means of a report not made public although it had come into the hands of the applicants and 'indeed it was likely that it would' (*per* Stuart-Smith L.J.).

[32] See, *e.g. R. v. Secretary of State for the Home Department, ex p. Silva*, The Times, April 1, 1994, CA (Home Secretary told deportees by mistake they had no right of appeal— later corrected. Leave refused because not unfair not to give right of appeal). See paras 7–063–7–066 below.

[33] For the extent to which a general representation may amount to a 'policy', see the fuller discussion at paras 5–098–5–099 above, and in relation to the substantive legitimate expectations see paras 12–029–12–033 below. See *Att.-Gen. for Hong Kong v. Ng Yuen Shiu*, n.94, above, and *R. v. Secretary of State for the Home Department, ex p. Asif Mahmood Khan*, n.94, above. Of course, an individual personally in receipt of a representation may be in a better position factually to establish a legitimate expectation than a member of a class: this explains the decision of the Divisional Court in *R. v. Secretary of State for the Home Department, ex p. Islam* [1990] C.O.D. 177, where lack of a personal assurance from the Home Office led to the conclusion that no legitimate expectation could arise, distinguishing *R. v. Secretary of State for the*

regular past practice not previously affecting the applicant and not directed at him personally could provide the basis for a legitimate expectation. It is of course necessary that the applicant is a member of the class of persons who are the subject of the representation while that representation is operative.[34]

Knowledge of the representation

Could an applicant claim the benefit of a representation contained in, say, a government circular which he had not seen until after the relevant decision had been made? The fact that the applicant is in the class to which the representation is directed but happens not to be aware of it should not, it is submitted, deprive him of the benefit of the representation.[35] To do so would involve unfair discrimination between those who were and were not aware of the representation and would benefit the well-informed or well-advised. It would also encourage undesirable administrative practice by too readily relieving decision-makers of the normal consequences of their actions.[36]

7–058

Reliance on the representation

There have been isolated suggestions that for the courts to protect a legitimate expectation, it is necessary for the applicant not only to

7–059

Home Department, ex p. Oloniluyi [1989] Imm. A.R. 135.

[34] *R. v. Inland Revenue Commissioners, ex p. Camacq Corp.* [1990] 1 W.L.R. 191, CA (where the revenue operates a practice to benefit one class of taxpayer, only someone within that class may have a legitimate expectation that it will continue). See also *R. v. Jockey Club, ex p. RAM Racecourses* [1993] 2 All E.R. 225, 238–39. See the controversial Australian case of *Minister for Immigration and Ethnic Affairs v. Teoh* (1995) 183 C.L.R. 273, where the High Court held that the UN Covenant on the Rights of the Child, which was not incorporated into Australian law, may nevertheless give rise to a legitimate expectation that the executive decision-maker would comply with it, at least to the extent of giving an affected person a hearing on the matter. For a critical article see Taggart (1996) 112 L.Q.R. 50. *Teoh* was followed by the CA in *R. v. Secretary of State for the Home Department, ex p. Ahmed (Mohammed Hussain)* [1998] 1 Imm. A.R. 375. Cf. *Behluli v. Secretary of State for the Home Department* [1998] 1 Imm. A.R. 407; *Thomas and Hilcare v. Babtiste*, Privy Council, March 17, 1999; *R. v. DPP ex p. Kebilene*, *The Times*, March 31, 1999.

[35] Correspondingly, a legitimate expectation may be revoked by a changed departmental circular properly communicated, though not necessarily known to the applicant. See discussion below, paras. 7-063–7-066, and *Hughes v. Department of Health and Social Security* [1985] A.C. 776, 788 *per* Lord Diplock.

[36] But see *R. v. Secretary of State for the Home Department, ex p. Akyol* [1990] Imm. A.R. 571; *Lloyd v. McMahon* [1987] A.C. 625, 696, 714, where their Lordships considered the effect of ignorance of the existing practice.

have been aware of the representation but also to have relied on it, and possibly to have acted to his detriment. In *R. v. Secretary of State for the Home Department, ex p. Oloniluyi*,[37] the Court of Appeal held that the applicant had a legitimate expectation, encouraged by passport stamps and the representations of an immigration official, that she would have no trouble returning to the United Kingdom. It was held that she had relied to her detriment on those representations as she would not have risked going abroad without the representations, and that the refusal of re-entry altered her rights of appeal and prejudiced her chances of obtaining permission to enter in the future.[38]

7–060   The suggestion that detrimental reliance might be necessary to found an application on legitimate expectation clearly draws sustenance from the parallel with the private law concept of estoppel.[39] The general principle justifying estoppel and the public law principle of legitimate expectation are superficially similar: in both cases it is regarded as inequitable for the promissor to act inconsistently, to renege on a representation, peremptorily to go back on a promise.[40] In important cases, however, a legitimate expectation has been founded in the absence of detrimental reliance,[41] and there are good reasons why this should be so. First, it should be noted that detrimental reliance is not required for all kinds of private law estoppel. It is not a necessary element in what is known as "equitable" or "promissory" estoppel.[42] Secondly, in relation to procedural fairness (substantive legitimate expectations will be considered separately below),[43] the question is not whether the authority is bound to honour the expectation it induced, but only whether the promissee should be entitled to argue for its fulfilment. The parallel with the concept of

---

[37] [1989] Imm. A.R. 135; [1989] C.O.D. 275.

[38] It is not clear whether and to what extent the members of the Court of Appeal regarded the finding of reliance as vital to their decision, but the fact of reliance was separately considered. See further, *R. v. Jockey Club, ex p. RAM Racecourses* [1993] 2 All E.R. 223, 236, 237 where Stuart-Smith L.J. suggested that reliance would be a precondition for the establishing of a legitimate expectation where an applicant 'is saying, 'You cannot alter your policy now in my case; it is too late' ".

[39] This will be discussed more fully below in relation to the substantive legitimate expectation. See Chap. 12, below.

[40] See, *e.g. R. v. Horseferry Road Magistrates' Court, ex p. Bennett* [1994] A.C. 42, 61, *per* Lord Griffith, citing *Chu Piuwing v. Att.-Gen.* [1984] H.K.L.R. 411, 417, *per* McMullin V-P.

[41] *e.g.* in the cases of *R. v. Secretary of State for the Home Department, ex p. Asis Mahmood Kahn* [1984] 1 W.L.R. 1337; *Att.-Gen. of Hong Kong v. Ng Yuen Shiu* [1983] A.C. 629; and *R. v. Secretary of State for the Home Department, ex p. Ruddock* [1987] 1 W.L.R. 1482.

[42] See G. Treitel, *The Law of Contract*, (8th ed., 1991), p. 105. Detrimental reliance is however required for 'proprietary estoppel'. *Ibid.* pp. 125–126. See *Crabb v. Arun D.C.* [1976] Ch. 179.

[43] See Chap. 12, para. 12–026.

estoppel is therefore inexact. Thirdly, there is good reason to assert that public bodies should suffer the consequences of their representations unless strongly competing considerations of public policy indicate otherwise.

The effect of a voluntary hearing

If a body which is entitled to reach a decision without any prior hearing elects to give a hearing before coming to its decision, can that decision be impugned on the ground that the hearing did not conform to the standards of fairness? Some older authority suggests that it cannot.[44] However on further reflection the position appears less clear. In other areas of the law the volunteer is at times burdened with the same duties as the conscript. I am under no obligation to give a hitchhiker a lift in my car, but if I choose to give him a lift I owe him the same duty of care as I would if he were a fare-paying passenger and I were a common carrier or bound by contract to convey him. 7–061

Whatever the position may have been in the past,[45] it seems clear today that by providing a voluntary hearing the decision-maker will have induced a legitimate expectation of fairness and the hearing will therefore have to conform to the standards appropriate to the decision being made.[46] 7–062

The revocation of a legitimate expectation

An expectation need not endure eternally. It may come to an end naturally or it may be cancelled. There are sound reasons why officials ought to be free to change their policies and practices, for otherwise their discretion would be fettered.[47] 7–063

---

[44] *Ex p. Death* (1852) 18 Q.B. 647, 659; *Green v. Blake* [1948] I.R. 242, 267; *Russell v. Duke of Norfolk* [1948] 1 All E.R. 488, 491; [1949] 1 All E.R. 109, 115; *Nakkuda Ali v. Jayaratne* [1951] A.C. 66, 77; *R. v. Bird* (1963) 38 D.L.R. (2d) 354. *Contra, R. v. Minister of Labour, ex p. General Supplies Ltd* (1965) 47 D.L.R. (2d) 189, applying a dictum in *R. v. Metropolitan Police Commissioner, ex p. Parker* [1953] 1 W.L.R. 1150, 1157.

[45] See the 4th edition of this work at pp. 237–238.

[46] Even in Canada, where "courts have displayed very little interest in using the notion of expectations as an explicit element of their reasoning about the threshold [of the fair hearing]. If an agency is not required to give a hearing, but undertakes to give one, it must be faithful to its undertaking." J.M. Evans, H.N. Janisch, David Mullan, R.C.B. Risk, *Administrative Law: Cases, Text and Materials* (1989), p. 94.

[47] A point made in *Findlay v. Secretary of State for the Home Department* [1985] A.C. 318; and *R. v. Secretary of State for Health, ex p. U.S. Tobacco International Inc.* [1992] 1 Q.B. 353, where it was held that the ministers were entitled to change their policy, in the public interest. See also *Hughes v. Department of Health and Social Security* [1985] A.C.

As with the creation of an expectation, its revocation may be effected by either an express or an implied representation. An express representation must be clear and unambiguous. A change in a departmental circular would, if properly communicated, although not necessarily personally to any particular individual, serve as an express representation for these purposes.[48] In some cases, however, the existing procedures of consultation may be so entrenched that they may be cancelled only after giving interested persons a "proper opportunity to comment and object".[49]

7–064   In the case of an implied representation, an event or series of events may cancel a previous expectation. For example, where a pattern or practice of consultation exists (for example, a practice of renewing licences or consulting neighbours), the point at which that pattern or practice is cancelled by implication will be a matter of "fact and degree".[50]

7–065   It should again be stressed that it is the representation *of the decision-maker* that cancels a legitimate expectation. The principle that supports the legitimate expectation generating an entitlement is that of legal certainty: a person should be able to rely on promises or representations. It follows that where the person who has made those representations unambiguously cancels them, and where that cancellation is known or ought to be known to the affected person, then the basis for reliance no longer exists. However, against persons who have already relied upon the representation, the decision-maker should be bound (at least to the extent of providing a fair hearing).[51] For the same reason it is wrong to suggest that a legitimate expectation can be forfeited, for example by unmeritorious conduct on

---

776 where Lord Diplock said that the liberty to change administrative policies is 'inherent in our constitutional form of government'. *Ibid.* at 788. See Chap. 10, below. And see the discussion of the revocation of a substantive expectation in Chap. 12, paras 12-029–12-033 below.

[48] 'When a change in administrative policy takes place and is communicated in a departmental circular ... any reasonable expectations that may have been aroused ... by any previous circular are destroyed and replaced.' *Per* Lord Diplock in *Hughes v. Department of Health and Social Security* [1985] A.C. 776, 788.

[49] *per* Glidewell L.J. in *R. v. British Coal Corp., ex p. Vardy* (1994) 6 Admin. L.R. 1.

[50] Wade and Forsyth suggest that the case of *Schmidt* [1969] 2 Ch. 149 involved the cancellation of a legitimate expectation (*Administrative Law,* 7th ed., 1994) p. 525). With respect, the student's right to a hearing (were he to be deported within the duration of his agreed stay in the United Kingdom) would have been based upon a deprivation of a right or interest. Lord Denning held that the student did not enjoy a legitimate expectation of remaining beyond that period. There was however no cancellation of any legitimate expectation in that case. See also *R. v. Secretary of State for the Home Department, ex p. Malh* [1991] 1 Q.B. 194.

[51] In relation to the expectation of a continuing benefit, see Chap. 12, below, paras 12-027 *et seq.*

the part of the applicant.[52] Unless the expectation were expressly made conditional upon the applicant's "good behaviour", the decision whether to rely on the expectation or to waive it lies with the applicant alone. It would also seem wrong to prejudge the merits of the applicant's present case on his previous wrongdoing.[53]

It should also be noted that although an entitlement to a fair hearing **7–066** based upon a legitimate expectation may be revoked by a counter-representation (express or implied), an entitlement to a fair hearing based upon the applicant's rights or protectable interests cannot be revoked at all. Thus where a person's entitlement to a hearing is based upon his need to protect his reputation, or his employment, a representation from the decision-maker to the effect that a hearing cannot be expected, or can no longer be expected, will be of no avail. This is because the hearing in such cases has nothing to do with the intention or grace or past practices of the decision-maker; it is required for the purpose of allowing the affected person the opportunity to defend his threatened rights or interests.[54]

---

[52] As is suggested by Wade, *op. cit.* n. 50 above, pp. 522–528. In *Cinnamond v. British Airport Authority* [1980] 1 W.L.R. 582, Lord Denning upheld the absence of a hearing on the ground of lack of legitimate expectation of a hearing due to the unmeritorious past conduct of the applicants. Brandon L.J. however based his decision upon the ground that a hearing 'would have availed the applicant nothing' (an exception considered in Chap. 9 below, paras 9–030 *et seq.*).

[53] The wrongdoing may however affect the question of whether a remedy is exercised in the discretion of the court: see para. 15–046.

[54] In a case like *Cinnamond*, above, the hearing would normally be required to protect the applicants' interests. Their unmeritorious conduct could of course be penalised by the failure to grant a discretionary remedy.

CHAPTER 8

PROCEDURAL FAIRNESS: CONTENT

Tucker L.J. in *Russell v. Duke of Norfolk*[1] said that "there are, in my view, no words which are of universal application in every kind of domestic tribunal ... whatever standard is adopted, one essential is that the person concerned should have a reasonable opportunity of presenting his case". 8–001

The content of fair procedures is therefore infinitely flexible. It ranges from mere consultation at the lower end, upwards through an entitlement to make written representations, to make oral representations, to a fully fledged hearing at the other extreme with most of the characteristics of a judicial trial. What is required in any particular case is incapable of definition in abstract terms. As Lord Bridge has put it: "the so-called rules of natural justice are not engraved on tablets of stone. To use the phrase which better expresses the underlying concept, what the requirements of fairness demand when any body, domestic, administrative or judicial, has to make a decision which will affect the rights of individuals depends on the character of the decision-making body, the kind of decision it has to make and the statutory or other framework in which it operates."[2] 8–002

The content of a hearing is easier to determine in cases where it is based upon a legitimate expectation of a hearing—but even in such a case the scope of the expected hearing may not be easy to define. Where the right to procedural fairness has a statutory source then substantial guidance as to what should be provided can be obtained, usually by construction of the legislation in question. Even in such a 8–003

---

[1] [1949] 1 All E.R. 109, 118.

[2] *Lloyd v. McMahon* [1987] A.C. 625, 702. For a recent example, see *R. v. Leicester Crown Court, ex p. Phipps* [1997] C.O.D. 299 (where there is no customary general practice, an individual judge will have to devise a procedure that is fair and just and meets the particular circumstances of the case). But for the dangers of excessive informality, see *Dyason v. Secretary of State for the Environment, Transport and the Regions* (1998) 75 P. & C.R. 506.

case, however, terms such as "consultation" need elaboration[3] and degrees of disclosure or candour will differ in different circumstances. Furthermore the courts may be prepared to supplement the statutory code. In the recent case of *Doody,*[4] Lord Mustill in summarising the effect of the authorities said: "The principles of fairness are not to be applied by rote identically in every situation. What fairness demands is dependent on the context of the decision, and this is to be taken into account in all its aspects. An essential factor of the context is the statute which creates the discretion, as regards both its language and the shape of the legal and administrative system within which the decision is taken." While the statute is an essential factor it is not the *only* feature and the courts will supplement the statutory code or if the statute is silent imply a code.[5]

PRIOR NOTICE OF THE DECISION

8–004   Procedural fairness generally requires that persons liable to be directly affected by proposed administrative acts, decisions or proceedings be given adequate notice of what is proposed, so that they may be in a position:

   (1) to make representations on their own behalf[6]; or

   (2) to appear at a hearing or inquiry (if one is to be held); and

   (3) effectively to prepare their own case and to answer the case (if any) they have to meet.

In disciplinary and analogous situations, there will often be a further reason why adequate prior notice should be given to the party

---

[3] See *R. v. Secretary of State for Social Services, ex p. Association of Metropolitan Authorities* [1986] 1 W.L.R. 1.

[4] *R. v. Secretary of State for the Home Department, ex p. Doody* [1994] 1 A.C. 531, 560.

[5] See *Doody* (above, n.4) esp. 562; *R. v. Parole Board, ex p. Wilson* [1992] 2 Q.B. 740; *Wiseman v. Bomeman* [1971] A.C. 297, 308, 311, 312, 317G and 320; *Lloyd v. McMahon* [1987] A.C. 625, 202H–703A, *per* Lord Bridge; *Pearlberg v. Varty* [1972] 1 W.L.R. 534, 551A–B *per* Lord Salmon. *cf.* Lord Hailsham 540C–D. To supplement the procedures must not frustrate the statutory scheme; *R. v. Birmingham C.C., ex p. Ferrero Ltd* [1993] 1 All E.R. 530, 542 (Taylor L.J.).

[6] *cf. Hoggard v. Worsbrough U.D.C.* [1962] 2 Q.B. 93 (insufficient warning given of what was proposed to be done to plaintiff's detriment; plaintiff's abstention from making immediate representations excusable because he was left under a misapprehension). See also *R. v. Secretary of State for the Home Department, ex p. Doody* [1994] 1 A.C. 531, 563 where Lord Mustill describes it as a proposition of common sense.

to be charged—to give him the opportunity of offering to resign[7] or (for example) surrender his licence rather than face the prospect of formal condemnation.

In a large majority of the reported cases where breach of the **8–005** requirements of fairness has been alleged, no notice whatsoever of the action taken or proposed to be taken was given to the person claiming to be aggrieved,[8] and failure to give him prior notice was tantamount to a denial of an opportunity to be heard.[9] The requirement that prior notice be given, therefore, usually follows automatically from a right to be consulted or heard (whether in writing or orally).

If there is a duty to give prior notice, it does not invariably follow **8–006** that notice must actually be served and received[10]; it is not uncommon for legislation to provide that it is sufficient if reasonable steps are taken to give notice.[11] If the number of persons affected is

---

[7] See the excellent comment, 'Judicial Control of Acts of Private Associations' (1963) 76 Harv.L.R., 983, 1028. Of course, it does not necessarily follow that the competent author is obliged to accept such a resignation or withdrawal.

[8] See, *e.g. Bagg's case* (1615) 11 Co.Rep. 93b; *Cooper v. Wandsworth Board of Works* (1863) 14 C.B.(N.S.) 180; *Ridge v. Baldwin* [1964] A.C. 40; *Glynn v. Keele University* [1971] 1 W.L.R. 487; *R. v. Havering JJ., ex p. Smith* [1974] 3 All E.R. 484. It should be noted, however, that as the knowledge of the basic requirements of fairness has increased among both potential Applicants and Respondents, the proportion of cases involving a complete failure to give notice or to hear has fallen, as compared to those cases involving a challenge to the extent or nature of the hearing.

[9] See *Annamunthodo v. Oilfield Workers' Trade Union* [1961] A.C. 945; *Maradana Mosque Trustees v. Mahmud* [1967] A.C. 13; *Lau Liat Meng v. Disciplinary Committee* [1968] A.C. 391 (notice given of proposed action on ground X but action taken on ground Y of which no notice, or inadequate notice, had been given); *Fairmount Investments Ltd. v. Secretary of State for the Environment* [1976] 1 W.L.R. 1255; and *Hadmor Productions v. Hamilton* [1983] 1 A.C. 191 at 233B–C. *Cf. R. v. Secretary of State for Health ex p. U.S. Tobacco International Inc.* [1992] Q.B. 353, 370F–G; *Chief Constable of North Wales Police v. Evans* [1982] 1 W.L.R. 1155; *R. v. Hampshire C.C., ex p. K* [1990] 2 Q.B. 71.

[10] But the general rule is that it must be: see, *e.g. Re Wykeham Terrace, Brighton* [1971] Ch. 204; *cf. R. v. Kensington and Chelsea Rent Tribunal, ex p. MacFarlane* [1974] 1 W.L.R. 1486 (notice served but not received: proceedings valid, but tribunal has discretion to reconsider its decision in light of representations subsequently made by absent party).

[11] *e.g.* under the Town and Country Planning Act 1990, s. 65, a local planning authority shall not entertain an application for planning permission unless the applicant has certified that he is the sole owner of all the land to which the application relates, or has notified the owner. Where, however, the applicant has been unable to identify the owner he must show that he has taken reasonable steps to do so and has published notice of the application in a local newspaper circulating in the locality. See also Town and Country Planning General Development Order 1988, Arts. 12 and 12A (S.I. 1988 No. 1813, subst. by S.I. 1992 No. 1493). It may still be wrong to proceed if it is known that notice has not in fact been received, at least where the statute makes the time at which notice is received important: *R. v. London County Q.S. Appeals Committee, ex p. Rossi* [1956] 1 Q.B. 682. *Cf. R. v. Devon and Cornwall Rent Tribunal, ex p. West* (1975) 29 P. & C.R. 316; *Willowgreen Ltd v. Smithers* [1994] 1 W.L.R. 832.

indeterminate,[12] to give public notice in a manner fairly and reasonably calculated to alert those likely to be interested in the subject-matter may be enough to satisfy the rule.[13] But where a person is likely to suffer particular loss from the decision, the duty of "candour" is that much higher.[14] If a person upon whom notice ought to be served, or his representative, obstructs service[15] or negligently fails to notify a change of address,[16] or if the matter is one of special urgency,[17] non-service of notice may be excused. Other possible exceptions to the general rule—where the person claiming to be aggrieved must be assumed to have known or did in fact know what was being alleged or what was likely to happen to him,[18] or that he suffered no real detriment by the omission[19] or impliedly waived the defect by appearing at a subsequent hearing[20]—must be viewed with some reserve.[21] Seldom will the absence of prior notice leave a person with an adequate opportunity of preparing his own case or his answers.

8–007   As the reason for imposing an obligation to give prior notice is usually to afford those who will be affected an opportunity to make representations, the notice must be served in sufficient time to enable representations to be made effectively.[22] If an oral hearing is to be

---

[12] And not merely large; *cf. Young v. Ladies Imperial Club Ltd* [1920] 2 K.B. 523 (irregularly constituted meeting; fact that a committee member was known to wish not to attend did not justify failure to summon her).

[13] See, *e.g. Wilson v. Secretary of State for the Environment* [1973] 1 W.L.R. 1083; *Waitemata County v. Local Government Committee* [1964] N.Z.L.R. 689, 698–699.

[14] *R. v. Secretary of State for Health, ex p. U.S. Tobacco International Inc.* [1992] Q.B. 353. *R. v. Ealing Magistrates' Court, ex p. Fanneran* (1996) 8 Admin. L.R. 351 (dog owner entitled to be heard before destruction order is made).

[15] *De Verteuil v. Knaggs* [1918] A.C. 557, 560–561.

[16] *James v. Institute of Chartered Accountants* (1907) 98 L.T. 225; *Glynn v. Keele University* [1971] 1 W.L.R. 487; *Al-Mehdawi v. Secretary of State for the Home Department* [1990] 1 A.C. 876 (where the negligence was that of the appellant's solicitor).

[17] *De Verteuil v. Knaggs*, above; Town and Country Planning Act 1971; s. 58(6), as inserted by s. 7(1) of the Town and Country Planning (Amendment) Act 1972 (affixing building preservation notice to building instead of service on owner and occupier permissible in case of urgency).

[18] *cf. Robinson v. Sunderland Corp.* [1899] 1 Q.B. 751, 757, 758; *Russell v. Duke of Norfolk* [1949] 1 All E.R. 109, 117–118; *Byme v. Kinematograph Renters Society Ltd* [1958] 1 W.L.R. 762, 785.

[19] *cf. Davis v. Carew-Pole* [1956] 1 W.L.R. 833, 838–840. See generally on this point, *John v. Rees* [1970] Ch. 345, 402.

[20] *Noakes v. Smith* (1942) 107 J.P. 101.

[21] See, *e.g. Hibernian Property Co. Ltd. v. Secretary of State for the Environment* (1973) 27 P. & C.R. 197, 213; *Fairmount Investments Ltd. v. Secretary of State for the Environment* [1976] 1 W.L.R. 1255, 1266. See also *Rees v. Crane* [1994] 2 A.C. 173, PC, and see the discussion in paras 9-030–9-035 below.

[22] *Lee v. Department of Education and Science* (1967) 66 L.G.R. 211; *R. v. Liverpool Corp., ex p. Liverpool Taxi Fleet Operators' Association* [1972] 2 Q.B. 299; *R. v. Thames Magistrates*

held, the time and place must be properly notified.[23] If charges are to be brought, they should be specified with particularity,[24] and in any event an interested party ought not to be taken by surprise by being expected to give an immediate answer to an important point raised for the first time at the hearing.[25] Nevertheless, sometimes domestic tribunals have been accorded a considerable degree of latitude in such matters.[26]

Statutory rules may set out in varying detail the requirements for the giving of notice and for consultation. There is no set form, and procedures will differ for different decisions, tribunals and statutory inquiries. For example, the requirements for the publicity of proposals for development plans have altered over time and are somewhat different for different types of plan. In relation to structure plans, the report of the Skeffington committee in 1969[27] proposed that authorities should ensure effective publicity for their structure plan proposals and should secure the participation of the public through public meetings, exhibitions and press conferences. Guidance issued by the Secretary of State urged authorities to regard the bare statutory provisions[28] as minimum requirements and to supplement them so as to conform   **8–008**

Court, ex p. Polemis [1974] 1 W.L.R. 1371 (refusal of an adjournment); *Brentnall v. Free Presbyterian Church of Scotland*, 1986 S.L.T. 471. *R. v. Guildford Justices, ex p. Rich* [1997] 1 Cr. App. R. (S) 49 (sufficient notice of distress order must be given to allow affected individual opportunity to make representations); *R. v. Devon County Council, ex p. Baker* [1995] 1 All E.R. 73 (insufficient notice given to residents of proposed closure of old people's home to enable proper representations or objections); *R. v. Secretary of State for the Home Department, ex p. Moon* (1996) 8 Admin. L.R. 477.

[23] *Hopkins v. Smethwick Board of Health* (1890) 24 QBD 712, 715; *Wilson v. Secretary of State for the Environment* [1988] 3 P.L. 520; cf. *Ostreicher v. Secretary of State for the Environment* [1978] W.L.R. 810 (date of hearing inconvenient for religious reasons).

[24] *Ex p. Daisy Hopkins* (1891) 61 L.J.Q.B. 240; *McDonald v. Lanarkshire Fire Brigade Joint Committee* 1959 S.C. 141. *R. v. LAUTRO, ex p. Tee* (1995) 7 Admin. L.R. 289; see further, the duty of adequate disclosure, below, at para. 8–018 *et seq.*

[25] *R. v. Rodney and Minister of Manpower and Immigration* (1972) 27 D.L.R. (3d) 756. *R. v. Chance, ex p. Coopers & Lybrand* (1995) 7 Admin. L.R. 821, 835H (surprise as the enemy of justice).

[26] See, *e.g. Sloane v. G.M.C.* [1970] 1 W.L.R. 1130; *Norman and Moran v. National Dock Labour Board* [1957] 1 Lloyd's Rep. 455 (imprecise charges); contrast *Stevenson v. United Road Transport Union* [1977] I.C.R. 893.

[27] *People and Planning*, (1969, HMSO).

[28] Under section 7 of the Town and Country Planning Act 1971, authorities were required to take such steps as they thought necessary to ensure that adequate publicity was given in their area to their draft proposals, to make the public aware of their opportunity to make representations about the proposals, and to provide them with an adequate opportunity to do so. The authority then had to submit to the Secretary of State a statement of the steps taken when the draft plan was submitted for his approval, and he had the power to reject the draft if not satisfied that the participation was adequately achieved.

with Skeffington's ideals.[29] In 1981 a change in policy was announced, advising authorities to do no more than achieve the bare statutory requirements.[30] These requirements were themselves amended from 1992.[31] Under new regulations[32] the authority is required to carry out consultations with a list of named consultees.[33] This duty carries with it a duty to "consider any representations made by the consultees before finally determining the contents of the proposal".[34] The authority is however no longer required to consult anyone else. If additional persons are however voluntarily consulted, the authority is required to prepare a statement of those consultees, and of any steps they took to publicise the proposals and to provide persons with an opportunity of making representations in respect of those proposals.[35]

8–009   By contrast, the duty to advertise applications for planning permission, or to consult neighbours or members of the public about development proposals, has expanded recently. Up until 1991 there was no general duty to advertise planning applications or to notify neighbours of their existence. That duty did however attach to "unneighbourly development" and to departures from the development plan[36] as well as development which would, in the opinion of the authority, affect the character or appearance of a conservation area or the setting of a listed building. In these cases the authority is obliged to publish a notice in a local newspaper and to post a site notice on or near the building,[37] and not to determine the application within 21 days of the publication and posting of the notice. Outside of these and other specially protected areas however there was no general requirement to publicise planning applications.[38] It was even held that, in a case where there had been an informal

---

[29] Department of the Environment, Circular 52/72.

[30] Department of the Environment, Circular 23/81.

[31] By the Planning and Compensation Act 1991, Sched. 4, para. 17, effective February 10, 1992 (S.I. 1991 No. 2905). See now Town and Country Planning Act 1990 s.33 (in respect of structure plans), s.12 (in respect of unitary development plans), and s.40 (in respect of local plans).

[32] Town and Country Planning (Development Plan) Regulations 1991 (No. 2794).

[33] *ibid.* reg. 10. The consultees include the Secretaries of State for the Environment and Transport, other local planning authorities for the area or adjacent areas, the National Rivers Authority, the Countryside Commission, the Nature Conservancy Council and the Historic Buildings and Monuments Commission.

[34] *ibid.* reg. 10(2).

[35] *ibid.* reg. 10(3).

[36] As listed in the former article 8 of the Town and Country General Development Order 1988.

[37] Planning (Listed Buildings and Conservation Areas) Act 1990, s.73.

[38] Although there is and has been a duty to consult with specified bodies about specified applications. See arts. 18–21 of the Town and Country Planning General Development Order 1988, and Department of Environment Circular 22/88, Appendix C.

practice of neighbour notification, that practice would not give rise to any legitimate expectation of notification on the part of a neighbour who was not notified because of an administrative error.[39]

In 1991 however the law was changed,[40] so that now all planning **8–010** applications must be publicised by the local planning authority, either by a site notice or notification of neighbours. In addition, an advertisement in a newspaper is required in some specified cases,[41] and in all cases of "major development".[42] These requirements of publicity are backed up by a duty to "take into account" any representations that are made in response to them, and the authority is forbidden from determining the application before 21 days from the posting of a site notice or 14 days from the date of the publication of a newspaper notice.[43]

Although the non-issue or the inadequacy of the notice can **8–011** invalidate the subsequent proceedings,[44] exceptions to the general rule have been introduced by statute. For example, under a number of statutes procedural defects will only be a ground for setting aside an order if a defect has resulted in the applicant being substantially

---

[39] *R. v. Secretary of State for the Environment, ex p. Kent* [1988] J.P.L. 124; [1988] 3 P.L.R. 17; upheld in the Court of Appeal [1990] J.P.L. 124.

[40] By section 16(2) of the Planning and Compensation Act 1991, amending section 71 of the Town and Country Planning Act 1990, and introduced by art. 12B of the Town and Country Planning General Development Order 1988 (inserted by the Town and Country Planning General Development (Amendment) (No. 4) Order 1992 (S.I. 1992 No. 1493)).

[41] Where the application is accompanied by an environment statement, departures from a development plan, or development affecting a public right of way. Art. 12B (above), para. 2.

[42] Defined under para. 7 of art. 12B above, with a further list suggested by Department of Environment Circular 15/92.

[43] Above, art. 22A.

[44] Statutorily prescribed details on giving notice may, however, be construed as directory; the court may then fall back on considerations of fairness to decide whether the notice was adequate: see, *e.g. R. v. Devon and Cornwall Rent Tribunal, ex p. West* (1974) 29 P. & C.R. 316. In *R. v. Bradford-on-Avon U.D.C., ex p. Boulton* [1964] 1 W.L.R. 1136 it was held that a factual error in the contents of an ownership certificate did not necessarily deprive the authority of jurisdiction to deal with the planning application. This rule was however set aside in *Main v. Swansea C.C.* (1984) 49 P. & C.R. 26, where the Court of Appeal refused to accept that all factual errors should be categorised as mere irregularities unless so gross as to make the certificate no certificate at all. Instead the Court would have regard to a number of circumstances, including the effect on other parties and the public. In *R. v. Lambeth B.C., ex p. Sharp* [1987] J.P.L. 440, CA, the local authority's grant of planning permission in respect of its own land was held invalid for failure to comply with the correct form of notice in a newspaper advertisement. See also *R. v. Doncaster M.B.C., ex p. British Railways Board* [1987] J.P.L. 444.

prejudiced thereby.[45] Non-service or inadequacy of a notice depriving the applicant of a proper opportunity to put his case will normally constitute substantial prejudice.

CONSULTATION AND WRITTEN REPRESENTATIONS

8–012   A fair "hearing" does not necessarily mean that there must be an opportunity to be heard orally. In some situations it is sufficient if written representations are considered. Where the words "hearing" or "opportunity to be heard" are used in legislation, they usually[46] require a hearing[47] at which oral submissions and evidence can be tendered. However, in a great many statutory contexts, a duty of "consultation" is placed upon the decision-maker. This is almost always interpreted by the courts to require merely an opportunity to make written representations, or comments upon announced proposals.

8–013   The language of "consultation" usually finds no place in the vocabulary of procedural protection where the entitlement derives from the common law duty of natural justice or fairness (except where the source of the entitlement is a legitimate expectation[48]). Nevertheless, in this situation too, the opportunity to make written representations may on occasions be held to be all that fairness

---

[45] See, *e.g.* section 288 of the Town and Country Planning Act 1990. In *Wilson v. Secretary of State for the Environment* [1988] J.P.L. 540, it was held that the failure by the authority to notify of an appeal those who were consulted or notified of the original proposal, or who had made representations, might not result in substantial prejudice. However in that case the applicant, being the leader of local opposition to the development, was substantially prejudiced by the authority's failure to notify him of the appeal. See also s. 176(5), *ibid.* which permits the Secretary of State of the Environment on an enforcement appeal to disregard a failure by the local authority to serve any person with an enforcement notice if neither the appellant nor that person has been 'substantially prejudiced' by the failure. In the absence of such express provision, however, the courts will not normally imply a requirement that prejudice be shown.

[46] But *cf. R. v. Housing Appeal Tribunal* [1920] 3 K.B. 334. See further, *R. v. Immigration Appeal Tribunal ex p. Jones (Ross)* [1988] 1 W.L.R. 477. (The expression 'hearing and determining appeals' in paragraph 11 of Schedule 5 to the Immigration Act 1971 did not necessitate an oral hearing in all circumstances; hence rule 20(c) of the Immigration Appeals (Procedure) Rules 1984 giving the tribunal discretion to dispense with an oral hearing was not *ultra vires*.) See also *Lloyd v. McMahon* [1987] A.C. 625, *R. v. Army Board of the Defence Council, ex p. Anderson* [1992] 1 Q.B. 169 and *cf. R. v. Hull Prison Board of Visitors, ex p. St Germain (No. 2)* [1979] 1 W.L.R. 1401.

[47] Not merely an informal meeting: *Ealing B.C. v. Minister of Housing and Local Government* [1952] Ch. 856.

[48] As for example, in *Council for Civil Service Unions v. Minister for the Civil Service* [1985] 1 A.C. 374.

requires.[49] For example, when considering a first application for an entertainments licence a local authority was held to be under no duty to give the applicant an oral hearing, although it was necessary to inform him of objections made and to give him an opportunity to reply.[50] A school governor could not be dismissed by his local authority without being given an opportunity to reply in writing to the complaints made against him.[51] And the Army Board of the Defence Council was entitled to deal with a complaint of racial discrimination by way of written representations.[52] The true question in every case is whether the decision-maker acted fairly in all the circumstances, and therefore written representations may be sufficient in a particular case although the nature of the right or interest affected would normally indicate that an oral hearing was necessary.[53] In many cases, it is the impracticality of requiring the decision maker to hold oral hearings which leads the courts to hold that written representations are sufficient. Thus in the case of the first-time applicant for an entertainment licence, the court could not but take account of the danger of requiring that oral hearings be held for a

---

[49] *R. v. Amphlett (J.)* [1915] 2 K.B. 223; *R. v. Central Tribunal, ex p. Parton* (1916) 32 T.L.R. 476; *R. v. Housing Appeal Tribunal* [1920] 3 K.B. 334; *Stuart v. Haughley Parochial Church Council* [1935] Ch. 452 *aff d.* [1936] Ch. 32); *R. (Cairns) v. Local Government Board* [1911] 2 I.R. 331; *Brighton Corp. v. Parry* (1972) 70 L.G.R. 576; *Kavanagh v. Chief Constable of Devon and Cornwall* [1974] Q.B. 624, 634; *Fairmount Investments Ltd v. Secretary of State for the Environment* [1976] 1 W.L.R. 1255, 1266; *Ayanlowo v. I.R.C.* [1975] I.R.L.R. 253; *R. v. Whalley, ex p. Bordin & Co.* [1972] V.R. 748. See generally *Local Government Board v. Arlidge* [1915] A.C. 120. If, however, the deciding body conveys the impression that it will accord an oral hearing but then determines the issue on the basis of preliminary written submissions, it may be held to have contravened natural justice: *R. v. Secretary of State for Wales, ex p. Green* (1969) 67 L.G.R. 560. See also *R. v. Liverpool Corp., ex p. Liverpool Taxi Fleet Operators' Association* [1972] 2 Q.B. 299 (no proper opportunity to make any submissions); *Lloyd v. McMahon* [1987] A.C. 625 (proceedings for surcharging councillors only given an opportunity to make written representations upheld).

[50] *R. v. Huntingdon D.C., ex p. Cowan* [1984] 1 W.L.R. 501 (decision quashed because of failure to give the applicant an opportunity to reply to the objections).

[51] *R. v. Brent L.B.C., ex p. Assegai* (1987) 151 L.G. Rev. 891 (*obiter*).

[52] *R. v. Army Board of the Defence Council, ex p. Anderson* [1992] 1 Q.B. 169; see also *R. v. Department of Health, ex p. Gandhi* [1991] 1 W.L.R. 1053 (Secretary of State hearing appeal from Medical Practices Committee under s.33(5) NHS Act 1977 on issue of racial discrimination could dispense with oral hearing).

[53] See, *e.g. Lloyd v. McMahon* [1987] A.C. 625, where the House of Lords held that a district auditor had not acted unfairly in not offering oral hearings to councillors before certifying that financial losses of the council were the result of their wilful misconduct, since the councillors had made extensive written representations. However, for at least some of their Lordships, the determining factor was that the applicants had not *requested* an oral hearing. 'If any had asked to be heard orally and the auditor had refused, there would have been clear ground for a complaint of unfairness', *per* Lord Bridge at 706F; see also Lord Templeman at 714D.

completely open-ended category of applicants.[54] Similarly, a series of recent cases have decided that fairness requires that the opportunity to make representations be afforded to prisoners in a number of situations; for example, mandatory[55] and discretionary[56] life sentence prisoners now have an opportunity to make representations before the "tariff" period is fixed, and high security "category A" prisoners may make representations before any review of the security classification.[57] In all such cases, it has been held that written representations are appropriate.

8–014   It should not be assumed that entitlement to an *oral* hearing means that the applicant can choose to make written representations instead. A litigant has no basic right to conduct his case in writing without attending the hearing, and a tribunal may therefore be justified in disregarding written submissions where an applicant has failed to appear.[58]

8–015   Statutory tribunals and inquiries may be required to conduct oral hearings.[59] Sometimes an appellant may be able to waive his right to an oral hearing in favour of a hearing by means of written representations.[60] In planning appeals a third alternative is an informal "hearing".[61] If a tribunal has a general discretion to proceed by way of written representations, it should not have an inflexible policy of declining requests for oral hearings, but must consider whether there are circumstances—for example substantial disputes on questions of fact—which should lead it to depart from its usual course of action.[62]

---

[54] *R. v. Huntingdon D.C., ex p. Cowan* [1984] 1 W.L.R. 501, above, n. 50.

[55] *R. v. Secretary of State for the Home Department, ex p. Doody* [1994] 1 A.C. 531.

[56] *R. v. Secretary of State for the Home Department, ex p. McCartney* [1994] C.O.D. 528; *R. v. Secretary of State for the Home Department, ex p. Chapman, The Times*, October 25, 1994.

[57] *R. v. Secretary of State for the Home Department, ex p. Duggan*, [1994] 3 All E.R. 277.

[58] *Banin v. MacKinlay* [1985] 1 All E.R. 842 (taxpayer who did not attend hearing of Special Commissioners but merely sent materials marked 'Pleadings and Affidavit' could not complain when the Commissioners dismissed his appeal solely on the evidence and arguments put forward by the Crown. There was no breach of natural justice, and a statutory privilege for barristers and solicitors (section 50(5) Taxes Management Act 1970) entitling them to plead in writing did not extend to litigants in person). *Per contra*, it may be unfair to require written evidence when the individual is not at liberty to provide it: *R. v. South Western Magistrates, ex p. Doyle* [1996] C.O.D. 309.

[59] See, *e.g.* Town and Country Planning Act 1990, ss. 78 and 79(2).

[60] See, *e.g.* Town and Country Planning (Appeals) (Written Representations Procedure) Regulations 1987 (No. 701).

[61] See Department of the Environment Circular 10/88 (Annex 2).

[62] *R. v. Army Board of the Defence Council, ex p. Anderson* [1992] Q.B. 169. The Secretary of State for the Environment has a discretion not to hold a public inquiry under the Highway Act 1980, instead merely entertaining written representations. But he may not refuse to hold a hearing simply because he considers that all the necessary information is before him and that the issues raised are clear to him; he must also be satisfied that he can properly weight any two or more conflicting issues, and that

Administrative convenience must not be allowed to override the exigencies of a particular case.[63] If there are contending parties before a tribunal and one is permitted to give oral evidence, the same facility must, of course, be afforded to the others.[64]

If a party who is entitled to request an oral hearing abstains from so doing, how far does he waive entitlement to other procedural protection—such as the opportunity to make written representations—which fairness would have afforded him? In one case it was indicated that he impliedly abandons his right to be apprised of and comment on evidential material obtained by the tribunal.[65] This may be a reasonable interpretation in special situations where the proceedings are essentially inquisitorial; it should not be accepted as a general principle of law.[66] Insofar as the statutory procedures for planning appeals by means of written representations now codify the common law, it should be noted that these require the exchange of representations between the local authority and appellant.[67] They also require the notification of all persons who were consulted or notified of the original application, or who made representations.[68]

8–016

When a duty to entertain written representations is imposed by statute, by way of a duty to consult, what is required of the decision maker in each case to comply with the duty will depend upon the statutory context. But the fundamental requirements of the duty of consultation have been well summarised by Webster J.:

8–017

"[I]n any context the essence of consultation is the communication of a genuine invitation to give advice and a genuine consideration of that advice. In my view it must go without saying that to

---

those with the right to make representations can have their representations properly taken into account: see *Binney v. Secretary of State for the Environment* [1984] J.P.L. 871 where it was held that the minister in question had misdirected himself as to the factors to take into account. See also, *Shorman v. Secretary of State for the Environment* [1977] J.P.L. 98. It was suggested by Webster J. in *Binney* (without so deciding) that it might be more important to allow objectors to a scheme to make oral representations to a scheme where that scheme had been proposed by the minister himself rather than by a local authority (at 873).

[63] *R. v. Department of Health, ex p. Gandhi* [1991] 1 W.L.R. 1053, 1063 *per* Taylor L.J.

[64] *R. v. Kingston-upon-Hull Rent Tribunal, ex p. Black* (1949) 65 T.L.R. 209.

[65] *R. v. Deputy Industrial Injuries Commissioner, ex p. Moore* [1965] 1 Q.B. 456, 476, 490.

[66] And see *Lloyd v. McMahon*, above, n.53, where there was no suggestion that the fact that the applicants had failed to request oral hearings meant that the district auditor was not under a duty to consider their written representations.

[67] Town and Country Planning (Appeals) (Written Representations Procedure) Regulations 1987 (No. 701). Under regs. 5 and 6 the local authority shall submit a questionnaire to the Secretary of State and all parties, to which (reg. 7) the appellant may reply within 17 days.

[68] *ibid.* reg. 6.

achieve consultation sufficient information must be supplied by
the consulting to the consulted party to enable it to tender helpful
advice. Sufficient time must be given by the consulting to the
consulted party. Sufficient, in that context, does not mean ample,
but at least enough to enable the relevant purpose to be fulfilled.
By helpful advice, in this context, I mean sufficiently informed
and considered information or advice about aspects of the form of
substance of the proposals, or their implications for the consulted
party, being aspects material to the implementation of the
proposal as to which the party consulted might have relevant
information or advice to offer."[69]

Essentially, in developing standards of consultation, and applying
those standards to particular statutory contexts, the courts are using
the general principles of fairness to ensure that the consulted party is
able properly to address the concerns of the decision-maker. However,
as is the case where written representations are required, the courts
may be in a poor position to ensure that the decision-maker considers
those representations. At the lowest, the courts will attempt to ensure
that all written representations are before the decision maker when the
decision is made, and will quash a decision made in disregard of
representations.[70] Nevertheless, where a large-scale consultation
exercise has been carried out, the courts may be effectively powerless
to ensure that representations have been read and digested—unless
the decision-maker is required to address representations received by
way of reasons.[71] Furthermore, where consultations are invited upon
detailed proposals which have already been arrived at, the duty of the

---

[69] *R. v. Secretary of State for Social Services, ex p. Association of Metropolitan Authorities*
[1986] 1 W.L.R. 1, 4. See further, *R. v. Gwent C.C. and Secretary of State for Wales, ex p.
Bryant* [1988] C.O.D. 19 (consultation arising from legitimate expectation), where
Hodgson J. considered the requirements of fair consultation, and stressed that the
process must take place at a sufficiently early stage in the decision making process
for the exercise to be meaningful. *Cf. R. v. Camden L.B.C., ex p. Cran* [1995] R.T.R. 346.
See also *R. v. Devon C.C., ex p. Baker* [1995] 1 All E.R. 73. *R. v. Lambeth L.B.C., ex p. N*
[1996] E.L.R. 299; *R. v. Secretary of State for Trade and Industry, ex p. UNISON* [1996]
I.C.R. 1003; *Desmond v. Bromley L.B.C.* (1996) 28 H.L.R. 518 (distinguishing *ex p.
AMA*); *R. v. Secretary of State for Transport, ex p. Richmond-upon-Thames L.B.C.* [1996] 1
W.L.R. 1460 (level of detail in consultation sufficient to enable representations)."

[70] See, *e.g. R. v. Manchester Metropolitan University, ex p. Nolan, The Independent*, July 15,
1993 (examination board's disciplinary decision taken in ignorance of written
testimonials and psychiatric evidence quashed, where applicant had no right to
attend and was "entirely dependent" on what was placed before the board).

[71] See below, paras. 8–039 *et seq.*

court to ensure that genuine consideration has been given to critical representations is taxed to the utmost.[72]

DUTY OF ADEQUATE DISCLOSURE

If prejudicial allegations are to be made against a person, he must **8–018** normally, as we have seen, be given particulars of them before the hearing so that he can prepare his answers.[73] In order to protect his interests he must also be enabled to controvert, correct or comment on other evidence or information that may be relevant to the decision; indeed, at least in some circumstances there will be a duty on the decision maker to disclose information favourable to the applicant, as well as information prejudicial to his case.[74] If material is available

---

[72] See, *e.g. R. v. Hillingdon Health Authority ex p. Goodwin* [1984] I.C.R. 800 for the extent to which a proposed scheme may be developed in advance of a consultation process; compare *Rollo v. Minister of Town and Country Planning* [1948] 1 All E.R. 13. But see *ex p. Cran* n. 69 above (consultation should have taken place before the Council's 'mind was made up').

[73] See para. 8–004 *et seq.*, above. See also *McDonald v. Lanarkshire Fire Brigade Joint Committee*, 1959 S.C. 141 (particulars of disciplinary allegations communicated only after undue delay); *R. v. Department of Health ex p. Gandhi* [1991] 1 W.L.R. 1053. In *Council of Civil Service Unions v. Minister for the Civil Service* [1985] A.C. 374, 415, Lord Roskill indicated that legitimate expectations can take many forms including, 'an expectation of being allowed time to make representations'. In *Hadmor Productions v. Hamilton* [1983] 1 A.C. 191, 233 Lord Diplock stated that 'one of the most fundamental rules of natural justice [is] the right ... to be informed of any point adverse ... that is going to be relied upon ... and to be given an opportunity of stating what his answer to it is'. See also Lord Diplock in *Bushell v. Secretary of State for Environment* [1981] A.C. 75, 96. Reference should also be made to the requirement to give reasons for a decision, below, para. 8–039 *et seq*. A reaffirmation of the courts' current approach was provided by the decision of a Divisional Court in *R. v. Secretary of State for the Home Department, ex p. Duggan* [1994] 3 All E.R. 277 where it was decided that a prisoner serving a life sentence for murder is entitled, subject to necessary exceptions due to public interest immunity, to be informed of the gist of any matter of facts or opinion relevant to his security recategorisation and to reasons for any decision to maintain him as a 'category A' prisoner. See also *R. v. Hampshire C.C., ex p. K and Another* [1990] 2 Q.B. 71, as to the duty of local authorities in child abuse cases to be open and to disclose all relevant material; and *R. v. Secretary of State for the Home Department ex p. Hickey* [1995] 1 W.L.R. 734 (disclosure of evidence obtained by Secretary of State in considering petition to refer a conviction to the Court of Appeal under section 17 of the Criminal Appeal Act 1968).

[74] See *R. v. Secretary of State for the Home Department, ex p. Abdi, The Times*, March 10, 1994, where Sedley J. held that because in asylum cases a very high procedural and substantive duty of fairness rests on the Home Secretary in coming to a conclusion that a claim for asylum is 'without foundation' under para. 5 of Sched. 2 to the Asylum and Immigration Appeals Act 1993 (see *Re Musisi* [1987] A.C. 514, 531, *per* Lord Bridge), it was incumbent upon the Home Secretary to disclose to a Special Adjudicator not only those facts supporting his conclusion, but also any factual material pointing in the opposite direction. However, the Court of Appeal: by a

before the hearing, the right course will usually be to give him advance notification; but it cannot be said that there is a hard and fast rule on this matter, and sometimes natural justice will be held to be satisfied if the material is divulged at the hearing, which may have to be adjourned if he cannot fairly be expected to make his reply without time for consideration.[75] In deciding whether fairness does or does not require an adjournment in order to allow further time to consider such material and to prepare representations, a court or other decision-maker should take into account the importance of the proceedings and the likely adverse consequences on the party seeking the adjournment; the risk that the applicant would be prejudiced; the risk of prejudice to any opponent if the adjournment were granted; the convenience of the Court and the interests of justice in ensuring the efficient despatch of business; and the extent to which the applicant has been responsible for the circumstances leading to the request for an adjournment.[76]

8–019 If relevant evidential material is not disclosed at all to a party who is potentially prejudiced by it, there is prima facie unfairness, irrespective of whether the material in question arose before, during or after the hearing. This proposition can be illustrated by a large number of cases involving the use of undisclosed reports by administrative tribunals and other adjudicating bodies.[77] If the deciding body is or has the trappings of a judicial tribunal and receives or appears to receive evidence *ex parte* which is not fully

---

majority, reversed the decision, principally on the basis that the courts should not supplement the statutory procedure in circumstances where the legislation was designed to achieve a very quick determination of appeals (*The Times*, April 25, 1994). The House of Lords has now upheld the decision of the Court of Appeal: see [1996] 1 W.L.R. 298. See also *Re D (Minors) (Adoption Reports: Confidentiality)* [1996] A.C. 593: ('It is a first principle of fairness that each party to a judicial process shall have the opportunity to answer by evidence and argument any adverse material which the tribunal may take into account when forming its opinion', *per* Lord Mustill at p. 603H); and *R v. Secretary of state for the Home Department, ex p. Fayed* [1998] 1 W.L.R. 763 (duty on Secretary of State to disclose his concerns in application for citizenship).

[75] See further para. 8–025 below.

[76] *R. v. Kingston-upon-Thames JJ., ex p. Martin* [1994] Imm. A.R. 172.

[77] See, *e.g. R. v. Milk Marketing Board, ex p. North* (1934) 50 T.L.R. 559; *R. v. Westminster (City of) Assessment Committee* [1941] 1 K.B. 53; *R. v. Milk Board, ex p. Tomkins* [1944] V.L.R. 187; *R. v. Architects' Registration Tribunal, ex p. Jaggar* [1945] 2 All E.R. 131; *Re Estate of Roscrea Meat Products Ltd* [1958] I.R. 47; *Low v. Earthquake Commission* [1959] N.Z.L.R. 1198; *R. v. Metropolitan Fair Rents Board, ex p. Canestra* [1961] V.R. 89; *Kanda v. Government of Malaya* [1962] A.C. 322; *R. v. Kent Police Authority, ex p. Godden* [1971] 2 Q.B. 662; *South Otago Hospital Board v. Nurses and Midwives Board* [1972] N.Z.L.R. 828; *Fairmount Investments Ltd v. Secretary of State for the Environment* [1976] 1 W.L.R. 1255. For the general rule, see *Board of Education v. Rice* [1911] A.C. 179, 182. And see *Shareef v. Commissioner for Registration of Indian and Pakistani Residents* [1966] A.C. 47 (inadequate disclosure of relevant reports). See also cases cited in n. 78 below.

disclosed, or holds *ex parte* inspections during the course or after the conclusion of the hearing, the case for setting the decision aside is obviously very strong; the maxim that justice must be seen to be done can readily be invoked.[78] If an appellate tribunal has communications with a tribunal of first instance with a view to altering the original decision, the parties to the proceedings before that tribunal ought to be notified so that they can make further submissions.[79] *A fortiori*, it is a breach of natural justice for an appellate authority, or a body receiving the report of the appellate authority, to hold private interviews with witnesses.[80] In relation to central government decision-making, especially on issues of policy, the duty of disclosure may be lessened in respect of information originating within the government department. When a minister considers whether to grant a planning application following a local inquiry and consequent report by the inspector, he is under no obligation to disclose to objectors or

---

[78] See, *e.g. R. v. Bodmin JJ., ex p. McEwen* [1947] K.B. 321; *Fowler v. Fowler* [1963] 2 W.L.R. 155 (courts); *R. v. Birmingham City Magistrate, ex p. Chris Foreign foods (Wholesalers) Ltd* [1970] 1 W.L.R. 1428 (magistrate condemning food); *Eastcheap Dried Fruit Co. v. N.V. Gebroeders Catz' Verecniging* [1962] 1 Lloyd's Rep. 283 (arbitrators); *R. v. Newmarket Assessment Committee* [1945] 2 All E.R. 371; *Barrs v. British Wool Marketing Board*, 1957 S.C. 72; *R. v. Deputy Industrial Injuries Commissioner, ex p. Jones* [1962] 2 Q.B. 677 (statutory tribunals); *Taylor v. National Union of Seamen* [1967] 1 W.L.R. 532 (trade unions) *R. v. Home Secretary, ex p. Georghiades* (1992) 5 Admin L.R. 457 (parole board). See also *Re Gregson and Armstrong* (1894) 70 L.T. 106 and *Goold v. Evans* [1951] 2 T.L.R. 1189; *Errington v. Minister of Health* [1935] 1 K.B. 249; *Hibemian Property Co. Ltd. v. Secretary of State for the Environment* (1974) 27 P. & C.R. 197; *Clark v. Wellington Rent Appeal Board* [1975] 2 N.Z.L.R. 24, 28–30 on the impropriety of *ex parte* views; *cf. Salsbury v. Woodland* [1970] 1 Q.B. 324 on the circumstances in which an unaccompanied view is permissible; *R. v. Lilydale Magistrates' Court, ex p. Ciccone* [1973] V.R. 122 on the suspicions of bias that may arise from the travelling arrangements; compare *R. v. Ely JJ., ex p. Burgess* [1992] Crim.L.R. 888; *R. v. Green* [1950] 1 All E.R. 38 and *R. v. Furlong, ibid.* at 636 on the impropriety of private communications between judge and jury: see also the discussion on bias in relation to the limits of propriety in communications between justices and their clerks in Chap. 11 below, esp. paras 11-024–11-025; and *Fisher v. Keane* (1879) 11 Ch.D. 353 on *ex parte* hearing in club expulsion cases.

[79] *R. v. Huntingdon Confirming Authority* [1929] 1 K.B. 698. *Cf. The Corchester* [1957] P. 84; *R. v. Secretary of State for Education, ex p. S* [1994] C.O.D. 200 where Sedley J. held that the decision of the Secretary of State should be quashed because he received additional advice as to educational needs of a child of which the parents were unaware.

[80] *Palmer v. Inverness Hospitals Committee*, 1963 S.C. 311; *Wilcox v. H.G.S.* [1976] I.C.R. 306. But where a minister legitimately declines to hold a public inquiry in respect of a planning application, it would appear that he need not give to objectors the written representations of those supporting the scheme: *Binney v. Secretary of State for the Environment* [1984] J.P.L. 871 (although Webster J. did not reach a final conclusion on the point); *Fairmount Investments Ltd v. Secretary of State for the Environment* [1976] 1 W.L.R. 1255, 1266 *per* Lord Russell (a person concerned has the right not to be 'taken by surprise in a relevantly unfair way by the conclusions of the inspector').

to give them an opportunity of commenting on advice, expert or otherwise, which he receives from the department in the course of making up his mind.[81] And where the Parliamentary Commissioner for Administration has produced a draft report pursuant to an individual's complaint passed to him by the complainant's Member of Parliament, the Ombudsman does not act unfairly or contrarily to natural justice in sending a copy of the draft report to the government department involved but not to the complainant, since it is the department rather than the complainant which is being investigated and which may have to justify its conduct before a Parliamentary select committee and face public criticism.[82]

8–020   To the general rule there are various exceptions, some of which have already been indicated. There are cases were disclosure of evidential material might inflict serious harm on the person directly concerned (*e.g.* disclosure of a distressing medical report to a claimant for a social security benefit)[83] or other persons, or where disclosure would be a breach of confidence or might be injurious to the public interest (*e.g.* because it would involve the revelation of official secrets, inhibit frankness of comment and the detection of crime, and might make it impossible to obtain certain classes of essential information at all in the future).[84] And where a committee is entitled to sit in private session, it is not obliged to disclose legal advice of its officers to persons with a right to be heard, or to invite representations on the

---

[81] *Bushell v. Secretary of State for the Environment* [1981] A.C. 75, 102, *per* Lord Diplock. Further, the House of Lords held that even where the post-inquiry evidence contradicts or modifies evidence given at the inquiry, the Secretary of State is not obliged to reopen the inquiry. However, if the new evidence is on a matter of central importance rather than (as in *Bushell*) on a matter held to be tangential or irrelevant to the inquiry, it is submitted that there would be a duty to reopen the inquiry, or to afford individuals the right to make further written representations; see *R. v. Secretary of State for Health, ex p. U.S. Tobacco International Inc.* [1992] Q.B. 353.

[82] *R. v. Parliamentary Commissioner for Administration, ex p. Dyer* [1994] 1 W.L.R. 621 (*sed quaere* whether in some circumstances the complainant's interest in receiving fair consideration of his or her complaint might not in fairness demand that the draft report be disclosed to him or her).

[83] See *R. v. Kent Police Authority, ex p. Godden* [1971] 2 Q.B. 662 (undisclosed official psychiatric report on police officer; court ordered disclosure to officer's own medical adviser but not to the officer himself). *Cf. Re W.L.W.* [1972] 2 W.L.R. 1207 (report on condition of mental patient).

[84] *R. v. Lewes JJ., ex p. Gaming Board of Great Britain* [1973] A.C. 388; *R. v. Secretary of State for the Home Department, ex p. Hickey* [1995] Q.B. 43, CA; but see *R. v. Poole B.C. ex p. Cooper, The Times,* October 21, 1994 (information received by local authority during statutory inquiries about homelessness of housing applicant could not be protected from disclosure on ground of confidentiality). See also *R. v. Joint Higher Committee on Surgical Training, ex p. Milner* (1995) 7 Admin L.R. 454 (Committee not obliged to disclose references to applicant for accreditation as surgeon; interests of confidentiality outweighed applicant's interest in disclosure).

advice.[85] In such situations the person claiming to be aggrieved should nevertheless be adequately apprised of the case he has to answer, subject to the need for withholding details in order to protect other overriding interests.[86] An argument relying upon mere administrative inconvenience—for example, in having to prepare and disclose summaries of evidence which cannot itself be disclosed—is unlikely to succeed.[87]

JUDICIAL AND OFFICIAL NOTICE

Against this background one must consider the concept of judicial **8–021** notice, which in administrative law shades off into what is known in the United States as "official notice".[88] Courts, which are required to decide cases on the basis of the rules of evidence, are also allowed to take judicial notice of matters of common knowledge, and these need not be put to the parties before them. How far judicial notice can properly extend is not altogether clear. The general principle is "that a person exercising judicial functions is not justified in noticing directly or indirectly by statement or otherwise facts within his private knowledge. He ought to be sworn and state them as a witness."[89] Exceptionally (if, for example, magistrates propose to take into account their impressions of a party before them, derived from earlier proceedings in which he was involved),[90] an adjudicator may be permitted to use his personal knowledge, provided that there is no real danger of bias and the matter to be taken into account is clearly disclosed to the party concerned.[91] In one case,[92] an appeal was lodged

---

[85] *Stoop v. Royal Borough of Kensington and Chelsea* [1992] 1 P.L.R. 58 (local authority planning and conservation committee).

[86] See esp. *R. v. Gaming Board for Great Britain, ex p. Benaim and Khaida* [1970] 2 Q.B. 417, on how much information ought to be disclosed to applicants for consents to run gaming clubs; *R. v. Home Secretary, ex p. Hosenball* [1977] 1 W.L.R. 766 (intelligence information and deportation); *R. v. Secretary of State for the Home Department, ex p. Duggan* [1994] 3 All E.R. 277 ('category A' prisoners should receive the 'gist' of reports submitted to the Secretary of State in determining all reviews of security classifications, where to disclose the full report would not be in the public interest).

[87] *R. v. Secretary of State for the Home Department, ex p. Duggan*, n. 86 above.

[88] For a critical survey of the American doctrine, see K.C. Davis, *Administrative Law Treatise* (2nd ed.), Chap. 15. See also J.A. Smillie. 'The Problem of 'Official Notice' " [1975] P.L. 64.

[89] *R. (Giant's Causeway, etc., Tramway Co.) v. Antrim JJ.* [1895] 2 I.R. 603. 649. See also *Re Frank Bros. Ltd and Hamilton Board of Police Cmrs* (1967) 63 D.L.R. (2d) 309.

[90] See *Thomas v. Thomas* [1961] 1 W.L.R. 1; *Brinkley v. Brinkley* [1965] P. 75; *cf. Munday v. Munday* [1954] 1 W.L.R. 1078; *Dugdale v. Kraft Foods Ltd* [1977] I.C.R. 487, 54–55.

[91] See Chap. 11 below.

[92] *Wetherall v. Harrison* [1976] Q.B. 773. The court did warn, however, against the expert's unduly pressing his opinion upon his non-expert colleagues.

against an acquittal by lay magistrates, on the ground that one of them had used his medical expertise during their retirement to consider their verdict, to persuade them to reject the only evidence given on a particular issue. The appeal was dismissed; such expertise may properly be used to evaluate evidence given, but not to contradict evidence or introduce new evidence that should be made available to the parties.[93] The degree of latitude conceded to liquor licensing justices to make use of undisclosed private knowledge has gone much further and is quite uncharacteristic of any form of litigation.[94] More characteristic of the standards appropriate for administrative adjudication was the attitude adopted towards arbitrators deciding workmen's compensation cases, who were permitted to draw on their own accumulated knowledge of general and local labour conditions to supplement evidence, but were obliged to disclose their thoughts to the claimant if non-disclosure would unfairly deprive him of his right to lead evidence or tender submissions on specific facts in issue.[95]

8–022 Statutory tribunals are set up because they already have or can be expected to acquire specialised expertise. Clearly they are entitled to use their expertise to draw inferences from evidence. If a tribunal is under an obligation to observe the rules of evidence it cannot use its own expert opinion as a substitute for evidence,[96] though it may still be able to rely on an extended concept of judicial notice to supplement evidence. But a number of special tribunals are not bound by the strict rules of evidence. They are charged with the task of actively finding the material fact by any appropriate means; they may be permitted to

---

[93] For a stricter approach to the problem, however, see *R. v. Prosser* (1836) 7 C. & P. 648. See also *R. v. Field, ex p. White* (1895) 64 L.J.M.C. 158. *Cf.* Minister's duty to disclose evidence upon which he relies when disagreeing with a finding of fact by an inspector in a planning or compulsory purchase appeal.

[94] *cf. R. v. Howard* [1902] 2 K.B. 363, 376; *Boyle v. Wilson* [1907] A.C. 45. In *Wetherall* (above n.92) it was stated that more latitude should always be given to lay adjudicators on the ground that, unlike professional judges, they could not be expected to approach the evidence without bringing to bear their own knowledge.

[95] See, *e.g. Peart v. Bolckow, Vaughan & Co.* [1925] 1 K.B. 399; *Reynolds v. Llanelly Associated Tinplate Co.* [1948] 1 All E.R. 140; and generally, *Learmonth Property Investment Co. v. Aitken,* 1971 S.L.T. 349, 356; on industrial tribunals, see *e.g. Dugdale v. Kraft Foods Ltd* [1976] 1 W.L.R. 1288, 1294–1295; *Adda International Ltd. v. Curcio* [1976] I.C.R. 407; *Spurling v. Development Underwriting (Vic.) Pty Ltd* [1973] V.R. 1, 10 *Bowman v. DPP* [1991] R.T.R. 263; *Norbrook Laboratories (GB) Ltd v. Health and Safety Executive, The Times,* February 23, 1998 (justices proposing to rely upon local knowledge should let both prosecution and defence know to give them opportunity to comment); and see *Mullen v. Hackney L.B.C.* [1997] 2 All E.R. 906, CA held judge entitled to take judicial notice of matters which were notorious, or clearly established, or susceptible of demonstration by reference to a readily obtainable and authoritative source. He could rely on his local knowledge provided he did so properly and within reasonable limits).

[96] *Moxon v. Minister of Pensions* [1945] K.B. 490.

adopt inquisitorial procedures,[97] undertake unaccompanied inspections,[98] consult experts[99] and use their own technical and local knowledge[1] and their past experience which may be based on evidence given in previous cases[2]; their final decision may, in some cases, be based on broad considerations of public policy. They are nevertheless obliged to act fairly. And this means that, in the absence of contrary intendment, they must not place a party at a disadvantage by depriving him of an adequate opportunity of commenting on material relevant to their decision if it is gleaned from an outside source[3] or in the course of their own investigations,[4] or from evidence given in earlier cases.[5] In other words, one may expect the doctrine of "official notice" to be more readily applicable where the information relied upon is drawn from the general, accumulated experience of the decision-maker, rather than from an identifiable source upon which he has relied, whether it be another person, particular documents or specific prior events. As yet the case law gives no clear indication of the extent to which they will be permitted to abstain from disclosing during the hearing their own expert opinions, or information relevant

---

[97] *cf. R. v. Medical Appeal Tribunal (North Midland Region), ex p. Hubble* [1958] 2 Q.B. 228, 240–241; *aff'd.* [1959] 2 Q.B. 408.

[98] *cf. R. v. Brighton & Area Rent Tribunal, ex p. Marine Parade Estates (936) Ltd* [1950] 2 K.B. 410. *Cf. Halsey v. Esso Petroleum Co.* [1961] 1 W.L.R. 683, 689; *Salsbury v. Woodland* [1970] 1 Q.B. 324 (unaccompanied view by judge). For recognition of the greater flexibility given in this respect to inspectors conducting public local inquiries, see *Fairmount Investments Ltd v. Secretary of State for the Environment* [1976] 1 W.L.R. 1255, 1264. And see *Hickmott v. Dorset C.C.* (1977) 35 P. & C.R. 195.

[99] *cf. R. v. Deputy Industrial Injuries Commissioner, ex p. Jones* [1962] 2 Q.B. 677. See also *Wislang v. Medical Practitioners Disciplinary Committee* [1974] 1 N.Z.L.R. 29 (no duty to disclose legal advice obtained from outside the tribunal on a point of law upon which the individual had addressed the tribunal).

[1] *Crofton Investment Trust Ltd v. Greater London Rent Assessment Committee* [1967] 2 Q.B. 955. See also *R. v. Brighton Rent Officers, ex p. Elliott* (1975) 29 P. & C.R. 456 (rent officer not required to disclose before the statutory consultation with the parties, the properties with which he proposed to compare the premises in question). And see *Kalil v. Bray* [1977] 1 N.S.W.L.R. 256 (specialist tribunal may rely on its own expertise to reject otherwise uncontradicted lay evidence).

[2] *cf. R. v. Deputy Industrial Injuries Commissioner, ex p. Moore* [1965] 1 Q.B. 456.

[3] As in *Jones's* case (above, n. 99); *Hibernian Property Co. Ltd v. Secretary of State for the Environment* (1974) 27 P. & C.R. 197 (views of occupiers favouring demolition of unfit houses).

[4] *R. v. Paddington & St Marylebone Rent Tribunal, ex p. Bell, London & Provincial Properties Ltd* [1949] 1 K.B. 666, 682 (important evidential point commented on during inspection but not properly put to landlords); *Crofton Investment Trust Ltd v. Greater London Rent Assessment Committee* [1967] 2 Q.B. 955, 968 (dictum); *Fairmount* (above, n. 98) at 1265 (inspection revealed evidence of an aspect of unfitness not relied upon at inquiry). See also *Hickmott v. Dorset C.C.* (above, n. 98).

[5] See *Moore's* case (above, n. 2) at 466–468, 489–490 (dicta). And see *Re Martin (John) & Co. Ltd* (1974) 8 S.A.S.R. 237, where on the facts an opportunity to rebut the evidence was found to have been given.

to the exercise of their discretion in so far as they can take public policy considerations into account.[6] But it is thought that the courts will lean in favour of imposing judicial standards as far as practicable,[7] so that if a party is misled as to the basis on which the tribunal is likely to decide and is thus placed at a material disadvantage in putting his case, he may be held to have been denied procedural fairness.[8]

RIGHT TO AN ORAL HEARING

8–023   A person who is entitled to be heard orally, or who is given an oral hearing as a matter of discretion under a power conferred by statutory or other formal rules,[9] must be allowed an adequate opportunity of putting his own case. As noted above, he will normally be entitled to that opportunity, particularly where there is some dispute as to material facts or other matter on which oral argument will be of assistance to the decision-maker.[10] If he has a right to appear, it will, of course, be a breach of that right, in addition to being unfair, for the

---

[6] *cf.* K.C. Davis's general position (above, n.88) that matters of policy and material affecting the exercise of discretion should, as far as is practicable, be disclosed but be controvertible by argument rather than the adduction of evidence.

[7] See, *e.g.* the *Learmonth* case, above, n. 95, and the *Brighton Rent Officers'* case, above, n. 1, (tribunal entitled to use local knowledge but not undisclosed knowledge of particular facts in issue). *Cf.* however, *Wetherall's* case, above, n. 92.

[8] *Shareef v. Commissioner for Registration of Indian and Pakistani Residents* [1966] A.C. 47 (applicant's advocate misled as to importance attached by tribunal to specific item of evidence; decision quashed); contrast *Drewitt v. Price Tribunal* [1959] N.Z.L.R. 21 (parties inadequately aware of basis of decision, but no fault attributable); and see last two cases cited at para. 8–013, n. 49 above, on misleading interested parties as to procedure to be aplied. See also *Société Franco-Tunisienne d'Ammement-Tunis v. Government of Ceylon* [1959] 1 W.L.R. 787 (arbitration; giving the decision on basis of point of law not raised at the hering is misconduct; *quaerc* whether this would be regarded as a breach of natural justice in proceedings before an administrative tribunal); *Re Chien Sign-Shou* [1967] 1 W.L.R. 1155; *Re Simeon* [1935] 2 K.B. 183. See also *R. v. Criminal Injuries Compensation Board, ex p. Ince* [1973] 1 W.L.R. 1334 at 1344–1345; *cf. British Oxygen Co. Ltd v. Board of Trade* [1971] A.C. 610.

[9] For the position in 'voluntary' hearings, see Chap. 7, para. 7–061 above, and for situations where there is no right to an oral hearing, see *Lloyd v. McMahon* [1987] A.C. 625 and para. 8–012 *et seq.* above.

[10] See *R. v. Criminal Injuries Compensation Board, ex p. Dickson* [1997] 1 W.L.R. 58 (applicant not entitled to oral hearing because no dispute as to primary facts); *R. v. Criminal Injuries Compensation Board, ex p. Cook* [1996] 1 W.L.R. 1037, CA; *cf. R. v. Criminal Injuries Compensation Board, ex p. Singh (Amrik)* [1996] C.O.D. 149. See also *R. v. Secretary of State for Wales, ex p. Emery* [1996] 4 All E.R. 1 (conflict of documentary evidence as to footpath should have been tested at public inquiry; Secretary of State acted unfairly in deciding without convening inquiry); *R. v. Secretary of State for the Home Department, ex p. Khanafer* [1996] Imm. A.R. 212; *R. v. Cardinal Newman's School, Birmingham, ex p. S* [1998] E.L.R. 304.

tribunal to refuse, deliberately or through inadvertence, to hear him[11] or even to allow him to be present.[12] His right to be heard must not be stultified by constant interruptions. Nevertheless, the right to an oral hearing does not in all cases confer the right to be personally present at the hearing, if the case is being conducted by a representative. Thus the Secretary of State was entitled to require a prisoner to meet the costs of his production at court for an application for judicial review, since there was no fundamental right to be present.[13]

The fact that there is a right to an oral hearing usually indicates that the hearing is to be in public. This enables the public to see that justice is done and plays a significant part in the maintenance of proper standards. In the case of judicial-type bodies the circumstances in which the public can be excluded from the substantive hearing are strictly circumscribed. This does not however apply to preliminary hearings, which are frequently held in private. When a hearing should normally be heard in public there is usually a discretion to exclude the public for good reason, such as national security, but the public should not be excluded to any greater extent than is necessary in the interests of justice.[14]

8–024

---

[11] *R. v. Birkenhead JJ., ex p. Fisher* [1962] 1 W.L.R. 1410; *R. v. Gravesend JJ., ex p. Sheldon* [1968] 1 W.L.R. 1699; *R. v. Kingston-upon-Hull Rent Tribunal, ex p. Black* (1949) 65 T.L.R. 209; *Chettiar v. Chettiar* [1962] 1 W.L.R. 279; *Malloch v. Aberdeen Corp.* [1971] 1 W.L.R. 1578; similarly where the tribunal will not hear a party on an essential issue: *Sheldon v. Bromfield JJ.* [1964] 2 Q.B. 573; *Hodgkins v. Hodgkins* [1965] 1 W.L.R. 1448; *R. v. Hendon JJ., ex p. Gorchein* [1973] 1 W.L.R. 1502 (*R. v. Woking JJ., ex p. Gossage* [1973] Q.B. 448 distinguished); and see *R. v. Hopkins, ex p. Haywood* [1973] 1 W.L.R. 965; *R. v. Worcester Justices, ex p. Daniels* (1997) 161 J.P. 121 (Magistrate appearing not to pay attention); *Jones v. Welsh Rugby Football Union, The Times*, March 6, 1997 (noted, [1997] P.L. 340) (arguable that failure by RFU to let applicant challenge by question or evidence the factual basis of the evidence against him, or to vary procedure for viewing video evidence, was unfair); *R. v. Clerkenwell Metropolitan Stipendiary Magistrate, ex p. Hooper* [1998] 1 W.L.R. 800 (oral hearing before bindover and/or order for surety).

[12] *R. v. Dewsbury Magistrates Court, ex p. K, The Times*, March 16, 1994; *R. v. Ely JJ., ex p. Burgess* [1972] Crim. L.R. 888 (the Divisional Court held that a view was part of a criminal trial, and that the absence of the accused, unless there were special circumstances, was a fatal matter. The fact that the justices travelled to the view in the same car as the prosecutor, even though there was no evidence that they discussed the issue, meant a fair trial was not possible, applying Ackner L.J. in *R. v. Liverpool City JJ., ex p. Topping* [1983] 1 W.L.R. 119).

[13] *R. v. Secretary of State for the Home Department, ex p. Wynne* [1992] 1 Q.B. 406, CA. See also *R. v. Morley* [1988] Q.B. 601.

[14] *Scott v. S.* [1913] A.C. 417; *Att.-Gen. v. Leveller Magazine Ltd* [1979] A.C. 440; *R. v. Malvern JJ., ex p. Evans* [1988] Q.B. 540 (unruly persons may be excluded from an inquiry); *Lovelock v. Minister of Transport* (1980) 39 P. & C.R. 468 and even a defendant who is disruptive and is appearing in person can be removed during his trial for a criminal offence: see *R. v. Morley* [1988] Q.B. 601.

8–025   An oral hearing will in some cases merely involve the right to deliver oral representations, untramelled by rules of evidence or rights to produce or cross-examine witnesses. In other cases, an oral hearing will be afforded in the context of a fully judicialised procedure. If the tribunal is obliged to observe the rules of evidence, in the past the rejection of relevant and admissible evidence was considered a mere "error of law", but nowadays it may constitute denial of a fair hearing according to the requirements of procedural fairness.[15] Again, natural justice may be violated by a refusal to allow a party (or his legal representative) to address the tribunal on the law or the facts[16] or, after a finding of guilt, on the penalty to be imposed.[17] Wrongful refusal of an adjournment to a party unable to attend the hearing[18] or requiring time to produce a witness or other important evidence may also be tantamount to a denial of justice.[19] It may also be contrary to the rules of natural justice for a tribunal to refuse to grant an adjournment where the continuation of the proceedings may prejudice the fairness of the trial of other proceedings, at least if there is a real risk of injustice.[20] In such a situation, the tribunal; or reviewing court, must balance the potential prejudice to the applicant against the public and/or private interest in the speedy determination of the proceedings.[21] However, it has been emphasised that the power to adjourn is one "which has to be exercised with great care and only when there is a real risk of serious prejudice which may lead to injustice".[22] It would appear that, in practice, the test is difficult to satisfy.[23]

---

[15] *General Medical Council v. Spackman* [1943] A.C. 627; *Bond v. Bond* [1967] P. 39.

[16] *Disher v. Disher* [1965] P. 31; *Mayes v. Mayes* [1971] 1 W.L.R. 679.

[17] *Ex p. Kelly, re Teece* [1966] 2 N.S.W.R. 674; *Ex p. Kent, re Callaghan* [1969] 2 N.S.W.R. 84; see also *Fullbrook v. Berkshire Magistrates' Courts Committee* (1970) 69 L.G.R. 75 (clerk dismissed for misconduct, entitled to opportunity to be heard on question whether pension should be forfeited).

[18] *Re M (an Infant)* [1968] 1 W.L.R. 1897; *Rose v. Humbles* [1972] 1 W.L.R. 33. See also *R. v. Llandrindod Wells JJ., ex p. Gibson* [1968] 1 W.L.R. 598; *Priddle v. Fisher & Sons, ibid.* 1478 where the tribunal should have granted adjournment though not expressly requested; *R. v. Kingston-upon-Thames JJ., ex p. Martin, The Times*, March 25, 1993.

[19] *R. v. Medical Appeal Tribunal (Midland Region), ex p. Carrarini* [1966] 1 W.L.R. 883; *R. v. Thames Magistrates' Court, ex p. Polemis* [1974] 1 W.L.R. 1371; *R. v. Panel on Takeovers and Mergers, ex p. Guinness plc* [1990] 1 Q.B. 146.

[20] *R. v. Panel on Takeovers and Mergers, ex p. Fayed* [1992] B.C.C. 524, 531; *R. v. Institute of Chartered Accountants, ex p. Brindle, The Times*, January 12, 1994.

[21] *Brindle* (n. 20 above), *per* Hirst L.J.

[22] *Fayed,* (n. 20 above), at 531, *per* Neill L.J.

[23] See, in addition to the above cases, *R. v. Chairman of the Regulatory Board of Lloyds Ltd, ex p. Macmillan, The Times*, December 14, 1994; *R. v. Chance, ex p. Smith, Coopers & Lybrand* (1995) 7 Admin. L.R. 821; *R. v. Executive Council of the Joint Disciplinary Scheme, ex p. Hipps* (unreported, June 12, 1996).

A party who is unable to understand the English language should be allowed to engage (and in serious cases ought to be provided with) an interpreter.[24]

RIGHT TO CALL WITNESSES

Where a party is entitled to an oral hearing before a decision is taken **8–026** which materially affects his rights or interests, he may be entitled to call witnesses to support his case.[25] A tribunal will normally have a discretion whether or not to grant such a request, but the discretion must be exercised reasonably and in good faith, so that, for example, the decision of a prison board of visitors at a disciplinary hearing not to allow a prisoner to call witnesses because of administrative inconvenience was held to be contrary to natural justice.[26] The failure of prosecution authorities to inform the defendant of potential witnesses may also invalidate a decision,[27] although such cases have recently been explained (at least in the criminal context) as resting not upon a breach of natural justice but upon a breach of duty owed by the prosecution to the court and defence.[28] Where magistrates declined to issue warrants for the arrest of reluctant defence witnesses whose evidence was plainly material, a defendant succeeded in establishing a breach of natural justice.[29] In child care cases, a local authority has a duty to weigh fairly and objectively its discretion to authorise or refuse a medical examination of a child requested by parents in the

---

[24] *cf. Re Fuld's Estate (No. 2)* [1965] 1 W.L.R. 1336; *R. v. Merthyr Tydfil JJ., ex p. Jenkins* [1967] 2 Q.B. 21, 23 (dictum) (see now Welsh Language Act 1967, s. 1).

[25] *Vye v. Vye* [1969] 1 W.L.R. 588. Natural justice does not require that witnesses be excluded while other witnesses are giving evidence; *Moore v. Lambeth County Court Registrar* [1969] 1 W.L.R. 141.

[26] *R. v. Board of Visitors of Hull Prison, ex p. St Germain (No. 2)* [1979] 1 W.L.R. 1401. Similarly, it was held that the attendance of witnesses could not be refused because the tribunal thought there was ample evidence against the prisoner. See also *R. v. Gartree Prison Visitors, ex p. Mealy*, The Times, November 14, 1981 (decision of prison board of visitors quashed where prisoner not allowed to question his own witness or to comment on the evidence presented); *cf. Cheung v. Minister of Employment and Immigration* [1981] 2 F.C. 764 (1981) 122 D.L.R. (3d) 41 (Immigration adjudicator wrong to refuse to allow applicant to call for purposes of cross-examination an immigration officer who had made a damaging statutory statement about the applicant.)

[27] *R. v. Leyland Magistrates, ex p. Hawthorn* [1979] Q.B. 283; *R. v. Blundeston Prison Board of Visitors, ex p. Fox-Taylor* [1982] 1 All E.R. 646.

[28] *Al-Mehdawi v. Secretary of State for the Home Office* [1990] A.C. 876, HL. See further Chap. 9, para. 9–039 below.

[29] *R. v. Bradford JJ., ex p. Wilkinson* [1990] 1 W.L.R. 692.

hope of obtaining expert evidence in their favour,[30] and the authority must also allow evidence to be brought and witnesses to be called at a hearing for an interim care order where the order is opposed.[31]

8–027   However, the courts will allow tribunals a certain latitude in deciding whether to permit witnesses to be called. In *R. v. Panel on Takcovers and Mergers, ex p. Guiness plc,* the Court of Appeal felt the "greatest anxiety" about the Panel's decision not to grant an adjournment to allow witnesses for Guinness to attend, but found it impossible to say that that decision was wrong, bearing in mind the "overwhelming" evidence in favour of the Panel's view, and the fact that the Panel did not see itself as exercising a disciplinary function, regarding its procedures as inquisitorial rather than adversarial.[32]

8–028   Even in disciplinary cases, there can be limitations on the right to allow witnesses to attend. A taxi driver suspended for life from a radio-paging service failed to impugn the proceedings of the Board hearing his case (in private law proceedings alleging a breach of natural justice), since the Board's refusal to grant an adjournment at the close of the proceedings to allow the applicant to seek possible witnesses did not breach the implied contractual right to natural justice, but was a proper exercise of its discretion.[33]

Finally, it may be a breach of procedural fairness for a tribunal to refuse to allow a party to call his witnesses in the order that he thinks best, if there is a real possibility of prejudice to the effective presentation of the case.[34]

RIGHT TO LEGAL REPRESENTATION

8–029   There is some authority for the proposition that a person who is entitled to appear before a statutory tribunal is also usually entitled, in the absence of express or implied provision to the contrary,[35] to be

---

[30] *R. v. Hampshire C.C., ex p. K* [1990] 2 Q.B. 71. And Magistrates' refusal of an adjournment to enable 'vital' defence witnesses to attend was held to have deprived the applicant of a reasonable opportunity to present his defence: *R. v. Hereford Magistrates Court, ex p. Rowlands* [1998] Q.B. 110.

[31] *R. v. Birmingham City Juvenile Court, ex p. Birmingham C.C.* [1988] 1 W.L.R. 337. This result was reached both, it would seem, on construction, and on natural justice grounds.

[32] [1990] 1 Q.B. 146. See Lord Donaldson M.R.'s comments on the 'remarkable' nature of the panel in general.

[33] *Bradman v. Radio Taxicabs Ltd* (1984) 134 New L.J. 1018. The driver had been told before the hearing began that he could call witnesses.

[34] *Briscoe v. Briscoe* [1968] P. 501; *Barnes v. B.P.C. (Business Forms) Ltd* [1975] 1 W.L.R. 1565.

[35] *Maynard v. Osmond* [1977] Q.B. 240 (disciplinary proceedings against police officer).

represented by a lawyer or by any other appropriate spokesman of his choice.[36]

However, for many bodies with a statutory basis, this puts the case **8–030** too high, and it is more accurate to say that the decision-maker possesses a discretion whether to allow legal representation. The courts may then scrutinise the exercise of that discretion according to the ordinary principles of review.[37] Thus in a series of cases concerning the right of prisoners to be represented at disciplinary hearings before Boards of Visitors, the courts have quashed decisions where there was a refusal to allow representation where the charge and potential penalty were particularly grave, or where relevant factors such as the ability of the prisoner to present his case, the availability of witnesses, the complexity of the case in fact and law, and the necessity for even-handedness between prisoners and prison officers had not been properly considered.[38] However, where the charge had a straightforward factual and legal basis,[39] and where the prisoner was intelligent, articulate and had a clear appreciation of the proceedings,[40] courts have declined to interfere with decisions not to allow representation.

As regards informal proceedings before a domestic tribunal, it is **8–031** similarly the case that such bodies possess a discretion as to whether

---

[36] *R. v. St Mary Abbotts Assessment Committee* [1891] 1 Q.B. 378; *R. v. Board of Appeal, ex p. Kay* (1916) 22 C.L.R. 183. See also Powers of Criminal Courts Act 1973, s.21 (1); *R. v. Birmingham JJ., ex p. Wyatt* [1976] 1 W.L.R. 260. The scope of the rule is not, however, clear either in England or in some other jurisdictions. See *Fraser v. Mudge* [1975] 1 W.L.R. 1132 (disciplinary proceedings against a prison inmate) and below, n. 40; *Maynard v. Osmond*, above, n. 35, at 253 (dicta); *cf. Robinson v. R.* [1985] A.C. 956 and *R. v. Board of Visitors Maze Prison, ex p. Hone* [1988] A.C. 379. And see *Golder v. U.K.* (1975), where the European Court of Human Rights upheld prisoner's right of access to his solicitor: see Graham Zellick (1975) 38 M.L.R. 683 *Murray v. United Kingdom* (1996) 22 E.H.R.R. 29 (lack of access to lawyer during first 48 hours in detention violated right to fair hearing under Article 6(1) and (3)). In some cases the matter is put more narrowly as being a matter of discretion for an adjudicator to allow the individual to appear in person or through an agent; see *R. v. Visiting Justice at Her Majesty's Prison, Pentridge, ex p. Walker* [1975] V.R. 883, where the principal authorities are considered. *Cf. Maynard v. Osmond* [1977] Q.B. 240 (appearance 'in person' does not include representation by a lawyer). See also *Alder* [1972] P.L. 278.

[37] See, *e.g. R. v. Secretary of State for the Home Department, ex p. Tarrant* [1985] Q.B. 251 (board of visitors' refusal to allow legal representation unreasonable on charge of mutiny): *R. v. Rathbone, ex p. Dikko* [1985] Q.B. 630. See further *R. v. Secretary of State for the Home Department, ex p. Vera Lawson* [1994] Imm. A.R. 58.

[38] *ibid.*; approved by the House of Lords in *R. v. Board of Visitors of H.M. Prisons, The Maze, ex p. Hone* [1988] A.C. 379.

[39] *R. v. Board of Visitors of HM Remand Centre Risley, ex p. Draper, The Times*, May 24, 1988.

[40] *R. v. Board of Visitors of Parkhurst Prison, ex p. Norney, The Times*, July 29, 1989; [1990] C.O.D. 133.

to allow representation, although the courts will be less willing to intervene where representation is refused,[41] even where the character of the hearing is disciplinary.[42] However, it may be that where the allegation is an "infamous" one, the tribunal can only reasonably exercise its discretion in one way, and there is therefore a duty to allow legal representation.[43]

8–032   No matter what the status or functions of the tribunal, it would be contrary to the requirements of procedural fairness to allow one side to be legally represented but to refuse the same right to the other. And where legal representation is permitted or granted, a party may be entitled to confer with non-legally qualified advisors, although such persons would be barred from fully representing the party.[44] Further, the right to legal representation will where appropriate extend beyond the courtroom or hearing venue, and will be subsumed into the general principle that every citizen has a right of unimpeded access to a court and to legal advice. Thus, prison rules which authorised a prison governor or officer designated by him, to open and read any communication to a prisoner, and to intercept any communication of objectionable content or inordinate length, were held to be *ultra vires* the Prison Act 1952 to the extent that they authorised intrusion beyond the minimum necessary to ensure that correspondence was bona fide legal correspondence.[45]

---

[41] *Re Macqueen and Nottingham Caledonian Society* (1861) 9 C.B.(N.S.) 793; *Enderby Town Football Club Ltd v. Football Association Ltd* [1971] Ch. 591, CA; *Pett v. Greyhound Racing Association Ltd (No. 2)* [1970] 1 Q.B. 46. See also *Ex p. Death* (1852) 18 Q.B. 647. There is some authority for the proposition that when a body has made no formal rule on the matter, it cannot refuse to exercise its discretion to consider allowing legal representation to a person whose ability to pursue his livelihood is in jeopardy: *Pett v. Greyhound Racing Association Ltd (No. 1)* [1969] 1 Q.B. 125, as explained by Lord Denning M.R. in the *Enderby Town* case (above) at 605–606. However, it would appear possible for legal representation to be excluded altogether, whether as of right or in the discretion of the tribunal, by the exercise of an express rule-making power; see, *e.g.* Cairns L.J. in *Enderby Town* (above) at 609; *Maynard v. Osmond* (above) at 252, 256, where it was held that legal representation had effectively been excluded by a rule made under a statutory power.

[42] *Tait v. Central Radio Taxis,* 1989 S.L.T. 217 (member of taxi radio company not entitled to representation before disciplinary committee which debarred him from membership).

[43] *Manchanda v. Medical Eye Centre Assn* (1987) 131 S.J. 47 (natural justice required that doctor be represented before Medical Eye Centre Association committee hearing allegation of unbecoming conduct).

[44] *R. v. Leicester City JJ., ex p. Barrow* [1991] 2 Q.B. 260, CA (poll tax protestors allowed to have non-legally qualified assistants in magistrates' court).

[45] *R. v. Secretary of State for the Home Department, ex p. Leech (No. 2)* [1994] Q.B. 198, CA; see now the Prison (Amendment) (No.2) Rules 1993, S.I. 1993 No. 3075 which permit a prisoner to correspond with his legal adviser and any court (including the European Commission and Court of Human Rights) without the correspondence being read, whether or not legal proceedings have commenced subject to restrictions

In considering whether procedural fairness implies a right to legal   **8–033**
representation (if a party is able to obtain it), it should be borne in
mind that only reasonable standards of fair adjudication, and not ideal
standards, are required. Whether, and if so when, legal representation
ought to be permitted before a tribunal can raise difficult questions of
policy. The reasons for excluding legal representatives (or permitting
them to appear only with the tribunal's consent) are various. It is said
that they tend to introduce too much formality and an inappropriate
adversarial element into the proceedings, which are apt to become
unnecessarily prolonged[46] they disturb witnesses and inexpert
members of the tribunal by asking awkward questions and making
"technical" points; their presence increases the likelihood of
subsequent proceedings in the courts to impugn the decision. This
recital suggests that, in general, legal representation of the right
quality before statutory tribunals is desirable, and that a person
threatened with social or financial ruin by disciplinary proceedings in
a purely domestic forum may be gravely prejudiced if he is denied
legal representation. Since the Franks Report the right to legal
representation before statutory tribunals has been extended[47]; and it
has begun to find its way into disciplinary procedures in universities
and national sporting organisations.[48] Development of the case law on
implied rights to legal representation in non-statutory environments
should be guided by a realistic appraisal of the interests of the person
claiming it, as well as of the interests of the organisation to which he
belongs.

---

where the governor has reason to believe the communication may contain an illicit
enclosure, or may endanger prison security, the safety of others, etc. *cf. Murray v.
United Kingdom* (1996) 22 E.H.R.R. 29; *R. v. Governor of Whitemoor Prison, ex p. Main*
[1997] C.O.D. 400 (search of correspondence did not prevent free flow of information
between applicant and solicitor); *cf. R. v. London Borough of Newham, ex p. Ajayi* (1996)
28 H.L.R. 25.

[46] An argument used in connection with the imposition of punishment on members of
disciplined organisations: see, *e.g. Fraser v. Mudge* [1975] 1 W.L.R. 1132. It may of
course also be argued that the appearance of unfairness in such proceedings may
have an equally deleterious effect upon morale and rehabilitation. See Harry
Whitmore (1970) 33 M.L.R. 481; Annual Report of the Council on Tribunals for 1970–
71, para. 60.

[47] For a right to legal aid in the context of a criminal trial or appeal, see the decision of
the European Court of Human Rights in *Boner v. United Kingdom* (1995) 19 E.H.R.R.
246, where the court found that the refusal of legal aid was a violation of art. 6(3)(c),
which provides for the right, for any person charged with a criminal offence, where
'he has not sufficient means to pay for legal assistance, to be given it free when the
interests of justice so require.'

[48] In 1972 legal representation was permitted at certain disciplinary hearings before the
stewards of the Jockey Club and the Greyhound Racing Association, and before the
Football Association authorities; see above, n. 41.

8–034   What, however, has happened at recent ministerial inquiries, does illustrate a change of emphasis in the role of the person conducting an inquiry. The traditional approach in the past, much favoured by planning inquiry inspectors, was to let anyone who had an interest appear, call every witness he wished, and be separately represented if he was prepared to meet the expenses involved. Now a much more "hands on" approach is sometimes adopted by the inspector or other person in charge of the inquiry. Thus in the case of both the Taylor Inquiry into the Hillsborough football disaster and the Woolf Inquiry into the Strangeways and other prison riots, only those persons whose actions were at risk of being criticised were allowed to be represented, witnesses were normally only called by counsel to the inquiry, who exercised his discretion as to who should be called, and cross-examination was strictly limited. Different techniques were used for different classes of evidence, only part was given orally (not all in public), other evidence was written and in the case of the Prison Inquiry even seminars were employed to canvass issues of wide-ranging nature. This departure from the usual common law adversarial nature of resolving issues of fact was used to save both time and resources and to avoid the inquiries being overwhelmed by material. It meant that reports were able to be produced within reasonable time limits, which was very much in the public interest, without any complaints of lack of fairness.[49] An even more restricted approach to the representation of witnesses was adopted in the case of the inquiry conducted by Scott L.J. into the Matrix Churchill, Arms to Iraq affair.[50]

RIGHT TO CROSS-EXAMINATION

8–035   Refusal to permit cross-examination of witnesses may amount to procedural unfairness,[51] especially if a witness has testified orally and

---

[49] As to techniques used at the Woolf Inquiry, see *Prison Disturbances*, section 2 Cm. 1456, February 1991, and Rod Morgan 'Woolf: In Retrospect and Prospect' (1991) M.L.R. 713.

[50] See Sir Louis Blom-Cooper [1994] P.L. 1.

[51] *Re Fremington School* (1846) 10 Jur. (O.S.) 512; *Osgood v. Nelson* (1872) L.R. 5 HL 636, 646, 660; *Marriott v. Minister of Health* (1936) 154 L.T. 47, 50; *R. v. Newmarket Assessment Committee* [1945] 2 All E.R. 371, 373; *Magistrates of Ayr v. Lord Advocate*, 1950 S.C. 102, 109. Refusal to permit cross-examination of a witness in proceedings in a court will be a denial of justice; see *R. v. Edmonton JJ., ex p. Brooks* [1960] 1 W.L.R. 697; *Blaise v. Blaise* [1969] 2 W.L.R. 1047; *cf.* though *R. v. Wells Street Stipendiary Magistrate, ex p. Seillon* [1978] 1 W.L.R. 1002 (refusal to permit cross-examination of witness in committal proceedings not reviewable by prerogative order prior to their termination). See also *Errington v. Wilson, The Times*, June 2, 1995. Procedural codes for statutory tribunals and inquiries normally give an express right of cross-

a party requests leave to confront and cross-examine him. The fact that the proceedings may be inquisitorial and informal is inconclusive.[52] As with the question of entitlement to legal representation, the matter is one for the discretion of the tribunal. However, where a "judicialised" procedure has been adopted and witnesses are called to give evidence, then the courts will be very ready in the absence of strong reasons to the contrary to find unfairness where a tribunal declines to allow those witnesses to be tested in cross-examination, and indeed it may be unfair for the tribunal not to grant an adjournment to allow witnesses to attend for the purpose of being cross-examined.[53] As Lord Edmund-Davies has pointed out, "there is a massive body of accepted decisions establishing that natural justice requires that a party be given an opportunity of challenging by cross-examination witnesses called by other parties on relevant issues."[54] The true question in every case is whether the absence of cross-examination renders the decision unfair in all the circumstances. If no useful purpose is likely to be served by allowing cross-examination then the courts will be slow to disturb that decision.[55] Thus in *Bushell v. Secretary of State for the Environment*, the

---

[52] *R. v. Brighton & Area Rent Tribunal* [1950] 2 K.B. 410, 419; *Ceylon University v. Fernando* [1960] W.L.R. 223, 235 (dicta). In the *Fernando* case (involving disciplinary charges) it was held that a fair hearing had been given although witnesses had been heard in Fernando's absence; he had been given a sufficient account of what they had said and he had not asked to confront or cross-examine them. But *quaere* whether it was reasonable in the circumstances to make Fernando's right to cross-examine contingent on his taking the initiative in making such a request; he was not legally represented. Nor, indeed, was he represented at the hearing of the appeal before the Privy Council. In *R. v., Commission for Racial Equality, ex p. Cottrell & Rothon* [1980] 1 W.L.R. 1580, it was held that a hearing held pursuant to section 58(5) of the Race Relations Act 1976 (where the C.R.E. was minded to issue a non-discrimination notice) was more investigative than judicial in character, and consequently fairness did not require that the applicants should have the opportunity to cross-examine witnesses.

[53] *R. v. Criminal Injuries Compensation Board, ex p. Cobb* [1995] C.O.D. 126.

[54] *Bushell v. Secretary of State for the Environment* [1981] A.C. 75, 116, there citing *Marriott v. Minister of Health* (1935) 52 T.L.R. 63, 67 *per* Swift J. (compulsory purchase orders inquiry); *Errington v. Minister of Health* [1935] 1 K.B. 249, 272 *per* Maugham L.J. (clearance order); *R. v. Deputy Industrial Injuries Commissioner, ex p. Moore* [1965] 1 Q.B. 465, 488, 490 *per* Diplock L.J.; *Wednesbury Corp. v. Ministry of Housing and Local Government (No. 2)* [1966] 2 Q.B. 275, 302 *per* Diplock L.J. (local government inquiry); *Errington v. Wilson, The Times*, June 2, 1995. (Outer House of the Court of Session, justices' food destruction order where conflicting scientific evidence).

[55] *Bushell v. Secretary of State for the Environment* [1981] A.C. 75, 108, *per* Viscount Dilhome.

majority of the House of Lords held that an inspector at a motorway planning inquiry had not acted unfairly in refusing to allow cross-examination of witnesses from the Department of Transport in relation to traffic flow forecasts, because such evidence "was Government policy in the relevant sense of being a topic unsuitable for investigation by individual inspectors upon whatever material happens to be presented to them at local inquiries held throughout the country."[56] It is submitted that there is no conflict of principle between such reasoning and the dicta of Lord Edmund-Davies, who dissented in the case. The difference between their Lordships simply concerned whether such evidence was indeed a "relevant issue" for the inquiry.

8–036   Even if cross-examination of some witnesses is permitted, a decision-maker is not necessarily obliged to allow cross-examination of every other witness by every party,[57] and there may exceptionally be valid grounds for disallowing questions to a witness on a particular matter.[58] It has been suggested that the proper approach of the courts to all these questions is to ask whether the tribunal's exercise of its discretion can be faulted on normal judicial review grounds—for example, has it, in considering whether to allow cross-examination, had regard to irrelevant considerations, or is its decision unreasonable?[59] However, such an approach is only justifiable in those situations where the decision in all the circumstances complies with the minimum requirements of procedural fairness. In respect of decisions which are subject to the requirements of procedural fairness, the decision-maker has no discretion to adopt a procedure which will not comply with the minimum standards of fairness applicable.

8–037   f a party to proceedings claims that he has suffered an injustice because the non-appearance of a witness has made it impossible to cross-examine him, an attack on the validity of the proceedings may seem to be justified but may well prove to be abortive. A tribunal may

---

[56] *ibid.*, at 100H–101A; see also *per* Lord Lane at 123A. It might be asked why, this being the case, it was that the inspector permitted evidence to be led at the inquiry in relation to the traffic forecasts. It is submitted that in an ordinary case, if a tribunal allows a witness to lead evidence which is not strictly relevant, it ought also to allow cross-examination on such evidence. *Bushell* is perhaps unusual in that the ultimate decision-maker was not the tribunal (the inspector) but the Secretary of State, who had indicated that such evidence was not a matter appropriate for the inquiry. There was therefore no prejudice in allowing the untested evidence to stand, since the decision-maker (the Secretary of State) appreciated that it was not relevant to the decision which he had to make.

[57] *R. v. London Regional Passengers Committee, ex p. Brent L.B.C., The Times,* May 23, 1985.

[58] As where questions are put to a civil servant on the merits of government policy (see *Bushell's* case, above, n. 54). The immunity from cross-examination conceded to the civil servant witness in *Re Trunk Roads Act 1936* [1939] 2 K.B. 515 seems to have been more extensive than this.

[59] *R. v. London Regional Passengers Committee, ex p. Brent L.B.C., The Times,* May 23, 1985.

be entitled to base its decision on hearsay, written depositions or medical reports.[60] In these circumstances a person aggrieved will normally be unable to insist on oral testimony by the original source of the information, provided that he has had a genuine opportunity to controvert that information.[61] It is the responsibility of the decision maker to make due allowance for the lack of an opportunity to cross-examine when assessing the evidence.

Three final points can be made. First, often a party cannot **8–038** effectively exercise his right to cross-examine unless he is represented by a lawyer. Secondly, in proceedings culminating in the imposition of a penalty, procedural fairness requires that after the case has been proved, or even if there is no dispute as to the law and facts in the first place,[62] that there should be a right to address the tribunal in mitigation[63] unless the penalty is automatic. Thirdly, there may well be questions of law or opinion on which a party cannot properly claim any right to lead evidence or to cross-examine witnesses but on which he can fairly claim an implied right to make submissions to the deciding body.

Right to Reasons

No general duty to give reasons?

It has long been a commonly recited proposition of English law that **8–039** there is no general rule of law that reasons should be given for administrative decisions.[64] On this view, a decision-maker is not

---

[60] See also, *R. v. Epping and Harlow JJ., ex p. Massaro* [1973] Q.B. 433 (prosecution not obliged to produce for cross-examination at committal proceedings witnesses who will be called at trial).

[61] *Wilson v. Esquimait & Nanaimo Ry.* [1922] 1 A.C. 202; *R. v. War Pensions Entitlement Appeal Tribunal, ex p. Bott* (1933) 50 C.L.R. 228. See also *Miller (T.A.) Ltd. v. Minister of Housing and Local Government* [1968] 1 W.L.R. 992 (enforcement notice appeal). In these cases the relevant evidential material was disclosed in writing. See also, *Kavanagh v. Chief Constable of Devon and Cornwall* [1974] Q.B. 624 (Crown Court, on an appeal from a refusal to register a person under the Firearms Act 1968, may, like the original decision maker, rely upon hearsay evidence). See, however, *Re W.L.W.* [1972] Ch. 456, where production of the author of a report for cross-examination was held to be a requisite of natural justice in a proceeding in a court of law.

[62] *Ridge v. Baldwin* [1964] A.C. 40, 68; *Burn v. National Amalgamated Labourers Union* [1920] 2 Ch. 364, 374; *Edgar v. Meade* (1917) 23 C.L.R. 29, 43; *cf. Weinberger v. Inglis* [1919] A.C. 606, 632.

[63] *Fullbrook v. Berkshire Magistrates' Court Committee* (1970) 69 L.G.R. 75.

[64] See, *e.g. R. v. Gaming Board of Great Britain, ex p. Benaim and Khaida* [1970] 2 Q.B. 417, 431 (where, however, the need to keep confidential the sources of the board's information was a paramount consideration); *Cannock Chase D.C. v. Kelly* [1978] 1 W.L.R. 1, 4; *McInnes v. Onslow-Fane* [1978] 1 W.L.R. 1520, 1532–1535 (a non-statutory

normally required to consider whether fairness or natural justice demands that reasons should be provided to an individual affected by a decision. This is because the giving of reasons has not been considered to be a requirement of the rules of procedural propriety. But the situation may now be changing.

8–040   The absence of a duty to give reasons has sometimes been explained as following from the fact that the courts themselves are not obliged at common law to give reasons for their decisions.[65] However, today not only the higher courts, but all courts, at least in relation to some of their decisions, are under such an obligation, for—

> "It is the function of professional judges to give reasons for their decisions and the decisions to which they are a party. This court would look askance at the refusal by a judge to give reasons for a decision particularly if requested to do so by one of the parties ... it may well be that if such a case should arise this court would find that it had power to order the judge to give his reasons for his decision."[66]

---

tribunal); *Payne v. Lord Harris of Greenwich* [1981] 1 W.L.R. 754, 764 *per* Brightman L.J. (prisoner not entitled to reasons for refusal of parole; now overruled by *R. v. Secretary of State for the Home Department, ex p. Doody* [1994] 1 A.C. 531); *R. v. Bristol, ex p. Pearce* (1984) 83 L.G.R. 711; *Antaios Compania Navicra S.A. v. Salen Rederiema A.B.* ("The Antaios") [1985] A.C. 191, 199 *per* Lord Diplock; *R. v. Secretary of State for Social Services, ex p. Connolly* [1986] 1 W.L.R. 421, 431, *per* Slade L.J. See also *Re Glendenning Motorways Inc. and Royal Transportation Ltd.* (1976) 59 D.L.R. (3d) 89; *Public Service Board of New South Wales v. Osmond* (1986) 60 A.J.L.R. 209, where the High Court of Australia finnly rejected the judgment of Kirby C.J. in the New South Wales Court of Appeal [1984] 3 N.S.W.L.R. 447. *Cf.* Taggart (ed.), *Judicial Review of Administrative Action in the 1980s*, pp. 53–69.

[65] See, for example, the fourth edition of this book, at p. 195: "Minimum standards [of fairness] cannot be higher than those prescribed by the courts for themselves. Courts are not obliged to give reasons ..."

[66] *R. v. Knightsbridge Crown Court, ex p. International Sporting Club* [1982] Q.B. 304, DC *per* Griffiths L.J. See also *Norton Tool Co. Ltd v. Tewson* [1973] 1 W.L.R. 45, 49; *Capital and Suburban Properties Ltd v. Swycher* [1976] Ch. 319, 326; *Tramountana Armadora S.A. v. Atlantic Shipping Co. S.A.* [1978] 2 All E.R. 870, 872; *Hoey v. Hoey* [1984] 1 W.L.R. 464 (reasons for decisions should be stated in custody cases); *Eagil Trust Co. v. Pigott-Brown,* below, n.68; *R. v. Crown Court at Harrow, ex p. Dave,* below n. 69; *R. v. Ministry of Defence, ex p. Murray* [1998] C.O.D. 134 (court-martial). However, *cf. Macdonald v. R.* [1977] 2 S.C.R. 665 (although judges are normally expected to give reasons for their decisions, the absence of reasons is not in itself a ground of appeal). See also, in relation to decisions of Magistrates, *R. v. Southend Stipendiary Magistrate, ex p. Rochford D.C.* [1995] Env. L.R. 1 (no general duty on Magistrates to give judgments or reasons for decisions); *R. v. Haringey Magistrates, ex p. Cragg* [1997] C.O.D. 160 (no general duty to give reasons, even where no appeal from Magistrates' decision); *Harrison v. Department of Social Security* [1997] C.O.D. 220. But see *R. v. Burton-upon-Trent Justices, ex p. Hussein* (April 29, 1996, unreported). (Magistrates obliged to give reasons where determining appeal by way of rehearing from licensing authority which was itself obliged to give reasons). See generally, Taggart (1983) 33 U.T.L.J. 1.

This obligation that the higher courts should give reasoned decisions is subject to well-established exceptions, such as in the exercise of a judge's discretion on costs, and on a judge's refusal of leave to appeal to the Court of Appeal from his decision to refuse leave to appeal from the decision of an arbitrator,[67] but apart from such exceptions, in the case of discretionary exercise, as in other decisions on facts of law, the judge should set out his reasons.[68] If he does not do so, his decision may be quashed and remitted for a rehearing.[69]

As a general proposition, it is still accurate to say that "the law does   **8–041** not at present recognise a general duty to give reasons for an administrative decision."[70] But the increasing number of so-called "exceptional" circumstances[71] in which fairness or natural justice does now require that reasons be afforded to an affected individual means that the general proposition is meaningful only in indicating that the mere fact that a decision-making process is held to be subject to the

---

[67] *Antaios Compania Naviera S.A. v. Salen Rederiema A.B. (The Antaios);* [1985] A.C. 191, HL (judges ought not to give reasons for such a refusal of leave).

[68] *Eagil Trust Co. v. Pigott-Brown* [1985] 3 All E.R. 119, 122, CA, *per* Griffiths L.J. (in application to strike out action for want of prosecution, judge should give sufficient reasons to show the Court of Appeal the principles on which he has acted and the reasons that have led to his conclusion).

[69] As is now the case in relation to Crown Court decisions (save perhaps for some interlocutory or procedural decisions): *R. v. Crown Court at Harrow, ex p. Dave* [1994] 1 W.L.R. 98; *R. v. Snaresbrook Crown Court, ex p. Lea, The Times,* April 5, 1994 (reasons for decision on licensing appeal). See also *R. v. Stafford Crown Court, ex p. Reid, The Independent,* March 13, 1995 (no duty to give reasons for Crown Court refusal to extend time for appealing against conviction before Magistrates); *R. v. Southwark Crown Court, ex p. Samuel* [1995] C.O.D. 249; *R. v. Winchester Crown Court, ex p. Morris* [1996] C.O.D. 104; *R. v. Southwark Crown Court ex p. Brooke* [1997] C.O.D. 7 (following *Dave*); *R. v. Bozat* (1997) 9 Admin. L.R. 125 (Crown Court Judge should give reasons for recommending deportation).

[70] *per* Lord Mustill, speaking for the House of Lords in *R. v. Secretary of State for the Home Department, ex p. Doody* [1994] 1 A.C. 531, 564; compare *R. v. Lambeth L.B.C., ex p. Walters* [1994] 2 F.C.R. 336, where Sir Louis Blom-Cooper Q.C., sitting as a deputy judge, suggested that English law has now arrived at a point where there is at least a general duty to give reasons wherever the statutorily impregnated administrative process is infused with the concept of fair treatment to those potentially affected by administrative action. But see *R. v. Kensington and Chelsea R.L.B.C. ex p. Grillo,* (1996) 28 H.C.R. 94, CA, where Neill L.J. doubted the proposition of the judge at first instance (also Sir Louis Blom-Cooper Q.C.) that there was a general duty to give reasons 'in every aspect of the homeless persons legislation'. Neill L.J. did, however, foresee that 'there may come a time when English law does impose a general obligation on administrative authorities to give reasons ...' (at p. 105); see further, Sir Louis Blom-Cooper Q.C. in *R. v. Islington L.B.C., ex p. Hinds* (1995) 27 H.L.R. 65; (1996) 28 H.L.R. 302, CA. But the general proposition was reaffirmed *R. v. Ministry of Defence, ex p. Murray* [1998] C.O.D. 134.

[71] In *R. v. Universities Funding Council, ex p. Institute of Dental Surgery* [1994] 1 W.L.R. 242 the Divisional Court rejected the contention that the duty to give reasons could any longer be described as an 'exceptional one'.

requirements of fairness does not automatically or naturally lead to the further conclusion that reasons must be given. However, it is certainly now the case that a decision-maker subject to the requirements of fairness should consider carefully whether, in the particular circumstances of the case, reasons should be given Indeed, so fast is the case law on the duty to give reasons developing, that it should now be added that fairness or natural justice will "often" require a decision-maker to give reasons for its decision, even in the absence of any statutory indication.[72]

The advantages of a duty to give reasons

8–042   The absence of a general duty to give reasons has long been condemned as a major defect of our system of administrative law. As the Justice-All Souls Committee concluded, "no single factor has inhibited the development of English administrative law as seriously as the absence of any general obligation upon public authorities to give reasons for their decisions".[73] The beneficial effects of a duty to give reasons are many. To have to provide an explanation of the basis for their decision is a salutary discipline for those who have to decide anything that adversely affects others.[74] The giving of reasons is widely regarded as one of the principles of good administration[75] in that it encourages a careful examination of the relevant issues, the elimination of extraneous considerations, and consistency in decision-making. Moreover, if published, reasons can provide guidance to others on the body's likely future decisions, and so deter applications which would be unsuccessful. Further, the giving of reasons may

---

[72] See *ex p. Murray*, above, n.66, which contains an important and valuable general summary of the present extent of the duty to give reasons, and records and reflects the 'perceptible trend towards an insistence on greater openness in the making of administrative decisions' (*per* Hooper J.). See also *R. v. Secretary of State for Education, ex p. G* [1995] E.L.R. 58, 67 (*per* Latham J.).

[73] Justice-All Souls Committee Report, *Administrative Justice, Some Necessary Reforms* (1988), p.71, quoting the earlier Justice Committee Report, *Administration Under Law* (1971), p.23. See generally the Justice-All Souls Committee's valuable review of the duty to give reasons, its advantages and disadvantages, in Chapter 3 of the report. See further, Wade and Forsyth, *Administrative Law* (7th ed., 1994) p. 541; Woolf, 41st Hamlyn Lectures, *Protection of the Public—A New Challenge* (1990), p. 92. For recent judicial consideration of the purpose and advantages of the duty to give reasons, see the important survey in *ex. p. Murray*, above, n.66. See also, *ex p. Hinds*, above, n.70.

[74] 'Having to give reasons concentrates the mind wonderfully' *per* Donaldson J. (who has been a leading judicial proponent of extending the legal duty to give reasons) in *Tramountana Annadora S.A. v. Atlantic Shipping Co. S.A.* [1978] 2 All E.R. 870, 872.

[75] See, for example, R. Gregory and P. Hutchinson, *The Parliamentary Ombudsman* (1975). p.288 (failure to give reasons can constitute maladministration). Compare G. Richardson, 'The Duty to Give Reasons: Potential and Practice' [1986] P.L. 437.

protect the body from unjustified challenges, because those adversely affected are more likely to accept a decision if they know why it has been taken.[76] In addition, basic fairness and respect for the individual often requires that those in authority over others should tell them why they are subject to some liability or have been refused some benefit.

It is because of these very real benefits which result from the giving **8–043** of reasons that a legal duty to give reasons has become an integral part of the model of administration that has dominated English administrative law since the publication of the Franks Report.[77] If those entitled to be heard have no right to know how a tribunal resolved the issues in dispute at the hearing, they may well regard as an empty ritual their legally conferred opportunity to be heard and to influence the tribunal by producing witnesses and other evidence to establish the relevant facts, advancing arguments on the proper exercise of any discretion and the resolution of any legal questions, and challenging their opponents' case. Unless the tribunal makes findings on disputes as to fact, explains the exercise of its discretion (by indicating the considerations that it has taken into account and relative weight assigned to them, for example) and gives its answers to any questions of law, there can be no assurance that the tribunal has discharged its obligation to base its decision upon the material presented at the hearing, rather than on extraneous considerations.[78]

In addition to helping to ensure the fairness of an initial hearing, a **8–044** requirement of reasons is of particular importance where decisions are subject to a right of appeal on questions of law.[79] A reasoned decision is necessary to enable the person prejudicially affected by the decision to know whether he has a ground of appeal; it will also assist the appellate court to scrutinise effectively the decision for relevant error,

---

[76] See, *e.g. R. v. Secretary of State for the Home Department, ex p. Singh, The Times,* June 8, 1987, QBD, where Woolf L.J. explained that it was highly undesirable for the Home Office not to give written notification of a decision on an application for asylum, not only because of the potential unfairness to the applicant, but because without notice, an applicant would be likely to receive leave to move for judicial review, whatever the real merits of his case, if he indicated that as far as he was aware no decision had been taken on his case.

[77] Cmnd. 218 (1957), para. 98; similar recommendations had been made 25 years earlier by the Donoughmore Committee Cmd. 4060 (1932) p.100, but they were not implemented. The U.S. Administrative Procedure Act's requirement of reasons applies principally to formal adjudication, although the courts have imposed a duty to make findings of fact and to state reasons in some other situations: see Davis, *Administrative Law Treatise* (2nd ed.), Chap. 14, pp.21–29. In contrast, all regulations, decisions and directives of the European Communities' Council and Commission must be supported by reasons.

[78] *Cf. R. v. Mental Health Review Tribunal, ex p. Clatworthy* [1985] 3 All E.R. 699 at 703–704.

[79] See, *e.g.* Tribunals and Inquiries Act 1992, s. 10.

345

without necessarily usurping the function of the tribunal by itself redetermining the questions of fact and discretion which Parliament entrusted to the tribunal.

The disadvantages of a duty to give reasons

8–045 There are, however, some significant objections which can be raised to the courts extending a general requirement to provide reasons and findings of fact to all administrative bodies that are in any case obliged by the duty of fairness to inform those whom they may prejudicially affect of the case that they have to meet and to offer them an opportunity to submit representations. These include the possibility that reasons, especially if published, will unduly increase "legalisation" and the formal nature of the decision making process,[80] place burdens upon decision makers that will occasion administrative delays, and encourage the disappointed to pore over the reasons in the hope of detecting some shortcoming for which to seek redress in the courts.[81] In addition, a reluctance to give reasons perhaps because they may occasion harm (by, for example, causing personal distress,[82] revealing confidences, or endangering national security[83]) could discourage the making of difficult or controversial decisions or result in the production of anodyne, uninformative and standard reasons. Nonetheless, apart from the exceptional case, the advantages of providing reasons so clearly outweigh the costs that fairness requires that the individual be informed of the basis of the decision.

---

[80] *cf. Verndell v. Kearney & Trecker Marwin Ltd* [1983] I.C.R. 683 at 694–695 (warning to tribunals not to reduce questions of facts, degree and discretion to legal propositions by excessively elaborate reasons).

[81] See *McInnes v. Onslow-Fane* [1978] 1 W.L.R. 1520, 1535; see also *R. v. Chief Registrar of Friendly Societies, ex p. New Cross Building Society* [1984] Q.B. 227, 245; (detailed reasons may tempt a reviewing court erroneously to assume an appellate of *de novo* jurisdiction). See also the disadvantages listed by Hooper J. in *ex p. Murray*, above, n. 66; and see *R. v. Mayor, Commonality and Citizens of the City of London, ex p. Matson* (1996) 8 Admin. L.R. 49, 70, where Swinton Thomas L.J. cast doubt upon the argument that it would be wrong to require a collegiate body to articulate a reason or set of reasons for its decision.

[82] *McInnes v. Onslow-Fane*, above, at 1533; *cf. Grundy (Teddington) Ltd v. Plummer* [1983] I.C.R. 367, 373–374.

[83] *cf.* Interception of Communications Act 1985, Sched. 1, para. 4(2) which forbids the Tribunal from giving reasons for its disposition of complaints of wiretapping or other forms of interception of communications. See *R. v. Secretary of State for the Home Department, ex p. Adams* [1995] All E.R. (E.C.) 177 (reasons not required where, to be meaningful, they would have to reveal sensitive intelligence information).

The distinction between the duty to give reasons and the duty of adequate disclosure

The duty to give reasons for a decision must be distinguished from the 8–046 fundamental principle of natural justice already considered[84] which imposes an obligation to provide information about the case which a party affected may want to answer. Some cases which appear to suggest that reasons are required by natural justice or fairness are in reality examples of this more basic requirement. For example, a local authority must not suspend a contractor from its list of approved contractors without giving detailed reasons immediately (or as soon as is practicable in a case where serious impropriety is suspected).[85] This is not an example of a case where reasons are required, but rather safeguards the contractor's right to make further representations: the authority must disclose the case against the contractor so that it may be able to answer the allegation as quickly as possible. Thus the right to information protects the right to make representations, but does not in itself entitle the contractor to a justification of the final decision.[86]

Circumstances in which reasons will be required

A failure to provide reasons may give grounds for challenging an 8–047 administrative decision on the ground that it amounts to procedural impropriety in the following circumstances.[87]

---

[84] Above, para. 8–004 *et seq.*

[85] *R. v. Enfield L.B.C., ex p. T.F. Unwin Ltd* [1989] C.O.D. 466. *Cf. Cinnamond v. British Airports Authority* [1980] 1 W.L.R. 582, 591.

[86] See also, *e.g. R. v. Secretary of State for the Home Office, ex p. Thirukumar* [1989] Imm. A.R. 270, CA (applicant for asylum should be made aware of reasons why his application is being at least provisionally refused; in reality so that he can make further representations); *cf. R. v. Secretary of State for Foreign and Commonwealth Affairs, ex p. Everett* [1989] Q.B. 811, CA, *per* O'Connor L.J. (Secretary of State did not have to afford applicant opportunity to be heard before refusing application for a passport, but 'was entitled to refuse the passport but to give his reason for so doing' and 'tell him that if there were any exceptional grounds which might call for the issue of a passport he would consider them'). See also the dicta of Lord Denning M.R. in *Breen v. A.E.U.* [1971] 2 Q.B. 175, 190–191 where he stated that fairness may require that a person who is being deprived of an important right should be given a hearing and reasons. This again may be understood as referring to disclosure of the case against the individual. An important recent example of the distinction is *R. v. Secretary of state for the Home Department, ex p. Fayed* [1997] 1 W.L.R. 228, CA (no duty to give reasons because of statutory exclusion, but duty to disclose to applicant the subject matter of the decision-maker's concern to allow meaningful representations.

[87] See Michael Akehurst, 'Statements of Reasons for Judicial and Administrative Decisions' (1970)33 M.L.R. 154.

(1) Reasons for a decision may be expressly or impliedly[88] required by statute. A duty to supply reasons when requested to do so is imposed by the Tribunals and Inquiries Act 1971 on a large number of statutory tribunals and on Ministers notifying decisions after the holding of a statutory inquiry or in cases where the person concerned could have required the holding of such an inquiry.[89] This duty, which is qualified by a narrow range of exceptions,[90] is enforceable by mandamus.[91] A similar duty has been imposed on various other tribunals and public bodies by statute or regulations.[92] There are indications, for example, that in deciding a planning appeal on the basis of written representations, an inspector is obliged to

---

[88] Useful articles on this topic include Michael Akehurst, (1970) 33 M.L.R. 154; J.W. Bridge in D. Lasok *et al.* (eds.), *Fundamental Duties*, Chap 7; Michael Taggart, (1980) 9 N.Z.U.L.R. 162; and see Geoffrey Flick, *Natural Justice* (2nd ed., 1979), Chap. 6.

[89] s. 12, Sched. 1. The duty may be extended to designated discretionary statutory inquiries or hearings (ss. 12(3), 19(1), (2)). In a number of instances procedural rules have imposed a duty to give reasons without a prior request (see, *e.g.* S.I. 1985 No. 16, Sched. 1, r. 9(3) (industrial tribunals).

[90] The duty does not apply to ministerial decisions in connection with orders and schemes of a legislative character. Where the duty applies, a statement of reasons may still be refused or restricted by the tribunal or Minister on grounds of national security; and it may also be withheld in the interests of a party to the decision if it is asked for by someone not primarily concerned with the decision. Orders may be made after consultation with the Council on Tribunals excluding particular classes of decisions from the scope of section 12; such Orders have been few. See also Civil Aviation Act 1982, s. 67(2), (3) and (4) (circumstances in which Civil Aviation Authority may or must refrain from giving reasons for air transport licensing decision).

[91] *Parrish v. Minister of Housing and Local Government* (1961) 59 L.G.R. 411, 418; *Brayhead (Ascot) Ltd v. Berkshire C.C.* [1964] 2 Q.B. 303, 313–314; *Mountview Court Properties Ltd v. Devlin* (1970) 21 P. & C.R. 689, 693.

[92] See, *e.g.* Town and Country Planning (Inquiries Procedure) Rules 1992 (S.I. 1992 No. 2038). See, *e.g. London Residuary Body v. Secretary of State for the Environment* (1989) 58 P. & C.R. 256 (Secretary of State's decision to grant planning permission for County Hall against advice of inspector was quashed because 'the letter ... plainly calculated to mislead ...' and therefore failed to give proper reasons for the decision as required by statute). See also *Leigh Estates (U.K.) Ltd v. Secretary of State for the Environment* [1996] J.P.L. 217 (duty to explain why grant of planning permission would prejudice preparation of development plan). But see *R. v. Aylesbury Vale D.C., ex p. Chaplin* [1998] J.P.L. 49 (Town and Country Planning Act 1990 did not impose on local planning authority a general duty to give reasons for *granting* application for planning permission). See also, outside the context of planning, *Berridge v. Benjies Business Centre* [1997] 1 W.L.R. 53, PC (adequacy of statutory reasons); *R. v. Secretary of State for Health, ex p. R.P. Scherer Ltd* (1996) B.M.L.R. 12 (requirement of reasons under E.C. Council Directive 89/105 was equivalent to common law duty to give reasons; Minister's decision letter sufficient); *R. v. Doncaster M.B.C., ex p. Nortrop* (1996) 28 H.L.R. 862 (failure of Housing Benefit Review Board to give sufficient reasons to discharge statutory duty); *R. v. Brent L.B.C., ex p. Baruwa* (1996) 28 H.L.R. 361.

give reasons dealing with the parties' major contentions, even though the statutory duty to give reasons without a request from a party applies only to decisions made after an inquiry.[93]

(2) Where statute or regulation provides a right of appeal from a decision, reasons may be required so as to enable the affected individual to exercise effectively that right. A right to reasons in these circumstances may be explained either by reference to the rules of natural justice or, more usually, by a necessary implication from the rules which provide for the appeal.[94] Thus in one group of cases, tribunals when stating a case on an award of costs have been required to give reasons if their award departs from normal practice.[95] And in another, licensing justices empowered to refuse liquor licences on specified grounds were held to have failed to hear and determine according to law when they failed to specify the ground for refusal.[96] The courts may even imply a right to

---

[93] See *Grenfell-Baines v. Secretary of State for the Environment* [1985] J.P.L. 256.

[94] See especially, *Norton Tool Co. Ltd v. Tewson* [1973] 1 W.L.R. 45, 49; *Alexander Machinery (Dudley) Ltd v. Crabtree* [1974] I.C.R. 120, 122 (in *R. v. Civil Service Appeal Board, ex p. Cunningham* [1992] I.C.R. 817; [1991] 4 All E.R. 310, 317, Lord Donaldson M.R. rejected the suggestion of Gibbs C.J. in *Public Service Board of New South Wales v. Osmond* [1987] L.R.C. (Const.) 681, 688, that the above two cases could be explained by the existence of a statutory duty to give reasons). Australian courts have gone further in requiring reasons to be given by judges when the appellant's right of appeal would otherwise be rendered nugatory: see, *e.g. Pettitt v. Dunkley* [1971] 1 N.S.W.L.R. 376; *Pinkstone v. Goldrick* [1979] 1 N.S.W.L.R. 279; *Australian Timber Workers Union v. Monaro Sawmills Pty Ltd* (1980) 29 A.L.R. 322; for a more cautious approach, see *R. v. Awatere* [1982] 1 N.Z.L.R. 644.

[95] *Smeaton Hanscomb & Co. Ltd v. Sassoon I. Setty, Son & Co. (No. 2)* [1953] 1 W.L.R. 1481; *Lewis v. Haverfordwest R.D.C.* [1953] 1 W.L.R. 1486 (arbitrator); *Pepys v. London Transport Executive* [1975] 1 W.L.R. 234 (Land Tribunal), disapproving dicta to the contrary in *Hood Investment Co. Ltd v. Marlow U.D.C.* (1964) 15 P. & C.R. 229, 232. *Cf. Westminster C.C. v. Great Portland Estates Plc* [1985] A.C. 661 (planning authority must give reasons for deciding exceptionally to take into account personal circumstances); *Ynyforgan and Glais Gypsy Site Action Group v. Secretary of State for Wales* [1981] J.P.L. 874 (particularly clear reasons to be given for departure from development plan). Recent cases have built on the suggestion (which may also be seen in *ex p. Cunningham,* below) that reasons may be required to explain a decision which departs from a policy or usual practice, or is otherwise unexplained, even if there is no general duty to give reasons: *R. v. Islington L.B.C., ex p. Rixon* [1997] E.L.R. 66 (authority should have given reasons for departing from statutory guidance).

[96] *R. v. Sykes* (1875) 1 QBD 52; *Ex p. Smith* (1878) 3 QBD 374; *Tranter v. Lancashire JJ.* (1887) 51 J.P. 454; *R. v. Thomas* [1892] 1 Q.B. 426. In *ex p. Gorman* [1904] A.C. 23, 28, Lord Herschell described the decision in *ex p. Smith* (where the applicant had not demanded that the justices give their reasons) as 'somewhat peculiar'. But see *Minister of National Revenue v. Wrights' Canadian Ropes Ltd* [1947] A.C. 109; and see Akehurst, 'Statements of Reasons for Judicial and Administrative Decisions' (1970) 33 M.L.R. 154, 156.

reasons into a well-developed statutory framework which is silent on the question of an entitlement to reasons.[97] The courts have recently demonstrated a greater willingness to intervene in such circumstances (provided always that they do not discern a statutory intention to *exclude* reasons) simply on the basis that procedural fairness requires that reasons be given.[98]

(3) Whether the above decisions are explainable on the basis of a statutory implication or not, it is now clear that natural justice or fairness may itself require, in a wide range of circumstances, that reasons be given. In a landmark decision, the Court of Appeal in *R. v. Civil Service Appeal Board, ex p. Cunningham* held that the Civil Service Appeal Board, a "judicialised" tribunal established under the royal prerogative, was under a duty to give outline reasons for its decisions, sufficient to show to what it has directed its mind and to indicate whether its decisions are lawful, and a failure to do so is a breach of natural justice.[99] This decision demonstrates the falsity of the argument that natural justice concerns only procedure *at* the hearing, and accordingly cannot require the provision of reasons, which are part of the form of the determination made *after* the hearing. Natural justice should not be viewed so narrowly; the form of a determination is part of the procedure of a hearing, and is no less subject to the requirements of natural justice than any other part.[1]

---

[97] *R. v. Secretary of State for the Home Department, ex p. Doody* (above, n. 70); compare *R. v. Secretary of State for the Home Office, ex p. Stitt*, The Times, February 3, 1987, DC (Secretary of State did not have to give reasons for conclusion that a person was 'concerned in the commission, preparation, or instigation of acts of terrorism' within the meaning of the Prevention of Terrorism (Temporary Provisions) Act 1976 and 1984 in making an exclusion order, in part because the 1976 Act accorded a comprehensive package of rights to candidates for exclusion, which did not include the right to reasons). In *R. v. Civil Service Appeal Board, ex p. Cunningham* (above, n. 94), Lord Donaldson M.R. rejected the argument that since Parliament had required some tribunals to give reasons by statute, therefore the common law was unable to impose a similar requirement upon other tribunals if justice so required.

[98] *ex p. Murray*, above, n.70. Interestingly, that case also suggested that the converse situation-*i.e.* where the statutory framework does not provide for any appeal-may *also* be a factor in favour of requiring the provision of reasons (relying on *ex p. Cunningham* and *Doody*, below).

[99] *R. v. Civil Service Appeal Board, ex p. Cunningham* [1991] 4 All E.R. 310; see Herberg [1991] P.L. 340.

[1] *ibid.*, at 322, *per* McCowan L.J. Dicta of Hobhouse L.J. in *R. v. Criminal Injuries Compensation Board, ex p. Cook* [1996] 1 W.L.R. 1037, 1051c (which were not essential to the decision), which appear to suggest that the giving of inadequate reasons does not constitute a procedural impropriety, must be treated with reserve.

One ground upon which fairness may require that reasons be provided in such a case is that reasons enable a person aggrieved by a decision to know not only whether he may appeal, but also—as in *Cunningham*[2]—whether he may maintain in action for judicial review on an independent ground such as illegality or irrationality.[3] But the House of Lords has recently made it clear that this is only one ground for the imposition of a duty to give reasons. In addition, their Lordships held, it may be that the very importance of the decision to the individual—for example, a decision concerning personal liberty—is such that the individual cannot be left to receive an unreasoned decision, as if "the distant oracle has spoken".[4] It is submitted that it is preferable not to attempt to separate out the different grounds upon which a duty to give reasons may arise; rather, there is a "unitary test"[5] which rests on familiar considerations of fairness[6]; within such a test,

---

[2] *R. v. Civil Service Appeal Board, ex p. Cunningham, ibid. R. v. Secretary of State for the Home Department, ex p. Chetta* [1996] C.O.D. 463, where the court criticised the practice of only given reasons after a challenge had been brought for this reason.

[3] The Australian Administrative Decisions (Judicial Review) Act, 1977, s.13 entitles applicants for judicial review to a statement of reasons from the decision maker; interestingly, the High Court has inferred from this duty to give reasons, an implied obligation to conduct a prior hearing for all decisions: see *Kiora v. Minister of Immigration and Ethnic Affairs* (1986) 62 A.L.R. 321.

[4] *per* Lord Mustill in *R. v. Secretary of State for the Home Department, ex p. Doody* [1994] 1 A.C. 531, 565; applied to security categorisation of prisoners in *R. v. Secretary of State for the Home Department, ex p. Duggan* [1994] 3 All E.R. 277. *R. v. Secretary of State for the Home Department, ex p. Follen* [1996] C.O.D. 169 (decision to refuse release on licence quashed where no adequate reasons for not following recommendations of Parole Board); *R. v. Secretary of State for the Home Department, ex p. Lillycrop, The Times,* December 13, 1996 (Parole Board should summarise in decision letter reasons why parole not recommended); *cf.* the penetrating analysis of Sedley J. in *R. v. Universities Funding Council, ex p. Institute of Dental Surgery* [1994] 1 W.L.R. 242 (reasons not required for decision of UFC where based upon 'pure academic judgment', even though the decision had substantial financial implications for the applicant). The 'oraccular' effect of an unreasoned decision will, naturally, be greater in a case where there is no right of appeal, and this has led to the suggestion that the fact that there is *no* right of appeal may be a factor in favour of requiring reasons: see *ex p. Murray,* above, n.70. The position would therefore appear to be that *both* the existence of a right of appeal (or judicial review), and the absence of any appeal, may be factors predisposing the courts to require reasons.

[5] *per* Sedley J. in *R. v. Universities Funding Council, ex p. Institute of Dental Surgery* (n.4 above).

[6] In *Cunningham* (above, n. 2). Lord Donaldson M.R. relied in his judgment upon the general words of guidance offered by Lord Bridge in *Lloyd v. McMahon* (above, n.9), and cited at the opening of this chapter, that the requirements of fairness in every case must be determined by a consideration of the character of the decision making body and the framework within which it operates (to which may be added, the effect which the decision is likely to have upon the affected individual).

regard may be had, where appropriate, to the multiple grounds which may exist, such as a need for reasons to know whether to challenge the decision (by appeal or judicial review); the importance of the decision on the individual's liberty or livelihood; the advantage of concentrating the decision-maker's mind and ensuring that the issues have been conscientiously addressed, the general nature of the adjudicating process,[7] and so on.

8–048 Since the duty to give reasons may now be seen simply as yet another aspect of the requirements of procedural fairness, it would be wrong to imagine that the duty may be artificially confined to situations in which the decision maker is acting in a "judicial" or "quasi-judicial" capacity. Although in *Cunningham*, some reliance was placed upon the fact that the Civil Service Appeal Board is a fully "judicialised" tribunal, and one that is almost unique among tribunals in not falling under a statutory duty to give reasons, subsequent decisions have made it clear that reasons may be required of a body exercising "quasi-judicial" functions, such as that of the Home Secretary in relation to the tariff period to be served by life sentence prisoners,[8] and "administrative" functions, such as a local authority making decisions regarding an individual's housing application.[9] The distinction between judicial, quasi-judicial and administrative functions may be consigned to history in this context, as well as more generally. As Sedley J. has put it, in rejecting such a submission in the context of the duty to give reasons, "In the modern state the decisions of administrative bodies can have a more immediate and profound impact on people's lives than the decisions of courts, and public law has since *Ridge v. Baldwin* been alive to that fact."[10]

---

[7] *per* Neill L.J. in *R. v. Kensington and Chelsea R.L.B.C., ex p. Grillo, The Independent,* June 13, 1995. (1996) 28 H.L.R, 94, CA, where the court, in holding that fairness did not require the provision of reasons, relied on the fact that the appellate procedure in question was voluntary. And see now *Murray Supra,* n.70.

[8] *R. v. Secretary of State for the Home Department, ex p. Doody,* and later cases above, n. 4.

[9] *R. v. Islington L.B.C., ex p. Trail* [1994] 2 F.C.R. 1261; *R. v. Lambeth L.B.C., ex p. Walters* [1994] 2 F.C.R. 336 (both decisions of Sir Louis Blom-Cooper Q.C.); but see *R. v. Bristol C.C., ex p. Bailey* (1995) 27 H.L.R. 307 (local authority subcommittee determining appeal against authority's refusal to award renovation grant not required to give reasons). See also, in the housing context, *R. v. Camden L.B.C., ex p. Adair* (1997) 29 H.L.R. 236 (nature of duty to give reasons under section 64 of the Housing Act 1985 for decision that applicant not in priority need); *R. v. Kensington and Chelsea R.L.B.C., ex p. Campbell* (1996) 28 H.L.R. 160; *R. v. Lambeth L.B.C. Housing Benefit Review Board, ex p. Harrington, The Times,* December 20, 1996 (duty to supply material facts and reasoning); *R. v. Housing Benefit Review Board of South Tyneside M.B.C., ex p. Tooley* [1996] C.O.D. 143.

[10] *R. v. Universities Funding Council, ex p. Institute of Dental Surgery* (above, n. 4), at 258. A host of recent examples can now be given of circumstances where reasons are

The standard of reasons required

It is clear that the reasons given must be intelligible and must **8–049**
adequately meet the substance of the arguments advanced.[11] However,
it is still difficult to state precisely the standard of reasoning the court
will demand. Much depends upon the particular circumstances and
the statutory context in which the duty to give reasons arises. The
courts have not attempted to define a uniform standard or threshold
which the reasons must satisfy. For example, it may be unrealistic to
require a tribunal faced with conflicting evidence on a matter that is
essentially one of opinion, to state much more than that on the basis
of what it has heard and of its own expertise it prefers one view to
the other or that it finds neither wholly satisfactory and therefore
adopts its own.[12] On the other hand, the reasons must generally state
the tribunal's material findings of fact (and, if the facts were disputed

---

required; see, for example, *R. v. Mayor, Commonality and Citizens of the City of London, ex p. Matson* (1996) 8 Admin. L.R. 49 (Court of Aldermen, in relation to decision not to confirm election of Alderman following victory in ward vote); *R. v. Secretary of State for the Home Department, ex p. Erdogan (Resul)* [1995] Imm. A.R. 430 (Home Secretary's decision not to extend exceptional leave to remain); *R. v. Islington L.B.C., ex p. Rixon* [1997] E.L.R. 66 (Council's decision as to community care and educational for disabled person, where Council was departing from guidelines); *R. v. Criminal Injuries Compensation Board, ex p. Cook* [1996] 1 W.L.R. 1037, CA (reasons for refusal of compensation; considering a number of earlier CICB cases); *Secretary of State for Social Security v. Richards* [1996] C.O.D. 507 (Pensions Appeal Tribunal). See, however, *R. v. Secretary of State for the Home Department, ex p. Owalabi* [1995] Imm. A.R. 400 (immigration; no reasons required for refusal to exercise extra statutory discretion); *R. v. Solicitor-General, ex p. Taylor and Taylor* (1996) 8 Admin L.R. (no reasons required for decision not to institute contempt proceedings against newspaper editors (*obiter*); *R. v. General Medical Council, ex p. Salvi, The Times,* February 24, 1998 (no reasons required for GMC's refusal to re-register doctor on register of GPs).

[11] *Re Poyser and Mills' Arbitration* [1964] 2 Q.B. 467, 477–478 is the most frequently cited judicial articulation of the test of the adequacy of reasons; approved in *Westminster C.C. v. Great Portland Estates Plc.* [1985] A.C. 661, 673; *cf. Save Britain's Heritage v. Number One Poultry Ltd* [1991] 1 W.L.R. 153, 165. See also *Edwin H. Bradley & Sons Ltd v. Secretary of State for the Environment* (1982) 47 P. & C.R. 374, where the same standard was applied despite the subjective element in the minister's duty under the Town and Country Planning Act 1971, s. 9(8) to give such statement as he considers appropriate of the reasons for his decision. *Bolton M.B.C. v. Secretary of State for the Environment (No. 2)* [1995] 3 P.L.R. 37.

[12] See, *e.g. Metropolitan Property Holdings Ltd v. Laufer* (1975) 29 P. & C.R. 172; *Guppys (Bridport) Ltd v. Sandoe* (1975) 30 P. & C.R. 69 (rent assessment committees); *cf,* the more demanding standard in *French Kier Developments Ltd v. Secretary of State for the Environment* [1977] 1 All E.R. 296 (planning). Scottish courts may scrutinise rent tribunal's reasons more closely: see, *e.g. Albyn Properties Ltd v. Knox,* 1977 S.L.T. 41; and see Young and Watchman, 1978 S.L.T. 201.

at the hearing, their evidential support[13]), and meet the substance of the principal arguments that the tribunal was required to consider. In short, the reasons must show that the decision maker successfully came to grips with the main contentions advanced by the parties,[14] and must "tell the parties in broad terms why they lost or, as the case may be, won."[15]

8–050   In the area of planning law, a reason that simply stated the statutory ground of decision was found to be adequate when considered against the background of the arguments advanced at an inquiry and the inspector's report[16]; in general, the test of adequacy is less helpful in this context than the question of whether the applicant has been substantially prejudiced by the deficiency of the reasons.[17]

8–051   Some general guidance may be derived from a consideration of the purposes served by a duty to give reasons. Thus, reasons should be

---

[13] But see *R. v. Secretary of State for the Home Department, ex p. Swati* [1986] 1 W.L.R. 477 (passenger refused entry entitled only to be told the ground for refusal; statement of facts required only after notice of appeal is given).

[14] In addition to *Re Poyser*, above, n. 11, authority for the proposition in the text can be found, for example, in *R. v. Immigration Appeal Tribunal, ex p. Khan* [1983] Q.B. 790; *Knights Motors Ltd. v. Secretary of State for the Environment* [1984] J.P.L. 584; *R. v. Mental Health Tribunal, ex p. Pickering* [1986] 1 All E.R. 99. See also, *Bolton M.B.C.,* n. 11 above; *MIT Securities Ltd v. Secretary of State for the Environment* [1998] J.P.L. 138; (1998) 75 P. & C.R. 188, CA; *S v. Special Educational Needs Tribunal* [1995] 1 W.L.R. 1627, 1636; *R. v. Immigration Appeal Tribunal, ex p. Jebunisha Patel* [1996] Imm. A.R. 161, 167; *Arulandandam v. Secretary of State for the Home Department* [1996] Imm. A.R. 587, 592; *R. v. Secretary of State for Education, ex p. G* [1995] E.L.R. 58, 67; *R. v. Lancashire C.C., ex p. Maycock* (1995) 159 L.G. Rev. 201 ('standard letter' with individual variations sufficient in circumstances); *R. v. Islington L.B.C., ex p. Hinds* (1996) 28 H.L.R. 302; *R. v. Criminal Injuries Compensation Board, ex p. Cook* [1996] 1 W.L.R. 1037, 1043; *R. v. Secretary of State for Transport, ex p. Richmond-upon-Thames L.B.C.* [1996] 1 W.L.R. 1460, CA.

[15] *per* Lord Donaldson M.R. in *UCATT v. Brain* [1981] I.R.L.R. 224, 228 (reasons required of industrial tribunal); see further *Piggott Brothers & Co. Ltd v. Jackson* [1991] I.R.L.R. 309, 313; *ex p. Ross, The Times,* June 9, 1994, CA (prison governor giving reasons for transfer of disruptive prisoner did not need to give 'chapter and verse' of prisoner's conduct relied upon.

[16] *Elliott v. Southwark L.B.C.* [1976] 1 W.L.R. 499. See also *Hope v. Secretary of State for the Environment* (1975) 31 P. & C.R. 120 (no general rule that reasons for decisions in planning appeals decided by inspectors need always only be brief); *Bolton M.D.C. v. Secretary of State for the Environment. The Times,* May 25, 1995, HL (Secretary of State must state his reasons in sufficient detail to enable the reader to know what conclusion he had reached on the principal important controversial issues, but he did not have to refer to every material consideration). *Cf. Ellis v. Secretary of State for the Environment* (1974) 31 P. & C.R. 130; *Save Britain's Heritage v. Number One Poultry Ltd,* above, n. 11. (Secretary of State adequately demonstrated substantial acceptance of inspector's report by singling out landmark points in inspector's reasoning process).

[17] *Save Britain's Heritage v. Number One Poultry Ltd,* above, n.11. The House of Lords explicitly rejected the view that a court must first decide whether reasons given were adequate, and then assess whether the inadequacy could conceal a flaw in the decision-making process.

sufficiently detailed as to make quite clear to the parties—and especially the losing party—why the tribunal decided as it did, and to avoid the impression that the decision was based upon extraneous considerations, rather than the matters raised at the hearing.[18] Reasons must also enable the court to which an appeal lies to discharge its appellate function, and when this is limited to questions of law, it will only be necessary to explain the exercise of discretion and to set out the evidence for the findings of fact in enough detail to disclose that the tribunal has not acted unreasonably.[19] Some decisions (such as the refusal of planning permission by an inspector) should be accompanied by reasons that are sufficiently precise to permit the individual to make the modifications necessary to secure a favourable decision in the future, or (where a Secretary of State disagrees with an inspector) to enable an objector to know what, if any, impact the planning considerations taken into account in a grant of planning permission may have in relation to the determination of future applications.[20] On the other hand, courts should not scrutinise reasons with the analytical rigour employed on statutes or trust instruments,[21] and ought to forgive obvious mistakes that were unlikely to have misled anyone.[22] Brevity is an administrative virtue, and elliptical reasons may be perfectly comprehensible when considered against the background of the arguments at the hearing.[23]

---

[18] See, *e.g. R. v. Mental Health Review Tribunal, ex p. Clatworthy* [1985] 3 All E.R. 699.

[19] See *Varndell v. Kearney & Trecker Marwin Ltd* [1983] I.C.R. 683, 693–694, criticising the possibly more stringent test propounded in *Alexander Machinery (Dudley) Ltd v. Crabtree* [1974] I.C.R. 120, 122; *cf. Thameside M.B.C. v. Secretary of State for the Environment* [1984] J.P.L. 180, where the court may have set a high standard to ensure that a peripheral consideration in the determination of a planning appeal had not been given undue importance. And see *R. v. Registrar of Friendly Societies*, above, n. 81.

[20] *Save Britain's Heritage*, above, n.11 at 167. A mental health review tribunal should give sufficiently precise reasons to enable patients and medical advisors to cover the matters on a renewed application.

[21] *Seddon Properties Ltd v. Secretary of State for the Environment* (1978) 42 P. & C.R. 26; *UCATT v. Brain* [1981] I.R.L.R. 224, 228.

[22] *Elmbridge B.C. v. Secretary of State for the Environment* (1980) 39 P. & C.R. 543, 547–548.

[23] See *Elliot v. Southwark L.B.C.* [1976] 1 W.L.R. 499; *R. v. Mental Health Tribunal, ex p. Pickering* [1986] 1 All E.R. 99; and see *Great Portland Estates plc v. Westminster City Council* [1985] A.C. 661, 673. The courts have recognised that the decision letters of inspectors are generally more succinct than the report and recommendations by inspectors together with letter of decision from the Secretary of State in non-devolved appeals. Nonetheless, in devolved decisions inspectors are held to much the same standard; see *Hope v. Secretary of State for the Environment* (1975) 31 P. & C.R. 120; *cf. Ellis v. Secretary of State for the Environment* (1974) 31 P. & C.R. 130. See also *Hatfield Construction Ltd v. Secretary of State for the Environment* [1983] J.P.L. 605. And see A. Barker and M. Couper, (1983) 6 *Urban Law and Policy* 363, 454–455, where the increase in court challenges to inspectors' decisions in the early 1980s is attributed to deficiencies in inspectors' skills in writing decision letters.

8–052   However, whilst concern for the quality of administrative justice does not require that all tribunals in all circumstances comply with some universally applicable standard, it is, nonetheless, essential that the courts do not allow the duty to give reasons to atrophy. In principle a remedy ought to lie for failure to give reasons, [24] although whether such an order would be made when the court is not satisfied that substantial prejudice has been caused to the applicant is more dubious.[25] Where reasons are given, they should be adequate and intelligible.[26]

8–053   Whatever standards are applied by judges to the adequacy of reasons given under a duty, it seems likely that reasons given voluntarily—where there is no duty—will be reviewed in accordance with the same standards as are applied to compulsory reasons.[27] It is no answer to an attack on the reasons for a decision on the grounds that they disclose a failure to take into account a relevant consideration or that an irrelevant consideration was taken into account or an error of law was made, that there is no requirements to give reasons. The unlawfulness in such a case lies not in the failure to give proper reasons, but in the unlawful nature of the decision, reasoning, or failure to reason, thereby disclosed.[28] On applications for

---

[24] On an appeal from a decision on a question of law the courts may well have an inherent jurisdiction to direct the Minister or tribunal to give adequate reasons although no formal application for mandamus has been made; see *Iveagh (Earl) v. Minister of Housing and Local Government* [1964] 1 Q.B. 395, 410. Contrast *Ex p. Woodhouse, The Times*, June 18, 1960; [1960] C.L.Y. 140, where inadequate reasons were given but leave to apply for mandamus for a fuller statement was refused.

[25] *R. v. Liverpool C.C., ex p. Liverpool Taxi Fleet Operators' Association* [1975] 1 W.L.R. 701, 706, but cf. *Preston B.C. v. Secretary of State for the Enviroment* [1978] J.P.L. 548 (omission of significant part of reasoning normally prejudicial); *Save Britain's Heritage*, above, n. 11. See further, para. 8–055. outside the planning field, however (where the requirement to demonstrate substantial prejudice is required by statute), the courts will not readily conclude that an applicant is not prejudiced by an inadequately reasoned decision. The test may be whether any other conclusion than that reached was realistically possible: *ex p. Murray*, n. 70, above, or whether it is 'obvious' that there is no injustice (*R. v. Winchester Crown Court, ex p. Morris* [1996] C.O.D. 104).

[26] For a discussion of the 'irrationality' of inadequate or incomprehensible reasons, see Chap. 12, below, paras 12-018–12-023.

[27] See *Elmbridge B.C. v. Secretary of State for the Environment* (1980) 39 P. misdirection on the evidence'); *Westminster C.C. v. Secretary of State for the Enviroment* [1984] J.P.L. 27, 29–30; see also *Grenfell-Baines v. Secretary of State for the Enviroment* [1985] J.P.L. 256. See however, *Kentucky Fried Chicken Pty Ltd v. Gantidis* (1979) 140 C.L.R. 675 In *R. v. Secretary of State for Transport, ex p. Richmond-upon-Thames L.B.C.*, the Court of Appeal ([1996] 1 W.L.R. 1460) did not rely upon the suggestion of Jowitt J. at first instance ([1996] 1 W.L.R. 1005) that there was no duty to give reasons in respect of a voluntary consulation.

[28] See, *e.g. R. v. Criminal Injuries Compensation Board v. Gambles*, [1994] P.I.Q.R. 314 (CICB's reasons contained a defect such that the decision could not stand, in failing to establish or disclose a rational and proportionate nexus between the conduct of the

judicial review it is the practice of government departments and public bodies to explain their reasons for their actions irrespective of any legal obligation to do so, where the outcome of the applications will depend on these reasons. As Lord Donaldson M.R. has said, judicial review "is a process which fails to be considered with all the cards face upwards on the table and the vast majority of the cards start in the authority's hands".[29] But in those cases where it is only because of the demands of natural justice or fairness that reasons are given, it may be that a lower standard applies; reasons may be as brief as a few sentences if that is enough to convey the substance of the decision.[30]

The implications which can be drawn from a failure to provide reasons

Where an applicant seeks to impugn a decision of an administrative authority other than by claiming non-compliance with a duty to give reasons—for example by challenging the legality or rationality of the decision—a failure by that authority to offer any answer to the allegations may justify an inference that its reasons were bad in law or that it had exercised its powers unlawfully. However, there is a conflict of authorities at the highest level as to the strength of the evidence of "collateral" unlawfulness which the applicant must adduce in order to benefit from the inference of unlawfulness if no justification of the decision is given. In *Padfield v. Minister of Agriculture, Fisheries and Food*, where the challenge was to the purpose to which the Minister had applied the regulations in question, the House of Lords suggested that if a prima facie case of unlawfulness was established by the applicant, then in the absence of reasons the court could infer that the power was exercised outside of the legislative purpose.[31] However, a more restrictive approach was adopted in *R. v. Secretary of State for Trade and Industry, ex p. Lonrho*, where, upon a challenge for irrationality, it was held that the absence of reasons could provide no support for the suggested irrationality of the decision unless, "if all other known facts and the circumstances appear to point overwhelmingly in favour of a different decision, the decision maker cannot complain if the court draws the inference that he has had no rational reason for his

8–054

---

applicant and the decision not to offer him even a discounted award). But see now *R. v. Criminal Injuries Compensation Board, ex p. Cook* [1996] 1 W.L.R. 1037, CA.

[29] *R. v. Lancashire C.C., ex p. Huddleston* [1986] 2 All E.R. 941.

[30] *R. v. Civil Service Appeal Board, ex p. Cunningham*, above, n. 2.

[31] [1968] A.C. 997, 1053, 1061, 1032–1033, 1049, *per* Lords Pearce, Upjohn, Reid and Hodson. See also dicta in *R. v. Brixton Prison Governor, ex p. Soblen* [1963] 2 Q.B. 243, 302, 307–308 *per* Lord Denning M.R. and Donovar L.J.

decision".[32] Although there is some support for the restrictive *Lonrho* test, at least where an authority has a specific exemption from a statutory duty to give reasons, (in which case the courts ought not to force the authority to choose between waiving the exemption and risking an adverse inference[33]) in general, recent authority has favoured the *Padfield* approach, even in cases where the ground of review is irrationality (as in *Lonrho*) rather than illegality. Thus where a local authority made a very meagre disclosure of reasons in response to an application for judicial review of a decision not to award a student grant, the Court of Appeal suggested that if the applicant could merely show that the facts were sufficient to obtain leave to apply for judicial review then, even though there was no obligation on the decision-maker to give reasons to the applicant, the authority would be under a duty to make full and fair disclosure to the court.[34] And where the Civil Service Appeal Board had awarded an inexplicably low sum in compensation for unfair dismissal, the failure of the Board to provide reasons to the court to dispel the "arguable" case of the applicant led the court to presume that the prima facie irrational decision was in fact irrational.[35] The *Padfield* approach can

---

[32] [1989] 1 W.L.R. 525, at 539. See also *Eagil Trust Co. Ltd v. Piggott-Brown* [1985] 3 All E.R. 119 (tribunal presumed to have acted properly when court can see how a point could have been answered, despite failure of reasons to deal with it expressly).

[33] *R. v. Secretary of State for Social Services, ex p. Connolly* [1986] 1 W.L.R. 421, CA. (Since social security commissioners have been specifically exempted by art. 2 of the Tribunals and Inquiries (Social Security Commissioners) Order 1980 from the general requirement under s.12(1) of the Tribunals and Inquiries Act 1971 to give reasons when refusing leave to appeal from a determination of the attendance allowance board, no adverse inference should be drawn from a failure to give reasons, and the court ought not to confront the commissioners with the embarrassing choice of either complying with the court's wishes and thus waiving their statutory exemption or declining to comply and thus running the risk of apparent discourtesy to the court and of adverse inferences being drawn, *per* Slade L.J.) *Cf. Coombs*, below, n. 36.

[34] *R. v. Lancashire C.C., ex p. Huddleston* [1986] 2 All E.R. 941. The court did not on the facts infer that the authority had erred in exercising its discretion or that it had acted irrationally. Parker L.J. and Sir George Waller did not share Lord Donaldson's unease about the lack of disclosure in the case, but 'I do not understand them to have disagreed with the principle' (*per* Lord Donaldson M.R. in *Cunningham*, above, n. 2). Compare *New Zealand Fishing Industry Assn. v. Minister of Agriculture and Fisheries* [1988] 1 N.Z.L.R. 544, CA (Minister's failure to file affidavit giving reasons for decision could serve to strengthen misgivings as to lawfulness of action).

[35] *Cunningham*, above, n.2. See also *R. v. Criminal Injuries Compensation Board, ex p. Cummins* [1992] C.O.D. 297 (although the CICB is not under statutory duty to give reasons, failure to show basis of fact on which it relied in making award to victim of crime rendered the award perverse); *R. v. Secretary of State for the Home Department, ex p. Sinclair* [1992] Imm. A.R. 293 (decision of Home Secretary to sign extradition warrant *Wednesbury* unreasonable); *R. v. Secretary of State for Education, ex p. Standish, The Times*, November 15, 1993 (ground upon which teacher debarred from his employment was not identified by the Secretary of State by reasons or by his

also be supported by reference to more general principles of the law of evidence. As Lord Lowry has pointed out, in another case concerning a challenge for irrationality in the absence of justification by the decision-maker:

"In our legal system generally, the silence of one party in face of the other party's evidence may convert that evidence into proof in relation to matters which are, or are likely to be, within the knowledge of the silent party and about which that party could be expected to give evidence. Thus, depending on the circumstances, a prima facie case may become a strong or even an overwhelming case."[36]

It should be noted, however, that in the absence of reasons it will often be difficult to establish a prima facie case that a wide discretionary power has been improperly exercised,[37] and thus an applicant will not be able to obtain leave and thereby pressure the decision maker to justify the decision to the court. The readiness of the courts to infer unlawfulness is therefore no substitute for a duty on public bodies to give reasons for their decisions to affected individuals. **8–055**

Conclusion

The courts have recently developed the principle that inherent in the duty to act with procedural fairness there is in some situations a limited implied obligation on administrative bodies to give reasoned decisions. It may be that now that the courts are free of the former **8–056**

---

affidavit, and hence the decision quashed for irrationality); *cf. R. v. Criminal Injuries Compensation Board, ex p. Gambles,* above, (reasoning which omitted one important step was defective and hence decision must be quashed).

[36] *R. v. Inland Revenue Commissioners, ex p. TC Coombs & Co.* [1991] 2 A.C. 283, 300. In fact it was held that the sparseness of evidence provided by the Revenue to justify a notice under s. 20(3) of the Taxes Management Act 1970 compelling the disclosure of documents should not lead to the conclusion that the Revenue had acted irrationally; however, it is suggested that the decision turned on special circumstances which justified the failure to provide reasons: the fact that the notice had been scrutinised by a Commissioner and hence the presumption of regularity *omnia praesumuntur rite et solenniter esse acta donec probelur in contrarium* applied; the fact that there was a general duty of confidentiality on the Revenue; and that on the facts there had been an express promise of anonymity and confidentiality.

[37] See, *e.g. Cannock Chase D.C. v. Kelly* [1978] 1 W.L.R. 1. *Cf. Secretary of State for Employment v. ASLEF (No. 2)* [1972] 2 Q.B. 455. See also *British Airways Board v. Laker Airways Ltd,* above, at p.432 (*ultra vires* difficult to establish in decision concerning international relations).

constraints of natural justice, they are prepared to look beyond the model of judicial-type decision-making (where the duty to give reasons does not always exist) in developing the requirements of fairness.

8–057 Legislation may be required before we are likely to see a general legal obligation on administrators to give reasons for their decisions. Nonetheless, both administrators and the courts are recognising in an ever growing number of situations that the requirements of good administration require reasons to be given (at least on request) and that in their absence injustice can result. As this appreciation increases it can be expected that there will be a progressive readiness on the part of the courts, in particular situations, to find inherent in the duty to act with procedural fairness an implied obligation that, at least on request, an administrative body should give reasons for its decisions.

8–058 The courts having developed a preference for the use of the term "fairness" to that of "natural justice" will now invariably infer a requirement of fairness in the decision-making process, in the absence of a clear contrary intent manifest in the relevant statutory or other framework. It is as part of that requirement of fairness that the obligation to give reasons is being extended by the courts pragmatically from one situation to another. At the time when new administrative processes are introduced they are likely to incorporate the same obligation.[38] In this way the absence of a general requirement should in time become progressively less important.

---

[38] There is anecdotal evidence from Australia that the existence of a statutory right to require reasons is increasingly causing administrators to provide reasons at the time the decision is made. For a recommendation that the requirement for reasons under the Administrative Decisions (Judicial Review) Act 1977 be extended, so as to be roughly co-extensive with decisions to which the Act applies, see Administrative Review Council, *Review of the Administrative Decision (Judicial Review) Act; Statements of Reasons for Decisions*, Report No. 33.

CHAPTER 9

PROCEDURAL FAIRNESS: EXCEPTIONS

We have seen in Chapter 7 that decision makers performing public **9–001** functions are always required to perform those functions fairly, where the decision may adversely affect a person's rights or interests or where a person has a legitimate expectation of fair treatment. Chapter 8 examined, in a variety of different circumstances, the content of that requirement. There are, however, in addition, situations where, although the requirements of procedural fairness are prima facie applicable, the decision-maker may be exempt from all or some of the procedural forms that would otherwise be required. This Chapter considers these exceptions. They should be distinguished from decisions which have been held to offend against procedural fairness but which are not set aside by the courts which refuse a remedy in the exercise of their discretion. The exercise of discretion by the courts in this way is considered in Chapter 15 below.

Express statutory exclusion of a fair hearing

Parliament may, by the use of apt but clear words, expressly dispense **9–002** with the need for notice to be given of a proposed decision, or for a hearing prior to the decision, where such notice or hearing would otherwise be required.[1] A statute may also permit the exercise of powers, *ex parte*.[2] In the interests of administrative efficiency and expedition the requirements of fairness have been excluded by statute which, for example, enables decision makers to refuse a hearing to an

---

[1] See discussion in Chap. 7 at paras 7-013–7-020 and Dean J. in *Haoucher v. Minister for Immigration and Ethnic Affairs* (1990) 169 C.L.R. 648.

[2] See, *e.g. Cheetham v. Mayor of Manchester* (1875) L.R. 10 C.P. 249; Town and Country Planning Act 1990, ss. 62–70.

interested party[3] or to decline to entertain particular kinds of representations[4] and objections.[5]

9–003   Subordinate legislation purporting to exclude a hearing should, however, be strictly construed.[6] Indeed, even when a discretion to hold a hearing or conduct an inquiry is conferred by a statute, a refusal to exercise it may constitute a denial of natural justice if fairness plainly demands that a hearing be held.[7] And an express statutory power to proceed without a hearing may not exclude the right to make informal or written representations.[8] Similarly, an express statutory provision excluding a duty to give reasons has been held not to exclude a duty to disclose the substance of the case so that an applicant for citizenship could make representation.[9]

Where the legislation expressly requires notice and hearing for certain purposes but imposes no procedural requirement for other purposes

9–004   We have considered above the circumstances in which the requirements of procedural fairness may be invoked to supplement statutory procedures. The obverse circumstances can exist and a

---

[3] Town and Country Planning Act 1990, s. 35B(4): No person shall have the right to be heard at an examination in public. Statutory rules of procedure have not been made for the examination in public of structure plans, but a non-statutory Code of Practice has been issued by the Department of the Environment. See Annex to Planning Policy Guidance, n.12. See also Dunlop [1976] J.P.L. 8, 75; Malcolm Grant, *Urban Planning Law,* (1982) p.99 *et seq.*

[4] See *Re Berkhamsted Grammer School* [1908] 2 Ch. 25; and for a more equivocal formula which was held to exclude any duty to observe the rule, *Patterson v. District Commissioner for Accra* [1948] A.C. 341. Contrast *R. v. British Columbia Pollution Control Board* (1967) 61 D.L.R. (2d) 221 (objector had no right to be "heard", but his right to lodge objections imposed certain implied procedural duties on the deciding body).

[5] Highways Act 1980, s.258 (objections to compulsory purchase order where objections based on urging alternative route).

[6] *R. v. Housing Appeal Tribunal* [1920] 3 K.B. 334, 342, 343, 346. See also *R. v. Local Government Board* [1911] 2 I.R. 331, 342–343; *Tauhara Properties Ltd v. Mercantile Developments Ltd* [1974] 1 N.Z.L.R. 584, 590, *cf.* decisions in which procedural rules contained in regulations have been held directory only in the absence of a specific statutory power to impose formal requirements by regulation: *Francis Jackson Developments Ltd v. Hall* [1951] 2 K.B. 488; *R. v. Devon and Cornwall Rent Tribunal, ex p. West* (1975) 29 P. & C.R. 316.

[7] *Fraser v. State Services Commission* [1984] 1 N.Z.L.R. 116, 122, 1225; *cf. Binney v. Secretary of State for the Environment* [1984] J.P.L. 871.

[8] See *Hundal v. Superintendent of Motor Vehicles* (1985) 20 D.L.R. (4th) 592; *cf. Nicholson v. Haldimand-Norfolk Regional Board of Commissioners of Police* [1979] 1 S.C.R. 311 (implied exclusion of a formal oral hearing). See generally Chap. 7 above, paras 7-013–7-020.

[9] *R. v. Secretary of State for the Home Department, ex p. Fayed* [1998] W.L.R. 763.

statutory procedural framework may be held impliedly to exclude the more extensive protection provided by common law means of application of the maxim *expressio unius est exclusio alterius.*[10]

Where disclosure of information would be prejudicial to the public interest

In the past English courts readily accepted the argument that to require Ministers to reveal to interested parties materials prepared or obtained in the course of departmental duties might unduly interfere with the administrative process by destroying the anonymity of the civil service, discouraging frank comment in official reports and undermining the principle of ministerial responsibility to Parliament.[11] In housing and town planning cases, the refusal of the courts to require the disclosure of inspectors' reports on inquiries and other relevant materials, even where the Minister's functions were recognised as including a judicial element, reduced but did not eliminate the area in which the duties of procedural fairness operated.[12]

9–005

But principles of fairness may still be modified, by legislation or judicial decision, for the protection of particular facets of the public interest—*e.g.* the maintenance of secrecy about aspects of national policy[13] or the sources of information leading to the detection of crime

9–006

---

[10] A number of recent decisions have sought to distinguish those cases where the omission of a procedural safeguard from a statutory framework represents a settled legislative intention that the procedural safeguard should be excluded, from the case of a 'mere omission' which may be filled by the courts: see, *e.g. R. v. Secretary of State for the Home Department, ex p. Abdi* [1996] 1 W.L.R. 298; *R. v. Secretary of State for Education and Employment, ex p. M* [1996] E.L.R. 162; *R. v. Secretary of State for Wales, ex p. Emery* [1996] 4 All E.R. 1; and see further, paras 7–013 to 7–020, above.

[11] See esp. the *Arlidge* case [1915] A.C. 120. And see *Laffer v. Gillen* [1927] A.C. 886, 895–896.

[12] See above, Chap. 6

[13] *Hutton v. Att.-Gen.* [1927] 1 Ch. 427, 439 (defence policy); *R. v. Home Secretary, ex p. Hosenball* [1977] 1 W.L.R. 766 (intelligence information); *Council of Civil Service Unions v. Minister for the Civil Service* [1985] A.C. 374; *R. v. Secretary of State for the Home Office, ex p. Stitt, The Times,* February 3, 1987, DC (Secretary of State did not have to give reasons for his conclusion that a person was 'concerned in the commission, preparation, or instigation of acts of terrorism' where there was bone fide evidence that security was involved, and the court would not examine the strength of that justification), and see *R. v. Secretary of State for the Home Department, ex p. H, The Times,* August 5, 1987, DC; *R. v. Director, Government Communications Headquarters, ex p. Hodges, The Times,* July 26, 1988, DC (question of whether an individual's positive vetting clearance should be removed was a matter to be decided with reference to national security considerations and as such could not be examined by the courts); *R.*

or other wrongdoing[14] or other information supplied in confidence for the purposes of government,[15] or the discharge of certain public functions.[16] In general, however, the climate of opinion has changed; the administrative process has become less opaque.[17]

9–007 The conception that secrecy may be in the public interest has not been confined to matters of administration. Where a bishop refused to agree to a proposed presentation to a living, and the patron, who appealed to the archbishop, was denied access to certain letters affecting the issue, the court declined to quash the proceedings, on the ground that the exercise of these powers might "require the nicest tact and discretion and involve the consideration of matters the publication of which would be of no use to anybody and might do an infinity of

---

v. Home Secretary, ex p. Cheblak [1991] 1 W.L.R. 890 (see further below); *R. v. Secretary of State for the Home Department, ex p. Chahal* [1995] 1 W.L.R. 526; (1997) 23 E.H.R.R. 413 (*sub nom. Chahal v. United Kingdom*) (European Court of Human Rights found violations of Art. 13 (read with Art. 3) and Art. 5(4) of the Convention).

[14] *R. v. Arndel* (1906) 2 C.L.R. 557, 575–577, 582, See also *Laffer v. Gillen* [1927] A.C. 886; *R. v. Gaming Board for Great Britain, ex p. Benaim and Khaida* [1970] 2 Q.B. 417; *R. v. Lewes JJ., ex p. Home Secretary* [1973] A.C. 388 (names of informants, details of information supplied to police and content of police reports in respect of applicants for gaming club consents). But see the House of Lords decision in *R. v. Chief Constable of the West Midland Police, ex p. Wiley* [1995] 1 A.C. 274 (no justification for imposing a general class public interest immunity on all documents generated by police complaints procedure).

[15] *Collymore v. Att.-Gen.* [1970] A.C. 538 (confidential information about industrial disputes and relations): *Crompton (Alfred) Amusement Machines Ltd v. Customs and Excise Commissioners (No. 2)* [1974] A.C. 405; *cf.* however, *Norwich Pharmacal Co. v. Customs and Excise Commissioners* [1974] A.C. 133 (confidential information supplied by traders to commissioners making inquiries). Confidential particulars relating to an informant's commercial or financial affairs supplied in connection with air transport licences must normally be withheld by the Civil Aviation Authority: Civil Aviation Act 1982, ss. 23 and 64–72. See also *R. v Teachers Tribunal, ex p. Colvin* [1974] V.R. 905 (references written in confidence about candidates for promotion); *R. v. Board of Visitors of Wandsworth Prison, ex p. Raymond, The Times* June 17, 1987, DC (there are circumstances which could justify withholding a welfare report made on prisoner for disciplinary hearing, although normally to ensure that "justice... be seen to be done", it should be disclosed); *R. v. Secretary of State for Health, ex p. U.S. Tobacco Ltd* [1992] 1 Q.B. 353, 371, Taylor L.J. (disclosure of scientific advice given to Secretary of State by independent experts in relation to proposed ban on oral snuff).

[16] *cf. D. v. NSPCC* [1978] A.C. 171; *Science Research Council v. Nasse* [1980] A.C. 1028.

[17] *cf. e.g.* the Town & Country Planning (Inquiries Procedure) Rules 1974 (S.I. 1974 No. 419) r. 10(4), which allowed an inspector of a planning appeal "not to require or permit the giving or production of any evidence... which would be contrary to the public interest." This provision has been removed from the Rules. (See now S.I. 1992 No. 2038.) However, see Pt IV of Circular 84 issued by the Department of the Environment which exempts from consideration planning proposals of the Crown involving national security. See *R. v. Secretary of State for Defence, ex p. Camden L.B.C.* [1995] J.P.L. 403. And see McCoubrey "Security Planning Regulations and Defence Establishments" [1994] J.P.L. 1075.

harm by perhaps wrecking the peace of a parish for a generation." In [18]a child custody case the House of Lords refused disclosure of confidential reports made to the court by the Official Solicitor because their disclosure to the parents concerned might damage children whose welfare it was the paramount duty of the court to protect; common-law duties to abide by the rules of natural justice were not ends in themselves, and where they did not serve the ends of justice, they could not be allowed to "become the master instead of the servant of justice."[19]

Where a threat to national security, in particular, is given as the reason for denying or restricting an individual's entitlement to procedural fairness, the Domestic Courts have, as yet, been unwilling under the common law to intervene by examining the strength of that justification—still less by insisting upon procedural fairness in the face of such a justification. National security has been treated as "the exclusive responsibility of the executive"[20]; it is "par excellence a non-   **9–008**

---

[18] *R. v. Canterbury (Archbishop), ex p. Morant* [1944] K.B. 282, 292.

[19] *Re K (Infants)* [1965] A.C. 201 at 238, *per* Lord Devlin. See also *Re D (Infants)* [1970] 1 W.L.R. 599 (local authority case records on children under care); *Re P. A. (an Infant)* [1971] 1 W.L.R. 1530 (report to court on adoption issue), though *cf. Re W.L.W.* [1972] Ch. 456 (report on condition of mental patient); *R. v. Kent Police Authority, ex p. Godden* [1971] 2 Q.B. 662 (disclosure of medical report to be restricted to applicant's own doctor); *Re M* [1973] Q.B. 108; *Re B (A Minor)* [1975] Fam. 127 (report to court on adoption issue); *Re F (D) (A Minor)* (1977) 76 L.G.R. 133, 142–143; *R. v. Norfolk C.C., ex p. M* [1989] Q.B. 619 (entry of H on the Council's child abuse register was judicially reviewable and could be struck down for breach of natural justice or fairness, although the courts would be reluctant to do so, given the confidential nature of the list, and the paramountcy of the child's interests); approved *R. v. Harrow L.B.C. ex p. D.* [1990] Fam. 133; [1991] 1 W.L.R. 395. See also *H. v. H.* [1974] 1 W.L.R. 595 (information supplied to judge in confidence by a child during custody proceedings); but see *B v. W* [1979] 1 W.L.R. 1041 (breach of natural justice not to disclose social workers report used by court to assess character of party in wardship proceedings).

[20] *per* Lord Donaldson M.R. in *R. v. Home Secretary, ex p. Cheblak* [1991] 1 W.L.R. 890, 902. See also *R. v. Secretary of State for the Home Department ex p. Mr and Mrs B., The Independent,* January 29, 1991 (deportation); *R. v. Secretary of State for the Home Department ex p. Al-Harbi* (Otton J., March 21, 1991) (asylum); *Hussain v. Secretary of State for the Home Department* [1993] Imm. A.R. 353, CA (asylum claim); *Balfour v. Foreign and Commonwealth Office* [1994] 1 W.L.R. 681, 688; *R. v. Secretary of State for the Home Department ex p. Gallagher, The Times,* [1995] E.C.R. I–4253, CA (exclusion order); *R. v. Secretary of State for the Home Department, ex p. Adams* [1995] All E.R. (EC) 177 (and see now *The Independent,* April 28, 1995 [1995] 3 C.M.L.R. 476); *R. v. Secretary of State for the Home Department ex p. McQuillan* [1995] 4 All E.R. 400, (Sedley J.) (exclusion order). But see now the decision of the European Court of Human Rights in *Chahal v. United Kingdom* (1997) 23 E.H.R.R. 413, which calls into question the common law position (see below).

In Australia national security has been less readily employed as a basis for excluding procedural fairness. See Hanks, 'National Security—A Political Concept' (1988) 14 Monash Univ. L.Rev. 114. See Lustgarten and Leigh, *In From the Cold;*

justiciable question"[21]—unless "the minister responsible has acted otherwise than in good faith or has in any way overstepped the limitations upon his authority which are imposed by the law".[22] As Lane L.J. has put it, in the context of a challenge to a deportation order:

> "There are occasions, though they are rare, when what are more generally the rights of an individual must be subordinated to the protection of the realm...In ordinary circumstances common fairness—you can call it natural justice if you wish—would demand that he be given particulars of the charge against him; that he is given the names of the witnesses who are prepared to testify against him and, indeed, probably the nature of the evidence which those witnesses are preprared to give...But there are counter-balancing factors...The alien certainly has inadequate information upon which to prepare or direct his defence to the various charges which are made against him, and the only way that could be remedied would be to disclose information to him which might probably have an adverse effect on the national security. The choice is regrettably clear: the alien must suffer, if suffering there be, and this is so on whichever basis of argument one choses."[23]

9–009   Nevertheless, the Courts have more recently emphasised that an invocation of national security does not lead to a complete judicial abdication of inquiry; it is not entirely a non-justiciable question. "If the decision is successfully challenged, on the ground that it has been reached by a process which is unfair, then the Government is under an obligation to produce evidence that the decision was in fact based

---

National Security and Parliamentary Democracy (1994), for an excellent account of national security in a number of countries.

[21] *per* Lord Diplock, in *Council of Civil Service Unions, ex p. Minister for the Civil Service* [1985] A.C. 374, 412. For New Zealand law see *Daganyasi v. Minister of Immigration* [1980] 2 N.Z.L.R. 130. However in *Petrocorp Exploration Ltd v. Butcher* [1991] 1 N.Z.L.R. 1 it was held that, although the Minister's claim to sole judge of the national interest would normally not be justiciable, the courts were entitled to decide whether his actions were "consistent with his commercial obligations and the elementary principles of fair play" *per* Cooke P.

[22] *per* Lord Donaldson M.R. in *R. v. Home Secretary, ex p. Cheblak*, above, n.20 at 907; *cf.* Lustgarten & Leigh (above, n.20) at p. 187.

[23] *R. v. Secretary of State for Home Affairs, ex p. Hosenball* [1977] 1 W.L.R. 766, 783–4. The Immigration Rules require the Secretary of State to take into account certain specified considerations before making a deportation order; see Statement of Changes in Immigration Rules (laid before Parliament on May 23, 1994) at para. 364.

on grounds of national security".[24] But such a requirement may be easily satisfied. The courts do not require evidence that the deposed risk to national security is real; they are in practice satisfied with evidence which, while more than "mere assertion", simply indicates in very broad terms the grounds upon which the Secretary of State considers that matters of national security have been raised.[25] Once this factual basis has been established, so that the Court is satisfied that the interest of national security is a relevant factor to be considered in the determination of the case, and was in fact so considered, then "the court will accept the opinion of the Crown or its responsible officer as to what is required to meet it, unless it is possible to show that the opinion was one which no reasonable minister advising the Crown could in the circumstances reasonably have held."[26]

Such a *Wednesbury* safeguard will usually be nugatory, since the court will *ex hypothesi* not have before it the evidence upon which the minister has come to his decision; it will accordingly be very difficult for the court to come to the conclusion that the minister's decision was not within the band of rational decisions.[27] It appears, however, that the courts are now prepared to require that the minister conducts a balancing exercise between on the one hand the requirements of national security and on the other the interests of the individual in the fairness of the decision,[28] or, particularly, in the protection of his

9–010

---

[24] *per* Lord Fraser, *Council of Civil Service Unions v. Minister for the Civil Service* [1985] 1 A.C. 374, 402 citing *The Zamora* [1916] 2 A.C. 77. In the words of Lord Roskill 'evidence, and not mere assertion, must be forthcoming', *ibid.*, at 421; *cf. per* Mann L.J. in *R. v. Secretary of State for the Home Department ex p. Mr B. and Mrs B.*, above, n. 20: 'Of course the Court requires more than mere assertion. Evidence is required'; *Balfour v. Foreign and Commonwealth Office* [1994] 1 W.L.R. 681, 688, *per* Russell L.J. See further *R. v. Ministry of Defence, ex p. Smith*, [1995] 4 All E.R. 427 where the Divisional Court rejected the argument that the policy of the armed forces of dismissing homosexuals from the services could be justified by reference to the danger to national security. That decision was affirmed by the Court of Appeal at [1996] Q.B. 517, where the argument from national security had *less prominence*.

[25] See, *e.g. Hussain*, above n. 20, at p. 357; *McQuillan*, [1995] 4 All E.R. 400,423; for even weaker formulations, see *Cheblak*, above and *Al-Harbi*, above. *Cf. R. v. Home Secretary ex p. Ruddock* [1987] 1 W.L.R. 1482, 1491–2, *per* Taylor L.J.

[26] *ibid.*, at 406, 412, 420, *per* Lords Scarman, Diplock and Roskill. In Israel it has been held that the right to be heard is not automatically excluded under emergency regulations which allow a military commander to demolish a house without judicial proceedings. See B. Bracha, 'Judicial Review of Security Powers in Israel: A New Policy of the Courts' (1991) 28 Stamford J. of Int. Law 39, 75–80. The fair hearing may however be excluded when 'urgent action is necessary to avoid serious consequences', *ibid.* at 77.

[27] See *per* Sedley J. in *McQuillan*, above, at 423.

[28] *per* Lord Fraser in *CCSU*, above n. 24, at p. 402.

fundamental rights, such as the right to life, to freedom,[29] or other rights protected by the European Convention on Human Rights.[30] It remains the case at present, however, that that balancing exercise is effectively unsupervised by the courts.[31] However, such an abstentionist stance by domestic courts may leave the United Kingdom in breach of its obligations under the European Convention. In *Chahal v. United Kingdom*,[32] the European Court of Human Rights held unanimously that the failure of the courts to carry out or supervise effectively a balancing test (weighing national security considerations) was a breach of Article 5(4), since Mr Chahal's deprivation of liberty had not been subject to any effective judicial control. The Court considered that it must be possible to employ techniques which both accommodated legitimate security concerns about the nature and sources of intelligence information and yet accorded the individual a substantial measure of procedural justice. The domestic case-law set out above must now be considered in the light of this more searching approach.

Where an obligation to give notice and opportunity to be heard would obstruct the taking of prompt action

Statutory relaxation of procedural propriety

9–011   Desirable though it may be to allow a hearing or an opportunity to make representations, or simply to give prior notice, before a decision is taken which interferes with a person's rights or interests, summary action may be alleged to be justifiable when an urgent need for

---

[29] *Chahal v. Secretary of State for the Home Department* [1995] 1 W.L.R. 526, declining to follow *NSH v. Secretary of State for the Home Department* [1988] Imm. A.R. 389; *ex p. McQuillan*, above.

[30] *Johnson v. Constable of the Royal Ulster Constabulary* [1986] 3 C.M.L.R. 240, 262 (decision of ECJ that provision of Northern Ireland Sex Discrimination Order requiring Tribunals to treat a national security certificate as conclusive evidence that conditions for derogating from the principle of equal treatment were fulfilled were contrary to the provision of effective judicial control laid down in Art. 6 of the Equal Treatment Directive; the Court relying upon principles of the European Convention on Human Rights).

[31] See, however, the suggestion in *ex p. McNeill* (Northern Ireland Court of Appeal, April 22, 1993, *per* Hutton L.C.J.) that the balancing exercise may be supervised or conducted by the courts (relying upon *Attorney General v. Leveller Magazine* [1979] A.C. 440); not followed in *McQuillan*, above.

[32] (1997) 23 E.H.R.R. 413.

protecting the interests of other persons arises.[33] For example, the purpose of giving the Executive powers to detain security suspects in wartime or grave emergency could be frustrated if the suspect were entitled to prior notice of its intentions.[34] The interests of public safety or public health have been made the justification for the summary interfences with property (or other) rights, as where an inspector from the Ministry of Agriculture destroys infected crops,[35] the abatement of a dangerous nuisance without notice in the exercise of common-law powers,[36] the prohibiting by administrative order of smoking in a theatre,[37] the cancellation or overturn of a residential care or nursing home's registration,[38] and the detaining or disposal by the Post Office of dangerous or obscene postal communication.[39] An authorised public officer may summarily suspend the licence of a public service vehicle or prohibit the driving of a goods vehicle which is dangerously

---

[33] See generally Chap. 7 above, para. 7–031. *Kioa v. West* (1985) 159 C.L.R. 550.

[34] In the English cases in time of war (see, *e.g. R. v. Halliday* [1917] A.C. 260; *Liversidge v. Anderson* [1942] A.C. 206) the applicability of the rules of procedural fairness were not in issue, but it was held that the functions of the Secretary of State were purely executive, and in Liversidge's case Lord Maugham observed *obiter* (at 221) that the Secretary of State was under no legal duty to give prior notice or opportunity to be heard. An advisory committee was set up by administrative action to review the case of detainees. In the Australian case of *Ex p. Walsh* (1942) 42 S.R. (N.S.W.) 125, 130 it was held that a similar internment power was not qualified by the rules of natural justice. On the application of natural justice to proceedings before an advisory committee in Northern Ireland, see (1972) 23 N.I.L.Q. 331; see now Northern Ireland (Emergency Provisions) Act 1978, Sched. 1 (not in force since its non-renewal after July 1980, under section 33 of the Act). Under the Prevention of Terrorism (Temporary Provisions) Act 1989, the Home Secretary may make an exclusion order prior to affording the affected person a hearing before an advisor appointed to hear any objection; for its compatibility with Art. 9(1) of E.C. Directive 64/221 (co-ordination of special measures concerning movement and residence of foreign nationals), see *R. v. Secretary of State for the Home Department, ex p. Gallagher* [1996] 1 C.M.L.R. 543 (ECJ): expulsion decision should not be taken before hearing save in cases of urgency. Summary action for the maintenance of public security or public order in normal times may also be permissible: see, *e.g.* the South African case, *Sachs v. Minister of the Interior* [1934] A.D. 11, 36, 38 (restriction of movement order). As to the entitlement to procedural fairness after summary action has been taken where national security considerations are in issue, see above, para. 9–011. In India the need for urgency has overidden the need for a fair hearing in cases, *e.g.* involving deportation or the impounding of a passport. See *Mareka Gandhi v. Union of India* A.I.R. [1978] S.C. 597. However, after the impounding of the passport in that case 'an opportunity of hearing, remedial in aim, should be given' *ibid.* 630. On the post-decisional hearing see below paras 9–019–9–023.

[35] Plant Health Act 1967, ss. 3, 4 (as amended).

[36] See *Lonsdale (Earl) v. Nelson* (1823) 2 B. & C. 302, 311–312: *Jones v. Williams* (1843) 11 M. & W., 766–767 (dicta).

[37] *R. v. Barry* (1949) 24 M.P.R. 290 (Can.).

[38] Registered Homes Act 1984, ss. 11, 30.

[39] Post Office Act 1953, ss. 8, 11 (as amended).

defective; there is a statutory procedure for review of the suspension.[40] Customs officials may also seize obscene works; they are forfeited after one month unless the owner lodges a notice of objection, in which case the question of forfeiture is determinable only in a judicial proceeding.[41] Food suspected of not complying with food safety requirements may be seized by an authorised officer of a food authority, but condemnation is a matter for a magistrate only; notice of the proceedings must be given and anyone liable to be prosecuted is entitled to be heard in these civil proceedings.[42] The owner of a building is not entitled to prior notice of its intended listing as being of architectural or historic interest.[43] Should he wish to alter the building, however, he is entitled to a hearing against a refusal of listed building consent.[44]

9–012   In some of these examples in which summary action needs to be taken without prior notice we can see illustrated a range of *ex post facto* safeguards provided by modern statute law. There are in fact remarkably few situations in which the enforcement powers of public authorities and administrative officers are exercisable without notice.[45] Some of the exceptional situations arise under the Public Health Acts. A local authority is empowered to examine and test sewers, drains and sanitary conveniences that it believes to be defective; to remedy

---

[40] Road Traffic Act 1988, ss. 69, 70, 72.

[41] Customs Consolidation Act 1876, s. 42; Customs and Excise Management Act 1979, s. 139, Sched. 3. See also. Obscene Publications Act 1959, s. 3(3).

[42] Food Safety Act 1990, s. 9. No appeal lies to the Crown Court, because the magistrate is not acting as a court (*R. v. Cornwall Q.S., ex p. Kerley* [1956] 1 W.L.R. 906). The denial of a right of appeal is obviously sensible, but *quaere* whether, as was stated *obiter* in that case (at 910, 911), the justices are acting in a purely administrative capacity. If they are, and the food is in fact fit for consumption, they might be liable for trespass. But it is thought that if necessary, they would be held to be acting judicially (*cf. R. v. Birmingham City JJ., ex p. Chris Foreign Foods (Wholesalers) Ltd* [1970] 1 W.L.R. 1428 (magistrate, though acting 'administratively' bound to 'act fairly': decision as to condemnation or quashed by certiorari)) and hence immune from civil liability in the absence of malice.
For a decision under a now repealed provision in which the *audi alteram partem* rule was held to be impliedly exluded for reasons of urgency in the condemnation and destruction of contaminated food, see *White v. Redfern* (1879) 5 QBD 15. But see *Errington v. Wilson, The Times,* June 2. 1995 (natural justice required and, in this case, denied for lack of opportunity to cross-examine).

[43] Planning (Listed Buildings and Conservation Areas) Act 1990 the Government rejected a recommendation that there should be such a right by The House of Commons Environment Select Committee in 1988 (*Observations on the first Report of the Environmental Committee in Session 1986 and 87*), H.C. 268 (1987–88) para. 2. However, informal notification of owners of listed building is now common practice.

[44] *ibid.* s. 20.

[45] See, *e.g.* the notices required for planning enforcement. Town and Country Planning Act 1990 s.172. See also the relatively recent 'Planning Contravention Notice', *ibid.* s. 171C.

stopped-up drains; to order the cleansing or destruction of filthy or verminous articles; and to remove to hospital an inmate of a common lodging house who is suffering from a notifiable disease giving rise to a serious risk of infection. Public health officers may destroy or deinfest verminous articles offered for sale.[46]

Even where a statutory power to give prior notice exists, legislation **9–013** may permit prior notice to be dispensed with if it is impracticable to give it, for example where direct action has to be taken to make a dangerous building safe.[47] Alternatively, powers of direct enforcement may become exercisable only by virtue of an order made by a magistrate upon an application made by a competent authority. In some of these cases the magistrate is expressly empowered to act *ex parte* if he deems it necessary—*e.g.* on applications for the removal of dead bodies from buildings in the interests of public health, for the removal of inmates of infected houses, for requiring persons to submit to medical examination in specified circumstances and for the detention in hospital of persons suffering from infectious diseases.[48] If the magistrate is not expressly empowered to act *ex parte* but no opportunity to be heard is expressly granted to persons affected, it is a question of construction and common sense whether such an opportunity ought to be implied.[49]

---

[46] Public Health (Control of Disease) Act 1984, s.41 (compare s.37); Public Health Act 1961, ss.17, 37. Other direct enforcement powers conferred by public health legislation are exercisable only when notice has been served on the persons affected—*e.g.* powers to pull down structures erected in contravention of building regulations, to cleanse, filthy and verminous premises, to require the vacation of these premises during deinfestation, to cleanse and disinfect premises and articles thereon in order to prevent the spread of infectious disease, and to destroy rodents which are overrunning premises: see the 1936 Act, ss. 15(1)(i)(b), 83: Public Health (Control of Disease) Act 1984, ss. 31–32; Public Health Act 1961, ss. 35, 36; Prevention of Damage by Pests Act 1949, s. 6.

[47] Building Act 1984, ss. 77, 78(1) and (2). The question whether it would have been more reasonable to apply to a magistrates' court for an order to be made against the owners can be determined in proceedings in which the recovery of expenses for the work executed is claimed (*ibid.*, s. 78(3) and (5)).

[48] Public Health (Control of Disease) Act 1984, ss. 48, 32, 35–36, 38. *Cf. dicta* in *R. v. Davey* [1899] 2 Q.B. 301, 305–306 on the implied right to act *ex parte* for reasons of urgency under earlier public health legislation.

[49] For decisions on the implied common-law right to be heard before justices before forfeiture of property, see *Gill v. Bright* (1871) 41 L.J.M.C. 22, *ex p. Francis* [1903] 1 K.B. 275; contrast *White v. Redfern* (1879) 5 QBD 15 (condemnation of food; but *cf.* n. 14 above), and *R. v. Davey* (above, n. 48). See also, *R. v. Havering JJ., ex p, Smith* [1974] 3 All E.R. 484 (service of notice upon occupiers of caravans required before justices made site clearance order, considerations of administrative inconvenience notwithstanding).

Judicial relaxation of procedural propriety for urgency

9–014   Urgency may warrant relaxing the requirements of fairness even where there is no statute or regulation by which this is expressly permitted.[50] Thus a local authority could, without any consultation, withdraw children from a special school after allegations of persistent cruelty and abuse without this involving any procedural impropriety. In such circumstances there exists an emergency in which the primary concern is as to the safety and welfare of the children.[51] The suspension without first affording an opportunity to be heard, of a Romanian Airline's flight permit, following the failure by five of its pilots of CAA examinations in aviation law, flight rules, and procedures, was not unfair where an immediate threat to air safety was apprehended.[52] Similarly where a self-regulatory organisation, the Life Assurance Unit Trust Regulatory Organisation, acted urgently with the object of protecting investors, it was not required to consider whether there was sufficient time to receive representations.[53] In general, whether the need for urgent action outweighs the importance of notifying or consulting an affected party depends on an assessment of the circumstances of each case on which opinions can differ.[54]

---

[50] *De Verteuil v. Knaggs* [1918] A.C. 557, 560–561. Thus a magistrate is under no obligation to heat a person other than the informant before issuing a search warrant: *R. v. Peterborough JJ., ex p. Hicks* [1977] 1 W.L.R. 1371. See for a broad statement, restricting the application of the rule in the interests of public health, *R. v. Davey* [1902] 2 Q.B. 301, 305–306.

[51] *R. v. Powys C. C., ex p. Horner* [1989] Fam. Law 320.

[52] *R. v. Secretary of State for Transport, ex p. Pegasus Holdings (London) Ltd* [1988] 1 W.L.R. 990. *Cf. Coutts v. Commonwealth* (1985) 59 A.L.R. 699 (no requirement in Australia where air force pilot compulsorily retired on medical grounds).

[53] *R. v. Life Assurance Unit Trust Regulatory Organisation, ex p. Ross* [1993] Q.B. 17, CA; see also *R. v. Birmingham City C.C., ex p. Ferrero Ltd* [1993] 1 All E.R. 530, CA. The rules of natural justice do not apply to the making a Notice of Intervention in a solicitor's practice on the ground of suspected dishonesty under the Solicitors Act 1974, so that there is no requirement to give particulars of the reasons for intervention in the Notice: *Giles v. Law Society* (1996) 8 Admin. L.R. 105, CA. However, the Act does afford a right of judicial consideration *ex post facto*.

[54] See, *e.g. Bishop v. Ontario Securities Commission* (1964) 44 D.L.R. (2d) 24; *R. v. Randolph* [1966] S.C.R. 260; *Venicoff's* case [1920] 3 K.B. 72, 79–80; *Gaiman v. National Association for Mental Health* [1971] Ch. 317, 336; *Furnell v. Whangarei High Schools Board* [1973] A.C. 660 (power to suspend teacher); *Amalgamated Investment and Property Co. Ltd v. John Walker and Sons Ltd* [1977] 1 W.L.R. 164, 174 (dicta that no notice is required before a building of architectural or historic importance is listed). But an *ex post facto* hearing may be required: see dicta in *Soblen's* case [1963] 2 Q.B. 243, 298, and *Schmidt's* case [1969] 2 Ch. 149, 170–171, 173–174. See further below, para. 9–025 *et seq.*

Where for other reasons it is impracticable to give prior notice or opportunity to be heard

We have seen that in the past the duty to act fairly did not normally **9–015** apply to decisions containing a substantial "policy" content or regarded as essentially "allocative".[55] In other jurisdictions, even after the demise of the old distinction between "judicial" and "administrative" decisions, the category of "legislative" decision has tended to survive.[56] As we have contended however,[57] "policy" or "legislative" decisions should not *ipso facto* be excused from the duty to act fairly. Indeed, in a number of cases that duty has been imposed in a policy setting,[58] although in others the content of the fair hearing may be relaxed.[59]

There may however, in a particular case, be good reasons why the **9–016** duty to act fairly should not apply where the decision involves policy formulation or rule making. The most convincing reason will be that the number of persons affected by a particular order, act or decision is so great as to make it manifestly impracticable for them all to be given an opportunity of being heard by the competent authority beforehand.[60] This is the reason why representations may not be required for the making of regulations of a legislative character.[61] But

---

[55] Chap. 7, para. 7–031 above.

[56] In Canada for example. See Le Dains J.'s definition in *Cardinal v. Director of Kent Institution* [1985] 2 S.C.R. 643.

[57] Chap. 7, para. 7–011 above.

[58] See, *e.g. R. v. Secretary of State for the Environment, ex p. Brent L.B.C.* [1982] Q.B. 593; *R. v. Secretary of State for Transport, ex. p. Greater London Council* [1986] Q.B. 556; *R. v. British Coal Corp. & Secretary of State for Trade & Industry, ex p. Vardy* [1993] I.C.R. 720, DC.

[59] *e.g.* in respect of the right to cross examination. See, *Bushell v. Secretary of State for the Environment* [1981] A.C. 75.

[60] *cf. Waitemata County v. Local Government Commission* [1964] N.Z.L.R. at 698–699. See also *Re Canadian Forest Products Ltd* (1960) 24 D.L.R. (2d) 753; *White v. Ryde Municipal Council* [1977] 2 N.S.W.L.R. 909, 921; *R. v. Secretary of State for Social Services, ex p. Child Poverty Action Group, The Times,* August 8, 1985, CA.

[61] See *Bates v. Lord Hailsham* [1972] 1 W.L.R. 1373; A similar case in Ireland is *Cassidy v. Minister for Industry & Commerce* [1978] I.R. 297 (no consultations with Vintners' association before making a statutory instrument fixing minimum prices for intoxicating liquor). Mason J. in *Kioa v. West* (1985) 159 C.L.R. 550 would exclude from the right to procedural fairness decisions having a quasi-legislative or 'policy' or 'political' character. But see *Bread Manufacturers of New South Wales v. Evans* (1981) 38 A.L.R. 93. In Canada the fact that a decision is contained in an instrument normally associated with legislative powers (*e.g.* a byelaw or regulation) is not determinative of the characterisation of the power as being exempt from a fair hearing. The legislative nature of a board's powers was however given as reason for keeping to a minimum the procedural content of an express statutory duty to conduct a hearing. See *Manitoba League of the Physically Handicapped Inc. v. Manitoba (Taxicab Board)* (1988) 56 D.L.R. (4th) 191.

a statute may impliedly require an opportunity to be given for representations to be made against local authority byelaws before they are confirmed by a Minister[62] and an Act can provide for notice and opportunity to be heard prior to statutory instruments being made.[63] We have noted above the contrast with the American experience, where extensive "rulemaking" procedurees are required for all subordinate law-making.[64] Another reason for excluding the fair hearing in such cases[65] may be that the decision maker is responsible to Parliament for the decision.

9–017   The large number of applicants competing for scarce resources may make it impracticable to offer each applicant a hearing. If, for example, there are 1,200 applicants for seventy places available in the Law Department of a university institution (or a corresponding ratio of applicants to available licences, permits or grants) it may be impossible to afford interviews (or hearings) to many of those who, from the particulars supplied with their written applications, appear sufficiently meritorious or suitable to warrant fuller personal consideration.[66] Criteria for selection should however be evolved and applied in an attempt to do justice as far as this is possible; but there will inevitably be persons who will reasonably feel aggrieved at having been denied an adequate opportunity of presenting their case. Where a hearing can be provided, considerations of administrative practicality may influence or determine the content of the procedure which is capable of being adopted.[67]

9–018   Even if the court finds that a breach of procedural fairness has occurred, administrative impracticability may still be relied upon as a reason for refusing a remedy in its discretion.[68] Courts should be unwilling to excuse a breach of procedural fairness merely upon the

---

[62] Local Government Act 1972, s. 236 (as amended).

[63] See Chap. 7, para. 7–032 above.

[64] *ibid.*

[65] See, *e.g. Essex C.C. v. Ministry of Housing & Local Government* [1967] 66 L.G.R. 23. *Cf. CREEDNZ v. Governor General* [1981] 1 N.Z.L.R. 172: *Kioa v. West* above, n. 61.

[66] See *Central Council for Education and Training in Social Work v. Edwards, The Times,* May 5, 1978, which supports the propositions contained in the text, but where a refusal to admit was declared invalid on the ground that the interview was conducted unfairly. See, in the context of licences, *McInnes v. Onslow Fane* [1978] 1 W.L.R. 1520, where Megarry VC's distinction between 'application' and 'revocation' cases may be explained as resting upon this basis; see further Chap. 7, paras 7–007–7010 above.

[67] See, *e.g. R. v. Birmingham C.C., ex p. Darshan Kaur,* [1991] C.O.D. 21, DC. (Lack of translator at public meeting not improper because it was administratively impossible to provide translators for every language spoken at the meeting.) *R. v. Secretary of State for Wales, ex p. Williams* [1996] C.O.D. 127 (Secretary of State, having consulted in relation to a proposal to close special schools, was not required to consult further in relation to representations of local authority made during consultation process; it was undesirable so to prolong the consultation process).

[68] See below, Chap. 15.

ground that to quash the decision would cause the decision maker administrative inconvenience: "even if chaos should result, still the law must be obeyed".[69] In *R. v. Sectretary of State for Social Services, ex p. Association of Metropolitan Authorities* (the *AMA* case)[70] Webster J. held that, although the Secretary of State had not complied with his statutory duty to consult, the housing benefit regulations under challenge should not be quashed, as delegated legislation is not normally revoked unless there are exceptional circumstances, and to revoke the existing regulations would result in confusion.[71] Fortunately, however, courts traditionally receive arguments based upon administrative impracticability with scepticism. Except where the difficulty caused to the decision maker is more than inconvenience, and approaches impracticability or where there is an overriding need for finality and certainty,[72] a remedy should not be refused solely upon this basis. Even if, contrary to Lord Atkin's dictum, convenience and justice are on speaking terms,[73] conversation between the two should be strictly limited.[74]

---

[69] *per* Lord Denning M.R. in *Bradbury v. Enfield L.B.C.* [1967] 1 W.L.R. 1311, 1324H: *R. v. Governors of Small Heath School, ex p. Birmingham C.C., The Times,* August 14, 1989; [1990] C.O.D. 23, CA.

[70] [1986] 1 W.L.R. 1, DC. See also *R. v. Gateshead Metropolitan B.C., ex p. Nichol* [1988] 87 L.G.R. 435, CA (Court refused to quash part-implemented school reorganisation scheme).

[71] Since a large number of local authorities had acted upon the regulations as promulgated by determining claims in accordance with their terms; see also *R. v. Secretary of State for Employment, ex p. Seymour-Smith* [1994] I.R.L.R. 448. See now also *R. v. Brent L.B.C., ex p. O'Malley; R. v. Secretary of State for the Environment, ex p. Walters* [1998] C.O.D. 121, where the Court of Appeal upheld the decision of Schiemann J. that notwithstanding that the extensive consultation process (relating to the redevelopment of council housing estates) carried out by the Respondents was flawed, no relief should be granted since there was overwhelming evidence that the granting of review would damage the interests of a large number of other individuals, and it would be 'absurd' to ignore such disbenefits; the courts' discretion to refuse relief was said to be a broad one to be exercised in the light of the particular circumstances. The Court rejected a submission that where there was no 'undue deay' under section 31(6) of the Supreme Court Act 1981, the court could not take into account substantial hardship or prejudice to third parties which would be caused by delay or abandonment of this scheme.

[72] See, *e.g. R. v. Monopolies and Mergers Commission, ex p. Argyll Group* [1986] 1 W.L.R. 763, where the Court of Appeal refused to grant a remedy for what was held to be an unlawful delegation of discretion because, among other reasons, commercial considerations dictated that decisions of the MMC should be speedy and final. The Court was influenced, however, by the fact that the unlawful decision had been approved by the Secretary of State; *cf. R. v. Panel on Takeovers and Mergers, ex p. Datafin* [1987] Q.B. 815, CA.

[73] *General Medical Council v. Spackman* [1943] A.C. 627, 638.

[74] The same principle may be seen in the jurisprudence of the European Court of Justice: *E.C. Commission v. Lisrestal* [1997] 2 C.M.L.R. 1 (right to be heard is fundamental principle of Community law which cannot be ignored for reasons of

Where a procedurally flawed decision has been followed by an *ex post facto* hearing or by an appeal which complies with the requirements of fairness

9–019   There are situations where the absence of procedural fairness before a decision is made can subsequently be adequately "cured". For example an adequate hearing may be provided on appeal. This is therefore of relevance when deciding whether it would be reasonable to require a person to pursue an appeal as an "alternative remedy". However if an appeal is incapable of "curing" a procedural error committed at first instance, it would be unfair to require the appeal to be pursued before the person applies to a court for relief.

9–020   A prior hearing may be better than a subsequent hearing, but a subsequent hearing, for example on appeal, is better than no hearing at all[75]; and in some cases the courts have held that statutory provisions for an administrative appeal[76] or even full judicial review on the merits[77] are sufficient to negative the existence of any implied duty to have a hearing before the original decision is made.[78] This approach may be acceptable where the original decision does not cause significant detriment to the person affected,[79] or where there is also a paramount need for prompt action, or where it is otherwise impracticable to afford antecedent hearings.

9–021   The question of whether a decision vitiated by a breach of the rules of fairness can be made good by a subsequent hearing does not admit

---

administrative inconvenience; decision that grant from European Social Fund should be repaid because of fraud, without consulting grantee, was annulled).

[75] *cf. Cinnamond v. British Airports Authority* [1980] 1 W.L.R. 582.

[76] *St. James and St John, Clerkenwell, Vestry v. Feary* (1890) 24 QBD 703; *R. v. Randloph* [1966] S.C.R. 260 (interim mail stop order). See also *Pearlberg v. Varty* [1972] 1 W.L.R. 534 (tax assessments): *Furnell v. Whangarei High Schools Board* [1973] A.C. 660 (suspension of teacher pending full hearing); see also *Maynard v. Osmond* [1977] Q.B. 240, 253 (right of legal representation on appeal a reason for not implying the same right in original proceedings). *Twist v. Randwick M.C.* (1976) 136 C.L.R. 106; *Marine Hull & Liability Insurance Co. v. Hurford* (1985) 67 A.L.R. 77.

[77] *Literature Board of Review v. H.M.H. Publishing Co. Inc.* [1964] Qd.R. 261 (order prohibiting distribution of *Playboy* magazine); *Twist v. Randwick M.C.* (1976) 136 C.L.R. 106. And see the discussion of enforcement powers below, para. 9–027.

[78] Similarly, a fair hearing may not be required at the second hearing of a two-stage process where the person affected had an adequate hearing at the first stage. See *South Australia v. O'Shea* (1987) 163 C.L.R. 378. *Cf. Haoucher v. Minister for Immigration and Ethnic Affairs* (1990) 169 C.L.R. 648.

[79] Although detriment may not be immediately obvious; it may be less easy to convince a decision maker that a decision already taken is wrong than to persuade the body initially of the merits of one's case. *Cf. R. v. Portsmouth C.C., ex p. Gregory* (1990) 89 L.G.R. 478, DC, where the determinations of a special council committee set up to investigate two councillors were irremediably flawed by the earlier investigations of a council subcommittee.

of a single answer applicable to all situations in which the issue may arise. Whilst it is difficult to reconcile all the relevant cases, recent case law indicates that the courts are increasingly favouring an approach based in large part upon an assessment of whether, in all the circumstances of the hearing and appeal, the procedure as a whole satisfied the requirements of fairness.

Of particular importance are (i) the gravity of the error commited at first instance,[80] (ii) the likelihood that the prejudicial effects of the error may also have permeated the rehearing, (iii) the seriousness of the consequences for the individual, (iv) the width of the powers of the appellate body and (v) whether the appellate decision is reached only on the basis of the material before the original tribunal or by way of rehearing *de novo*.[81]

It is possible to detect an increased willingness on the part of the courts in recent years to accept that an appeal has "cured" a defective decision. In *Calvin v. Carr*,[82] the Privy Council doubted that there was a general rule[83] that a failure of fairness at the initial hearing is not to be cured by procedurally correct appeal; in particular, it was suggested, a more latitudinarian attitude should be taken towards the proceedings of domestic tribunals whose authority is derived from the

9–022

---

[80] Thus an original decision vitiated by bias will normally not be allowed to stand: *Anderton v. Auckland C.C.* [1978] 1 N.Z.L.R. 657, 700.

[81] *e.g. Pillai v. Singapore C.C.* [1968] 1 W.L.R. 1278, 1286; *Wislang v. Medical Practitioners Disciplinary Committee* [1974] 1 N.Z.L.R. 29; *Reid v. Rowley* [1977] 2 N.Z.L.R. 472; *Calvin v. Carr* [1980] A.C. 574; *Lloyd v. McMahon* [1987] A.C. 625; *Twist v. Randwick M.C.* (1976) 136 C.L.R. 106; *R. v. LAUTRO, ex p. Tee* (1995) 7 Admin. L.R. 289; *R. v. Legal Aid Board, ex p. Donn & Co. (a firm)* [1996] 3 All E.R. 1 (Area Committee's unfairness in failing to consider full representations of solicitors seeking legal aid contract not cured by chairman subsequently confirming individually with six of seven members of committee that full representations made no difference to their decision). In India it has been held that a post-decisional hearing cannot normally cure an act that is a nullity for want of natural justice. See *State of Orissa v. Bina Pani*, AIR 1967 S.C. 1269, 1271 and cases cited by S. Sorabjee, 'Obliging Government to Control Itself: Recent Developments in Indian Administrative Law' [1994] P.L. 39, 41. However in some cases a post-decisional hearing has been applied. But in *K.I. Shepherd v. Union of India* 1987 (4) SCC 431 the court said that 'It is common experience that once a decision has been taken, there is a tendency to uphold it and a representation may not yield any fruitful purpose'. In some cases the United States courts uphold the principle of a 'post-decisional hearing'. See, *e.g. Annie G. Philips v. Commissioner of Internal Revenue*, 283 U.S. 589. See also South African cases under the Apartheid security legislation, *e.g. Momopiat and Naidoo v. Ministry of Law & Order* 1986 (2) S.A. 264 (W) (per Goldstone J.).

[82] [1980] A.C. 574. but *cf. Rees v. Crane* [1994] 2 A.C. 173, 192, where Lord Slynn, having referred to the 4th ed. of this book, went on to say 'the courts should not be bound by rigid rules' and to stress in that case the respondent could not rely on urgency or administrative inconvenience.

[83] As proposed by Megarry J. in *Leary v. National Union of Vehicle Builders* [1971] Ch. 34 (trade union expulsion case).

consensual rules of a voluntary association. Thus, in that case, an appeal to the Committee of the Australian Jockey Club was held, for this reason, to cure a defective decision of race stewards who had disqualified the owner of a horse alleged to have been raced improperly. In *Lloyd v. McMahon*,[84] the House of Lords confirmed this trend outside the context of domestic tribunals. It was held that the decision of a district auditor to surcharge councillors for failure to set a valid rate, without according them oral hearings would, had it been procedurally defective, have been cured by the statutory appeal from the auditor's decision to the High Court. It should be noted, however, with reference to the criteria set out above, that the scope of the appeal was very wide, all the evidence being susceptible of re-examination, including the merits of the decision.[85]

9–023   It would seem that these considerations may be relevant both to establishing whether a breach of the requirements of fairness has occurred and to the exercise by the court of its discretion to award particular forms of relief. There may also be situations in which, although the provision of a right of appeal is not required, a court will be satisfied that nothing short of compliance with the requirements of procedural fairness at both stages will afford to the individual the standards of fairness demanded in the particular context.[86]

Where the decision complained of is only a preliminary to a decision subject to procedural fairness

9–024   In what circumstances must the rules of procedural fairness be observed by persons entrusted with the conduct of an investigation but having no power to give a binding decision? This is one of the most troublesome problems in relation to procedural fairness. The authorities often appear to be, and sometimes are, in conflict with one another. When one comes across a judicial formulation of general legal principle it is not infrequently misleading because the court has in mind only a limited range of contexts in which the problem arises. Again, some of the best-known dicta have been uttered in cases where no allegation of unfairness was made, and one can never be certain

---

[84] [1987] A.C. 625.

[85] It was expressly suggested that the situation might be different if the appellate body was bound by findings of fact, or restricted to questions of law (*per* Lord Templeman at 891); this suggests that a rehearing by way of judicial review would not be sufficient (see *per* Lord Bridge at 884).

[86] See *Leary v. National Union of Vehicle Builders* [1971] C. 34; *Denton v. Auckland City* [1969] N.Z.L.R. 256. Neither of these cases should now be regarded as authority for the wider proposition that defects may never be cured by a fair hearing at an appeal: *Calvin v. Carr* (above n. 81).

that the same words would have been used if that issue had been before the court. Nor is it always possible to assess how far the form of the proceedings has influenced the approach adopted by the court. If certiorari is sought to quash a non-binding report, the court may well look askance[87]; if prohibition is sought to prevent the investigation from going further, the court may be more easily persuaded.[88] Many of the considerations relevant in this context are also in play where the court is invited to refuse permission to apply for judicial review because an applicant has failed to pursue an alternative remedy.[89] However, the case law considered here is distinctive because the courts are considering a prior question; namely, are the procedural framework and effects of the preliminary decision such that it would be unfair to the affected person to hold that his entitlement to be heard at a later stage, or his entitlement to challenge the preliminary decision, means that no hearing or other procedural protection is required in respect of the preliminary decision?

Even if we ignored the existing authorities altogether, and the problem is examined entirely in the light of the need for fairness to be shown to individuals and for efficiency to be displayed in the conduct of public affairs, it is unlikely that any neat set of answers will emerge. It may not be very difficult to give the best available answer to a problem set in a given legislative and factual context; it is very difficult to supply satisfactory answers couched in general terms. However, the following tentative observations, based on principle as well as authority, are offered.

9–025

Proximity between investigation and act or decision

The degree of proximity between the investigation in question and an act or decision directly adverse to the interests of the person claiming entitlement to be heard may be important. Thus, a person empowered or required to conduct a preliminary investigation with a view to recommending or deciding whether a formal inquiry or hearing (which may lead to a binding and adverse decision) should take place is not normally under any obligation to comply with the rules of

9–026

---

[87] See, *e.g. R. v. St Lawrence's Hospital, Caterham, Statutory Visitors, ex p. Pritchard* [1953] 1 W.L.R. 1158; but note that the non-binding nature of a decision is no longer (if it ever was) a bar to judicial review; see *Gillick v. West Norfolk and Wisbech Area Health Authority* [1986] A.C. 112; *R. v. Secretary of State for the Environment, ex p. Greenwich L.B.C.* [1989] C.O.D. 530, DC; see further, Chap. 7, para. 7–031.

[88] See below, paras 9–026–9–027, where the authorities are listed.

[89] See paras 14–007–14–009 below.

fairness.[90] But he may be placed under such an obligation if his investigation is an integral and necessary part of a process which may terminate in action adverse to the interests of a person claiming to be heard before him[91]; for instance, the principles of fairness must be observed by magistrates conducting a preliminary investigation in respect of a charge of an indictable offence.[92] Although "prosecuting"

---

[90] See, *e.g. Beetham v. Trinidad Cement Co.* [1960] A.C. 132; *Medical Board of Queensland v. Byrne* (1958) 100 C.L.R. 582; *R. v. Saskatchewan College of Physicians and Surgeons, ex p. Samuels* (1966) 58 D.L.R. (2d) 622; *R. v. Ministry of Education, ex p. Southampton School District* (1967) 59 D.L.R. (2d) 587; *Parry-Jones v. Law Society* [1969] 1 Ch. 1; *R. v. British Columbia College of Dental Surgeons, ex p. Schumacher* (1970) 8 D.L.R. (3d) 473. *Cf. ex p, Tango; Re Drummoyue M.C.* (1962) S.R. (N.S.W.) 193 (no implied duty to give prior notice and opportunity to be heard before giving early warning of future intention to restrict use of property) *Moran v. Lloyd's* [1981] 1 Lloyd's Rep. 423 (inquiry by Lloyd's which recommended that Lloyd's should exercise its disciplinary powers against M under section 20 of the Lloyd's Act 1871 was not subject to the rules of natural justice; Lord Denning M.R. stated that the rules of natural justice 'have no application to a preliminary inquiry of this kind' because 'it does not decide anything in the least. It does not do anything which adversely affects the man concerned or prejudices him in any way' (at 427)). For a further discussion on prosecutorial discretion see Chap. 5, para. 5–043 above and Chap. 10, para. 10–007 below. See also *Giles v. Law Society* (1996) 8 Admin. L.R. 105, 114 (decision to issue notice of intervention against solicitor).

[91] *Wiseman v. Borneman* [1971] A.C. 297, esp. *per* Lord Wilberforce at 317 (preliminary steps towards tax assessment; requirements of fairness satisfied by statutory procedure); *cf. Pearlberg v. Varty* [1972] 1 W.L.R. 534 (no duty to observe natural justice). See also *Balen v. Inland Revenue Commissioners* [1978] 2 All E.R. 1033. Statutory provision is made for a hearing before the Consumer Advisory Committee and the Monopolies and Mergers Commission: Fair Trading Act 1973, s. 81. But *cf. Rees v. Cranel* [1994] 2 A.C. 173. In *Re Att.-Gen. Canada and Canadian Tobacco Manufacturers' Council* (1986) 26 D.L.R. (4th) 677 it was held that the duty of fairness applied to a power to recommend if, as a result of the recommendation, adverse consequences for the applicant are 'probable or close to probable'. In Ireland suspensions from *e.g.* trade unions do not require a fair hearing when made not as a way of punishment but by way of a holding operation pending full investigation of the complaint (*e.g. Quirke v. Bord Luthcleas Na H, Eireann* [1988] I.R. 83).

[92] See *R. v. Botting* (1966) 56 D.L.R. (2d) 25, and esp. Laskin J.A. at 30–42; and see *R. v. Coleshill JJ., ex p. Davies* [1971] 1 W.L.R. 1684, and *R. v. Colchester Magistrates, ex p. Beck* [1979] 2 W.L.R. 637, 645; though *cf. ex p. Coffey, re Evans* [1971] 1 N.S.W.R. 434. A further reason for requiring observance of natural justice in a preliminary investigation by magistrates is that the investigation may end with a remand in custody or a requirement that bail be furnished. But because of the limited purpose of the hearing the accused is not entitled to confront and cross-examine all the witnesses who may be called by the prosecution at trial; *R. v. Epping and Harlow JJ., ex p. Massaro* [1973] Q.B. 433; but *cf.* the duty of fairness imposed upon the prosecution in a trial to call or to reveal to the accused beforehand the identity of material witnesses: *R. v. Leyland JJ., ex p. Hawthorn* [1979] Q.B. 283 (although *quaere* whether this decision should properly be seen as resting upon a duty of fairness: *R. v. Secretary of State for the Home Department, ex p. Al Mehdawi* [1990] 1 A.C. 876, and para. 9–035; *R. v. Lucas* [1973] V.R. 693; see further *Re Van Beelen* (1974) 9 S.A.S.R. 163, 243–250. However, the defendant has the right to give evidence after the magistrates

decisions—whether in the criminal or disciplinary sphere—are clearly reviewable,[93] it would only be in a wholly exceptional case that the prosecutor might come under a duty to hear or consult either the prospective accused, the complainant, or any other party, before coming to a decision as to whether or not to prosecute.[94]

Preliminary investigations subject to procedural fairness

Exceptionally, it may be necessary to import the rules of fairness into the conduct of an inquiry or investigation, the holding of which is not a prerequisite of further proceedings or action. Since the hearings and report of a judicial tribunal or inquiry set up to investigate an alleged public scandal attract a great deal of publicity, it may be unfair to deny a person against whom damaging allegations may be made before the tribunal the procedural protection accorded to a defendant in legal proceedings.[95] On the other hand, even where the report of

9–027

---

have rejected his submission of no case to answer: *R. v. Horseferry Road Stipendiary Magistrate, ex p. Adams* [1977] 1 W.L.R. 1197. Courts may be reluctant to intervene in the conduct of preliminary examinations before their conclusion: *R. v. Wells Street Stipendiary Magistrate, ex p. Seillon* [1978] 1 W.L.R. 1002 (refusal of cross-examination); and see *R. v. Wells Street Stipendiary Magistrate, ex p. Deakin* [1980] A.C. 477.

[93] See *R. v. Metropolitan Police Commissioner, ex p. Blackburn* [1968] 2 Q.B. 118; *R. v. General Council of the Bar, ex p. Percival* [1991] 1 Q.B. 212. In the Canadian case of *Re Peel Board of Education and B* (1987) 59 O.R. (2d) 654 it was held that a school principal must give a pupil an opportunity to be heard before suspending for misconduct. See also *Knight v. Indian Head School Division No. 19* (1990) 69 D.L.R. (4th) 489 (education director entitled to notice and fair opportunity to respond before being dismissed, even though dismissable without cause and the opportunity of subsequent review by a board). See generally Mold 'Employment during good behaviour and at pleasure' (1989) 2 Can., J. of Admin. L. and Practice 238.

[94] In *Selvarajan v. Race Relations Board* [1975] 1 W.L.R. 1686, 1696, Lawton L.J. suggested that the courts might be entitled to interfere with the DPP's discretion to initiate a prosecution if he acted 'unfairly' but there was no suggestion that fairness might require consultation, See further, *Blackburn* (above); *R. v. Police Complaints Board, ex p. Madden* [1983] 1 W.L.R. 447 (where it was accepted that the Board was under a duty to act 'fairly' in considering complaints); *Percival* (above); *Brooks v. DPP of Jamaica* [1994] 1 A.C. 568 (decision of DPP to prefer indictment, or of Judge to consent to preferral, was a purely procedural step and neither principles of fairness nor Jamaican Constitution entitled person indicted to be given prior notice of DPP's decision, or to attend before Judge).

[95] Tribunals of Inquiry (Evidence) Act 1921; Cmnd. 3121 (1966) (the Salmon Report), 16–18. See also *Re Ontario Crime Commission* (1962) 133 C.C.C., 116. But procedural irregularities in a report may be raised collaterally in proceedings to declare invalid an instrument for the making of which a valid report was a prerequisite: *Hoffmann-La Roche (F.) & Co. AG v. Secretary of State for Trade and Industry* [1975] A.C. 295, 354, 365. In *Syndicat des employés de production du Québec et de l'Acadie v. Canada (Canadian Human Rights Commission)* (1989) 62 D.L.R. (4th) 385, the Supreme Court of Canada stated, *obiter*, that complainants are entitled to know the substance of evidence

such an inquiry may be expected to contain criticism of particular persons, it may be that the efficient conduct of the inquiry requires that rights to legal representation and particularly cross-examination be dispensed with.[96] The case for requiring a Department of Trade inspector conducting a formal investigation into a company's affairs[97] to observe the detailed rules of fairness has been thought to be perhaps less strong; here again the report may lead to judicial proceedings (including a petition for a winding-up order[98]), but is not a prerequisite of the institution of such proceedings; the inspector's report may at the discretion of the Secretary of State be published,[99] but the investigation is carried out in private. The balance is still a fine one, inasmuch as the investigation (to which officers or agents of the company, or any other person whom the inspectors believe may be in possession of information relating to any matter which they believe is relevant to the investigation may be compelled to attend and to answer questions and produce documents[1]) and report expose persons to a legal hazard[2] as well as potentially damaging publicity. It has accordingly been held that the rudiments of natural justice or fairness must be observed, in so far as the inspector must, before publishing a report containing serious criticisms and allegations against a person, put to that person the substance of them and given him an

---

contained in the investigative report and to comment on it before their complaint of discrimation is dismissed. And in *Federation of Women's Teachers' Association of Ontario v. Ontario (Human Rights Commission)* (1988) 67 QR (2d) 492 it was held that the Commission, before deciding whether to refer a complaint of discrimation for adjudication, was required to inform those under investigation of the substance of the case against them.

[96] In relation to the procedure adopted at Scott L.J.'s inquiry into the 'Arms to Iraq' affair, See Sir Louis Blom-Cooper, Q.C. 'Witnesses and the Scott Inquiry' [1994] P.L. 1. In New Zealand natural justice has been held to apply to preliminary decisions. See, *e.g. Birss v. Secretary for Justice* [1984] 1 N.Z.L.R. 513; *Fraser v. State Services Commission* [1984] 1 N.Z.L.R. 116.

[97] Companies Act 1985, ss.431–434; 436–439, 441, 446 (as amended by the Companies Act 1989).

[98] Companies Act 1985, s.60 (Now partially repealed by the Financial Services Act 1986).

[99] Companies Act 1985, s.437(3)(c).

[1] Companies Act 1985, s.434.

[2] *cf. Testro Bros Pty Ltd v. Tait* (1963) 109 C.L.R. 353, 370, per Kitto J., *Wiseman v. Borneman* [1971] A.C. 297, 317; *R. v. Cheltenham JJ., ex p. Secretary of State for Trade* [1977] 1 W.L.R. 95; *London and County Securities Ltd v. Nicholson* [1980] 1 W.L.R. 948; *Savings and Investment Bank Ltd v. Gasco Investments (Netherlands) BV* [1984] 1 W.L.R. 271. As to the effect of the privilege against self-incrimination, see *McClelland, Pope & Langley Ltd v. Howard* [1968] 1 All E.R. 549n, HL. In *Re London United Investments Plc* [1992] Ch. D 578 (privilege is impliedly excluded by 1985 Act). But see now *Saunders v. United Kingdom* (decision of European Commission, May 10, 1994, Application 19187/91): use at trial of material obtained under inspectors powers was a breach of Art. 6(1) of the Convention. See now 23 E.H.R.R. 30.

opportunity of rebutting them.[3] However it has been held that the inspector is not required to allow the cross-examination of witnesses, nor is he required to recall the person to rebut allegations subsequently made by other witnesses, nor to submit his tentative conclusions to the "accused" before sending his report to the Minister (although it is in fact the usual practice of inspectors to submit draft conclusions to affected individuals).[4] The Minister is under no implied procedural duty to entertain representations or to disclose the information that he has acquired before exercising his discretion to appoint inspectors to conduct an inquiry.[5] The weight of judicial authority on investigations of the kind conducted under the Companies Act has laid heavy emphasis on their non-judicial character, the importance of an expeditious conclusion and the difficulty of the investigative task.[6] This view has recently also been taken by the European Court of Human Rights, on a challenge to an inspectors' report on the ground that it violated the applicants' rights to honour and reputation under Art. 6(1) of the Convention, and denied them effective court access.[7] The Court held that the functions performed by the inspectors was essentially investigative, in that they did not adjudicate either in form or in substance, nor make a civil or criminal adjudication concerning the applicants' rights. Even though

---

[3] *Re Pergamon Press Ltd* [1971] Ch. 388.

[4] *Maxwell v. Department of Trade and Industry* [1974] Q.B. 523. See also *R. v. Chettenham JJ., ex p. Secretary of State for Trade* [1977] 1 W.L.R. 95 (witness summons, issued to inspector to reveal evidence given in confidence at an inquiry, quashed); but see below for the position under the European Convention. As was done by the Scott Inquiry (n.96, above).

[5] *Norwest Holst Ltd v. Department of Trade* [1978] Ch. 201.

[6] See, *e.g. Re Grosvenor & West-End Ry. Terminus Hotel Co.* (1897) 76 L.T. 337: *Hearts of Oak Assurance Co. v. Att.-Gen.* [1932] A.C. 392; *O'Connor, v. Waldron* [1935] A.C. 76; *St John v. Fraser* [1935] S.C.R. 441; *Re Imperial Tobacco Co.* [1939] O.R. 627; *R. v. Coppel, ex p. Viney Industries Ltd* [1962] V.R. 630; *Testro Bros Pty Ltd v. Tait* (above, n. 2). See, however, the dissenting judgments of Kitto and Menzies JJ. in the last-named case, pointing out that adverse legal consequences for the person who had been denied a proper hearing could flow directly from the report in question; and see a critical article by Gerard Nash (1964) 38 A.L.J. 111. See also *Re SBA Properties Ltd* [1967] 1 W.L.R. 799; *R. v. Race Relations Board, ex p. Selvarajan* [1975] 1 W.L.R. 1686. But in *Tampion v. Anderson* [1973] V.R. 321 at 715 judicial immunity for words spoken in the course of proceedings was conferred upon a board of inquiry as well as counsel and witnesses appearing before it; and see *Trapp v. Mackie* [1979] 1 W.L.R. 377 (HL, Sc.). Compare s. 236 of the Insolvency Act 1986, under which a person may be compelled to answer questions without the benefit of the privilege against self-incrimination: In *British & Commonwealth Holdings plc (Joint Administrators) v. Spicer and Oppenheim* [1993] A.C. 426 [1992] 3 W.L.R. 854; *Bishopsgate Investment Management v. Maxwell* [1993] Ch. D 1.

[7] *Fayed v. United Kingdom*, E.C.H.R., Case No. 28/1993/423/502, September 21, 1994; *The Times*, October 11, 1994.

the report may have led to uncompensated damage to the applicants' reputations, it was held that the potential remedy of judicial review, while limited, provided sufficient guarantees for the persons affected.

Binding nature of preliminary decision

9–028 In a number of cases in which the proceedings of investigating bodies have been impugned (mainly on grounds other than non-compliance with the principles of fairness) the courts have refused to intervene unless the investigation does or can culiminate in a determination or order which has binding force or will itself acquire binding force upon confirmation or promulgation by another body or which otherwise controls the decision of that other body.[8] To put the matter in another way, an investigating body is under no duty to act fairly if it cannot do more than recommend or advise on action which another body may take in its own name and in its own discretion.[9] This proposition cannot be accepted without qualification. Whilst it would be absurd to impose judicial standards on every body that advises a government department as to the exercise of its executive functions, justice will sometimes demand—as the courts are increasingly recognising—that an investigation preceding a discretionary administrative decision be conducted in accordance with the requirements of procedural fairness.[10] Inspectors holding inquiries in respect of compulsory purchase orders are undoubtedly obliged to act fairly,[11] although their findings and recommendations are in no way binding on the Minister when he decides whether or not to confirm the order. If express procedural duties are cast upon an investigating authority this in itself may support the view that a common-law duty to observe the

---

[8] See, *e.g. Ex p. Mineral Deposits Pty Ltd, re Claye and Lynch* (1959) S.R. (N.S.W.) 167 and *R. v. Ontario Labour Relations Board, ex p. Kitchener Food Market Ltd* (1966) 57 D.L.R. (2d) 521, where the authorities are reviewed.

[9] See, *e.g. R. v. Macfarlane, ex p. O'Flanagan and O'Kelly* (1923) 32 C.L.R. 518 (not a natural justice case); *R. v. St Lawrence's Hospital, Caterham, Statutory Visitors* [1953] 1 W.L.R. 1158; *Guay v. Lafleur* [1965] S.C.R. 12; *de Freitas v. Benny* [1976] A.C. 239. Cf. *Rees v. Crane* [1994] 2 A.C. 173.

[10] Whether or not the function may be characterised as 'judicial'; see *Re Pergamon Press Ltd* [1971] Ch. 388; *R. v. Race Relations Board, ex p. Selvarajan* [1975] 1 W.L.R. 1686; *R. v. Commission for Racial Equality, ex p. Cottrell and Rothon* [1980] 1 W.L.R. 1580, 1587. See, on this point, *Re Mackey* (1971 N.I. unreported); Gibson J. held that internee in Northern Ireland entitled to natural justice when his case was considered by advisory committee. But the requirements of fairness may be reduced to the merest procedural shell: *R. v. Home Secretary, ex p. Hosenball* [1977] 1 W.L.R. 766 (hearing before advisory committee pending deportation on national security grounds); *R. v. Home Secretary ex p. Cheblak* [1991] 1 W.L.R. 890.

[11] See above, para. 9–011.

requirements of fairness attaches to the investigations.[12] And even where statute expressly accords a great degree of procedural latitude to the Parliamentary Commissioner for Administration, the courts recognise that a report containing criticisms of a government department should be sent in draft to the department for comments.[13] However, it has been held that a person whose complaint initiated the Commissioner's investigation—and who may be offered financial recompense as a consequence of his report—is not entitled to a copy of the draft report, because although the complainant's rights are affected by the decision, it is the department and not the complainant who is being investigated and who is liable to face public criticism for its acts.[14] Furthermore, a duty of procedural fairness is imposed upon the proceedings of the Parole Board both by statute and by the common law, inasmuch as a decision by the Home Secretary to revoke the licence of a released prisoner and recall him to gaol may be contingent upon the receipt of a recommendation by the Board to that effect.[15]

---

[12] See, *e.g. Saulnier v. Quebec Police Commission* [1976] 1 S.C.R. 572.

[13] The obligation to give the official against whom a complaint is made and his departmental head an opportunity of commenting on the allegations may be regarded as importing a more general duty to act fairly with respect to those officials; but, this apart, he enjoys the widest freedom of action in relation to matters within his competence (Parliamentary Commissioner Act 1967, s. 7). See also Health Service Commissioner Act 1993 see also Local Government Act 1974, ss. 28, 29 (Commission for Local Government). See too *Grunwick Processing Laboratories Ltd v. ACAS* [1978] A.C. 655 where an express statutory duty to ascertain workers' opinions was construed as mandatory; although it is virtually inconceivable that this would ever require a formal hearing to be held, some of the judgments referred to the body's function as judicial and to its procedural duty to comply with the rules of natural justice.

[14] *R. v. Parliamentary Commissioner for Administration, ex p. Dyer* [1994] 1 W.L.R. 621; *cf. R. v. Commissioner for Local Administration, ex p. Eastleigh B.C.* [1988] Q.B. 855; *R. v. Commissioner for Local Administration, ex p. Croydon L.B.C.* [1989] 1 All E.R. 1033.

[15] Criminal Justice Act 1991, s. 34 and Crime (Sentences) Act 1997, s. 28; *Thynne, Wilson and Gunnell v. United Kingdom* (1990) 13 E.H.R.R. 666; *R. v. Parole Board, ex p. Wilson* [1992] 1 Q.B. 740. However, where the Parole Board merely reviewed (as an extra-statutory practice) and confirmed the decision of the Secretary of State to recall to prison a discretionary life sentence prisoner who had been released on licence, prior to a full statutory review, the Court of Appeal held that the requirements of full hearing do not apply, because that review was only intended to be 'tentative and provisional': *R. v. Parole Board, ex p. Watson* [1996] 1 W.L.R. 906 (*per* Sir Thomas Bingham M.R.); *cf. R. v. Secretary of State for the Home Department, ex p. Seton* (April 25, 1996, unreported).

Duty to observe principles of fairness

9–029　In special situations, persons entrusted with a duty to conduct a statutory inquiry and collect information may be obliged to observe the principles of fairness, although they are not even entitled to submit recommendations to the deciding body.[16] Such a situation can arise because the type of inquiry conducted is one in which members of the public have come to expect certain minimum procedural standards to be maintained. In this situation, as in some of the others reviewed in this chapter, the observance of the *audi alteram partem* rule may be called for because non-observance would give the appearance of injustice. This was the position with the preliminary investigation into the conduct of a judge. A suspension of a judge, even temporarily, was a matter of such significance that he should be given the opportunity of making representations before it happened.[17]

Where the defect of natural justice has made no difference to the result; where to require fairness or natural justice would be futile; where no prejudice has been caused to the applicant

9–030　The courts are not infrequently invited to decline to grant judicial review for an alleged failure to comply with the requirements of procedural fairness on the ground that to grant a remedy would make no difference to the ultimate result. The invitation may be phrased in a number of different ways: any remedy would be pointless, because it would not benefit the applicant, who has already received all that he would obtain by way of relief; the applicant has not suffered any real prejudice; the decision would have been no different if the decision maker had followed the precepts of natural justice (either because the merits of the case are weak or because the applicant is undeserving). In each case, the court is in some measure invited to look beyond the narrow question of whether the decision was taken in a procedurally improper manner, to the wider question of whether a decision properly taken would or could have benefited the applicant.

9–031　　The response of the courts to this argument, in its many forms, is still uncertain. In some cases the courts have refused to grant relief when satisfied that the outcome could not have been different had natural justice been fully observed.[18] These decisions have been sought

---

[16] *Wednesbury Corp. v. Ministry of Housing and Local Government (No. 2)* [1966] 2 Q.B. 275, 302–303, *per* Diplock L.J.

[17] *Rees v. Crane* [1994] 2 A.C. 173. *Cf.* the majority decision in *Furnell v. Whangerei High School Board* [1973] A.C. 660.

[18] *Glynn v. Keele University* [1971] 1 W.L.R. 487, 496; *Lamond v. Barnett* [1964] N.Z.L.R. 195, 203–204; *Donatelli Shoes Ltd v. Labour Relations Board of Quebec* [1964] C.S. (Que.)

to be explained on the ground that the relief sought was discretionary,[19] or on the ground that breach makes an order voidable rather than void.[20] It is submitted that neither explanation is sufficient. As to the former, it is right to note that a refusal of relief on the ground that it would make "no difference" may be explained either as an exercise of the courts' discretion as to the grant of relief, or as a part of the consideration of whether the principles of fairness have in fact been infringed at all. However, this in itself goes no way towards an identification of those cases in which the courts are prepared to refuse relief, as a matter of discretion or otherwise. As to the latter, it is clear that the court may still have discretion to refuse the statutory remedy even though the decision is void.[21] There are also cases, arising in various contexts, in which it has been assumed that the inadequacy of the hearing is in itself sufficient for the decision to be set aside: in those instances the courts have declined to embark upon a speculative inquiry about the possible impact of the procedural irregularity upon the decision.[22]

193, 203; *R. v. Law Society of Alberta, ex p. Demco* (1967) 64 D.L.R. (2d) 140; *Cinnamond v. BAA* [1980] 1 W.L.R. 582; *R. v. Chief National Insurance Commissioner, ex p. Connor* [1981] Q.B. 758; *R. v. Monopolies and Mergers Commission, ex p. Argyll* [1986] 1 W.L.R. 763; *R. v. Bristol C.C., ex p. Pearce* (1984) 83 L.G.R. 711; *R. v. Criminal Injuries Compensation Board ex p. Aston* [1994] C.O.D. 500. See also *Davis v. Carew-Pole* [1956] 1 W.L.R. 833, 840; *Byrne v. Kinematograph Renters Society Ltd* [1958] 1 W.L.R. 762, 785; *Durayappah v. Fernando* [1967] 2 A.C. 337, 350. *Fulop (Imre) v. Secretary of State for the Home Department* [1995] Imm. A.R. 323, CA ('no possibility' of a different decision since missing documents unhelpful to applicant); *R. v. London Borough of Camden, ex p. Paddock* [1995] C.O.D. 130 (case 'falls within the narrow margin of cases in which the court can say with confidence that the [unfairness] has caused no actual injustice'); *R. v. Islington L.B.C., ex p. Degnan* [1998] C.O.D. 46, CA ('exceptional case'; judge 'near to certainty' that the flawed decision made no difference to the result).

[19] See esp. *Glynn's* case (above); *R. v. Aston University Senate, ex p. Roffey* [1969] 2 Q.B. 538 (certiorari; undue delay); *Fullbrook v. Berkshire Magistrates' Courts Committee* (1970) 69 L.G.R. 75 (declaration; unreasonable conduct of plaintiff). Since in a large majority of cases the plaintiff or applicant is seeking a discretionary remedy, this type of question frequently arises.

[20] In *Stevenson v. United Road Transport Union* [1977] I.C.R. 893, the characterisation of the decision as void or voidable was stated to be relevant only to the court's approach to its exercise of discretion to grant relief, in that case a declaration.

[21] See *Miller v. Weymouth and Melcombe Regis Corp* (1974) 27 P. & C.R. 468,480–481 (not a natural justice case, but where the court declined to quash a void decision for lack of prejudice to the applicant; see J. E. Alder (1975) 91 L.Q.R. 10. See also *Kent C.C. v. Secretary of State for the Environment* (1977) 75 L.G.R. 452, 460–461. Contrast *Goddard v. Minister of Housing and Local Government* [1958] 1 W.L.R. 1151, 1153; *Savoury v. Secretary of State for Wales* (1976) 31 P. & C.R. 344, 347.

[22] *R. v. Registrar of Building Societies* [1960] 1 W.L.R. 669, 684; *Annamunthodo v. Oilfield Workers' Trade Union* [1961] A.C. 945, 956; *Kanda v. Government of Malaya* [1962] A.C. 322, 327; *John v. Rees* [1970] Ch. 345, 402; *R. v. Thames Magistratres' Court, ex p. Polemis* [1974] 1 W.L.R. 1371, 1375–1376. See also *R. v. Devon and Cornwall Rent Tribunal, ex p. West* (1975) 29 P. & C.R. 316, 320–321. See also the *Fairmount* case, above, and see the

9–032   Whether a person who has been denied an adequate hearing must also establish that this affected the ultimate decision is particularly relevant when proceedings are brought for the statutory remedy to quash, for example, a planning appeal or a compulsory purchase order. Relief may be granted either if there has been a failure to comply with statutory requirements and the applicant has been substantially prejudiced thereby, or if the decision or order in question was not one that the authority was empowered to make.[23] In some cases where it has been assumed that a breach of the rules of natural justice falls under the first limb, the applicant has been granted relief upon showing that had he been afforded the hearing to which he was entitled, the decision might have been different.[24] In other cases, however the courts have treated the defect as falling under the second limb, but have defined a breach of natural justice to include the risk that the irregularity might have affected the outcome, although no clear guidance has emerged on the closeness with which a court should scrutinise the facts.[25] Once again, it may be questioned, however, whether such categorisation does more than mask the principles upon which the courts act. It appears clear that in planning

---

cautionary dicta of Lord Hailsham in *London & Clydeside Estates Ltd v. Aberdeen D.C.* [1980] 1 W.L.R. 182, 189.

[23] *e.g.* Town and Country Planning Act 1990, s. 288; Acquisition of Land Act 1981.

[24] See *e.g. Wilson v. Secretary of State for the Environment* [1973] 1 W.L.R. 1083, 1095–1096 (if adequate notice had been given, representations might have been made and an inquiry might have been held); *Leighton and Newman Car Sales Ltd v. Secretary of State for the Environment* (1976) 32 P. & C.R. 1: *semble, Davies v. Secretary of State for Wales* [1977] J.P.L. 102; and see *George v. Secretary of State for the Environment* (1979) 250 E.G. 339 (relief denied); *R. v. Mayor of Greenwich L.B.C., ex p. Patel* (1985) 51 P. & C.R. 282 (real as opposed to remote or fanciful loss or prejudice must be shown) *R. v. Canterbury City Council, ex p. Springimage Ltd* (1994) 68 P. & C.R. 171 (relief denied because 'no real possibility' of different decision). That doubts persist whether a breach of the rules of natural justice renders a decision void for the purpose of the second limb of the statutory formula is attributable to the judgments of Maugham and (*semble*) Roche L.JJ. in *Errington v. Minister of Health* [1935] 1 K.B. 249, 279–280, 282, although their Lordships seem virtually to have regarded the breach *ipso facto* to have caused substantial prejudice to the applicant's interests. Nowadays, courts may normally be expected to characterise a breach of the rules of natural justice as going to the power of the Minister to make the decision: *Fairmount Investments Ltd v. Secretary of State for the Environment* [1976] 1 W.L.R. 1255, 1263. See also *Lithgow v. Secretary of State for Scotland*, 1973 S.L.T. 81.

[25] See *Hibernian Property Co. Ltd v. Secretary of State for the Environment* (1974) 27 P. & C.R. 197, 212, 214; *Lake District Special Planning Board v. Secretary of State for the Environment* [1975] J.P.L. 220; *Performance Cars Ltd v. Secretary of State for the Environment* (1977) 34 P. & C.R. 92; *General Accident Fire & Life Assurance Corp. Ltd v. Secretary of State for the Environment, ibid.* at 588. See also *R. v. Visiting Justice at Her Majesty's Prison, Pentridge, ex p. Walker* [1975] V.R. 883 (magistrate's failure to realise that he had a discretion to allow legal representation did not prejudice applicant); *George v. Secretary of State for the Environment*, above, n.24.

cases, where a failure to comply with a statutory requirement is alleged, substantial prejudice must be shown.[26] In other circumstances, however, the position is less clear although courts are unlikely to interfere with decisions where the results, however irregular, are of trivial importance, or wholly speculative[27] or remote.

The courts have rightly cautioned against the suggestion that no prejudice has been caused to the applicant because the flawed decision would inevitably have been the same. It is not for the courts to substitute their opinion for that of the authority constituted by law to decide the matters in question.[28] As it has recently been put, in a case involving a destruction order under the Dangerous Dogs Act 1991,

    9–033

> "the notion that when the rules of natural justice have not been observed, one can still uphold the result because it would not have made any difference, is to be treated with great caution. Down that slippery slope lies the way to dictatorship. On the other hand, if it is a case where it is demonstrable beyond doubt that it would have made no difference, the court may, if it thinks fit, uphold a conviction even if natural justice had not been done"."

Further, "natural justice is not always or entirely about the fact or substance of fairness. It has also something to do with the appearance of fairness. In the hallowed phrase, 'Justice must not only be done, it must also be seen to be done'."[29] These cases support the view that the fundamental principle at stake is that public confidence in the fairness of adjudication or hearing procedures may be undermined if decisions are allowed to stand despite the absence of what a

---

[26] See *R. v. Mayor of Greenwich L.B.C. ex p. Patel*, above, n. 24.

[27] Although in such cases the applicant for judicial review is unlikely to be granted standing to sue on the grounds of lack of sufficient interest. See Chap. 2, above. In India it has been held that a prior hearing is required when an administrative action is 'prejudicial to the citizen'. *The Scheduled Caste and Weaker Sections Welfare Assoc. v. State of Karnataka* AIR 1991 S.C. 1117.

[28] *per* Lord Hailsham in *Chief Constable of the North Wales Police v. Evans* [1982] 1 W.L.R. 1155, 1160; see also *per* Lord Brightman, 1173. See also *John v. Rees* [1970] Ch. D 345, 582; *R. v. Secretary of State for the Environment, ex p. Brent L.B.C.* [1982] Q.B. 593, 734; *R. v. Secretary of State for Education ex p. Prior* [1994] I.C.R. 877 *per* Brooke J.

[29] *R. v. Ealing Magistrates' Court, ex p. Fanneran* (1996) 8 Admin. L.R. 351, 358, *per* Staughton L.J. A possibly more extreme formulation was set out by Rougier J. in the same case (at p. 359):

'...no one can ever say for certain what must have happened in the circumstances which have not, in fact, arisen. The robing rooms up and down this land are full of strange tales of seemingly impregnable cases foundering on some unforseen forensic reef. It is not, in my opinion, for this court to employ its imagination to postulate facts which might or might not have occurred or arguments which might or might not have succeeded had the rules of natural justice been followed'.

reasonable observer might regard as an adequate hearing, rather than that injustice lies only in holding an individual bound by a decision whose substantive reliability is cast in doubt by the existence of procedural irregularities.[30]

9–034   But on the whole judges have declined to commit themselves unequivocally to the proposition that intervention will never be withheld when they are satisfied that no amount of procedural propriety would have affected the outcome.[31] Thus a decision by school governors refusing to correct an inaccurate statement in a consultation paper, and refusing to extend the consultation period was not unfair because the error in question could not have led a person reading the pamphlet to have reached a different conclusion.[32] A decision by the chairman of the Monopolies and Mergers Commission to recommend to the Secretary of State that a take-over reference be laid aside, while beyond his powers, should not, in the discretion of the court, be quashed because there was little doubt that a properly constituted committee would have reached the same decision.[33] The result may be the same where the remedy sought by the applicant would be of no practical use; where, for example, it was sought to quash a decision to disclose a report which had, by the date of

---

[30] *Cheall v. Association of Professional, Executive, Clerical and Computer Staff* [1983] Q.B. 126, *per* Donaldson L.J. On the facts, relief was refused on the ground that although the applicant had been denied a fair hearing, the Court held that he could not 'feel unfairly treated'. effectively because the decision maker did not have a discretion to decide in his favour. *Cf. R. v. Inner West London Coroner ex p. Dallaglio* [1994] 4 All E.R. 139.

[31] See *e.g. Ridge v. Baldwin* [1964] A.C. 40, 68; *Maradana Mosque Trustees v. Mahmud* [1967] 1 A.C. 13, 24–25; *Malloch v. Aberdeen Corp.* [1971] 1 W.L.R. 1578, 1582–1583, 1600; *Re B (Minors)* [1973] Fam. 179, 189; *Wislang v. Medical Practitioners Disciplinary Committee* [1974] 1 N.Z.L.R. 29, 42; *Scott v. Aberdeen Corp.*, 1976 S.L.T. 141; *Hickmott v. Dorset C.C.* (1977) 35 P. & C.R. 195; *R. v. Hull Prison Board of Visitors, ex p. St Germain* [1979] Q.B. 425, 450–451; *Stininato v. Auckland Boxing Association (Inc.)* [1978] 1 N.Z.L.R. 1, 29. *Cf. Bhardwaj v. Post Office* [1978] I.C.R. 144 (appeal from industrial tribunal dismissed because no real likelihood that chairman's overly strict attitude towards the appellant would have affected the result: but the tribunal's order of costs against appellant was allowed). An employee who alleges that he was dismissed unfairly because he was given no opportunity to be heard may recover less statutory compensation if the industrial tribunal decides that he contributed to his own dismissal by his conduct, but the tribunal should not consider whether he would have been dismissed, absent the unfair treatment, in any event: *Polkey v. A.E. Dayton Services Ltd.* [1987] 1 W.L.R. 1147.

[32] *R. v. Haberdashers' Aske's Hatcham School Governors, ex p. ILEA, The Times,* March 9, 1989.

[33] *R. v. Monopolies and Mergers Commission, ex p. Argyll* [1985] 1 W.L.R. 763 (the Court of Appeal also took into account the needs of good public administration); *cf. R. v. Secretary of State for Education and Science, ex p. ILEA* [1990] C.O.D. 319; *R. v. Bristol C.C. ex p. Pearce* (1984) 83 L.G.R. 711 (food hawkers not shown objections; but those objections could not possibly have motivated decision).

judgment, already been disclosed.[34] Whether the requisite flexibility is to be found in the definition of a breach of the *audi alteram partem* principle, in the statutory requirement of "substantial prejudice" or in the court's discretion over the remedy will generally be immaterial (except where the relief sought is non-discretionary, for example, an appeal[35] or a claim for damages).

In some cases it has been suggested that an applicant who is for   **9–035**
some reason underserving forfeits his right to fair hearing.[36] The forfeiture may be based upon a prejudgment of their merit as applicants, or a prejudgment of the likelihood of their wining the sympathy of the decision maker. We have already suggested[37] that a legitimate expectation which is derived from the representation of the decision-maker, should not be forfeited by the conduct of the applicant, however unmeritorious. It is also wrong for a hearing to be conditional upon the "good behaviour" of the applicant, and risky to prejudge the merits of the applicant's present case upon his previous wrongdoing. The same reasoning applies to the right to a fair hearing based upon a right or interest.[38]

Where the absence of a hearing is not due to any fault on the part of the decision-maker

Where alleged procedural unfairness is not the fault of the tribunal or   **9–036**
other decision-maker, is an applicant still entitled to have the decision quashed on the basis that he has not been accorded procedural fairness? Until recently, the answer to this question was not clear. Where, on an *inter partes* hearing, the absence of procedural fairness is due to the conduct of, or a failure by, the other party to the hearing, it had for some time been thought that the courts have a discretion to

---

[34] *R. v. Sunderland Juvenile Court, ex p. G* [1988] 1 W.L.R. 398; *cf. R. v. NW Thames Regional Health Authority, ex p. Daniels* [1993] 4 Med. L.R. 364.

[35] *cf. Ottley v. Morris* [1979] 1 All E.R. 65 (whether refusal of adjournment constituted ground of appeal on point of law depended on whether appellant might thereby have suffered a substantial injustice). *Hickmott v. Dorset C.C.* (1977) 35 P. & C.R. 195 (evidence improperly received in breach of *Judi alteram partem* rule could not have affected the result: appeal dismissed in absence of miscarriage of justice).

[36] *e.g. Cinnamond v. British Airports Authority* [1980] 1 W.L.R. 582 (minicab drivers at Heathrow Airport previously prosecuted frequently for breach of byelaw thus not entitled to fair hearing because no legitimate expectation (Lord Denning) or because it would have 'availed them nothing' (Lord Brandon).

[37] See Chap. 7, para. 7–065.

[38] Although the behaviour of the applicant may well influence the court's exercise of discretion in relation to the award of a remedy.

quash the decision.[39] Thus, where prison authorities had failed to make known to a prisoner charged with an offence against discipline the existence of a witness to the alleged offence, the determination of the prison board of visitors was quashed on the grounds of unfairness, albeit that this was not caused by the board of visitors themselves.[40] Where an important prosecution witness on a charge of shoplifting deceived the court as to his reason for resigning from the Metropolitan Police (being in fact required to resign following disgraceful conduct including a conviction), it was held that his deliberate concealment constituted unfairness, so that the conviction should be quashed.[41]

9–037   It has been suggested, however, that these decisions should be viewed not as resting on principles of fairness, but as based upon the alternative principle that "fraud unravels everything", or because the "process leading to conviction" has been distorted and vitiated as a result of a breach of duty owed to the court and to the defence by a prosecutor.[42] The principles of fairness, in contrast, are "concerned solely with the propriety of the procedure adopted by the decision-maker."[43] But this approach, it is submitted, risks leaving uncorrected procedural errors which are the responsibility of the prosecution or respondent, but which cannot be characterised as fraud or breach of duty. As Bingham L.J. has said, "If a procedural mishap occurs as a result of misunderstanding, confusion, failure of communication, or perhaps even inefficiency, and the result is to deny justice to the applicant, I should be very sorry to hold that the remedy of judicial review was not available".[44]

---

[39] *R. v. Blundeston Prison Board of Visitors, ex p. Fox-Taylor* [1982] 1 All E.R. 646; *R. v. Leyland J., ex p. Hawthorn* [1979] Q.B. 283; *R. v. Bolton JJ. ex p. Scally* [1991] 1 Q.B. 537; but see *Al Mehdawi*, below, n. 42.

[40] *R. v. Blundeston Prison Board of Visitors, ex p. Fox-Taylor* [1982] 1 All E.R. 646.

[41] *R. v. Knightsbridge Crown Court, ex p. Goonatilleke* [1986] Q.B. 1 (since the witness in question had presented the defendant for prosecution, and had ensured that he was prosecuted, it is suggested that he was effectively in the position of a prosecutor or respondent rather than a true third party).

[42] *per* Lord Bridge in *Al Mehdawi v. Secretary of State for the Home Department* [1990] A.C. 876, 895–896, Lord Bridge's reinterpretation of the earlier decisions is not entirely satisfactory, because it is not clear that in all such cases there has been anything approaching a breach of duty owed to the Court or to the defence, let alone fraud. For example, in *R. v. Bolton JJ., ex p. Scally* (above, n. 39), evidence led by the Crown Prosecution Service of blood alcohol levels in a drink-driving case was held to be unreliable due to 'an ordinary lack of care'. The Court held that certiorari would lie, because the prosecution's error had 'corrupted the process leading to conviction in a manner which was unfair' (*per* Watkins L.J.), but it would not appear that anything approaching fraud or breach of duty was established. See further, Herberg [1990] P.L. 467.

[43] *ibid.*, p. 894c.

[44] *Bagga Khan v. Secretary of State for the Home Department* [1987] Imm. A.R. 543–555.

As a general rule, a person who has himself impeded or frustrated   9–038
the service of notice of impending action cannot afterwards be heard
to complain that he did not receive actual notice.[45] But where the
mistake is due to the conduct of the applicant's legal representatives,
the position was until recently unclear. The question was expressly left
open in *R. v. Immigration Appeal Tribunal, ex p. Enwia.*[46] In *R. v.
Immigration Appeal Tribunal, ex p. Rahmani,*[47] the Court of Appeal held
that where an immigrant applicant's solicitors had negligently failed to
proceed with an appeal from a refusal of an application for an
extension of stay, the applicant was entitled to judicial review of the
dismissal of her appeal, since she had been denied a basic opportunity
to be heard, and the applicant herself was wholly innocent of
responsibility for this. Although the House of Lords in *Rahmani*
upheld the decision of the Court of Appeal, it did so on different
grounds and did not approve or reject the Court of Appeal's view

However, in *R. v. Secretary of State for the Home Department, ex p. Al*   9–039
Mehdawi,[48] the House of Lords did directly consider the Court of
Appeal's decision in *Rahmani*, and came to a very different conclusion.
In *Al Mehdawi*, the applicant had lodged an appeal against the Home
Sectetary's decision to make a deportation order against him. Notice of
the appeal was sent to his solicitors, who misaddressed the letter
when sending it on to the applicant, who consequently never received
notice of the appeal. The appeal was therefore dismissed in his
absence. On an application for judicial review of the decision to
dismiss the appeal, on the ground that the applicant had been denied
a fair (or any) hearing, the House of Lords held that a party cannot

---

[45] *De Verteuil v. Knaggs* [1918] A.C. 557, 560–561; see also *James v. Institute of Chartered
Accountants* (1907) 98 L.T. 225; *Glynn v. Keele University* [1971] 1 W.L.R. 487, 495
(failure to notify change of address); *R. v. Newport Justices, ex p. Carey,* (1996) 160 J.P.
613; Div. Ct (applicant's absence from hearing his own fault); *R. v. Secretary of State
for the Home Department, ex p. Kikaka* [1996] Imm. A.R. 340 (applicant had chosen to
represent herself).

[46] [1984] 1 W.L.R. 117, CA. At first instance, Comyn J. held that the court could grant
relief in such circumstances, although his judgment was reversed on the facts by the
Court of Appeal.

[47] [1985] Q.B. 1109, CA; [1986] A.C. 475, HL (*sub nom Rahmani v. Diggiues*).

[48] [1990] 1 A.C. 876. See also *Hassan v. Secretary of State for the Home Department* [1994]
Imm. A.R. 482, CA. See also, all following *Al Mehdawi: Secretary of State for the Home
Department v. Mohammed Yasin* [1995] Imm. A.R. 118, 121–122 (failure of applicant's
advisors to draw Tribunal's attention to brother's case); *Samuel Dele Adeniyi v.
Secretary of State for the Home Department* [1995] Imm. A.R. 101 (failure of solicitors to
send notice of appeal to correct address); *R. v. Governors of Sheffield Hallam University,
ex p. R* [1995] E.L.R. 267 (failure of applicant's solicitor to seek sufficient adjournment
to consider new material); *R. v. Secretary of State for the Home Department, ex p: Osei
Yaw Yeboah* [1995] Imm. A.R. 393 (applicant not represented at appeal through fault
of solicitor); *R. v. Monopolies and Mergers Commission, ex p. Stagecoach Holdings Plc, The
Times,* July 23, 1996.

complain of a denial of a fair hearing where he has failed to make use of an opportunity to be heard through the fault of his own advisers, even if he himself is not responsible in any way for that failure. Lord Bridge drew an analogy with the position in private law, where a party who lost the opportunity to have his case heard through the negligence of his legal advisers would be left with no remedy except against those advisers. Their Lordships were clearly influenced by the fear that to allow review in such circumstances could open the way for manipulation of hearings, and would hinder the dismissal of abandoned appeals by administrative bodies. It may thus now confidently be stated that the courts will not intervene to correct an alleged procedural defect which arose from the fault of the applicant or his representatives, unless, perhaps, the tribunal were also at fault.[49]

---

[49] On the other hand, fault by an applicant's legal advisers may be a 'good reason' for delay in bringing an application for judicial review; see *R. v. Secretary of State for the Home Department, ex p. Oyeleye* [1994] Imm. A.R. 268; *R. v. London Borough of Newham ex p. Gentle* (1994) 26 H.L.R. 466.

CHAPTER 10

PROCEDURAL FAIRNESS: FETTERING OF DISCRETION

FETTERING OF DISCRETION BY SELF-CREATED RULES OF POLICY

A decision-making body exercising public functions which is entrusted **10–001** with a discretion must not, by the adoption of a fixed rule of policy, disable itself from exercising its discretion in individual cases. It may not "fetter" its discretion. A body that does fetter its discretion in that way may offend against either or both of two grounds of judicial review: the ground of legality and the ground of procedural propriety. It offends against legality by failing to use its powers in the way they were intended, namely, to employ and to utilise the discretion conferred upon it. It offends against procedural propriety by failing to permit affected persons to influence the use of that discretion. By failing to keep its "mind ajar", by "shutting its ears" to an application, the body in question effectively forecloses participation in the decision-making process.

Because the "no fettering" rule is mostly employed as a means of **10–002** keeping open the possibility of meaningful participation in the decision-making process, we deal with it in this section of the book as a species of the genus procedural fairness. The overlap with illegality (and even irrationality) should, however, be borne in mind. As we have said, the so-called "grounds" of review are by no means entirely self-contained.

The rule against fettering discretion by no means forbids bodies **10–003** upon which discretionary power has been conferred to guide the implementation of that discretion by means of a policy or a rule. It directs attention to the *attitude* of the decision-maker, who must simply be prepared to make an exception to that rule or policy in a deserving case. Nor does the rule against fettering discretion focus upon the content of the hearing which must be afforded to persons interested in changing the decision-maker's mind. The decision-maker must allow interested individuals the opportunity to persuade him to amend or deviate from the rule or policy, but, unlike the principle of natural justice or fair hearing, the rule against fettering is not concerned with any particular form of hearing or with any particular technique of making or receiving representations.[1]

10–004   The underlying rationale of the rule against fettering discretion is to ensure that two perfectly legitimate administrative values, those of legal certainty and consistency, may be counteracted by another equally legitimate administrative value, namely, that of responsiveness. While allowing rules and policies to promote the former values, it insists that the full rigour of certainty and consistency be tempered by the willingness to make exceptions, to respond flexibly to unusual situations, and to apply justice in the individual case.[2]

10–005   Thus, a tribunal which has power to award costs fails to exercise its discretion if it fixes specific amounts to be applied indiscriminately to all cases before it[3]; but its statutory discretion may be wide enough to justify the adoption of a rule not to award any costs save in exceptional circumstances,[4] as distinct from a rule never to award any costs at all. A body to which discretion has been entrusted may also, of course, have been expressly authorised to make regulations that in some way affect its exercise of discretion. To the extent that it has exercised its statutory rule-making power it must decide individual cases by reference to any relevant provision in its regulations, rather than by applying the terms of the empowering Act.[5] But otherwise

---

[1] In *R. v. Secretary of State for the Environment, ex. p. Brent L.B.C.* [1982] Q.B. 593 the decision of the Secretary of State was held unlawful both for fettering of discretion and for failing to provide a fair hearing.

[2] See further, D.J. Galligan, 'The Nature and Functions of Policy Within Discretionary Power' [1976] P.L. 332 pp. 21–31. And see H.J. Elcock, *Administrative Justice*, Chaps 1, 2 and 5. For an analysis of the advantages and disadvantages of creation by various administrative techniques, criteria to regulate the exercise of discretion, see J. Jowell, 'The Legal Control of Administrative Discretion' [1973] P.L. 178; *Law and Bureaucracy* (1975); D.J. Galligan, *Discretionary Powers, A Legal Study of Official Discretion* (1986). See also K.C. Davis, *Discretionary Justice* (1969). See also the works cited in Chap. 5, above, paras 5–004 and 5–006, nn. 3 and 5. On the distinction between rules and objectives, see *Oddy v. Transport Salaried Staff's Association* [1973] I.C.R. 524. See also Henry L. Molot, 'The Self-Created Rule of Policy and Other Ways of Exercising Administrative Discretion' (1972) 18 McGill L.J. 310. See also *R. v. Secretary of State for the Home Department, ex p. Venables* [1997] 3 W.L.R. 23, 47, where Lord Browne-Wilkinson restated the distinction between a proper policy and an over-rigid or inflexible one, and referred to the passage in the text.

[3] *R. v. Merioneth JJ.* (1844) 6 Q.B. 153; *R. v. Glamorganshire JJ.* (1850) 19 L.J.M.C. 172.

[4] *Re Wood's Application* (1952) 3 P. & C.R. 238; *R. v. Secretary of State for the Environment, ex p. Reinisch* (1971) 70 L.G.R. 126. Indeed, when a tribunal departs from its normal rule it may be required to give clear reasons for its decision: *Pepys v. London Transport Executive* [1975] 1 W.L.R. 234; *R. v. Wreck Commissioner, ex p. Knight* [1976] 3 All E.R. 8.

[5] See, *e.g.* Betting, Gaming and Lotteries Act 1963, Sched. 6 (as amended by the Act of 1968, Sched. 11, Pt II, para. 3), empowering local authorities to resolve not to grant or renew licences for certain forms of gambling on premises of a specified class: see

discretion may not generally be validly exercised by a public body solely on the basis of some policy or rule that it had informally previously adopted.[6] The more specific the statutory criteria to be applied by the tribunal, the less likely are courts to conclude that the tribunal may legitimately give effect to its own policies.[7]

The courts have often been called upon to consider the **10–006** circumstances in which licensing justices and other licensing authorities may lay down general principles for the exercise of their own discretion in relation to applications before them. It would be going too far to say that a licensing tribunal must "put aside preconceived opinions and previous resolutions."[8] A local licensing authority is entitled to have regard to the special requirements of the neighbourhood and in dealing with individual applications it may be justified in adopting and following a general rule that the total number of licences in its area ought to be reduced,[9] or that, unless exceptional circumstances are present, it will not grant any further licences to enable residential hotels to serve liquor to non-residents,[10] or that it will normally give priority to those applicants for licences, for which demand exceeds supply, who do not already have one.[11] It is obvious the rule that it formulates must not be based on considerations extraneous to those contemplated by the enabling Act; otherwise it has exercised its discretion invalidly by taking irrelevant

---

R. v. Herrod, ex p. Leeds C.C. [1976] Q.B. 540, 559–560, 563–564. See also *Re Ricard and Unemployment Insurance Commission* (1976) 64 D.L.R. (3d) 190 (raising the question of distinguishing between power to make rules respecting proof of, rather than definition of, eligibility for benefit). And see the difficult case of *Re War Amputations of Canada and Pension Review Board* (1975) 55 D.L.R. (3d) 724 on the implications of the exercise by an administrative tribunal of a statutory power to interpret legislation.

[6] For an example of the imposition of a statutory duty to establish criteria for the exercise of discretion, see Housing Association Act 1985, s.5(1) and (2) (criteria to be satisfied by housing associations for registration with Housing Corporation).

[7] See *Green v. Daniels* (1977) 51 A.L.J.R. 463.

[8] *R. v. Brighton Corp , ex p. Tilling (Thomas) Ltd* (1916) 85 L.J.K.B. 1552, 1556. The general principles to be applied are summarised by the Court of Appeal in *R. v. Windsor Licensing JJ., ex p. Hodes* [1983] 1 W.L.R. 685; the Justices cannot properly determine an application simply by reference to a preordained policy without reference to the particular facts of the application before them.

[9] *Boyle v. Wilson* [1907] A.C. 45 (liquor licences); *R. v. Prestwich Corp., ex p. Gandz* (1945) 109 J.P. 157 (taxicab licences); Local Government (Miscellaneous Provisions) Act 1982, Sched. 3, para. 12(3)(c) and (4), empowering local authorities to refuse licenses for sex establishments solely on the basis that it is considered that the number of establishments in the locality equals or exceeds the number considered appropriate; *cf. R. v. Bournemouth B.C., ex p. Continental Books Ltd, The Times,* May 19, 1994.

[10] *R. v. Torquay Licensing JJ., ex p. Brockman* [1951] 2 K.B. 784. See also *R. v. Holborn Licensing JJ., ex p. Stratford Catering Co.* (1926) 136 L.T. 278.

[11] *R. v. Tower Hamlets L.B.C., ex p. Kayne-Levenson* [1975] Q.B. 431, 446, 452. See also *Perilly v. Tower Hamlets L.B.C.* [1973] Q.B. 9 (rule that licences granted in order of application upheld).

considerations into account.[12] However, a factor that may properly be taken into account in exercising a discretion may become an unlawful fetter upon discretion if it is elevated to the status of a general rule that results in the pursuit of consistency at the expense of the merits of individual cases.[13] Indeed, the Court of Appeal has warned the Transport Tribunal (in its capacity as a transport licensing appellate authority) against developing a body of rigidly binding precedent.[14] *A fortiori*, the authority must not predetermine the issue, as by resolving to refuse all applications,[15] or all applications of a certain class,[16] or all applications except those of a certain class[17] and then proceeding to refuse an application before it in pursuance of such a resolution[18]; although it is not obliged to consider every application before it with a fully open mind, it must at least keep its mind ajar. Similarly, whilst the Supplementary Benefits Commission was entitled to assess an applicant's resources on the assumption that if he is a university student he is in receipt of a parental contribution bringing his grant up to the maximum awarded by local authorities, it cannot calculate the applicant's resources on this basis when the facts of the particular

---

[12] As in *R. v. Police Commissioner, ex p. Randall* (1911) 27 T.L.R. 505 and *R. v. Rotherham Licensing JJ., ex p. Chapman* [1939] 2 All E.R. 710 (as explained in *R. v. Torquay Licensing JJ.* (n.10, above)). Nor must the rule be applied capriciously: see n. 34, below.

[13] *R. v. Flintshire C.C. County Licensing (Stage Plays) Committee, ex p. Barrett* [1957] 1 Q.B. 350 (committee adopted general rule that no alcoholic liquor or tobacco be sold in a theatre if adequate drinking facilities were available near by, irrespective of the past record of the theatre, and having imposed this condition on one theatre imposed it on the applicants in the interests of consistency).

[14] *Merchandise Transport Ltd v. British Transport Commission* [1962] 2 Q.B. 173, 186, 192–193. The decisions of planning inspectors have until recently not been regarded as even relevant considerations in assessing the merits of planning applications. But see now *North Wiltshire D.C. v. Secretary of State for the Environment* [1992] J.P.L. 955, CA.

[15] *R. v. Walsall JJ.* (1854) 3 W.R. 69.

[16] *R. v. L.C.C., ex p. Corrie* [1918] 1 K.B. 68 (local authority resolved to refuse all further permits, without exception, to distribute literature in public parks); *cf. Sharp v. Hughes* (1893) 57 J.P. 104. See also *Sagnata Investments Ltd v. Norwich Corp.* [1971] 2 Q.B. 614; *R. v. Tower Hamlets L.B.C., ex p. Kayne-Levenson* [1975] Q.B. 431; *R. v. Wakefield Crown Court, ex p. Oldfield* [1978] Crim.L.R. 164; *R. v. Rochdale M.B.C., ex. p. Cromer Ring Mill Ltd* [1982] 3 All E.R. 761.

[17] See also *R. v. Sylvester* (1862) 31 L.J.M.C. 93 (refusal to issue any beerhouse licences except to applicants who agreed to take out an excise licence for sale of spirits also); *R. v. Barry D.C., ex p. Jones* (1900) 16 T.L.R. 556 (refusal to issue any new taxicab licences except to two proprietors and their drivers).

[18] Ordinarily, any challenge to a resolution will occur at the stage of the application of that resolution to a particular case, rather than in the form of a general challenge to the making of the resolution itself. Nevertheless, in an appropriate case, where the difficulties of establishing *locus standi* can be overcome, the resolution itself may be challenged by way of an application for declaratory relief or otherwise; see *Re Findlay* [1985] A.C. 318.

case show that the assumed contribution has not been made.[19] The relevant principles were well stated by Bankes L.J. in a case in which the Port of London Authority had refused an application for a licence to construct certain works, on the ground that it had itself been charged with the provision of accommodation of that character.

> "There are on the one hand cases where a tribunal in the honest exercise of its discretion has adopted a policy, and, without refusing to hear an applicant, intimates to him what its policy is, and that after hearing him it will in accordance with its policy decide against him, *unless there is something exceptional in his case* ... if the policy has been adopted for reasons which the tribunal may legitimately entertain, no objection could be taken to such a course. On the other hand there are cases where a tribunal has passed a rule, or come to a determination, not to hear any application of a particular character by whomsoever made. There is a wide distinction to be drawn between these two classes."[20] (Bankes L.J.'s emphasis.)"

It is obviously desirable that a tribunal should openly state any general principles by which it intends to be guided in the exercise of its discretion. The courts have encouraged licensing justices to follow this practice,[21] and when a tribunal is required to give an individual an opportunity to be heard, it may be a denial of natural justice not to disclose the principles upon which the tribunal proposes to exercise its discretion.[22]

---

[19] *R. v. Barnsley Supplementary Benefits Appeal Tribunal, ex p. Atkinson* [1977] 1 W.L.R. 917; see also *R. v. Greater Birmingham Appeal Tribunal, ex p. Simper* [1974] Q.B. 543 for another instance in which the Commission was found to have applied its working rules too strictly.

[20] *R. v. P.L.A., ex p. Kynoch Ltd* [1919] 1 K.B. 176, 184. The vital words here italicised (by the author of the first edition of this work) are omitted from the report of Bankes L.J.'s judgment in other series of reports; see 88 L.J.K.B. at 559, 120 L.T. at 179, 83 J.P. at 43. The judgment appears to have been substantially rewritten for the purpose of publication in the Law Reports.

[21] *R. v. Holborn Licensing JJ., ex p. Stratford Catering Co.* (1926) 136 L.T. 278, 281; *R. v. Torquay Licensing JJ., ex p. Brockman* (above, n. 10) at 788. See generally Robson, *Justice and Administrative Law* (3rd ed., 1951), pp. 611–614, 629. See also the "structuring of discretion", proposed by K.C. Davis (above, n. 2).
Open prescription or specification of the principles that are to govern the exercise of discretion is to be found in other areas also—*e.g.* by publication of instructions to immigration officers concerning the exercise of their powers and duties under immigration legislation; and various publications and statements issued by the Department of the Environment relating to planning control.

[22] *R. v. Criminal Injuries Compensation Board, ex p. Ince* [1973] 1 W.L.R. 1334, 1345. In Canada it has been held that precise standards may be required. See *Re Garden Gulf Court & Motel Inc. v. Island Telephone Co.* (1981) 126 D.L.R. (3rd) 281. See also *Re Irving Oil Ltd v. Public Utilities Commission* (1986) 34 D.L.R. (4th) 448.

10–007 Many of the cases illustrating the principles now under consideration have been concerned with the discretionary grant of licences and permits; but the ambit of these principles is not confined to this class of function.[23] In 1858 the Court of Appeal in Chancery sternly reproved a sanitary authority for having laid down a general rule that all cesspits and privies in its area should be replaced by water-closets, instead of having dealt with each case individually on its merits.[24] There the authority was treated as a body analogous to a tribunal exercising a judicial discretion. But similar principles can be applied to other functions of public bodies, without drawing artificial analogies with tribunals, or resorting to the obsolete distinction between judicial, quasi-judicial and administrative bodies. In a Scottish case it was assumed that the Secretary of State, in deciding whether to approve an appointment to the office of chief constable, was not entitled to adopt a rigid rule never to approve the appointment of an officer who was already a member of the local police force in question.[25] The Secretary of State for the Environment was held to have fettered his discretion in adopting a policy of disallowing all purely local objections to the allocation of land for gypsy sites.[26] Local

---

[23] This statement of the law was approved by the Divisional Court in *R. v. Secretary of State for the Environment, ex p. Brent L.B.C.* [1982] Q.B. 593, 642. See also *Lavender (H.) & Son Ltd v. Minister of Housing and Local Government* [1970] 1 W.L.R. 1231; *cf. Stringer v. Minister of Housing and Local Government, ibid.* 1281 (local authority fettered its planning policy by agreement but Secretary of State on appeal not so fettered).

[24] *Tinkler v. Wandsworth Board of Works* (1858) 27 L.J.Ch. 342. This decision is a singular illustration of the principle that an Englishman's home is his castle. See also *Wood v. Widnes Corp.* [1898] 1 Q.B. 463.

[25] *Kilmarnock Magistrates v. Secretary of State for Scotland*, 1961 S.C. 350 (held, entitled to adopt a general policy to that effect, subject to willingness to make exceptions in special cases).

[26] *R. v. Secretary of State for the Environment, ex p. Halton D.C.* (1983) 82 L.G.R. 662; compare *R. v. Home Secretary, ex p. Bennett, The Times,* August 18, 1986 (Home Secretary's criteria for approval of police rent allowance was over-rigid). The Secretary of State for the Home Office was held (by a majority of the House of Lords) to have fettered his discretion in setting a 'tariff' period of 15 years for a person sentenced to be detained at Her Majesty's Pleasure, because the 'tariff' period did not permit review on grounds other than those relating to the circumstances of the commission of the crime and the applicant's state of mind, contrary to the Secretary of State's statutory power which was not fettered in this way: see *R. v. Secretary of State for the Home Department, ex p. Venables* [1997] 3 W.L.R. 23, *per* Lord Browne-Wilkinson (45e–50g), Lord Steyn (69c–73d, although his Lordship did not use the language of fettering of discretion) and Lord Hope (80c–f, 82d–84f). Compare, in the Court of Appeal, [1997] 2 W.L.R. 67 at 90b–e, *per* Lord Woolf M.R. See also *R. v. Secretary of State for the Home Department, ex p. Zulfikar* [1996] C.O.D. 256 (blanket policy of strip-searching prisoners after every visit not unlawful); *R. v. Secretary of State for the Home Department, ex p. Hastrup* [1996] Imm. A.R. 616 (Minister's discretion as to whether to deport a person married to a British citizen with a British child not fettered by Home Office policy document). *

authorities must be prepared, at least when an objection is expressly raised,[27] to make exceptions, after considering the merits of individual cases, to their general rules about allocating children to denominational schools,[28] abolishing secondary schools that admit children on the basis of ability,[29] evicting tenants of council houses who are in arrears with their rent,[30] making payments for the provision of temporary housing accommodation,[31] refusing applications for housing by children of those "intentionally homeless"[32] or referring tenancies to a rent tribunal[33] or refusing applications for requests for assessments of a child's special educational needs.[34] A chief constable ought not to adopt a rigid rule not to institute any prosecution at all for an anti-social class of criminal offence[35] nor should he fetter his discretion by treating the

---

[27] *Smith v. Inner London Education Authority* [1978] 1 All E.R. 411.

[28] *Cumings v. Birkenhead Corp.* [1972] Ch. 12.

[29] *Smith's* case (above, n. 27).

[30] *Bristol D.C. v. Clark* [1975] 1 W.L.R. 1443, 1448 (dicta); *R. v. Tower Hamlets L.B.C., ex p. Khalique, The Times,* March 17, 1994 (rule that cases where rent arrears greater than £500 would be rendered 'non-active' went well beyond the bounds of a lawful policy since it permitted no flexibility whatsoever). See also *R. v. Lambeth L.B.C. ex p. Njomo* (1996) 28 H.L.A. 737. *Cf. Elliott v. Brighton B.C.* (1980) 79 L.G.R. 506 (fettering of discretion to recondition substandard houses after failure to comply with improvement notice).

[31] *Roberts v. Dorset C.C.* (1977) 75 L.G.R. 462.

[32] *Att.-Gen. ex rel. Tilley v. Wandsworth L.B.C.* [1981] 1 W.L.R. 854 (Templeman L.J. went further in suggesting that even a policy resolution hedged around with exceptions might not be entirely free from attack (p. 858)).

[33] *R. v. Barnet & Camden Rent Tribunal, ex p. Frey Investments Ltd* [1972] 2 Q.B. 342, explaining *R. v. Paddington & St Marylebone Rent Tribunal, ex p. Bell London & Provincial Properties Ltd* [1949] 1 K.B. 666 as a case of a capricious reference made without consideration of relevant matters.

[34] *R. v. Hampshire C.C., ex p. W* [1994] E.L.R. 460.

[35] *R. v. Metropolitan Police Commissioner, ex p. Blackburn* [1968] 2 Q.B. 118 (gaming offences in clubs); but a large measure of discretion must be conceded to the police as prosecutors: *Buckoke v. G.L.C.* [1971] Ch. 655; *R. v. Metropolitan Police Commissioner, ex p. Blackburn (No. 3)* [1973] Q.B. 241. See also *R. v. Race Relations Board, ex p. Selvarajan* [1975] 1 W.L.R. 1686, 1697 (dicta that exercise of discretion by Director of Public Prosecutions is reviewable in the courts); *R. v. General Council of the Bar, ex p. Percival* [1991] 1 Q.B. 212; *R. v. DPP, ex p. Langlands-Pearse* [1991] C.O.D. 92; *R. v. Inland Revenue Commissioner, ex p. Mead* [1993] 1 All E.R. 772; *R. v. Chief Constable of Kent, ex p. L* [1993] 1 All E.R. 756; *R. v. DPP ex p. C* [1995] 1 Cr. App. R. 136; (1995) 7 Admin L.R. 385. The effect of these decisions is that the power to review a decision of the CPS or DPP not to prosecute is only to be exercised sparingly; only (*per* Kennedy L.J. in *ex p. C,* above) where the decision has been taken (i) because of some unlawful policy; or (ii) because of a failure to act in accordance with a settled policy; or (iii) perversely. A prosecution unreasonably or unfairly instituted may be struck out as an abuse of process or may result in an absolute discharge or a reduced sentence (*Buckoke v. G.L.C.* (above) at 668, 670–671; *Smedleys Ltd v. Breed* [1974] A.C. 839, 856–857, 861; *R. v. Arrowsmith* [1975] Q.B. 678, 689–691); and see *DPP v. Humphrys* [1977] A.C. 1; *cf. Johnson v. Phillips* [1976] 1 W.L.R. 65 (limited discretion of

decision of the Director of Public Prosecutions that there was insufficient evidence to justify the prosecution of an officer, as determinative of the question of whether to dismiss for unfairness disciplinary charges against that officer based on substantially the same facts.[36] The Law Society was entitled to have policies governing claims against the Compensation Fund (including a policy excluding compensation for consequential loss) provided that such policy admitted of exceptions in appropriate cases, and that any special reasons put forward were considered.[37] The House of Lords has even applied these basic principles to the discretionary award of investment allowances to industrialists by a government department.[38]

10–008   The courts may be prepared to scrutinise closely the conduct of a decision-maker in assessing whether or not he has unlawfully fettered his discretion. A course of conduct involving the consistent rejection of applications belonging to a particular class may justify an inference that the competent authority has adopted an unavowed rule to refuse all.[39] Further, where a departmental handbook on its face fettered the discretion of the Ministry, the courts were prepared to go behind a claim that the handbook was not in fact relied upon in reaching the impugned decision, the handbook was on the basis that "so much a

---

police officer to commit technical offences in the execution of duty to protect life and property); see also *Donnelly v. Jackman* [1970] 1 W.L.R. 562; *Squires v. Botwright* [1972] R.T.R. 462 (apparent extensions of the powers of police officers to stop suspects); see David Lanham, 'Arrest, Detention and Compulsion' [1974] Crim.L.R. 288. See generally, K.C. Davis, *Discretionary Justice: a Preliminary Inquiry* (1969); A.F. Wilcox, *The Decision to Prosecute* (1972); K.C. Davis, *Police Discretion* (1975) and *Discretionary Justice in Europe and America* (1976). See also Bernard M. Dickens, 'The Attorney-General's Consent to Prosecutions' (1972) 35 M.L.R. 347; Roger Hood (ed.), *Crime, Criminology and Public Opinion* (1974), 161–195 (D.G.T. Williams).

[36] *R. v. Chief Constable Thames Vally Police, ex p. Police Complaints Authority* [1996] C.O.D. 324.

[37] *R. v. Law Society, ex p. Reigate Projects Ltd* [1993] 1 W.L.R. 1531.

[38] *British Oxygen Co. Ltd v. Board of Trade* [1971] A.C. 610; *cf. R. v. Secretary of State for Transport, ex p. Sheriff & Sons Ltd, The Times*, December 18, 1986.

[39] *cf. Macbeth v. Ashley* (1874) L.R. 2 H.L.Sc. 352, 357. This passage was expressly approved in *R. v. Warwickshire C.C., ex p. Collymore* [1995] E.L.R. 217 where Judge J. held that where, over a period of three years, 300 appeals from decisions of the council to refuse discretionary student grants had all failed, it could be inferred that the policy to refuse to award discretionary grants save in 'most extraordinary' circumstances had been applied far too rigidly. The judge did not decide, however, whether the mere fact the council's policy admitted of exceptions only in the 'most extraordinary' circumstances itself constituted an unlawful blanket policy; compare *R. v. Warwickshire C.C., ex p. Williams, The Independent*, February 15, 1995, where Schiemann J. held that the council was entitled to have a policy to make no discretionary education grants save in 'exceptional circumstances'.

part of the Department's thinking" that its influence could not be dismissed.[40]

The courts may not always have been consistent in their willingness **10–009** to allow administrative tribunals to formulate and apply rules or policies to regulate their exercise of discretion.[41] In some cases the courts have taken a strict view. For example, domestic tribunals have been said to act improperly in refusing to allow a party to appear at the hearing with a legal representative solely because it has never been their practice to permit it.[42] And tribunals have been taken to task for elevating to the status of binding legal rules their own decisional criteria, instead of using them as no more than working rules or rebuttable presumptions to guide them in the exercise of their statutory discretion or in their application of the relevant statutory standards.[43] An error of this kind may also be characterised as a failure to answer the question remitted by the legislation by taking into account irrelevant considerations or by ignoring the relevant.[44] At the other extreme, however, are powers that enable the decision maker to consider so wide a range of policy considerations that it becomes difficult to set any effective limit on the principles by which their exercise may be guided. Thus, a policy decision by the Home Secretary to exclude without exception alien students of scientology has been held to be legally unimpeachable.[45] However, the courts have

---

[40] *R. v. Secretary of State for Transport, ex p. Sheriff & Sons, The Times,* December 18, 1986. Compare *R. v. Southwark L.B.C., ex p. Udu* (1996) 8 Admin. L.R. 25 (local authority entitled to have general policy of not funding courses at private colleges and postgraduate courses, subject to 'exceptional cases').

[41] See D.J. Galligan [1976] P.L. 332, 348–355.

[42] *e.g. Pett v. Greyhound Racing Association (Ltd) (No. 1)* [1969] 1 Q.B. 125; *Enderby Town Football Club Ltd v. Football Association Ltd* [1971] Ch. 591, 605–606.

[43] *e.g. R. v. Greater Birmingham Appeal Tribunal, ex p. Simper* [1974] Q.B. 543; *R. v. Barnsley Supplementary Benefits Appeal Tribunal, ex p. Atkinson* [1977] 1 W.L.R. 917; *R. v. Criminal Injuries Compensation Board, ex p. R.J.C. (an Infant)* [1978] Crim. L.R. 220.

[44] *e.g. R. v. Criminal Injuries Compensation Board, ex p. Ince* [1973] 1 W.L.R. 1334; *Saggers v. British Railways Board* [1977] 1 W.L.R. 1090 (*cf. Re Funk and Manitoba Labour Board* (1976) 66 D.L.R. (3d) 35); *R. v. Criminal Injuries Compensation Board, ex p. Clowes* [1977] 1 W.L.R. 1353. See also *Green v. Daniels* (1977) 51 A.L.J.R. 463 (tribunal had no discretion in the interests of administrative efficiency to add to the statutory conditions of eligibility for benefit).

[45] *Schmidt v. Home Secretary* [1969] 2 Ch. 149. See also the concurring judgment of Viscount Dilhorne in *British Oxygen Co. Ltd. v. Board of Trade* [1971] A.C. 610, 630–631. *Cf. R. v. Minister of Transport, ex p. Grey Coaches Ltd* (1933) 77 S.J. 310. See too *R. v. Secretary of State for the Environment, ex p. Friends of the Earth, The Times,* April 12, 1994 (Secretary of State did not fetter his ability to take enforcement action against water authorities by accepting undertakings from the authorities, because acceptance of undertakings furthered purpose of Water Industry Act 1991, and undertakings did not in fact impede further enforcement action). See *R. v. National Rivers Authority ex p. Moreton* [1996] Env.L.R. 234. Similar considerations might also have applied in 1977 and 1978 to the policy decision to withhold export credit guarantees from companies

in recent years been more prepared, particularly in the context of local government, to intervene in matters of policy-making and policy-implementation, to ensure that there is no improper fettering of discretion; to ensure, for example, that a manifesto commitment is not blindly implemented following an election victory.[46]

10–010   In determining the validity of the exercise of discretion that falls between these extremes particular importance may be attached to the fact that before the agency applied its rules or policy an opportunity was afforded the individual affected to make representations. It will be rare that the repository of discretion will be held to have fettered its exercise unlawfully if it has been addressed on the applicability of the non-statutory criterion to the particular case, on whether an exception to the rules or policy should be made in that instance and on the soundness of the standard that has been adopted.[47] On the other

---

that had infringed the guidelines of the Government's incomes policy. (See para. 6–036 above.) It has also been held that a Minister (or other public body) does not fetter his discretion in incurring expenditure in anticipation of legislation, so long as he does not bind himself as to decisions to be taken pursuant to the legislation after it has received the Royal Assent and come into force: see *R. v. Secretary of State for Health, ex p. Keen* [1990] C.O.D. 371.

[46] *R. v. G.L.C., ex p. Bromley L.B.C.* [1983] 1 A.C. 768 (the 'Fares Fair' case). Lords Diplock and Brandon, in particular, criticised the G.L.C. for implementing its manifesto commitment to introduce a subsidy policy automatically after the election. Compare *R. v. Merseyside C.C., ex p. Great Universal Stores Limited* (1982) 80 L.G.R. 639, where the Fares Fair case was distinguished on the ground, *inter alia*, that the Merseyside C.C. had considered its manifesto commitment afresh after the election, before implementing the policy; *cf. R. v. Waltham Forest, L.B.C., ex p. Baxter* [1988] Q.B. 419 (councillors entitled to regard manifesto as very important factor in reaching decision). And see Chap. 12, para. 12-062–12-064 below.

[47] *e.g. Boyle v. Wilson* [1907] A.C. 45; *British Oxygen* case (above, n. 38) at 625, 631; *Malloch v. Aberdeen Corp. (No. 2)*, 1974 S.L.T. 253; *Smith v. Inner London Education Authority* [1978] 1 All E.R. 411. *Cf.*, however, *R. v. Rotherham Licensing JJ., ex p. Chapman* [1939] 2 All E.R. 710.

One reason why the courts have rarely impugned for fettering ministerial dispositions of planning appeals, proposals for compulsory acquisition of land and other matters that are decided after a public inquiry has been held, is that individuals affected by these decisions will have had an opportunity to bring to the Minister's attention considerations that may mitigate against a mechanical application of some rule of thumb. See, *e.g. Franklin v. Minister of Town and Country Planning* [1948] A.C. 87; *Stringer v. Minister of Housing and Local Government* [1970] 1 W.L.R. 1281. Another reason for judicial reluctance to intervene is the wide range of policy considerations relevant to the exercise of the statutory powers in question. It will require a decision letter worded with particular infelicity or the adoption by the court of an unduly narrow construction of it (*e.g. Lavender (H.) and Son Ltd v. Minister of Housing and Local Government* [1970] 1 W.L.R. 1231) to lead the court to the conclusion that the Minister, in effect, viewed the inquiry and the inspector's report with the utmost cynicism. It may also be noted that there are dicta in the majority judgments in *Sagnata Investments Ltd v. Norwich Corp.* [1971] 2 Q.B. 614, 632, 633, 639 that lend support to the view that even after a hearing, an administrative discretion may not be exercised solely on the basis of a policy decision to grant no more licences of

hand, the duty not to fetter a discretion continues after representations have been entertained, up to the time that the decision is taken, and accordingly, it may well be an unlawful fetter for a decision-maker to refuse to entertain a delegation who have already been heard, if the decision-maker does not ascertain whether they have any new representations to make.[48]

Although there is little authority on the point, it may be that a body **10–011** that has administratively reduced the scope of its discretion may thereby attract to itself a duty to hear that would not otherwise have been imposed upon it. A hearing of some sort might be thought to be appropriate in these circumstances to guard against any improper fettering of discretion,[49] and because the adoption of more specific criteria may give rise to disputes for the resolution of which a hearing would be appropriate.[50]

Moreover, when an agency openly prescribes the criteria upon **10–012** which it proposes to decide it may thereby engender a legitimate expectation in one who satisfies them, and thereby create an interest that in fairness should be given some procedural,[51] or even substantive,[52] protection. Thus there are circumstances in which an authority will not be permitted to depart from its previously announced policy without affording a hearing to those adversely affected by it.[53] And whilst it is clear that an administrative body will

---

specified types. However, in that case the court was primarily considering the legality of a decision of Quarter Sessions, to which an appeal lay by way of rehearing from the licensing authority, rather than whether the original decision to refuse the licence was *ultra vires* the local authority. Moreover, an unimpeachable finding of fact by the Recorder was treated as virtually amounting to an assertion that the hearing had been treated by the council as a mere formality.

[48] *R. v. Secretary of State for the Environment, ex p. Brent L.B.C.* [1982] Q.B. 593 (Secretary of State fettered discretion in refusing to entertain new representations from affected local authorities).

[49] See, *e.g.* the *British Oxygen* case (above, n. 38); *cf. Re Innisfil (Township of) and Vespra (Township of)* (1978) 23 O.R. (2d) 147.

[50] *e.g. R. v. Holborn Licensing JJ., ex p. Stratford Catering Co. Ltd* (1926) 42 T.L.R. 778, 781; *R. v. Criminal Injuries Compensation Board, ex p. Ince* [1973] 1 W.L.R. 1334, 1345 (tribunals that are in any event required to conduct a hearing should disclose the principles upon which they propose to make their decision). See also *Salemi v. MacKellar (No. 2)* (1977) 137 C.L.R. 396, for conflicting dicta on whether, before deciding to deport an alien on the ground that he did not fall within the terms of an amnesty for certain classes of prohibited immigrants, the Minister must allow representation to be made. But see *Birdi v. Home Secretary* (1975) 119 S.J. 322.

[51] See Chap. 7 paras 7–037 *et seq.*

[52] See Chap. 12 paras 12–025 *et seq.*

[53] *R. v. Liverpool Corp., ex p. Liverpool Taxi Fleet Operators' Association* [1972] 2 Q.B. 299; *Att.-Gen. of Hong Kong v. Ng Yuen Shiu* [1983] 2 A.C. 629; *R. v. Secretary of State for the Home Department, ex p. Asif Mahmood Khan* [1984] 1 W.L.R. 1337; see further the cases cited at para. 12–028 below. See also paras 5–098–5–099 above. There is as yet little indication that English courts are prepared to go further and require that interested

normally be free from substantive restrictions upon its ability to change its policy[54] (if otherwise *intra vires*), the courts have on occasions been willing to hold public bodies to declared existing policies, on the basis that the policy has engendered a legitimate expectation, even where the effect is effectively to grant the applicant "substantive" relief.[55] Further, the courts should be receptive to the argument that when an administrative body has purported to apply, not to abandon, its own rules or policies, but has manifestly applied them erroneously, the resulting decision may be set aside as an unreasonable exercise of discretion.[56] This question is dealt with more fully in Chapter 13 below, but here we should note a subtle change in the argument and in the interests and values advanced. Up to now we have seen the public authority seeking, in the interest of legal certainty (and perhaps also of efficiency) to operate a known and certain rule or policy. The applicant wishes to persuade the authority to depart from

---

parties are entitled to participate in the original formulation of standards (unless, of course, the decision maker has encouraged an expectation to that effect), even though it could be argued that their adoption limits the opportunities of those entitled to be heard to influence the decision when the discretion is exercised; moreover, non-statutory rules are not normally subject to the political scrutiny given to statutory instruments and byelaws.

[54] *Laker Airways Ltd v. Department of Trade* [1977] Q.B. 643, 708–709, 728; *R. v. Secretary of State for the Home Department, ex p. Asif Mahmood Khan* [1984] 1 W.L.R. 1337; *cf.*, however, *H.T.V. Ltd v. Price Commission* [1976] I.C.R. 170 (tribunal may not depart from an interpretation of a statutory provision to the detriment of a party who has relied upon it).

[55] *R. v. Secretary of State for the Home Department, ex p. Asif Mahmood Khan*, above; *R. v. Secretary of State for the Home Department, ex p. Ruddock* [1987] 1 W.L.R. 1482; *R. v. Inland Revenue Commissioners, ex p. Preston* [1985] A.C. 835; *Matrix Securities Ltd v. Inland Revenue Commissioners* [1994] 1 W.L.R. 334. See further, Chap. 12, para. 12–027 et seq.

[56] See *Salemi's* case (above, n. 50) at 456, and the cases cited above relating to the doctrine of legitimate expectation. *Cf. R. v. Home Secretary, ex p. Hosenball* [1977] 1 W.L.R. 766, 781, 788 on the legal effect of a statement by the Home Secretary on the procedure to be followed before a person was deported on grounds that gave no right to a statutory appeal. It has been said that the Government may at any time amend the terms of the non-statutory Criminal Injuries Compensation Scheme (*R. v. Criminal Injuries Compensation Board, ex p. Lain* [1967] 2 Q.B. 864 at 885) the Secretary of State however, could not amend the Scheme by introducing an entirely new "tariff" scheme in circumstances where he had a continuing obligation to consider whether to bring into force a statutory scheme enacted by Parliament under the Criminal Justice Act 1988: *R. v. Secretary of State for the Home Department, ex p. the Fire Brigades Union,* [1995] 2 A.C. 513, HL and the courts have quashed decisions by the Criminal Injuries Compensation Board in which the Board has erred in its construction of the scheme, although it may be appropriate for the courts to adopt a more flexible approach to its intereptation than it would were it contained in a formal legislative instrument: see *R. v. Criminal Injuries Compensation Board, ex p. Schofield* [1971] 1 W.L.R. 926, 931 (*per* Bridge J., dissenting); *R. v. Criminal Injuries Compensation Board, ex p. P* [1995] 1 W.L.R. 845, especially *per* Neill L.J. at 855–858.

the rule or policy in the interest of responsive administration, so as to provide justice in the individual case. In the situation we are now considering it is the applicant who, in the interest of legal certainty, wishes the public body to abide by its policy and to fulfil expectations engendered by its representations. And it is the authority that wishes to be free to depart from its previous announcements in the interest of responsive administration and in order to fulfil its public duties.

It has been held by the Court of Appeal that the Home Office might **10–013** not disappoint an expectation, arising out of a circular, which set out the criteria for the adoption of children from abroad.[57] And the House of Lords has made it clear that the Inland Revenue Commissioners may be bound by representations made to individual taxpayers and that to disappoint an expectation based on such a representation may amount to an "abuse of power".[58] However, the principles of legitimate expectation and the no-fettering principle came into conflict in a case concerning the Home Secretary's policy in relation to the parole of prisoners.[59] Following an abrupt change in that policy, two life sentence prisoners claimed a legitimate expectation that the original policy should have been followed in their case. The House of Lords held that the Home Secretary was entitled to change his policy, provided that his discretion had been lawfully exercised. Lord Scarman said that "Any other view would entail the conclusions that the unfettered discretion conferred by the statute on the Minister can in some cases be restricted so as to hamper, or even prevent, changes of policy."[60] There is no doubt that a public body must be unhampered in the pursuit of its lawful purposes, but, as will be seen

---

[57] *R. v. Secretary of State for the Home Department, ex p. Asif Mohammed Khan* [1984] 1 W.L.R. 1337.

[58] *per* Lord Templeman in *Re Preston* [1985] A.C. 835, 867. See also *Matrix Securities Ltd v. Inland Revenue Commissioners* [1994] 1 W.L.R. 334.

[59] *Re Findlay* [1985] A.C. 318; *R. v. Gaming Board of Great Britain, ex p. Kingsley* [1996] C.O.D. 241 (there could be no reasonable, and hence no legitimate, expectation that Gaming Board would fetter its discretion by agreeing not to take account of certain matters in deciding, as required to do by statute, whether the applicant was a fit and proper person). *Cf.* the Canadian case of *Gregson v. National Parole Board* [1983] 1 F.C. 573, TD. For Australia see *Ansett Transport Industries (Operations) Pty Ltd v. Commonwealth* (1977) 139 C.L.R. 54; *Minister for Immigration v. Kurtovic* (1990) 92 A.L.R. 93.

[60] *ibid.* at 338. See also Lord Diplock in *Hughes v. Department of Health and Social Security* [1985] A.C. 776, 788: 'The liberty to make such change [of administrative policy] is something which is inherent in our form of constitutional government' (compulsory retirement of civil servants changed from 65 to 60). See also *R. v. Secretary of State for Health, ex p. U.S. Tobacco International Inc.* [1992] 1 Q.B. 353 (change of policy *re* manufacture of 'oral snuff' due to belief that it endangered health).

below,[61] there may be circumstances where an authority's right to change its policies may be inhibited by expectations which it has legitimately induced.

UNDERTAKING NOT TO EXERCISE A DISCRETION

10–014 A public authority cannot effectively bind itself not to exercise a discretion if to do so would be to disable itself from fulfilling the primary purposes for which it was created. It has been said that "if a person or public body is entrusted by the Legislature with certain powers and duties expressly or impliedly for public purposes, those persons or bodies cannot divest themselves of these powers and duties. They cannot enter into any contract or take any action incompatible with the due exercise of their powers or duties."[62] So to act would be "to renounce a part of their statutory birthright."[63] Clearly this cannot be understood to mean that a public authority is never competent to limit its discretion by entering into commercial contracts[64] or restrictive covenants[65]; the principle must be stated more conservatively. Breaking it down into a series of neat propositions presents problems: formulations are not uniform, the decided cases have arisen in a variety of contexts and not all are reconcilable with one another. However, some generalisations may be offered:

> (1) A public authority cannot effectively disable itself by contractual or other undertakings from making[66] or enforcing[67] a byelaw, refusing or revoking a grant of planning permission,[68] or exercising any other statutory power of

---

[61] Chap. 12, paras 12-029–12-033.

[62] *Birkdale District Electricity Supply Co. v. Southport Corp.* [1926] A.C. 355, 364. See also para. 12–026 below.

[63] *ibid.,* at 371. See also *Ayr Harbour Trustees v. Oswald* (1883) 8 App.Cas. 623, 634. For a critical and comparative survey, see J.D.B. Mitchell, *Contracts of Public Authorities.* See also Peter W. Hogg, *Liability of the Crown* (2nd ed., 1989), pp. 129–140; Colin Turpin, *Government Procuremental Contracts* (1989); Paul Rogerson [1971] P.L. 288; J.M. Evans (1972) 35 M.L.R. 88; Enid Campbell (1971) 45 A.L.J. 338.

[64] See, *e.g.* the *Birkdale* case (above, n. 62); though *cf. York Corp. v. Henry Leetham & Son* [1924] 1 Ch. 557. See also *R. v. G.L.C., ex p. Burgess* [1978] I.C.R. 991 (Local Government Act 1972, s.111 wide enough to enable local authority to enter into a closed shop agreement).

[65] See, *e.g. Stourcliffe Estates Co. v. Bournemouth Corp.* [1910] 2 Ch. 12.

[66] *Cory (William) & Son Ltd v. City of London Corp.* [1951] 2 K.B. 475; *Winter v. City of Saskatoon* (1965) 47 D.L.R. (2d) 53. But see *Commission of the European Communities v. Council of the European Communities* [1973] E.C.R. 575.

[67] *Bean (William) & Sons Ltd v. Flaxton R.D.C.* [1929] 1 K.B. 450.

[68] *Ransom & Luck Ltd v. Surbiton B.C.* [1949] Ch. 180, 195, 198; *Stringer v. Minister of Housing and Local Government* [1970] 1 W.L.R. 1281 (though in this case the planning

primary importance[69] such as a power of compulsory
purchase,[70] nor can it effectively bind itself to exercise such a
power in any particular way. Similarly, it cannot be estopped
by its inertia or acquiescence from fulfilling a duty to exercise
a power when the occasion arises for it to be exercised.[71] And
these principles apply *a fortiori* to fettering the effective
discharge of public duties.[72]

(2) More specifically, a body endowed with statutory powers and
duties exercisable for public purposes in relation to land
cannot disable itself from fulfilling those purposes by
dedicating or granting the land or interests therein in a

authority did not purport to fetter itself absolutely); *Windsor and Maidenhead R.B.C. v.
Brandrose Investments Ltd* [1983] 1 W.L.R. 509 (planning authority cannot bind itself by
contract to grant planning permission; relief refused in court's discretion). See,
however, *R. v. Sevenoaks D.C., ex p. Terry* [1985] 3 All E.R. 226 (council which granted
planning permission to developer did not act unlawfully in resolving previously to
sell site to developers, since formal sale agreement not entered into until after grant
of planning permission) (*Steeples v. Derbyshire C.C.* [1985] 1 W.L.R. 256 not followed).
Decisions such as *Terry* are susceptible to an analysis in terms of bias; see *Terry, R. v.
St Edmundsbury B.C., ex p. Investors in Industry Commercial Properties Ltd* [1985] 1
W.L.R. 1168, and see further paras 11-040–11-047 below. On the use of planning
agreements between local authorities and developers, see M. Grant [1975] J.P.L. 501; J.
Jowell [1977] J.P.L. 414. See also *Jones v. Secretary of State for Wales* (1974) 28 P. & C.R.
280; *Beaconsfield D.C. v. Gams* (1974) 234 E.G. 49; (1976) 237 E.G. 657; and see
Hildenborough Village Preservation Association v. Secretary of State for the Environment
[1978] J.P.L. 708 (applicant estopped from impugning the validity of a condition
dealing with a matter included in a planning agreement, on the strength of which
permission was granted); and see the correspondence provoked by this decision in
[1978] J.P.L. 806 and [1979] J.P.L. 166.
[69] *Ayr Harbour Trustees v. Oswald* (1883) 8 App.Cas. 623; *Ski Enterprises Ltd v. Tongariro
Board* [1964] N.Z.L.R. 884; contrast the *Stourcliffe* case (above, n. 65), where the power
restricted was of a subsidiary nature. Cf. *R. v. Secretary of State for the Home Department,
ex p. Fire Brigades Union* [1995] 2 A.C. 513. (Home Secretary could not disable himself
from ability to bring statutory scheme into effect by adopting alternative scheme having
consequence that statutory scheme 'will not now be implemented').
[70] *Triggs v. Staines U.D.C.* [1969] 1 Ch. 10. Cf. *Sovmots Investments Ltd v. Secretary of State
for the Environment* [1977] Q.B. 411, 420–421, 479–480; [1979] A.C. 144, 185–186 (local
authority did not unlawfully fetter its discretion when, on its compulsory acquisition
of leasehold interest, it undertook to obey the covenants and not to seek unilaterally
to acquire the freehold).
[71] *Yabbicom v. R.* [1899] 1 Q.B. 444 (power to prosecute for breach of byelaw). For the
circumstances in which assurances (including assurances given by officials) may
possibly operate as an estoppel, see para. 12–026 below.
[72] *Sunderland Corp. v. Priestman* [1927] 2 Ch. 107, 116; *Maritime Electric Co. v. General
Dairies Ltd* [1937] A.C. 610; *Customs and Excise Commissioners v. Hebson Ltd* [1953] 2
Lloyd's Rep. 382; *Society of Medical Officers of Health v. Hope* [1960] A.C. 551, 568, 569;
Union S.S. Co. v. Inland Revenue Commissioners [1962] N.Z.L.R. 659; *Smith v. Att.-Gen.*
[1973] 2 N.Z.L.R. 393, 397; *Northwest County D.C. v. Case (J.I.) (Australia) Pty. Ltd*
[1974] 2 N.S.W.L.R. Cf. George Spencer Bower and A.K. Turner, *Estoppel by
Representation* (3rd ed., 1977), pp. 149–150.

manner or for a purpose incompatible with the fulfilment of the primary purposes.[73] Whether a proposed new purpose is compatible with the primary purposes may raise questions of interpretation, fact and reasonably foreseeable probability; incompatibility cannot be established by mere conjecture.[74] Contracts for the sale of council houses have been specifically enforced even after the local authority has changed its policy on this matter[75]; similarly, a resolution by a Conservative-dominated local authority authorising the sale of a council-owned block of flats on terms including a restrictive covenant preventing the authority from letting vacant flats in council-retained neighbouring blocks was held (by a majority of the Court of Appeal) to be a lawful resolution not fettering the exercise by the council of its housing powers, because the policy was consistent with the purposes of the housing legislation.[76]

---

[73] *Ayr Harbour Trustees* case (above, n. 69); *Patterson v. Provost of St Andrews* (1881) 6 App.Cas. 833; *R. v. Leake (Inhabitants)* (1833) 5 B. & Ad. 469, 478; *British Transport Commission v. Westmorland C.C.* [1958] A.C. 126; *Dowty Boulton Paul Ltd v. Wolverhampton Corp. (No. 2)* [1976] Ch. 13 (with which, contrast *Dowty Boulton Paul Ltd v. Wolverhampton Corp.* [1971] 1 W.L.R. 204) but compare *R. v. Hammersmith and Fulham L.B.C., ex p. Beddowes* [1987] Q.B. 1050. *Cf.* the *Stourcliffe* case (above, n. 65; restriction upon discretion to use land for a subordinate purpose held binding); *Blake v. Hendon Corp.* [1962] 1 Q.B. 283, 301–303 (statutory power to let was subordinate to primary power to make land available as a public park and would not therefore be lawfully exercisable unless compatible with that power).

[74] *Westmorland* case (n. 73 above). *Cf.* the curious decision of the Court of Appeal in *British Railways Board v. Glass* [1965] Ch. 538, where the board was held to be bound by a right of way across the lines conferred by a predecessor in title, although there was evidence that the right of way gave rise to danger and inconvenience; *Rogerson* [1971] P.L. at 293–294.

[75] See *Storer v. Manchester C.C.* [1974] 1 W.L.R. 1403; *Gibson v. Manchester C.C.* [1978] 1 W.L.R. 520 (*rev'd.* [1979] 1 W.L.R. 294 on other grounds). In 1976 the Conservative-controlled Greater London Council announced that it would grant to the tenants of its council houses an option to purchase, exercisable at any time within 10 years; *quaere* whether this would amount to an unlawful fettering of the powers of the authority. Note, now, the 'right to buy' registration: Housing Acts 1980–1986.

[76] *R. v. Hammersmith and Fulham L.B.C., ex p. Beddowes* [1987] Q.B. 1050. However, as the dissent of Kerr L.J. suggests, it should not of itself be sufficient answer to a charge of unlawful fettering to establish that the policy implemented is within the four corners of the empowering legislation; where the legislation leaves open a choice of policy alternatives it may, it is submitted, be an unlawful fetter to resolve in advance of the decision to adopt a particular policy approach. See, *e.g. R. v. Legal Aid Board, ex p. R. M. Broudie & Co. (a firm)* [1994] C.O.D. 435 (guidance to taxing officer as to choice of circumstances which could be regarded as 'exceptional' in determining uplift to solicitor's costs was unlawful as restricting taxing officer's discretion where words of legislation ('all the relevant circumstances') were unlimited.

(3) Contracts and covenants entered into by the Crown are not to be construed as being subject to implied terms that would exclude the exercise of general discretionary powers for the public good; on the contrary, they are to be construed as incorporating an implied term that such powers remain exercisable.[77] This is broadly true of other public authorities also, but the status and functions of the Crown in this regard are of a higher order. Indeed, it still possibly remains the law that the Crown's general power to dismiss its servants cannot be ousted even by the express terms of a contract,[78] unless sanctioned by statute. However, assertions such as that the Crown is incapable of so contracting as to fetter its future executive action in any way, or that in all contracts entered into by the Crown there is an implied term that the Crown may repudiate its obligations whenever in its opinion executive necessity so demands, must be viewed with reserve today.[79] The Crown cannot be allowed to tie its hands completely by prior undertakings and the courts will not allow the Crown to evade compliance with ostensibly binding obligations whenever it thinks fit.[80] How and where the line is to be drawn is anything but clear. If a public authority lawfully repudiates or departs from the terms of a binding contract in order to exercise its overriding discretionary powers, or if it is held never to have been bound in law by an ostensibly binding contract because the undertakings would improperly fetter its general discretionary powers, the other

---

[77] *Crown Lands Commissioners v. Page* [1960] 2 Q.B. 274 (no covenant for quiet enjoyment to be implied in Crown lease so as to preclude Crown from exercising statutory requisitioning powers). See also *Molton Builders Ltd. v. City of Westminster L.B.C.* (1975) 30 P. & C.R. 182, 188 (applicability of the doctrine of derogation from grant to exercise by Crown Estate Commissioners of their statutory power to consent to enforcement notice left open). And see *Cudgen Rutile (No. 2) Ltd v. Chalk* [1975] A.C. 520 (contract to lease Crown land other than in accordance with statutory provisions invalid).

[78] *Riordan v. War Office* [1959] 1 W.L.R. 1046, 1053–1054. See now Employment Protection (Consolidation) Act 1978, s.138 (as amended). It is now reasonably clear that civil servants have contracts of employment with the Crown. See *R. v. Lord Chancellor's Department, ex p. Nangle* [1992] 1 All E.R. 897.

[79] The rule ambiguously formulated in *Rederiaktiebolaget Amphitrite v. R.* [1921] 3 K.B. 500 is one of open texture. For a critical discussion, see *Ansett Transport Industries (Operations) Pty Ltd v. Commonwealth* (1977) 17 A.L.R. 513. Specific relief in civil proceedings is in any event not available directly against the Crown.

[80] See the very lucid statement of the issues by Devlin L.J. in *Crown Lands Commissioners v. Page* [1960] 2 Q.B. 274, 291–294. See also *H.T.V. Ltd v. Price Commission* [1976] I.C.R. 170, 185G–H per Lord Denning M.R. and *R. v. Inland Revenue Commissioners, ex. p. Preston* [1985] A.C. 835, 865 per Lord Templeman and *R. v. Secretary of State for Home Department, ex. p. Doody* [1994] 1 A.C. 531.

party to the agreement has no right whatsoever to damages or compensation under the general law, no matter how serious the damage that party may have suffered. There is a case for providing an appropriate remedy by way of an award of compensation determinable by a judicial body.[81]

---

[81] See Mitchell, *op. cit.* above, n. 63, *passim.* Such provisions exist in French administrative law. *Contra,* Hogg, *op. cit.,* above, n. 63, arguing against the validity of the *Amphitrite* principle and urging that there should be a remedy in damages; but see Campbell, *loc. cit.,* pointing out objections of principle to the latter view.

CHAPTER 11

PROCEDURAL FAIRNESS: BIAS AND INTEREST

INTRODUCTION

Procedural fairness demands not only that those whose interests may **11–001** be affected by an act or decision should be given prior notice and an adequate opportunity to be heard. It also requires that the decision-maker should not be biased or prejudiced in a way that precludes fair and genuine consideration being given to the arguments advanced by the parties.[1] Although perfect objectivity may be an unrealisable objective, the rule against bias thus aims at preventing a hearing from being a sham or a ritual or a mere exercise in "symbolic reassurance",[2] due to the fact that the decision-maker was not in practice persuadable. The rule against bias is concerned, however, not only to prevent the distorting influence of actual bias, but also to protect the integrity of the decision-making process by ensuring that, however disinterested the decision-maker is in fact, the circumstances should not give rise to the appearance or risk of bias.

In defining the scope of the rule against bias and its content, at least **11–002** three requirements of public law are thus in play: The first seeks accuracy in public decision-making and the second seeks the absence of prejudice or partiality on the part of the decision-maker. An accurate decision is more likely to be achieved by a decision-maker who is in fact impartial or disinterested in the outcome of the decision and who puts aside any personal prejudices. The third requirement is for public confidence in the decision-making process. Even though the decision-maker may in fact be scrupulously impartial, the appearance of bias can itself call into question the legitimacy of the decision-making process. In general, the rule against bias looks to the

---

[1] Bias has been defined as 'an operative prejudice, whether conscious or unconscious': *R. v. Queen's County JJ.* [1908] 1 I.R. 285, 294, *per* Lord O'Brien C.J.

[2] See M. Edelman, *The Symbolic Uses of Politics* (1967).

413

appearance or risk of bias rather than bias in fact, in order to ensure that "justice should not only be done, but should manifestly and undoubtedly be seen to be done."[3]

11–003 This Chapter will begin with a consideration of the early background to the concept of bias in judicial and administrative settings. If then considers:

(1) The test of bias. Various tests have been advanced in the past, varying from that of "reasonable suspicion" of bias to "probability" of bias. The House of Lords in *R. v. Gough*[4] adopted a test of "real danger" of bias.

(2) Situations which will normally disqualify a decision-maker for bias.

(3) Situations which will not normally disqualify a decision-maker for bias.

Early background

11–004 Bracton wrote that a judge was not to hear a case if he was suspected of partiality because of consanguinity, affinity, friendship or enmity with a party, or because of his subordinate status towards a party or because he was or had been a party's advocate.[5] These principles, which Bracton set out as if they were already part of the common law, were in fact the canon law rules for recusation of suspected judges,[6] which were applied in the English ecclesiastical courts[7] and also, it seems, in medieval Scottish courts.[8] They bear a close resemblance to the grounds for disqualification of judges for likelihood of bias in modern English law. It might well be supposed, therefore, that they were imported into the common law in its early formative period by Bracton himself, or by his contemporaries or predecessors. Indirect support for an opinion that they were received into the common law might be derived from the fact that the grounds of exception for

---

[3] *per* Lord Hewart C.J. in *R. v. Sussex JJ., ex p. McCarthy* [1924] 1 K.B. 256, 259.

[4] [1993] A.C. 646.

[5] *De Legibus*, f. 412.

[6] For the grounds of exception to the *suspectus judex* in canon law (pecuniary interest, advocacy, kinship, friendship, great enmity), see *Codex Juris Canonici*, canons 1613–1614; and Naz (ed), *Traite de Droit Canonique*, iv, 95–98. There is a legend that a Pope (subsequently canonised) once condemned himself to be burned to death for his sins ((1430) Y.B. 8 Hen. 6, Hill. pl. 6).

[7] F.W. Maitland, *Roman Canon Law in the Church of England* (1898), 114.

[8] Lord Cooper (ed.), *Regiam Majestatem and Quoniam Attachiamenta*, (1947) 324–325.

interest and bias to the competency of witnesses in courts Christian had been applied from the earliest times to the challenge of jurors of the grand assize[9] and the possessory assizes.[10] Moreover, at least as early as the fourteenth century, common-law judges were held to be incompetent to hear cases in which they were themselves parties.[11] Yet there seems to be no evidence that Bracton's broad statement of canon law doctrine as common law was accepted and acted upon by his successors. On the contrary, it was laid down that favour was not to be presumed in a judge.[12] The principle that a judge was disqualified from adjudicating whenever there was a real likelihood that he might be biased was not unequivocally established until the 1860s.[13] Bracton is not cited in any of the leading English cases on the matter. One must conclude that the balance of probability is titled against the view that the canon law rules were ever directly incorporated in the common law. The common-law judges came to adopt principles substantially the same as those of the canon lawyers, not by way of conscious imitation, but by moving independently towards a just and reasonable solution.

The reluctance of the common lawyers to recognise the concept of **11–005** disqualification of judges for interest or bias is illustrated by Coke's bald assertion[14] that judges and justices, unlike jurors, could not be challenged—an assertion reiterated by Blackstone, who thought it a

---

[9] Glanvill, *De Legibus*, Bk. II, c. 12 (transl. Pound and Plucknett, *Readings on the History and System of the Common Law* (3rd ed.), 143). For the canon law rules, see *Wigmore on Evidence* (3rd ed.), ii, 678, n. 14; see also Naz, *op. cit.* n. 6 above, iv, 483–484; Harrington (1954) 14 *The Jurist* at 297. The canon law rules were later applied in a modified form to determine competency of witnesses at common law: Wigmore, *op, cit.*, ii, 675–683; Holdsworth, *History of English Law*, ix, 185 *et seq.*

[10] Bracton, *De Legibus*, ff. 143b, 185. See (1354) 28 Lib.Ass. 18 (juror challengeable because member of commonalty that was party to suit); (1481) Y.B. 21 Edw. 4, Mich. pl. 3 (juror challengeable in assize brought by dean and chapter of Lincoln, because he was brother of a prebendary of the chapter). The King could judge his own causes, with the exception that he could not be both actor and judex in cases of high treason: Bracton, *op. cit.*, f. 119; L, Ehrlich, *Proceedings Against the Crown (1216–1377)*, 47–49.

[11] See, *e.g.* (1371) 45 Lib.Ass. 3, where a party in a case at assizes that had to be heard before two judges was himself appointed judge upon the death of one of the two justices of assize: held, he could not judge his own cause. References to early Yearbook cases are collected by S.E. Thorne (ed.), *Egerton's Discourse upon the Statutes*, 73n. See also 2 Roll Abr. 92–93.

[12] See dictum in *Brooks v. Earl of Rivers* (1668) Hardres 503 (Chamberlain of Chester not disqualified from hearing an action in which his brother-in-law was a party).

[13] Blackburn J.'s judgment in *R. v. Rand* (1866) L.R. 1 Q.B. 230 is regarded as the *locus classicus*.

[14] Co.Litt. 294a.

salutary rule of public policy.[15] Long before Blackstone's day, however, Sir Nicholas Bacon,[16] the Earl of Derby[17] and the Mayor of Hereford (who was laid by the heels by the Court of King's Bench)[18] had discovered that the common law did not permit a judge to determine a matter in which he had a direct pecuniary or proprietary interest.[19] And it was Coke himself who had elevated to a fundamental principle of the common law the proposition that no man should be a judge in his own cause. In *Dr Bonham's* case, when examining the claim of the College of Physicians to fine its memebers for malpractice, he said that the censors of the College "cannot be judges, ministers, and parties ... quia aliquis non debet esse judex in propria causa ... and one cannot be judge and attorney for any of the parties." Moreover, "when an Act of Parliament is against common right or reason, or repugnant, or impossible to be performed, the common law will controul it, and adjudge such Act to be void." So "if any Act of Parliament gives to any to hold, or to have conusans of all manner of pleas arising before him within his manor ... yet he shall have no plea, to which he himself is party; for, as hath been said, iniquum est aliquem suae rei esse judicem".[20] Similar views were expressed by Hobart[21] and Holt.[22] It is doubtful whether a court ever held a statute to be void solely because it made a man a judge in his own cause[23] and it has been argued that Coke was merely laying down that statutes framed in such terms were to be strictly construed to avoid what would appear to be an obvious absurdity.[24] That Parliament is competent to make a person a judge in his own cause has long been indisputable[25] but the

---

[15] Comm., iii, 361. 'For the law will not suppose the possibility of bias or favour in a judge, who is already sworn to administer impartial justice, and whose authority greatly depends upon that presumption and idea.'

[16] *Sir Nicholas Bacon's* case (1563) 2 Dyer 220b.

[17] *Earl of Derby's* case (1613) 12 Co.Rep. 114.

[18] *Anon.* (1697) 1 Salk, 396 (facts given in *Wright v. Crump* (1702) 2 Ld.Raym. 766).

[19] For other early reported cases, see the *Foxham Tithing* case (1705) 2 Salk. 607 (surveyor adjudicated as justice in matter concerning his office); *Company of Mercers and Ironmongers of Chester v. Bowker* (1725) 1 Str. 639 (member of company became mayor and member of court before judgment). Though *cf. Markwick v. City of London* (1707) 2 Bro. P.C. 409: *Great Charte v. Kennington* (1742) 2 Str. 1173 (justices in removal case interested as local ratepayers).

[20] (1610) 8 Co.Rep. 113b, 118. See also Co.Litt. 141a.

[21] *Day v. Savadge* (1614) Hob. 85, 86, 87.

[22] *London (City of) v. Wood* (1701) 12 Mod. 669, 686–688.

[23] See the illuminating article by T.F.T. Plucknett. 'Bonham's Case and Judicial Review' (1926) 40 Harv.L.R. 30.

[24] MacKay, 'Coke—Parliamentary Sovereignty or the Supremacy of Law' (1924) 22 Mich. L.R. 215; S.E. Thorne. 'Dr. Bonham's Case' (1938) 54 L.Q.R. 543; J.W. Gough, *Fundamental Law in English Constitutional History*, (1955) 31–39.

[25] *Great Charte v. Kennington* (n.19 above) (dictum); *Lee v. Bude & Torrington Junction Ry.* (1871) L.R. 6 C.P. 576, 582, where Willes J. described Hobart C.J.'s dicta in *Day v.*

courts continue to uphold the common-law tradition by declining to adopt such a construction of a statute if its wording is open to another construction.[26]

Later developments

In developing the modern law relating to disqualification of judicial officers for interest and bias, the superior courts have striven to apply the principle enumerated by Lord Hewart C.J. that it "is of fundamental importance that justice should not only be done, but should manifestly and undoubtedly be seen to be done",[27] without giving currency to "the erroneous impression that it is more important that justice should appear to be done than that it should in fact be done."[28] The emphasis thus shifted from the simple precepts of the law of nature to the need to maintain public confidence in the administration of justice.[29] No person who was a party to proceedings or who had any direct pecuniary interest in the result was qualified at common law to adjudicate in those proceedings. If, however, it was alleged that the adjudicator has made himself partisan, by reason of his words or deeds or his association with a party who was instituting or defending the proceedings before him, the courts would not hold him automatically to be disqualified.

11–006

Savadge (n. 21 above) as "a warning, rather than an authority to be followed." See also *Rich v. Christchurch Girls' High School Board of Governors (No. 1)* [1974] 1 N.Z.L.R. 1, 9, 18–20.

[26] Bl.Comm. i, 91; *Mersey Docks & Harbour Board Trustees v. Gibbs* (1866) L.R. 1 H.L 93, 110; *Wingrove v. Morgan* [1934] Ch. 423, 430; *Rice v. Commissioner of Stamp Duties* [1954] A.C. 216, 234; and *University of Edinburgh v. Craik*, 1954 S.C. 190, 195, with which contrast *R. v. Minister of Agriculture & Fisheries, ex p. Graham* [1955] 2 Q.B. 140 and *Wilkinson v. Barking Corp.* [1948] 1 K.B. 721. See also *Jeffs v. New Zealand Dairy Production and Marketing Board* [1967] 1 A.C. 551.

[27] *R. v. Sussex JJ., ex p. McCarthy* [1924] 1 K.B. 256, 259. In *R. v. Essex JJ., ex p. Perkins* [1927] 2 K.B. 475, 488, Avory J. suggested that "be seen" must be a misprint for "seem".

[28] *R. v. Camborne JJ., ex p. Pearce* [1955] 1 Q.B. 41, 52. Contrast *R. v. Byles* (1912) 77 J.P. 40, where Avory J. said: "It is as important (if not more important) that justice should seem to be done, as that it should be done": but compare *Shrager v. Basil Dighton Ltd* [1924] 1 K.B. 274, 284, *per* Atkin L.J.: "Next to the tribunal being in fact impartial is the importance of its appearing so." *Cf,* Lord Scarman in *R. v. Atkinson* [1978] 1 W.L.R. 425, 428 "in this sensitive area, the appearance of justice is part of the substance of justice" (sentence quashed on appeal on the ground that comments made by the judge could have given rise to a reasonable suspicion that he had discussed with counsel during a pre-trial review the possibility that a plea-bargain should be struck).

[29] See *Serjeant v. Dale* (1877) 2 QBD 558, 567.

An adjudicator may indeed seldom achieve "the icy impartiality of a Rhadamanthus",[30] and the idea that "by taking the oath of office as a judge, a man ceases to be human and strips himself of all predilections, becomes a passionless thinking machine,"[31] is doubtless a myth. The common law nevertheless disqualifies a judge, magistrate or independent arbitrator from adjudicating whenever circumstances point to a risk that he would have a bias in relation to a party or an issue before him. The test for bias will now be considered.

THE TEST OF BIAS

11–007 There are some circumstances where public confidence would inevitably be shaken if the decision were allowed to stand. Such are cases where the decision-maker has a pecuniary or proprietary interest in the outcome of the proceedings. These cases clearly breach the maxim that nobody may be judge in his own cause[32] and "attract the full force [of the requirement that] justice must not only be done but manifestly be seen to be done".[33]

11–008 A decision may always be invalidated if actual bias on the part of a decision-maker was proved.[34] In some situations, however, especially with regard to criminal justice, the court will not be concerned to investigate evidence of actual bias. It is no doubt desirable that all adjudicators, like Caesar's wife, should be above suspicion,[35] but it

---

[30] Coke, *Institutes* iii 35: Rhadamanthus, the cruel judge of Hell, punished before he heard. *Cf. Jackson v. Barry Ry.* [1893] 1 Ch. 238, 248. *per* Bowen J. But even Rhadamanthus was not, apparently, conversant with the *audi alteram partem* rule.

[31] *Re J. P. Linahan*, 138 F. 2d 650 (1942), *per* Jerome Frank J. See also *R. v. Barnsley Licensing JJ.* [1960] 2 Q.B. 167, *per* Devlin L.J., on unconscious bias; and see generally, for a sophisticated analysis with special reference to international adjudication. Thomas M Franck, *The Structure of Impartiality*, and (1967) 19 Stanford L.R. 1217.

[32] See, *e.g. R. v. Rand* (1866) L.R. 1 Q.B. 230, 232: "Any pecuniary interest, however small, in the subject matter of the inquiry, does disqualify a person from acting as a judge in the matter", *per* Blackburn J. See also *Dimes v. Proprietors of Grand Junction Canal* (1852) 3 H.L. Cas. 759, 793 *per* Lord Campbell.

[33] *per* Lord Goff in *R. v. Gough* [1993] A.C. 646, 661. The above passage was approved in *R. v. Bow Street Metropolitan Stipendiary Magistrate, ex p. Pinochet Ugarte (No. 2)* [1999] 1 All E.R. 577 where it was held by the House of Lords that a judge (Lord Hoffmann) was automatically disqualified from hearing a matter in a case where his decision could lead to the promotion of a cause in which the judge was involved with one of the parties (in this case the judge was a director of a charity closely associated to a party and sharing its objectives).

[34] See, *e.g. R. v. Burton, ex p. Young* [1897] 2 Q.B. 468, 471; *R. v. Tempest* (1902) 86 L.T. 585, 587. And see the persuasive decision of the Manitoba Court of Appeal in *Re Gooliah and Minister of Citizenship and Immigration* (1967) 63 D.L.R. (2d) 224 (deportation order quashed because hearing officer showed actual bias); see too *Anderton v. Auckland City Council* [1978] 1 N.Z.L.R. 657, 687.

[35] *Lesson v. G.M.C.* (1889) 43 Ch D 366, 385.

would not be desirable to inquire into the mental state of a judge, a member of a jury or justices or their clerk because of the confidential nature of the judicial decision-making process. Nor would it be useful to do so because in many cases bias may be unconscious in its effect.[36] For those reasons, the courts look at the circumstances of the particular case to see if there is an appearance of bias.

Various tests have been applied to establish the limits of apparent **11–009** bias. At the one extreme, the courts disallow any decision where there has been a "reasonable suspicion of bias".[37] At the other extreme, a decision-maker will only be disqualified where there is a "real likelihood of bias".[38] "Real likelihood" can refer to either the possibility or the probability of bias. In respect of either test, there are two variants: Under the first, the suspicion or likelihood of bias is derived in the circumstances of the case from the point of view of the "reasonable man".[39] Under the second variant, the courts themselves decided the matter, based upon the impression they have of bias in the circumstances of the case.

---

[36] The courts have frequently laid down that they are not concerned with the question whether an adjudicator was in fact biased. See *Allinson v. G.M.C.* [1894] 1 Q.B. 750, 758; *R. v. Queen's County JJ.* [1908] 2 I.R. 285, 306; *R. v. Halifax JJ., ex p. Robinson* (1912) 76 J.P. 233, 234–235; *R. v. Caernarvon Licensing JJ., ex p. Benson* (1948) 1 13 J.P. 23, 24; *R. v. Barnsley Licensing JJ.* [1960] 2 Q.B. 167, 187.

[37] *R. v. Sussex JJ., ex p. McCarthy* [1924] 1 K.B. 256: "Nothing is to be done which creates even a suspicion that there has been an improper interference with the course of justice", *per* Lord Hewart C.J. at 259: See also *R. v. Huggins* [1895] 1 Q.B. 563; *Cottle v. Cottle* [1939] 2 All E.R. 535. *Metropolitan Properties Co. (F.G.C.) Ltd v. Lannon* [1969] 1 Q.B. 577, 599 "The court does not look to see if there was a real likelihood that he would, or did, in fact favour one side at the expense of the other. The court looks at the impression which would be given to other people", *per* Lord Denning. See also Edmund Davies L.J. at p. 606: it was enough if there is *"reasonable* suspicion of bias". And see Danckwerts L.J. at pp. 601–602. After *Lannon* the reasonable suspicion test was applied by Lord Widgery C.J. in *R. v. Uxbridge JJ., ex p. Burbridge, The Times,* June 21, 1972, and *R. v. McLean, ex p. Aikens* (1974) 139 J.P. 261. But he was more uncertain in *R. v. Altrincham JJ., ex p. N. Pennington* [1975] Q.B. 549. See also *R. v. Liverpool City JJ., ex p. Topping* [1983] 1 W.L.R. 119; *R. v. Morris (orse Williams)* (1990) 93 Cr. App. R. 102.

[38] *R. v. Barnsley Licensing JJ., ex p. Barnsley & District Licensed Victuallers' Association* [1960] 2 Q.B. 167, 187, *per* Devlin L.J. See also *R. v. Rand* (1866) L.R. 1 Q.B. 230, *per* Blackburn J.; *Frome United Breweries Co. Ltd v. Bath JJ.* [1926] A.C. 586, 591; *R. v. Camborne JJ., ex p. Pearce* [1955] 1 Q.B. 41.

[39] *per* Lord Denning M.R. in *Metropolitan Properties Co. v. Lannon* (n. 37 above). See also *R. v. Sunderland JJ.* [1901] 2 K.B. 357, 373. See also *Hannam v. Bradford Corp.* [1970] 1 W.L.R. 937, 942 (*per* Sachs L.J.), 949 (*per* Cross L.J.). See also *ex p. Quantas Airways Ltd, re Horsington* [1969] 1 N.S.W.R. 788; *R. v. Peacock, ex p. Whelan* [1971] Qd.R. 471; *R. v. Lilydale Magistrates' Court, ex p. Ciccone* [1973] V.R. 122; *R. v. Watson, ex p. Armstrong* (1975) 136 C.L.R. 248, 258–263. Compare the formulation of the test adopted in *R. v. Commonwealth Conciliation and Arbitration Commission, ex p. Angliss Group* (1969) 122 C.L.R. 546, 553, and approved in *Whitford Residents etc. Association (Inc.) v. Manukau City Corp.* [1974] 2 N.Z.L.R. 340, as "a suspicion of bias reasonably—and not

11–010   The various tests of bias thus range along a spectrum. At the one end a court will require that, before a decision is invalidated, bias must be shown to have been present. At the other end of the spectrum, the court will strike at the decision where a reasonable person would have a reasonable suspicion from the circumstances of the case that bias might have infected the decision. In between these extremes is the "probability of bias" (this being closer to the "actual bias" test), and the "possibility of bias" (this test being closer to that of reasonable suspicion).

11–011   In the recent case of *R. v. Gough*[40] the House of Lords considered these various tests in relation to an allegation of bias on the part of a juror in a criminal trial.[41] Having carefully considered the authorities, it was held that direct pecuniary or proprietary interest always disqualified the decision-maker. Outside of that category, it was held that the correct test is whether, in the circumstances of the case, the court considers that there appeared to be a "real danger of bias". In such a case, the decision should not stand. This test is similar to that of the "real likelihood of bias" and it was made clear that it refers to the *possibility*—not probability—of bias.[42] The "reasonable suspicion test" was thus rejected. It was also held that the same test should be applied in all cases of apparent bias (whether concerning justices, members of inferior tribunals, arbitrators, justices' clerks or jurors). It was held too that the "real danger" test should be applied from the point of view of the court, not from that of the "reasonable man". Lord Goff said:

> "Since however the court investigates the actual circumstances, knowledge of such circumstances as are found by the court must

---

fancifully—entertained by responsible minds.' See also *Ardahalian v. Unifert International S.A. (The Elissar)* [1994] 2 Lloyd's Rep. 84; *Bremer Handelsgesellschaft M.B.H. v. Ets. Soules et Cie* [1985] 1 Lloyd's Rep. 160, [1985] 2 Lloyd's Rep. 199.

[40] [1993] A.C. 646.

[41] The appellant was indicted on a single count of conspiring with his brother to commit robbery. The brother had been discharged, but after conviction it was discovered that the brother's neighbour had served on the jury.

[42] The expression 'real danger' of bias had been adopted by Lord Ackner in *R. v. Spencer* [1987] A.C. 128, approving *R. v. Sawyer* (1980) 71 Cr. App. R. 283, 285. See also *R. v. Puttnam* (1991) Cr. App. R. 281. The *Gough* test has been recently followed in *R. v. Gaming Board for Great Britain, ex p. Kingsley* [1996] 10 C.L. 113 (CA, July 4, 1996)—it was common ground that there was evidence establishing the appearance of bias, but there was no evidence of a real danger of injustice arising from it, nor could the decision lawfully be delegated to an independent tribunal; *R. v. Secretary of State for the Environment, ex p. Kirkstall Valley Campaign* [1996] 3 All E.R. 304 (*Gough* test accepted for bodies whether judicial or administrative). But *cf. David Eves v. Hambros Bank (Jersey) Ltd* [1996] 1 W.L.R. 251, PC (where the body was not asked to decide any question between the parties, the fact that a member of the court had an interest in the bank would not vitiate the proceedings on the ground of bias).

be imputed to the reasonable man; and in the results it is difficult to see what difference there is between the impression derived by a reasonable man to whom such knowledge has been imputed, and the impression derived by the court, here personifying the reasonable man.[43]"

The test of bias has been settled by *Gough*—at least in relation to criminal adjudications. However, the test cannot be mechanically applied to a particular case and it is now necessary to consider some particular situations in which a decision-maker may be disqualified for bias.

DISQUALIFICATION FOR BIAS

Direct pecuniary or proprietary interests

As was made clear in *Gough*,[44] no person is qualified to adjudicate in any judicial proceedings in the outcome of which he has a direct pecuniary interest. The rule applies no matter how exalted the tribunal—a decree made by a Lord Chancellor with respect to a company in which he was a shareholder was held to be void able[45]— or how trivial the interest.[46] Nor is it material that the judge could not reasonably be suspected of having allowed himself to be influenced by

11–012

---

[43] *ibid.* at pp. 667–668. In *Auckland Casino Ltd v. Casino Control Authority* [1995] 1 N.Z.L.R. 142, the New Zealand Court of Appeal noted that since *R. v. Gough and Webb v. R.* (1994) 122 A.L.R. 41 there was, as to the test for apparent bias, a conflict of approach between the House of Lords and the High Court of Australia, but said that once it is accepted that the hypothetical reasonable observer must be informed, the distinction between the real danger and reasonable suspicion tests becomes very thin. In the South African case *BTR Industries v. Metal & Allied Workers Union* 1992 (3) S.A. 673(A) it was held that for 'judicial' situations a 'reasonable suspicion' test applies while 'real likelihood' of bias applies to all other cases. In *Pinochet (No. 2)* (above, n. 33) the majority seemed to prefer the Australian approach to *Gough*, although that matter was not directly decided.

[44] Above, n. 40.

[45] *Dimes v. Grand Junction Canal Co. Proprietors* (1852) 3 H.L.C. 759. *Cf. Sir Nicholas Bacon's* case (1563) 2 Dyer 220b; *Earl of Derby's* case (1613) 12 Co.Rep. 114. There can be no real doubt that interest as a creditor will normally disqualify: *Jeffs v. New Zealand Dairy Production and Marketing Board* [1967] 1 A.C. 551; *Barker v. Westmorland C.C.* (1958) 56 L.G.R. 267 (dicta).

[46] Justices who were shareholders in a railway company were held to be disqualified from hearing charges against persons accused of travelling on the railway without a proper ticket: *Re Hopkins* (1858) E.B. & E. 100; *R. v. Hammond* (1863) 9 L.T. (N. S.) 423, where Blackburn J. observed: 'The interest to each shareholder may be less than 1/4d. but it is still an interest.' But in *Auckland Casino Ltd v. Casino Control Authority* [1995] 1 N.Z.L.R. 142, 148, the New Zealand Court of Appeal was prepared to accept that the *de minimis* rule could apply.

disqualified from voting on any question on which they have more than an insignificant pecuniary interest.[63] More detailed prohibitions apply to members of education authorities.[64] Officers of local authorities must disclose a direct or indirect pecuniary interest in any contract of a local authority.[65]

Participation in appeal against own decisions

11–017 Normally there will be a breach of natural justice where an adjudicator takes part in the determination of an appeal against one of his own decisions, unless he is expressly authorised to do so by statute.[66] At

---

[63] Local Government Act 1972, ss. 94–98. The Secretary of State for the Environment has the power to remove this disability in any case where the number of members disqualified would be so large as to impede the transaction of business or where it is in the interests of the local inhabitants to do so. See also the *National Code of Local Government Conduct*, Department of Environment Circular 94/75, which requires disclosure of pecuniary and some non-pecuniary interests such as kinship, friendship or membership of an association that might influence a councillor's judgment. Many local authorities have introduced their own register of members' pecuniary interests. Where this is introduced, completion of the register is normally a condition of membership of committees, a practice which was upheld in *R. v. Newham L.B.C., ex p. Haggerty* (1986) 85 L.G.R. 48. See also *The Conduct of Local Authority Business* Cmnd. 9797 (1986), para. 6.45. (And see the recommendations of that Committee (under the Chairmanship of Mr David Widdicombe Q.C.) in relation to statutory registers of members interests, at para. 6.56.)

[64] See, *e.g.* Education (School Government) Regulations 1987, Reg. 14 and Sched. 2, para. 2 setting out the circumstances in which members are prohibited from (a) attending meetings, (b) taking part in discussion and (c) voting where they have any direct or indirect pecuniary interest in any contract, proposed contract or other matter. See *Bostock v. Kay* (1989) 1 Admin. L.R. 73, CA (failure to withdraw from meeting deciding to close down two schools and replace them by a City Technology College held unlawful as there was a 'very real chance' that the change would affect the pecuniary interests of the governor, whose son and wife were employed in the school). See also *R. v. Governors of Small Heath School, ex p. Birmingham City Council* [1990] C.O.D. 23, CA (governors disqualified from participating in a decision to change a school to grant-maintained status but remedy not granted in court's discretion). See also *R. v. Governors of Bacon's School, ex p. I.L.E.A.* [1990] C.O.D. 414. But see *Noble v. I.L.E.A.* (1983) 82 L.G.R. 291 (teacher-governor wrongly participated in resolution to dismiss another teacher which could result in a vacant post for which he might be eligible and conceivably a 'potential candidate').

[65] Local Government Act 1972, s. 117. See also Public Bodies Corrupt Practices Act 1889 and the Prevention of Corruption Acts 1906–16. Local Authorities (Members' Interests) (Amendment) Regulations 1996 [S.I. 1996 No. 1215] in force July 1, 1996 amend the Local Authorities (Members' Interests) Regulations 1992.

[66] Authorisation by rules of a voluntary association may be inadequate, for these can be declared to be contrary to natural justice. No question of invalidity was raised in *Herring v. Templeman* [1973] 3 All E.R. 569 about the terms of a trust deed establishing a teacher-training college which authorised the principal to recommend a student's dismissal and nominated him chairman of the academic board which assessed the student's record.

best he is likely to incline towards affirming his earlier decision; at worst he can be depicted as a judge in his own cause. In both cases there is likely to be a real danger of bias. Yet the superior judges declined to apply such a principle to the exercise of their own appellate functions.[67] In general, however, a decision-maker must not participate or indeed give the impression of participating in such an appeal.[68] Thus a clerk to a statutory tribunal ought not to act as clerk to a tribunal hearing an appeal against that decision if he takes part in the appellate tribunal's deliberations.[69]

Practical problems are liable to arise where a body exercising **11–018** licensing or disciplinary functions refers a particular case to a committee or sub-committee of its members for hearing and report, and the report is then considered and the issue decision by the parent body. Are the members who made the report disqualified from sitting on the parent body when it makes its decision? There has been surprisingly little discussion of the question in the reported English cases,[70] and disqualification attaches only if members of the sub-committee show active partisanship as members of the parent body,[71] or possibly if the report of the sub-committee was in effect a decision

---

[67] See *R. v. Lovegrove* [1951] 1 All E.R. 804, CCA. See also R.E. Megarry, *Miscellany-at-Law* (1955), 314; H.H. Marshall, *Natural Justice* (1959), 36–38. See Supreme Court of Judicature (Consolidation) Act 1925, s.68(4); Criminal Appeal Act 1966, s.2(3). See also Crown Court Rules 1971 (S.I. 1971 No. 1292), r. 5.

[68] For magisterial law, see *R. v. Lancashire JJ.* (1906) 75 L.J.K.B. 198. For administrative law, see *R. v. Brixton I.T.C.* (1913) 29 T.L.R. 712 (tax appeal); *Cooper v. Wilson* [1937] 2 K.B. 309 (*dist'd.* in *Kilduff v. Wilson* [1939] 1 All E.R. 429) (police disciplinary appeal); *R. v. North-East Surrey Assessment Committee, ex p. Woolworth (F.W.) & Co.* [1933] 1 K.B. 776 (*dist'd.* in *Middlesex County Valuation Committee v. West Middlesex Asst. Cttee.* [1937] Ch. 361); *Barrs v. British Wool Marketing Board*, 1957 S.C. 72 (valuation appeals) (see J. Bennett Miller, 1958 J.R. 39); *R. v. Alberta Securities Commission* (1962) 36 D.L.R. (2d) 199; *Re Glassman and Council of the College of Physicians and Surgeons* (1966) 55 D.L.R. (2d) 674; *R. v. Mullins, ex p. Stonehouse* [1971] Qd.R. 66. See also *Hannam v. Bradford Corp.* [1970] 1 W.L.R. 937.

[69] *R. v. Salford Asst. Cttee., ex p. Ogden* [1937] 2 K.B. 1 (where a strict rule was applied). Contrast *Re Lawson* (1941) 57 T.L.R. 315; *R. v. Architects' Registration Tribunal, ex p. Jaggar* [1945] 2 All E.R. 131; *R. v. Liverpool Dock Labour Board, ex p. Brandon* [1954] 2 Lloyd's Rep. 186. See also *R. v. Minister of Agriculture and Fisheries, ex p. Graham* [1955] 2 Q.B. 140. *R. v. South Worcestershire Magistrates, ex p. Lilley* [1995] 1 W.L.R. 1595. Lay justices heard and rejected PII application and then went on to hear prosecution. The procedure was such that 'a reasonable and fairminded person could reasonably have suspected the applicant could not have a fair trial'. (HL refused leave to appeal: see [1996] 1 W.L.R. 481). *R. v. Parole Board, ex p. Watson* [1996] 1 W.L.R. 906, CA (no bias in extra-statutory practice).

[70] *Osgood v. Nelson* (1872) L.R. 5 H.L. 636 was decided on the assumption that participation in the final decision by the members concerned was unexceptionable. See also *Jeffs v. New Zealand Dairy Production and Marketing Board* [1967] 1 A.C. 551.

[71] As in *R. v. L.C.C., ex p. Akkersdyk* [1892] 1 Q.B. 190.

and the proceedings before the parent body were in effect an appeal.[72] But a report will normally include a statement of findings and recommendations, which may be controverted before the parent body; and in such a case the participation of members of the sub-committee in the final decision may be of dubious validity, depending upon whether there is a real danger of bias.

11–019   There have been a number of recent cases where a member of a board or bench had previously been involved in an application by the same party. In one such case it was held that a president of a mental health review tribunal, who had sat on the case of a patient seeking discharge from a mental health institution, was not disqualified by statute from sitting on a later application by the same patient.[73] Nor was a licensing justice disqualified from sitting on an appeal against a refusal of a wine bar licence when he had sat on the decision to refuse a previous application by the applicant.[74] However, a magistrate who had convicted a defendant of threatening to kill his wife was disqualified from sitting on the bench which a month later tried the defendant for a separate offence.[75] It was made clear, however, that in such a case the mere knowledge of the defendant's previous convictions did not necessarily preclude a fair trial; that only arose when the knowledge was disclosed in a way which might lead to real danger of bias.[76]

---

[72] But see *French v. Law Society of Upper Canada* [1975] 2 S.C.R. 767; *cf. Re Merchant and Benchers of the Law Society of Saskatchewan* (1972) 32 D.L.R. (3d) 178; *Re Prescott* (1971) 19 D.L.R. (3d) 446; *Re Dancyger and Alberta Pharmaceutical Association* (1971) 17 D.L.R. (3d) 206 (recommendations, not decisions). Where an initial decision is taken by body X, and members of body X participate in the proceedings of body Y which has to determine whether to uphold it, the distinction is clearer (see *Hannam v. Bradford Corp.* [1970] 1 W.L.R. 937); but *cf. Ward v. Bradford Corp.* (1971) 70 L.G.R. 27 (where this distinction was obscured, partly because the governors who had sat on the disciplinary committee were excluded from the governing body when it dealt with on appeal).

[73] *R. v. Oxford Regional Mental Health Review Tribunal, ex p. Mackman, The Times*, June 2, 1986.

[74] *R. v. Crown Court at Bristol, ex p. Cooper* [1990] W.L.R. 1031, CA.

[75] *R. v. Downham Market Magistrates' Court, ex p. Nudd,* [1989] R.T.R. 169; [1989] Crim. L.R. 147. *Cf. Huchard v. DPP* [1994] C.O.D. 451 show the bench details of a previous conviction of the same offence (drink driving) but application refused as the applicant had pleaded guilty and the previous conviction was only relevant to sentence and in addition the bench had itself concluded the knowledge was not prejudicial.

[76] The term 'suspicion of bias' was used in *Nudd,* but after *R. v. Gough,* n. 40 above, real danger of bias would be the test. See also J. N. Spencer (1986) 150 J.P. 307.

Likelihood of bias because of personal attitudes and relationships

Personal hostility

It has been said that mere personal prejudice, even resulting from a   **11–020**
previous dispute or altercation, is not comprehended within the term
"a challenge to the favour" of a tribunal and is therefore not a ground
for setting aside its decision.[77] This dictum cannot be supported as a
general principle of law, but it is appropriate to the context in which it
was uttered, an action arising out of expulsion from a trade union.
Behind the expulsion of a member from a voluntary association there
often lies a history of friction between the member and leading
officials. The ground of expulsion may be opposition to the declared
policies of the association.[78] The rules of the association permit the
committee to act, in a sense, as judges in their own cause. The
expelled member may not, therefore, succeed in having the decision
set aside by the courts merely by demonstrating that the committee
were not, or were not likely to be, impartial towards him; he will have
to prove that members of the committee did not fairly consider his
case and had made up their minds to expel him before they heard
him,[79] or that, for example, the union secretary was both in form and
in substance prosecutor and judge.[80] It is reasonable, however, for the
law to require a greater measure of detachment from members of a
professional disciplinary tribunal, which can have grave consequences
upon a person's right to a livelihood.[81]

---

[77] *Maclean v. Workers' Union* [1929] 1 Ch. 602, 625.

[78] As in *White v. Kuzych* [1951] A.C. 585 (expulsion of opponent of union's closed shop policy). See E. F. Whitmore (1952) 30 Can. B.R. 1.

[79] *White v. Kuzych* (n. 78 above) at 595–596; *R. v. Brewer, ex p. Renzella* [1973] V.R. 375. In *Dickason v. Edwards* (1910) 10 C.L.R. 243 the Australian High Court imposed a stricter standard of impartiality; but in that case the member expelled was accused of having directed personal abuse against the officer who presided over the committee, and there was, moreover, evidence that the committee had predetermined the issue.

[80] *Taylor v. National Union of Seamen* [1967] 1 W.L.R. 532; *Roebuck v. National Union of Mineworkers* [1977] I.C.R. 573. See also *Australian Workers' Union v. Bowen (No. 2)* (1948) 77 C.L.R. 601, where the union secretary had taken an active part in instituting the proceedings against the plaintiff and was 'invincibly' biased against him but nevertheless sat as a member of the committee to judge his case.

[81] See *Law v. Chartered Institute of Patent Agents* [1919] 2 Ch. 276; *Thompson v. B.M.A. (N.S.W. Branch)* [1924] A.C. 764, 779–781; *R. v. Optical Board of Registration, ex p. Qurban* [1933] S.A.S.R. 1; *cf. R. v. Medical Board of South Australia, ex p. S.* (1976) 14 S.A.S.R. 360, where, on the facts, the identification of the adjudicators with the prosecutors was held to be insufficiently close to disqualify. Contrast, however, *R. v. Liverpool Dock Labour Board Appeal Tribunal, ex p. Brandon* [1954] 2 Lloyd's Rep. 186 (dismissed docker complained of bias on ground of his unpopularity with his union which was represented on the appeal tribunal; held immaterial, partly on ground that the whole disciplinary machine depended on union representation on the tribunal).

11–021   There can be no doubt that in the ordinary courts strong personal animosity towards a party disqualifies a judge from adjudicating if it gives rise to a real danger of bias. Thus, a conviction by an Irish magistrate was quashed when it was shown, by an uncontradicted affidavit, that very bad feeling (originating in a trespass by a fowl) existed between him and the defendant's family, and that shortly after the conviction he had used words indicative of enmity towards the defendant.[82] In Canada a magistrate was held to be disqualified from hearing a charge against a person with whom he had recently come to blows.[83] But the evidence must be compelling; the courts are reluctant to conclude that any judicial officer's judgment is likely to be warped by personal feeling.[84] General expressions of hostility towards a group to which a party belongs (*e.g.* poachers or motorists[85]) have not acted as a disqualification. A teetotaller was competent to sit as a licensing justice the courts declined to accept the view that his principles were likely to prevent him from dealing fairly with applications before him.[86] Where, however, an adjudicator expressed his general sentiments so vehemently as to make it likely that he would be incapable of dealing with an individual case in a judicial spirit (as where a licensing justice who was a proselytising teetotaller wrote that he would have been a traitor to his principles if he had voted for the granting of a particular licence,[87] or where an arbitrator said that in his experience all persons of the nationality of one of the parties before him were untruthful witnesses[88]), the courts have held him to be disqualified. Again, where an adjudicator manifested open hostility

---

[82] *R. (Donoghue) v. Cork County JJ.* [1910] 2 I.R. 271. See also *R. (Kingston) v. Cork County JJ.* [1910] 2 I.R. 658; *R. (Harrington) v. Clare County JJ.* [1918] 2 I.R. 116 (X, a participant in a political procession, charged Y, a police officer, with assault arising out of a clash with the procession; Z, also a participant in the procession, held disqualified from hearing the summons against Y).

[83] *R. v. Handley* (1921) 61 D.L.R. 656.

[84] See, however, *R. v. Abingdon JJ., ex p. Cousins* (1964) 108 S.J. 840, where the court, applying a test of suspicion of bias, set aside the conviction of an unsatisfactory former pupil of the chairman of the Bench (who was a headmaster).

[85] *Ex p. Wilder* (1902) 66 J.P. 761.

[86] *R. v. Dublin JJ.* [1904] 2 I.R. 75; *Goodall v. Bilsland*, 1909 S.C. 1152; *M'Geehen v. Knox*, 1913 S.C. 688 (members of and subscribers to bodies that include opposition to grant of new licences among their objects are not disqualified); *R. v. Nailsworth Licensing JJ., ex p. Bird* [1953] 1 W.L.R. 1046, 1048.

[87] *R. v. Halifax JJ., ex p. Robinson* (1912) 76 J.P. 233. See also *R. v. Rand* (1913) 15 D.L.R. 69 for prejudgment of a case.

[88] *Re "Catalina" v. "Norma"* (1938) 61 Ll.Rep. 360 (actual bias shown). See also *ex p. Schofield, re Austin* (1953) 53 S.R. (N.S.W.) 163 (magistrate, in convicting X and Y for obstructing Z in the course of his duty, called X and Y perjurers; he immediately heard and dismissed summonses brought by X and Y against Z for assault; *held,* disqualified from adjudicating in second case). *R. v. Horseferry Magistrates' Court, ex p., Bilhar Chima* [1995] C.O.D. 317 (clerk made racist remark).

to a party or his advocate[89] at the hearing, the only reasonable conclusion may be that a fair hearing has not been granted. When the chair of the bench of magistrates produced a note to be used as a basis for passing sentence of the defendants before all the evidence had been called, it was held that the not had promoted the appearance of bias.[90] In a recent case it was held that when a coroner used the terms "unhinged" and "mentally unwell" to describe relatives of the deceased, these expressions indicated a real possibility that he had unconsciously allowed himself to be influenced against the applicant's argument that the inquest should be reopened.[91]

If members of a tribunal have formed an unfavourable impression   **11–022** of a party in previous proceedings before them, it may be unrealistic to insist that it is contrary to natural justice for them to adjudicate.[92] But a close scrutiny of the conduct of the proceedings may be justified if he complains that he has been denied a fair hearing.[93]

The legal effect of personal hostility by members of administrative bodies ought in general[94] to be determined by reference to the same criteria as those adopted for courts, subject to the proviso that it may sometimes be reasonable to disregard the hostility of a small number of members of a large public body.

---

[89] *R. v. Magistrate Taylor, ex p. Ruud* (1965) 50 D.L.R. (2d) 444; *Re Elliott* (1959) 29 W.W.R. (N.S.) 579; *Re Golomb and College of Physicians and Surgeons of Ontario* (1976) 68 D.L.R. (3d) 25; *cf. Re College of Physicians and Surgeons of Ontario and Casullo* [1977] 2 S.C.R. 2 (vigorous questioning of an evasive witness justifiable); and see *R. v. Watson, ex p. Armstrong* (1976) 136 C.L.R. 248 (statement by judge in the course of proceedings that he did not believe the evidence of either party held to be vitiating bias).

[90] *R. v. Romsey JJ., ex p. Gale* [1992] Crim. L.R. 451. See *Ellis v. Ministry of Defence* [1985] I.C.R. 257 (held that a preliminary or tentative indication of the decision-maker's view is permissible, provided that it does not give the impression of being a concluded decision at a stage when evidence is still to be received and arguments heard).

[91] *R. v. Inner West London Coroner, ex p. Dallaglio* [1994] 4 All E.R. 139. *Dallaglio* was applied in *R. v. Highgate Magistrate's Court ex p. Riley* [1996] C.O.D. 12.

[92] *Re B. (T.A.) (an Infant)* [1971] Ch. 270, 277–278; *Ewert v. Lonie* [1972] V.R. 308. But extreme cases may arise, creating a likelihood of bias or prejudice: *Munday v. Munday* [1954] 1 W.L.R. 1078, 1082; see also *R. v. Grimsby Borough Q.S., ex p. Fuller* [1956] 1 Q.B. 36. And see *R. v. Board of Visitors of Frankland Prison, ex p. Lewis* [1986] 1 W.L.R. 130 (Chairman of Board of Visitors trying prisoner for drug offence had previously been a member of the local review committee considering his application for release on licence. *Held:* no bias.

[93] See: 'Disqualification of Judges for Bias in the Federal Courts' (1966) 79 Harv.L.R. 1435. See also 'State Procedures for Disqualification of Judges for Bias and Prejudice' (1967) 42 N.Y.U.L.R.

[94] Though *cf. R. v. Liverpool Dock Labour Board Appeal Tribunal, ex p. Brandon* [1954] 2 Lloyd's Rep. 186.

Personal friendship

11–023 Normally close personal friendship will give rise to a real possibility of bias. The English reports are almost wholly destitute of decisions on the point,[95] but there is no reason for doubting that such a rule exists. In Australia the decision of a tribunal was set aside because a member of the tribunal was a personal friend of an applicant's husband.[96]

11–024 Members of local tribunals are, of course, often acquainted with the parties who appear before them. A member who is a close friend of a party will normally think it proper not to sit if a quorum can be formed without him. In *Gough*[97] the fact that a juror was a neighbour of the defendant's brother was held, on the facts of that case, not to have provided a real danger of bias.

Family relationship

11–025 Kinship has always been recognised as a ground for challenging a juror, and in 1572 a court went so far as to uphold an objection to proceedings in which the sheriff who had summoned the jury was related in the ninth degree to one of the parties.[98] Despite a seventeenth-century decision that kinship did not operate as a disqualification for a judge,[99] it is now well established that it does disqualify wherever it is close enough to cause a likelihood of bias.[1] Family relationship between judge and counsel does not appear to be exceptionable, but it has been suggested that judges are disqualified from sitting in cases where near relatives are witnesses.[2] There is no reason for differentiating between the courts and administrative tribunals in these matters. In a Canadian case the decision of a

---

[95] In *Cottle v. Cottle* [1939] 2 All E.R. 535 a Divisional Court ordered a rehearing of a matrimonial case where the magistrate was a friend of the wife's family and the wife's mother had given the husband to understand that the magistrate would be biased in her favour. This is a marginal case; there was no finding of any real likelihood of bias.

[96] *ex p. Blume, re Osborn* (1958) 58 S.R. (N.S.W.) 334.

[97] *R. v. Gough* [1993] A.C. 646.

[98] *Vernon v. Manners* (1572) 2 Plowd. 425.

[99] *Brookes v. Earl of Rivers* (1668) Hardres 503. Cf. *Bridgman v. Holt* (1693) 1 Show.P.C. 111, where Holt C.J. withdrew from a case in which his brother was a party.

[1] *R. v. Rand* (1866) L.R. 1 Q.B. 230, 232–233; *R. (Murray and Wortley) v. Armagh County JJ.* (1915) 49 I.L.T. 56. See also *Becquet v. Lempriere* (1830) 1 Knapp 376 (jurat of Royal Court of Jersey held by Privy Council to be disqualified from hearing case in which deceased wife's nephew a party). Cf. *Auten v. Rayner* [1958] 1 W.L.R. 1300.

[2] Sir Alfred Denning (1954) 71 S.A.L.J. 345, 355.

tribunal was set aside because the chairman was the husband of an executive officer of a body which was a party to proceedings before the tribunal.[3]

Professional and vocational relationship

A reasonable apprehension of bias may arise because of the professional[4] business[5] or other vocational relationship of an adjudicator with a party before him. It is unlikely that proceedings could be successfully impugned on this ground unless the community of interest between judge and party (or the conflict of interest between them)[6] was directly related to the subject-matter of the proceedings.[7]   **11–026**

Professional relationships between magistrates' clerks (who may still be solicitors in private practice) and parties before the magistrates' court may render the proceedings vulnerable. Just as it is improper for the one person to act as judge and advocate,[8] so is it improper for the   **11–027**

---

[3] *Ladies of the Sacred Heart of Jesus v. Armstrong's Point Association* (1961) 29 D.L.R. (2d) 373. *R. v. Wilson and Sprason* (1996) 8 Admin. L.R. 1 (wife of prison officer on jury); *R. v. Salt* (1996) 8 Admin. L.R. 429 (son of usher on jury).

[4] In the United States there has been much discussion of the qualification of judges to hear cases argued by members of law firms to which they formerly belonged; see Frank, 'Disqualification of Judges' (1947) 56 Yale L.J. 605. On the competence of a barrister to rule as arbitrator on the misconduct of solicitors with whom he had had close professional relations, see *Bright v. River Plate Construction Co.* [1900] 2 Ch. 835. And see *Ghirardosi v. Minister of Highways for British Columbia* [1966] S.C.R. 367 (determination quashed because arbitrator in proceedings to which a government department was a party was, unknown to the other party, solicitor to the department); *cf. Re Marques and Dylex Ltd* (1977) 81 D.L.R. (3d) 554 (member of labour board not disqualified because his law firm had acted for one of the parties). See also *R. v. Peacock, ex p. Whelan* [1971] Qd.R. 471 (magistrate issuing summons was employee of solicitors acting for complainant authority).

[5] See *Sziland v. Szasz* [1955] S.C.R. 3 (arbitrator business associate of one party, unknown to the other party); *Veritas Shipping Co. v. Anglo-Canadian Cement Ltd* [1966] 1 Lloyd's Rep. 76.

[6] See *R. v. Huggins* [1895] 1 Q.B. 563 (one member of bench belonged to small class of licensed river pilots; defendant charged with infringement of their privileges; conviction of defendant quashed, despite no finding that there had been real likelihood of bias). Contrast *R. v. Burton, ex p. Young* [1897] 2 Q.B. 468. See also *West End Service (Innisfail) Ltd v. Innisfail Town Council* (1958) 11 D.L.R. (2d) 364 (garage proprietor applied to council for exemption from early closing byelaw: application refused; decision held invalid since three councillors were competitors and likely to be biased).

[7] *Stevens v. Stevens* (1929) 93 J.P. 120 (validity of matrimonial proceedings unaffected by fact that one of the justices was member of husband's trade union). *Cf. R. v. Barnsley Licensing JJ.* [1960] 2 Q.B. 167, where a decision to grant an off-licence to a co-operative society was upheld although all but one of the justices were members of the society. Contrast *Metropolitan Properties Co. (F.G.C.) Ltd v. Lannon* [1969] 1 Q.B. 577.

[8] Though conceptions of judicial propriety were still fluid in the nineteenth century: R.E. Megarry, *Miscellany-at-Law*, 7–8; *Thellusson v. Rendlesham* (1859) 7 H.L.C. 429.

relationship between an adjudicator and the "victim" of the person appearing before him is readily liable to disqualify the adjudicator, whether or not his personal advancement is involved.[20]

Possibility of bias because of attitudes towards the issue

11–030 Disqualification for bias may exist where a decision-maker has an interest in the issue by virtue of his identification with one of the parties, or has otherwise indicated partisanship in relation to the issue.

Two main classes of cases may arise, although they are by no means exhaustive. The first is where an adjudicator is associated with a body that institutes or defends the proceedings. The courts have refused to hold that a person is disqualified at common law from sitting to hear a case merely on the ground that he is a member of the public authority, or a member of or subscriber to the voluntary association, that is a party to the proceedings,[21] unless he has personally taken an active part in instituting the proceedings, or has voted in favour of a resolution that the proceedings be instituted,[22] for he is then in substance both judge and party.

---

[20] *R. v. Altrincham JJ., ex p. Pennington* [1975] Q.B. 549 (magistrate disqualified from hearing charges of deliveries of goods of short weight to local authority schools; the magistrate was a member of the local authority's education committee).

[21] *R. v. Handsley* (1882) 8 QBD 383 (member of local authority not disqualified for likelihood of bias from adjudicating in proceedings brought by the authority; see, however, the statutory disqualification now imposed by the Justices of the Peace Act 1949, s. 3); *R. v. Camborne JJ., ex p. Pearce* [1955] 1 Q.B. 41 (clerk to justices was member of council instituting proceedings); *R. v. Deal JJ.* (1881) 45 L.T. 439 (justices subscribers to R.S.P.C.A., who were prosecutors); *R. v. Burton, ex p. Young* [1897] 2 Q.B. 468 (justice member of Incorporated Law Society, who were prosecutors); *Leeson v. G.M.C.* (1889) 43 Ch D 366; *Allinson v. G.M.C.* [1894] 1 Q.B. 750 (members of G.M.C. hearing charges of professional misconduct against doctors were members of the Medical Defence Union which had initiated the proceedings, but they had themselves taken no part in initiating them); *R. v. Pwllheli JJ., ex p. Soane* [1948] 2 All E.R. 815 (justice member of fishery board who were prosecutors; he had taken no part in resolution to prosecute; see now, however, Justices of the Peace Act 1949, s. 6); *Barnsley* case, n. 19 above (licensing justices granted off-licence to co-operative society of which they were members); *R. v. Altrincham JJ., ex p. Pennington* [1975] Q.B. 549 (magistrate not disqualified by her membership of local authority from hearing case in which an officer of the authority was the prosecutor); *Hanson v. Church Commissioners for England* [1978] Q.B. 823 (Lord Chief Justice and Master of the Rolls not disqualified from hearing appeal from rent assessment committee by virtue of their *ex officio* status as Commissioners, the landlords of the appellant).

[22] *R. v. Milledge* (1879) 4 QBD 332; *R. v. Winchester JJ.* (1882) 46 J.P. 724; *R. v. Lee* (1882) 9 QBD 394 (justices had, as members of local authority, supported resolution to prosecute; *held*, disqualified despite statutory removal of disqualification for membership of local authority); *R. v. Gaisford* [1892] 1 Q.B. 381 (disqualification of justice who had set proceedings in motion); *R. v. Allan* (1864) 4 B. & S. 915; *R. v.*

The second class of case (which is not always clearly distinguishable **11–031** from the first) is where a decision-maker has shown partisanship in a corporate or private capacity. Thus, when the Council of the Chartered Institute of Patent Agents expelled a member after having previously made an unsuccessful application to the Board of Trade for the erasure of the member's name from the register, it was held that the expulsion was vitiated by the council's earlier conduct, which gave rise to a reasonable suspicion that it would be biased in making its decision.[23] Most of the cases are concerned with magistrates who have adjudicated after having substantially committed themselves by actively opposing or supporting the cause of a party or applicant before them. Licensing justices who have been present at meetings where it has been resolved to oppose the applications that are to come before them have been held to be incompetent to hear those applications.[24] Yet in two cases justices who had signed petitions for the grant of a licence were held to be qualified to sit to grant the licences afterwards.[25]

In certain respects, however, licensing justices stand in a peculiar **11–032** position. They are entitled to adopt a general policy, based on their own investigations and private knowledge and their assessment of local requirements, with regard to the granting and renewal of public house licences in their area.[26] They are sometimes members of the local authority, which may have adopted town planning policies that will affect the future location of public houses.[27] They may themselves

---

Henley [1892] 1 Q.B. 504 (fishery board cases). See also *R. v. Barnsley M.B.C., ex p. Hook* [1976] 1 W.L.R. 1052. See also *R. v. Meyer* (1876) 1 QBD 173; *R. v. Optical Board of Registration, ex p. Qurban* [1933] S.A.S.R. 1 (members of Board, having arranged for collection of evidence against Q, held disqualified for sitting in proceedings to remove him from register). See also *Stollery v. Greyhound Rating Control Board* (1972) 128 C.L.R. 509, *cf.*, however, *R. v. Altrincham JJ.,* n. 21 above (mere membership of a local authority or of a police authority is not a disqualification from adjudicating in a case in which a council official or a police officer is the prosecutor). See also *Re French and Law Society of Upper Canada (No. 2)* (1976) 57 D.L.R. (3d) 481. See also *Rees v. Crane* [1994] 2 A.C. 173; *R. v. Highgate Magistrate's Court, ex p. Riley* [1996] C.O.D. 12 (remark indicating that police officer's evidence likely to be treated more favourably than defendants).

[23] *Law v. Chartered Institute of Patent Agents* [1919] 2 Ch. 276, 293 where Eve J. adopted the language of Farwell L.J., who had once said that he could not trust the whole bench of bishops to do justice under such conditions. See also *R. v. Optical Board of Registration, ex p. Qurban* [1933] S.A.S.R. 1.

[24] *R. v. Fraser* (1893) 57 J.P. 500; *R. v. Caernarvon Licensing JJ., ex p. Benson* (1948) 1 13 J.P. 23; see also *R. v. Ferguson* (1890) 54 J.P. 101 (justice disqualified who had privately campaigned against grant of licence).

[25] *R. v. Taylor, ex p. Vogwill* (1898) 62 J.P. 67; *R. v. Nailsworth Licensing JJ., ex p. Bird* [1953] 1 W.L.R. 1046. *Cf. R. v. Crown Court at Bristol, ex p. Cooper* [1990] 1 W.L.R. 1031.

[26] See, *e.g. R. v. Howard* [1902] 2 K.B. 363; *R. v. Torquay Licensing JJ., ex p. Brockman* [1951] 2 K.B. 784.

[27] *cf. R. v. Sheffield Confirming Authority* [1937] 3 All E.R. 114.

initiate an objection to the renewal of a licence and then proceed to sit and vote on the application as members of the compensation authority.[28] But they have been disqualified if they have already taken such active steps to oppose the renewal as to give rise to a real likelihood that they will not be capable of hearing and determining the application in a judicial spirit.[29]

11–033 Somewhat similar principles governing the common-law disqualifications for bias may be applied to other licensing authorities. Individual members of the authority should not take sides with or against the applicant before the hearing, but the legal effect of such partisanship may depend upon the degree of partisanship,[30] and possibly the number of partisans and the size of the authority. But where three members of a London County Council committee who had voted against an application for the renewal of a music and dancing licence instructed counsel to oppose the application before the full council, it was held that their presence at the hearing before the council affected the validity of the council's decision to refuse renewal, although they had not voted.[31] In another case, where a single councillor was alleged to be likely to be biased in connection with a similar application, there was a divergence of opinion on the question whether, if the allegations had been made out, the decision of the council would have been automatically tainted.[32]

11–034 On principle, a member of a court or tribunal ought to be held disqualified if he gives evidence for or against a party to the proceedings; but, surprisingly enough, there is no clear authority to that effect,[33] and it has been held that a justice of the peace who has

---

[28] *R. v. Leicester JJ., ex p. Allbrighton* [1927] 1 K.B. 557; see also *R. v. Howard* (n. 26 above); Licensing Act 1964, ss. 13, 14, 16, Sched. 3.

[29] *Frome United Breweries Co. v. Bath JJ.* [1926] A.C. 586 (licensing justices instructed solicitor to appear before compensation authority on their behalf; they then sat and voted as members of compensation authority). See further, on prejudgment as a disqualification, *R. v. Sunderland JJ.* [1901] 2 K.B. 357; *cf. Leeds Corp. v. Ryder* [1907] A.C. 420. And see *R. v. Crown Court at Bristol, ex p. Cooper* (n. 25 above).

[30] *R. v. Australian Stevedoring Industry Board* (1953) 88 C.L.R. 100, 116; see also *Barrier Reef Broadcasting Pty Ltd v. Minister for Post and Communications* (1978) 19 A.L.R. 425 (refusal to permit cross-examination of witness on a particular issue gave rise to a reasonable suspicion that the tribunal had already made up its mind on that point).

[31] *R. v. L.C.C., ex p. Akkersdyk* [1892] 1 Q.B. 190. See also *Hannam v. Bradford Corp.* [1970] 1 W.L.R. 937 (decision could not stand though only three out of 10 members disqualified for likelihood of bias).

[32] *R. v. L.C.C., ex p. Empire Theatre* (1894) 71 L.T. 638, 639, 640 (*per* Charles and Wright JJ.); contrast *R. v. Hendon R.D.C., ex p. Chorley* [1933] 2 K.B. 696 (disqualifying effect of pecuniary interest of single councillor).

[33] *cf.* dicta in *Mitchell v. Croydon JJ.* (1914) 78 J.P. 385, 387. At the trial of the Earl of Essex before the Court of the Lord High Steward, Popham C.J. gave evidence against the accused and then acted as a judicial adviser to the court: Catherine Bowen, *The Lion and the Throne*, 123, 128–129.

been subpoenaed as a witness is not necessarily disqualified from adjudicating in the same case.[34] But if a magistrates' clerk (who is only an adviser to the court) ought not to officiate in proceedings in which he has been called as a witness,[35] members of the bench should, *a fortiori*, refrain from adjudicating when placed in such a position.

If a tribunal is entitled to act on the personal or expert knowledge   **11–035**
of its members, there may be no legal objection to a member's giving evidence in a case and then taking part in the decision unless it appears from the evidence that he has predetermined the issue.[36] But such a situation is liable to create the danger of unfairness.

SITUATIONS WHERE BIAS WILL NOT APPLY

Waiver

A party may waive his objections to a decision-maker who would   **11–036**
otherwise be disqualified on the ground of bias.[37] Objection is generally deemed to have been waived if the party or his legal representative knew of the disqualification and acquiesced in the proceedings by failing to take objection at the earliest practicable opportunity.[38] But there is no presumption of waiver if the disqualified adjudicator failed to make a complete disclosure of his interest,[39] or if

---

[34] *R. v. Tooke* (1870) 34 J.P. 773; *R. v. Farrant* (1880) 20 QBD 58. In the former case the evidence given was not indicative of partisanship. The decision in the latter case, however, is remarkable, in view of the magistrate's association with the prosecutor.

[35] *Jolliffe v. Jolliffe* [1957] P. 6, 12–13, 14–15 (dicta)

[36] *cf. Wetherall v. Harrison* [1976] Q.B. 773. And see *R. v. Colchester Stipendiary Magistrate, ex p. Beck* [1979] Q.B. 674 (submission of documents (both admissible and inadmissible) prejudicial to accused by prosecution prior to hearing of committal proceedings not breach of natural justice).

[37] *R. (Giant's Causeway, etc., Tramway Co.) v. Antrim JJ.* [1895] 2 I.R. 603.

[38] *R. v. Byles* (1912) 77 J.P. 40. In *R. v. Richmond JJ.* (1860) 24 J.P. 422 and *ex p. Ilchester Parish* (1861) 25 J.P. 56 it was held that an applicant for certiorari had to specify in his affidavits that neither he nor his advocate knew of the objection at the time of the hearing or acquiesced in it. *Sed quaere* whether such an omission ought to be so seriously regarded. *Cf. R. v. Essex JJ.*, n. 41 below, and *R. v. Williams*, n. 43 below. See also *R. v. Lilydale Magistrates' Court, ex p. Ciccone* [1973] V.R. 122, 131–136 where the authorities are reviewed. A more recent review of English, Australian and New Zealand authorities on waiver of objections for bias was undertaken by the New Zealand Court of Appeal in *Auckland Casino Ltd v. Casino Control Authority* [1995] 1 N.Z.L.R. 142. It was held that, although confronted with an agonising choice, the party ultimately complaining in that case had waived the objection by delaying until the decision was known. It was accepted, however, that displays of blatant bias, likely to undermine public confidence in the justice system, should not necessarily be capable of private waiver; while in criminal cases private waiver should not normally be possible at all.

[39] *R. v. Cumberland JJ.* (1882) 52 J.P. 502.

the party affected was prevented by surprise from taking the objection at the appropriate time,[40] or if he was unrepresented by counsel and did not know of his right to object at the time.[41] Where the disqualification is statutory, it may be waived if it is merely declaratory of a common-law disqualification.[42] In what circumstances a new statutory disqualification is capable of being waived is not entirely clear,[43] but even if the decision is to be regarded as void the court, in deciding whether to grant the particular remedy sought, may be entitled in its discretion to take account of the delay, acquiescence or misconduct of the party impugning the decision.[44]

11–037   Recent cases have raised the question of the proper behaviour expected of an inspector following a planning inquiry.[45] There is little doubt that an inspector who accepts hospitality or a lift to the site visit from one party in the absence of the other would be disqualified for bias, but this would not be the case where the inspector had asked the appellant if he objected to this behaviour and the appellant had not objected.[46]

Statutory or contractual exemptions

11–038   Parliament may provide by express words or necessary implication,[47] or the parties to a contract or the members of an organisation may agree, that power to decide disputes shall be committed to a person or

---

[40] *R. (Harrington) v. Clare County JJ.* [1918] 2 I.R. 116.

[41] *R. v. Essex JJ., ex p. Perkins* [1927] 2 K.B. 475.

[42] *Wakefield Local Board v. West Riding & Grimsby Ry.* (1865) L.R. 1 Q.B. 84.

[43] That such a defect may render the proceedings void is indicated by *R. v. Williams, ex p. Phillips* [1914] 1 K.B. 608; compare Scrutton J.'s dicta in *R. v. Simpson* [1914] 1 K.B. 66, 75, but contrast the dicta of Ridley and Bailhache JJ. in that case (73, 76–77). See further, R. B. Cooke (1955) 71 L.Q.R. 100, 106–107; A.G. Davis (1955) 18 M.L.R. 495.

[44] See, *e.g. R. v. Williams, ex p. Phillips* (n. 43 above), a case on the discretionary nature of certiorari. See also *R. v. Inner London Q.S., ex p. D'Souza* [1970] 1 W.L.R. 376. 378–379. A statute may expressly provide that adjudication by justices subject to certain statutory disqualifications does not affect the validity of the proceedings in which they have taken part. *e.g.* Justice of the Peace Act 1949, s. 5; Licensing Act 1964, s. 193(6). See, *e.g. R. v. Barnsley Licensing JJ.* [1960] 2 Q.B. 167.

[45] *Fox v. Secretary of State for the Environment and Dover D.C.* [1993] J.P.L. 448; *Cottrell v. Secretary of State for the Environment* [1991] J.P.L. 1155. See also *Halifax Building Society v. Secretary of State for the Environment* [1983] J.P.L. 816.

[46] *Fox,* and *Cottrell,* n. 45 above.

[47] See above; *Re Ashby* [1934] O.R. 421, 431; *Re Public Accountancy Act and Stoller* (1960) 25 D.L.R. (2d) 410; *Jeffs v. New Zealand Dairy Production & Marketing Board* [1967] 1 A.C. 551; *Rich v. Christchurch Girl's High School Board of Governors (No. 1)* [1974] 1 N.Z.L.R. 1; *Re W. D. Latimer Co. Ltd and Bray* (1974) 52 D.L.R. (3d) 161; *Ringrose v. College of Physicians and Surgeons of Alberta* [1977] 1 S.C.R. 814; *Re McArthur and Municipal District of Foothills* (1977) 78 D.L.R. (3d) 359.

an authority interested in the result. In such cases the disqualifying effect of the particular forms of interest covered by the statute or agreement may be treated as having been wholly or substantially removed,[48] though in some of these situations disqualification may still attach if on the facts there appears to be a real danger of bias.[49] Local planning authorities are, under the terms of the planning legislation,[50] permitted to reject an inspector's recommendations after a public inquiry into the authority's local plans. Despite the safeguards surrounding this power (such as the power of the Secretary of State for the Environment to "call in" the plan),[51] it has been held to allow the authority to be judge in its own cause.[52]

Necessity

A person who is subject to disqualification at common law may be required to decide the matter if there is no other competent tribunal or if a quorum cannot be formed without him.[53] Here the doctrine of necessity is applied to prevent a failure of justice.[54] So, if proceedings

11–039

---

[48] For restrictive interpretation of the effect of statutes removing certain common-law disqualifications, see *R. v. Milledge, R. v. Winchester JJ., R. v. Lee, R. v. Gaisford* and *R. v. Henley,* cited at para. 11–030, n.22 above. See also *Roebuck v. National Union of Mineworkers* [1977] I.C.R. 573 (union rules required members of committee to attend council meeting at which the committee's decision was considered; but they did not require the area president (who had, in effect, instituted the disciplinary proceedings) to participate in the adjudication); and see *R. v. Wadley, ex p. Burton* [1976] Qd.R. 286.

[49] *Barnsley* case (n.44 above). Similarly, where a statute prohibits bias of a particular kind (say a pecuniary interest), this does not prevent the court from extending that prohibition to other forms of bias. The *expressio unius* maxim will not normally apply. See, *e.g. R. v. Crown Court at Bristol, ex p. Cooper* [1990] 2 All E.R. 193, 201, *per* Bingham L.J. *Cf.* Chap. 7 above, paras 7-013–7-018 for discussion of statutory provision or exclusion of the *audi alteram partem* rule. Compare *Reza v. General Medical Council* [1991] 2 A.C. 182, HL (G.M.C. committee held inquiry into two groups of charges. Having found the appellant guilty of some of the charges in Group A they refused to reconstitute the committee to hear Group B. *Held:* Permitted by the Professional Conduct Rules *and* no real likelihood of bias.)

[50] Town and Country Planning Act 1990, ss. 33–44.

[51] *ibid.,* ss. 35A and 44.

[52] *R. v. Hammersmith and Fulham L.B.C., ex p. People Before Profit Ltd* [1981] J.P.L. 869.

[53] *cf.* Lamond, 'Of Interest as a Disqualification in Judges' (1907) 23 S.L.R. 152–153, citing a Scottish case of 1744 where withdrawal of the interested judges would have left the court without a quorum. See R.R.S. Tracey, 'Disqualified Adjudicators: The Doctrine of Necessity in Public Law' [1982] P.L. 628.

[54] But the doctrine has been applied very sparingly in modern English law. It was not invoked (though it could have been) in the *Barnsley* case (n. 44 above). See also *Lower Hutt City Council v. Bank* [1974] 1 N.Z.L.R. 545; *Laytons Wines Ltd v. Wellington South Licensing Trust (No. 2)* [1977] 1 N.Z.L.R. 570, 576–578. *Cf. R. v. Peterborough Commrs., ex*

were brought against all the superior judges, they would have to sit as judges in their own cause.[55] Similarly, a judge may be obliged to hear a case in which he has a pecuniary interest.[56] A colonial governor could validly assent in the Queen's name to a Bill indemnifying him against the legal consequences of his own conduct, since there was no other officer who could have done so.[57] The judges of Saskatchewan were held to be required *ex necessitate* to pass upon the constitutionality of legislation rendering them liable to pay income tax on their salaries.[58] Again, if a member of a professional or other organisation has so conducted himself that no disciplinary tribunal can address itself impartially towards his case, he will not inevitably be able to establish immunity from disciplinary proceedings on that ground.[59] But the rule of necessity ought not to be mechanically applied if its enforcement would be an affront to justice (*e.g.* where all members of the only statutory body empowered to revoke a licence are subject to disqualifications), and it may be right for a court to scrutinise the actual conduct of the proceedings closely if the rule cannot be wholly circumvented.[60] If it is possible to constitute a different tribunal unaffected by interest or bias, no difficulty arises. When in 1925 a case came before the Supreme Court of Texas involving an organisation called the Woodmen of the World, of which all the judges of the court were members, the Governor neatly solved the problem by appointing an *ad hoc* court of three women.[61]

11–040 What would be the position in English administrative law if a Minister were to be called upon to decide whether or not to confirm an order made by a local authority affecting his own property? He

---

p. *Lewis* [1965] 2 O.R. 577 (doctrine applied). See further *R. v. Cawthorne, ex p. Public Service Association etc.* (1977) 17 S.A–S.R. 321, 337–338.

[55] 2 Roll.Abr. 93, pl. 6; see also 16 Vin.Abr. (2nd ed.), 573 *et seq.*, citing fifteenth century cases.

[56] *Great Charte v. Kennington* (1742) 2 Str. 1173; *R. v. Essex JJ.* (1816) 5 M. & S. 513; *Grand Junction Canal Co. v. Dimes* (1849) 12 Beav. 63; *Dimes v. Grand Junction Canal Proprietors* (1852) 3 H.L.C. 759, 778–779, *Ranger v. Great Western Ry.* (1854) 5 H.L.C. 72, 88.

[57] *Phillips v. Eyre* (1870) L.R. 6 Q.B. 1.

[58] *The Judges v. Att.-Gen. for Saskatchewan* (1937) 53 T.L.R. 464. See also *Willing v. Hollobone (No. 2)* (1975) 11 S.A.S.R. 118 (magistrates not disqualified for bias, *inter alia*, because the ground applied to all magistrates); *Re Caccamo and Minister of Manpower and Immigration* (1977) 75 D.L.R. (3d) 720 (alleged disqualification applicable to all immigration officers).

[59] *cf. Brinkley v. Hassig*, 83 F. 2d 351 (1936) (cited 23 N.Y.U.L.Q.R. 132). See also Robert M. Sedgewick (1945) 23 Can. B.R. 453, 467. This was the course taken by the Privy Council in *Rees v. Crane* [1994] 2 A.C. 173 as to allegations of bias by the Chief Justice of Trinidad and Tobago in relation to the suspension of a High Court judge.

[60] See K.C. Davis, *Administrative Law Treatise*, ii, v. 164–166; *R. v. Optical Board of Registration, ex p. Qurban* [1933] S.A.S.R. 1, 13.

[61] Cited by Frank (1947) 56 Harv. L.R. 605, 611, n. 21.

could not lawfully transfer to another Minister his duty to decide. He might depute one of his own officials to make the decision; the decision would nevertheless be made in the Minister's name. It is submitted that the validity of the decision could not be challenged merely on the ground that the Minister was in a sense judge in his own cause; for the legal duty to decide the class of matter to which this belonged had been cast upon him, and upon him alone.[62] If it were possible to show that the Minister had in fact failed to consider the merits of the order for reasons of personal interest, his decision could be successfully challenged.

Necessity may also play a part in excusing an appearance of bias where it would not be impossible for anyone else to make the decision but where the particular administrative structure makes it inevitable that some appearance of bias will occur. Thus where inspectors authorised by the Secretary of State for Trade investigated the affairs of a company of which the applicant was chairman, and some of the same inspectors had previously investigated another company of which he was chairman, it was held that the terms of the inspectors' powers permitted them to have "suspicions" about matters to be investigated.[63] Where a board of prison visitors found a prisoner guilty of having a controlled drug in his cell, the prisoner alleged the presence of bias because the chairman of the board had been a member of a local review committee which had earlier considered the prisoner's release on licence under the parole system. The application was dismissed because the functions of the board of visitors were such that they would inevitably have considerable knowledge of a prisoner charged with a disciplinary offence.[64] For similar reasons, the president of a mental health review tribunal who had previously sat on the case of an applicant seeking discharge from an institution was not disqualified from sitting on a later application by the same patient,[65] and a licensing justice was not barred from hearing an application although he had sat on the bench which had refused the applicant's previous application. It was held that licensing justices were bound to and entitled to bring to bear their local knowledge on licensing matters.[66]

11–041

---

[62] *cf. Auten v. Rayner* [1958] 1 W.L.R. 1300.

[63] *R. v. Secretary of State for Trade, ex p. Perestrello* [1981] 1 Q.B. 19.

[64] *R. v. Board of Visitors of Frankland Prison, ex p. Lewis* [1986] 1 W.L.R. 130.

[65] *R. v. Oxford Regional Mental Health Review Tribunal, ex p. Mackman, The Times*, June 2, 1986.

[66] *R. v. Crown Court at Bristol, ex p. Cooper* [1990] 2 All E.R. 193, CA. See also *CREED N.Z. v. Governor-General (N.Z.)* (1981) N.Z.L.R. 172 (no 'predetermination' when decision taken by Executive Council).

Policy and bias

11–042 Closely related to the doctrine of necessity is that which permits public officials to exhibit certain kinds of bias in the exercise of their judgment or discretion on matters of public policy. Ordinary members of legislative bodies are entitled, and sometimes expected, to show political bias. They ought not to show personal bias, or to participate in deliberations on a matter in respect of which they have a private pecuniary interest, but their participation in such circumstances may not in itself affect the validity of a legislative instrument.[67]

11–043 Where a councillor had previously indicated his opposition in general to the existence of sex establishments, he was not disqualified from sitting on a panel to license sex establishments,[68] provided he gave genuine consideration to the decision.[69] Nor was a Minister disqualified from determining a planning application on a site where he had previously (as a Member of Parliament) supported an opponent of planning permission.[70]

11–044 However, if the personal interests of members participating in a decision affecting individual rights or interests (such as a decision to grant planning permission) preclude them from acting fairly, the decision can be declared to be invalid on the motion of a person aggrieved.[71] It has been held, however, that a builder was not disqualified from sitting on a local authority planning committee on

---

[67] If a member of the House of Commons votes on a matter on which he has a private pecuniary interest, his vote may be disallowed; but the rule is not at all exacting, and no vote has been disallowed on such a ground since the nineteenth century: Erskine May, *Parliamentary Practice* (21st ed.), 354–359; Select Committee on Members' Interests (Declaration) (H.C. 102 (1974–75)), para. 28. The matter of MPs' interests was the subject of an investigation by Lord Nolan. See the Nolan Committee Report, Cm. 2850 (1995). For the duties of local authority members and officers to declare pecuniary interests, see paras 11-015–11-016 above. The failure to declare a non-pecuniary interest may justify an adverse report of maladministration by the Commissioner for Local Administration. See, *e.g. R. v. Commissioner for Local Administration, ex p. Blakey* [1994] E.G.C.S. 49; C.O.D. 345 .

[68] *R. v. Reading B.C., ex p. Quietlynn Ltd* (1987) 85 L.G.R. 387. See also *R. v. Tower Hamlets L.B.C., ex p. Khatun, The Times,* December 8, 1994, CA. (An interview *re* intentional homelessness not flawed as conducted by council employee aware of local housing conditions.)

[69] See also *R. v. Chesterfield B.C., ex p. Darker Enterprises Ltd* [1992] C.O.D. 466.

[70] *London and Clydeside Estates Ltd v. Secretary of State for Scotland,* 1987 S.L.T. 459. See also *CREED N.Z.* (n. 66 above).

[71] See *R. v. Hendon R.D.C., ex p. Chorley* [1933] 2 K.B. 696 (certiorari issued to quash a grant of planning permission vitiated by a councillor's pecuniary interest: the legislation then in force made provision for rights of objection to an application). See now Local Government Act 1972, ss. 94–98.

the ground of his being a commercial rival of the applicant for planning permission.[72]

When an authority is expressly empowered to make a provisional **11–045** decision, and is then empowered to entertain representations or consider objections against it with a view to deciding whether or not to give it final effect, it is absurd to expect that authority to be totally impartial between itself and the objectors; the authority is naturally likely to be biased in favour of the proposal that it has initiated.[73]

Members of tribunals exercising discretionary regulatory powers, **11–046** such as planning inspectors, will normally be entitled, indeed expected, to adopt and follow general policy guidelines. These guidelines will influence their decisions in individual cases. But by announcing their intention to follow those guidelines they ought not, in general, to be regarded as disqualified for bias unless they have committed themselves so firmly as to make it impracticable for them to deal fairly with subsequent cases on their merits.[74]

In some situations those who have to make decisions can hardly **11–047** insulate themselves from the general ethos of their organisation; they are likely to have firm views about the proper regulation of its affairs, and they will often be familiar with the issues and the conduct of the parties before they assume their role as adjudicators. Licensing justices are entitled to bring their local knowledge to bear on their decisions, including information they may have obtained about an applicant during a previous hearing.[75] Applications of the rules against interest and bias must be tempered with realism; educational institutions, trades unions, clubs and even professional associations are apt to present special problems and it may be right to require evidence of actual bias, rather than mere danger of bias, before a decision is set aside by a court in these settings.[76]

---

[72] *R. v. Holderness D.C., ex p. James Roberts Developments Ltd* (1993) 157 L.G.R. 643. Butler-Sloss L.J. considered that architects or surveyors would also not be disqualified in these circumstances.

[73] As in the *Stevenage* case (*Franklin v. Minister of Town and Country Planning* [1948] A.C. 87). See also *Lim v. Minister of the Interior, Malaya* [1964] 1 W.L.R. 554, 566 (deprivation of citizenship order). But *audi alteram partem* may still be required: *Lower Hutt City Council v. Bank* [1974] 1 N.Z.L.R. 545 (council had precluded itself from fairly considering objections to its own proposed scheme by entering into a contract to carry out the work contemplated by the scheme).

[74] See the discussion on government policy as a material or relevant consideration in Chap. 5, paras 5–098–5–099 above. See also *R. v. Commonwealth Conciliation and Arbitration Committee, ex p. Angliss* (1969) 122 C.L.R. 546; *New Zealand Public Service Association v. Lee* [1970] N.Z.L.R. 317; *Turner v. Allison* [1971] N.Z.L.R. 833; *R. v. Pickersgill, ex p. Smith* (1971) 14 D.L.R. (3d) 717.

[75] *R. v. Crown Court at Bristol, ex p. Cooper* [1990] 1 W.L.R. 1031.

[76] But see a case where latitudinarianism was carried too far: *Ward v. Bradford Corp.* (1971) 70 L.G.R. *Cf. Hannam v. Bradford Corp.* [1970] 1 W.L.R. 937, CA (three out of 10 members of Education Authority Committee governors of school from which

11–048   The normal standards of impartiality applied in an adjudicative setting cannot meaningfully be applied to a body entitled to initiate a proposal and then to decide whether to proceed with it in the face of objections. What standards should be imposed on the Secretary of State for the Environment when he has to decide whether or not to confirm a compulsory purchase order or clearance order made by a local authority or to approve a local planning authority's structure plan or to allow an appeal against refusal of planning permission? It would be inappropriate for the courts to insist on his maintaining the lofty detachment required of a judicial officer determining a *lis inter partes*.[77] The Secretary of State's decisions can seldom be wrenched entirely from their context and viewed in isolation from his governmental responsibilities.[78]

11–049   In some situations it will even be perfectly proper for a public body to make a particular decision for its own pecuniary advantage (as distinct from the pecuniary advantage of individual members or officers). It has been held to be a "material" planning consideration that the developer will contribute some of the profits of the development to a benefit or advantage for the local community.[79] However, in *Steeples v. Derbyshire C.C.*[80] a local planning authority had entered into an agreement with a developer which provided that the authority would be liable for liquidated damages if it failed to use its "best endeavours" to procure planning permissions. The decision was invalidated on the ground of bias. Later cases, however, have made it clear that the courts will not lightly interfere with a planning decision made on the basis of a predetermined policy so long as the authority gives genuine consideration to the application. Thus where the majority party group had met and decided in advance to support an application for a development, it was held that the members of the group were not disqualified from subsequently sitting on the

---

applicant dismissed. *Held:* disqualification because of real likelihood of bias). *Cf. Rees v. Crane* [1994] 2 A.C. 173 where the Privy Council thought right to take into account the distinguished nature of the members of the Judicial and Legal Service Commission and say of them that 'their professional backgrounds are such that an assumption of bias should not be lightly made'.

[77] A point conceded by implication by the report of the Franks Committee on Administrative Tribunals and Enquiries (Cmnd. 218 (1957)), 5, 59–61, 88–83. Contrast the unrealistic views of the Committee on Ministers' Powers (Cmd. 4060 (1932)), 78. on disqualification for 'departmental bias'. See also *Whitford Residents etc. Association (Inc.) v. Manukau City Corp.* [1974] 2 N.Z.L.R. 340.

[78] *Re Manchester (Ringway Airport) Compulsory Purchase Order* (1935) 153 L.T. 219.

[79] See, *e.g. R. v. Westminster City Council, ex p. Monahan* [1990] 1 Q.B. 87 and see Chap. 5 above, para. 5–097 on the limits of 'planning gain'. Local planning authorities can determine their own applications, even where they are engaged in joint ventures.

[80] [1984] 3 All E.R. 468.

committee which determined the application. Politics was held to play so large a part in local government that, if disqualification was to be avoided, the planning committee would have had to adopt impractical standards.[81]

Other cases have held that a local authority was not disqualified **11–050** from granting a planning permission on a site in which the authority had an interest where the decision was properly considered, was by no means a foregone conclusion[82] and the council had not acted in such a way that it "could not exercise proper discretion".[83]

---

[81] *R. v. Amber Valley D.C., ex p. Jackson* [1985] 1 W.L.R. 298. See also *R. v. Waltham Forest L.D.C., ex p. Baxter* [1988] Q.B. 419 (local authority councillor entitled to give weight to views of party colleagues and party whip but could not abdicate responsibility by voting blindly in support of party policy. On the evidence, discretion not fettered by party whip). In *R. v. Secretary of State for the Environment ex p. Kirkstall Valley Campaign Ltd* [1996] 3 All E.R. 304 Sedley J. carefully considered to what extent participation in proceedings would amount to bias. He concluded that the person need not necessarily withdraw from discussion, but it would be 'wise advice' to do so. See also, *R. v. Buckinghamshire County Council ex p. Milton Keynes B.C.* (1997) 9 Admin. L.R. 159 (Conservative party members had not been 'instructed' to vote, on proposals for the establishment of a grammar school, in a manner inconsistent with what was lawfully allowed in the interest of party unity as set out in *Baxter*).

[82] *R. v. Sevenoaks D.C., ex p. Terry* [1985] 3 All E.R. 226; *R. v. St Edmundsbury B.C., ex p. Investors in Industry Commercial Properties Ltd* [1985] 3 All E.R. 234; *R. v. Carlisle City Council, ex p. Cumbrian Co-operative Society Ltd* (1985) 276 E.G. 1161; [1986] J.P.L. 206. See also *R. v. Merton L.B.C., ex p. Burnett* [1990] P.L.R. 72; [1990] J.P.L. 354; *R. v. Canterbury C.C., ex p. Springimage Ltd* [1995] J.P.L. 20.

[83] *per* Glidewell J. in *R. v. Sevenoaks D.C., ex p. Terry*, n. 82 above, at 233. This test was followed in *R. v. City of Wakefield M.D.C and British Coal Corp., ex p. Warmfield Co. Ltd* [1994] J.P.L. 341.

CHAPTER 12

THE UNREASONABLE EXERCISE OF POWER

INTRODUCTION

We now turn to the third general ground of review, which is variously **12–001** known as unreasonableness or, increasingly, irrationality, and sometimes as the abuse of power. Under this ground the question asked is not whether the decision-maker strayed outside the purposes defined by the governing statute (the test of "illegality"), nor whether the decision was procedurally unfair (the test of "procedural propriety"). The question here is whether the power under which the decision-maker acts, a power normally conferring a broad discretion, has been *improperly exercised*.

The terms employed to identify this ground of review are imprecise **12–002** and misleading. The famous formulation by Lord Greene in the *Wednesbury* case,[1] that the courts can only interfere if a decision "is so unreasonable that no reasonable authority could ever come to it",[2] attempts, albeit imperfectly, to convey the point that judges should not lightly interfere with official decisions on this ground. Its tautological definition,[3] however, fails to guide us with any degree of certitude.[4]

---

[1] *Associated Provincial Picture Houses Ltd v. Wednesbury Corp.* [1948] 1 K.B. 223. See also the statement of Griffiths L.J. in *R. v. Commission for Racial Equality, ex p. Hillingdon L.B.C.* [1982] Q.B. 276.

[2] *ibid.* at 229–230.

[3] Because it defines the negative term unreasonableness by both a negative and positive reference to itself: 'so unreasonable that no reasonable body should so act'.

[4] '...we still adhere to [the *Wednesbury* definition of unreasonableness] out of usage if not affection'. *Per* Glidewell L.J. in *R. v. Inland Revenue Commissioner, ex p. Taylor (No. 2)* [1989] 3 All E.R. 353, 357. Recent writings setting out the scope of *Wednesbury* review include: Lord Irvine Q.C., 'Judges and Decision-Makers: the theory and practice of Wednesbury review' [1996] P.L. 59; Martin Norris, 'Ex parte Smith: irrationality and human rights' [1996] P.L. 590; Paul Walker, 'What's Wrong with Irrationality?' [1995] P.L. 556; Deryck Beyleveld, 'The Concept of a human right and incorporation of the ECHR' [1995] P.L. 577; Sir Robert Carnwath 'The reasonable limits of local authority powers' [1966] P.L. 2440.

12–003   "Unreasonableness" is sometimes used to denote particularly extreme behaviour, such as acting in bad faith, or a decision which is "perverse",[5] or "absurd"—implying that the decision-maker has "taken leave of his senses".[6] In the *GCHQ* case,[7] Lord Diplock preferred to use the term "irrational", which he described as applying to "a decision which is so outrageous in its defiance of logic or accepted moral standards that no sensible person who had applied his mind to the question to be decided could have arrived at it".[8] This formulation is at least candid in its acknowledgment that courts can employ both logic and accepted moral standards as criteria by which to assess official decisions, but it does not assist in elucidating any more specific categories of legally unacceptable substantive decisions. In addition, as has been recently pointed out, the term irrationality has the drawback that it casts doubt on the mental capacity of the decision-maker,[9] whereas many decisions which fall foul of this head have been coldly rational. Recent attempts to reformulate the ground as denoting "a decision so unreasonable that no person acting reasonably could have come to it",[10] or a decision which elicits the exclamation: "My goodness, that is certainly wrong!"[11] perhaps help to give an

---

[5] *per* Lord Brightman in *Pulhofer v. Hillingdon L.B.C.* [1986] A.C. 484, 518.

[6] *per* Lord Scarman in *R. v. Secretary of State for the Environment, ex p. Notts C.C.* [1986] A.C. 240, 247–248.

[7] *Council of Civil Service Unions v. Minister for the Civil Service* [1985] A.C. 374.

[8] *ibid.* at 410. *Cf.* Diplock L.J.'s earlier definition of an unreasonable decision which is *"exercised in a manner which no reasonable man could consider justifiable"* (emphasis added): *Luby v. Newcastle-upon-Lyme Corp.* [1964] 2 Q.B. 64, 72. Under the 1994 Interim Constitution of South Africa where *"administrative justice"* is enshrined as a fundamental right, it was provided that every person shall have the right to *"administrative action which is justifiable* in relation to the reasons given for it where any of his or her rights is affected or threatened." Chap. 3. Article 24(d). (Reasons are required for decisions affecting rights or interests in Article 24(c).) (Emphasis added.) But see now section 63 of the South African Constitution.

[9] 'I eschew the synonym of 'irrational', because, although it is attractive as being shorter than *Wednesbury* unreasonable, and has the imprimatur of Lord Diplock ... it is widely misunderstood by politicians, both local and national, and even more by their constituents, as casting doubt on the mental capacity of the decision-maker, a matter which in practice is seldom, if ever, in issue...' *Per* Lord Donaldson M.R. in *R. v. Devon C.C., ex p. G* [1988] 3 W.L.R. 49, 51. See Lord Cooke's criticism of *Wednesbury* in *R. v. Chief Constable of Sussex ex p. International Trader's Ferry Ltd.* [1999] 1 All E.R. 129.

[10] *per* Lord Lowry in *Champion v. Chief Constable of the Gwent Constabulary* [1990] 1 W.L.R. 1, 16.

[11] *per* May L.J. in *Neale v. Hereford & Worcester C.C.* [1986] I.C.R. 471, 483 (not in the context of judicial review, but employed by the Master of the Rolls in *R. v. Devon C.C., ex p. G* (n. 9 above), and in *Piggott Brothers & Co. Ltd v. Jackson* T.L.R. May 20, 1991.

indication of the flavour of the conduct which qualifies as being within the concept of unreasonableness, but are no more helpful as guides to its precise parameters.

In 1898 a relatively specific account of unreasonableness in the context of a review of local authority byelaws was provided in the case of *Kruse v. Johnson*.[12] Lord Russell of Killowen C.J. expressed the view there that byelaws should be benevolently interpreted by the courts, but could be struck down for unreasonableness: "If, for instance, they were found to be partial and unequal in their operation between different classes; if they were manifestly unjust; if they disclosed bad faith; if they involved such oppressive or gratuitous interference with the rights of those subject to them such as could find no justification in the minds of reasonable men." Lately, however, if we seek more definite criteria of the unreasonable or irrational decision, however defined, we are usually confronted with a cascading list of administrative sins which does little to allay the confusion. Lord Greene in *Wednesbury* provided such a list, all the items on which he considered to "overlap to a very great extent" and "run into one another".[13] These included: bad faith, dishonesty, attention given to extraneous circumstances, disregard of public policy, wrong attention given to irrelevant considerations, and failure to take into account matters which are bound to be considered. Some of these instances, particularly those referring to the taking into account of irrelevant considerations (or failing to take them into account) we have seen in Chapter 5 are today more appropriately considered as instances of illegality rather than unreasonableness,[14] because they are extraneous to the objects or purposes of the statute under which the power is being exercised, taking the decision outside the "four corners" of the governing statute.

This Chapter deals with the variety of senses variously attributed to decisions which have been called unreasonable, or irrational, or simply instances of an abuse of power. The terms will be used interchangeably, for they each have in common the fact that they refer to the improper exercise of power. It is important to recognise, however, that concealed beneath all of the appellations are three distinct ways in which power may be improperly exercised:

(1) First, there is the case where there has been material defect in the decision-making *process*. The assessment here focuses upon the motives or reasoning underlying or supporting the

12–004

12–005

---

[12] [1889] 2 Q.B. 291.

[13] n. 2 above. *Ibid.*

[14] *cf.* H.W.R. Wade and C. F. Forsyth, *Administrative Law* (1994), pp. 399–400.

decision; upon the factors taken into account on the way to reaching the decision, or upon the way the decision is justified or reasoned. We shall examine here:

(a) decisions taken in bad faith;
(b) decisions based on considerations which have been accorded manifestly inappropriate weight; and
(c) strictly "irrational" decisions, namely, decisions which are apparently illogical or arbitrary, or supported by inadequate evidence or by inadequate or incomprehensible reasons.

(2) Second, are decisions taken in violation of common law or constitutional principles governing the exercise of official power. These principles apply even where discretion has been conferred in the widest terms. Two principles will be considered:

(a) the principle of legal certainty (which requires the protection of substantive legitimate expectations); and
(b) the principle of equality (which requires decisions to be consistently applied and prohibits measures which make unjustifiable or unfair distinctions between individuals).

It might be noted here that these two principles correspond to two of the "general principles of law" which, in European Community law, apply to the exercise of all public functions.[15] There is another such principle, that of "proportionality", which could be included at this point but which is perhaps better viewed as a test of the exercise of power under all of the three categories which are set out here. Proportionality will therefore be examined at the end of this chapter, after the three categories have been considered.

(3) The third category contains what might be called oppressive decisions. The focus here is upon the end-product of the decision; upon its affect on individuals (and not upon the process by which the decision was reached). Decisions may be impugned under this head because of the unnecessarily onerous impact they have on the rights or interest of persons affected by them.

12–006   Any decision may of course violate more than one of these categories, but it is important to appreciate that the general ground of

---

[15] See Chap. 17 below, and see J. Schwartze, *European Administrative Law*, (1992).

unreasonableness is applied in three very different situations, each focusing on a different aspect of the decision-making process and each looking at very different ways in which power may be abused.

Before considering these categories in turn, we should note that **12–007** interference under any one of them presents a conceptual difficulty for judges since, in exercising their powers of judicial review, they ought not to imagine themselves as being in the position of the competent authority when the decision was taken and then test the reasonableness of the decision as against the decision they would have taken. To do so would involve the courts in reconsidering the merits of the decision—a process which is inappropriate to judicial review because it involves the court acting as if they were themselves the recipients of the power. Lord Greene in *Wednesbury*[16] thought that an unreasonable decision under his definition "would require something overwhelming" (such as a teacher being dismissed on the ground of her red hair).[17] Whether or not that is so, what the courts have to guard against is having to second-guess administrators who are entitled to a "margin of appreciation"[18] of the facts or merits of a case. This margin, and the corresponding intensity of review will also be considered below. We shall see that it may well vary in accordance with the nature of the power concerned, the type of decision made, and the rights or interests at stake.

Finally, we should consider the justification for the courts **12–008** intervening at all in official decisions which are neither procedurally improper nor contravene the terms of a statute and are not therefore invalid on the ground of illegality. As was discussed in the Introduction to this work,[19] judicial review involves the courts in a task that is wider than the interpretation of statutory power. Some powers (*e.g.* prerogative and contractual powers) do not have statutory sources. And the exercise of all power, statutorily conferred or not, is presumed by the courts to operate in the context of common law or constitutional principles, unless Parliament expressly provides to the contrary. The courts therefore imply the requirement that all discretion should be exercised as reason directs[20] and in accordance with

---

[16] n. 1 above.

[17] *ibid.* at 229. The illustration is from *Short v. Poole Corp.* [1926] Ch. 66. Previous editions of this work considered that cases in the 1960s had shorn the *Wednesbury* formula of its unnecessary reference to "overwhelming" proof.

[18] The term *marge d'appreciation* is employed in European Community law and in the law of the European Convention of Human Rights. The correct translation is probably "margin of assessment", or "margin of discretion". Since the term has now been used frequently in English law it will be employed here unless a more exact meaning is required.

[19] Chap. 1, para. 1–030 *et seq.*

[20] "[Courts] should assume, unless the contrary unmistakably appears, that the legislature was made up of reasonable persons pursuing reasonable purposes

standards governing their exercise which are appropriate to any constitutional democracy—irrespective of whether the constitution is set out in a formal written document. These standards will now be examined.[21]

DEFECTS IN THE DECISION-MAKING PROCESS

12–009 The first category of unreasonable decision contains some defect in the process of arriving at the decision; in the way the decision was reached or in the manner by which it has been justified. The focus here is thus upon the factors taken into account by the decision-maker on the way to making the decision; on the motives and upon the factors or evidence by which the decision was influenced. We shall first look at decisions infected with bad faith, then at decisions where the considerations taken into account are wrongly balanced, and finally at strictly "irrational" decisions, namely, those that are based upon the lack of ostensible logic, inadequate evidence or inappropriate reasons.

Bad faith

12–010 Fundamental to the legitimacy of public decision-making is the principle that official decisions should not be infected with motives such as fraud (or dishonesty), malice or personal self-interest. These motives, which have the effect of distorting or unfairly biasing the decision-maker's approach to the subject of the decision, cause the decision to be taken in bad faith or for an improper purpose (the term "improper" here bearing a connotation of moral impropriety). Some of the decisions based on bad faith will also violate the ground of illegality, as the offending motive may take the decision outside the "four corners" of the authorised power. Irrespective of whether this be so, any ingredient of bad faith may in itself cause a decision to be invalid.[22]

---

reasonably." H. Hart and A. Sacks, *The Legal Process; Basic Problems in the Making and Application of Law* (10th ed., 1958), p. 1415.

[21] Where a decision is infected with unreasonableness it may be possible for the courts to sever the bad parts from the good (the reasonable from the unreasonable). In such a case, the same principles apply that were discussed in relation to the severability of illegal decision in Chap. 5, above, paras 5-100–5-101. See, *e.g. R. v. Immigration Appeal Tribunal, ex p. Manshoora Begum* [1986] Imm. A.R. 385 (severance of offending part of immigration regulation).

[22] The duty to act in good faith has sometimes been distinguished from the duty to act reasonably. Scrutton L.J. observed that; "Some of the most honest people are the most

A power is exercised *fraudulently* if its repository intends to achieve **12–011** an object other than that which he claims to be seeking. The intention may be to promote another public interest or private interests. A power is exercised *maliciously* if its repository is motivated by personal animosity towards those who are directly affected by its exercise.

Examples of cases involving fraudulent or dishonest motives include **12–012** those where a local authority acquired property for the ostensible purpose of widening a street or redeveloping an urban area but in reality for the purpose of reselling it at a profit[23]; or preventing the owner from reaping the benefit of the expected increment in land values[24]; or giving an advantage to a third party.[25] Licensing powers cannot be used to augment public funds.[26] An authority, purporting to exercise powers of compulsory acquisition for the purpose of widening streets, proposed to widen a street only to a minute extent, its true purpose being to alter the street level.[27] A local authority

---

unreasonable; and some excesses may be sincerely believed in but yet be quite beyond the limits of reasonableness.' *R. v. Roberts, ex p. Scurr* [1924] 2 K.B. 695, 719. Lord MacNaghton, however, in *Westminster Corp. v. L. & N. Ry.* [1905] A.C. 426, 430, suggested that the duty to act reasonably was implicit in the duty to act in good faith. The previous edition of this work considered that the duty to act in good faith was a general principle of administrative law; de Smith, *Judicial Review* (4th ed.), p. 347. But we now have the three 'grounds' of judicial review and it is submitted that bad faith fits comfortably into the ground of unreasonableness. *Pace* Lord MacNaghton, bad faith is implicit in the duty not to act unreasonably, or in the duty not to abuse official power (although it has not always been explicitly articulated as such).

[23] *Gard v. Commissioners of Sewers for the City of London* (1885) 28 Ch D 486; *Donaldson v. South Shields Corp.* [1899] W.N. 6; *Fernley v. Limehouse Board of Works* (1899) 68 L.J. Ch. 344; *Denman (J.L.) & Co. v. Westminster Corp.* [1906] 1 Ch. 464, 475; *R. v. Minister of Health, ex p. Davis* [1929] 1 K.B. 619, 624. Contrast *C.C. Auto Port Pty Ltd v. Minister for Works* (1966) 113 C.L.R. 365. But see the puzzling decision, *Robins (E.) & Son Ltd v. Minister of Health* [1939] 1 K.B. 520 where the Court of Appeal held the local authority had an unfettered discretion in its choice of method (clearance or demolition) of dealing with compulsorily acquired land. Mackinnon L.J. (at 537–538) also observed that, even had the property owners succeeded in establishing that the local authority had adopted the method of compulsory purchase in order to be able to resell the land to the owners (who wished to develop it) at a high price, that would not have affected the validity of the decision. *Cf. Merrick v. Liverpool Corp.* [1910] 2 Ch. 449, 463.

[24] *Sydney Municipal Council v. Campbell* [1925] A.C. 338. See, further, *Grice v. Dudley Corp.* [1958] Ch. 329 and other authorities there cited at 341–342.

[25] *Bartrum v. Manurewa Borough* [1962] N.Z.L.R. 21.

[26] *R. v. Bowman* [1898] 1 Q.B. 663; *R. v. Birmingham Licensing Planning Committee, ex p. Kennedy* [1972] 2 Q.B. 140. See also *R. v. Shann* [1910] 2 K.B. 418, 434.

[27] *Lynch v. Commissioners of Sewers for the City of London* (1886) 32 Ch D 72. Attempts to impugn compulsory purchase orders in the English courts for improper purpose were successful in *Grice v. Dudley Corp.* (n. 24 above), *London & Westcliff Properties Ltd v. Minister of Housing and Local Government* [1961] 1 W.L.R. 519, *Webb v. Minister of Housing and Local Government* [1965] 1 W.L.R. 755, *Meravale Builders Ltd v. Secretary of*

empowered to acquire unfit houses purported to do so in order to provide temporary accommodation pending their demolition, but in reality intended to render them fit for habitation and add them to its permanent housing stock.[28] An authority purporting to dismiss school-teachers on educational grounds, in reality dismissed them for reasons of economy.[29] An authority claiming to raise the salaries of its employees to reflect an increase in their duties, in reality did so in order to grant an employee an increase unrelated to the changes in his duties.[30] A police authority which called its former chief constable, who was living abroad, ostensibly for medical examination (and cancelled his pension when he failed to appear) in reality called him so as to facilitate the execution of a warrant of arrest issued against him by the Bankruptcy Court.[31] A local authority sought to acquire land for its benefit, when its true motive was to remove gypsies from the land.[32]

12–013 A decision based on malice is usually one that is directed *ad hominem*—*e.g.* where a byelaw or order has been made especially to

---

the *Environment* (1978) 36 P. & C.R. 87, and *Victoria Square Property Co. Ltd v. Southwark L.B.C.* [1978] 1 W.L.R. 463; and unsuccessful in *Hanks v. Minister of Housing and Local Government* [1963] 1 Q.B. 999, *Simpsons Motor Sales (London) Ltd v. Hendon Corp.* [1964] A.C. 1088 and *Moore v. Minister of Housing and Local Government* [1966] 2 Q.B. 602. See also *Birmingham & Midland Motor Omnibus Co. v. Worcestershire C.C.* [1967] 1 W.L.R. 409 (diversion of traffic for unauthorised purpose).

[28] *Victoria Square Property Co. Ltd v. Southwark L.B.C.* (n. 27 above).

[29] *Hanson v. Radcliffe U.D.C.* [1922] 2 Ch. 490; *Sadler v. Sheffield Corp.* [1924] 1 Ch. 483. See also *Smith v. McNally* [1912] 1 Ch. 816, 825–826; *Martin v. Eccles Corp.* [1919] 1 Ch. 387, 400 ('grounds connected with the giving of religious instruction'). Contrast *Price v. Rhondda U.D.C.* [1923] 2 Ch. 377; *Short v. Poole Corp.* [1926] Ch. 66.

[30] *R. (Wexford C.C.) v. Local Government Board* [1902] 2 I.R. 349. See also the Australian case *Brownells Ltd v. Ironmongers' Wages Board* (1950) 81 C.L.R. 108, esp. 120, 130 (wages board fixed high overtime rates in reality to bring about closure of shops at hours different from those required by statute).

[31] *R. v. Leigh (Lord)* [1987] 1 Q.B. 582. See also *R. v. Brixton Prison Governor, ex p. Soblen* [1963] 2 Q.B. 243 where it was unsuccessfully alleged that the true purpose of deportation was to comply with a request for extradition. See also *R. v. Secretary of State for the Environment, ex p. Ostler* [1977] Q.B. 122 where the applicant was issued with false information which misled him not to appear at a public inquiry. But judicial review was excluded by an ouster clause. In other cases it has been said that where bad faith is established, the courts will be prepared to set aside a decision procured or made fraudulently, despite the existence of a formula purporting to exclude judicial review. See, *e.g. Lazarus Estates Ltd v. Beasley* [1956] 1 Q.B. 702, 712–713, *per* Denning L.J. See also *ibid.* at 722, *per* Parker L.J.: fraud 'vitiates all transactions known to the law of however high a degree of solemnity.' See also cases cited by counsel in *Smith v. East Elloe R.D.C.* [1956] A.C. 736, 740 where it was held that the statutory language was sufficiently clear to exclude challenge for bad faith to a compulsory purchase order outside the short statutory limitation period. See *further* above, Chap. 4 para. 4–014 *et seq.*

[32] *Costello v. Dacorum D.C.* (1980) 79 L.G.R. 133; and see Wade and Forsyth, n. 14 above, p. 880.

thwart an individual application for a permit.[33] The malice may arise out of personal or political animosity built up over a series of past dealings.[34] For instance, in a Canadian case the cancellation of a liquor licence was held to be an abuse of power where the decision was prompted by the proprietor's support of a religious sect who were considered a nuisance by the police.[35] In another Canadian case the court inferred *mala fides* from the fact that a byelaw was made for the compulsory purchase of land which was the subject of pending litigation between the owner and the local authority.[36] And in a third it was held that a local authority cannot use its licensing power to prohibit lawful businesses of which it disapproves.[37] In an English case the decision of the Derbyshire County Council to cease advertising in journals controlled by Times Newspapers which had written articles critical of its councillors was explicitly held to have been motivated by bad faith and therefore declared invalid for that reason alone.[38]

The balance of relevant considerations

When the courts review a decision they are careful not readily to interfere with the balancing of considerations which are relevant to the   **12–014**

---

[33] *Lubrizol Corp. Pty Ltd v. Leichhardt Municipal Council* [1961] N.S.W.R. 111; *Boyd Builders Ltd v. City of Ottawa* (1964) 45 D.L.R. (2d) 211.

[34] The allegation by Mrs Smith in *Smith v. East Elloe R.D.C.* [1986] A.C. 736. Personal animosity towards a party may also disqualify an adjudicator: *R. (Donoghue) v. Cork County JJ.* [1910] 2 I.R. 271; *R. (Kingston) v. Cork County JJ.* [1910] 2 I.R. 658; *R. (Harrington) v. Clare County JJ.* [1918] 2 I.R. 116; *Law v. Chartered Institute of Patent Agents* [1919] 2 Ch. 276; *R. v. Handley* (1921) 61 D.L.R. 656; *Re "Catalina" and "Norma"* (1938) 61 Ll. Rep. 360.

[35] See *Roncarelli v. Duplessis* (1959) 16 D.L.R. (2d) 689, 705. For further proceedings see [1959] S.C.R. 121.

[36] *Re Burns and Township of Haldimand* (1966) 52 D.L.R. (2d) 101.

[37] *Prince George (City of) v. Payne* [1978] 1 S.C.R. 458. In any event a power to regulate will not normally be constructed to allow total prohibition: *Tarr v. Tarr* [1973] A.C. 254, 265–268. For another interesting Canadian case, see *Re Doctors Hospital and Minister of Health* (1976) 68 D.L.R. (3d) 220 (power to revoke approval as public hospital wrongfully exercised in the interests of economy).

[38] *R. v. Derbyshire C.C., ex p. The Times Supplement Ltd and Others* [1991] C.O.D. 129. In *R. v. Ealing L.B.C., ex p. Times Newspapers Ltd* (1986) 85 L.G.R. 316 the London borough councils imposed a ban on purchasing the publications of the Times Newspapers in their libraries. Watkins L.J., without going so far as to label the 'shadowy' reasons for imposing the ban (to punish a 'tyrannical employer') as bad faith—he called them 'a transparent piece of camouflage'—did hold the decision both irrational and an abuse of power (as well as illegal—as discussed in Chap. 5 para. 5–072, above). Cf. *R. v. Lewisham L.B.C., ex p. Shell U.K. Ltd* [1988] 1 All E.R. 938 (ban on purchasing Shell's products to pressure parent company to sever links with South African subsidiary illegal but not unreasonable, although 'very near the line').

power that is exercised by an authority.[39] The balancing and weighing of relevant considerations is primarily a matter for the public authority and not for the courts. Courts have, however, been willing to strike down as unreasonable decisions where manifestly excessive or manifestly inadequate weight has been accorded to a relevant consideration.[40]

12–015   For example, a local authority, or the Secretary of State on appeal, may, in considering whether to grant a permission for the change of use of a building, have regard not only to the proposed new use but also to the existing use of the building and weigh the one against the other. The courts are concerned normally to leave the balancing of these considerations to the planning authority. However, where the refusal of planning permission is based on the preference for the preservation of the building's existing use, the refusal may be struck down in the extreme case where there is in practice "no reasonable prospect" of that use being preserved.[41] In effect, in such a case the courts are holding that the existing use is being accorded excessive weight in the balancing exercise involved. The courts have also interfered with the balancing of "material" planning considerations, by holding that excessive weight had been accorded to a planning permission that had long since expired.[42] Although planning authorities are required, in deciding whether to grant or refuse planning permission, to have regard to government circulars, or to development plans,[43] a "slavish" adherence to those (relevant and material) considerations may render a decision invalid.[44]

12–016   Similarly, in many cases involving the eviction of gypsies from local authority sites it has been held that the weighing of the various considerations relevant to the exercise of the power (such as nuisance,

---

[39] See, *e.g.* Lord Scarman's speech in *United Kingdom Association of Professional Engineers v. Advisory, Conciliation and Arbitration Services* [1981] A.C. 424. See generally, G. L. Peiris, "*Wednesbury* Unreasonableness: the Expanding Canvas" (1987) C.L.J. 53; *Pulhofer v. Hillingdon L.B.C.* [1986] A.C. 484 (re local authority's duty to house the homeless).

[40] de Smith (4th ed.) p. 499 regarded this head as constituting the substance of the case against the local authority in *Wednesbury*.

[41] *London Residuary Body v. Lambeth L.B.C.* [1990] 1 W.L.R. 744. See *Westminster City Council v. British Waterways Board* [1985] A.C. 676, where Bridge L.J. said that "In a contest between the planning merits of two competing uses, to justify refusal of permission for use B on the sole ground that use A ought to be preserved, it must, in my view, be necessary at least to show a balance of probability that, if permission is refused for use B, the land in dispute will be effectively put to use A."

[42] *South Oxfordshire D.C. v. Secretary of State for the Environment* [1981] 1 W.L.R. 1092.

[43] See Chap. 5 paras 5-098–5-099.

[44] *Simpson v. Edinburgh Corp.* 1960 S.C. 313; *Niarchos (London) Ltd v. Secretary of State for the Environment* (1977) 35 P. & C.R. 259. The weight attached to a planning obligation has recently been held to be a matter essentially for the planning authorities and not for the courts, but subject to *Wednesbury* unreasonableness. *Tesco Stores v. Secretary of State for The Environment* [1995] 1 W.L.R. 759, HL.

obstruction, or danger) against the council's legal duty to provide adequate accommodation for gypsies[45] is primarily a matter for the local authority.[46] However, where the local authority had for over 10 years ignored its duty to provide adequate accommodation for gypsies in its area, the assumption was made that insufficient weight had been accorded to that relevant consideration, and the decision to evict was held void for unreasonableness.[47]

In licensing cases it has also been held that too much weight had been placed by an authority upon recent precedent refusing refreshment licences, and too little upon the 50-year previous enjoyment of the licence by the applicant.[48]

In cases involving the Home Secretary's discretion to release life **12–017** prisoners who had served their "tariff", it is normally for the Home Secretary to balance the various considerations relevant to the decision. However, it has been held that the weight attached by the Home Secretary to minor crimes or misdemeanours the prisoner committed some time ago when on temporary release was excessive, rendering the decision not permanently to release the prisoner "perverse".[49] Excessive weight attached to expressions of expert opinion (in the form of a medical certificate,[50] counsel's opinion,[51] or even the opinion of the Chief Justice about the release of a prisoner) can similarly render a decision unreasonable,[52] as can the reliance

---

[45] Under section 6 of The Caravan Sites Act 1968.

[46] *e.g. R. v. Avon C.C., ex p. Rexworthy* (1988) 87 L.G.R. 470.

[47] *W. Glamorgan C.C. v. Rafferty* [1987] 1 W.L.R. 457 ('The decision...required the weighing of the factors according to the personal judgment of the Councillors but the law does not permit complete freedom of choice assessment...': *per* Ralph Gibson L.J.).

[48] *R. v. Flintshire County Licensing Committee, ex p. Barrett* [1957] 1 Q.B. 350.

[49] See *R. v. Secretary of State for the Home Department, ex p. Benson*, The Times, November 21, 1988; [1989] C.O.D. 329; *R. v. Secretary of State for the Home Department, ex p. Cox* (1993) Admin. L.R. 17; [1992] C.O.D. 72. (These decisions could equally be decided on the ground that the excessive weight attached to the minor crimes and misdemeanours amounted to the taking into account of considerations that were irrelevant to the statutory purpose because they did not address the question of the prisoner's dangerousness. In *Cox* both tests were applied.) See *R. v. Secretary of State for the Home Department ex p. Zulfikar* [1996] C.O.D. 256, where it was held that 'undue weight' should not have been given to a parole requirement that the offender 'address his offending', where the offender continued to deny the offence.

[50] *R. v. Devon C.C., ex p. G* [1988] 3 W.L.R. 49.

[51] *R. v. Lancashire C.C., ex p. Hook* [1980] 1 Q.B.

[52] *R. v. Home Secretary, ex p. Handscomb* (1988) 86 Cr.App.R. 59; *R. v. Home Secretary, ex p. Walsh*, [1992] C.O.D. 240. But see *R. v. The Council of Legal Education, ex p. Vine et al.* (unreported) Transcript No. CO 1223–94, QBD, where applicants to the Council of Legal Education's legal practice course challenged the decision to assess applications *inter alia* by failing to have regard to A level results. The challenge of unreasonableness on those grounds failed largely because the Council had 'consulted experts at every stage'.

upon an immaterial mistake in an application for legal aid as a ground of refusal.[53]. In *R. v. Secretary of State for the Home Department ex p. Venables* the House of Lords held[54] that, in fixing the tariffs for young offenders and deciding the part of the sentence required for punishment and deterrence, the Home Secretary had wrongly taken into account irrelevant material derived from public petitions and via the media. Lord Steyn held that the Home Secretary's decision was also *procedurally* flawed by "the credence and weight" which he gave to the public clamour for an increase in the level of the tariff.

The exercise of balancing relevant considerations is primarily a matter for the decision-maker. The courts, however, do properly

---

[53] *R. v. Law Society, ex p. Gates & Co., The Times,* March 31, 1988. See also *R. v. Legal Aid Committee No. 10 (East Midlands), ex p. McKenna* (1990) 2 Admin. L.R. 585 (cost of litigation in grant of legal aid should not be the sole or even decisive factor). In *Secretary of State for Education and Science v. Tameside M.B.C.* [1977] A.C. 1014, 1048 Lord Wilberforce said that the 'mere possibility' of disruption by the unions of the local authority's plan to reintroduce grammar schools could not be a ground for the Secretary of State's issuing a direction to abandon the plan. He said that 'The ultimate question in this case, in my opinion, is whether the Secretary of State has given sufficient, or any weight to this particular factor in the exercise of his judgment'. The threat of disruption of live animal exports was held, in the interest of the rule of law, not to be relevant to the decision of ports authorities to ban such exports. *R. v. Coventry Airport & others, ex. p. Phoenix Aviation,* [1995] 3 All E.R. 37, *Cf. R. v. Chief Constable of Sussex, ex p. Int. Trader's Ferry Ltd,* [1996] Q.B. 197. The Court of Appeal has since held that the Chief Constable's decision to provide policing on only two days a week to protect the transport of livestock where animal rights protestors were demonstrating was not unreasonable or disproportionate under domestic and E.C. law because of restraints on resources, and there being no reasonable prospects of those resources being increased: [1997] 3 W.L.R. 132. This judgment was upheld by the House of Lords: [1998] 3 W.L.R. 12. See also *R. v. Camden L.B.C., ex p. H (a minor)* [1996] E.L.R. 306, CA (committee of governors had failed to consider sufficiently what effect the reversal of the headteacher's decision to expel pupils would have on the maintenance of discipline in the school and what effect the reinstatement of X and Y would have on the victim himself). But see *R. v. Secretary of State for the Home Department, ex p. Singh (Rabhbir)* [1995] Imm. A.R. 447 (although there was no evidence to show that an appropriate balancing exercise had been carried out to ensure that the risk to the individual had been balanced against the public interest, the Secretary of State would carry out such an exercise in the course of S's asylum application). See also *Raziastaraie (Mansour Ali) v. Secretary of State for the Home Department* [1995] Imm. A.R. 459 (*R. v. Secretary of State for the Home Department, ex p. Chahal* [1995] 1 W.L.R. 526 was distinguished, House of Lords dismissed the appeal: [1996] 2 W.L.R. 766). See also *R. v. Southwark LBC ex p. Cordwell* (1995) 27 H.L.R. 594 (closure order under Housing Act 1985. No evidence of error in the calculation of the proper weight to be given to occupier's wishes); *R. v. Kensington & Chelsea RLBC ex p. Ben-el-Mabrouk* (1995) 27 H.L.R. 564; *R. v. Mid-Hertfordshire Justices ex p. Cox* (1996) 8 Admin. L.R. 409 (unreasonable failure to place weight on fact that poll tax defaulter could not afford to pay fine because destitute).

[54] [1997] 3 W.L.R. 23.

intervene to correct a manifest imbalance where disproportionate weight has been accorded to one or other relevant consideration.[55]

Rationality: logic, evidence and reasoning

Although the terms irrationality and unreasonableness are these days **12–018** often used interchangeably, irrationality is only one facet of unreasonableness.[56] A decision is irrational in the strict sense of that term if it is unreasoned; if it is lacking ostensible logic or comprehensible justification. Instances of irrational decisions include those made in an arbitrary fashion, perhaps "by spinning a coin or consulting an astrologer".[57] "Absurd" or "perverse" decisions may be presumed to have been decided in that fashion, as may decisions where the given reasons are simply unintelligible. Less extreme examples of the irrational decision include those in which there is an absence of logical connection between the evidence and the ostensible reasons for the decision, where the reasons display no adequate justification for the decision, or where there is absence of evidence in support of the decision.

We have seen that the absence of reasons for a decision may **12–019** constitute a breach of a fair hearing.[58] Irrationality may also sometimes be inferred from the absence of reasons.[59] When reasons are required, either by statute or by the growing common law requirements, or where they are provided, even though not strictly required, those reasons must be both "adequate and intelligible". They must therefore

---

[55] See, *e.g. R. v. Housing Benefit Review Board of the London Borough of Sutton* [1992] C.O.D. 450, where Potts J. held that, in refusing the applicant housing benefit, the Board 'had attached a wholly disproportionate weight to the fact that the applicant could not meet her liability to pay rent'. Proportionality will be discussed at para. 12–068 *et seq.* below.

[56] 'I would accordingly incline to accept the Secretary of State's argument on this point, while observing that decisions reached by him are susceptible to challenge on any *Wednesbury* ground, of which irrationality is only one'. *per* Sir Thomas Bingham M.R. in *R. v. Secretary of State for the Home Department, ex p. Omibiyo* [1996] 2 All E.R. 901.

[57] *R. v. Deputy Industrial Injuries Commissioner, ex p. Moore* [1965] 1 Q.B. 456 at p. 488, *per* Diplock L.J. *R. v. Lambeth L.B.C., ex p. Ashley* (1997) 29 H.L.R. 385 (points scheme for the allocation of housing was plainly 'illogical and irrational'). See also *R. v. Islington L.B.C. ex p. Hassan* (1995) 27 H.L.R. 485 (finding of intentional homelessness illogical).

[58] Chap. 8, para. 8–039 *et seq.*

[59] *Padfield v. Minister of Agriculture Fisheries and Food* [1968] A.C. 997, 1932; 1049; 1053–1054; 1061–1062; *Lonrho plc v. Secretary of State for Trade and Industry* [1989] 1 W.L.R. 525, 539; *R. v. Civil Service Appeal Board, ex p. Cunningham* [1991] 4 All E.R. 310. But it may not be possible for the court to infer unreasonableness from the lack of reasons. See, *e.g. R. v. Secretary of State for the Home Department, ex p. Adams* [1995] E.C.R. 177 (*per* Steyn L.J. and Kay J.).

both rationally relate to the evidence in the case,[60] and be comprehensible in themselves.[61] The reasons will not be construed in the same way as courts would construe a statute, but a decision may be struck down where an applicant can show substantial prejudice resulting from a failure on the part of the decision-maker to demonstrate how an issue of law had been resolved or a disputed issue of fact decided, or by "demonstrating some other lack of reasoning which raised substantial doubts over the decision-making process".[62]

12–020   Substantial doubt over what is intended may also result in a provision being held invalid for uncertainty. As is the case with contracts, decisions in public law can be void for uncertainty. A byelaw or statutory instrument may be pronounced invalid for uncertainty where it fails to indicate adequately what it is prohibiting.[63] However, in the recent case of *Percy v. Hall*[64] the Court of Appeal conducted an

---

[60] In *Re Poyser and Mills' Arbitration* [1964] 2 Q.B. 467, Megaw J., speaking of the duty to give reasons imposed by s.12 of the Tribunals and Inquiries Act 1958 said, at p. 478, that the required reasons 'must be read as meaning that proper adequate reasons must be given ... which deal with the substantial points that have been raised.' See also Lord Scarman in *Westminster City Council v. Great Portland Estates Plc* [1985] A.C. 661, at 673.

[61] See Phillips J. in *Hope v. Secretary of State for the Environment* (1975) 31 P. & C.R. 120, 123, referring to a decision of a planning inspector which 'must be such that it enables the appellant to understand on what grounds the appeal has been decided and be in sufficient detail to enable him to know what conclusions the inspector has reached on the principal important issues'. See also *Ward v. Secretary of State for the Environment* (1989) 59 P. & C.R. 486, 487 where Woolf L.J. said that "With regard to the requirement to give reasons it suffices to say that the reasons must be ones which are understandable to those who will receive those reasons", and cited with approval in *Save Britain's Heritage v. Number 1 Poultry Ltd* [1991] 1 W.L.R. 153, 165 (*per* Lord Bridge). See also: *Bolton M.D.C. v. Secretary of State for the Environment* (1996) 71 P. & C.R. 309. In *R. v. Hammersmith & Fulham L.B.C., ex p. Earls Court Ltd, The Times,* September 7, 1993, it was held that a condition imposed upon an entertainment licence which was so obscure that it necessitated the issue of a construction summons was 'unreasonable in the *Wednesbury* sense'; *per* Kennedy L.J.

[62] *Save Britain's Heritage v. Number 1 Poultry Ltd* [1991] 1 W.L.R. 153, 168 *per* Lord Bridge, emphasising, however, that the adequacy of reasons depended upon the legislative context and could not be answered *in vacuo*.

[63] Byelaws were held void for uncertainty in *Nash v. Finlay* (1901) 20 Cox C.C. 101, *United Bill Posting Company v. Somerset C.C.* (1926) 42 T.L.R. 537, 538 (Lord Hewart C.J.). *Cf. R. v. Fenny Stratford JJ., ex p. Watney Mann (Midland) Ltd* [1976] 1 W.L.R. 1101 (condition attached to nuisance abatement order). See also *Re Dartmouth and SS Kresge Co. Ltd* (1966) 58 D.L.R. (2d) 229 (S.C. of Nova Scotia). See generally, D.G.T. Williams, 'Criminal Law and Administrative Law: Problems of Procedure and Reasonableness', in *Essays in Honour of J. C. Smith* (1987) at 170. In *McEldowney v. Forde* [1971] A.C. 632, the majority of their Lordships assumed that the test of uncertainty applied to regulations as well as byelaws. See also *Staden v. Tarjanyi* (1980) 78 L.G.R. 614, 623–624.

[64] [1997] Q.B. 924.

exhaustive survey of the authorities (*per* Simon Brown L.J.) and reached the conclusion that a byelaw would be treated as valid unless it was so uncertain in its language as to have no ascertainable meaning or was so unclear in its effect as to be incapable of certain application. Mere "ambiguity" would not suffice.[65] Uncertainty is a ground for invalidating conditions annexed to grants of planning permission and site licences. Such conditions may be void for uncertainty if they can be given no meaning at all, or no sensible or ascertainable meaning.[66]

As was discussed in Chapter 4,[67] courts in judicial review will not **12-021** normally interfere with an administrator's assessment of fact. In two situations, however, they may do so: first, where the existence of a set of facts is a condition precedent to the exercise of a power,[68] and second, when the decision-maker has taken into account as a fact something which is wrong or where he has misunderstood the facts upon which the decision depends,[69] Similarly, if there is "no evidence" for a finding upon which a decision depends,[70] or where the evidence,

---

[65] *cf. Kruse v. Johnson* [1898] 2 Q.B. 473.

[66] *cf. Fawcett Properties Ltd v. Buckingham C.C.* [1961] A.C. 636; *Hall v. Shoreham-by-Sea U.D.C.* [1964] 1 W.L.R. 240; *Mixnam's Properties Ltd v. Chertsey U.D.C.* [1964] 1 Q.B. 214; [1965] A.C. 735; see *David Lowe and Sons Ltd v. Musselburgh Corp.,* 1974 S.L.T. 5 (condition incapable of any certain or intelligible interpretation). In *Bizony v. Secretary of State for the Environment* (1976) 239 E.G. 281, 284 the test of uncertainty applied to a planning condition was limited to linguistic ambiguity or uncertainty in meaning: mere difficulty in determining whether the condition had been breached on particular facts was not enough. In *Shanley M.J. Ltd (In liquidation) v. Secretary of State for the Environment* [1982] J.P.L. 380 it was held that a condition favouring local people was void for uncertainty. But in *Alderson v. Secretary of State for the Environment* [1984] J.P.L. 429 the Court of Appeal held a condition limiting occupation of premises to persons 'employed locally in agriculture' was not uncertain. See Department of Environment, Circular 11/97. See also *Bromsgrove D.C. v. Secretary of State for the Environment* [1988] J.P.L. 257 (difficulty of enforcement does not invalidate for uncertainty). In *R. v. Barnett L.B.C., ex p. Johnson* [1989] C.O.D. 538 (conditions attached to grant-aid for a community festival prohibiting 'political activity' were held 'meaningless').

[67] Para. 4–055 *et seq.*

[68] See *R. v. Secretary of State for the Home Department, ex p. Khawajah* [1984] A.C. 74.

[69] See, *e.g. Hollis v. Secretary of State for the Environment* (1984) 47 P. & C.R. 351 (incorrect conclusion by inspector that land never had green belt status a ground for quashing the decision). See also Lord Wilberforce's suggestion in *Secretary of State for Education and Science v. Tameside M.B.C.* [1977] A.C. 1014. And see Jones 'Mistake of Fact in Administrative Law' [1990] P.L. 507. In *R. v. Legal Aid Committee No. 10 (E. Midlands) ex p. McKenna* (1990) 2 Admin. L.R. 585, the court struck down the refusal of legal aid where the decision was based upon a 'demonstrably mistaken view of the facts'. The Australian Administrative Decisions (Judicial Review) Act 1977, s.5(3)(b) provides for judicial review where 'the person who made the decision based on the decision on the existence of a particular fact, and that fact did not exist'. See also *ibid.* section 6(3)(b).

[70] *Ashbridge Investments Ltd v. Minister of Housing and Local Government* [1965] 1 W.L.R. 1320; *Coleen Properties Ltd v. Minister of Housing and Local Government* [1971] 1 W.L.R. 433 (on which see J.M. Evans (1971) 34 M.L.R.). For more recent planning decisions

taken as a whole, is not reasonably capable of supporting a finding of fact, the decision may be impugned.[71] Again, these decisions are surely best described as strictly "irrational".[72]

where decisions have been invalidated for lack of evidence see *Archer and Thompson v. Secretary of State for the Environment and Penwith D.C.* [1991] J.P.L. 1027; *Hertsmere B.C. v. Secretary of State for the Environment and Percy* [1991] J.P.L. 552. In *R. v. Secretary of State for Home Affairs ex p. Zakrocki* [1996] C.O.D. 304, Carnwath J. held that there had been no evidential basis for the assertion that arrangements could have been made for care in the community of an immigrant and, therefore, the decision of the Home Secretary was unreasonable. And see *Methodist Church of New Zealand v. Gray* [1996] 2 N.Z.L.R. 554, 558 (successful appeal on question of law when decision based on view of facts which could not reasonably be entertained). See also *R. v. Newbury District Council v. ex p. Blackwell* [1988] C.O.D. 155 (planning committee's failure to obtain evidence of likely increase in road use on safety 'unreasonable in the Wednesbury case'.

[71] See, *e.g. Allinson v. General Council of Medical Education and Registration* [1894] 1 Q.B. 750, 760, 763; *American Thread Co. v. Joyce* (1913) 108 L.T. 353; *Smith v. General Motor Cab Co.* [1911] A.C. 188; *Doggett v. Waterloo Taxi Cab Co.* [1910] 2 K.B. 336; *Jones v. Minister of Health* (1950) 84 L.I.L.Rep. 416; *Cababe v. Walton-on-Thames U.D.C.* [1914] A.C. 102, 114; *Rowell v. Minister of Pensions* [1946] 1 All E.R. 664, 666; *Davies v. Price* [1958] 1 W.L.R. 434, 441–442; *R. v. Birmingham Compensation Appeal Tribunal, ex p. Road Haulage Executive* [1952] 2 All E.R. 100; *Maradana Mosque Trustees v. Mahmud* [1967] 1 A.C. 13; *Global Plant Ltd v. Secretary of State for Social Services* [1972] 1 Q.B. 139, 155.

[72] Decisions unsupported by evidence have been held to be unreasonable in *Osgood v. Nelson* (1872) L.R. 5 HL 636; *R. v. Att.-Gen., ex p. Imperial Chemical Industries plc* (1986) 60 Tax Cas. 1. *R. v. Birmingham City Council, ex p. Sheptonhurst Ltd* [1990] 1 All E.R. 1026 (no evidence in licensing decision *re* sex establishment 'irrational'); *R. v. Housing Benefit Review Board of the London Borough of Sutton ex p. Keegan* [1992] C.O.D. 450; 27 H.L.R. 114 (lack of evidence of failure to pay rent rendered decision 'unreasonable'). See also *Piggott Bros and Co. Ltd v. Jackson* [1992] I.C.R. 85 where Lord Donaldson M.R., in the context of employment law, held that, to find a decision 'perverse', the appeal tribunal had to be able to identify a finding of fact unsupported by any evidence. In *Peak Park Joint Planning Board v. Secretary of State for the Environment* [1991] J.P.L. 744, a conclusion which 'flew in the face of the evidence' and was 'based on a view of the facts which could not reasonably be entertained' was held to be 'perverse'. Sometimes such decisions have been held to involve excess of jurisdiction (*e.g. Ashbridge Investments,* n. 70 above). Lord Diplock occasionally held that the principles of natural justice required a decision to be based on 'evidential material of probative value'. See, *e.g. Att.-Gen. v. Ryan* [1980] A.C. 718; *R. v. Deputy Industrial Injuries Commissioner, ex p. Moore* [1965] 1 Q.B. 456. See also *Mahon v. Air New Zealand Ltd* [1984] A.C. 808. In Australia the Australian Administrative Decisions (Judicial Review) Act 1977 authorises review on the independent ground that there was 'no evidence or other material' to justify the decision. The United States Administrative Procedure Act 1946, s.10(e) requires findings to be supported by 'substantial evidence on the record as a whole'. See also *R. v. Secretary of State for the Home Department ex p. Abdi* [1966] 1 W.L.R. 298 certification that minister had knowledge of immigration policies in Spain amounted to 'sufficient evidence' on which adjudicators were entitled to decide the question on asylum; but see the dissents of Lords Slynn and Mustill. *cf. R. v. Highbury Corner Magistrates, ex p. Rabhani* (unreported February 19, 1996) (Magistrates acted unreasonably on evidence before them); *R. v. Epping Magistrates, ex p. Howard and Leach* [1997] R.A. 258 (compensation ordered by magistrates following distraint mistakenly levied. Held, granting the application: the

It should not, however, be assumed that in our legal system the failure of a party to adduce evidence will lead the court necessarily to infer that the silence should be converted into proof against that party. As was recently said by Lord Lowry, "if the silent party's failure to give evidence...can be explained...the effect of his silence in favour of the other party may be either reduced or nullified".[73]

12–022

Where a decision would otherwise be unreasonable, the question of evidential support arises starkly where national security is asserted as a justification for interfering with a person's rights or interests. In some kinds of case it is the duty of the courts to strike the balance between those two interests themselves, if necessary by sitting *in camera*.[74] In *R. v. Home Secretary, ex p. Hosenball*[75] it was held that the decision as to whether national security was threatened was one for the Home Secretary, not for the courts.

12–023

---

method used by the Magistrates, particularly their valuation of a skip, was unexplained and appeared to be a guess. The Magistrates had acted unreasonably as there was no evidence to justify the valuations. A rehearing of the claim for compensation was ordered); *R. v. Secretary of State for the Environment and Rich Investments Ltd ex p. Bexley L.B.C.* (1995) 70 P. & C.R. 522 (the Planning Inspector was wrong to conclude that the failure to arrive at a negotiated resolution of the appeal was wholly attributable to B. He ignored the fact that R had originally agreed to assume their own costs and then resiled from that agreement and thus had acted unreasonably and reached a decision which was perverse). But see *R. v. Secretary of State for the Home Department, ex p. Ellaway* [1996] C.O.D. 328; *Re Neal (Coronor: Jury)* [1996] C.O.D. 190 (Staughton J. held, refusing an application to quash an open verdict, that 'it could not be said that the coroner had reached a verdict, that no reasonable coroner could have reached').

[73] *R. v. Inland Revenue Commissioners, ex p. T.C. Coombs and Co.* [1991] 2 A.C. 283, 300. See also *Gouriet v. Union of Post Office Workers* [1978] A.C. 435, 486 (*per* Lord Dilhorne). And expert evidence may be rejected without evidence to contradict it where the matter is within the professional experience of the Inspector. See *Kentucky Fried Chicken (GB) Ltd v. Secretary of State for the Environment* (1978) 245 E.G. 839; *Ainley v. Secretary of State for the Environment* [1987] J.P.L. 33. Lack of reasons may, however, permit an interference of irrationality. See the cases cited above at n. 59 above. The wrongful rejection of evidence by an inferior tribunal may amount either to a failure to take into account a relevant consideration (and thus render the decision 'illegal'; see, *e.g. Grunwick Processing Laboratories Ltd v. ACAS* [1978] A.C. 655) or to a failure to afford procedural propriety, as the hearing may not comply with the *audi alteram partem* rule of natural justice. See, *e.g. R. v. Wood* (1855) 5 E. & B. 49 (conviction after refusal to hear submission that byelaw contravened was *ultra vires*); *G.M.C. v. Spackman* [1943] A.C. 627 (doctor struck off register after G.M.C. had refused to receive evidence by him to disprove adultery with patient); *R. v. Kingston-upon-Hull Rent Tribunal, ex p. Black* (1949) 65 T.L.R. 209 (tribunal reduced rent after failing to give landlady opportunity to be heard on the substantial issue); *R. v. Birkenhead JJ., ex p. Fisher* [1962] 1 W.L.R. 1410; *Bond v. Bond* [1967] P. 39.

[74] *e.g.* criminal cases, or civil cases where public interest immunity certificates are issued, or cases under section 10 of the Contempt of Court Act 1981.

[75] [1977] 1 W.L.R. 766.

In the *GCHQ* case,[76] however, it was held that the government "is under an obligation to produce evidence that the decision was in fact based on grounds of national security".[77] Lord Scarman said that:

> "Though there are limits dictated by the law and common sense which the court must observe when dealing with the question, the court does not abdicate its judicial functions. If the question arises as a matter of fact, the court requires evidence to be given."[78]

The question as to what evidence is sufficient for these purposes is not, however, clear. In *R. v. Home Secretary, ex p. Cheblak*[79] it was held that there was sufficient particularity in "a statement that the applicant was known to have links with an unspecified [terrorist] organisation".[80] At present the courts may be unwilling to go behind a certificate of this kind to read the documents for themselves.[81]

PRINCIPLES GOVERNING THE EXERCISE OF OFFICIAL POWER

12–024 We have seen in a number of situations how the scope of an official power cannot be interpreted in isolation from general principles governing the exercise of power in a constitutional democracy.[82] The

---

[76] [1985] A.C. 374.

[77] *per* Lord Fraser, *ibid.* at 402.

[78] *ibid.* at 404. Lord Scarman went on to say that once the factual basis was established by evidence, the opinion of the Crown as to what is required to meet it would be accepted 'unless it is possible to show that the opinion was one which no reasonable minister ... could ... reasonably have held'. *Ibid.* at 406.

[79] [1991] 2 All E.R. 319.

[80] Lord Donaldson M.R. at 331–332 quoted Geoffrey Lane L.J. in *Hosenball*, n. 75 above, to the effect that if the alien had 'inadequate information on which to prepare or direct his defence. ... The choice is regretably clear: the alien must suffer, if suffering there be ...'.

[81] As in *Balfour v. Foreign and Commonwealth Office* [1994] 1 W.L.R. 681. In the recent case *R. v. Secretary of State for the Home Department, ex p. Kevin McQuillan* [1995] All E.R. 400; Sedley J., in view of recent precedent, felt unable to investigate the statement of the Home Secretary that the applicant's exclusion was 'expedient' and that further details could lead to the discovery of sources of information that would compromise the lives of informants. But see the 'balancing' of national security considerations required by the Court of Appeal in *Chahal v. Home Secretary* [1995] 1 W.L.R. 526. See also *R. v. Secretary of State for the Home Department, ex p. Adams* [1995] All E.R. (E.C.) 177. Note also that in *Chahal v. U.K.* (1997) 23 E.C.H.R. 413 it was held that the procedures before the '3 wise men' advisory review panel violated Article 5(4) of the European Convention on Human Rights. The Court held that 'it was possible to employ techniques which both accommodated legitimate security concerns about the nature and sources of intelligence information and yet accorded the individual a substantial measure of procedural justice'.

[82] See Chap. 1, para. 1–023 *et seq.*

courts presume that these principles apply to the exercise of all powers and that even where the decision-maker is invested with wide discretion, that discretion is to be exercised in accordance with those principles unless Parliament clearly indicates otherwise. One such principle, the rule of law, contains within it a number of requirements such as the right of the individual to access to the law and that power should not be arbitrarily exercised. The rule of law above all rests upon the principle of legal certainty, which will be considered here, along with a principle which is partly but not wholly contained within the rule of law, namely, the principle of equality, or equal treatment without unfair discrimination.

Legal certainty and substantive legitimate expectations

The requirement that a person's "legitimate expectations" should not be disappointed is, as we have seen above,[83] a basic feature of the rule of law. In European Community law, the basic principle of "legal certainty" fulfils the same objective. Some aspects of legal certainty are deeply embedded in English law, such as the principle that there shall be no punishment in the absence of the breach of an established law.[84] The courts have invalidated decisions of public authorities which impose penalties for actions which are not unlawful.[85] In Chapter 8 above we saw that a legitimate expectation can, under certain circumstances, found a right to a fair hearing. We shall now consider

12–025

---

[83] Chap. 7, para. 7–037 *et seq.* See also para. 5–053.

[84] See Blackstone's *Commentaries of the Laws of England* (1765) Vol. 1 p. 44. Maitland said that 'Known general laws, however bad, interfere less with freedom than decisions based on no previous known rule.' *Collected Papers*, vol. 1 (1911) p. 81. Maitland equated arbitrary power with power that is 'uncertain' or 'incalculable'; *ibid.*, p. 80. See also the Roman Law principle that the Praetor could not depart from the published terms of his edict. See Asconius, *in Comelianum*, 52 and *Dio Cassius* 36.40. See A. Watson, *Law Making in the Later Roman Republic* (1974) 93–94. Closer to home is the recently published version of Bentham's 'disappointment-prevention principle' as an element of his greatest happiness principle. This requires more than 'regret', but the loss of an 'expectation'. See P. Schofield, *Official Aptitude Maximised; Expense Minimised* (1993), Appendix B 'On Retrenchment'. See also J. Rawls, *A Theory of Justice* (1972), pp. 235–243. For the principle of legitimate expectation, 'vertrauensschutz', in European law see generally J. Schwartze, *European Administrative Law* (1992) p. 867 *et seq.* See also Chap. 17 below, paras 17–069–17–071 and the review of the case law by Sedley J. In *R. v. Ministry of Agriculture, Fisheries and Food, ex p. Hamble Fisheries Ltd* [1995] 2 All E.R. 714, 725–28.

[85] *e.g., Congreve v. Secretary of State for Home Affairs* [1976] 1 Q.B. 629 (punishment of (lawful) overlapping licence fee-holders); *Wheeler v. Leicester City Council* [1985] A.C. 1054 (withdrawal of licence to rugby football facilities because of (lawful) contacts of some players with South Africa). See the further discussion of these two cases in Chap. 5 above, para. 5–077.

the legitimate expectation in its substantive sense: in what circumstances may a decision which disappoints an expectation of a substantive benefit or advantage be held invalid on that account?

12–026   The following principles may be asserted in respect of public law powers:

(1) A public body with limited powers cannot bind itself to act outside of its authorised powers; and if it purports to do so it can repudiate its undertaking, for it cannot extend its powers by creating an estoppel.[86]

(2) A body entrusted with duties or with discretionary powers for the public benefit effectively may not avoid its duties or fetter itself in the discharge of its powers (including duties to exercise its powers free from extraneous impediments).[87]

(3) The general rules of agency apply in public law, except that an agent (a) cannot bind his principal to do what is *ultra vires* and probably (b) cannot bind his principal by exceeding his own authority if that authority is circumscribed by statute.[88]

---

[86] *Fairtitle v. Gilbert* (1787) 2 T.R. 169 (invalid mortgage), *Rhyl U.D.C. v. Rhyl Amusements Ltd* [1959] 1 W.L.R. 465 (invalid lease); *Cudgen Rutile (No. 2) Pty Ltd v. Chalk* [1975] A.C. 520, PC (invalid contract to lease); *Co-operative Retail Services Ltd v. Taff-Ely B.C.* (1980) 39 P. & C.R. 223 (unauthorised communication of void planning permission cannot estop local authority from denying the permission); *Rootkin v. Kent C.C.* [1981] 1 W.L.R. 1186 (council not estopped from denying factual error which would have prevented it from exercising its statutory discretion). *R. v. West Oxfordshire D.C., ex p. Pearce Homes Ltd* [1986] J.P.L. 522 (council not estopped from resiling from previous resolution granting permission because notification of that permission had been qualified by a condition not yet accepted). See also *R. v. Yeovil B.C., ex p. Trustees of Elim Pentacostal Church* 23 P. & C.R. 39. And see paras 12–029–12–033 below.

[87] See *Customs and Excise Commissioners v. Hebson Ltd* [1953] 2 Lloyd's Rep. 382, 396–397; *Sovmots Investments Ltd v. Secretary of State for the Environment* [1977] Q.B. 411, 437, 479–480; rev'd. on other grounds [1979] A.C. 144; *Laker Airways Ltd v. Department of Trade* [1977] Q.B. 643, 708, 728 (*cf.* the somewhat ambiguous formulation on Lord Denning M.R. at 707); *Turner v. DPP* (1978) 68 Cr.App.R. 70. In *Hughes v. Department of Health and Social Security* [1985] A.C. 776, 788 *per* Lord Diplock: 'The liberty to make such changes [in policy] is inherent in our constitutional form of government'. See also *Re Findlay* [1985] A.C. 318, 338, *per* Lord Scarman; *R. v. Secretary of State for Health, ex p. US Tobacco International Inc.* [1992] 1 Q.B. 353, 369, *per* Taylor L.J. And see paras 12–029–12–033 below.

[88] Although the existing case law on this subject is equivocal. See, *e.g.* G.H. Treitel [1957] P.L. 321, 335–339; Colin Turpin, *Government Contracts*, 33–36; *cf.* Griffith and Street, *Principles of Administrative Law* (5th ed., 1973), 261, n. 2. See also P.P. Craig (1977) 93 L.Q.R. 398. See *Att.-Gen. for Ceylon v. Silva* [1953] A.C. 461, involving an erroneous representation by a Crown servant as to the scope of his own authority. It is not clear from the Privy Council's judgment whether the Crown would have been bound if the Crown had held him out as possessing the necessary authority (which was, however, limited by statute); or indeed whether the doctrine of 'usual' authority has any application at all in public law, see *Western Fish Products Ltd v. Penwith D.C.*

(4) Purported authorisation, waiver, acquiescence and delay do not preclude a public body from reasserting its legal rights or powers against another party if it has no power to sanction the conduct in question or to endow that party with the legal right or immunity that he claims.[89] However, there are dicta to the effect that planning authorities may waive certain defects in formal procedural requirements,[90] perhaps so long as third parties are not adversely affected.

(1978) 38 P. & C.R. 7; [1981] 2 All E.R. 204. And see *R. v. Home Secretary, ex p. Choudhary* [1978] 1 W.L.R. 1177 (Home Secretary not bound by leave to enter granted by immigration officer inconsistently with the Act or immigration rules); but see *R. v. Home Secretary, ex p. Ram* [1979] 1 W.L.R. 148, doubting whether this applied where leave had not been obtained through fraud or misrepresentation. See now *Onoluyi v. Secretary of State for Home Affairs* [1989] Imm.A.R. 135 (oral assurances that Nigerian student would have no difficulty returning to U.K. after visit home for Christmas. Refusal of entry on return invalid). Cf. *R. v. Secretary of State for Home Affairs, ex p. Patel* (1990) Imm.A.R. 89. See also *Matrix Securities Ltd v. Inland Revenue Commissioners* [1994] 1 W.L.R. 334 (assurances by local inspector of taxes did not bind Revenue when it was made clear that the scheme should have been approved by the Financial Division of the Revenue.) But see *R. v. Southwark L.B.C., ex p. Bannerman* (1990) 2 Admin. L.R. 381 (lack of delegation to official but assumed 'that those who write letters on behalf of their superiors have the authority to do so'). See also the discussion in relation to *Lever Finance*, below.

[89] See, *e.g. Islington Vestry v. Homsey U.D.C.* [1900] 1 Ch. 695 (informal agreement to receive sewage could be repudiated; no binding contract to that effect could validly have been concluded); *Minister of Agriculture and Fisheries v. Matthews* [1950] 1 K.B. 149, applying *Minister of Agriculture and Fisheries v. Halkin*, CA unreported (Minister could not create tenancy of requisitioned land, hence occupier could be dispossessed; power could not be extended by estoppel); *Yabbicom v. R.* [1899] 1 Q.B. 444 (ostensible but invalid approval of building plans by local authority; plans not conforming to byelaw; local authority not precluded from prosecuting for contravention of byelaw); *Redbridge L.B.C. v. Jaques* [1970] 1 W.L.R. 1604; *Cambridgeshire & Isle of Ely C.C. v. Rust* [1972] 2 Q.B. 426 (local authority entitled to prosecute for obstruction of the highway, despite long acquiescence in the obstruction; it had no power to license the obstruction). See also *R. v. Arrowsmith* [1975] Q.B. 678 (letter from DPP stating that the accused would not be prosecuted for her conduct on one occasion provided no defence to a prosecution for subsequent similar conduct; but her mistaken reliance upon the letter justified reduction in sentence). The other side of the coin is that validity cannot be conferred on an invalid administrative order merely by the acquiescence of the party to whom it is addressed; he will not be estopped from subsequently asserting its invalidity: *Swallow and Pearson v. Middlesex C.C.* [1953] 1 W.L.R. 422; *semble, Bucknell (Frank) and Sons Ltd v. Croydon L.B.C.* [1973] 1 W.L.R. 534; cf., however, *Portsmouth Corp. v. Ali* [1973] 1 W.L.R. 173, 175–176; see also *Hildenborough Village Preservation Association v. Secretary of State for the Environment* [1978] J.P.L. 708 (applicant estopped from denying validity of condition covering an issue included in an undertaking on the strength of which permission had been granted).

[90] Lord Denning in *Wells v. Minister of Housing and Local Government* [1967] 1 W.L.R. 1000, 1007; *Lever Finance Ltd v. Westminster L.B.C.* [1971] Q.B. 222. This aspect of *Lever Finance* was approved in *Western Fish Products Ltd v. Penwith D.C.* (1978) 38 P. & C.R. 7; [1981] 2 All E.R. 204.

(5) In respect of unauthorised and erroneous assurances or advice given by officials upon which members of the public rely to their detriment, there have been two approaches. At one time it could be safely said that they were simply nugatory (unless they fell within the scope of agency in contract), although a negligent misstatement or course of conduct causing economic loss might give rise to liability in tort.[91] Thus if a local government officer to whom the necessary powers have not been delegated assures a builder that planning permission is not required for what he proposes to do, this assertion, though acted upon by the inquirer, does not affect the power of the local authority to arrive at and act on an opposite decision.[92] However, another line of cases, attributable in large part to the efforts of Lord Denning, held that in some circumstances when public bodies and officers, in their dealings with a citizen, take it upon themselves to assume authority on a matter concerning him, the citizen is entitled to rely on their having the authority that they have asserted if he cannot reasonably be expected to know the limits of that authority; and he should not be required to suffer for his reliance if they lack the necessary authority.[93] Thus, public authorities have

---

[91] See generally, B.S. Markesinis and S.F. Deakin, *Tort Law* (3rd ed., 1993) pp. 86–95.

[92] *Southend-on-Sea Corp. v. Hodgson (Wickford) Ltd* [1962] 1 Q.B. 416; *Western Fish Products Ltd v. Penwith D.C.* (1978) 77 L.G.R. 185; see also *Princes Investments Ltd v. Frimley and Camberley U.D.C.* [1962] 1 Q.B. 681. *A fortiori*, where an official erroneously notifies the applicant that permission has been granted but the builder incurs no expense before being informed of the error: *Norfolk C.C. v. Secretary of State for the Environment* [1973] 1 W.L.R. 1400. Whether or not it would be necessary to create an estoppel in an analogous private law situation to establish a detrimental reliance by the representee, it almost certainly always is in public law. See also *Re a Holiday in Italy* [1975] 1 C.M.L.R. 184 (national insurance commissioner held that a person who acted on erroneous advice of official that a holiday abroad would not prejudice his right to sickness benefit was nonetheless ineligible); and see *Re an Absence in Germany* [1978] 2 C.M.L.R. 603, 607.

[93] *Robertson v. Minister of Pensions* [1949] 1 K.B. 227, 223, *per* Denning J.; *Falmouth Boat Construction Co. v. Howell* [1950] 1 K.B. 16, 26, *per* Lord Denning. See also *Re L. (A.C.) (an Infant)* [1971] 3 All E.R. 743 (local authority, having misled mother into believing that she need not lodge a second formal objection to the authority's application for parental rights, not entitled to rely on her failure to lodge the second objection in due time); *cf. Hanson v. Church Commissioners for England* [1978] Q.B. 823 (tenant denied a hearing before rent assessment committee as a result, in part, of misleading advice given to him by the clerk to the committee). See also *R. v. Tower Hamlets L.B.C., ex p. Kayne-Levenson* [1975] Q.B. 431 (local authority misled licensee into thinking that she could not nominate the applicant to be her successor: Lord Denning M.R. (at 441) appeared to think that the local authority was not bound to treat the applicant as though he had been nominated). *Cf. Suthendran v. Immigration Appeal Tribunal* [1977] A.C. 359 (erroneous intimation by Home Office that appellant had a right of appeal caused no prejudice); *R. v. Melton and Belvoir JJ., ex p. Tynan* (1977) 75 L.G.R. 544. For

been held bound by assurances given in disregard of a formal statutory requirement, upon which an individual relied to his detriment.[94] The Court of Appeal in *Lever Finance* applied this principle to a determination by a planning official, even though the power to decide had not been delegated to him in proper form.[95] The general principle remains, however, that a public authority may not vary the scope of its statutory powers and duties as a result of its own errors or the conduct of others. Judicial resort to estoppel in these circumstances may prejudice the interests of third parties.[96] For example, the neighbouring property owners in *Lever Finance*, who found that houses had been built closer to their boundary line than had been allowed under the original planning permission, might well feel aggrieved that they had had no opportunity to object to the form of the permission that ultimately bound the

---

an example of the estoppel where no question of *vires* was raised, see *Crabb v. Arun D.C.* [1976] Ch. 179. See generally P.P. Craig (1977) 93 L.Q.R. 398.

[94] *Wells v. Minister of Housing and Local Government* [1967] 1 W.L.R. 1000 (informal determination that planning permission not required); but see the *Western Fish* case (n. 92 above) where *Wells* was narrowly distinguished; *Re L. (A.C.) (an Infant)* [1971] 3 All E.R. 743 (*Wells's* case followed in different context): *English-Speaking Union of the Commonwealth v. Westminster (City) L.B.C.* (1973) 26 P. & C.R. 575.

[95] *Lever Finance Ltd v. Westminster (City) L.B.C.* [1971] 1 Q.B. 222, CA (oral assurance by borough architect that planning permission not required). This decision, applying *Robertson v. Minister of Pensions and Wells'* case (nn. 93 and 94 above) cannot be reconciled with *Southend-on-Sea Corp. v. Hodgson (Wickford) Ltd (D.C.)* (n. 92 above), or with the observations in *Howell v. Falmouth Boat Construction Co. Ltd* [1951] A.C. 837, 845, 847. For the difficulties implicit in the judgments, see J.M. Evans (1971) 34 M.L.R. 335. See also A.W. Bradley [1971] C.L.J. 3; B.C. Gould (1971) 87 L.Q.R. 15; *cf. R. v. Yeovil Corp., ex p. Elim Pentecostal Church Trustees* (1971) 70 L.G.R. 142 (absence of written determination by town clerk prevented his communication to applicants for having binding force); *Morelli v. Department of Environment* [1976] N.I. 159 (procedural error by clerk invalidated planning permission purportedly granted to plaintiff). See also, J.E. Alder [1974] J.P.L. 447; Michael Albery (1974) 90 L.Q.R. 351. The problems raised by the *Lever* case were alleviated by the wider powers of delegation to local officials conferred by the Town and Country Planning Act 1971, s.4 (formerly the Town and Country Planning Act 1968, s.68). Still wider powers of delegation to officials have been conferred by the Local Government Act 1972, s.101. See also *Norfolk C.C. v. Secretary of State for the Environment* [1973] 1 W.L.R. 1400, 1405 (authority may be bound by terms of notification served upon person who has relied upon it, even though it does not, through clerical error, accurately embody the authority's decision).

[96] And may drastically curtail the willingness of public officials to give informal advice: See *Brooks and Burton Ltd v. Secretary of State for the Environment* (1976) 75 L.G.R. 285, 296, where the *Lever* case was described as 'the most advanced case of the application of the estoppel doctrine, and one not to be repeated.' On appeal, the Court of Appeal stated that an estoppel could not be established on the facts: [1977] 1 W.L.R. 1294, 1300.

planning authority.[97] Despite the cases to the contrary, it seems today that, in general, authority that is unlawfully assumed will not bind a public authority. Even Lord Denning appeared to have relented when he said in respect of a purported grant of a planning permission by a town clerk unauthorised to grant the permission, that:

"The protection of the public interest is entrusted to the representative bodies and to the ministers. It would be quite wrong that it should be preempted by a mistaken issue by a clerk of a printed form—without any authority in that behalf ... when the result would be to damage the interests of the public at large."[98]

The two lines of authority are not easily reconciled. However, in general, both recent authority and principle assert that a public authority cannot be estopped from denying its lawful duties and powers.[99] Nor can estoppel be pleaded by a public authority against an individual who has apparently accepted the benefits of an unlawful act or provision.[1] There are, however, two exceptions to these rules. The first exception arises when the authority has power to delegate authority to an official and there are special circumstances justifying the

---

[97] *Quaere* whether they could recover damages from the local authority by establishing that the officer was careless and that the permission would not have been granted had it been originally applied for in its subsequently amended form.

[98] *Co-operative Retail Services Ltd v. Taff-Ely B.C.* (1980) 39 P. & C.R. 223, 239–240. See also *R. v. Yeovil B.C., ex p. Trustees of Elim Pentacostal Church* (1971) 23 P. & C.R. 39; *R. v. W. Oxfordshire D.C., ex p. Pearce Homes Ltd* [1986] J.P.L. 523 (formal notification of a decision has no effect if the notification is contrary to the terms of the decision). See also *R. v. Secretary of State for Education & Science, ex p. Hardy, The Times*, July 28, 1988 (decision to approve scheme could be revoked because it was not a 'formal precise and published' decision). But see *Costain Homes Ltd v. Secretary of State for the Environment* [1988] J.P.L. 701. See also *R. v. Southwark L.B.C., ex p. Bannerman* (1990) 2 Admin. L.R. 381 (despite lack of formal delegation to official it is 'to be assumed that those who write letters on behalf of their superiors have the authority to do so').

[99] *Western Fish Products Ltd v. Penwith D.C.* (1978) 38 P. & C.R. 7; [1981] 2 All E.R. 204. *Tandridge D.C. v. Telecom Securicor Cellular Radio* [1996] J.P.L. 128 refusal to grant planning permission to erect a multi-antenna mast for mobile telephone service. *Lever* [1971] 1 Q.B. 222; *Western Fish Products* [1981] 2 All E.R. 204; *Camden* (1994) 67 P. & C.R. 59 considered on question of whether estoppel arose. (No evidence of detrimental reliance). See also, *R. v. Criminal Injury Compensation Board ex p. Keane & Marsden* [1988] C.O.D. 128.

[1] *City of Bradford M.C. v. Secretary of State for the Environment* [1986] J.P.L. 598, CA. *Cf. Hidenborough Village Preservation Society v. Secretary of State for the Environment* [1978] J.P.L. 708.

applicant in believing that the officer concerned had power to bind the authority (*e.g.* where there was evidence of a widespread practice of delegation of powers to officers, to authorise immaterial modifications of approved plans).[2] The second exception arises where the authority waives a formal procedural requirement. In such a case it may be estopped from relying on its absence.[3]

Where a person who has relied to his detriment upon erroneous advice has suffered loss, and where the doctrine of estoppel will not come to his aid, administrative redress will in any event often be a more appropriate remedy than judicial review, and complaints can be investigated by the appropriate Ombudsman as allegations of injustice caused by maladministration.[4]

---

[2] *Lever Finance* was followed, despite the qualifications of *Western Fish*, presumably under this exception, in *Camden L.B.C. v. Secretary of State for the Environment* (1993) 67 P. & C.R. 59 (authority held to the terms of a letter written by officer representing that a proposed roof extension did not require planning permission. *Held:* officer had actual or ostensible authority). See also *Gowa v. Att.-Gen.* [1985] 1 W.L.R. 1003 (the Crown estopped, by letter from colonial governor 30 years earlier, from denying registration of British citizenship; see also *The Times*, December 27, 1984).

[3] *ibid.*, citing *Wells v. Minister of Housing and Local Government* [1967] 1 W.L.R. 1000. A. Bradley, 'Administrative Justice and the Binding Effects of Official Acts' [1981] C.L.P. 1; M. Akehurst, 'Revocation of Administrative Decisions' [1982] P.L. 613.

[4] A related question to that of estoppel in the sense discussed above is that of 'issue estoppel' or *res judicata* in public law. To what extent may legal certainty be protected by estopping the repeated litigation of an issue which has already been determined? See generally, G. Ganz, 'Estoppel and *Res Judicata* in Administrative Law' [1965] P.L. 237; Wade and Forsyth, *Administrative Law* (1994) pp. 278–283. Cases have held that issue estoppel could not be relied on in judicial review or habeas corpus proceedings. See, *e.g. R. v. Secretary of State for the Environment, ex p. Hackney L.B.C.* [1983] 1 W.L.R. 524, [1984] 1 W.L.R. 592; approved in *R. v. Secretary of State for the Home Department, ex p. Momin Ali* [1984] 1 W.L.R. 663. Compare issue estoppel in planning decisions. *Thrasyvoulou v. Secretary of State for the Environment* [1990] 2 A.C. 233 (decision to grant planning permission—but not refusal of permission—creates rights which should be protected by issue estoppel). See C. Crawford (1990) M.L.R. 814. See also *Watts v. Secretary of State for the Environment* [1991] J.P.L. 718 (in order that an earlier decision upon the evidence or admission by a party could operate as an issue estoppel in relation to a subsequent issue in subsequent proceedings, the following conditions must be fulfilled: (a) the issue must have been fully argued; (b) the tribunal must have addressed the matter fully; (c) the tribunal must have made an unequivocal decision on the matter; (d) the above three matters must be clear on the face of the record, and (e) there must have been a finding essential and not incidental to the conclusion). *R. v. Secretary of State for the Home Department, ex p. Alakesan,* [1997] Imm. A.R. 315 (A unsuccessfully argued that the Home Secretary was bound by *res judicata* to follow the immigration adjudicator's recommendations and that the decision was therefore unlawful. *Held:* provided the Home Secretary gave reasons for

Lawful representations and substantive legitimate expectations

12–027 Where a public authority is acting within the lawful scope of is authority, can it be held to its undertakings or promises—express or implied? As we have seen, an undertaking that a prescribed procedure will be followed creates a legitimate expectation that must not be thwarted.[5] The fulfilment of substantive expectations have also been upheld. For example, the Court of Appeal held that the Home Office could not disappoint an expectation, contained in the terms of a Home Office circular, setting out the conditions for the adoption of children from abroad.[6] In *Re Preston*[7] the applicant taxpayer claimed that the Inland Revenue

---

departing from the recommendations of the adjudicator and considered the recommendations fairly, there was no case for arguing that *res judicata* bound the Minister). *R. v. Secretary of State for Education, ex p. C* [1996] E.L.R. 93 (held: dismissing the application: it was not irrational for the same person to reach a different decision when reconsidering the same facts); *A & T Investments v. Secretary of State for the Environment* (1996) 72 P. & C.R. 540; issue estoppel; *Thrasyvoulou* considered); *Hammond v. Secretary of State for the Environment* (1997) 74 P. & C.R. 134; *The Times*, February (estoppel *per rem judicatam*; *Thrasyvoulou* considered. A decision of a planning inspector gave rise to an estoppel and where subsequently different inspectors reached contradictory decisions, the first in time prevailed); *cf. R. v. South West Thames Mental Health Review Tribunal, ex p. Demetri* [1997] C.O.D. 44; *Porter v. Secretary of State for Transport* [1996] 3 All E.R. 693. (No issue estoppel in relation to alternative development certificate. Decision lacked the necessary element of finality. A refusal of planning permission not determinative as a fresh application could be made). But see *Barber v. Staffordshire County Council* [1996] 2 All E.R. 748 (issue estoppel in respect of to industrial tribunal application; *Arnold v. National Westminster Bank plc* [1991] 2 A.C. 93 applied.

[5] *R. v. Liverpool City Council, ex p. Liverpool Taxi Fleet Operators' Association* [1972] 2 Q.B. 299; *Att.-Gen. of Hong Kong v. Ng Yuen Shiu* [1983] 2 A.C. 629. And see Chap. 7 above, paras 7-037–7-066.

[6] *R. v. Secretary of State for the Home Department, ex p. Asif Mohammed Khan* [1984] 1 W.L.R. 1337. Parker L.J. considered, following the *Hong Kong* case, n. 5 above, that the Secretary of State having induced a reasonable expectation that the circular advice would be followed, could not 'resile from that undertaking without affording interested persons a hearing and then only if the overriding public interest demanded it'. Dunn L.J. held that, although the circular letter did not create an estoppel, the Home Secretary reached his decision on irrelevant considerations, having failed to take into account his own rules, and had therefore acted unreasonably.

[7] [1985] A.C. 835. For discussion of the substantive legitimate expectation see, *e.g.* G. Ganz, 'Legitimate expectation: A confusion of concepts' in C. Harlow (ed.), *Public Law and Politics* (1986), Chap. 8; R. Baldwin and D. Horne, 'Expectations in a joyless landscape' (1986), 49 M.L.R. 685; P. Elias, 'Legitimate expectation and judicial review' in J. Jowell and D. Oliver (eds), *New Directions in Judicial Review* (1988), pp. 37–50; C.F. Forsyth, 'The Provenance and Protection of Legitimate Expectations' [1988] C.L.J. 238; B. Hadfield, 'Judicial Review and the concept of legitimate expectation' (1988) 39 N.I.L.Q. 103; P.P. Craig, 'Legitimate Expectations: a Conceptual Analysis' (1992) 108 L.Q.R. 79. P.P. Craig, 'Substantive Legitimate Expectations in Domestic and Community Law' [1996] C.L.J. 289; Lester, 'Government Compliance with

Commission should honour an agreement with him not to pursue tax claims. It was held on the facts that the agreement did not bind the Revenue, but Lord Templeman made it clear that, in principle, conduct equivalent to a breach of contract or breach of representation could amount to an "abuse of power" on the part of the tax authorities.[8] Subsequent cases have held that the doctrine of legitimate expectation, as propounded in the *GCHQ* case[9] as founding a duty to act fairly in the procedural sense, is by no means so confined.[10] Recently the House of Lords unanimously accepted that it may be an abuse of power for the Revenue to seek to extract tax contrary to an advance clearing given by the Revenue.[11]

The protection of a substantive legitimate expectation is now fully   **12–028** accepted in English law as a principle governing the exercise of discretion. Decisions of public bodies "may not be internally inconsistent".[12] To qualify for protection—to be "legitimate"—the expectation of a substantive benefit or advantage must contain the following qualities:

---

international human rights law: a new year's legitimate expectation' [1996] P.L. 187— comment on *Minister for Immigration and Ethnic Affairs v. Teoh* (1995) 69 A.L.J.R. 423. Michael Taggart, 'Legitimate expectation and Treaties in the High Court of Australia' (1996) 112 L.Q.R. 50; Ryszard Piotrowicz, 'Unincorporated treaties in Australian Law' [1996] P.L. 190; Rabinder Singh and Karen Steyn, 'Legitimate Expectation in 1996. Where Now?' (1996) 1 Judicial Review 17; C. Himsworth, 'Legitimately expecting proportionality?' [1996] P.L. 46.

[8] *ibid.* at 867. See also Lord Scarman at 851–852 and his speech extolling the virtues of consistency in *H.T.V. Ltd v. Price Commission* [1976] I.C.R. 170.

[9] *Council of Civil Service Unions v. Minister for the Civil Service* [1985] A.C. 374.

[10] See, *e.g. R. v. Secretary of State for the Home Department, ex p. Ruddock* [1987] 1 W.L.R. 1482 (legitimate expectation that circular establishing procedures for telephone tapping should be fulfilled—but held that it was); *R. v. Board of Inland Revenue, ex p. M.F.K. Underwriting Agencies Ltd* [1990] 1 W.L.R. 1545 (ruling on tax consequences of scheme could create expectation of fulfilment, but not on the facts of this case); *R. v. Secretary of State for Health, ex p. U.S. Tobacco International Inc.* [1992] 1 Q.B. 353 (change of policy led to manufacture of 'oral snuff' being banned. Held no substantive—but only procedural—legitimate expectation in the circumstances); *Olonilvyi v. Secretary of State for Home Affairs* [1989] Imm.A.R. 135 (representation that applicant would be able to re-enter U.K. must be fulfilled). But see *R. v. Secretary of State for Home Affairs ex p. Patel* [1990] 3 Imm.A.R. 89; *R. v. Croydon JJ., ex p. Dean* [1993] Q.B. 769 (expectation that would not be prosecuted). See also *R. v. Lord Chancellor, ex p. Hibbit and Saunders* [1993] C.O.D. 326 (unfair to fulfil a legitimate expectation where applicants who had previous long-standing contracts as court shorthand writers not given opportunity to submit lower tender in new tender procedure. But not amenable to judicial review as 'private law'). But see *R. v. Walsall M.B.C., ex p. Yapp, The Times*, August 6, 1993 (council able to seek fresh tenders for building works and no legitimate expectation that own workforce would be favoured).

[11] *Matrix Securities Ltd v. Inland Revenue Commissioners* [1994] 1 W.L.R. 334, *per* Lord Browne-Wilkinson.

[12] *R. v. Inland Revenue Commissioners, ex p. M.F.K. Underwriting Agencies Ltd* [1990] 1

(1) The expectation must be induced by the decision-maker either expressly—by means of a promise or undertaking, or implicitly—by means of settled past conduct or practice.[13]

(2) An express promise or undertaking can take the form of (a) a general representation, issued either to "the world" or to a class of beneficiaries; or (b) a specific representation addressed to a particular individual or individuals.[14]

(3) A general representation may take various forms, including that of a circular letter or other statement of policy.[15] It can

---

W.L.R. 1545, 1569, DC, *per* Bingham L.J.

[13] The position is the same in European Community law. See J. Schwartze, *European Administrative Law* (1992) pp. 1134–1135. For a reference to the legitimate expectation in the case law of Australia, Canada, India, Ireland, New Zealand and South Africa see Chap. 7 above, para. 7–038 and n. 85. Note that the legitimate expectation can arise in any one case from both a promise and practice. See, *e.g. ex p. Ruddock*, n. 10 above. And see *R. v. IRC, ex p., Unilever plc* [1996] C.O.D. 369; [1996] S.T.C. 681, CA. Claim for tax relief made in similar form to that accepted in previous years and therefore unfair for the Inland Revenue Commission to resile from previous practice without notice. Note also the controversial Australian Case of *Minister for Immigration and Ethnic Affairs v. Teoh* (1995) 183 C.L.R. 273, where the High Court held that the International Covenant on the Rights of the Child, which was not incorporated into Australian law, may nevertheless give rise to a legitimate expectation that executive decision-makers will comply with it, at least to the extent of giving a person affected by a decision not to act in accordance with the Convention the right to a hearing on the matter. See also the discussion above, in the notes to Chap. 5, paras 5–049–5–051. And see Taggart (1996) 112 L.Q.R. 50. *Teoh* was followed in *R. v. Secretary of State for the Home Department, ex p. Ahmed (Mohammed Hussain)* [1998] Imm.A.R. 375, but not by the Privy Council in *Thomas and Hilaire v. Babtiste*, March 17, 1999. In *R. v. DPP, ex p. Kebilene, The Times*, March 31, 1999 it was held that there was no legitimate expectation to have the provisions of the ECHR enforced in advance of the bringing into force of the relevant provisions of the Human Rights Act 1998.

[14] Compare the position in relation to estoppel in private law. Spencer, Bower and Turner, *Estoppel by Representation* (1977), p. 117, distinguish a representation to a 'specific person whom the representor intended the representation to reach and affect', and a representation to 'the world', namely, to a member of the public or section of the community. See also *R. v. Jockey Club, ex p. RAM Racecourses Ltd* [1993] 2 All E.R. 225 at 238–239.

[15] *Quaere* whether a legitimate expectation can arise from a statement made in Parliament during the course of the passage of a bill. After *Pepper v. Hart* [1993] A.C. 593 (discussed at Chap. 5 above, para. 5–069) the parliamentary record may be consulted to resolve an ambiguity in a statutory provision. Normally the statement relied on will be relevant to the intent or purpose of the statute—a matter distinct from the legitimate expectation. However, it may also be relevant to the manner in which a discretion will be exercised. The statement has to be considered in the context of the full statutory scheme. In *R. v. Secretary of State for the Home Department, ex p. Sakala*, [1994] Imm.A.R. 227, the applicant contended that the Home Secretary should be bound by a statement made in Parliament during the passage of the Immigration Bill 1988, that he would, in a decision about political asylum, 'invariably accept the recommendations of a special adjudicator', unless the decision was perverse or

also include published decisions about advance clearance, or extra-statutory concessions.[16] A person who seeks to rely upon a representation must be one of the class to whom it may reasonably be expected to apply. Thus a report from the Jockey Club announcing the intended availability of new licensed racecourses, which was sent to existing racecourse owners, was held not to apply to prospective new racecourse owners who spent money on a new site in reliance upon the report.[17]

Whether a general representation will be held to give rise to a legitimate expectation does not depend upon the intention of the decision-maker. The question is whether the representation may reasonably induce a person within the class to rely on it.[18] The context of the representation is therefore important. For example, a departmental circular letter setting out the criteria for the adoption of children from abroad may induce a legitimate expectation that its detail will be followed.[19] But other circulars may be more in the nature of advisory documents, purporting to interpret the law or the likely implementation of government policy and therefore less likely to induce binding expectations (for example, Planning Policy Guidance notes issued by the Department of the Environment on diverse matters, including policy in relation to affordable housing, or to permissible conditions attached to planning permissions).

(4) A specific representation may take the form of a letter, or another considered assurance, undertaking or promise of a

---

unlawful. It was held that he was not so bound. See further para. 5–069 above.

[16] The Inland Revenue Commissioners may give advice through official published statements and unofficial private 'rulings' and advance clearances. The Inland Revenue also has discretion to disapply the law by means of extra-statutory concessions under its powers of 'wide managerial discretion'. See, *e.g. R. v. Inland Revenue Commissioners, ex p. National Federation of Self-Employed and Small Businesses Ltd* [1982] A.C. 617; *Vestey v. Inland Revenue Commissioners (Nos. 1 & 2)* [1980] A.C. 1148; *R. v. Inspector of Taxes, ex p. Fulford Dobson* [1987] 1 Q.B. 978 at 988.

[17] *R. v. Jockey Club, ex p. RAM Racecourses Ltd* [1993] 2 All E.R. 225. See also *R. v. Inland Revenue Commissioners, ex p. Camacq Corp.* 1 W.L.R. 191 (Applicant not within the class of intended beneficiaries of tax clearance).

[18] See Sedley J. in *R. v. Ministry of Agriculture Fisheries and Food, ex p. Hambles Fisheries (Offshore) Ltd* [1995] 2 All E.R. 714. See further on that nature of 'policy', paras 5-098–5-099 above.

[19] *R. v. Secretary of State for the Home Department, ex p. Asif Mohammed Khan* [1984] 1 W.L.R. 1337. See also *R. v. Secretary of State for Defence, ex p. Camden L.B.C.* [1995] J.P.L. 403.

benefit or advantage or course of action which the authority intend to follow.[20] To be binding, the representation must fulfill the following conditions:

(a) The representation must be based upon full disclosure. Thus where a person is seeking advance clearance for a scheme from the tax authorities he must be frank about what is being sought and put "all his cards face up on the table", giving full details of the specific transaction on which a ruling is required, the ruling that is sought, and the use intended to be made of it.[21]

(b) The representation must be made by a person with actual or ostensible authority to make the representation. The authority will not be bound if the promisee knew, or ought to have known, that the person making the representation had no power to bind the authority.[22]

(c) The representation must be "clear unambiguous and devoid of relevant qualification".[23] Whether or not the representation is binding is a matter of construction as to which the intention of the promissor may be relevant but not determinative. The test should be whether it is reasonable to assume that the promisee intended the representation to be binding.[24]

---

[20] Where the Revenue have entered into an agreement under section 54(1) of the Taxes Management Act 1970 with a taxpayer in relation to a scheme, it has been held that they are precluded from litigating the subject-matter of the agreement, even if it is based upon an error of law. *Cenlon Finance Co. Ltd v. Elwood* [1962] A.C. 782; *Olin Energy Systems Ltd v. Scorer* [1985] A.C. 645 at 658 (*per* Lord Keith).

[21] *per* Bingham L.J. in *ex p. M.F.K. Underwriters*, n. 12 above, at 1569–1570. Lack of full disclosure also vitiated the expectation in *Matrix Securities*, n. 11 above.

[22] See, *e.g. ex p. Matrix Securities*, n. 11 above, where the assurance was given by a local inspector of taxes, but should have been given by the Financial Division of the Revenue.

[23] *per* Bingham L.J. in *ex p. M.F.K. Underwriters*, n. 12 above, at 1570. See *R. v. Shropshire County Council, ex p. Jones* (1996) Admin. L.R. 625 (applicant for student grant given to understand he has a very good chance of securing an award does not acquire a legitimate expectation). *See also R. v. IRC, ex p. Unilever plc* [1996] C.O.D. 369; [1996] S.T.C. 681, CA. And see *R. v. Gaming Board of Great Britain, ex p. Kingsley* [1996] C.O.D. 241.

[24] See, *e.g. R. v. Secretary of State for the Home Department, ex p. Silva, The Times,* April 1, 1994 (letters sent to two Colombian citizens erroneously informing them of their right to appeal against deportation orders made against them held by Court of Appeal to be 'misinformation' which did not create a legitimate expectation as it was not 'unfair or inconsistent with good administration for the Home Secretary to pursue their deportation without an appeal'. *Per* Simon Brown L.J.).

(5) Despite dicta to the contrary,[25] it is not necessary for a person to have changed his position or to have acted to his detriment in order to obtain the benefit of a legitimate expectation. In a number of leading cases it has been held that a legitimate expectation should have been fulfilled in a situation where detrimental reliance had not taken place or was not appropriate or required in the circumstances.[26] For example, the applicant may legitimately seek the promised benefits of a tax scheme without having expended funds on promoting the scheme,[27] and individuals might legitimately seek the enforcement of a policy about the tapping of telephones[28] or the criteria for the adoption of children from abroad,[29] without incurring expenditure or otherwise acting to their detriment. Private law analogies from the field of estoppel are, we have seen, of limited relevance where a public law principle requires public officials to honour their undertakings and respect legal certainty, irrespective of the loss incurred by the individual concerned.[30]

Although detrimental reliance should not therefore be a condition precedent to the protection of a substantive legitimate expectation, it may be relevant in two situations: first, it might provide evidence of the existence or extent of an expectation. In that sense it can be a consideration to be taken into account in deciding whether a person was in fact led to believe that the authority would be bound by the

---

[25] *Rootkin v. Kent C.C.* [1981] W.L.R. 1186; *R. v. Jockey Club, ex p. RAM Racecourses Ltd* [1993] 1 All E.R. 225; *R. v. Inland Revenue Commissioners, ex p. Camacq* [1990] 1 W.L.R. 191.

[26] *R. v. Ministry for Agriculture, Fisheries and Foods, ex p. Hamble Fisheries (Offshore Ltd)* n. 18 above Sedley J. said at 725J, that 'the decision-maker's knowledge or ignorance of the extent of reliance placed by the applicant upon the factors upon which the expectation is founded has no bearing upon the existence or legitimacy of the expectation'.

[27] Note that Bingham L.J. in *ex p. M.F.K. Underwriting Agencies*, n. 12 above, did not require detrimental reliance but said that 'if a public authority so conducts itself so as to create a legitimate expectation that a certain course will be followed it would *often be unfair* if the authority were permitted to follow a different course to the detriment of one who entertained the expectation *particularly if he relied on it*' (emphasis added). *Ibid.* at 1569–1570.

[28] *ex p. Ruddock,* n. 10 above.

[29] *ex p. Asif Khan,* n. 19 above.

[30] *cf.* the discussion in relation to legitimate expectations and procedural propriety at Chap. 7 above, paras 7-037–7-063 in relation to private law estoppel. See generally, G. Treitel, *The Law of Contract* (8th ed., 1991), pp. 105, 125–126.

representations. Second, detrimental reliance may be relevant to the decision of the authority whether to revoke a representation—an issue which we now consider.

Revocation of a legitimate expectation

12–029 A number of cases have emphasised that, by declaring a policy, a decision-maker "cannot preclude any possible need to change it."[31] In one such case two life sentence prisoners claimed that they should have been released under the terms of a policy in relation to parole announced by the Home Secretary but which had since been suddenly changed. In the House of Lords it was held that the prisoners' expectations were not "legitimate".

12–030 Lord Scarman, with whom the other members of the House concurred, said that:

> "Given the substance and purpose of the legislative provisions governing parole, the most that a convicted prisoner can legitimately expect is that his case will be examined individually in the light of whatever policy the Secretary of State sees fit to adopt provided always that the adopted policy is a lawful exercise of discretion conferred upon him by statute. Any other view would entail the conclusions that the unfettered discretion conferred by the statute on the minister can in some cases be restricted so as to hamper, or even prevent, changes of policy."[32]

12–031 A similar view was expressed in a case where the applicants had been encouraged through a government grant to manufacture their product, "oral snuff", in the United Kingdom. Shortly after their factory opened the Minister was advised to ban the product on the ground of its danger to health. The applicants claimed that the decision infringed their legitimate expectations to continue to manufacture their product. It was held, however, that the Minister's"

---

[31] *R. v. Secretary of State for the Home Department, ex p. Ruddock* [1987] 1 W.L.R. 1982. *Per* Taylor L.J. at 1497. Although a hearing may have to be provided before changing it (see Chap. 7 above, paras 7–063–7–066).

[32] *Re Findlay* [1985] A.C. 318, 338. And see Lord Diplock in *Hughes v. Department of Health & Social Security* [1985] A.C. 776 at 788 where Lord Diplock said: 'The liberty to make such change [of administrative policy] is something which is inherent in our form of constitutional government.' (Compulsory retirement of civil servants at 65 changed to 60.)

moral obligations" to the applicants could not fetter his discretion and could not therefore "prevail over the public interest".[33]

Given the duty of a public body not to fetter its discretion,[34] under **12–032** what circumstances will a legitimate expectation be protected in the face of a change in policy? Clearly the change in policy must be a "lawful exercise of discretion".[35] The body's discretion to alter its policy must therefore be exercised after taking into account relevant considerations, and ignoring the irrelevant. The body must also pursue authorised and not extraneous purposes. These considerations and purposes can include matters such as the need to maintain national security[36] and matters of public policy.[37] Nor should the discretion be exercised unreasonably—for example, simply in order to confound the recipient of the expectation, or in bad faith. The conduct of the recipient of the representation should not be relevant to a decision to revoke the representation.[38]

The potential antithesis between the object of the protection of the **12–033** legitimate expectation (legal certainty) and the object of the "no-fettering" doctrine (flexibility) may not, however, always be resolved in favour of the latter. Although free to alter its policy, the authority is by no means free to ignore the existence of a legitimate expectation. Now that the legitimate expectation has been accepted in law as an interest worthy of protection, its existence becomes a relevant consideration which must be taken into account in the exercise of a discretion. It is placed upon the scale and must therefore be properly weighed. The weighing is, as we have noted many times, a matter principally for the authority, but the courts may intervene where the expectation is entirely ignored or given manifestly improper weight.[39] It is at this point that the fact that the promisee

---

[33] *R. v. Secretary of State for Health, ex p. United States Tobacco International Inc.* [1992] 1 Q.B. 353 at 368, *per* Taylor L.J. See also Moreland J. at 372. The legitimate expectation did, however, found a right on the part of the applicants to a fair hearing. *Knopt v. Johannesburg City Council* 1995 (2) 3AJ(19).

[34] See Chap. 10 above.

[35] *per* Scarman L.J. in *Findlay*, n. 32 above.

[36] As in *Council of Civil Service Unions v. Minister for the Civil Service* [1985] A.C. 374.

[37] As in *ex p. U.S. Tobacco International Inc.* n.33 above where the expectation was disappointed in the interest of protecting public health.

[38] As it was held to be in *Cinnamond v. British Airport Authority* [1980] 1 W.L.R. 582, *per* Lord Denning M.R. Except of course if appropriate conduct could be implied as a condition of the fulfilment of the expectation. The conduct could of course be taken into account in the decision of the court as to whether, in its discretion, to award the applicant a remedy.

[39] See paras 12–014–12–017, above. This was surely Bingham L.J.'s point in *M.F.K. Underwriting Agencies Ltd* (n.12 above), when he said that breach of an expectation may be unfair 'particularly' if the promise acted upon it. *Cf.* the approach of Laws J. in *Secretary of State for Transport, ex p. Richmond-upon-Thames L.B.C.* [1994] 1 W.L.R. 74 where he felt that, because discretion could not be fettered, and therefore the

treated differently and different situations not to be treated in the same way unless such treatment is "objectively justified".[46] A British executive decision or even primary legislation may thus be set aside if it conflicts, on the ground of inequality, with a directly effective Treaty provision or with directly effective Community legislation.[47] National measures taken in implementation or fulfilment of the requirements of Community law may also be set aside on that ground,[48] even when a Community provision leaves a discretion to the Member States as to how to implement the requirement.[49]

12–037   Article 14 of the European Convention on Human Rights provides that: "The enjoyment of the rights and freedoms set forth in this Convention shall be secured without discrimination on any ground such as race, colour, language, religion, political or other opinion, national or social origin, association with a national minority, property, birth or other status." Article 14 does not confer a substantive right in itself. It is a guarantee not of equal treatment *per se* but of equal fundamental rights as set out in the Convention. It is said to come into play by "piggy-backing" on another Article of the Convention; for example, by setting a limit on the derogations from the rights provided in the Convention.[50] Unequal treatment under the Convention requires "objective and reasonable justification". Under this test the apparent inequality that is being challenged must, to be valid,

---

criteria relied on to identify their sex were no longer appropriate. Held, refusing the applications: that although recent medical research into gender identity dysphoria showed that a person's sex might be determined by the construction of the brain, while uncertainties remained, the Registrar General could not be said to have acted irrationally, nor was his decision contrary to Art. 5 E.C.H.R.)

[46] Case 139/77 *Denkavit* [1978] E.C.R. 1317.

[47] *R. v. Secretary of State for Employment, ex p. Equal Opportunity Commission* [1995] 1 A.C. 1 (legislative provisions allowing differential unfair dismissal and redundancy compensation for part-time workers with less than five years' service held indirectly to discriminate against women.)

[48] See *Rienks* [1983] E.C.R. 4233.

[49] See Case 202/85, *Klensch* [1986] E.C.R. 3477, 3508. In *R. v. Ministry of Agriculture, Fisheries & Food ex p. First City Trading Ltd* [1997] C.M.L.R. 250, Laws J. conducted an exhaustive analysis of the case law of the E.C.J. in relation to the principle of equality as it applied to the British beef ban. He came to the conclusion that the test under E.C. law, requiring a substantive justification of discrimination, was different from the *Wednesbury* test.

'By our domestic law, if a public decision-maker were to treat apparently identical cases differently there would no doubt be a prima facie Wednesbury case against him, since on the face of it such an approach bears the hallmark of irrationality ... The court would look for an explanation of the difference; but the justification offered would in the ordinary way only be rejected on the grounds of perversity.'

[50] It does not require an actual breach of the Convention to come into play. It is sufficient that the facts of the case fall 'within the ambit' of the rights guaranteed by the Convention. See, *e.g. Belgian Linguistics Case* 1 E.H.R.R. 241; February 9, 1967, Series A, No. 5.

pursue a "legitimate aim" and, in addition, the means pursued to achieve the end must be proportionate. The "margin of appreciation" given to national governments will vary, depending upon the issue. Discriminatory provisions against women[51] will receive stricter scrutiny than those against certain ranks in the army.[52] In so far as the European Convention applies directly in our law,[53] equality of treatment will apply as a principle to be observed.

Independently of European Community law and the law relating to the European Convention, equality of treatment has shown itself to be a principle of lawful administration in English law. We have already seen that in the nineteenth century Lord Russell considered that byelaws could be held unreasonable because of "partial and unequal treatment in their operation as between different classes".[54] Although subsequent cases did not articulate the principle with equivalent clarity, unequal treatment has justified a number of instances where the courts have struck down a decision or provision which infringes equality in either its formal or its substantive sense. English common law has traditionally placed ancient duties, requiring equality of treatment, upon common carriers, inn-keepers and some monopoly enterprises such as ports and harbours, obliging them to accept all travellers.[55] In addition the courts have occasionally invoked notions of "public policy" to strike down discriminatory provisions. In *Nagle v. Fielden*[56] the Jockey Club's refusal of a horse trainer's licence to a woman was held to be against public policy, and in *Edwards v. SOGAT*,[57] a case involving a challenge to the withdrawal of collective bargaining rights, Lord Denning said that our courts "will not allow a power to be exercised arbitrarily or capriciously or with unfair

12–038

---

[51] See, *e.g. Abdulaziz* 7 E.H.R.R. 471; May 28, 1985, Series A No. 94.

[52] *Engel v. Netherlands* (No. 1) [1976] E.H.R.R. 647.

[53] See the discussion in Chap. 5 at paras 5-049–5-051.

[54] *Kruse v. Johnson* (1889) 2 Q.B. 291. In *Re City of Montreal and Arcade Amusements Inc.* (1985) 18 D.L.R. (4th) 161 it was held that a byelaw prohibiting minors from entering amusement halls was void on the ground that the power to make byelaws does not include a power to enact discriminatory provisions.

[55] "and others who are in a reasonable fit condition to be received". *Rothfield v. N.B. Railway* (1920) S.C. 805; *Pidgeon v. Legge* (1857) 21 J.P. 743. Similar principles have applied to the providers of some utilities. See, *e.g. South of Scotland Electricity Board v. British Oxygen Ltd* [1959] 1 W.L.R. 587.

[56] [1966] 2 Q.B. 633.

[57] [1971] Ch. 354. The reach of public policy was not sufficient to prohibit certain forms of discrimination which were thus made unlawful through legislation passed in the 1960s. The governing statutes are now the Race Relations Act 1976 and the Sex Discrimination Act 1975. See also the Equal Pay Act 1970. See generally, A. Lester and G. Bindman, *Race and the Law* (1972); D. Feldman, *Civil Liberties and Human Rights in England and Wales* (1993) Chap. 18.

discrimination, neither in the making of rules or in the enforcement of them" (a statement which addresses itself to both substantive and formal equality).

12–039   Formal equality in the sense of consistency in the implementation of the law has been applied in a number of recent cases. In holding that the test of whether an applicant for a student grant was "ordinarily resident in the United Kingdom" should be consistently applied, the Master of the Rolls said that "it is a cardinal principle of good public administration that all persons in a similar position should be treated similarly".[58] The Home Secretary, in considering the remission of a prisoner's sentence, must have regard to the length of time served by his codefendants.[59] It is well established that planning permission may be refused on the ground that a grant of permission would create a precedent from which, as a practical matter, it would be difficult for the authority to depart without creating an impression of unfairness.[60] And it is material to the grant of planning permission that permission was granted in other similarly situated cases.[61]

---

[58] *R. v. Hertfordshire C.C., ex p. Cheung, The Times*, April 4, 1986, *per* Lord Donaldson M.R.

[59] *R. v. Home Secretary, ex p. Walsh, The Times*, December 17, 1991. See also *Doody v. Secretary of State for the Home Department* [1994] A.C. 531. See also *R. v. Secretary of State for the Home Department, ex p. Stroud* [1993] C.O.D. 75 (Home Secretary's policy on release of life-sentence prisoners from hospitals must be applied so that any distinction between those prisoners and other life prisoners had a 'legitimate reason'.) But see *R. v. Special Adjudicator, ex p. Kandasamy, The Times*, March 11, 1994 where Hidden J. held (in relation to two applicants for political asylum whose cases were identical but who were treated differently) that 'there was no principle of inconsistency in public law on which the applicant could rely in the absence of procedural unfairness amounting to an abuse of power'. A number of cases have considered the question as to whether selective enforcement or selective concessions (*e.g.* concessions to individuals or groups of taxpayers by the Inland Revenue) violates equal treatment, or whether to cease a previously unfair practice is unfair to those who were previously unfairly treated. In general, selective enforcement of the law has been held not to breach the principle of equal treatment in view of the limited resources available to the prosecuting officials and the legitimacy of exemplary prosecutions. See, *e.g. Vestey v. Inland Revenue Commissioners* [1980] A.C. 1148; *R. v. Inland Revenue Commissioners, ex p. National Federation of Self-Employed and Small Businesses Ltd* [1982] A.C. 617; *R. v. Inland Revenue, ex p. Mead* [1993] 1 All E.R. 772; *Woods v. Secretary of State for Scotland*, 1991 S.L.T. 197. But for dicta indicating equality of treatment may be applied in the tax field, see *J. Rothschild Holdings v. Inland Revenue Commissioners* [1988] S.T.C. 435; *R. v. Inland Revenue Commissioners, ex p. Warburg* [1994] S.T.C. 518, 541.

[60] See, *e.g. Collis Radio v. Secretary of State for the Environment* (1975) P. & C.R. 390; *Tempo Discount v. Secretary of State for the Environment* [1979] J.P.L. 97; *Poundstretcher Ltd v. Secretary of State for the Environment & Liverpool Council* [1989] J.P.L. 90. Thus upholding the notion of consistency and equality of treatment as a 'material consideration' in planning.

[61] *Ynys Mon Isle of Anglesey B.C. v. Secretary of State for Wales and Parry Bros.* [1984] J.P.L. 646. In *R. v. Secretary of State for the Home Department ex p. Urmaza* [1996] C.O.D. 479,

Although until recently the decisions of planning inspectors were **12–040** not considered "material considerations" which should be followed in like cases, they have now been accorded the status of precedent in the interest of consistency and equality of treatment.[62] Where a London borough council devolved its powers to allocate housing to the homeless to seven neighbourhoods, and where this arrangement resulted in the application of variable standards for letting housing to the homeless, this was held to be "unfair and irrational".[63] The preferential allocation of council housing to a councillor, in order to put her in a better position to fight a local election in her own constituency, was held to be an "abuse of power" because it was unfair to others on the housing list.[64] It has been held that a decision to renew a licence should not disregard the fact that licences were recently granted in other like cases.[65]

The courts have also struck down instances of substantive **12–041** inequality; invalidating byelaws, rules or decisions on the ground of their discriminatory effect. In *Board of Education v. Rice*,[66] a case noted for its application of natural justice, the substantive issue was the authority's power to fund church schools less favourably than other schools. Lord Halsbury, who felt that the differential treatment was based upon hostility to the church schools said: "... it is clear that the local education authority ought to be as impartial as the rate collector

---

Sedley J. held that where a government department publishes a policy document, the 'legal principle of consistency in the exercise of public powers' (citing paras 12–034 to 12–043 of this work) creates a presumption that the Minister will follow his own policy. If there is a departure from the policy, there must be good reason for it (almost certainly supported by the giving of reasons). Sedley J. added that the principle of consistency, in the eye of the law, does not extend to being consistently wrong about the proper interpretation of the policy in accordance with its objects. See also *R. v. DPP, ex p. C*; [1995] 1 Cr.App.R. 136 the Court can interfere with a decision not to prosecute where the prosecutor fails to follow the settled policy set out in the Code for Crown Prosecutions); *R. v. Commissioner of Police for the Metropolis, ex p. P* (1996) 8 Admin. L.R. 6 (police where liable to judicial review if they gave a formal caution in clear breach of the guidelines in H.O. Circular 18/1994, even if the breach was unintentional). These cases deal with consistency as an aspect of legal certainty rather than equality, for which see above. See also the Canadian case *British Columbia Telephone Co. v. Shaw Cablesystems (B.C.) Ltd*, [1995] 2 S.C.R. 739 where two administrative bodies had given inconsistent decisions and the Supreme Court of Canada held that, if each decision was in itself not unlawful, the courts have jurisdiction to declare one of the decisions inoperative. The Supreme Court based the decision on 'the presumption of legislative coherence'.

[62] *North Wiltshire D.C. v. Secretary of State for the Environment* [1992] J.P.L. 955, CA *per* Mann L.J. This approach has recently been confirmed in *Aylesbury Vale D.C. v. Secretary of State for the Environment and Woodruff* [1995] J.P.L. 26, QBD.

[63] *R. v. Tower Hamlets L.B.C., ex p. Ali* (1992) 25 H.L.R. 158, 314.

[64] *R. v. Port Talbot B.C. and others, ex p. Jones* [1988] 2 All E.R. 207, QBD.

[65] *R. v. Birmingham City Council, ex p. Steptonhurst Ltd* [1990] 1 All E.R. 1026.

[66] [1911] A.C. 179.

who demands the rate without reference to the peculiar views of the ratepayer."[67] In *Prescott v. Birmingham Corp.*[68] the corporation, which had power to charge "such fares as they may think fit" on their public transport services introduced a scheme for free bus travel for the elderly. The decision was declared to be an improper exercise of discretion because it conferred out of rates "a special benefit on some particular class of inhabitants [and] would amount simply to the making of a gift or present in money's worth to a particular section of the local community at the expense of the general body of ratepayers."[69] Planning conditions that favour "locals only" in the allocation of housing or office space may also fall foul of the principle,[70] as may the discrimination in the allocation of school places to children living outside the school's catchment area.[71]

12–042 The House of Lords has held that the adoption by a local authority of the statutory criterion of pensionable age (65 for men and 60 for women) as the qualification for free admittance to a leisure centre is a breach of the statutory prohibition against sex discrimination.[72] In

---

[67] *ibid.* at 186. In *Maynard v. Osmond* [1977] Q.B. 240, 254, 258–259 it was assumed that a statutory instrument would be invalid if its provisions unfairly discriminated between senior and junior officers.

[68] [1955] 1 Ch. 210.

[69] Clearly the notion of equality applied in *Prescott* would not suit all theories of equality. Local authorities were given power ultimately to allow certain classes of free travel by the Travel Concessions Act 1964. In *Roberts v. Hopwood* [1925] A.C. 578 the House of Lords confirmed the view of the district auditor that the attempt of Poplar Borough Council to raise the level of wages of both men and women employees to an equal level was unlawful. Lord Atkinson considered that the council was guided by 'eccentric principles of socialistic philanthropy, or feminist ambition to secure the equality of the sexes'. Despite its headnote, the case was not decided on unreasonableness but on the ground of illegality, there being no 'rational proportion' between the rates paid to women employees and the going market rate. See Ormrod L.J. in *Pickwell v. Camden L.B.C.* [1993] Q.B. 962, 999–1000. See also Sir David Williams, 'Law and Administrative Discretion' (1994) Indiana J. of Global Legal Studs, 191. See further paras 5-094–5-096 above.

[70] See M. Grant, *Urban Planning Law* (1982) pp. 349–351; *Slough Industrial Estates Ltd v. Secretary of State for the Environment* [1987] J.P.L. 353; *Kember v. Secretary of State for the Environment* [1982] J.P.L. 383. Such conditions may be void for uncertainty, see above, para. 12–020. For unreasonably discriminatory taxi licence conditions (giving advantages to Hackney cabs) see *R. v. Blackpool B.C., ex p. Red Cab Taxis and Others, The Times*, May 13, 1995. See also *R. v. Avon C.C., ex p. Terry Adams Ltd* [1994] Env.L.R. 442 (discrimination in tenders for waste contracts).

[71] *R. v. Greenwich L.B.C., ex p. Governors of the John Ball Primary School* (1989) 88 L.G.R. 589; *R. v. Kingston-on-Thames L.B.C., ex p. Kingwell* [1992] 1 F.L.R. 182; *R. v. Bromley L.B.C., ex p. C & Others* [1992] 1 F.L.R. 174; *R. v. Rochdale M.B.C., ex p. Schemet,* (1993) 91 L.G.R. 425; *R. v. Devon C.C., ex p. G* [1989] A.C. 573.

[72] *James v. Eastleigh B.C.* [1990] 2 A.C. 751. But see *R. v. Secretary of State for Health, ex p. Richardson*, unreported, May 5, 1994, DC (pensionable age not discriminatory as a criterion for provision of drugs without charge under regulations under section 77(1) of the National Health Service Act 1977).

New Zealand, a regulation which discriminated between male and female married teachers in its conditions as to payment for removal expenses was struck down irrespective of anti-discrimination legislation.[73] Cooke J. said that:

"In modern times discrimination on the ground of sex alone is so controversial, and so widely regarded as wrong, that I would not be prepared to infer authority to introduce it from such general language as is found in [the relevant regulation]."[74]

A very clear recent application of the principle of substantive **12–043** equality was provided in relation to a challenge to immigration regulations. Lord Russell's formulation of unreasonableness as, *inter alia*, involving "partial and unequal" treatment[75] was cited in support of the striking down of the regulations which restricted the admission of dependent relatives to those having a standard of living "substantially below [their] own country". Simon Brown J. held that these regulations, which would benefit immigrants from affluent countries, were therefore "manifestly unjust and unreasonable".[76] In a more recent case, the court of Appeal accepted the principle of equality as being applicable to the question of the exclusion of homosexual men & women from the armed forces. The policy was not, however, held to be irrational.[77]

---

[73] *Van Gorkum v. Att.-Gen.* [1977] 1 N.Z.L.R. 535.

[74] *ibid.* at 541. See also the Australian case, *Leeth v. Commonwealth* (1992) 107 A.L.R. 672 (*per* Deane, Toohey, Gaudron JJ.)

[75] *Kruse v. Johnson*, n. 54 above.

[76] *R. v. Immigration Appeal Tribunal, ex p. Manshoora Bugum* [1986] Imm.A.R. 385. The offending provision was severed from the rest of the regulations. On discrimination on the basis of affluence see also *R. v. Secretary of State for Home Affairs, ex p. Wynne* [1992] 2 All E.R. 301, CA (prisoner's right to attend court hearing should not depend upon his ability to pay); *R. v. Legal Aid Committee No. 10 (East Midlands), ex p. McKenna* [1990] C.O.D. 358, 360 (cost of litigation irrelevant to grant of legal aid since it "would place multinational corporations in a position of advantage *vis-a-vis* individual claimants which, in my opinion, such commercial concerns ought not to enjoy", *per* Roch J.). See also *R. v. General Medical Council, The Times,* February 17, 1995 (G.M.C.'s entry qualification for foreign-qualified doctors unlawful).

[77] *R. v. Ministry of Defence, ex p. Smith* [1996] Q.B. 517. And see *R. v. Secretary of State for Social Security, ex p. Armstrong* (1996) 8 Admin. L.R. 626 (the test in section 72 Social Security Contributions and Benefits Act 1992, for entitlement to the care component of disability living allowance which was whether a disabled person could prepare a cooked meal, was not necessarily discriminatory against women, as it was not to be applied only to those who could already cook. Those applicants who could not cook must be assumed to be ready to learn); *Hughes v. Secretary of State for the Environment and New Forest D.C.* (1996) 71 P. & C.R. 168. (Application for judicial review from planning inspector's decisions refused. The inspector refused to grant planning permission for a mobile home to house a gypsy family. H argued unsuccessfully that: there was a blanket policy against the provision of gypsy sites which was the policy

OPPRESSIVE DECISIONS

12–044 Official decisions may be held unreasonable when they are unduly oppressive because they subject the complainant to an excessive hardship or an unnecessarily onerous infringement of his rights or interests. As we shall see, the principle of proportionality directs itself to the evaluation of the permitted degree of infringement of rights or interests, and we shall consider whether the specific application of proportionality may sharpen that evaluation in English law. However, whether or not proportionality is expressly applied, this aspect of substantive review is well known to English law.

12–045 The focus of attention in these cases will be principally the *impact* of the decision upon the affected person. The outcome or end-product of the decision-making process will thus be assessed, rather than the way the decision was reached (although the factors taken into account in reaching the decision may also be—or may be assumed to be— incorrectly weighed). Since the claim is essentially abuse of power, in the sense of excessive use of power, each case must be considered in the context of the nature of the decision, the function of the particular power and the nature of the interests or rights affected. We shall see, therefore, that the intensity of review (the margin of appreciation allowed the decision-maker) will differ in different circumstances, and that the courts impose particularly anxious scrutiny in cases where fundamental human rights have been infringed.

12–046 Town and country planning provides countless examples where planning conditions have been held unreasonable because of their unnecessarily onerous impact. Although the legislation permits the local authority, or the Secretary of State on appeal, to attach conditions to planning permissions as they may "think fit",[78] conditions have been held unreasonable which, in effect, require the developer to dedicate part of his land for public use[79] or otherwise require the

---

was partial, unequal and discriminatory against a national minority and destructive of a traditional way of life and therefore *ultra vires* and it was contrary to the common law and Article 8 E.C.H.R.); *R. v. Secretary of State for Foreign and Commonwealth Affairs, ex p. Manelfi* [1996] 12 C.L. 65 (judicial review of decision that M was ineligible for employment at GCHQ because of the foreign nationalities of his parents—M claimed application of the rules without waiver were *Wednesbury* unreasonable and contrary to the common law and the International Covenant on Civil and Political Rights 1996, Article 26. Held, dismissing the application: the decision in the making of the rules and their application were made in the interests of national security and were nonjusticiable). For a full statement of the extent to which equality is considered "a general axiom of rational behaviour", see *Matadeen v. Pointu* [1999] A.C. 98, PC; *cf. Hugo v. President of the Republic of South Africa* 1996 (4) SA 1012 (D).

[78] Town & Country Planning Act 1990, s.70(1).

[79] *Hall & Co. Ltd v. Shoreham-by-Sea U.D.C.* [1964] 1 W.L.R. 240. The purpose of the

developer to provide the off-site physical infrastructure necessary to unlock the development.[80] Similarly, a planning condition was held unreasonable which, in effect, required the developer to construct housing to local authority standards and rents, and to take tenants from the council's waiting list.[81] Conditions attached to similar broad powers to license caravan sites were held by the House of Lords to be unreasonable because they were "a gratuitous interference with the rights of the occupier".[82] A condition attached to the reopening of a public inquiry by the Secretary of State for the Environment was held to be unreasonable because it resulted in "considerable expense, inconvenience and risk to the applicant".[83] The Secretary of State's refusal to renew a temporary planning permission was struck down because it would be "unreasonably burdensome" on the applicant.[84]

The exercise of compulsory purchase powers has similarly been held **12–047** unreasonable when the authority already possessed, or was able to acquire voluntarily, other equally suitable land.[85] Where a local authority acquired land for one purpose (such as a wall to protect the coast), it was held unreasonable for it to acquire more land than it needed.[86]

---

condition was to ensure safe access to the site—a purpose well within the 'four corners' of the legislation.

[80] *City of Bradford M.C. v. Secretary of State for the Environment* [1986] J.P.L. 598. But such a condition may survive if framed in negative terms. See *Grampian R.C. v. City of Aberdeen* [1984] J.P.L. 590; (1983) 47 P. & C.R. 633, HL. Although the House of Lords have recently held that a negative condition may even survive even if there is no 'reasonable prospect' of the development being carried out. *British Railways Board v. Secretary of State for the Environment* [1994] J.P.L. 32, HL.

[81] *R. v. Hillingdon L.B.C., ex p. Royco Homes Ltd* [1974] 1 Q.B. 720. For an older case holding it unlawful to seek developers' contributions, see *R. v. Bowman* [1898] 1 Q.B. 663. But where these contributions are provided by means of what are now called 'planning obligations' (and used to be called planning agreements or 'planning gain') under section 106 of the Town and Country Planning Act 1990, developers' contributions may be upheld. See further Chap. 5 above, para. 5–036.

[82] *Mixnam's Properties Ltd v. Chertsey U.D.C.* [1965] A.C. 735. The conditions provided, *inter alia*, for security of tenure, no premium charged, and no restrictions on commercial or political activity. See also *R. v. North Hertfordshire D.C., ex p. Cobbold* [1985] 3 All E.R. 486 (oppressive condition attached to licence for pop concert); *R. v. Barnett L.B.C., ex p. Johnson* (1989) 89 L.G.R. 581 (condition prohibiting political parties and activities at community festival held unreasonable).

[83] *R. v. Secretary of State for the Environment, ex p. Fielder Estates (Canvey) Ltd, The Times,* June 10, 1988. See also *Niarchos (London) Ltd v. Secretary of State for the Environment* (1980) 79 L.G.R. 264.

[84] *Niarchos Ltd v. Secretary of State for the Environment* (1977) 35 P. & C.R. 259.

[85] *Brown v. Secretary of State for the Environment* (1978) 40 P. & C.R. 285; *Prest v. Secretary of State for Wales* (1982) 81 L.G.R. 193. But see *R. v. Secretary of State for Transport, ex p. de Rothschild* [1989] 1 All E.R. 933 (discussed further below at para. 12–057).

[86] *Webb v. Minister of Housing and Local Government* [1965] 1 W.L.R. 755. See also *Gard v. Commissioners of Sewers of City of London* (1885) 28 Ch.D. 486. See also *Leader v. Moxon* (1773) 3 Wils.K.B. 461 (Paving Commissioners empowered to execute street works in

to the earlier case of *Congreve v. Home Office*,[1] where the Home Secretary's decision to withdraw television licences from those who had failed to pay a higher fee (but were nevertheless within their rights so to do) was held by the Court of Appeal to be unlawful because it imposed a punishment which related to no wrong. In both cases, the courts refused to countenance the achievement of a legitimate end (the raising of revenue in *Congreve* and the promotion of good race relations in *Wheeler*) by means which were excessive (punishing, in each case, where the individual had done no legal wrong).[2]

12–052   Similar reasoning was employed in a case where some London local authorities decided to withdraw their subscriptions to all publications in their public libraries published by the Times Newspapers group. Following an acrimonious labour dispute, the action was taken in an attempt to impose sanctions on the newspaper proprietors. This consideration was held to be extraneous to the statutory duty of providing a "comprehensive and efficient library service."[3] The imposition of the sanctions was also held to be unreasonable and an abuse of the councils' powers.[4]

'procedural impropriety' to describe the lack of relation between the penalty and the council's legitimate objectives.

[1] [1976] 1 Q.B. 629.

[2] There may be different explanations of the grounds on which both *Congreve* and *Wheeler* were decided. One ground may be the infringement of the principle of legal certainty, which was discussed in para. 12–025 *et seq.* above. Another may be that the decisions were 'illegal' in that both the council in *Wheeler* and the Home Secretary in *Congreve* acted for an improper purpose (namely, the imposition of a punishment). See further, Chap. 5, paras 5–072–5–077 above. Compare the approach of Browne-Wilkinson L.J. in his dissenting judgment in the Court of Appeal, *ibid.* at pp. 1064–1065, where he raised the conflict between 'two basic principles of a democratic society', one that allowed a 'democratically elected body to conduct its affairs in accordance with its own views' and the other 'the right to freedom of speech and conscience enjoyed by each individual'. Basing his decision on illegality rather than on unreasonableness (the council having taken a 'legally irrelevant factor' into account), he came close to deciding the matter on the ground of the council's acting inconsistently with 'fundamental freedoms of speech and conscience'. See also *R. v. Lewisham L.B.C., ex p. Shell U.K. Ltd* [1988] 1 All E.R. 938 (boycott of the products of the Shell company in order to bring pressure on one of its subsidiary companies to withdraw its (lawful) business from South Africa held illegal). *Cf.* the New Zealand decision of *Ashby v. Minister of Immigration* [1981] 1 N.Z.L.R. 222 where the refusal of admission of the South African rugby football team into New Zealand was upheld on the ground that the public interest (a relevant consideration in the context of the Minister's power) allowed it.

[3] The Public Libraries and Museums Act 1964, s.7(1).

[4] *R. v. Ealing L.B.C., ex p. Times Newspapers* (1986) 85 L.G.R. 316. It was not explicitly stated that the decision amounted to an excessive and unnecessary infringement on freedom of expression. The case raises interesting questions as to the reasonableness of decisions to cease subscriptions to, or remove books from the library of 'politically incorrect' material. Another case involving a local authority. In *R. v. Liverpool City*

THE INTENSITY OF REVIEW

The willingness of the courts to strike down a decision on the ground **12–053** that it is unreasonable or an abuse of discretion will be influenced in part by the administrative scheme under review; for example, by the existence of internal administrative review or of alternative appeal structures or the extent of the expertise of the initial decision-maker.[5] The threshold of intervention or margin of appreciation afforded the decision-maker is, however, particularly influenced by the subject matter of the decision. At one extreme are managerial and policy decisions, and on the other are cases involving infringements of fundamental human rights.

Managerial and policy decisions

In two notable cases the House of Lords refused to hold unreasonable **12–054** decisions of the Secretary of State for the Environment in the exercise of powers to control the expenditure of local authorities.[6] In both cases the threshold of unreasonableness was held to be "extreme" and was formulated to include decisions "so absurd that [the decision maker] must have taken leave of his senses."[7] In *ex p. Hammersmith and Fulham L.B.C.*, the question concerned the power of the Secretary of State to cap the local authority's community charge if the authority's budget was set at a level which he considered "excessive" in accordance with principles determined by him. Lord Bridge held that the setting of a norm of local government expenditure was a matter of national economic policy, and therefore a matter "depending essentially upon political judgment". Outside of "the extremes of bad faith, improper motive or manifest absurdity", the question whether a local authority's budget for a year is "excessive" could not, it was said, be judged by any "objective criterion".[8]

Council, ex p. Secretary of State for Employment (1988) 154 L.G.R. 118, the council sought to boycott the Government's Employment Training Scheme, despite the fact that it was voluntary. The council did this outside of any statutory framework, by imposing a standard condition on all grant aid that the organisation to be aided took no part in the scheme. The purpose, punishment of the organisations, was held to be unlawful.

[5] See, *e.g. R. v. Home Secretary, ex p. Swati* [1986] 1 W.L.R. 477; *R. v. Chief Constable of the Merseyside Police, ex p. Calveley* [1986] 1 Q.B. 424; *Pulhofer v. Hillingdon L.B.C.* [1986] A.C. 484. See also *R. v. Secretary of State for Social Services, ex p. Stitt* [1990] C.O.D. 288.

[6] *R. v. Secretary of State for the Environment, ex p. Nottinghamshire C.C.* [1986] A.C. 240; *R. v. Secretary of State for the Environment, ex p. Hammersmith and Fulham L.B.C.* [1991] 1 A.C. 521.

[7] *ibid., per* lord Bridge at 596–597.

[8] *ibid.*

12–055   These two cases do not entirely rule out the possibility of a finding of unreasonableness in decisions that are in the general area of social and economic policy,[9] but they do show that the intensity of review in such cases will be low. It should, however, be noted that both these cases were coloured by the fact that the House of Commons had, by resolution, approved the Secretary of State's decisions.[10]

12–056   The rationales of both cases have a sound constitutional basis: budgetary decisions are quintessential policy decisions involving calculations of social and economic preference. Such questions are more suited to decision by elected representatives than by the courts. Nevertheless, the courts have in the past intervened in decisions about local authority expenditure—in relation to the setting of transport fares, for example,[11] or the payment of salaries and wages to employees.[12] The ground of the court's intervention in these cases, as we have seen,[13] was, normally, illegality, rather than unreasonableness.[14] In *Pickwell v. Camden L.B.C.* the council's allegedly over-generous wage settlement was held not, on the facts available to the court, to be unlawful. As to whether it was unreasonable, Ormrod L.J. said:

---

[9] See the discussion of "justiciable" decisions at paras 5–029–5–036. A similar reserve was expressed by the House of Lords in regard to questions of "social and ethical controversy" (in respect of the guidance on contraception from the Department of Health) in *Gillick v. W. Norfolk and Wisbech Area Health Authority* [1986] A.C. 112, 194, 206 (Lords Bridge and Templeman). See also *Airedale NHS Trust v. Bland* per Lord Mustill at 887–888; Hoffmann L.J. in the Court of Appeal at 824 *et seq.; R. v. Lord Chancellor, ex p. Maxwell* [1997] 1 W.L.R. 104 (substitution of trial judge for another judge not irrational act of Lord Chancellor. Deployment of judicial resources justiciable, but the decision, involving allocation of resources between different courts, is almost always for Lord Chancellor alone); *R. v. Lord Chancellor ex p. Stockler* (1996) 8 Admin. L.R. 590; *R. v. Radio Authority ex p. Bull* [1997] 3 W.L.R. 1094 (authority's ban on Amnesty International's broadcasts should only be interfered with where "manifest breach" of principles). *Cf. R. v. Coventry City Council, ex p. Phoenix Aviation* [1995] 3 All E.R. 37. (Public authorities operating air and sea ports were not entitled, in the absence of an emergency, to ban the flights or shipments of livestock by animal exporters so as to avoid the disruptive consequences of unlawful protesters. To do so would infringe the rule of law. Nor (*per* Simon Brown L.J.) were the legitimate interests of the exporters sufficiently considered); *R. v. Chief Constable of Sussex, ex p. International Trader's Ferry Ltd* [1998] 3 W.L.R. 1260, HL (not unreasonable for the Chief Constable to reduce effective policing of the export traders to two days per week in the face of lack of sufficient resources).

[10] Discussed at para. 12–065 below.

[11] See, *e.g. Bromley L.B.C. v. Greater London Council* [1983] 1 A.C. 768. See discussion in Chap. 5 paras 5–094–5–096 above.

[12] *Roberts v. Hopwood* [1925] A.C. 579.

[13] Chap. 5 above, paras 5–094–5–096.

[14] As suggested by Ormrod L.J. in *Pickwell v. Camden L.B.C.* [1983] Q.B. 962, 999–1000. See also *Westminster City Council v. Greater London Council* [1986] A.C. 668.

"The question for this court is not whether Camden made a bad bargain for the ratepayers, or were precipitate in making the offer to the strikers, or could have achieved a cheaper settlement by waiting, or made a better bargain by different tactics. These are matters for the electorate at the next election."[15]

Decisions infringing fundamental rights

We have seen in Chapter 5[16] how fundamental rights may be implied **12–057** in the common law through different routes: through the provisions of the European Convention when they are presumed to apply as a treaty obligation, or through the common law when they may be protected in the absence of a statute containing express words indicating the contrary. When the Human Rights Act comes into effect then the relevant provisions of the European convention on Human Rights will apply directly in England law.[17]

The presumption of statutory interpretation in favour of fundamental rights does, however, possess limits as a device to control their infringement. In some areas, the statute is simply not consistent with a fundamental right, since interference with the right is integral to the statute's aims. For example, statutes authorising deportation, or restricting immigration, inherently sanction the interference with freedom of movement. A presumption against that interference cannot, therefore, easily be made. Similarly, the over-riding purpose of the planning statutes is to curtail the right to develop land and, in the British discretionary regulatory system, to confer wide discretion on authorities to grant or refuse planning permission and to impose conditions as they "think fit".[18] Those challenges to planning conditions which have resulted in their being struck down as unreasonable by the courts[19] would have been unlikely to succeed if the presumption against interference with property rights had been the only argument relied upon, since the statute clearly intended to

---

[15] *ibid.* Compare the approach of the Court of Appeal in the area of economic regulation in *R. v. Monopolies and Mergers Commission, ex p. Argyll Group plc* [1986] 1 W.L.R. 763 where the Secretary of State, rather than the court, was said by the Master of the Rolls to be the primary 'guardian of the public interest'.

[16] At paras 5-047–5-057.

[17] For an excellent account of the extent of the use of human rights in English courts see Murray Hunt, *Using Human Rights Law in English Courts* (1997). And see M. Beloff and H. Mountfield, 'Unconventional Behaviour? Judicial Uses of the European Convention on Human Rights in England and Wales' 1996 E.H.R.L.R. 467.

[18] s.70(1) Town and Country Planning Act 1990.

[19] See above, para. 12–046.

diminish or extinguish those rights. For example, a condition requiring the dedication of the developer's land for public access[20] falls squarely within the statute's purpose (access being a perfectly proper material consideration in planning). In such a case, however, the exercise of the power can be unreasonable, rather than illegal, with the focus of inquiry not upon the purpose of the power (which has been fulfilled) but upon its impact upon the complainant and the claim that the interference with his property rights are excessive. Statutes permitting compulsory purchase also fall into this category; it cannot be presumed that their "draconian" infringement of property rights is not intended, yet a compulsory purchase order may be overturned for unreasonableness where the decision is not "sufficiently justified".[21]

Furthermore if, as was held in *Brind*,[22] the conferral of wide discretionary power rebuts a presumption of conformity with a treaty obligation, then it surely follows that such a power similarly rebuts the presumption against the infringement of fundamental rights in domestic law alone.

12–058 Despite these limitations, the courts have been, even in the absence of the domestic enactment of legislation incorporating specific human rights, increasingly affording special protection to fundamental rights in the following ways:

> (1) As we have seen in the case of *Leech*[23]; where a statutory power does not clearly authorise the infringement of a fundamental right (whether the source of that right lies in a treaty *or* an implied "constitutional right"[24] the courts will make the inference that the statutory intent was not to infringe that right.[25]

---

[20] *Hall v. Shoreham-by-Sea U.D.C.*, n. 79 above.

[21] *e.g. Secretary of State for Transport and others, ex p. de Rothschild and another* [1989] 1 All E.R. 993, CA. See also *Brown v. Secretary of State for the Environment* (1978) 40 P. & C.R. 285; *Prest v. Secretary of State for Wales* (1982) 81 L.G.R. 193, CA.

[22] [1991] A.C. 696. *Cf. Brind* with the approach of the Israel Supreme Court in *Kahane v. Broadcasting Authority*—media coverage of PLO. See I. Zamir & I. Zysblat, *Public Law in Israel* (1996), p. 74.

[23] *R. v. Secretary of State for the Home Department, ex p. Leech (No. 2)* [1994] Q.B. 198.

[24] *ibid., per* Steyn L.J. See also, in the context of private law, Lord Diplock in *Bremer v. South Indian Shipping Co. Ltd.* [1981] A.C. 909, 917.

[25] The approach in *Leech* was expressly followed by Laws J. in *R. v. Lord Chancellor, ex p. Witham* [1997] 2 All E.R. 779 where it was held that excessive court fees deprived a citizen of his constitutional right of access to the courts. Such rights not 'the consequence of the democratic political process but would be logically prior to it'. Leech was also followed in *R. v. Secretary of State for the Home Department, ex p. Simms, O'Brien, The Times* [1997] C.O.D. 217 (prohibition on use by a journalist of material gathered on a visit to a prisoner violated prisoners' right to free speech and the restriction not necessary or justified). The Court of Appeal overruled this judgment, *ex p. Simms* (1998) 95 L.S.G. 23. The House of Lords (July 8, 1999) then

(2) Where a statute does confer discretionary power to interfere with a fundamental right (and thus, according to *Brind*[26] is not ambiguous in its intent), the courts nevertheless require the power to be reasonably exercised. Unreasonableness in such cases is not, however, synonymous with "absurdity" or "perversity". Review is stricter and the courts ask the question posed by the majority in *Brind*,[27] namely, "whether a reasonable Secretary of State, on the material before him, could reasonably conclude that the interference with freedom of expression was justifiable".[28] This test lowers the threshold of unreasonableness. In addition, it has been held that decisions infringing rights should receive the "most anxious scrutiny" of the courts.[29]

---

reversed the CA. *Cf. R. v. Secretary of State for the Home Department ex p. Maby* C.L.D. June 1996. *Leech* was taken a step further in *R. v. Secretary of State for Social Security ex p. Joint Council for the Welfare of Immigrants* [1997] 1 W.L.R. 275 where it was held that regulations excluding from income support entitlement those who sought asylum otherwise than on immediate arrival in the United Kingdom or whose claims were rejected and awaiting appeal, both conflicted with and rendered rights in other legislation nugatory and were so Draconian to an extent that 'no civilised nation can tolerate.' (*per* Simon Brown L.J. citing Lord Ellenborough C.J. in *R. v. Eastbourne (Inhabitants)* (1803) 4 East. 103 at 107, 102 E.R. 769 at 770 'the law of humanity, which is anterior to all positive laws obliges us to afford (poor foreigners) them relief, to save them from starving'). And see also Lord Steyn's acceptance of the concept of 'substantive fairness' in *Pierson v. Secretary of State for the Home Department* [1998] A.C. 539.

[26] n. 22 above.

[27] n. 22 above. *Per* Lords Bridge, Roskill and Templeman.

[28] See also *R. v. Secretary of State for the Environment, ex p. NALGO, The Times,* December 2, 1992.

[29] *per* Lord Bridge in *Bugdaycay v. Home Secretary* [1987] A.C. 514, 531, speaking of the right to life in a deportation case. Such decisions, he said would be subject to a 'more rigorous examination', Lord Templeman at 537–538. See also *National and Local Government Officers Association v. Secretary of State for the Environment and Another* (1993) Admin L.R. 785 applying the test to the restriction on the political activities on local government officers. In *Prest v. Secretary of State for Wales* (1982) 81 L.G.R. 193, Watkins L.J. said that compulsory purchase decisions must be 'carefully scrutinised', and Lord Denning M.R. said the Secretary of State must in such cases show that the public interest 'decisively demands' the compulsory purchase order. See also *R. v. Ministry of Defence ex p. Smith* [1996] Q.B. 517 where Bingham M.R. accepted that, in relation to an unreasonable decision, 'the more substantial the interference with human rights, the more the court will require by justification before it is satisfied that the decision is reasonable.' Note the reversal of the usual *Wednesbury* burden of proof. See also *Tan Te Lam v. Superintendent of Tai A Chav Detention Centre* [1997] A.C. 97, PC where it was accepted that in respect of the lawfulness of the detention of a migrant in Hong Kong 'very clear words' would be needed to authorise continued detention; *R. v. Secretary of State for the Home Department, ex p. Launder* [1997] 1 W.L.R. 839 (it was normally open to the Court to review the exercise of the Home Secretary's discretion under the Extradition Act 1989, s.12). The fact that a decision was taken on policy grounds of an important or sensitive nature and involving delicate relations between foreign states did

12–059   In *Brind*, the majority indicated that a decision-maker who exercises broad discretion must show that such an infringement can only be justified by an "important competing public interest".[30] In extradition cases it has been held that such a test does not reverse the onus of proof and place it on the Home Secretary.[31]

12–060   In cases of compulsory purchase the Court of Appeal has held that although the confirmation of a compulsory purchase order must be "sufficiently justified" by the Secretary of State,[32] it is not appropriate to use the expression "onus of proof" in such a situation where there is no *lis inter partes*.[33]

12–061   In contrast to cases involving managerial or policy decisions, where judicial intervention will be sparingly undertaken, the courts will look significantly harder at cases involving infringements of human rights, but without reversing the onus or burden of proofs or necessarily abandoning all of the *Wednesbury* reserve.[34] Once, however, the Human Rights Act has been brought into effect, the courts will be able directly to enforce provisions of the European Convention on Human Rights in respect of the exercise of public functions. In respect of legislation, however, courts would only be

---

not affect the court's duty to ensure the applicant was afforded proper protection, although the court would be mindful of both the limitations of its constitutional role and the need in such a case for "anxious scrutiny"; *R. v. Secretary of State for the Home Department, ex p. Norney* (1995) 7 Admin. L.R. 861 (unlawful to delay referring cases of discretionary life prisoners to parole board until the end of tariff period. This policy was unreasonable in the *Wednesbury* sense. It flouted the principles of common law and the European Convention on Human Rights). But see: *R. v. Parole Board, ex p. Martin* [1996] C.O.D. 236 (decision not to release mandatory life prisoner on licence was not perverse).

[30] *per* Lords Bridge and Roskill in *Brind*, n. 22 above, at 749–751.

[31] See *R. v. Home Secretary, ex p. Osman, The Independent,* September 10, 1992. However, although no reasons are required for the Home Secretary's decision the court "could expect [him] to file an affidavit disclosing the basis on which the decision was taken" (*per* Woolf L.J.).

[32] *R. v. Secretary of State for Transport, ex p. de Rothschild* [1989] 1 All E.R. 933.

[33] "To talk of questions of onus of proof when so many competing factors have to be taken into the balance [such as questions of landscape and other amenity, feasibility, cost and delay] seems to me not only inappropriate but a somewhat difficult concept", *per* Slade L.J. in *de Rothschild*, n. 32 above.

[34] Compare the threefold standard of review employed by the United States Supreme Court to test allegations of discriminatory state action under the "equality" clause (14th Amendment to the U.S. Constitution). Where the discrimination is on the basis of a "suspect classification", such as race or national origin (where discrimination implies "inferiority in civil society") or where the classification burdens "fundamental rights", strict scrutiny is applied (see, *e.g. Palmore v. Sidoti* (1984) 466 U.S. 429). Where the alleged discrimination refers to social and economic policy and the matter is not justiciable, it will survive challenge if "rationally related to furthering a legitimate government objective". (See, *e.g. Massachusetts Board of Retirement v. Murgis* (1976) 427 U.S. 307.) In between these is a third category, that of "quasi-suspect classification" under which sex discrimination has fallen (see, *e.g. Michael M v. Superior Court of Sonoma County* (1981) 450 U.S. 464).

permitted to issue a "declaration of incompatibility" with the Convention and it would thus lie with Parliament whether to remedy the incompatibility.

Obtaining a democratic mandate

Is it "relevant" to the question of reasonableness (a) that the decision **12–062** of a local authority was supported by a democratic "mandate" in the sense that it apparently gained the support of the electorate at a recent election? Or (b) that an executive decision or policy was approved by parliamentary resolution?

Mandate of local authority

On the question of the mandate of a local authority, the cases appear **12–063** at first sight to differ. In the *Bromley* case[35] the Greater London Council justified a 25 per cent reduction in transport fares partly on the basis that they were supported by the electorate at the recent election. It was argued that the council therefore possessed a "mandate" to lower the fares in the way the successful majority party had promised in its electoral manifesto. The House of Lords disagreed; those elected had to consider the interests of all the inhabitants of the area, in the light of their legal duties. In the *Tameside* case[36] the local authority introduced a scheme, promised at a recent local election, to abolish certain recently established comprehensive schools and to reintroduce grammar schools by a process of selection—all in a period of four months. The Secretary of State sought to intervene under section 68 of the Education Act 1944 which permitted him to do so when "he was satisfied" that a local authority were acting "unresaonably". The House of Lords held that the Secretary of State did not in those circumstances have the power to intervene because the council had not acted unreasonably in the *Wednesbury* sense. This decision was considerably influenced by the fact that the local authority was recently elected, with a mandate to reintroduce grammar schools.

While superficially contradictory, these two cases were decided on **12–064** different grounds. The *Bromley* case was decided on the basis of the council's exceeding the particular powers established in the governing statute. It is therefore authority for the correct proposition that no "mandate" from the electorate can serve as a justification for an illegal

---

[35] *Bromley B.C. v. G.L.C.* [1983] 1 A.C. 768.
[36] *Secretary of State for Education and Science v. Tameside M.B.C.* [1977] A.C. 1014.

act.[37] In *Tameside*, although the scope of the governing statute was in issue, the case turned on the unreasonableness of the local authority's behaviour. A manifesto commitment may be relevant evidence of the unreasonableness of a decision which permits a range of lawful courses of action. It should never, however, be taken as conclusive proof of reasonableness, as other factors may be weighed against it.[38]

Approval by parliamentary resolution

12–065 In two cases the House of Lords regarded it as relevant to the reasonableness of a decision of a Minister that the decision had by resolution been approved by one or both Houses of Parliament.[39]

While these resolutions of course fall short of statutory authority, they may constitute strong evidence of the reasonableness of a decision. But such evidence should not be regarded by the courts as conclusive proof of unreasonableness.[40] While it is understandable that the courts should adopt this approach in the interests of unity between the courts and Parliament, the resolutions cannot make what is unreasonable, reasonable. The resolutions do not have the

---

[37] In *Bromley*, Lord Denning, in the Court of Appeal, [1982] 2 W.L.R. 62 said that a manifesto should "not be taken as gospel... When a party gets into power, it should consider any proposal or promise afresh, and on its merits...". And see his reservations about the doctrine of the mandate in *The Changing Law* (1953) where he wrote: "Some people vote for [a member] because they approve of some of the proposals in his party's manifesto, others because they approve of others of the proposals. Yet others because, while they do not really approve of the proposals, they disapprove still more of the counter-proposals of the rival party, and so forth. It is impossible to say therefore that the majority of the people approve of any particular proposal, let alone every proposal in the manifesto" (pp. 8–10). To the extent that *Bromley* was influenced by the breach of the council's 'fiduciary' duty to the ratepayers, see Chap. 5, paras 5-094–5-096 above. See also *R. v. Merseyside C.C., ex p. Great Universal Stores Ltd* (1982) 80 L.G.R. 639. And see para. 10–009 n. 46 above.

[38] See also *R. v. Somerset C.C., ex p. Fewings* [1995] 1 All E.R. 513 where (in relation to the council's ban on stag-hunting) Laws J. held that the fact that the council were an elected body would not influence the court to interpret "benevolently" whether the decision was within the permissible scope of the statute, "as may be the approach in the case of an assessment of the reasonableness of the exercise of a discretionary power". See further, Chap. 5, para. 5–073 above.

[39] *R. v. Secretary of State for the Environment, ex p. Nottinghamshire C.C.* [1986] A.C. 240, 247 (*per* Lord Scarman); *R. v. Secretary of State for the Environment, ex p. Hammersmith & Fulham L.B.C.* [1991] 1 A.C. 521, 597 (*per* Lord Bridge).

[40] The Home Secretary's directives in *Brind* (n. 22 above) were also approved by both Houses of Parliament. Yet the directives that were held partially invalid in *R. v. Immigration Appeal Tribunal, ex p. Begum Manshoora, The Times*, July 24, 1986, had also been laid before Parliament.

imprimatur of statutes and so do not excuse the courts from performing their proper role and the courts do declare unlawful regulations approved by Parliament.[41]

Statutory unreasonableness

What is the standard of unreasonableness, or degree of intensity of review, in cases where the term "unreasonable" is contained in a statute?[42] In the *Tameside* case,[43] the Secretary of State had the power to issue directions to the local authority "if [h]e is satisfied" that the local authority is "acting unreasonably".[44] Despite this seemingly subjective formulation, the House of Lords read the term "unreasonably" as expressing the *Wednesbury* formulation. The Secretary of State could therefore issue directions only where the local authority were acting so unreasonably that no reasonable authority would so act.[45]

12–066

It has been argued[46] that the extreme reserve of *Wednesbury*, which was devised to inhibit the powers of *courts* to intervene in the merits of an administrative decision, should not apply to the formulation of unreasonableness in the Education Act 1944 in respect of the decision of a Minister, whose constitutional position is entirely different. The matter surely, however, depends upon the administrative scheme established by a particular statute. It could be argued that the Education Act 1944 has as an important purpose the placing of education policy primarily with the local authority, with the Minister having power to intervene only in extreme cases. In the case of other administrative schemes, however, the statute may pose the Minister with fewer obstacles to intervention.[47] For example, section 9 of the

12–067

---

[41] As they were in *Commissioners of Customs and Excise v. Cure and Deeley* [1962] 1 Q.B. 340; *ex p. Leech*, n. 23 above. The same argument applies to moneys allocated with parliamentary approval to a specific project that may not be lawful. In *Chief Adjudication Officer v. Foster* [1993] A.C. 754, Lord Bridge left open the question of whether to follow the *Nottinghamshire case* in the matter of Parliamentary approval. *Cf. City of Edinburgh D.C. v. Secretary of State for Scotland*, 1985 S.L.T. 551, 556.

[42] Compare the discussion in Chap. 5 paras 5-016–5-020 above where the standard of reasonableness is contained in a statute.

[43] [1977] A.C. 1014—described above, para. 12–063.

[44] Section 68 of the Education Act 1994.

[45] A second aspect of *Tameside* was the possible mistake of material fact, discussed above, Chap. 4. para 4–067. For a critical account of the *Tameside* case, see D. Bull, "*Tameside* Revisited: Prospectively 'Reasonable'; Retrospective 'Maladministration'" (1987) 50 M.L.R. 307.

[46] P. Craig, *Administrative Law*, (3rd ed., 1994) p. 435.

[47] Sometimes by permitting the Minister to exercise default powers even in the absence of unreasonable behaviour on the part of a local authority. See, *e.g.* the formulation under the Housing Act 1980, which permits the Secretary of State to intervene to

Education Act 1981 places a local authority under a duty to comply with a request from a parent for an assessment of their child's special needs unless the request is in the opinion of the authority "unreasonable". In a recent case it was held that the "public law test" of reasonableness which was "intended to protect the local authority...against interference by the Secretary of State" was not applicable to section 9, which required a "strightforward factual test" of unreasonableness, "based on all the material before the authority".[48] This clearly implies that the *Wednesbury* formulation may be appropriately applied in cases such as that of *Tameside*, but is not appropriate to all statutes where the term unreasonable is employed.[49] The term "unreasonable", in its *Wednesbury* or any other sense, is no magic formula; everything must depend upon the context.

PROPORTIONALITY

12–068   Proportionality is a recognised "general principle of law" applied both by the European Court of Justice and the European Court of Human Rights. Originating in Prussia[50] in the nineteenth century, proportionality has been recommended for adoption in the Member States of the European Community by a resolution of the Committee

---

exercise the local authority's powers to sell council housing 'where it appears to the Secretary of State that tenants ... have or may have difficulty in exercising their right to buy effectively and expeditiously'. *R. v. Secretary of State for the Environment, ex p. Norwich C.C.* [1982] Q.B. 808. See also the scheme for the management of the Social Fund, with its system of internal reviews both by officers and an independent inspectorate, and which the courts have held should not easily be subjected to external interference: *R. v. Secretary of State for Social Services, ex p. Stitt* [1990] C.O.D. 288; *R. v. Social Fund Inspector, ex p. Waris Ali* [1993] C.O.D. 263. See T. Mullens 'The Social Fund—Cash Limiting Social Security' (1989) 52 M.L.R. 64.

[48] *R. v. Hampshire C.C., ex p. W, The Times,* June 9, 1994 (*per* Sedley J.).

[49] See, *e.g.* the wide discretion of a legal aid committee to refuse legal aid 'if it appears unreasonable in the particular circumstances of the case': *R. v. Legal Aid Committee No. 1 (London), ex p. Rondel* [1967] 2 Q.B. 482. But see *R. v. Legal Aid Committee No. 10 (East Midlands), ex p. McKenna* (1990) 2 Admin. L.R. 585 where the committee's decision was flawed because it was based upon a demonstrably mistaken view of the facts.

[50] The principle of *Verhaltnismassigkeit* was invoked by the Prussian Supreme Administrative Court to check the discretionary powers of police authorities. See M.P. Singh, *German Administrative Law: A Common Lawyer's View* (1985), pp. 88–101. For an account of the principle of proportionality in German and French law, European Community Law, European Human Rights law and its application in English law see J. Jowell and A. Lester, 'Proportionality: Neither Novel nor Dangerous' in Jowell and Oliver (eds) *New Directions in Judicial Review* (1989), p. 51. For a full account of proportionality in European Community Law and in that of many of the Member States, see J. Schwartze, *European Administrative Law* (1992), Chap. 5.

of Ministers of the Council of Europe.[51] It was defined there as requiring an administrative authority, when exercising a discretionary power, to—

"maintain a proper balance between any adverse effects which its decision may have on the rights, liberties, or interests of persons and the purpose which it pursues."

Proportionality was suggested by Lord Diplock in the *GCHQ* case as a possible fourth ground of judicial review in English law.[52] It is explicitly applied by British courts in respect of directly effective Community law.[53]

The principal opposition to proportionality in England is based on **12–069** the view that it lowers the threshold of judicial intervention and involves the courts considering the merits and facts of administrative decisions.[54] However, in *Att.-Gen. v. Guardian Newspapers Ltd (No. 2),*[55] Lord Goff said that:

"It is established in the jurisprudence of the European Court of Human Rights that...interference with freedom of expression should be no more than is proportionate to the legitimate aim pursued. I have no reason to believe that English law, as applied in the courts, leads to any different conclusion."[56]

In judicial review, proportionality has been explicitly applied in a **12–070** few cases.[57] It was pleaded in the *Brind* case, and, although not there applied, future application was not ruled out.[58] Whether or not

---

[51] Adopted March 11, 1980.

[52] *Council for Civil Service Unions v. Minister of State for the Civil Service* [1985] A.C. 374, 410.

[53] See, *e.g. R. v. Minister of Agriculture, Fisheries and Food, ex p. Roberts and Others* [1991] 1 C.M.L.R. 555; *Thomas v. Adjudication Officer* [1991] 2 Q.B. 164, CA; *Stoke-on-Trent C.C. v. B&Q plc* [1991] 1 Ch. 48.

[54] See Lord Lowry's arguments against proportionality in *Brind* [1991] A.C. 696, at 766–767. See also Lord Ackner at 762. See also S. Boyron, 'Proportionality in English Administrative Law: A Faulty Translation?' [1992] O.J.L.S. 237.

[55] [1990] 1 A.C. 109.

[56] *ibid.* at 283. See also Lord Griffiths at 273.

[57] *per* Lords Denning and Scarman in *R. v. Barnsley M.B.C., ex p. Hook* [1976] 1 W.L.R. 1052 (disproportionate punishment for street trader); *R. v. Brent L.B.C., ex p. Assegai, The Times,* June 18, 1987 (banning from council meeting out of proportion to what the applicant had done, *per* Woolf L.J.): *R. v. Secretary of State for Transport, ex p. Pegasus Holidays (London) Ltd and Airbro (U.K.) Ltd,* August 7, 1987, Transcript CO/1377/87, QBD.

[58] [1991] 1 A.C. 696, *per* Lords Bridge, Roskill and Templeman. See M. Beloff, 'Judical Review—2001: A Prophetic Odyssey' (1995) 58 M.L.R. 143, 151. But see Neill L.J. in the *NALGO* case, n. 28 above, who considered *Brind* to have rejected proportionality.

explicitly applied, proportionality provides an implicit explanation for some of the existing judicial interventions under the guise of *Wednesbury* unreasonableness. It is especially apposite as a tool for assessing two categories which we have identified as categories of the unreasonable decision, namely, those challenged (a) for being unreasonably onerous or oppressive and (b) for a manifestly improper balance of relevant considerations. Under the first of these, the courts in effect evaluate whether there has been a disproportionate *interference* with the applicant's rights or interests. Under the second, the exercise of balancing relevant considerations involves the courts in effect evaluating whether manifestly disproportionate *weight* has been attached to one or other considerations relevant to the decision.

12–071 As it is applied in its European context (by the European Court of Justice, the European Court of Human Rights and in some of the Member States of the European Union), there are two principal formulations by which proportionality is tested.[59] These are: (a) the balancing test and (b) the necessity test. There is also a third test which is occasionally applied, namely, (c) the suitability test.

> (1) *The balancing test* requires a balancing of the ends which an official decision attempts to achieve against the means applied to achieve them. This exercise requires an identification of the ends or purposes sought by the official decisions. In addition, it requires an identification of the means employed to achieve those ends, a task which frequently involves an assessment of the impact of the decision upon affected persons.[60] Different

---

NALGO was followed on this point by Simon Brown L.J. in *ex p. Smith*, at first instance: [1995] 4 All E.R. 427. Lord Templeman willing to apply proportionality if appropriate (which it was not) in *R. v. Independent Television Commission, ex p. TSW Broadcasting Ltd* [1996] E.M.L.R. 291.

[59] See paras 17–051 and 17–085 below for a fuller account of proportionality in E.C. law.

[60] In France the development of the principle of proportionality arose out of the case of *Ville Nouvelle Est. Ministre de l'équipement et du logement contre Fédération de défense des personnes concernées par le project actuellement denommée Ville Nouvelle Est.* C.E. Mai 28, 1971, Rec. 410 Concl. Braibant, in which compulsory purchase procedures were set in motion to acquire a site for a single residential and academic complex for the University of Lille. Although the Conseil d'Etat upheld the Minister's decision, it required the carrying out of a balance of costs and benefits (*le bilan coût-advantages*). Without interfering in the merits (*opportunités*) of the decision, it was stated that the Minister could not declare an operation to be in the public interest unless 'the interference with private property, the financial costs, and, where they arise, the attendant social inconveniences are not excessive having regard to the needs of the operation.' See also C.E. Octobre 20, 1972, *Societé Civile Sainte-Marie de l'Assumption*, Rec. 657, Concl. Morisot; R.D.P., 1973, 843, where the construction of a slip-road off an autoroute was held unlawful because regard had not been had to the interests of the inmates of a psychiatric hospital who would be disturbed by the use of the road on that site.

ends or purposes and different means will be accorded different weights. For example, in the context of European Community law, it would appear that where the purpose of an infringement of a fundamental norm, such as Article 28 of the E.C. Treaty,[61] is the protection of consumers,[62] or the health of animals,[63] then these purposes may be accorded less weight than a purpose such as the protection of human health.[64] Similarly, if the means pursued to achieve a measure involve a breach of a human right or the deprivation of a person's livelihood,[65] these factors are likely to be weighed more heavily than one that affects individuals in a more trivial manner. The application of the balancing test is well illustrated by the case of *Bela-Muhle Josef Bergmann v. Grows-Farm*,[66] where the Court of Justice held unlawful a Council Regulation[67] which made compulsory the use of skimmed milk powder in the feeding of livestock. The purpose of the Regulation was to diminish the surpluses of skimmed milk powder, but its effect, which was to make the cost to users three times that of the equivalent amount of vegetable feeding stuffs, was held disproportionate.

(2) *The necessity test* requires that, where a particular objective can be achieved by more than one available means, the least harmful of these means should be adopted to achieve a particular objective. Like the United States' principle of the "least restrictive alternative",[68] this aspect of proportionality requires public bodies to adopt those regulatory measures which cause the minimum injury to an individual or community. It only applies where more than one means is

---

[61] Which prohibits 'quantitative restrictions on imports and all measures having an equivalent effect.'

[62] Case 120/78 *Cassis de Dijon* [1979] E.C.R. 649.

[63] Case 40/82 *Commission v. U.K.* [1984] E.C.R. 2793.

[64] Case 266/267/87 *A.P.I.* [1989] E.C.R. 1295.

[65] Case 44/79 *Hauer* [1979] E.C.R. 3727.

[66] Case 114/76 [1977] E.C.R. 1211. See F. Snyder, *The Law of the Common Agricultural Policy* (1985) at 39, 56–60, 143–153.

[67] Regulation 563/76, [1976] O.J. L67/18.

[68] See Tribe, *American Constitutional Law* (1978), pp. 341–342. Professor Charles L. Black has argued expressly that the principle of proportionality applies to the interpretation of the American Bill of Rights: see 'On Reading and Using the Ninth Amendment' in *The Humane Imagination* (1986), at pp. 196–197. See the interesting case law on whether the Eighth Amendment to the U.S. Constitution, prohibiting 'cruel and unusual puris humeur' requires the application of a proportionality test. See esp. *Harmelin v. Michigan* III S.Ct. 2680 (1991). See (1992) 27 Harv. Civil Rts. & Civil Libs. L. Rev. 262.

available to implement the law's objective.[69] For example, in *Cassis de Dijon*[70] the Court of Justice held that a German measure totally prohibiting the marketing of a black-currant liqueur whose alcohol content fell below a required percentage was disproportionate. It was held that other measures, such as labelling the product, could achieve the same result by less restrictive means.

(3) *The suitability test* requires authorities to employ means which are appropriate to the accomplishment of a given law, and which are not in themselves incapable of implementation or unlawful. For example, in a case in Germany it was held that the police may not require the owner of kennels to reduce noise by keeping the dogs in closed rooms, in a manner inconsistent with the law relating to the protection of animals.[71]

12–072   Proportionality is also employed by the European Commission and Court of Human Rights as a general principle of law to interpret the provisions of the European Convention of Human Rights.[72] Two cases involving the United Kingdom will suffice to give an impression of the use of the principle: Article 10(1) of the Convention guarantees the right to freedom of expression and the right to receive and impart information and ideas "without interference by public authority." These rights may be limited under Article 10(2) by "such formalities, conditions, restrictions or penalties as are prescribed by law and are necessary in a democratic society,. . .".[73]

12–073   In the *Sunday Times (Thalidomide)* case,[74] the "necessity" of the House of Lords' injunction preventing the publication and dissemination of an article and information about pending Thalidomide litigation was examined using the test of proportionality. The Strasbourg Court had

---

[69] Thus in German law an innkeeper could not be fined for excessive noise emanating from his premises if the noise could be effectively controlled by advancing his closing hours. Decision of March 16, 1907, 17 BWVGHE 227.

[70] Case 120/78 *Cassis de Dijon* [1979] E.C.R. 649. See also Case 104/75 *de Peijper* [1976] E.C.R. 613; Case 33/74 *Binsbergen* [1974] E.C.R. 1299; Case 36/75 *Rutili* [1974] E.C.R. 1219.

[71] Decision of October 30, 1970, 27 OVG Luneburg E321.

[72] Cmd. 8969.

[73] "[I]n the interests of national security, territorial integrity or public safety, for the prevention of disorder or crime, for the protection of health or morals, for the protection of the reputation or rights of others, for preventing the disclosure of information received in confidence, or for maintaining the authority and impartiality of the judiciary."

[74] *Sunday Times v. United Kingdom* (1979–80) 2 E.H.R.R. 245.

to decide whether the "interference" complained of corresponded to a "pressing social need" and was "proportionate to the legitimate aim pursued" and in particular "necessary" in a democratic society to protect the authority of the judiciary. The Court held that the restraint imposed upon the applicants' freedom of expression "proves not to be proportionate to the legitimate aim pursued; it was not necessary in a democratic society for maintaining the authority of the judiciary."[75]

In *Lithgow and Others*,[76] the Court considered the adequacy of compensation paid to shipbuilding companies for the taking of their property under United Kingdom nationalisation legislation, in the light of Article 1 of the First Protocol to the European Convention. The principle of proportionality had been expressed in an earlier case, *Sporrong and Lönnroth*[77] in terms of the concept of "fair balance" required to be struck between the demands of the general interest of the community and the protection of the individual's fundamental rights. It was held in that case that such a balance would not be found if the person concerned had to bear "an individual and excessive burden."[78]

12–074

In *Lithgow*, the Court observed that:

12–075

> "Clearly, compensation terms are material to the assessment whether a fair balance has been struck between various interests at stake and, notably, whether or not a disproportionate burden has been imposed on the person who has been deprived of his possessions."[79]

In summary, the principle of proportionality as employed in the European context is essentially a device to evaluate two aspects of a decision:

12–076

(1) whether the relative merits of differing objectives or interests were appropriately weighed or "fairly balanced" (*e.g.* was the right to information fairly balanced against the need to protect the authority of the judiciary?);

(2) whether the measure in question was in the circumstances excessively restrictive or inflicted an unnecessary burden on affected persons (*e.g.* was the increased cost of skimmed milk

---

[75] Para. 67.

[76] *Lithgow v. United Kingdom*, May 22, 1984, Series A, No. 102.

[77] *Sporrong and Lönnroth v. Sweden*, September 23, 1982, Series A, No. 52.

[78] *Lithgow, op. cit.* n. 76 above, para. 120, p. 50.

[79] *ibid.*

powder unnecessarily burden-some on users? Could the measure have been achieved by a less restrictive alternative?).[80]

Intensity of review for proportionality

12–077 Does proportionality as applied in the various European contexts amount to a test of the merits of a decision, a test inappropriate to English judicial review? Does it, in other words, permit the court to balance the relative merits of a decision and then decide the question as if they, not the administrators, were the recipients of the power?

12–078 The principle of proportionality cannot, as Schwartze points out,[81] be equated with the principle of achieving the right balance. However, in some contexts the application of proportionality, in particular by the use of the test of "necessity" or "least restrictive alternative", as outlined above, might involve the courts, in some types of case, in a more intense evaluation of the merits of a case than they now exercise.

12–079 Recent cases challenging the British legislation prohibiting Sunday trading demonstrate the profound difficulties involved in the application of the pro-portionality test, even under European Community Law, in certain contexts. In *Stoke-on-Trent*,[82] holding that the Sunday trading legislation did not infringe the principle of proportionality, Hoffmann J. said that the "compromise adopted by the United Kingdom Parliament" (between the aim of preventing shop workers from feeling under an obligation to work on Sundays, as against inconvenience and loss of trade for the economy) was not "untenable", and was "capable of forming the rational basis for

---

[80] Compare the similar approach taken in the important Canadian case *R. v. Oakes* (1986) 26 D.L.R. (4th) 200. Section 1 of the Canadian Charter guarantees the rights and freedoms there set out 'subject only to such reasonable limits prescribed by law as can demonstrably be justified in a free and democratic society'. It was held by Dickson J. that s.1 required a 'proportionality test', containing three components: (1) the measures must be 'carefully designed to achieve the objective in question'; (2) the means, 'even if rationally connected' to the objective should impair 'as little as possible' the right in question; and (3) there must be proportionality between the effects of the measures and the objective. See Mullender, 'The Principle of Proportionality in Canadian Charter Adjudication', (1993) Bracton L.J. 25; Beatty, *Talking Heads and The Supremes: The Canadian Production of Constitutional Review* (1990); P. Hogg, 'Interpreting the Charter of Rights' (1990) 28 Osgoode Hall L.J. 817. But see A. Hutchinson 'Waiting for Coraf' (1991) 41 U. of Toronto L.J. 350.

[81] J. Schwartze, *European Administrative Law* (1992), p. 860.

[82] *Stoke-on-Trent City Council and Norwich City Council v. B & Q plc* [1991] Ch. 48.

legislation".[83] The *Wednesbury*-like formulation of this test met with the strong disapproval of Advocate-General van Gerven[84] and was not applied by the European Court of Justice, although the Court did not disagree with Hoffmann J.'s conclusions on the merits of the case.[85]

Under proportionality, different margins of appreciation apply in **12–080** different circumstances. Varying levels of the intensity of review will be appropriate in different categories of case and this will, in turn, correspond to the different formulations of the test (balancing, necessity, suitability) outlined above. In many cases, decision-makers enjoy a wide margin of appreciation and courts will strike down a decision on the grounds of proportionality only when the balance was manifestly inappropriate or when the rights or interests of the complainant have been subjected to an unnecessarily excessive burden.

Under European Community law the margin of appreciation will be **12–081** lower (and thus the intensity of review greater) where what is in issue involves a breach of a fundamental norm. Thus, when a national measure offends a fundamental provision of the Treaty, such as the prohibitions against free movement of goods or workers, all derogations will be interpreted restrictively.[86] In a sense the courts are involved here in the assessment of "legality", simply deciding whether the decision amounts to a breach of a provision of the Treaty, in the same way as an English court would decide whether a decision is in breach of a power authorised by a statute. In contrast, when what is in issue is a breach of a less fundamental provision (such as a directive of the Commission under the Common Agricultural Policy) the Court

---

[83] *ibid.* at 63–65, Hoffmann J. felt that these were 'essentially legislative questions involving balance of interests and the judiciary cannot do more than decide whether the view of the legislature is one which could be reasonably held. 'He also said that' the function of the court is to review the acts of the legislature but not to substitute its own policies or values', *ibid.* See also Case 145/88 *Torfaen B.C. v. B & Q plc* [1990] 2 Q.B. 19.

[84] *Stoke-on-Trent City Council and Norwich City Council v. B & Q plc* [1993] A.C. 900, 944–45.

[85] See Arnull (1991) 16 E.L.Rev. 112. For a useful account of the Sunday trading cases, see R. Rawlings, 'The Eurolaw Game: Some Deductions from a Saga' (1993) J. Law and Soc. 309. In Cases C-267 & 268/9 *Keck* [1993] E.C.R. 1 6097, the Court took all 'selling arrangements' outside of the scope of Art. 30 [now renumbered Art. 28] altogether. Perhaps this will (and perhaps it was designed to) avoid forcing national courts in the future to apply proportionality in making 'legislative' choices.

[86] See, for example, Case 36/75 *Rutili v. French Minister of the Interior* [1975] E.C.R. 1219, where an Italian resident in France who had allegedly indulged in subversive activities was issued with a residence permit subject to a prohibition on residence in certain Departments. The Court held that the exceptions in Art. 48(3) to the right to the free movement of workers—on grounds of public policy, public security or public health—must be interpreted strictly, and that interference with this right could be justified only by a 'genuine and sufficiently serious threat to public policy necessary for the protection of those interests in a democratic society'.

may allow the decision-maker a wider margin of appreciation.[87] More significantly, in respect of measures involving the European Commission in complex economic assessment, such as in the implementation of anti-dumping measures, the European Court has established that it will not simply substitute its own discretion for that of the Commission. Instead, the Court tends to grant to the Commission a wide margin of assessment in such a context and only attacks the substance of a measure on the grounds that it infringes a general principle of law (including the principle of proportionality) if it can be shown that the conclusions of the Commission were manifestly or patently wrong.[88] Thus one recent survey has noted that, in the application of the principle of proportionality in Community anti-dumping law, the European Court has shown "extreme self restraint."[89]

12–082   In the context of the law relating to the European Convention, when a fundamental human right such as free speech has been breached, the interference must be positively justified by a "pressing social need".[90] The margin of assessment permitted the decision-maker in this context is, similarly, not uniform. It will depend upon the subject matter, that is the nature of the interests in question.[91]

---

[87] See, *e.g.* Case C-331/88 *Fedesa* [1990] E.C.R. I-4023, where the Court held that, in respect of judicial review of a directive under the Common Agricultural Policy, legality could only be affected if 'the measure is manifestly inappropriate having regard to the objective which the competent institution is seeking to pursue.' See also Case C-280/93 *Germany v. Council (Bananas)* [1994] E.C.R. I-4973 at 5068, 89–98. For a fuller exposition of this interesting argument in relation to E.C. law, see Gráinne de Burca, 'The Principle of Proportionality and its Application in E.C. Law' (1993) 13 *Yearbook of European Law* 105; P. Craig, *Administrative Law* (1994) pp. 418–421; N. Emiliou, *The Concept of Proportionality in European Law* (1995).

[88] See Case 57/72 *Westzucker v. EVS Zucher* [1973] E.C.R. 321; Case 136/77 *Rache v. HZA Mainz* [1978] E.C.R. 1245.

[89] A. Egger, 'The Principle of Proportionality in Community Anti-dumping Law' (1993) 18 E.L. Rev. 367.

[90] *Sunday Times v. U.K.* n. 74 above.

[91] In some cases two fundamental rights may be in conflict (such as the right to impart information and the protection of life). See, *e.g. Open Door and Dublin Well Women v. Ireland*, A/246 (1992) 15 E.H.R.R. 244 where the Court of Human Rights held that the Irish Supreme Court's injunction forbidding information about abortions offended Art. 10 of the Convention in spite of a 'wide margin of appreciation' enjoyed by national authorities in matters of morals and the nature of human life; *cf.* Case C-159/90 *Society for the Protection of Unborn Children Ireland Ltd v. Stephen Grogan and Others* [1991] 3 C.M.L.R. 849.

Proportionality in English law?

The following propositions may now be advanced: **12–083**

(1) To the extent that Community law is directly effective, and to the extent to which the European Convention applies as a treaty obligation, proportionality is a principle of law which is and must be applied by the English courts.

(2) Proportionality is already applied, albeit mostly implicitly, as a standard by which to assess the lawfulness of certain administrative decisions. English law does, on occasion, already incorporate proportionality in each of its meanings: (a) an appropriate balancing between means and ends; (b) necessity, or least restrictive alternative; and (c) suitability.

    (a) *The balancing test*
        This formulation of proportionality is applied in two situations, both of which coincide with those applied in the context of European Community law and as applied by the European Court of Human Rights.[92] The situations involve: (i) excessively onerous penalties or infringements of rights or interests and (ii) manifest imbalance of relevant considerations.

        (i) *Penalties and infringements on rights or duties* When the English courts review a decision on the ground of its oppressive impact on affected parties,[93] they have sometimes expressly used the language of proportionality. It has always been used in the area of sentencing, where the punishment must fit the crime,[94] but proportionality has been alluded to

---

[92] See para. 12–071 above.

[93] See paras 12-044–12-052 above.

[94] See generally, A. Ashworth, *Sentencing and Criminal Justice* (1992), Chap. 4. See, *e.g. R. v. Admiralty Board of the Defence Council ex p. Coupland* [1996] C.O.D. 147 (sentence of dismissal from service wholly disproportionate to offence); *R. v. Highbury Corner Magistrates, ex p. Rabhani* [1996] 7 C.L. (magistrates acted *Wednesbury* unreasonably and made a decision that no reasonable magistrates properly directing themselves could have reached on the evidence before them in refusing a downward variation of maintenance order). But see *R. v. Secretary of State for the Home Department, ex p. Tremayne,* May 2, 1996 (unreported). (Home Secretary's decision to introduce random urine sampling of prisoners was not irrational. The approach balanced the interests of prisoners against the need to address the problem of drug taking). See further, *R. v. Secretary of State for the Home Department ex p. Singh (Manvinder)* [1996] Imm. A.R. 41; *Kalunga v. Secretary of State for the Home Department* [1994] Imm. A.R. 585; *Whitchelo v. Secretary of State for the Home Department,* unreported, April 2, 1996.

more recently in the context of administrative penalties as well.[95]

Lord Denning would have struck down a decision suspending a stallholder's licence on the ground that "the punishment is altogether excessive and out of proportion to the occasion"[96] A resolution of a local authority banning a member of the public from local authority property was held to be "out of proportion to what the applicant had done",[97] and proportionality was expressly used to test the government's suspension of the permits of Romanian pilots.[98] Recently Laws J. held that when justices were determining what sentence to impose upon a person who had failed to pay his nondomestic rates, "sufficient regard should be had to the principle of proportionality".[99] He also refused to prohibit the publication of a report critical of the applicant by the Advertising Standards Authority pending a judicial

---

[95] In India it has recently been held (in a case concerned with the quantum of punishment imposed by a court martial) that 'The doctrine of proportionality, as part of the concept of judicial review, would ensure that even on an aspect which is otherwise within the exclusive province of the Court-Martial, if the decision of the Court even as to sentence is an outrageous defiance of logic, then the sentence would not be immune from correction'. Per Venkatachalia J. in *Ramjit Thakur v. Union of India*, A.I.R. 1987 S.C. 2386, 2392. S. Sorabjee says that this decision 'Lays the seeds of the proportionality principle in Indian administrative law without recourse to any constitutional provision': see 'Obliging Government to control itself: Recent Developments in Indian Administrative Law' [1994] P.L. 39, 48.

[96] *R. v. Barnsley M.B.C., ex p. Hook* [1976] 1 W.L.R. 1052, 1057. The offence was urinating in the street and using offensive language. The Court of Appeal struck down the suspension on the ground of the lack of a fair hearing. See also *R. v. Secretary of State for the Home Department, ex p. Benwell* [1984] I.C.R. 723, 736 where Hodson J. said that 'in an extreme case an administrative or quasi-administrative penalty can be attacked on the ground that it was so disproportionate to the offence as to be perverse'. And see J. Beatson 'Proportionality' (1988) 104 L.Q.R. 180.

[97] *R. v. Brent L.B.C., ex p. Assegai* (1987) 151 L.G.R. 891. The reason for the ban was the applicant's unruly behaviour at previous meetings.

[98] *R. v. Secretary of State for Transport, ex p. Pegasus Holidays (London) Ltd and Airbro (U.K.) Ltd* [1988] 1 W.L.R. 990.

[99] *R. v. Highbury Corner JJ., ex p. Uchendu, The Times*, January 28, 1994. In a different area of law, the Court of Appeal (*per* Neill L.J.) has recently held that juries in libel actions 'should be asked to ensure that any award was proportionate to the damage which the plaintiff had suffered.' In the circumstances an award of £250,000 was excessive 'by any objective standards of reasonable compensation or necessity or proportionality'. *Rantzen v. Mirror Group Newspapers and Others* [1994] Q.B. 670. See also *Commissioner of Customs and Excise v. Peninsular & Oriental Steam Navigation Company* [1994] S.T.C. 259, where it was held in relation to a penalty imposed for a serious misdeclaration of VAT that only in the most limited circumstances will the doctrine of proportionality be applied to penalties provided for by national law.

review unless there was a "pressing ground, in the language of Strasbourg, a pressing social need to restrain the public body from carrying out its functions in the ordinary way."[1]

Mention has been made above to conditions attached to planning permissions struck down because unduly onerous or oppressive.[2] Another test of a valid condition is that it should "fairly and reasonably relate" to the development for which permission is given. This requirement is separate from the requirement that the condition not be unreasonable.[3] In the *Newbury* case,[4] planning permission was obtained for the change of the use from an aircraft hangar to storage. A condition required the building to be demolished before a given date. The condition survived a challenge for both illegality (the demolition served a proper planning purpose of improving the appearance of the area) and unreasonableness (it was not in the circumstances oppressive). The condition, however, failed "fairly and reasonably to relate to the development", presumably because the requirement of demolition, a "building operation" under the Act, was too remote, or insufficiently connected, to the mere change of use which was sought and granted. Perhaps a more precise way of expressing this concept is that a condition must have a proportionate relationship to the permission.[5]

---

[1] R. v. Advertising Standards Authority Ltd, ex p. Vernon Organisation [1992] 1 W.L.R. 1289.

[2] Para. 12–046 above.

[3] The test was first approved in Pyx Granite Co. v. Ministry of Housing and Local Government [1958] 1 Q.B. 554 and accepted by the House of Lords in Fawcett Properties Ltd v. Buckingham C.C. [1961] A.C. 636 and applied by the House of Lords in Newbury D.C. v. Secretary of State for the Environment [1980] A.C. 528.

[4] ibid. But this test has recently been held by the House of Lords not to apply to planning obligations. Tesco Stores Ltd v. Secretary of State for the Environment [1995] 2 All E.R. 636.

[5] The notion of fair and reasonable relation may also arise in the context of the question whether a consideration taken into account in deciding whether to grant a planning permission is 'material'. In R. v. Westminster City Council, ex p. Monahan [1990] 1 Q.B. 187 it was held that a planning advantage or gain obtained through a planning obligation (in that case the profits from the proposed adjacent development being applied to improve facilities at Covent Garden opera house) were material to planning. However, if the advantage offered was at the other end of town, it may fail to be material because too remote or insufficiently connected to the site in question. In the United States, conditions attached to the equivalent of planning permissions

(ii) *Manifest imbalance of relevant considerations* We have seen that the courts do intervene, albeit sparingly, where excessive or manifestly inadequate weight is accorded to a relevant consideration.[6] Proportionality is here applied as a test to ensure that the proper *process* of decision-making was carried out; that the relevant considerations were properly balanced. Recent decisions on deportations, although employing the language of *Wednesbury* make it clear that the courts might in a suitable case interfere with the Home Secretary's decision if the required "balancing exercise" (weighing the deportation as "conducive to the public good" against the deportee's "well founded fear of prosecution" in the country to which he is removed) was not properly carried out. The Court of Appeal held that a decision could be invalidated if some "trivial danger to national security" was invoked to justify a deportation where there was a present threat to the life of the deportee if the deportation took place.[7]

(b) *The necessity test*

As in the case law of the European Community, proportionality in English law has greatest potential force in connection with infringements of fundamental human rights. Many of these rights are necessary for the preservation and the vitality of a democratic society. The courts will wish to guard against any unnecessary interference with those rights and will exercise a close scrutiny upon any derogations. In cases involving human

---

which have no 'nexus' with the permission granted may violate a constitutional right not to have property 'taken' without compensation. In *Dolan v. City of Tizard*, No. 93–518, 62 U.S.L.W. 4576 (June 24, 1994), the Supreme Court held that such a condition should have a 'rough proportionality' to the impact of the proposed development.

[6] See paras 12-014–12-017. In *R. v. Chief Constable of Sussex, ex p. International Trader's Ferry* [1997] 3 W.L.R. 132, Kennedy L.J. said that in that case proportionality and irrationality would 'in practice yield the same result'. And see the cases cited under 12–058 above. See also *R. v. Secretary of State for Health, ex p. R.P. Scherer Ltd*; Rt Hon. Lord Hoffmann 'A Sense of Proportion', (1997) The Irish Jurist, 49.

[7] *R. v. Secretary of State for the Home Department, ex p. Chahal* [1995] 1 W.L.R. 526 (on the facts the decision was held to be properly balanced.) See also *R. v. Housing Benefit Review Board of Sutton L.B.C., ex p. Keegan* [1992] C.O.D. 450 (Board's refusal of housing benefit unreasonable because it had attached a 'disproportionate weight' to applicant's inability to pay rent.)

rights, the courts may do well to use the "necessity test", demanding that the infringement of the human right in question be the least restrictive alternative.

The reserve expressed towards proportionality in *Brind*,[8] was not shared in the recent case of *Leech*.[9] We have seen[10] that in that case the Court of Appeal upheld the "constitutional right" of the prisoner to access to the courts. The question was whether the interference with a prisoner's mail permitted by the regulations was broad enough to infringe that right. The test adopted by Steyn L.J. to decide that question was whether there was a "self-evident and pressing need"[11] for such a power. None was demonstrated. The language of proportionality was thus explicit and the Court of Appeal even went so far as to consider the jurisprudence of the European Court of Justice on the matter which, although not directly binding, "reinforces a conclusion that we have arrived at in the light of the principles of our domestic jurisprudence".[12]

Other cases, outside of the field of human rights, have also used the test of necessity. For example, planning conditions have been struck down because a less restrictive or less onerous alternative could be provided— such as would permit compensation to be paid to the owner of the land.[13] In another case, compulsory purchase of land has been invalidated because the authority was able voluntarily to acquire other equally suitable land.[14]

---

[8] Above, n. 22 and paras 12-057–12-061 and 12-070. Had a proportionality test been applied in *Brind* it might well have been held that the ban on direct broadcasting was not disproportionate. After all, the end pursued by the directives was the weighty prevention of terrorism and the means used to obtain it were carefully circumscribed. (Whether the means were an effective measure is another question.)

[9] *R. v. Secretary of State for the Home Department, ex p. Leech (No. 2)* [1994] Q.B. 198, CA.

[10] Above, para. 12-058.

[11] *ibid.* at 550. Also referred to as 'objective need' or 'demonstrable need'. *Ibid.* at 551.

[12] *ibid.* at 554, *per* Steyn L.J. The case referred to was *Campbell v. U.K.* (1993) 15 E.H.R.R. 137.

[13] See *Hall and Co. v. Shoreham-by-Sea U.D.C.* [1969] 1 W.L.R. 240 (condition requiring dedication of access road to public); *R. v. Hillingdon L.B.C., ex p. Royco Homes Ltd* [1974] 1 Q.B. 720 (conditions in effect requiring applicant to provide council housing when alternative powers under the Housing Acts would allow compensation to be paid). But for a case where alternative powers permitting compensation were not required, see *Westminster Bank v. Beverley B.C.* [1971] A.C. 508. See also *Hovering Gravels Ltd v. Secretary of State for the Environment* [1975] Q.B. 754; *R. v. Exeter C.C., ex p. J.L. Thomas and Co. Ltd* [1989] 3 P.L.R. 61.

[14] *Brown v. Secretary of State for the Environment* (1978) 40 P. & C.R. 285. See also *Prest v. Secretary of State for Wales* (1982) 81 L.G.R. 193. But see *R. v. Secretary of State for Transport, ex p. de Rothschild* [1989] 1 All E.R. 933. See also *Webb v. Minister of Housing*

In a recent case it was held that the decision to delist a company, as opposed to "lesser measures" (such as the continuation of the suspension of the shares) was, in the circumstances, and having taken into account the interests of the shareholders, "not disproportionate to the damage which it was designed to prevent either at common law or under Community law."[15]

(c) *The Suitability Test*

English law has applied a test analogous to suitability. One instance involved a byelaw being held invalid because its implementation was not possible.[16]

(3) The intensity of review under the principle of proportionality need not necessarily eliminate or even reduce the reserve the *Wednesbury* test in relation to interference with the merits of an official decision. The so called "margin of appreciation" is not, in many cases, obviously different from the threshold under

---

and Local Government [1965] 1 W.L.R. 755 (unreasonable for local authority to acquire more land than needed).

[15] *R. v. International Stock Exchange of the United Kingdom and the Republic of Ireland, ex p. Else (1982) Ltd* [1993] Q.B. 534, *per* Popplewell J. Proportionality was applied here as 'an aspect of rationality'. See also the example given by Zamir from an Israeli case, *Laor v. Board of Censorship for Films and Plays* (1987) 41 (1) P.D. 421, where a total ban on a film causing 'near certainty of substantial damage' to public order was held disproportionate where less restrictive measures (such as the cutting out of certain scenes) could have dealt with the problem. I. Zamir, 'Unreasonableness, Balance of Interests and Proportionality' (1993) Tel-Aviv Studies in Law 131. Recently, proportionality has been formally recognised by the Supreme Court of Israel as a separate ground (different from unreasonableness) for the review of administrative action. The Court held that the proportionality test consists of three elements. First, the means adopted by the authority in exercising its power should rationally fit the legislative purpose. Secondly, the authority should adopt such means that do not injure the individual more than necessary. And thirdly, the injury caused to the individual by the exercise of the power should not be disproportional to the benefit which accrues to the general public. Under this test the Court recently invalidated some administrative decisions. See, for example *Ben-Atiya v. Minister of Education* (1995) 49 (5) P.D. 1. And see I. Zamir and Z. Zysblat, *Public Law in Israel* (1996), especially sections 2, 3 and 11. See also *R. v. Tamworth JJ., ex p. Walsh, The Times,* March 3, 1994. (Justices acted unreasonably in committing to custody a solicitor who criticised the listing system in court. Three alternative measures were available: ordering his removal; reporting him to the Law Society, or adjourning the matter. They had used 'a sledgehammer to crack a nut'). See also *R. v. Camden L.B.C., ex p. Cran* [1995] R.T.R. 346 (consultation with residents about car-parking scheme deficient because 'there had been no recognition of the possibility let alone the fact that a number of the beneficial results of introducing full controls might have been well achieved by other means', *per* McCullogh J.).

[16] *Arlidge v. Mayor etc. of Islington* [1909] 2 K.B. 133 (the byelaw requiring the annual cleaning of lodging houses unreasonable when access not possible). And see further para. 12–053 above.

the *Wednesbury* formulation. Outside of the field of human rights, proportionality should normally only be applied if the means are manifestly or grossly out of balance in relation to the end sought. The judicial exercise remains in the nature of review rather than appeal.

We have seen that the margin of appreciation in respect of the *Wednesbury* test is not uniform. It differs in accordance with a number of different factors, with a wide margin accorded the decision-maker in cases involving the allocation of resources[17] and a low margin in cases involving an infringement of fundamental human rights.[18] Such a distinction appears to be paralleled in European law, where, as we have seen, the courts reduce the margin of appreciation in respect of a derogation from a fundamental norm (such as a derogation of or exception of a fundamental provision of the E.C. Treaty or of the European Convention of Human Rights)[19] and widen the margin of appreciation in respect of delegated decision-making involving complex economic assessment.[20]

(4) Should proportionality be explicitly adopted in English law, as a separate ground of review, or as a particular test of *Wednesbury* unreasonableness? As we have seen, acceptance of proportionality does not necessarily imply an abandonment of the judicial restraint associated with the *Wednesbury* formulation. It would, however, provide a useful instrument to delineate more precisely its scope. Since the principle is already applied in the large and probably growing area of directly effective Community law, and in respect of human rights questions where the Convention applies directly, and since the test is already applied in other cases without explicit mention, the coherence and comprehensibility of administrative law would surely be improved by an explicit recognition of its application.

---

[17] See paras 12-054–12-056 above.
[18] See paras 12-057–12-061 above.
[19] See para. 12–081 above.
[20] Para. 12–081 above.

CONCLUSIONS

12–084 (1) There are three distinct ways in which power may be unreasonably exercised or abused:

(a) Where there is a defect in the decision-making process—in the way the decision was reached or the factors taken into account in reaching the decision. These include:

(i) decisions taken in bad faith;
(ii) irrational decisions—those which are arbitrary, or inadequately justified or reasoned;
(iii) decisions where relevant considerations are manifestly inappropriately balanced.

(b) Where there is an infringement of principles governing the exercise of power in a constitutional democracy. These include:

(i) the principle of legal certainty (which requires the fulfilment of legitimate expectations);
(ii) the principle of equality (which requires decisions to be consistently applied and prohibits the making of unjustifiable distinctions between individuals).

(c) Where the impact of the decision is oppressive or an unnecessarily onerous infringement of a person's rights or interests.

(2) The intensity of review; or margin of appreciation, differs in accordance with the kind of decision made. Review is most intense in cases where human rights are infringed and least intense where decisions involve matters of social and economic policy.

(3) Obtaining an electoral "mandate" for a decision, or the approval by resolution of Parliament, may provide evidence of the reasonableness of a decision (but not of its legality). But such evidence should not be regarded as conclusive.

(4) Where the standard of unreasonableness is provided by statute, the intensity of review will depend upon the context of the statutory scheme as a whole.

(5) The principle of proportionality applies as a test in the evaluation of decisions subject to directly effective European Community law and to the provisions of the European Convention of Human Rights where it applies as a treaty obligation. Proportionality requires the following:

(a) appropriate balancing between means and ends;

(b) necessity, or the use of the least restrictive alternative; and (rarely)

(c) suitability.

(6) Proportionality in all of the above senses is already effectively applied in English law, normally under the name of *Wednesbury* unreasonableness, irrationality, abuse of power or other terms. It is particularly apposite to evaluate decisions which:

(a) involve a manifest imbalance of relevant considerations (item (1)(a)(iii) above); or

(b) involve oppressive or excessively onerous penalties or infringements of rights or interests (item 1(c) above).

(7) The intensity of review under proportionality in European Community law and under the law pertaining to the European Convention on Human Rights varies in accordance with the issue, in a way that is not markedly different from that in English law in comparable situations.

(8) The express application of proportionality in English law would not imply an abandonment of the restraint appropriate to the judicial review of discretionary powers. It would have the advantage of creating a unity between the standards of review under directly effective European Community law and other English law, and would make more explicit and comprehensible the tests already applied.

PART III

PROCEDURES AND REMEDIES

PART III

PROCEDURES AND
REMEDIES

INTRODUCTION

A modern system of judicial review requires not only principles to set **III–001** the boundaries of lawful official action, but also to secure their effective implementation by means of adequate procedures and remedies. The importance of procedural or adjectival rules and principles is shown by the long-standing interest in their reform. While the principles of judicial review have been ignored, procedures and remedies have been considered twice by the Law Commission of England and Wales[1]; by JUSTICE, the British Section of the International Commission of Jurists[2]; and by Lord Woolf in the *Access to Justice* report which presaged the radical new Civil Procedure Rules which came into force in April 1999. The chapters which follow are primarily concerned with stating and evaluating the formal powers, procedural rules and practices of the court. Their context must, however, be recognised. First, as can be seen from Chapter 13, the starting point for understanding the development of remedies and procedures in English law public law cannot be first principles or rational design. Rather it is to be gleaned from an understanding of the piecemeal development from a system of monarchical government where the King's courts exercised discretion to dispense justice to deserving supplicants. Even when modernisation came in the twentieth century, it was, in typical English fashion, carried out by reference to what went before it, not by starting afresh.

A second important context is an understanding of what actually **III–002** happens outside the courts and the formal procedural rules. Only very recently has there begun to be any empirical investigation of these matters, yet they are clearly of vital importance if we are to know how effective any proposed further reforms will be. For instance, in practice, access to the courts may be determined as much by the

---

[1] See para. 13–063 *et seq.*
[2] See para. 13–065.

availability of legal aid as by the rules of standing or the requirement that an applicant for judicial review under Order 53 must first obtain the permission of the court. We must avoid a situation where in practice only the very poor, the very rich or those supported by interest groups or other bodies such as the Equal Opportunities Commission can afford to incur the financial burdens of public law litigation. The relationship between the formal procedural rules and the process of negotiated settlement is also of great importance, though little is known about it.

III–003   A third context for the adjectival rules and practices are the values and public policies which underpin them. Procedures and remedies of public law are by no means neutral in their intent or result. Different emphasis may be given to facilitating access to the courts; assisting in the management of the court's caseload; protecting the executive from unmeritorious challenges or from the grant of remedies which, though desired by an aggrieved person, may be detrimental to the wider public interest.[3]

Remedies

III–004   What remedies should be at the disposal of a court supervising the public law functions of the modern state?[4] First, the court should be able to set aside (quash) an unlawful decision. Secondly, it should be able to refer the matter back to the decision maker for further consideration in the light of the court's judgment. In some circumstances it might be desirable to permit the court, even though it is exercising review rather than appeal powers, to substitute its own decision for that of the impugned one.[5] Thirdly, the court should be able to declare the rights of the parties, perhaps also on an interim basis until it is able to consider the matter fully. Fourthly, the court needs power to direct that any of the parties do, or refrain from doing, any act in relation to the particular matter. In addition, compensation or restitution may be needed where a citizen has suffered loss as the result of unlawful administrative action. Finally, effective interim remedies—to "hold the ring" until full determination of the matter—are essential.

III–005   Most, but not all, of these remedies are available in the High Court in England and Wales, though they are often known by antiquated

---

[3] See further para. 14–040 *et seq.*

[4] For a clear statutory statement, see s. 30 of [Queensland's] Judicial Review Act 1991. Discussed by T.H. Jones (1993) 12 C.J.Q. 256

[5] See Law Commission Consultation Paper No. 126, Chap 13; *Administrative Law: Judicial Review and Statutory Appeals*, Law Com. No. 226, para. 3.16.

names which may sometimes be apt to confuse. The prerogative orders (certiorari, prohibition and mandamus) are now merely forms of relief and most of the technical rules governing their availability have rightly been abandoned. The space devoted to detailed consideration of these remedies in this edition of this work is accordingly much reduced.[6] The same process of simplification is also evident in relation to injunctions and declarations in public law proceedings. Gaps remain. For many reformers, one of the largest is the limited rights to compensation in English law for unlawful administrative acts.

Procedures

Most common law jurisdictions have modernised the procedures through which aggrieved persons can enforce public law rights or duties owed to them. In England and Wales reforms have been piecemeal and there is sometimes a bewildering array of routes into court for a person challenging the validity of a decision of a body exercising public law functions. **III–006**

This book focuses on the main public law litigation procedure—Order 53 now contained in Schedule 1 to the Civil Procedure Rules.[7] There are, however, many other procedures including applications for the writ of habeas corpus, various kinds of appeals from tribunals and ministers to the High Court and statutory applications to quash certain orders of local authorities and ministers.[8]

In April 1999, a "revolutionary set" of Civil Procedure Rules (CPR) came into force governing all civil cases in the High Court and county courts.[9] This new procedural code was made by statutory instrument under the terms of the Civil Proceedure Act 1997 in order to implement recommendations made by Lord Woolf's inquiry into improving civil litigation procedures in England and Wales.[10] The revolution did not at its outset sweep away the existing High Court public law procedures. As with some other specialised forms of

---

[6] The purpose of the technical limitations on the availability of the prerogative orders was to set boundaries to the types of decision which fell within the court's supervisory jurisdiction. A different, but equally complex body of case law—the public/private divide considered in Chap. 3—now performs this role.

[7] Prior to April 1999, Order 53 was part of the Rules of Supreme Court, the procedural rules which used to govern litigation in the High Court.

[8] For detailed consideration of all of these, see further Richard Gordon *et al, Judicial Review and Crown Office Practice* (1999). The historical development of some of these procedures are considered in Chap. 13, below.

[9] R.L. Turner, *The Civil Procedure Rules: a White Book Service* (1999), p. vii.

[10] *Access to Justice: a final report to the Lord Chancellor* (1996).

litigation, the procedures contained in the former Rules of the Supreme Court for making applications for judicial review (along with other public law procedures) are retained in the CPR with only minor drafting amendments.[11] Judicial review in England and Wales therefore continues to be governed by "Order 53", though many of the broad principles contained in the CPR now apply to applications for judicial review.[12]

For an area of law often concerned with the vindication of group rights, and with the public interest, the procedures that currently exist are curiously wedded to procedural models developed in private law—not least in the failure to provide any effective mechanism for the wider public interests (apart from the interests of the particular applicant and respondent) to be represented before the court.

The impact of Europe on remedies and procedures

III–007   A major challenge for the future is to reconcile the different traditions and values of the English procedures and remedies with those of the European Community and European Convention on Human Rights. Both organisations have found English procedures lacking. The writ of habeas corpus does not provide an "effective remedy" under the Convention.[13] Rules that prevented coercive remedies being granted against the Crown have been held to impair the effectiveness of Community law.[14] Other disparities seem bound to occur in the future, perhaps in the context of time-limits or the rules of standing. As with developments in the substantive principles of judicial review,[15] there is little to commend the development of different rules of public law litigation in England and Wales, with one set of procedures and remedies applying to Community law matters, another to litigation under the Human Rights Act, 1998 and another to purely domestic issues. Reconciling these differences will be a key challenge in the coming years.

---

[11] CPR, Pt 50(3) and Schedule 1.

[12] See para. 14–001, below.

[13] *X v. United Kingdom* (1982) 4 E.C.H.R. 188.

[14] See Chap. 17.

[15] See Chap. 12.

CHAPTER 13

THE HISTORICAL DEVELOPMENT OF JUDICIAL REVIEW REMEDIES AND PROCEDURES

INTRODUCTION

This Chapter explains, in outline, the historical development of the **13–001** procedures for initiating what we now call "judicial review" and the remedies at the disposal of the court. While many other countries whose legal systems are based on those of England and Wales have undertaken root and branch reform to the supervisory jurisdiction of their courts, the process of modernising judicial review remedies and procedures in England and Wales has so far been piecemeal and more superficial. Section 29(1) of the Supreme Court Act 1981, which puts the High Court's general power of judicial review on a statutory footing, does so by reference to the pre-existing common law powers of the court:

"The High Court shall have jurisdiction to make orders of mandamus, prohibition and certiorari in those classes of cases in which it had power to do so immediately before the commencement of this Act."[1]

To understand why the current procedural and remedial arrangements are as they are, one therefore needs to delve back in time.

THE WRIT SYSTEM

One of the central characteristics of the English common law was the **13–002** writ. In the earliest times, the royal writs were sealed governmental documents, drafted in a crisp, business-like manner, by which the

---

[1] This re-enacts section 7 of the Administration of Justice (Miscellaneous Provisions) Act 1938 which turned the prerogative 'writs' of mandamus, prohibition and certiorari—explained below—into 'orders'.

King conveyed notifications or orders.[2] Certiorari[3] was essentially a royal demand for information; the King, wishing to be certified of some matter, orders that the necessary information be provided for him. Thus, the King wishes to be more fully informed of allegations of extortion made by his subjects in Lincoln, and therefore appoints commissioners to inquire into them.[4] The Calendar of Inquisitions mentions numerous writs of certiorari, addressed to the escheator[5] or the sheriff, to make inquisitions; the earliest are for the year 1260.[6] When Parliament grants Edward II one foot-soldier for every township, the writ addressed to the sheriffs to send in returns of their townships to the Exchequer is a writ of certiorari.[7] It was, in fact, one of the King's own writs, used for general governmental purposes.

13–003   In early times, the King also issued countless innominate writs that included the word "mandamus"—"the autocratic head of a vast administrative system will have occasion to 'mandamus' his subjects many times in the course of a day"[8]—but it seems probable that the connection between most of these royal mandates and the modern judicial writ was verbal only. Moreover, the writs called mandamus that appear in the early law books are concerned not with private grievances at all, but with steps to be taken by the escheator or the sheriff in connection with possible accretions to the royal revenues.

13–004   Subjects unattracted to the justice dispensed by the "antiquated and archaic process" of the local courts came in increasing numbers to seek a remedy from the King himself, in the form of a royal writ. In this way, it has been noted, "arbitrary, even irresponsible interventions in law suits" took place.[9] By the middle of the twelfth century, such royal interventions became judicialised and redress was obtained through the King's Court rather than from the King himself. Eventually, writs came to be issued in certain standard forms, collected in the Register of Writs. Each was designed to deal with a particular type of grievance. New forms of writs were capable of creation only by the

---

[2] R.C. Van Caenegem, *Royal Writs in England from the Conquest to Glanville: Studies in the Early History of the Common Law* (Seldon Society, 1959), p. v. and Part Two.

[3] The word is not, apparently, of classical origin: Du Cange, *Glossarium Mediae et Infimae Latinitatis*, Vol. 2.

[4] *Placitorum Abbreviatio* 155 (49 Hen. 3).

[5] *Cf. Register of Original Writs, et seq.*, 293, 296; for history of the escheator, see W.A. Morris and J.R. Strayer, *The English Government at Work, 1327–36* (1947), Vol. ii, pp. 109–167.

[6] *Calendar of Inquisitions*, Vol. i, pp. 130, 131.

[7] *Inquisitions and Assessments Relating to Feudal Aids*, Vol. i, p. 16; see also Introduction, p. xxiii.

[8] Jenks (1923) 32 Yale L.J. 530.

[9] See, generally, R.C. Van Caenegem, *The Birth of the English Common Law* (2nd ed., 1988), esp. p. 30.

Chancellor. By the time of Bracton,[10] it could be said that a remedy from the King's Courts could be obtained only if an appropriate writ existed. The development of the writ system, therefore, has about it a hint of paradox for modern administrative law: what began as *executive* commands aimed at *avoiding* judicial proceedings became in turn the central mechanism for the judicial *control* of executive action.

The term "prerogative writs"

When and why did some of these judicialised writs come to be called, **13–005** individually and then later collectively, "prerogative" writs? Although this term for the writs of certiorari, mandamus, prohibition and habeas corpus is well known wherever the language of the common law is spoken, there is no entirely satisfactory answer to these questions. The use of the phrase prerogative writs to refer *collectively* to these four writs emerges only surprisingly late in the history of writs generally, in the time of Blackstone and Mansfield in the mid-eighteenth century. The origins of the term can, however, be traced to the political inclinations of certain Royalist judges in the seventeenth century who were keen to associate the beneficent remedy of habeas corpus with the King's personal solicititude for the welfare of his subjects.[11]

Few judges were more ardently Royalist than Montagu, who **13–006** succeeded Coke[12] as Chief Justice of the King's Bench after Coke had been removed by the King in 1617. It is in a case decided by Montagu and three brethren not noted for their independence of the Crown that habeas corpus is for the first time reported as being called a prerogative writ. In Montagu's words it is "a prerogative writ, which concerns the King's justice to be administered to his subjects; for the King ought to have an account why any of his subjects are

---

[10] Henry de Bracton (d. 1268). His *De Leqibus et Consuetudinibus Angliae* (hereinafter *De Legibus*) was the first systematic treatise on English law.

[11] The theory that the prerogative writs were in origin peculiar to the King himself is valid only with respect to certain obsolete and obsolescent writs. The earliest appearances of certiorari and mandamus in judicial proceedings were often as the result of applications made by subjects.

[12] Sir Edward Coke (1552–1634). He was successively Solicitor General, Speaker of the House of Commons, Attorney-General, Chief Justice of Common Pleas and Chief Justice of the King's Bench. He was removed from the last named post by the King in 1617. To the displeasure of the King, he asserted the jurisdiction of the common law courts over royal power: he held that a royal proclamation could not change the law and doubted the King's prerogative to control the conduct of litigation which involved royal interests. His *Institutes* (hereinafter 'Co. Inst.') were the first treatises on the modern common law.

imprisoned".[13] His primary purpose was to emphasise that the writ would run to the Cinque Ports in spite of the fact that they were an exempt jurisdiction to which writs relating to ordinary suits between subjects would not run. Even so, it is reasonable to ascribe his use of the word "prerogative" to his political inclinations. Habeas corpus was a beneficent remedy, and it was sound politics to associate its award with the King's concern for his subjects. Its value became enhanced during the constitutional struggles of the seventeenth century–albeit, paradoxically, as a safeguard of the liberty of the King's political opponents–and it came to be regarded, with Magna Carta,[14] as the greatest bastion of individual liberty.

13–007   Though the four writs had acquired their "prerogative" characteristics by the middle of the seventeenth century, strangely it was not until a century later, in 1759, that anybody (Mansfield) seems to have thought of classifying the writs as a group.[15] Those shared characteristics included the following:

> (1) They were not writs of course which could be purchased by or on behalf of any applicant from the Royal Chancery; they could not be had for the asking, but proper cause had to be shown to the satisfaction of the court why they should issue.

> (2) The award of the prerogative writs usually lay within the discretion of the court. The court was entitled to refuse certiorari and mandamus to applicants if they had been guilty of unreasonable delay or misconduct or if an adequate alternative remedy existed, notwithstanding that they have proved a usurpation of jurisdiction by the inferior tribunal or an omission to perform a public duty. But although none of the prerogative writs was a writ of course, not all were discretionary. Prohibition, for example, issued as of right in certain cases; and habeas corpus *ad subjiciendum*, the most famous of them all, was a writ of right which issued *ex debito justitiae* when the applicant had satisfied the court that his detention was unlawful. These two writs, therefore, were not in the fullest sense writs of grace.

---

[13] *Richard Bourn's* Case (1620) Cro. Jac. 543. See also the judgments of his brethren reported in Palm. 54 for like language. Similar reasoning was used in two slightly earlier cases in 2 Roll. Abr. 69; but the word 'prerogative' is not mentioned there.

[14] Habeas Corpus was often said to be founded on Magna Carta: Holdsworth, *The History of English Law*, Vol. i. p. 228. So, too, was mandamus: *R. v. Heathcote* (1712) 10 Mod. 48, 53; *Tapping on Mandamus*, (1848) pp. 2, 5.

[15] *R. v. Cowle* (1759) 2 Burr. 834, 855–856, *per* Mansfield. This seems to be the first reference to certiorai as a prerogative writ.

(3) The prerogative writs were awarded pre-eminently out of the Court of King's Bench. Bracton described the emergent court as *"aula regia* where the King's justices *proprias causas regis terminant."*[16] This jurisdiction belonged peculiarly to the King's Bench; the court held–at one time in reality, later only in theory[17]—*coram rege ipso.*[18] It comprised the hearing of pleas of the Crown and the examination and correction of the errors of other courts.

(4) At common law they would go to exempt jurisdictions (*e.g.* the Counties Palatine, the Cinque Ports), to which the King's writs did not normally run.

The late recognition that the prerogative writs formed a group **13–008** distinct from other writs is perhaps the oddest feature of their history. Although a relationship between the writs was assumed to exist, its nature was not defined; there was no Bracton to undertake the task of systematic analysis and rationalisation. After Coke and until Mansfield and Blackstone no common lawyer except Hale[19] was able to survey the whole field of the law with scholarship and insight. And by the time that Mansfield had perceived the close relationship between the writs and had chosen to link them verbally with the rights of the Crown, each writ had developed piecemeal its own special characteristics, so that to define the class with precision in terms of characteristics common to all its members had become virtually impossible. But it is easy enough to explain why Mansfield[20] and Blackstone,[21] who were good King's men, should have insisted on the prerogative character of habeas corpus. And if these were the qualities which in their eyes entitled habeas corpus to classification as a prerogative writ, they were shared in large measure by mandamus, "a command issuing in the King's name from the court of King's Bench" and "a writ of a most extensively remedial nature".[22] The writ of

---

[16] *De Legibus, f.* 150b.

[17] *Prohibitions del Roy* (1607) 12 Co.Rep.63.

[18] Holdsworth, *History of English Law,* Vol. i, pp. 204–206.

[19] Sir Matthew Hale (1609–76) wrote prolifically. Perhaps most important is his *History of the Common Law* (1713).

[20] Earl Mansfield (William Murray), 1705–93 was Chief Justice of the King's Bench from 1756.

[21] Sir William Blackstone, 1723–80, first Vinerian Professor of English law in the University of Oxford. His *Commentaries on the Law of England* (hereinafter 'Commentaries') were published between 1756–69.

[22] Blackstone, *Commentaries,* Vol. iii, p. 110.

mandamus, moreover, expressly alleged a contempt of the Crown[23] consisting in the neglect of a public duty; and it was a writ of grace. The "prerogative" characteristics of prohibition and certiorari were still more obvious. Prohibition had always been associated with the maintenance of the rights of the Crown. Certiorari was historically linked with the King's person as well as with the King's Bench; it was of high importance for the control of inferior tribunals, particularly with respect to the administration of criminal justice; it was a writ of course for the King but not for the subject.

13–009   Mansfield and Blackstone, then, were responsible, if not for the invention of the term "prerogative writ", at least for its acceptance as part of the lawyer's vocabulary. We may now turn to examine in more detail the separate development of each of the prerogative writs.

The origins of the writ of certiorari

13–010   From about 1280, the judicial forms of the writ of certiorari were in common use, issuing on the application of ordinary litigants. The breadth of the issues that could be thus raised is amply illustrated in the edited volumes of King's Bench cases for the reigns of Edward I and his six successors.[24] The conception then prevailing was well expressed in a modern Canadian case:

> "The theory is that the Sovereign has been appealed to by some one of his subjects who complains of an injustice done him by an inferior court; whereupon the Sovereign, saying that he wishes to be certified—certiorari—of the matter, orders that the record, etc., be transmitted into a court in which he is sitting."[25]

Much of this very broad remedial jurisdiction passed from the courts of common law to the Court of Chancery, and in the Tudor and early Stuart periods the writ of certiorari frequently issued to bring the proceedings of inferior courts of common law before the Chancellor.[26] Later, however, the Chancery confined its supervisory functions to inferior courts of equity.

13–011   From the fourteenth century until the middle of the seventeenth century the following seem to have been the main purposes served by certiorari:

---

[23] See the form of the writ in *Bagg's* case (1615) 11 Co. Rep. 93b. The phrase also appeared in some modern forms of the writ: Short and Mellor, *Practice on the Crown Side* (2nd ed., 1908), pp. 518, 591 *et passim*.

[24] Seldon Soc., Vols. 55, 57, 58, 74, 76, 82, 88, edited by G.O. Sayles.

[25] *R. v. Titchmarsh* (1915) 22 D.L.R. 272, 277–278.

[26] Cowell, *Interpreter*, M2; Spence, *Equitable Jurisdiction*, Vol. i, pp. 686, 687.

(1) To supervise the proceedings of inferior courts of specialised jurisdiction—for example, the Commissioners of Sewers, the Courts Merchant, the Court of Admiralty, the Courts of the Forests—by bringing up cases to Westminster for trial or, if necessary, retrial or review.

(2) To obtain information for administrative purposes; for example, the sheriff is told to find out whether one who has been granted the King's protection is tarrying in the city instead of journeying forth in the King's service; the escheator must certify into the Chancery the value of knights' fees and advowsons which have escheated to the King.

(3) To bring into the Chancery or before the common-law courts judicial records and other formal documents for a wide diversity of purposes. The Register of Writs gives many examples.

(4) To remove coroners' inquisitions and indictments into the King's Bench.

The origins of the writ of prohibition

Prohibition is one of the oldest writs known to the law. From the first its primary function seems to have been to limit the jurisdiction of the ecclesiastical courts. It later came to be used as a weapon by the common law courts in their conflicts with the Courts of Chancery and Admiralty. Disobedience to a prohibition was conceived of as a contempt of the Crown. Since it was "the proper power and honour of the King's Bench to limit the jurisdiction of all other courts"[27] the writ usually issued out of that court; but it could also be awarded by the Chancery and the Common Pleas.   **13–012**

The "prerogative" character of the writ has been repeatedly stressed. Fitzherbert says that "the King for himself may sue forth this writ, although the plea in the spiritual court be betwixt two common persons, because the suit is in derogation of his Crown."[28] That the protection of private interests is only a secondary function of the writ is brought out in the comparatively modern case of *Worthington v. Jeffries*, where it was said that: **13–013**

---

[27] *Case of the Company of Homers in London* (1642) 2 Roll.R. 471.
[28] Fitzherbert, *Natura Brevium*, p. 40 E.

"the ground of decision in considering whether prohibition is or is
not to be granted, is not whether the individual suitor has or has
not suffered damage, but is whether the royal prerogative has
been encroached upon by reason of the prescribed order of the
administration of justice having been disobeyed."[29]

Hence it has been said that even a complete stranger to the
proceeding in the other court could have the writ.

The expansion of government

13–014   Before elected borough and county councils were established by the
Municipal Corporations Acts 1835 and 1882, local government
functions were carried out by the Justices of the Peace. J.P.s were
drawn almost exclusively from the ranks of the landed gentry and
their duties included the regulation of wages and prices, the
implementation of the Poor Law as well as the administration of petty
justice. With the vast increase in the non-judicial duties of the J.P.s
after 1660, certiorari acquired a new importance. By whom and by
what means were the decisions of J.P.s to be subjected to judicial
review? The conciliar courts had gone, and no new governmental
organ had arisen to take their place. The Court of King's Bench, which
had always been associated with the work of government and which
had retained a supervisory jurisdiction over the work of the justices in
sessions and of other local bodies during the heyday of the Council
and the Star Chamber, was manifestly the proper superintending
authority. But it could not exercise its authority by means of the writ
of error, for although error lay to impeach the record of a judgment
given on an indictment it would not lie to quash convictions and
orders made in summary proceedings. Persons aggrieved by summary
convictions and orders might bring applications for habeas corpus or
civil actions for trespass or replevin in order to obtain redress; but
these modes of proceeding were not always appropriate, and in any
event collateral attack was available only for acts done without
jurisdiction.[30] After a period of doubt and vacillation, the court
ultimately committed itself to the proposition that the appropriate
remedy in all cases where an inferior statutory tribunal had exceeded
its jurisdiction or drawn up a conviction or order that was bad on its
face was a writ of certiorari to quash the conviction or order. The
process by which this proposition came to be established is still not

---

[29] (1875) L.R. 10 C.P. 379, 382.
[30] A. Rubinstein, 'On the Origins of Judicial Review' (1964) 1 U. of B.C. Law Rev. 1 at
3–7.

free from obscurity; but by 1700 it was possible for Holt C.J., in the famous case of *Groenvelt v. Burwell*,[31] to proclaim the grand generalisation that: "It is a consequence of all jurisdictions to have their proceedings returned here by certiorari to be examined here ... Where any court is erected by statute, a certiorari lies to it ..."

Thereafter the King's Bench became inundated with motions for certiorari to quash rates and orders made by justices and other bodies exercising administrative functions under semi-judicial forms. It became, in effect, a superior administrative court, supervising much of the business of local government by keeping subordinate bodies within their legal limitations by writs of certiorari and prohibition, and ordering them to perform their duties by writs of mandamus. The modern High Court has succeeded to much of this jurisdiction, and there can be no doubt that the absence in the common law systems of a distinct body of public law, whereby proceedings against public authorities are instituted only before special administrative courts and are governed by a special body of rules, is directly traceable to the extensive use of prerogative writs by the Court of King's Bench.   **13–015**

Certiorari and prohibition established themselves as the most important remedies in administrative law because in the latter part of the seventeenth century local administration was free from effective supervision by the central government. The role of supervisor was assumed by the Court of King's Bench, which had declared that it would "examine the proceedings of all jurisdictions erected by Act of Parliament ... to the end that ... they keep themselves within their jurisdictions".[32] Apart from their formal ministerial duties, whatever the justices had to do was "the exercise of a jurisdiction".[33] It was assumed that the writs of certiorari and prohibition, by which they were controlled in their capacity as courts of summary jurisdiction, were equally appropriate devices for superintending the exercise of their multifarious governmental functions.   **13–016**

With the coming of industrialisation, urbanisation and democratic reform, the J.P.s shed many of their general local government functions.[34] A new phase opened in the history of certiorari and prohibition during the 1830s. Two legal issues (still a source of controversy in judicial review proceedings today) engaged the courts during this period. The first was the question of which of the newly created government bodies were amenable to certiorari and prohibition. Ad hoc bodies and elected local government authorities,   **13–017**

---

[31] (1700) 1 Ld.Raym. 454, 459 (certiorari to review disciplinary decisions of the censors of the College of Physicians).

[32] *R. v. Glamorganshire Inhabitants (Cardiff Bridge Case)* (1700) 1 Ld.Raym. 580.

[33] F.W. Maitland, 'The Shallows and Silences of Real Life,' *Collected Papers*, Vol. i, p. 478.

[34] See W.R. Cornish and G. de N. Clark, *Law and Society in England 1750–1950* (1989), p. 21.

clothed with extensive regulatory powers over persons over persons and property, were set up to administer the expanding functions of government. Auditors were invested with statutory powers to disallow illegal payments made out of public funds.[35] Parliament not infrequently provided a statutory method of challenging the decisions of these authorities by way of certiorari.[36] It was natural that the courts should take the view that common law certiorari and prohibition could properly issue to other authorities discharging similar functions where Parliament had made no express provision for a method of challenge.[37]

13–018   With the accumulation of precedents, the courts took a step further and held (after some vacillation) that the orders of central government departments and ministers[38] (but not of the Crown as such) were amenable to certiorari and prohibition. No longer was the availability of the writs limited to courts *stricto sensu*, or even to bodies that closely resembled the courts.

The writ of mandamus

13–019   Today the main role of the order of mandamus is to compel inferior tribunals to exercise jurisdiction that they have wrongfully declined, and to enforce the exercise of statutory duties and discretion in accordance with the law. The origins of the writ are rather later than those of certiorari and prohibition. Although the history and qualities of certiorari and prohibition well qualified them for inclusion in a "prerogative" group of writs, the claims of mandamus were less obvious. Not until 1573 do we find a reported case that centres around a judicial writ of mandamus serving purposes substantially similar to

---

[35] See William A. Robson, *The Development of Local Government* (1954) for an account of the development of the office of District Auditor.

[36] *e.g.* Poor Law Amendment Act 1834, ss.105, 106; Municipal Corporations (General) Act 1837, s.44; Tithe Act 1837, s.3; Poor Law Amendment Act 1844, s.35. In some instances statutory certiorari was apparently intended to take the place of an appeal to the courts and to enable the courts to review the merits of the order impugned: *Re Dent Tithe Commutation* (1845) 8 Q.B. 43, 59; *R. v. Roberts* [1908] 1 K.B. 407. See also *The State (Raftis and Dowling) v. Leonard* [1960] I.R. 381.

[37] See, *e.g. R. v. Arkwright* (1848) 12 Q.B. 960 (certiorari to church building commissioners for order stopping up churchyard paths); *R. v. Aberdare Canal Co.* (1850) 14 Q.B. 854 (certiorari to ad hoc commissioners for sanction given to building of a bridge); *Re Crosby-upon-Eden Tithes* (1849) 13 Q.B. 761 (prohibition to tithe commissioners); *Church v. Inclosure Commissioners* (1862) 11 C.B. (N.S.) 664 (prohibition to inclosure commissioners).

[38] For a useful judicial survey of the development of remedies against Ministers, see *M. v. Home Office* [1994] 1 A.C. 377.

those of the modern writ[39]—it was issued to restore a citizen of London to his franchise of which he had been illegally deprived. The modern writ of mandamus did not, however, begin to emerge till the early years of the seventeenth century; and for practical purposes its history can be said to have begun with *Bagg's* case.[40] The writ in this case is shown to have issued out of the King's Bench and to have been attested by Coke as Chief Justice; it recited that Bagg, a capital burgess of Plymouth, had been unjustly removed from his office by the mayor and commonalty, and commanded them to restore him unless they showed to the court good cause for their conduct. They failed to satisfy the court and a peremptory mandamus was issued to restore Bagg. From then onward many such writs issued to compel restitution[41] to offices and liberties. By the early years of the eighteenth century it had become—thanks largely to the work of Holt—something more comprehensive than a writ of restitution. It would go, on the application of a party aggrieved, to compel the performance of a wide range of public or quasi-public duties, performance of which had been wrongfully refused. It would issue, for example, to compel the admission (as well as the restoration) of a duly qualified alderman to a corporation,[42] or to compel the holding of an election to the office,[43] and it became a valuable device to prevent the unlawful packing of corporations.[44] More important still, it would issue to inferior tribunals that wrongfully declined jurisdiction.[45] Through the writ of mandamus, the King's Bench compelled the carrying-out of ministerial duties incumbent upon both administrative and judicial bodies.

Lord Mansfield's contribution to mandamus

The rules governing the issue of the writ gradually took shape until they were fully stated by Lord Mansfield in a series of cases.[46] What is   **13–020**

---

[39] *Middleton's* case, 3 Dyer 332b. The writ in this case was modelled after one issued in an earlier unreported case of a similar character: *Anable's* case, temp. Henry VI. Miss Henderson has observed (*Foundations of English Administrative Law*, pp. 49, 53–54) that the writ in *Middleton's* case was analogous to a writ of privilege. In the 17th century mandamus lost its connection with privilege (*ibid.* pp. 75–76).

[40] (1615) 11 Co. Rep. 93b.

[41] In the 17th century the writ was often called a writ of restitution: *e.g.* 1 Bulst. 174; Poph. 133, 176; Style 32; 3 Salk. 231; Hale's, *Analysis of the Law*, 60.

[42] *R. v. Norwich (Mayor)* 2 Ld.Raym. 1244.

[43] *R. v. Evesham (Mayor)* 7 Mod. 166.

[44] It was regularly used after 1688 by the Whigs to secure admission to the Tory-packed borough corporations.

[45] See, *e.g. Groenvelt v. Burwell*, 1 Ld.Raym. 454; *R. v. Montague*, Sess.Cas. 106.

[46] See, esp. *R. v. Blooer* (1760) 2 Burr, 1043; *R. v. Barker* (1762) 3 Burr. 1265; *R. v. Askew*

particularly interesting about Mansfield's judgments is that he persistently refers to mandamus as a "prerogative" writ.[47] Thus, in a typical passage, he calls it "a prerogative writ flowing from the King himself, sitting in his court, superintending the police and preserving the peace of this country."[48] Speaking in 1762, Mansfield observed that within the past century mandamus had been:

> "liberally interposed for the benefit of the subject and advancement of justice....It was introduced, to prevent disorder from a failure of justice, and defect of police. Therefore it ought to be used upon all occasions where the law has established no specific remedy, and where in justice and good government there ought to be one."[49]

Already by that time the primary function of the writ was to compel inferior tribunals to exercise jurisdiction and discretion according to law. But it issued also for what Blackstone called "an infinite variety of other purposes"[50] large and small—to compel the town of Derby to fulfil its obligations under the Militia Acts,[51] to order the election, admission or restoration of a party aggrieved "to any office or franchise of a public nature whether spiritual or temporal",[52] to secure the use of a meeting-house, to obtain production, delivery and inspection of public documents, to compel local officials to pay over sums due and to perform a variety of other public duties, to compel justices of the peace to issue warrants, make rates, appoint overseers and pass accounts, to compel a body corporate to surrender its regalia or to affix its common seal.

13–021   By the middle of the nineteenth century the body of case law had swollen to grotesque proportions. In 1848 Thomas Tapping incorporated in his exhaustive and unreadable treatise on the writ,[53] an analysis of all the cases, arranged alphabetically according to subject-matter. The list, which ranged from Abbot through Bastards, Corpse, Scavenger and Swordbearer down to Yeoman of Wood Wharf,

---

(1768) 4 Burr. 2186.

[47] *e.g.* in *R. v. Cowle* (1759) 2 Burr. 834, 855; *R. v. Barker* (1762) 1 Wm.B1. 352; *R. v. Vice-Chancellor (of Cambridge University)* (1765) 3 Burr. 1647, 1659. For a similar early reference to mandamus, see *Knipe v. Edwin* (1694) 4 Mod. 281; *cf. R. v. Patrick*, 1 Keb. 610.

[48] *R. v. Barker* (1762) 3 Burr. 1265.

[49] *R. v. Barker* (1762) 3 Burr. 1265, 1267.

[50] Blackstone, *Commentaries*, Vol. iii, p.110.

[51] Holdsworth, *H.E.L.*, Vol. x, p. 156.

[52] Blackstone, *loc. cit.*

[53] Entitled 'The Law and Practice of the High Prerogative Writ of Mandamus, as it obtains both in England, and in Ireland'.

ran to 252 pages. But the heyday of mandamus was by then nearly over, and its significance was to dwindle almost as swiftly as it had risen.

The decline of mandamus

After 1835 the corrupt oligarchies which had controlled the boroughs **13–022** were superseded by local councils elected on broad franchise. Half a century later the broom of reform swept through the counties, and for most administrative purposes elected local authorities replaced the county justices and the parish vestries. The new regime made for a more orderly system of local government, in which the delays and irregularities which had evoked so many applications for mandamus were less likely to occur. Central administrative control, exercised by means of district audit of accounts, inspection of services, powers to act in default, and a host of other regulatory devices, became the normal agency for securing the proper discharge of local duties. In respect of acts and decisions by local authorities affecting individual rights, Parliament adopted the practice of providing persons aggrieved with a right of complaint, objection or appeal to a central government department; and by supplying these efficacious alternative remedies it indirectly took away the right of the individual to obtain a mandamus. The decline of mandamus was also expedited by such factors as reform in the administration of other classes of corporations, and the gradual disappearance of the concept of freehold office in which the holder was quasiproprietary rights enforceable by mandamus.[54] For these and other reasons[55] the area of public activity and inactivity within which mandamus can play an effective part has diminished. So, while reform of local government leads to an increasing role for certiorari and prohibition,[56] it spelt a diminishing importance for mandamus.

The writ of habeas corpus

Finally, we turn to the prerogative writ of habeas corpus *ad* **13–023** *subjiciendum*.[57] Though it is the most renowned contribution of the English common law to the protection of human liberty, its origins

---

[54] The holder of a freehold office was removable only for misbehaviour, and had the right to be heard in his own defence before removal.

[55] Some of which referred to in Shortt, *Informations, Prohibition and Mandamus* (1887), pp. 271–272.

[56] See above, para. 13–014.

[57] Other forms of habeas corpus are now practically obsolete.

were modest.[58] The earliest writs of habeas corpus were used in mesne process; they were commands addressed to royal officials to bring before one of the King's courts the body of a person whose presence was required for the purpose of a judicial proceeding. In this form habeas corpus preceded Magna Carta. The connection, readily discerned by seventeenth-century writers, between the text of the Charter and the development of the writ owes less to historical fact than to partisan imagination and wishful legend.

13–024   In the fourteenth century there emerged the writ of habeas corpus *cum causa*, requiring the person who already had custody of a prisoner to produce him before the court, together with the ground for the detention. A means of testing the legality of the detention, this was the immediate ancestor of the modern writ.[59] It was used by the common law courts at Westminster to protect, assert and extend their own jurisdiction against their various rivals by securing the release of litigants and others from custody.[60] It was also used by private litigants to procure an order for release from wrongful imprisonment; and in this way it came to assume high constitutional importance as a device for impugning the validity of arbitrary imprisonment by the Executive. The decision in *Darnel's* case,[61] that a warrant certifying a committal to be "by the special command of the King" disclosed a sufficient ground for imprisonment, was overruled by the Petition of Right in the following year. But the machinery for removing the abuse of lengthy imprisonment without trial was still defective. Reforms were introduced by the Habeas Corpus Act 1679: if a person was held on a serious criminal charge, he was to be given release on bail or a speedy trial in pursuance of an application for habeas corpus.[62] Severe financial penalties (which are still in force) were imposed on judges wrongfully refusing to issue the writ, on gaolers evading service of or compliance with the writ and on persons recommitting a prisoner who had already been discharged on a habeas corpus.

13–025   In 1816 the Act was extended to cases of civil detention and the judges were empowered to inquire into the truth of the facts set out in the gaoler's return to the writ in such cases. Given a relatively temperate political climate, with an alert body of informed opinion and an independent Judiciary, habeas corpus flourished while liberty in many lands languished. Efficiency was its virtue: habeas corpus really worked. "When Dicey declared that the Habeas Corpus Acts

---

[58] Maxwell Cohen (1938) 16 Can.B.R. 92; R.J. Sharpe, *The Law of Habeas* (2nd ed., 1989), Chap. 1.

[59] Cohen (1940) 18 Can.B.R. 10, 172. See also Holdsworth, *History of the Laws of England*, Vol. ix, pp. 24–51; E. Jenks (1902) 18 L.Q.R. 64.

[60] In some situations its effect was analogous to that of a writ of prohibition.

[61] (1627) 3 St.Tr. 1.

[62] s.6. This section was repealed by the Courts Act 1971, s.56(4), Sched. 11, Pt.iv.

were 'for practical purposes worth a hundred constitutional articles guaranteeing individual liberty'[63] he spoke for the mass of English constitutional lawyers."[64] Substantive guarantees unaccompanied by any effective procedural technique for enforcing them are, indeed, often worthless. But a number of modern constitutional bills of rights incorporate not only entrenched substantive guarantees but also entrenched procedures for enforcement in the courts.[65] This new emphasis on the importance of judicial remedies can be regarded as an indirect recognition of English experience.[66] It has, however, been doubted whether habeas corpus serves any useful purpose today, given the expansion in the scope of judicial review under Order 53.[67]

INJUNCTIONS[68]

After the labyrinthine by-ways of the common law prerogative writs one has a sense of greater freedom in the fields of equity. The injunction and the declaratory order were more flexible and adaptable instrument of judicial control than the common law remedies. They were less burdended by precedent. They were comparatively free from the abstruse technicalities and hair-splitting distinctions besetting certiorari, prohibition and mandamus. They could be awarded against bodies whose functions contained no judicial element. However, historically the instrusions of equity upon the domain of public law were desultory and selective. The injunction, still pre-eminently a private law remedy, did not come to play a significant part in public law until the nineteenth century. And although declarations have equitable roots, the remedy is better seen as a statutory one. By the time the equitable remedies had begun to extend their reach, the prerogative writs were recognised as the principle methods of obtaining judicial review of administrative action, and they were too securely entrenched to be readily ousted by newcomers. The expectations of those who looked for a dramatic increase in the part played by equitable remedies in administrative law have not been

13–026

---

[63] *Introduction to the Study of the Constitution* (10th ed. 1959), p.199.

[64] S.A. de Smith, *The New Commonwealth and its Constitutions*, (1964), p.167.

[65] *e.g.* Constitution of India, Arts. 19, 21, 22, 32, 226; Constitution of Jamaica (S.I. 1962 No. 1550, Sched. 2), ss.15, 20, 25, 49, 50.

[66] England was not the only country to devise an effective judicial remedy for obtaining release from wrongful imprisonment. Thus, similar remedies were evolved in Scots law, Roman-Dutch law and some Latin American systems. But habeas corpus has attracted special attention overseas.

[67] A.P. Le Sueur, 'Should we Abolish the Writ of Habeas Corpus?' [1992] P.L. 13; *cf.* M. Shrimpton 'In Defence of Habeas Corpus' [1993] P.L. 24 and Law Com. No. 226, Part XI.

[68] On modern law and practice relation to injunctions in judicial review proceedings, see below, para 15–016.

fulfilled. Nevertheless, the equitable sector, which until recently was little more than a miscellany of loosely connected topics, has acquired cohesion and substance through the creative activity of individual judges; and the creative impulse is by no means spent.[69] Moreover, a consequence of the procedural reforms of 1977, considered below, that enable an applicant for judicial review to request a declaration or an injunction (or both), alone or combined with one or more of the prerogative orders, is that these remedies have moved closer to the mainstream of administrative law.

The Court of Exchequer

13–027 The Court of Exchequer assumed a general equitable jurisdiction during the course of the sixteenth century.[70] In the it exercised equitable powers incidentally to its capacity as a court of revenue.[71] In the exercise of this ancillary jurisdiction it entertained English informations filed by the Attorney-General to secure the protection and enforcement of the proprietary and fiscal rights of the Crown against subjects.[72] The relief awarded included injunctions and declaratory orders. The English information may well have been the earliest form of equitable proceeding lying predominantly within the field of public law. Its procedural rules were unwarrantably favourable to the Crown, and a belated recognition of this injustice was one reason why it had fallen into desuetude some years before it was abolished by Parliament in 1947.[73]

13–028 A more beneficent and important contribution made by the Court of Exchequer to public law was its practice of awarding equitable relief against the Crown, represented by the Attorney-General.[74] For this purpose it does not seem that the court differentiated between cases where the interests of the Crown were indirectly affected and cases

---

[69] See, esp. Lord Denning's own dicta in *Lee v. Showman's Guild of Great Britain* [1952] 2 Q.B. 329, 346; *Barnard v. National Dock Labour Board* [1953] 2 Q.B. 18 at 41–44; *Taylor v. National Assistance Board* [1957] P. 101, 111; *Pyx Granite Co. v. Ministry of Housing and Local Government* [1958] 1 Q.B. 554, 571.

[70] Holdsworth, *History of the Laws of England*, Vol. i, p. 241. It was described as 'an ancient though originally usurped jurisdiction' in *Att.-Gen. v. Halling* (1846) 15 M. & W. 687, 694, where the history of the several sides to the court's equitable jurisdiction is traced. See also Holdsworth, *op. cit.* Vol. xii, pp. 456–458.

[71] See *Att.-Gen. v. Halling* (1846) 15 M. & W. 687, 694.

[72] G.S. Robertson, *Civil Proceedings by and against the Crown*, pp. 234 *et seq.*

[73] Crown Proceedings Act 1947, s. 13; Sched. 1, para. 1.

[74] Preceding the award of such relief by the Court of Chancery: Holdsworth. 'History of Remedies against the Crown' (1922) 38 L.Q.R. at 280–281. See also H.G. Hanbury, *Essays in Equity* pp. 114–120.

where the interests of the Crown were directly affected.[75] Judgment in favour of the subject usually took the form of a declaratory order. After 1841 the practice of suing the Attorney-General in an action for a declaration (except under special statutory provisions or upon a petition of right) fell temporarily into abeyance.[76] But this dormant jurisdiction of the Court of Exchequer passed to the High Court of Justice of 1873; and, as we shall see, it was revived in 1911 in a notable case[77] which gave a new impetus to the action for a declaration in public law.

The Court of Chancery

In its early days the Court of Chancery appears to have had little concern with matters of public law, save in so far as its jurisdiction to issue common injunctions to restrain persons from proceeding in the courts of common law and enforcing judgments obtained at common law[78] incidentally raise questions of constitutional importance. The chronology of its interventions in the field of public law cannot be traced with assurance. One can say that the blurred outlines of its jurisdiction were taking shape soon after the Restoration, that they had become more distinct by the middle of the eighteenth century and that the process of clarification did not end with the Judicature Acts; but much must be left to conjecture. Blackstone's account of equitable jurisdiction was inadequate, but it would appear that by his time the Court of Chancery was entertaining at least four classes of proceedings that have a bearing on our inquiry. First, the Crown could sue in Chancery as an alternative to bringing an English information in the Exchequer.[79]

Secondly, a Crown grantee or other person claiming rights under the Crown was permitted to sue in the King's name in order to take advantage of the prerogative. If he sued in his own name in a proceeding that touched the rights of the Crown he had to join the Attorney-General as co-plaintiff.[80] From these beginnings there emerged a general principle that in matters of equitable jurisdiction in

13–029

13–030

---

[75] G.E. Robinson, *Public Authorities and Legal Liability* (1925), pp. xxxvii–xxxix (introductory chapter on remedies against the Crown by J.H. Morgan).

[76] See Court of Chancery Act 1841.

[77] *Dyson v. Att.-Gen.* [1911] 1 K.B. 410.

[78] Substantially abolished with respect to proceedings in the superior courts by the Supreme Court of Judicature Act 1873, s.24(5). See Supreme Court of Judicature (Consolidation) Act 1925, s.41.

[79] Robertson. *op. cit.* pp. 237, 238.

[80] *ibid.* p. 464.

which the King's interest were involved the Attorney-General was competent to sue at the relation of a private plaintiff, the relator bearing the costs and receiving the benefit of the court's award.[81]

13–031   Thirdly, the court would issue injunctions to restrain the commission or continuance of public nuisances[82] though this was a power more frequently exercised by the Court of Exchequer.[83] Such an injunction could be addressed even to the members of an inferior court whose order had been responsible for creating the nuisance.[84] In Hardwicke's time it was established that an information by the Attorney-General was the proper mode of proceeding,[85] unless an individual had suffered particular damage by reason of the nuisance, in which case the intervention of the Attorney-General was unnecessary.

13–032   Fourthly, during the seventeenth century the Attorney-General was bringing information in the Court of Chancery to secure the establishment and due administration of charitable or public trusts.[86] This class of proceeding was of major historical importance; it was the commonest, and possibly the first, of the early forms of relator actions in equity.[87] It was founded on the status of the Crown as *parens patriae;*

---

[81] *Att.-Gen. of Duchy of Lancaster v. Health* (1690) Prec.Ch. 13; *Att.-Gen. v. Oglender* (1740) 1 Ves. Jun. 246, 1 Ves.Jun.Supp. 105.

[82] The general jurisdiction of the Court of Chancery to restrain nuisances goes back to Elizabethan times; *Att.-Gen. v. Richards* (1788) 2 Anst. 608; *Story on Equity* (2nd English ed.), para. 921. See generally W.J. Jones, *The Elizabethan Court of Chancery.*

[83] *Att.-Gen. v. Cleaver* (1811) 18 Ves. 211, 217.

[84] *Box v. Allen* (1727) Dick. 49 (injunction to Commissioners of Sewers); *Att.-Gen. v. Forbes* (1836) 2 My. & Cr. 123 (injunction to magistrates at quarter sessions).

[85] *Baines v. Baker* (1752) Amb. 158, 159.

[86] The view that the Attorney-General's intervention preceded the Statute 43 Eliz. c.4 seems to be erroneous. His intervention is traceable to the time of Charles I and became common in the second half of Charles II's reign: Gareth Jones, *History of the Law of Charity, 1532–1827,* pp. 21–22, 34f.

[87] It was the only form of equitable relator action mentioned by Blackstone, *Commentaries,* Vol. iii, p. 427. An early example of a proceeding by way of Attorney-General's information and private bill with respect to a charity was *Att.-Gen. v. Newman* (1670) 1 Ch.Cas. 157, where the appropriateness of the bill was doubted. For early examples of the settled form of relator action, see *Att.-Gen. v. Hart* (1703) Prec. Ch. 225; *Att.-Gen. v. Bains* (1708) Prec.Ch. 270. For the limits of the court's intervention, see Fonblanque, *Treatise of Equity* (3rd ed.), Vol. ii, pp. 205–206; *Att.-Gen. v. Smart* (1748) 1 Ves.Sen. 72. At common law the informer who was permitted to bring a civil action upon a penal statute (see Holdsworth, *H.E.L.,* Vol. ii, pp. 453–454; Vol. iv, pp. 355–359), or a *qui tam* information for a penalty to be shared by himself and the Crown, was also called a relator (see 21 Jac. 1, c.4). In the eighteenth century a criminal information could be exhibited either by the Attorney-General *ex officio* or by the Master of the Crown Office at the relation of an informer (*H.E.L.,* Vol. ix, pp. 237–246). In civil proceedings at common law the only class of relator action corresponding with the relator action in equity was the information in the nature of a *quo warranto;* see, *e.g.* 9 Anne c.20, s.4.

and it was the progenitor of new types of proceedings brought by the Attorney-General as the Crown's representative in matters especially appertaining to the public welfare.

The Sovereign, as *parens patriae*, is responsible for the **13–033** superintendence of infants, idiots, lunatics and charities.[88] The Chancellor, as the keeper of the King's conscience, was the appropriate officer to dispense this prerogative jurisdiction, and the Attorney-General, as the King's forensic representative, was the appropriate officer to appear for the Crown in the Chancellor's court. If the funds of a public body were deemed to be impressed with a charitable trust, it was clearly appropriate for the Attorney-General to go to the Court of Chancery to seek an injunction against their misapplication. Thus the Attorney-General came to bring information to restrain unlawful expenditure of borough funds.[89]

The concept of a *parens patriae* had still larger implications. The **13–034** Crown, as *parens patriae*, had a vistatorial authority over those charitable and ecclesiastical corporations which lacked founders or visitors. A municipal corporation had no visitor; then let the Crown be its visitor and supervisor.[90] At common law the visitatorial power was exercised by bringing *quo warranto* informations and applications for writs of mandamus and *scire facias* in the King's Bench. Most of these proceedings arose out of defaults other than the misuse of corporate funds. Since the Crown was empowered, in a proper case, to sue in such of its courts as it thought fit, it could and did elect to take proceedings in equity generally to secure the observance of the law by municipal corporations.[91] This trend of development could well end with a broad proposition that the Attorney-General, representing the Crown, could properly apply to the Court of Chancery to restrain the execution of illegal acts committed not merely by corporations which held property on trust for public purposes but also by other bodies, of statutory as well as of non-statutory origin, where such illegalities tended to injure the public welfare. So, indeed, it did end, but not without a long period of judicial hesitation.[92]

Gradually, during the course of the nineteenth century, a group of **13–035** general principles crystallised. The Attorney-General could proceed *ex proprio motu* (*i.e.* of his own motion) in any action in which he might

---

[88] *Chitty on Prerogative*, Chap. IX. Lord Nottingham referred to the King as *pater patriae*: Reports of Cases by Lord Nottingham, Vol. 1 (Selden Soc., Vol. 73, ed. D.E.C. Yale), 209. The prerogative jurisdiction has been partly superseded by statute.

[89] *Att.-Gen. v. Aspinall* (1837) 2 M. & Cr. 613.

[90] *Cf.* Roscoe Pound, 'Visitatorial Jurisdiction over Corporations in Equity' (1936) 49 Harv.L.R. 369.

[91] As in *Att.-Gen. v. Galway Corp.* (1828) 1 Molloy 95.

[92] See H. A. Street and S. Brice, *Ultra Vires*, (1930), pp. 265–266.

appear at the instance of a relator[93]; the relator need not show any personal interest in the subject-matter of the suit, for the proceedings were the Attorney-General's[94]; the right of the Attorney-General to intervene depended upon the public consequences of the act complained of, not on the intrinsic characteristics of the defendant body[95]; the right of an individual to sue without joining the Attorney-General depended on whether his own legal interests were more particularly affected than those of the public in general. In essence, the general right of the Attorney-General to seek the repression of *ultra vires* acts tending to injure the public grew out of a broad conception of the prerogative of protection, and the details of the rules governing *locus standi* were substantially borrowed from the law of public nuisance.

13–036   In recent years there has been only the most tentative relaxation of the rules governing *locus standi* in relation to injunctions,[96] and the function of the Attorney-General as protector of the public interest, enabling him to obtain an injunction to restrain breaches of the criminal law, has been extended.[97] But the main factor conductive to an expansion of the role of the injunction in public law has been its close association with the declaratory judgment. It is quite common for injunctive and declaratory relief to be claimed in the same proceedings, and in such cases the courts tend to refrain from drawing fine distinctions between the permissible scope of the two remedies.

DECLARATIONS[98]

13–037   The potentialities of the declaration in public law have been realised only during the twentieth century. But the greatest authority on the action for a declaration has said that "All that is new about declaratory judgments

---

[93] *Att.-Gen. v. Dublin Corp.* (1827) 1 Bli. (N.S.) 312, 337–338.

[94] *Att.-Gen. v. Vivian* (1825) 1 Russ. 236.

[95] See, *e.g. Att.-Gen. v. Oxford, Worcester & Wolverhampton Ry.* (1854) 2 W.R. 330; *Att.-Gen. v. Cockermouth Local Board* (1874) L.R. 18 Eq. 172.

[96] In *Gouriet v. Union of Post Office Workers* [1978] A.C. 435, the House of Lords reaffirmed the requirements that an injunction to restrain a breach of the criminal law will only be granted to an individual who can establish that the defendant's conduct either endangers private legal right or may occasion him special loss not suffered by members of the public at large.

[97] In a number of recent cases local authorities have been accorded a similar role as guardians of the public interest in their locality by virtue of the Local Government Act 1972, s.222. In *Gouriet's* case (above, n. 96), however, a warning was sounded about the dangers of a regular resort to injunctions for this purpose).

[98] On the modern law and practice relating to declarations in judicial review proceedings, see below, 15–030.

is the name—the phenomenon itself is as ancient as the administration of justice by courts" and that "Anglo-American statues have from time immemorial authorised and courts have rendered judgments purely declaratory in form and effect."[99] To question these assertions with reference to English law may be presumptuous, especially as the development of declaratory orders in English legal history has never been thoroughly investigated; yet it would seem that in England the purely declaratory judgment is a comparatively modern institution.

Judicial resistance to declaratory relief

From its earliest days the Court of Chancery did indeed issue declaratory orders.[1] But the books on Chancery practice are silent on the matter of purely declaratory judgments. And if a general practice of rendering purely declaratory judgments had ever existed, it had certainly been abandoned by the 1840s. Thus, Bruce V.-C. observed in 1847[2]: "Nakedly to declare a right, without doing or directing anything else relating to the right, does not, I conceive, belong to the functions of this Court." This view is supported by many other judicial dicta[3] and the contrary view would make nonsense of Lord Brougham's prolonged agitation for importing the main features of the Scots action of declarator into English law.[4]

13–038

More significant for the development of the action for a declaration in public law was the practice of the Court of Exchequer, which, uninhibited by the restraints that the Court of Chancery had imposed upon itself, had long awarded equitable relief against the Crown, represented by the Attorney-General, on bills filed by subjects.[5] Its jurisdiction to grant relief against the Crown was derived from a statute of 1841,[6] its judgments were usually declaratory in form.

13–039

---

[99] E.M. Borchard, *Declaratory Judgments* (1st ed.), pp. 62, 73. The author fails to cite any relevant English authority in support of his assertions. In the second edition the former passage is reworded to read: "All that is new about the declaratory judgment is its name and its broad scope—the phenomenon itself is as old judicial history" (p. 137).

[1] G. Spence, *Equitable Jurisdiction*, Vol. i, p. 390. See also Comment, "Developments in the Law—Declaratory Judgments, 1941–1949" (1949) 62 Harv. L.R. 787.

[2] *Clough v. Ratcliffe* (1847) 1 De G. & S. 164, 178–179.

[3] See, *e.g.* *Elliotson v. Knowles* (1842) 11 L.J.Ch. 399, 400.

[4] See Borchard, *op. cit.* (2nd ed.), pp. 125–128, for an account of the rules of Scots law and Brougham's campaign.

[5] The view taken by the Chancery has been that since equity acts *in personam* it would be indecent to command the Crown and, moreover, the court's command would be nugatory, since it could not be enforced by attachment or sequestration (Clode, *op. cit.* pp. 142–143). This does not sufficiently explain the refusal to make purely declaratory orders against the Crown. The explanation is to be found in the general practice of the court not to make such orders against any person.

[6] Crown Debts Act 1541 (33 Hen. 8, c.39); see esp. s.79 (repealed). The leading cases on equitable relief against the Crown in the Exchequer include *Sir Thomas Cecil's Case*

Whether its jurisdiction extended to declaring that the Crown was under an obligation (*e.g.* to pay money) to the plaintiff is very dubious.[7] In 1841 its general equitable jurisdiction passed to the Court of Chancery,[8] but it seems probable that its jurisdiction to give equitable relief against the Crown was incidental to its capacity as a court of revenue and did not, therefore, pass to the Court of Chancery.[9] But whatever may be the correct view, it appears to have ceased to exercise this jurisdiction after 1841 and the Court of Chancery was never called upon to determine whether it had succeeded to it. Not until 1911 was its jurisdiction to award declaratory judgments in ordinary civil actions against the Crown, represented by the Attorney-General, rediscovered and revived[10] and all the precedents cited on that occasion were Exchequer precedents.

Legislative reforms

13–040 The Judicature Acts of 1873–75 transferred the jurisdiction of the superior courts of common law and equity to the High Court, and empowered the Rule Committee to make rules regulating the practice and procedure of the court. Order 25, rule 5, made in 1853 provided:

> "No action or proceeding shall be open to objection, on the ground that a merely declaratory judgment or order is sought thereby, and the Court may make binding declarations of right whether any consequential relief is or could be claimed, or not.[11]"

13–041 The concluding words of the rule were designed to rectify the unsatisfactory state of affairs that had arisen through the restrictive interpretation given to the 1852 Act. But the courts, while recognising

---

(1598) 7 Co.Rep. 18b; *Pawlett v. Att.-Gen.* (1668) Hardres 465; *Casberd v. Att.-Gen.* (1819) 6 Price 411; *Deare v. Att.-Gen.* (1835) 1 Y. & C.Ex. 197; *Hodge v. Att.-Gen.* (1839) 3 Y. & C.Ex. 342.

[7] See *Tito v. Waddell (No. 2)* [1977] Ch. 106, 256–259, where the plaintiffs were unable to proceed under the Crown Proceedings Act 1947 in so far as their claim against the Crown was held not to arise "in respect of His Majesty's Government in the United Kingdom" (s.40(2)(b)). It was further stated that even if jurisdiction to grant declaratory relief in such circumstances did exist, this statutory exemption of the Crown from liability should normally lead the court in its discretion to refuse relief.

[8] Court of Chancery Act 1841.

[9] See *Att.-Gen. v. Halling* (1846) 15 M. & W. 687, 698–699. No clear finding on this point was made in *Dyson v. Att.-Gen.* [1911] 1 K.B. 410. If the revenue jurisdiction passed to the High Court under s.10 of the Judicature Act 1873 and was exercised by the Queen's Bench Division after 1881, the point is an academic one.

[10] *Dyson v. Att.-Gen.* [1911] 1 K.B. 410.

[11] Order 15, r.16 in the final version of the Rules of the Supreme Court.

that Order 25, rule 5, had introduced "an innovation of a very important kind",[12] still showed a curious reluctance to award declarations save in cases where other relief might have been claimed for a legal wrong, and they insisted that the jurisdiction should be exercised with great caution. The turning point came in 1911. The Inland Revenue Commissioners issued to Dyson, a taxpayer, a form and notice requiring him under penalty to submit certain particulars. Relying on the pre-1842 Exchequer precedents and Order 25, rule 5, he sued the Attorney-General for declarations that the requisition was unauthorised and that he was under no obligation to comply with it inasmuch as it was *ultra vires* the Finance Act. The Court of Appeal held that this form of proceeding was a proper one,[13] and subsequently granted the declarations sought.[14] The judgments in the first *Dyson* case were founded partly on a misreading of legal history[15]; the court failed, moreover, to consider the question whether Order 25, rule 5, bound the Crown[16] and the decision raised the difficult problem whether, and if so, how far, the action for a declaration against the Attorney-General could be employed, when a petition of right against the Crown would have been an appropriate remedy.[17] But the decision was of the highest importance in the

---

[12] *Ellis v. Duke of Bedford* [1899] 1 Ch. 494, 515; *Chapman v. Michaelson* [1909] 1 Ch. 238, 243.

[13] *Dyson v. Att.-Gen.* [1911] 1 K.B. 410.

[14] *Dyson v. Att.-Gen.* [1912] 1 Ch. 159. The *Dyson* principle was applied in *Burghes v. Att.-Gen.* [1911] 2 Ch. 139 (*aff'd.* [1912] 1 Ch. 173).

[15] The court erroneously assumed (see also *Esquimalt & Nanaimo Railway Co. v. Wilson* [1920] A.C. 358, 365–368) that the Exchequer precedents were equally applicable to the Court of Chancery. For an attempt to explain away this aberration, see *Bombay & Persia Steam Navigation Co. v. Maclay* [1920] 3 K.B. 402, 407. But Cozens-Hardy M.R. observed ([1911] 1 K.B. 410, 417): 'The absence of any precedent does not trouble me.'

[16] See H. Street, *Governmental Liability,* p. 134, pointing out that as the rule was not expressed to bind the Crown the decision can be defended only on the assumption that the Exchequer precedents alone were being relied on; the Chancery practice had been to refuse to award declarations against the Crown except on a petition of right. For the present application of the Rules of the Supreme Court to proceedings by and against the Crown, see RSC, Ord. 77, r. 1; *Franklin v. The Queen (No. 2)* [1974] Q.B. 205.

[17] *Semble,* where the rights of the Crown were directly affected and a petition of right was a proper remedy, an action for a declaration against the Attorney-General as the representative of the Crown would not lie: *Att.-Gen. for Ontario v. MacLean Gold Mines Ltd* [1927] A.C. 185. The controversy surrounding this question (for which see Street, *op. cit.* pp. 132–133; Glanville Williams, *Crown Proceedings,* p. 90) has become largely irrelevant since the Crown Proceedings Act 1947, which abolished the petition of right procedure for almost all purposes; though *cf.* Colonial Stock Act 1877, s.20; *Franklin v. Att.-Gen.* [1974] Q.B. 185. And see *Tito v. Waddell (No. 2)* [1977] Ch. 106, 259–260 (declaratory relief should not be granted when an action under the Crown Proceedings Act 1947 could be instituted).

development of the action for a declaration. In the first place, the members of the court not merely upheld the propriety of the form of proceeding adopted but gave it their warm approval.[18]

13–042   Secondly, this was a case in which the plaintiff had no "cause of action" that would have entitled him to any other form of judicial relief; the threat to his interests created by the unlawful demand that had been made upon him could be directly averted only by the award of a binding declaration.[19]

Thirdly, the plaintiff could have waited until he was sued for penalties for non-compliance with the requisition and then set up its invalidity by way of defence; nevertheless, the court declined to regard that procedure as the only permissible method of determining the issue.

13–043   In 1915 the principle laid down in *Dyson*'s case was buttressed by a further decision of the Court of Appeal in which it affirmed its power to make a declaration that plaintiffs were not under a legal obligation (to repay money paid to them in respect of certain bills of exchange) to which the defendants (who had instituted proceedings against the plaintiffs in the United States) claimed them to be subject.[20] In this case the defendant had contended that Order 25, rule 5, was not *ultra vires*.

The Rule Committee had statutory power to make rules for practice and procedure with respect to all matters over which the Supreme Court had jurisdiction[21]; it had admittedly no power to extend the jurisdiction of the court. The Court of Appeal held, however, that the rule had not conferred any new jurisdiction upon the court and was, therefore, *ultra vires*. Jurisdiction to give purely declaratory judgments, even in cases where there was no independent cause of action and no possibility of granting consequential relief, had (so the court held) always resided in the Court of Chancery although the court had

---

[18] See, esp., *per* Farwell L.J. [1911] 1 K.B. 410, 420; *per* Fletcher Moulton L.J. [1912] 1 Ch. 158, 168.

[19] It would seem that the legal right asserted by Dyson was his privilege to decide what information to supply to the Commissioners in the absence of any legally enforceable duty of the kind alleged by them. In *Gouriet v. Union of Post Office Workers* [1978] A.C. 435, 502, Lord Diplock suggested that the relevant interest of Dyson was that an unlawful demand had been made for a penalty payable for non-compliance, which, had the plaintiff succumbed, he could have sued to recover; *cf.* his Lordship's analysis of the applicant's rights affected in *R. v. Criminal Injuries Compensation Board, ex p. Lain* [1967] 2 Q.B. 864, 888–889. See now *Woolwich Equitable Building Society v. Inland Revenue Commissioners* [1993] 1 A.C. 70.

[20] *Guaranty Trust Co. of New York v. Hannay & Co.* [1915] 2 K.B. 536, *per* Pickford and Bankes L.JJ., Buckley L.J. dissenting. The plaintiffs were eventually successful in obtaining the declarations they had sought: see [1918] 2 K.B. 623. See also *Russian Commercial & Industrial Bank v. British Bank for Foreign Trade Ltd* [1921] 2 A.C. 438.

[21] Judicature Act 1873, ss.16, 23; Judicature Act 1925, s.17.

adopted a settled practice of refusing to render such judgments.[22] Seldom has the elastic concept of jurisdiction been more judiciously stretched. And Bankes L.J. expressed the view that the rule "should receive as liberal a construction as possible."[23]

The growth in use of the declaration

During the present century the action declaration has become one of the most popular forms of proceedings in the High Court. As early as 1917 an American authority was able to write that the practice of making declarations of right had completely revolutionised English remedial law.[24] Most of the declaratory judgments to which he referred were given in proceedings instituted by originating summons in the Chancery Division for the determination of questions arising out of the administration of estates and trusts or for the construction of various classes of written instruments. Proceedings instituted by writ under Order 25, rule 5, were not frequent until after the *Dyson* case. In those areas of administrative law where statutory tribunals and inquiries do not operate, it has come to be more widely used against public authorities than the older and less flexible non-statutory remedies. Flexibility is, indeed, the greatest merit of the declaratory judgment.

13–044

LEGISLATIVE REFORM OF PROCEDURES

So far this historical survey has focused on the development of remedies rather than procedures. As we have seen, the fundamental characteristics of the remedies available to challenge governmental action in the High Court were largely settled by the early years of the twentieth century; the major concerns since then have been with the search for effective, efficient and flexible procedures.

13–045

In the context of public law, the procedural rules and practices of the High Court can be seen as attempting to achieve a number of goals. First, they may seek to assist the court in achieving the efficient flow of cases through what is today called the Crown Office List.[25] The concerns about how best to cope with growing numbers of applications are not new, but stretch back at least as far as the 1930s.

13–046

---

[22] [1915] 2 K.B. 563–564. This interpretation of the effect of r. 5 is not easily reconcilable with the observations on its effect referred to above, n. 94.

[23] At p. 572.

[24] E. R. Sunderland (1917) 16 Mich.L.R. 69, 77.

[25] On the Crown Office, see below, para. 14–001.

Secondly, the form of procedures may seek to protect the interests of the respondents (usually, of course, governmental bodies) and third parties from unmeritorious or tardy challenge. Thirdly, the procedures may seek to promote access for applicants, for example, by having relatively relaxed rules as to who has standing to apply for judicial review and ensuring that the procedural regime is as simple as possible. The complex array of public law procedures that exist today can be seen as an attempt to accommodate all these goals in differing degrees.[26]

Statutory applications to quash

13–047 Today, the term "statutory judicial review" is a rather confusing misnomer, for the whole judicial review jurisdiction of the High Court—with the exception of applications for the writ of habeas corpus—now has a statutory, rather than common law, foundation.[27] Nevertheless, the term is appropriate to describe the origins of this procedure in 1930. Statutory review clauses provide that within a strict time limit, usually six weeks, any person aggrieved by a specified administrative order, notice, scheme, action or other decision made may challenge its legality in the High Court. The procedural regime for so doing is entirely distinct from that of Order 53; for example, in addition to the different time limits, there is no general requirement that the applicant obtain the leave of the court.[28]

13–048 The first statutory review clause was enacted by section 11 of the Housing Act 1930 which dealt with challenges to slum clearance orders. The innovatory new procedure was prompted by a series of cases during the preceding years in which successful applications for certiorari had been made to quash orders of local authorities when the schemes had been almost brought into operation and after great expense had been incurred. The clause was presented by the government during its passage through Parliament as "a most important and valuable provision. It is the greatest safeguard you can afford to the individual and at the same time provides a method by which questions of right can be determined at the earliest possible moment."[29]

---

[26] Some have argued that the third goal at facilitating access to the courts has been given insufficient weight: see Lord Scarman [1990] P.L. 490, 492; Le Sueur and Sunkin [1992] P.L. 102 p. 127.

[27] For an account of the modern practice and procedure on statutory applications to quash, see para. 15–058 of the 5th ed. of this text.

[28] See para. 14–001 of the 5th ed. of this text.

[29] But s.289 of the Town and Country Planning Act 1990 provides an *appeal* to the High Court against an enforcement notice upheld by the Secretary of State for the

There has been an expansion in the subject areas in which statutory **13–049** review is used. At first confined to compulsory purchase and land use planning,[30] clauses[31] have come to be used increasingly in the field of regulation of industry.[32] The introduction of the statutory review procedure can clearly be seen as instigated by dissatisfaction with the operation of the common law prerogative orders. From the perspective of the respondents—particularly local authorities—the prerogative writs and procedures had failed to provide sufficient safeguards, particularly from tardy challenges.[33] Typically, however, the reforms implemented were piecemeal and designed to deal with one particular context only, namely slum clearance orders. It was to be another three years before the general inadequacies of the prerogative writ procedures were tackled.

Procedures for applying for prerogative writs[34]

Throughout the 1930s, the courts and government continued to be **13–050** concerned that the procedures for obtaining the prerogative writs were unacceptably inefficient; they were wasteful of court time and the delays that ensued had a capacity to frustrate administrative action.

Introduction of the leave requirement[35]

Until 1933, an applicant for any of the prerogative writs applied first **13–051** for an order (or rule) nisi. At this hearing, before a Divisional Court of three judges, the court considered the applicant's case in full and determined whether the writ sought should issue. If the applicant

---

Environment on appeal. The Planning and Compensation Act 1991 introduced a requirement (now the new s.289(6)) that an appeal may only be brought under that section with the leave of the court. This limitation was proposed by Robert Carnwath Q.C. in his report, *Enforcing Planning Control* (1989).

[30] H.L. Deb., cols. 461–463 (July 15, 1930). See also H.L. Deb., cols. 582–583 (July 21, 1930).

[31] See, *e.g.* the modern provisions in the: Town and Country Planning Act 1990, ss.287, 288; Local Government and Planning Act 1980, Sched. 32, Pt. I (designation of Enterprise Zones); Ancient Monuments and Archaeological Areas Act 1975, s.55; Highways Act 1980, Sched. 2.

[32] See, *e.g.* Petroleum Act 1987, s.14; Airport Act 1986, s.49; Telecommunications Act 1984, s.18; Medicines Act 1968, s.107.

[33] The Association of Municipal Councils played an important role in advocating introduction of the new review procedure.

[34] For an account of the modern practice and procedure under RSC Ord. 53, see Chap. 14.

[35] For a more detailed account of the history of the leave requirement, see Le Sueur and Sunkin [1992] P.L. 102. In the Civil Procedure Rules introduced in 1999, 'leave' was renamed permission.

satisfied the court that his case had merit, the order nisi was granted. The onus then lay on the *respondent* to show cause, at a second hearing before a Divisional Court, why the order should *not* be made absolute. Both government and the courts became dissatisfied with this procedure. From the government's perspective, it was seen as inappropriate that at the second hearing applicants could "sit back" and watch the respondent try to get the order nisi discharged. The court's dissatisfaction lay in what was seen as a duplication of efforts at the nisi and absolute hearings; at both stages a Divisional Court considered the merits of the application.

13–052   Following recommendations of the Hanworth Business of the Court Committee,[36] legislation was introduced to modernise procedures on the Crown Side of the King's Bench Division, though leaving the writ of habeas corpus, and the procedure for obtaining it, untouched; it was apparently thought that to meddle with it might be construed as subversive activity.[37] The Administration of Justice (Miscellaneous Provisions) Act 1933 abolished the two stage nisi and absolute procedure and introduced a requirement that an applicant first obtain the leave of the court before an application for a prerogative writ be made. The leave hearing continued to be an *ex parte* hearing before a Divisional Court. The real significance of the reform was that, leave having been granted, the burden remained on the applicant at the second hearing to prove his case. The 1938 Act of the same name replaced the writs of certiorari, prohibition and mandamus by orders of the same names. The change of designation reflected only a simplification of procedure.

Reform agendas

13–053   Thirty years later, dissatisfaction with the public law procedures and remedies of the High Court persisted. During the intervening period, branches of administrative law other than judicial review had undergone important reforms: the Crown Proceedings Act 1947 had more or less put the Crown in the same position as that of the ordinary defendant in private law litigation; the Tribunals and Inquiries Act 1958 had implemented many of the recommendations of the landmark Franks Committee Report; and the office of Parliamentary Commissioner for Administration had been created. In contrast, High Court procedure for judicial review—despite the limited reforms of the 1930s—were little different to those that had operated a century before.

---

[36] The Business of the Courts Committee: Interim Report, Cmd, 4265 (1933).

[37] See R. M. Jackson, *Machinery of Justice in England* (6th ed.), pp. 45–46.

In 1966 the Law Commission[38] began to take soundings on administrative law reform, with special reference to the role of the courts. In 1967 it published an exploratory working paper, and after extensive consultations it formally recommended to the Lord Chancellor in May 1969 that a wide-ranging inquiry be conducted by a Royal Commission or a body of similar status into the following questions: **13–054**

(1) whether the form and procedure of existing judicial remedies in administrative law needed to be altered;

(2) whether changes in the scope of judicial review were required;

(3) how far remedies in respect of administrative acts and omissions should include the right to damages;

(4) whether special principles should govern administrative contracts and torts; and

(5) how far changes should be made in the organisation and personnel of the courts for the purposes of administrative law.[39]

At this time the civil service was beginning to receive the impact of the Parliamentary Commissioner for Administration and was also about to undergo reconstruction in the light of the recommendations of the Fulton Committee.[40] Many prominent civil servants, moreover, were uneasy at the spontaneous revival of judicial activism. And some lawyers thought that procedural reform was too urgent to be deferred till the conclusion of a large-scale inquiry.

In December 1969 the Lord Chancellor rejected the Law Commission's recommendations and requested it to undertake its own inquiry into question (1), the form and procedure of judicial remedies; changes in the scope of review were to be outside the Commission's terms of reference.[41] **13–055**

In 1971, while the Law Commission was carrying out its investigation, Justice (the British Section of the International Commission of Jurists) published its own report entitled *Administration under Law*, in which it examined some of the basic issues shelved by the Government. Among its proposals were the extension of duties to **13–056**

---

[38] Constituted as a permanent advisory body on law reform in pursuance of the Law Commissions Act 1965. For a short account of the Commission's method of work see R.M. Jackson, *op. cit.* (6th ed.), pp. 538–545; and see, generally, J.H. Farrar, *Law Reform and the Law Commission*.

[39] Cmnd. 4059 (1969).

[40] Report of the Committee on the Civil Service, Cmnd. 3638 (1968).

[41] H.L. Deb., Vol. 306, cols. 189–190 (December 4, 1969).

provide official information and reasons for decisions, the creation of new machinery to enable a court to ascertain the facts on which administrative decisions were based, and the conferment of power to award damages to persons aggrieved by decisions tainted with procedural or substantive irregularity in circumstances where there is no cause of action for damages under the law as it now stands. The detailed recommendations were open to criticism on various grounds,[42] particularly in view of the burden they would impose on the public service, but the suggestions for compensation and damages pinpointed an important weakness inherent in the present scope and effect of judicial review. Since this was a report by an unofficial body, it could be and was conveniently ignored by the Government.

The creation of a new RSC Order 53

13–057 The Law Commission, impeded by the unfortunately restrictive nature of its brief, produced its final report in 1976,[43] some four and a half years after the publication of a detailed working paper.[44] The principal proposal of the Commission was that all the existing non-statutory administrative law remedies should be capable of being claimed in a unified application for judicial review. Again, as in the reforms of the 1930s, no consideration was given to the status of the writ of habeas corpus. The Commission's main recommendation was implemented, with an expedition which was previously absent, by amendments to the Rules of the Supreme Court that took effect in January 1978.[45] The new RSC Ord. 53 provided for a single procedure for obtaining the prerogative orders, injunctions, declarations and damages in public law proceedings. The leave requirement was retained. The Divisional Court of the Queen's Bench continued to hear both applications for leave[46] and substantive hearings. The limited nature of the reforms is revealed by the fact that they were implemented by means of a series of amendments to the Rules of Court. Only several years later, after questions were raised as to the *vires* under which the Rule Committee had acted, was the application for judicial review put on a statutory

---

[42] See *e.g.* (1972) 12 J.S.P.T.L. (N.S.) 72.

[43] Cmnd. 6407 (1976).

[44] *Remedies in Administrative Law* (Law Com. No. 40). A similar working paper on the corresponding remedies in Scots law was issued by the Scottish Law Commission (Memorandum No. 14). The working paper's modest proposals evoked a surprising amount of criticism both on technical grounds and because they would indirectly expand the scope of judicial review, which would be undesirable.

[45] RSC (Amendment No. 3) 1977, (S.I. 1977 No. 1955) (L. 30). *Cf.* Judicature (Northern Ireland) Act 1978, ss.18–25.

[46] Except during Vacation, when the application was to a judge in chambers.

footing.[47] The aspects of the Commission's proposals (in particular that interim declaratory relief be available against the Crown) which clearly required to be introduced by statute remained unimplemented.[48]

Problems with the new Order 53

The new Order 53 was to some extent a victim of its own success: the **13–058** availability of a streamlined procedure was one reason for the rapid growth in the number of applications for judicial review. Soon there were considerable delays in determining cases on the Crown Office List. In 1980, two years after the major reform, a number of further extensive and fundamental changes were made to Order 53. Provision was made for both leave and substantive applications to be heard by single judges rather than the Divisional Court[49] and applications for leave could now be made "on paper" without the need for any hearing.

In 1985, the government attempted to take a further step to make **13–059** Order 53 more efficient. By clause 43 of the Administration of Justice Bill, it sought to abolish the applicant's right to renew a leave application to the Court of Appeal. Judges of the Court of Appeal took the unprecedented step of speaking against this proposal while giving judgment[50] and during the committee stage of the Bill in the House of Lords, Lord Denning described the proposal as a "constitutional monstrosity". The clause was defeated, reintroduced in an amended form (allowing renewal to a Divisional Court including a Lord Justice of Appeal), but that too was defeated.

For a period, the modified Order 53 enabled applications for judicial **13–060** review to be determined with acceptable dispatch. By the close of the 1980s, however, the Crown Court List was again beset with delays which continue to this day.

Justice/All Souls Review

Undeterred by the lack of government interest in its earlier report, **13–061** Justice again picked up the gauntlet of administrative law reform. In

---

[47] Supreme Court Act 1981, s.31.

[48] For comments, see H.W.R. Wade (1978) 94 L.Q.R. 179; Carol Harlow [1978] P.L. 1; J. Beatson and M.H. Matthews (1978) 41 M.L.R. 437; and see the commentary on Order 53 in *The Supreme Court Practice.*

[49] A Divisional Court continues to hear applications for leave and substantive applications in 'criminal causes or matters'. See, further, para. 14–011.

[50] *R. v. Income Tax Special Commissioner, ex p. Stipplechoice Ltd.* [1985] 2 All E.R. 465, 467, *per* Ackner L.J. See also the comment by A.W. Bradley [1986] P.L. 361.

1978, a committee was established in conjunction with All Souls College, Oxford charged with devising practical proposals for reform with the aim of giving administrative law clarity, coherence, comprehensibility and accessibility.[51] Ten years later, it published its report.[52] It made several recommendations in relation to judicial review remedies and procedures. First, that the leave requirement in Order 53 proceedings should be abandoned. In its place there should be a procedure for striking out hopeless or bogus applications or, alternatively, a two-stage procedure similar to that in Scotland should be introduced.[53] Secondly, the three month limitation period should be repealed and undue delay should be a barrier only in so far as it causes substantial prejudice or hardship to others or would be detrimental to good administration.[54] Thirdly, discovery and cross-examination should be permitted more liberally; the general rule should be that documents which are relevant to contested issues between the parties should be disclosed. Fourthly, the Committee supported the increasingly liberal grant of *locus standi*.[55]

13–062   The Committee's report attracted considerable interest and no less criticism. Given its commitment to promoting access to justice rather than the safeguarding of respondents or to efficiency, it never looked likely to find favour with government.

Reconsideration by the Law Commission

13–063   During the early 1990s the Law Commission once again turned its attention to judicial review procedures and remedies.[56] Its recommendations were cautious. The liberal interpretation of *O'Reilly v. Mackman*[57] and its principle of procedural exclusivity, already accepted by the House of Lords,[58] was approved. The report recommended that the leave stage in Order 53 proceedings ought to be retained, though renamed the "preliminary consideration" and that

---

[51] For a critique of the Committee's methodology, see Dawn Oliver and R.C. Austin [1991] P.L. 441; Carol Harlow (1990) 40 J.L.S. 85.

[52] Report of the Committee of the Justice/All Souls Review of Administrative Law in the United Kingdom, *Administrative Justice—Some Necessary Reforms* (1988).

[53] *Op. cit.* Chap. 5.

[54] *Loc. cit.*

[55] *Op. cit.* para. 7–050.

[56] See: Law Commission Fifth Programme of Law Reform. Law Com. No. 200 (1991); Law Commission Consultation Paper No. 126 (1993); *Administrative Law: Judicial Review and Statutory Appeals*. Law Com. No. 226 (October 1994); R. Gordon Q.C., [1995] P.L. 11.

[57] See further Chap. 3 above.

[58] *Roy v. Kensington and Chelsea and Westminster Family Practitioner Committee* [1992] 1 A.C. 624.

the test be whether the application discloses a serious issue which ought to be determined.[59] The Law Commission endorsed the continued existence of a requirement of standing, but argued that the court should have a discretion to allow applications where the applicant was not directly affected by the impugned decision but it was nevertheless in the public interest that the application proceed.[60]

In relation to the forms of relief, the report recommended that the Latin names for the prerogative writs (certiorari, prohibition and mandamus) be replaced with plain English ones.[61] Interim and advisory declarations should be available to the court.[62] No proposals were made for the reform of habeas corpus, though the Law Commission argued against the narrow approach to the scope of review adopted by the Court of Appeal in recent applications for habeas corpus.[63]
 13–064

The Civil Procedure Rules

The latest "history" of reform of public law procedures cannot yet be written. As this book is being written in May 1999, the new Civil Procedure Rules have recently come into force. The rules, made under powers conferred by the Civil Procedure Act 1997, provide a single code for litigation in the county courts, the High Court and Court of Appeal. They implement many of the recommendations made by Lord Woolf's inquiry into civil justice in England and Wales conducted during the mid-1990s.[64] There was not, alas, sufficient time to revise thoroughly the procedural rules governing public law litigation in the High Court. Those rules, including Order 53, have for the time being been re-enacted with only minor drafting amendments in Schedule 1 to the Civil Procedure Rules. New public law procedural rules will be made in due course. The committee responsible for drafting the new rules are under a duty to exercise their powers "with a view to securing that the civil justice system is accessible, fair and efficient."[65]
 13–065

One of Lord Woolf's recommendations was, however, implemented speedily. Applications for judicial review against local authorities by homeless persons accounted for over a third of cases initiated in 1995. The Housing Act 1996 enacted a requirement that local authorities
 13–066

---

[59] See below, para. 14–020.

[60] See above, para. 2–025.

[61] See below, para. 15–003.

[62] See below, para. 15–030.

[63] See paras 15–036 *et seq.* of the 5th ed. of this text.

[64] See *Access to Justice: a final report to the Lord Chancellor* (1996). Chapter 18 of the report deals specifically with public law proceedings.

[65] Civil Procedure Act 1997, s.1(3).

establish internal complaints procedures for dealing with such complaints; and where a dispute cannot be resolved in this way, an appeal on points of law may be taken to the county courts.[66]

---

[66] Housing Act 1996, ss.202, 204.

CHAPTER 14

THE APPLICATION FOR JUDICIAL REVIEW

INTRODUCTION

This Chapter describes and evaluates the main procedure for raising **14–001** issues of public law in England and Wales. The legal basis of the procedures for making an application for judicial review is sections 29, 31 and 43 of the Supreme Court Act 1981 and Order 53. Until April 1999, Order 53 was part of the Rules of the Supreme Court, the procedural code which used to govern the conduct of litigation in the High Court. Order 53 now forms part of the Civil Procedure Rules (CPR) that apply to all litigation in county courts, the High Court and Court of Appeal (Civil Division). When the CPR were first made, there was not sufficient time to carry out any thorough-going reform of Order 53. It was therefore re-enacted, with some changes in terminology, in Schedule 1 to the CPR.[1] Everything provided for in Order 53 must now be interpreted and applied in the light of "revolutionary" culture which underpins the new CPR—the "overriding objective of enabling the court to deal with cases justly".[2] More particularly[3]:

"Dealing with a case justly includes, so far as practicable—

(a) ensuring that the parties are on an equal footing;

(b) saving expense;

(c) dealing with the case in ways which are proportionate—

   (i) to the amount of money involved;
   (ii) to the importance of the case;
   (iii) to the complexity of the issues; and
   (iv) to the financial position of each party;

---

[1] See also the *Practice Direction*.
[2] CPR, r. 1.1(1).
[3] CPR, r. 1.1(2).

(d) ensuring that it is dealt with expeditiously and fairly; and

(e) allotting to it an appropriate share of the court's resources, while taking into account the need to allot the resources to other cases."

Most of the practices and procedures for making an application for judicial review are not, however, greatly affected by the enactment of the CPR. The two main features which distinguish Order 53 from other forms of litigation remain as they were before:

(i) An applicant may not commence an application for judicial review without first obtaining the permission (formerly "leave") of the High Court to do so. Other types of civil proceedings are started when the court issues a claim form at the request of a claimant.[4]

(ii) There is a requirement that applications for permission be made "promptly, and in any event within three months from the date when grounds for the application first arose unless the court considers there is a good reason for extending the period within which the application shall be made".[5] The time periods for commencing claims in tort and breach of contract are set out in the Limitation Act 1980, typically six years from the date on which the cause of action arose.

Applications for judicial review are dealt with separately from the other forms of litigation handled within the Queen's Bench Division. Pending judicial review applications are placed on the Crown Office List and are determined by one or more of the specialist High Court judges "nominated" by the Lord Chief Justice for the purpose. The number of nominated judges has grown from four to 25. They spend only some of their time on Crown Office litigation; like other High Court judges they also try other civil and criminal cases. These arrangements represent a compromise: while recognising the need for expert judges in the field of public law, it maintains the English tradition that everyone, including public bodies and office-holders, ought to be subject to justice in the ordinary courts.[6]

14–002   Order 53 provides for a single procedure for seeking and obtaining one or more of the prerogative remedies of certiorari, prohibition and

---

[4] CPR, Part 7. There is also an alternative procedure for starting claims in Part 8.

[5] Order 53, r. 4(1), discussed below at para. 14–013.

[6] See A.V. Dicey, *Introduction to the Study of the Law of the Constitution* (10th ed., 1959), p. 193: Dicey's second meaning of the rule of law was that 'every man, whatever his rank or condition, is subject to the ordinary law of the realm and amenable to the jurisdiction of the ordinary tribunals'.

mandamus.[7] An applicant may also seek an injunction[8]; a declaration[9] and damages in the same application.[10] The Order 53 procedure has acted as an important catalyst in the growth of judicial review and the development of legal principle in the field of administrative law. The procedure usually consists of two, but there can be three or four stages:

(1) the application for permission of the court to commence proceedings;

(2) an interlocutory stage;

(3) the hearing of the substantive application; and finally

(4) any appeal.

OBTAINING THE PERMISSION OF THE COURT[11]

The requirement that a person wishing to make a public law challenge   **14–003** to a public body must first obtain the permission (or leave) of the court is a controversial one. There have been calls both for its abolition[12] and in support of its retention.[13]

The purpose of the permission stage

The permission stage in Order 53 proceedings serves a number of   **14–004** purposes. First, it may safeguard public authorities by deterring or eliminating clearly ill-founded claims without the need for them to become a party to litigation. The requirement may also prevent administrative action being paralysed by a pending, but possibly

---

[7] Order 53, r. 1(1). See also the Supreme Court Act 1981, s. 31(1), (2). For an account of the historical development of the prerogative orders, see para. 13–005; and on the grant of prerogative orders, para. 15–003.

[8] Para. 15–016.

[9] Para. 15–030.

[10] See Chap. 16.

[11] Supreme Court Act 1981, s. 31(3), (6); Order 53, r. 3. Prior to the CPR, the term used was 'leave' rather than 'permission.' See, generally, A.P. Le Sueur and M. Sunkin, 'Applications for Judicial Review: The Requirement of Leave' [1992] P.L. 102.

[12] See, *e.g.* Justice/All Souls Review, *Administrative Justice—Some Necessary Reforms* (1988), p. 157; Lord Scarman [1990] P.L. 490.

[13] Woolf, *Protection of the Public—A New Challenge* (1990), p.20 and Law Com. No. 226, Part V.

spurious, legal challenge.[14] Secondly, for the High Court, the permission procedure provides a mechanism for the efficient management of the growing judicial review caseload. A large proportion of applications can be disposed of at the permission stage with the minimum use of the court's limited resources.[15] Thirdly, for the applicant the permission stage, far from being an impediment to access to justice, may actually be advantageous since it enables the litigant expeditiously and cheaply to obtain the views of a High Court judge on the merits of his application.[16]

Criteria on which permission is granted or refused

14–005 No comprehensive statement of the criteria for determining applications for permission exists. Section 31 of the Supreme Court Act 1981 and Order 53 refer expressly to only two grounds on which permission should be refused: where there has been delay in applying to the court[17]; or where the applicant does not have a sufficient interest in the matter to which the application relates.[18] It has been held, however, that these issues of delay[19] and *locus standi*[20] should ordinarily be left to be dealt with at the full hearing; in practice, only in the clearest cases will permission be refused on either of these grounds alone.[21] In addition to having sufficient interest, in some recent cases it has been held that an applicant must have legal personality; permission may therefore be refused where an unincorporated association brings proceedings in its own name.[22]

14–006 Permission will be refused where applications are:

(1) "frivolous, vexatious or hopeless"[23]

(2) made by "busybodies with misguided or trivial complaints of administrative error"[24];

---

[14] See Lord Diplock, *Inland Revenue Commissioners v. National Federation of Self-Employed and Small Businesses* [1982] A.C. 617, 643.

[15] See CPR, r.1(1)(2)(e), set out in para. 14–001 above.

[16] See Woolf, *Protection of the Public—A New Challenge* (1990), p. 21.

[17] s. 31(6), (7) and r. 4. See below, para. 14–013.

[18] s. 31(3) and r. 3(7). On standing generally, see above, Chap. 2.

[19] See *Caswell v. Dairy Produce Quota Tribunal for England and Wales* [1990] 2 A.C. 738. *Cf. R. v. Secretary of State for Trade and Industry, ex p. Greenpeace Ltd* [1998] Env. L.R. 415.

[20] *Inland Revenue Commissioners v. National Federation of Self-Employed and Small Businesses* [1982] A.C. 617; *R. v. Somerset County Council, ex p. Dixon* [1997] C.O.D. 323 at 327.

[21] Le Sueur and Sunkin [1992] P.L. 102, pp. 120–121.

[22] See para. 2–023.

[23] See *The Supreme Court Practice 1998*, para. 53/1–14/30.

[24] *Inland Revenue Commissioners v. National Federation of Self-Employed and Small Businesses* [1982] A.C. 617 at 643.

(3) "misconceived";

(4) "unarguable" or "groundless";

(5) where there is a more appropriate alternative procedure[25]; or

(6) where an application for judicial review is an inappropriate procedure.[26]

Uberrimae fides is required, and permission will not be granted, or may later be set aside, if there has been deliberate misrepresentation or concealment of material facts in the applicant's written evidence.[27] Permission has sometimes been refused on grounds of policy, principally that to subject certain sorts of decision to judicial review challenge would be detrimental to effective administration.[28] It has been suggested that it is wrong for such a broad discretion to be exercised at this preliminary stage of the litigation process, if only because important issues of principle may often emerge only late in the litigation process.[29] Concern has also been expressed about variation in the rates of grant of permission between different subject areas of judicial review and also between different judges.[30]

Exhaustion of alternative remedies

One of the most common grounds upon which permission to apply for judicial review is refused is that an applicant has failed to pursue a   **14–007**

---

[25] See para. 14–007.

[26] If the matter is a private law one, the court rather than refusing the application for permission, may order that the case continue as if begun by claim form in CPR, Pt 7.

[27] *R. v. Kensington I.T.C.* [1917] 1 K.B. 486; *R. v. Stevens, ex p. Callender, The Times,* October 26, 1956.

[28] In *R. v. Secretary of State for the Home Department, ex p. Swati* [1986] 1 W.L.R. 772, the Court of Appeal laid down that leave should be granted only in "exceptional circumstances" where applicants were persons refused admission to the U.K. on the ground that an immigration officer was not satisfied that they were genuine visitors. In *R. v. Harrow L.B.C., ex p. D.* [1990] Fam. 133, Butler-Sloss L.J. in the Court of Appeal said, in considering a challenge by a mother of a decision to place her and her children's names on a child protection register: "The important power of the court to intervene should be kept very much in reserve, perhaps confined to the exceptional case which involves a point of principle which needs to be resolved, not only for the individual case but cases in general so as to establish that [case conferences] are not being conducted in an unsatisfactory manner. In the normal case where criticism is made of some individual aspect of the procedure which does not raise any point of principle, leave [*i.e.* permission] should be refused."

[29] *e.g.* as in *R. v. Norfolk C.C., ex p. M* [1989] Q.B. 619. See Le Sueur and Sunkin [1992] P.L. 102, p. 125.

[30] M. Sunkin, L. Bridges and G. Mészáros, *Judicial Review in Perspective* (1995).

more appropriate method of pursuing the grievance.[31] For the court to require the alternative procedure to be exhausted prior to resorting to judicial review is in accord with judicial review being very properly regarded as a remedy of last resort. It is important that the process should not be clogged with unnecessary cases which are perfectly capable of being dealt with in another tribunal. It can also be the situation that Parliament, by establishing an alternative procedure, indicated either expressly or by implication that it intends that procedure to be used. In exercising its discretion the court will attach importance to the indication of Parliament's intention and the general policy of the CPR to encourage alternative dispute resolution.[32] A third reason for requiring an alternative procedure to be used is that the alternative body may have a special expertise in determining the issues involved.

14–008 The applicant will not however be required to resort to some other procedure if that other procedure is less convenient or otherwise less appropriate.[33] The other body may for example lack the power to deal with the issue.[34] The other procedure may be less expeditious and if a matter is urgent the court may allow the application to proceed.[35] Where the alternative procedure is an appeal, this will usually indicate that it is more appropriate, as the powers on the appeal are likely to be at least as extensive as those of the court and the appeal procedure will usually include machinery which ensures that the proper material is available for the purpose of determining the appeal. Thus on appeal from magistrates, the "case stated procedure" is usually more appropriate than judicial review.[36] The case stated contains the

---

[31] Such alternative remedies have been held to include: persuing an appeal to a statutory tribunal (*e.g. R. v. Secretary of State for the Home Department, ex p. Swati* [1986] 1 W.L.R. 722; *R. v. Chief Constable of Merseyside Police, ex p. Calveley* [1986] 1 Q.B. 424; *R. v. Ministry of Defence, ex p. Sweeney* [1999] C.O.D. 122); an offer of a rehearing by the respondent public body (*e.g. R. v. London Beth Din, ex p. Bloom* [1998] C.O.D. 131); commencing a private prosecution (*e.g. R. v. DPP, ex p. Camelot Group plc* (1998) 10 Admin.L.R. 93); making a complaint to the Local Commissioner for Administration (*R. v. Lambeth LBC, ex p. Crookes* (1997) 29 H.L.R. 28).

[32] See, *e.g. R. v. Chief Constable of Merseyside, ex p. Calveley* [1986] 1 Q.B. 424; *R. v. Secretary of State for Home Affairs, ex p. Swati* [1986] 1 W.L.R. 477; Bradley 'Judicial Review by Other Routes' [1988] P.L. 169; Lewis 'The Exhaustion of Alternative Remedies in Administrative Law' [1992] C.L.J. 138.

[33] *R. v. Hillingdon L.B.C., ex p. Royco Homes Ltd* [1974] Q.B. 720; *R. v. Chief Immigration Officer, ex p. Kharrazi* [1980] W.L.R. 1396 (not practicable to use the machinery under s. 13 Immigration Act 1971 as applicant would have to return to Iran to exercise his right of appeal and would be caught in a war).

[34] *Leech v. Deputy Governor of Parkhurst Prison* [1988] A.C. 533 (at that time the Home Secretary lacked the power to remove a disciplinary finding in relation to a prisoner from his record).

[35] See, *e.g. R. v. Hillingdon L.B.C., ex p. Royco Homes Ltd.*, n. 33 above.

[36] But *cf. R. v. Hereford Magistrates Court, ex p. Rowlands* [1998] Q.B. 110.

findings of the magistrates which would not otherwise normally be available.[37] If, of course, the issue cannot be determined on appeal then there will be no valid objection to judicial review. Questions as to whether an applicant should have resorted to another procedure will normally arise on the application for permission and not after the hearing on the merits. Once the court has heard the merits there is little purpose in requiring the parties to resort to some other tribunal.[38]

It is also necessary to distinguish the situation where the existence **14–009** of a second tier appeal cures a defect in the previous procedures—for example, where a subsequent appeal provides the required degree of fairness which was missing from the original procedure. Here again no question of discretion is involved.[39]

Applying for permission

The application for permission must be in the form of a full statement **14–010** that identifies and describes the applicant, sets out the relief sought and the grounds on which it is sought,[40] and be supported by written evidence verifying the facts relied on.[41] The applicant may choose to apply for permission in one of two ways: by a wholly written application, or by a short hearing in open court.[42]

Applications for permission are dealt with on paper unless an oral **14–011** hearing is requested on Form 86A. Written applications for permission are invariably determined by a single nominated judge. When there is a hearing in non-criminal causes or matters,[43] permission applications

---

[37] *R. v. Poole Magistrates, ex p. Benham* [1991] R.V.R. 217 but fact that applicant required bail altered the situation. See also *R. v. Special Commissioner, ex p. Napier* [1988] All E.R. 166.

[38] See *ex p. Calveley*, above, n. 32.

[39] See above, para. 9–019 *et seq.*

[40] In Prescribed Form 86A.

[41] Order 53, r. 3(2).

[42] r. 3(3). Applications for permission are listed on the footing that they will take no more than 20 minutes and any reply by the respondent will take no more than 10 minutes: see *Practice Note* [1991] 1 W.L.R. 280.

[43] In Order 53 proceedings, for some purposes distinction is drawn between 'criminal' and 'civil' applications. For a definition of criminal cause or matter see *Amand v. Secretary of State for Home Affairs* [1943] A.C. 147, 156, *per* Viscount Simon L.C.: proceedings '... the direct outcome of which may be trial of the applicant and his possible punishment for an alleged offence by a Court claiming jurisdiction to do so'; see also *Carr v. Atkins* [1987] Q.B. 963 and *R. v. Blandford JJ., ex p. Pamment* [1990] 1 W.L.R. 1490. The main practical consequence is that in Ord. 53 renewed permission hearings and full hearings of criminal applications are dealt with by a Divisional Court and there is no appeal to the Court of Appeal but an appeal with permission to the House of Lords: Supreme Court Act 1981, s. 18(1)(a) and Administration of

are usually determined by a single judge, or, exceptionally, by a Divisional Court.[44] Where the application relates to a criminal matter (*e.g.* judicial review of a decision of magistrates in criminal proceedings), the hearing is usually before a Divisional Court as when in a criminal cause of matter heard by a single judge an applicant has the right to renew before a Divisional Court.

14–012   Oral applications tend to be used where the facts are complex, the legal submissions subtle or the applicant has delayed making the application for permission. A hearing may also be a more effective way of generating publicity for an applicant's cause. Where interim remedies are sought there must be an oral application of which all affected parties should normally have had notice.[45] In other cases, even if an applicant does not request an oral hearing, the court may order there to be one. It has been suggested that an oral application on notice should be made in cases involving school closures and analogous issues.[46] Written applications have the advantage of being less costly for the applicant; there is no need to instruct counsel to appear. It is sensible to make applications in writing where it is quite clear that leave should be granted.[47]

The timing of the application for permission

14–013   An application for permission may be refused if it is made tardily or if it is premature. Applications for permission must be made "promptly and in any event within three months from the date when grounds for the application first arose unless the court considers there is good reason for extending the period within which the application should

---

Justice Act 1960, s. 1(2).

[44] The allocation of a civil case (at the leave stage or the full hearing) to a Divisional Court of two or more judges may be made by the Crown Office where particularly complex or politically sensitive issues are raised by an application. The difference between a Divisional Court and a hearing before a single judge is that while the latter is before a High Court judge alone, the Divisional Court will be presided over by a Lord Justice who will normally sit with one, but sometimes two, High Court judges.

[45] *R. v. Kensington and Chelsea R.L.B.C., ex p. Hammell* [1989] Q.B. 518.

[46] *R. v. Northamptonshire C.C., ex p. K* [1994] C.O.D. 28.

[47] It has been suggested that the requirement of leave should be dispensed with when both parties agree: Woolf, [1992] P.L. 221, 232.

be made."[48] Where certiorari[49] is sought in respect of any judgment, order, conviction or other proceedings, time begins to run from the date of that judgment, etc.[50] Apart from certiorari there is no such legislative formula to guide the court. Factors taken into account include: whether the applicant had prior warning of the decision complained of[51]; and whether there has been a period of time between the taking of the decision impugned and its communication to the applicant.[52] The fact that a breach of a public law duty is a continuing one does not necessarily make it irrelevant to take into account the data at which the breach began in considering any question of delay.[53] The primary requirement is always one of promptness and permission may be refused on the ground of undue delay even if the application is made within three months.[54] The mere fact that permission is given does not mean that an extension of time for making the application is given; an express application for extension of time must be made.[55] If time is extended at the permission stage, the question of delay remains relevant to the discretion of the court to grant or refuse relief at the full hearing.[56]

The criteria governing the exercise of the court's discretion to extend time has caused problems because of the different form of words inadvertently used in Order 53, r.4(1) and section 31(6) of the Supreme Court Act.[57] Under the Rules the court may extend time if the applicant shows there is "good reason" for the delay. Even if satisfied that there is such a good reason, the court may still refuse permission on the ground of delay because under section 31(6) the court may consider whether the granting of relief would "be likely to cause substantial hardship to, or substantially prejudice the rights of, any person or would be detrimental to good administration." In all but the

14–014

---

[48] Order 53, r. 4(1); Alistair Lindsay, 'Delay in Judicial Review Cases: a Conundrum Solved?' [1995] P.L. 417; M.J. Beloff, 'Time, time, time it's on my side, yes it is' in C. Forsyth and I. Hare (eds), *The Golden Metwand and the Crooked Cord* (1998), p.267.

[49] On the order of certiorari generally, see below, para. 15–012.

[50] Order 53, r. 4(1).

[51] *R. v. Secretary of State for Transport, ex p. Presvac Engineering Ltd* (1992) 4 Admin. L.R. 121, CA.

[52] *R. v. Redbridge L.B.C., ex p. Gurmit Ram* [1992] 1 Q.B. 384.

[53] *R. v. Essex C.C., ex p. C* [1993] C.O.D. 398; *R. v. Secretary of State for Trade and Industry, ex p. Greenpeace Ltd* [1998] Env. L.R. 415.

[54] e.g. *R. v. Secretary of State for Health, ex p. Alcohol Recovery Project* [1993] C.O.D. 344.

[55] *R. v. Lloyd's of London, ex p. Briggs* [1993] 1 Lloyd's Rep. 176.

[56] See paras 15–046–15–048.

[57] A *circulus inextricabilis* (*Caswell v. Dairy Produce Quota Tribunal for England and Wales* [1990] 2 All E.R. 434, *per* Lloyd L.J., [1989] 1 W.L.R. 1089, 1094F) is created because Order 53, r. 4(1) and (3) are expressed to be without prejudice to any statutory provision which has the effect of limiting the time within which an application for judicial review is made: and s. 31(2) is expressed to be without any prejudice to any enactment or rule of the court which had that effect.

clearest cases, the court will, however, normally postpone consideration of hardship, prejudice and detriment to good administration until the full hearing.[58]

14–015   The following have been held to be "good reasons" for undue delay: time taken to obtain legal aid[59]; the importance of the point of law at stake[60]; the pursuit of alternative legal remedies.[61] The following have been held not to be good reasons: tardiness on the part of an applicant's non-legal advisor[62]; time taken pursuing avenues of political redress, such as organising a lobby of Parliament, before applying for leave.[63]

14–016   The courts have been loathe to define with precision any definition or description of what constitutes detriment to good administration,[64] in part because the need for finality may be greater in one context than another. The criteria set out in section 31(6)—substantial hardship, substantial prejudice and detriment to good administration—are to be read disjunctively.[65]

14–017   In numerical terms, the fact that an application for permission is made prematurely is almost as important a ground for refusing permission as is delay.[66] Where permission is sought to apply for certiorari to quash any judgment, order or conviction or other proceedings which is subject to appeal and a time is limited for bringing an appeal, the court may adjourn the application for permission until the appeal is determined or the time for appealing has expired.[67]

---

[58] *Caswell v. Dairy Produce Quota Tribunal for England and Wales* [1990] 2 A.C. 738; *cf. R. v. Secretary of State for Trade and Industry, ex p. Greenpeace Ltd* [1998] Env. L.R. 415.

[59] *R. v. Stratford on Avon D.C., ex p. Jackson* [1985] 1 W.L.R. 1319.

[60] *R. v. Secretary of State for the Home Office, ex p. Ruddock* [1987] 1 W.L.R. 1482; *R. v. Collins and others, ex p. S (No.2)* [1998] 1 F.L.R. 790.

[61] See, *e.g. R. v. Stratford on Avon D.C., ex p. Jackson* [1985] 1 W.L.R. 1319; *R. v. Rochdale M.B.C., ex p. Cromer Ring Mill Ltd* [1982] 2 All E.R. 761; *R. v. Secretary of State for the Environment, ex p. West Oxfordshire D.C.* [1994] C.O.D. 134.

[62] *R. v. Tavistock General Commissioners, ex p. Worth* [1985] S.T.C. 564. (Overruled on other grounds by the House of Lords in *R. v. Criminal Injuries Compensation Board, ex p. A* [1999] 1 W.L.R. 974).

[63] See *e.g. R. v. Secretary of State for Health, ex p. Alcohol Recovery Project* [1993] C.O.D. 344 and *R. v. Redbridge L.B.C.* [1991] C.O.D. 398.

[64] *Caswell v. Dairy Produce Quota Tribunal* [1990] 2 A.C. 738.

[65] *ibid.*

[66] Le Sueur and Sunkin [1992] P.L. 102, p. 123; see further Jack Beatson, 'Prematurity and ripeness for review' in C. Forsyth and I. Hare (eds), *The Golden Metwand and the Crooked Cord* (1998), p. 221.

[67] Order 53, r. 3(8).

Challenging the grant or refusal of permission

There has been a growing trend for litigants to challenge the decision **14–018** of the court made at the permission stage: applicants by renewing their applications to another judge or the Court of Appeal; respondents by applying to set aside the grant of permission. If, on a written application permission is refused or granted on terms unacceptable to the applicant, he may renew his application within 10 days to a judge in open court where it will be dealt with *de novo*.[68] Where the application is in a civil cause or matter, there is a further right to renew an application to the Court of Appeal within seven days.[69] In both civil and criminal matters no appeal lies to the House of Lords against the refusal of permission.[70] A significant proportion of renewed applications for permission are successful.[71]

Where permission has been granted, a respondent may apply to set **14–019** aside a grant of permission on the grounds that the application discloses absolutely no arguable case[72] or that there had not been frank disclosure by the applicant of all material matters both of fact and law.[73] However, except in very clear cases such applications are not looked on with favour by the courts.[74]

Reform of the permission stage

In its 1994 report, the Law Commission considered it to be essential **14–020** that a procedure such as the permission requirement be retained to filter out hopeless applications.[75] It nevertheless recognised that a number of reforms to the existing arrangements were necessary. First, the permission stage should be called the "preliminary consideration". Secondly, all preliminary considerations should be determined without an oral hearing, except where interim remedies are claimed or a hearing is desirable in the interests of justice. As in the present procedure, an applicant would be able to renew an initially unsuccessful application in open court. Thirdly, the Law Commission

---

[68] Order 53, r. 3(4).

[69] CPR, Sched. 1, Order 59, r. 14(3).

[70] See *Re Poh* [1983] 1 W.L.R. 2.

[71] M. Sunkin (1987) 50 M.L.R. 432, 456; L. Bridges *et al, Judicial Review in Perspective* (2nd ed., 1995), Chap. 7.

[72] See *R. v. Secretary of State for the Home Department, ex p. Khalid Al-Nafeesi* [1990] C.O.D. 106.

[73] What is material is to be decided by the court and not by the assessment of the applicant or his legal advisors: see generally *R. v. Jockey Club Licensing Committee, ex p. Wright* [1991] C.O.D. 306.

[74] See, *e.g. R. v. Secretary of State for the Home Department, ex p. Chinoy* [1991] C.O.D. 381.

[75] Law Com. No. 226. Parts V and IX. For comment, see R. Gordon Q.C. [1995] P.L. 11.

accepted that the Rules should be redrawn to provide express criteria to be applied in determining preliminary considerations. It also recommended that the general requirement of "an arguable case" should be reformulated and the Rules should state that "the judge shall consider whether the application discloses a serious issue which ought to be determined".[76]

14–021   Under the Law Commission's proposals, it would be possible for the judge determining the preliminary consideration to invite the putative respondent to give information on a prescribed form on matters such as its decision-making procedure prior to the impugned decision, any internal review undertaken, what alternative remedies are available to the applicant and any other reasons why it is considered that the application should not proceed to a substantive hearing.[77] It remains to be seen whether the committee responsible for revising Order 53 in the new CPR will accept the Law Commission's recommendations.

THE INTERIM STAGE

Service

14–022   Permission to apply having been granted, the substantive application is commenced by issuing a claim form under Part 7 of the CPR, which must be served on all persons who are directly affected.[78] In addition,

---

[76] Law Com. No. 226, para. 5.15. This new formula should not be regarded as in any way increasing the threshold for the applicant. The idea was taken from a package of recommendations made by Le Sueur and Sunkin in 'Applications for Judicial Review: The Requirement of Leave' [1992] P.L. 102, 128; the authors intended this form of words to incorporate into the leave stage the general approach used by the courts in determining whether to grant interim injunctions following *American Cyanamid v. Ethicon* [1975] A.C. 396 where the House of Lords recognised that: 'It is no part of the court's function at [the interlocutory stage] of the litigation to try to resolve conflicts of evidence on affidavits as to facts on which the claim of either party may ultimately depend nor to decide difficult questions of law which call for detailed argument and mature consideration. These are matters to be dealt with at trial.' (*Per* Lord Diplock at 407.) See also R. Gordon Q.C. [1995] P.L. 11, 14.

[77] Law Com. No. 226, paras 4.8–4.11.

[78] Order 53, r. 5(3). The meaning of 'persons directly affected' was considered by the House of Lords in *R. v. Rent Officer Service, ex p. Muldoon; R. v. Rent Officer Service, ex p. Kelly* [1996] 1 W.L.R. 1103. Lord Keith held 'that a person is directly affected by something connotes that he is affected without the intervention of any intermediate agency'. In the instant case the Secretary of State for Social Security, who applied to be joined as a respondent to applications for judicial review challenging a failure to determine claims for housing benefit, was only indirectly affected (his department ultimately paid 95 per cent of the cost of this benefit by way of subsidy to the local authority) as it was the local authority which would have to pay the applicants directly if the applications for judicial review were successful.

at the hearing the court may allow any person who desires to be heard in opposition, and who appears to be a proper person to be heard, but who has not been served with the notice or summons, to be so heard.[79] There are, however, no express provisions for third parties (*e.g.* a pressure group) to intervene in *support* of an application. Given that these are public law proceedings, this is an odd omission. The court has however, a discretion to allow third parties to intervene and to be represented.[80]

The respondent has 56 days to file written evidence in reply. Extensions in time will be granted only in circumstances which are wholly exceptional and for the most compelling reasons.[81]

Interim remedies[82]

When the relief sought includes an order of certiorari or prohibition, **14–023** the grant of permission will, if the court so directs, operate as a stay of proceedings impugned until the determination of the application or until the court otherwise orders.[83] The term "stay of proceedings" is not confined to proceedings of a judicial nature, but encompasses the process by which any decision challenged has been reached, including the decision itself.[84] When any other sort of relief is requested, the court may at any time grant interim remedies in accordance with Part 25 of the CPR.[85] Although a stay of proceedings and an interim injunction perform the same function of preserving the status quo until the full hearing, there are conceptual and practical differences between the two forms of relief. While the injunction protects the interest of the litigant in dispute with another, the stay is not addressed to an "opposing" party but rather is directed at suspending the operation of a particular decision. While the grant of an interim injunction is usually conditional upon the applicant giving a

---

[79] Order 53, r. 9(1).

[80] *e.g. R. v. Secretary of State for the Home Department, ex p. Sivakumaran (U.N. High Commissioner for Refugees intervening)* [1988] 1 A.C. 958 (intervention in appeal to the House of Lords). Lord Goff noted "it was not until counsel for the intervener ... made his submissions that the substance of the argument became clear". See further Justice/Public Law Project, *A Matter of Public Interest* (1996) and Sir Konrad Schiemann, 'Interventions in Public Interest Cases' [1966] P.L. 240.

[81] *Practice Note (Judicial Review: Affidavit in reply)* [1989] 1 W.L.R. 358.

[82] Interim injunctive remedies are considered in more detail at para. 15–018.

[83] Order 53, r. 3(10).

[84] See *R. v. Secretary of State for Education and Science, ex p. Avon County Council* [1991] 1 Q.B. 558.

[85] Order 53, r. 3(10)(b).

cross-undertaking in damages,[86] there appears to be no such requirement or practice in relation to a stay of proceedings.

14–024   One interlocutory form of relief identified as ripe for reform by the Law Commission in 1976 and 1994 was the need for the court to have power to grant interim declaratory orders, especially against the Crown. The CPR now contain such a power.[87]

Disclosure

14–025   Order 53 explicitly provides for the making of interlocutory applications in respect of disclosure of documents and cross-examination of people who have been given written evidence.[88] These were innovations of the 1977 reforms, and they might have amounted to a potentially significant development. This has not been the reality. In practice, unless the applicant can show a prima facie breach of public duty, disclosure will not usually be granted.[89] The courts have, however, encouraged public bodies to adopt the practice of filing written evidence which discloses all relevant matters.[90]

14–026   Where the challenge is on the ground of *Wednesbury* irrationality, full disclosure of the type which is a matter of routine in general civil proceedings will seldom be ordered.[91] Applications for disclosure "in the hope that something might turn up" are regarded as an illegitimate exercise, at least in the absence of a prima facie reason to suppose that the deponent's evidence is untruthful.[92] Generally, disclosure to go behind the contents of a person's written evidence will be ordered only if there is some material before the court which

---

[86] The Crown and other public bodies carrying out law enforcement functions do not need to give such an undertaking: *F. Hoffmann-La Roche & Co. A.G. v. Secretary of State for Trade and Industry* [1975] A.C. 295 and *Kirklees M.B.C. v. Wickes Building Supplies Ltd* [1993] A.C. 227.

[87] CPR, r. 25.1(1)(a).

[88] Order 53, r.8. Disclosure means stating that a document relevant to legal proceedings exists and the right of other parties to inspect it.

[89] See *R. v. Inland Revenue Commissioners, ex p. National Federation of Self-Employed and Small Business Ltd* [1982] A.C. 617, 654E, per Lord Scarman.

[90] Sir John Donaldson M.R. in *R. v. Lancashire C.C., ex p. Huddleston* [1986] 2 All E.R. 941, 945: "... if and when the applicant can satisfy a judge of a public law court that the facts disclosed by her entitle her to apply for judicial review of the decision [t]hen it becomes the duty of the respondent to make full and fair disclosure."

[91] See *R. v. Secretary of State for the Environment and Other, ex p. Smith* [1988] C.O.D. 3. Cf. *R. v. Secretary of State for Transport, ex p. A.P.H. Road Safety Ltd* [1993] C.O.D. 150.

[92] See, *e.g. R. v. Secretary of State for the Environment, ex p. Doncaster B.C.* [1990] C.O.D. 441; *R. v. Secretary of State for the Environment, ex p. Islington L.B.C. and London Lesbian and Gay Centre* [1992] C.O.D. 67; *R. v. Secretary of State for Foreign and Commonwealth Affairs, ex p. World Development Movement Ltd* [1995] 1 W.L.R. 386.

suggests that it is not accurate.[93] Even reports referred to in affidavits, routinely inspected in general civil proceedings, will not be the subject of disclosure under Order 53 unless the applicant shows that the production of the documents is necessary for fairly disposing of the matter before the court.[94]

Opinion is divided as to whether disclosure should become more routinely available in judicial review proceedings or whether a strict (or stricter) approach should be maintained.[95]

Withdrawal

Approximately half of all applications for judicial review granted leave are withdrawn before the full hearing.[96]   **14–027**

THE FULL HEARING

In civil causes or matter,[97] the full hearing of the substantive   **14–028** application will be before a single judge or, where the Crown Office directs, a Divisional Court. In criminal causes or matters,[98] the application is always before a Divisional Court. If the application for permission has been successfully renewed to the Court of Appeal, the substantive application will be heard by a Divisional Court unless the Court of Appeal directs that it will hear the application itself (*e.g.* where the court below is bound by an authority which is said to be wrongly decided).[99]

Although the court has a discretion to order cross-examination,   **14–029** unlike in general civil proceedings cross-examination is not used as a matter of course. Rarely has cross-examination of people on their

---

[93] See *R. v. Secretary of State for the Home Department, ex p. B.H.* [1990] C.O.D. 445; *Brien v. Secretary of State for the Environment and Bromley L.B.C.* [1995] J.P.L. 528. In its 1994 report, the Law Commission considered that this approach was unduly restrictive and undermined the basic test of relevance and necessity laid down in *O'Reilly v. Mackman:* see Law Com. No. 226, para. 7.12.

[94] *R. v. Inland Revenue Commissioners, ex p. Taylor* [1989] 1 All E.R. 906.

[95] See Law Commission Consultation Paper No. 126, *Administrative Law: Judicial Review and Statutory Appeals*, para. 8.10. In its 1994 report, the Law Commission made no recommendations for amendments of the Rules dealing with disclosure (or 'discovery' as it was known before the CPR): see Law Com. No. 226, para. 7.12.

[96] See M. Sunkin, 'Withdrawing: a Problem in Judicial Review?' in P. Leyland and T. Woods (eds), *Administrative Law Facing the Future* (1997).

[97] Order 53, r. 5(2).

[98] Order 53, r. 5(1). On the meaning of 'criminal cause or matter', see above, para. 14–011.

[99] See *Practice Direction (Judicial Review: Appeals)* [1982] 1 W.L.R. 1375.

14–036   Unfortunately, there are many situations in which there can be disputes as to the assessment of facts between the individual citizen and public body where there is no or no adequate alternative fact-finding mechanism to the court, such as an appeal body. A written procedure is unsuited to resolve "disguised" appeals as to the merits of the decisions of this nature and the courts on judicial review can do no more than decide whether on the evidence which the public body contends was available it was entitled to come to the decision which it did. Yet such issues continue to form a significant proportion of the public law caseload. There is, therefore, a need for a more effective fact-finding procedure. One alternative would be for the court to be more ready to allow cross-examination and disclosure as happens now when the courts have to determine the existence of precedent fact, but this would involve changing the nature of the ordinary judicial review hearing from a reviewing role and making the procedure more protracted and expensive and adding to the existing delays in obtaining a decision from the court. A preferable solution would be for those cases which regularly give rise to factual issues to have those factual issues initially determined by a tribunal and for its decisions to be subject to review by the court. Alternatively, the High Court could be given the power to refer issues of fact to another body, possibly the Parliamentary Commissioner for Administration or the county court, for determination.

14–037   The most acute problems arise where judges are required to make decisions which involve their evaluating public policy considerations. Although it is usually accepted by judges that policy-making is for the administration and should be eschewed by the courts,[9] it is clear that the courts do often justify their decisions simply in terms of what is socially desirable rather than on any legal principle. For example, in a series of decisions the courts have laid down that a more stringent test for permission to apply for judicial review under Order 53 should be applied to certain categories of complaint (notably immigration and homelessness decisions and challenges to child protection work of local authorities) on the ground that subjecting these types of decisions to judicial review challenge would be detrimental to good public administration.[10] Again, from time to time, the court has justified applying statutory provisions in a way different to their apparently literal effect for reasons of public policy.[11]

---

[9] See Chap. 1.

[10] See above, para. 14–006, n. 24.

[11] See, *e.g. R. v. Registrar General, ex p. Smith* [1991] 2 Q.B. 393 (adopted person refused access to original birth certificate to trace natural mother despite apparently absolute entitlement under s. 51 of the Adoption Act 1976 on ground that the person would be a potential menace to mother). *Cf. X (A Minor) (Adoption Details: Disclosure)* [1994] 3 All E.R. 372.

Again, policy decisions are taken by the court when it exercises **14–038** discretion as to whether to grant a remedy for unlawful action. In judicial review under Order 53 and statutory review a remedy does not follow as of right and relief can be refused even if the court finds the action or decision tainted by unlawfulness. Relief has been refused on the ground, for example, that to grant the order sought would result in unacceptable administrative disruption[12] or the absence of prejudice to an applicant. The court, therefore, takes cognisance of the practical impact of their decisions, yet it may not necessarily be fully informed of what this is likely to be.

It is, therefore, not surprising that it has been argued that at the **14–039** present time we have the worst of two worlds: a judiciary which is becoming increasingly interventionist which is confined by procedures and practices which exclude from their consideration certain information and factual investigation which would enable them to make more appropriate decisions as to when and how to intervene. A possible solution which has been proposed is the creation of an Advocate-General or Director of Civil Proceedings whose duty would be to present evidence of the public interest to the court,[13] and a movement from adversarial towards inquisitorial procedures.

The different interests of those affected by judicial review

The different participants involved in proceedings for judicial review **14–040** may well attach importance to different aspects of the present procedures. The applicant will not be interested in the safeguards which are built into the procedure which are justified by the need to avoid abuse. However, the respondent public body will attach the greatest importance to their retention since otherwise its activities may be unnecessarily disrupted which would not be in the interests of good administration. The courts are also attaching greater importance to the existence of the safeguards to help them alleviate the problems created by their increasing case load which is subjecting the court system to unwelcome strain.

Neither the applicant nor the respondent will necessarily welcome **14–041** the involvement of third parties since their presence may complicate the proceedings and lead to additional expense and delay. However, the presence of the third party may be of the greatest assistance to the

---

[12] *e.g. R. v. Gateshead B.C., ex p. Nichol* [1988] C.O.D. 97.

[13] J.A.G. Griffith, "Judicial Decision-Making in Public Law" [1985] P.L. 564; Woolf, *Protection of the Public—A New Challenge* (1990), pp. 109–113; Sir Jack Jacob, "Safeguarding the Public Interest in English Civil Proceedings" (1982) 1 C.J.Q. 312, esp. pp. 316–319.

court since otherwise the court may be totally unaware of a consequence of its decision which would be prejudicial to the public at large.

14–042 While the interests of the court, the parties and other interested bodies may appear to be in conflict, closer examination may indicate that their interests are much closer than they realise. An applicant who has a meritorious case usually will have no difficulty in surmounting the hurdle of obtaining permission, but he could be seriously prejudiced if his case is substantially delayed because of the court having to deal with unmeritorious applications which should have been dealt with at the outset by a refusal of permission. The third party who can be affected by the proceedings may have no desire to incur the expense of being involved in the proceedings. His sole concern could well be that the proceedings should be completed as soon as possible so that, for example, a property which is subject to planning blight may be sold.

14–043 What is required is a procedure which reconciles these interests to the greatest extent possible. A procedure which allows the citizen ready access to a system of justice that he can afford and provides, where he has been unfairly or unreasonably or unlawfully treated, an effective remedy. A system which, while protecting the public from abuse of power is not so interventionist that it is inconsistent with good administration because it is over-intrusive. Devising a system which reconciles these objectives is by no means easy. It requires a careful balancing of the respective interests involved. The present procedure of judicial review is a substantial improvement on the previous situation, but it is now apparent that further changes are needed.

CHAPTER 15

REMEDIES IN JUDICIAL REVIEW

INTRODUCTION

The court's powers to grant relief on an application for judicial review **15–001** are now contained in section 31 of the Supreme Court Act 1981. The court may be called upon to make a variety of remedial orders. Before the full hearing of an application is heard, an applicant may seek an interim order in the form of an interim injunction a stay of proceedings to prevent the respondent public body continuing with its disputed conduct, or an interim declaration.[1] At the conclusion of the full hearing, a successful applicant may request the court to grant an order of mandamus,[2] certiorari or prohibition[3] (for historical reasons known collectively as "prerogative orders"[4]), an injunction[5] or a declaration.[6] The court may grant these remedial orders singly or in combination.[7] A distinctive feature of all these remedies is that the court has discretion to withhold them from an applicant even if the respondent public body is held to have acted unlawfully.[8] Prior to the procedural reforms to judical review in 1978,[9] a plethora of technical rules restricted the circumstances in which applicants could be granted each particular remedial order. Since then, however, the courts have shown a marked reluctance to let the former intricacies and obscurities hamper the provision of effective redress to aggrieved persons and the courts now encourage flexibility. For almost all purposes, the orders of mandamus and prohibition can now be regarded as indistinguishable

---

[1] Para. 15–018.
[2] Para. 15–005.
[3] Para. 15–012.
[4] Para. 13–005.
[5] Para. 15–016.
[6] Para. 15–013.
[7] Supreme Court Act 1981, s. 31(5); Order 53, r. 2 (contained in Civil Procedure Rules, Sched. 1).
[8] Para. 15–048.
[9] Para. 13–057.

in their effect from final injunctions[10]: all three remedies "direct any of the parties to do, or refrain from doing, any act in relation to the particular matter".[11] In its 1994 report *Administrative Law: Judicial Review and Statutory Appeals,* the Law Commission argued that the Latin names for the prerogative orders obscured their functions to non-lawyers; it recommended that the Supreme Court Act 1981 be amended to rename the remedies "mandatory orders", "prohibiting orders" and "quashing orders".[12] This suggestion was not accepted by Lord Woolf in *Access to Justice.*[13]

15–002   A claim for damages may also be included in an application for judicial review, but these will be awarded only if the applicant proves that an actionable tort has been committed by the respondent public body.[14] In practice, any claim for damages is usually adjudicated upon at a separate hearing after the public law issues have been determined.

PREROGATIVE ORDERS

15–003   The scope of the prerogative orders reflects the general principle that it is not the role of the High Court in judicial review proceedings to substitute its decision for that of the original decision-maker.[15] So, where mandamus is ordered against a tribunal which has refused to entertain an application, it will be in the form of "mandamus to hear and determine according to law" rather than to reach a particular decision, except where the circumstances are such that only one decision can be reached as a matter of law, namely that stated by the court. Where an order of certiorari is issued to quash a decision that

---

[10] *M v. Home Office* [1994] 1 A.C. 377, 415E.

[11] Words used in the Australian Administrative Decisions (Judicial Review) Act 1977, s. 30 which introduced a flexible range of remedies to replace prerogative writs with a view to freeing 'judicial review from its emphasis on the character of the remedy sought, instead allowing the court to consider the substance of the applicant's grievance' (Electoral and Administrative Review Commission, Issues Paper No. 4, 1990); see further T.H. Jones, 'The Reform of Judicial Review in Queensland' (1993) 12 C.J.Q. 256.

[12] Law Com. No. 226, para. 8.3.

[13] See para. 13–065.

[14] See Chap. 16, below.

[15] The Law Commission recommended that, in the case of decisions by an inferior court or tribunal, the reviewing court should be empowered to substitute its own decision, provided that: (a) there was only one lawful decision that could be arrived at; and (b) the grounds for review arose out of an error of law: see Law Com. No. 226, para. 8.16. For an illustration of the type of situation where the 'blunt instrument' of the prerogative orders could usefully be supplemented by a power to make a substitute order, see *R. v. Tower Hamlets L.B.C., ex p. Tower Hamlets Combined Traders Association* [1994] C.O.D. 325.

has been made, the High Court may at the same time remit the matter back to the court, tribunal or authority concerned with a direction to reconsider it and reach a decision in accordance with the judgment of the court.[16] One specific exception to this principle of the court not formally substituting its own decision, is where an applicant seeks certiorari to quash a sentence of a magistrates' court or the Crown Court on the grounds that the court had no power to pass the sentence; the High Court may, instead of quashing the sentence and remitting the matter back, pass any sentence which the former courts could have passed.[17]

The prerogative orders may be granted either singly or in **15–004** combination.[18] Where, for example, an applicant is aggrieved by a decision, certiorari may be sought to quash it, together with an order of mandamus to compel the decision-maker to determine the issue in accordance with law.

The court may award a prohibition *quousque*—an order that is operative until the decision-maker or inferior tribunal has corrected its conduct by containing itself within the bounds of its jurisdiction.[19]

MANDAMUS[20]

Not all public duties cast upon public authorities are potentially **15–005** enforceable by mandamus. Some are, in the eyes of the law, duties of imperfect obligation[21]—general statutory obligations too vague to be susceptible to judicial enforcement.[22] Latitude will also often be given to a public body with respect to the manner and extent of their performance of their duties, particularly when resources are insufficient to satisfy all claims upon them; in these circumstances, judicial enforcement tends to be limited to situations in which

---

[16] Supreme Court Act 1981, s. 31(5); Order 53, r. 9(4).

[17] Supreme Court Act 1981, s. 43.

[18] *ibid.* s. 31(2); Order 53, r.2.

[19] *e.g. R. v. Liverpool Corp., ex p. Liverpool Taxi Fleet Operators' Association* [1972] Q.B. 299 (prohibition against a local authority to restrain it from acting on a resolution to increase the number of taxi-cab licences until it had entertained representations by interested parties).

[20] For an account of the historical development of mandamus, see para. 13–019.

[21] *cf. R. v. Governor of South Australia* (1907) 4 C.L.R. 1497, 1511.

[22] *e.g.* National Health Service Act 1977, s. 1(1): 'It is the Secretary of State's duty to continue the promotion in England and Wales of a comprehensive health service designed to secure improvement—(a) in the physical and mental health of the people of those countries, and (b) in the prevention, diagnosis and treatment of illness, and for that purpose to secure the effective provision of services in accordance with this Act.'

reasonable efforts to perform had not been made.[23] Moreover, the court will not intervene in the exercise of a power which is permissive rather than mandatory.[24]

15–006   Mandamus will not, of course, lie to compel the performance of a mere moral duty,[25] or to order anything to be done that is contrary to law. No action or proceeding shall be begun or prosecuted against any person in respect of anything done in obedience to an order of mandamus.[26] Many of the narrow technicalities which once applied to the grant of mandamus, for example, that it would not lie for the purpose of undoing that which has already been done in contravention of statute,[27] no longer restrict the remedy.[28] Mandamus will not, however, be granted to enforce a civil obligation to make restitution to a third party, even where it is the grant of certiorari which gives rise to that obligation.[29]

Demand and refusal

15–007   It is preferable for the applicant to be able to show that he has demanded performance of the duty and that performance has been refused by the authority obliged to discharge it.[30] An applicant, before

---

[23] See, *e.g. R. v. Inner London Education Authority, ex p. Ali* (1990) 2 Admin. L.R. 822 where the question arose whether a local education authority was in breach of duties to secure the availability of sufficient schools for providing primary and secondary education to all pupils under the Education Act 1944, s. 8. It was held that the duty was neither absolute nor was it a matter entirely for the authority to decide what steps it should reasonably take in seeking to fulfil the duty. An authority which was faced with a situation where, without any fault on its part, it has for a limited period not complied with the standard which the section set was not automatically in breach of duty. Furthermore, even where there was a breach, the court in its discretion may not intervene if the authority was doing all that it reasonably could to remedy the situation. *Cf. R. v. Governor of South Australia* (1907) 4 C.L.R. 1497, 1511.

[24] See generally *Padfield v. Minister of Agriculture, Fisheries and Foods* [1968] A.C. 997.

[25] *e.g.* to make good a military officer's pay: *Ex p. Napier* (1852) 18 Q.B. 692.

[26] Order 53, r. 10.

[27] See the fourth edition of this work, p. 542.

[28] See also C. Lewis, *Judicial Remedies in Public Law* (1991), p. 171.

[29] *R. v. Barnet Magistrates' Court, ex p. Cantor* [1998] 2 All E.R. 333.

[30] See, generally, Tapping, *On Mandamus* pp. 282–286. For consideration of these requirements, see *The State (Modern Homes (Ireland) Ltd) v. Dublin Corp.* [1953] I.R. 202, 213–216; *R. v. Board of Commissioners of Public Utilities, ex p. Halifax Transit Corp.* (1971) 15 D.L.R. (3d) 720. *Cf.* Lewis, *op. cit.*, p. 171 ('There is old authority requiring the applicant to have made an express demand for the authority to act and for the authority to have refused. In modern times this formalistic approach is unlikely to be required.') Whatever the formal position now on 'demand and refusal' the matter may be rather academic as an applicant who fails to write an appropriate 'letter before action' prior to seeking permission to apply for judicial review is unlikely to be granted permission: see *R. v. Horsham D.C., ex p. Wenman* [1995] 1 W.L.R. 680.

applying for judicial review, should address a distinct and specific demand or request to the respondent that he perform the duty imposed upon him.[31] There are cases where the mere fact of non-compliance with a duty is a sufficient ground for the award of a mandamus—for example, where the applicant has been substantially prejudiced by the respondent's procrastination.[32] Delay in complying with the demand or request,[33] the indication of readiness to comply only subject to conditions,[34] or persistent temporising and failure to give a direct answer,[35] may well be tantamount to refusal.

Interrelationship between mandamus and other remedies

An order of mandamus is only one of a number of remedies for 15–008 securing the performance of public duties. In many Acts dealing with the provision of services by bodies such as local authorities, default powers may be available when, in the opinion of the relevant Secretary of State, a body has failed to discharge the public responsibility with which it was entrusted.[36] The existence of such a default power will not usually prevent a person aggrieved by the non-performance from applying for judicial review.[37] Not all Acts expressly

---

[31] *cf. R. v. Bristol & Exeter Ry.* (1843) 4 Q.B. 162, where the only demand made was premature. And see *R. v. New Westminster (City), ex p. Canadian Wirevision Ltd* (1965) 48 D.L.R. (2d) 219, where the application or demand (which had been refused) had never been made in the prescribed form.

[32] *R. v. Secretary of State for the Home Department, ex p. Phansopkar* [1976] Q.B. 606.

[33] See *R. v. Richmond (City), ex p. May (E.B.) Pty Ltd* [1955] V.L.R. 379 (mandamus to grant a permit where the competent authority had, erroneously but in good faith, failed to give its decision before the statutory period had expired). *cf. R. v. Secretary of State for the Home Department, ex p. Phansopkar* [1976] Q.B. 606 (respondent required to consider on their merits applications for certificate of partiality addressed to Home Office in London rather than to government officials abroad, despite any explicit statutory provision to this effect: the court was concerned by the impediment that would be imposed upon the exercise of the right of entry if applicants were forced to apply in their country of origin, a requirement that would involve a substantial delay). From the applicant's perspective, it must be remembered that an application for permission to apply for judicial review must normally be made promptly and in any event within three months 'from the date when grounds for the application first arose': Order 53, r. 4(1).

[34] See *R. v. Lancaster (Inhabitants)* (1900) 64 J.P. 280 (where unlawful conditions had been attached).

[35] *City Motor Transit Co. v. Wijesinghe* (1961) N.L.R. 156. And see *R. v. Tower Hamlets L.B.C., ex p. Kayne-Levenson* [1975] Q.B. 431 (local authority required to determine licence application: whilst placing applicant on waiting list equivalent to a refusal, applicant could not appeal until application formally refused).

[36] *e.g.* Education Act 1944, s. 99.

[37] *e.g. R.v. Inner London Education Authority, ex p. Ali* (1990) 2 Admin. L.R. 822 (the fact that the Secretary of State had power to give directions under the Education Act

provide that the duty shall be enforceable by mandamus on an application for judicial review by the Secretary of State, but the minister's power to do so is implicit.[38] This judicial sanction is in fact rarely invoked; a minister is likely to prefer the simpler and swifter course of assuming the relevant functions him or herself or transferring them to another authority or, if there is power to do so, to threaten to withhold a central grant.

15–009   What is the relationship between mandamus and the other public law judicial remedies? Many of the former technicalities relating to the relationship between the judicial remedies are now in practice regarded as obsolete. But it would seem that mandamus is not the proper means of enforcing a duty to abstain from acting unlawfully. Thus, if a public authority or officer threatens to act *ultra vires*, the appropriate remedy will be prohibition, an injunction or a declaration, and not an application for mandamus not to exceed the powers conferred by law. If an inferior tribunal exceeds its jurisdiction, prohibition and not mandamus lies to compel it to stay its hand, and certiorari, not mandamus, lies to prevent it from acting upon its final order. In some situations, however, mandamus has been granted to undo what has been done; the courts merely treat the unlawful act as a nullity and order the competent authority to perform its duty as if it had refused to act at all in the first place.[39] An excess of jurisdiction was sometimes styled a refusal of jurisdiction in respect of which mandamus will issue. Again, distinctions between duties to act

---

1944, s.99, and can do so on complaint, creates no inference that the ordinary jurisdiction of the court is ousted, though it is very relevant to the exercise of the court's discretion) *cf. R. v. Westminster C.C., ex p. P* (1999) 31 H.L.R. 154 (applicants should have applied to Secretary of State to exercise his default powers under Local Authority Social Services Act 1970, s. 7D). On the broad question of exhausting alternative remedies before seeking judicial review, see para. 14–007.

[38] As under the Education Act 1944, s. 68; *cf. R. v. Leicester Guardians* [1899] 2 Q.B. 632; *Secretary of State for Education and Science v. Tameside M.B.C.* [1977] A.C. 1014, 1046. *Quaere* whether the court has that degree of discretion over the remedy normally associated with mandatory orders once it has found the direction to have been lawfully given: see *Lord Advocate v. Glasgow Corporation*, 1973 S.L.T. 33, 36, 38, HL where a negative answer was given. *Semble* even refusal to exercise a mere power will be enforceable by mandamus, for once the minister has taken advantage of his statutory right to order the authority to act, the authority is then placed under a legal duty to exercise the power.

[39] In *R. v. Paddington Valuation Officer, ex p. Peachey Property Corp. Ltd* [1966] 1 Q.B. 380, 402–403, 413, Lord Denning M.R. and Dankwerts L.J. held that mandamus could issue to order the preparation of a proper valuation list even if the original list was only *voidable* (pending the award of certiorari to quash). Salmon L.J. (at 418–419) and the Divisional Court ([1964] 1 W.L.R. 1186) inclined to the view that certiorari would have to issue as well as mandamus unless the list was a nullity.

lawfully and duties not to act unlawfully may be very fine. But given that certiorari and mandamus may now be sought in a single application these technical distinctions are of little importance today.

To what extent does mandamus occupy the field covered by **15–010** certiorari? Certiorari will lie to quash a determination made in excess of or without jurisdiction. A person who is aggrieved by such a determination will normally be content to have it quashed and will seldom seek a fresh determination even if the vitiating jurisdictional defect is capable of being rectified. If he does wish to have the matter determined afresh he will usually apply for both certiorari and mandamus.[40]

There is no doubt that mandamus will lie to compel a tribunal to **15–011** state a case[41] and to give reasons for its decision when it is required to do so by statute.[42] Where the giving of reasons is required by statute, mandamus will lie to compel the tribunal to give adequately intelligible reasons.[43]

CERTIORARI AND PROHIBITION

Historically, the orders of certiorari and prohibition have had so many **15–012** characteristics in common that they may be discussed together. The one significant difference between them is that prohibition may, and usually must, be invoked at an earlier stage than certiorari. Prohibition will not lie unless something remains to be done that a court can prohibit. Certiorari will not lie unless something has been done that a court can quash. But it is sometimes appropriate to apply for both orders simultaneously—certiorari to quash an order made by a tribunal in excess of its jurisdiction, and prohibition to prevent the tribunal from continuing to exceed its jurisdiction.

For a century or more it was generally assumed that certiorari and **15–013** prohibition would issue only in respect of "judicial acts" or administrative acts in the performance of which the competent

---

[40] *e.g.* as in *R. v. Panel on Takeovers and Mergers, ex p. Datafin plc* [1987] Q.B. 815. See also the power of the court, when granting certiorati, also to remit the matter back to the court, tribunal or other body with a direction to reconsider it and reach a decision in accordance with the findings of the court: Supreme Court Act 1981, s. 31(5); Order 53, r. 9(4).

[41] *R. v. Watson, ex p. Bretherton* [1945] K.B. 96. *Aliter* if, because of expiry of a time limit, the duty has become a mere power: *R. v. Northumberland Q.S., ex p. Williamson* [1965] 1 W.L.R. 700. See now Supreme Court Act 1981, s. 29(4).

[42] *Brayhead (Ascot) Ltd v. Berkshire C.C.* [1964] 2 Q.B. 303, 313–314; *Parrish v. Minister of Housing and Local Government* (1961) 59 L.G.R. 411, 418.

[43] In *Iveagh (Earl) v. Minister of Housing and Local Government* [1964] 1 Q.B. 395, 410, Lord Denning M.R. observed that the court could order a minister to make good his omission to give adequate reasons. On reason-giving more generally, see para. 8–039.

authority was under an express or implied duty to "act judicially" (or fairly). Because certiorari and prohibition were the main judicial remedies in administrative law it used to be very important to be able to identify "judicial acts" and situations where the courts could be expected to hold that there was a duty to act judicially. However, a judicial recognition that the rules of natural justice do not import an inflexible procedural code of uniform applicability and the increasing frequency with which judges fall back upon the vaguer duty to act fairly have shifted the focus of the argument from whether there are any implied procedural obligations to be complied with before a power may lawfully be exercised in determining their content in the particular context. It is now beyond doubt that certiorari and prohibition are not confined to reviewing decisions of a judicial nature.[44]

15–014   It has been held that the orders will not issue to persons who take it upon themselves to exercise a jurisdiction without any colour of legal authority; the acts of usurpers are to be regarded as nugatory. Where a tribunal which had power to grant cinematograph licences adopted a practice of approving building plans before the application for a licence was made, on the understanding that it would later grant the licence if it approved the plans, the courts held that certiorari and mandamus would not go to the tribunal for a refusal to approve plans, since the tribunal had no legal authority whatsoever to make provisional decisions.[45] However, today, in order to remove uncertainty, a court would issue the orders to bodies that purport to be acting in pursuance of lawful authority.[46] In relation to a void decision, an order of certiorari *in effect* declares that it was ineffective *ab initio;* in the case of a voidable decision, certiorari will deprive the decision of legal effect.[47]

Certiorari may now be ordered to quash subordinate legislative instruments.[48]

---

[44] See, *e.g. R. v. Hillingdon L.B.C., ex p. Royco Homes Ltd* [1974] Q.B. 720.

[45] *R. v. Barnstaple JJ., ex p. Carder* [1938] 1 K.B. 385. See also *Re Daws* (1838) 8 A. & E. 936; *R. v. Maguire and O'Sheil* [1923] 2 I.R. 58; and *Re Clifford and O'Sullivan* [1921] 2 A.C. 570 (no prohibition to court martial in state of martial law, for it is not a body exercising legal jurisdiction but an instrument for executing the will of the military commander). But for a more satisfactory result see *Steve Dart Co. v. Board of Arbitration* [1974] 2 F.C. 215 (prohibition issued to a tribunal purporting to act under legislation that did not empower its creation).

[46] A.T. Markose, *Judicial Control of Administrative Action in India,* pp. 199–201; see also Amnon Rubinstein, *Jurisdiction and Illegality,* pp. 83–85.

[47] See above para. 4–039 *et seq.* on the distinction between 'void' and 'voidable'. Also, see P. Cane, *An Introduction to Administrative Law* (3rd ed., 1996), pp. 62–63.

[48] In *R. v. Secretary of State for Social Security, ex p. Association of Metropolitan Authorities* [1986] 1 W.L.R. 1 certiorari was assumed to be available to quash a statutory instrument on housing benefit but was refused by the court in its discretion.

It is still not altogether clear what is the earliest stage at which an **15–015** application for an order for prohibition may be made. If want of jurisdiction is apparent, prohibition may be applied for at once. If want of jurisdiction is not apparent, the application must wait until the tribunal has actually stepped outside its jurisdiction (as by continuing the hearing after an incorrect determination of a jurisdictional fact) or is undoubtedly about to step outside its jurisdiction (as where it has announced its intention to entertain matters into which it has no power to inquire).[49] This is the generally accepted doctrine; but doubts have sometimes been expressed about the power to award prohibition for an anticipatory excess of jurisdiction.[50] On the other hand, there have been modern decisions in which applications for prohibition have been considered even before the inferior tribunal has had the opportunity to address itself to the disputed question of its jurisdiction.[51] In any event, a doubt as to whether an application for prohibition is premature is likely to be resolved in the applicant's favour if the final order of the tribunal may be protected by statute from challenge.[52] The right to apply for prohibition remains as long as something remains to be done, by or under the authority of the tribunal, that the court can effectively

---

Certiorari was granted in *R. v. Secretary of State for Health, ex p. U.S. Tobacco International* [1992] 1 Q.B. 353. Prior to this decision only declaratory relief had ever been granted in relation to statutory instruments.

[49] *Re Zohrab v. Smith* (1848) 17 L.J.Q.B. 174, 176; *London Corp. v. Cox* (1867) L.R. 2 HL 239; *R. v. Electricity Commissioners* [1924] 1 K.B. 171; *R. v. Minister of Health, ex p. Villiers* [1936] 2 K.B. 29. See also *R. v. Local Commissioner for Administration for North and East Area of England, ex p. Bradford Metropolitan City Council* [1979] Q.B. 287 (*rev'd.* in CA), where on an application to prohibit a local commissioner from investigating certain matters, a declaration was granted that the Commissioner should not investigate complaints that did not prima facie amount to allegations of maladministration.

[50] *Re Ashby* [1934] O.R. 421, 431.

[51] *R. v. Tottenham & District Rent Tribunal, ex p. Northfield (Highgate) Ltd* [1957] 1 Q.B. 103, 107–108, *per* Lord Goddard C.J. And see *R. v. Galvin, ex p. Metal Trades Employers' Association* (1949) 77 C.L.R. 432, 445; *Bell v. Ontario Human Rights Commission* [1971] S.C.R. 756. But a court may decline to exercise its discretion to issue prohibition before the tribunal has had an opportunity to explore the factual issues upon which its jurisdiction may depend: *Maritime Telegraph and Telephone Co. Ltd v. Canada Labour Relations Board* [1976] 2 F.C. 343. See further, P. W. Hogg (1971) 9 O.H.L.J. 203.

[52] See *R. v. Minister of Health, ex p. Davis* [1929] 1 K.B. 619, DC.

prohibit[53]; but an applicant who has been guilty of delay may be refused leave to apply for judicial review.[54]

INJUNCTIVE RELIEF[55]

15–016   An injunction is an order of a court addressed to a party requiring that party to do or to refrain from doing a particular act. Hence an injunction may be prohibitory or mandatory. Until late in the nineteenth century all injunctions were worded in a prohibitory form (*e.g.* not to allow an obstruction to continue to interfere with the plaintiff's rights), but the direct mandatory form (*e.g.* to remove the obstruction) may now be used. An injunction may be a final order granted at the conclusion of proceedings or an interim order. A final injunction granted on an application for judicial review is normally indistinguishable in its effect from an order of prohibition and mandamus[56]: injunctions may be granted to prevent *ultra vires* acts by public bodies[57] and to enforce public law duties.[58] The main importance of the injunction in Order 53 proceedings is that, unlike the prerogative orders, it may be granted at an interlocutory stage on an interim basis to preserve the status quo until a final hearing.

15–017   The jurisdiction of the High Court to grant injunctions on an application for judicial review rests on section 31(2) of the Supreme Court Act 1981[59] which gives the court power to grant an injunction in any case where it appears just and convenient to do so having regard to:

> (1) the nature of the matters in respect of which relief may be granted by a prerogative order;

---

[53] *Re London Scottish Permanent Building Society Ltd* (1893) 63 L.J.Q.B. 112, 113; *Estate & Trust Agencies (1927) Ltd v. Singapore Improvement Trust* [1937] A.C. 898, 917–918; *cf. Re Poe* (1833) 5 B. & Ad. 681; *Chabot v. Lord Morpeth* (1844) 15 Q.B. 446, 457–458; *Re Clifford and O'Sullivan* [1921] 2 A.C. 570; *Ex p. Mineral Deposits Pty. Ltd, re Claye and Lynch* (1959) S.R.(N.S.W.) 167 (tribunals *functi officio*); Markose, *Judicial Control of Administrative Action in India*, p. 282; and Ross A. Sundberg (1970) 7 Melb.U.L.Rev. 507, aptly criticising some of the decisions for excessive technicality.

[54] See above, para. 14–013.

[55] Detailed references to authorities for basic propositions of law relating to injunctions are omitted: see, generally, David Bean, *Injunctions* (7th ed., 1996).

[56] See *M. v. Home Office* [1994] 1 A.C. 377, 415E.

[57] *e.g. R. v. North Yorkshire C.C., ex p. M.* [1989] Q.B. 411; *Re Cook* [1986] N.I. 242, 272–274, QBD, 274, 280–282, CA.

[58] *e.g. R. v. Kensington and Chelsea R.L.B.C., ex p. Hammell* [1989] 1 Q.B. 518.

[59] See s. 30 in relation to injunctions restraining a person not entitled to do so from acting in a public office. On the High Court's general jurisdiction to grant injunctions, see s. 37.

(2) the nature of the persons and bodies against whom relief may be granted by such orders; and

(3) all the circumstances of the case.

The court may grant an injunction on such terms and conditions as it thinks fit. Although the discretion conferred is very broad, it will be exercised in accordance with recognised principles.[60]

Interim injunctive orders

Where a court concludes that a public body's decision is susceptible to judicial review, a concomitant to granting leave will, if necessary, be to "hold the ring"[61] pending the determination of the full application. Interim relief may be granted in the form of: **15–018**

(1) an interim injunction or

(2) a stay of proceedings.

In many cases, no formal injunctive order is made, the respondent instead giving an undertaking to the court.

Interim injunction

An interim injunction is one granted before trial, for the purpose of preventing any change in the status quo from taking place until the final determination of the merits of the case.[62] Interim injunctions may be mandatory[63] or prohibitory. **15–019**

The test applied in determining whether or not to grant an interim injunction in an application for judicial review is said to be broadly **15–020**

---

[60] See below, para. 15–020.

[61] An expression used in *R. v. Cardiff City Council, ex p. Barry* [1990] C.O.D. 94 and *M. v. Home Office* [1992] 1 Q.B. 270, 139J, CA.

[62] CPR, Pt 25 (which applies to Order 53 proceedings). It is not always immediately obvious what the status quo is. In Canada, an employee who was forcibly retired under the terms of a collective agreement with the Crown airline, Air Canada, sought and was granted an injunction. On appeal, the Divisional Court set it aside on the ground that the injunction altered the status quo rather than maintaining it: *Stevenson v. Air Canada* (1982) 35 O.R. (2d) 68.

[63] *Ex p. Hammell* (above, n. 58). *Cf. Shepherd Homes Ltd v. Sandham* [1971] Ch. 340. See also *Meade v. Haringey L.B.C.* [1979] 1 W.L.R. 637 (in the case of an injunction to perform public duties, the court must be able to specify with precision what the authority needs to do; an injunction will not be granted if close supervision is required to ensure that duty being observed).

similar to that now applied in general law proceedings.[64] In 1975, the House of Lords held that a claimant need no longer establish a prima facie case, but instead merely demonstrate that there is a serious issue to be tried, *i.e.* a claim that is not frivolous or vexatious and discloses a reasonable prospect of success.[65] The aim is to avoid the court having to consider difficult questions of law or fact at the interim stage. In practice effect, however, the old prima facie case test continues to apply in many judicial review cases[66] because a prerequisite to the grant of an interim injunction is the grant of permission, where the threshold often approximates more to the need to show a prima facie case than merely a potentially arguable one.[67] Also, in judicial review proceedings, unlike many general civil proceedings, the court will often determine applications for interim relief by reference to its prediction of the final outcome of the Order 53 application.[68] As in proceedings concerned purely with private law issues,[69] where the grant of an interim injunction would effectively bring the matter to a close, a strong prima facie case will probably have to be shown.

15–021 The claimant having shown that there is, at the least, a serious issue to be tried, the court will then consider whether it is just and convenient to grant an interim injunction. This involves the court deciding whether there is an adequate alternative remedy in damages, either to the claimant seeking the injunction[70] or the defendant in the event that an injunction is granted against him.[71] The availability of a remedy in damages to the claimant will normally preclude the grant to him of an injunction. Even if damages are available, they may not be an adequate remedy.[72] If there is doubt about either or both the claimant's and/or the defendant's remedy in damages the court will

---

[64] *Factortame Ltd v. Secretary of State for Transport (No. 2)* [1991] A.C. 603, HL.

[65] *American Cyanamid Co. v. Ethicon Ltd* [1975] A.C. 396.

[66] But not all: see *e.g. R. v. Secretary of State for the Home Department, ex p. Doorga* [1990] C.O.D. 109; *Scotia Pharmaceuticals International Ltd v. Secretary of State for Health* [1994] C.O.D. 241.

[67] Particularly where a mandatory injunction is sought, the courts appear to look for a strong prima facie case. See, *e.g. Ex p. Hammell* (above, n. 58). On the relationship between the thresholds for permission and for interim injunctive relief, see further above, paras 14–005 and 14–021, n. 76.

[68] See below, para. 17–012.

[69] See, *e.g. Office Overload v. Gunn* [1977] F.S.R. 39; *Patrick Chadwick v. Brimley Business Centre Inc.* (1989) 35 C.P.C. (2d) 152 (H.C.J.).

[70] *i.e.* in the event of the interim injunction being refused, but the claimant succeeding at trial.

[71] *i.e.* if the interim injunction is granted but the claimant fails at trial. The grant of an interim injunction is usually conditional on the claimant/applicant giving an undertaking to pay damages in these circumstances: see para. 15–025 below.

[72] *e.g. R. v. Kensington and Chelsea R.L.B.C., ex p. Hammell* [1989] 1 Q.B. 518.

proceed to consider what has become known as the "balance of convenience". The factors to be taken into consideration will vary from case to case.

The nature of applications for judicial review will often require there **15–022** to be some modifications of the usual guidelines for the exercise of the court's discretion at the interim stage. First, questions as to the adequacy of damages as an adequate alternative remedy will usually be less relevant. In judicial review, there will often be no alternative remedy in damages because of the absence of any general right to damages for loss caused by unlawful administrative action *per se*.[73] It follows that in cases involving the public interest, for example, where a party is a public body performing public duties, the decision to grant or withhold interim injunctive relief will usually be made not on the basis of the adequacy of damages but on the balance of convenience test.[74] In such cases, the balance of convenience must be looked at widely, taking into account the interests of the general public to whom the duties are owed.[75]

Another difference from private law proceedings is that in judicial **15–023** review, there is less likely to be a dispute of issues of fact. Where the only dispute is as to law, the court may have to make the best prediction it can of the final outcome and give that prediction decisive weight in resolving the interlocutory issue.[76]

Others factors that may be taken into account in determining the **15–024** balance of convenience include the importance of upholding the law of the land and the duty placed on certain authorities to enforce the law in the public interest.[77] In the case of a challenge to the validity of a law, the court should not exercise its discretion to restrain a public authority by interim injunction from enforcing apparently authentic law unless it is satisfied, having regard to all the circumstances, that the challenge to the validity of the law is, prima facie, so firmly based as to justify so exceptional a course being taken.[78] The general principle that expression of opinion or the expression and the

---

[73] See below, Chap. 16.

[74] *R. v. Secretary of State for Transport, ex p. Factortame Ltd (No. 2)* [1991] 1 A.C. 603, 672–673.

[75] *ibid.*; see also *R. v. H.M. Treasury, ex p. British Telecommunications plc* [1995] C.O.D. 56. Cf. *R. v. Secretary of State for Health, ex p. Generics (U.K.) Ltd* [1997] C.O.D. 294.

[76] *Factortame (No. 2)* (above, n. 74) at 660 (*per* Lord Bridge).

[77] *ibid.* at 672.

[78] *ibid.* at 673 (*per* Lord Goff). In *ex p. British Telecommunications plc* (above, n. 75), the Court of Appeal indicated that where an interim injunction is sought pending the reference of a question to the E.C.J. under Art. 234 of the E.C. Treaty, in most cases the court will be able to conclude little more than that the plaintiff's case is arguable or strongly arguable: it is not sensible for a national court to consider in depth a question, which by referring, it declares itself unable to resolve.

dissemination of information will not be restrained by the courts except on pressing grounds applies as much to a public body which is under a duty to express an opinion as to a private individual.[79]

15–025   The discretionary bars to the award of an injunction are applied with particular stringency to the applicant for interlocutory relief, and he is in any event usually required to give an undertaking in damages lest at the trial the interim injunction is shown to have been wrongly granted and the defendant has suffered loss as a result. Many applicants are legally aided and have insufficient means to give an effective undertaking in damages. This is not a bar to the grant of interim relief,[80] for the requirement of a cross-undertaking is a matter of discretion for the court. Neither the Crown nor local authorities have any special exemption from giving cross-undertakings in damages, but a court is unlikely to exercise its discretion to require one where an injunction is sought in a law enforcement action.[81]

Stay of proceedings

15–026   Under Order 53,[82] the court is empowered to grant a stay of proceedings where the applicant is seeking final relief in the form of an order of prohibition or certiorari. Authorities are divided as to the scope and effect of such a "stay". The Court of Appeal has held that the term is apt to include executive decisions and the process by which the decision was reached and may be granted to prevent a minister from implementing a decision.[83] More recently, however, the

---

[79] *R. v. Advertising Standards Authority Ltd, ex p. Vernons Organisation Ltd* [1993] 1 W.L.R. 1289; *cf. R. v. Advertising Standards Authority, ex p. Direct Line Financial Services Ltd* [1998] C.O.D. 20 (interim injunction granted restraining ASA from publishing adjudication).

[80] *Ex p. Hammell* (above, n. 72); *Allen v. Jambo Holdings Ltd* [1980] 1 W.L.R. 1252; Purchas L.J. suggested in *R. v. Lambeth L.B.C., ex p. Sibyll Walter* (February 2, 1989, unreported) that the court may have jurisdiction to grant an injunction without any cross undertakings in damages. In *R. v. Secretary of State for the Environment, ex p. Rose Theatre Trust Company* [1990] 1 Q.B. 504, however, Schiemann J. held the court should be extremely slow to do so.

[81] *F. Hoffmann-La Roche & Co. A. G. v. Secretary of State for Trade and Industry* [1975] A.C. 295; *Director General of Fair Trading v. Tobyward Ltd* [1989] 1 W.L.R. 517; *Kirklees M.B.C. v. Wickes Building Supplies Ltd* [1993] A.C. 227; *Coventry City Council v. Finnie* (1997) 29 H.L.R. 658.

[82] r. 3(10)(a).

[83] *R. v. Secretary of State for Education and Science, ex p. Avon C.C.* [1991] 1 Q.B. 558, 561, 563 (*per* Glidewell and Taylor L.JJ.) (decision of minister to make order giving school grant maintained status.) See also Lord Donaldson M.R. in *R. v. Secretary of State for the Home Department, ex p. Muboyayi* [1992] 1 Q.B. 244, 258 (declines to express opinion on whether *Avon* will survive an appeal to the House of Lords) and *R. v. Advertising Standards Authority Ltd, ex p. Vernons Organisation Ltd* (above, n. 79) (application for stay 'in truth' an application for an injunction).

Privy Council held, *obiter*, that a stay of proceedings is merely an order which puts a stop to the further conduct of proceedings in court or before a tribunal at the stage which they have reached, the object being to avoid the hearing or trial taking place; and that it could have no possible application to an executive decision which has already been made.[84] The position awaits clarification by the House of Lords.[85]

Given the fundamental conflict of authorities over the basic nature of the order, it is difficult to describe with any certainty the principal features of a stay of proceedings: **15–027**

(1) Unlike an injunction it is an order directed not at a party to the litigation but at the decision-making process of the court, tribunal or other decision-maker. It may not, therefore, be an order capable of being breached by a party to the proceedings, or anyone else, and may not be enforceable by contempt proceedings.[86]

(2) A decision made by an officer or Minister of the Crown can be stayed by an order of the court.[87] Now that it is clear that interim injunctive relief can be ordered against officers and Ministers of the Crown,[88] this characteristic of the stay is of less importance.

(3) Although the court has a general discretion to grant a stay of proceedings subject to any conditions it considers appropriate, cross-undertakings in damages will not normally be required.

---

[84] *per* Lord Oliver in *Minister of Foreign Affairs, Trade and Industry v. Vehicles and Supplies Ltd* [1991] 1 W.L.R. 550, 556. The Board was considering section 564B(4) of the Jamaican Civil Procedure Code which is in similar terms to Order 53, r. 3(10)(a). *Ex p. Avon* (above, n. 83) was neither referred to nor cited in argument.

[85] The Law Commission has recommended that 'proceedings' in this context ought to be given a narrow meaning. This is in light of the fact that injunctions are now available against ministers on an application for judicial review and the suggestion that the court ought to be empowered to grant interim declarations: see Law Com. No. 226, para. 6.26.

[86] *Minister of Foreign Affairs, Trade and Industry v. Vehicles and Supplies Ltd* (above, n. 84) at 71 (*per* Lord Oliver). *Pace* C. Lewis, *Judicial Remedies in Public Law* (1992), p. 157 ('A stay is an order of the court. Breach of a stay will be punishable as a contempt of court.').

[87] *R. v. Secretary of State for Education and Science, ex p. Avon C.C.* [1991] 1 Q.B. 558, 562 (*per* Glidewell L.J.). *cf. R. v. Secretary of State for the Home Department, ex p. Kirkwood* [1984] 1 W.L.R. 913; *R. v. Secretary of State for the Home Department, ex p. Mohammed Yacoob* [1984] 1 W.L.R. 920. In the two House of Lords' decisions in the *Factortame* cases ((*No. 1*)) [1990] 2 A.C. 85; (*No. 2*) [1991] 1 A.C. 603), no mention was made of the question whether the court had power to grant a stay of proceedings against Ministers; it had been suggested that this omission was no accident: see Woolf, *Protection of the Public—a New Challenge* (1990), p. 65.

[88] *M. v. Home Office* [1994] 1 A.C. 377.

Final injunctions

15–028 A final injunction is granted at the conclusion of the proceedings and is definitive of the rights of the parties, but it need not be expressed to have perpetual effect; it may be awarded for a fixed period, or for a fixed period with leave to apply for an extension, or for an indefinite period terminable when conditions imposed on the defendant have been complied with; or its operation may be suspended for a period-during which the defendant is given the opportunity to comply with the conditions imposed on him, the plaintiff being given leave to reapply at the end of that time. The elasticity of form and content that characterises the injunction is, indeed, one of its main advantages over orders of mandamus and prohibition.

15–029 In general, a mandatory injunction will not issue to compel the performance of a continuing series of acts—for example, the execution of building or repair works[89] or the operation of a ferry service[90] or the delivery of mail that has been interrupted by an industrial dispute [91]—which the court is incapable of superintending. This rule cannot be expressed without qualification, for the court has jurisdiction to order the abatement of a nuisance although compliance with its order may entail the execution of extensive works over which the court would not be capable of maintaining effective superintendence[92] and it can award a prohibitory injunction to restrian the discontinuance of a public service.[93] It is doubtful whether a mandatory injunction will issue at the suit of a private plaintiff to compel a public body to carry out its positive statutory duties, unless the statute is to be interpreted

---

[89] *Att.-Gen. v. Staffordshire C.C.* [1905] 1 Ch. 336, 342 (a case where a declaration was sought in respect of liability to maintain and repair a highway).

[90] *Att.-Gen. v. Colchester Corp.* [1955] 2 Q.B. 207; *cf. Gravesham B.C. v. British Railways Board* [1978] Ch. 379, 403–405. See also *Att.-Gen. v. Ripon Cathedral (Dean & Chapter)* [1945] Ch. 239; *Morton v. Eltham Borough* [1961] N.Z.L.R. 1 (gas supply); *Dowty Boulton Paul Ltd v. Wolverhampton Corp.* [1971] 1 W.L.R. 204, 211–212 (maintenance of airfield; injunction prohibitory in form but mandatory in substance). *Semble* in Scots law a wider range of public duties may be enforced by a remedy analogous to a mandatory injunction: see *Docherty (T.) Ltd v. Burgh of Monifieth*, 1971 S.L.T. 13; Court of Session Act 1868, s. 91 (duty to construct sewers); and this may issue despite the existence of an alternative administrative remedy *(ibid.)*.

[91] *Stephen (Harold) & Co. Ltd v. Post Office* [1977] 1 W.L.R. 1172; *cf. Fairfax (John) & Sons Ltd v. Australian Telecommunications Commission* [1977] 2 N.S.W.L.R. 400.

[92] See, *e.g. Pride of Derby & Derbyshire Angling Association Ltd v. British Celanese Ltd* [1953] Ch. 149. Other Limited exceptions to the general rule are mentioned in *Att.-Gen. v. Colchester Corp.* [1955] 2 Q.B. 207, 216

[93] *Warwickshire C.C. v. British Railways Board* [1969] 1 W.L.R. 1117 (railway service; not followed in *Prestatyn U.D.C. v. Prestatyn Railway Ltd* [1970] 1 W.L.R. 33, but only on the question of *locus standi*).

as giving the plaintiff a private right of action for breach of those duties; the more appropriate judicial remedy (if any) will be a prerogative order of mandamus.[94]

DECLARATIONS

A declaration is a formal statement by the court pronouncing upon the **15–030** existence or non-existence of a legal state of affairs. It declares what the legal position is and what are the rights of the parties. A declaration is to be contrasted with an executory, in other words, coercive judgment which can be enforced by the courts. In the case of an executory judgment, the courts determine the respective rights of the parties and then order the defendant to act in a certain way, for example, to pay damages or to refrain from interfering with the claimant's rights. If the order is disregarded, it can be enforced by official action, usually by levying execution against the defendant's property or by imprisoning him for contempt of court. A declaration, on the other hand, pronounces upon the existence of a legal relationship but does not contain any order which can be enforced against the defendant.[95] The court may, for example, declare that the

---

[94] *Glossop v. Heston & Isleworth Local Board* (1879) 12 Ch.D. 102; see also *Att.-Gen. v. Clerkenwell Vestry* [1891] 3 Ch. 527, 537 (dictum) (alleged breach of duty in failing to provide proper drainage system). *Semble* even an application for mandamus would have been inappropriate, for Parliament had provided another specific remedy: *Pasmore v. Oswaldtwistle U.B.C.* [1898] A.C. 387. See also *Att.-Gen. v. Pontypridd Waterworks Co.* [1908] Ch. 388. For an illustration of a mandatory injunction issuing to compel the performance of a semi-private nature, see *Holland v. Dickson* (1888) 37 Ch.D. 669 (statutory duty of company to permit stockholder or shareholder to inspect its books). And see *Meade v. Haringey L.B.C.* [1979] 1 W.L.R. 637, where a right to sue for damages does not appear to have been regarded as a condition precedent to the award of a mandatory injunction in that case.

[95] In *Webster v. Southwark L.B.C.* [1983] Q.B. 698, Forbes J. decided that although there had been only a declaration and no injunction granted and although a declaration was not a coercive order the court had an inherent power to make an order of sequestration where the interests of justice demanded compliance. In that case, the appellant refused to provide a hall for an election meeting in clear breach of s. 82 of the Representation of the People Act 1949. Sir William Wade and C.F. Forsyth express reservations about the case in *Administrative Law* (7th ed., 1994), p. 592. Whilst there is substance in that criticism as long as there is express or implied liberty to apply to the court, there is no reason why, if it is appropriate, the court should not subsequently make an executory order and then enforce that order. In addition, it is arguably a contempt of court deliberately to interfere with a legal situation declared by the courts. If, for example, the courts have declared that an individual has the right to remain in this country, it could be contempt for the Home Office to remove him after having had notice of the declaration. This was accepted to be the position by counsel for the Home Secretary in *M. v. Home Office* [1994] 1 A.C. 377.

plaintiff is a British subject or that a notice served upon him by a public body is invalid and of no effect. The declaration pronounces on what is the legal position.

15–031   The fact that a declaration is not coercive is one of its advantages as a public law remedy. Because it merely pronounces upon the legal position, it is well suited to the supervisory role of administrative law in England. In addition, by careful draftsmanship the declaration can be tailored so as not to interfere with the activities of public bodies more than is necessary to ensure that they comply with the law. In many situations all that is required is for the legal position to be clearly set out in a declaration for a dispute of considerable public importance to be resolved. It usually relates to events which have already occurred. However, as will be seen, it is increasingly being used to pronounce upon the legality of a future situation and in that way the occurrence of illegal action is avoided. The courts have jurisdiction to grant an anticipatory injunction, *quia timet*, where this is the only way to avoid imminent danger to the plaintiff but the courts are extremely cautious about granting such relief and the necessity for it can be avoided by granting a declaration instead.

15–032   During the 1970s litigants applied with increasing frequency for declarations in order to obtain relief against the activities of the Crown and other public bodies. Many of the landmark decisions which Lord Diplock regarded as constituting the "progress towards a comprehensive system of administrative law [which was] the greatest achievement of the English courts in [his] judicial lifetime"[96] were decided in civil proceedings in which the plaintiff sought a declaration. For example, in perhaps the most important decision of all, *Ridge v. Baldwin*[97] Lord Reid concluded his historic speech by announcing: "I do not think that this House should do more than declare that the dismissal of the appellant is null and void and remit the case to the Queen's Bench Division for further procedure." Similarly, in the almost equally important decision of *Anisminic v. Foreign Compensation Commission*,[98] in restoring the decision of Browne J. which had been reversed by the Court of Appeal, the House of Lords granted a declaration that a provisional determination by the Commission was made without, or in excess of, jurisdiction and was a nullity.

---

[96] *R. v. Inland Revenue Commissioners, ex p. National Federation of Self-Employed and Small Businesses Ltd* [1982] A.C. 617, 641.

[97] [1964] A.C. 40.

[98] [1969] 2 A.C. 147.

Declarations in an application for judicial review

The jurisdiction of the court on an application for judicial review **15–033** depends on the terms of Order 53, rule 1(2), and section 31 of the Supreme Court Act 1981. The language of these provisions links the jurisdiction to that which exists in the case of prerogative orders. However, Order 53, rule 1(2), and section 31 of the Supreme Court 1981 do not say that the jurisdiction shall be the same as that in the case of the prerogative orders[99] but merely require the courts to have regard to "the nature of the matters in respect of which relief may be granted by way of" those orders. In view of this language, it would be possible to argue that the jurisdiction to grant declarations or injunctions on applications for judicial review could be more extensive than that in relation to the grant of the prerogative orders. However, in practice, no distinction has been drawn between a claim for one form of relief or another (except for damages).[1] This is no doubt for a very good reason. The jurisdiction in relation to the prerogative orders is now so wide that there is no need to draw any distinction between the position as to the prerogative orders and declarations. Where the problems occur is because the wrong procedure may have been used because the issue is not regarded as one involving questions of public law and as so being appropriate for judicial review.[2]

Non-justiciable issues

There are certain matters in respect of which it is inappropriate for **15–034** any court to adjudicate. In the case of declaratory relief because of its flexible nature, relief can be granted at the very boundaries of the court's jurisdiction. However, even in the case of declarations, purely moral or political issues will not be determined by the courts nor will the courts grant declaratory relief in respect of obligations arising under international treaties where they are not part of the domestic law.[3] The position with regard to parliamentary proceedings and

---

[99] As to the prerogative orders, see para. 15–003. The jurisdiction is subject to the same statutory restrictions. Therefore a declaration cannot be granted contrary to s. 29(5) of the Supreme Court Act 1981: *R. v. Crown Court at Chelmsford, ex p. Chief Constable* [1994] 1 W.L.R. 359.

[1] See Chap. 16.

[2] See above para. 3–046.

[3] In *Malone v. Metropolitan Police Commissioner (No. 2)* [1979] Ch. 344, Megarry V.-C. refused a declaration that there had been a breach of the European Convention of Human Rights; but *cf. R. v. Secretary of State for Foreign Commonwealth Office, ex p. Indian Association of Alberta* [1982] Q.B. 892; *Re Molyneux* [1986] 1 W.L.R. 331; *Blackburn v. Att.-Gen.* [1971] 1 W.L.R. 1037; *MacWhirter v. Att.-Gen.* [1972] C.M.L.R. 882; and *R. v. Secretary of State for Health, ex p. Imperial Tobacco Ltd* [1999] C.O.D. 138.

legislation is very similar to that in relation to injunctions.[4] Except in cases where an Act of Parliament is incompatible with European Community Law, or now under the terms of the Human Rights Act 1998,[5] no Act of Parliament, however repugnant to the rules of common law or natural justice, can be declared illegal or void.[6] Similarly the courts cannot inquire into the legislative process of Parliament, for example, they cannot stay a declaratory action on the ground that a Bill before Parliament would, if passed, relieve the defendants from their statutory obligation.[7] However, the courts do have jurisdiction to scrutinise resolutions of either House of Parliament with the exception of resolutions concerning parliamentary privilege. Parliamentary resolutions are not laws. Therefore, if they are incompatible with the law or purport to alter it, they are of no legal effect, and so the courts have power to declare that this is the situation. However, they have in the past, as a matter of discretion, expressed considerable reluctance about declaring that parliamentary resolutions are void.[8] But even if a resolution is not itself declared void, there can be little doubt that a court will grant a declaration which makes clear the limited effect in law of a resolution.[9] The fact that delegated legislation has been approved by Parliament does not prevent it being challenged. However, it will influence the courts' willingness to declare that the legislation is invalid.[10]

---

[4] See the 5th ed. of this work at para. 17–038 *et seq.*

[5] *R. v. Department of Transport, ex p. Factortame (No. 1 and No. 2)* [1990] 2 A.C. 85; [1991] 1 A.C. 603.

[6] *Pickin v. British Rail Board* [1974] A.C. 763. *Cf.* the courts' possible jurisdiction to determine whether what purported to be an Act of Parliament was, as a matter of fact, an authentic expression of Parliament's sovereign will. The position is different in those countries where the legislature is limited by a written constitution: *Rediffusion (Hong Kong) v. Att.-Gen. of Hong Kong* [1970] A.C. 1136, 1154–1155 and Wade, *op. cit.*, p. 671.

[7] *Willow Wren Carrying Co. Ltd v. British Transport Commission* [1956] 1 W.L.R. 213,216. But see *Ching Garage Ltd v. Chingford Corp.* [1960] 1 W.L.R. 947, 955; [1961] 1 W.L.R. 470, HL (in deciding whether to grant declaratory relief the court may take account of an Act which is on the Statute Book even if it is not yet in force).

[8] *Bradlaugh v. Gossett* (1884) 12 QBD 271 esp. 282, *per* Stephens J.

[9] *Bowles v. Bank of England* [1913] 1 Ch. 57.

[10] *Hoffmann-La Roche v. Secretary of State for Trade and Industry* [1975] A.C. 295, esp. 344, 354, 365; *Laker Airways v. Department of Trade* [1977] 1 Q.B. 643, esp. 703, *per* Lord Denning M.R.; *R. v. Her Majesty's Treasury, ex p. Smedley* [1985] Q.B. 657. 666–667 and 670; *R. v. Inland Revenue Commissioners, ex p. Woolwich Equitable Building Society* [1990] S.T.C. 862; *Nottinghamshire C.C. v. Secretary of State for the Environment* [1986] A.C. 240, 250.

The effect of the existence of non-statutory alternative remedies

The existence of non-statutory remedies will generally not exclude the **15–035** jurisdiction of the courts to grant declaratory relief. So far as the prerogative orders are concerned, the position is made clear as a result of section 31(2) of the Supreme Court Act 1981 and Order 53 which provides that one of the factors to be taken into account in deciding whether it is "just and convenient" to grant declaratory relief is whether the issues raised are "matters in respect of which relief may be granted by orders of mandamus, prohibition and certiorari." So the availability of an alternative prerogative remedy is a factor in favour of, not against the grant of, a declaration.[11]

Interlocutory and interim declarations

A declaration can be described as "interim" because it is granted at **15–036** that stage of the proceedings. Nevertheless, it may be a final declaration and therefore it is to be contrasted with an "interim" declaration which is only granted until final judgment. The grant of an interim injunction in support of a claim for a declaration is not a decision on the merits of the claim and is therefore not tartamount to an interim injunction.[12] Following recommendations by the Law Commission and in Lord Woolf's *Access to Justice* report, an express power to grant interim declarations was included in the CPR when they were enacted in April 1999.[13]

Negative declarations

The courts can be unwilling to grant a negative declaration. By a **15–037** negative declaration is meant a declaration in negative terms, that is of no right or no liability. It can also be a declaration as to the absence of any right or power in a defendant or respondent. In order to decide whether a declaration is a negative declaration, it is necessary not

---

[11] However, in relation to Visitors of Universities and other eleemosynary corporations the internal laws of the organisation gave an exclusive jurisdiction to the Visitor as long as the Visitor was acting within his jurisdiction. If he was not then the courts' supervisory jurisdiction would remain: *R. v. Hull University Visitor, ex p. Page* [1993] A.C. 682 and para. 3–032.

[12] *Newport Association Football Club Ltd v. Football Association of Wales Ltd* [1995] 2 All E.R. 87.

[13] CPR, r.25.1(1)(b).

merely to examine the terms of the declaration but also its substance since by a careful use of language, what is in fact a negative declaration can be drafted in positive terms.

15–038   There are probably two reasons which explain the reluctance of the court to grant negative declarations.[14] The first is very similar to the reason that explains the opposition to granting declarations as to theoretical issues, if the objective is to anticipate possible proceedings, those proceedings may never occur. The second reason is that they can be used for the purposes of forum shopping.[15] Where there is no existing proceedings, the court will usually want to be satisfied that there is some bona fide reason for commencing them but if there is the court will then be prepared to decide on the merits whether declaratory relief should be granted.[16]

Utility

15–039   One of the most important characteristics of judicial review is that it is a practical procedure which does not readily provide a remedy just because someone has technically succeeded on an application. It will not provide a remedy if it will serve no purpose. Events can overtake proceedings. For example, a licence, the validity of which is challenged in the proceedings, may have expired by the hearing. Similarly an activity under challenge may have ceased before a remedy has been granted.[17] Even a declaration may serve no purpose in those circumstances.

15–040   Sometimes when there has been a breach of natural justice the court will refuse relief because the defect is subsequently cured, for

---

[14] Reflected both in the judgment of Pickford L.J. in *Guaranty Trust Co. of New York v. Hannay & Co.* [1915] 2 K.B. 536, 564–565, he said. "I think that a declaration that a person is not liable in an existing or possible action is one that will hardly ever be made, but that in practically every case the person asking it will be left to set up his defence in the action when it is brought" and *Dyson v. Att.-Gen.* [1911] 1 K.B. 410, 417.

[15] See *Camilla Cotton Oil Co. v. Granadex S.A.* [1976] 2 Lloyd's Rep. 10 and the speech of Lord Wilberforce.

[16] See *Rediffusion (Hong Kong) Ltd v. Att.-Gen. of Hong Kong* [1970] A.C. 1136, 1156; *British Airways v. Laker Airways* [1985] A.C. 58; *Staffordshire Moorlands D.C. v. Cartwright* (1991) 63 P. & C.R. 285 (the Court of Appeal granted declarations that planning permission had not been implemented by the defendants, but Mustill L.J. indicated that it was an exceptional case and normally resort should be had to enforcement proceedings).

[17] In *Williams v. Home Office (No. 2)* [1981] 1 All E.R. 1211 and [1982] 2 All E.R. 564, a prison unit had closed.

example, by an appeal. However, this is strictly speaking not a matter of discretion but substance. If the appeal fulfils the requirements of the principles of fairness, then the applicant has no grounds of complaint.

If the applicant has not been prejudiced by the matters on which he **15–041** relies then the court may refuse relief, even though he has succeeded in establishing some defect. The literal or technical breach of an apparently mandatory provision in a statute may be so insignificant as not in effect to matter. In those circumstances the court may in its discretion refuse relief.[18] Courts have sometimes been prepared to take into account the fact that the decision would in any event have been the same even if the defect had not existed.[19] Here it is important to proceed with a considerable degree of caution. As the Law Commission has pointed out, in assuming inevitability of outcome the court is prejudging the decision and thus may be in danger of overstepping the bounds of its reviewing functions by entering into the merits of the decision itself.[20]

Nullity and *ultra vires* and discretion

The result of a decision being unlawful is considered fully elsewhere.[21] **15–042** However, if (which is doubtful) for the purposes of public law a decision can ever be categorised as being a nullity. then that will be relevant to the exercise of discretion to grant or withhold relief. There can be no purpose in purporting to keep alive a decision which is devoid of all content. Subject to there being some purpose in obtaining the decision of a court, if a court comes to the conclusion that a decision is totally invalid and of no effect, it will normally readily be prepared to grant a declaration to this effect. Strictly speaking there is nothing to be achieved in the case of a decision which is a nullity in making an order of certiorari. You cannot quash something which is already a nullity. However, in practice adopting a pragmatic approach and so avoiding becoming involved in issues as to the quality and status of an invalid administrative decision, the court will be prepared

---

[18] See, for example *R. v. Dairy Produce Quota Tribunal, ex p. Davies* [1987] 2 C.M.L.R. 399, *R. v. Lambeth L.B.C., ex p. Sharp* (1988) 55 P. & C.R. 232. *R. v. Governors of Small Heath School, ex p. Birmingham City Council* [1990] C.O.D. 23, and *R. v. Governors of Bacon's School, ex p. I.L.E.A.* [1990] C.O.D. 414.

[19] See *e.g. Cinnamond v. British Airports Authority* [1980] 1 W.L.R. 582.

[20] Law Commission 226, *Administrative Law: Judicial Review and Statutory Appeals*, para. 8.18. See also Clark, 'Natural Justice: Substance and Shadow' [1975] P.L. 27 and the statement of Megarry J. in *John v. Rees* [1970] Ch. 345, 402.

[21] See Chap. 4 above and *Anisminic Ltd v. Foreign Compensation Commission* [1969] 2 A.C. 147, 171; *London and Clydeside Estates Ltd v. Aberdeen D.C.* [1980] 1 W.L.R. 182, 189, 203; *Chief Constable of North Wales Police v. Evans* [1982] 1 W.L.R. 1155, 1163; *Hoffmann-LaRoche & Co. v. Secretary of State for Trade and Industry* [1975] A.C. 295.

to make an order of certiorari without resolving the complex issue as to whether or not this is strictly necessary. This is subject to the case being one in which the court would in any event have granted relief, if this were necessary, in the form of an order of certiorari.

Theoretical issues and advisory declarations

15–043 If an issue is theoretical, then in ordinary civil proceedings that is a compelling factor against the grant of relief and that remains the situation even if one of the parties has a perfectly legitimate reason for seeking clarification of the legal situation.[22] In proceedings for judicial review, however, there have now been a number of cases in which the courts have given advisory opinions, in the form of a declaration, where it was clearly desirable that they should do so. The declaratory opinions are given in circumstances where no other remedy would be appropriate. Sir John Laws categorises these situations where it is appropriate for the courts to grant declarations as being "hypothetical". They can equally appropriately be described as raising *theoretical* issues. A hypothetical question is a question which needs to be answered for a real practical purpose, although there may not be an immediate situation on which the decision will have practical affect. A "hypothetical" question has to be distinguished from an "academic" question. An academic question is one which need not be answered for any visible practical purpose, although an answer would satisfy academic curiosity, for example, by clarifying a difficult area of the law. Sir John considers that it would be wrong for the court to grant relief in order to answer academic questions.[23]

15–044 While obtaining advisory declarations from the courts has implications for judicial resources, because of the benefit which can accrue to the public at large and to good administration from the grant of advisory declarations, it is desirable that the courts adopt a generous approach to the grant of advisory relief. Support for this approach can be found in the recent decision of the House of Lords *Equal Opportunities Commission and Another v. Secretary of State for*

---

[22] See *Sun Life Assurance v. Jervis* [1944] A.C. 111. 114. *per* Viscount Simon L.C.: 'the appellants are concerned to obtain, if they can, a favourable decision from this House because they fear that other cases may arise under similar documents in which others who have taken out policies of endowment assurance with them will rely on the decision of the Court of Appeal, but if the appellants desire to have the view of the House of Lords on the issue on which the Court of Appeal has pronounced, their proper and more convenient course is to await a further claim and to bring that claim. if necessary, up to the House of Lords with a party on the record whose interest it is to resist the appeal.'

[23] See Laws, 'Judicial Remedies and the Constitution' (1994) 57 M.L.R. 213 pp. 214–219.

Employment.[24] In that case relief in respect of a complaint of discrimination was refused to an individual applicant but granted to the Equal Opportunities Commission. The contention of both parties was that the differing threshold provisions, contained in the Employment Protection (Consolidation) Act 1978 which full-time and part-time workers had to fulfil in order to qualify for unfair dismissal and redundancy, were incompatible with Article 119 of the EEC Treaty. In his speech in that case Lord Browne-Wilkinson[25] made clear that the courts possessed powers enabling them to grant a declaration as to public rights even if there were no decision which could be the subject of a prerogative order. There is therefore no question of the court not having the necessary jurisdiction to grant an advisory declaration. He did not regard the declaratory power of the Chancery Court as being any less extensive than that of a judge engaged in judical review.

RELIEF AGAINST THE CROWN

Judicial review developed from remedies by which the monarch's **15–045** court supervised the decisions and conduct of inferior courts and administrative bodies. It is well-accepted that in judicial review proceedings, prerogative orders cannot be granted against the Crown[26] directly. This is "both because there would be an incongruity in the Queen commanding herself to an act, and also because disobedience to a writ of mandamus is to be enforced by attachment".[27] This presents few practical problems as statutes rarely place duties on "the Crown".[28] Most statutory and prerogative powers of central government are exercised by Secretaries of State and judicial review proceedings may be brought against ministers in their official capacity. The one difficulty that used to face applicants seeking a remedy against a minister was that, until relatively recently, Part II of the Crown Proceedings Act 1947, which restricts the circumstances in which injunctions may be granted against ministers, was held to apply

---

[24] [1995] 1 A.C. 1.

[25] At 36, and see also Lord Keith at 27.

[26] On the Crown generally, see para. 3–034.

[27] *R. v. Powell* (1841) 1 Q.B. 352, 361 *per* Lord Denman C.J., quoted with approval by Lord Woolf in *M v. Home Office* [1994] 1 A.C. 377 at 415. *Cf. Page v. Hull University Visitor* [1993] A.C. 682 where the House of Lords appears to have accepted without argument that certiorari could lie against the Queen "as visitor" to a University.

[28] For an example of a statute placing a public law power directly on the Crown, see the Import, Export and Customs Powers (Defence) Act 1939, s. 9(3): "This Act shall expire on such date as His Majesty may declare by Order in Council to be the end of the emergency that was the occasion of the passing of this Act" (discussed by Gabriele Ganz, "Delegated Legislation: a necessary evil or a constitutional outrage?", Chap. 3 in P. Leyland and T. Woods (eds), *Administrative Law Facing the Future* (1997).

not only to private law proceedings against central government but also to restrict the court's powers to grant injunctions on applications for judicial review. In other words, the 1947 Act, which had been passed to make litigation against central government less hampered by outdated technical protections against "the Crown", was believed to qualify the plain words in section 31 of the Supreme Court Act 1981 giving power to the court to grant injunctive relief during an application for judicial review.[29] The bar on injunctive relief against ministers could pose significant practical difficulties for applicants as injunctions are the only form of remedial order which, on an application for judicial review, the court is able to grant on an interim basis pending the full hearing of the case. It is now clear, however, that the court does indeed have jurisdiction to grant injunctions against ministers on applications for judicial review. First, the House of Lords held, following the European Court of Justice, the court had power to grant interim injunctions against ministers where this was necessary in order to protect rights under Community law.[30] Secondly, the House of Lords held that Part II of the 1947 Act applies only to "civil proceedings," as defined by section 38(2), not to applications for judicial review.[31] In practice, however, an injunction against a minister can be no more than a peremptory declaration because the Rules of Court provide for special arrangements for the execution and satisfaction of such remedial orders.[32] Even though it is now clear that the courts possess jurisdiction to grant injunctions against ministers and other officers of the Crown, this power is exercised only in the most limited of circumstances. A declaration will continue to be regarded as the most appropriate remedy on an application for judicial review involving officers of the Crown.[33]

DISCRETION TO WITHHOLD REMEDIES

15–046   The prima facie approach is that an applicant who succeeds in establishing the unlawfulness of administrative action is entitled to be granted a remedial order. The court does, however, have discretion to

---

[29] The case law was uncertain: see *R. v. Secretary of State for the Home Department ex p. Herbage* [1987] Q.B. 872; *R. v. Licensing Authority, ex p. Smith Kline & French Laboratories Ltd (No. 2)* [1990] Q.B. 574; both overruled by *R. v. Secretary of State for Transport, ex p. Factortame Ltd (No. 1)* [1990] 2 A.C. 85.

[30] Case C-214/89 *R. v. Secretary of State for Transport, ex p. Factortame Ltd (No. 2)* [1991] A.C. 603, 658 and [1992] Q.B. 680.

[31] *M. v. Home Office* [1994] 1 A.C. 377.

[32] RSC, Ord. 77, r. 1(2).

[33] *M. v. Home Office* [1994] 1 A.C. 377, 412.

withhold a remedy altogether[34] or to grant a declaration[35] (rather than a more coercive orders of certiorari, prohibition, mandamus or an injunction[36] which may have been sought by the applicant). There are well-established situations where the court will depart from the prima facie position. This may be because of the applicant's own conduct or because of the adverse consequences to third parties or the public interest.

Delay

Delay is distinct from the other grounds upon which the court may **15–047** withhold a remedy in that it is expressly recognised in section 31(6) of the Supreme Court Act 1981 which provides that where there has been undue delay in making an application for judicial review:

> "the court may refuse to grant–(a) leave [*i.e.* permission] for making the application, or (b) any relief sought on the application if it considers that the grant of the relief sought would be likely to cause substantial hardship to, or substantial prejudice to the rights of, any person or would be detrimental to good administration."

Order 53, r. 4(1) states that applications for permission must be made "promptly and in any event within three months from the date when grounds for the application first arose".[37] Delay is thus relevant both at the permission stage and in relation to the grant of relief after the court has determined the merits of the applicant's case. The court regards these as distinct stages and in relation to the latter, delay is a factor to be considered in deciding whether or not to withhold a remedy *only* if to grant relief would be likely to cause hardship, prejudice or detriment to the respondent or a third party within the meaning of section 31(6)(b). At the full hearing the court is not concerned with the question whether there is "good reason" to extend time for seeking permission under Order 53, rule 4(1).[38]

The courts have tended to avoid formulating any precise description **15–048** of what constitutes detriment to good administration. This is because

---

[34] *R. v. Lincolnshire C.C. and Wealden D.C., ex p. Atkinson, Wales and Stratford* (1996) 8 Admin. L.R. 529 at 550, *per* Sedley J.: "To refuse relief where an error of law by a public authority has been demonstrated is an unusual and strong thing; but there is no doubt that it can be done."

[35] Para. 15–030.

[36] On injunctions, see para. 15–028.

[37] See para. 14–013.

[38] *R. v. Criminal Injuries Compensation Board, ex p. A* [1999] 2 W.L.R. 974, HL; on Order 53, r.4(1), see para. 14–011, above.

applications for judicial review arise in many different situations and the need for finality may be greater in one context than another. It has, however, been observed that "there is an interest in good administration independently of hardship, or prejudice to the rights of third parties".[39] In relation to the leave stage, a court may take the view the it is self-evident that a delay has caused detriment to good administration without requiring specific evidence that this has in fact occurred,[40] but in relation to withholding relief evidence may be required.[41]

---

[39] *R. v. Dairy Produce Quota Tribunal, ex p. Caswell* [1990] 2 A.C. 738. See also *R. v. Monopolies and Mergers Commission, ex p. Argyll* [1986] 1 W.L.R. 763, 774; *Coney v. Choyce* [1975] 1 W.L.R. 422, 436; *R. v. Panel on Takeovers and Mergers, ex p. Guinness plc* [1990] 1 Q.B. 146, 177.

[40] *R. v. Newbury D.C., ex p. Chieveley Parish Council* (1998) 10 Admin.L.R. 676. (unexplained delay in applying out of time for judicial review of major planning proposal).

[41] *R. v. Secretary of State for the Home Department Ex p. Oyeleye (Florence Jumoke)* [1994] Imm. A.R. 268 (no evidence of detriment to good administration had been put before the court and accordingly the court could not be satisfied that there was any such detriment).

CHAPTER 16

TORT DAMAGES AND JUDICIAL REVIEW

INTRODUCTION

This Chapter is concerned with the tortious liability of public bodies **16–001** and officials under domestic law[1] to provide compensation for loss and damage caused by unlawful administrative action.

A fundamental tenet of English law is that the failure of a public **16–002** body to act in accordance with public law principles *of itself* gives no entitlement at common law to compensation for any loss suffered. Nor does the careless performance of a statutory duty in itself give rise to any cause of action in the absence of a common law duty of care in negligence or a right of action for breach of statutory duty.[2] To recover damages, a recognised cause of action in tort must be pleaded and proved. In short, while in some cases it may be a necessary[3] condition, it is never a sufficient one for the award of damages that the act or omission complained of be "unlawful" in a public law sense.

English common law generally sets its face against the development **16–003** of any special body of rules for the tortious liabilities of officials and government bodies (though until the enactment of the Crown Proceedings Act 1947, certain procedural difficulties stood in the way of a person wishing to sue the Crown). Where the common law does acknowledge the public status of a defendant in a private law action, this recognition tends merely to be in the form of adaptations to the general framework of the ordinary rules of liability. Professor A.V. Dicey, writing at the turn of the last century, elevated this characteristic of English law to the status of an aspect of the rule of law. In Dicey's words, "every man, whatever be his rank or condition, is subject to the ordinary law of the realm and amenable to the

---

[1] For an account of monetary remedies for loss arising from unlawful action under European Community law, see below, para. 17–036 *et seq.*

[2] *Geddis v. Proprietors of Bann Reservoir* (1878) 3 App. Cas. 430 as explained by the House of Lords in X *(Minors) v. Bedfordshire County Council* [1995] 2 A.C. 633.

[3] See below, para. 16–025.

jurisdiction of the ordinary tribunals."[4] Dicey then alleges that the law reports of his time abounded with cases in which officials were brought before the courts and made, in their personal capacity, liable to the payment of damages for acts done in their official capacity.[5] For Dicey, the function of tortious liability here was principally to provide a mechanism for controlling governmental power.

16–004   In   modern   administrative   law   in   England,   however,   the development of principles of judicial review, and latterly the principle of procedural exclusivity,[6] have diminished the importance of actions for damages as a way of controlling executive action within the confines of the law. Today the major question is whether a system of remedies in administrative law can be complete without the provision of rights to compensation and restitution to people harmed by *ultra vires* acts or omissions of public bodies. If compensation and restitution are to be provided for at least some of the losses caused by such actions of government, the question arises as to how best this can be achieved. The orthodox common law approach, described by Dicey, is still applied with vigour in the courts and enjoys some support among academic writers.[7] Others, however, now question whether this model is appropriate for handling losses caused by governmental action and there have been calls for a distinctly public law of tort.[8]

Procedural matters

16–005   The High Court has power to award damages on an application for judicial review if the applicant claims damages.[9] This power is designed to prevent multiplicity of proceedings and does not affect the rule that there is no right to damages for unlawful administrative action *per se.*[10] The Order 53 procedure, which rarely includes

---

[4] *Introduction to the Law of the Constitution* (10th ed., 1959), p. 193.

[5] *ibid.* In his exposition, Dicey chose to ignore the special position of the Crown (see para. 3–034) and also the existence of judicial immunity (see para. 16–013).

[6] See para. 3–046.

[7] See, *e.g.*, P.W. Hogg, *Liability of the Crown* (2nd ed., 1989), p. iv ('in my view, the government ought usually to be subject to the same rules of legal liability as the subject. I reject the European-derived alternative of a distinctive public law of governmental liability, administered by special courts. My approach leads me to criticise most of the immunities and privileges that still apply to the Crown.') and p. 119; Carol Harlow, *Compensation and Government Torts* (1982), p. 80; H.W.R. Wade, *Constitutional Fundamentals* (1980), p. 663.

[8] See, *e.g.* David Cohen and J.C. Smith, 'Entitlement and the Body Politic: rethinking negligence in public law' (1986) 64 Can.B.R. 1; B. Hepple, Chap. 6 in P.B.H. Birks (ed), *Frontiers of Liability: vol. II* (1994).

[9] Supreme Court Act 1981, s. 31(4); Order 53, r. 7(1) (CPR, Sched. 1).

[10] See para. 16–002.

opportunities for testimony from witnesses, is not well-suited to dealing with some of the issues which may arise in a tort claim (for instance whether a person has been negligent). It is therefore common practice for the court to first deal with public law issues and then, if the applicant is successful, to order the damages claim to be determined at a separate hearing. The question whether a person seeking damages from public body for actions or omissions allegedly to be legally invalid may proceed directly to make a claim for damages in general civil proceedings without first initiating an application for judicial review has been considered elsewhere.[11]

Relationships between grounds of judicial review and tort liability

The correlation between a finding that action taken by a public body is, as a matter of public law, flawed and a person's right in private law to damages is not straight-forward. The position may be summarised as follows:

    (1) It has recently been held that it is neither helpful nor necessary to introduce public law concepts as to the validity of a decision into the question of a public body's liability at common law for negligence.[12] Nevertheless, issues as to the lawful scope of a public body's discretion do remain important to questions of tortious liability in relation to negligence, breach of statutory duty, misfeasance in public office and other torts. A duty of care will not be imposed which will be inconsistent with, or fetter, a statutory duty. Where a statute confers a discretion on a public body as to the extent to which, and the methods by which, a statutory duty is to be performed, only if the decision complained of is outside the ambit of the lawful discretion may a duty of care be imposed; in relation to "policy" decisions[13] of a public body, a finding that the act or omission was unlawful is normally viewed as a precondition for common law liability in tort.[14] Holding a decision to be unlawful does not involve a finding that it was taken negligently; a decision without legal authority may nevertheless have been the product of very careful consideration by a decision-maker.[15] Unlawfulness (in the judicial

16–006

---

[11] See para. 3–035.

[12] *X (Minors) v. Bedfordshire C.C.*, [1995] 2 A.C. 633.

[13] The distinction between policy decisions and operational activities of public bodies is considered below at para. 16–021. 'Operational' activities are not normally the subject of applications for judicial review.

[14] Below, para. 16–022.

[15] See P.P. Craig, 'Negligence in the Exercise of a Statutory Power' (1978) 94 L.Q.R. 428, 448.

review sense) and negligence are conceptually distinct[16] and so negligence cannot be inferred by a process of "relating back" from a finding of invalidity.[17]

16–007   There is no special affinity between any particular grounds of judicial review and cause of action for damages; whether there is a cause of action will depend on the particular facts. This may be illustrated in the following ways:

(1) Where a decision-maker takes into account an irrelevant consideration, as well as providing grounds for quashing the decision, this may create a right to damages for misfeasance in public office if it can be proved that the action complained of was done knowingly or maliciously.[18] But the fact that a consideration was taken into account which is irrelevant says nothing about whether the decision-making process which led to the error involved any failure to take reasonable care—a necessary element for recovery in the tort of negligence.[19]

(2) An official's statement, in addition to creating a legitimate expectation according to the principles of judicial review, may possibly, if untrue and given in response to a specific request, also give an action in damages for negligent misstatement.[20]

(3) The failure of a public body, contrary to the principles of natural justice, to give a person a proper hearing before making a decision does not, of itself, give rise to a cause of action for damages.[21] Where a contract exists between the parties, such as a contract of employment, contravention of a principle such as *audi alterem partem* may amount to a breach of an express or implied term of the contract; but where there is a contractual relationship of this sort, judicial review will not normally lie.[22] In order to recover damages in the public law arena, the aggrieved person will need to show that the

---

[16] See Lord Diplock in *Dunlop v. Woollahra Municipal Council* [1982] A.C. 158, 171–172.

[17] See P.P. Craig, "Compensation in Public Law" (1980) 96 L.Q.R. 413, 425.

[18] Below, para. 16–028.

[19] See Craig (1978) 94 L.Q.R. 428, 448.

[20] See, *e.g. Davy v. Spelthorne D.C.* [1984] A.C. 262; para. 16–026, below.

[21] See *Dunlop v. Woollahra Municipal Council* [1982] A.C. 158, 171–172, PC and *Welbridge Holdings Ltd v. Metropolitan Corp. of Greater Winnipeg* [1971] S.C.R. 957 (no duty of care owed to person damnified through reliance on validity of council byelaw later held invalid for breach of natural justice). *Cf. Maharaj v. Att.-Gen. for Trinidad and Tobago (No. 2)* [1979] A.C. 385, PC (constitutional provision for the redress for breach of fundamental rights held to include award of damages for committal for contempt without complying with the requirements of natural justice).

[22] See para. 3–018.

procedural impropriety or other unlawful administrative action also constituted an actionable breach of statutory duty, misfeasance in public office or other recognised civil wrong.

(4) Delay in making a decision may result in an order of mandamus on an application for judicial review[23] and, possibly, a claim for damages—though delay of itself does not found a cause of action.[24] Negligence or actionable breach of statutory duty will have to be argued.

(5) Although the term "reasonableness" may be used to define both the standard of care imposed by the tort of negligence and as a ground of judicial review, the terminology does not always bear a consistent meaning between the two branches of law. It does not follow that because a decision is held unlawful as *Wednesbury* unreasonable, the decision taker was negligent, *i.e.* he failed to take reasonable care coming to the decision; it may well have been reached only after very careful deliberation. A court may, however, infer that a decision was *so unreasonable* that it could *only* be explained by the presence of malice.[25]

DEFENDANTS IN MONETARY CLAIMS RELATING TO JUDICIAL REVIEW

In the context with which we are concerned, the person against whom the claim for a pecuniary remedy is made will usually be the   **16–008**

---

[23] See, *e.g.*, *R. v. Gloucestershire C.C. ex p. P* [1993] C.O.D. 303 (alleged unreasonable delay by education authority in providing statement of special educational need under the Education Act 1981 not found on the facts).

[24] See, *e.g.*, *R. v. H.M. Treasury, ex p. Petch* [1990] C.O.D. 19. (There was an implied duty owed to a civil servant under the Superannuation Act 1972 to consider his claim for a pension timeously and failure to do so could give rise to damages for breach of statutory duty and in common law negligence—though on the facts there had been no breach. In an unreported decision on January 15, 1990, the Court of Appeal dismissed the plaintiff's appeal on the facts without hearing argument on the law.) In *Calveley v. Chief Constable of Merseyside Police* [1989] A.C. 1228, HL police officers were suspended on full pay pending investigation of complaints made against them. They alleged the disciplinary proceedings were misconducted and there had been undue delay. It was held that there was no actionable breach of statutory duty because Parliament did not intend to confer on police officers subject to disciplinary proceedings under the Police (Discipline) Regulations 1977 any right to damages; nor was there a common law duty of care as no loss was foreseeable.

[25] See, *e.g. Jones v. Swansea C.C.* [1990] 1 W.L.R. 1453, 1461F (misfeasance in public office).

respondent in judicial review proceedings. However, direct and vicarious liability in tort may make it necessary for some other person to be joined as a party where compensation is sought.

The principle espoused by Dicey,[26] that an individual official is personally liable for torts committed in the course of his official duties, remains good today.[27] Usually the official's employer will be vicariously, and so jointly and severally, liable[28]; but an employer of an official will not be vicariously liable for a person who is a public officer given independent statutory powers or duties in his or her own right.[29] A public authority may be vicariously liable for its officers who commit misfeasance in public office providing that the employee is engaged in a misguided and unauthorised method of performing his or her duties rather than an unauthorised act so unconnected with his or her authorised duties as to be quite independent of and outside those duties.[30] Police officers are neither Crown servants nor employees of the local police authority; the Chief Constable of each police force in the U.K. is, however, made by statute vicariously liable for the acts and omissions of his officers and any damages awarded against an officer will be paid out of the police fund.[31]

---

[26] Above, para. 16–003.

[27] *e.g. Lonrho plc v. Tebbit* [1992] 4 All E.R. 280 (minister and officials alleged to have negligently failed to release plaintiff company from undertakings not to acquire more than 30 per cent of another company following investigation by Monopolies and Mergers Commission). Mr Tebbitt was the Secretary of State for Trade and Industry at the time. In practice, the Crown will pay any damages awarded against a minister or official.

[28] *e.g. Home Office v. Dorset Yacht Co. Ltd* [1970] A.C. 1004. *Cf.* the position of a minister who is not vicariously liable for acts or omissions for civil servants in his or her department; they are not his employees or agents, but the Crown's. On the position of public employees generally, see Arrowsmith, *Civil Liability of Public Authorities* (1992), Chap. 4 and S. Fredman and G. Morris, *The State as Employer: Labour Law in the Public Services* (1989).

[29] *e.g.*, the council would not have been responsible for their employee, Mr Sharp, the local land charges registrar in *Ministry of Housing and Local Government v. Sharp and Hemel Hempstead R.D.C.* [1970] 2 Q.B. 223. *Per* Lord Denning M.R.: 'In keeping the register and issuing the certificates, [Mr Sharp] is not acting for the council. He is carrying out *his* own statutory duties [as the 'proper officer' under the Land Charges Act 1925] on *his* own behalf. So he himself is responsible for breach of those duties and not the council: see *Stanbury v. Exeter Corp.* [1905] 2 K.B. 838.' The council was, however, vicariously liable for the subordinate clerk employed by them who actually carried out the negligent search. The council did not seek to rely on the fact that the minor clerk, although their employee, was seconded to the registrar and so part of *his* staff.

[30] *Racz v. Home Office* [1994] 2 A.C. 45.

[31] Police Act 1964, s. 48. This rule does not apply to a Chief Constable himself who, in theory at least, remains personally liable for damages arising from his own tortious acts. For a detailed treatment of police liability, see R. Clayton and H. Tomlinson, *Civil Actions Against the Police* (2nd ed., 1992).

Local authorities are statutory corporations given specific powers to **16–009** defend any legal proceedings.[32] The burgeoning use of "contracting out" and other market-based mechanisms for the delivery of public services[33] has not yet been followed by the development of any new general principles of civil liability. So on normal principles,[34] where service delivery has truly been contracted out to an independent contractor, the public body will not be vicariously liable for the tortious acts of that contractor (unless statute provides otherwise).[35] The public body may, however, owe some non-delegable duty to the plaintiff in these circumstances. But many "bodies" delivering services, such as executive agencies in central government[36] have no separative legal personality apart from that of their parent organisation which will remain directly liable for tortious acts.

The Crown as a defendant[37]

As with the prerogative orders and injunctions for *ultra vires* acts[38] the **16–010** Crown (as distinct from its servants and agents) needs special consideration in relation to pecuniary remedies. Following the enactment of the Crown Proceedings Act 1947, many (but not all) of the Crown's former immunities from suit for damages in tort enjoyed by central government have been removed and to a large extent it now stands in a broadly (but not wholly) similar position to a private person of full age and capacity in relation to its liabilities.[39]

In relation to tort, section 2 of the 1947 Act places the Crown in the **16–011** same position as other defendants for certain categories of liability, namely: (i) vicarious liability; (ii) direct liability to its employees; (iii) direct liability arising from breaches of duties attaching to the ownership, occupation, possession and control of property; and (iv) direct liability for breach of a statutory duty.[40] This approach has been

---

[32] Local Government Act 1972, s.222.

[33] Above, Chap. 1.

[34] Criticised by Ewan McKendrick (1990) 53 M.L.R. 770.

[35] Under section 85 Criminal Justice Act 1991, any contracted-out remand prison must have a "controller", a Crown Servant appointed by the Secretary of State; presumably the Crown will be vicariously liable for the tort of this officer under section 2(1) Crown Proceedings Act 1947.

[36] See Hepple, above, n. 8 in particular p. 78.

[37] For a comprehensive treatment of the subject, see Peter W. Hogg, *Liability of the Crown* (2nd ed., 1989).

[38] See Chap. 15.

[39] Crown Proceedings Act 1947, s. 2(1).

[40] This does not make the Crown liable for damages for breach of public law statutory duties possessed by it alone; there is liability only in respect of statutory duties "binding also upon persons other than the Crown and its officers": see s. 2(2).

criticised as it may leave the Crown with unintended immunity where no individual Crown servant is negligent (so the Crown is not vicariously liable), yet the duty owed by the Crown directly does not fall within one of the specified categories.[41]

16–012   Those who carry on the activities of government in the various bodies which collectively constitute the Crown are servants or agents of the Crown. For the purposes of civil proceedings, the 1947 Act states that, unless the context otherwise requires, "agents" includes an independent contractor employed by the Crown and "officer" in relation to the Crown includes any servant of Her Majesty and accordingly includes a minister of the Crown.[42] In relation to liability of the Crown for tort, the Act provides that an "officer" is someone who has been directly or indirectly appointed by the Crown and who is, at the material time, being paid in respect of his duties as an officer of the Crown solely out of the consolidated fund, monies provided by Parliament, or any other fund certified by the Treasury.[43] In accordance with section 17, the Treasury publishes a list of authorised government departments for the purpose of identifying the department by and against which civil proceedings may be brought. The list is not exhaustive and where a body, which is part of the Crown, is not identified on the list or where there is doubt as to which of the authorised departments on the list is the appropriate one, the proceedings can be brought against the Attorney-General.

Judges and Tribunals

16–013   Many judicial review challenges are against the decisions of judges, magistrates, coroners, tribunals or others taking decisions of a judicial nature. In an important exception to the general principle of treating state officials similarly to private persons, the law confers an extremely high degree of immunity from tortious liability on those exercising judicial functions.[44]

---

[41] See Hogg, *op. cit.*, pp. 102–104.

[42] s. 38(2).

[43] s. 2(6).

[44] On judicial immunity generally, see Abimbola Olowofoyeku, *Suing Judges: a study of judicial immunity* (1993) and J.F. Clerk and W.H.B. Lindsell, *Clerk and Lindsell on Torts* (1995) Chap. 27; M. Brazier, 'Judicial Immunity and the Independence of the Judiciary' [1976] P.L. 397.

TORTIOUS LIABILITY GENERALLY

This section outlines possible grounds for seeking damages in tort **16–014** against a public body in circumstances where judicial review may also lie. Many of the difficulties which face any plaintiff pursuing an action in tort are exacerbated where what is being claimed is compensation for loss due to the activities with which this book is concerned. This is especially the case where the decisions relate to the allocation of resources, licensing, inspection and other forms of regulation.

First, the loss suffered by the plaintiff as a result of a public **16–015** authority's negligent acts or omissions[45] will often be economic loss, which is not consequential on any damage to property or personal injury, a kind of loss in respect of which the courts are reluctant to provide a remedy in the absence of a contract.[46] Secondly, in many cases, the complaint will be that a public body failed to prevent a third party inflicting loss on the complainant, for instance by approving plans or inspecting buildings carelessly[47] (where the breach of duty can be characterised as the failure of a public body to control the acts or omissions of builders or architects), licensing of financial services (supervision of deposit takers)[48] or in the context of the criminal justice system, failing to detect and prevent the acts of criminals.[49] English tort law is generally hostile to the notion of imposing a duty of care for acts of independent third parties.[50]

In addition, it is rare for the common law to impose a duty to take **16–016** positive action, in the absence of a special relationship, to protect a stranger from being harmed. In the perennial illustration of this principle, a man may stand by and watch a child drown in a shallow pool without committing any tort. The main policy justifications for

---

[45] The position in relation to negligent misstatements and economic loss is rather different: since *Hedley Byrne & Co. Ltd v. Heller & Partners Ltd* [1964] A.C. 465 pure economic loss arising from negligent information and advice has, in some circumstances, been recoverable. This cause of action is considered separately, below, para. 16–026.

[46] On economic loss generally, see *Clerk and Lindsell on Torts*, paras 10–49–10–50.

[47] *Anns v. Merton L.B.C.* [1978] A.C. 728 (now largely overruled); *Murphy v. Brentwood D.C.* [1991] 1 A.C. 398; *Curran v. Northern Ireland Co-ownership Housing Association Ltd* [1987] A.C. 718.

[48] *Yuen Kun-yeu v. Att.-Gen. of Hong Kong* [1988] A.C. 175.

[49] *Hill v. Chief Constable of West Yorkshire* [1989] A.C. 53 (no duty owed by police to victim for alleged failure promptly to apprehend unknown perpetrator of a crime). *Cf. Home Office v. Dorset Yacht Co. Ltd* [1970] A.C. 1004 (Home Office vicariously liable for negligence of prison officers who permitted borstal boys in their control to escape and cause damage to the plaintiff's property).

[50] See *e.g. X (Minors) v. Bedfordshire C.C.* [1995] 2 A.C. 633 at 751, *per* Lord Browne-Wilkinson "In my judgment, The courts should proceed with great care before holding liable in negligence those who have been charged by parliament with the task of protecting society from the wrong-doings of others."

distinguishing between failing to act (nonfeasance) and acting wrongfully (misfeasance) are, first, that the imposition of affirmative duties is normally more burdensome on an individual in terms of time, trouble, risk and money than are negative duties and, secondly, the difficulty in some cases of identifying the person to be sued.[51] The courts have found it difficult to develop satisfactorily the law in the case of nonfeasance by public bodies; in particular this raises the question whether a public body may be liable in tort for the non-exercise of permissive statutory powers—as opposed to non-performance of duties—such as those enabling it to inspect or regulate or confer benefits such as licences or financial grants. It was at one time thought that a public authority did not incur liability for failing to exercise a power, or even for exercising it dilatorily, although a foreseeable injury to person or property would have been averted by a proper exercise of the power.[52] One reason for this view was that if the authority was under no duty to act, a failure to act (or the taking of action that caused no more loss than would have occurred had nothing been done) was within the discretion statutorily conferred. It is now clear, however, that this simple analysis incompletely states the law.[53] Courts are nowadays slow to construe discretion as absolute, with the result that a failure on the part of a public authority to act consistently with the underlying purposes for which a discretion was conferred may not only amount to a breach of a public law duty but also give rise to liability in tort to those who as a result suffer

---

[51] See Peter Cane (ed.), *Atiyah's Accidents, Compensation and the Law* (4th ed., 1987) pp. 82–86, who goes on to argue that there is no really satisfactory reason for distinguishing between misfeasance and nonfeasance (pp. 102–1030: 'this distinction is based on irrational misconceptions about causal principles on the one hand, and an exaggerated fear of the burdensomeness of affirmative obligations on the other.')

[52] *East Suffolk Rivers Catchment Board v. Kent* [1941] A.C. 74 (board had powers, but no duty, under the Land Drainage Act 1930 to repair and maintain drainage works; it carried out dilatory repairs of river banks after flooding which resulted in plaintiff's land being flooded for much longer than it needed to be), considered by the House of Lords in *Stovin v. Wise* [1996] A.C. 923 and the Court of Appeal in *Capital & Counties plc v. Hampshire C.C.* [1997] Q.B. 1004.

[53] *Anns v. Merton L.B.C.* [1978] A.C. 728. This case, in so far as it relates to the duty of care owed by local authorities for the negligent exercise or non-exercise of statutory powers to approve plans or inspect building works, has been overruled by *Murphy v. Brentwood D.C.* [1991] 1 A.C. 398. No duty is owed by a local authority to the owner or purchaser of a building in respect of the cost of repairing the building itself as this is pure economic loss. *Murphy*, however, leaves open the question whether a duty of care is owed for a negligent exercise or non-exercise of statutory powers which result in injury to a person or physical damage to property other than the buildings itself. *Anns* therefore remains authority on the issue of liability for omissions: *Murphy* has not been followed in New Zealand: see *Invercargill City Council v. Hamlin* [1996] A.C. 624, PC.

foreseeable loss.[54] It has been argued that the justification for not creating positive duties to act, breach of which will give rise to liability, do not apply in the case of public bodies where they are under a public law duty to consider whether and how to exercise a statutory power, and therefore the courts should consider each case on its merits without adopting a presumption for or against liability.[55] However, the circumstances in which inaction on the part of a public body when exercising such a discretion will render it liable to pay damages are likely to be rare.

The causation of damage also creates particular problems in respect **16–017** of the imposition of tortious liability on public authorities for unlawful administrative action.[56] It is trite law that judicial review is not concerned with the merits of administrative decisions and the court should ordinarily avoid substituting its own opinion for that of the public body as to how precisely a discretion should be exercised. How, then, is a court to approach a case where, for example, a plaintiff alleges that a breach of natural justice activated by malice has caused him loss (such as the refusal of a licence to trade) or the decision maker negligently failed to take into account a relevant consideration? The court may avoid second-guessing what decision the public authority would have reached had the decision not been tainted by illegality by saying that the plaintiff has at most lost *an opportunity* to obtain a benefit. Probability will be defined by, among other facts, the degree of discretion possessed by the decision maker. As Harlow points out,[57] whilst in most cases a court may attempt to place a value on a lost chance,[58] special difficulties arise in relation to damages claims associated with judicial review because this exercise would necessarily involve the court substituting its own discretion for that of the decision maker.[59] A solution is to defer the action for damages until after the outcome of the application for judicial review is known and the public body has complied with the decision. However, even if

---

[54] Providing, of course, that the foreseeable loss is otherwise recoverable, *e.g.* as not being pure economic loss.

[55] Arrowsmith, *Civil Liability of Public Authorities* (1992), pp. 183–184.

[56] See generally *Clerk and Lindsell on Torts*, paras 1–103 and 10–142 *et seq.* In the context of damages in the public law context, see Harlow, *Compensation and Government Torts* (1982), p. 93. *Cf.* Justice/All Souls, *Administrative Justice—Some Necessary Reforms* (1988) para. 11.86, who did not see causation as a major problem. See further McBride [1979] C.L.J. 323, 334–340.

[57] *ibid.*

[58] See *Chaplin v. Hicks* [1911] 2 K.B. 786 (a case in contract); whether this principle is applicable in tort was expressly left open by the House of Lords in *Hotson v. East Berkshire A.H.A.* [1987] A.C. 750.

[59] Again, the Justice/All Souls review saw no problem in the court considering whether an authority might validly have refused the benefit and taking that into account in determining damages (*op. cit.*, para. 11.86).

the court considering the damages claim waits for the decision maker to reconsider the decision in accordance with law, conceptual problems may still arise if a decision is characterised as void (rather than voidable)[60]; in these circumstances what will have caused the plaintiff's loss? One answer, arguably, is the act of taking a void, or the omission to take a valid, decision. If practical steps have been taken to implement a void decision, *e.g.* by entering onto the plaintiff's land or seizing his goods, then that physical act may of itself constitute the tort rather than the underlying invalid decision.[61] But often there will be no such steps to execute a decision, *e.g.* as when a licence to carry on a trade is revoked negligently or in a manner which amounts to misfeasance in public office. In a number of cases, it has been held that a plaintiff ought to have ignored an invalid decision,[62] with the result that damage has been held to have arisen not from the unlawful administrative decision, but the plaintiff's own voluntary compliance with it. This approach has rightly been criticised as unrealistic,[63] and the courts have on occasion explicitly or implicitly accepted that a person's act in obeying an invalid order was a reasonable response.[64]

16–018   A final difficulty with tort liability for unlawful administrative action lies in the application of the rules as to remoteness of damage,[65] particularly in relation to economic damage.[66] Given the fact that governmental actions will often, of their very nature, foreseeably affect a great many people, it is not clear that the applications of ordinary principles on remoteness will adequately protect public authorities from being subject to crushing liability. As already stated, a person who has suffered loss as a result of unlawful administrative conduct has to plead and establish liability under a recognised cause of action in tort to recover damages; a public body has no pecuniary liability for maladministration or invalid administrative action *per se.*[67] Negligence, negligent misstatement, breach of statutory duty, misfeasance in public office, false imprisonment, trespass and nuisance are probably the

---

[60] See Chap. 4.
[61] *e.g. Cooper v. Wandsworth Board of Works* (1883) 14 C.B. (N.S.) 180.
[62] See *e.g. Dunlop v. Woollahra M.C.* [1982] A.C. 158, PC; *Scott v. Gamble* [1916] 2 K.B. 504; *O'Connor v. Isaacs* [1956] 2 Q.B. 288.
[63] See Hogg. *op. cit.*, p. 110, n. 158, citing *McClintock v. Commonwealth* (1947) 75 C.L.R. 1. See further Rubenstein, *Jurisdiction and Illegality* (1965), p. 322.
[64] See, *e.g. Farrington v. Thomson* [1959] V.R. 286; *Roncarelli v. Duplessis* (1959) 16 D.L.R. (2d) 689, 708. See further McBride [1979] C.L.J. 323.
[65] See generally, *Clerk and Lindsell on Torts*, para. 1–129 *et seq.*
[66] *Op. cit.*, para. 10–162.
[67] See above, para. 16–002

most obvious causes of action in this context, but there is no reason why others may not provide a route to compensation if the necessary elements can be established on the facts of the case.

LIABILITY FOR UNLAWFUL ADMINISTRATIVE ACTION UNDER DIFFERENT TORTS

Negligence[68]

In general, liability for negligent acts and omissions will be imposed **16–019** by a court where:

(1) the defendant owes the plaintiff a duty of care. This will exist if: (i) the harm suffered by the plaintiff was reasonably foreseeable; (ii) the relationship between the defendant and plaintiff was sufficiently "proximate"; (iii) the imposition of a duty of care would be just and reasonable.[69] This involves the court considering broad questions of public policy;

(2) the defendant was in breach of the standard of care required in the circumstances;

(3) the plaintiff suffered damage as a result of the breach. The damage in question must normally include physical damage to property[70] or the person or economic loss arising from such damage.[71]

In recent years, English law has turned its back on the search for general principles of negligence liability, and instead the law is set to develop incrementally, on a case by case basis. In novel situations, arguments based on analogies to previously decided cases, rather than appeals to principle, are likely to find more favour in the courts.[72]

In many instances, the application of such general rules of liability **16–020** to public bodies presents little difficulty: when a pedestrian is struck down by a negligently driven van it is of no importance whether the

---

[68] For a detailed account of the general law of negligence, see R.A. Percy and C.T. Walton (eds), *Charlesworth on Negligence* (1997) and *Clerk and Lindsell on Torts*, Chap. 10.

[69] See *Clerk and Lindsell on Torts*, para. 10–48.

[70] On the need to show damage to property other than to the negligently constructed building or manufactured chattel itself, see *Murphy v. Brentwood D.C.* [1991] 1 A.C. 398.

[71] See *Clerk and Lindsell on Torts*, para. 10–49.

[72] See, *e.g.*, Lord Keith in *Murphy v. Brentwood D.C.* [1991] 1 A.C. 398, 461.; *X (Minors) v. Bedfordshire C.C.* [1995] 2 A.C. 633 at 735D.

driver is on the business of a commercial enterprise or a public authority. Where, however, allegations of negligence are made in relation to the way in which a public body has performed some public function—such as the state regulation of financial services, social work or the investigation of crime—greater difficulties may arise. Ultimately any judicial decision on whether to impose a duty of care in a novel situation is one of policy. Because of the nature of public functions— which give special powers and impose responsibilities on administrators—some policy factors not usually relevant, or less important, where the defendant is a private person come into play. Regrettably, much effort has been spent deliberating *how* such policy considerations are to be taken into account by the common law, rather than in the examination of *what* they are and *when* they are to apply.

16–021   Much of the debate in the case law and academic literature is over whether there needs to be a special framework for determining the existence of a duty of care in respect of governmental activities or whether the general test (described above) is sufficiently flexible to be used in this context. In many cases in which the courts have had to decide whether a public body owes a plaintiff a duty of care in respect of its public functions, the courts have proceeded simply by the application of the general legal framework.[73] In other cases, the courts have adopted a different and more elaborate approach[74] to determining whether a duty arises in respect of functions which contain an element of "planning" or "policy", as opposed to merely "operational" activities.[75] Those who advocate the need for a special framework suggest it is needed for two broad types of reason. First, the general test is inadequate to accommodate the special policy factors that need to be taken into account in relation to certain public functions. Secondly, application of the general test will, it is thought by some, result in liability being imposed in too many cases,[76] or alternatively that it will result in too large an area of immunity for public bodies.

---

[73] Thus, in cases where the plaintiff has alleged that an Adjudication Officer negligently determined his entitlement to unemployment benefit: *Jones v. Department of Employment* [1989] 1 Q.B. 1; or that the Crown Prosecution Service failed to ensure that a magistrates' court was informed that offences for which he had been bailed had subsequently been taken into consideration by the Crown Court: *Welsh v. Chief Constable of the Merseyside Police and the Crown Prosecution Service* [1993] 1 All E.R. 692. See also *Bennett v. Commissioner of Police* [1995] 1 W.L.R. 488.

[74] Harlow, *Compensation and Government Torts* (1982), p. 55, describes it as "incredibly complex".

[75] For a critical survey of decisions which have applied, ignored or distinguished the policy/operational text between 1978 and 1985, see S.H. Bailey and M.J. Bowan, "The Policy/Operational Dichotomy—A Cuckoo in the Nest" (1986) 45 C.L.J. 430. See also *X (Minors) v. Bedfordshire C.C.* [1995] 2 A.C. 633 at 7374–738.

[76] See, *e.g.* Woolf, *Protection of the Public* (1990), p. 60.

In *Anns v. Merton L.B.C.*,[77] Lord Wilberforce distinguished policy   **16–022**
aspects of a local authority's functions from its operational ones and
said that a duty of care was more likely to be imposed in respect of
the latter. The terms "policy" and "operational" are misleading in that
they may suggest a distinction between making a decision and
carrying out a decision. It is clear that some stages of the
implementation process involve a policy aspect, and so are unlikely to
give rise to a duty of care situation.[78] Various synonyms are used:
"administrative" or "business powers"[79] instead of operational;
"planning" decisions instead of "policy". Lord Salmon drew no such
distinction in *Anns*, holding more straightforwardly that every person
whether discharging a public duty or not, is under a common law
obligation to some persons in some circumstances to conduct himself
with reasonable care so as not to injure those persons likely to be
injured by his lack of care.

Where the policy/operational dichotomy has been used, the   **16–023**
following have been held to be "operational" decisions[80]: a decision by
a local authority to place a boy with known pyromaniac tendencies in
an insecure home,[81] the decision of a highway authority not to put up
road signs at a particular location[82]; and a decision of a minister not to
release a company promptly from certain undertakings it had been
required to give during an investigation by the Monopolies and
Mergers Commission.[83]

The general status of the House of Lords' decision in *Anns* is now   **16–024**
greatly diminished, it now having been overruled by *Murphy* in so far
as it was authority for imposing a duty of care in respect of defects in
work which has not caused damage to the property or person of the
plaintiff.[84] In *Murphy* nothing was said, however, about the policy/
operational approach, and it can be assumed that this aspect of the

---

[77] [1978] A.C. 728. So far as English law is concerned, the origins of the policy/
operational dichotomy lie in Lord Diplock's speech in *Home Office v. Dorset Yacht Co.
Ltd* [1970] A.C. 1004. For an account of the notion, and its roots in the U.S.A. see
Aronson and Whitmore, *op. cit.*, p. 36.

[78] *e.g.* decisions as to the staffing levels at a regulatory agency.

[79] See *Rowling v. Takaro Properties Ltd* [1988] A.C. 473, 500.

[80] For further illustrations of the application of the distinction, see: *Clerk and Lindsell on
Torts*, para. 10–174; Arrowsmith, *Civil Liability of Public Authorities* (1992), 172–174;
Barrett v. Enfield L.B.C. [1998] Q.B. 367; *X (Minors) v. Bedfordshire C.C.* [1995] 2 A.C.
633 at 748 H.

[81] *Vicar of Writtle v. Essex C.C.* (1979) L.G.R. 656.

[82] *Bird v. Pearce* [1979] R.T.R. 369 (failure to put up temporary signs warning of absence
of road markings); *Lavis v. Kent C.C.* (1994) 90 L.G.R. 416 (failure to erect sign
warning of sharp bend).

[83] *Lonrho plc v. Tebbit* [1991] 4 All E.R. 973 (Browne-Wilkinson V.-C.); [1992] 4 All E.R.
280, CA.

[84] *Murphy v. Brentwood D.C.* [1991] 1 A.C. 398.

decision was not intended to be overruled[85] though the usefulness of the distinction has been doubted by the Privy Council. In determining the question whether a minister who had allegedly misconstrued regulations so as to cause loss to the plaintiff was liable, their Lordships in *Rowling v. Takaro Properties Ltd* inclined to the views, expressed in the academic literature, that the distinction did not provide a touchstone for liability,[86] but rather was expressive of the need to exclude altogether those cases in which the decision under attack is of such a kind that a question whether it had been made negligently was not justiciable. Lord Keith, citing Craig,[87] gave as illustrations discretionary decisions on the allocation of scarce resources and the distribution of risks. The categorisation of a decision as one of policy or planning may exclude liability; but a conclusion that it did not fall within that category did not mean that a duty of care will necessarily exist. The Privy Council, having considered all the circumstances and applied the general test, held that there was no duty of care. Subsequent cases have also doubted the utility of the policy/operation distinction.[88]

16–025   Wrangling over the forensic approach has deflected attention from the heart of the matter: what, if any, policy factors are uniquely or commonly determinative of public bodies' liability in negligence in respect of their public law functions? An exhaustive list of considerations is, of course, impossible, as all the relevant circumstances of a case will need to be considered.[89] Some of the following may be relevant.

> (1) Many powers and duties of a governmental nature must necessarily contain a large "policy" element and it is for the public body, not the courts, to decide what policy to pursue.[90]

---

[85] *X (Minors) v. Bedfordshire C.C.* [1995] 2 A.C. 633 at Lord Browne-Wilkinson said that this part of the decision in Anns had largely escaped criticism in later cases.

[86] [1988] A.C. 473. Of course, establishing that a decision is an 'operational' one is only a precondition to recovering damages for tort—a duty, breach and damage will have to be proved.

[87] See now P.P. Craig, *Administrative Law*, (3rd. ed., 1994) pp. 620–625 for a discussion of justiciability in relation to duties of care in tort law.

[88] See, *e.g. Osman v. Ferguson* [1993] 4 All E.R. 344; *Stovin v. Wise* [1996] A.C. 923 (Lord Hoffmann describes distinction as 'inadequate').

[89] *Rowling v. Takaro Properties Ltd* (above, n. 86), *per* Lord Keith.

[90] Justice/All Souls, para. 11.22. For an illustration of a situation in which a duty of care was denied because the plaintiff public bodies were carrying out a public duty involving balancing the public interest, see *Bennett v. Commissioner of Police of the Metropolis and Others* [1995] 1 W.L.R. 488 (Secretary of State signing public interest immunity certificate); *X (Minors) v. Bedfordshire C.C.* [1995] 2 A.C. 633 at 738G.

This may apply both to the question of whether a duty of care is imposed and the setting of the standard of care required.

(2) It may be desirable for the law of torts and the grounds of judicial review to set broadly consistent standards as to the conduct required of public authorities.[91] For instance, if a decision which is amenable to judicial review is "reasonable" in the *Wednesbury* sense, it may be undesirable to categorise it as negligent. As Harlow has put it, many judges believe that there must be an exact correspondence between negligence liability and "unlawful" exercise of discretionary power in public law.[92] It is unfortunate that the term "unreasonable" is used both in judicial review and negligence; it usually means different things in each context.[93]

(3) Usually the damage caused by invalid administrative action will be pure economic loss not consequential on any physical damage. For a variety of policy reasons the law of negligence in general denies recovery for such loss[94]; many of these are as applicable to determining the liability of public authorities for their public functions as elsewhere.

(4) The concern that exists that the imposition of liability may have a chilling effect on the quality of administrators' actions.[95]

(5) Where the defendant is performing a specific statutory function the purpose for which the power or duty was conferred is regarded as being relevant in determining the existence and extent of any common law duty of care.[96] Thus where the purpose of the duty is to protect health and safety this is seen as impliedly excluding any greater common law duty (*e.g.* to prevent economic loss arising from a defective building). Arguably this confuses and blurs the boundaries between the tort of negligence and the tort of breach of

---

[91] See above, para 16–007.

[92] Harlow, *Compensation and Government Torts* (1982), p. 53.

[93] [1978] A.C. 728.

[94] See *Clerk and Lindsell on Torts*, para. 10–50; *Davis v. Radcliffe* [1990] 1 W.L.R. 821 (action by depositors against the Finance Board and Treasury of the Isle of Man) but *cf. Allen v. Bloomsbury Health Authority* [1993] 1 All E.R. 651 (action against health authority for economic loss due to failure to sterilise).

[95] Below, para. 16–051.

[96] See *Governors of the Peabody Donation Fund v. Sir Lindsay Parkinson and Co. Ltd* [1985] A.C. 210, HL; *X (Minors) v. Bedfordshire C.C.* [1995] 2 A.C. 633, 739C; *Stovin v. Wise* [1996] A.C. 923.

statutory duty[97] and unduly restricts the development of negligence liability. Since the duty of care in negligence arises from a relationship between the parties, not by virtue of a statute as in breach of statutory duty, the purpose for which the public body was given certain powers by statute should at most be no more than a matter to be considered as part of the relationship. In any event the pursuit of identifying a precise implicit legislative purpose is often a fruitless exercise as it is relatively easy to ascribe a variety of objects or purposes to statutes conferring powers.[98]

(6) The existence or absence of an alternative method of redress for the plaintiff is often regarded as relevant to determining whether or not a common law duty of care exists. Thus, where the plaintiff may appeal to a tribunal or official against a decision, and the appellate body has power to order compensation, that will indicate that the court ought not impose a tortious liability on the original decision maker.[99] There are comments in the authorities justifying the same inference being drawn because of the existence of the right to apply for judicial review.[1] However, judicial review is available in respect of all administrative action and accordingly no special significance can be attached to its availability.

(7) The courts will be slow to regard the misinterpretation of legislation as indicating negligence on the part of the decision

---

[97] On which, see para. 16–034 below. See further K.M. Stanton, *Breach of Statutory Duty in Tort* (1986), pp. 29–30.

[98] See further J.J. Doyle in P.D. Finn (ed.), *Essays on Torts* (1989), pp. 223–234; R. O'Dair (1991) 54 M.L.R. 561.

[99] See, *e.g. Jones v. Department of Employment* [1989] 1 Q.B. 1 (plaintiff had no cause of action in negligence against an officer who underestimated his entitlement to a welfare benefit. The plaintiff had successfully appealed against the determination and had received back-payments, though no interest); *X (Minors) v. Bedfordshire C.C.* [1995] 2 A.C. 633 at 751A-B; *Barrett v. Enfield L.B.C.* [1998] Q.B. 367.

[1] See, *e.g. Rowling v. Takaro Properties Ltd* [1988] A.C., 473, 501–502 where it was held that the only effect of the allegedly negligent decision by the minister (in misconstruing legislation and so refusing consent) was delay. *Per* Lord Keith: 'This is because the processes of judicial review are available to the aggrieved party; and assuming that the alleged error of law is so serious that it can properly be described as negligent, the decision will assuredly be quashed by a process which, in New Zealand as in the United Kingdom, will normally be carried out with promptitude.' See also *Calveley v. Chief Constable of the Merseyside Police* [1989] A.C. 1228 at 1237f where, in relation to a claim for breach of statutory duty. Lord Bridge refers to judicial review as an alternative remedy justifying the refusal of tortious liability and *Curran v. Northern Ireland Co-Ownership Housing Association Ltd* [1987] A.C. 718.

maker.[2] There is often room for more than one construction of a statutory provision and only a court can give a conclusive interpretation.

Negligent misstatement[3]

Liability for careless false statements of fact and opinion which **16–026** cause a plaintiff economic loss is based on somewhat different principles than liability for types of loss caused by careless acts and omissions.[4] In this area of law, no material distinction appears to have been drawn between the liability of administrative bodies and other persons.[5] It is clear that not every false statement made by a public official will attract liability. A duty of care will be owed only where a statement was both intended to be relied upon for a particular purpose[6] or transaction and it was actually so relied upon and there is a sufficiently proximate relationship between the parties.[7] Even as between private persons the courts are very slow to superimpose a common law duty of care on a defendant who is disseminating information in order to comply with a statutory requirement[8]; a similar approach will certainly be adopted in the public law context. The defendant also had to know that what he said would be communicated to the plaintiff or a class of persons of which the plaintiff was a member. In the public law context, liability is most likely to lie against officials giving answers to specific questions. *e.g.* planning officers who gave erroneous assurances that the operation of an enforcement notice would be suspended for three years.[9]

---

[2] See, *e.g.*, *Rowling v. Takaro Properties Ltd* (above, n. 1) and *Dunlop v. Woollahra M.C.* [1982] A.C. 158, PC.

[3] See further, *Clerk and Lindsell on Torts*, para. 10–24 *et seq.*

[4] *Hedley Byrne & Co. v. Heller* [1964] A.C. 465 and *Caparo Industries plc v. Dickman* [1990] 2 A.C. 605. *Cf. James McNaughton Paper v. Hicks Anderson* [1991] 2 Q.B. 113, *per* Neill L.J. that, in the light of later decisions, detailed reference to *Hedley Byrne* serves little purpose.

[5] See, *e.g. Ministry of Housing and Local Government v. Sharp* [1970] 2 Q.B. 223.

[6] For analysis of the problems entailed in identifying the 'purpose' for which a statement is made, see B. Hepple and R. O'Dair (1992) 45 C.L.P. Annual Review 151 *et seq.*

[7] *Yuen Kun-Yeu v. Att.-Gen. of Hong Kong* [1988] A.C. 175 *per* Lord Keith at 194.

[8] See. *e.g.*, *Caparo v. Dickman* [1990] 2 A.C. 605 accounts audited pursuant to Companies Act); *Deloitte Haskins & Sells v. National Mutual Life Nominees Ltd* [1993] 2 All E.R. 1015 (duty to report under Securities Act 1978).

[9] *Davy v. Spelthorne B.C.* [1984] A.C. 262; *Welton v. North Cornwall D.C.* [1997] 1 W.L.R. 570; *Lambert v. West Devon B.C.* [1997] J.P.L. 735. *Cf. Tidman v. Reading B.C.* [1994] 3 P.L.R. 72; *R. v. Hounslow L.B.C., ex p. Williamson* [1996] E.G.C.S. 27.

16–027   Both in the case of negligent misstatement and other forms of negligence it must be accepted that as a result of the recent decisions of the House of Lords and the Privy Council already cited, the circumstances in which liability for negligence for administrative default will be limited to special situations. Unless and until there is legislative intervention or a change of heart on the part of the House of Lords, little progress in developing additional situations where damages will be payable can be expected.

Misfeasance in public office[10]

16–028   As a general rule, in determining questions of tortious liability the motives of the defendant are immaterial. But proof of improper motive may be fatal to a defence of statutory authority to commit an act that is prima facie tortious.[11] Moreover, improper motive (or malice or bad faith) is an essential ingredient in several specific torts such as malicious prosecution. In addition there is the developing tort of misfeasance in public office, the precise scope of which is not yet settled[12]: this is the subject matter of this section.

16–029   A public authority[13] or person holding a public office[14] may be liable for the tort of misfeasance in public office where:

(1) there is an exercise or non-exercise of public power, whether common law, statutory or from some other source;

---

[10] See further: Arrowsmith, *op. cit.*, pp. 226–234; Aronson and Whitmore, *op. cit.*, pp. 120–131; Hogg, *op. cit.*. pp. 81–85: R.C. Evans (1982) 31 I.C.L.Q. 640: Gould (1972) 5 N.Z.U.L.R. 105: McBride [1979] C.L.J. 323.

[11] *cf. Westminster Corp. v. L. & N.W. Railway* [1905] A.C. 426 (where the allegations of improper motives were not, however, made out).

[12] The tort does, however, have an ancient pedigree. For a useful account of the historical development of the tort, see R.C. Evans, 'Damages for Unlawful Administrative Action: The Remedy for Misfeasance in Public Office' (1982) 31 I.C.L.Q. 640. Revival of interest in the tort dates from a series of Commonwealth decisions: *Farrington v. Thomson and Bridgland* [1959] V.C. 286 (wrongful order to close hotel); *Roncarelli v. Duplessis* [1959] S.C.R. 121 (Can.); *David v. Abdul Cader* [1963] 1 W.L.R. 834 (PC, Ceylon); *Dunlop v. Woollahra M.C.* [1982] A.C. 158, PC and see also *Northern Territory v. Mengel* (1995) 60 A.L.J.R. 527.

[13] Whether directly or vicariously. After some initial hesitation as to whether a public authority could be vicariously for the misfeasance of its servants, the House of Lords has now confirmed that they may be: *Racz v. Home Office* [1994] 2 A.C. 45.

[14] A person who is paid out of public funds and who 'owes duties to members of the public as to how the office shall be exercised': see *Tampion v. Anderson* [1973] V.R. 715, 720. Also *Henley v. Mayor of Lyme* (1828) 5 Bing. 91, 107. *Quaere* whether the officer has to be paid out of public funds: see McBride, *op. cit.*, 326.

(2) which is either[15] (a) affected by malice towards the plaintiff[16] or (b) the decision maker knows is unlawful[17]; and

(3) the plaintiff is in consequence deprived of a benefit or suffers other loss.[18]

It is unclear whether the tort is confined to those actions or decisions which are capable of being characterised as the exercise of "public" power or whether it extends to decisions taken by a public body in capacities such as the plaintiff's landlord or in the exercise of contractual powers.[19] But a police officer investigating suspected disciplinary offenses alleged to have been committed by another officer who makes a written report to his superior officer was held not to have done an "act" amounting to an exercise of power or authority for the purposes of this tort.[20]

16–030

A power is exercised maliciously if its repository is motivated by personal animosity towards those who are directly affected by its exercise.[21] Where misfeasance is alleged against a decision-making

16–031

---

[15] The term 'malice' is sometimes used to describe both of the alternative states of defendants' mind. As Harlow points out (*op. cit.*, p. 60) malice is used in tort law in two senses: objectively to mean intentional wrong-doing; and subjectively; to mean malevolence or spite. Although there is a substantial overlap between the two categories, Arrowsmith (*op. cit.*, p. 229) rightly urges that they should be treated as distinct. See now *Three Rivers D.C. v. Bank of England (No. 3)* [1996] 3 All E.R. 558.

[16] That is, an intent to injure the plaintiff: see *Bennett v. Commissioner of Police of the Metropolis* [1995] 1 W.L.R. 488, 501.

[17] *Bourgoin S.A. v. Minister of Agriculture, Fisheries and Food* [1986] Q.B. 716 (it was alleged, *inter alia*, that minister knew that a refusal of licence to import turkeys from France was contrary to the Treaty of Rome).

[18] As the tort's historical antecedents lie in actions on the case (rather than trespass) where actual damage had to be pleaded and found, damage is a necessary element of the tort: see, *e.g., Farrington v. Thomson and Bridgland* [1959] V.R. 286, 297 and *Wood v. Blair and Helmsley R.D.C., The Times*, July 5, 1957 (noted Beatson and Matthews, *Administrative Law: Cases and Materials* (1983), p. 428). See also R.C. Evans (1982) 31 I.C.L.Q. 640, 641 and Clayton and Tomlinson, *op. cit.*, p. 369. Loss of liberty or damage to reputation are sufficient types of damage: see *Brayser v. Maclean* (1875) L.R. 6 P.C. 398, 404. *Cf.* Arrowsmith who argues that the tort is probably actionable *per se* (*Civil Liability of Public Authorities* (1992), p. 233) and also *Clerk and Lindsell on Torts*, para. 1-101–1-102 (where reference is made to certain old authorities on breach of duty by public officer in the absence of proof of damage).

[19] See Lord Lowry, speaking *obiter*, in *Jones v. Swansea C.C* [1990] 1 W.L.R. 1453, 1458 (the plaintiff needed both planning permission and the council's permission *as her landlord* for the change of use of premises). The point is open to be decided in future cases.

[20] *Calveley v. Chief Constable of the Merseyside Police* [1989] A.C. 1228, 1240. Such a report may however give rise to a cause of action for defamation.

[21] In *Roncarelli v. Duplessis* (above, n. 12) at 141, Rand J. defined malice more widely. as 'acting for a reason and purposed knowingly foreign to the administration.' There is no need to adopt uniform terminology.

body, it is sufficient to show that a majority of its members present had made the decision with the object of damaging the plaintiff.[22] Often there may be no direct evidence of the existence of malice, and in these circumstances the court may make adverse inferences, *e.g.* from the fact that a decision was so unreasonable that it could *only* be explained by the presence of such a motive.[23] A court will not entertain allegation of bad faith or malice made against the repository of a power unless it has been expressly pleaded and properly particularised.[24]

16–032   As an alternative to pleading malice in the subjective sense just described, the tort may be established by proof that the public power was exercised by a person knowing (or possibly, reckless as to whether) it was contrary to law.[25] There is no reason to confine the unlawfulness to acts *ultra vires* in a judicial review sense; the action may, for example, be contrary to European Community law[26] or in contempt of an order of a court.

16–033   In few English cases so far has the tort been established on the facts and therefore the courts have not had to concern themselves with the principles that govern the award of damages.[27] On the current state of the authorities it appears that exemplary damages are not available for the tort.[28]

---

[22] *Jones v. Swansea C.C.* (above, n. 19).

[23] See, *e.g. Jones v. Swansea C.C.* (above.n. 19)—the court could make no such inference as there were rational grounds for the decision.

[24] *Demetriades v. Glasgow Corp.* [1951] 1 All E.R. 457, 460, 461, 463; *Campbell v. Ramsay* (1968) 70 S.R. (N.S.W.) 327.

[25] In *Three Rivers D.C. v. Bank of England (No. 3)* [1996] 3 All E.R. 558 it was held, following the majority in *Northern Territory v. Mengel* (n. 12 above) that it was not sufficient to prove simply knowledge of the unlawful nature of the act and that the act caused the plaintiff's loss. Per Clarke J. at 582: 'For the purposes of the requirement that the officer knows that he has no power to do the act complained of, it is sufficient that the officer has actual knowledge that the act was unlawful or, in circumstances in which he believes or suspects that the act is beyond his powers, that he does not ascertain whether or not that is so, or fails to take such steps as would be taken by an honest and reasonable man to ascertain the true position. For the purposes of the requirement that the officer knows that his act will probably injure the plaintiff or a person in a class of which the plaintiff is a member it is sufficient that the officer has actual knowledge that this act will probably damage the plaintiff or such a person, if he does not ascertain whether or not that is so, or he fails to make such inquiries as an honest and reasonable man would make as to the probability of such damage.'

[26] As in *Bourgoin S.A. v. Minister of Agriculture, Fisheries and Food* [1986] Q.B. 716. In such situations today, liability may arise independently of the tort of misfeasance in public office: see Joined Cases C-46 and C-48/93 *Brasserie du Pecheur S.A. v. Germany; R. v. Secretary of State for Transport, ex p. Factortame (No. 2)* [1996] Q.B. 404 (considered at para. 17–036 below).

[27] See para. 16–041.

[28] See para. 16–042.

Breach of statutory duty[29]

Questions of liability for the negligent exercise of statutory powers **16–034** have already been examined[30]; here we need to consider whether the breach of a statutory duty, *in itself* and without proof of negligence, may give rise to an action in damages for English law has witnessed "the painful emergence of a nominate tort" of breach of statutory duty.[31]

Some statutory provisions expressly create rights of action for **16–035** damages in tort against public bodies in breach of a statutory duty[32] and here few problems arise. More difficult is the more common situation where the legislation is silent on the issue whether breach entitles a person who suffers loss due to non-compliance with the statutory duty to commence an action for damages. The question is always approached as one of statutory construction to ascertain whether the legislature intended to provide for such private law claims for monetary compensation and for this reason it is difficult to discuss the tort in terms of generally applicable principles.[33] This judicial technique has rightly been criticised: "The failure of the judges to develop a governing attitude means that it is almost impossible to predict, outside the decided authorities, when the courts will regard a civil duty as impliedly created. In effect the judge can do what he likes, and then select one of the conflicted principles stated by his predecessors in order to justify his decision."[34]

Most statutory duties in the public law context are owed to the **16–036** public at large rather than to private individuals. Where the legislation in question establishes an administrative system to promote the social welfare of the community, exceptionally clear statutory language will be needed to show a parliamentary intention to create a right to damages.[35] Categorising a duty as being in broad and general terms in

---

[29] See further K. Stanton, *Breach of Statutory Duty in Tort* (1986), esp. pp. 73–84; *Clerk and Lindsell on Torts*, Chap. 14.

[30] Below, para. 16–039.

[31] *per* Dixon J., *The Queen in Right of Canada v. Saskatchewan Wheat Pool* (1983) 143 D.L.R. (3d) 9, (Sup. Ct. of Canada). For the purposes of awards of exemplary damages (see para. 16–042 below), breaches of different statutory duties are to be regarded as *sui generis* torts rather than there being a single nominate tort of branch of statutory duty: see *A.B. v. South West Water Services Ltd* [1993] Q.B. 507 and G. Pipe (1994) 57 M.L.R. 91 at 94.

[32] See, *e.g.* Highways Act 1980, s.57.

[33] *Hague v. Deputy Governor of Parkhurst Prison* [1992] 1 A.C. 58 *per* Lord Bridge.

[34] Glanville Williams. "The Effect of Penal Legislation in Tort" (1960) 233 M.L.R. 23, 246.

[35] See *X (Minors) v. Bedfordshire County Council* [1995] 2 A.C. 633; *O'Rouke v. Camden L.B.C.* [1998] A.C. 188.

this way is fatal to a claim for damages, even on judicial review. On this basis a breach of section 8 of the Education Act 1944 was held to give no right of action.[36]

16–037   It is therefore a necessary, but not sufficient, precondition to liability to establish that the particular statutory duty was intended to protect a certain class of person (rather than the public at large) from a particular type of damage.[37] Factors which may raise a presumption of no legislative intention to create private rights to compensation include: the existence of a penalty or other remedy (including judicial review) for non-compliance[38]; the fact that the aggrieved person had opportunities to participate in the decision-making process and had appeal rights[39]; by whom the duty is owed[40]; and the anticipated policy consequences of imposing liability.[41] Where the duty in question arises from a statutory instrument, the court will examine the enabling Act to see whether it gives power to the minister to create private rights[42] By way of illustration, breach of the Prison Rules has been held to give no right of action in damages to a prisoner[43]; nor the Police (Discipline) Regulations to an officer facing disciplinary action.[44]

False imprisonment[45]

16–038   Claims arising from *ultra vires* actions which lead to the unlawful confinement of the plaintiff are most likely to arise in connection with government functions such as the criminal justice system, immigration control and the treatment of the mentally ill.

16–039   The tort of false imprisonment has two elements[46]: (a) the fact of complete deprivation of liberty for any time, however short[47] and (b)

---

[36] *R. v. Inner London Education Authority, ex p. Ali* (1990) 2 Admin. L.R. 822 (local education authority had failed to provide school places for a large number of children in the Stepney area of London).

[37] *Hague's* case (above, n. 33), *per* Lord Jauncey at 750.

[38] See, *e.g. Lonrho plc v. Shell Petroleum Co. (No. 2)* [1982] A.C. 173; *Hague* (above, n. 33); *Calveley v. Chief Constable of the Merseyside Police* (above, n. 1).

[39] See *X (Minors) v. Bedfordshire C.C.* [1995] 2 A.C. 633.

[40] So, if the duty is imposed only on a public authority, rather than also on private persons, there may be a presumption against an intention to create liability in damages; see T. Weir, 'Compensation in Public Law' [1989] P.L. 40, 53.

[41] *Clegg Parkinson & Co. Ltd v. Earby Gas* [1896] 1 Q.B. 592.

[42] *Hague's* case (above, n. 33), *per* Lord Jauncy at 751.

[43] *Hague's* case (above, n. 33).

[44] *Calveley v. Chief Constable of the Merseyside Police* [1989] A.C. 1228.

[45] See further, *Clerk and Lindsell on Tort*, para. 17–15.

[46] *Hague's* case (above, n. 33), *per* Lord Bridge at 743d.

[47] See *R v. Bournewood Community and Mental Health NHS Trust, ex p. L* [1998] 3 W.L.R. (autistic patient incapable of consenting to medical treatment not deprived of liberty when kept on an unlocked ward since he had not made any attempt to leave).

the absence of lawful authority to justify it.[48] In the public law field, questions of unlawful detention may arise in contexts such as prison discipline, immigration control and detention under mental health legislation. Where a person is allegedly unlawfully detained by a public body, a challenge may be made either under Order 53 or by way of an application for a writ of habeas corpus. In the former proceedings, a claim for damages for false imprisonment may be included; if habeas corpus is sought, separate proceedings for damages will have to be commenced. Where a public body is concerned, it is uncertain whether a plaintiff may proceed directly to make a claim for damages in a private law action, or whether it is necessary first to have the issue of the legality of the detention determined in judicial review proceedings.[49]

It is not necessary to prove physical incarceration; rather the gist of the tort is restraint (over and above that imposed by the general law or a binding contract) so that a person has no liberty to go at all times to all places where he wishes.[50]

Section 12(1) of the Prison Act 1952 provides lawful authority for **16–040** the restraint of prisoners within the defined bounds of the prison by the governor of the prison. A prisoner has no cause of action for false imprisonment if he is confined for a particular time within a particular part of the prison, for example, he is segregated and held in solitary confinement, even if the restraint was not in accordance with the Prison Rules 1964.[51] Where, however, a prison officer acts in bad faith by deliberately subjecting a prisoner to restraint which he knows he has no authority to impose he may render himself personally liable to an action for false imprisonment.[52] An otherwise lawful imprisonment is not rendered unlawful by reason only of the conditions of detention, however intolerable they may be.[53]

---

[48] *Clerk and Lindsell on Tort*, para. 17–15, quoted with approval by Lord Jauncey in *Hague's* case (above, n. 33) at 753d. As to what amounts to lawful authority, see *Olutu v. Home Office* [1997] 1 W.L.R. 328 (person detained after expiry of custody time limit set by Prosecution of Offences Act 1985 was lawfully detained); *R. v. Governor of H.M. Prison Brockhill, ex p. Evans (No. 2)* [1999] 1 W.L.R. 103 (unlawful detention of convicted prisoner after date for relase based on calculation in accordance with Divisional Court judgment which was later overruled); *Percy v. Hall* [1997] Q.B. 924 (the fact that byelaws were later declared void for uncertainty did not render tortious the actions of police officers who, at the relevant time, reasonably believed that byelaw offences were being committed).

[49] Above, para. 16–005.

[50] *Hague's* case (above, n. 33), *per* Lord Jauncey, 753.

[51] *Hague's* case (above, n. 33).

[52] *Hague's* case (above, n. 33).

[53] *Hague's* case (above, n. 33).

MEASURE OF DAMAGES[54]

16–041 Generally, the aim of damages is to compensate the plaintiff for loss caused by the defendant's conduct. In tort, damages put the plaintiff as nearly as possible into the position he would have been in had the tortious act not occurred. "Aggravated damages"—compensation for mental distress or injured feelings—may also be awarded.

16–042 Very exceptionally, the court may award exemplary damages in tort to deter and condemn the defendant's conduct rather than merely to compensate the plaintiff.[55] Such damages are generally viewed as anomalous and courts take a restrictive approach, awarding exemplary damages only if:

(1) the case falls within one of three categories (based on nature of the defendant's tortious conduct) set out by Lord Devlin in *Rookes v. Barnard*[56]; and

(2) exemplary damages were awarded in a case before 1964 in respect of the tort upon which the plaintiff bases his claim.

Considerable doubt existed as to whether both these tests, described further below, have to be satisfied or whether it is sufficient for the plaintiff to comply with one. The Court of Appeal has now held, though not without some hesitation, that both conditions do have to be satisfied.[57]

Nature of defendant's conduct test

16–043 It is a necessary, but not sufficient, condition that the plaintiff's case falls within one of three categories, based on the quality of the defendant's act, set out by Lord Devlin in *Rookes v. Barnard*.[58] The first is "oppressive, arbitrary or unconstitutional action by the servants of the government". In this context, government servants includes all those who by common law or statute are exercising functions of a governmental character such as local authorites and the police as well

---

[54] For a more detailed account of damages generally, see H. McGregor and J. Mayne (eds) *McGregor on Damages* (16th ed., 1997).

[55] See generally Law Commission, *Aggravated, Exemplary and Restitutionary Damages* (Law Com. 247); *Thompson v. Commr. of Police for the Metropolis* [1998] Q.B. 498 (in actions against police, £50,000 is the absolute maximum award appropriate for exemplory damages).

[56] [1964] A.C. 1129.

[57] *per* Sir Thomas Bingham in *A.B. and Others v. South West Water Services Ltd* [1993] Q.B. 507. See further A.S. Burrows (1993) 109 L.Q.R. 358.

[58] Above, n. 56

as Crown servants. The boundary between "governmental" and "private" functions is drawn differently in relation to the award of exemplary damages than it is for the purposes of the public/private divide under RSC Ord. 53[59] and so, for instance, exemplary damages have been awarded against a local authority guilty of racial discrimination in selecting an employee.[60] However, torts committed in the course of carrying out commercial operations, such as the supply of water, fall outside this category.[61]

The meanings of oppressive, arbitrary and unconstitutional are not settled, though it is clear that the three elements are to be read disjunctively.[62] Doubt has been expressed in the Court of Appeal as to whether every *ultra vires* act is unconstitutional and the absence of aggravating features is something which ought to be taken into account in deciding whether to award exemplary damages.[63] Conduct which is merely negligent is probably insufficient.[64]   16–044

The second category of case is where the defendant committed the tortious act having calculated that the economic benefits to him flowing from the action would be greater than any damages he might be liable to pay. The third category contemplated by Lord Devlin is where there are circumstances in which the award of exemplary damages was expressly authorised by statute, none of which are particularly relevant in the public law context.   16–045

The cause of action test

Even if a case falls within one of Lord Devlin's categories, exemplary damages will only be available if the plaintiff's claim arises from a tort in which such damages had been awarded prior to the House of Lord's decision in *Rookes v. Barnard* in 1964[65]; this (according to the Court of Appeal in *A.B. and Others v. South West Water Services Ltd*[66]) appears to be the effect of the House of Lord's decision in *Cassell & Co*   16–046

---

[59] On which see Chap. 3 above.

[60] *Bradford C.C.v. Arora* [1991] 2 Q.B. 507. Following the Court of Appeal decision in *A.B. and Others v. South West Water Services Ltd* (above, n. 57) exemplary damages are no longer available in cases of racial or sex discrimination and to this extent *Arora* is no longer good law. See *Deane v. Ealing L.B.C.* [1993] I.R.L.R. 209 (E.A.T.) where *South West Waters* was applied so as to deny exemplary damages for racial discrimination. *cf.* cases of sex discrimination contrary to E.C. law. *Marshall (No. 2)* [1993] I.R.L.R. 445 requires damages which are a 'real deterrent to the employer'.

[61] *A.B. and Others v. South West Water Services Ltd* (above, n. 57).

[62] *Holden v. Chief Constable of Lancashire* [1987] Q.B. 380.

[63] *per* Purchas L.J. in *Holden v. Chief Constable of Lancashire* (above).

[64] See *Barbara v. Home Office* (1984) 134 N.L.J. 888.

[65] Above, n. 56.

[66] Above, n. 57.

v. Broome[67] where it was held that Lord Devlin intended to restrict, not expand, the scope of exemplary damages. The torts which satisfy the test include trespass to the person[68] and property,[69] false imprisonment,[70] malicious prosecution, private nuisance[71] and defamation; but negligence, deceit,[72] and public nuisance do not.[73] A surprising, and perhaps unforeseen, consequence of the strict application of the precedent-based cause of action test appears to be that exemplary damages cannot be recovered where a plaintiff pleads misfeasance in public office even though the tort falls four-square within Lord Devlin's first category of oppressive, arbitrary and unconstitutional action.[74] Cases in which exemplary damages have been awarded for race or sex discrimination have subsequently been doubted.[75] Exemplary damages will not be awarded where there are a large number of plaintiffs.[76] Claims for exemplary damages must be specifically pleaded and particularised.[77]

REFORM AND THE IMPACT OF LIABILITY

16–047 Some people take as their starting point a belief that public bodies and officials should provide compensation for damage caused by their unlawful administrative conduct. Certainly, it can seem unfair that an aggrieved person is left to shoulder loss where a court finds the administrative action which caused it unlawful and grants judicial review. This is especially so where the public body erred while carrying out a regulatory function (*e.g.* by means of licensing) designed to benefit the community as a whole and where it was not practicable for the adversely affected person to insure against the risk of damage.[78] In such circumstances why should it not be the

---

[67] [1972] A.C. 1027.

[68] *Huckle v. Money* (1763) 2 Wils. 205.

[69] *Wilkes v. Wood* (1763) Lofft. 1. See also *R. v. Reading JJ., ex p. South West Meats Ltd.* [1992] Crim. L.R. 672 (entry to premises under invalid search warrant).

[70] See *Att.-Gen. of St Christopher v. Reynolds* [1980] A.C. 637.

[71] *Bell v. Midland Railway Co.* (1861) 10 C.B. (N.S.) 287, considered in *A.B. and Others v. South West Water Services Ltd* (above, n. 57) at 621.

[72] *Cassell & Co. v. Broome* [1972] A.C. 1027.

[73] *A.B. and Others v. South West Water Services Ltd* (above, n. 57).

[74] It will be necessary to show a case of 'misfeasance in public office' where prior to 1964 exemplary damages were awarded. It is not easy to know when this tort became established in English law (see n. 40 above) and arguably this happened only after 1964.

[75] *A.B. and Others v. South West Water Services Ltd* (above, n. 57).

[76] *A.B. and Others v. South West Water Services Ltd* (above, n. 57).

[77] RSC, Order 18, r. 8(3).

[78] Many tort actions against central and local government are, in reality, brought by insurance companies exercising their rights of subrogation under policies. T. Weir has

community *qua* taxpayers—rather than the individual who suffers damage as a result of unlawful administration—which bares the loss? The imperfect interface in English law between notions of unlawful acts in judicial review proceedings and rights to damages in tort means that some victims of bureaucratic error currently go uncompensated,[79] though in the absence of empirical data it is unclear how extensive the problem really is.

Judges, pressure groups and political parties in England have attempted or called for reform but none have yet been successful. In 1966, three members of the High Court of Australia, in a case where the defendant council unlawfully[80] extracted gravel from a river bed thereby preventing the plaintiff using his right under licence to pump water to irrigate his farmland, asserted the proposition that "by an action for damages upon the case, a person who suffers harm or loss as the inevitable consequence of the unlawful, intentional and positive acts of another, is entitled to recover damages from that other".[81] But this principle has since been rejected by the House of Lords[82] and doubted by the Privy Council,[83] and recently overruled by the High Court of Australia.[84] **16–048**

In 1988, the Justice/All Souls Review recommended that even in the absence of an actionable tort or other ground for claiming damages in private law, there should be a right to damages for unlawful administrative action or omission which causes a person loss.[85] Four years earlier, the Committee of Ministers of the Council of Europe had also adopted a principle of rights to compensation: **16–049**

---

argued that claims in respect of damage covered by a solvent insurer should be barred absolutely: see "Governmental Liability" [1989] P.L. 40 at 59.

[79] As in, *e.g., R. v. Knowsley M.B.C., ex p. Maguire, The Times,* June 26, 1992.

[80] It had failed to obtain the necessary permit or certificate of authority, contrary to regulations.

[81] *Beaudesert District Shire Council v. Smith* (1966) 120 C.L.R. 145, 156. In line of early English cases damages were awarded on the basis of the unlawfulness of an act in itself: see, *e.g. Ashby v. White* (1704) 1 Brown 62 (returning officers liable for rejecting vote of qualified elector without proof of malice).

[82] *Lonrho Ltd v. Shell Petroleum (No. 2)* [1982] A.C. 173, 188.

[83] *Dunlop v. Woollahra Municipal Council* [1982] A.C. 158.

[84] *Northern Territory of Australia v. Mengel* (1995) 60 A.L.J.R. 527.

[85] Report of the Committee of the Justice/All Souls Review of Administrative Law in the United Kingdom, *Administrative Justice—Some Necessary Reforms* (Oxford, 1988), para. 11.83: "compensation shall be recoverable by any person who sustains loss as a result of ... (a) any act, decision, determination, instrument or order of a public body which materially affects him and which is for any reason wrongful or contrary to law; or (b) unreasonable or excessive delay on the part of any public body in taking any action, teaching any decision or determination, making any order or carrying out any duty". An earlier report by Justice, *Administration under Law* (1971) had also advocated the power to award damages to persons aggrieved by decisions tainted with procedural or substantive irregularity in circumstances where there is no cause

"Reparation should be ensured for damage caused by an act due to a failure of a public authority to conduct itself in a way which can reasonably be expected from it in relation to the injured person. Such a failure is presumed in case of transgression of an established legal rule."[86]

16–050 In a document published in 1990, the Liberal Democrats indicated that they would amend the Crown Proceedings Act 1947 and the Supreme Court Act 1981 so that "a person injured by maladministration would be entitled to damages without having to prove negligence or malice."[87] And in 1991 the Institute for Public Policy Research in its draft constitution for the U.K. included provision for an Act of Parliament to provide for "effective remedies (including the payment of compensation) in cases where applications for judicial review are upheld",[88] though this stops short of requiring the creation of a right of action for damages of unlawful administrative action *per se*. Neither of the major political parties in the U.K. have made commitments to enacting legislation for compensation in this context. What is most likely to prompt such legislative reform is the growing divergence between rights to compensation for *ultra vires* acts under European Community law[89] and those in the purely domestic law sphere.

16–051 In the absence of new legislation, reform through the courts will be difficult: the general principle of "no damage in the absence of a recognised tort" is now probably too entrenched in domestic case law to permit any far-reaching change of direction by the judges. In any event, the dominant judicial attitude during the 1980s and early[90]

---

of action for damages under the law as it now stands. *Cf.* the criticisms of Woolf, *Protection of the Public—A New Challenge* (1990), p. 58.

[86] Principle I contained in Recommendation No. R (84) 15 Relating to Public Liability (adopted by the Committee of Ministers on September 18, 1984 at the 375th meeting of the Ministers' Deputies). The aim of the recommendation, which of course is non-binding, is to encourage uniformity among the member states of the Council of Europe. The Justice/All Souls Report (para. 11.63) argued that this formula probably adds little to the existing heads of liability in English Law.

[87] "'We, The People...'—Towards a Written Constitution", Federal Green Paper No. 13 (1990).

[88] *The Constitution of the United Kingdom*, Article 118.1.3.

[89] See above, n. 33.

[90] There have, however, been hints to the contrary. In *R. v. Secretary of State for Transport, ex p. Factortame Ltd and others (No. 5)* [1998] C.O.D. 381, 383 Lord Woolf M.R., giving judgment in the Court of Appeal on a claim for *Francovich* damages for breach of Community law said "we leave for consideration on another occasion the circumstances, if any, which, quite apart from any requirement of Community law, our law will give a remedy for damage caused by legislation enacted in breach of a superior legal rule. Traditionally this remedy has not been available in our law. Now that it is undoubtedly available in circumstances which contain a Community law element it may be right on

1990s has been one of hostility towards attempts to extend any further the liability of public authorities, even within the confines of the current framework of tort law. The main fear appears to be that to do so would inhibit effective decision taking by public bodies. Thus, duties of care have been denied in relation to the work of a financial services regulatory agency,[91] social workers[92] and in respect of investigations by the police[93] in part in concern that liability would lead to "detrimentally defensive" administration. In *Rowling v. Takaro Properties Ltd,* Lord Keith spoke of the danger of "overkill"[94] and suggested that following the House of Lord's decision in *Anns v. Merton L.B.C.,*[95] (where council inspectors carrying out statutory functions of inspection of the safety of new building were held to be negligent in approving defective foundations) the cure had been worse than the disease. Building inspectors of some local authorities had reacted by simply increasing, unnecessarily, the requisite depth of foundations, thereby imposing a substantial and unnecessary financial burden on members of the community.[96] A similar danger, Lord Keith believed, arose in relation to the imposition of a duty of care on a minister (as in *Rowling*) not to misconstrue legislation. Similar concerns have been expressed extrajudicially.[97] The judicial view is not, however, monolithic.[98] In *Home Office v. Dorset Yacht Co. Ltd.*[99] Lord Reid had no hesitation in dismissing a policy argument that imposing vicarious liability on the Home Office for damage caused as a result of prison officers negligently allowing borstal boys to escape from custody would curtail continued experimentation with minimum security regimes which were an important aspect of rehabilitation schemes. His experience led him to believe that "Her Majesty's

---

some future occasion to re-examine that tradition'. Note also the possibility of a claim for damages under the Human Rights Act 1998, s. 8.

[91] *Yuen Kun-yeu v. Att.-Gen. of Hong Kong* [1988] A.C. 175, 196; [1987] 2 All E.R. 705. 714. In England, statutory immunity has in some circumstances been given to those exercising regulatory functions, *e.g.,* under s. 187 of the Financial Services Act 1986 and s. 14 of the Lloyd's Act 1982.

[92] *X (Minors) v. Bedfordshire C.C.* [1995] 2 A.C. 633.

[93] *Hill v. Chief Constable of West Yorkshire* [1988] 1 A.C. 53. *Per* Lord Keith: 'The general sense of public duty which motivates police forces is unlikely to be appreciably reinforced by the imposition of such liability so far as concerns their function in the investigation and suppression of crime...In some instances the imposition of liability may lead to the exercise of a function being carried out with a detrimentally defensive frame of mind.'

[94] [1988] A.C. 473, 502.

[95] [1978] A.C. 728.

[96] See also G. Ganz [1977] P.L. 306.

[97] Woolf, *Protection of the Public—A New Challenge* (1990), p. 58.

[98] On the contradictory 'academic and judicial musing...regarding the instrumental affect of state liability', see further D. Cohen and J.C. Smith, (1986) 64 Can.B.R. 1.

[99] [1970] A.C. 1004.

servants were made of sterner stuff' than the public servants of New York who had been granted immunity in *Williams v. New York State*.[1] In any event, it is now clear that an immunity from tort actions, conferred by law for reasons of public policy in relation to the investigation and suppression of crime by the police, is contrary to Article 6(1) of the European Convention on Human Rights.[2]

16–052 A number of questions emerge from the assertion that the further imposition of liability to pay damages for invalid administrative action would have a detrimentally chilling effect on decision makers. First, the arguments often fail to identify *who* will be liable and in what sense: is the liability directly that of the public body, its vicarious liability for the acts of employees, or the personal liability of individual administrators? It has been argued that vicarious and personal liability is undesirable and may indeed have a detrimental impact on decision-making; and that direct state liability is at least disadvantageous.[3] But in practice even if an individual civil servant or minister is a named defendant in a successful action for damages, the award will be paid out of public funds. Any impact on an administrator's behaviour therefore comes not from anxiety of personal financial inconvenience or ruin flowing directly from the damages award as such.

16–053 Why then is the problem of self-protection by administrators more significant in relation to damages awards than public law remedies? A sharp distinction has sometimes been drawn between remedies such as prohibition and certiorari, which are said to have a beneficial impact on administrative behaviour and liability for damages which has an undesirable effect.[4] In its broadest sense, however, "judicial review of administrative action" is not confined to the public law grounds of illegality, procedural propriety and unreasonableness. The present function of tort law is not confined to retrospective

---

[1] (1955) 127 NE (2d) 545. See also *Osman v. Ferguson* [1993] 4 All E.R. 344.

[2] *Osman v. United Kingdom* [1999] Crim.L.R. 82 (European Court of Human Rights).

[3] See D. Cohen and J.C. Smith *op. cit.*, esp. pp. 9, 16; Peter H. Schuck, *Suing Government: Citizen Remedies for Official Wrongs* (USA, 1980). These authors point out that the assumptions about rational economic behaviour of private individuals and firms in reaction to tort liability often cannot be applied to government bodies. As Cohen and Smith state succinctly at p. 8: 'To the extent that private tort law doctrines are premised on deterrent objectives they may be singularly ineffective when applied to the state.'

[4] See *e.g.*, the speech of Lord Bridge in *Hague v. Deputy Governor of Parkhurst Prison* [1992] 1 A.C. 58 where it was said that 'the availability of judicial review as a means of questioning the legality of action purportedly taken in pursuance of the Prison Rules is a beneficial and necessary jurisdiction which cannot properly be circumscribed by considerations of policy or expediency in relation to prison administration'—in contrast to the 'wholly different question' of the availability of damages.

compensation for harm inflicted; the substantive rules of tort also set standards of acceptable administrative behaviour and so too would any expanded liability for damages. In the absence of more cogent empirical evidence on the effects of imposing (or not imposing) a more extensive liability to pay damages on public officials than currently exists[5], it would be rash to oppose damages for unlawful acts on this ground alone. But equally, even if greater compensation for invalid administrative acts is desirable, it does not inevitably follow that creating a new action for damages is the most appropriate mechanism for providing it. Alternatives include greater use of the ombudsmen to recommend, or require, compensation to be paid or the creation of a fund analogous to that administered by the Criminal Injuries Compensation Board to which the victim of unlawful administrative action causing loss may apply.

---

[5] A handful of small-scale empirical studies have been carried out in England see: G. Ganz [1977] P.L. 306; Tony Weir [1989] P.L. 40,60.

PART IV

EUROPEAN COMMUNITY LAW AND JUDICIAL REVIEW

CHAPTER 17

EUROPEAN COMMUNITY LAW IN JUDICIAL REVIEW

INTRODUCTION

The United Kingdom's membership of the European Community has brought with it significant changes to the law and practice of judicial review in England and Wales.[1] In the High Court, applicants for judicial review may now in some circumstances challenge national measures on the ground of breach of European Community law.[2] Less commonly, applications for judicial review may also raise questions about the validity of administrative decisions and legislation made by the institutions of the European Community themselves.[3] Moreover, European Community law has had an impact on the basic methods of work of national courts, including their approach to interpreting legislation,[4] the procedures to be followed by litigants and the nature of the remedies available to protect people's rights under Community law.[5]

17–001

The two courts of the European Community—the European Court of Justice and the Court of First Instance—have important roles. When a national court or tribunal requests it to do so, the European Court gives authoritative rulings on questions of interpretation of Community law.[6] Both courts also have powers to determine actions brought directly to them alleging that Member States or institutions of the Community have breached Community law.[7]

17–002

---

[1] For fuller accounts of Community law and institutions, see Paul Craig and Gráinne de Búrca, *EU Law: Text, Cases and Materials* (2nd ed., 1998) and Trevor Hartley, *The Foundations of European Community Law* (4th ed., 1998).

[2] The grounds for review of national measures are considered at para. 17–073 *et seq.*

[3] See para. 17–044; a national court cannot, however, declare an European Community measure to be unlawful.

[4] See para. 17–031.

[5] See para. 17–032 *et seq.*

[6] See para. 17–040.

[7] See para. 17–041 *et seq.*

THE NATURE OF COMMUNITY LAW

17–003 Rules of Community law have their main sources in the treaties which establish the Community and the European Union, in secondary legislation made by the institutions of the Community, and in the general principles of law developed by the European Court. Early on in the development of the Community legal system, the European Court propounded the doctrine that any rule of Community law, whatever its source, prevails over inconsistent rules of national law in Member States.[8] The primacy of Community law is absolute. It applies whether the rule of Community law came into being before or after the rule of national law. It applies to all forms of national law. Where a person before an inferior court or tribunal seeks to rely upon a rule of Community law which is irreconcilable with national law, *that* court or tribunal is obliged immediately to disregard the national law: under Community law, it has "the power to do everything necessary at the moment of its application to set aside national legislative provisions which might prevent Community rules from having full force and effect".[9] In England and Wales, primacy therefore means that all courts and tribunals must "disapply" any provision in an Act of Parliament or statutory instrument that is irreconcilable with Community law.[10] This leads to a peculiar situation. As we have already seen, English law generally requires public law issues to be dealt with exclusively by the High Court using the Order 53 application for judicial review procedure.[11] Questions about the validity of legislation are *par excellence* issues of public law. Community law, however, requires that they be dealt with by the court or tribunal in which they first arise during the ordinary course of legal proceedings. This may result in a bench of lay magistrates or an inferior tribunal adjudicating on the applicability of an Act of Parliament. Applications for judicial review are thus only one of many types of legal proceedings in which the primacy principle operates.

---

[8] Case 6/64 *Costa v. ENEL* [1964] E.C.R. 585.

[9] Case 106/77 *Simmenthal* [1978] E.C.R. 629.

[10] See para. 17–025 below.

[11] This is the 'procedural exclusivity' rule first propounded by the House of Lords in *O'Reilly v. Mackman* [1983] 2 A.C. 237; see above, para. 3–035 *et seq.* Note also that questions of the compatibility of Acts of Parliament and statutory instruments with the provisions of the Human Rights Act 1998 are dealt with exclusively by the High Court in England and Wales.

The treaties

Community law stems from the treaties which establish the European **17–004**
Union and the European Community. Each time the Member States
have agreed at intergovernmental conferences to change the
institutional framework and scope of the European Union and
European Community, so these treaties have been revised. This was
done most recently in June 1997 by the "Treaty of Amsterdam
amending the Treaty on European Union, the Treaties establishing the
European Communities and certain related Acts".[12] The Treaty of
Amsterdam came into force throughout the fifteen Member States on
May 1, 1999. In an attempt at simplification, provisions in earlier
versions of the treaties have been renumbered. Care must therefore
now be taken to understand whether an Article number is given in
reference to a treaty provision before or after the Amsterdam
revisions.[13]

For our purposes, there are two main treaties. The Treaty on **17–005**
European Union[14] (as amended by the Treaty of Amsterdam) sets out
the broad decision-taking framework for the Union in which there are
three broad "pillars," or spheres of public policy. The first pillar is the
European Community; the powers and institutional structures of the
Community are set out principally in a distinct treaty, the E.C. Treaty
(as amended by the Treaty of Amsterdam).[15] The second pillar of the
European Union is common foreign and security policy.[16] The third
pillar is police and judicial co-operation in criminal matters.[17]
Decision-taking and law-making powers in the Community are
significantly different from those in the other two pillars, and it is
with the Community that this Chapter is concerned.

Early on in the development of the Community legal system, the **17–006**
European Court held that some provisions of the treaties may be
relied upon directly by litigants in national courts (the doctrine of
"direct effect") even though they may not have been specifically
incorporated into a Member States' domestic legal system.[18] It can
now be said that direct effect extends to all provisions in the E.C.

---

[12] Cm. 3780.

[13] *e.g.* Article 177 of the E.C. Treaty becomes Article 234. In this Chapter, new Article
numbers are given followed by the previous number in square brackets, thus: Article
234 [177].

[14] Also known as the Maastricht Treaty or T.E.U.

[15] Also known as the Treaty of Rome.

[16] Treaty on European Union, Title V.

[17] Treaty on European Union, Title VI.

[18] Case 26/62 *Van Gend en Loos* [1963] E.C.R. 1. The relationship between national law
and treaty obligations varies between the Member States according to the constitution
of each.

Treaty which create rights and obligations sufficiently complete, clear and precise to be judicially enforceable. The provisions which meet these criteria may be relied upon by litigants in national courts and tribunals both "vertically" against state institutions and also "horizontally" against other citizens and business enterprises. In England and Wales, the treaties have all been specifically incorporated into national law by successive Acts of Parliament,[19] and so there has been no conflict between Community law and English law on the application of the direct effect doctrine.

Community secondary legislation

17–007 An unusual feature of the Community, in comparison with other international organisations, is that legislative powers have been conferred on its institutions by the E.C. Treaty[20]:

> "In order to carry out their task and in accordance with the provisions of this Treaty, the European Parliament acting jointly with the Council, the Council and the Commission shall make regulations and issue directives, take decisions, make recommendations or deliver opinions.
>
> A regulation shall have general application. It shall be binding in its entirety and directly applicable in all Member States.
>
> A directive shall be binding, as to the result to be achieved, upon each Member State to which it is addressed, but shall leave to the national authorities the choice of form and methods.
>
> A decision shall be binding in its entirety upon those to whom it is addressed.
>
> Recommendations and opinions shall have no binding force."

These forms of legal instruments were devised at the inception of the Community. The practical distinctions between regulations and directives has lost some of its significance. This is in part because of a legislative practice of often drafting regulations and directives with a similar degree of detail; in part because of the development in the case law of the European Court of the notion of direct effect of directives.[21] Nevertheless, important differences remain.

---

[19] European Communities Act 1972 (considered at para. 17–018 below).
[20] E.C. Treaty, Article 249 [189].
[21] See para. 17–014 below.

Regulations

As has been seen, all regulations are "directly applicable". Regulations **17–008**
thus become part of national law without any need for the Member
State to adopt implementing measures. Indeed it will often be
unlawful for Member States to transpose Community regulations into
national law. This is so in particular where such transposition may
obscure or distort the Community provisions, or have the effect of
concealing their Community character.[22] Moreover, in some fields the
Community will be regarded as having exclusive legislative
competence, so that the adoption of Community regulations will
preclude Member States from adopting any legislative measures in the
field occupied by the regulations.[23]

Community regulations may however sometimes be incomplete in **17–009**
that they do not specify, for example, the administrative measures
necessary for their application or the penalties to be imposed in the
event of non-compliance. In such cases Member States, far from
being prohibited from acting, are under a duty to adopt the
legislative measures necessary to make the regulations fully
effective.[24]

Since regulations are, by virtue of Article 249 [189] of the Treaty, **17–010**
directly applicable, it is not usually necessary to consider separately
the question of their direct effect. But direct effect is distinct from
direct applicability. Not all provisions of regulations have direct effect,
just as not all provisions of Acts of Parliament create rights and duties.
However, where the provisions of regulations are by their nature and
wording directly enforceable, they will readily be held to have direct
effect.[25]

Directives

Directives, as has been seen, are binding on Member States as to the **17–011**
result to be achieved, but leave to the national authorities the choice of

---

[22] See Case 39/72 *Commission v. Italy* [1973] E.C.R. 101; Case 34/73 *Variola* [1973] E.C.R.
981, 991. *Cf.* Case 272/83 *Commission v. Italy* [1985] E.C.R. 1057, para. 27.

[23] See, *e.g.* Case 74/69 *Hauptzollamt Bremen v. Krohn* [1970] E.C.R. 451, 458. *Cf.* Case
40/69 *Bollman* [1970] E.C.R. 69, 79. This is reminiscent of the notion of pre-emption in
U.S. constitutional law, where the expression 'occupying the field' is used of U.S.
federal legislation.

[24] Case 128/78 *Commission v. United Kingdom (Tachographs)* [1979] E.C.R. 419.

[25] See Case 93/71 *Leonesio v. Ministero dell' Agricoltura e Foreste* [1972] E.C.R. 287, para.
22.

forms and methods. Directives, therefore, in contrast to regulations,[26] require that national measures should be adopted to give effect to them.

17–012   In principle, a directive must be implemented by legislation, not by mere changes in administrative practice. Implementation must fully satisfy the requirement of legal certainty; Member States must therefore transpose their terms into national law as binding provisions.[27] Moreover it is a general requirement of Community law, following from the principles of legal certainty and legal protection of the individual, that Member States' laws "should be worded unequivocally so as to give the persons concerned a clear and precise understanding of their rights and obligations and enable national courts to ensure that those rights and obligations are observed."[28]

17–013   Legislative action may not be necessary where the existence of general principles of constitutional or administrative law renders implementation by specific legislation superfluous:

> "provided ... that those principles guarantee that the national authorities will in fact apply the directive fully and that, where the directive is intended to create rights for individuals, the legal position arising from those principles is sufficiently precise and clear and the persons concerned are made fully aware of their rights and, where appropriate, afforded the possibility of relying on them before the national courts. That last condition is of particular importance where the directive in question is intended to accord rights to nationals of other Member States because those nationals are not normally aware of such principles."[29]

Failure to implement a directive may render the Member State liable in damages, giving those affected a Community right to sue in the national courts.[30]

17–014   Although directives are not "directly applicable" (in the sense that they are not intended to have the force of law in the absence of national implementing measures), nevertheless they may—like some treaty provisions[31]—have "direct effect". This means that litigants before national courts and tribunals may rely directly on provisions

---

[26] See above, para. 17–008.

[27] See Case 239/85 *Commission v. Belgium* [1986] E.C.R. 3645, para. 7. See further, on the limits of the Member State's discretion, Case 143/83 *Commission v. Denmark* [1955] E.C.R. 42.

[28] Case 257/86 *Commission v. Italy* [1988] E.C.R. 3249, para. 12.

[29] Case 29/84 *Commission v. Germany* [1985] E.C.R. 1661, para. 23.

[30] Joined Cases C-16/90 and C-19/90 *Francovich* [1991] E.C.R. I-5357, below at para. 17–036.

[31] On direct effect of treaty provisions, see para. 17–006 above.

contained in a directive if certain conditions are satisfied. First, the time limit set for Member States to implement the directive must have expired. Secondly, the Member State must have failed to implement the directive into national law properly or at all. Thirdly, the directive must create justiciable rights or obligations (this criterion is similar to that for the direct effect of treaty provisions): the provision relied upon must be unconditional and sufficiently precise.[32]

There is an important difference between the operation of the **17–015** principle of direct effect in relation to treaty provisions and directives. Treaty provisions which are directly effective may be relied upon by a litigant against any other litigant, including fellow citizens and business enterprises. The principle of direct effect allows directives, in contrast, to be relied upon only "vertically" against "emanations of the State". However, the notion of the State is broadly defined for this purpose; a body is an emanation of the State if it "was subject to the authority or control of the State or had special powers beyond those which result from the normal rules applicable to relations between individuals".[33] It includes, for example, a public utility such as British Gas prior to privatisation.[34] The obligation to give effect to directives is one incumbent on all authorities of the Member States, including local authorities,[35] and the governing body of a profession where "entrusted with a public duty".[36] It therefore seems likely that most bodies which are subject to judicial review in the English courts would be regarded as a manifestation of the State for the purpose of permitting an individual to invoke a directive against them.

The limitation on the effect of directives is mitigated by the requirements that national legislation must be construed wherever

---

[32] In *Evans v. Motor Insurers Bureau and other appeals* [1999] Lloyd's Rep. 30, 1988 a claimant argued that the Motor Insurers Bureau Agreement was incompatible with Directive 84/5 and they were entitled to compensation under the Directive. The Court of Appeal held that, even though the provisions of the Directive might be unconditional and sufficiently precise in terms of identifying the persons entitled to compensation, the Directive did not identify the person liable to provide the compensation. The claim therefore failed.

[33] Case C-188/89 *Foster v. British Gas Plc* [1990] E.C.R. I-3313, para. 18; and see the discussion of 'public functions' at para. 3–021 above.

[34] *Foster*, see n. 33; House of Lords in [1991] 2 A.C. 306; contrast *Doughty v. Rolls Royce*, CA [1992] I.C.R. 538. In *Griffin v. South West Water Services Ltd* [1995] I.R.L.R. 15, Blackburn J. held, applying *Foster*, that a privatised water company is a State authority against which directives can be enforced directly. He stated that the material criterion for the purposes of direct effect is not whether the body in question is under the control of the State but whether the public service which it performs is under State control.

[35] Case 103/88 *Costanzo v. Comsene di Milano* [1989] E.C.R. 1839.

[36] Case 56/83 *Rienks* [1983] E.C.R. 4233.

possible so as to conform to directives.[37]

Decisions

17–016   Under provisions of the E.C. Treaty and of Community legislation, the Council or the Commission are empowered to adopt binding decisions, addressed to Member States or to individuals. In accordance with Article 249 of the E.C. Treaty, decisions are binding in their entirety upon those to whom they are addressed. A decision addressed to a Member State may often impose obligations on it: such a decision might require it, for example, to abolish an unlawful tax or an unlawful State aid. Such decisions may have direct effect where their terms are clear and precise, and so confer rights on individuals enforceable in the national courts.[38]

General principles of law

17–017   An important source of Community law is the general principles of law applied by the European Court. These principles stem from the legal systems of the Member States and have been used by the European Court, by a process analogous with the development of the common law by the English courts, to supplement and refine the Community Treaties and Community legislation. In order for the Court to apply such a principle, it is not necessary that it is recognised in the domestic law of all Member States; and even where it is so recognised, its scope in Community law may be different from its scope in national law. Where a Community measure infringes a general principle, such as the principle of non-discrimination (or equality), it may be annulled by the European Court[39]; it may also give rise to an action in the European Court for damages against the Community under Article [215(2)] of the Treaty. Further, the Court uses the general principles as an aid for the interpretation of Community acts. The general principles of law are binding not only on the Community institutions but also, within the scope of Community law, on the Member States and a national measure may be held invalid on the ground that it is incompatible with such a principle.[40]

---

[37] Case 169/80 *Administration des Douanes v. Gondrand Frères* [1981] E.C.R. 1931, para. 17; Joined Cases 212–217/80 *Salumi* [1981] E.C.R. 2735, para. 10; Case 70/83 *Kloppenburg* [1984] E.C.R. 1075, para. 11.

[38] See Case 9/70 *Grad v. Finanzont* [1970] E.C.R. 825.

[39] See below, para. 17–043.

[40] See below, para. 17–025.

European Communities Act 1972

So far as the courts and tribunals of England and Wales are concerned, **17–018** the sources of Community law are incorporated into English law by virtue of the European Communities Act 1972 and its subsequent amendments.

The European Communities Act 1972 seeks to give legal effect in the United Kingdom to the principles of primacy and direct effect. The scheme of the Act is straightforward; apart from limited amendments to the law, it contains in section 2, two principal provisions, section 2(1) and section 2(2), which enable the entire corpus of Community law to be given effect in the United Kingdom.

Section 2(1) provides in substance that all directly effective **17–019** Community law should have such effect in the U.K.:

> "All such rights, powers, liabilities, obligations and restrictions from time to time created or arising by or under the Treaties, and all such remedies and procedures from time to time provided for by or under the Treaties, as in accordance with the Treaties are without further enactment to be given legal effect or used in the United Kingdom shall be recognised and available in law, and be enforced, allowed and followed accordingly; and the expression 'enforceable Community right' and similar expressions shall be read as referring to one to which this subsection applies."

The wording makes it clear that the question whether a particular provision has direct effect[41] is determined by Community law.

Section 2(2) makes provision for the implementation of Community **17–020** law in the United Kingdom by means of subordinate legislation.[42] Implementation is either by Order in Council or by regulation made by a Minister or department designated for the purpose by Order in Council.[43]

Implementing measures, which will take the form of a statutory **17–021** instrument,[44] will be submitted for approval by Parliament. If not approved by each House, they will be subject to annulment by negative resolution of either House.[45] In the case of statutory instruments made under section 2(2) of the Act, therefore, and in contrast to the usual case, the Government has a choice of which

---

[41] Elegantly rendered by s. 2(1) as: to be given legal effect, etc., without further enactment.

[42] For the interpretation of section 2(2), see *R. v. Secretary of State for Trade and Industry, ex p. Unison* [1997] 1 C.M.L.R. 459.

[43] European Communities (Designation) Order 1973, S.I. 1973 No. 1889.

[44] Sched. 2. para. 2(1) and s. 1(1) of the Statutory Instruments Act 1946.

[45] Sched. 2. para. 2(2).

parliamentary procedure to apply: namely either an "affirmative" procedure which requires a vote of approval by each House, or a "negative" procedure which requires merely that the instrument is laid before Parliament without a subsequent resolution of annulment being passed.

17–022   Section 2(4) of the Act provides that implementing measures made under section 2(2) may include "any such provision (of any such extent) as might be made by Act of Parliament". It would seem therefore that such measures are not subject to the limitations normally applicable to delegated legislation and that they may override Acts of Parliament.[46]

17–023   Section 3(1) of the Act provides as follows:

> "For the purposes of all legal proceedings any question as to the meaning or effect of any of the Treaties, or as to the validity, meaning or effect of any Community instrument, shall be treated as a question of law (and, if not referred to the European Court, be for determination as such in accordance with the principles laid down by and any relevant decision of the European Court)."

Thus the case law of the European Court is expressed to be binding on United Kingdom courts and tribunals.

THE ROLE OF NATIONAL COURTS IN JUDICIAL REVIEW

17–024 In judicial review as in other types of litigation, national courts and the European Court and Court of First Instance[47] have separate and

---

[46] See *Factortame (No. 1)* [1990] A.C. 85, 140 *per* Lord Bridge; P.P. Craig. "Sovereignty of the UK Parliament after *Factortame*." (1991) Y.E.L. 221.

Implementing measures made under s. 2(2) may not, however, by Schedule 2:
   (a) impose or increase taxation:
   (b) enact retroactive legislation:
   (c) sub-delegate legislative power (except to make rules of procedure for any court or tribunal);
   (d) create any new criminal offence punishable with imprisonment for more than two years or punishable on summary conviction with imprisonment for more than three months or with a fine of more than, £400 (if not calculated on a daily basis) or with a fine of more than £5 per day.

[47] The Court of First Instance was created in 1988 (E.C. Treaty, Article 225 [168a]) to determine some types of case. The CFI hears cases brought by individuals against Community institutions. It does not give preliminary rulings under Article 234 [177], on which see para. 17–040.

different roles in adjudicating upon issues of Community law. In England and Wales, an applicant for judicial review in the High Court may seek to utilise rules of Community law in various ways.

Challenging a national measure in a national court

An applicant for judicial review may argue that an act or omission by a public authority in England and Wales is in breach of Community law.[48] By virtue of the principle of primacy, all national measures—including Acts of Parliament—may be challenged as being contrary to any rule of Community law. Community law is thus a broad "chapter head" of judicial review in addition to those of illegality, procedural impropriety and irrationality propounded by Lord Diplock.[49] The constituent parts of this chapter head will be considered in more detail below.[50] Where a Member State makes delegated legislation or takes administrative action to implement Community provisions, such national measures may be open to challenge on the ground that the Community provisions are themselves invalid.[51] A statutory instrument made pursuant to section 2(2) of the European Communities Act 1972 may also be challenged on the ground that it is contrary to *English* law if it goes beyond the enabling provision by purporting to do more than is required to implement the Community measure.[52]

17–025

Arguments based on Community law cannot be used in all cases. An applicant for judicial review needs to show that the act or omission of the public authority which is complained about is required or permitted by Community law. If the impugned decision is authorised solely by national law—that is, it is wholly internal to a Member State—then Community law has no application.[53] If, however,

17–026

---

[48] On what constitutes a public authority (or a body exercising public functions), see Chap. 3 above. Note that the Community law concept of 'emanation of the state', used to determine against whom directives may be directly effective, is formulated in different terms: see para 17–015, above.

[49] *Council of Civil Service Unions v. Minister for the Civil Service* [1985] A.C. 374, 410 discussed above in para. III-001 *et seq.*

[50] See para. 17–073 *et seq.*

[51] *e.g. R. v. Minister of Agriculture, Fisheries and Food, ex p. FEDESA* [1988] 3 C.M.L.R. 661. This ground of challenge presumably does not apply to Acts of Parliament. Note that a national court has no power to determine that a Community measure is invalid (though it may declare that it is valid): see para. 17–029 below.

[52] See *Hayward v. Cammell Laird Shipbuilders (No. 2)* [1988] A.C. 894.

[53] *e.g. R. v. Ministry of Agriculture, Fisheries and Food, ex p. First City Trading Ltd* [1997] 1 C.M.L.R. 250 (general principles of Community law could not be used as ground of review of U.K.'s Beef Transfer Scheme, which granted emergency aid to slaughterhouses in the wake of the BSE crisis, because the Scheme was not adopted

a Member State implementing Community law has chosen to apply it also to purely internal situations, then the European Court has jurisdiction to give a preliminary ruling on the interpretation of Community law if a national court from that Member State requests it to do so.[54]

17–027   It is difficult to describe succinctly what fields of government decision-making have a Community element to them (thus opening up potential judicial review challenges on the ground of breach of Community law). Some indication of the broad range of policy areas which fall within the ambit of Community law can be seen from Article 3 [3] of the E.C. Treaty[55]:

1. For the purposes set out in Article 2, the activities of the Community shall include, as provided in this Treaty and in accordance with the timetable set out therein:

   (a) the prohibition, as between Member States, of customs duties and quantitative restrictions on the import and export of goods, and of all other measures having equivalent effect;

   (b) a common commercial policy;

   (c) an internal market characterised by the abolition, as between Member States, of obstacles to the free movement of goods, persons, services and capital;

   (d) measures concerning the entry and movement of persons as provided for in Title IV;

   (e) a common policy in the sphere of agriculture and fisheries;

   (f) a common policy in the sphere of transport;

   (g) a system ensuring that competition in the internal market is not distorted;

   (h) the approximation of the laws of Member States to the extent required for the functioning of the common market;

---

pursuant to Community law and the U.K. government did not have to rely upon any Community law permission in order to implement it): *Krasniqi v. Chief Adjudication Officer* [1999] C.O.D. 154 (entitlement to welfare benefits of Kosovan refugee in U.K. a matter wholly internal to U.K. so, despite its literal wording, Community Regulation on Application of Social Security Schemes 1408/71 did not apply).

[54] C-28/95 *Leur-Bloem v. Inspecteur der Belastingdienst/Ondernemingen Amsterdam 2* [1998] Q.B. 182 (Netherlands had legislated to align purely domestic situations with Directive 90/434 on taxation of shares). The preliminary ruling procedure is described at para. 17–040 below.

[55] These Community policies are spelt out in more detail in E.C. Treaty, Part Three.

  (i) the promotion of co-ordination between employment policies of the Member States with a view to enhancing their effectiveness by developing a co-ordinated strategy for employment;

  (j) a policy in the social sphere comprising a European Social Fund;

  (k) the strengthening of economic and social cohesion;

  (l) a policy in the sphere of the environment;

 (m) the strengthening of the competitiveness of Community industry;

  (n) the promotion of research and technological development;

  (o) encouragement for the establishment and development of trans-European networks;

  (p) a contribution to the attainment of a high level of health protection;

  (q) a contribution to education and training of quality and to the flowering of the cultures of the Member States;

  (r) a policy in the sphere of development co-operation;

  (s) the association of the overseas countries and territories in order to increase trade and promote jointly economic and social development;

  (t) a contribution to the strengthening of consumer protection;

  (u) measures in the spheres of energy, civil protection and tourism.

In some of these areas of governance, the Community has exclusive **17–028** policy-making and legislative competence.[56] Where this is so and the Community makes regulations, Member States are prohibited from passing national legislation on the same subject matter.[57] Where the Community has such sole competence, schemes will nevertheless normally be given practical implementation by national institutions such as H.M. Customs and Excise and the Ministry of Agriculture, Fisheries and Food in England and so applicants may challenge the legality of the steps taken to administer Community policy and law. In many other areas of policy-making and legislation, Member States and the Community share competence—both are permitted, within limits, to pursue their own goals.[58] Some spheres of governance remain

---

[56] *e.g.* regulation of imports into the European Union of goods from non-Member States and compliance with international conservation and management measures by fishing vessels on the high seas.

[57] *e.g.* Case 74/69 *Hauptzollamt Bremen-Freihafen v. Waren-Import-Gesellschaft Krohn & Co.* [1970] E.C.R. 451 (to the extent that Member States have assigned legislative powers in tariff matters to the Community in order to ensure the proper operation of the common agricultural market, they no longer have the power to make autonomous provisions in this field).

[58] *e.g.* the regulation of competition and the imposition of Value Added Tax.

matters wholly internal to Member States and Community law has no application. However, even in areas of government where Member States retain competence, such as for foreign and security policy, they have to respect common Community policy which touch upon that area.[59]

Challenging a Community measure in a national court

17-029 Most applications for judicial review in which issues of Community law arise are concerned with attempts to argue that a public authority in the United Kingdom has acted contrary to Community law, as outlined in the previous sections. Occasionally, however, the intent is different and the applicant seeks to argue that a Community regulation,[60] directive[61] or a decision,[62] or a rule contained within it, is itself invalid. This may be a necessary step in an attempt to challenge a national measure (*e.g.* an argument that a statutory instrument is ineffective because the directive which it purports to transpose into English law is, as a matter of Community law, invalid) or the aim may bluntly be the Community measure in and of itself.[63] The grounds for arguing that Community measures are invalid are considered below.

17-030 There are obvious problems in allowing national courts to adjudicate upon the efficacy of rules of Community law—not least the practical ones that courts in Member States may reach different conclusions and the judgments of the courts in one Member State have no binding precedent in others. To avoid these difficulties, the following arrangements have been devised. National courts are allowed to examine the validity of a Community measure and, if they decide that the arguments advanced to challenge its validity are unfounded, they may conclude that the Community measure is valid. National courts are not, however, permitted to declare measures adopted by Community institutions invalid: if the national court is minded to do

---

[59] C-124/95 *R. v H.M. Treasury, ex p. Centro-Com Srl* [1997] Q.B. 683 (Member States retained competence in the area of foreign and security policy, but had to respect the Community's common commercial policy in whatever foreign and security measures were taken).

[60] See para. 17–008.

[61] See para. 17–011.

[62] See para. 17–016.

[63] The High Court has recently granted permission to apply for judicial review to an applicant seeking a declaration that a directive, as yet not implemented into the laws of the United Kingdom, was invalid: *R. v. Secretary of State for Health, ex p. Imperial Tobacco Ltd* [1999] C.O.D. 138. No reference was made in that case to C-408/95 *Eurotunnel SA v. SeaFrance* [1998] B.T.C. 5200 (European Court holds that a natural or legal person may challenge before a national court the validity of provisions in directives).

this, it must refer the question to the European Court for a preliminary ruling on the correct interpretation of Community law.[64] The European Court has sole jurisdiction to rule definitively on the validity of actions and omissions of the Community institutions.[65] Pending the European Court's ruling, a national court may grant interim remedies. Where the contested Community measure (*e.g.* a directive) has been incorporated into national law by national legislation, the national court may grant interim remedies to suspend the operation of the national measure.[66] Exceptionally, a national court may suspend the application of the Community measure (*e.g.* a regulation or decision) in the Member State in question by the grant of an interim remedy.[67]

Interpretation by national courts

In the course of an application for judicial review, as in other forms of legal proceedings, national courts may have the task of interpreting national legislation which deals with the same subject matter as Community law. They have an obligation to interpret national   **17–031**

---

[64] On the procedure by which national courts obtain preliminary rulings, see para. 17–040.

[65] C-314/85 *Firma Foto-Frost v. Hauptzollamt Lubeck-Ost* [1987] E.C.R. 4199.

[66] C-143/88 *Zuckerfabrik v. Süderdithmarschen AG v Hauptzollant Itzehoc* [1991] E.C.R. I-415. The conditions to be satisfied in order for a national court to grant interim relief by way of suspension of the national measure are: (a) serious doubts must exist as to the validity of the Community legislation; (b) the national court must set out its reasons why the legislation must be held invalid; (c) the suspension must be necessary in order to prevent serious and irreparable harm; (d) the damage to the applicant must be liable to materialise before the European Court could rule on the validity of the measure; (e) the damage must be irreversible; (f) the national court must take account of the Community; and (g) the national court should examine whether the Community legislation would be deprived of effectiveness if it were not immediately implemented. In *R. v. Secretary of State for Health, ex p. Macrae Seafoods Ltd* [1995] C.O.D. 369 Laws J. held that the merits of an applicant's challenge in these circumstances should have a higher threshold than that required for permission to apply for judicial review (on which, see para. 14–010 above). He stated that the test of "serious and irreparable harm" meant that an applicants needed to demonstrate that their economic interests would be fatally or at least gravely undermined beyond recovery.

[67] C-465/93 *Atlanta Fruchthandelsgesellschaft mbH v. Bundesamt fur Ernahrung und Forstwirtschaft* [1996] All E.R. (E.C.) 31 Such relief will be granted only where: (a) the national court entertains serious doubts about the validity of the contested measure; (b) interim relief is necessary to avoid serious and irreparable harm and not merely financial damage the party seeking relief; (c) the national court takes account of Community interests including damage to the legal regime established by the regulation, and financial risk of interim relief, and (d) the national court respects the decisions of the European Court on the lawfulness of the regulation or on any application for similar interim relief at Community level.

legislation in a manner which is consistent with and gives effect to the rules of Community law. This is an incident of the general duty placed on all national institutions in Member States to[68]:

"take all appropriate measures, whether general or particular, to ensure fulfilment of the obligations arising out of this Treaty or resulting from action taken by the institutions of the Community. They shall facilitate the achievement of the Community's tasks.

They shall abstain from any measure which could jeopardise the attainment of the objectives of this Treaty."

Thus, national legislation must be construed in the light of the aims of any relevant Articles of the E.C. Treaty.[69] National courts are also required to interpret national law in the light of wording and purpose of any pertinent directives.[70] This is so even if a Member State has failed to transpose a directive into national law by the due date, or it has failed to do so fully.[71] The interpretative obligation applies whether the national legislation was passed before or after the directive in question and whether or not the national legislation was passed specifically to implement the directive.[72] In 1990 the European Court stated the interpretative obligation in its strongest terms yet[73]:

"in applying national law, whether the provisions were adopted before or after the directive, the national court is called upon to interpret it is required to do so, as far as possible, in the light of

---

[68] E.C. Treaty, Article 10 [5].

[69] *e.g.* C-165/91 *Van Munster v. Rijksdienst voor Pensionen* [1994] E.C.R. I-4661 (where, for the purpose of applying a provision of its domestic law, a national court has to characterise a social security benefit awarded under the statutory scheme of another Member State, it should interpret its own legislation in the light of the aims of Articles 48–51 of the E.C. Treaty and, as far as is at all possible, prevent its interpretation from being such as to discourage a migrant worker from actually exercising his Community law right of freedom of movement).

[70] As the House of Lords has done in *e.g. Litster v. Forth Dry Dock & Engineering Co Ltd* [1990] 1 A.C. 546 (the U.K.'s Transfer of Undertakings (Protection of Employment) Regulations 1981 were made in order implement Directive 77/187 and had to be construed to give effect to the purpose of the directive); *Pickstone v. Freemans* [1989] A.C. 66 (employee's claim to be doing work of equal value to a more highly paid employee of the opposite sex not barred by the fact that other employees of the opposite sex are employed on the same terms as the claimant).

[71] Case 14/83 *Von Colson and Kamann v. Land Nordrhein-Westfalen* [1984] E.C.R. 1891.

[72] C-106/89 *Marleasing SA v. La Comercial Internacional de Alimentacion SA* [1990] E.C.R. I-4135 (Spanish Civil Code had to be interpreted in the light of Directive 68/151).

[73] *Marleasing*, para 8. Article 189 has been renumbered Article 249 and is set out at para. 17–007 above.

the wording and purpose of the directive in order to achieve the result pursued by the latter and thereby comply with the third paragraph of Article 189 [now Article 249] of the Treaty."

Since then doubts have arisen about what this requires—does "as far as possible" require a national court to distort the clear meaning of national legislation? The European Court has subsequently stated, rather opaquely, that the interpretative duty should not result in an imposition "on an individual of an obligation laid down by a directive which has not been transposed".[74]

Effective procedures and remedies[75]

Where Community rights fall to be enforced in the national courts, the question arises to what extent Community law governs the procedural rules applicable and the remedies available. In principle it is the national law which applies, for Community law and national law are independent systems of law, each operating autonomously in its own sphere. However, exceptions may occur where a rule of national law in some way impedes the effective enforcement of Community rights.

    17–032

The issue has frequently been put before the Court in references from national courts themselves. The answers given by the Court show a marked evolution. In the early cases the Court was content to accept that the exercise of Community rights was subject to national rules, provided that those rules were not less favourable than those governing the same right of action on an internal matter and that they did not make it impossible in practice to exercise the Community rights. More recently the emphasis has shifted to the need for Community rights to be effectively enforced, the overriding requirement of an effective remedy, and the displacement if necessary of all procedural and other obstacles to the protection of Community rights. Thus national courts may be required not to apply any rule of national law whose effect is to preclude immediate enforcement of a Community right.[76]

The European Court, in spelling out in its case law the obligations of national courts, has relied in particular on Article 10 [5] of the

---

[74] C-168/95, *Criminal Proceedings against Arcaro* [1996] E.C.R. I-4705, para. 42.

[75] For a more detailed account, see T. Tridimas, *The General Principles of E.C. Law* (1999).

[76] The first clear statement of this principle was in *Simmenthal*, above, para. 17–009. See further M. Hoskins, 'Tilting the Balance: Supremacy and National Procedural Rules' (1996) 21 E.L.Rev. 365; A. Ward, 'Effective Sanctions in EC Law: A Moving Boundary in the Division of Competence' (1995) 1 E.L.J. 205.

Treaty, which it has viewed as embodying a principle of cooperation requiring the national courts to ensure the effective protection of rights arising under Community law.[77]

Limitation periods

17–033 The issue thus arises how far the exercise of Community rights is subject to procedural rules laid down by national law. In numerous cases, national courts in Member States have had to consider this in relation to limitation periods for bringing legal action, and there have been references to the European Court for preliminary rulings. In one case where a claimant sought to recover charges having equivalent effect to customs duties, levied in breach of the E.C. Treaty, and the defendant sought to plead the expiry of a 30-day limitation period prescribed by national law, the European Court stated:

> "... in the absence of any Community rules, it is for the national legal order of each Member State to designate the competent courts and to lay down the procedural rules for proceedings designed to ensure the protection of rights which individuals acquire through the direct effect of Community law, provided that such rules are not less favourable than those governing the same right of action on an internal matter. [...] In default of ... harmonisation measures, the rights conferred by Community law must be exercised before the national courts in accordance with the rules of procedure laid down by national law. The position would be different if those rules and time-limits made it impossible in practice to exercise rights which the national courts have a duty to protect. This does not apply to the fixing of a reasonable period of limitation within which an action must be bought. The fixing, as regards fiscal proceedings, of such a period is in fact an application of a fundamental principle of legal certainty which protects the authority concerned and the party from whom payment is claimed."[78]

The European Court expressed no view as to whether the 30 day time limit constituted a "reasonable" period of limitation, leaving this

---

[77] See, *e.g.* Case 47/76 *Cornes* [1976] E.C.R. 2043; Case 33/76 *Rewe* [1976] E.C.R. 1989; Case 811/79 *Amministrazione delle Finanze dello Stato v. Ariet.* [1980] E.C.R. 2545; Case 826/79 *Amministrazione delle Finanze dello Stato v. MIRECO* [1980] E.C.R. 2559; Case C-213/89, *Factortame* [1990] E.C.R. I-2433, 2473–2474; see also John Temple Lang, "Community Constitutional Law: Article 5 EEC Treaty" (1990) C.M.L. Rev. 645.

[78] Case 45/76 *Comet v. Prodktschap voor Siergewassem* [1976] E.C.R. 2043; see also Case 33/76 *Rewe v. Landwirtschaftskammer Saarland* [1976] E.C.R. 1989.

issue to be decided by the national court which made the reference. In recent years, the requirements of Community law have been applied more strictly, with the result that national provisions may have to be applied *more* favourably to a claimant where a Community right is in issue than in a case of a purely internal character.[79] In principle, it might in appropriate circumstances be possible for an applicant for judicial review in England and Wales to seek to argue that the requirement in Order 53, rule 4 that applications for permission to apply for judicial review be made "promptly and in any event within three months from the date when grounds for the application first arose"[80] is an unreasonable impediment to exercising Community rights. Such an argument is unlikely to succeed, however: first, the court has discretion which it would surely exercise to extend the period for applying for permission if it "considers there is good reason"; and secondly the European Court's own limitation period for receiving direct actions challenging the legality of Community measures is only two months.[81]

Effective judicial review

The European Court lays considerable stress on the requirement that Member States provide effective means of judicial review. In *Les Verts*,[82] it emphasised that the Community "is a Community based on the rule of law, inasmuch as neither its Member States nor its institutions can avoid a review of the question whether the measures adopted by them are in conformity with the basic constitutional charter, the Treaty." The national courts may be required to ensure the effective protection of rights created by the Treaty or by Community legislation. In *Johnston v. Chief Constable of the Royal Ulster Constabulary*[83] in 1986, the Court spelt out the requirements of effective judicial review under Community law. The reference to the Court raised the question whether, in the field of national security, the issue   **17–034**

---

[79] *e.g.* Case 208/90 *Emmott v. Minister for Social Welfare* [1991] E.C.R. I-4269 (until such time as a directive had been properly transposed, a defaulting Member State might not rely on an individual's delay in initiating proceedings against it in order to protect rights conferred on her by the directive; a period laid down by national law within which proceedings had to be initiated could not begin to run before that time). *Emmott* applies only where the national rules deprive the applicant of any opportunity whatever to rely on his right arising from Community law: C-188/95 *Fantask A/S and others v. Industriministeriet (Erhvervsministeriet)* [1997] E.C.R. I-6783.

[80] See para. 14–013, above.

[81] See para. 17–043 below.

[82] Case 294/83 *Partie Ecologiste (Les Verts) v. European Parliament* [1986] E.C.R. 1339, para. 23.

[83] Case 222/84, [1987] Q.B. 129.

of a certificate by the executive purporting to be definitive and so to exclude the jurisdiction of the courts could preclude reliance on directly effective rights under Community law. Because a number of police officers had been assassinated, the Chief Constable decided that while male officers of the RUC would carry fire-arms, female members of the RUC Reserve would not be issued with firearms or receive firearms training. On this basis he refused to renew the contracts of female members of the RUC full-time Reserve, except when the duties could only be undertaken by a woman. Alleging unlawful sex discrimination, Mrs Johnston challenged the refusal to renew her full-time contract and her exclusion from firearms training. The Sex Discrimination (Northern Ireland) Order 1976[84] made it unlawful for an employer to discriminate against a woman either by refusing to offer her employment or in the way he afforded her access to opportunities for training, except where being a man was a genuine occupational qualification for the job. However, Article 53(1) of the Order provided that none of its provisions rendered unlawful an act done for the purpose of safeguarding national security or of protecting public safety or public order. Article 53(2) stated that a certificate signed by the Secretary of State certifying that an act was done for these purposes was conclusive evidence that those conditions were fulfilled. Before the hearing of the case, the Secretary of State issued a certificate, as provided for in Article 53 of the Order, stating that the refusal to offer full-time employment to Mrs Johnston in the RUC Reserve was for the purpose of safeguarding national security and protecting public safety and public order. Mrs Johnston conceded that the issue of that certificate deprived her of a remedy under that Order. Instead she relied on the equal treatment directive,[85] Article 6 of which provides:

> "Member States shall introduce into their national legal systems such measures as are necessary to enable all persons who consider themselves wronged by failure to apply to them the principle of equal treatment within the meaning of Articles 3, 4 and 5 to pursue their claims by judicial process after possible recourse to other competent authorities."

17–035   On a reference from the Industrial Tribunal, the Court ruled that the principle of effective judicial review laid down in Article 6 of the directive reflected a general principle of law which underlay the

---

[84] 1976 No. 1042 (N.I. 15).

[85] Council Directive 76/207 on the implementation of the principle of equal treatment for men and women as regards access to employment, vocational training and promotion, and working conditions. [1976] O.J. L39 at 40.

constitutional traditions common to the Member States and was also laid down in Articles 6 and 13 of the European Convention on Human Rights. That principle did not allow a certificate issued by a national authority stating that the conditions for derogating from the principle of equal treatment for men and women for the purposes of protecting public safety were satisfied to be treated as conclusive evidence so as to exclude the exercise of any power of review by the courts. The provision contained in Article 6 to the effect that all persons who considered themselves wronged by sex discrimination must have an effective judicial remedy could be relied on by individuals as against a Member State which had not ensured that it was fully implemented in its internal legal order.

State liability in damages for breach of Community law

The requirement to provide effective remedies for the protection of Community rights may also include the obligation to provide adequate compensation. It is a principle of Community law that Member States are obliged to pay compensation for harm caused to individuals by breaches of Community law for which they are held responsible. Where there is a dispute over payment of such compensation, it is national courts which adjudicate on the issues.[86] The harm in question may be caused in many ways—for instance, by the failure to transpose a directive into national law within the required period; by incorrectly transposing a directive[87]; by enacting primary legislation contrary to the provisions of the E.C. Treaty[88]; or by officials taking administrative action such as refusing an export licence in breach of Community law.[89] In *Francovich v. Italy*, the European Court (giving a preliminary ruling to an Italian court) held that the full effectiveness of Community rules would be impaired and the protection of rights

17–036

---

[86] Only those courts in the United Kingdom which have power to award damages generally may grant damages for breach of Community law; where a statutory tribunal, such as an employment tribunal, lacks that power, a claimant will have to start pursue a claim in the county courts or the High Court in the ordinary way: *Potter v. Secretary of State for Employment* [1998] Eu L.R. 388. An application for judicial review made under Order 53 (see Chap. 14, above) may include a claim for damages.

[87] e.g. C-392/93 *R. v. HM Treasury, ex p. British Telecommunications plc* [1996] Q.B. 615 (incorrect transposition of Directive 90/531 on procurement procedures of enterprises operating in the water, energy, transport and telecommunications sector).

[88] e.g. C-48/93 *R. v. Secretary of State for Transport, ex p. Factortame Ltd and others* [1996] Q.B. 404 (enactment by United Kingdom Parliament of Merchant Shipping Act 1988, Part II contrary to provisions in the E.C. Treaty).

[89] e.g. C-5/94 *R. v. Ministry of Agriculture, Fisheries and Food, ex p. Hedley Lomas (Ireland) Ltd* [1997] Q.B. 139 (refusal, contrary to E.C. Treaty, of export licence for live sheep destined for Spanish slaughterhouse).

which they granted would be weakened if individuals were unable to obtain compensation when their rights were infringed by breach of Community law for which a Member State was responsible.[90] The possibility of compensation by the Member State was particularly indispensable where (as on the facts of the case) the full effectiveness of Community rules was subject to prior action on the part of the State and, consequently, individuals could not, in the absence of such action, enforce the rights granted to them before the national courts. Further foundation for the Member States' obligation to pay compensation for such harm was to be found in Article 10 [5] of the E.C. Treaty.[91]

17–037   In *Francovich* and subsequent cases in which national courts have requested preliminary rulings, the European Court has laid down the broad principles for liability. In the absence of Community legislation, it is a matter for the internal legal order of each Member State to develop more specific conditions. Synthesising the pronouncements of the European Court, it may now be said that there is an entitlement to compensation where the following conditions are met by a claimant.

(a) The rule of Community law which has been infringed (i) must be intended to confer rights on individuals and (ii) where the complaint is that a directive has not been transposed, the content of that those rights must be able to be identified on the basis of the provisions of the directive itself.[92] The right conferred by Community law may[93] or may not be directly effective.

---

[90] C-69/90 *Francovich v. Italy* [1991] E.C.R. I-5357. Italy had failed to transpose Directive 80/987, guaranteeing employees a minimum level of protection in the event of an employer's insolvency, into national law. Member States were required to set up institution which would provide specific guarantees of payment of unpaid wage claims. The European Court held that provisions in the Directive were not sufficiently precise and unconditional (see para. 17–014 above) to be directly effective.

[91] See para. 17–031, above.

[92] These conditions were specified in *Francovich*, n. 90 above. In *Bowden v. South West Water Services Ltd* [1998] Env.L.R. 445 a fisherman claimed that the United Kingdom had breached Directive 91/492 (on the health conditions for the production and the placing on the market of live bivalve molluscs) by making a statutory instrument prohibiting the harvest shellfish from a certain part of the coastline. The High Court held that the claimant had failed to demonstrate that the Directive involved the 'grant of rights to individuals'.

[93] In C-48/93 *R. v. Secretary of State for Transport, ex p. Factortame (No. 4)* [1996] Q.B. 404 the successful claim against the United Kingdom was that the Merchant Shipping Act 1988 breached a directly effective provision in the E.C. Treaty prohibiting discrimination on the ground of nationality. The European Court rejected an argument that *Francovich* was concerned only 'to fill a lacuna in the system for safeguarding the rights of individuals' and so limited to situations were the Community law right was not directly effective.

(b) The breach of Community law must be "sufficiently serious". A failure by a Member State to transpose a directive within the prescribed period is *per se* a serious breach of Community law and the circumstances of the failure is not relevant to determining liability.[94] So also will a breach of Community law if it persists despite a judgment of the European Court establishing the infringement in question. Where the breach, whether intentional or otherwise, is of a fundamental principle of the E.C. Treaty, such as the prohibition on discrimination on the grounds of nationality, this will almost invariably give rise to liability in damages.[95] In other circumstances, the following factors will be material in determining whether an infringement passes the threshold of seriousness[96]: (i) the clarity and precision of the rule breached[97]; (ii) the measure of discretion left by that rule to the national authorities[98]; (iii) whether the infringement and damage caused was intentional or involuntary; (iv) whether any error of law was excusable or inexcusable[99]; (v) the fact that the position taken by a

---

[94] C-178, C-179, C-188–190/94 *Dillenkofer and others v. Germany* [1997] Q.B. 259 (Germany had failed within the prescribed time to transpose the Package Travel Directive 90/314/EEC which sought to protect tourists in the event of the insolvency of the travel operator).

[95] *R. v. Secretary of State for Transport, ex p. Factortame Ltd (No.5)* [1998] C.O.D. 381, CA.

[96] C-46, C-49/93 *Brasserie du Pêcheur S.A. v. Germany; R. v. Secretary of State for Transport, ex p. Factortame Ltd and others (No. 4)* [1996] Q.B. 404.

[97] In C-392/93 *R. v. HM Treasury, ex p. British Telecommunications plc* [1996] Q.B. 615 the European Court held that incorrect transposition of part of Directive 90/531 on procurement did not amount to a serious breach because the Article in question was imprecisely worked and was reasonably capable of bearing the interpretation given to it by the United Kingdom in good faith. The interpretation was shared by other Member States and was not manifestly contrary to the wording of the Directive and the objectives pursued by it. Also, no guidance had been available from the European Court. Finally, the Commission did not raise the matter when the implementing legislation was adopted.

[98] *e.g.* in C-5/94 *R. v. Ministry of Agriculture, Fisheries and Food, ex p. Hedley Lomas (Ireland) Ltd* [1997] Q.B. 139 the United Kingdom imposed a general ban on the export of live animals to Spain for slaughter, contrary to E.C. Treaty, Article 28 [30] on the free movement of goods. The European Court held that here the national authorities had not been called upon to make any legislative choices and had only reduced discretion, or even no discretion. In such a situation the mere infringement of Community law may be sufficient to establish the existence of a sufficiently serious breach.

[99] *e.g.* in *R. v. Secretary of State for Transport, ex p. Factortame Ltd (No.5)* [1998] 1 All E.R. 736 (Note), the High Court held that the damage caused by the enactment of the Merchant Shipping Act 1988, Part II was sufficiently serious because: (1) discrimination on the ground of nationality contrary to the E.C. Treaty was the intended effect of the criteria; (2) the government was aware that those criteria would necessarily injure the applicants who would be unable to fish against the British quota; (3) the Act was constructed to ensure it would not be delayed by legal

Community institution may have contributed towards the omission; (vi) the adoption or retention of national measures or practices contrary to Community law. If a decision by an official would have been the same even if no breach of Community law had occurred, this may be insufficiently serious to warrant compensation.[1]

(c) There is a causal link between the breach of the Member State's obligation and the harm sustained by the injured party. This condition is to be decided in accordance with national rules on liability, provided that national law is not less favourable than those relating to a similar purely domestic claim and they are not such, as in practice to make it impossible or excessively difficult to obtain effective reparation for loss or damage resulting from breach of Community law.

17–038   Where these conditions are satisfied, the quantum awarded must be commensurate with the loss or damage sustained. A national court may not totally exclude loss of profit as a head of damage. If exemplary damages are available in domestic claims, these may be awarded in similar situations for breach of Community law.[2]

THE ROLES OF THE EUROPEAN COURT OF JUSTICE AND COURT OF FIRST INSTANCE

17–039   The roles and powers of the European Court of Justice and Court of First Instance are relevant to judicial review in two main ways. First, the European Court issues definitive guidance on the interpretation of Community law to national courts under the preliminary rulings

---

challenges and this made it impossible for the applicants to obtain interim relief without the European Court's intervention; and (4) the Commission had been consistently hostile to the proposed legislation.

[1] *R. v. Secretary of State for the Home Department, ex p. Gallagher* [1996] 2 C.M.L.R. 951, CA (order excluding applicant from entering Great Britain was made under the Prevention of Terrorism (Temporary Provisions) Act 1989 without following the rules of procedural fairness set out in Directive 64/221, but the breach was not sufficiently serious to merit an award of compensation as there was no evidence to suggest that the Secretary of State would have reached a different conclusion had he received the applicant's representations at an earlier stage).

[2] In *R. v. Secretary of State for Transport, ex p. Factortame Ltd (No.5)* [1998] 1 All E.R. 736 (Note), the High Court held that liability for a breach of Community law could best be compared with breach of statutory duty (on which see para. 16–034 above), as it was not possible to compare the United Kingdom's actions with the tort of misfeasance (see para. 16–028). Under English law, a breach of statutory duty only gave rise to exemplary damages if there was express statutory provision for them and no such provision existed in this case.

procedure set out in Article 234 [177] of the E.C. Treaty. Secondly, the European Court and Court of First Instance have their own powers to adjudicate directly on challenges to the legal validity of legal instruments, acts and omissions of the Community institutions (but not of national measures).

References to the European Court from national courts

Any national court of tribunal is empowered to refer questions on the interpretation of Community law to the European Court. In relation to application for judicial review in England and Wales, this means the High Court, Court of Appeal and House of Lords may, and in some situations must, refer questions of law to the European Court of Justice. Article 234 states[3]:

17–040

> "The Court of Justice shall have jurisdiction to give preliminary rulings concerning:
>
> (a) the interpretation of this Treaty;
> (b) the validity and interpretation of acts of the institutions of the Community and of the ECB;
> (c) the interpretation of the statutes of bodies established by an act of the Council, where those statutes so provide.
>
> Where such a question is raised before any court or tribunal of a Member State, that court or tribunal may, if it considers that a decision on the question is necessary to enable it to give judgment, request the Court of Justice to give a ruling thereon.
>
> Where any such question is raised in a case pending before a court or tribunal of a Member State against whose decisions there is no judicial remedy under national law, that court or tribunal shall bring the matter before the Court of Justice."

Where an applicant or respondent in an application for judicial review in England and Wales raises an issue about the correct interpretation of a rule of Community law which is critical to the High Court's final decision, "the ordinary course is ordinarily to refer the issue to the European Court unless the High Court can with complete

---

[3] See also *Note for Guidance on References by National Courts for Preliminary Rulings* [1997] All E.R (E.C.)1 (issued by the European Court) and *Practice Direction (Supreme Court: References to the Court of Justice of the European Communities)* [1999] 1 W.L.R. 260 (issued in England and Wales).

confidence resolve the issue itself".[4] If the question of interpretation is "already decided or obvious" national courts may proceed to give judgment without seeking a preliminary ruling.[5] In judicial review proceedings the House of Lords is the final court of appeal, and it is therefore compulsory for it to make a reference for a preliminary ruling unless the point of Community law is *acte clair*.[6] It will also be compulsory for a national court to seek a preliminary ruling where it is intending to question the validity of a Community act (for example a Regulation or Directive).[7]

In giving a preliminary ruling, the European Court does not decide issues of fact or national law. After the European Court has given its preliminary ruling the national court must apply the rule of Community law, as interpreted by the European Court, to the facts of the case before it.[8] The ruling given by the European Court is binding in subsequent cases on all courts before which the same question arises—unless the national court seeks to obtain a fresh ruling from the European Court in which the question can be reconsidered.

Direct actions in the European Court and Court of First Instance

17–041   Detailed consideration of the work of the European Court and Court of First Instance in determining actions made directly to them fall outside the scope of this book, except insofar as it has an impact on the manner in which the High Court in England and Wales exercises its own function of judicial review. Two main types of proceedings are relevant.

Enforcement actions

17–042   The Commission, or under certain conditions a Member State, may bring an action directly before the European Court against a Member State for failure of the latter to fulfil an obligation under the treaty.[9] The European Court has no power to adjudicate on complaints from

---

[4] *Per* Sir Thomas Bingham M.R., *R. v. International Stock Exchange of the United Kingdom and the Republic of Ireland Ltd, ex p. Else Ltd* [1993] Q.B. 534, 545.

[5] C-283/81 *CILFIT Srl v. Ministry of Health* [1982] E.C.R. 3415. This is the doctrine of *acte clair*.

[6] As was presumably the case in *Equal Opportunities Commission v. Secretary of State for Employment* [1995] 1 A.C. 1 (statutory provisions on rights of part-time workers declared to be inconsistent with Community law).

[7] See para. 17–030, above.

[8] See European Communities Act 1972, s. 3(1).

[9] E.C. Treaty, Articles 226–228 [169–171].

individuals against Member States.[10] If the European Court finds that the defendant Member State has infringed Community law, it must take the necessary measures to comply with the judgment of the Court. The European Court may impose a financial penalty on a Member State. In England and Wales, applications for judicial review by a person against a public authority, alleging breach of Community law, are sometimes conducted at the same time as the Commission brings an enforcement action before the European Court. Thus in relation to provisions of the Merchant Shipping Act 1988, the Spanish trawler owners commenced judicial review against the Secretary of State for Transport in the High Court and the Commission brought proceedings against the United Kingdom in the European Court.[11] Attempts of the United Kingdom government to comply with a ruling of the European Court in enforcement proceedings may themselves be subject to judicial review,[12] though the Commission also monitors compliance by Member States.

Review of legality

One the main functions of the European Court and Court of First   **17–043** Instance is to review the legality of secondary legislation and actions[13] and failures to act[14] of the Community institutions. Where the applicant in such an action is an institution of the Community or a Member State, the action is dealt with by the European Court. Where the applicant is an individual, business enterprise or pressure group, the Court of First Instance has jurisdiction. The courts may annul a measure adopted by a Community institution or require a Community institution to adopt a measure. Individuals and legal persons such as businesses and pressure groups may also, in some circumstances, have standing to bring an action. This is so where an action is brought to challenge the validity of decisions addressed to such a person.[15] The standing of such people (often referred to as "non-privileged applicants") to question the legality of a decision addressed to another or a regulation is, however, very limited: people have standing only to

---

[10] It is however open to an aggrieved person to lodge a complaint with the Commission inviting the Commission to institute proceedings under Article 226 [169]; but the individual cannot compel the Commission to institute such proceedings and cannot challenge any failure or refusal by the Commission.

[11] See [1991] 1 A.C. 603 and [1992] Q.B. 680 (E.C.J).

[12] *R. v. Secretary of State for the Environment, ex p. Friends of the Earth Ltd* (1995) 7 Admin. L.R. 793.

[13] E.C. Treaty, Article 230 [173].

[14] E.C. Treaty, Article 232 [175].

[15] For the definition of a 'decision', see para. 17–016 above.

the extent that the measure is "of direct and individual concern" to them.[16] The European Court and Court of First Instance have taken a very restrictive view of this requirement. People have no right to bring proceedings questioning the legality of a directive.[17] The time limit for bringing actions is only two months. The grounds upon which actions may be brought are "lack of competence, infringement of an essential procedural requirement, infringement of this Treaty or of any rule of law relating to its application, or misuse of powers".[18] These are considered further below.[19]

A person with standing to challenge the legality of decision or failure to act before the Court of First Instance, but who fails to do so within the two month time limit, is precluded from questioning the validity of that decision before a national court.[20]

GROUNDS OF JUDICIAL REVIEW AGAINST COMMUNITY MEASURES

17–044 Community law provides grounds for challenging both the legality of Community measures and of national measures. The next two sections of the Chapter consider each of these situations in turn. As we have already noted, Community measures may be challenged either directly in the European Court and Court of First Instance,[21] or (with restrictions) in proceedings before a national court.[22] The grounds of review are broadly the same in each situation and in outline they are the following:

  (i) lack of adequate reasoning;

  (ii) failure to state, or state correctly, the provisions of the treaty under which the measure was adopted;

  (iii) failure to hear a person affected before adopting the measure;

  (iv) failure to consult other bodies where consultation is required;

  (v) breach of the general principles of law developed by the European Court — including proportionality, non-discrimination, respect for fundamental rights, legal certainty, and protection of legitimate expectations.

---

[16] E.C. Treaty, Article 230 [173].
[17] The only option is to challenge the directive in a national court: see para. 17–029.
[18] E.C. Treaty, Article 230 [173].
[19] See para. 17–044 *et seq.*
[20] C-178/95 *Wiljo NV v. Belgium* [1997] All E.R. (E.C.) 226.
[21] See para. 17–041.
[22] See para. 17–029.

So extensive are the grounds of review that it is now probably more **17–045** helpful to indicate the grounds on which the European Court will *not* annul a measure. These include:

(1) A minor procedural irregularity which is not regarded as sufficiently serious to justify annulment of the measure,[23] or which has not prejudiced the applicant.[24]

(2) An alleged misjudgment by the Council or Commission in an area where the institution concerned enjoys a wide power of appraisal in assessing a complex economic situation.[25]

The grounds of review are thus wider than those under English law. **17–046** A ground of challenge recognised under English law will probably be available under Community law; while some grounds available in Community law, for example lack of adequate reasoning, are not yet generally available under English law. In any case in which the validity of a Community measure is in issue in the English courts, the court may have to consider whether the question of validity should be referred to the European Court under Article 234 [177]. The English court will thus have to give preliminary consideration to a challenge based on any of the grounds indicated above, in order to decide whether a reference is justified.

General principles of law[26]

The general principles of Community law constitute a considerable **17–047** limitation on the policy-making powers of the Community institutions. What follows gives a brief account of the most important of those principles.

---

[23] See *e.g.* Joined Cases 156/79 and 51/80 *Gratreau v. Commission* [1980] E.C.R. 3943, paras 23 to 24 of the judgment.

[24] See *e.g.* Joined Cases 209 to 215, 218/78 *Van Landewyck v. Commission* [1980] E.C.R. 3215, para. 47. For a similar point in English law see *R. v. Commissioners of Customs and Excise, ex p. Cooke and Stevenson* [1970] 1 All E.R. 1068.

[25] Case 331/88 *FEDESA and others* [1990] E.C.R. I-4203, para. 14.

[26] See further T. Tridimas, *The General Principles of EC Law* (1999); John A. Usher, *General Principles of EC Law* (1998).

Equality

17–048   Although certain provisions of the E.C. Treaty provide for the principle of equal treatment with regard to specific matters,[27] the European Court has held that the principle of equality is a general principle of law of which those provisions are merely specific expressions and which precludes comparable situations from being treated differently unless the difference in treatment is objectively justified.[28] It also prohibits different situations from being treated in the same way unless such treatment is objectively justified.[29]

17–049   In order to determine whether two products or two undertakings are in a comparable situation, the Court may have recourse to the criterion of competition. Thus, in the case of products, the Court will consider whether the one can be substituted for the other in the specific use to which the latter is traditionally put. Where two products are interchangeable they are in a comparable competitive position and, in principle, should be treated in the same manner.[30] By contrast, products which have different applications are not in a comparable situation and a difference in their treatment will not normally amount to prohibited discrimination. In the case of undertakings, the Court may have regard to their production[31] or to their legal structure[32] with a view to determining whether their competitive positions are comparable.

17–050   Difference in treatment between comparable situations is not prohibited, however, where it is objectively justified. Whether that is so depends on the particular circumstances of each case, account being taken of the objectives of the measure in question. In general, the Court has interpreted the notion of "objective justification" broadly.[33]

---

[27] See, *e.g.* Art 12 [6] (prohibition of discrimination on the grounds of nationality); Art. 34(3) [40(3)] (prohibition of discrimination between producers and consumers in the common agricultural policy); Art. 141 [119] (equal pay for equal work for men and women).

[28] See, *e.g.* Case 810/79 *Überschär v. Bundesversichorungsanstalt für Angestellte* [1980] E.C.R. 2747, para. 16; Joined Cases 117/76 and 16/77 *Ruckdeschel v. Hauptzollamt Hamburg St Annen* [1977] E.C.R. 1753, para. 7; Case 84/87 *Erpelding v. Secrétaine d'Etat à l'Agriculture et à la Viticulture* [1988] E.C.R. 2647, para. 29.

[29] Case 106/83 *Sermide v. Cassa Conguaglio Zucchero* [1984] E.C.R. 4209, para. 28.

[30] See, *e.g.* Joined Cases 117/76 and 16/77 *Ruckdeschel*; Joined Cases 124/76 and 20/77 *Moulins Pont-à-Mousson v. Office Interprofessionnel des Céréales* [1977] E.C.R. 1795.

[31] Case 222/84 *Johnston v. Chief Constable of the Royal Ulster Constabulary* [1986] E.C.R. 1651.

[32] Joined Cases 17 and 20/61 *Klöckner v. High Authority* [1962] E.C.R. 325, 345.

[33] Thus, it has been held that the discrimination which arises from the fact that a Council Regulation grants aid for sugar in transit between two approved warehouses situated in a single Member State but refuses such aid for sugar in transit between two approved warehouses situated in different Member States is objectively justified on the ground that the supervisory measures which would be necessary if the aid

Proportionality

The principle of proportionality requires that action taken by the **17–051** Community must be proportionate to its objectives.[34] It requires, in particular, that "the individual should not have his freedom of action limited beyond the degree necessary in the public interest".[35] In order to establish whether a provision of Community law is consonant with the principle of proportionality, it is necessary to establish, first, whether the means it employs to achieve the aim correspond to the importance of the aim and, secondly, whether they are necessary for its achievement.[36]

The principle of proportionality enables the Court to review not only **17–052** the legality but also the merits of legislative and administrative measures taken by the Community institutions.[37]

---

were to be granted in the case of international aid would involve disproportionate administrative costs (Case 2/82 *Wagner v. BALM* [1983] E.C.R. 371). The Court has also held that where a trader's milk production has been significantly reduced by an exceptional event throughout the years which, according to Community law, may be taken as reference years and, as a result, that trader has been unable to obtain an individual quota based on a representative production, the Community rules treat that producer adversely in comparison with other producers who are able to rely on a representative production but that such an effect is justified by the need to limit the number of years which may be taken as reference years in the interests of both legal certainty and the effectiveness of the quota system (Case 84/87 *Erpelding*, above n. 29, para. 30).

[34] The principle is often said to be derived from the principle known in German law as *Verhältnismässigkeit*, a principle which in the case law of the *Bundesverfassungsgericht* (Federal Constitutional Court) has been held to underlie certain provisions of the German *Grundgesetz* (Basic Law). Compare the scope of the principle in areas of English law where Community law does not apply. See further Schwarze, *European Administrative Law*, Chap. 5; Jowell and Lester, 'Proportionality: neither novel nor dangerous' in J. Jowell and D. Oliver (eds) *New Directions in Judicial Review* (1988), 51; de Búrca, 'The Principle of Proportionality and its Application in E.C. Law' (1993) 13 Y.E.L. 105; N. Emiliou, *The Principle of Proportionality in European Law* (1996).

[35] Case 11/70 *Internationale Handelsgesellschaft v. Einfuhr- und Vorratsstelle Getreide* [1970] E.C.R. 1125, 1147 *per* de Lamothe A.-G. Note, however, that the principle may also be invoked by Member States: see, *e.g.* Case 116/82 *Commission v. Germany* [1986] E.C.R. 2520.

[36] Case 66/82 *Fromancais v. Forma* [1983] E.C.R. 395, para. 8; Case 15/83 *Denkavit Nederland v. Hoofdproduktschap voor Akkerbouwprodukten* [1984] E.C.R. 2171, para. 25.

[37] In Case 240/78 *Atalanta v. Produktschap voor Vee en Vless* [1979] E.C.R. 2137, the Court was concerned with the interpretation of Art. 5(2) of Commission Regulation (EEC) 1889/76 laying down detailed rules for granting private storage aid for pigmeat which provides that 'The security shall be wholly forfeit if the obligations imposed by the contract are not fulfilled'. The Court held that the absolute nature of Art. 5(2) ran counter to the principle of proportionality because it did not permit the penalty to be made commensurate with the degree of failure to implement the contractual obligations or with the seriousness of the breach of those obligations. In *Maas*, (Case 21/85 *Mass v. Bundesantalt für Landwirtschaftliche Marktordnung* [1986] E.C.R. 3537—see also Case 181/84 *Man (Sugar) v. IBAP* [1985] E.C.R. 2889), the Court was concerned

17–053   The principle of proportionality is applied throughout the field of economic law. The Court has held[38] that the lawfulness of the prohibition of an economic activity is subject to the condition that the prohibitory measures are appropriate and necessary in order to achieve the objectives legitimately pursued by the legislation. Where there is a choice between several appropriate measures recourse must be had to the least onerous and the disadvantages caused must not be disproportionate to the aims pursued.

17–054   This principle has however been qualified in cases where the institution has a wide margin of appraisal. For example, in relation to a measure concerning the common agricultural policy the Court stated:

> "... with regard to judicial review of compliance with those conditions it must be stated that in matters concerning the common agricultural policy the Community legislature has a discretionary power which corresponds to the political responsibilities given to it by Articles 40 and 43 [now 34 and 37] of the Treaty. Consequently, the legality of a measure adopted in

---

with the validity of Art. 20(1) of Commission Regulation (EEC) 1974/80 laying down implementing rules in respect of certain food aid operations involving cereals and rice. Maas, which had been declared successful tenderer for the supply of food aid to Ethiopia, transported the goods to the intended destination but the intervention agency declared the security furnished forfeit on the ground that Maas had not shipped the goods within the period laid down by Community law and also on the ground that it had used vessels which were more than 15 years old, contrary to Community rules. The Court held that forfeiture of the security was not justified since the shipment period had been exceeded by only a short time. It also held that Art. 20(1) of Regulation 1974/80 infringed the principle of proportionality in so far as its effect was that the security had to be declared wholly forfeit where the goods were transported in vessels which were more than 15 years old since that requirement was not of such importance as to justify total forfeiture of the security. *cf.* Case C-104/94 *Cereol Italia v. Azienda Agricola Castello* [1995] E.C.R. I-2983. In that case the Court found that penalties which went as far as forfeiture of entitlement to aid for two marketing years, where a producer deliberately or by reason of serious negligence failed to notify the Commission of changes in the area sown, were proportionate in view of the importance of the obligation of notification for the operation of the aid system. By contrast, in Case C-296/94 *Pietsch v. Hauptzollamt Hamburg-Waltershof* [1996] E.C.R. I-3409 the Court annulled a Commission regulation which imposed a charge on the import of mushrooms from third world countries equal to 90 per cent of their value, on the ground that the level of the charges was disproportionate and amounted effectively to a prohibition of imports. Also, in Case C-295/94 *Hüpeden & Co KG v. Hauptzollamt Hamburg-Jonas* [1996] E.C.R. I-3375 the Court annulled a Council regulation holding that a flat-rate charge set at a very high level (150 per cent of the value of the goods) and levied on all traders who exceeded the import quota regardless of whether they did so inadvertently of fraudulently was excessive.

[38] C-331/88 *R. v. Ministry of Agriculture, Fisheries and Food, ex p. FEDESA* [1991] 1 C.M.L.R. 507.

that sphere can be affected only if the measure is manifestly inappropriate having regard to the objective which the competent institution is seeking to pursue."[39]

The Court has also held that although, in exercising their powers, the Community institutions must ensure that the amounts which commercial operators are charged are no greater than is required to achieve the aim which the authorities seek to accomplish,[40] it does not necessarily follow that that obligation must be measured in relation to the individual situation of any one particular group of operators since, given the multiplicity and complexity of economic circumstances, such an evaluation would not only be impossible to achieve but would also create perpetual uncertainty in the law.[41]   **17–055**

In summary, although the principle of proportionality permits the Court to substitute its own evaluation of the exercise of discretion there are cases where the margin of appraisal allowed to the decision-making institution is wider than others.

Legal certainty and legitimate expectations

The principles of legal certainty and of the protection of legitimate expectations require that the effect of Community legislation must be clear and predictable for those who are subject to it.[42] One of the most important manifestations of the principle of legal certainty is the principle of non-retroactivity. According to the established case law of the Court, a Community measure, other than a criminal measure, may take effect from a point in time before its publication provided that two conditions are fulfilled: the purpose to be achieved by the measure so demands and the legitimate expectations of those concerned are duly respected.[43] With regard to criminal provisions, however, the prohibition of retroactive application is absolute.[44]   **17–056**

---

[39] *FEDESA*, see above n. 25. See also Case 265/87 *Schräder v. Hazptzollamt Gonau* [1989] E.C.R. 2237, paras 21 and 22; Case C-159/90 *Society for the Protection of Unborn Children—Ireland Ltd v. S. Grogan and Others* [1991] E.C.R. I-4685.

[40] See, *e.g.* Case C-26/90 *Wünscher* [1991] E.C.R. I-4961.

[41] See, *e.g.* Case 5/73 *Balkan-Import-Export v. Hauptzollamt Berlin-Pacewf* [1973] E.C.R. 1091, para. 22; Case 9/73 *Schlüter v. Hauptzollampt Lörrach* [1973] E.C.R. 1135, para 22; Joined Cases 154/78, etc. *Valsabbia v. Commission* [1980] E.C.R. 907, para. 118.

[42] See the Advocate-General's Opinion of December 9, 1992 in Case C-168/91 *Konstantinidis* [1993] E.C.R. I-1191.

[43] See, *e.g.* Case 98/78 *Racke* [1979] E.C.R. 69, para. 20; Case 99/78 *Decker* [1979] E.C.R. 101, para. 8; Case 108/81 *Amylum v. Council* [1982] E.C.R. 3107, paras 4–17; Case C-368/89, *Crispoltoni* [1991] E.C.R. I-3695, para. 17.

[44] See Case 63/83 *R. v. Kirk* [1984] E.C.R. 2689, paras, 21–22.

17–057   Legitimate expectations may arise out of conduct of the Community institutions[45] or out of previous legislation.[46] A striking example of the application of the principle is provided by the milk quota cases. With a view to curbing excess milk production, the Council enacted Regulation No. 1078/77 offering a premium to producers who undertook not to market milk products for a period of five years and those who undertook to convert their dairy farms to meat production for a period of four years. Subsequently, Council Regulation 857/84 introduced a levy payable on quantities of milk delivered beyond a guaranteed threshold known as reference quantity. It did not provide, however, for the allocation of a reference quantity to producers who, pursuant to an undertaking under Regulation 1078/77, had not delivered milk and who, upon the termination of their undertaking, were willing to resume milk production. The Court held that the total exclusion of those producers from the allocation of a reference quantity ran counter to the principle of legitimate expectations.[47] Regulation 857/84 was subsequently amended so as to provide that those producers were entitled to a reference quantity equal to 60 per cent of the quantity of milk delivered by the producer during the 12 calendar months preceding the month in which his application for the non-marketing or conversion premium under Regulation 1078/77 was made. The Court held, however, that the ceiling of 60 per cent was also contrary to the principle of legitimate expectations and therefore invalid:

> "It must be made clear ... that where a reduction ... is applied, the principle of the protection of legitimate expectations precludes the rate of reduction from being fixed at such a high level, by comparison with those applicable to producers whose reference quantities are fixed pursuant to ... Regulation No. 857/84, that its application amounts to a restriction which specifically affects them by very reason of the undertaking given by them under Regulation No. 1078/77."[48]

17–058   A legitimate expectation will not be protected, however, unless it is reasonable. Thus, the Court has emphasised that traders cannot have an expectation that an existing situation which is capable of being altered by the Community institutions in the exercise of their

---

[45] See, *e.g.* Case 81/72 *Commission v. Council* [1973] E.C.R. 575; Case 127/80 *Grogan v. Commission* [1982] E.C.R. 869.

[46] See, *e.g.* Case C-152/88 *Sofrimport v. Commission* [1990] E.C.R. I-2477.

[47] Case 120/86 *Mulder v. Minister van Landbouw en Visserij* [1988] E.C.R. 2321; Case 170/86 *Von Deetzen v. Hauptzollamt Hamburg-Jonas* [1988] E.C.R. 2355.

[48] Case C-189/89 *Spagl* [1990] E.C.R. I-4539, para. 22; Case C-217/89 *Pastätter* [1990] E.C.R. I-4585. para. 13.

discretionary power will be maintained.[49] Also, a trader cannot have a legitimate expectation to derive an advantage from a particular measure if that measure was never intended to bestow that advantage.[50]

Human rights[51]

The E.C. Treaty does not provide for a catalogue of fundamental human rights. In its seminal judgment in *Internationale Handelsgesellschaft*, however the Court pronounced[52]: **17–059**

"respect for fundamental rights forms an integral part of the general principles of law protected by the Court of Justice. The protection of such rights, whilst inspired by the constitutional traditions common to the Member States, must be ensured within the framework of the structure and objectives of the Community."

In *Nold*[53] the Court stated that it cannot uphold measures which are incompatible with fundamental rights recognised and protected by the Constitutions of the Member States. It also identified as a source of human rights international treaties for the protection of human rights on which the Member States have collaborated or of which they are signatories. In subsequent cases, it accepted that the European Convention on Human Rights has special significance in this respect.[54] **17–060**

The rights which have been expressly recognised by the Court so far as forming part of the Community legal order include the right to property, the right freely to choose and practise a trade or profession,[55] freedom of trade,[56] the right to an effective legal remedy before the national courts[57]; freedom of trade union activity,[58] prohibition of discrimination based on sex,[59] religious equality,[60] freedom of **17–061**

---

[49] Case C-350/88 *Delacre and Others v. Commission* [1990] E.C.R. I-395.
[50] Case 2/75 *Mackprang v. Commission* [1975] E.C.R. 607.
[51] See Lammy Betten and Nicholas Grief, *EU Law and Human Rights* (1998). For human rights as a ground of challenge to national measures in Community laws, see para. 17–079.
[52] *Internationale Handelsgesellschaft v. Einfuhr-und Vorrarsstelle Getreide*, see above, n. 36.
[53] Case 4/73 *Nold v. Commission* [1974] E.C.R. 491.
[54] Case 222/84 *Johnston v. Chief Constable of the Royal Ulster Constabulary* [1986] E.C.R. 1651; Case C-260/89 *ERT v. Pliroforisis* [1991] E.C.R. I-2925.
[55] *Nold*, see above, n. 54; Case 44/79 *Hauer* [1979] E.C.R. 3727.
[56] Case 19/92, [1993] E.C.R. I-1663.
[57] *Johnston v. Chief Constable of the Royal Ulster Constabulary*, see above, n. 32.
[58] Case 175/73 *Union Syndicate v. Council* [1974] E.C.R. 917.
[59] Case 149/77 *Defrenne v. Sabena* [1978] E.C.R. 1365.
[60] Case 130/75 *Prais v. Council* [1976] E.C.R. 1589.

expression[61] and the right to respect private life and medical secrecy.[62]

17–062 It is not easy to identify in the abstract the exact content of a right recognised by the Court as forming part of the Community legal order. The Court has held, for example, that the right to property and the individual's right freely to choose and practise a trade or profession do not constitute unfettered prerogatives but must be viewed in the light of their social function.[63] On this basis, the Court has held that those rights may be restricted, for example, in the context of a common organisation of the market, provided that those restrictions correspond to objectives of general interest pursued by the Community and that they do not constitute a disproportionate and intolerable interference which infringes upon the very substance of the rights guaranteed.[64] It may be concluded that, in general, provided that the substance of a right is respected, certain aspects of it may have to give way to the attainment of Community objectives or may be sacrificed in order to safeguard an overriding interest.[65]

17–063 It will be noted that although the E.C. Treaty does not provide for a catalogue of fundamental rights, the principle of respect of fundamental rights has been endorsed in subsequent texts, notably in the preamble to the Single European Act,[66] in the Treaty on European Union,[67] and more recently the Treaty of Amsterdam.[68]

The right to be heard[69]

17–064 Among the fundamental rights recognised by the Court is a person's right to be heard before a decision affecting him is taken. This right, and related procedural rights, are also referred to as the rights of the

---

[61] Case C-260/89 *ERT*, see above, n. 55. C-219/91, *Ter Voon* [1992] E.C.R. I-5485.

[62] Case 136/79 *National Panasonic v. Commission* [1980] E.C.R. 2033; Case C-62/90 *Commission v. Germany* [1992] E.C.R. I-2575; Case C-404/92P *X v. Commission* [1994] E.C.R. I-4737.

[63] *Nold*, see above, n. 54, *Hauer*, see above n. 56.

[64] See Hartley, *op. cit.*, Chap. 9 and Anderson, *Preliminary References* (1995). Note also that the Treaty of Amsterdam introduced a special preliminary reference procedure in relation to Title IV of the E.C. Treaty (Arts 61–69) on Visas, Asylum, Immigration and other policies related to the Free Movement of Persons.

[65] See, *e.g.*, in relation to the freedom of trade, *Procureur de la République v. ADBHU*, see above, para. 12, and in relation to the freedom of expression, *Ter Voort*, see above, para. 38.

[66] [1987] O.J. L/169.

[67] See Article F, para. 2.

[68] See T.E.U. Articles G and 7 as amended by the Treaty of Amsterdam.

[69] For procedural propriety as a general challenge to purely domestic situations in English law, see Chaps 6–9 above.

defence (in French, *droits de la défense*).[70] The Court has held that respect for the rights of the defence, in all proceedings which are initiated against a person and which are liable to culminate in a measure adversely affecting that person, is a fundamental principle of Community law which must be guaranteed even in the absence of any specific rules.[71] The rights of the defence include, in particular, the right to be heard, the right in certain circumstances to be assisted by a lawyer,[72] and legal professional privilege.[73] The right to be heard seems first to have been examined in cases brought against the Community by its own employees, but has subsequently been recognised as an inherent right of undertakings in competition proceedings, of Member States in proceedings relating to Article 86 [90] of the Treaty and in proceedings under Article 88 [93] on State aids, and of parties to, and of persons liable to be affected by, many other types of proceedings.

(i) Right to be heard in competition proceedings

In competition law, the Court examined the right to a fair hearing in the *Transocean Marine Paint* case.[74] There, the Commission exempted from the prohibition provided for in Article 81(1) [(85(1)] of the Treaty an agreement concluded between the members of the Transocean Marine Paint Association but made the exemption subject to a condition, in relation to which the Association considered that the Commission had not given it the opportunity to make its views known in advance. The Commission argued that Regulation 99/63, which required the Commission to inform undertakings and associations of undertakings of the objections raised against them, did not relate to the conditions which the Commission intended to attach to a decision granting exemption. The Court accepted that argument but continued[75]:

17–065

"It is clear, however, both from the nature and objective of the procedure for hearings, and from Articles 5, 6 and 7 of Regulation

---

[70] See Ole Due, "Le respect des droits de la défense dans le droit administratif communautaire", *Cahiers de droit européen* (1987) p. 383. For an extensive treatment, see Schwarze, *European Administrative Law*, pp. 1243–1371, esp. 1320 *et seq.*

[71] Case 234/84 *Belgium v. Commission* [1986] E.C.R. 2263, para. 27; Case C-301/87 *France v. Commission* [1990] E.C.R. I-307, para. 29: Joined Cases C-48/90 and C-66/90 *Netherlands and others v. Commission* [1992] E.C.R. I-565, paras, 37, 44.

[72] See, *e.g.* Case 115/80 *Demont v. Commission* [1981] E.C.R. 3147.

[73] Case 155/79 *AM & S v. Commission* [1982] E.C.R. 1575.

[74] Case 17/74 *Transocean Marine Paint v. Commission* [1974] E.C.R. 1063.

[75] *Op. cit.*, para. 15 of the judgment.

No. 99/63, that this Regulation ... applies the general rule that a person whose interests are perceptibly affected by a decision taken by a public authority must be given the opportunity to make his point of view known. This rule requires that an undertaking be clearly informed, in good time, of the essence of conditions to which the Commission intends to subject an exemption and it must have the opportunity to submit its observations to the Commission. This is especially so in the case of conditions which, as in this case, impose considerable obligations having far reaching effects."

17–066   In competition proceedings, the right to a hearing requires the Commission to inform the undertaking concerned of the facts upon which the Commission's adverse decision is based. However, the requirement to disclose the necessary information may come into conflict with the obligation of "professional secrecy"[76] incumbent upon Community officials. Consequently, the Commission may not use to the detriment of an undertaking facts or documents which it is under an obligation not to disclose, where the failure to make such disclosure adversely affects the undertaking's opportunity to be heard.[77] In *Orkem*[78] the Court was confronted with the question whether, in the absence of any right to remain silent expressly embodied in the relevant provisions of Community law, the general principles of Community law included the right of an undertaking not to supply information capable of being used in order to establish against it an infringement of Community competition law—the privilege against self-incrimination. The Court held that the Commission is entitled to compel an undertaking to provide all necessary information concerning such facts as may be known to it and to disclose to the Commission all relevant documents which are in its possession, even if the latter may be used to establish, against it or another undertaking, the existence of anti-competitive conduct. However, the Commission may not, by means of a decision calling for information, undermine the rights of defence of the undertaking concerned and therefore it may not compel an undertaking to provide it with answers which might involve an admission on its part of the existence of an infringement, which it is incumbent upon the Commission to prove. On that basis, the Court annulled certain questions contained in the contested decision addressed by the Commission to the undertaking concerned. The Court thus took an extensive view of the privilege against self-incrimination, although that

---

[76] See Art. 214 of the E.C. Treaty and Art. 20 of Reg. 17.

[77] Case 85/76 *Hoffmann-La Roche v. Commission*, [1979] E.C.R. 461, para. 14.

[78] Case 374/87 *Orkem v. Commission* [1989] E.C.R. 3283.

privilege is generally recognized by the laws of the Member States only for natural persons and only in the context of criminal proceedings.[79]

(ii) Right to be heard in anti-dumping proceedings

In *Al-Jubail,*[80] the Court held that the right to a fair hearing must be **17–067** respected in anti-dumping proceedings before anti-dumping measures are adopted, even though such measures are adopted by way of regulation rather than decision. The basic anti-dumping legislation must therefore be interpreted so as to take account of the requirements stemming from the right to a fair hearing. In performing their duty to provide information, the Community institutions must act with all due diligence by seeking—

> "to provide the undertakings concerned, as far as is compatible with the obligation not to disclose business secrets, with information relevant to the defence of their interests, choosing, if necessary on their own initiative, the appropriate means of providing such information. In any event, the undertakings concerned should have been placed in a position during the administrative procedure in which they could effectively make known their views on the correctness and relevance of the facts and circumstances alleged and on the evidence presented by the Commission in support of its allegation concerning the existence of dumping and the resultant injury."

However, the rights do not apply to all aspects of the anti-dumping proceedings. The Court has held that it is within the discretion of the Council to choose any one of the methods provided for by the Community rules for the purposes of calculating the export price and therefore the Council is under no obligation to give the undertaking concerned the opportunity to present its observations in advance on the method selected.[81]

---

[79] Compare the decision of the House of Lords in *Westinghouse Uranium Contract* [1978] A.C. 547.

[80] Case C-49/88 *Al-Juhail Fertilizer Company v. Council* [1991] E.C.R. I-3187, para. 17.

[81] Case C-178/87 *Minolta v. Council* [1992] E.C.R. I-15.

(iii) Right to be heard in other proceedings

17–068 The right to be heard now appears to extend to administrative proceedings generally.[82] In *Fiskano v. Commission* the right was recognised in proceedings relating to an alleged infringement by a Swedish vessel of a Fisheries Agreement between the Community and Sweden.[83] There the Court reaffirmed that "observance of the right to be heard is, in all proceedings initiated against a person which are liable to culminate in a measure adversely affecting that person, a fundamental principle of Community law which must be guaranteed even in the absence of any rules governing the procedure in question".[84] There the proceedings in question were regarded as involving the imposition of a penalty, but it seems that the principle applies to all proceedings which might result in an adverse decision of any kind. Thus in *Technische Universität München*[85] the Court held, departing from its previous case law, that undertakings which seek duty-free import of scientific instruments have the right to be heard on objections to their application before the Commission takes a decision.

The requirement to state reasons[86]

17–069 Article 253 [190] of the E.C. Treaty requires that binding acts of the European Parliament, the Council and the Commission must state the reasons on which they are based and that they must refer to any proposals or opinions which were required to be obtained pursuant to the Treaty. Insufficient reasoning constitutes a breach of an essential procedural requirement. The requirement of reasoning has a threefold objective[87]: it seeks to give an opportunity to the parties involved of defending their rights, to the European Court of exercising its supervisory functions and to the Member States and third persons of ascertaining the circumstances in which the enacting institution has applied the E.C. Treaty.

17–070 Although, as a general rule, the statement of reasons must disclose in a clear and unequivocal fashion the reasoning of the enacting

---

[82] See further C-32/95P *Listertal* [1996] E.C.R. I-5377;

[83] Case C-135/92, [1994] E.C.R. I-2885.

[84] Para. 39 of the judgment.

[85] Case C-269/90, [1991] E.C.R. I-5469.

[86] For reasons as a ground of challenge to national measures in Community law, see para. 17–077; and in purely domestic situations, see paras 8-039–8-099 above.

[87] Case 24/62 *Germany v. Commission* [1963] E.C.R. 63, 69; Case 294/81 *Control Data v. Commission* [1983] E.C.R. 911, para. 14.

authority,[88] the extent of the duty to state reasons depends on the nature of the act in question and the context in which it was adopted.[89] A distinction is drawn between acts of general application and decisions.[90] With regard to general acts, especially regulations, it is sufficient if the reasons given explain in essence the measures taken without need for a specific statement of reasons in support of all the details which might be contained in such a measure, provided that such details fall within the general scheme of the measure as a whole.[91] With regard to individual decisions, the Court has stated that the purpose of the requirement of reasoning is to enable the Court to review the legality of the decision and to provide the person concerned with details sufficient to allow him to ascertain whether the decision is well founded or is vitiated by a defect which will allow its legality to be contested.[92] A decision must therefore refer to the matters of fact and law on which the legal justification for the measure is based.[93]

The extent of the reasoning required also depends on the context in **17–071** which the act in question was adopted and the legal rules governing the matter. Thus, it is accepted that, although the reasons on which a decision following a well-established line of decisions is based may be given in a summary manner, for example by a reference to those

---

[88] Case 108/81 *Amylum v. Council* [1982] E.C.R. 3107, para. 37; C-350/88 *Delacre and Others v. Commission* [1990] E.C.R. I-395, para. 13.

[89] Case 13/72 *Netherlands v. Commission* [1973] E.C.R. 27, para. 11; Case 819/79. *Germany v. Commission* [1981] E.C.R. 21, para. 19.

[90] See, the Opinion of Advocate-General Van Gerven in Case C-137/92 *Commission v. BASF* [1994] E.C.R. I-2555, 2571 *et seq.*

[91] Case 166/78 *Italy v. Commission* [1979] E.C.R. 2575, para. 8.

[92] See, *e.g.* Case 32/86 *Sisma v. Commission* [1987] E.C.R. 1645, para. 8; Case C-269/90 *Technische Universität München* [1991] E.C.R. I-5469, para. 26 and Opinion of Advocate-General Jacobs at 5492–3.

[93] See, *e.g.* Case 322/81 *Michelin v. Commission* [1983] E.C.R. 3461, para. 14; Case 41/69 *ACF Chemiefarma v. Commission* [1970] E.C.R. 661, para. 78; Case C-358/90 *Compagnia Italiana Alcool v. Commission* [1992] E.C.R. I-2457. For a recent case where the Court annulled a Commission decision on State aid, see Joined Cases C-329/93, 62/95 63/95 *Germany, Hanseatische Industrie-Beteiligungen GmbH and Bremer Vulkan Verbund AG v. Commission* [1996] E.C.R. I-5151. See also Case T-95/94 *Sytraval and Brink's France S.A.R.L. v. Commission* [1995] E.C.R. II-2651. By contrast, in Case C-166/95 P *Commission v. Daffix* [1997] E.C.R. I-983, the Court of Justice found that on the circumstances of the case the decision of the Commission to remove an official from office on grounds of misconduct was sufficiently reasoned and quashed the judgment of the CFI (Case T-12/94 [1995] E.C.R.-SC II-233). Similarly, in *Parliament v. Innamorati*, the Court held that in a competition for recruitment of Community officials, the criteria for marking adopted by the selection board are secret so that failure to communicate those criteria to an unsuccessful candidate does not breach the requirement to give reasons. Case C-254/95 *Parliament v. Innamorati* [1996] E.C.R. I-3423, reversing the decision of the Court of First Instance in Case T-289/94 [1995] E.C.R.-SC II-393.

decisions, the enacting authority must give an explicit account of its reasoning if the decision goes appreciably further than the previous decisions.[94] However, when a decision is addressed to a Member State and that State has been closely involved in the process by which the decision was made and is therefore aware of the reasons which led the enacting institution to adopt the decision, there is no need for extensive reasoning.[95] The European Court has stated that the degree of precision of the statement of the reasons for a decision must be weighed against practical realities and the time and technical facilities available for making the decision.[96] Thus, when the Commission issues a decision rejecting an application for assistance from the European Social Fund for a vocational training course it is sufficient for that decision to contain a concise statement of reasons. That is an unavoidable consequence of the processing of a large number of applications for assistance upon which the Commission must adjudicate within a short period.[97] By contrast, where an application for assistance from the European Social Fund has been accepted, a decision of the Commission which reduces the amount of the assistance initially granted has more grave adverse consequences for the person concerned and must state clearly the reasons which justify that reduction.[98]

17–072   In principle, an act must state in its preamble the legal basis on which it was adopted. Failure to refer to a precise provision of the Treaty need not constitute an infringement of an essential procedural requirement, however, when the legal basis of the measure can be determined from other parts of that measure.[99]

GROUNDS FOR JUDICIAL REVIEW OF NATIONAL MEASURES

17–073   Since in most fields Community measures are implemented by the authorities of the Member States, issues of legality will usually arise between the individual and those authorities, rather than between the individual and the Community institutions themselves. The standard case is that in which the individual claims a right under Community law, contending that the national measures fail to give effect to that right. The failure alleged may be either non-implementation or

---

[94] Case 73/74 *Papiers Peints v. Commission* [1975] E.C.R. 1491, para. 31.
[95] *Netherlands v. Commission*, see above, n. 90, para. 11; *Germany v. Commission*, see above, n. 90, para. 19.
[96] Case 16/65 *Schwarze v. Einfuhr- und Vorratsstelle Getreide* [1965] E.C.R. 877, 888; *Delacre and Others v. Commission*, see above, n. 89, para. 16.
[97] Cas C-213/87 *Gemeente Amsterdam and VLA v. Commission* [1990] E.C.R. I-221.
[98] Case C-181/90 *Consorgan v. Commission* [1992] E.C.R. I-3557.
[99] Case 45/86 *Commission v. Counat* [1987] E.C.R. 1493, para. 9.

implementation which purports to give effect to Community rights but does so incorrectly. Because of the direct effect of many provisions of Community law the individual will often be able to rely on Community provisions notwithstanding the absence of implementing measures and indeed even in the presence of conflicting national provisions.[1] Such cases will be brought in the national court, and although the national court has no jurisdiction to declare Community measures invalid[2] it can of course declare a national measure unlawful and grant appropriate remedies.[3] It may do so, if the Community law is clear, without a reference to the European Court.[4]

By relying upon the direct effect of Community law, the individual **17–074** may be able to challenge national measures and have them declared unlawful.[5] Thus a deportation order will be quashed if it is found contrary to Community law.[6] There are frequent examples of challenge to measures imposing restrictions on imports from other Member States contrary to Articles 28 to 30 [30 to 36] of the E.C. Treaty. [7] Such cases may arise whether or not the individual has a directly enforceable right under Community law. In other cases, an individual may not rely on the direct effect of Community provisions, but simply contend that the national authorities have acted unlawfully, independently of the question whether the Community provisions have direct effect.[8]

As a result of developments in the case law of the European Court, **17–075** the grounds on which national measures may be challenged as being unlawful under Community law correspond closely (although not exactly) with the grounds on which Community measures may be challenged.[9] Thus national measures may be challenged not only as infringing the Treaty or Community legislation, but also, where giving effect to Community provisions, as infringing the general principles of law recognised in Community law: for example the principle of proportionality, the principle of non-discrimination, the principle of respect for fundamental rights, and the principle of protection of legitimate expectations.

---

[1] See paras 17–003, 17–006, 17–014 above.

[2] See para. 17–029.

[3] For remedies, see Chap. 15 above and para. 17–032.

[4] See above, para. 17–054.

[5] On direct effect of treaty provisions, see para. 17–006; on direct effect of directives, see para. 17–014.

[6] *R. v. Secretary of State for the Home Department, ex p. Dannenberg* [1984] Q.B. 766.

[7] *R. v. Secretary of State for Social Services, ex p. Bomore Medical Supplies Ltd* [1986] 1 C.M.L.R. 228 (decision of minister on reimbursement of pharmacists).

[8] *e.g. Twyford Parish Council and Others v. Secretary of State for the Environment* [1992] 1 C.M.L.R. 276 and *R. v. H.M. Treasury, ex p. Smedley* [1985] Q.B. 657.

[9] See above, para. 17–044.

It is now clearly established that where Community law is applicable, the grounds on which national measures may be challenged in the national courts are not the same as those on which national measures may be challenged in English law. The situations in which Community law may arise are so varied that no definitive general statement is possible; the following points should be treated as illustrative only.

Review of discretion

17–076 Where Community rights are in issue, the discretion of the administration will be limited and the Wednesbury case-law has no application; and the English court must if necessary make its own findings of fact in deciding whether the measures challenged are lawful.[10] The court may be required to find that a measure is unlawful even though it would not be invalidated on the *Wednesbury* approach.[11]

Failure to state reasons

17–077 Where a decision of the national authorities has the effect of denying a fundamental Community right, such a decision must be open to challenge by judicial proceedings so that its legality under Community law can be reviewed; accordingly the person concerned must be able to ascertain the reasons for the decision so that he can decide whether to take proceedings with full knowledge of the relevant facts.[12] It is therefore not sufficient for him to be informed of the reasons for a decision only after legal proceedings have been commenced.

General principles of law

17–078 A national measure may be struck down on the ground that it runs counter to a general principle of law. Examples will be given here by

---

[10] See *R. v. MAFF, ex p. Bell Lines and Anor* [1984] 2 C.M.L.R. 502, 509–511.

[11] *R. v. Secretary of State for Social Services, ex p. Schering Chemicals Ltd* [1987] 1 C.M.L.R. 277; *R. v. Minister of Agriculture, Fisheries and Food, ex p. Roberts* [1991] 1 C.M.L.R. 555.

[12] Case 222/86, *UNECTEF v. Heylens* [1987] E.C.R. 4097; Case C-340/89 *Vlasspoulou v. Ministerium für Justiz, Bundes- und Europaangelegenheitem Baden-Württemberg* [1991] E.C.R. I-2357; Case C-104/91 *Colegio Oficial de agentes de la Propiedad Inmobiliaria v. Agicure Borrell and Others* [1992] E.C.R. I-3003; Case C-19/92 *Kraus v. Land Baden-Württemberg* [1993] E.C.R. I-1663.

reference to the principle of protection of fundamental rights, the principle of proportionality, the principle of equality, and the principle of protection of legitimate expectations.

Fundamental rights

In the context of review of national measures[13] the principle of protection of fundamental rights has been applied in two distinct situations: first, in reviewing measures taken by the Member States when implementing Community law; secondly, in reviewing measures taken by the Member States not directly acting within the field of Community law, but where such measures fall within the scope of the Treaty and are covered by an explicit derogation.   **17–079**

The first category may be illustrated by cases in the field of agriculture, where the Member States implement Community legislation. Since the Community institutions are bound by the principle of respect for fundamental rights and their legislation must be interpreted accordingly, it follows that the national authorities, in implementing that legislation, are also so bound.[14] Thus, in *Wachauf*,[15] Mr Wachauf was a tenant farmer who had received a milk quota under the applicable Community rules. Upon the expiry of his tenancy, he requested compensation for the definite discontinuance of milk production but his request was refused on the ground that the lessor had not given his consent as required by Community law. It was argued that if the Community rules in question were interpreted as meaning that, upon the expiry of the lease, the lessee's milk quota must be returned to the lessor, they could have the effect of precluding the lessee from benefiting from the system of compensation for discontinuance of milk production if the lessor were opposed to it. That is because in so far as the milk quota corresponding to the farm in question returns to the lessor, it cannot be taken into account for the purposes of granting compensation. It was argued that such a consequence would be unacceptable if the lessor had never engaged in milk production since the lessee, who would have acquired the milk quota by his own labour, would then be deprived, without compensation, of the fruits of that labour.   **17–080**

---

[13] For the application of the principle in the context of review of Community measures, see above, para. 17–059; for human rights in purely domestic situations, see para. 5–047 *et seq.* above.

[14] Joined Cases 201 and 202/85 *Klensch v. Secrétaire d'Etat à l'Agriculture et à la Viticulture* [1986] E.C.R. 3477.

[15] Case 5/88 *Wachauf v. Bundesamt füt Emährung und Forstwirtschaft* [1989] E.C.R. 2609. *Cf.* Case C-2/92, *Bostock* [1994] E.C.R. I-955.

17–081   After recalling its judgment in *Hauer*, the Court stated[16];

> "Community rules which, upon the expiry of the lease, had the effect of depriving the lessee, without compensation, of the fruits of his labour and of his investments in the tenanted holding would be incompatible with the requirements of the protection of fundamental rights in the Community legal order. Since those requirements are also binding on the Member States when they implement Community rules, the Member States must, as far as possible, apply those rules in accordance with those requirements."

In the circumstances of the case, the Court found that the Community rules left the competent national authorities a sufficiently wide margin of discretion to enable them to apply those rules in a manner consistent with the requirements of the protection of fundamental rights.

17–082   Even where Member States are not implementing Community measures, similar principles may apply. The effect of the European Convention on Human Rights on the review of national measures is demonstrated by the European Court's judgment in *ERT*, which concerned certain exclusive television rights under Greek law. The Court considered the issue of restrictions on the freedom to provide services and the justification for such restrictions under Articles 46 [Article 56] and 55 [66] of the Treaty, and devoted a section of its judgment to the issue raised under Article 10 of the European Convention on Human Rights (E.C.H.R). It stated that where national legislation falls within the scope of Community law, the Court must supply all the elements of interpretation necessary for the national court to assess the conformity of that legislation with the fundamental rights protected by the Court, as they derive, in particular, from the E.C.H.R. Where a Member State invokes the combined provisions of Articles 46 and 55 to justify legislation liable to impede the exercise of the freedom to provide services, that justification, provided for by Community law, must be interpreted in the light of the general principles of law and in particular of fundamental rights; thus the national legislation in question may only benefit from the exceptions provided for by the combined provisions of Articles 46 and 55 if it is in conformity with fundamental rights.[17]

17–083   It followed, the Court concluded, that in such a case it was the duty of the national court and, where appropriate, the European Court to assess the application of those provisions having regard to all the rules

---

[16] *Wachauf*, n. 16 above, para. 19.
[17] C-260/89 *ERT v. Pliroflorisis* [1991] E.C.R. I-2925, paras 42–43.

of Community law, including the freedom of expression enshrined in Article 10 of the E.C.H.R., as a general principle of law protected by the Court.[18]

Thus, the case law of the Court in this area appears to be evolving.[19] **17–084** Although this development should not be presented too schematically, it seems that the review by the European Court of compliance with human rights has developed from a review of Community measures adopted by the Community institutions themselves, to a review of measures adopted by Member States in implementing Community measures, and more recently to a review of measures adopted by Member States which, in one way or another, fall within the scope of Community law.[20]

The principle of proportionality

The principle of proportionality[21] can also be used as the basis for **17–085** challenging national measures and for claiming rights in the national courts. It applies across the whole field of Community law, but its precise effect will depend upon the context. In general terms, it requires that the obligations imposed on a citizen by a measure must not go beyond what is strictly necessary to attain the objectives pursued by that measure. It also requires that a measure must not be manifestly disproportionate to the objective, in that it goes beyond any reasonable relationship between the end and the means.

Many of the applications of the principle to national measures **17–086** concern the scope of exceptions to the basic freedoms of movement of goods and persons under the Treaty. For example, restrictions on the free movement of goods are permitted on such grounds as public health under Article 30 of the Treaty, but such grounds must not result in under restrictions. Where the national measure is tested against a basic Treaty freedom, such as the free movement of goods, strict scrutiny will be applied to the national restriction. Thus the Court has struck down measures which enable pharmaceutical companies to

---

[18] Para. 44.

[19] Compare the earlier judgments in Case 149/77 *Defrenne v. Sabena* [1978] E.C.R. 1365; Case 60/84 *Cinéthèque v. Fédération nationale des cinémas français* [1985] E.C.R. 2605; Case 12/86 *Demirel* [1987] E.C.R. 3719; but see for an early decision Case 36/75, *Rutili* [1975] E.C.R. 1219 at paras 31 and 32.

[20] See the Advocate General's Opinion of December 9, 1992 in Case C-168/91, *Konstantinidis* [1993] E.C.R. I-1191.

[21] In relation to Community measures, see para. 17–051; and for proportionality as a ground in purely domestic situations, see para. 12–068 *et seq.*

limit imports from other Member States to their own main distributors and to exclude "parallel imports" from other Member States, in the absence of a compelling public health justification.[22]

The Court has also held that a Member State may not impose on nationals of other Member States, exercising their right to freedom of movement, the obligation to make a declaration of residence within three days of entering the State's territory, subject to a penal sanction for failure to comply, since the timelimit of three days cannot be regarded as reasonable.[23]

17–087 Criminal penalties imposed by national law are strictly subject to the test of proportionality. As the Court stated in *Casati*[24]:

> "In principle, criminal legislation and the rules of criminal procedure are matters for which the Member States are still responsible. However, it is clear from a consistent line of cases decided by the Court, that Community law also sets certain limits in that area as regards the control measures which it permits the Member States to maintain in connection with the free movement of goods and persons. The administrative measures or penalties must not go beyond what is strictly necessary, the control procedures must not be conceived in such a way as to restrict the freedom required by the Treaty and they must not be accompanied by a penalty which is so disproportionate to the gravity of the infringement that it becomes an obstacle to the exercise of that freedom."

17–088 Thus, the Court has held that national legislation which penalises offences concerning the payment of value added tax on importation from another Member State more severely than those concerning the payment of value added tax on domestic transactions is incompatible with Article 90 [95] of the Treaty in so far as that difference is disproportionate to the dissimilarity between the two categories of offences.[25] The Court has also held that seizure or confiscation of a product imported illegally could be considered disproportionate, and therefore incompatible with Article 28 [30], to the extent to which the return of the product to the Member State of origin would be sufficient.[26]

---

[22] Case 104/75 *De Peijper v. The Netherlands (Ministére public)* [1976] E.C.R. 613.

[23] C-265/88 *Criminal Proceedings against Messner* [1989] E.C.R. 4209.

[24] Case 203/80 E.C.R. 2595, para. 27.

[25] Case 299/86 *Drexl* [1988] E.C.R. 1213.

[26] Case C-367/89 *Aime Rizhardr* [1991] E.C.R. I-4621; See further Case 41/76, *Donckvnwolcke v. Procureur de la République* [1976] E.C.R. 1921; Case 179/78 *Procureur de la Republique v. Rivoira* [1979] E.C.R. 1147. On confiscation, see also *Leifer* [1995] E.C.R. I-3231; Case C-84/95 *Bosphorus Hava Yollari Turizm ve Ticaret AS v. Minister for*

The test of proportionality is clearly a stringent one, especially when   **17–089**
the need for the national measure falls to be weighed against a
fundamental Treaty freedom. Similarly, derogations from directives
providing for equal treatment must be strictly construed. *Thomas*[27]
concerned the scope of the derogation under Article 7(1)(a) of the
equal treatment directive from the principle of equal treatment for
men and women in matters of social security. According to Article
7(1)(a) the directive was to be without prejudice to the right of the
Member States to exclude from its scope the determination of
pensionable age for the purposes of granting old-age and retirement
pensions and "the possible consequences thereof for other benefits."
The Court held that that derogation was limited to the forms of
discrimination existing under the other benefit schemes which are
necessarily and objectively linked to the difference in retirement ages.

The application of proportionality is, however, far from   **17–090**
straightforward. In some cases the answer seems quite obvious; yet in
other cases, it may be more subjective, or in other ways not suited to
judicial determination.[28] For example; the question whether the
measure is reasonably likely to attain its objective may be a matter in
which expertise is required and expert evidence may conflict; but
when in addition the question is asked whether other less restrictive
measures might be used to achieve the same objective, a court may
find it not merely difficult, but impossible, to answer.[29]

The difficulties are compounded where the issue is not resolved by   **17–091**
the European Court itself but is in effect referred back to the national
court. For example in *De Peijper*,[30] a case concerning the marketing of
pharmaceutical products, the European Court held that a particular
national rule or practice (which had the effect of impeding parallel
imports and so raised the issue of restricting trade between Member
States contrary to Articles 28 to 30 [30 to 36] of the Treaty) could not
be maintained "unless it is clearly proved that any other rule or

---

Transport and the Attorney-General [1996] E.C.R. I-3953; Case C-177/95 *Ebony Maritime SA v. Prefetto della Provincia di Brindisi and Others* [1997] E.C.R. I-1111.

[27] Case C-328/91 *Secretary of State for Social Security v. Thomas and Others* [1993] E.C.R. I-1247.

[28] But see, for a readiness to apply the principle, *Thomas* (Court of Appeal); on appeal, referred by House of Lords: above n. 29.

[29] Although in order to determine whether a national measure complies with the principle of proportionality the Court will take into account whether other less restrictive measures exists, a restriction imposed by a Member State on a fundamental freedom will not necessarily fail the test of proportionality merely because another Member State imposes a less severe restriction. If that were so, Member States would need to align their legislation with the Member State which imposes the least onerous requirements. See Case C-384/93 *Alpine Investments* [1995] E.C.R. I-1141; Case C-3/95 *Reisebüro Broede v. Gerd Sandker* [1996] E.C.R. I-6511.

[30] Case 15/74 *De Peijper v. Sterling Drug Inc.* [1974] E.C.R. 1147.

practice [presumably, less restrictive of trade between Member States but achieving the same public health objectives] would obviously be beyond the means which can reasonably be expected of an administration operating in a normal manner".

17–092 The difficulties in leaving to national courts the application of the principle of proportionality were clearly illustrated in the protracted Sunday trading litigation, in which English supermarket chains sought to evade the prohibition on Sunday trading by relying on Article 28 [30] of the Treaty.[31]

17–093 It should also be noted that even if the difficulties could be resolved in the national courts, such an approach would scarcely serve the purpose of securing the uniform interpretation and application of Community law in all the Member States. The difficulties are not confined to the application of the principle of proportionality; similar difficulties may arise in applying human rights principles.[32]

17–094 In conclusion, the application of proportionality can go beyond the English ground of unreasonableness or irrationality and is most strictly applied when the need for a national measure falls to be weighed against a Treaty freedom. However, its application and the margin of appraisal permitted to the decision making authority may vary, in accordance with different situations.

Equality[33]

17–095 The principle of equality, like the principle of proportionality, is binding not only on the Community institutions but also, within the field of Community law, on the Member States. Thus where Community rules leave Member States free to choose between various methods of implementation, a Member State may not choose an option whose implementation in its territory would be liable to create, directly or indirectly, discrimination prohibited by Community law.[34] One of the most fundamental principles of the Treaty is the prohibition

---

[31] See especially *Stoke-on-Trent C.C. and Norwich C.C. v. B & Q* [1991] Ch. 48 (Hoffmann J.) and the Opinion of Advocate-General Van Gerven in Case C-169/91 *B & Q.* [1992] E.C.R. I-6635. See also the disturbing critique by Richard Rawlings, 'The Eurolaw Game: Some Deductions from a Saga' (1993) *Journal of Law and Society* 309. The scope of Art. 30 was reconsidered by the Court in Joined Cases C-267/91 and C-268/91 *Keck and Mithouard* [1993] E.C.R. I-6097. For a Sunday trading case decided subsequently, see Joined Cases C-69/93 and C-258/93 *Punto Casa Spa v. Sindaco del Comune di Capena* [1994] E.C.R. I-2355.

[32] See Clapham, 'A human rights policy for the European Community' (1990) Y.E.L. 309, 328–332.

[33] On equality as a ground of challenge in E.C. law to Community measures, see 17–048.

[34] *Klensch v. Secrétaire d'Etat*, see above, n. 15.

of discrimination on the grounds of nationality.[35] That prohibition covers indirect discrimination, that is to say, discrimination which although it is ostensibly made by the application of other criteria leads effectively to the same result.[36] Thus, depending on the circumstances, discrimination on the ground of residence may result in indirect discrimination. [37]

There is a close affinity between the principle of equal treatment **17–096** and the protection of fundamental rights. In *P v. S and Cornwall County Council*[38] the applicant in the main proceedings was dismissed from his employment following his decision to undergo gender reassignment by surgical operation. The question was referred to the Court whether the Equal Treatment Directive precludes dismissal of a transexual for reasons related to a gender reassignment. The Court held that, in view of sex equality as a fundamental human right, the scope of the directive cannot be confined to discrimination based on the fact that a person is of one or other sex. It stated that discrimination arising from gender reassignment is based essentially, if not exclusively, on the sex of the person concerned. Where a person is dismissed on the ground that he or she has undergone gender reassignment, he or she is treated unfavourably by comparison with persons of the sex to which he or she was deemed to belong before undergoing gender reassignment. The Court concluded (at para. 22) that:

"To tolerate such discrimination would be tantamount, as regards such a person, to a failure to respect the dignity and freedom to which he or she is entitled, and which the Court has a duty to safeguard."

The case provides a prime example of the way the Court views the **17–097** principle of equality as a general principle of Community law transcending the provisions of Community legislation. In effect, the Court applied a general principle of unwritten Community human

---

[35] The general prohibition is contained in Art 12 [6]. It is implemented in relation to specific domains by other provisions of the Treaty, *e.g.* Art 39 [48] (free movement of workers), Art 43 [52] (freedom of establishment) and Art. 49 [59] (freedom of services). Art. 6 applies independently only to situations with regard to which there is no specific prohibition: see Case 9/73 *Schlüter* [1973] E.C.R. 1135 and Case C-357/89 *Raulin* [1992] E.C.R. I-1027, Case C-295/90 *European Parliament v. Council* [1992] E.C.R. I-5299 and Case C-92/92 *Phil Collins v. Imtrat Handelsgesellschaft* [1993] E.C.R. I-5145.

[36] Case 152/73 *Sotgiu v. Deutsche Bundesport* [1974] E.C.R. 153; Case 71/76 *Thieffry* [1977] E.C.R. 765; Case 15/69 *Südmilch v. Ugliola* [1969] E.C.R. 363.

[37] See Arts 92, 93(2) of the Treaty and Case 52/84, *Commission v. Belgium* [1986] 1 E.C.R. 89.

[38] Case C-13/91 [1996] E.C.R. I-2143.

rights law, according to which discrimination on arbitrary criteria is prohibited, rather than the provisions of the Equal Treatment Directive, a literal interpretation of which does not seem to support the Court's finding. By contrast, in[39] *Kalanke v. Freir Hansestadt Bremen*[40], the Court found that the Bremen Law on Equal Treatment which provided for positive discrimination in favour of women was incompatible with Article 2(4) of the Equal Treatment Directive.

Protection of legitimate expectations[41]

17–098 National authorities responsible for applying Community law are bound to observe the principle of protection of legitimate expectations. The principle is best illustrated in the context of the recovery by national authorities of aid paid by Member States in breach of Community rules. Where for example the Commission finds that aid which has been granted by a State to an undertaking is incompatible with the common market, and thus unlawful under Article 87 [92] of the Treaty, it may require the national authorities to recover that aid.[42] In general, the Court has been reluctant to accept that the principle provides a good defence against an order to recover unlawfully paid state aid. In one case,[43] the undertaking concerned claimed that the Commission's order to the national authorities to recover the aid was incompatible with the principle of protection of legitimate expectations on the ground that it had received the aid on the basis of definitive decisions and on the ground that it had used it in relation to a product which was not subject to the guidelines notified to the Member States by the Commission. The Court rejected those arguments stating that failure to include that specific product in the guidelines could not justify a legitimate expectation on the part of the undertaking, since the guidelines could not derogate from Articles 87 [92] and 88 [93] of the Treaty which prohibited the granting of the aid. In another case, however, the Court accepted that the Commission's unreasonable delay in requiring the recovery of State aid gave rise to a legitimate expectation on the part of the undertaking which prevented

---

[39] Case C-450/93.
[40] [1995] E.C.R. I-3051.
[41] Case 5/82 *Hauptzollarnt Krefeld v. Maizena* [1982] E.C.R. 4601, para. 22. For legitimate expectations as a ground for challenging Community measures, see para. 17–056.
[42] See. *e.g.* Case C-5/89 *Commission v. Germany* [1990] E.C.R. I-3437.
[43] Case 310/85 *Deufil v. Commission* [1987] E.C.R. 901.

the Commission from requiring the national authorities to order the refund of the aid.[44]

In the context of agricultural aids, the Court has held that Community law does not prevent national law from having regard, in excluding recovery of unduly paid aids, to the need to protect legitimate expectations, provided that the same procedural rules are applied to the recovery of purely national financial benefits and that the interests of the Community are taken fully into account.[45]　**17–099**

A practice of a Member State which infringes Community law may never give rise to legitimate expectations on the part of an economic operator[46]; and that is so even where a Community institution has failed to take the necessary action to ensure that the State in question correctly applies the Community rules.[47]　**17–100**

---

[44] Case 223/85 *RSV v. Commission* [1987] E.C.R. 4617. But see Case C-301/87 *France v. Commission* [1990] E.C.R. I-307.

[45] Joined cases 205–215/82 *Deutsche Milchkontor v. Germany* [1983] E.C.R. 2633, para. 33.

[46] Case 316/86 *Hauptzollarnt Hamburg-Jonas v. Krücken* [1988] E.C.R. 2213, para. 23.

[47] Case 5/82 *Hauptzollarnt Krefeld v. Maizena* [1982] E.C.R. 4601, para. 22.

INDEX

References are to paragraph numbers

Index

Index

Index